D0618278

twayne

companion to contemporary world literature

from the editors of *world literature today*

twayne

companion to contemporary world literature

from the editors of *world literature today*

pamela a. genova
editor

volume

2

parts VI–VIII

appendices
index

TWAYNE
PUBLISHERS™

New York • Detroit • San Diego • San Francisco • Cleveland • New Haven, Conn. • Waterville, Maine • London • Munich

Twayne Companion to Contemporary World Literature: From the Editors of *World Literature Today*

Pamela A. Genova

Twayne/Gale
Frank Menchaca, Publisher, Twayne Publishers
Stephen Wasserstein, Senior Editor

Project Editor
Ken Wachsberger

Proofreading, Copyediting
Bill Kaufman
Gina Misiroglu

Indexer
J. Naomi Linzer

Data Capture
Gwen Tucker

Permissions
Shalice Shah-Caldwell

Product Design
Michelle DiMercurio

Imaging and Multimedia
Lezlie Light
Kelly Quin
David G. Oblender
Dan Newell
Leitha Etheridge-Sims

Composition
Evi Seoud

Manufacturing
Rhonda Williams

LIBRARY OF CONGRESS CATALOG-IN-PUBLICATION DATA

Twayne companion to contemporary world literature : from the editors of World Literature Today / edited by Pamela A. Genova.
      p. cm.
Includes bibliographical references and index.
   ISBN 0-8057-1700-5 (hard : set) — ISBN 0-8057-1701-3 (v. 1) — ISBN 0-8057-1702-1 (v. 2)
   1. Literature, Modern—20th century—History and criticism. I. Genova, Pamela Antonia, 1961- II. World Literature Today.

   PN771 .T93 2003
   809'.04—dc21

2002152498

Revised

Printed in the United States of America
10 9 8 7 6 5 4 3 2 1

Contents

■ VOLUME 2

VI. Eastern Europe, Russia, and the Balkans

Eastern Europe, Russia, and the Balkans

ALBANIA

Albanian Nationalism and Socialism in the Fiction of Ismail Kadare

Ismail Kadare (b. 1936) is the only modern Albanian writer who is known widely outside his own country. Although he writes both poetry and prose fiction, he is known primarily for the latter. Thematically, Kadare's fiction contains strains of Albanian nationalist thinking and of twentieth-century socialist thought. But Kadare avoids the idolatry of nationalism and socialism by disavowing the notion that the deeds of the traditional "old man" or of the socialist "new man" are sufficient, *independently,* to secure the well-being of the nation. The strengths of socialism must redeem the weaknesses of national traditions; and conversely, the virtues of national thought must overcome the imperfections of socialist practice. In Kadare's works collectively, the old national symbol is hence resurrected, but Kadare endows the two heads of the eagle with fresh significance and the eagle itself with unfamiliar vitality.

Of his numerous works, three are rich in Kadarean conceptions: the novel *Gjenerali i ushtrisë së vdekur* (The General of the Dead Army; 1963), the collection of short stories *Qyteti i jugut* (The Southern City; 1964) and the novel *Dasma* (The Wedding; 1968). In *Gjenerali* a nameless Italian general is sent to Albania by his government in order to recover the bones of Italian soldiers who had died and were buried there during World War II. A priest, also nameless, accompanies the general on his mission. These two are in an uncomfortable relationship: they dislike each other; only necessity binds them together. Although characterization of the men is sympathetic, what they symbolize is unlovable. While the general is a symbol of militarism, he is also more than that: he stands for Western attitudes toward life and love, the indestructible matters of human existence.

The priest epitomizes the religious support which is accorded Western views. In the general's precise and diligent search for the bones of dead men, and in the sad consequences of this search for himself—anxiety, insomnia, nightmares and alcoholism—Kadare wants us to discover a terrifying aspect of Western ways, namely, that these ways serve the forces of death, not life.

The life-promoting forces are found in Albanian character and in socialist action. As the general and his partner move from one locality to the next in their search for bones, they encounter Albanians of different ranks. In these encounters Kadare develops the contrast between the two antagonistic modes of thought and living; but he does not over-ideologize the distinction, for he never explicitly mentions socialism, capitalism or Westernism. Albanians are portrayed as vigorous, self-controlled, altruistic and proud in contrast to Westerners, who are debilitated, sexually lawless, selfish and greedy. Whatever vice exists among Albanians is imported.

Despite so much national commendation, however, *Gjenerali* is not a piece of nationalistic propaganda promoting the tired but attractive notion that the West is corrupt while Albania is pure. Kadare weakens the allure of this notion by showing that while vice is unevenly distributed, suffering is not. The wartime intruders and their descendants do not suffer any more on account of their corruption, nor do the Albanians suffer any less because of their virtue. One episode will suffice to support this point; the situation is recalled from the war years. Against the protest of local Albanians, the occupation sets up a bordello, run by foreign girls and patronized by the occupiers. A young Albanian, succumbing to the lure of the brothel, stains his and his family's reputation. The boy's father avenges the family by murdering the leading temptress. But the father is quickly apprehended and hanged within a few days for his act of revenge. He is not even given time to celebrate the manly pride which motivated his deed.

For all that, Western ways remain inherently punitive, for they spell the destruction of moral character,
while Albanian ways remain life-promoting, because
they sustain moral character. Thus, while Albanians too
can count their dead, there is no Albanian equivalent
of the demoralized, nameless General of the Dead
Army. This idealistic picture of Albanian character starts
to fade, however, in *Qyteti i jugut* and in *Dasma*. In these
later works the foreign intruder is not so conspicuous;
and in taking a more relaxed view of the character of
Albanian society, Kadare uncovers indigenous, not imported, evils against which he warns his countrymen.

Katrina, the heroine of *Dasma*, is a peasant girl from
the mountains. In accordance with the custom of arranged marriages, she was engaged at a young age and
was expected from that time on to begin learning the
skills which would prepare her to be a wife. However,
the hopes of her father are disappointed several years
later when the authorities send Katrina, along with
other students, to southern Albania in order to work at
a railroad camp. (The location is significant, for southern Albania has been regarded as more cultivated than
the mountainous north, within whose formidable fast-
nesses the mountaineers have been able to preserve ancient customs. Not surprisingly, the Albanian Communist movement began in the south.) The trip to the
south is Katrina's first encounter with the world outside
her village. Her father opposes her exposure to this
world, but the wishes of the local Party authorities over-
rule him.

In her new surroundings Katrina becomes acquainted with what she calls "paja e partisë" (the dowry
of the Party), which does not involve clothes and linen,
but freedom and knowledge for women. She begins to
despise her background and to pity her father for his
submission to a social system which relies for its survival upon conformity, violence and the oppression of
women. Katrina breaks her engagement, and not long
thereafter she falls in love with a young worker named
Xheviti, who wishes to marry her. She consents; and
through this independent course of action, she not only
severs herself from her family, but also compromises
her family's integrity: for since the traditional marriage
is really a marriage of families, the moral failure of one
individual affects many others. This is why, as the novel
makes clear, the engagement period is frequently attended by the anxious hope of the negotiating parties
that neither side will suffer the misfortune of moral failure or a breach of trust.

The wedding (*dasma*) of Katrina and Xheviti, a
wedding which they have arranged themselves, is the
central event of the novel. The guests include humble
well-wishers, friends of the married couple, local Party

personnel and several intellectuals. The guests represent, in short, every stratum of Albanian culture.
Through a series of subplots Kadare explores the character of relationships between the sexes in Albania. The
novel is a condemnation of traditional marriage, its patriarchal basis and its indifference to the happiness of
the young. It also attacks the matchmaking negotiations, which barter lives as though people were on a
level no higher than that of sheep, donkeys and goats.
Finally, the novel denounces the violence which is often
used to avenge a serious breach of trust.

In Katrina's and Xheviti's case, trust has been
breached, for the girl's parents had promised her to another. The tension pervading the novel arises from the
unarticulated understanding of everyone that sooner or
later a broken promise will be avenged. But the newlyweds are not afraid; they know that their personal rights
are protected by the Party. The shades of tragedy which
have clouded the marriage festivities materialize when
the father and the matchmaker unexpectedly appear. In
the dark woods near the wedding hall, they attack each
other, then mysteriously disappear, "si dy përbindësha
të plagosur" (like two wounded monsters), leaving
drops of blood on the ground as evidence of their savage encounter. But the wedding joy is undiminished,
and when the long celebration ends at daybreak, the
sun rises on yet another couple to be married with their
own consent in socialist Albania.

The message is clear: the old customs are vicious
and will crumble under the weight of their own contradictions, without in the least hindering the establishment of more humane relationships between men and
women.

In this message, are we hearing the voice of Kadare
or the collective voice of the Albanian Labor (Communist) Party denouncing female bondage, patriarchalism
and social conservatism? This is a legitimate question,
for in *Dasma* the writer appears to have reversed the
picture which emerged in *Gjenerali*. *Dasma*'s picture of
the suppression of women is the antithesis of *Gjenerali*'s
celebration of the purity and stability of male-female relationships. And the violent tendencies of Albanian
men, deplored in *Dasma,* are either lauded in *Gjenerali*
as examples of Albanian masculine pride, or else ex-
cused as excrescences alien to the true character of Albanians. The traditional Albanians in *Gjenerali* are portrayed as noble, while many of those in *Dasma* are
pictured as ignoble. It is as though Kadare were describing two different peoples. But he is not. They are the
same; it is the basis of evaluation which differs in the
two novels. For in *Gjenerali* Albanians measure up well
when they are compared against the militaristic and debilitated West, but these same Albanians are found

wanting when their customs are evaluated against professed socialist ideals.

The test of an honest observer lies in his willingness to subject even his ideals to scrutiny. Kadare passes the test in *Qyteti i jugut*. *Qyteti* is a collection of short stories, many of which are set in or around the "southern city." This would be Gjirokastër, Kadare's birthplace, in southern Albania. Many of the stories are autobiographical and recount impressions (sometimes through the eyes of a small boy) of wartime and socialist Albania.

Love and marriage reappear in *Qyteti*. "Në kafe" (In the Café) is the account of two fathers conducting matchmaking negotiations. Because these have become illegal, the fathers must negotiate stealthily. They have met in the café in order to settle the issue of the bride price. The bride-to-be is the same Katrina who appears in *Dasma*. Kadare exposes the materialistic thinking which often governs arranged marriages. Concerned to get the highest price for his daughter, Katrina's father is callous as he reflects on what the future probably holds for her. At thirty, "Katrina do të ketë marrë fund si grua" (Katrina will be finished as a woman). At forty-five, "Katrina do të jetë krejt e plakur. Rrudhat do ta kenë mbuluar prej kohësh fytyrën e saj. Në to do të jetë shkruar si në një libër të ri mërzia e viteve dhe vuajtja" (Katrina will have aged completely. For a long time her face will have been covered with wrinkles, in which would be written, as in a new book, suffering and the misery of years). At forty-seven: "Ndoshta vdekja? S'është çudi" (Death, maybe? Not surprising). The negotiations are abruptly halted by Party officials who had been secretly observing them.

In contrast to this picture of Party diligence, "Sezoni dimëror i Kafe Rivierës" (Winter Season at the Café Riviera) depicts a leadership which is apathetic in the face of arranged marriages. In this story a young idealistic waiter loses his job for speaking out against the participation of Party members and enthusiasts in arranged marriages. The criticism is open and unambiguous, but it is not a criticism of socialism. On the contrary, Kadare's point is that the leadership is not living up to the socialist ideal of freedom for women.

But *Dasma*'s notion that relationships in the new society are invariably better than those in the old is shattered in "Historia," which relates a brief romantic encounter between two students. The girl is appealing, but her immodesty, frivolity and shallow urbanity distress the moral young man who is attracted to her. Through rediscovering the beauty inherent in his country's struggle to shape its history, and most of all through realizing that he is necessary to that struggle, the young man is delivered from bewilderment and from shallow attach-

ment. "Historia" is therefore also a lesson on the obligation of the new man to maintain zealous commitment to socialist freedom. But this commitment must not be tainted with self-seeking. This is the lesson of "Shërbimi i parë" (The First Assignment), which concerns a dairy manager whose dedication to his work, which he genuinely loves, is undermined through his growing fascination with the publicity and attention that he begins to enjoy as a result of the very usefulness of his work to the new society.

Besides narratives of socialist life, *Qyteti* also includes stories which explore several aspects of Albanian national character. Especially in the narratives which are set during World War II, we are shown a brave and proud people trying to survive against formidable odds. But these narratives also indicate that while courage and pride are adequate to form a strong nationality, they are insufficient to construct a strong *nation*. For this latter purpose Albanians must overcome ignorance, backwardness and superstitious trusts.

In summary, Kadare's major works reveal a remarkable writer who is appreciative of both his countrymen and his nation. Yet he is spared the temptation of self-congratulatory nationalism by Albanian history, which provides too many tragic warnings of the impotence of national virtue unsupported by progressive thinking. At the same time, although the author is committed to socialism, his awareness of its failures and of its ambiguous successes restrains the thoughtless exuberance that too frequently attends ideological allegiance.

Janet Byron, Autumn 1979

Evolution and Revolution in Modern Albanian Literature

Tehut e shpatës kemi ecur rrufe.
Pastaj shpata ka ecur mbi ne.

(The blade of the sword we came down in a dash.
The sword then came down upon us in a flash.)

▦ XHEVAHIR SPAHIU

Establishing a literary culture in Albania has never been an easy task, though not for want of artistic endeavor and creative impulses. All too often the tempestuous course of Albanian history has nipped the flowers of Albanian literature in the bud and severed the roots of intellectual culture.

Early Albanian literature of the sixteenth and seventeenth century, with its primarily biblical focus religious translations and devotional texts (beginning with the "Missal" of Gjon Buzuku in 1555), might have provided a foundation for literary creativity in the age of the Counter-Reformation under the somewhat ambiguous patronage of the Catholic Church, had not the banners of Islam soon been destined to bear the full brunt of the Turkish invasion. The Ottoman colonization of Albania, which had begun as early as 1385, was to split the country into three spheres of culture, all virtually independent of one another: 1) the cosmopolitan traditions of the Islamic Orient using initially Turkish, Persian, and Arabic as their media of expression and later Albanian in a stylized *Aljamiado* literature, i.e. the so-called poetry of the *Bejtexhinj;* 2) the lingering Byzantine heritage of Greek Orthodoxy in southern Albania, which produced a number of religious and scholarly works in Greek script in the eighteenth century; and 3) the awakening culture and literature of the Arbëresh (Italo-Albanians) in southern Italy, nourished by a more favorable social, political, and economic climate and by the fertile intellectual soil of Italian civilization.

The stable foundations of an Albanian national literature were finally laid in the second half of the nineteenth century with the rise of the nationalist movement striving for Albania's independence from a decaying Ottoman Empire. The literature of this so-called *Rilindja* period of national awakening was one of romantic nationalism and provides an excellent key to an understanding of the Albanian mentality even today. As so often in the history of Albanian literature, writing in Albanian, by its very existence, constituted an act of defiance against the foreign powers ruling the country or dominating it culturally. Indeed, the Sublime Porte rightly regarded most Albanian cultural and educational activity as subversive, and as such saw fit to ban Albanian-language schools and the publication of all books and periodicals in Albanian. With no access to education in their own language, only a small minority of Albanians could hope to break through the barriers to literary creativity and intellectual thought.

At the beginning of the twentieth century the Catholic education facilities set up by the Franciscans and Jesuits in Shkodër (Scutari) under the auspices of the Austro-Hungarian *Kultusprotektorat* paved the way for the creation of an intellectual elite in Albania, which in turn produced the rudiments of a more sophisticated literature that expressed itself primarily in poetry. The culmination of Albanian literature before World War II is seen in the works of the talented Franciscan pater Gjergj Fishta (1871–1940), once lauded as the national poet of Albania, though from 1945 to 1990, for reasons more political than literary, ostracized from the Albanian Parnassus.

Indeed, virtually the whole literature of prewar Albania was swept away by the political revolution that took place in the country during and after World War II, to be replaced by a radically proletarian and socialist literature in its infancy. The first minister of education and culture of the "new" Albania, Sejfullah Malëshova (1901–c. 1970), a self-styled "rebel poet" who used the pseudonym Lame Kodra, nevertheless followed a relatively liberal course in order to encourage the reintegration of noncommunist writers and forces into the new structures of power. His success was limited, though, as he very soon fell into disgrace as an "opportunist" and was eliminated by Enver Hoxha (1908–85) in a power struggle in 1946. Malëshova, strangely enough, survived his fall. This left-wing idealist, who had once been a member of the Soviet Comintern, spent his later life in internal exile as a humble stock clerk in Fier, where, for years on end, not a single inhabitant of the town dared speak to him. His only social contact was to play soccer with the children. Whenever anyone approached, he would pinch his lips with his fingers, betraying the vow of eternal silence that ensured his survival. Malëshova died of appendicitis in unimaginable isolation.

Most other writers and intellectuals who had not left the country by 1944 suffered a similar or worse fate. The Catholic writers of the north were of course among the first to be eliminated by the new regime: the poet Lazër Shantoja (1892–1945) was shot in the spring of 1945; the poet Bernardin Palaj (1897–1947) died in prison in Shkodër around 1947; Vinçenc Prennushi (1885–1949), poet, folklorist, and Archbishop of Durrës, was tortured to death in Durrës prison in February 1949; Ndoc Nikaj (1864–1951), often called the father of twentieth-century Albanian prose, was arrested in 1946 at the age of eighty-two on the absurd charge of planning to "use violence to overthrow the government" and died in Shkodër prison five years later. Repression was not confined to the Catholics, however. The dramatist Kristo Floqi (1873–1951) died in 1951 after several years in prison. The talented short-story writer Mitrush Kuteli (1907–67), whose real name was Dhimitër Pasko, was sentenced to fifteen years in prison and spent at least three years in a Tiranë jail and doing forced labor in the notorious swamp of Maliq near Korçë. With him in Tiranë was Andrea Varfi (b. 1914), later to be celebrated as a classic author of early socialist realism. The novelist and Spanish Civil War veteran Petro Marko (b. 1913) was invited to Hollywood after the war by Billy Wilder to do film scripts. He was hindered in his reply to the invitation by a stay in prison in Tiranë from 1947 to 1950, where he was often suspended in chains.

Enver Hoxha was deeply suspicious of Albanian writers and intellectuals and remained so to the end of his days. The intellectual freedom which had existed, ironically enough, under the prewar Zog dictatorship and during the Italian occupation was snuffed out completely. The party demanded nothing less than absolute obedience. The simplest means of eliminating questionable writers was to deny them access to publication. As a result, many a talented quill turned nolens volens to translating. The pantheistic poet Lasgush Poradeci (1899–1987), a twentieth-century classic, is said to have preferred to break his pencil in two rather than write the kind of poetry "they" wanted. Instead, he rendered Burns, Pushkin, Lermontov, Goethe, Heine, and Brecht into fluid Albanian before dying in absolute poverty. The respected Petro Zheji (b. 1929), spiritual father to a whole generation of Albanian intellectuals, is an admired translator of Aragon, Cervantes, Asturias, Goncharov, and Sciascia but never had access to publishing facilities for his own works, imbued with symbolism; Jusuf Vrioni, Kadare's talented translator into French, spent over a decade in prison because of his aristocratic origins before being allowed to work. A handful of prewar authors did manage to adapt. Sterjo Spasse (1914–89) from Lake Prespa, for instance, whose early novels *Pse?!* (Why?!; 1935), with its strongly nihilistic overtones, and *Afërdita* (1944) portrayed the dilemma of the young intellectual in a backward rural society, wrote prose in the vein of socialist realism but never published anything convincing in his later years. The same is true of the satirist Nonda Bulka (1906–72).

The persecution of intellectuals—in particular of those who had been abroad before 1944—and the break with virtually all cultural traditions created a literary and cultural vacuum in Albania that lasted until the sixties, the results of which can still be felt today. No one will ever know how many gifted writers and artists were dispatched to do menial chores in dangerous branches of industry or banished to the provinces forever, to internment in some isolated mountain village with no hope of return.

With Albania's integration into the Soviet bloc during the fifties, Soviet literary models were introduced and slavishly imitated. The verse, short stories, and novels produced by the first generation of postwar Albanian writers were nevertheless for the most part not literary publications at all. They were politically motivated and educative in nature, often to the point of being cumbersomely didactic. Patriotism and the "right" political convictions counted for much more than literary sophistication. *Lumi i vdekur* (The Dead River; Tiranë, 1965) by Jakov Xoxa (1923–79) from Fier, one of the rare works

of the period with any literary merit, was modeled on the Russian novel *Tikhii Don* (1928–40; Eng. *And Quiet Flows the Don*) by Mikhail Aleksandrovich Sholokhov (1905–84) and his *Juga e bardhë* (The White South Wind; Tiranë, 1971) on the latter's *Podniataia tselina* (1932–60; Eng. *Virgin Soil Upturned*). *Një vjeshtë me stuhi* (Stormy Autumn; Tiranë, 1959) by Ali Abdihoxha (b. 1923) was a complete imitation of *Molodaia Gvardiia* (1945; Eng. *The Young Guard*) by Aleksander Aleksandrovich Fadeyev (1901–56). Among other representative authors of this period of Albanian literature were Dhimitër S. Shuteriqi (b. 1915) from Elbasan, now a preeminent literary historian; Shevqet Musaraj (1914–86) from the Vlorë region; Fatmir Gjata (1922–89) from Korçë; and the poets Aleks Çaçi (1916–89), Mark Gurakuqi (1922–77), Luan Qafëzezi (b. 1922), and Llazar Siliqi (b. 1924), none of whom was able to express much particular talent.

The writers of the fifties and early sixties started from scratch. They were inspired, if at all, by revolutionary pathos and an awareness of being the very first generation of a new literature and of a new Albania. The link between this literature and Marxist politics had been firmly cemented, and the political message was the essential for those who wished to survive. Writers were encouraged to concentrate their creative energies on specific themes such as the partisan struggle of the "national liberation war" and on the building of socialism. Subjects devoid of any redeeming educational value in Marxist terms were considered alien and taboo, and indeed still have been up to the present. "L'art pour l'art" is quite unthinkable in modern Albania. Socialist realism gave writers the tools with which to create, but, as an absolute value, it allowed them no alternatives. As a result, the vast body of writing churned out in the fifties and sixties proved in general to be sterile and exceptionally conformist. The subject matter of the period was repetitious, and unelaborate texts were spoonfed to the reader time and again without much attention to basic elements of style. Political education and fueling the patriotic sentiments of the masses were considered more important than esthetic values. Even the formal criteria of criticism such as variety and richness in lexicon and textual structure were demoted to give priority to patriotism and the political message.

A turning point came in the stormy year 1961, which on the one hand marked the political break with the Soviet Union—and thus with Soviet literary models—and on the other hand witnessed the publication of a number of trend-setting volumes, in particular of poetry: *Shekulli im* (My Century) by Ismail Kadare, *Hapat e mija në asfalt* (My Steps on the Pavement) by Dritëro Agolli, and, in the following year, *Shtigje poetike*

(Poetic Paths) by Fatos Arapi. It is ironic to note that whereas Albania had broken with the Soviet Union to save socialism, leading Albanian writers, educated in the Eastern bloc, took advantage of the rupture to part not only with Soviet models but also with socialist realism itself. The attempt made to broaden the literary horizon in search of something new inevitably led to a hefty literary and of course political controversy on 11 July 1961 at a meeting of the Albanian Union of Writers and Artists. The debate, conducted not only by writers but also by leading party and government figures, was published in the literary journal *Drita* (The Light) and received wide public attention in the wake of the Fourth Party Congress of that year. It pitted writers of the older generation—such as Andrea Varfi, Luan Qafëzezi, and Mark Gurakuqi, who voiced their support for fixed poetic standards and the solid traditions of socialist Albanian literature and opposed new elements such as free verse as un-Albanian—against a new generation led by Ismail Kadare, Dritëro Agolli, and Fatos Arapi, who were in favor of a literary renewal and a broadening of the stylistic and thematic horizon. The road to renewal was given the green light by Enver Hoxha himself, who saw that the situation was untenable.

Though it constituted no radical change of course, no political "thaw" in the Soviet sense, 1961 set the stage for a quarter of a century of trial and error, which has now led to much greater sophistication in Albanian literature. Themes and styles diversified, and more attention was paid to formal literary criteria and to the question of individuality.

This first attempt to liberalize Albania's rigid literature and culture somewhat reached its peak in the early seventies in the wake of China's Cultural Revolution, an echo of which had been felt in Albanian letters. Heading the so-called liberal movement were the dramatist Fadil Paçrami (b. 1922), party secretary for ideological affairs in Tiranë, and Todi Lubonja, director of radio and television broadcasting. They encouraged liberal trends and permitted some Western ideas and influence to penetrate Albanian culture (more interesting plays and the broadcasting of Italian pop music and the Beatles on radio). The eleventh song festival on 25 December 1972 served as a pretext in this in actual fact rather harmless movement to keep writers and and artists, and consequently the whole country, in tow. At the Fourth Plenary Session of the Central Committee on 26–28 June 1973 Enver Hoxha took the offensive and presented a report that must now be regarded as a hallmark in the annals of European obscurantism: "Të thellojmë luftën ideologjike kundër shfaqjeve të huaja e qëndrimeve liberale ndaj tyre" (Let Us Strengthen the Ideological Struggle Against Foreign Manifestations and Liberal At-

titudes Toward Them). The liberal movement was swiftly crushed and its two figureheads mercilessly condemned for their sins as deviationists and enemies of the people. Todi Lubonja was released from prison in June 1987, and Fadil Paçrami was finally freed from Kosovë e Madha prison near Elbasan on 17 March 1991, two weeks before Albania's first multiparty elections.

What followed from 1973 to at least 1975 was a virtual reign of terror against Albanian writers and intellectuals, comparable in spirit at least to the Stalinist purges of the 1930s. These years constituted the major setback in the development of Albanian literature and culture. Poets and prose writers began vying with one another in the proclamation of their revolutionary fervor and in their rejection of foreign and liberal influences. Those who were less convincing or whose publications were found to be tainted with liberality were banned to the provinces or landed in prison. The more fortunate simply lost their right to publish. Almost all major authors had a work withdrawn from circulation and "turned into cardboard." Learning foreign languages was effectively banned, and those who already had the misfortune of knowing French or Italian found themselves in dangerously embarrassing positions. Artists and painters such as Maks Velo (b. 1938), Edison Gjergo (b. 1938), Ali Oseku (b. 1944), Edi Hila (b. 1946), and Abdullah Cangoni (c.1920–88) were denounced at the Fourth Plenary Session and sent to prisons and concentration camps such as the notorious copper mines at Spaç for agitation and propaganda—i.e., for having expressed a vague interest in Pablo Picasso, Salvador Dalí, or Max Ernst.

The frenzy had largely subsided by 1978, but no deviation from the ideological course set by the party was dared until the death of Enver Hoxha on 11 April 1985. With the notable exception of Ismail Kadare, no Albanian writers were allowed to express any negative views or even to leave the country. In April 1986 the prose writer Koço Kosta (b. 1944) raised an eyebrow or two when he published the first part of a realistic short story, "Ata të dy e të tjerë" (The Two of Them and the Others), in the Tiranë literary periodical *Nëntori* (November), which contained some indirect criticism of the system. The author disappeared, banned to the tiny village of Greshicë near Fier, and was denied rights to publish for three years "pour encourager les autres." The second part of his short story, scheduled for publication in the May 1986 edition of *Nëntori,* was torn out at the last minute and replaced with something more acceptable. The watchful eye of the party continued to channel all literary creativity in the "right direction" up to December 1990, which finally saw the first tentative steps toward pluralism and democratization in Albania.

Despite the constraints of socialist realism, Stalinist dictatorship, and corruption at all levels of society, Albanian literature made much progress in the seventies and eighties. The best example of creativity and originality in contemporary Albanian letters is Ismail Kadare (b. 1936), still the only Albanian writer to enjoy a broad international reputation. Kadare's talents both as a poet and as a prose writer have lost none of their innovative force over the last three decades, and his courage in attacking literary mediocrity within the system brought about a degree of flexibility in socialist realism which enabled it to survive.

Born and raised in the museum city of Gjirokastër, Kadare studied at the Faculty of History and Philology of the University of Tiranë and subsequently at the Gorky Institute of World Literature in Moscow until 1960, when relations between Albania and the Soviet Union became tense. From the start, Kadare enjoyed a privileged relationship with Enver Hoxha, also from Gjirokastër, which enabled him to pursue literary and personal objectives for which other writers would certainly have been sent into internal exile or to prison. He had begun his literary career in the 1950s as a poet with verse collections such as Ëndërrimet (Dreams; Tiranë, 1957) and Shekulli im (My Century; Tiranë, 1961), which gave proof not only of his youthful inspiration but also of talent and poetic originality in the vein of the Russian poets Yevgeni Yevtushenko (b. 1933) and Andrei Voznesensky (b. 1933). Kadare's poetry was less bombastic than previous verse and gained direct access to the hearts of the readers, who saw in him the spirit of the times and appreciated the diversity of his themes.

Kadare's international reputation up to the present rests entirely upon his prose, in particular his historical novels and short stories. His first prose work, and perhaps still his best known, Gjenerali i ushtrisë së vdekur (Tiranë, 1963; Eng. The General of the Dead Army), dealt with the immediate postwar years as seen through the eyes of an Italian general in the company of a priest on a mission to Albania to exhume and repatriate the remains of his fallen soldiers. The novel was published in a revised edition in 1967, and after the success of the French-language edition (Paris, 1970), it was widely translated (English, German, Italian, Romanian, Spanish, Portuguese, Danish, Swedish, Polish, Czech, Hungarian, Russian, Greek, et cetera) and laid the foundations for Kadare's deserved renown abroad.[1]

Kadare's works are a strict reflection of the vicissitudes of Albanian political life. In the seventies he turned increasingly to historical prose, a safer haven, and became an unrivaled master of the genre. Kështjella (The Castle; Tiranë, 1970), a work reminiscent of Dino Buzzati's novel Il deserto dei Tartari (1940; Eng. The Tar-

tar Steppe), takes us back to the fifteenth century, the age of the Albanian national hero Scanderbeg (1405–68) and in minute, carefully composed detail depicts the siege of a medieval Albanian fortress—symbolic of Albania itself—by the Turks during one of their numerous punitive expeditions to subdue the country. The allusion to the political events of the 1960s seen by many critics was not unintentional. In 1961 Albania had stubbornly broken ties with the mighty Soviet Union, and after the 1968 invasion of Czechoslovakia it felt the very real possibility of a Soviet incursion to bring the country back into the fold. No Albanian reader, at any rate, could be unaware of the analogy construed between the Sublime Porte and the Kremlin.

Next came Kronikë në gur (Tiranë, 1971; Eng. Chronicle in Stone), a forceful novel set in Kadare's native Gjirokastër. Nëntori i një kryeqyteti (November of a Capital City; Tiranë, 1973), set in Tiranë under Italian occupation in 1940, was, like Dasma (The Wedding; Tiranë, 1968), less successful, a reflection of the 1973–75 purge. Dimri i madh (The Great Winter; Tiranë, 1977) constitutes a literary digestion of the traumatic rupture of relations with the Soviet Union. In Ura me tri harqe (The Bridge with Three Arches; Tiranë, 1978) Kadare returned to the mythical origins of Albania's haunted history to bring to life one of the most awesome motifs of Balkan legendry, that of immurement; the work has been interpreted as an Albanian response to the Serbian Nobel Prize winner Ivo Andrić's novel Na Drini ćuprija (1959; Eng. Bridge on the Drina). Kadare is at his best with Balkan themes.[2]

Kadare's subsequent short stories and shorter novels were published in three collections: Emblema e dikurshme (Signs of the Past; Tiranë, 1977), Gjakftohtësia (Cold-Bloodedness; Tiranë, 1980), and Koha e shkrimeve (Epoch of Writings; Tiranë, 1986), the latter two volumes being decidedly nonconformist by Albanian standards. The shorter novels appeared here in the form of short stories for editorial reasons. Among the best prose works contained in these books were: Kush e solli Doruntinën? (Who Brought Doruntine Back?), in which he once again revived his country's legendary past; Sjellësi i fatkeqësisë (The Bearer of Evil Tidings), also known as "The Caravan of Veils"; Viti i mbrapshtë (The Dark Year), set in the turbulent and ominous year of 1914, a cautious allusion to modern Albania; Krushqit janë të ngrirë (The Wedding Procession Turned to Ice), a moving description of the Kosovo tragedy as experienced by a Prishtinë surgeon; the excellent Nëpunësi i pallatit të ëndrrave (The Official of the Palace of Dreams); and Prill i thyer (Eng. Broken April). In contrast to these shorter novels and short stories was the 700-page novel Koncert në fund të dimrit (Concert at the End of Winter; Tiranë, 1988), a monumental review of Albania's dramatic break with post-Mao China in 1978, with overt criticism of the depersonalization of the individual under socialism; it returned to the epic proportions of "The Great Winter," with which it has many parallels.

Ismail Kadare did his utmost to emancipate Albanian literature, over which, in view of his talent and his close personal relationship with Enver Hoxha, he reigned as an absolute monarch in the seventies and eighties. His unexpected departure from Albania and application for political asylum in France in October 1990 caused a good deal of consternation, but he will no doubt return to his homeland when the time is right.

Kadare's overriding position in contemporary Albanian literature, compounded by his international reputation, has cast a shadow over all other contemporary Albanian writers. One of these who has had a far from negligible influence on the course of contemporary literature is Dritëro Agolli (b. 1931), head of the Albanian Union of Writers and Artists since the purge of Paçrami and Lubonja in 1973. Like Kadare, he made his name originally as a poet before turning to prose and is widely admired in both genres. His first verse collections, *Në udhë dola* (I Went Out on the Street; Tiranë, 1958), *Hapat e mija në asfalt* (My Steps on the Pavement; Tiranë, 1961), and *Shtigje malesh dhe trotuare* (Mountain Paths and Sidewalks; Tiranë, 1965), introduced him to the reading public as a sincere lyric poet of the soil and evinced masterful verse technique. One senses the influence of his training in the Soviet Union in this early verse, the spirit of Eduard Bagritsky (1895–1934) and Dmitri Kedrin (1907–45) in particular. An attachment to his roots came to form the basis of Agolli's poetic credo, especially in *Devoll, Devoll* (Tiranë, 1964), which begins as follows:

Po, Devoll,
    i tillë qenkam unë,
Paskam marrë baltën tënde arave,
Në një trastë leshi
    ndënë gunë,

Për t'ia sjellë
    Lidhjës së Shkrimtarëve.

(Yes, Devoll,
    I'm one of them,
I gathered your mud from the fields
in a woollen sack
    under my coat,
to carry it
    to the Writers Union.)

With the volume *Baballarët* (The Fathers; Tiranë, 1969) Agolli's verse, however, lost much of its sponta-

neity and tilted toward "official" poetry in the service of ideology. A prime example of such party panegyrics enjoying wide publicity and official acclamation was *Nënë Shqipëri* (Mother Albania; Tiranë, 1974). By the time he became a member of the Central Committee and head of the Writers Union, Agolli's talent as a poet was well on the decline.

Like Kadare, Agolli turned increasingly to prose in the seventies. His strength lies in the short story rather than in the novel, although an exception can be made for his satiric novel *Shkëlqimi dhe rënia e shokut Zylo* (The Splendor and Fall of Comrade Zylo; Tiranë, 1973), now available in a French translation (Paris, 1990). Zylo is the epitome of the bureaucrat in a socialist society who uses his position to wield influence and to save his own skin. With subtle wit and often folksy humor, Agolli traces the day-to-day activities of Comrade Zylo and his companion Demka in all their absurdity. An earlier collection of his short stories, *Zhurma e ererave të dikurshme* (The Noise of Winds of the Past; Tiranë, 1964), had the distinction of being banned and "turned into cardboard."

Among other major contemporary prose writers are the abovementioned Petro Marko from Dhërmi on the Himaran coast, who paved the road to modernity before Kadare and is now being rediscovered; the historical novelist Sabri Godo (b. 1924) from Delvinë; the short-story writer Naum Prifti (b. 1932) from Kolonjë; the novelist Dhimitër Xhuvani (b. 1934), born in Pogradec on Lake Ohrid; Skënder Drini (b. 1935) from Korçë, much influenced in style by Kadare; Teodor Laço (b. 1936);[3] Kiço Blushi (b. 1943); the abovementioned Koço Kosta (b. 1944) from the Lunxhëria region; Nasi Lera (b. 1944) from the Korçë region, noted as an excellent stylist; Zija Çela (b. 1946); Valter File (b. 1954) from Ersekë; the short-story writer and poet Preç Zogaj (b. 1956); Teodor Keko; and the short-story writer Elena Kadare (b. 1943) and the novelist Diana Çuli (b. 1951), no doubt the best among the women prose writers.

The gradual refinement of style and the diversification of themes in Albanian prose of the seventies and eighties have been paralleled in modern poetry too. The esthetic appeal of poetic language, the relative freedom of expression offered by verse, and the opportunity to pursue one's fantasies in a society which has been seemingly obsessed with industrial output, manufacturing statistics, and the construction of dams continue to attract a good many Albanian writers to poetry rather than to prose.

The best known of the contemporary poets of Albanian to have solved the dilemma of the poet with a fixed mission is Fatos Arapi (b. 1930) from the port city of Vlorë, author of philosophical verse, love lyrics, and poignant elegies on death. His first two collections, *Shtigje poetike* (Poetic Paths; Tiranë, 1962) and *Poema dhe vjersha* (Poems and Verse; Tiranë, 1966), evinced a more modern verse form than that of his contemporaries. A child of the Ionian coast, Arapi has never lost his fascination with the sparkling waters of the sea, the tang of the salt air, and the intensity of Mediterranean light, all of which flood his verse. Indeed, beyond the echoing pathos of much of his revolutionary verse production on industrial and political themes in later volumes, his true poetic vocation can be seen in the creation of an equilibrium between the harmony of the waves and the rhythmic impulses of his being. Criticized in the 1973 purge for the volume *Më jepni një emër* (Give Me a Name; Tiranë, 1973), which was "turned into cardboard" too, he withdrew and fell silent as the poet he is until 1989.

Other leading poets are: Koçi Petriti (b. 1941) from Korçë; Kosovo-born Adem Istrefi (b. 1942), whose more traditional poetry is imbued with the epic traditions of Kosovo oral verse; Ndoc Gjetja (b. 1944), a transparent lyric poet from Lezhë; Ndoc Papleka (b. 1945) from Tropojë in the north; the passionate Xhevahir Spahiu (b. 1945) from Skrapar, the enfant terrible of Albanian letters; Natasha Lako (b. 1948) of Korçë; Bardhyl Londo (b. 1948) from Lipë near Përmet; the archeologist Moikom Zeqo (b. 1949) of Durrës, whose highly intellectual and metaphorical verse has been inspired in good part by the lost grandeur of his ancient Dyrrachium; Preç Zogaj (b. 1956); and the gifted Rudolf Marku (b. 1950) from Lezhë, whose recent collection *Udhëtim për në vendin e gjërave që njohim* (Voyage to the Place of Things We Know; Tiranë, 1989) was well received. Of the younger poets who have made a promising start, mention may be made of Mimoza Ahmeti (b. 1963) from Krujë and of Erind Pajo (b. 1972) and Ervin Hatibi (b. 1974), both of Tiranë.[4]

Still, the literature of Albania itself is only half the story of Albanian literature. In Yugoslavia, Albanian is spoken by at least two million people (as opposed to three million in Albania), the language now being second there only to Serbo-Croatian. The center of the Albanian population is the tormented Autonomous Socialist Region of Kosovo (Alb. *Kosova*), where the Albanians with their extremely high birthrate now make up over 90 percent of the population. Prishtinë, the capital of Kosovo, has up to the present been able to vie with Tiranë in almost every way as a focal point for Albanian literary and cultural activity and as a publishing center for Albanian literature. The future of Albanian culture in Yugoslavia is, however, uncertain.

The Albanian literature of Kosovo was late to develop. It was the founding in 1949 of the literary periodical *Jeta e Re* (New Life) that gave voice to the young generation of Albanian writers in Yugoslavia and served as an initial forum for literary publication. Although some monographs were published in the fifties, it was not until the midsixties that Albanian and Kosovo Albanian literature began to appear in print in Yugoslavia on a significant scale. The extreme political divergence between Yugoslavia and Albania that erupted in 1948 made it evident to Kosovo Albanians from the start that they could not look to Tiranë for more than moral support in culture and education. The preservation and fostering of Albanian culture in Yugoslavia under often hostile conditions was of necessity to be the concern of Yugoslav Albanians themselves. The formidable problems posed by widespread illiteracy and dire poverty among the Albanians in Kosovo, as in Albania, were compounded substantially by an unwillingness on the part of the Serbian authorities in Belgrade for many years to give the Albanians access to education and cultural facilities in their own language. Full cultural autonomy was first achieved after much delay under the constitution of 1974, though only in Kosovo itself. In 1989–90, however, Kosovo de facto lost its limited autonomy and freedom and was placed under direct Serbian military occupation. Immediately after the dissolution of the Kosovo parliament in the summer of 1990 the only Albanian-language daily newspaper was banned, as was all Albanian radio and television broadcasting in Kosovo. The situation has been particularly dire for Albanian writers and intellectuals there. They constitute the greatest threat to Serbian rule over the region under the populist leader Slobodan Milošević, who has shown nothing but contempt for the demands of equality and human rights for the Albanian minority.

Desiring to overcome the cultural isolation from which it suffers and which has increased dramatically since the repression of the 1981 and 1989 uprisings, the present generation of young Kosovo writers is eager to lap up foreign influence and currents of contemporary European thought that have been rejected offhand in Tiranë. At the same time, this much more eclectic literature has lost surprisingly little of its traditional Albanian flavor. Its strength and dynamism are a direct result of the need perceived by Kosovo Albanians to defend their cultural values in a region plagued by ethnic conflict, political turmoil, and economic collapse. Despite such overwhelming problems, Kosovo Albanians have always enjoyed and taken full advantage of intellectual freedom and liberty of expression at the cultural level, which has enabled Albanian culture in Kosovo to develop much more rapidly and freely over the last two decades than in Albania itself.

Among the classic prose writers of the first generation were the humorist Sitki Imami (1912–83) from Gjakovë (Djakovica); Hivzi Sulejmani (1912–75) from Mitrovicë, who helped bring early Kosovo literature out of its regional focus and provinciality; Ramiz Kelmendi (b. 1930) from Pejë (Peć); and the writer and dissident Adem Demaçi (b. 1936) of Prishtinë, finally released in April 1990 after twenty-eight years in Serbian prison camps.[5]

One of the leading contemporary prose writers of Kosovo is Rexhep Qosja (b. 1936), who is not only one of the most eminent and prolific literary critics in the Balkans, an academician, and the former director of the Albanological Institute in Prishtinë, but also the editor of anthologies and author of numerous scholarly monographs, including a three-volume history of Albanian literature of the romantic period. Qosja has published one of the most widely admired and translated novels of recent years, *Vdekja më vjen prej syve të tillë* (Death Comes from Such Eyes; Prishtinë, 1974). It is a work of original narrative technique and composition, "thirteen tales which might constitute a novel." The protagonist Xhezairi i Gjikës is a professional writer caught up in a frightening web of political intrigue, secret police, interrogation, and torture, a world evincing definite yet subtly couched political allusions to the very real desperation felt by present-day Albanian intellectuals in Kosovo.

Among other prose writers of talent are the hermetic Anton Pashku (b. 1938); Nazmi Rrahmani (b. 1941), a prolific and popular novelist of Kosovo village life; Teki Dërvishi (b. 1943) of Gjakovë, who, like Pashku, has penetrated the psyche of modern man with his novels and short stories; Mehmet Kraja (b. 1952) of Kështenjë in the coastal Kraja region of Montenegro; Musa Ramadani (b. 1944) from Gjilan; the humorist Arif Demolli (b. 1949), who, since his imprisonment for a couple of years after the 1981 uprising, has been able to publish little of his prose on the realities of Kosovan life; Zejnullah Rrahmani (b. 1952) from Ballovc near Podujevë, whose novel *Sheshi i Unazës* (Ring Square; Prishtinë, 1978) centers on the Kosovan obsession with liberty, on the death and resurrection of a city-state; and Jusuf Buxhovi (b. 1946) of Pejë, whose novel *Shënimet e Gjon Nikollë Kazazit* (The Notes of Gjon Nikollë Kazazi; Prishtinë, 1982) evokes the figure of the eighteenth-century Gjakovan scholar who discovered the only surviving copy of the first Albanian book, Buzuku's *Meshari* (1555). The principal motif of Buxhovi's work, however, is not the life of Kazazi but the dramatic spread of the plague in eighteenth-century Gjakovë, an account not unsimilar to Albert Camus's in *La peste* (1947; Eng. *The Plague*).

Poetry has always been the vanguard of literature in Kosovo and has enjoyed more popularity among writers and the reading public there than prose. The writer widely considered to be the father of modern Albanian poetry in Yugoslavia, Esad Mekuli (b. 1916), was born not in Kosovo itself but in the legendary Montenegrin village of Plava on the Albanian border, where national traditions are still held high. Mekuli, founder of the abovementioned literary periodical *Jeta e Re*, whose editor-in-chief he remained until 1971, is a committed poet of social awareness whose outrage at social injustice, violence, genocide, and suffering mirrors that of the prerevolutionary verse of Migjeni (1911–38) of Shkodër. Among the other "classics" of modern verse in Kosovo are: the pensive Enver Gjerqeku (b. 1928) of Gjakovë; Din Mehmeti (b. 1932); the tender lyric poet Adem Gajtani (1935–82); Fahredin Gunga (b. 1936) of Mitrovicë; Azem Shkreli (b. 1938), from the Rugova mountains near Pejë, who is head of Kosovo Film Studios in Prishtinë; Rrahman Dedaj (b. 1939) of Podujevë; the versatile Ali Podrimja (b. 1942) of Gjakovë, probably the best Albanian poet of all, if one were to venture a qualitative classification; Eqrem Basha (b. 1948) from Dibër; and the critics Sabri Hamiti (b. 1950) and Agim Vinca (b. 1947), the latter from Veleshtë near Struga in Macedonia, a writer whose popular verse is firmly anchored in the soil of his place of birth.

In Yugoslavia, where the situation is now eminently precarious for the very survival of Albanian culture, writers and intellectuals have taken the lead, as elsewhere in Eastern Europe. The literary critic Ibrahim Rugova (b. 1945) now heads the Kosovan League for Democracy and Human Rights, the fledgling Kosovan alternative to the Serbian police state, and Rexhep Qosja has nolens volens become the father figure and the spokesperson of the nation's psyche. Over the past ten years since the 1981 uprising, Albanian writers and intellectuals in Yugoslavia have been intimidated, humiliated, physically mishandled, and imprisoned, with or without trial, on an almost systematic basis. Should multiparty elections and a democratic government ever come to Kosovo—which at present seems doubtful—these two writers could once again evince the predominance of literary and cultural activity in the process of democratization and renewal in Eastern Europe.

In Albania itself, which has often been referred to by the press as the "last bastion of Stalinism," political change in 1990 was as dramatic as it had been in the other countries of Eastern Europe the year before. December 1990 saw the introduction of political pluralism and the first tentative steps toward democracy after decades of "dictatorship of the proletariat" and isolation.

Has there ever been dissent in modern Albanian literature? Yes and no. In a "pro memoria" addressed to Enver Hoxha, the writer Kasëm Trebeshina (b. 1926) warned the Albanian leader as early as 5 October 1953 that his cultural policies were leading the nation down the road to disaster. After seventeen years in prison (a comparatively light sentence, as he notes) and twenty years of silence, Trebeshina has now resurfaced with a handful of other writers and artists—among whom are Lazër Radi (b. 1916), Kapllan Resuli (b.1935), Frederik Reshpja, Fatos Lubonja (b. 1951), Visar Zhiti (b.1953), and Bashkim Shehu (b. 1955)—to see his prediction come true. Dissent there was: rare acts of self-destruction and unspoken thoughts in the hidden recesses of the minds of every intellectual. But opposition? No. In an interview with the Voice of America in February 1991, Dritëro Agolli stated that all Albanian writers were conformists. In a sense he is right, and understandably so in view of the level of political control over the actions and very thoughts of all intellectuals, a control unparalleled in Europe and perhaps anywhere on earth. Every volume of poetry went through the hands of ten to fifteen politically vigilant reviewers before publication, every drama at least thirty (which helps explain the absence of good Albanian theater). Never has there been an Albanian *samizdat* or even a publishing house in exile. Ties with the outside world were reduced by the party to an absolute minimum, and no Albanian writers, with the exception of Ismail Kadare, were ever permitted to go abroad. For forty-five years Albania was a different planet, cut off from the world we know. Splendid isolation? No! There is now so much to catch up on and many uncertainties about what the future holds. But one thing can be said for sure: the most interesting period in the history of Albanian literature has just begun.

Robert Elsie, Spring 1991

[1] On Kadare, see Janet Byron, "Albanian Folklore and History in the Fiction of Ismail Kadare: A Review of Two French Translations," *WLT* 58:1 (Winter 1984), pp. 40–42.

[2] Several of these individual works by Kadare have been reviewed in this journal: *Chronicle in Stone* in *WLT* 61:4 (Autumn 1987), p. 669; *Der große Winter* in *WLT* 62:3 (Summer 1988), p. 493; *Koha e shkrimeve* in *WLT* 61:4 (Autumn 1987), p. 666; *Qui a ramené Doruntine?* in *WLT* 61:2 (Spring 1987), p. 331; *Koncert në fund të dimrit* in *WLT* 63:2 (Spring 1989), p. 347; *Eschyle ou l'éternel perdant* in *WLT* 63:3 (Summer 1989), p. 519; and *Broken April* in this issue, p. 343.

[3] On Teodor Laço, see *WLT* 63:1 (Winter 1989), p. 147.

[4] On Bardhyl Londo and Mimoza Ahmeti, see *WLT* 64:1 (Winter 1990), p. 174. On Natasha Lako, see this issue, p. 344.

[5] On Adam Demaçi, see *WLT* 65:1 (Winter 1991), p. 165.

[6] Several of these Kosovo poets and critics have been reviewed in this journal: Din Mehmeti in *WLT* 63:2 (Spring 1989), p.

348; Azem Shkreli in *WLT* 63:1 (Winter 1989), p. 148; Rrahman Dedaj in *WLT* 64:2 (Spring 1990), p. 342; Ali Podrimja in *WLT* 62:4 (Autumn 1988), p. 708; Sabri Hamiti in *WLT* 64:3 (Summer 1990), p. 508; and Agim Vinca in this issue, p. 345.

BULGARIA

1981 Nobel Laureate Elias Canetti: A Writer Apart

At first glance, if it was at the *New York Times,* the news that the 1981 Nobel Prize in Literature was awarded to Elias Canetti would seem to belie Ivar Ivask's observation that, in vying for recognition, "major writers from major languages have more support than major authors from minor literatures" (*WLT* 55:2, p. 198). The *Times's* front-page article bore the heading "Bulgarian Wins the Nobel Prize for Literature," and the continuation was captioned "Bulgarian Writer Wins Nobel Prize" (16 October 1981). The content of the article made evident, however, that Canetti belongs not in the second but in the first category. He is a major German-language writer and, one must insist, no more a Bulgarian writer than I. B. Singer, the 1978 laureate (see *WLT* 53:2, pp. 197–201), is a Polish writer, or Czesław Miłosz, last year's prize recipient (see *WLT* 52:3, pp. 357–425 and 55:1, pp. 5–6), a Lithuanian writer—however great the debt of these authors to their birthlands may be.

To be sure, Elias Canetti was born in Bulgaria (in 1905), but he did not acquire its language as his mother tongue. Rather, his first language was Ladino, the Old Spanish of the Sephardic Jews, and whatever Bulgarian he had learned he soon lost when he was taken to England as a child of six. Moreover, while his mother stemmed from one of the country's oldest Sephardic families, his paternal grandparents had moved to Bulgaria from Adrianople, and like many of the Sephardim, they retained Turkish citizenship. Canetti too was a Turkish subject.[1] Nevertheless, the problem of where he belongs as a writer can be resolved simply if it is conceded that someone who writes in German is a German author. Yet the question of this author's personal identity, of his "nationality," which is not German, cannot be dismissed. It touches upon the heart of his work and the fascination he has exercised on an international audience that has grown ever larger through the years. This identity is inseparably linked with a life history that, if it is to be properly understood, must be traced back almost five centuries to Inquisitional Spain.

The surname Canetti is, of course, neither Slavic nor Germanic. It is an Italianized form of the place-name Canete and derives from the city of the family's origins between Cuenca and Valencia. Before the mass emigration of Bulgarian Jews to Israel after World War II—to its lasting honor, Bulgaria had saved them from annihilation—such names as Canetti, Arditti (the maiden name of the laureate's mother), Morenzi or Almosino were hardly uncommon in the larger towns of the Kingdom. They could, in fact, be encountered throughout the Balkans and still farther reaches of the Turkish domain to which thousands of Spanish Jews had fled from the terror of the Inquisition, among them the writer's own forebears. But Canetti was fated to become a *German* writer, and in the German-speaking countries, where he spent his most formative years, such names are rare. They catch both the eye and the ear and mark their owner as an outsider, all the more when they are identified, as the name Canetti is today, with an art so profoundly expressive of a nation's history and character as its literature.

The conjecture may be warranted that the rarity of the name itself and exotic appeal such rarity creates inspired the fairly consistent cover and dust-jacket designs of Canetti's books. Particularly the American editions, but also the German originals, forcefully display the author's surname, alone, in imposingly bold type across the front and back, so that it greatly overshadows the title. But despite its prominence, the name does not jump out to greet the viewer. It stands commandingly on its threshold, as it were, declaring the presence of a writer who challenges more than he invites the reader to venture acquaintance with him. Whoever takes up this challenge discovers an author who has secured for himself an elevated and very distinct place in German letters on terms of his own. He requires of the reader a high degree of concentration; he demands too the readiness to relinquish what is familiar and assuring and to follow him, the writer, on paths that may lead into realms of absurdity and madness. The reader must be willing to persist with him in his unconventional pursuit of themes and interests that resist traditional modes of portrayal: the hateful tyranny of death over human existence, the dynamics and interplay of crowds and power, the world of myth and magic, the essence and authority of literary genius.

In citing Canetti's "original and most vigorously profiled personality," the Swedish Academy confirmed what has become a universally accepted view. Also, the interviews that have appeared during the past two decades attest to these same qualities, consistently revealing an artist-thinker of striking originality and commanding presence. Even so individual and formidable a discussion partner as Theodor Adorno pales and seems disadvantaged in conversation with him.[2] Indeed, there appears to exist no discrepancy between the man and the writer; Canetti's personal presence and the presence projected in his books are equally intense and absorbing. The acquaintance with the oeuvre would genuinely seem to represent a full and authentic acquaintance with the author's personality itself. Thus the evident displeasure with which the laureate declined to grant interviews after the award was publicized—"Whoever wants to know something should read my books"[3]—reflected a readily experienced truth and can find justification on grounds that lie beyond the sheer desire for privacy.

■ ■ ■

Canetti's fascination as an artist-intellectual is starkly revealed in the two major works that established his literary eminence—which until today remains the eminence of the solitary outsider; they are the novel *Die Blendung* (translated as *Auto-da-Fé*), first published in 1935, and the encyclopedic study *Masse und Macht* (*Crowds and Power*), on which he labored for twenty years before it finally appeared in 1960. The extraordinary claim he made for the latter work, namely that in it he had "succeeded in grabbing this century by the throat," can be applied to the novel also—if *Auto-da-Fé* is viewed as an artistic-symbolic portrayal of the unspoken but clearly underlying thesis of *Crowds and Power:* that the two great calamities of the twentieth century, Hitlerism and Stalinism, arose from the dialectical interaction of human masses, which tyrants can create and exploit, and the problem of power and paranoia. The accomplishment of the novel lies in Canetti's narrative transformation of this thesis, which he was to elaborate in *Crowds and Power* only years later. In the story of the private scholar Peter Kien he portrayed an intellectual so estranged from reality—the "Head Without a World"—and so hostile to it that he could end only in self-destruction. The flames that engulf the "greatest Sinologist of his time" amid the gigantic mass of his books—the novel teems with symbolic masses—forebode the ruin that was soon to descend on Canetti's Europe.

Auto-da-Fé has gained its author a respected place within the cosmopolitan Central European narrative tradition that is represented by the Austrian novelists Kafka, Musil and Broch, with whom he is most often associated. It has been recognized also as a precursor of trends that were to culminate only twenty years later in the literature of the absurd. It has been described as an "experimental novel without stylistic experiments," and as such it demonstrates Canetti's originality in the most telling way. He discussed the book's narrative strategy in the following manner:

One day, the thought came to me that the world should not be depicted as in earlier novels, from one writer's standpoint, as it were; the world had *crumbled,* and only if one had the courage to show it in its crumbled state could one possibly offer an authentic conception of it. However, this did not mean that one had to tackle a chaotic book, in which nothing was comprehensible anymore; on the contrary, a writer had to invent extreme individuals with the most rigorous consistency, like the individuals the world consisted of, and he had to place these extreme individuals next to one another in their separateness.[4]

The total elimination of "one writer's standpoint" contributes more than any other narrative device to the novel's stunning effect. Canetti succeeded fully in neutralizing his narrator: he has been given no authoritative and distinguishing voice, but rather he becomes the ever-changing echo of the sundry voices that inhabit the story; he accompanies its "extreme individuals" on a compulsive course through their micro-cosmic world as though they, and their world, were whole and not "crumbled." For the narrator, unlike the author, Kien and his tormentors are seemingly unexceptional; his tone betrays no judgment, and he offers no guidance. The reader is directly faced with the madness of this world—which is conjured up, moreover, in a language that is wholly lucid and concrete—and left to fend for himself in its threatening midst. Such abandonment is unaccustomed and very probably helps to account for the frequently heard criticisms that the novel is "too difficult" (or even incomprehensible), that reading it is disturbing or eerie. *Auto-da-Fé* surely is difficult, but its essential difficulties are not formal and stylistic ones. Rather, they are difficulties that arise from the novel's inherent demand that the reader consciously confront as real, and reject, the madness it portrays and for which it offers no antidote.

The 1947 American edition of *Auto-da-Fé* was significantly titled *The Tower of Babel,* thus reflecting the narrative's chaotic world of extreme individuals in the unbridgeable separateness that Canetti embodied in the peculiarities of their speech. Still other titles, these of his own choosing, underscore the prime function in his writing of individualized speech, of what he has termed the "acoustic citation." A collection of grotesque satirical character sketches is called *Der Ohrenzeuge* (1974; translated as *Earwitness,* 1979); in the portrait devoted to the title character, the "Earwitness" himself, the reader learns that "his ear is better and more faithful than any gadget, nothing is erased, nothing is blocked, . . . he accurately registers even things he does not understand and delivers them unaltered if people wish him to do so." The first volume of Canetti's autobiography is entitled *Die gerettete Zunge* (1977; *The Tongue Set Free,* 1979), and the second *Die Fackel im Ohr* (1980), literally "The Torch in the Ear." This latter title—which the planned American translation will reportedly not bear—refers to the journal *Die Fackel* (The Torch), which the Viennese satirist and polemicist Karl Kraus edited and wrote from 1899 until his death in 1936. For some five years, in Vienna, Kraus exercised a spiritual and intellectual dictatorship over Canetti, who found himself merged into the "hunting pack" that he perceived in the enthralled audiences at Kraus's celebrated readings. In order to regain the freedom of his own judgments, Canetti was compelled to liberate himself from this powerful hold; but he confessed lasting gratitude to Kraus for the gift of *hearing* that he had received from him: "Since hearing him, it has not been possible for me not to do my own hearing."[5]

The start of work on *Auto-da-Fé* coincided with Canetti's self-liberation from the oppressive sway of Karl Kraus and suggests that Kraus's inspiration had been internally set free and could now become productive. The kinship of Canetti's novel with Kraus's gigantic drama of World War I, *Die letzten Tage der Menschheit* (*The Last Days of Mankind;* 1919), is evident. It is not a kinship that arises from imitation but rather a kinship of artistic and ethical persuasion. In countless variants of human speech, captured in their subtlest pitches and shadings, Kraus had brought to life and condemned the same "crumbled" world that Canetti now undertook to evoke in *Auto-da-Fé*—by means of what he called the "acoustic mask." For Canetti, it is through speech that people assume shape and form, are clearly delineated from every angle, are differentiated one from another. "A person's speech-shape," he explained, "the stable character of his speech, this language that arose with him, that he alone possesses, that will pass with him, is what I call his acoustic mask."[6] Canetti has left no doubt that his sensitivity for this phenomenon was honed by Karl Kraus. But he must have been uncommonly receptive to the nuances of individual speech from his earliest years on.

Not only was his mother tongue, Ladino, not the language of his birthplace, it was also not the sole language of his home. To each other his parents spoke German, which he was unable to comprehend. What is better suited to stir curiosity and awaken the desire for initiation and possession than the secrets parents withhold from their children! Indeed, Canetti's resentment toward his mother for such exclusion vanished only when she began teaching him German in his ninth year. From his grandfather, moreover, he heard songs in Turkish, and from the peasant girls who lived in his home as serving women he heard fairy tales in Bulgarian (which he later mysteriously retained only in German).

And to complicate these circumstances further, there were the Hebrew prayers, readings and songs on holidays, in which the boy participated with a feeling of importance though without understanding the ancient language. Upon this multilingual beginning followed two years in England, from 1911 to 1913, when the young Canetti started school and read his first books, in English. From 1913 until he completed the gymnasium eleven years later, he changed countries three times and lived successively in Vienna, Zürich and Frankfurt—each city with its own peculiarities of German idiom. Against this background it is no wonder that Canetti became an "earwitness," a master of the "acoustic citation," and that, in addition, he acquired the cosmopolitan sensitivities that enabled the encompassing vision not only of *Auto-da-Fé* but also of his second major work, *Crowds and Power.*

The title of this massive study—which is as strikingly original as *Auto-da-Fé* and likewise reveals Canetti as a writer apart—announces its theme with self-assured succinctness. But its method and scope cannot be characterized without the help of an ungainly procession of academically robed adjectives such as: *anthropological, ethnological, sociological, philosophical, psychological.* In a spectacular feat of intellectual synthesis Canetti joined the disciplines to which they apply and produced an absolutely novel inquiry into the interdynamics of masses and power. Not only did he accomplish this in a language that is clear and concrete to the same degree that the subjects of his investigation are dark and elusive, but he did it also in declared independence of the scientific-theoretical schools that have shaped our contemporary view of these subjects. To both the praise, if not to say amazement, and the skepticism of Canetti's commentators, *Crowds and Power* refers nowhere to either Sigmund Freud or Karl Marx, nor does it show any debt to them. Canetti consciously excluded them from his reflections, in part because of critical doubts and a goodly measure of personal rejection, but more significantly because he was determined to start anew, as it were, to go at his task, as he stressed, in a "completely naïve" way, to develop his own terminology and to attain his own results. The richness and complexity of his study frustrate the attempt to define these results within a common conceptual framework or to distill some single theory from them.

Praise for *Crowds and Power,* which has been acclaimed as a revolutionary work, has usually centered on the author's intellectual breadth, imagination and originality rather than on the practical or theoretical value of his findings. He had set out to seize his century by the throat, but the century, as a historical and political reality, is absent from his book. Its undeniable her-

metic quality has elicited the criticism that *Crowds and Power* is "lost," "unscientific," "idiosyncratic." Such criticism, which has sometimes amounted to rejection, must be seen as a consequence of the book's most-cited characteristic, its originality. Whether this work will ultimately be regarded as a grand curiosity or accepted as a valid contribution to the analysis of mass behavior and the politics of tyranny, and thus to human survival, will be decided by the kinds of thought and ideas it proves itself able to stimulate. Will Canetti's insights be incorporated into the systems of knowledge that help to determine social and political planning? Can they be employed to help reconcile the destructive global rivalries between West and East and, increasingly, North and South? Canetti himself demonstrated in his essay "Hitler, According to Speer" that such questions need not be academic, that they possess genuine content, and that *Crowds and Power,* for all its seeming exoticism, may bear directly on the most crucial problems of contemporary existence.[7]

■ ■ ■

The awarding of the Nobel Prize to Canetti produced news reports that showed considerable uncertainty or, in some instances, plain helplessness. Inherent in much of the commentary was the not unfamiliar question on this annual occasion: Who *is* he? Or perhaps, Who's *he!* Yet Canetti is not new to the American literary scene. In fact, he had achieved recognition in America—and even more in England—before he gained prominence in Germany. Both *Auto-da-Fé* and *Crowds and Power* were acknowledged early as remarkable works by an unusually gifted author. There were three successive printings of *Auto-da-Fé* in England in 1946–47 and four more between 1962 and 1973; during the years 1947–79 there were four printings in America. *Crowds and Power* first appeared in both countries in 1962, and in America it has been issued three times since. Starting in 1978, Seabury Press in New York has published another five of Canetti's works in translation. Nonetheless, it is fair to say that since the early 1960s his repute has grown most steadily and his stature has been acknowledged most firmly in Germany—although he did not reach a popular audience there until *Die gerettete Zunge* appeared in 1977.

Canetti himself will probably not be impressed by his new prominence; fame has never been his goal. But now that it has come, the intriguing question arises of what country, or countries, will want to share it with him; and along with this question there arises once again that of his identity. The answer given at the outset still holds: As a writer in German, Canetti is—like Kafka, the German-speaking Jew from Czech Prague whom he esteems—a German writer. But again like Kafka, he is one who evades neat categorization. The term "writer in exile" has often been applied to him, but its validity is not apparent. From what homeland was Canetti exiled? Given his personal history, the answer that he had found his sole homeland in the German language is more than just metaphorical. Although he was forced to flee from Austria—where he had lived from 1924 to 1938—when it was joined to the Greater Germany of the Third Reich, he did not permit himself to be banished from the realm of the German language. Perhaps the most moving statement he has made in this context is the following from the year 1944:

> The language of my intellect will remain German—because I am Jewish. Whatever remains of the land which has been laid waste in every way—I wish to preserve it in me as a Jew. *Their* destiny too is mine; but I bring along a universal human legacy. I want to give back to their language what I owe it. I want to contribute to their having something that others can be grateful for.[8]

This is not the declaration of a writer in exile, but of one for whom language and vocation together have created an identity that lies beyond any geographical or national-political boundaries. Yet even within the cultural sphere of the German language and its literature, it is the identity of a writer who comprehends himself as an outsider. Both in defiance and gratitude he wishes to return to *their* language what he owes it.

Even when Canetti himself speaks of "the two great expulsions" in his past, that of his forebears from Spain and that of the Jews from Nazi Germany, the one appears to be as close to him and as vivid as the other; he is not evoking an exile that can be translated into the terms of literary history and national identities. Rather, he is placing himself within a tradition that permits identifications of mythical dimension. At the end of an insightful discussion with the novelist Horst Bienek, Canetti said:

> Sometimes I think myself to be a Spanish poet in the German language. When I read the old Spaniards, for example *Celestina* or Quevedo's *Sueños*, I believe that I myself am speaking in them. No one knows who he really is. It gives me strength to know at least this much.[9]

The persuasion that no one has full knowledge of his identity does not imply a diminution but rather an enrichment of the self—which for Canetti is the product of millennia of human experience. He intends it quite literally when he claims affinity with the old Spanish poets. He, the German writer, is the offspring of untold ancestors who emerged from the obscurity of history in medieval Spain and who remain present in his personality five centuries later. Their becoming and being are an inseparable part of his own; their cultural experience is alive in him.

Fundamental to this belief and indeed to Canetti's entire thought is the concept of transformation, a phenomenon in which he sees the origins of mankind as well as the essence of human existence. Nowhere does the boldness of this concept, as he has interpreted it, become so apparent as in his assertions that "man is the sum of all the animals into which he transformed himself in the course of his history."[10] But less drastically, Canetti has applied it also to his view of work and profession in the life of each individual, stating his conviction that "the individual, and really every individual, possesses a totality of natural bents and that in the last analysis many of these bents derive from the rich store of old transformations. No one is really a unity and should live as a unity."[11] It is this belief in the multiple character of the self that underlies Canetti's often-cited opposition to the "division of labor" and helps to explain one of the most salient characteristics of his writing: its unusual range and diversity.

At seventy-six, Canetti has hardly concluded his oeuvre. A sequel to *Crowds and Power*—whose tentative appearance he has announced more than once—has been awaiting its definitive form for at least a decade. During the same period he has been cautiously withholding from publication several works of fiction. They are said to include two more novels and some plays, all in advanced stages of completion. The two volumes of his autobiography, which appeared within three years of each other, in 1977 and 1980, extend only to 1931; thus a third volume would seem likely, perhaps in the near future. With a writer so thoroughly distinctive as Canetti, all predictions are precarious but for one: that from his solitary place, outside the traditional literary categories, he will continue to fascinate a steadily growing readership with works of high originality and challenging symbolic vision.

Sidney Rosenfeld, Winter 1982

▪ ELIAS CANETTI'S WORKS IN ENGLISH

Auto-da-Fé. Joachim Neugroschel, tr. New York, Seabury, 1979.

The Conscience of Words. Joachim Neugroschel, tr. New York, Seabury, 1979.

Crowds and Power. Carol Stewart, tr. New York, Seabury, 1978.

Earwitness: Fifty Characters. Joachim Neugroschel, tr. New York, Seabury, 1979.

The Human Province. Joachim Neugroschel, tr. New York, Seabury, 1978.

Kafka's Other Trial. Christopher Middleton, tr. New York, Schocken, 1974.

The Tongue Set Free: Remembrance of a European Childhood. Joachim Neugroschel, tr. New York, Seabury, 1980.

The Voices of Marrakesh: A Record of a Visit. J. A. Underwood, tr. New York, Seabury, 1978.

[1] See Elias Canetti, *The Tongue Set Free*, p. 104. Unless otherwise noted, all references will be to works by Canetti currently available in English and listed in the bibliography below. Translations from works in German are my own.

[2] See "Gespräch mit Theodor W. Adorno" in Elias Canetti, *Die geteilte Zukunft*, Munich, Hanser, 1972, pp. 66–92.

[3] *The New York Times,* 18 October 1981.

[4] Elias Canetti, "The First Book," in his *The Conscience of Words,* p. 210.

[5] Elias Canetti, "Karl Kraus: The School of Resistance," in his *The Conscience of Words,* p. 34.

[6] Quoted in Peter Laemmle, "Macht und Ohnmacht des Ohrenzeugen," *Canetti lesen: Erfahrungen mit seinem Büchern,* H. G. Göpfert, ed., Munich, Hanser, 1975, pp. 54–55.

[7] See Canetti's "Hitler, According to Speer," in his *The Conscience of Words,* pp. 145–52. For a stimulating discussion of the concrete significance of *Crowds and Power* see Dagmar Barnouw's essay "Elias Canettis poetische Anthropologie," in *Canetti lesen,* pp. 11–31, and also her excellent monograph *Elias Canetti,* Stuttgart, Metzler, 1979, pp. 109–13.

[8] Elias Canetti, *The Human Province,* p. 53.

[9] Elias Canetti, "Gespräch mit Horst Bienek," in his *Die geteilte Zukunft,* p. 103.

[10] Ibid., p. 97.

[11] Elias Canetti, "Gespräch mit Joachim Schickel," in his *Die geteilte Zukunft,* p. 126.

CROATIA

The Ex(centric) Mind of Europe: Dubravka Ugrešić

Two introductory notes: first, I gave this paper (about a novel that is a satire of a literary conference) at the annual literary conference of the American Comparative Literature Association. More specifically, Dubravka Ugrešić's *Fording the Stream of Consciousness* is a satire of people like me—Western critics—who are interested in people like her: an author from the "other" Europe. Second, I would like to thank Michael Heim, the translator of *Fording the Stream,* for his invaluable assistance. Professor Heim met Ugrešić at a literary conference in Zagreb, the very same conference that was the inspiration for the novel which he later translated.

In one of the most famous statements of High Modernism, "Tradition and the Individual Talent" (1919), T. S. Eliot hypothesizes that all European literature exists in a synchronic order. Past geniuses are in dialogue with the present in an ever-shifting canon that constitutes "the mind of Europe." Eliot's modernism is rid-

dled with polyglot practices, but which "mind" does *The Waste Land* reflect? German, French, Greek, Latin, Italian, and a little Sanskrit are the remnants of one version of Western Civilization from Eliot's Harvard education. But what would the "mind of Europe" look like to contemporary literary critics?

One answer might be the fiction of Dubravka Ugrešić, from Zagreb, Croatia. Her linguistic toolbox is eclectic, including "major" European languages such as French and Russian, but she also employs Czech, Hungarian, and her native Croatian, languages untouched by Eliot, Pound, or Joyce. Of course, this gesture questions the very idea of a "major" language, of a "center," at the same time that it recognizes the dilemmas of a writer in a "minor" language. This paper will examine how Ugrešić's novel *Fording the Stream of Consciousness* (orig. *Forsiranje romana-reke,* 1988) both parodies and engages serious problems of cultural identity in an incisive and witty satire of an international literary conference.

In the opening pages of the novel, the narrator (presumably Ugrešić herself) arrives at the dormitory for the Iowa Writers Conference—she has a room on the international floor, mostly Third World— only to discover that the previous cosmopolitan parade of characters who traipsed through left her with a rather unglamorous pile of dirty dishes. She and her roommate Helga set to work: "Giving the pots and pans a tender once-over, I thought of tradition in Eliot's sense of the term and evolution in Tynyanov's" (5).[1] And from a handful of prosaic details and diary entries, Ugrešić launches into a fanciful satire of an actual literary conference. In 1988 this was the pretext for a lively and clever novel; reality, of course, took a different turn when the former Yugoslavia was not invaded by literati, but occupied by an international force of UN troops to hold rival factions of Serbs, Moslems, and Croatians at bay. The war, with its tangled politics and its ferocious varieties of nationalism, is not the subject of this paper; but it does inescapably affect the text, its subsequent reception, and Ugrešić's position as a "Yugoslav" writer once that referent is no longer a self-evident fact. These are points to which I will return; first, on to the conference.

The novel is a literary "matryoshka"; like the set of colorful nested dolls, it is a composite of varied forms. In using the analogy of the "matryoshka," a Russian term, to allude to the idea that "writers are all one big family," however, the narrator Dubravka quickly falls out of her roommate Helga's frame of reference: "What's a ma-tryosh-ka?" And in fact, this continual stumbling in and out of cultural frames of reference provides the hilarious baseline rhythm, the semantic and linguistic sidestep that keeps the reader off-balance.

Viewed as a whole, the novel is a formal exercise in irony, an experimental tour de force somewhere between Borges and Bakhtin, comparable to Calvino's *If on a Winter's Night a Traveler*. Ugrešić, a scholar of Russian literature, is a critic who has written a novel for and about critics. Its formal aspects coincide with Bakhtin's prescriptions for carnivalesque literature (in *Problems of Dostoevsky's Poetics*), above all in her use of "comic effect" but also in her "extraordinary freedom of plot and philosophical invention, bold and unrestrained use of the fantastic," and "wide use of inserted genres."[2] A rough sketch of the novel will provide an approximate idea of her fictional antics. The novel contains a number of genres—diary entries, letters, and standard third-person narration—all centered on a fictional conference. The conference, in turn, is a chance meeting place for a number of improbable plot lines including the accidental death of José Ramón Espeso (who tragically slips and kills himself while climbing out of the hotel swimming pool), a stolen novel (from the unfortunate Czech Jan Zdražil, who succeeds in smuggling it out of the country only to have it pilfered from his hotel room), the sex-capades of the Minister and his mistress Vanda (she pulls slips of paper containing the names of suggestive games out of a hat—a parodic echo of Kundera's *Unbearable Lightness of Being*), the emigration-to-the-West plot (a lithe spy seduces one of the Russian conference-goers), the revenge of the feminists versus the stodgy male critic, the literature-conspiracy theory and the nefarious ATCL, the Agency for the Totalitarian Control of Literature.

Carnivalesque confusion at the level of plot is replicated on the linguistic level. When Jan Zdražil's novel is stolen, the news sets off a chain reaction in the conference room as the translation earphones deliver the same lines in Czech ("Lidé! Ukradli mi román! Moje životní dílo!"), German ("Man hat mir meinen Roman gestohlen! Mein Meisterwerk!"), French ("On m'a volé mon roman! Mon chef-d' œuvre!"), Russian ("U menia ukrali roman! Moi shedevr!"), and English: "My novel's been stolen! My masterpiece!" (71). Zdražil, who only speaks Czech, has to struggle through interpreters to make anyone take his predicament seriously. In these multilingual scenes, the Czech is at a distinct disadvantage; Michael Heim, the translator, has conveyed the absurdity of Zdražil's position by giving the English-language audience a tiny Czech lesson: each time Zdražil says "Ano," a student helpfully adds "'Yes,' he says,'" producing an odd language echo-chamber. Zdražil, in despair over the loss of his novel, has trouble even engineering his own suicide due to linguistic misunderstanding.

Dubravka Ugrešić (*Robert H. Taylor*)

After unsuccessful ventures into German ("Sprechen-SieDeutsch?"), English ("DoyouspeakEnglish?"), and Russian ("Po-russki?"), he resorts to an absurd pantomime and receives an assortment of medicines that will not do the trick.

One needs to bear in mind that this multilingual farce was originally composed in Croatian, since the text poses very real problems of translation at the same time that it satirizes the dilemma itself. Heim had the substantial task of making the novel accessible to an English-language audience, since the original edition was distinctly Slavic in its linguistic orientation: Croatian, Czech, and Russian, with shorter digressions into French and practically no English at all. To reproduce the cosmopolitan feel of the novel, and to compensate for the loss of longer passages in Czech, Heim has added German. Czech occupies a curious status in the work, since Ugrešić does not know the language and hired a translator for these sections. Nevertheless, Czech is comprehensible to Croatian readers in a way unavailable to English speakers, since these languages are as similar as French is to Spanish. What I find especially pertinent in all of this linguistic play, however, is that Czech, as a marker of difference and a certain exoticism, is to the original Croatian novel what the Croatian novel is to the rest of the world (even more so). If we follow the path of a Borgesian *mise-en-abîme*, *Fording the Stream of Consciousness* is that "minor" novel brought to a Western audience to mock itself and us. In a sense, the novel is the revenge of a "minor" language upon the "major" languages, for although Ugrešić parodies the Western academic establishment and American cultural stereotypes (among others), she rarely uses English (only for proper names, slogans, or lyrics, but not for dialogue or description), even though she is a fluent speaker. This inversion makes few concessions to English-speakers (obviously not her originally intended audience), which leaves to the translator the task of rendering the text linguistically and culturally comprehensible.

The status of a "minor" literature is poignantly satirized in the friendship between Marc, an American, and his Croatian counterpart Pipo Fink, a thirtysomething who could have just stepped out of Gombrowicz's homage to immaturity, *Ferdydurke*. They swap stereotypes, an international language of references, in the hotel bar. "Ken Kesey," offers Marc. "Jack Kerouac," counters Pipo, who has read *On the Road* in translation and "every word J. D. Salinger had ever written" (55). Pipo's dilemma can be summed up in the following paradox: his desire to be the Yugoslav Kerouac and the absolute impossibility of ever doing so. Or the Yugoslav Vonnegut: he invents a cool line of Vonnegut prose, "I'm just a coot from the cape and I smoke a pack of Pall Malls a day," and attempts the translation into his own culture, "I'm just a coot from Virovitica and I smoke a pack of Dravas a day" (91), judging it as entirely unsatisfactory. The quote is not authentic Vonnegut, and both of these lines are originally in Croatian. Despite the fact that the text alludes to the dominance of American culture (Vonnegut is popular in Zagreb), Croatian obviously maintains the linguistic upper hand, pastiching the American author.

Pipo's "national inferiority complex"—"How can I write a major novel if I live a minor life?"—is undermined by the cleverness of the novel itself (150). Of course, Pipo is wrong, since his question is an existential one and not a matter of national identity. The point of this paper, however, is not to install Yugoslav literature in the pantheon of "minor" or "Third World" literatures (Pipo fantasizes about this and then dismisses the idea [207–8]) but rather to question our overhasty assumptions about what a "minor" literature is. More specifically, Ugrešić challenges our facile notions of East versus West.

While Pipo and Marc are sitting in a café, Marc suddenly whips out a pair of binoculars and his *Guide to European Songbirds*. Metaphorically, Pipo feels transformed into an exotic oddity, an Eastern specimen under the scrutiny of the Western gaze. Ugrešić ruthlessly satirizes Russian-literature Fulbrights who go to the dark and dangerous East, taking photos of Lenin's tomb, marketplaces, slogans, "each of them not only sublimely certain that they were the first to see it all but also, once they have turned their genuine grotesqueries

into unbearable kitsch, shamelessly forcing their 'authentic,' 'ironic,' or 'completely unbiased' angle on us, on us Russians" (49).[3] How should one respond to cultural stereotypes? In another twist, the novel offers the cynical option: exploit them, work them for all you can. Ivan Ljuština and Ranko Leš, fictional critics at the conference, agree that "Mitteleuropa" is "in": "How can you compare Miller and Mailer to the likes of Musil and Mahler, to the likes of Freud, Kafka and Krleža—to mention only a few?" (89). In her 1992 essay "Parrots and Priests" Ugrešić playfully advises her imaginary writer friend Petar Petrović to change his name so that it starts with a *K* in order to ride the Central European fad with Kundera, Konrad, Klima, Krleža, and Kiš. They eventually settle on "Kefka," just different enough from "Kafka" to be respectable.

In the former Yugoslavia, cultural identity is fraught with complications that defy such Western labels as "East European," "Central European," or even "Yugoslav," now that Yugoslavia has been replaced by five independent republics: the Republic of Bosnia-Herzegovina, the Federal Republic of Yugoslavia, and the Republics of Croatia, Slovenia, and Macedonia. It is not a simple matter to categorize Ugrešić as "Central European," because, as she noted at a 1992 literary conference, she did not share the "Central European clichés like 'Communism, Iron Curtain, censorship, repression, totalitarianism, socialist realism.'"[4] Writers in Tito's Yugoslavia were not constrained by the kind of censorship prevalent in Poland, Czechoslovakia, or Hungary, but enjoyed a relatively free, if isolated, publishing marketplace. On the very margin of the "East," the Yugoslav writer still had access to a wealth of translations from literatures outside; within Yugoslavia, the literary domain flourished, with authors writing in Serbian, Croatian, Macedonian, and Slovene (Ugrešić, 1992, 11). This multicultural utopia, this liberal Iron Curtain exception, crumbled under self-destructive nationalisms, as we know, in the spring of 1992.

What are the qualities of a "minor" literature? According to Deleuze and Guattari's *Towards a Minor Literature* (1975), "minor" literatures share three basic qualities: deterritorialized language, an immediate connection to politics, and status as a "collective enunciation." The "collective enunciation" occupies a critical position in relation to the larger society the writer inhabits: "If the writer is in the margins or completely outside his or her fragile community, this situation allows the writer all the more possibility to express another possible community and to forge the means for another consciousness and another sensibility" (17). The writer of the "minor" literature thus designates a utopian alternative to the "major" culture from which it dissents.

There is also the assumption that literature in general, as Sartre maintains, is on the side of freedom, animated by indignation toward injustice. Ugrešić offers a deliberately banal version of this in her mock introduction to the Zagreb Literary Colloquium: "All of you—poets, novelists, artists—contribute freely of your labors to the cause of peace, breaking down geographic, political and ideological barriers to form a neutral ground of the written word where you can wield that proverbial pen which is stronger than the sword" (38).

But what if the poets, novelists, and artists contribute freely of their labors not to the cause of peace but to its opposite? And what is the role of nationalism and language in this debate? In the period before the outbreak of the war, linguistic battle lines were drawn when Croatian President Franjo Tudman outlawed Serbian Cyrillic script in Krajina (14), while Latin script was outlawed by Serbs in Belgrade (43). In her "Parrots and Priests" essay Ugrešić laments the role of writers in stirring nationalist fires rather than quelling them: "Intellectuals, among them our fellow writers, have taken a stand at the side of their rulers, presidents and governments, their official politics, at least the great majority have." Many writers have assumed nationalistic mantles: Dobrica Ćosić (Serb),[5] Vuk Draković (anti-Milošević Serb),[6] and Radovan Karadžić. Even those who do not support a particular faction have been adopted by rival parties: Ivo Andrić, the 1962 Nobel Prize winner, was posthumously claimed by the Serbs (despite the fact that he was born in Croatia)[7] and Milan Kundera by the Slovenes. Ugrešić herself refuses to declare a nationality, preferring the innocuous category "other" (Have a Nice Day, 1993), which represents a total refusal to accept any identity imposed by the "Great Manipulators," as she calls them. When asked by a journalist, "What are you, technically?" she eventually feels obliged to concede that she is "a Balkan."

Ugrešić is often expected by Western interviewers to act as the spokesperson for her country. At a 1992 conference on the topic "Intellectuals as Leaders," she comments that the Yugoslav writer has traditionally not been called upon to be the voice of the people, and never really wanted that role (679). There is something tedious and predictable about questions posed to Yugoslav writers who are considered politically "interesting" rather than esthetically valuable. Danilo Kiš imagines what a Western audience, uncensored and politically incorrect, might say to him, a Yugoslav writer in the tradition of Borges: "Why don't [you] stick to [your] politico-exotico-Communistski problems and leave the real literature—the maid of all work, the sweet servant of childhood—to us?" (76).

For Kiš, as for Ugrešić, speaking for the collective has been tainted by nationalists who claim to be "of the people and for the people" (Kiš, 17). In her introduction to Café Europa, a series of essays on postcommunist Yugoslavia, Slavenka Drakulić describes her violent aversion to the use of the first-person plural. She associates "we" with kindergarten, communist youth organizations, politicians, and May Day parades. Her revulsion takes on a nearly physical quality as she imagines being crushed in a crowd on May Day or Tito's birthday: "I can feel the crowd pushing me forward, all of us moving as one, a single body—a sort of automatic puppet-like motion because no one is capable of anything else" (2). And yet she must use that pronoun to situate herself culturally, first as Yugoslav and second as postcommunist. She describes the embarrassment of being at a literary roundtable on Eastern Europe (not unlike "Intellectuals as Leaders") and suddenly realizing the division between "us and them," despite the fact that she did not know the languages of the other speakers (23).

A Danish critic vehemently reproached Ugrešić in 1993 for Fording the Stream of Consciousness, misreading the work as an offensive satire of the war. The critic accused her of engaging in a crass form of literary escapism when she actually had other pressing concerns like the "bloody war" raging at home. Whether in response to these criticisms or (more likely) because of her own preoccupations, Ugrešić's last two books, Have a Nice Day (1993) and Kultura Laži (1995; partially translated in Balkan Blues), are a move away from fiction and into essays on culture and problems of national identity. Even when she is ostensibly writing about American culture, she sees everything "in double exposure," as she explains to her "shrink": "I talk about Socialism, about our mentality, collectivism, about the collective we, instead of the individual I, about the we who is never responsible, in the name of whom a bright future is promised us, in the name of whom people are slaughtering each other now" (55). No amount of Yoga or self-help (her therapist's advice) can change her simultaneous and conflicting consciousness of both realities at home and in the United States. Atleast for now, Ugrešić's writing leaves her no alternative: her personal life is political.

In Third World Literature in the Era of Multinational Capitalism (1986) Fredric Jameson claims that nationalism is "fundamental in the third world (and also in the most vital areas of the second world)" and plays a central role in its culture (65). More specifically, he understands literature as a form of national allegory that draws attention to "us," "the people." But who is this subject of this idealized collective enunciation if you do not accept any national label? Can you have a national allegory without a nation? Aijaz Ahmad, in his answer to Jameson, suggests that the opposition between "third world" (national allegory) and "first world" (postmodernity) does not hold, since no country is insulated from the reach of global markets; this is what constitutes the condition of "postmodernity" in the first place. *Fording the Stream of Consciousness* cannot be categorized as simply belonging to a "national" literature, because it is concerned with an international literary conference at which literary critics are satirized, particularly those who study "minor" literatures; neither is it "realist," since it encompasses a wide range of genres and styles. Ugrešić's novel, multilingual and experimental, fails to fit into the "minor" literature box.

How should Ugrešić's work be classified, if neither "Eastern Europe" nor "Central Europe" is apt to describe her cultural location? Northwestern University Press avoids this confusion by placing her in the "Writings from an Unbound Europe" series with a collection of authors from postcommunist countries: David Albahari, Bora Ćosić, and Borislav Pekiš (Serb); Josef Hirsal (Czech), Norman Manea (Romanian), and Evgeny Popov (Russian). Andrew Wachtel, the editor of the series, claims Ugrešić is "postmodern," "insofar as [she] employs Borgesian techniques of overt citation and parody while blurring the boundaries between high and low culture, and between art and life" (ix). In this case, she might be listed with such international postmodernists as Gabriel García Márquez, Italo Calvino, Umberto Eco, and Salman Rushdie. Or should she be included in a compilation of women writers who address gender difference? Her short story "Steffie Speck in the Jaws of Life" parodies "women's writing" at the same time that it embodies it. Whatever category is chosen will appear insufficient for one reason or another.

However one reads the novel, its play on linguistic misunderstanding glaringly highlights the fact of its translation. Although the plot of the novel suggests ways in which the "minor" takes revenge on the "major," there is no escaping the irony that we read it in English, a "major" language and the language of global culture. Ugrešić satirizes the dilemma in "Steffie Speck" when the unlucky, unattractive heroine, on vacation in St. Tropez, finally meets her dream man, a celebrated film director. He is intellectual, handsome, and whisks her away to Hollywood. All obstacles to their love conveniently vanish: Steffie survives a plane crash on her way to Hawaii, and the director's wife conveniently dies of leukemia. But the most improbable part of the story is that he "happens to speak Croatian"; the fairy tale stalls before it can get started (39–40). Untranslated, *Fording the Stream* would reach five million speakers of Croatian; in English, the novel has a potential audience of one and a half billion English speakers. For writers in "minor" languages, English is the ticket to global currency. What are the implications of using English as an international medium? In a pamphlet titled "The Future of English," the British Council predicts that "within a decade or so, the number of people who speak English as a second language will exceed the number of native speakers." Which leads to the fascinating prospect that native speakers "will become, so to speak, minority shareholders in a global resource" (31).

Jean-Paul Flagus, a parody of Sartre and the cult of Flaubert (*Fla*-Flaubert, *gus*-Gustav), and his able computer-wizard sidekick Raúl unveil their vision for the "total control of literature" before the hapless Minister of Culture in one of the final chapters of *Fording the Stream*. Flagus and Raúl scour the globe on a mission to chart the literary achievement of the unmarked regions of the world in order to translate, control, and contain local geniuses. It is all a question of "literary production, regulated by a large army of literary critics and theoreticians" (186).

> A critic with a comparative background will always question the claim of a writer to be new, unique; he'll always throw him together with some group or other, some movement, some model. . . . I have no doubt that some day soon our position of total control will enable us to alter the very face of literature, to guide the efforts of its creators, create our own prefabricated works, award them prizes, make them bestsellers, raise up lowly writers and strike down the mighty, in other words, regulate the course of literary history, be its movers and shakers, so to speak. The total control of literature is a monumental idea, the road to literary engineering. Global literary engineering! (187).[8]

She is on to us. And it occurred to me that the American Comparative Literature Association is only one letter removed from the ATCL, the Agency for the Totalitarian Control of Literature, Flagus and Raúl's literary conspiracy. I will not classify Ugrešić as the tragic representative of a "minor" literature, but rather as a clever author and critic who can negotiate the treacherous territory of cultural identity both East and West.

Martha Kuhlman, Summer 1999

■ WORKS CITED

Ahmad, Aijaz. "Jameson's Rhetoric of Otherness and the 'National Allegory.'" *Social Text,* Fall 1986, pp. 3–25.

Bakhtin, Mikhail. *Problems of Dostoevsky's Poetics.* Minneapolis. University of Minnesota Press. 1984.

Deleuze, Gilles, and Felix Guattari. *Kafka: Towards a Minor Literature.* Minneapolis. University of Minnesota Press. 1986.

Drakulić, Slavenka. *Café Europa: Life After Communism.* New York. Norton. 1996.

Glenny, Misha. *The Fall of Yugoslavia.* New York. Penguin. 1996.

Hawkesworth, Celia. "Dubravka Ugrešić: The Insider's Story." *Slavonic and East European Review,* 68:3 (July 1990).

Jameson, Fredric. "Third World Literature in the Era of Multinational Capitalism." *Social Text,* Fall 1986, pp. 65–88.

Kiš, Danilo. "The Gingerbread Heart, or Nationalism." *Homo Poeticus.* New York. Farrar, Straus & Giroux. 1995.

McCrum, Robert. "Se Habla Inglés." *New York Times Book Review,* 8 March 1998, p. 31.

Ngugi wa Thiong'o. "Moving the Centre: Towards a Pluralism of Cultures." In his *Moving the Centre.* London. James Currey. 1993.

Ugrešić, Dubravka. *Fording the Stream of Consciousness.* Michael Henry Heim, tr. Evanston, Il. Northwestern University Press. 1993.

———. *In the Jaws of Life and Other Stories.* Andrew Wachtel, ed. Celia Hawkesworth and Michael Henry Heim, trs. Evanston, Il. Northwestern University Press. 1993.

———. *Have a Nice Day: From the Balkan War to the American Dream.* Celia Hawkesworth, tr. New York. Viking. 1994.

———. "Parrots and Priests." *Times Literary Supplement,* 15 May 1992, pp. 10–12.

———. "Intellectuals as Leaders" [roundtable discussion]. *Partisan Review,* 59:4 (1992).

———. "Balkan Blues." *Balkan Blues Out of Yugoslavia.* Joanna Labon, ed. Evanston, Il. Northwestern University Press. 1995.

Taylor, Neil. "A Post-Modern Profession." *Times Literary Supplement,* 27 July 1990, p. 798.

[1] Tynyanov theorizes that literary works change in form and function through history. His dialectical theory of literature would clash with T. S. Eliot's conception of literature as timeless and universal.

[2] In fact, Bakhtin's fourteen elements of Menippean satire (chapter 4) read surprisingly like a recipe for the novel: point 4, slum naturalism; 9, scandal scenes; 10, chance encounters; 12, genres; 13, mixture of high and low styles; 14, topicality. "Does this mean that Dostoevsky proceeded directly and consciously from the ancient Menippea? Of course not," writes Bakhtin (121). Does this mean that Ugrešić proceeded directly and consciously from Bakhtin? Well, why not? It is only so much grist for the postmodern mill. But whether she really did use Bakhtin as a model is ultimately not so important.

[3] Ironically enough, Ugrešić indulges in the same kind of generalizations in *Have a Nice Day* (1993) when she turns her Eastern gaze on the American cult of the "organizer," joggers, television, advertising, and an all-pervasive, gratingly superficial American happiness.

[4] "Petar Petrović, in consternation, leafs through a foreign anthology containing his work: on the title page is a photograph of tired, gray people waiting in line for sauerkraut in Bucharest. 'But I didn't wait in lines!' objects Petar Petrović" ("Parrots and Priests," 1992).

[5] "By raising the flag of Serbia's ancient obsession, Kosovo, [Milošević] won considerable sympathy among nationalist in-

tellectuals guided by the novelist, historian and erstwhile dissident, Dobrica Ćosić. Ćosić and some like-minded academics had been behind a notorious document called the Memorandum which was published in 1986. This bitter attack on the Kosovo policy of the (former) communist authorities anticipated the atmosphere of national intolerance which was about to smother reason in Yugoslavia" (Glenny, 33).

[6] "A novelist and journalist himself, Drasković renounced Yugoslavia from the start in favor of his conception of a Greater Serbian state" (Glenny, 39).

[7] "Since the war began, Andrić has once again become a symbol not of majestic writing but of Serbia's greatness, particularly among Serbs in Bosnia. It is Andrić who articulated with great fluency the history, suffering and historical mission of the Serbs in Bosnia. With all the irony that this opaque conflict can muster, it is usually forgotten that Andrić was a Croat" (Glenny, 22). Nevertheless, it is true that Andrić writes in the Serbian variant of Serbo-Croatian (Heim).

[8] In her afterword she compares Flagus's project for the control of literature to the contemporary state of publishing, which seems to produce the same "literary hamburgers" everywhere. Another contemporary example might be the Internet, but in this case the prognosis is somewhat better for writers from less prosperous countries. "Ugrešić" yields 132 hits on Altavista, most of which are related to journals in Serbo-Croatian, but also English-language publishers of her books; Miroslav Krleža yields 326, and Ivo Andrić, the 1962 Nobel Prize winner, scores 1,200.

CZECH REPUBLIC AND SLOVAKIA

Václav Havel: A Writer for Today's Season

In the course of the last fifteen years the name of Václav Havel has been appearing in Western newspapers and journals with increasing frequency. However, the contents of the references have undergone a subtle but significant shift. During the early seventies Havel's image abroad was that of the author of witty, intelligent plays which assess in a surprisingly original and, at the same time, irresistibly humorous way certain problematic issues of modern life. On first sight one recognizes in them the morally destructive pressures which a totalitarian system exerts on an individual, but on closer acquaintance with these multileveled texts one finds that they also portray the more subtle pressures emerging from a modern-day democracy.

For example, Havel's first play, *Zahradní slavnost* (*The Garden Party*), written in 1963 when the playwright was only twenty-seven, was produced within the first three years of its appearance in twenty West German theatres as well as in Austria, Switzerland, Sweden, Finland and Hungary. It was also translated into French and Italian. Less than fifteen years later, in the fall of 1980, Havel's German publisher lists performances of his last three plays (written between 1975 and 1977) in half a dozen German theatres, as well as in Austria, Switzerland, Holland, Iceland, Great Britain, not to speak of worldwide radio and television performances from Israel to Canada. Within the relatively brief period of his activity as a writer (1963–78) Václav Havel's name became internationally known, and he is counted today among the leading contemporary playwrights.

But the image of Havel as a playwright underwent a basic change about four years ago when it took on a new dimension. Not only did he emerge as one of the three spokesmen for the ill-fated human rights movement in Czechoslovakia known as "Charter 77," but he also drew attention to himself by his "Open Letter to President Husak" dated October 1975, an eloquent statement of fearless adherence to the truth. In fact the "Open Letter" is more than that: it is a fine attempt to formulate the deep-seated dangers to the average man's psyche arising from the daily pressures of a totalitarian system. The danger is rooted in a basic emotion, shared by most human beings—fear. Havel defines this ubiquitous fear in a deeper sense, "an existential sense, if you will, namely, the more or less conscious participation in the collective awareness of a permanent and ubiquitous endangerment; anxiety about what is being, or might be, endangered; becoming gradually used to this threat as a substantive part of the actual world; the ever-increasing degree to which, even more skillfully and matter-of-factly, we go in for our various kinds of external adaptation as the only effective method of self-defence."[1] With a lucidity which comes with ethical conviction, founded on clear philosophical assumptions, Havel argues how the most brutal forms of subjugation exerted by the authorities upon the public, though now seemingly past history, have become more subtle and "moved into the sphere of existential pressure." Imperceptibly the image of the playwright merges into that of a public figure, the characters on his stage are superseded by his living contemporaries, his humorous artifacts become merely the fictional equivalent of his searching arguments based on real experience in an existing social system.

The third change in Havel's image abroad occurred in the autumn of 1979, when he and some other writers and professionals underwent a trial for "subversive activities." By now the playwright who appealed to audiences from Stockholm to Tel Aviv, from Zürich to Toronto, the author of lucid speculative prose, has become—much more tangibly than before—a victim of an oppressive regime. We are not likely to read a new work by Václav Havel before the mid-1980s. Surely his older works are bound to gain increasingly wider audiences, but for the moment his opus is closed off. Dem-

onstrations of sympathizers, worldwide petitions by theatre people and writers, a public staging of a verbatim replica of the court trial at which he was sentenced—all these efforts of solidarity have solidified Havel's image as the "dissident," the victim, the martyr for freedom. Here lies a strange problem. Were Václav Havel a second-rate writer, such a turn of events would have been much to his advantage. But since Havel is a first-rate writer, a man of only partly tapped genius, the literary world might need a reminder that concern for Havel as a suffering human being must not obscure the literary importance of his work for our contemporary world.

Some of the most well-known people in theatre today have realized this before it is said here. Tom Stoppard, who feels a kindred spirit to Havel and whose successful play *Jumpers* (1972) is a sort of sister play to Havel's *Ztížené možnosti soustředění* (*The Increased Difficulty of Concentration;* 1969), dedicated his scintillating dramatic satire *Professional Foul* to Havel with the explicit comment that he had in mind "not just the Chartist" but the playwright, and that his dedication is to "a fellow writer. . . in admiration";[2] Harold Pinter read the main parts in the 1977 BBC production of Havel's one-act plays *Audience* and *Vernissage;* the French actress Simone Signoret, the actor Yves Montand, the German filmmaker Volker Schlöndorff and other personalities took part in a remarkable documentary performance in Munich in February 1980, conceived by the French director Patrice Chéreau, which replayed, with only minimally adjusted scenario, the Prague trial of October 1979 during which Havel and five others were given lengthy prison sentences. Since then Havel's name has become surrounded by an aura of admiration for the artist victimized by totalitarianism. And he is denied pencil and paper to prove that he is more than that. In the following brief remarks I would like to tell what, I feel, this "more" consists of and sketch three aspects of Havel's work which seem to me to represent his particular contribution to modern literature.

■ ■ ■

Much of contemporary literature has been influenced by Ludwig Wittgenstein's inquiry into the relation between language and reality. While writers like Marshall McLuhan and Norman O. Brown have in different ways voiced rejection of our overly verbal consciousness, others like George Steiner have stressed the importance of the spoken word in its unique capacity to "translate" phenomena into "rational" perceptions. The Czechs are in a peculiarly sensitive position with regard to language. Having spent centuries under various regimes (after all, Czechoslovakia as an independent state existed for only twenty-one years, from 1918 to 1939), their language and literature became modes of preserving the national identity. Since, under the rigors of their present regime, they are once again faced daily with an official language which takes on the rigid nature of sacred texts, they—and in particular the spokesmen of their sensibilities, their writers—are bound to cope with the constant awareness that this language has little to do with the reality to which it claims to refer. With the "official" language there goes an "official" consciousness which is outside the daily life of an average person. The process of constant pigeonholing of everything as either good or bad, the unshakable value judgments which go with these words (examples like "enemy of the people," "subversive bourgeois revisionists" or "lackeys of Imperialism" will suffice) have created a chasm between everyday language and the official language; and this has resulted in a sort of linguistic schizophrenia of every person who has some sort of official post.[3] In this connection one is bound to remember Orwell's concept of "Newspeak," which was intended to subjugate the mind by linguistic means.

Havel has brought this phenomenon to the stage for the first time and in an inimitable way. The three plays *The Garden Party* (1963), *Vyrozumění* (*The Memorandum;* 1965) and *Horský hotel* (*The Mountain Hotel;* 1974), are examples of this. The first play is about a young man, Hugo Pludek, who acquires a new consciousness through learning the official language. At the beginning of the play he is a monosyllabic, surly son to his hovering parents; at the end of the play he has gained a high office in the government by having learned how to speak the "correct" language. This learning process makes for entertaining theatre: the audience watches Hugo's rise to power as he begins to declaim snappy proverbs which are rhythmically perfect but make no logical sense, as his self-assurance grows when he spoons out arguments in circular logic, as he achieves agility in balancing false syllogisms and prefabricated phrases like a sword-juggler. Thought is no longer needed—and indeed, in true "Newspeak" style, to be avoided—if the acrobatics of linguistic devices hold the floor.

At the end of the play Hugo Pludek, by now perfectly versed in the officially sanctioned lingo, has arrived at the peak of a steep career as civil servant. Having dispensed with individual memory, with commonsense reference to reality, with simple human logic, he makes his exit from the stage with a firework of abstract rhetorics: "Today we all know very well that A may be often B as well as A; that B may just as well be A; that B may be B, but equally it may be A and C . . . and in certain circumstances even F may become

Q, Y, and perhaps also H. . . . Truth is just as complicated and multiform as everything else in the world."[4] Hugo has become a talking machine, a robot, repeating language which has become independent of its user. He has become a well-functioning particle in a system.

Havel's next and possibly best-known play, *The Memorandum* (1965), takes up the same theme; but by now language (or "Newspeak") has become, as it were, the central character, and the human figures around it seem to exist only in relationship to that center, which is both the most explicit as well as the most alienating aspect of the play, because the author has performed the dramatic feat of having literally created a new synthetic language. Despite the humor of the play, however, the tone is a shade grimmer than that of *The Garden Party.* The learning of a new language is no longer seen as a tool for a career but has become a necessity for survival. The setting is a huge bureaucratic establishment where coffee breaks punctuate activities with the regularity of a metronome, where certain writing desks go with certain positions and the human figure which fills the chair at a certain desk is arbitrary and exchangeable. In order to make official communication allegedly more precise (but in fact absurdly complex and inappropriate), the head office has implemented the use of a new synthetic language, Ptydepe, which is to be used by all employees (Ptydepe lessons given by a "ptydometh," a teacher, are an absolute must). Josef Gross, the hapless director of one division who has worked in the office for years and grown accustomed to its smooth mechanized workings, faces one morning an existential problem: the memorandum which lies on his desk (as countless memoranda have in the past) is written in a language which he does not understand. This is the beginning of his downfall, since it makes him the outsider to the whole establishment already well versed in the new form of communication. Gross's director's chair is filled by another person, and his fortunes go rapidly downhill. The fact that in the second half of the play they begin to rise again in proportion to the dwindling fortunes of Ptydepe and that he is reinstalled in the director's seat once again—a jerky puppet's travesty of an archetypal hero's quest—stresses the mechanistic quality of the play, which could be expanded ad infinitum, using the same patterns of cause and effect. Everything is predictable; any particle of the set pattern of events (be it another figure or another synthetic language) could easily be substituted.

The Mountain Hotel (1976) takes this notion to its dramatic as well as philosophical conclusion. The author himself called it a play which becomes "its own single theme."[5] The mechanizing of communication has become the very subject of the play. A number of phrases pertaining to food, joy, the weather, memory, sex, hope, disappointment, et cetera have been distributed regularly throughout the play, as if a computer had ordered input data in a certain way. Then certain characters are attached to the phrases and made to speak them at various times. Of course, since the regular reappearance of the phrases is the first concern of the play, the characters are secondary and are shuffled around so that each of them gets to say a certain phrase at a certain time. The result is a perfectly constructed "well-made play," except that its form is inverted. Phrases and movements have become autonomous, and the characters have become interchangeable. The play is perhaps the only literary work setting up one consistent portrayal of what we call modern man's disintegration of personality.

Another aspect of Havel's work in which he touches an essential fiber of contemporary consciousness is his startling treatment of a theme which has become the trusty war-horse of academic research projects—the dynamics of man's life in groups, namely the "tension between the individual and society." In Havel's work there are three distinctly original molds of this perennial literary theme, which range from comedy achieved with a moody computer to a new lusty version of *Žebrácká opera* (The Beggar's Opera). With his "Stoppardian" work *The Increased Difficulty of Concentration* Havel has written a play around a man whose life seems stretched to the breaking point between his intellectual endeavors (he is trying to write a treatise on the nature of ethics) and his actual daily life (he is hamstrung between two women—three at the end of the play, and if we added another, predictable act, there would be four). His mental efforts consist of circular arguments, and his physical ones lead him constantly along the same circular path: i.e., back to the place from which he started. This hapless character, whose thoughts lead him to conclusions such as "various people have in various circumstances and at various times various needs"[6] and whose private life consists of gaining more expertise in coping with the predictable form of emotional pressure exerted by the alternating women in his life, finds out that he has been selected as a random sample of behavioral patterns which are to be ordered and analyzed by a computer-oriented research team. The model sample of individual behavior patterns is so mechanized that it seems to be a stencil rather than a sample. The individual "sample" turns out to be a particle of completely predictable events, of Pavlovian reactions to equally predictable stimuli, so that only the computer, endearingly disturbed and refusing to cooperate with these predictable scraps of reality—foreshadowing R2D2, the affable computer-character of *Star Wars*—remains exempted

from the general signal-response-bound nature of the society.

Spiklenci (The Conspirators; 1971), which had its premiere in Germany in 1974, is a starker version of the self-propelled circuit of social endeavor. The play could be called a computerized study of revolution. In their systematic struggle for power the four main figures, representatives of public guidance and safety (the Heads of the Police, the Military, the Law and Culture), are choreographed through a series of steps of a dance of power, nourished by greed and triggered by deceit, the movements of which become entirely foreseeable by the second act and inevitably lead back to the initial constellation.

Havel's next work, written only a few months after he had completed *The Conspirators* (which he himself found too abstract in nature), is a completely different play, colorful, erotic, full of verbal wit and teeming with energy, namely a recasting of John Gay's *The Beggar's Opera*. This is extraordinarily theatrical material which has the unique distinction of laying claim to three politically scandalous premieres two-and-a-half centuries apart and under totally different regimes (a monarchy in 1727, a precarious republic in Brecht's adaptation in 1927, and a "people's democracy" in 1977 when the Czech unofficial "premiere" in a village resulted in severe repercussions for all those connected with it). As we know, this play too is about a version of the power game. The basic message of "dog eats dog," which seems as true in eighteenth-century England as it is in a modern state from Right to Left, is given an added dimension by Havel, one which, though very amusing on the stage, strikes a fearful undertone. The audience no longer knows who is what kind of dog and who eats whom. They no longer know who only plays the dog in order to protect the law or who protects the law in order to be able to pursue his canine activities under that guise. The unethical guise for an ethical reason and the ethical guise for an unethical reason can no longer be distinguished. Like the skins of an onion, the layers of morality and amorality in society can be peeled off one by one, and nothing remains at the center.

Havel's last three short plays, *Audience, Vernissage* and *Protest,* were all written between 1975 and 1978. These three plays, which have been performed and televised all over the Western world and have had a considerable impact on Western countries, have one remarkable feature in common. They are all built around one and the same character: a semi-autobiographical figure, a quiet, thoughtful, shy man named Vaněk who is faced with different situations to which he responds in his own particular way; his figure takes on a reality which goes far beyond the time and place of the actual stage play. If the character itself is semi-autobiographical, the situations he gets into are entirely realistic in that they deal with various facets of what the West has come to call a "dissident"[7] writer under a totalitarian regime. In *Audience* Vaněk, a writer considered "subversive" by the regime, has been assigned to the coldest and toughest job in a brewery. The play consists of a conversation between the brewmaster and Vaněk during which the former, after lengthy, theatrically amusing "social" niceties and carefully aimed small talk, finally asks Vaněk (whom he thinks pretty handy at inventing stories) to write up some stuff—a short paragraph would do—on his, Vaněk's, subversive activities. He, the brewmaster, was really hard up for information to give to the state police for their files, and how could he, a simple, harmless fellow, be expected to continue to think up classified information? He would be glad to repay Vaněk by moving him to a softer job. The deal falls through, for moral and also for dramatic reasons, and the action—as in most of Havel's plays, could start all over again.

In *Vernissage,* which is often performed together with *Audience,* Vaněk visits a couple of friends who, serving delicacies in their newly furnished luxury apartment, are also out to exert some kind of pressure on Vaněk. Their "well-meant" arguments—Vaněk can't get a word in edgewise—range from advice to go to the sauna and live a more healthy life, to come to terms with himself, to start a family—in other words, to become integrated and, if you wish, normalized. Again these arguments are ultimately shown in a different light when the couple launch a violent attack at the moment he tries to leave quietly. What they needed was an audience for their "happiness," for their objets d'art as well as for their love scenes. Lest these remarks imply that the play has a moralistic touch, it should be added that again Havel brings in one of his by now famous dramatic twists at the end which alienate the content and stress the formal aspect, bringing home the "artifact" nature of the play.

It is of particularly poignant significance that Havel's last play before he went to serve his prison sentence is one about political dissidence. He takes up the complex, burning issue of freedom of speech and molds it into a remarkable one-act play with two characters and a briefcase, some brandy glasses, a pair of slippers and a magnolia tree as the only props. The content of the play revolves around the signing of a petition which lands in the furnace at the end of the play. Vaněk comes with the document in his briefcase to another writer who is getting along well and whose plays are performed all over the country because he is accommodating to the rules of the regime and writes only what is "allowed." The intellectual and dramatic highlight lies in the final speech with which the successful writer explains to Vaněk why—in the interests of the common good and "relentless objective reflection" on the issue rather than "subjective inner feeling"—he could not possibly sign the human rights petition to free a recently imprisoned composer-singer.[8] The singer is freed for other reasons before the end of the play, and the tangible value of the petition is nullified. However, we have witnessed an argument on social ethics which Havel has left as a sort of interim legacy for the theatres of the world. It is food for thought for directors and actors just as much as for philosophers and social scientists—and above all, perhaps, for thinking human beings under any regime.

■ ■ ■

And so Václav Havel's work, though reflecting in a unique way the features of his own society, contains startling resources for the Western consciousness and emerges in all its artistic and philosophical importance, if considered in the context of contemporary international literature. His figure Vaněk (which has already been taken up by two other Czech playwrights, Pavel Kohout and Pavel Landovský, who have used the character in two of their own plays and have thus given it continuum and an additional realistic dimension) is a sort of ethical, incorruptible Alice in a dubious land where reasoning and actions are based on the attempt to survive within a system whose nature is accepted without question. As to the issue of the Individual versus Society, Havel's work reveals the relativism of ethical standpoints in Western literature (examples from Pinter to Robbe-Grillet, from Beckett to Pynchon abound). Havel's MacHeath, the gallant crook who does wrong in order to fight a greater wrong in Gay's and Brecht's plays, becomes a cynic who gives in to the ways of a world where the relativism between good and evil forms so complex a pattern that an ethical choice becomes impossible. Havel's explorations of language as a tool of power relates as much to the West German playwright Peter Handke's angry study of a man molded linguistically into a social system, as it illuminates a burning problem of Central-Eastern European writers and cultures: namely, that the struggle for a free language is in fact a struggle for political and social independence.[9]

These remarks began with a comment on what I take to be Václav Havel's "image" in the Western world today. Without forgetting that he is a man of unusual fortitude and ethical courage, one should look beyond the situation at hand—as he always does himself—and stress the realization that he is not only a playwright who gives shape to some of the most important issues of our time but also a thinker who from his small place in a small country in the heart of Europe sends forth an eloquent artistic diagnosis of men living in social groups East or West. More than that. While imparting his diagnosis of our ills, he makes us laugh—which, they tell me, is half the cure.

Marketa Goetz-Stankiewicz, Summer 1981

¹ Václav Havel, "An Open Letter," *Encounter,* September 1975, p. 15.

² Tom Stoppard, "Introduction" to his *Every Good Boy Deserves Favour and Professional Foul,* London, Faber, 1978, p. 9.

³ In this connection see also Henry Kučera, "The Language Dilemma of a Czech Writer," *WLT,* 54:4 (Autumn 1980), pp. 577–81.

⁴ Václav Havel, *The Garden Party,* Vera Blackwell, tr., London, Cape, 1969, p. 74.

⁵ Václav Havel, "Dovětek autora," in *Hry* 1970–76, Toronto, Sixty-Eight, 1977, p. 309.

⁶ Václav Havel, *The Increased Difficulty of Concentration,* Vera Blackwell, tr., London, Cape, 1968, p. 29.

⁷ The writers themselves dislike the term *dissident.* In his searching essay "The Power of the Powerless" Havel calls it "a ghost that haunts Eastern Europe which is called 'dissidentism' in the West" and defines it as "the inescapable result of the contemporary phase of the system" (Václav Havel et al., *O svobodě a moci,* London, 1980, p. 11). Similarly, Milan Kundera says that he does not like "the word dissident, particularly when applied to art," because he feels it is an act of "politicising literature" which does not do justice to the literary work (*Index on Censorship,* 6:6, November-December 1977).

⁸ Václav Havel, *Protest,* Gabriel Laub, tr., Reinbek, Rowohlt, 1978, p. 51. The Czech original is circulating in Czechoslovakia in typescript as a publication of Edice Petlice (Padlock Editions).

⁹ See e.g. the Polish writer Andrzej Luczaj, "Zniewolony jezyk" [The Captive Language], *Kultura,* 12:339, December 1980.

The World of Jaroslav Seifert

Jaroslav Seifert[1] appeared on the cultural and political scene in 1920, at the age of nineteen, with the publication of his first book of poems, *Město v slzách* (The City in Tears). He was one of the writers, most of them poets of the same generation, who banded together in an organization called Devětsil. Despite the fact that "épater les bourgeois" was written large in their program, the impact of bourgeois culture penetrated into every nook and cranny of their existence. It was Karel Čapek's translation of Apollinaire's poem "Zone" which became of inestimable importance to that very fertile generation of young Czech poets. Devětsil was remarkably international. The group's publications contained articles by foreign writers in foreign languages, even in German, al-

though German was almost taboo in many circles. The members' poetry, however, kept its distinctly Czech character. Jiří Wolker, Vítězslav Nezval, Jaroslav Seifert—they all wrote about the simplest things, experiences of daily life, utensils, plants, and snow, only occasionally crossing over from literal meanings to metaphorical ones.

Whereas Seifert's writings underwent subtle changes in the course of time, with the exception of his poetist period, which will be discussed shortly, his themes remained relatively constant: the beauty of Prague, beautiful young women, his friendships, and, again and again, his mother. Closely linked to his mother were his detailed memories of his parents' home in Žižkov, a poor working-class neighborhood of Prague. Although he is regularly referred to as coming from a working-class family, his father was actually an unsuccessful businessman. His early phase is generally referred to as proletarian, but little of it actually is, apart from enthusiastic exclamations about the Soviet Union and expressions of solidarity with the poor. Thus the poem "Slavnostní den" (A Festive Day), which demands that workers also be able to eat the dishes one finds in gourmet restaurants, a poem that was severely criticized, shows him more as a would-be bourgeois than as a proletarian.

As some of his Marxist critics charged, Seifert was waiting for the revolution but was not engaged in bringing it about. The focus of Devětsil was not primarily political but poetic. Insofar as it was political, as in the case of the popular, self-professed communist poet Jiří Wolker (1900–24), its Marxism was moralistic and nostalgic. Purity and gentleness, love of man, not for his heroism but for his weakness and humiliation, were the essence of its poetry. However, even Wolker's gentle moralism was attacked by Vítězslav Nezval (1900–58), one of the most prominent members of the group, who claimed that art had no purpose beyond being art. This was the first step which was to lead to poetism, the one ism which originated in Czech literature.

The poet and authority figure around whom the young leftists such as Wolker gathered in the years immediately following World War I was Stanislav K. Neumann (1875–1947), who in 1921 published an anthology of verse by various poets called *Sovětské Rusi* (For Soviet Russia), to which Seifert also contributed. Neumann proclaimed that contributions must be clear and understandable to the average reader and must identify ideologically with the socialist world and the socialist revolution. After the model of the Soviet organization Proletkult, a Czech counterpart was founded in 1921. The Czech phase of proletarian literature was brief, however. By 1922 Devětsil, under the leadership of the critic Karel Teige, turned to poetism, which was to combine a philosophy stressing the joy of life, turning life itself into poetry, and the struggle for a communist revolution. It was to encompass not only poetry but all the arts. Teige stressed the role of fantasy, fun, and the absurd as outlets of man's irrational side. The poetists now withdrew from political poetry, but not from politics.

Predictably, the carnival atmosphere did not last, and already in Seifert's collection of 1925, *Slavík zpívá špatně* (The Nightingale Sings Badly), death, battlefields, and gas masks, along with love and nature, are among his themes. Death also is the climax in "Akrobat," a poem published by Nezval in 1927. As was often the case with the poetists earlier, the setting is a circus, but rather than gaiety, the mood here is one of disaster. The proletarian phase of Devětsil was followed by disillusionment and, more accurately in some cases, by relief that after years of devotion to the cause, the still-young poets could consider their own enjoyment part of their program. From efforts to look at the shortcomings of the world, they turned to feelings and the subconscious, thus preparing the way for surrealism. They turned from discipline to an attitude of "enjoying the moment." Although the models of proletarian poetry had originated in Russia, the poetist ones were to be found in the West, particularly in France. The intoxication of the senses and adventures of the imagination were stressed and not German *Innerlichkeit* or the "Russian soul."

The most outstanding of the poetists was Nezval. Talented, imaginative, and sensuous, he led a bohemian, anarchic life and combined childlike playfulness with a terror of the supernatural. In comparison with Seifert, Nezval's poetry was more varied, more fantastic, and richer in surprises. Seifert in his poetist collection *Na vlnách TSF* (On the Radio Waves; 1925) no longer dreamed of socialism but experienced the many symbols of the exotic world: Paris, Italy, the sea. Nonetheless, did the many paraphernalia of dissembling—masks, costumes, makeup—which we find in Nezval's contemporary poems as well as in Seifert's not suggest different faces behind the smiling ones not only with Nezval but also with Seifert?

It was in 1922 that Seifert gave a lecture at a public meeting which was to have a strong impact first on Nezval and then on Devětsil as a whole. There he pointed out that for poetry to have an impact on workers, it not only has to be intelligible to them but also enjoyable as entertainment. Cowboy films, circuses, and soccer would qualify, and it was up to the artists to bridge the gap between intellectuals and proletarians. The proper function of poetry was to be an outlet for emotions, and its former function, persuasion, could be taken over by

posters and caricatures. The poetry of the poetists revealed a kinship to dada. Seifert and Teige called for a break with older esthetic traditions. Modern art was to be sought not in the studios of painters but in dance bars with the sounds of the first jazz bands, in coffeehouses and music halls, and in the lights of Paris boulevards. Seifert nevertheless saw in this art a pre-image of the world of socialism. With the October Revolution in the background of their consciousness, the majority of young poets and artists in the Devětsil circle then believed that a new social transformation was beginning, and many of them, including Seifert, were members of the Communist Party. As the whole world was to become poetic, painting and the writing of poems were to be replaced by picture poems and photomontages. Together with constructivism, poetism implied the belief that, with the help of modern technology, revolutions would lead to the beauty of which they dreamed.

Despite his professed allegiance to the Devětsil movement and his flirtations with Mallarmé, Rimbaud, and Verlaine, Seifert remained a very traditional and even primitive poet. František X. Šalda, the most respected critic of the time, wrote: "Seifert's poetic world in *Samá láska* [All Love; 1923] is in no fundamental respect different from the simple world of a little Prague official: film, sports, engineering, longing for Paris, of which he has the same kind of ideas which every little suburban dressmaker could have."[2]

It seems surprising that in spite of their turn to poetism, the members of Devětsil continued to consider themselves communists. In 1929 seven writers, including Seifert, signed a manifesto rejecting the new leadership under Klement Gottwald, who was to become President of Czechoslovakia in 1948, and were expelled from the party. Though some later reapplied for membership, Seifert became a Social Democrat and, with the exception of a brief period in 1948, seems to have remained one in spirit. His volume of poems *Osm dnů* (Eight Days; 1937), written on the occasion of President Masaryk's death, underscores his strong identification with the beloved president and the republic. In 1929 Seifert was also dropped from Devětsil for reasons which are not entirely clear.

In the late twenties and thirties the mood of Czech poetry reflected an atmosphere of death, nightmares, and ugliness, for which no satisfactory explanation has been given; it came before the economic depression hit Czechoslovakia with full force and before the Nazis began to threaten its existence. Seifert seemed little affected by this mood. In fact, it was in 1933 that he published *Jablko z klína* (An Apple from the Lap), in which the main theme is love. With these simple, sometimes balladesque poems, Seifert reached new heights of popularity, while Nezval gradually became the almost total-ly isolated standard-bearer of surrealism. In the thirties and early forties the pendulum of Czech literature swung back to tradition. Social themes generally gained ground at the expense of personal poetry, and concern about national survival moved into the foreground. By then the energy of the Czech avant-garde was spent, and the formal dissolution of the surrealist group in 1938 was merely a gesture after the fact. The disaster which struck the Czechoslovak Republic was reflected in some of Seifert's best collections, such as *Zhasněte světla* (Turn Off the Lights; 1938), *Světlem oděná* (Dressed in Light; 1940), referring to Prague, *Kammen most* (The Stone Bridge; 1944), and others, which reas-serted his attachment to the national heritage. With his genuinely positive temperament, Seifert increasingly has been for many Czechs a rock of security to whom they looked in times of adversity ever since he spoke out at the writers' association meeting in 1956 on behalf of imprisoned and silenced writers. This view is also re-flected in the many enthusiastic tributes to him from all over the world since he received the 1984 Nobel Prize; only the press in Czechoslovakia has limited itself to brief factual statements.

A politically very different group with which Devětsil actually had many points of contact was "Pátečníci," the "Friday group," also known as the "pragmatic group" around President Masaryk, which met on Fridays at the "Castle" or in the home of Josef and Karel Čapek (1887–1945; 1890–1938) and includ-ed both Čapeks and the leftist novelist Vladislav Vančura (1891–1942), a member of Devětsil. The Čapeks, who had spent their apprenticeships in France and Germany respectively, contributed considerably to the international dimension of Czech literature. A cos-mopolitanism analogous to that of the Friday group and of Devětsil could also be found mutatis mutandis in the Catholic group of writers, including Jaroslav Durych (1886–1962) and Jan Čep (1902–74), influenced by Gabriel Marcel and Paul Claudel. With all of them, a universalist note predominated until the threat of Na-zism brought about a turn to national themes. At the same time the old Czech tradition of satire continued. The political cabaret, *Červená sedma* (The Red Seven), under the direction of Eduard Bass, flourished in the early years of the Republic. Despite censorship, a prac-tice which was difficult to reconcile with democracy, sa-tiric magazines of various political orientations were published. Seifert was the editor of one, *Sršatec* (The Porcupine), from 1923 until 1925; in addition, artists from Seifert's circle such as Adolf Hoffmeister (1902–73) and František Bidlo drew political caricatures. Jaroslav Hašek (1883–1923) and his *Adventures of the*

Good Soldier Schweik are too well known to be discussed in this brief summary.

A unique institution in Prague from the second half of the twenties until the Munich Accord was "Osvobo-zené divadlo," the "Liberated Theatre." Strongly influ-enced by American movies, dada, and the Soviet revolu-tionary theatre, it stressed nonconformist, militant social and political satire. One innovative feature of the "Liberated Theatre" was the combination of theatre, dance, and song, another the clever dialogues of Jiří Voskovec (1905–81) and Jan Werich (1905–80). The audiences were primarily left-wing intellectuals, and it goes without saying that Seifert and his friends saw every one of the programs. Of similar importance was the composer, dramatist, and producer, Emil František Burian (1904–59), a member of Devětsil who became the artistic director of D-34 (D = *divadlo* [theatre]; "34" became "35" et cetera in successive years). Influenced by Brecht and the poetists, his repertory included—before the theatre was closed in 1938—not only Czech works such as *Schweik* but also, for example, Georg Büchner's *Leonce und Lena* and *Villon,* a play based on the French poet.

A much more intimate picture of Seifert than that gathered from his poetry is found in his only major prose work, a book of reminiscences, published in To-ronto in 1981 and in Prague in a somewhat shortened version in 1983 under the title *Všecky krásy světa* (All the Beauties of the World). The title, originally a phrase in Smetana's *Bartered Bride,* came to Seifert via Teige's introduction to the volume Devětsil (1922), in which he stated that all the beauties of the world should be the subject of poetry. The book for the most part consists of reminiscences written in haphazard order as they seem to have occurred to him, with extended digres-sions. Events are only rarely placed in time, so that the reader has to rely on a knowledge of the Czech cultural scene.

There are two main differences between Seifert's prose and his poetry. First, whereas the poetry generally hovers *above* mundane reality, the prose deals with what moved the poet—and with "what was in the air" at different times of his life. Second, although the poetry reflects his longing for beauty and goodness in the midst of evil, the reminiscences concentrate almost en-tirely on the positive. Memories of conviviality, of the warmth of his childhood home despite its poverty, and of love and beauty in nature far outweigh the episodes of Nazi terror and the references, only hinted at, to the situation after 1948. The negative note which does ap-pear concerns the quick passage of time, the increasing-ly frequent deaths of his friends, and the expectation of his own death. Despite the infirmities of old age, among the themes on which he dwells most fondly are detailed memories of food and drink, and, repeatedly, his delight in beautiful young women.

Prague is the central focus of Seifert's work, and he sees it as one, with layers of the 1970s superimposed on those of the 1910s and 1950s. Being conservative by temperament, he resents modernizations which obstruct or merely change beautiful views. The Žižkov he loves is the old workers' section of the city with its *pavlače* (wooden corridors which run along the backs of many Prague houses on every floor), dirt, smells, and often quaint characters. Much of the housing referred to in Kafka's *Trial* is clearly located in the same Žižkov. Undoubtedly Seifert and Kafka saw the same scenes, only with different eyes. In stream-of-consciousness fashion, Seifert moves from subject to subject within chapters. The one called "Důvěrné sdělení" (Confidential Communication), for example, begins with Seifert's being interviewed by a young woman editor. Her first naïve question—when did his love for Prague begin— leads him to reminisce about his trips to relatives in nearby Kralupy and the view of the Prague skyline along the way. Then, without transition, he moves on to a sketch of the classic poet of Prague, Jan Neruda, and Neruda's view of Prague. This leads him to an account of demonstrations he witnessed in Žižkov against increases in the price of bread as well as to scenes in church and at political meetings, which are followed by a detailed paragraph about the parklike slope Petřín on the left bank of the Moldau and the lovers in Letná Park. When he refers to the disaster which befell other European cities, he may have in mind the problematic question of Czechoslovakia's twice in recent times offering no organized resistance to aggression but thereby saving Prague, the most precious national possession. Despite the statement of his avant-garde days, the beauty he reminisces about in this quasi-summary of his life is not inspired by poetism but by the traditions of nineteenth-century literature, including its leisurely narration and its *Kleinmalerei*.

In spite of Seifert's nostalgia for the past, his reminiscences reveal no tension between past and present, only the realization that by now most of the beauty of his life lies in his memories. He grinds no axes, fights no battles, unlike the other writers remembering the same period, and only subtly identifies himself with good and against evil in whatever form. In contrast, the memoirs of Vítězslav Nezval, who obviously comes to mind, are filled with tensions between communists and pragmatists, between individuals, and even between Nezval's bohemian life in the city and the bucolic country life of his parents. Karel Honzík, who in *Ze života avantgardy* (From the Life of the Avant-garde; 1963) left

us one of the liveliest pictures of the Czech avant-garde, contrasts its excitement and inventiveness with the dull passivity of the Western world, which watched indifferently as Czechoslovakia was sacrificed to an illusory world peace. Because of its depiction of minute details of life from pre–World War I days on, "All the Beauties of the World" is an invaluable source for the kind of information to which not even the fashionable "history from below" school pays much attention, whether it be the description of a delicatessen window, Seifert's father's businesses, or the cafés, bars, and back rooms where early twentieth-century literati congregated.

One could say much more about "All the Beauties of the World" than the present framework permits. The very genesis of the book, which originally was to be a text for a volume of photographs, is interesting. As Jan Vladislav wrote in a recent letter, it contains not a single negative portrait, even of persons such as Marie Majerová (1882–1967), about whom Seifert had no illusions. There is a thematic parallelism among "All the Beauties of the World," the 1929 essay collection *Hvězdy nad rajskou zahradou* (Stars over Paradise Garden), and Seifert's recent *Býti básníkem* (To Be a Poet). Together with his poetry, his reminiscences might be viewed as a detailed, documented ode to life.

In the speech which he prepared for the Swedish Academy upon receiving the Nobel Prize, Seifert explained his view of himself as a lyric poet and of the lyrical position within his world view. He explained the unusually strong interest in lyric poetry among the Czechs as an outgrowth of Czech history, with its periods during which direct political expression was silenced and religious expression was problematic. However, though lyrical expression flowing from the emotions and senses of the individual and identifying with external objects not only suits the Czechs generally but him as a lyric poet in particular, he is seriously concerned about its exclusiveness. Convinced that a tension among the three approaches—rational, lyrical, and pathetic—is necessary, he views the rational, i.e. the conceptual, as dominant in the present world to a dangerous extent. The component he finds lacking, especially in Czech life and culture, is that of pathos, which represents a volitional-moral perspective. The most striking expression of this deficiency to Seifert is the absence, or near absence, of tragedy. Therefore, despite his personal emphatic identification with the conciliatory, harmonious lyric spirit, he wishes for the inner vibration and movement of will which would result in taking stands "for what we consider just and against what is, but should not be."

When we trace Seifert's poetry from its beginning in 1920 to "To Be a Poet" (1983), his last collection to have appeared so far, we see a development, via some pirouettes, toward increasing simplicity and artlessness, almost prose. Seifert's poetry, at all stages of his work, is easy to understand. In fact, its very simplicity and lack of sophistication would alienate the type of person who reads poetry in the West and appeal all the more to the Czech readers. The questionable validity of the notion of universality as a criterion of the quality of literature becomes clear if we consider the fact that Seifert's cycle of poems titled *Maminka* (Mother; 1954) is extremely popular in Czechoslovakia but would be unacceptable to Western readers. In the abstract, translatability of literature is considered a criterion of value; but actually, in concrete terms, we know that this is not the case. There are substantial parts of the codex of world literature which do not translate well, so that the position of many specific works of literature is different in each national scale of values.

The awarding of the Nobel Prize to Seifert came as a surprise to many. Unlike Havel, Kundera, and Vaculík,[3] he has, with negligible exceptions, not been translated into Western languages. However, his kind of poetry and relationship to a broad readership may constitute a valuable challenge to the Western esoteric poets whose works are the objects of academic explications rather than of love.

Wilma A. Iggers, Winter 1986

---

[1] On Seifert's selection as the 1984 Nobel laureate, see *WLT* 59:2, pp. 173–75.

[2] František X. Šalda, *O nejmladši poesii české* (About the Latest Czech Poetry), Prague, 1928, p. 53.

[3] On Václav Havel, Milan Kundera, and Ludvík Vaculík, see respectively *WLT* 55:3, pp. 389–93, *WLT* 57:2, pp. 206–209, and *BA* 49:1, pp. 7–12.

1968: Prague, Paris, and Josef Škvorecký

When in September of 1968, with my eyes still filled with the image of Russian tanks parked along Prague streets, I arrived for a few days in the West, a rather sympathetic young man asked me with an aggressiveness he did not try to conceal, "What exactly do you Czechs want? Are you already tired of socialism? Would you have preferred our society of mass consumption?" Today, over ten years later, the Western Left is almost unanimous in its approval of the Prague Spring. But I am not certain that the misunderstanding has been cleared up.

The Western intellectual in his proverbial egocentricity often takes interest in certain issues not so much

in order to have a thorough knowledge of them as to integrate them, like a pebble, into the mosaic of his own theoretical speculations. Alexander Dubček is thus confused, according to the situation, sometimes with Allende or Trotsky and sometimes with Lumumba or Che Guevara. The Prague Spring is acknowledged and placed—but really it remains unknown.

I would like, above all, to emphasize this fact: the Prague Spring did not come as a revolutionary explosion succeeding the night of the Stalinist era; it had been prepared by a whole process of liberalization, long and intense, that developed during the sixties. It is even possible that it all started slightly earlier, maybe in 1956 with the revelations of the Twentieth Congress in Moscow, or even in 1948, at the birth of Czech Stalinism. Its origins were with the critical minds that gradually decomposed the dogmas of the regime, called Marx to witness against Marxism, common sense against ideological delirium, humanist sophisms against inhumane ones. By dint of laughing at the system they led the system to be ashamed of itself; sustained by an overwhelming majority of the population, they slowly but inevitably laid the guilt at the feet of the state which was gradually less and less capable of believing in itself and in its truth.

At home we would say cynically that the ideal political regime is a dictatorship in decomposition; the oppressive machinery functions more and more defectively, and yet its existence alone suffices to keep the national spirit in a maximally creative tension. A dictatorship in decomposition, that was the sixties. When I look back I see us as incessantly dissatisfied and protesting, but at the same time filled with optimism. We were certain that the cultural traditions of the nation (its skepticism, its sense of reality, its deeply rooted incredulity) were stronger than the oriental political system imported from abroad, and that sooner or later they would overcome it. We were the optimists of skepticism: we believed in its subversive strength and its eventual victory.

It was during the summer of 1967, after the explosive writers' congress, that the heads of state, estimating the decomposition of the dictatorship had gone too far, tried to enforce a harsh policy. But they could not succeed. The process of decomposition had already spread even to a guilt-ridden central committee that in January 1968 refused the proposed political hardening and decided to allow itself to be led by the unknown Dubček. What we now call the Prague Spring began as follows: the critical spirit, until then limited to corrosive criticism, exploded; the country refused the way of life imported from Russia, censorship disappeared, and the borders were opened; all the social organizations (syndicates, unions, associations) originally intended to transmit unquestioningly the Party's will to the masses became independent and began to change into the unexpected instruments of the unexpected democracy. A system was thus born (more or less without any preconceived plan) that was really without precedent: an economy completely nationalized, an agriculture in the hands of the cooperatives, a relative equality without castes, without rich and poor, and without the stupidity of money-grabbing. We had, at the same time, the freedom of expression, a plurality of opinions and an extremely dynamic cultural life that was the motive force of the whole movement. (The exceptional influence of culture—of literature, theatre and magazines—gives to the whole of the sixties a character that is special and irresistibly attractive.) I do not know to what extent this system was viable and what were its prospects; but I do know the moment during which it existed, and that moment was superb.

Since today's Western Left defines its goal as a *socialism in freedom,* it is logical that the Prague Spring has become part of its political discourse. I am made, aware, more and more often, that the Prague Spring is compared to the Parisian May as if the two events had been analogous and convergent. The truth, however, is not so simple. I do not want to speak of the difference, almost too evident, between the lengths of time that the two lasted. (In Prague we had an unprecedented political system for eight months; its destruction in August signified a tragic turning point in the nation's history.) Similarly, I have no intention of sinking into "politological" speculations about the two events. Such speculations bore me; and worse still, I find them repugnant, for I have spent twenty years of my life in a country whose official doctrine regarding any human problem knew no better than to reduce it to a political question. This doctrinaire passion for the reducing of man is the evil that anyone who comes from "over there" has learned to detest the most. All I want to do is narrow down a few reasons, without concealing their hypothetical character, that explain why in spite of the same nonconformity, in spite of the same desire for change, a difference in "climate" separated the two springs.

May 1968 was a revolt of youth. The initiative of the Prague Spring was within the hands of adults who were basing their action on their historical experience and disappointment. Youth, indeed, played an important role during the Spring, but not a predominating one. To claim the contrary is a myth fabricated *a posteriori* with a view to appending the Prague Spring to the pleiad of worldwide student revolts. The Parisian May was an explosion of revolutionary lyricism. The Prague Spring was the explosion of a postrevolutionary skepti-

cism. That is why the Parisian student looked toward Prague with distrust (or rather with indifference) and why the Prague citizen had but a smile for the Parisian illusions, which he considered, rightly or wrongly, as discredited, comical or dangerous. (A paradox on which one should reflect: the only successful realization—again ephemeral—of a socialism in freedom was not achieved in revolutionary enthusiasm but in skeptical lucidity.)

The Parisian May was radical. That revolt which, during long years, had prepared the explosion of the Prague Spring was a popular one of the moderates. Like the headmistress in Škvorecký's *Mirákl* (Miracle in Bohemia) who replaced Marx's most offensive statements with less objectionable ones, everyone tried to dull, lessen and lighten the weight of the political system. "Thaw," the actual word one sometimes uses to designate that process, is very significant. It was a question of melting the ice, of softening what was hard. If I speak of moderation, I do not think of a precise political conception but of a human reflex that is deeply rooted: radicalism as such, whatever it was, was an irritant rather like an allergy; for most Czechs it was tied in the subconscious to their worst memories.

The Parisian May questioned what one calls European culture and its traditional values. The Prague Spring was a passionate defense of the European cultural tradition in the broadest and most tolerant sense of the term. It was a defense as much of Christianity as of modern art, since that state denied both to us in a similar manner. We have all fought to have a right to that tradition, threatened in Czechoslovakia by the anti-Western messianism of Russian totalitarianism.

The Parisian May was a revolt of the Left. As for the Prague Spring, the traditional concepts of left and right do not really apply. This division of right wing and left wing still has a very real sense when applied to the lives of people in the West. From the viewpoint of worldwide politics, however, it no longer does. Is totalitarianism left-wing or right-wing? Is it progressive or reactionary? These questions make no sense. Russian totalitarianism is above all a different culture—thereby also a political culture—where the European distinction between those of the Left and those of the Right loses all its significance. Was Khrushchev to the left or to the right of Stalin? The Czech citizen is confronted today neither with a leftist terror nor a rightist one, but with a new totalitarian culture that is foreign to him. If some of us consider ourselves as rather left-wing or right-wing, we can only become aware of this distinction in relation to the problems of the West, but not at all in relation to the problems of our own country, which are already of a different order.

The Western reader can only be surprised by Škvorecký's novel. Surely he expects that a Czech writer who emigrated after the invasion of 1968 will write a plea for the Prague Spring? It is precisely because Škvorecký is a child of his country and remains faithful to the spirit which produced the Prague Spring that his look at it is charged with a constant irony. Immediately apparent in "Miracle in Bohemia" is his criticism, primarily through anecdotes, of all the revolutionary gestures and illusions that, as the weeks passed, forced themselves upon the scene of the Prague Spring. In Czechoslovakia the look that Škvorecký casts upon the Spring has already triggered violent polemics. In Bohemia not only is his book prohibited (as is all of his work), but he is also criticized by numerous opponents of the Husák regime who, while living in trying and tragic circumstances, are no longer capable of looking at themselves ironically. Under the circumstances this is understandable. Each of us is free to engage in a polemic with this novel, but only on this understanding; one must not forget that Škvorecký's book is the fruit of a rich experience and in the best spirit of the realist tradition.

Everything in "Miracle in Bohemia" bears the stamp of truth, and Škvorecký's fictional characters and events have their real-life counterparts. That also applies to the principal plot, a "miracle" staged by the police, who later murder the priest involved and mount a violent anti-religious campaign. The village's name has been transformed from Číhošť to Písečnice. Ivana the Terrible, headmistress of a girls' school who selected the least offensive quotations from Marx, is one of the true and unheralded heroines of the "moderation"—and I have known dozens like her. She led a silent struggle against a given radicalism (the Communist revolution of 1948) only to become a victim of the opposing radicalism. (By the way, no Communist author has managed to create a Communist character more moving than the one Škvorecký, a convinced non-Communist, has given us here.) The poet Vrchcoláb, the dramatist Hejl, the chess master Bukavec are portraits of individuals actually alive and well known in Europe. I do not know if this is true of Arachidov, the Russian novelist; but whether or not he is based on a real-life model, he seems to be more real than reality itself. And if you believe his character to be exaggerated, I can assure you that reality exaggerates much more than does Škvorecký. If all these portraits are marvelously mischievous, even wicked, the hero of the novel, Daniel Smiřický—a stylized self-portrait of the author—is far from being simply a representative of the truth and a "positive hero." Even though Smiřický often appears in an attractive light, Škvoreck doesn't spare him from the irony which pervades the

novel. All this created a spiritual atmosphere a little different from the one with which the revolutionaries to the west of the Elbe were acquainted, and Josef Škvorecký recreates this atmosphere better than any other writer.

Škvorecký made his debut in literature with *The Cowards,* an exceptionally mature novel written just after the war when he was only twenty-four. The book sat in his drawer for a very long time and was published only during the thaw that followed the revelations of 1956. Its publication immediately let loose a violent ideological campaign against Škvorecký in the newspapers as well as at various writers' meetings, where he was vilified and slandered. The book was banned, and he had to wait for another "thaw," the one of the sixties, before it was reprinted in an edition of a hundred thousand copies. No only did Škvorecký become the first "bestselling" author of the young postwar Czech literature, he also became the symbol of a free and anti-official literature.

But why, exactly, had there been a scandal? *The Cowards* denounced neither Stalinism nor the Gulag, and it didn't really correspond to what one calls in the West dissident literature. The novel tells the story of a young schoolboy who plays in a jazz band and attempts, not without some bad luck, to make love to a reluctant girlfriend. Everything takes place during the last days of the war, and everything is described from the point of view of a disrespectful, often sarcastic young man. And this is precisely what was found to be so objectionable: the novel was a non-ideological discourse which dealt with sacred topics—the Liberation today has its place in the golden showcase of all the museums of Europe—without the obligatory gravity and respect.

If I have lingered over Škvorecký's first novel, published in 1958, it's because the author is already completely present in it; he's the same writer we meet in "Miracle in Bohemia," written twenty-five years later in Canada: in both he shows us a way of looking at history from below, a look ingenuously plebeian, a harsh humor in the tradition of Jaroslav Hašek's *The Good Soldier Schweik,* an extraordinary sense of the anecdote, mistrust of history's ideologies and myths, little taste for the affectations of modern prose, and a simplicity that borders on the provocative while simultaneously giving evidence of a very refined culture—in short, allow me to say it, an anti-revolutionary spirit.

I hasten to explain that term: Škvorecký is not a reactionary and would doubtlessly never have wished that the nationalized factories be returned to their former owners or that the agricultural cooperatives be dissolved. If I associate him with an anti-revolutionary spirit, I mean that his works present a criticism of the spirit of the revolution, with its myths, its eschatology, its attitude of "all or nothing." That criticism is not concerned with claims and concrete revolutionary platforms but with the revolutionary attitude in general as one of the basic attitudes man adopts with regard to the world. For now, "Miracle in Bohemia" is the only work that gives a comprehensive account of the extraordinary story of the Prague Spring.

Jan Palach's suicide by fire in January 1969 to protest the fate of country—an act as foreign to Czech history as the appearance of the Russian tanks—brought an end to a historical period. Besides, is what I have said just now about the spirit of the Prague Spring really true? Can one still speak today of the revolt of the moderates? The Russian invasion was too terrible by far.[2] Moreover, the state power is no longer what it was in Bohemia. It is no longer fanatical, as it was during the fifties, nor guilt-ridden, as it was during the sixties, but openly cynical. Can a plebeian cynicism contend with a power more cynical than itself? The time has come when Josef Škvorecký, the skeptical ironist, no longer has a place in his own country.

Milan Kundera, Autumn 1980, translated by Anne-Marie La Traverse

Milan Kundera *(Vera Kundera)*

Ed. Note: Milan Kundera's essay originally appeared as a preface to the French edition of Josef Škvorecký's novel *Mirákl,* entitled *Miracle en Bohême* (Paris, Gallimard, 1978) and translated by Petr Král. The present English version of the article was first published in the August 1979 issue of *Canada Forum,* pp. 6–9. We are grateful to Kundera, Gallimard and the editors of *Canada Forum* for permitting *us to reprint the essay* here.

Milan Kundera: Dialogues with Fiction

Skepticism does not annihilate the world; it merely turns it into questions. That is why it is the most fruitful attitude I know.[1]

Milan Kundera writes fiction in order to ask questions. Could that have actually happened? Why was he so ashamed of her anyway? Then why did he make it all up? Why did he lie? Why is she so nervous? Has Mirek ever understood her? These questions, part of a dialogue between narrator and reader, or perhaps between narrator and author, are taken from the first pages of Kundera's latest novel, *Kniha smíchu a zapomnění (The Book of Laughter and Forgetting;* 1980).[2] They are characteristic of his approach, as are some of

the chapter headings from the same book: "Who Is Krystyna?" "What is Litost?" "Who is Voltaire?"

Kundera interrogates his characters, poses questions to his various narrator-personae, engages his readers and puzzles them into questioning themselves. He is after clarity, definition, with a French faith in lucidity and a Czech mistrust of absolutes. The devil laughs at God because of His inscrutability; angels laugh with God at the simplicity of creation. Kundera, with an ironic smile, constructs fictional worlds in which patient investigation by narrator, characters and readers is rewarded by glimpses into the rules of the game.

Kundera is an astonishingly inventive author who uses a variety of structural ways to question his themes. In his first novel, *Žert (The Joke;* revised version, 1982),[3] he used the technique of multiple narration. By cross-examining the accounts of the story furnished by four narrators, Kundera exposed their "overlapping delusions," to use the memorable phrase of critic Elizabeth Pochoda.[4] In prewar Czech literature this technique was favored by Karel Čapek. But whereas Čapek the relativist showed that each man has his own truth, Kundera the skeptic shows that each man has his own falsehood.

A related technique employed by Kundera is the multiple point of view on the author's part, resulting in shifts of perspective and of the relative scale of importance. Kundera's metaphor for this purpose is the movable observation tower. The author discusses it with his readers in his second novel, *Život je jinde* (*Life Is Elsewhere; 1974*).

> Our book is like you. It, too, yearns to be all the other novels it could have been. That is why we are constantly dreaming about erecting other observatories. How about putting one up in the middle of the artist's life, or perhaps in the life of the janitor's son or that of the redheaded girl? After all, what do we really know about these people?[5]

The observatory is mentioned again in *The Book of Laughter and Forgetting,* along with several closely related images: the window of Kundera's Prague apartment, with its view of the castle above and the police courtyards below; and the window on the top floor of a French high-rise, from which the exiled novelist contemplates his homeland, the tears in his eyes magnifying the past like the lenses of a telescope. In this novel about memory and awareness, background and foreground, past and present, the recollected trivia and forgotten loves are ever shifting and sliding past each other. Russian tanks invade the country, and Mother is thinking about some pears the pharmacist promised her. Shocking. Or is it? In a beautiful image Kundera describes Mother's perspective: "A big pear in the foreground and somewhere off in the distance a tank, tiny as a ladybug, ready at any moment to take wing and disappear from sight. So Mother was right after all: tanks are mortal, pears eternal" (*BL,* 29).

Are tanks more important than pears? Questions, and still more questions. The very structure of *The Book of Laughter and Forgetting* is a question, for, as Kundera explains, the book is not so much a novel as a book of variations—and what are variations if not a spiral of questions about a single theme? In a broader sense, Kundera's prose writings as a whole can be seen as variations on a few related themes: awareness and self-deception, the power of human lucidity and its limits, the games of history and love.

Kundera's fiction is a game of wits in which deception is one of the main strategies. Ludvík, the hero of *The Joke,* feigns love for Helena as part of his scheme of revenge. *The Farewell Party* is a comedy of deception, while *The Book of Laughter and Forgetting* and many of Kundera's short stories are ironic dissertations on the arts of erotic trickery. The distinctive feature of Kundera's fiction, however, is not merely that his characters resort to guile in order to outwit fate and each other; his heroes and heroines also frequently deceive themselves. In fact, self-deception is such a striking element

in Kundera's stories and novels that his protagonists could really be divided into two moral types: those who are satisfied to remain self-deluded and those struggling for a measure of self-awareness.

Self-deception is often unmasked when a character is called upon to take action. In Kundera's world a crucial step is frequently taken without clear motivation or deliberation, impulsively, catching the psyche exposed like a sudden, involuntary glimpse of one's face in a mirror. In *The Farewell Party*—a book about death and birth, yet Kundera's most playful novel—a pivotal point occurs when the pregnant Růžena reaches for a pill held in the palm of her adversary Jakub. Růžena believes the pill to be a tranquilizer, but as Jakub knows perfectly well, it actually contains poison: "Jakub stared into her eyes, then slowly, ceremoniously, he opened his hand."[6] For a moment he is vouchsafed a searing flash of insight into the meaning of his behavior.

> Raskolnikov experienced his act of murder as a tragedy, and staggered under the weight of his deed. Jakub was amazed to find that his deed was weightless, easy to bear, light as air. And he wondered whether there was not more horror in this lightness than in all the dark agonies and contortions of the Russian hero. (*FP,* 195)

In a masterpiece of concise irony, the narrator describes Jakub's meditation on guilt: "The One testing him (the nonexistent God) wished to learn what Jakub was really like and not what he pretended to be like. And Jakub decided to be honest in the face of his examiner, to be the person he really was" (*FP,* 153). Who, then, is Jakub? The one *pretending* to be Jakub, or the one who *decided* to be Jakub? Can someone deciding to be honest at the same time *be* honest?

One form of self-deception to which Kundera's protagonists are prone may be called "bad faith," a moral syndrome reminiscent of the *mauvaise foi* first diagnosed in the modern consciousness by Jean-Paul Sartre. This bad faith is consciously induced self-deception whereby people pretend to themselves to be unaware of certain realities in order to postpone the need for making decisions. The example cited by Sartre is that of a woman who is physically attracted to a certain man but wishes to postpone making a decision about permitting physical intimacy. The man touches her arm, but she pretends to herself to be quite unaware of this contact, or she tells herself that it happened accidentally. By willing to separate herself from her body's experience, she becomes a victim of her own insincerity.

Mauvaise foi is a philosophical concept, and its applicability to literary characters is only implicit. Yet there are remarkable parallels between Sartre's paradigm and several situations in Kundera's novels. In *Life Is Elsewhere* the artist kisses Maman, and "subsequent reflection could not change what had happened but only establish the fact that something wrong had taken place. But Maman could not be sure even of that, and so she postponed solving the problem until some future time" (*LE,* 38). In *The Farewell Party,* during a romantic interlude at a country inn,

> Mrs. Klima felt the director's calf pressing against her left leg. She was perfectly aware of it, but did not withdraw her leg. It was contact which established a significantly flirtatious connection between them, but at the same time a contact which could have happened accidentally, a gesture so trivial that she need pay no attention to it. (*FP,* 140)

Similarly, in *The Book of Laughter and Forgetting,* Tamina—perhaps the most attractive and intriguing of Kundera's heroines—tries to suppress her awareness of sexual intimacy with Hugo by concentrating on vacations spent with her late husband, a mental effort Kundera compares to an exercise in irregular verbs. "But why did Tamina refuse to defend herself?" asks the narrator. *He* (not *she*—Czech grammar is clear about the gender of anonymous narrators) is puzzled, for it is not only the protagonists or readers who struggle for awareness; the narrator too begins in a state of partial ignorance and gains knowledge slowly, painfully, as the story progresses. As Czech critic Milan Blahynka put it: "The narrator is not immune to self-deception, but must struggle like the rest of us for every bit of understanding."[7]

Why is self-awareness so difficult to achieve? Kundera does not look to Freud for the answer. People fool themselves because truth is elusive and fragmented, and because they are losing touch with memory and history. Civilization, filled with ever newer means for recording the instant moment, is reaching a kind of amnesiac senility, an innocent second childhood: individuals forget who they are; nations lose their history and die.

The hero of *The Joke* still had a name and a tradition, was rooted in a specific time and place. Memory, in *The Joke,* has an ambiguous significance: the loss of tradition, as exemplified by the banalization of the ancient Ride of the Kings, is to be deplored, but forgetfulness is also a necessary means of healing and reconciliation. Nothing will be forgiven, writes Kundera, but everything will be forgotten.

However, by the time the cycle of novels has culminated in *The Book of Laughter and Forgetting* (and the 1968 invasion of his land has faded from the world's conscience), amnesia has become for Kundera a clear-cut metaphor for individual and national destruction. After *The Joke* Kundera's novels grow more ahistorical and parodic, with characters designated by first names or occupational categories. *The Farewell Party* takes place in a spa, far from Prague and close to the border of national and geographic anonymity. In *The Book of Laughter and Forgetting* Kundera shifts back and forth from a very real Prague to a painfully recollected homeland and finally to an Atlantis of blissful amnesia, an innocent island suggestive of a miniature America as well as the land of Lilliput.

The discontinuity with the past, the generational amnesia, is reflected in several of Kundera's novels by the search for a missing parent—more specifically a missing father, the *pater absconditus.* In *Life Is Elsewhere,* commenting on the youthful poet's desire for freedom, the narrator explains: "He is free who is unaware of his origin. He is free who is born of an egg dropped in the woods" (*LE,* 113). In this novel Kundera examines the lyric element in life and art, the poet as artist and revolutionary, and it is his contention that lyric poets come predominantly from homes in which the father is absent or subordinate—forgotten. From the very beginning the poet Jaromil's paternal background is presented as vague, questionable. The opening sentence of the novel raises a question about Jaromil's origin: "Exactly where and when was the poet conceived?" (*LE,* 2). Jaromil's father considered the premarital conception a mistake and urged Maman to undergo an abortion. Even after the birth of Jaromil, the theme of abortion as canceled paternity continues to be sounded. A statuette of Apollo in Maman's bedroom is used by Maman and by her husband as a symbolic expression of negated fatherhood. Maman daydreams of the possibility that Apollo rather than the engineer might have been her real lover, and she feels "an intoxicating longing for the child to be called Apollo, a name which meant 'he who has no human father.'" The motif of the vitiation of the young poet's paternity—neither having a father nor being one—echoes repeatedly through the novel, and in one of the final scenes the dying and delirious Jaromil searches in vain for his father's picture, which his mother has taken off the wall.

In *The Farewell Party* paternity once again becomes an important element (see a recently published symposium on Czech literature).[8] In contrast to the previous novels, which trace the quests of fatherless sons, *The Farewell Party* is a waltz of sonless fathers, a battleground of love and procreation. The locale is a spa specializing in the treatment of childless women, yet for the men fertility is a threat to be countered by a variety of strategies, from abortion to homicide. The ultimate parody on the separation of Eros and procreation is performed by the spa's physician, who achieves a kind of Apollonian paternity by mechanically injecting women with sperm-bank samples of his own semen. The human link between the generations is broken, and the only memory is the biological memory locked within the genes.

And what of the paternal links in *The Book of Laughter and Forgetting*? The only paternal figure of any prominence is Kundera's own father. He is described in a touching, sympathetic way, but he is dying, losing his memory and his power of speech, and thus once again represents the loss of fatherhood, the rift in continuity. Through an act of love, Kundera tries to recall his father and to divine the meaning of the latter's cryptic words. But the sound of his father's voice is blurred by the inane commonplaces of the mock father of the country—the President of Forgetting—resounding from a nearby loudspeaker. The voice of a father receding into the past, the voice of a despised leader speaking from historic Prague Castle and heard from far away by the exiled author—a revealing image of the human and literary fate of Milan Kundera.

From his high-rise tower in Brittany, from his Paris window, Milan Kundera is still looking east toward Prague, toward his Moravian birthplace, toward the Central Europe he considers his spiritual home. What is there in his work that is descended from Czech literary traditions? The novel of ideas has never taken root in Czech culture, nor has the kind of intellectual game Kundera plays with Eros and politics, fiction and reality. Czech readers are more used to laughing than to exploring the sources of laughter, and pure jeu d'esprit has appeared in modern Czech literature only rarely and belatedly.

Kundera's real literary roots are in the eighteenth century, in the digressive storytellers, in Sterne and especially in the French ironists and Encyclopedists. In his recent works, particularly *The Book of Laughter and Forgetting,* as Kundera leaves the land of Bohemia and views the little figures of the world panorama from an ever higher observatory, his irony often changes to Swiftian satire, and to Swiftian pessimism. Among modern writers, he has expressed an affinity for Thomas Mann, for Anatole France, for the existentialists, for the Central European writers with a philosophical bent. As he put it in a 1963 interview: "Precision of thought moves me more than precision of observation. In literature, I like unconcealed intellect, whether it manifests itself as reflection, analysis, irony or compositional playfulness."[9]

The bulk of Kundera's work has never been published in his homeland, but he does not bewail the necessity of writing for foreigners. He thinks the era of pa-

rochial national literatures is over, and he believes in the Goethean concept of a world community of letters. The knowledge that he is dependent on translators has affected Kundera's style, inducing him to make his expression clearer, more decisive, less subject to misinterpretation. He once stated in a newspaper interview: "The need for translations prodded me to wash my tongue, to strip my words down to their most basic meaning."[10]

Kundera's purely literary paternity may be European rather than specifically Czech, but he has many qualities which have come to be associated with Czech culture: skepticism, dislike of hubris and gigantism, insistence on a human scale as the ideal measure of values, the use of humor as a means of demystification. Very much in the Czech tradition too is the writer as teacher and moralist. The need of Czech authors to exhort and educate their own people and the outside world has often had ambiguous—if not destructive—effects on literature. It is hard to say just what effects Kundera's strong political engagement has on his fiction. There is no doubt that his fervor and the associated lyrical emotions he is at such pains to suppress have added power to his high-energy writing and have given his fiction its unusual interplay of polis, Eros and Thanatos. Of course, there is a price to be paid when ironic detachment and inquisitive attitude are replaced by assertions, particularly when those assertions are questionable. Is the cultural impact of the East really so one-sidedly detrimental? What are the origins of the triviality, amnesia, infantility of the modern world? Or its genocidal propensities? As the genially insane physician of *The Farewell Party* so hilariously—and chillingly—shows, superrationality is never very far from irrationality.

In interviews and statements Kundera may engage in polemics, but in his novels, stories and plays this great author's most personal voice sounds a dialogue with the truth. After publication of *The Joke,* Czech novelist and playwright Ivan Klíma wrote: "In his passionate desire to reach the truth, no matter how bitter; to resist every illusion, no matter how modestly formulated; to eradicate all myths, no matter how innocent-looking, Milan Kundera has gone further than anyone in the history of Czech prose."[11] This is still true today.

Peter Kussi, Spring 1983

[1] Antonín J. Liehm, *The Politics of Culture,* Peter Kussi, tr., New York, Grove, 1967, p. 142.

[2] Milan Kundera, *The Book of Laughter and Forgetting,* Michael H. Heim, tr., New York, Knopf, 1980. Subsequent references use the abbreviation *BL.* For reviews see *WLT* 54:1, p. 131 (French edition) and 56:2, p. 366 (Czech).

[3] Milan Kundera, *The Joke,* Michael H. Heim, tr., New York, Harper & Row, 1982.

[4] Elizabeth Pochoda, "Overlapping Delusions," *The Nation,* 2 October 1976, p. 312.

[5] Milan Kundera, *Life Is Elsewhere,* Peter Kussi, tr., New York, Knopf, 1974, p. 254. Subsequent references use the abbreviation *LE.* For reviews see *BA* 49:4, p. 806 (English edition) and *WLT* 54:1, p. 131 (Czech).

[6] Milan Kundera, *The Farewell Party,* Peter Kussi, tr., New York, Knopf, 1976, p. 129. Subsequent references use the abbreviation *FP.* For reviews see *WLT* 52:4, p. 663 (English edition) and 54:4, p. 670 (Czech).

[7] Milan Blahynka, "Milan Kundera prozaik," *Plamen,* 1 (1967), p. 45.

[8] *Czech Literature Since 1956: A Symposium,* William E. Harkins and Paul I. Trensky, eds., New York, Bohemica, 1980, pp. 56–61.

[9] Helena Kostková, "Nejhůře střežené státní tajemství—prozaik Milan Kundera," *Svědectví,* 15:60 (1980), p. 703.

[10] Milan Kundera, interview in *Le Monde,* 23 January 1976.

[11] Ivan Klíma, "Žert a Sekyra," *Orientace,* 1 (1967), p. 87.

GREECE

Yannis Ritsos (*Kimon Friar*)

The Predominance of Poetry in Greek Literature

To discuss the relative importance of poetry and prose in Greek literature seems unnecessary, since the conclusion is so obvious. Five Greek writers have received international recognition in this century: Cavafy, Seferis (Nobel Prize, 1963), Ritsos (Lenin Prize, 1977), Elytis (Nobel Prize, 1979), and Kazantzakis (Peace Prize, 1956). The first four are not only poets but *exclusively* and doctrinairely so, dedicated to the poetic genre over and above literature in its alternative modes; the fifth, a much more eclectic man of letters who won fame as a novelist, nevertheless considered himself primarily a poet and denigrated his "prosaic" achievements.

Still, the preeminence of poetry, so obvious in 1985, could not have been predicted in, say, 1930. On the contrary, the aftermath of Greece's first great trial in this century, her defeat by Turkey in Asia Minor and the consequent flow of Anatolians into Helladic Greece, seems to have created a great desire for prose. "Pezá thélume, pezá" (We need prose, prose), cried, in 1927, the influential demoticist and novelist Yannis Psiharis,[1] who for several decades had been insisting that "the crucial time for a nation is the time when it begins to write prose."[2] What he meant by this is clear. First, the novel would resolve the infamous "language question" in favor of demotic, not because poetry had failed to ally itself with demoticism (the opposite is true, except for

Cavafy), but because the novel would reach so many more readers and would therefore extend and clinch what poetry had already begun. That was only a prediction. André Mirambel, however, looking back on the same situation in the 1940s, argued that the prediction had come true: "In Greece, more than any other country, the novel was connected with the language," he claimed, and he went on to assert that the novel's development coincided with the most crucial period of the language question and played such a strong role in forming the nation's linguistic sensibility that it in fact put an end to the language question in the field of letters.[3]

These claims are surely exaggerated, chiefly because Psiharis's own novels, and later those of Myrivilis and Kazantzakis (for example), employed idiosyncratic versions of demotic somewhat tributary to the mainstream literary language as it actually evolved, more under the influence of the prose writings of Solomos, Palamas and Seferis—all of them paradoxically poets— than under the influence of novels. Psiharis was nonetheless correct in assuming that novels would reach more readers than would poetry, which leads to the second meaning of his insistence that a nation's crucial time is when it begins to write prose. Psiharis's belief was that a national culture presupposes a reading public and that a reading public of any size can be developed only through prose. The condition to which he aspired actually came to pass, according to Mirambel: the novel made writers important factors in molding national opinion because this genre connected them more pervasively with a literate public. Again, the claim seems parochial, since Greece possessed a national culture long before novels were written there and indeed while the greater part of the population was illiterate.

Lurking behind Psiharis's doctrine, however, is a third factor that gives it more weight. This is the urbanization of Greece that was accelerated by the colossal influx, after 1922, of refugees from Anatolia. Psiharis and the other advocates of prose saw the novel, in Greece as elsewhere, as the natural form for the bourgeoisie. Lastly, the novel seemed destined to become predominant by default because of poetry's inability—before the 1930s—to speak to a Greece vastly changed by the Asia Minor Disaster (Cavafy, though he had been addressing the new conditions for decades, was still not "discovered" in Helladic Greece). "The new generation," writes I. M. Panayotopoulos, could not respond to the "love of decoration . . . of the ornamentation that delighted people of quieter eras."[4] And George Theotokas, distinguished advocate and practitioner of the urban novel (himself a transplant from Constantinople), wrote in his manifesto Eléfthero pnévma in 1929: "As much as we love our poets, we cannot live in the twentieth century by lyricism alone. . . . We demand a real discussion of ideas, a real theatre, a real novel."[5] Thus we have at least four different areas which lend meaning to Psiharis's cry, "Pezá thélume, pezá": demoticism, the need for a reading public, urbanization, and poetry's failure (so far) to adapt. No wonder that the critic Kleon Paraschos could assert in 1937:

> The strong advance that the writing of novels exhibits in Greece today is not a fashion imported . . . from Europe, nor can it be assigned to the ambitions of a few who long to be read by as large a public as possible, but to a much more organic reason in that it reflects . . . our intellectual and social realities. . . . No other form but the novel can express this complex world.[6]

Why, then, has poetry rather than prose remained predominant in Greece, contrary to all predictions? The answer obviously derives from what happened to poetry in the 1930s and afterward, but also from a specific problem inherent in Greek prose. We should look at this problem first, because it will help to explain why poetry made such a strong comeback, especially during and after Greece's second great trial in this century, in the 1940s.

The specific problem with prose was that it had no truly viable, all-pervasive roots in the Greek literary tradition. There is, of course, the genre called the Greek novel or prose romance, dating from the second and third centuries A.D. and represented by works such as Longus's Daphnis and Chloë and Achilles Tatius's Leucippe and Cleitophon. The ancient "novel" influenced the many romances of Byzantine times[7] and, through them, the seventeenth-century Cretan romance and even Solomos; so we have a direct line of descent to the nineteenth century. The trouble, however, is that a) the descent is eventually into verse, and b) the romantic nature of this material was precisely what post-1922 Greek literature was trying to escape. If any ancient writers of prose were to provide viable roots for the antiromantic novelists of the twentieth century, these were quasi-literary ones: specifically Plato, an obvious influence on Kostas Varnalis's satire I alithiní apologhía tu Sokráti (Socrates' True Apology; 1931), and the Evangelists, very much present in Kazantzakis's Christ Recrucified and even more so in The Last Temptation. Plato and the Gospels were not enough, however. Nor were other quasi-literary compositions such as saints' lives (sinaksária), Byzantine chronicles, or folktales. As for early nineteenth-century works of prose, Andhonios Matesis's O vasilikós (1830?) was a stage play, Solomos's I yinéka tu Zákithos (1826) remained unknown, and Makriyannis's Memoirs were waiting to be first truly appreciated by a poet, Seferis, in the midtwentieth century.

It should not be surprising, therefore, that the modern Greek novel began, and continued, chiefly under foreign influence, despite its attempts at Greekness. Indeed, the actual beginning was a spate of translations, always of romantic works—for example, Mme de Staël's Corinne (1835), a prose rendering of Edward Young's Night Thoughts (also 1835), lots of Walter Scott, and so forth. In order to marry all this to Greekness, authors devised romantic plots involving Greece's recent struggle for freedom (e.g., Stefanos Ksénos's I iroís tis ellinikís epanastáseos [The Heroine of the Greek Revolution; 1852]) or focused on farmers in the village (e.g., Pavlos Kallighas's Thános Vlékas [1835]), whence, eventually, the ithoghrafikó novel so roundly condemned by George Theotokas. The most important, and artificial, means by which all this was supposedly fastened to Greek roots was that of an archaizing language. Thános Vlékas, important in the history of modern Greek prose as the first social novel, attempted a realistic portrayal of peasant life, yet its language, intended to uplift the reader because it evoked ancient Greece, is totally unreal. A jug of cool water becomes an angheíon psihrú ídhatos, and even the villagers' sighs have been purified from their natural (and Turkish!) "Ach!" to the Attic "Ai!" Alexander Rankavis in his history of Greek literature (1877) says nonetheless that Kallighas "écrit dans un style qui peut servir du modèle"![8]

Of course there are bright spots where an exceptional talent breaks through, despite everything, to produce a novel or short story that is more than imitative: Roidhis and Papadhiamandhis in the nineteenth century, Myrivilis and Tahtsis in the twentieth, to cite only the most obvious. In addition, the genre possessed self-corrective powers. Prodded by Psiharis, it cured itself of archaizing and also, through the popular and prolific Ghrighorios Ksenopoulos, of its aversion to urban settings. Its foreign orientation remained, however. Psiharis himself, we should remember, lived in France and reflected European ideas more than Greek ones. Translations continued their decisive role. It was Kamboúroghlou's rendering of Zola's *Nana* in 1880, for instance, that signaled a shift to naturalism. Kazantzakis's first novel was modeled on D'Annunzio, his later ones on Dostoevsky, Tolstoy, and Gorky. The overall history of Greek prose is that of successive European trends: romanticism, realism, naturalism, symbolism, modernism, postmodernism. This is not bad in itself (and not untrue of poetry, either); the trouble is that the Greek roots to which these pan-European trends were connected could not be comprehensive, because there is no continuous tradition of Greek prose. So we are left with occasional—and sometimes extremely successful—connections merely with discrete, disparate elements from tradition: Varnalis's with Plato, mentioned earlier; Myrivilis's with the folktale in *O Vasílis o Arvanítis;* Kazantzakis's with the *sinaksária* in the novel originally entitled "The Saint's Life of Alexis Zorbas."

This kind of limited relationship with a discrete, disparate past turned out to be insufficient for Greek letters, especially after 1940. The limitation, however, was specific to prose, as we have seen. Poetry was able to overcome the probem and to relate effortlessly to a large, interconnected stystem of viable roots pervading every era of the Greek literary tradition. This, I believe, is why poetry has remained predominant in Greece, contrary to all predictions.

We should ask now why such a connection with all-pervasive roots mattered so much in Greece. A similar connection does not seem to be a universal need evidenced in the poetry of England, for example, or France, or the United States. But the Greek situation was different. Greek intellectuals in the early 1940s became obsessed with the subject of *Ellinikótita* (Greekness). Their questioning had of course begun earlier, but from 1941 to 1944 they experienced a kind of stoppage of time because of the German Occupation and used it for protracted introspection. The emptiness they felt had peaked after the first great trial of the century, the Asia Minor Disaster; it had been extended by the political instability of the midwar years; now it was con-firmed by Greece's helplessness under a new foreign domination, putting the country back where it had been under the Turks before the revolution. Then a belief in liberty and democracy as the essences of Greekness had given Hellenes a sense of identity (or, rather, had been given to them by European philhellenes and Greeks resident abroad in a desperate effort to instill some identity in them). Now, however, this same definition of Greekness was received largely (though not wholly) with mockery, because the intellectuals refused to blind themselves to the truths of Greek history since independence, knowing that their compatriots had failed several times to maintain democracy and had instead produced dictators to curtail their own liberty.

In short, Greekness could no longer be defined politically, nor could it be defined in any other way that involved external power. The only thing left was inwardness, an area in which Greeks experiencing massive emptiness *could* regain a sense of themselves as something set apart—could, in other words, gain identity. This is because Hellenism possesses a more continuous, more extensive, and at the same time coherent record of inwardness than any other culture in the West. And where is this record best displayed if not in Greek poetry from Homer and Hesiod down to the present?

Thus the 1940s, Greece's second great period of trial in this century, produced a distinct challenge to the nation's poets that could never be met in a pervasive way by her prose writers. The poets could quote lines, employ key vocabulary, repeat prosodic and stanzaic arrangements, and allude in diverse other ways to archaic, classic, Hellenistic, Roman Occupation, Byzantine, Turkish Occupation, Cretan, Ionian, and modern verse—all without the slightest artificiality. In this way they could pull themselves up by their own bootstraps, filling Greece's external emptiness with a glorious inwardness that could easily be brought into congruence with twentieth-century reality, since Greece's inward, poetic tradition is so often a record of the nation's outward, political failings.

The poetic rejuvenation that eventually captured one Lenin and two Nobel prizes for Greece actually began in the 1930s, which saw Seferis, Ritsos, and Elytis acquire their individual voices.[9] The rejuvenation involved the appreciation of Cavafy, that eccentric genius whose situation in Alexandria had directed him, several decades earlier, away from externals toward Greek inwardness and furthermore toward the coherence and continuity of that inwardness (since he believed that every era was an equivalent of every other era). It involved the rejection of ornamentation, inspired in part—at least for Seferis—by admiration for the functional *prose* of Makriyannis at a time when poetic models of sparseness were not available in Greek (except for Cavafy and Karyotakis) and when Greek novels, paradoxically, were still often ornamental in style. It involved either the extirpation of lyricism (Seferis), the assimilation of an unacceptable lyricism to an acceptable Greek elegiac tradition (Ritsos), or the freshening of lyricism through surrealism (Elytis). This preparation in the 1930s enabled the poets to respond creatively to the new challenges offered by the 1940s and eventually to give us masterpieces of rootedness such as Seferis's "Helen," Ritsos's *Philoctetes,* and Elytis's *Axion Esti.*

We should remember that Greek writers, perhaps precisely because their outward circumstances made them feel so little, aspired to be very big. For the poets, the form for this aspiration was ready-made: it was the splendid poetic tradition that they were continuing. This was a given, both in Greece and outside: no one had to waste any time assuring himself of the importance of Homer, Sophocles, Romanos the Melodist, the folk songs, or Solomos. The novelists, by contrast, had nothing equivalent—certainly nothing within Greece. Thus we find Kazantzakis, early in his career, protesting that he did not aspire to become another Ksenopoulos or Karkavitsas, but rather another Homer, Dante, or Shakespeare,[10] while later in his career, even after he had won international fame as a novelist, he still denigrated prose and continually assumed that he did his best work only in poetry or drama—*because those were in the Greek tradition.*

Though much has been accomplished in Greek prose, poetry is still clearly predominant in Greece as the twentieth century draws to its close. This is because poetry, in ways that prose could not duplicate, enabled its practitioners to reach back into their own national inwardness while at the same time avoiding insularity—since the Greek poetic tradition which granted them their identity belongs as well to the entire Western world.

Peter Bien, Spring 1985

[1] *Politeía* [newspaper], 16 October 1927. Cited in K. Dhimaras, *Istoría tis neoellinikís loghotehnías,* 3rd ed., Athens, Ikaros, 1964, p. 375.

[2] *Ródha ke míla,* vol. 4, Athens, 1907, p. 254. Cited in Dhimaras, p. 376.

[3] "Yíro sto neoellinikó mithistórima," *Eléfthera Ghrámata,* 15 September 1946, pp. 267–68. Compare Mirambel's *La littérature grecque moderne* ("Que sais-je?" no. 560), Paris, Presses Universitaires de France, 1965, pp. 59–70.

[4] *Ta prósopa ke ta kímena,* vol. 2, Athens, 1943, p. 35. Cited in Thomas Doulis, *Disaster and Fiction,* Berkeley, University of California Press, 1977, p. 157.

[5] Cited in Doulis, p. 167. In fact, Theotokas was inveighing less against poetry than against the traditional *ithoghrafikó* novel that ignored urban life and concentrated on the Greek village.

[6] "I néa ellinikí pezoghrafía," *To Néon Krátos,* September 1937, p. 69. Cited in Doulis, p. 169.

[7] For a meticulous examination of a twelfth-century prose romance's borrowings from *Leucippe and Cleitophon,* see Margaret Alexiou, "A Critical Reappraisal of Eustathios Makrembolites' *Hysmine and Hysminias,*" *Byzantine and Modern Greek Studies,* 3 (1977), pp. 23–43.

[8] A. R. Rangabé, *Précis d'une histoire de la littérature néohellénique,* vol. 2, Berlin, 1877, p. 271. Cited in Peter Bien, *Kazantzakis and the Linguistic Revolution in Greek Literature,* Princeton, N.J., Princeton University Press, 1972, p. 68.

[9] On the three major poets discussed in this essay, see the following: on Seferis, see *BA* 41:1 (Winter 1967), pp. 37–38, and 42:2 (Spring 1968), pp. 190–98; on Ritsos, see *BA* 48:1 (Winter 1974), pp. 15–20, *WLT* 53:4 (Autumn 1979), pp. 639–40, and 57:3 (Summer 1983), pp. 416–18; on Elytis, see *BA* 49:4 (Autumn 1975), pp. 627–716, and *WLT* 54:2, pp. 189–201. On other poets see the 780-page anthology *Modern Greek Poetry,* Kimon Friar, ed. & tr., New York, Simon & Schuster, 1973 (reviewed in *BA* 48:1 [Winter 1974], p. 198).

[10] Elli Alexiu, "Enas meghálos," *Néa Estía,* Christmas 1977, p. 31.

Tyranny and Myth in the Plays of Four Contemporary Greek Dramatists

The coup d'état by the Greek colonels in 1967 put a damper on the traditionally lively Athenian theatre scene. Strict censorship, imposed by the military government, seemed to foreclose any possibility of its being revived. Theatre forms traditionally popular in Athens were ill-suited to the political realities, and as a result, the Greek theatre was compelled to transform itself. Its apparently comatose state in the late sixties proved to be only a transitional stage. Censorship played a greater role in determining the nature of the Greek theatre during the final years of the dictatorship than did the idiosyncrasies of individual playwrights, the traditional preferences of the audience and even an apparent theoretical leaning toward the ideas of Brecht and Piscator. Among the most striking characteristics of the new theatre was the production of plays which fulfill the criteria for myth and ritual described in *The Theater and Its Double* by Antonin Artaud.

In these plays there are no anthropomorphic gods typical of classical myth. Instead there are new mythical figures representing man-made forces—economic, social, political—which, having achieved superhuman proportions, have turned on their makers to oppress them. The protagonists of these contemporary myths usually do not have the unique, individualistic traits common in realistic drama; instead they are typical, Everyman characters representative of humanity in general.

Despite their obvious debt to contemporary Western dramatic theory, the new Greek playwrights did more than imitate foreign models. Each work bears the individual stamp of the dramatist's imagination and talent as well as reflecting the influence of the censor. In addition, these plays appealed, as their immense popularity during the time of the dictatorship and only during that time indicates, to an indigenous transformation of the Greek theatregoer's sensibility. The theatre dealt with social and political needs by means of the esthetic experience. Incapable of changing the external world of the spectator, the theatrical performance provided a sublimation, a consolation and, ultimately, the source of a heightened awareness of common spiritual needs denied by the physical reality to which the Greek was obliged to conform.

In the fifties and early sixties, before the imposition of the dictatorship, the Athenian theatre offered four basic choices: situation comedies; melodramas; revues with topical satire, music and plump dancers; and, from the West, serious plays. A typical theatre season, that of 1963–64, for example, offered the most successful plays from New York, London and Paris in addition to important revivals. Bolt's *A Man for All Seasons,* Pirandello's *Tonight, We Improvise* and Genet's *The Balcony* were among the imports. In their variety of interests, the Athenian theatregoers resembled their counterparts in any democratic country.

Reflecting the circumstances created by the dictatorship, the taste of the Greek theatregoer changed radically. In part, the change is evident in the kind of foreign plays which began to draw large and enthusiastic audiences. Considering the traits shared by their governments with the Athens regime, it should not be surprising that Central Europe became an important source for new plays. Two of the biggest hits of the 1973–74 season were *Tango* by Polish playwright Slawomir Mrozek and *The Holders of the Keys* by the Czech Milan Kundera. Other plays were Havel's *Memorandum* and an adaptation of Jaroslav Hašek's *Good Soldier Schweik.* Pavel Kohout, another Czech, had two plays, *Poor Murderer* and *Augustus, Augustus,* running concurrently. Many of the plays which came from the West during the same season were part of the dramatic tradition, described by Rosette Lamont as "metaphysical farce," which inspired the Central European plays. Among these plays were Ionesco's *The Thirst and the Hunger,* Jean-Paul Sartre's *No Exit,* Roger Vitrac's *Victor, or The Children Take Power* and two different presentations of Alfred Jarry's *Ubu Roi.* Some of the plays mentioned above had been previously performed in Greece, but their revival during the 1973–74 season along with similar plays reinforces the impression that their return was due not to chance but to the fact that they served certain compelling needs of the audience.

Further evidence of the reorientation of the Greek theatre audience is the acceptance of plays by serious contemporary Greek playwrights. Between 1970 and 1974 over fifty-two new plays by Greek dramatists were produced, something unheard of in modern Greece where audiences have normally preferred their "quality" theatre to bear a foreign signature. Prominent among the many dramatists produced during this period are Yiorghos Kampanellis, who differs from the others in that he had produced several successful plays before 1967, Yiorghos Skourtis, Marietta Rialdi and Stratis Karras, whose plays will be discussed here.

Kampanellis's "Our Great Circus" is a series of historical vignettes loosely tied together with songs and placards which underline their common significance. The scenes are set in classical Greece and in the Byzantium of 1821, the time of the Greek revolution. Greek history is presented as a ritual repetition of a modern Cronus myth whose motifs include internecine strife, revolt and betrayal. In "Our Great Circus" history and myth become one in a recurring nightmare of momentary glory subverted by treachery and transformed into defeat and subjugation. As in the ancient myth, Cronus swallows his children, but in Kampanellis's version of the myth, instead of a Zeus waiting in the wings to overthrow his tyrant father, there are brave persons willing to sacrifice themselves in a foredoomed insurrection against oppression. Kampanellis's play provides a dramatic paraphrase of Ernst Cassirer's statement, "The myth of a people does not determine but is its fate." The fruit of the struggle is always snatched from those who fight. They are set aside and forgotten until long after their deaths, when they are no longer a threat. Then they are transformed by those who betrayed them into inoffensive symbols of patriotism, and statues are raised in their honor.

In the first scene agents of Philip of Macedon bribe the priests to set up a new Pythia at Delphi in order to secure a favorable oracle against Demosthenes and those who support the idea of uniting the city-states against the outsiders. Romios (the Greek) and Romiaki (the little Greek), the ringmaster-interlocutors who oversee the "circus" and occasionally participate in it, make feverish preparations to receive Philip's agents at Delphi. Romiaki plays the replacement for the High Priestess of Delphi (the old one having been done away with in order to increase the likelihood of oracles favorable to Philip). Romiaki and Romios frequently cross the line between their scenes of "historical" make-believe, and their function as observers, like the rest of the audience, is one of history. As in plays by Genet and

Brecht, the manipulation of the "real" and the "make-believe" serves to emphasize the abstract context of the situation.

Romiaki is both Romiaki and the new High Priestess. Simple soul that she is, she cannot believe that such underhanded skullduggery as she is called upon to perform is possible. She is terrified of being punished by Zeus for impersonating a priestess (until Romios, playing a priest in the pay of the Macedonians, assures her that Zeus too has been bought off), and at the same time she fears the consequences of failing her new masters. To bring herself and her nerves under control, the new High Priestess gets drunk and almost bungles her first oracle. Finally Philip gets what he wants, and the High Priestess is the first to give herself to his representatives.

Kampanellis's audiences did not miss the mythical allusions to their own political experience. They were sure to associate the corrupt oracle and the contemporary affairs of the Greek Orthodox Church. Both dictators, George Papadopoulos and Dimitris Ioannidis, who overthrew the former, having taken secular affairs in hand, did not neglect the Greek Church. They had their men "elected" Archbishop of Athens and made certain that the official incense carried prayers on their behalf.

Byzantium provides the setting for another reenactment of the myth. A beggar lavishes praise on Andronicus, the usurper of the Byzantine throne, while revealing that Constantinople has been sold piecemeal to "allies" who have acquired port facilities and are greedily preparing for more. The revolutionary heroes of 1821 liberate Greece with their blood and in good faith greet the new king imposed on them by their "Christian protectors" of the Holy Alliance. They live to see the land they fought for divided up among Bavarian fortune hunters and obsequious Greeks who failed to fight. Those who resist too much are permanently disposed of with the gift donated by their French protectors, the guillotine. The choice left to the heroes of 1821 is between death and servitude as porters for the rich and the powerful.

In the manner of Brecht, Kampanellis links the scenes of his play with songs which summarize the action and focus on its meaning. Underlying each scene are the motifs of the Cronus myth. All mythical heroes must struggle against the crushing forces of nature or, in Kampanellis's case, against the movement of history. What is reasserted, as each mythical hero takes arms against the forces which will eventually destroy him, is the indomitable nature of humanity. The myth is cyclical because there is always a new hero to rise up against the tyrants, whoever they are. Thus "Our Great Circus" is redeemed by those who never forget their pride or sell out. Because they renew a foredoomed struggle, Kampanellis gives these heroes a special dignity.

Conspiratorial euphoria and camaraderie dominated performances of "Our Great Circus" and of Skourtis's "Karaghiozis, Almost a Vizir." Whereas Kampanellis uses ancient Greek myth for the basic structure of "Our Great Circus," Skourtis taps the popular folk art of the shadow theatre. Its characters with their simple, caricatural personalities are archetypes of the Greek experience. Hadjiavatis is the bearded worshiper of authority and the constant companion of Karaghiozis. Stavrakas is the swaggering but cowardly tough who represents the lowlife of harbor cities. The Turks, including Mustafa Bey, Veligekas and the Vizir, are as powerful and capricious as the forces of nature. Karaghiozis, the Hellenized hero of the Turkish shadow theatre, needs all his cunning to survive in a world of injustice and violence. In using traditional folk characters and situations to make a commentary on the present, Skourtis participates in a tradition of sedition typical of shadow theatre in Mediterranean countries once part of the Ottoman Empire.

The traditional setting of plays about Karaghiozis presents the palace of the local Turkish dignitary on one side of the screen and Karaghiozis's hovel on the other. Most of Skourtis's play is set in the Vizir's throne room. However, in re-creating the traditional struggle between the haves and the have-nots, Skourtis does not permit us to forget for one moment that Karaghiozis and his friends live their lives in misery and poverty.

The lives they are forced to lead have left indelible evidence in their personalities and their physical appearance. Their typically exaggerated gestures, their unmotivated and endless violence and an atmosphere charged with greed and conspiracy all recall the puppet-like figures of Jarry's Ubu roi. Karaghiozis's hump (the symbol of oppression and countless beatings) and an exceptionally long arm (to provide a longer reach when he is stealing, begging or pummeling Hadjiavatis or one of his sons) describe his nature and condition as vividly as Ubu's pear-shaped frame. Karaghiozis's adventure begins because the Vizir is beset by his own courtiers who seek to overthrow him. To save his throne he calls upon the ever-ravenous and cunning Karaghiozis and his friends, who through sheer blundering luck manage to drive out the rebels and find themselves the possessors of an empty throne vacated by the terrified Vizir. Karaghiozis places himself on the throne and discovers its ability to provide him and his party with abundant food. His scepter, quite appropriately, is a large soup ladle (which recalls Jarry's more audacious use of a toilet cleaning brush for the same purpose). Power is the source of food, and soon Karaghiozis and his cohorts are groaning with distended stomachs.

In the meantime the Vizir, reconciled with his chastened lieutenants, returns to recapture the privileges abandoned to the common people. The unprepared Karaghiozis is as decisive a leader as Ubu when he comes under strong attack. He quickly finds himself dethroned and hungry again. The parallel with the almost bloodless coup of 21 April 1967 is clear. Anyone who wants power must be organized enough and willing enough to hold on to it.

Those who cannot hold power must learn to live with it; this is the subject of "Oust," Marietta Rialdi's tragic satire. "Oust" opens with the scene of a dreamlike bourgeois party. The actors' words are drawn out and meaningless. Only Eriphili's crawling around the small stage bare-breasted while muttering incomprehensibly enlivens the scene. The dream becomes a nightmare with the entry of Ok. Wearing a long, double-breasted overcoat, beard, glasses and a military top, Ok announces that the City has just been saved. Of course everyone is grateful, but beyond that, they are also curious. They would like to know who has been saved and from whom. Ok refuses to go into details.

When Ok leaves there are new efforts to simulate lighthearted gaiety. However, the rather feeble effusiveness evaporates as the guests begin, without reason, to suspect one another of being linked to those from whom the city has been rescued. The party is interrupted a second time by Ok, who is pursuing a fugitive said to be responsible for allegedly threatening to create a disturbance at the railway station. The suspect must be apprehended in order to restore civic calm and confidence in the government. Ok appeals to Xenophon's patriotism and cupidity to stand in for the guilty party. Cooperation with the new regime will mean a short stay in jail, but the City will be saved and a substantial reward will be waiting for Xenophon when he is released from prison. Some of the other guests are induced to testify against him. After the undercover hero has been led to prison, the guests, reviewing the evening's events, come to believe that he is truly guilty.

Adelaïda and Hippocrates, the hosts, decide to play along with the new government, as they did with those which preceded it. They spy on their neighbors and show up at public meetings to applaud the leader and jeer at those out of favor. They take care of the government and the government takes care of them. As he must, the Leader eventually falls, and the City is rescued by new saviors in search of new scapegoats and collaborators. Accustomed as they are to tyranny, the citizens of the City easily fall in step. Only Eriphili, who is young and beautiful, cannot survive living permanently in a prison, and the final scene becomes her death rite.

"Oust" is a nightmarish charade of the real world. Each regime, whatever its pretensions, is like the one it overthrows. Each revolutionary government seeks to legitimize its oppressive and irrational existence by resorting to the claim that the security of the state is in peril. It seeks and creates scapegoats from among the innocent and uninvolved populace. Operating on the principle that those who are not for it are against it, the government coerces citizens to become informers and perjurers in exchange for material rewards and security.

Apart from the obvious political allusions in the play, its effect is to magnify the horror of the mechanism of oppression contained in "Oust"'s central myth. Rialdi's characters and their situations are too vague and too changeable to be ascribed to a specific source. At the same time the audience is led to the unavoidable consciousness of its own fears and insecurities in a world where heroes and traitors are manufactured from among its members in order to sustain the organized irrationality of the colonels.

Whereas Rialdi creates a bizarre, dreamlike world whose horror is mitigated by humor, the plays of Stratis Karras engender anguish without relief. In Karras's "The Troupers" there is endless waiting for events which fail to take place and suffering because of unwanted events which do occur. The effect of "The Troupers" is cumulative, a bit like seeing a particularly nasty dream several nights in a row. Karras's characters, seedy sideshow performers, earn their insecure livelihoods by brutally punishing themselves in order to entertain others. There are two sets of performers with similar acts competing for work from the same impresario. The competition between these characters increases their anguish and leads them to even more self-destructive behavior. Their competitive and insecure status is a gruesome parody of the world of the Greek worker: a world of unemployment and extreme competition for the few places which do exist, made even more unbearable by a tyrannical state.

Miltos and Melpos perform short skits in which Melpos impersonates a woman. Miltos is the first to enter the rural café where they have supposedly been hired to perform. When he enters he is happy, but the café is filled with threatening objects. He finds placards and is unable to determine whether they are for or against the "situation." Their discovery might lead to the cancellation of the performance. Worse yet, he could be punished if he is caught near them. Is it a trap? Obviously there is room for fear, but it cannot be defined or discussed. A blind man rides a bicycle onstage, but his answers to Miltos's questions only add to the confusion.

Melpos adds his nervous sense of unpreparedness to the scene. He and Miltos must set up the stage and rehearse. Next Londos, whose gimmick is the systematic devouring of an automobile, comes in with his mother. Londos suffers terribly because digesting automobile parts worsens his ulcer, but it is the only work he knows. The three performers wait with feverish anticipation for the Impresario who engaged them. For all of them work will mean an end to their suffering.

The Impresario never appears. Instead the blind cyclist returns from time to time to add to their anxiety with his cryptic words. To make matters worse, performers with acts paralleling those of Miltos, Melpos and Londos arrive. They claim to have been hired by the same Impresario and boast of their superior talents. Melpos, Miltos and Londos redouble their efforts to impress their employer. The play ends unresolved as the stage lights slowly fade out on the frantic preparations of the six actors.

Karras and his fellow dramatists create ritual and myth, as Artaud suggested it should be, from the obsessions of their contemporaries. Their abstract characters and situations are expressions of recurring elements in the history of the Greek nation which the military dictatorship only served to accentuate. If it is possible to gauge the atmosphere which prevailed in Greece during the dictatorship, surely the plays which I have discussed and others like them are an accurate measurement.

With the fall of the dictatorship in 1974, the needs of the audience changed. The restoration of democracy in Greece brought about the abolition of most forms of censorship and resulted in a so-called "crisis" in the theatre. Theatres which had enjoyed a large and growing patronage suddenly found themselves empty. Audiences became unpredictable once again and sought variety where previously they could only be satisfied with variations on the theme of oppression.

The 1975–76 season saw the comeback of the revue. The dictatorship and the new political situation provided ample material for their satirical skits. There was a backlog of previously forbidden material to perform. Playwrights such as Kampanellis and Skourtis were still looking for their bearings. Kampanellis's "The People Are the Enemy," although it drew large crowds attracted by the playwright's reputation, a musical score by the previously banned Mikis Theodorakis and a first-rate cast, lacked the power of "Our Great Circus." The social and political situation can be blamed for part of the lessened audience response, but once possessing the freedom to be more realistic and to appeal to the intellect, Kampanellis might be said to have neglected his ability to touch the emotions. Likewise Skourtis's "The

Strike" with its simplistic, agitprop construction is only a boring lecture in comparison with the fierce humor of his adaptation of the Karaghiozis tradition. Only Rialdi's "Concentration Camp City" retains the mythical and ritual elements typical of her previous plays, despite the use of more explicit political and sexual humor.

What are the conclusions one can draw from this account of the development of Greek theatre? One can say that the playwrights discussed here were forced by the limits of censorship to seek new ways of communicating with their audiences. In the resultant flowering of Greek drama they discovered not only that they were capable of creating compelling drama despite the limitations imposed upon them (perhaps because of them), but that there exist large audiences capable of appreciating what they produced. Perhaps the present crisis of the Greek theatre should not be attributed to the Athenian audience, which is accused of having deserted it for television and other lesser forms of entertainment, but to the dramatists themselves, who failed to learn from their success with the abstract, indirect forms of myth and ritual and have instead strayed from their audiences.

E. D. Karampetsos, Spring 1979

The Stream of Consciousness in Greek Fiction

If it is true that the stream-of-consciousness technique in Anglophone fiction came as a natural, perhaps inevitable, development of the interior-monologue method,[1] one must assert that a comparable phenomenon occurred in Greek literature as well. All three of the greatest practitioners of stream of consciousness in English—Virginia Woolf, James Joyce, and William Faulkner—began their careers by writing in rather conventional forms, gradually turned to the interior monologue in works on introspective heroes with artistic inclinations or great sensitivity, and finally reached out and plunged into the waves of the consciousness of special characters, recording the complex workings of their psyches and minds in a freer and looser register of human experience. Thus, Woolf's novel *The Voyage Out* (1915) came before *Jacob's Room* (1922) and *Mrs. Dalloway* (1925), Joyce's *Dubliners* (1914) and *A Portrait of the Artist as a Young Man* (1915) predated *Ulysses* (1922) and *Finnegans Wake* (1939), and Faulkner's *Sound and the Fury* (1929) or *As I Lay Dying* (1930) and the Snopes trilogy were preceded by *Soldier's Pay* (1926) and *Mos-*

quitoes (1927). This chronological development is not absolute, of course, since Woolf and the American returned to traditional forms in later phases of their careers.

Certainly in the background of these works of fiction looms the presence of the French masters of psychological novels—Flaubert, Proust, even Gide—and, undoubtedly, the shadow of the great Russian analysts of the human soul: Dostoevsky, Tolstoy, Chekhov, and others. With the popularization of the psychological theories of Freud and Jung, novelists found in psychology a more solid and real foundation to erect the edifice of their fictional cosmos.

In Greece literary developments had reached a degree of intellectual maturity in the 1930s, a whole century after the establishment of a free Greek state (1830) and following two generations of historical and folkloric fiction whose main concern was the assertion of the essential Greekness and the national identity of the modern Greeks. Sociopolitical issues in Europe around the turn of the century, Greece's costly involvement in liberation wars (1912–22), the final collapse of Great Idea politics (1922), and the subsequent arrival of destitute refugees from Asia Minor and other lands radically altered the hitherto agrarian and idyllic village ethic of the country and underscored the rapid growth of urban centers with their first large-scale industries and new sociological phenomena and ensuing problems.[2]

The Greek intelligentsia had always kept their eyes on the achievements of the Europeans, as the British and Americans had on the French and other continentals. Thus, Greek novelists of the famous Generation of the 1930s—Myrivilis, Politis, Terzakis, Theotokas, Panayotopoulos, Venezis, Doukas, Akritas, Petsalis, Tsirkas, Hadzis, Sotiriou, et alia—started publishing then fairly mature works of psychological fiction with a good dose of social realism, although in these developments they had been preceded by the novels of K. Hadjopoulos and A. Papahiamandhis, who had bridged, as it were, the chasm between the folkloric and the more problematic aspects of Greek life a generation earlier.

Writers in Athens and Salonika, the Macedonian capital liberated by the Greeks in 1912, followed artistic developments in Europe via the medium of the French language, then being taught in secondary schools. French cultural magazines such as *Les Nouvelles Littéraires, Nouvelle Revue Française,* and later the *Revue de Deux Mondes* and *Le Figaro* became the vehicles via which the Greeks mostly secured access to French and, generally, European artistic, literary, philosophic, and sociopolitical manifestations and thoughts. Also, they could read French literature in the original, and English

Odysseus Elytis *(AP/Wide World Photos)*

and other texts through French translations. Very few knew English, but that did not matter much, since even Greece's national bard during the revolution era (1821–30), Dionysios Solomos, had developed his awareness and information primarily through Italian translations of seminal books of the period.

It seems that the Salonikan intelligentsia were bent on surpassing their Athenian fellow artists in terms of showing awareness of what was *en vogue* in Paris and the sophisticated European capitals; they therefore took their French readings more seriously and responded to their novelties more creatively than did the Old Greece authors. This perhaps accounts for the fact that most of the writers who "discovered" the avant-garde fiction of Woolf, Joyce, Mansfield, Proust, and Gide were all members of the Salonika circle of energetic writers, translators, and critics in the 1930s.[3]

These men were impressed by the interior-monologue method and, generally, by the kind of fiction that featured sensitive and introverted loners trying to cope with their problems, anxieties, or neuroses. They were also interested in radical attitudes vis-à-vis the questionable endurance of established moral, social, and esthetic standards—a touch of André Gide. These Salonikans produced a number of books employing similar methods of conveying primarily the inner world of their characters. Stelios Xefludas published "The Notebooks of Pavlos Photinos" (1930), "Men of Myth" (1946), and a few other books; Alkis Yannopoulos published one novel, "The Salamander" (1959), plus a number of stories in a comparable vein; George Delios wrote the novels "Nostalgic Men" (1934), "In the Tracks of the Unknown God" (1937), and "Family" (1957), plus stories and a good deal of literary criticism. All three have passed away, but the novelty of their interior-monologue method and of their up-to-date themes in presenting introspective "heroes" was noticed by academics teaching in the progressive university of their city; thus Linos Politis[4] and Apostolos Sahinis include short paragraphs on them in their literary histories or reviews.[5] Constantine Dimaras, the other noted cultural historian, refers to them very briefly or just registers their names.[6] I do not think that he was wrong or biased, for their books are rather tedious and not very carefully written, all esthetic presuppositions considered; to boot, few people read them. The fact remains, however, that these were the pioneers who blazed the trail which soon afterward led Greek fiction to the stream of consciousness proper and to more artistic work by others. In addition, Delios translated a few short stories by Woolf and Mansfield and wrote a long introduction in his published edition of these works. There, as in his earlier treatise on the contemporary novel (1940), Delios proved that his research had not been limited to the pages of the French magazines—especially in the case of his presentation of the two British ladies in 1963.[7] Later he wrote about Faulkner and others too.

The fourth, greatest, and still-active Salonikan pioneer, Nikos Gabriel Pentzikis (b. 1908), is a French-trained pharmacist who dedicated his life and inexhaustible energy to the cultural enrichment of his native city by means of an endless stream of literary publications, critical commentaries, translations, paintings, and lectures. He also holds the honor of being the first serious exponent of Joyce's *Ulysses,* acting either in a team of local translators or by himself. Moreover, Pentzikis had translated Edouard Dujardin's 1887 work *Les lauriers sont coupés,*[8] the very text that the Irishman had claimed as the model for his stream-of-consciousness technique.

Pentzikis's early novel *Andhreas Dhimakoudhis* (1935) belongs to the same introverted climate that conditioned the fiction of Xefludas and the other less-popular writers of that genre, but it is artistically superior, as is his later work, "Mrs. Ersi's Novel" (1966). These novels, as well as the better-known work "The

Dead and the Resurrection" (1944; rev. ed. 1970), follow the interior-monologue fashion and even expand it almost to the limits of the stream-of-consciousness method.[9] All in all, the truth is that no artist in Greece has done as much as Pentzikis to naturalize the stream of consciousness in fiction of typically Greek flavor and concerns. For the sake of history, I must mention here that the interior monologue, in a dramatic form variation, reached its apotheosis in the incomparable and popular novel *The Third Wedding Wreath* (1962) by Costas Taktsis, as its excellent translator John Chioles brilliantly showed in his introduction to it (1985). Its first British translation was by Leslie Finer (1967).

To complete the record of the establishment of this genre of fiction in Greece, one must also take a look at the texts of Woolf, Joyce, and Faulkner that appeared in Greek and observe *who* translated them and *when.* This examination may sound pedantic, but it is the only way to ascertain facts that will help one accept the 1960s as the period of this genre's coming of age in Greek literaure, since most Greek readers and reviewers read their first stream-of-consciousness specimens in translation.[10]

A partial list of Joyce translations begins in 1936 with Takis Papatsonis's version of the opening part of Molly Bloom's monologue. Pentzikis, alone or with his Salonikan team, published many excerpts from *Ulysses* in 1945–46 and later; Yannis Thomopoulos and Leonidas Nikolouzos, primarily the former, published the whole novel during the period 1969–76.[11] Pentzikis's sister Zoë Karelli is probably responsible for "Interior Monologue" (1935). Sophia Mavroidi-Papadaki translated "The Dead," and Menis Koumandareas "Evelyn" (1960). *A Portrait of the Artist as a Young Man* was done by M.S.(?) in 1965, *Dubliners* by Cosmas Politis in 1972 and Mando Aravandinou in 1971 and 1977; the latter also rendered excerpts from *Finnegans Wake* (1974–76), plus *Giacomo Joyce* and "The Cat and the Devil" (1977), as well as two popular studies of Joyce's life and knowledge of Greek (1977, 1983). It must be noted here that Papatsonis, Papadaki, Karelli, and Aravandinou are first-rate poets, whereas Politis, Pentzikis, and Koumandareas are excellent prose writers. They certainly must have absorbed some Joycean elements as they were laboring over his texts. Aravandinou even learned to employ stream-of-consciousness tactics in her esoteric free verse.

A partial list of Woolf's works in Greek starts with Delios's pieces from *The Death of the Moth* and *A Writer's Diary* (1963); K. Mitropoulou then translated *Mrs. Dalloway* in 1967, as did P. Kalantzis in 1973; Myrto Anagnostopoulou translated "Three Guineas," Mina Dalamanga *A Room of One's Own* (1980), and Elli Marmara

To the Lighthouse (1981). English scholar Olympia Karayorga marked the sad anniversary of Woolf's death with a biographical-critical study published in 1981. Once again, two of the translators, Delios and Mitropoulou, were already novelists of some note.

Faulkner's partial list is longer. Nikos Bakolas heads it with his version of *The Sound and the Fury* (1963), a work also rendered by Takis Mendrakos (1974). Yannis Lamizas translated *Sanctuary* (1965), Basil Kazantzis *The Reivers* (1966), D. P. Kostelenos *The Hamlet* (1969, 1982), Menis Koumanadeas *As I Lay Dying* (1970), Cosmas Politis *The Wild Palms* (1971), and Elli Marmara *Absalom, Absalom!* (1980). Several others translated some of Faulkner's stories in 1970 and afterward. Greek studies of Faulkner were published by the Cypriot A. Christophidis (1966) and the late George Delios (1974), an admirer of Woolf and Mansfield. Again we note distinguished names here, including Koumandareas and Politis, even Bakolas, who did a few original novels later on. Koumandareas was directly influenced by the American, as we shall see, whereas Politis had already reached the end of his creative career, having published good traditional novels in the 1930s and later.

The major point I wish to make in terms of chronology is that, with the exception of the appearance of parts of *Ulysses* in the decade 1936–46 (in limited-circulation magazines), the bulk of translations of such stream-of-consciousness works grew dramatically in the early 1960s. By 1980 several seminal novels had appeared, whereas before 1970 two bona fide stream-of-consciousness novels had followed the lead of Pentzikis's earlier work, with noticeable improvements. The year 1960 may therefore be taken as the *terminus post quem* in the Hellenization of this avant-garde technique.

At this juncture a digression should be made to emphasize the fact that after 1960, additional paragons began to bear on further developments in avant-garde narrative techniques in psychological and "cerebral" fiction: namely, the *nouveau roman* and *anti-roman* in France, with Alain Robbe-Grillet, Nathalie Sarraute, Michel Butor, and Claude Simon in the forefront of experimentation since the early 1950s. Greek translations followed a few years later, and critical commentaries were published by competent specialists such as A. Karandonis, A. Sahinis, and many others after 1965.[12] Translations of Robbe-Grillet's *Instantanés* and Sarraute's *Tropismes* were published in a joint edition by Tatiana Tsaliki-Milioni in 1970 featuring short fiction samples from both.

Since almost all the Greek novelists and translators I have cited so far know French much better than English—and often translate from French translations or use them as guides[13]—it would have been unscholarly and unfair if I were not to mention the impact of "the French connection" in this respect. Then again, most of these French innovators were well versed in the work of the three Anglophone masters, plus Durrell and Beckett; so the scheme of influences seems to form a complete circle.

In all probability, the first bona fide stream-of-consciousness novel was published in 1963 by Tatiana Gritsi-Milliex, the cosmopolitan wife of a French literary critic: ". . . And Behold a Pale Horse," which, although it reminds us of Faulkner's writings and concerns, must owe something to other influences as well. It is the sad story of Helen, a widow, who bravely faces the hardships of war and the German Occupation in an Athens suburb, reminiscing about sufferings, loves, hopes, and traumas. Each new chapter complicates the plot with the addition of new characters and their adventures. As this happens, the focus shifts to their viewpoints, although the controlling sensibility remains young Helen's. Thus, her initial interior monologues turn into stream of consciousness, with events and characters floating, as it were, at several points in time and place. The critic Alexander Kotzias insightfully commented that the novel is successful in its purpose to explore the inner world of the heroine, "because everything that happens is filtered through memory. A memory, though, that does not start at a fixed point in time, and from an already settled situation, or from one person only" (my translation).[14]

Helen's mental and physical pains make a moving story as Gritsi-Milliex manipulates her material. Some critics and readers, however, have found her stylistic mannerisms and form somewhat artificial, if not contrived. For instance, her title and epigraph from the Book of Revelations (6:8) were judged rather exaggerated even by Kotzias. As a woman, however, and as a veteran novelist since 1947, she is entitled to view that sad period and its innocent victims as an apocalypse of horror not unlike that of Francis Ford Coppola's film *Apocalypse Now*. A woman's sensitivity ranges beyond the limits of men's awareness. A woman writer has the right to see her heroine from the viewpoint of a fellow sufferer. Since the characters in ". . . And Behold a Pale Horse" had done nothing to invite any form of metaphysical punishment, the absurdity of man's malice toward man can be treated in terms of an incomprehensible apocalyptic vision of unfathomable horror.

After a few years, another bona fide stream-of-consciousness text appeared: Menis Koumandareas's fine novella "The Burnt Ones" (1972). Remember that in 1960 this talented man had translated Joyce's "Evelyn" and in 1970 Faulkner's *As I Lay Dying*. Evidently Koumandareas's close reading of this American novel did not leave him unaffected as a young artist. I quote here from what I wrote then about his novella:

> In "The Burnt Ones" Koumandareas transformed the dreary details of a fatal accident that claimed the lives of two simple and irresponsible youths to a little masterpiece. Seldom had character delineation been done more effectively and without direct commentary, and seldom has the atmosphere of a small industrial town been evoked in a more telling and economical manner. Events past and present, questions, answers, and comments are all reported indirectly and registered in the mind of a bored newspaperman who comes from the capital to cover the accident. The shifting of point of view from paragraph to paragraph, and the interchange of subject and object—the first narrator becomes the subject-matter in the subsequent paragraph, and so on—are much more sophisticated devices than the conflicting points of view in *Rashomon* or the different narrators and their varying and overlapping accounts of the happenings in Faulkner's *As I Lay Dying*. . . . "The Burnt Ones" isn't easy reading, but the patient reader will experience great satisfaction in reading it.[15]

Indeed, as I reread the work, I could not help thinking of Faulkner's Dewey Dell, Darl, and Anse and of their level and kind of life, their predicaments and expectations, their adventures on the road, and the interference of outsiders and sudden events. Koumandareas's equivalents (Tsihlias, Marinos, Paraskevas) belong to a similarly low intellectual and social level. Their lives, vices, and problems are somehow analogous to those of Faulkner's poor whites in the American South. Before this wonderful novella, Koumandareas had written nothing so original in form and technique, although he had been a meticulous stylist from the beginning. Apparently he felt that stream-of-consciousness narration did not suit his purposes, so he gave it up and continued doing well with novels in rather conventional forms.

Another good writer who wrote a dramatic novel that must owe something to Faulkner is Nikos Kasdaglis. Less sophisticated and accomplished as an artist, Kasdaglis released "The Thirst" (1970), a novel in which the narrative is much more dramatic than meditative and the instances of interior monologue and stream of consciousness are rather limited and short. An alternating viewpoint and the titling of chapters after the names of the characters are present, however. Also, Kasdaglis's thematic concerns verge on those in *As I Lay Dying* (out-of-wedlock pregnancy, exploitation, brutality, human

and social corruption, and the like). His characters "thirst for life" (hence the title), just like the American Southerners thirsted for their goal in life. "The Thirst" is a challenging novel, but Kasdaglis, like Koumandareas, has since opted for more traditional forms in his work. Of the two, the latter's novella is the much better integrated piece of avant-garde fiction.

While discussing the Joyce-Faulkner impact on Greek fiction of this kind, I must expand the focus by turning my attention to Cypriot writers as well, since they, as former British "colonials," knew English better and had more direct access to English culture than did the Hellenic novelists of their generation. Here again, one notices writers who used instances of interior monologue—and even stream of consciousness—in their otherwise rather traditional fiction; one will also discover at least two major novels employing a bona fide stream-of-consciousness technique. Foremost in the first category is Panos Ioannidis; dominant in the second is Hebe Meleagrou.

In his intriguing *Apographe*—*Historema* (Census: A Narrative; 1973), Ioannidis achieves an indirect but keen commentary on situations and characters whose conscience and behavior were conditioned by more or less ominous developments in their small macrocosm and in their inner microcosms. The story is fairly complex and long, but the end result is that of an accomplished craftsman. However, the catastrophe that "Census" foreshadows occurred a little later (1974), and the author has since exploited those sorry events in literature of a more conventional nature, probably to reach a larger readership.

The best exemplar, however, of the stream-of-consciousness method in Cypriot letters, and perhaps in Greek literature as an ethnic whole, is Hebe Meleagrou, a well-read and ambitious innovator in the realm of political or engaged fiction. In her first novel, the successful "Eastern Mediterranean" (1969), Meleagrou had utilized personal experiences and the historical circumstances that had engendered them to compose a genuine stream-of-consciousness text containing a rich gallery of local and foreign characters, whose lives and vicissitudes constitute an oblique record of what was happening and a prophecy as to what may lie in store for their island and themselves in the near future. Hers was a decisive plunge into the stream of events and of people's consciousness quite beyond the range and depth of Ioannidis in Cyprus. Expanding on the number of her characters and their walks of life, taking advantage of momentous events and of ensuing social, political, psychological, and moral themes, Meleagrou released in 1981 her masterpiece, "The Last Epoch but One," a novel in which the stream-of-consciousness

technique reached the perfection that distinguishes mature and sophisticated art. In my *World Literature Today*
review of the work (56:4, p. 732) I wrote:

> Through the dexterous use of flashback, interior
> monologue, dramatic scenes and a stream-of-
> consciousness technique reminiscent (but not
> imitative) of Joyce's and Faulkner's narrative
> methods, the Cypriot writer obliquely alludes to
> events, thoughts, actions and emotions that are
> experienced by the characters, in a constant shift-
> ing of time from the present day to various mo-
> ments in the past. Thus her mostly anonymous
> and representative characters act out their self-
> creation as they dramatize the events of the plot.
> Caught in a conflict involving forces beyond their
> ken, the characters envisage dynamic solutions
> whose consequences they anticipate on a shaky
> basis of wishful thinking motivated by chauvin-
> ism, or else they commit the Dantean sin of omis-
> sion and indifference. Mr. Ion, the Theologian,
> the Policeman, Margarita, Ioanna, Lucas, Emin
> Aga, the Army Commander and a host of other
> men and women from many walks of life become
> the unknowing agents of personal and even na-
> tional catastrophe, or are passively carried away
> by the momentum of unleashed powers leading
> to an inevitable as well as inexorable climax with-
> out a catharsis. . . . Seen, felt, dramatized and ex-
> perienced from within—from the center of con-
> sciousness of the persons who animate it—
> *Próteleftea epohí* is an impressive and demanding
> novel with no easy match in recent Hellenic liter-
> ature.

I would only add now that the overwhelming public
concern in Cyprus, the agony and anxiety vis-à-vis the
Greek Cypriots' survival as an ethnic group on their
home island and as individual units in it, seems to have
perfectly harmonized content and form in "The Last
Epoch but One" by the gifted and politically minded
Hebe Meleagrou.[16]

Returning to the fiction of Greece proper since
1960, one can distinguish two broad categories of novels employing comparable avant-garde methods: those
inspired by the agony of the individual in search of an
identity amid the collapsing moral edifice in the social
milieu; and those involving an indentical search by individuals who feel lost among the roles (real or imaginary) they think they must play in order to cope with
a crisis forced upon them by external factors. Although,
generally speaking, both categories consist of psychological novels, the first is obviously more political in nature—like Meleagrou's—whereas the second focuses
mainly on esthetic considerations and even mental aberration or disorientation. Authors in both seem obsessed with the tormenting process of giving utterance

to, and finding proper forms to express, the terror of
their gradual alienation. The Anglophone echoes in
them are few and faint. Topical and typical Greek circumstances have inspired them.

One of the best political novelists now active in
Athens is Alexander Kotzias, a prolific translator, author, and reviewer with a firm reputation. Even his earliest novel, "The Siege" (1953), attests to his sociopolitical sensitivities. I am concerned, though, with his
fine novel "The Brave Telemachus" (1972) and his more
recent work, "Encroachment of Authority" (1979).
Since both have been analyzed elsewhere,[17] I will only
mention that Kotzias employs in both works shifting
viewpoints, recording events and reactions to them
through the consciousness of the protagonists and main
agents of action in each episode. Interior monologues
occur frequently, and at times, as memory and intense
thinking overwhelm the actual event, the narrative acquires a stream-of-consciousness quality, though it
never reaches the complexity of, say, *Ulysses*. The latter,
however, may have suggested both the title and the central theme of "The Brave Telemachus," whose troubled
hero is shown in search of a father figure—analogous
to the Stephen Daedalus-Leopold Bloom situation—
since he wishes to reject his natural sire on account of
the latter's corruption. The circumstances and numerous characters that enhance the plot development have
to do with postwar machinations, economics, and politics, the civil war in Greece, and all manner of unsavory
details, both human and societal. The young hero,
though, struggles to retain his personal integrity amid
the chaos he senses around him.[18]

The same overall technique, with noticeable improvement in its effects, is used in "Encroachment of
Authority," Kotzias's indirect commentary on the moral
and social dereliction during the Junta years. The central hero and his friends experience the external social
storm from within, while their foes, brutal police and
paramilitary scum, perform their nefarious acts to per-
petuate the anomaly of the Colonels who had usurped
the state authority with their help. Again, all events are
reported through shifting centers of consciousness;
even the diabolical agents of this encroachment of
power are given the chance to voice their sick ideals and
attempt to justify their methods. The workings of tormented and tormenting minds and souls—agents and
their victims alike—subtly approximate the hell that
had descended upon the country. The stream-of-
consciousness technique enabled the author to harmonize form and content and to avoid sounding like a
preacher. As was the case with Meleagrou's political fiction, these novels achieved their desired objectivity and
convincing realism thanks to Kotzias's esoteric narra-

tive—a success that lesser writers of the militant left failed to secure because of their overt propaganda. His novels, nonetheless, lack the scope of Meleagrou's dissection of the sick and rotten body politic in Cyprus.

The young female narrator in Maro Douka's "Ancient Rust" (1979), one of the best novels on the same shameful period in Greece, functions as a woman who suffers. Her concerns, however, are more personal and immature, as she reminisces, after the collapse of the dictatorship, about her loves, her family, her friends, and the trials and tribulations they all went through, some of them losing their integrity in the process—her parents and several fanatical or indifferent friends included. As Peter Mackridge commented in the Autumn 1978 issue of *WLT* (54:4, p. 678): "Myrsine realizes her own faults, particularly an inability to communicate emotionally with other people (her mind is constantly overworking, so that even in her intimate moments she is observing herself, constructing scenarios of future developments, or simply fantasizing). The very writing itself shows this clearly: the other characters are not depicted vividly." Not as overtly political as Kotzias's "Encroachment of Authority," Douka's "Ancient Rust" is a novel that deals with the maturation process of Myrsine and other impressionable young students and mere workers, and with the inability of some to undergo any change for the better despite the imprisonments, tortures, and all manner of hardships they experienced. The narrative constantly shifts focus, as several levels of action or thought are reported in a rapid succession of chronological periods and locales in Myrsine's stream of consciousness, whose chaotic form approximates the outer confusion with which she has to cope. The stains of "the old rust" seem to have rubbed off on her skin as well. Finally, she emerges hurt but wiser, feeling cleansed and ready to start picking up the pieces of her shattered world and self. Mackridge's comments, though, may help us relate the nature of this novel to those of other women, who, much like Douka, begin their fictions with comparable political events and soon advance their key concerns to identity quests by young, tormented, imaginative women.[19]

Helen Ladia is an erudite lady who has published some very original collections of stories, fine translations of Orphic and Homeric hymns (with the poet D. P. Papaditsas), the extraordinary sequence of prose pieces titled "The Schizophrenic God" (1983), and the wonderful novel "Fragmentary Relationship" (1983), a work that brought her to the forefront of creative experimentation in prose fiction. I say "experimentation" because her writing style and plot structure differ tremendously from book to book, even when she rewrites the same story over and again, as in the case of "Fragmen-

tary Relationship." Having nothing in common with the Anglophone specimens I have cited so often, and not really much more in common with the *nouveau roman* and its French variations, Ladia's Muse is inspired by Kafkaesque nightmares and devices, and by Dostoevskian introspection. Ladia achieves a "supreme fiction"— to paraphrase Wallace Stevens—as she creates illusory "deceptions" for her reader, and for her narrating sensibilities too. To set her art in motion, she utilizes the intellectuals' anti-Junta activities and the 1974 Turkish invasion of Cyprus: i.e., a solid historical foundation upon which she builds a personal "fable." Her political considerations end with this surface element, however, for she is primarily concerned with the inner world(s) of her heroine(s) in the process of realizing an identity.

This predilection brings Ladia's fiction closer to the field of modern esthetics and to the theme of how literature is created—a process akin to John Barth's. She writes about the memories, thoughts, and adventures in the life of a young divorced woman, whose stream of consciousness involves a number of other persons in various locations and at various times, all within the same historical period and most of them fictitious and unreal. To boot, this tour de force is achieved in a rather vague and indefinite epistolary form without dates, addresses, full names, and other paraphernalia we have known since Richardson, Smollett, and their disciples. All these fabricated women, however, bear some relationship to their creator, the original narrator, and the narrator's inventor, Helen Ladia.[20] This secret is actually revealed on page 247, where the author concludes with the following confessional question: "And how will the Work that I have in my mind be written? What will I name you? Myrto, Thaleia, Haricleia, or otherwise?"

I implied earlier that it takes a feminine refinement of sentiment and intricate thinking to achieve this creative shifting of focus from the *external* (the factual details on the political plane) to the *internal* (their impact on the sensitive individual) world of the heroine—one of the author's masks. We saw how Kotzias emphasized the social condition, and how Douka subtly edged her concerns onto the existential becoming of her protagonist. With Ladia, this becoming is the dominant theme, because today's women, liberated as they are, still have to cope much more than men with a series of roles not of their own choice, or chosen wrongly on account of inexperience. The case of Kostoula Mitropoulou is even more challenging.

After an early start in 1958, a literary prize in 1962, and some thirty novels, dramas, and story collections to her credit by 1985, this energetic lady, who has translated texts by Virginia Woolf, Harold Pinter, Tennessee Williams, and other Anglophone artists, is now the most dynamic exponent of French-fashion avant-garde fiction. Mitropoulou's concern with politics was underscored with her novels "The Culprit" (1966), "Countdown" (1970), and "The Execution" (1973), plus, of course, her joining the 1973 student uprising at Athens Polytechnic University. A very sensitive, emotional, and traumatized lady, Mitropoulou has made her literary and theatre interests a means of self-vindication. Disillusioned with intimate relations, unsatisfied with the sociopolitical conditions in Greece, she has found therapy in virtually living her books and the theatre arts. Some of her best works—in very complex and involved stream of consciousness inspired by the *nouveau roman* and strange texts like Robbe-Grillet's *Dans le labyrinthe* (1959) and similarly labyrinthine narrative structures—have attracted the attention of professional scholars, who feel intrigued by her spectacular success. Her sales figures are high, and some of her books have gone through second or even third editions. In her scholarly monograph on Mitropoulou, Ritsa Frangou-Kikilia has expertly discussed the author's affinities with *les nouveaux romanciers* and has identified four main cycles of thematic concern in her work: numbers, fragmentation, music, and theatre.[21] These are best illustrated in the trilogy "This Theatre Was Him" (1982), "The Enlargement" (1983), and "Performance for One" (1985). Here is what she has to say about these three novels:

> In the first part of the trilogy, "This Theatre Was Him," *fragmentation* is the most characteristic element of the book; a fragmentation of objects, persons, body, soul, emotions. In "The Enlargement," the second part of the trilogy, the *abolished* dominates, not only with the abolition of others, but with the very feeling of *futility* at the moment something is being created and simultaneously has been abolished—an act of love, a dream, a myth, a person, the dominant passion. In "Performance for One" all these elements together are gathered in *one person,* the Author, who alone *stages* the performance with the abolished passion as *starting point,* and as *contents* the catalytically new of a love which is only "a performance for lovers who were abolished by their very reality." In the middle of such a *performance,* which is the whole "Cosmos in One," the Author will see his work being refuted, moment by moment; thus his very Life is refuted as well, together with the persons who were unexpectedly *contained* in a "Performance for One." (My translation, her italics.)

This dust-jacket statement gloriously reveals the esotericism of her thematic *problématique* and the kind of style and linguistic peculiarities Mitropoulou employs in her obsessive exploration of the real, the imaginary, the present, the absent, and all the states of the creative intellect and the tormented soul that her concerns inevitably invite. This makes for a tall order, and at least two American-trained comparatists have objected to her excessive complexity and not too careful working out of all details. Reviewing her "Performance for One" for *WLT* (58:1, p. 145), Thymios Karampetsos misread "a schizophrenic tropism" uniting writing and theme. Elsewhere, judiciously commenting on technique in the later collections of stories, "The Bench" (1984), Mara Yanní-Hadgopoúlou specified:

> The narrative technique in *O pángos* shows that Mitropoúlou is well aware of innovations in the art of fiction, for she experiments boldly with point of view, interior monologue, and time sequence. The final result, however, at times leaves the impression that the author has not mastered the proper technique for what she sets out to do. Lack of control in the point of view is an obvious weakness. Transitions from the perspective of an omniscient narrator to the center of a hero's consciousness are not always done smoothly; careless paragraph organization and the indiscriminate use of quotation marks in recalled speech or in actual expostulation often confuse even the professional reader.[22]

Yanní-Hadgopoúlou must be right, for in my own critique of Mitropoulou's unified collection of prose pieces, "Oscar, or the Smile in the Fresco" (1983), I had concluded that "there is a limit to what a short text can be and can bear. In my opinion, her undeniably great creative talent and energy will be served best by a greater degree of restraint and a lesser degree of artistry."[23] My advice implies that, like Ladia, Mitropoulou must learn to drop a hint here and there in the vagaries of her protean narrative to help her well-meaning fan follow her otherwise commendable stream-of-consciousness itineraries. Other scholars, however, have been more generous in assessing her skills. For instance, C. D. Gounelas liked her "Four Solitudes" (1981), and George Giannaris was impressed by "Life with the Others" (1982), mostly on account of her uniqueness of writing and thematic orientation.[24] Athenian commentators, as a whole, seem to enjoy this lady's radical innovations, despite minor peccadillos.

■ ■ ■

In retrospect, one must observe that the stream of consciousness in Greek letters has found its best expression in novelists who were primarily or initially motivated by political factors, with some of them eventually expanding their scope of awareness to the exploration of the mental and psychological processes of creating art (literature, theatre). The smooth transition was from the world *without* to the world *within*. One must also applaud the quality of women writers, who overwhelm the men at least in number, as their higher degree of sensitivity and emotional reaction to external stimuli has inspired them to experiment with esoteric and highly delicate issues quite impressively. The personal and environmental pressures that women experience in their now less-protected lives, as they become more liberated and thus more responsible for their decisions and behavior, have enabled creative women to achieve degrees of sophistication and excellence in psychological fiction of this kind which are normally reserved only for the seasoned masters among men.

One should also mention that, as with the celebrated Anglophone and Francophone achievements in this genre of prose fiction, the whole thing started with dogged experiments—by men like Xefludas, Delios, Yannopoulos, and Pentzikis almost half a century ago—in the application of interior-monologue sensibility to the indirect analysis of introspective individuals and eccentric characters. In time, authors' methods became bolder, just like Joyce's transition from *Dubliners to Ulysses.* Equivalents to the techniques of Woolf, Joyce, and Faulkner were approximated and, in a few cases, matched. The additional exposure of the Greeks some two decades later to the novelties of Robbe-Grillet, Sarraute, Butor, Simon, and other European and American writers motivated them to enlarge and enrich their artistic scope. It should also be emphasized that from the very beginning, no Greek novel in this avant-garde mode ever sounded unoriginal or imitative of alien models, at least no more than George Seferis's poetry is "imitative" of T. S. Eliot's or Odysseus Elytis's is of Paul Eluard's.

Koumandareas, Kotzias, Gritsi-Milliex, Meleagrou, Mitropoulou, Ladia, and Douka—to name only the most popular and rightfully acclaimed—now hold in the field of modern Greek fiction a place of distinction, a place almost as prominent as that of *les nouveaux romanciers* in France. After all, the French masters also had the same Anglophone masters as the Greeks of the first generation in the formative 1930s.

Marios Byron Raizis, Summer 1986

[1] This is inferred from a comparison of entries for these terms in manuals such as Harry Shaw's *Concise Dictionary of Literary Terms,* New York, McGraw-Hill, 1976. William James coined the phrase "stream of consciousness" in his 1890 treatise *Principles of Psychology.*

[2] Consult Thomas Doulis's excellent study *Disaster and Fiction: Modern Greek Fiction and the Impact of the Asia Minor Disaster of 1922,* Berkeley, University of California Press, 1977. Subsequent references use the abbreviation *DF.* For a review, see *WLT* 52:2 (Spring 1978), p. 324.

[3] See the poet George Th. Vafopoulos's fascinating *Aftovioghrafikes selidhes* (Autobiographical Pages); Athens, Estia, 1970–75, 4 vols. for numerous references to the Salonikan scene during four decades.

[4] Linos Politis, *A History of Modern Greek Literature,* Oxford, Clarendon, 1973, pp. 261–62.

[5] A. Sahinis in his review of Xefludas's "Cycle" (1944) relates the author's thematic affinities and psychological sensitivity to those of Woolf, although he notes diametrical differences too. *I pezoghrafi tis Katohis* (The Prose Writers of the Occupation), Athens, Ikaros, 1948, pp. 129–34.

[6] C. Th. Dimaras. *A History of Modern Greek Literature,* Mary Gianos, tr., Albany, Suny Press, 1972. p. 494.

[7] *Dhio aglidhes pezoghrafi* (Two English Women Prose Writers), Athens, Fexis, 1963, pp. 9–70.

[8] George Thaniel, *Homage to Byzantium: The Life and Work of Nikos Gabriel Pentzikis,* Minneapolis. North Central, 1983, p. 12. For a review, see *WLT* 57:4 (Autumn 1983), p. 673. I am indebted to Thaniel and Vafopoulos for my comments on Pentzikis.

[9] Stavros Deligiorgis, the translator of a chapter from Pentzikis's book *The Dead and the Resurrection,* commented to me, "It's actually a metaphysical monologue whose thematic concerns remind us of Dostoyefsky; while its stream-of-consciousness technique somehow resembles the more esoteric passages of Joyce's *Ulysses,* or the less involved ones in *Finnegans Wake.*" I incorporated this on p. 257 of my introduction, "The Literary Renaissance in Post-War Greece," *The Literary Review: Greece,* 16:3 (Spring 1973). Pentzikis's text in Deligiorgis's translation appears on pp. 268–72.

[10] Findings of research in the card catalogues of the National Library, the Parliament Library, and the University Library, all in Athens.

[11] Iakovos Pairidis, a small Athenian publisher with artistic inclinations, released this Hellenized *Ulysses* in ten thin books, which were later bound in three larger volumes (1969–76).

[12] For example, A. Sahinis's *To neo mythistorima* (The New Novel), Salonika, Konstantinidhis, 1972.

[13] Joyce's translator Yannis Thomopoulos admitted this, as did others, when I pointed out major or minor errors in their versions.

[14] A. Kotzias, *Metapolemiki pezoghrafi* (Postwar Prose Writers), Athens, Kedhros, 1982, p. 85.

[15] See p. 262 of my introduction in *The Literary Review: Greece* (note 10) and pp. 357–86 for Deligiorgis's translation of this novella.

[16] Meleagrou's novel was enthusiastically reviewed by the daily and periodical press, and by radio and television commentators in Nicosia and Athens, who interviewed her. I participated in her Athens television appearance and was interviewed by K. Serezis. The rector of the Panteios School of Political Science in Athens organized a panel discussion of this novel, with the author and myself as keynote speakers. The book received one of Greece's 1982 literary awards.

[17] See M. Byron Raizis, "Alexander Kotzias: A Portrait of a Man of Principle," *Greek World* (New York), July-August 1977, pp. 41–42.

[18] A chapter from "The Brave Telemachus" titled "Going Home" was included (in S. Kafatou's translation, pp. 37–51) in *Eigh-*

teen Texts: Writings by Contemporary Greek Authors, Willis Barn-
stone, ed., Cambridge, Ma., Harvard University Press, 1972.
The same volume contains Koumandareas's "Holy Sunday on
the Rock" in Deligiorgis's translation (pp. 161–66), the companion piece to "The Burnt Ones," in their combined Athens
edition. "Athos" by N. Kasdaglis is also included in N. G. Ger-
manakos's translation, pp. 135–51, as are texts by fifteen other
famous authors who defied the Junta.

[19] "The Ancient Rust" was recently made into a good television
serial, in which the director and actors employed Bergman-like
cinematic devices to render its stream-of-consciousness atmosphere. Koumandareas's later novel "Mrs. Koula" was also
turned into a fine television drama.

[20] See my *WLT* review in 58:4 (Autumn 1984), pp. 641–42. Because of its letterlike form, Ladia's narrative achieves Butor-like
effects in the opening paragraphs, where the inventive and restless narrator addresses her monologues to the recipient of her
communications—namely, the attractive girl she is in the process of creating as she undergoes identity changes herself. This
may be warranted, however, by the quasi-epistolary form and
its "mechanical" means of achieving smooth transitions between episodes.

[21] *I Kostoula Mitropoulou ke to anti-mythistorima* (Kostoula
Mitropoulou and the Anti-Novel), Athens, Theoria, 1984, p.
19. For a review, see *WLT* 58:3 (Summer 1984), p. 452.

[22] Cited from *WLT* 59:3 (Summer 1985), p. 468.

[23] Cited from *WLT* 58:2 (Spring 1984), p. 307.

[24] See *WLT* 56:4 (Autumn 1982), p. 733, and 57:1 (Winter
1983), p. 146 respectively.

HUNGARY

Desperate but Not Serious: The Situation of Hungarian Literature in the Nineties

All this to illustrate how tough it is to be Hungarian. And
that is not going to get any easier, even if, as they
promise, The Russians Leave.

▧ **PÉTER ESTERHÁZY**[1]

If Péter Esterházy wrote this before 1991, he was not
just indulging in the national sport of complaining wittily about Hungary's situation but was a prophet. Even
if he had the benefit of hindsight, he is more accurate
than those Hungarians, and not just writers, who expected that after the end of communism, as one critic
puts it, the West would come in and turn all the Central
European countries into Denmark overnight, or at least
in not more than four years. Of course, the Russians
have been gone for a while and had stopped paying
much attention to Hungarian intransigence even before
1989.

There is some good news along with the bad news.
The good news is that writers can say anything they

Ottó Orbán (*Robert H. Taylor*)

want to. The bad news is that they have trouble getting
it into print and even greater trouble getting paid. That
is one reason why, speaking of the state of literature in
Hungary, an editor in Budapest referred to the pre-1989
period as "the good old bad old days," and while no one
else in the Hungarian literary community whom I spoke
to during my recent stay there used quite the same language, the sentiment was echoed by those who produce
and publish creative work in print and on the air and
with varying degrees of lesser strength by writers.

First, some more bad news. Publishers went
through a very rough period. For example, before "the
changes," Corvina was a leading publisher of Hungarian
literature in translation and also published other literatures in Hungarian as well as lavishly illustrated art
books, guides, history books, cookbooks, and other
works related to Hungary. As many as 150 staff members occupied fifteen offices in a modern building at the
end of the most fashionable or at any rate most expensive street in Pest and produced 250 titles a year.

Corvina and the other twenty or so state-approved
publishing houses in Hungary—and in the rest of the
Warsaw Pact countries, for that matter—didn't have to

worry about the bottom line because they had no bottom line. As P. Hiemstra and László Kúnos put it, "The government decided on volumes, printing costs, market discounts and salaries. In this way the whole sequence of publishing and selling of books could be seen as being in the hands of one single nation-sized company: an overstaffed, overregulated, slow and bureaucratic company."[2] Print runs used to be artificially high. Júlia Lázár, who translated Sylvia Plath's *Journals,* said that the reader's report, made before the changes of 1989, recommended a printing of 50,000 copies, about average for the period. Now a print run even 10 percent of that is unusual. The Plath *Journals* were published in 1996 in an edition of not more than 2,000. New, smaller publishers of original Hungarian writing may publish ten books a year, and sometimes they have a run as large as 1,500 copies, though most are smaller, perhaps 500 for poetry. And that is hardly profitable. Some small publishers use two or three different names for different lines, partly for tax purposes, and they sell out, regroup, and emerge under other names.

The good news in the old days was that books were carefully edited. As many as seven people saw a manuscript through production, checking textual quality as well as political orthodoxy. The bad news is that now an author is lucky if one person is responsible for checking the accuracy of the text. And books were (artificially) cheap and readily available—unless they sold out, in which case reprinting was impossible because of lockstep schedules set three to five years in advance. Now, under free-market conditions, books are so expensive that the diminishing number of serious readers cannot afford them. The most difficult year for publishers, according to one editor, was 1993—another says 1996—when privatization occurred through a long and complex process. Employees were encouraged to bid for their company, especially if there was not a large gap between management and staff; but anyone could bid, and in any case employees had to seek financing. In one publishing company, the three top managers got 51 percent of the stock and the other employees 49 percent, a lesson that it is not just socialism under which some animals are more equal than others. The system of privatization, and not just in publishing, was felt to benefit those who had been in power under the communists.

This transition was less painful than the one in 1990, when the government decided to abandon control of publishing and nearly two thousand so-called publishing houses were founded. Some were get-rich-quick, one-book publishers, often of pornography which they sold on street corners, and even now there are many hurried and bad translations of very bad American genre fiction issued in hope of making a quick profit. Like the thirty or forty political parties which emerged in the fall of 1989, not all of these publishers survived the neo-Darwinian processes of the free market, but they radically altered the situation. Some of the old mammoth publishing houses like Gondolat, which had published several hundred books a year before the change, could not adjust under its Socialist Party managers and did not survive. A French publisher considered buying Gondolat, but, after looking at its padded payroll and other problems, backed out. Publishing houses that did survive, László Kúnos says, "understood that unavoidable steps had to be taken."

In Corvina's case, this meant reducing staff and new titles per year by roughly two-thirds. And the nature of the list has changed. While Corvina still publishes illustrated and art books, they have become too expensive to produce without careful attention to the market, and far fewer are issued. Corvina now depends more heavily on upper-level textbooks for high schools, especially guides summarizing the subjects of the final examinations that all students take at the end of their schooling. Another line features handbooks and textbooks for university students, mostly in the humanities, and a third offers language teaching, especially English, German, and French.

As this summary indicates, publishers in the past had to be careful about ideology. Today they have to be careful about the balance sheet, and as a result are less inclined to take chances with quality work that might have high production costs. One press refused to consider issuing a translation of *Angela's Ashes* because it was twice as long as any novel they had published. Another asked Éva Tóth, a leading translator, to do something for them, but not poetry or drama. And when radio producer Márton Mesterházi tried to interest publishers in translations he had commissioned of three Yeats plays, he was laughed at.

This is not good news, but things are changing. Some of the best news can be found in the Balassi Bookshop near the Buda end of the Margaret Bridge. Founded in 1991, Balassi publishes, on average, eighty titles per year, most of them so academic as to be hopelessly uncommercial: classical Hungarian literature, art history, sociology, cultural history, reproductions of eighteenth- and nineteenth-century typefaces and printers' and paper-makers' watermarks, dual-language editions of classic Chinese texts like *Master Sun on the Art of War,* catalogues of medieval and Renaissance libraries in Hungary. But with print runs between 500 and 3,000, publishers like Balassi and Argumentum cannot maintain this kind of list without subsidies.

Some funds are available, primarily but not exclusively for books that would not otherwise see print. The major sources to date are the National Cultural Fund and the Hungarian Book Foundation, both linked to the Ministry of Culture, which has some funds of its own; the Soros Foundation; the Attila József Foundation, run by the MSZP or Socialist Party; and the newest and perhaps the largest, the Higher Education Textbook Foundation, which, out of its 400 million forint budget (about $170 million, using, as in all later conversions, the exchange rate of early May 1999), can fund even books which might plausibly be used as supplementary texts.

The National Cultural Fund distributed about 2.7 billion forints ($14 million) in 1997, drawing funds from a trash tax on material in print and other media not judged to be of high quality and on "culture-related consumer-electronic goods" like TV sets, copying machines, floppy disks (not more than 1 percent each), and toy weapons (10 percent). Besides books and periodicals, it supports film, theater, music, visual and folk arts, and cultural institutions like libraries and museums.

Soros, which predates the change by five years and has many programs that are not specifically cultural, is a major supporter of publishers like Balassi. It puts about 80 million forints a year ($350,000) into big publishing projects. Until recently, Soros's Hungarian branch, like other foundations, gave grants directly to publishers. Now, in a unique program, Soros money supports specific titles and is intended to benefit readers who would otherwise not buy books because of the cost. In effect, Soros prefinances the production of quality manuscripts which, in the judgment of a board composed of a literary historian and representatives of three major libraries, meet the very broad criteria of reflecting the values of an open society. These include accessibility of ideas and equality of opportunity, which explains why a book on modern art led even *The Scenario of the Change of the Regime* in this year's selections. Then, after surveying as many as four thousand librarians about the needs and desires of their clients, Soros will buy and distribute, at no cost, between two hundred and three thousand copies.

The Soros Foundation has a number of smaller programs. One, in cooperation with the Open Society Institute (comprising thirty foundations in the area of the post-Soviet empire), selects ten to fifteen titles in the political and human sciences suggested by each foundation and arranges for their translation into the various national languages. In one program, which began before 1989, classic Anglo-Saxon philosophical works are translated—so far about 350 titles. In the other, East Translates East, important books from the human sciences in the past ten years are translated into the various languages. This is important because, as György Orbán of Balassi says, intellectuals in these countries almost certainly know what is going on in Paris, London, and New York, but someone in Budapest may not know what is going on in Bucharest or Warsaw.

All of these programs are intended to provide the reading audience with material that, because of slender or even negative margins between production cost and selling price, would otherwise be unavailable. In 1997, the last year for which figures have been published, Soros received 602 applications to produce original manuscripts and funded 162. Balassi received fourteen of these grants, Magvető, Ozirisz, and Seneca were accorded ten each. Nine of seventeen applications to translate foreign works were funded; Ozirisz and Balassi got three each. Of twenty-four applications to publish the first books of young writers, eight were accepted. And Soros has begun a competitive program to encourage the production of literary biography, until now not a significant Hungarian genre.

As the concentration of grants might suggest, some people in the literary world have the impression that the foundations, especially Soros and the National Cultural fund, are dominated by a clearly defined group of interests, with an unhealthy overlap between board members and people on the lists of editorial boards—either before or after grants are given. A controversy arose in 1999 because the current government included in its budget a line to subsidize, at a million forints per title, cheap new editions of 150 classics of Hungarian literature to celebrate the millennium. The publisher chosen was Ozirisz, which has very close ties to the administration. The decision was widely protested, and the latest word is that five publishers will be chosen for the project, though it is not clear how the spoils will be divided. It *is* clear that Hungarians have embraced a certain strain of democratic behavior familiar to Americans.

These cheap editions and those subsidized by Soros may help a little to ease the pressure on libraries. The good news, one editor says, is that they are jammed. The bad news, a librarian counters, is that library budgets are shrinking even as book prices, especially of foreign books, are growing, so that libraries can afford to buy fewer books for the use of patrons who now cannot afford to buy books they used to have in personal libraries. Another problem is the change in the book-deposit law. Formerly, publishers were required to supply sixteen copies of each title issued, and these would be distributed to the country's important libraries. Now only six copies are required—and often not sent, either because new publishers don't know about the law or because they go out of business so rapidly that what enforcement there is cannot catch up with them.

The Soros Foundation realizes that these grants, even combined with others, will not solve publishers' problems, and they are encouraged to pursue cross-financing—that is, to find income from other sources. One publisher survives partly because of its very popular magazine on dogs. Balassi runs a series of bookshops, including two at museums in the Buda Castle. But there are still cash-flow problems, and Soros will lend money at half the national bank rate to publishers whose lists meet open-society standards. In 1997, Soros had thirty-one applications and made thirteen loans. Almost a quarter of the 60.5 million forints (just under $300,000) went to Balassi. (Balassi also sponsors art exhibitions, but they are an attempt to re-create the coffee-house culture of the past rather than to make money.)

Publishers clearly need this kind of help. As László Kúnos of Corvina says, patterns of incomes and finances have changed. Books now have to be priced realistically, inflation has cut discretionary income, the distribution system had to be reinvented, and the number of bookstores dropped by 50 per cent in the 1990s. Moreover, as university librarian Nóra Deák and various others agree, the younger generation doesn't read as much as its predecessors, perhaps because of television, disaffection, or other cultural shifts, but at least partly because of the cost of books. At any rate, it is harder to move the product than it used to be. And when people do read, it is clear that their tastes have changed. Some of the worst trash has disappeared, but it was probably true that Hungary had been, in András Török's words, "an over-cultured country," partly because government control had kept out Western genre trash. Now the street-corner booksellers have ten or twenty Heather Grahams, Harold Robbinses, and Wilbur Smiths to one Vonnegut, Mailer, or Rushdie.

In another kind of attempt to foster a culture based on quality literature, the National Cultural Fund and the Soros Foundation support literary and other journals—Soros, fifteen of what it considers the most important cultural journals with liberal attitudes toward free expression of opinion. Gabriella Szilárd, director of Cultural Programs, says that Hungary is a country of journals, that every town of more than forty or fifty thousand has a journal, and that new writers find in them a first avenue into print. In 1997, forty-five of 145 applications were funded.

Soros and other granting agencies apparently try to be even-handed among competing ideologies, so much so that the editor of a nonpartisan magazine that has never received a subsidy was advised, perhaps partly in jest, to sell it to the Smallholders Party and get seven million forints in the next distribution. Clearly there is not as much money to go around as there was in the good/bad old days, partly because, according to one source, there are now 140 literary journals, though only seventy-three are listed in *Magyar Irodalom*. Those that have survived have had to learn to be at least as flexible and ingenious as the publishing houses. A case in point is *Nagyvilág* (Great World). It was first published—though planned earlier—in October 1956, an exact contemporary of the Revolution, to bring world literature, which had been ignored by Marxist critics, to the Hungarian audience. After the Revolution was suppressed, the party allowed it to continue, at first freely and then under supervision, as one of the concessions to Hungarian intellectuals. It featured for the first time translations of work by Pasternak, Brecht, Sartre, and other writers more controversial, from the party point of view, than the last two. It became one of the most popular journals in Hungary, read by everyone who claimed to be an intellectual, publishing 30,000 copies a month. It had a staff of twenty full-time employees, including the ideological supervisor, many of whom showed up only to collect their salaries. It had the funds to subscribe to all the leading journals and many newspapers throughout the world.

When the change came, each new interest group wanted its own journal, and there was more conflict over shrinking subsidies. *Nagyvilág* and many other government-controlled journals had been under the direction of the parent company, Pallas. When that went under, a smaller company, controlling twenty-two journals, was formed. That lasted two or three years, and when it sank, several journals went with it. *Nagyvilág* was close to sinking, and many of the staff left for other jobs. Those remaining formed a foundation for friends of the journal, invested a month's salary each, and sent letters inviting writers and readers to join the foundation. The journal survived—with a staff of four, all part-time, and a print run of 3,000.

Subscriptions and sales won't keep the journal going, so the editors have applied, with indifferent success, for foundation support. They turned to special monographic issues devoted to individual writers and national literatures and received support (e.g., from Argentina for a Borges issue) from various embassies. And they began to publish books, beginning with three a year and currently nine, including a popular series of short stories from various national literatures—American, Italian, Swedish, French, Japanese, British—which have previously appeared in the journal. They also publish, besides translations of books by writers like Camus, Hamsun, Silone, and Unamuno, original work by contemporary Hungarian poets and critics. This program has received support from Soros and other foundations, including foreign ones. As a result of these efforts, *Nagyvilág* is surviving. But it is hardly thriving, because, as editor Anikó Fázsy says, world literature is beyond or beneath everyday politics. To broaden its base, the magazine has begun to sponsor literary evenings in which writers confront critics or various sides debate issues like postmodernism, the crisis of values, or a new book like Győző Ferencz's *Hol a költészet mostanában?* (Where Is Poetry Now?). These meetings have drawn crowds which are not just standing-room-only but spill down the staircase, a situation that helps to account for Fázsy's optimism about the prospects for literature.

Of course, applying for subsidies means paperwork at both ends of the publishing process, the grant and the report, and the process and all the other shifts to raise money necessarily (in two senses) take time away from the business of creating and producing real work. Still, according to Miklós Vajda, editor of *Hungarian Quarterly,* quality publishing is making a comeback. An even more optimistic account of publishing and indeed of the general cultural situation is András Török's in the *Budapest Review of Books:* taking everything into account, he says, "subsidies [in 1998] are as much as 160 percent higher than those of last year."[3] It should be said that Török was secretary of state in the previous government's Ministry of Culture and may have been exaggerating its accomplishments. Other accounts are less rosy, and one should remember the Hungarian riddle: "'What is the difference between an optimist and a pessimist?' 'The pessimist is better informed.'"

Some of the good news about publishing is, according to several critics, bad news because, as Török says, they think that, even under difficult circumstances, so many literary journals have sprung up "that it is too easy to get a manuscript published and that this is harmful to the intrinsic development of literature." The poets I spoke to did not, naturally, share this view, though one of them, Győző Ferencz, agrees that it is easier to publish and that sheer volume may make it more difficult for readers to find the best work. But in the eighties, he says, it was no easier to find the best writers, because many could not get published at all. There were two monthly outlets and one weekly for poetry in Budapest and four or five in the provinces. All were government-run, and all had the same political/esthetic policies, so that if a poet was rejected by one, there was no chance with the others. Furthermore, there was a kind of cronyism to which Americans are not strangers. If a new poet took a poem to a literary magazine, it would probably be rejected. Never, of course, on ideological

grounds. Some other excuse would be given, or the editors would simply lose it or make the poet wait years for rejection.

Now things are better—for poets. Dramatists are in worse shape. According to Márton Mesterházi, a drama editor at Hungarian Radio for thirty years, the largest and most important theaters have become almost purely commercial, producing West End and Broadway hits and musicals. New Hungarian plays are produced, if at all, in theaters with two to three hundred seats—or in the provinces. András Török paints a characteristically rosy picture of provincial theater, where the "Young Turks" have established themselves as "the ruling elite in the current theater." And he points to a program of the National Cultural Fund "to pay repertory theater companies in the country that are willing to book (alternative) studio productions." However, his glowing report about the National Theater, supposedly under construction when he wrote in 1998, must be qualified. There is a very large hole next to the main bus station and the junction of the three metro lines in downtown Pest, but the government formed in the autumn of 1998 seems to have plans to build it elsewhere. One man very active in the literary world asks, rather sourly, whether a national theater is a building or a company of players—and, he says, Hungary already has the latter.

Mesterházi is no happier about the state of radio drama than of conventional productions. At one point he worked on 135 adaptations of classic drama from Aeschylus to Sean O'Casey, many put into Hungarian for the first time. Now, he says, all divisions of Hungarian Radio are bankrupt. No one in top management seems interested in the work itself or seems to have a sense of what good public radio should be. They want government subsidies for public radio while coveting the profits of commercial radio in "a euphoric state of marketing."

Marketing is an area not really open to writers, who have little control over the process. In the past, writers may not have had a great deal of power vis-à-vis the government, but at least they were organized—because everyone had to be organized. The Hungarian Writers Association was instituted by the communists, and in 1989 some argued that this Stalinist institution did not deserve to survive. Others argued that it did help to effect change and was a major force in the Revolution of 1956. In any case, the argument continues, even a liberal government would channel funds through and at the suggestion of this and other organizations. The organization now has about six hundred members. And the prediction was correct: the Ministry of Culture asks for recommendations about the distribution of literary prizes. Several years ago a dozen or so writers founded another organization in order to have a voice. And there is a postmodernist organization on one end of the literary-political spectrum and the so-called Populists (or "Popular" or "Folk" group) on the other, with the Hungarian Writers Association somewhere in the middle. But none of the new organizations has much power or money or importance for the communication of ideas—which may amount to the same thing.

Győző Ferencz, who has belonged to several of these organizations but says he refuses to join new ones and is getting out of the old ones, adds that he has found little advantage in them. He did get an invitation to a conference in Washington, D.C., that turned out to be sponsored by the followers of the Reverend Moon, and he enjoys an occasional family vacation at Szigliget, the Art Fund's retreat on the north shore of Lake Balaton. And even that is open for shorter periods than in the past.

Hungarian writers may not have effective organizations, but that doesn't stop them from choosing sides. A number of people I spoke to were less interested in discussing organizations than in lamenting the factionalism that blights the literary landscape. The basic split is between what are called, respectively, rural and urban writers. Some call the rural camp "populists," but Miklós Vajda prefers the Hungarian word *népi,* "of the people" or "of the village," as more accurate. He traces their heritage to Dezső Szabó, a novelist and essayist in the 1930s who responded to the effects of the Treaty of Trianon, which transferred huge slices of Hungarian territory and population to Slovakia, Romania, and Yugoslavia. Szabó was ultranationalist, anti-German, and anti-Semitic. The anti-German strain was also notable in the work of László Németh, who in *Tanú* (Witness), a periodical he wrote single-handed, advocated a "revolution of quality," a return to Magyar roots, and peoples' academies in every village.

At the end of the twentieth century, Vajda says, the ideology is an anachronism, and in fact the *népi* authors are united by little more than a solidarity of background. Both Vajda and Éva Tóth, who describes herself as an urban populist, think that the key to understanding this group is Ferenc Juhász's long poem, "The Boy Changed to a Stag Cries Out at the Gate of Secrets," based, like poems by József Erdélyi and László Nagy, on a Transylvanian folktale. The theme is like Thomas Wolfe's "you can't go home again" in that the provincial cannot return to the old way of life but also does not fit in with the liberal intellectual world of Budapest. The *népi* writers tend not to orient themselves toward Budapest, tend not to know English, and tend to be ignored by translators, so that I was not able to talk to any of them.

Before 1989, Vajda says, there were groupings but no animosity. Since then, with the rise of multiparty politics, rivalry and resentment have increased, breaking formal associations, friendships, even marriages. The *népi* authors regard the urbanites as arrogant because of their advantages in education, travel, and knowledge of languages—a gap that it will take a generation or more to close. Urban liberals think it unfair to label all *népi* writers as anti-Semitic, but they assume that the rural group is burdened by ideology and by an inferiority complex or complexes. Mesterházi cites as typical his experience with Menyhért Tamás, with whom he had a long relationship at Hungarian Radio. Tamás writes short novels which he then turns into radio plays—or plays which he turns into novels. The last project the two men worked on was "Stations," dealing with four Hungarians from Voivodina, Slovakia, the Ukraine, and Hungary proper. The four are confined to a railway carriage whose windows are blocked, and they must rely on station loudspeakers for information as to their whereabouts. Each has his secrets and neuroses, and in the course of fifty-five minutes these are explored in a kind of Hungarian *No Exit.*

Mesterházi did none of the writing, but he cut, prodded, tried to curtail irrelevancy and didacticism, and, as he said, hit Tamás with a ruler. The play was, he thought, quite successful in its 1995 production. A year later, he received a copy of the novel with a dedication. It had the same title and the core of the radio script. But on page 3, Mesterházi says, Tamás started preaching and never stopped. Clearly, Tamás has different esthetic views than his editor, who holds that the best Hungarian drama follows István Örkény in employing irony and "radical contempt of pathos." Perhaps irony and detachment are primarily urban qualities; certainly they are not prominent in early stages of committed literature, as demonstrated by proletarian and early feminist writing in the United States. And obviously, Tamás would not agree with Mesterházi's view of Hungarian drama. But at least Mesterházi and Tamás were for a time able to work together. This is rare, and the factionalism affects every area of literary life. Győző Ferencz says that he never tries to write at Szigliget because of the atmosphere. The rural group drinks upstairs; the urbanites drink downstairs; and the Transylvanian Hungarians march up and down the staircase between the two. The same kind of self-segregation occurs on the beach.

A number of Hungarians in Western Europe and North America continue to write in their native language, but it is not clear how deeply involved they are in literary politics. As for Hungarian writers in other regions cut off from Hungary by Trianon, one scholar/

poet says that most of the Hungarian writers in Voivodina have moved north of the Yugoslav border. Transylvanian writers tend to get favorable reception because they were persecuted for years under the Ceauşescu regime and because, cut off from the shifts in language, they supposedly speak and write an older, purer Hungarian. Still, while the Hungarian government periodically protests the treatment of Hungarians in Slovakia, the situation of writers seems enviable by comparison with those in Transylvania and Voivodina. Lajos Grendel has been president of Slovak PEN and is currently chair of the Association of Slovak Writers. Kalligram publishes about seventy-five books a year. But Grendel came to Budapest to launch his latest novel for the obvious reason that the Hungarian national audience is crucial to his and others' success.

Grendel says that the rural-urban split is not characteristic of the eighty to ninety Hungarian writers in Slovakia; rather, there is a generational disagreement about the nature and purpose of writing between older authors, who tend to write like nineteenth-century realists and as socially responsible moralists, and most younger writers, who are postmodernists. This seems partly true of writers in Hungary proper. Béla Pomogáts, president of the Hungarian Writers Association, admits that there are more traditional writers but is concerned that "the postmodern trend in Hungarian literature has started with the creative personality heeding no values outside literature and often replacing the traditional narrative with reflection, focusing mainly on language and modes of discourse."

Some writers, like the novelist Ferenc Temesi, recognize the existence of the urban/népi, traditional/modernist/postmodernist splits but have grown impatient with labels. Temesi's most popular novel, the two-volume Por (Dust), written in the form of a dictionary (A-K, L-Z), is obviously, as he claims, postmodern. But he also calls it "a historical, family, and autobiographical novel" covering six generations from 1833 to 1973, though not in chronological order. And being from Szeged, which one poet calls the most conservative city in Hungary and Temesi calls the nation's heart and real capital, he has affinities with the népi authors and has written the novel in the dialect of that city. It is therefore, he says, not really translatable. The mixture of elements is essentially Hungarian, like the mustard-colored building facing the bus station which has elements that are Turkish, Byzantine, Babylonian, classical, with some unidentifiable and idiosyncratic touches. Both volumes of the novel were best sellers; Temesi's father, after strong initial misgivings, helped to find material and was pleased with the result; and Temesi can go home to Szeged. Now, however, he says

that he has stopped being a postmodernist and has decided that novels need plot, event, resolution. Some younger writers seem to feel the same way and are presumably post-postmodern or neotraditionalists.

At any rate, divisions and schools still exist, and most of the people I interviewed think that the most important division is urban/populist. It is generally agreed that writers who publish in magazines of one faction don't even submit to opposition counterparts. Books by urban writers aren't reviewed by populists, and vice versa. And within the various camps, magazines have more or less prestige—a situation which of course changes. In 1989 two of the most influential magazines were Kortárs (Contemporary) and Új Írás (New Writing). The latter lost support under the new minister of culture and disappeared; the former survives. Élet és Irodalom (Life and Letters), referred to simply as És (And), was more influential before 1989 but survives as what some regard as an organ of the Free Democratic Party. Some literary people think it in the great tradition; others think it too neoliberal. Its rival, Magyar Napló (Hungarian Journal), began as an urban, postmodern venue, then was taken over by the Writers Association and then by the Populists and has lost so many readers that it struggles to survive. Other magazines mentioned with varying degrees of enthusiasm are 2000; Parnasszus, edited by István Turczi and devoted to poetry; Holmi (Thing), edited by Szabolcs Varády; Jelenkor, from a publishing house of the same name; and Kalligram, another publishing house and magazine in Slovakia. County governments put money into journals: Műhely (Workshop) in Győr is a good example. Many of the newer magazines tend to be devoted to a particular kind of literary politics, and their life is precarious. Orpheus has appeared again after a two-year hiatus due to financial difficulties; unlike 2000, És, Holmi, Jelenkor, and Kalligram, it did not receive a Soros subsidy in 1997.

Speaking of financial difficulties, all but a few writers have almost given up expecting any financial reward for their work. There are some exceptions: Péter Esterházy gets half a million forints per book from his publisher; Péter Nádas is able to live on his writing because of royalties from Germany. (Hungarian writing is currently popular in Germany and France, and writers translated into these languages are then accessible to publishers elsewhere.) Most writers, however, are not fortunate enough to gain foreign attention and royalties. Győző Ferencz, described as a fine poet by people from three different generations, published two books of poems and two collections of essays in the 1990s—and has yet to receive a forint in royalties. László Kúnos of Corvina Publishers and Miklós Vajda of the Hungarian Quarterly testify that this is not unusual. Most writers make their living teaching, translating, or doing reader reports—or all three and more. Some younger poets make a living writing soap-opera scripts. Translators at least get paid—currently 15,000 forints (about $63) for every twenty pages.

There are various grants and stipends for writers. The Soros Foundation gives noncompetitive grants to writers at several stages of their careers: for a body of work, for midcareer authors, and for young writers. These vary from 1.4 million forints at the top to 40,000 forints. The Ministry of Culture gives direct grants of double the minimum wage to writers under thirty-five, about 60,000 forints per month for ten or eleven months. The National Cultural Fund has grants and twenty to thirty annual prizes, and it supports former Kossuth Prize winners in return for electronic rights to all work, past and future. But one writer complains that, except for the Kossuth support, the same names keep appearing in different order in the various prize lists, and in any case, there is and never will be enough money to go around.

Hungarian and Slovak authors and probably writers in other former Soviet bloc countries regard this situation as unusual. Gustáv Murín is writing an article about pay for writers in Slovakia and says that his colleagues complain about lack of compensation and insist that "If I were in America. . . ." Americans have in this case a rare opportunity to disillusion Central Europeans. Most American writers get very little from their work, and editors in the U.S. complain about the lack of time, personnel, and resources to do the kind of careful work that was characteristic of the good old days.

This and much other anecdotal evidence demonstrates that what my Central European friends regard as a postapocalyptic situation is in fact nothing more than the normal operation of capitalism. (The obvious difference is that American academics are fairly well paid.) Or, as László Kúnos puts it, the changes since 1989 have been a big shock for Hungarian writers and the literary public. They have to accustom themselves to the idea that literature is less important to society and the general culture than it used to be. Kúnos refers primarily to the economic situation. Ferenc Temesi puts it more bluntly: in Central and Eastern Europe, "literature, in one moment, lost its importance, its role." Béla Pomogáts asks the more relevant question about what the writer is to do now. "Does literature. . .still belong in part to the political sphere, or is it solely art?" Should writers enter politics, or it is it possible that we don't need another Havel? Pomogáts does say that "the sense of importance rooted in [literature's] responsibility for public and national issues. . .has been shattered" along with "the impoverishment of literary institutions and a perceivable loss of the prestige accorded to writers and their creative work" (43, 44).

One reason for this, Frederick Turner argues, is that unlike Sándor Petőfi in the revolution of 1848 (and, Irén Kiss adds, many writers in 1956), the ideas and energy for the revolution of 1989 came not from writers but from bureaucrats, accountants, and other nonliterary types who saw that the old system had failed and so worked to modify and to change it. "How," Turner asks, "does one celebrate the patient growing of wealth and culture, the slow process of cultivation, virtuous discipline, democratic compromise, economic federalism, wide environmental management, the evolutionary chaos of the market?" All these are not only inconsistent with but antipathetic to much of Hungarian and indeed of other Western literature.

That may be arguable, but it is obvious that most of the stories in *Give or Take a Day* (Corvina, 1997) and *Thy Kingdom Come* (Noran/Palatinus, 1998) look backward, often in great and justifiable bitterness, rather than forward. Perhaps, at the end of the twentieth century, the idea of a prophetic writer seems more than a little ridiculous. Think of the attitude toward Norman Mailer. But Irén Kiss calls for a return to the sense of the strength of the writer's personality and for the preservation and renewal of the roots of Hungarian language and culture—not in a racial or racist sense but in terms of their pan-European, pan-Asian connections. If, she says, writers are not able to take these risks, then they deserve to be marginalized. In her recent collection of plays, *Tiszták, hősök, szentek* (Innocents, Heroes, Saints), she turns to historical figures like Cardinal Mindszenty and Saint Elizabeth of Hungary for inspiration. And Ferenc Temesi, after being a 1960s Hungarian Beatnik (rock and roll instead of progressive jazz, as in the American 1950s) and a postmodernist innovator, now says that a nation needs strong novels if it is to mature and hopes that his generation of writers has helped to create it. Poets like Éva Tóth and Ottó Orbán, now in their sixties, think of tradition in a different way, concentrating on the complex history of their time and its effect on themselves and their families. This is true in more oblique fashion of the stories of György Spiró, Adam Bodor, László Márton, Sándor Tar, and Emese Medgyesi, where the weight of communism is everywhere felt but rarely mentioned, as if it were atmospheric pressure. These writers witness rather than prophesy. Pomogáts calls for the great novel about the 1956 Revolution; Éva Tóth says that Tamás Benedicty (formerly Horváth) may have produced such a novel in his *Souvenir.*

Hungarians need to come to terms with the communist era, and it will probably be a dominant theme for some time. But in "Dust" and in *Halászóember* (The Fishing Man), Ferenc Temesi and Imre Oravecz have, in prose and poetry respectively, gone back to an earlier Hungary, before World War II, before the turn of the century, in order to use the perspective of history to place and judge recent events. Two writers are not necessarily a trend, but their strategies offer new possibilities. And both books were best sellers.

These writers offer new and exciting possibilities. And there is other good news. Despite the financial, factional, and artistic struggles, Hungarian writers continue to produce good work. Márton Mesterházi points to the heirs of István Örkény's ironic stance in plays like those of György Spiró (though Spiró has said that he will write no more plays). Ákos Németh and Géza Bereményi are also doing interesting work in drama.[6] Esterházy, Nádas, and Imre Kertész are, Mesterházi thinks, the novelists best known, and deservedly so, in the West. Miklós Vajda and others have high praise for Adam Bodor, a Transylvanian who escaped years of persecution in Romania, who links short stories in the manner of Sherwood Anderson's *Winesburg, Ohio*. And though Vajda as a member of the older generation thinks that the postmodernists sound alike, he singles out for praise Lajos Parti-Nagy's absurdist stories satirizing the Kadar-era petite bourgeoisie living on intellectual morsels dropped from above. Unfortunately, Vajda thinks, the stories are untranslatable not merely because English does not lend itself to Hungarian linguistic play, but also because the English audience does not share the experience recounted. Still, Parti-Nagy has been published in German—not notably more flexible than English.

Lajos Grendel speaks highly of the Slovak Hungarian poets Arpád Tőszér, the experimental László Cselényi and, in the younger generation, István Bettes. Among prose writers, the punk author Attila Győry is a cult figure among young readers. And almost everyone I spoke to singles out Grendel as one of the finest novelists writing today. Irén Kiss chided me about my ignorance of Hungarian putting me in a (very large) linguistic ghetto and singled out for special praise Endre Szkárosi and Anna Kiss, who have not been translated into English and who don't speak it. Anikó Fázsy mentions the poets Magda Székely, Zsuzsa Takács, Péter Dobai, and Zsófia Balla and the fiction writers Nádas and Sándor Tar.[7]

Ferenc Temesi, who is scheduled to become head of the Nyugat publishing house, now in the planning stages, says that there is a new generation of writers who are very exciting. Miklós György Száraz is in his forties; Norbert Haklik is twenty-two and, Temesi hopes and in fact insists, will one day be a great writer. If so, he will have to learn, like Márton Mesterházi, that persistence may pay off better than blazing prophecy. After being laughed out of publishers' offices several years ago, Mesterházi was asked to edit a collection of Yeats's plays, perhaps because 1999 is the sixtieth anniversary of Yeats's death. This would, he says, have been unthinkable three years ago. The rows of books at the Balassi office were heartening evidence that scholarly and historical writing are very much alive. And older writers continue to produce and young ones to knock at the door.

On a trip to Budapest earlier in 1999, I sat in a restaurant near two would-be filmmakers pitching ideas to each other. The American had a story about a wonder drug that cured ingrained Hungarian pessimism. Perhaps a drop or two has fallen into the Budapest water supply. Júlia Lázár brightened near the end of our interview. Good work is being published, she admitted. And her own work had been going not that badly. György Orbán was even more hopeful, saying "It can be done!"

Márton Mesterházi has something better than a wonder drug. The biggest mistake writers can make, he says, is to die too soon. It's important to outlive the fools. Many were silenced, by death or exile, under communism, a loss that no one in the East can forget and no one in the West should be allowed to forget. Those young and old who managed to outlive communism now have to find ways to outlive the capitalists. Perhaps they can fall back on irony—and on the spirit evidenced in the joke about Austrian and Hungarian commanders leading Hapsburg troops in battle. The Austrian wires headquarters, "Situation serious but not desperate." The Hungarian wires, "Situation desperate but not serious." His descendants may complain, but this spirit seems to enable them to go on writing and publishing.

Robert Murray Davis, Winter 2000

[1] Péter Esterházy, "The Miraculous Life of Prince Bluebeard," trs. Paula Balo and Martha Cowan, in *The Kiss: 20th Century Hungarian Short Stories*, Budapest, Corvina, 1995.

[2] P. Hiemstra and László Kúnos, "Restructuring of the Publishing Sector in Hungary," in *The Change: Dutch Business Experience in Supporting Central and Eastern Europe*, eds. Julia Djarova and Wim Jansen, The Hague, Delwel, 1996.

[3] András Török, *Budapest Review of Books*, 8:1 (Spring 1998), p. 45.

[4] Béla Pomogáts, "Literature and the New Democracy," *Hungarian Quarterly*, 39 (Autumn 1998), p. 47.

[5] See W. L. Webb, "Once Upon a Time in Central Europe," *Hungarian Quarterly*, 40 (Spring 1999), pp. 123–28, for a review of this and two other recently translated books of fiction.

[6] Plays by Spiró and Bereményi can be found in *Three Contemporary Hungarian Plays*, Boston/Budapest, Forest/Corvina, 1992.

Gyula Illyés (*Robert H. Taylor*)

[7] Nádas, Tar, Grendel, and eighteen other contemporary writers of fiction are translated inthe two story collections *Give or Take a Day* (Corvina, 1997) and *Thy Kingdom Come* (Noran/Palatinus, 1998).

Literature and Revolution in Hungary

1. In few European countries has poetry had so much fascination with the spirit of revolution as in Hungary. The story begins with the Spring of the Peoples and the role played in it by the then twenty-five-year-old Sándor Petőfi. Opinions may differ about his place in European or Hungarian literature, as to whether he was a populist firebrand "lacking in intellectual profundity" or a plebeian romantic admirably translating his ideals into revolutionary action. One thing remains unquestionable, however: his influence on political events. Thanks to a unique moment in nineteenth-century Hungarian history Petőfi could firmly link his social demands with the struggle for Hungarian independence (from Austria), and his poem "National Song," written for 15 March 1848, remained one of those rousing manifestos in

verse which survive along with the "Marseillaise" or Casimir Delavigne's "Warszawianka." Petőfi dreamed of "world-freedom," a term he borrowed from the radical French democrats and pre-Marxian socialists of the period, and he saw complete independence for a thoroughly reformed Hungary as the precondition to a free world of republics. In this idealistic and perhaps Utopian struggle for "world-freedom" he assigned a leading role to poets: "In our days God has ordered poets / to be the fiery pillars and / so to lead the wandering people / into Canaan's promised land."[1] He did not have much time to put this program into practice; during the March revolution at Pest he played the part of the "fiery pillar," but only a few months later during the parliamentary elections he clashed with some boorish representatives of the newly enfranchised "people." Having failed to be elected as a deputy, he enlisted in the Hungarian revolutionary army, served as aide-decamp to General Bem, and died on the battlefield at Segesvár in July 1849.

Petőfi died, but the "Petőfi model" lived on long after his death. After all, he fulfilled the romantic requirement of uniting word and deed. His example was somewhat marginalized by the Compromise of 1867, which created the dual monarchy of Austria-Hungary under Franz Joseph (in a somewhat notorious poem Petőfi had demanded that *all* kings should be hanged for the salvation of mankind), but as soon as the usefulness of the Compromise had run its course, the revolutionary model reemerged. It was revived in the first decade of the twentieth century by Endre Ady, whose *Új versek* (New Poems) and subsequent collections challenged both the political and the cultural status quo of conservative Hungary. True, in Ady one finds traces of decadence and also a strong death wish—hence his unusual emphasis on Life and Vitality—but politically he is almost as radical as Petőfi. In a famous essay, "Petőfi Bargains Not," he evokes the spirit of the revolutionary poet in these words: "Petőfi was the best representative of our premature national and social ambitions . . . he was a prophet."[2] Ady thought that Petőfi's program, the democratic revolution which leads to equal rights for everyone, had not been fully realized; moreover, the situation in the meantime had become more complicated, because the national issue (relations between Austria and Hungary and between Hungary proper and its national minorities) was hindering the introduction of radical social reforms. Complete independence from Austria would have meant the end of historical Hungary, yet a Central European confederation of equal nations could be created only on the ruins of the Monarchy. Ady hoped for and, in some poems, called for a revolution which would transform and thus stave off the complete collapse of historical Hungary. However, World War I intervened, and when at its end the Austro-Hungarian Monarchy did implode, its nationalities carved up the old territory without giving much thought to Ady's dreams or to the plans of the Hungarian radical democrat Oszkár Jászi; instead of a confederation, ferocious and, on the whole, authoritarian little nation-states were created with new national minorities.[3]

Ady was too ill to play any part in the Hungarian democratic revolution of 1918 and died soon afterward, but his poetry influenced generations to come, both with its radical social program and with its brooding, tragic perception of the "Magyar spirit." Between the two world wars many young people embraced his ideas in Hungary, and he became one of the spiritual fathers of the populist (*népi*) movement of the 1930s. Still, the poet who most faithfully followed Petőfi's line (not style!) and the model of the "committed" poet was not a country-born populist but a metropolitan socialist, Attila József. His life was a succession of social failures and astonishing poetic achievements.[4] First an anarchist rebel, then an underground communist, and finally a democratic socialist with a keen interest in Freudian psychoanalysis, he was the last major Hungarian poet who could still believe (at least for some years) in a revolutionary solution. József thought that the authoritarian, conservative Horthy regime, which perpetuated an anachronistic social system, could be destroyed only by a socialist revolution. Later with the rise of German National Socialism his priorities changed and he wrote, "Come, oh Freedom, *you* bear me Order!," putting human rights before complete equality and broad Leftist values before the worldwide victory of the proletariat.

It is not difficult to see in retrospect that the so-called revolutionary model functioned in Hungarian literature on the basis of diminishing returns. Petőfi may have been frustrated in some of his political ambitions, but he had his moment of glory in March 1848 and came to fulfill his earlier promise/prophecy of violent death in the service of Freedom. The gap between Ady's words and deeds and between his admonitions and practical possibilities was greater, and as for Attila József, he felt desperately isolated in his striving for socialism "with a human face": the masses either turned fascist or were mesmerized (and thoroughly terrorized) by Big Brother Stalin's benign gaze. Revolutions produced monsters and vicious counterrevolutions; should the poet uphold the idea of a "pure" revolution just for its own sake? József's life ended in schizophrenia and suicide on a railway track; in a sense he was overrun by the roaring "locomotive of History"—or so it seemed in 1937.

2. In a sense the "Petőfi model" of politically committed Hungarian poetry came to an end with Attila József's death. After World War II, however, this model was resurrected and expropriated by the Hungarian Communist Party, which came to power in 1948 with radical democratic slogans and with the help of deeply undemocratic methods. So, while venerating the three great revolutionary poets (Petőfi, Ady, Attila József) of the past, it tried to harness writers and poets into the service of the state, which was held up as both a result and a torchbearer of the socialist revolution. Socialist realism demanded a revolutionary posture on all issues of "progress," complete loyalty to the Soviet Union and the cause of Marxism-Leninism, and an appropriately hostile attitude toward the "reactionary" West. A tortuous kind of dialectics was used to solve the internal contradictions of this fundamentally conformist model.

By overstressing the "revolutionary line" in Hungarian poetry, communist cultural policy was openly discriminating against those poets who were apolitical or did not possess the same highly developed sense of social justice as Petőfi or Attila József. This was particularly true in the case of the poets of the first and second *Nyugat* generation; Babits and Kosztolányi were liberals with strong antifascist views, but their "bourgeois" label automatically assigned them to the second rank. The best apolitical poet of the entire post-1945 period, Sándor Weöres, and many others suffered the same fate: for seven years they were unable to publish original work and had to resort to translations and/or writing children's verse. After 1956 this situation changed for the better, but they had to wait until the seventies to gain full recognition in their native land.

As a matter of fact, relaxations of strict ideological controls began to take place already after Stalin's death in 1953. At that time the "revolutionary model" still exerted much influence on young Hungarian poets. Most of them believed, at least initially, in the poet's special role in society and in his social and national responsibility. László Nagy and Ferenc Juhász are names which stand for a whole generation. This is why they took part in the famous "writers' revolt" against the communist leadership in 1955–56, alongside such older poets as the populist socialist Gyula Illyés and the revisionist communist László Benjámin. Illyés, the author of an excellent prewar biography of Petőfi, already had in his desk drawer a powerful poem, "One Sentence on Tyranny," which was to be published only during the 1956 revolution. As for Benjámin, he started a remarkable anti-Stalinist poem with a motto from Petőfi and went on to express his moral revulsion against the crimes of the Communist Party in these words: "I have learned that. . .there is no man who can be / inhuman for the sake of humanity, / unjust for the sake of truth, / dishonest for honesty."[5]

The pull of the "revolutionary model" was great in other respects too. There was no *conscious* revolutionary plotting in Hungary in the years preceding the 1956 revolution; the so-called counterrevolutionary plot was invented post factum by shattered and vengeful communist functionaries. The anti-Stalinist movement aimed at correcting the mistakes of the regime, putting reformist communists into power instead of diehards; nobody believed that revolution was possible. The symbols and the slogans of 1956 were, however, borrowed from the Hungarian populist and democratic revolutionary tradition. It is a well-known fact that the party-controlled Thaw became a veritable avalanche through the debates of the Petőfi Circle, the debating forum of the reform-minded young intelligentsia. On the day of the revolution itself, 23 October 1956, the mass demonstration of Budapest students started at Petőfi's statue by the Danube with the recital of the poet's "National Song," mentioned above. This gave a somewhat nineteenth-century flavor to the whole event, to the popular uprising that followed. I am sure some of my fellow students (I was a student at the University of Budapest in those days) profusely quoted Endre Ady; and our newspaper published at the Faculty of Philology had Attila József's motto on the masthead: "Come, oh Freedom, *you* bear me Order!" Revolutions, for all the chaos and bloodshed they produce, tend to be romantic affairs, and the 1956 revolution in Hungary was perhaps the most romantic of all recent revolutions.

3. The demise of the "revolutionary model" in Hungarian literature took place slowly and not without opposition. What the restored communist regime needed most after 1956 was peace and quiet and at least a minimum of consensus. This could not have been achieved with pseudorevolutionary slogans extolling "proletarian internationalism" (read: pro-Soviet sentiments) and the unity of an allegedly procommunist but in fact harshly punished working class. (Most of the death sentences handed down by Kádár's courts between 1957 and 1960 were against young workers.) So, from its very beginnings the Kádár regime encouraged apolitical literature while jailing a number of ex-communist writers (Déry, Háy, Tardos, Zelk, and others) for their allegedly "antistate" activities. However, once these writers were released from jail and works cautiously critical of the regime were published (in the midsixties), Hungarian literature regained some of its autonomy and its capacity to revise earlier literary models. Although some poets of the older generation, notably Gyula Illyés and László Benjámin, remained faithful to their earlier ideals of a broadly "committed" poetry, there was a general movement toward apolitical literature and, in poetry, toward modernism.

During the 1970s two processes took place in Hungarian literature, both of which increased the erosion of the "revolutionary model" and even the model of socially committed poetry. First, some of the finest apolitical poets such as Sándor Weöres and János Pilinszky were at last recognized by the authorities and given the appropriate distinctions, including state awards. This underlined the incontrovertible fact that great poetry can be written by an apolitical, nonsocialist, or even Christian author. Second, a wave of new Hungarian fiction invaded the mind of the readers, pushing aside (and in a sense absorbing) poetry. Because of the impact of television, people read relatively less in the seventies than in the sixties, and they read more fiction and essays than verse. Moreover, as the extraliterary role of poetry has diminished, so "prose fiction has come to the fore and with it the stressing of literature *as* literature, which does not . . . mean indifference to public life necessarily."[6] In the 1970s and early 1980s a whole group of new writers emerged: after György Konrád (whose novel *The Case Worker* was a milestone in the development of new Hungarian fiction) came Esterházy, Nádas, Lengyel, Kornis, and Krasznahorkai, to mention only a few. As for the retreat of poetry from public affairs, the case of Sándor Csoóri is symptomatic. Csoóri, after a short phase of "committed" poetry, turned toward the private sphere and produced an abundance of personal lyrics, rich in imagery; at the same time he devoted numerous (and very influential) essays to Hungary's national and social problems. Today he is a political figure not because of his poetry but, in a sense, in spite of it.

Although by the 1980s the "revolutionary model" had disappeared, socially rebellious poetry continued to be written. György Petri is a case in point. He began writing poems in the 1970s which completely ignored the existence of party censorship as well as of social conventions, an attitude which forced him into *samizdat*. Almost alone among the poets of his generation, Petri wrote openly and with a harsh, biting, debunking irony about questions which, as a friendly critic put it, "other intellectuals discuss only in private":[7] the victims of 1956, the Polish upheaval of 1980–81, the lie of the sham consensus propping up the Kádár years, the opportunism pervading Hungarian society throughout the whole period. Still, saying to the communists in 1980, "Your innumerable doctrines, baseness is their basis, / have failed, are bankrupt,"[8] did not make Petri a revolutionary, only a rebel, a dissident, a marginal intellectual who reached only a very limited audience at the time. It was not until 1989 that Petri's work became legally publishable in Hungary, by which time he had matured into something of a "*samizdat* classic." Incidentally, his former *samizdat* publisher Gábor Demszky has recently been elected mayor of Budapest.

Can we then say in conclusion that the gradual revolution of 1989–90 which led to Hungary's first free elections in March 1990 was achieved without the active participation of Hungarian writers and poets? That would not be true either. Although poetry ceased to be a central force of political change, prose fiction, essays, and journalism all helped in undermining and then demolishing the crumbling monolithic structure of the one-party system. The December 1986 congress of the Hungarian Writers Association was in a sense a turning point in the strained relationship between the communist regime and the writers. The latter defended their autonomy and their right to fundamental criticism as vigorously as they did back in 1955–56 but were careful not to challenge directly the terminally ill yet still quite powerful authoritarian system. The last few years of the Kádár regime were rent by a number of "scandals"—publication bans on the poet Sándor Csoóri and on the playwright-essayist István Csurka, the suspension of the Szeged periodical *Tiszatáj* (on account of a politically sensitive poem by Gáspár Nagy)—but during this period the communist overseers of culture were already unwilling or unable to restore order by naked force. In this volatile situation *samizdat* publications (e.g., the review *Beszélő*) as well as sociological and political essays published in Paris and in the United States (e.g., by *Magyar Füzetek* and by Béla Király's publications) were eagerly read in Hungary and had a much greater effect than in earlier, less perturbed years. Writers criticizing the system "from within," from the ranks of the "democratic opposition," or even from abroad had all contributed to the logic of events that finally forced the communists to yield power to society peacefully. The recent changes are not all beneficial to Hungarian culture; but the preconditions to free creative work have been established, and—a good omen!—the first president of the new Republic of Hungary, proclaimed on 23 October 1989, is none other than a writer, Árpád Göncz. So Hungary too has its Havel, and its writers, perhaps for the first time in recent history, can at last forget about revolution.

George Gömöri, Spring 1991

[1] *Rebel or Revolutionary? Sándor Petőfi,* Budapest, Corvina, 1974, p. 177. The excerpt quoted was translated by Edwin Morgan.

[2] Endre Ady, *Válogattot cikkei és tanulmányai,* Budapest, 1954, p. 296.

[3] For much misfortune in Central Europe the responsibility lies squarely with the Allied Powers, especially France, and the blatantly unjust treaties of Versailles/Trianon.

[4] On Attila József, see *BA* 48:1 (Winter 1974), pp. 58–63.

[5] László Benjámin, *Egyetlen élet,* Budapest, 1956, p. 62.

George Konrád *(Courtesy: Harcourt Brace Jovanovich)*

[6] Péter Balassa, in *Formations,* 3:1 (Spring 1986), p. 152.

[7] Sándor Radnóti, in *Formations,* 3:1 (Spring 1986), p. 151.

[8] György Petri, in *Index on Censorship,* 12:2 (April 1983), p. 10. The translation is by George Gömöri and Clive Wilmer.

Freedom's Captives: Notes on George Konrád's Novels

Like most contemporary Eastern European novelists, the Hungarian György (George) Konrád deals with historical givens, unique social and political configurations, unalterable realities; yet the questions he poses in his works, the dilemmas and confrontations he describes, tend to be universal and therefore comprehensible to a larger readership. For example, his first novel, *The Case Worker* (A látogató, 1969), depicts the trials and tribulations of a Hungarian social worker and offers a devastating picture of Budapest lowlife. But as Irving Howe pointed out in his by now well-known review of the novel, communist Budapest, except for the absence of drugs, "seems very much like capitalist Manhattan,"[1] and in a recent review we read that Konrád is "one of the Eastern European writers most accessible to Western readers."[2] Perhaps because he is a Jew who lived through World War II as an impressionable child, or because as a student of literature he is mindful of the unity of Western culture, Konrád does view his country's problems from a supranational perspective. In recent years he has become an outspoken opponent of Hungarian socialism, though his real enemy is not ideology but political and cultural provincialism.

Of course there are those Hungarian critics of Konrád who feel that as a politically oriented writer he is too accessible—that he is in fact writing for the West, and the real reason he is acclaimed there is that the Western reader responds above all to his dissident political views.[3] These charges are usually made in Hungary with the assumption that if a writer is also a political dissenter, a troublemaker, he cannot be a serious artist. Although Konrád personally dislikes the label "dissident" (and said so in his lecture at the 1977 Venice Biennale on Cultural Dissent),[4] he has made a name for himself in recent years as a publicist and essayist, and his newer essays *have* been more combative in tone, more political in theme than novelists' essays generally are. But the truth of the matter is that Konrád's essays are inseparable from his fiction. Like many of his fellow writers, he realized long ago that in Eastern Europe there is no—there cannot be any—apolitical literature. Politics in that region, he has said in an interview, is "like money in the Western world; regardless of whether you like it or not, you have an ongoing relationship." He feels that his latest novel, *The Loser* (*A cinkos,* 1982), is a "book about politics, though . . . not a political book; it doesn't take a stand in favor of A against B. It's about the passion of politics, which is like romantic passion or the passion for money. It's about a disease . . . but one that a whole intellectual class suffered from."[5]

It is quite true that *The Loser* is the first Konrád novel to deal explicitly with Hungarian political reality and, not so coincidentally, the first not to be published in Budapest. *The Case Worker,* in comparison, is far less rooted in a specific time and place—as Howe suggested, the Budapest described in it could indeed be any metropolis. The hero of this novel is a universal figure, a lonely, doubt-ridden man trying to comprehend the scope and texture of human misery. At once compassionate and detached, he listens to his "clients'" horror stories and does what he can, which is not much. "With a stroke of the surgical knife it might be possible to cut short the propagation of human weaknesses," he muses, "but just as a living body rejects alien matter, so everyday life evacuates all peremptory regulations, cozily dogmatic verdicts—in a word, everything that is strictly logical and consistent—and then proceeds to solve its problems by quiet trickery and always in the most unexpected way." Yet Konrád's social worker is not merely a dispassionate observer and recorder. His daily dealings with the dregs of society—hopeless misfits, morons, would-be suicides, perverts, maniacs—do not make him indifferent; they simply teach him the limits of his effectiveness, turn his anguish into quiet melancholy and make him more aware of his wards' grotesqueries.

The Case Worker, finally, is a book about despair that is not altogether despairing; in fact it may even be called a moral triumph. Not that we are overwhelmed by optimism. The harried social worker does not believe that he will ever be anything but a "skeptical bureaucrat," or that he will ever leave the city, to which he is "bound inexorably by habit." And he does not believe in panaceas, "in antitechnological, anti-conformist, anticommunist, anticapitalist, anti-bureaucratic, and antirationalist salvation." The only thing he really believes is that sometimes, for brief spells, it is possible to alleviate suffering. "Even a frail branch can catch a suicide in his fall," he tells one of his clients.

Konrád's first critics were impressed not only by his moral seriousness but also by his style, by his unrelenting enumerations and spellbinding perorations. Indeed, what makes *The Case Worker* the extraordinary achievement it is—what transforms the sociological content of the work into art—is the author's success in revealing, with his physical descriptions even more effectively than with the actual case histories, the true state of his charges. In dingy workers' flats, evil-smelling bars, fortresslike marketplaces, cavernous railroad stations—wherever his rounds take him—the case worker becomes acutely aware of his surroundings, of sights and sounds and, most of all, things. Konrád, almost in the manner of the French *nouveau roman,* constructs a world of precisely observed objects; but his objects speak, and their tales of woe remain vivid.

The City Builder (*A városalapító,* 1977), Konrád's second novel, is even more experimental and elusive than *The Case Worker.* Here the author tries consciously to extend the boundaries of fiction by condensing and telescoping events and substituting free-floating meditation for narration. The novel outlines the political, social and economic history of an unnamed Eastern European city, where rulers and ruling classes kept changing but where the intoxication with power remained constant. The central consciousness is that of an architect who sees everything from the vantage point of his profession. He comes from a long line of builders; but whereas his forebears—ruthless, driven men—tried to impose their will on a convulsive world and sought stability in brick and stone, he is a technocrat in a socialist society, a "servant of law and order, agent of an open future, wizard of upward-soaring graphs, and self-hating hawker in an ideology shop, all in one." As a young city planner he had been "eager to sketch out the most daring visions of our collective history"; as a middle-aged, middle-echelon executive, however, he is content with his modest share of power and is glad that years of repression and regimentation have not dehumanized him completely.

Though filled with subtle allusions to recent as well as more distant events in Hungarian history, *The City Builder* too can be read as a series of universal life situations and archetypal confrontations. The hero is, in a way, Everyman: we see him as husband, lover, father, son, as bourgeois, rebel and trusted technocrat. Elaborately described scenes of birth and death and of natural and man-made disasters mark important turning points in his life. Even his profession is a curiously ambivalent, all-inclusive metaphor. On the one hand the planner is the artist, the creator, the preserver of civilization; but obsessed with his goals, he is also a ruthless and amoral manipulator. The novel makes it clear that in modern societies planners are the ultimate technicians who "benefit from each change in ideology" and are indispensable wherever "systems become complex and the stakes too risky." It is the narrator's voice we hear throughout, though the true protagonist of the novel is the city itself, whose main square, with its impressive public buildings and statuary, is a memorial to mock-heroism and real suffering. The narrator finds his city at once cozy and confining, irreplaceable and detestable, "an Eastern European showcase of devastation and reconstruction" that "can welcome the enemy with salt and bread, and, having taken crash courses in the art of survival . . . change its greeting signs, statues, scapegoats—its history."

In *The City Builder* Konrád once again proves his stylistic agility, though in this novel too the verbal abandon, the stunning fusion of abstract and concrete, adds up to more than a self-conscious tour de force. Konrád may have learned a great deal from the giants of literary modernism and the avant-garde of more recent vintage, but like other accomplished Eastern European experimenters, he eschews the impersonality of modernist fiction. In both novels cynicism and quiet despair yield periodically to anguished litanies, appeals, exhortations. In one particularly effective recital the city builder speaks not only for himself and his fellow citizens in a repressive Eastern European society, but for all peoples yearning for a freer, more human life.

> I don't want a city in which pedestrians are chased by warning signs amid ruined or abandoned walls; where nothing is allowed, nothing is possible, nothing is worth the trouble; where ready-made regulations stare at me from shopwindows. I don't want a city where everything stays the same, where suspicion oozes from plaster walls, squares are contaminated by idiotic monotony and a heap of garbage on the corner reminds me of my deformities. I don't want a city where I cower to avoid being snapped at, until I am snapped at for cowering; where greatness is an obtrusion, cowardice is peace, and talk is conspiracy; where I have to like the way things are because they cannot be otherwise; where cunning nobodies search the bunkers of wasted years, and humanity is an irritable substance, a graphic illustration of inattention, the refutation of my hopes, where streetcorner lottery-ticket vendors represent transcendence.[6]

I should note that the stylistic peculiarities of Konrád's fiction—his predilection for rhetorical flourishes, long verbal arias and set pieces and his disregard for more conventional narrative techniques—have also mystified a number of critics. Some feel that in *The City Builder,* at least, the author stretches the boundaries of fiction writing too far, thereby reducing its impact. In Pearl K. Bell's formulation, Konrád "pares the flesh of his book down to a bone of enraged abstraction that comes close to denying the very being of literature."[7]

But for a writer like Konrád, each work is a new adventure. His third and most recent novel, *The Loser,* is very different in both style and substance. Here abstraction yields to concretion, reverie and meditation to crisp exposition. The work fairly teems with narrative; scores upon scores of self-contained stories as well as realist mini-novels crowd its pages. Yet in its own way *The Loser* is also an experimental piece of fiction. Its pseudo-realism becomes apparent when one realizes that the main story line is not credible in the ordinary sense, that the plethora of subplots and masterfully compressed life histories are potential scenarios, the innumerable vignettes carefully drawn allegories. The novel is an attempted synthesis of Eastern European history; everything important that happened in Hungary in the last sixty-odd years is somehow worked into the novel. The hero—whom we see alternately as a pampered child, an underground communist, a prisoner, a cabinet minister, an academic, a mental patient—is a composite figure and unreal in that too many things happen to him; he lives through too many ordeals. Nevertheless, *The Loser*'s surface realism makes the novel Konrád's most anecdotal and most accessible to date, despite the fact that the events described are for the most part further removed from the author's personal experience than are those of *The Case Worker* and *The City Builder.* Whereas the first two works grew out of activities in which Konrád himself was involved (he was a superintendent in a child-welfare agency when he wrote *The Case Worker,* and he later worked at the Institute of Urban Planning in Budapest), *The Loser* chronicles the life and times of an older generation of radical intellectuals. "My life would probably have developed differently," Konrád has said in connection with the writing of the novel; "I would have been involved in many of the things they were involved in, had I been old enough, although in that case I would have been less suited to write this book which they, in all probability, could not have written."[8]

The author reports that he gathered much of the material for *The Loser* from old and often disgraced party members, retired functionaries, crusty veterans: "A regularly recurring event of my life in recent years has been to visit these people and listen to their stories. These, then, are their stories. . . . They are true stories, for the most part."[9] Konrád may be working with well-known material in *The Loser,* but he recasts the familiar elements with the subtle tools of a novelist, the perspicacity of an Eastern European sociologist and the concern of a modern moralist. Crucial historical sequences follow one another in quick succession, events are condensed, scenes fuse and separate, and the familiar idols and icons of recent decades appear new again in these fictional reenactments. The description of the outbreak of the 1956 revolt illustrates well Konrád's technique as a novelist: his knack for compression as well as his propensity for abstraction, his eye for detail and also for the underlying essence.

October 23, 1956

You could walk down the street with a flag before this day, too, but only on national holidays, passing by a reviewing stand and cheering the party leaders. It's a natural wonder: within a matter of hours, the populace became a people. The lethargy vanished, we are strong once again; they are scared of us, not we of them, and yes, we have a right to be on the street. The unruly and disobedient are celebrating now; what was forbidden only yesterday is suddenly allowed—simply because we do it and don't ask for permission. Let's tear off the straitjacket of fear, let's speak the truth for a change. Until now we used the lingo of the powerful to lie to one another; now we exchange words as though we were making love, and will not have our sentences approved by the censor enthroned in our heads. We are walking utopias; on a piece of paper we write down what we like and post it on the first tree. A whole system of rhetoric has crumbled, language has rebelled, everyone is a writer, the whole city a bulletin board. The whip can go on cracking, but the horse refuses to pull the cart.

The Loser may be more openly political than *The Case Worker* and *The City Builder,* but all three are simi-

lar in that they are novels about intellectuals. Konrád's aim is always to objectify his heroes' perceptions, to freeze their fleeting thoughts in sharp-featured images. And the more we learn about his characters, the more we realize that propelling each of them is an intense longing for freedom. In *The Case Worker,* according to one Konrád critic, "the ideal of freedom is off on a practice run."[10] Indeed, the quest for freedom—the "temptation of autonomy," as Konrád put it in one of his essays[11]—is the main theme of all his writings. "I would like to consider myself an independent writer," Konrád said in his Biennale lecture, "realizing that it is a lifelong struggle to strive for intellectual integrity in a world where official cultures, commercial considerations, fashions, prod me toward the commonplace, the archenemy of literature."[12] (The same idea is expressed even more forcefully and graphically by the hero of *The Case Worker:* "Minute air bubbles immured in limestone; such are the neglected opportunities of the free will.") Konrád considers his newest hero yet another Eastern European who, "as far as his circumstances permit it," is an independent intellectual. And he quickly adds: "This has always been my temptation."[13] But because the main character of *The Loser,* called simply T., wants to remain independent, he necessarily antagonizes the ubiquitous agents of power: the prewar Hungarian secret police and the Russian NKVD, as well as the more "civilized" security forces of present-day Hungary.

The tragedy of Konrád's heroes—the tragedy of an entire generation of fighter-intellectuals and, to a certain extent, of every human being—is that they are eager to identify themselves with a cause, a group, an individual, yet also cherish their privacy and insist on personal freedom. Their struggles are futile, because even as they yearn for a sense of release and wish they could dissolve their individual psyches in a kind of impersonal, collective consciousness, they realize that to reach this state each must not only sacrifice his personal autonomy but renounce his very personality as well. The hero of *The Loser* enters a mental hospital more or less voluntarily because he wants to be freed of the compulsion of thoughts, judgments, actions, of his own ambitions and vanities. He is ready to cut his ties with family and friends, to carry less weight and thus be able to get closer to the great redeemer—death. "A few more days, a few more years, and I'll stray into death's realm," he says wistfully. ("Nothing interests me now as much as this second birth of mine, my release from the clasp of existence," declared the narrator of *The City Builder.*) T. welcomes the mental hospital, for here he can at last become one with his surroundings, with the burned-out, dehumanized and still so human patients, with the very walls and columns. In this haven, "what I call 'I' has dried up, like water from a can. I and the world are two names for the same thing. . . . The gate is raised between me and the world of objects; I pass over into my friends and then recede from them." This resignation and passivity, which contrast sharply with the resolve often shown by Konrád's characters, do not, however, take T. past all hope. He would have reason enough to take his own life but does not, though he does reluctantly sanction the suicide plans of his reckless brother Dani. He even agrees to assist him; but at the very end of the novel, when Dani slips the noose around his neck and asks his brother, "You don't want to come with me?" T. says no. This "no" is his way of saying yes to life, though he knows that life for him is going to mean little more than the stale warmth of the mental asylum.

■ ■ ■

Some of Konrád's critics have noted with surprise that his heroes often talk of the "heroic age," the "idealist phase" of Eastern European socialism—in novels that unsparingly expose the arbitrariness and cynicism of state socialism. These critics at times raise the question: Did these revolutions ever have idealistic phases?[14] The narrators of *The City Builder* and *The Loser* would probably answer in the affirmative. What both of them suggest ultimately is that an ideal cannot pass through the crucible of experience unscathed; the ideal either is destroyed or, if it survives, is deformed. There is a scene in *The Loser* in which T., a tattered World War II forced laborer, makes it across Russian lines in heavy crossfire and immediately asks to be trained as an anti-Fascist activist. The battle-hardened Soviet officers are unimpressed, and T. is shipped unceremoniously to a POW camp. The scene is almost grotesquely ironic, for the more T. insists on proving his political loyalty, the more suspicious his captors become. We should stress that all this happens at a time when T. is still very much a believer in communism. Years later, in recalling his lost faith, he says: "Communism for me was a metaphysical future, a second creation, the work of man replacing God, the axis of all known human values—the thing we would accomplish together, correcting our errors as we went along, an open alternative to open oppression. I felt that if this experiment turned out to be a mistake, the human race would have lost its reason for being."

After the war, as the zealous propagandist of the new regime, T. still believes what he preaches, enjoys his power and understands and condones the incipient abuses. "I loved crowds the way I love women who yield to my shaping will," he says about this period of his life. "It was great to improvise and test my wit on Sunday mornings in my shabby radio studio. For six days my countrymen worked, and on the seventh they sat around and listened, and I fed them; the menu included just the right blend of music and propaganda." During this first stage of his country's social transformation, T. gladly forgoes the comforts of middle-class life, readily giving up his share of the family fortune. In this he is very much like the narrator of *The City Builder,* who also came from a bourgeois background and who, in discarding his former mythology, "cared little if the Persian rugs flew with it." T. wanted to be a truly committed, thus a consistent, ruthless revolutionary. Every daring experiment was an intellectual challenge for him—and a source of almost sensuous pleasure. He believed that "until now we had been a provincial theater in the middle of Europe; now our country could become a stage for experimental drama." In those heady, postwar days he had had kind feelings even for the Russians.

> If suffering is the greatest power on earth, for it gives rise to sacrifice, then they suffered enough for Eastern Europe. They were wild, but not cruel; they appeared fallible and clumsy even when grappling with our women. . . . These people, who were moved by children and old women, brought us civilization that could not be any more wicked than the one represented by the Germans, who, as far as I could tell, were not one bit moved by children and old women.

T.'s sympathy for the Russian people, his understanding of the Russian "soul," may bespeak the author's own attraction. Early in his career Konrád worked for a Budapest publishing house and edited a new Hungarian translation of Tolstoy's works. In addition, he wrote essays on Goncharov, Gogol, Gorky. It is also undeniable that Konrád the social scientist has been greatly influenced by Marxism.[15] His fictional heroes are disillusioned communists who are nevertheless busy offering Marxist analyses of society. But because their reformist zeal often borders on religious passion, these characters, especially *The Loser*'s T., express their erstwhile political commitment—and present disenchantment—in terms of religious concepts and images. Konrád himself is a humanist who views literature as a kind of secular religion. His gloomy novels, heavy with suffering, are made easier to bear by what one critic called the "sense of the sheer uncontainability of humanity."[16] "I am buoyed by the realization that nothing human can be clearly defined," says T. in the mental asylum. (Konrád is thought of as an unconventional novelist, an experimentalist, though he rejects the programmatic avant-garde. In one of his essays he has this to say about the theory of the *nouveau roman:* "[It] tried with positivist ambition to impose the methodological criteria of the natural sciences on literature. Actually, this scientific theory is the twin sister of Marxist aesthetics, which also condemned literature to mirroring reality. Poor literature, what else can it do? As though it were our *task* as people to live on Planet Earth. Where else could we live? We can think of nothing that is not part of reality.")[17] Konrád is also somewhat old-fashioned in believing in the moral value of literature, in "maintaining light against the threatening dark," as Stanley Kauffmann has written in his essay on the novelist.[18] A few years ago Konrád summed up his ars poetica, which could easily pass for a confession of faith.

> On the door of a Budapest church a simpleminded priest put up this sign: "Spend a half hour with your soul." I liked to go into this church for a half hour, which I felt I did spend with my soul. If somebody reads, he is in a better state of mind than if he is jostled on the subway. He may have a moment of self-discovery. If the light the author sheds on his own self is strong enough, it may illuminate his reader's mind. A concentrated, terrible, and serene moment is what literature really is.[19]

Ivan Sanders, Spring 1983

[1] Irving Howe, *The New York Times Book Review,* 27 January 1974, p. 1.

[2] Richard Sennett, "A Dark Novel of Eastern Europe," *The New York Times Book Review,* 26 September 1982, p. 1.

[3] See for example Sándor Fekete's article on "internal exiles," "Emigránsok, kint és bent," in *Új Tükör,* 18 April 1982, pp. 18–19; and journalist Péter Rényi's scathing attack on Konrád's "subversive activities" in the Hungarian Communist Party daily *Népszabadság,* 11 December 1982, p. 7.

[4] See George Konrád, "The Long Work of Liberty," *The New York Review of Books,* 26 January 1978, pp. 38–41.

[5] "The Novelists: George Konrád," interview in *The New Republic,* 5–12 January 1980, p. 26.

[6] George Konrád, *The City Builder,* Ivan Sanders, tr., New York, Harcourt Brace Jovanovich, 1977 (see *WLT* 52:1, p. 151 for a review of the Hungarian edition). Also available in English from HBJ are *The Case Worker* (Paul Aston, tr., 1974; see *BA* 49:1, p. 164) and *The Loser* (Ivan Sanders, tr., 1982). All quotations are from these editions. Translations not otherwise indicated are my own.

[7] Pearl K. Bell, in *Commentary,* 70 (December 1980), p. 66.

[8] "The Novelists: George Konrád," p. 25.

[9] Ibid., p. 26.

[10] Endre Bojtár, "Az irodalmi mű jelentése—Konrád Gyorgy: A látogató," *Irodalomtörténeti Közlemények,* 82 (1978), p. 229.

[11] See György Konrád, *Az autonómia kísértése,* Paris, Magyar Füzetek, 1980.

[12] Konrád, "The Long Work of Liberty," p. 40.

[13] "The Novelists: George Konrád," p. 25.

[14] See for example Jack Beatty, "Konrád's City Builders Lay Foundation for Modern Tyranny," *Politicks,* 8 May 1978, p. 7.

[15] Without some background in Hegel, Marx and Lukács, it is impossible to appreciate fully the provocative sociological analysis in *The Intellectuals on the Road to Class Power* (Andrew Arato and Richard E. Allen, trs., New York, Harcourt Brace Jovanovich, 1979), a treatise Konrád coauthored with Iván Szelényi.

[16] See Elisabeth Jakab, "Lying Low in Budapest," *The Nation,* 18 December 1982, p. 661.

[17] George Konrád, "Face and Mask," *Dissent,* Summer 1979, p. 300.

[18] *Salmagundi,* no. 57 (Summer 1982), p. 87.

[19] "The Novelists: George Konrád," p. 28.

POLAND

Presentation of Czesław Miłosz to the Jury

I have no hesitation whatsoever in stating that Czesław Miłosz is one of the greatest poets of our time, perhaps the greatest. Even if one strips his poems of the stylistic magnificence of his native Polish (which is what translation inevitably does) and reduces them to the naked subject matter, we still find ourselves confronting a severe and relentless mind of such intensity that the only parallel one is able to think of is that of the biblical characters—most likely Job. But the scope of the loss experienced by Miłosz was—not only from purely geographical considerations—somewhat larger.

Miłosz received what one might call a standard East European education, which included, among other things, what's known as the Holocaust, which he predicted in his poems of the late thirties. The wasteland he describes in his wartime (and some postwar) poetry is fairly literal: it is not the unresurrected Adonis that is missing there, but concrete millions of his countrymen. What toppled the whole enterprise was that his land, after being devastated physically, was also stolen from him and, proportionately, ruined spiritually. Out of these ashes emerged poetry which did not so much sing of outrage and grief as whisper of the guilt of the survivor. The core of the major themes of Miłosz's poetry is the unbearable realization that a human being is not able to grasp his experience, and the more that time separates him from this experience, the less become his chances to comprehend it. This realization alone extends—to say the least—our notion of the human psyche and casts quite a remorseless light on the proverbial interplay of cause and effect.

It wouldn't be fair, however, to reduce the significance of Miłosz's poetry to this theme. His, after all, is a metaphysical poetry which regards the things of this world (including language itself) as manifestations of a certain superior realm, miniaturized or magnified for the sake of our perception. The existential process for this poet is neither enigma nor explanation, but rather is symbolized by the test tube: the only thing which is unclear is what is being tested—whether it is the endurance of man in terms of applied pain, or the durability of pain itself.

Czesław Miłosz is perfectly aware that language is not a tool of cognition but rather a tool of assimilation in what appears to be a quite hostile world—unless it is employed by poetry, which alone tries to beat language at its own game and thus to bring it as close as possible to real cognizance. Short-cutting or, rather, short-circuiting the analytical process, Miłosz's poetry releases the reader from many psychological and purely linguistic traps, for it answers not the question "how to live" but "for the sake of what" to live. In a way, what this poet preaches is an awfully sober version of stoicism which does not ignore reality, however absurd and horrendous, but accepts it as a new norm which a human being has to absorb without giving up any of his fairly compromised values.

Joseph Brodsky, Summer 1978

Czesław Miłosz *(Gil Jain)*

Wisława Szymborska and The Importance of the Unimportant

I am no longer certain that what is important is more important than the unimportant.

▪ "NO TITLE REQUIRED"

For the second time in sixteen years, a Polish poet has been awarded the Nobel Prize in Literature. This is not a coincidence: the decision of the Swedish Academy to bestow the world's most prestigious literary award on Czesław Miłosz in 1980[1] and on Wisława Szymborska in 1996 is tribute to the exceptional vitality and prominence of contemporary Polish poetry. More than anyone else, it is Czesław Miłosz who gave Polish poetry its international visibility, both as a poet and translator and its enthusiastic promoter in America. It is Miłosz's seminal anthology *Postwar Polish Poetry,* first published in 1965, that contained—together with twenty other poets—the first English translations of Szymborska's verse. But Miłosz's significance is even deeper, and lies in the impact he has had on the shape of postwar Polish poetry. More than any other twentieth-century poet, Miłosz has created a model and a yardstick against which younger poets have to measure themselves. Wisława Szymborska is the one who has done so with the greatest success.

To most readers outside Poland, Szymborska's Nobel Prize came as a surprise. Long recognized in her native country as a leading voice in contemporary poetry, Szymborska has not achieved the same popularity in the English-speaking world enjoyed by other poets of her generation such as Zbigniew Herbert, Tadeusz Różewicz, and Miron Bialoszewski. Not a political poet (though some of her early poems were written according to the precepts of socialist realism), Szymborska drew little attention at a time when Western interest in Eastern Europe had a largely political motivation. She defied the "mold" used to describe literature "behind the iron curtain." However, a number of English translations of her poetry had appeared: Miłosz's anthology was followed in 1981 by the translations of Magnus Kryński and Robert Maguire, published as *Sounds, Feelings, Thoughts: Seventy Poems;*[2] Adam Czerniawski brought out *People on a Bridge*[3] in England in 1990; and in 1995 there appeared the comprehensive collection *View with a Grain of Sand,* a set of award-winning translations by Stanislaw Barańczak and Clare Cavanagh. It is only with this most recent publication that Szymborska's poetry came fully into the view of the English-speaking audience.

In contrast, Szymborska's reputation in Poland has been steadily growing ever since her third volume, *Wolanie do Yeti* (Calling Out to Yeti), appeared in 1957. The publication of each successive volume—*Sól* (Salt; 1962), *Sto pociech* (No End of Fun; 1967), *Wszelki wypadek* (Could Have; 1972), *Wielka liczba* (A Large Number; 1976), *Ludzie na moście* (1986; Eng. *People on a Bridge*), and *Koniec i początek* (The End and the Beginning; 1993)—has been an important poetic event, win-

Wisława Szymborska (*AP/Wide World Photos*)

personal effusions and an emotional tone. Absent as a person, she is nevertheless strongly present as a voice—a voice which is unmistakably her own and impossible to confuse with that of any other poet. It is a voice of a Cartesian consciousness and of a cognitive subject, a voice that narrates and at the same time reflects upon the meaning and implications of its own narrative. Often the very structure of Szymborska's poems reproduces the cognitive process, and the poems become a direct and unrhetorical form of "thinking aloud."

It has come to this: I'm sitting under a tree
beside a river
on a sunny morning.
. . . .
And since I'm here
I must have come from somewhere,
and before that
I must have turned up in many other places.
(175)

They may search memory, as in "May 16, 1973": "One of those many dates / that no longer ring a bell. // Where I was going that day, / what I was doing—I don't know" (199). Most often, they pose a question: "Maybe all this / is happening in some lab? / Under one lamp by day / and billions by night?" (201).

Szymborska's reflection rarely takes the form of categorical statements, and this is especially true of her later poetry. Reluctant to provide definitive answers, the poet prefers a margin of uncertainty. It is the initial premise of Descartes's formula, the "dubito" that describes best her philosophical attitude. But unlike the French philosopher, the Polish poet is unwilling to cross the threshold of uncertainty and step into the bright light of certitude: "certainty is beautiful, / but uncertainty is more beautiful still," she admits (197). Szymborska's reluctance is not the result of a lack of moral determination, but rather an expression of openness. It is an awareness that truth is complex and ambiguous, that reality is thick and consists of a myriad details, all of which need to be taken into account. In Szymborska's version of the well-known biblical story, Lot's wife looks back not only out of curiosity but with a number of different motives: regret, fear, anger, shame, the desire to go back. The poet shuns the didactic clarity of the biblical account in favor of a more tentative conclusion, but one closer to the complexity of psychological truth: "It's not inconceivable that my eyes were open. / It's possible I fell facing the city" (102).

In another poem Szymborska praises ignorance: "We're extremely fortunate / not to know precisely / the kind of world we live in" (213). What appears to be an

ning the author an ever-widening audience. Szymborska's ability to speak in simple language has made her poetry accessible and attractive to an unusually broad spectrum of readers.

Paradoxically, Szymborska's very simplicity and directness present the greatest challenge to a critic, and probably also account for a relative dearth of studies about her poetry. The analytic language of literary criticism often seems powerless and inadequate when dealing with these deceptively transparent poems; it is heavy-handed and clumsy in comparison with the lightness and agility of the poetic lines. Attempts at description and analysis frequently end in a frustrating realization of failure and the necessity to go back to the poems themselves, to let the poet speak with her own voice and defend herself against the awkward approximations of the critic. An important and integral part of her poetics, Szymborska's apparent ease conceals a conscious and determined effort. Her simplicity is careful, a result of struggle, and is hard to trace since the poet covers her tracks: "I borrow weighty words, / then labor heavily so that they may seem light."[4]

Szymborska is a poet of philosophical reflection. Like most Polish poets of her generation, she avoids ironic, tongue-in-cheek statement has in fact a deeper meaning, for the choice of ignorance is tantamount to an acceptance of the human condition, together with all its temporal, spatial, and cognitive limitations. It is a choice of the human over the inhuman, the concrete over the abstract, the particular over the universal. Szymborska's island of Utopia, where "all is elucidated" and dominated by "Unshaken Confidence," is uninhabited. Footprints point toward the sea, "As if all you can do here is leave / and plunge, never to return, into the depths" (128). Written in the 1970s, the poem can be read as an allusion to communist ideology and a depiction of the totalitarian state. It functions beyond its political context, however, and expresses the author's dislike of easy solutions and categorical assertions. Avoiding anything that might smack of dogmaticism or didacticism, Szymborska prefers to conclude her poems with an admission of ignorance or doubt: "I am," she says, "a question answering a question" (174).

This philosophical option explains also her predilection for paradox, a stylistic figure that undermines accepted truths and leaves questions open. For example, "To change so that nothing changes," reads a line from the poem "A Feminine Portrait." Elsewhere we find: "You expected a hermit to live in the wilderness, / but he has a little house and a garden, / surrounded by cheerful birch groves, / ten minutes off the highway. / Just follow the signs" (114). In "Elegiac Calculations," a metaphysical poem about death, each statement is followed by a parenthetic clause in the conditional mode.

How many of those I knew
(if I really knew them),
men, women
(if the distinction still holds)
have crossed that threshold
(if it is a threshold)
passed over that bridge
(if you can call it a bridge)—

The poem concludes on a note of uncertainty: "I've been given no assurance / as concerns their future fate" (188).

One of the most striking features of Szymborska's poetry is that reflections are prompted not by abstract ideas but by concrete and ordinary experiences: the sight of the sky, sitting on the shore of a river, looking at a painting, a visit to the doctor. Like Bialoszewski, although in a different idiom, Szymborska extols the everyday and the ordinary: her "miracle fair" is made up of barking dogs, trees reflected in a pond, gentle breezes, and gusty storms—the world "ever-present." At the theater she is moved by a glimpse of actors caught beneath the curtain more than by tragic tirades. The very triviality of these experiences betrays a philo-

sophical *parti pris* on the part of the poet, who questions and at the same time reverses the accepted opinion of what is important and what is unimportant. The usual hierarchies are stood on their head. Is the death of an insect less important than our own? Only if seen from "high above," that is from a human perspective, according to which "important matters are reserved for us" (103). Metaphysics are not above everyday reality, and need not be sought in the "starry night" of the philosophers; they pervade every aspect of our existence. In a series of paradoxes, Szymborska questions the division into the high and the low, the meta- and the physical, the earth and the sky.

Even the highest mountains
are no closer to the sky
than the deepest valleys.
There is no more of it in one place
than another.
The sky weighs on a cloud
as much as on a grave.
A mole is no less in seventh heaven
than the owl spreading her wings.
The object that falls in an abyss
falls from sky to sky.
(173)

In Szymborska's poetry, reality is "democratized," and "anniversaries of revolutions" are much less prominent than "ants stitching in the grass" and "the pattern of a wave." Szymborska pitches ontology against history and politics, the private and the individual against the public and the collective, and here she reveals a deep affinity with Czesław Miłosz. Common and humble reality is put forward at the expense of history and politics: "Even a passing moment has its fertile past, / its Friday before Saturday, / its May before June. / Its horizons are no less real / than those that a marshal's field glasses might scan" (175).

For Szymborska, man's life is short and marked by suffering and death. No historical event can alter or has altered this basic existential condition: "Nothing has changed. / The body still trembles as it trembled / before Rome was founded and after, / in the twentieth century before and after Christ" (151). On the contrary, history has only added to human suffering through wars and oppression. In her early and well-known poem "Breughel's Two Monkeys" she wrote:

This is what I see in my dreams about final exams:
two monkeys, chained to the floor, sit on the
  windowsill,
the sky behind them flutters,
the sea is taking its bath.

The exam is History of Mankind.

I stammer and hedge.

One monkey stares and listens with mocking disdain,
the other seems to be dreaming away—
but when it's clear I don't know what to say
he prompts me with a gentle
clinking of his chain.
(3)

History is not a manifestation of the human spirit, or an extension of the individual and man's projection into time, but a force inimical to man. A deeply humanistic poet, Szymborska sees history as the principal source of evil. Disrespectful of human life, it fails to account for the number of its victims, as it "rounds out skeletons to the nearest zero" ("A Hunger Camp at Jaslo"). It provides fertile ground for hatred, as in the poem "Hatred": "Gifted, diligent, hard-working. / Need we mention all the songs it has composed? / All the pages it has added to our history books? / All the human carpets it has spread / over countless city squares and football fields?" (182).

The sharpest edge of Szymborska's irony is reserved for politics. In an age which she ironically describes as "political," everything becomes "food" for politics.

To acquire a political meaning
you don't even have to be human.
Raw material will do,
or protein feed, or crude oil,

or a conference table whose shape
was quarreled over for months:
Should we arbitrate life and death
at a round table or a square one.
(150)

A pacifist, Szymborska sides with ordinary people against history: "I prefer the earth in civilian clothes. / I prefer conquered rather than conquering countries. /. . . . / I prefer Grimm's fairy tales to the first pages of newspapers" ("Possibilities").

Szymborska has a deep respect for reality and a sense of wonder at its diversity and inexhaustible richness. This once again brings her close to Miłosz: "So much world all at once—how it rustles and bustles!" (79). This is accompanied by a realization that there is a disparity between the unlimited vastness of reality and the limitations of the poetic imagination: "Four billion people on this earth, / but my imagination is still the same" (95). The mathematical value of π comes closer to expressing the infinite richness of the universe than does the poetic imagination: "It can't be comprehended *six five three five* at a glance, / *eight nine* by calculation, / *seven nine* or imagination, / not even *three two three*

eight by wit, that is, by comparison" (129). Art can seize only individual facts and existences, a fraction of reality.

On the hill where Troy used to be
seven cities have been discovered.
Seven cities. Six too many
for a single epic poem.
What can be done with them? What can be done?
The hexameters are bursting.
("Population Census")

The poet describes her own imagination as one that is moved not by "large numbers" but by what is particular, by that which can be described only in the singular. Even her dreams, she concedes, are not populous and "hold more solitude than noisy crowds." With a touch of irony, she speaks of herself as "a mouse at the foot of the maternal mountain," as a "jester" who prefers "Thursday over infinity" (119). Poetry, marked by insufficiency and imperfection, is a selection, a renunciation, a passing over in silence, and a "sigh" rather than a "full breath." Like anyone else, the poet is unable to step outside her own "I," her own particular existence. Being herself, she cannot be what she is not: "My apologies to everything that I can't be everywhere at once. / My apologies to everyone that I can't be each woman and each man. / I know I won't be justified as long as I live, / since I myself stand in my own way" (92).

Faced with a task that is impossible, Szymborska makes a choice—to describe what is immediate and accessible, the ordinary and the small: "Inexhaustible, unembraceable, / but particular to the smallest fiber, / grain of sand, / drop of water — / landscapes" (19). After all, every particle reflects the whole, every drop of water contains the entire universe: "A drop of water fell on my hand, / drawn from the Ganges and the Nile, // from hoarfrost ascended to heaven off a seal's whiskers, / from jugs broken in the cities of Ys and Tyre" (28).

In the opposition between reality and art, life and intellect, the poet declares herself on the side of reality and life. Ideas are most often pretexts to kill, a deadly weapon whether under the guise of an artistic experiment ("Experiment"), a political Utopia ("Utopia"), or ideological fanaticism ("The Terrorist, He Watches"). Even poetry is "a revenge of a mortal hand" ("The Joy of Writing"). Szymborska sides with reality against art and ideology, and this choice situates her in the mainstream of postwar Polish poetry alongside Miłosz, Herbert, and Bialoszewski.

Despite its familiarity and ordinariness, Szymborska's poetry is neither relaxing nor comforting. It is permeated by a consciousness of death, temporariness, and human vulnerability.

Nothing's a gift, it's all on loan.

I'm drowning in debt up to my ears.
I'll have to pay for myself
with my self,
give up my life for my life.

. . . .

Every tissue in us lies
on the debit side.
Not a tentacle or tendril
is for keeps.

The inventory, infinitely detailed,
implies we'll be left
not just empty-handed
but handless, too.
(206)

Not only do we live on credit, but life is a constant improvisation, a rehearsal in an unfamiliar setting, a play
without a script. What is more, the rehearsal is also the
only performance we are granted, and all our actions—
regardless how tentative—acquire the permanence of a
perfective tense: "And whatever I'll do, / will turn for
ever into what I've done" ("Instant Living").

In Szymborska's world, man is alone and distinct
from the world of nature and objects; the division between the human and nonhuman world is unbridgeable, as in "Conversation with a Stone."

I knock at the stone's front door.
"It's only me, let me come in.
I want to enter your insides,
have a look round,
breathe my fill of you."

"Go away," says the stone.
"I'm shut tight.
Even if you break me to pieces,
we'll all still be closed.
You can grind us to sand,
we still won't let you in."
(30)

The ontology of objects is beyond man's reach, and giving them anthropomorphic features is a misunderstanding. Consciousness is a human attribute; nature is unaware of itself. The sense of time, place, and purpose,
colors, shapes, sounds, and names are products of
human consciousness alone.

We call it a grain of sand,
but it calls itself neither grain nor sand.
It does just fine without a name,
whether general, particular,
permanent, passing,
incorrect, or apt.

Our glance, our touch mean nothing to it.
It doesn't feel itself seen and touched.

And that it fell on the windowsill
is only our experience, not its.
(135)

There is a contrast between nature's pure externali-
ty and its lack of self-awareness, on the one hand, and
man's tortured consciousness on the other: "Our skin
is just a coverup / for the land where none dare go, /
an internal inferno, /. . . . / In an onion there's only
onion / from its top to its toe" (120). Because it lacks
consciousness, nature is spared existential despair and
metaphysical anxiety, and seems to us to be edenic. The
communication between man and the external world is
one-way, from human consciousness toward external
reality, from man to objects. But the two realms remain
distinct and strange to each other.

Szymborska's poetry is one of existential terror, but
what makes it even more terrifying is that it avoids spectacular decorations and a tragic tone. Szymborska's tone
is matter-of-fact, constantly kept in check: "if you, then
with a touch of fear; / if despair, then not without some
quiet hope" (144). The tragic content is attenuated by
humor, wit, and an abundance of verbal games and
puns: "Life, however long, will always be short. / Too
short for anything to be added" (144). The situations
are trivial, and the effect is often a result of contrast between the triviality of the scene and the metaphysical
dimension of the event.

A dead beetle lies on the path through the field.
Three pairs of legs folded neatly on its belly.
Instead of death's confusion, tidiness and order.
The horror of this sight is moderate,
its scope is strictly local, from the wheat grass to the
  mint.
The grief is quarantined
The sky is blue.
(103)

Death is banal and inscrutable in its mystery. The
room of a suicide gives no clues to the man's tragedy.

I'll bet you think the room was empty.
Wrong. There were three chairs with sturdy backs.
A lamp, good for fighting the dark.
A desk, and on the desk a wallet, some newspapers.
A carefree Buddha and a worried Christ.
Seven lucky elephants, a notebook in a drawer.
You think our addresses weren't in it?
(122)

In one of her most popular and finest poems, "Cat
in an Empty Apartment," the poet describes grief—and
the sense of emptiness after the death of someone
close—from the perspective of a cat.

Die—you can't do that to a cat.

Since what can a cat do
in an empty apartment?
Climb the walls?
Rub up against furniture?
Nothing seems different here,
but nothing is the same.
Nothing has been moved,
but there's more space.
And at nighttime no lamps are lit.
(189)

Wisława Szymborska is not a prolific writer, and her poetic oeuvre consists of only some two hundred poems. Each poem, however, is a masterpiece. In crystalline and carefully wrought language, with a tone that is unpretentious, this poetry speaks to everyone and is about everyone. The ostensibly "unimportant" questions it poses prove to be the only questions that truly matter.

Bogdana Carpenter, Winter 1997

[1] On Miłosz, see *WLT* 52:3 (Summer 1978), pp. 357–425, and *WLT* 55:1 (Winter 1981), pp. 5–6.

[2] Wisława Szymborska, *Sounds, Feelings, Thoughts: Seventy Poems,* trs. Magnus J. Kryński and Robert A. Maguire, Princeton (N.J.), Princeton University Press, 1981. For a review, see *WLT* 56:2 (Spring 1982), p. 368.

[3] Wisława Szymborska, *People on a Bridge,* tr. Adam Czerniawski, London, Forest Books, 1990. For a review, see *WLT* 66:1 (Winter 1992), p. 163.

[4] All quotations referred to by page number come from Wisława Szymborska, *View with a Grain of Sand,* trs. Stanisław Barańczak and Clare Cavanagh, New York, Harcourt Brace, 1995. Citations without page references are my own translations.

The Poetic Phenomenology of a Religious Man: About the Literary Creativity of Karol Wojtyła

Polish thinkers always have been willing to express themselves in literary forms of communication. Our greatest thinkers are writers: poets, novelists, essayists, authors of political and ideological works. This phenomenon is very characteristic of Polish literature; it is both more important and more organically developed than the basically superficial, quasi-political character of our culture, which has been caused by a servitude of 150 years as well as by an early and persisting threat to our independence. Therefore literature may not have served solely as a "vicarious" force, but it may also, to a greater extent, have had "simultaneous functions" by

helping the institutions of national life that were not well developed. Who knows why it all happened that way? Actually, the Polish philosophical style is literary: it is non-systematic; it is oriented toward the life experience of the individual; it is willing to use metaphors, symbols, fictional examples and artistic tales (narration). Maybe this is above all a personalistic style: i.e., it focuses on the problems of a real, unique person, and its investigations are made in an individual, personal way.

It is not by chance that the greatest Polish mystics are poets: Benislawska, Mickiewicz, Norwid, the great innovator of theology. The leading political thinkers are poets too: Mochnacki, Krasiński, Brzozowski. And in return we observe a reciprocal movement: the most eminent philosophers engage in literature. Focusing on the Polish writers of this century, we find: Znaniecki, the author of such lyric poems as "Cheops"; Witkacy, who was possiblly more of a literary person than a philosopher; Kotarbiński, the author of numerous poetic miniatures; Leszek Kolakowski, the creator of several volumes of short stories and parables; and finally, the author of "The World of Human Hope," the master of spoken literature, Józef Tishner.

Within this circle inevitably there has to be one more philosopher and theologian. Astronomers can deduce from theoretical calculations the existence of a celestial sphere that is still invisible. The researcher of the revolution of literary spheres could operate in the same way. The star of a religious-mystical poet should revolve in postwar Polish poetry. Our theoretician would even have a candidate for that role: it could be a young priest, later Bishop of Cracow, then Cardinal Karol Wojtyla—a man predisposed to write meditative lyrics like few others, a philosopher who unites his interest in the works of mystics with the practice of the philosophy of action, a theologican with an inclination toward ethics and personalism, and an ecclesiologist, yet in addition, a former student of Polish (he attended Pigon's and Wyka's classes), an actor, a man of prayer and a protector of the arts. Should the observer of human and divine laws not desire to reach the fullness of life by serving the Good, the True and the Beautiful, about which he writes repeatedly? And if our erudite theoretician rummaged through the old issues of Catholic magazines (it is a pity that literary critics and scholars look there so seldom), he would find there the confirmation of his abstract considerations. He would submit the proposition that the shepherd of many souls Karol Wojtyla and the poet Andrzej Jawień are the same person. And he would be right.

■ ■ ■

Andrzej Jawień appears on the literary scene of his country at age thirty as a "mature poet" who knows what he expects from literature, who has his own poetic language and his own problems to solve. He starts from the great artistic forms: in 1950–52 three of his poems appear in the columns of *Tygodnik Powszechny* (Universal Weekly). It is probably the suspension of the newspaper until the end of 1956 that made the publication of his next poems impossible. From the moment of his debut with the publication of "Song of the Brightness of Water" until "Considerations on Death" in 1975 (signed with the pseudonym Stanislaw Gruda), a homogeneous poetic world has developed. The lyrical edifice enriches itself as the years pass; it blossoms out slowly while in substance remaining the same. The resemblance shows even in the most external aspect: in the form of the message, a long declaration that includes several parts; in an objective monologue-meditation; in identical central images and in poetic styles that remain similar.

As one attempts to characterize the works of Jawień that share a similarity of genre, the author himself lends a helping hand, for the titles of the poetic texts assign them accurately enough to well-defined traditional genres. In two of the eight titles of Jawień's important literary pieces the word *rozważanie* (consideration) appears; in the subtitle of a poetic drama appears the word *medytacya* (meditation); in another title we find *myśl* (thought or mind), and in the subtitles of both parts of "The Birth of Confessors" we find "thought" again. The information given by the author therefore situates those works as belonging to meditative literature, which is extremely important for European literary culture. This literature is not uniform; three groups can be signalized. First, at least for Jawień, is the *meditation*—i.e., the religious consideration on Christ's suffering and death. This genre was most frequent in the Middle Ages and bore exquisite fruit in Polish literature as well as in others. Two of Jawień's poems refer directly and wholly to this model: "Considerations on Death," whose theme is the problem of human mortality, and "The Quarry," whose theme is the factual circumstance of a worker's death. Secondly, the name "meditation" is also used to characterize a certain type of philosophical work, such as Descartes's *Meditationes de Prima Philosophia* (1641). Here again we find a connection with our poet, since philosophical discourse constitutes a characteristic feature of all Wojtyla's literary texts. They give a perfect example of the expression through words of a complex thought, of getting deeper into a vitally significant problem. Thirdly, reflective lyrics are called, somewhat more metaphorically, meditations. This genre has been used

frequently, most of all during the Baroque, the romantic period and our own times: one cannot omit Rilke, Eliot and Valéry, to quote only the greatest names.

Jawień does not choose an emotional-imaginative style of meditative creation, but rather an intellectual one, sparingly administering the figures of thought and style. If we add to this the extensive dimensions of his declarations, the rigor and accuracy of his discourse (which does not always mean intelligibility, because the substance of his considerations is mysterious and at the limits of the expressible), an extensive syntax that usually employs subordinate clauses, and many philosophical and theological terms, then it is impossible not to notice the affinity between Wojtyla's poems and the treatise. This seemingly old-fashioned poetic form was revived at the end of the forties through the efforts of Czesław Miłosz, author of "The Moral Treatise." The seed for this genre was sown in well-prepared soil. Karol Wojtyla wrote his doctoral dissertation on the literary output of St. John of the Cross, the Mystic Doctor, and his first scholarly publications as a young thinker were devoted to the Spanish mystic. St. John's works—a "mystical tetralogy," according to Wojtyla's beautiful definition—are in fact theological treatises which, in addition, comment on poetical verses. Moreover, they draw generously from literary funds. In the essay "On the Humanism of St. John of the Cross" Wojtyla writes: "His works were written in his native Spanish, doubtless constituting a singular phenomenon at the time. Besides that, they have the reputation of being, in the history of Spanish literature, historical events in the full meaning of the word. They are characterized not only by the great accuracy and strict logic of their theological message, but also by a real imaginativeness of poetic inspiration. . . . Poetry doubtless made it much easier for the author in a field that does not lend itself to expression either in the framework of colloquial prosaic language, or within the fetters of strictly scientific terminology" (HSJ, 8).[1]

If this characterization of the writings of the Doctor of the Night (the expression is from Jacques Maritain) is considered as the self-commentary of the Polish poet-theologian, one can ascertain that Wojtyla's decision to write poetry was dictated by his awareness of the insufficiency of scientific language to communicate religious experience. This awareness does not mean a total rejection of scientific and philosophical language. In Jawień's creation one can see a constant effort to *synthesize various forms of personal communication*. His poetry has the character of an objective report: the inner impulses are controlled; the characters do not show direct emotional reactions, but try to transform them into durable values shared by several individuals. In his poetry the expression of emotions is curtailed. This is perhaps why they are so powerful; since they appear seldom and discreetly, they work more efficiently. In such a conception of the lyrical "I" the philosophical position stands out; it is the position of an active personalism that aims toward controlling one's own psychological life, toward becoming freer, thus toward being the originator and the subject of one's actions and of one's inner life. Thanks to that, the monologues are seemingly alyrical, with little subjective and emotional coloration. Their instruments are reflection, a calm confession, reportage, images as the equivalent of emotions.

Since the word *equivalent* (*równoważnik*) has been uttered, some comment must be made about the ties of Jawień's poetry with the rules of neoclassical poetic technique (Eliot's "objective correlative") and with Cracow's avant-garde and its theory of the equivalence of feelings. As with the images, the "equivalent"—let me stress that Jawień does not use it too often—reminds us at first of the extensive and difficult metaphors of the Cracow avant-garde; it then clarifies itself and serves to bring close referents together. Three examples will testify to the dynamics of the images:

. . . the human wall opens from time to time—a face
a passage—then the lights of windows carry it
to another place nearby.
(SBW, 1)

I shall never forget the lakes that surprised us on our
    way
they were like two cisterns of light sleep.
Mixed with the gleam of
the clear August night, the metal was asleep.
(FJS)

. . . not only the tombstone, but the entire earth
is laid open,
death transforms the places of our passage.
(CD)

■ ■ ■

In Jawień's poetry one can discover symbolic images and objects that appear constantly and carry on the central ideas of his weltanschauung. I shall call these "themes," in accordance with the meaning conferred on that expression by French thematic criticism—i.e., repeatable images serving as the main devices by which the writer grasps the world. Examples of such central themes, which organize deep human experience into the material of linguistic signs, are: shining objects, the depth of the soul, a picture that cannot be lifted, the brightness of water, a reflecting and absorbing mirror, spiritual space, reaching beyond oneself, personal unification, a shining and enlightening window. Basically,

one can assume that these themes have not been gathered by chance and freely brought together in a given poetic message. It is therefore worth trying to reconstruct the order in which they are presented and the particular kind of syntax that brings the basic elements together into "clause-poems." In anticipation of what follows, it must be said that the rules which give an order and a dynamic to Jawień's themes of poetic meditation remind one of the rules by which a man proceeds in searching for and experiencing God; these rules—elaborated, ingrained in oneself, obtained by prayer through a centuries-long experience—are those that guided the way of the great mystics of our Western culture.

The Water of Life—the Work of Grace. Let us start at the beginning of the soul's journey and at the beginning of Jawień's literary creation. The latter is an absolute beginning which precedes even the first words written by the poet: we are speaking here of the title and the motto of the first of the future Pope's poetic communiqués. The title explains that the "brightness of water" will be the fundamental theme of the work; and in order to avoid leaving the reader in uncertainty, Jawień adds as a motto a passage from the Gospel according to John which contains Jesus's encounter with the Samaritan woman and in which Jesus speaks about the water of eternal life that provides for all human desires. Thus the poem "Song of the Brightness of Water" is all about the possibility of Union with God through the gift of the water of eternal life, which is interpreted in Catholic theology as a symbol for the Holy Ghost. We also know that, according to St. John of the Cross, the soul in search of the Beloved can be united with Him solely through the gift of the Holy Ghost.

The first literary work known to have been signed with the pseudonym Andrzej Jawień is constructed on the schema of the event related in John 4:5–42; it consists of monologues by the narrator and principal character of the poem, the Samaritan woman whom Jesus met at the well in Sychar. The beginning of the poem mentions tired eyes in which "the night's dark waters flowed into the words of prayer" and ends with the happy song and spontaneous cry of the Union with Him: "O, how good this is!" A fragment of the sixth poem, entitled "The Samaritan Woman," is the woman's confession of her encounter with Jesus (it would be more appropriate to say "her Encounter"); it informs us that we should interpret this event not so much realistically as mystically: "This well united me with you, / this well led me into you" (SBW).[2] In the twentieth chapter of *The Dark Night of the Soul* St. John of the Cross writes about the entrance of the soul into the Divine Union, in the terminal phase of "the passive night of the soul":

"The ninth step of love causes the soul to burn with sweet rapture. This is the state of perfection, that is, the state of those perfect souls who are aflame with the sweet love of God. This blissful flame of love is caused by the Holy Ghost, by virtue of the union which these souls have with God."[3]

The Inner and Outer Night. Let us come back now to the first steps of the journey. A digression forward was necessary to show that, from the very beginning, the human creature searches because he has been found, that he goes forward because he is attracted by Absolute Being, that he achieves heroic actions because he does not act in total solitude. Nonetheless, the road is long and arduous; only the most courageous of those who make the journey arrive at their destination. It is not without reason that in "Song of the Brightness of Water" the poet speaks of "the dark waters of the night" and that the action takes place at night. The same is true of the poetical drama "In Front of the Jeweler's Shop," where mysterious voices coming from within the mountains—and undoubtedly acting as signals of some sort—reach from the abysses of "the night of *Bieszczady* which is full of nature's secrets" (FJS, 1568). In the poem "The Mind Is a Strange Territory," even though there are no direct indications, the events also must happen at dusk, since the "luminosity of things" is granted such an important function in the poem.[4]

Solitary Suffering. "The Mind Is a Strange Territory" informs us of another drawback in the pilgrimage toward Unification, and this drawback is the solitary journey. At the beginning the narrator says that "no word, no gesture or sign will convey the whole image that we must enter alone, in order to struggle like Jacob." It becomes clear toward the end of the poem that this solitude is an indispensable condition for attaining the goal.

You must carry the image within yourself, so that
  you are completely transformed into its substance
which is promoted by silence and solitude,
solitude possible in man.
Possible because death takes no one away from her.

This solitude is favorable for conveying the image. It is a solitude so perfect that it overcomes death; therefore it cannot be anything but a symbol for the purification of subjectivity and its passing beyond the area of common experience. The Mystic Doctor was quite aware of it when he wrote that love is the reconciliation of solitary creatures, that it fulfills itself in solitude (*Spiritual Canticle*). Not only darkness and solitude accompany this wandering toward God, but also suffering, for the speaking subject of "The Mind Is a Strange Territory" says that "man suffers most because he is deprived

of vision," because religious passion has already been kindled while the moment of satisfaction and appeasement is still far off. Hope is what sustains the energies, but often it breaks down. "Considerations on Death" recalls the crisis of this theological virtue prior to the administering of supernatural aid: "My hope is not confirmed within me/by any layer of just my own memories,/hope in the mirror of encounters does not portray anything" (CD, 275).

The Vision of the Soul. The man in search of God does not long remain suspended in this painful stage; he soon receives support. This step along the mystical road is treated in the "shining eyes" theme, which appears to be most developed in "The Mind Is a Strange Territory." This poem, which shows the journey toward Eternal Being, is of all Jawień's works the most impregnated by mystical elements, the most consciously obfuscated, the most mysterious. The lyrical "I" reveals the way to overcome obstacles. It reminds us of the fact that "this strange, deep world exchanges eyes with him," and also that the eye "by its clear core saturates itself with reality and transforms it." The Samaritan woman, with the same determination, indicates this way of experiencing, although instead of exchanging eyes (the masters of inner life would say that here sensory vision is replaced by the vision of the soul), she proposes a change in the way of seeing: "To open the eyes in a different way from the usual and not to forget the vision in which the eyes once delighted." The eyes, shining by a light coming from without, changed, illuminated by their own clear core and transforming reality, have the faculty of seeing unusual things and of helping the other powers of the soul.

Opening Consciousness and Space. The protagonist in "The Mind. . ." is someone who at certain moments seems to represent the essence of humanity—he is not individualized—and who at other moments becomes the biblical Jacob, who was certainly the only mortal to see God "face to face." The choice of this figure was dictated by the logic of the work, since Jacob was, in the tradition of the Church Fathers, the model of a man whom God was inclined to bless, the symbol of the victorious spiritual fight. Andrzej Jawień took upon himself the very difficult poetical task of depicting the moment at which consciousness opens up before the Divine Personage arrives.

Someone—the same—opened his consciousness to
  the full,
in the same way as a child, a sheep or a tool, yet
  differently,
yet he did not crush them, he did not push them, he
  only embraced them,

and all trembled lightly in Him, revealing their inner fear.

The opening of consciousness precedes and certainly makes possible the opening of space and the subject's entrance into regions that were up to that point inaccessible to knowledge and existence: "And Jacob also trembled in Him, for never before / had reality so suddenly opened itself to him." In this phase other forms of space also open: not only inner space, but also wide worlds like the cosmic realms surrounding man. One might mention other examples of man's contact with spiritual regions. In the extensive meditation entitled "The Church," written during the Vatican II Council, we are asked to pay attention to the abyss that "every man bears within himself." Before she intones the song of the water of life and of the fulfillment of desires, the Samaritan woman confesses, in the part just preceding the end of "Song of the Brightness of Water," how uplifted she was by "the simple opening of the wall, through which I often passed, not knowing that it divided me from myself—and not only from myself."

Incomplete Knowledge. In the structure of Jawień's work the theme of cognition together with its symbolic image—the mirror—plays the leading role. The knowledge of ultimate questions is a long-lasting process, a strenuous one that never ends. Everyone who has wrestled with it knows about it. All the things and events that give us so much pleasure in our earthly existence become an obstacle when we arrive at the point of understanding the questions related to the Divine. How many grievances and complaints, groans and tears, do we find in the pages written by the scholars, the artists, the saints and all those whose torment was the impossibility of grasping the fundamental questions of life by means of the senses and the mind. This experience of some ultimate ignorance unites very disparate writers: Pascal, the exceptionally intellectual thinker, and St. Teresa of Avila, who possessed the most impassioned imagination; Thomas Aquinas, the titan who created a whole system of theology, and the Hebrew Prophets, who experienced premonitions and feelings. The characters populating Jawień's poetic world are also troubled by a hunger for knowledge of metaphysical problems. In "Considerations on Death" we find a sad cry about the One who hides Himself: "I wander on the narrow sidewalk of Earth, / I do not turn my attention from Your face, / which the world does not reveal to me" (CD, 275).

One can find encouragement in the knowledge that Someone Else who knows man facilitates the mutual recognition. The Samaritan woman gives the following account of her experience of the Holy Reality:

None of us dares to look so deep into himself.

He knew differently. He almost never lifted His eyes.
He had gathered great knowledge. . . .
He did not need to lose His control, nor lift His eyes
  to find out.
He saw me within Himself. He possessed me within
  Himself.
(SBW)

As the Church Fathers teach, God can see us completely, and He knows us without any restriction. In his lifetime man never achieves that. In Christian tradition the theme of the partial knowledge that is accessible to humanity has been made symbolical in the image of the mirror, and this was introduced into the Christian imagination by St. Paul. His well-known views about how we see "as in a mirror, faintly; but someday we will see face to face" have been taken up an incalculable number of times by artists and thinkers of the Western world. The mirror also appears in a majority of the literary texts of the future John Paul II; it is found in a variety of contexts and is used in many semantic forms. In the drama "In Front of the Jeweler's Shop" the characters hold their dialogues not only in front of the window exhibit of a mysterious jeweler but, above all, in front of the mirror behind which he stands. At a certain point Andrzej, the main figure in the first part of the drama, observes that "it was not an ordinary plane mirror, but some lens absorbing its object. We were not only reflected, but absorbed. It felt as though I was seen and recognized by someone who hid himself in the depth of this shop window" (FJS, 1577).

The Divine Light. Mirrors, multiplied in nature and within man, indeed constitute a world that reflects—albeit in an illusory and indistinct way—the lights proclaiming the proximity of the Desired One. Therefore one finds numerous references to "the brightness of objects" and "the brilliance of things" in "The Mind Is a Strange Territory." Likewise, in the Samaritan woman's relation of her mystical experience one finds this sentence: "I cannot take you all in me. But I wish that You would stay, just as leaves and flowers remain in the mirror of the well." The cited verses telling of luminous signs proclaim the coming of the final act, which is the same in all the literary texts quoted and discussed above. This act is presented in several different ways: as the reunion of the Samaritan woman with Jesus, of the Mother with the Son, of the dying man with the Resurrected, of the Shepherd with the Sheep, of man with his Creator. In the most revered and most reliable of the records preserved in man's collective memory, phenomena of light accompany the coming of this moment. The Prophet Isaiah says (58:9–10): "Thou shalt cry, and he shall say, Here I *am*. . . . Then shall thy light rise in obscurity, and thy darkness *be* as the noon day."

Communion. In the partly illuminated night, in the semi-darkness of the divine-human encounter, persons whose existence was totally opposed are united. Jacob is in Him with other things that "slightly trembled in Him," and so are the Samaritan woman, and the man receiving the Sacrament of Confirmation who "does not feel in himself the weight of hours." Although, as has already been mentioned several times, the human soul cannot look at God in a full light nor unite itself with Him completely, it reaches unusual heights, despite these limitations: as St. John of the Cross writes, the highest or tenth level of mystical love "causes the soul to become wholly assimilated to God. . . . Not because the soul will have the capacity of God, for this is impossible; but because all that the soul is will be like to God, so that the soul will be *God by participation.*"[5] The philosopher Karol Wojtyla, interpreting the lesson of the Spanish mystic from its factual, concretely psychological side, explains in the following way the need of engaging oneself in the process of uniting the human creature with the Divine, and the religious and philosophical meanings that result from it: "If one can express it in that way—life itself must explain Revelation. . . . St. John of the Cross explains the very substance of his experiences in an extremely convincing manner. It is convincing because he shares their dimension; he explains them precisely when he leaves the moment of experience, the experimental moment" (HSJ, 19–20). Thus, why not understand Karol Wojtyla's literary creation as a poetic phenomenology created to testify in an "extremely convincing" manner about the sequence and substance of religious experiences?

▪ ▪ ▪

In his philosophical works Karol Wojtyla several times expressed the conviction that the categories of *esse* and *fieri,* of being and becoming, are the basis on which man's nature should be conceived. The two are indissolubly tied together. Becoming is possible only to the man who is, and at the same time being is the first act of becoming—the destination of our poet-philosopher's weltanschauung can be explained in that extremely abbreviated form. This point is particularly clear and articulate in "Man and Action," a work that belongs to the realm of philosophical anthropology. The author writes: "The man who once existed essentially through what he did and also through what happened in him—*through these two aspects of a particular dynamic*—this man also becomes more and more 'someone,' and even to some extent more and more 'somebody'" (MA, 101).

One may say the same thing about Jawień's literary oeuvre, which, while preserving its original identity, has never stopped growing, progressing, developing. This expansion of artistic penetration was caused by the poet's evolution from the phenomenology of mystical experiences to the phenomenology of human experiences, by the shifting of the accents from mystical to active personalism. In Wojtyla's philosophical and literary works the center of interest is the active man; it is not so much the inner mechanisms of action or its material, social and cultural results that are considered, as it is the ontological and anthropological aspects. This "dynamic totality" called "man of action" should reveal the real essence of man. The originality of the author of "Sign of Resistance" lies in his awareness of man's activity. This awareness does not hide the existence of man; it testifies through action and in action to man's presence.

In the theses of "Man and Action" Wojtyla writes that reflection upon man's activities "allows us to attain the most precise insight into the human being and to understand it in the most complete way" (MA, 14). He examined these problems in his literary writings before he did so in his philosophical works. They are already clearly expressed in "The Quarry," a 1956 poem which is an example of a work that unites meditation with activist attitudes, religious and philosophical recollections with the narration of dramatic events, objective descriptions with personal memories. (The biographical background of these fragments is certainly the period during which St. Peter's future successor worked in the quarries near Cracow.) Skillfully the author unites abstraction and epic narration while deepening through artistic means the insight into the problem of labor, whose multifaceted profundity he observes. The collective subject of this labor is a social group fighting physically to obtain the right of existence for their community. The author of "The Quarry" depicts in a realistic way the harshness and murderous hardship of physical labor; the influence of these rigors is devastating, but there is also a certain pathos inseparable from the production of material values which lie at the basis of any other construction. Directly and courageously Jawień tells of the dignity and drama of the workers' destiny, a topic on which Stanislaw Brzozowski spoke clearly and truthfully decades earlier, again in the context of Polish culture: Brzozowski, the brilliant philosopher and author who evolved from Nietzscheism to Catholicism through Marxism and nationalism, used the startling metaphor of "the bloody pillar of muscular effort" which he saw as sustaining the edifice raised by humanity.

It is easy to isolate the key words in "The Quarry": hands, heart, work, pain, hammer, explosion, rending, blow, current, stone, love, anger. The action of the poem consists in the narration of a fatal work accident. Part four of the piece, dedicated to "the memory that accompanies work," shows how natural and social elements are entangled in the life and death of a muscular worker, how "suffering and some kind of injury came from it." Physical labor has not only energy-related and technical dimensions, but also the power to create a person. Jawień's metaphor "the hands are the heart's landscape" beautifully expresses that idea, as does his poetic formula: "And a thought grows in me, grows day after day: / the greatness of work is inside man" (EV, 25). The process of labor is thus considered in its whole richness: it is defined not only by contact with nature and by the gaining of material values, but also, to an equal if not greater extent, by its influence on the individual's personality and the formation of interpersonal relations.

Jawień's ensuing literary texts broaden the themes and structures of his work. In them, interest focuses on the human creature, living and acting in society. Reflection upon man and the character of human relationships starts to dominate, and the context that was made by sacral and natural time is now completed by historical time. "The Church," a poem made of many sections which one may read as an artistic commentary written by a participant in Vatican II, examines the universality of Catholicism, the problems caused by multiple nationalities and the resulting cultural differences in the Church, the personal models that are most needed by the contemporary Christian, and the duties that are incumbent on every believer in Christ's religion. In Jawień's lyrical vision, St. Peter's basilica becomes a microcosm representing the sanctuary—erected like an art work—of the Church's community, as well as the sanctified and renewed cosmos.

In the poem events also occur in the setting of a southern Polish mountain village, at a time when Confirmation is being celebrated. Despite the length of the narration, the naturalistic quality of the scenes and the unequivocal character of the discourse, this poetry deepens the metaphysical dimensions of existence. The truth accessible to man in the world of history and nature motivates him to resistance and to effort. It perturbs and distresses. Partly recognized truth provokes a greater desire: "Truth doesn't drip oil into wounds to stop the burning pain, / or sit you on a donkey to be led through the streets; / truth must be hurtful and hide" (EV, 61). As in the poet's earlier, more mystical period, hope takes on the appearance of faith in the protection of a Transcendental Personage interested in man, turned toward him and seeking him: "For there are invisible Hands that hold us / so that it takes great effort to carry the boat, / whose story, despite the shallows, follows its course" (EV, 62).

The poetic drama "In Front of the Jeweler's Shop" is the longest of the literary works which Karol Wojtyla has published to date. The linked destinies of three loving couples—the time is either the present or the immediate past—follow contrapuntal lines established by their declarations or by the declarations of others who are involved in the drama and who relate their actions. The reflections made by the characters mainly concern love. Is the subject of love a being who seems unable to grow from nature to the dimension of his calling by love? Andrzej's monologue dramatically shows the situation and the potentialities of man.

Here is man! He is not transparent
he is not monumental,
nor is he simple;
he is rather poor.
This is one man—two
four, a hundred, a million—
Multiply all of them
(and multiply this magnitude by weakness),
you obtain a number of people,
a number of human life.
(FJS, 1574)

The full meaning of the drama may be understood as a polemic between the basic conceptions of love that dominate our world: hedonistic and individualistic. Love, in Jawień's conception, is an encounter of persons, a mutual gift of oneself to the other, a perfect unification. In this perspective, it must be the gift of man as a whole, in his biological, axiological and temporal dimensions. Love most certainly reveals itself in the form of the total and ultimate unification of two human beings. This direction of Wojtyla's thinking, while giving action its dynamics, agrees with the philosophical standpoint expressed in his "Appraisal of the Possibility of Building a Christian Ethics on the Philosophy of Max Scheler." In the previous twenty years Karol Wojtyla took upon himself the task of establishing a philosophical position that would synthesize phenomenology and personalism. Starting with Scheler, he went in the direction of St. Thomas's personalism, while enriching his methodology with Husserl's phenomenology and with contemporary anthroposciences. The foundations of his new philosophy could not be, as with Scheler, emotion and experience, but *ethical action*. Man is considered in his totality as a subject capable of actions that bring empirically verifiable results. This constitutes an extremely important step in helping overcome the objective-subjective division which characterizes the philosophy of the last hundred years.[6]

In his literary endeavors Wojtyla constructed a weltanschauung which we shall call *active personalism,* sometimes doing so even earlier than in his philosophical work. In considering the poet's language at the level of syntax and semantic figures, an attentive reader will notice right away the preponderance of relative clauses, long sentences and a logical narrative sequence. This has a particular esthetic and ideological meaning. The hypotaxis unites into a coherent whole relatively long fragments of the text and establishes contact between widely separated words and expressions. This syntactic structure, as well as the construction of the whole in terms of composition (the repetition of motifs and of thematic images, the refrains), all make us perceive the characters' actions in their entirety, in organically related sequences. Less often sentences are joined by a coordinate conjunction; then they are set in a logical progression that stresses their temporal sequence. Usually parataxis is employed in literary declarations dealing with the atemporal world, no matter how it is understood. Hypotaxis places the protagonists of a poetical dialogue in the reality of action. Objects or persons belonging to this earthly world thus are subjects or initiate the process of becoming—we find here the literary reality of *fieri* and *esse* at the same time.

We are dealing here with a poetry that presents the concrete experience of human beings living in their time. The essence of such an experience and its poetic transcription is the sacral reality that lies beyond the duration of nature and history. This experience is signaled in the aforementioned texts by the intervention of visual elements, by the use of parallelism and by paradox. Paradox appears in Jawień's earlier texts, but only in "Considerations on Death" has it been given the main role. The structure of the poem is supported by paradox. The theme of death/resurrection and the schema of death leading to life are two of the most important paradoxes in Christianity. In Wojtyla's most recently published work there are many semantic figures based on antithesis: "maturity, descending into the hidden essence"; "passing is also gathering"; "the dying world reveals its life anew"; "the body of my soul and the soul of my body are united again." Words with antithetical meanings are linked in a dialectic tension: maturation/regression, word/silence, body/persistence, death/hope. Dynamically, and at several levels, stylistics once again gives this poem-meditation a meaning synchronized with Wojtyla's philosophical inquiries. To a certain extent the poem completes the philosophical inquiries; it embodies in artistic form the intuitions and the conclusions of the thinker. Poetry and philosophy thus complement each other. In poetry thought is permeated with intuition: "I still think precisely of what my heart hunts / and I do not know what fills me more: / Emotion or knowledge" (CD).

In today's literary culture an anti-genetic and *eo ipso* anti-biographical current predominates. Generally ignorance or knowledge about the author as a real person neither disturbs nor helps. We know far too well that literature is not the writing of memoirs or the collecting of documents, whatever they might be. Therefore we focus our attention on the works themselves, assuming that they contain everything the author wants to tell us. But in the present instance we must depart from that rule. The unusual influence of Karol Wojtyla's work results from our awareness of who the author is. The tension between the historical and literary roles played by the author is so important that to forget about it would be unpardonably thoughtless. By linking the category of "sender of a literary message"—an activity that belongs to literary criticism—with the personality of the author, we do not, in this particular case, diminish the perception of Wojtyla's poetry. On the contrary, we increase the esthetic effect and give an unusual resonance to the meaning of his work. The first poems to be written by a Pope-poet since Aeneus Sylvius Piccolomini five centuries ago, while retaining all their artistic value, gain the status of being literary documents of our time.

Krzysztof Dybciak, Spring 1980, translated by Alice-Catherine Carls

[1] Abbreviations in parentheses refer to the following works by Karol Wojtyla: CD = "Rozważania o śmierci" [Considerations on Death], *Znak,* 1975, no. 3, pp. 271–76; FJS = "Przed sklepem jubilera: Medytacja o sakramencie małżeństwa, przechodząca chwilami w dramat" [In Front of the Jeweler's Shop: Meditation on the Sacrament of Marriage; publ. in March 1980 by Random House as *The Jeweler's Shop*], *Znak,* 1960, no. 12, pp. 1564–1607; HSJ = "O humanizmie Sw. Jana od Krzyza" [On the Humanism of St. John of the Cross], *Znak,* 1951, no. 1, p. 8; MA = *Osoba i czyn* [Man and Action], Cracow, 1969; PST = "Personalizm tomistyczny" [The Personalism of St. Thomas], *Znak,* 1961, no. 5, pp. 668–69; SBW = "Pieśń to blasku wody" [Song of the Brightness of Water], *Tygodnik Powszechny,* 1950, no. 19, p. 1; MST = "Myśl jest przestrzenią dziwną" [The Mind Is a Strange Territory], *Tygodnik Powszechny,* 1952, no. 42, p. 4 (republished in the same journal, 1979, no. 5, p. 4). All translations are by Alice-Catherine Carls unless otherwise noted.

[2] The lines quoted are from the poem "The Samaritan Woman," which can be read in English translation in Karol Wojtyla, *Easter Vigil and Other Poems,* Jerzy Peterkiewicz, tr., New York, Random House, 1979, p. 12. The translation here is by Alice-Catherine Carls, however. Subsequent citations from this volume will use the abbreviation EV.

[3] St. John of the Cross, *The Dark Night of the Soul,* Kurt F. Reinhardt, tr. and ed., New York, Ungar, 1957, p. 216.

[4] Peterkiewicz renders the title as "Thought-Strange Space" and offers three excerpts in *Easter Vigil,* pp. 19–21.

[5] St. John of the Cross, p. 216.

6 In his essay "The Personalism of St. Thomas" Wojtyla writes about this process of contemporary thought: "We gradually observe in this philosophy a process which I would call the hypostasis of consciousness: consciousness becomes an independent subject of action and, indirectly, of existence; the latter emerges, so to speak, alongside the body, alongside its material structure submitted to the laws of nature. . . . This solution is radically different from that of St. Thomas. According to him, consciousness and self-consciousness are a derived product, something like the fruit of a thinking nature that would exist in man."

Eroticism and Exile: Anna Frajlich's Poetry

■ INTRODUCTION

Anna Frajlich is not only a Polish émigré poet; she is also a poet of emigration and an émigrés' poet—i.e., a poet truly respected and admired by other émigrés. One finds in Frajlich's verse a persistent preoccupation with the themes of exile, emigration, dislocation, and adaptation to new cultural contexts. Her poems are sensitive and penetrating notations of her changing attitudes toward emigration, of the complexities and ironies of émigré existence. The exilic motif dominates her writing. A poet who reached her poetic maturity as an émigré, Frajlich expresses in her poems a subtle interior exploration of herself in the context of the exilic condition. Emigration has become for Frajlich the crucible in which she is able to examine questions of deracination, cultural dislocation, homesickness for an elusive home, the search for a new sense of identity, the pain of loss or dispossession, and, ultimately, the reconfiguration of her identity and reintegration.

Because these themes are so central to her work, Anna Frajlich is not only a notable émigré poet, but, arguably, she is the most prominent Polish *woman* émigré poet of her generation. My reference to her as "an émigrés' poet" is borne out by many enthusiastic reviews of her work by critics and scholars who themselves are émigrés and who recognize the astuteness of her insights as well as the poetic power in her mapping of the stages of an émigré's transformation in and adaptation to exile. The chorus of her admirers includes, among others, the scholar and playwright Jan Kott, who labeled her "a poetess of exile"; the dean of Polish émigré poets, Stanislaw Baliński; and such literary critics as Maja Elżbieta Cybulska, herself an émigré in England, or Joanna Rostropowicz and Maya Peretz in the United States.¹ To cite one more emphatic expression of admiration, in his letter from Israel dated 15 February 1988, Stanislaw Wygodzki, another émigré writer, then in his eighties—who didn't know Anna personally at the time—wrote rather effusively: "Za tamte wiersze kocham Cię, moja droga Anno, kocham, naprawdę kocham" (For those poems I love you, my dear Anna. I love you, truly love you).²

To those unfamiliar with the history of Eastern Europe, Anna Frajlich's biography may appear very exotic. (Alas, her saga echoes in its "exoticism" the sagas of many who tried to elude Nazi terror.) Born in the village of Katta Taldyk in the Osh region of Kirghizia, whither her mother escaped from Lwów during the second world war, Anna was reunited with her father in Lysva, in the Ural Mountains, a year later, and in 1946 her family settled in Szczecin (Stettin) on the Baltic Sea, a city that became Polish at the end of the war, when Poland's borders were moved west. It was in Szczecin that she spent her childhood. Having graduated with an M.A. in Polish literature from Warsaw University in 1965, Anna began her career as a journalist at a newspaper for the blind. That same year she married. Two years later she gave birth to a son. Her new nuclear family left Poland in November 1969, in the aftermath of the 1968 anti-Semitic campaign, and after brief stays in Vienna and Rome, they settled in New York City in 1970.

In the United States, having tried her hand at several professions (writing for Polish-language newspapers, reporting for Radio Free Europe, working in an epidemiology lab), Frajlich enrolled in the doctoral program in Slavic studies at New York University and a few years later defended her Ph.D. thesis. Since 1982, she has been teaching Polish language and literature at Columbia University.

Frajlich is the author of ten volumes of poetry published on both sides of the Atlantic, as well as numerous scholarly and journalistic writings, and is a recipient of the prestigious Koscielski Foundation literary prize, bestowed on her in Switzerland in 1981. In 1993, after a twenty-four-year hiatus, she returned triumphantly to Poland, where four volumes of her poetry have since been published—*Ogrodem i ogrodzeniem* (1993), *Jeszcze w drodze* (1994), *W słońcu listopada* (2000), *Znów szuka mnie wiatr* (2001)—all of them enjoying a very positive reception.³ Indeed, the collection *W słońcu listopada* (In the November Sun) was among those works considered by readers of the very popular Warsaw daily *Rzeczpospolita* as a Polish book of the year.

■ THE POETRY OF EXILE

As her biography clearly indicates, Frajlich has experienced several moves and cultural transplantations. In one of her relatively early poems, "Kraj utracony" (The Lost Land), she expressed her painful predicament of being a "wandering Jew" (this and all subsequent translations here are my own): "Driven out of many a land / For Jacob's and Abraham's sin / My forefathers / My parents and I / To this day we are wandering" ("Z niejednego wygnani kraju / za Jakuba grzech i Abrahama / prarodzice moi / i rodzice / Do dziś dnia się błąkamy").[4] Expulsion from one's native land inevitably triggers emotional turmoil, a sense of loss and rejection, and leads to the questioning of one's identity. Several of Frajlich's poems written shortly after she had left Poland reflect the pain of exile and the bewilderment resulting from expulsion. In "Emigracja" (Emigration), for example, she wrote:

We—how come?—islanders
In the very heart of winds
In the odd school of humility
Where the elements teach
I still remember
The silence of continents
Frost on the wire fence
And the road to school.

(My—skąd nagle?—wyspiarze
w samym sercu wiatrów
w dziwnej szkole pokory
gdzie żywioły uczą
ciągle jeszcze pamiętam
cisze stałych lądów
szron na drucianym płocie
I drogę do szkoly)[5]

She presents herself as a windswept and humiliated émigré, an islander longing for the solid land mass of the continent she was forced to leave behind. The poem conjures in one's mind a powerful image of instability and a lack of both physical and emotional rootedness. Yet, in a speech delivered on 10 September 1998 in Helsinki, Finland, at the 65th International PEN Club Congress, which Frajlich attended as the delegate of the American branch of the Center for Writers in Exile, the poet made a rather striking statement: "I am a Polish poet who was exiled from Poland thirty years ago because I am a Jew. I am a Polish Jew who escaped the worst [she is referring to the Holocaust, of course] because I was born in Soviet Kirghizia, which now is independent Kyrgyzstan. I write Polish poetry in the United States, where I also teach Polish language and literature. In my soul my three beings—Jewish, Polish, and now American—are now one. Indivisible."

Frajlich's writing is an expressive personal record of her dispossession and reintegration, and delineates the strategies by which the poet arrived at her sense of "indivisible" identity. She herself admits that writing poetry had a therapeutic value for her in the early stages of her adaptation to exile.

■ LOVE AND EXILE

Unlike many other émigré writers, whose works consistently reflect negativity, pain, and their lack of acceptance of exile, Frajlich's stance is to challenge herself to accept, or even love, exile. In a poem dedicated to her son, a poem titled "Jesienna kolysanka" (Autumnal Lullaby) and composed shortly after her departure from Poland, Frajlich wrote: "Sleep my little son / and the wayfarers [travelers] / will come to love their pathless tracks. Sleep"[6] ("Śpij syneczku / i podróżni / pokochają swe bezdroża. Śpij"). The poem reflects her maternal affection and tenderness, but also her effort to appease *herself* while appeasing her son. It may well be read as a hint at another survival technique. She is telling her son—and convincing herself—that coming to love and accept one's exilic fate is the way to survive. "Pokochać bezdroża," "to come to love one's pathless tracks," the bewildering paths of one's existence, is the lesson Frajlich is imparting. In a sense, this statement may be read as her existential credo.

■ EROS AND EXILE

Still, seeing Anna Frajlich as merely a poet of exile would be a reductionist view. In the context of exploring her life in exile, she writes poems which examine her experiences as both an émigré and a woman. Her poetry also constitutes a consistent trail of testimonials recording the experience of a woman in its full range and complexity and in the multiplicity of her roles, from childhood to maturity, from the awakening of love and passion to its ending, from motherhood to menopause. Her extreme honesty and openness may well be the "fringe benefits" of emigration. Among the cognitive privileges she gained as a result of emigration was the realization that she no longer needed to be attentive to local norms, values, and taboos, that she could flaunt her uniqueness and individuality. In an untitled poem she wrote:

I am separate
The leaf that falls for me
So unusually places itself at my feet
Nobody sees it with my eyes
I am separate
—no part of a system
nobody's property
nor cog in a machine
separately I measure mountains on the moon . . .

The poem concludes:

I may break down—may
Stop suddenly
May fall in love—may
Suddenly leave
And while dying consecrate with my lips

A separate name of a separate God.[7]

As this poem clearly reveals, through love and life Anna Frajlich is determined to chart her own course. The assertive attitude is also reflected in other ways. The female persona of her poetry, for instance, is an equal partner in the erotic relationship, the subject and not merely the object of desire.

Eroticism infused with "exilic pain" and "eroticized" exile are the leitmotivs of Frajlich's poetry. On the one hand, her poems addressing erotic encounters are replete with implications that "exile" is embedded in love, whether in the form of physical or emotional distance and separation, or as anticipation and the bemoaning of the inevitable parting of ways. On the other hand, the poet "eroticizes" exile—that is, presents it as ultimately acceptable and, potentially, yielding benefits and rewards.

Eroticism and exile are strongly intertwined in Frajlich's verse. Not only does the poet explore both themes on the basis of her personal experience and treat them with utmost honesty; she also views them within the same context of challenges and inevitable transformations. They are her driving forces. Exile may equal freedom, but freedom is bound with notions of responsibility, decision making, abandonment to one's own devices, and also anguish, fear, and dread. Frajlich masterfully explores these issues in her poem "Rozmyslania Wyzwolenca" (Meditations of a Freed Man). The poem begins rather perversely—"Sweet is the yoke of enslavement / and bitter the fruit of freedom" ("Slodkie jest jarzmo niewoli / i gorzki owoc wolności")—but ends on an explicitly somber note: "and the freedman whose master / used to take care of his wants / wanders at huge risk / in the kernel of freedom encased / for one can die in rags [literally: under a fence] / or become Diocletian's father" ("i dziwi się wyzwoleniec / który mial wszystko u pana / jakie ogromne ryzyko / kryje się w jądrze wolności / bo można umrzeć pod plotem / lub ojcem byc Dioklecjana").[8] Freedoms gained as a result of exile can spell failure, loneliness, death in dire poverty, or grandeur (as in the case of the Roman slave Diocletian, who became the father of an emperor).

Love, like exile, also implies risk, anguish, and often difficult maneuvers and decisions. Eros inevitably leads to clashes, to the struggle between intellect and instinct, to breaking out from well-defined patterns and constantly crossing barriers. All this, however, leads to greater self-realization. Without these clashes and tensions prompted by Eros, an individual's libido and psyche would remain safe but passive, and would never achieve self-definition. Likewise, without exile and the challenges, tensions, and clashes generated by it, the cognitive process of arriving at one's sense of identity is likely to be impoverished. Potentially, at least, exile can lead to a cognitive drama resulting in a more profound cognitive denouement.[9]

A significant number of Frajlich's poems, including some of the most erotically charged ones, convey such tensions and sentiments. In love, as in exile, there is often a sense of loss, of a lack of attainment, of not connecting with the other person, of not reaching the yearned-for yet elusive goal or "home." Much of Frajlich's love poetry is what I would call in Polish "poezja niespełnienia," the poetry of unattainment or unfulfillment.

Eroticism is rendered with much subtlety in Frajlich's verse. Many of her love poems, though ostensibly placid, pulsate with subterranean erotic energy, sometimes implied by just a few words. In such erotically charged poems as "Renoir's Women" ("Kobiety Renoira"), "New York, November and a Rose" ("Nowy York, listopad i róża"), or "The Ocean Divides Us" ("Między nami ocean"), and many others, she traverses the field of erotic tensions, identifying them, musing on them, and devising survival strategies.[10] She does so without resorting to explicit descriptions, and certainly never comes close to vulgarity. "The Telephone" ("Telefon"), a poem quoted below in its entirety, reveals the subtlety of Frajlich's artistic means.

Telefon
Zmieniony
w dzwonki
i pierścionki drutów
sklebionych gdzieś pod ziemią
jesteś
—jak mnie uczono w szkole—
częstotliwóscia drgan na blaszcze
moge cię mieć
za siedem cyfr
i za guziczek
za swiatelko
moge mieć
drganie na membranie.
A chcialabym w wysokiej trawie
gdzie chodzą zuczki biedroneczki
a chcialabym cię mieć na sianie
—śmieszne zdziebelka w twoich wlosach
i chcialabym cię mieć w karecie
gdzie zasunięte firaneczki
klusem
donikąd spiesza konie
a ty calujesz moje dlonie
i moje usta
moje piersi
i nie ma siedmiu kpiących cyfr

jest tylko siedem gwiazd na niebie
i siedem gór
i siedem nocy . . .

Telephone
Changed
into jingling bells
and rings of wire
whirled somewhere under the ground
you are
—as I was taught at school—
the frequency of vibrations on tin
I can have you
for seven digits
and for a button
for a light
I can have
a vibrant strain of the membrane
And I would rather have you in tall grass
where ladybugs and beetles take their walks
and I would rather have you in the hay
—with funny little stalks stuck in your hair
and I would have you in a horse-drawn carriage
with curtains pulled together
trotting to nowhere
the horses would rush
and you'd place kisses on my hands
my lips
and breasts
and there would be no seven mocking digits
but only seven stars upon the skies
and seven mountains
and seven nights. . .[11]

At times the eroticism in Frajlich's poetry extends even to the sphere of nature and cosmology. In the poem titled "A Cosmic Prognosis for February 29th" ("Prognoza Kosmiczna na 29.II.") Frajlich personifies the planet Venus, presenting it as lying in an erotic pose not far from the planet Saturn, and writes of the inevitability of their separation.[12] In yet another recent untitled poem, the eroticism of nature merges with that of the poetic persona: "yet the lunar blood / rises in a tide / and in the stalks / in the arteries / in the milky ways / I rise" ("a przecież księżycowa krew / przypływem wzbiera / i w lodygach / w tetnicach / w mlecznych drogach / wschodzę").[13]

In the poem "Indian Summer," the erotically charged lines "and to pass in fullness / with clamor / and the boiling of pigment in blood" ("I przemijać pełnią / z loskotem / gotowaniem pigmentu we krwi") reflect both the short-lived ecstatic state and the sense of transitoriness of love and life.[14] Frajlich revisits repeatedly the theme of the inevitable exits from love and the re-

lentless passage of time. Exile becomes a metaphor for love, for life, or for human experience in general.

■ **FROM ADAPTATION TO ACCEPTANCE**
Yet Frajlich does not see exile as a bane, nor does she despair. On the contrary, her poetry gives repeated evidence of self-consolation, of adaptation through an active cognitive involvement, through an intellectual probing of circumstances, which leads to acceptance and to a re-creation of her self, so that she can cope. Perhaps that is the salient feature of her verse which makes it so appealing to other émigrés. She has recorded in her poems the slow, painful, complicated process of adaptation to exile, but has not ignored the rewards. She has shown that acceptance is possible. The poet has rendered her resulting redefinitions in personal as well as philosophical and, occasionally, political terms.

Frajlich's untitled poem beginning with the lines "Love exists, / but hidden under moss. / One needs to find it, dig it up, blow on it" ("Miłość jest, / lecz ukryta pod mchem. / Trzeba znaleźć odkopać odchuchać") can be read in no other way but as an affirmation of love and its presence.[15] Her views on emigration have also metamorphosed into willing acceptance. From a homeless and bewildered person fearful of forgetting the landscapes of her native land (and bemoaning the need to forget and yet the impossibility of forgetting), she moved through the stage of recognition that she is a person without a permanent address, and—while recognizing that Polish culture is closest to her heart—ultimately accepted the United States as her existential homeland. Even mere fragments of her poems indicate the significant transitions and her apparent reconciliation with exile. In an early poem titled "Acclimatization" she wrote: "I forget meticulously / I forget scrupulously / my native landscape / my daily landscape" ("Zapominam dokładnie / zapominam sumiennie / mój krajobraz ojczysty / mój krajobraz codzienny").[16]

Frajlich's poem "Bez adresu" (Without an Address), in which she refers to I. B. Singer's statement that each writer should have an address (his has consistently been Krochmalna Street in pre-World War II Warsaw), records another stage of her adaptation. The poem includes these lines:

I, too, am looking for my street
the one and only
in my waking hours, in my dreams, in my despair
between dreams and wakefulness
in the magic kaleidoscope
various streets mingle
their smell, their crowds I have under my skin
and the nocturnal hue of their silence
hangs over the window sill

like threads of Indian summer
but their names have faded
and numbers over the doors fell off
who knows
what's mine what belongs to others
. . . .

and which address
is the address.[17]

But in an untitled poem included in her volume *Który las* (Which Forest; 1986), she establishes a contrast between a city from her past, which she declares no longer hers, and her current domicile, New York City, which she presents as her own. Here we read: "*Mine* is the island cut into squares of streets / the crowd / winds blowing from the bay / winds from the rivers" ("Moja jest wyspa na kwadraty pocięta ulic / tłum / wiejące od zatoki wiatry / od rzek wiatry"; my emphasis—R.G.).[18]

While the past is always with her and makes its presence palpable in her poetry, it no longer has a devastating grip. In a recent poem titled "Taniec-Miasto" (Dance-City), Frajlich presented her childhood city of Szczecin as her Arcadia. The opening lines run as follows:

My Arcadia put together hastily
between one exile and the other
is just as beautiful, just as noble
as an ancient manor with pear and linden trees
my Arcadia built of boards left by the Germans
with each plate from a different set
holds in it the silence of fullness—the fullness of
  silence

(Moja Arkadia sklecona naprędce
pomiędzy jednym a drugim wygnaniem
jest równie piękna, jest równie dostojna
jak dwór prastary z gruszą i lipami
moja Arkadia z poniemieckich desek
z każdym talerzem z innego serwisu
ma w sobie cisze pełni—pełnie ciszy)[19]

This poem is a testimony to the poet's integration of her legacy, of having made her past an integral and acceptable part of her self. Frajlich's sense of identity has undergone a significant evolution. From a Polish Jew bemoaning the loss of her Polish homeland, she has evolved into a mature individual with a complex yet integrated sense of her own identity.

The ultimate acknowledgment of Frajlich's rootedness in the United States, of the fact that she is finally "placed" rather than displaced, is the speech she delivered a few years ago at the New York cemetery where her father is buried. The occasion was the unveiling of her father's monument. Here is the pertinent passage from her speech:

The dictionary states that the word *monument* is related to memory, it is to remind. . . . It is lasting evidence of someone or something. Of course, we the family don't need the monument to remember someone we loved. We are the walking monuments of this person, often without realizing it. We emulate him in our being. And we transport his essence to our children. But our memory disappears with us, and this is probably why we need this stone. For us this stone has one more significance. This is the first marked grave of my father's entire family. His mother, his sisters, and his half-brother were killed by the Nazis during the war, and they had no grave. The cemetery where his father was buried before World War II was razed. So in this context it is a celebration of hope that this memorial stone will not be upturned, and it will testify to my father's memory for a long time. Also, in a strange way it marks *our rooting in this soil.* (My emphasis—R.G.)

■ **CONCLUSION**

Despite the declared "rooting," the credo "pokochać bezdroża" (to come to love the pathless tracks) is still one that Frajlich must follow. Recognition of who one is tends to be an ongoing process, whether one is geographically settled in a concrete place or not. Just as in the sphere of erotic relationships there is never a lasting status quo, so life in general is in a state of constant flux. Thus, it is not surprising that Frajlich continues to fluctuate and evolve. In December 1998, for instance, she wrote a poem titled "Wiersz noworoczny" (A New Year's Poem), in which she delighted in a sense of calm, of having arrived, of having a peaceful home. Yet only a few months later, in an untitled poem of July 1999, Frajlich revealed a very different and a much more unsettled mood: "everything is a punishment / for having thought / I've already arrived" ("Wszystko jest karą / Za to że myślalam / Ze już dotarlam").[20]

Frajlich inscribes in her poetry the changing nature of her awareness. She isolates and describes her fleeting emotions, their flavors and shadings. Her inner world and her wisdom shine through her highly autobiographical work, revealing the evolving concept of herself as a full-blooded woman and an émigré. The poem "Thanatos and Eros" points up the limits of the evolution.

I shall die where I've been sown
where fate has tossed me
the earth will absorb my body
I'll absorb the earth with my body
as if I came to love it.
Yes.
As if I came to love it.

(Umrę tam gdzie mnie posiało

gdzie mnie rzucil los
ziemia wchlonie moje cialo
ziemie wchlonę swoim cialem
tak jak gdybym pokochala.
Tak.
Jak gdybym pokochala.)[21]

This poem, like much of Anna Frajlich's oeuvre, demonstrates most effectively the inextricable connection between eroticism and exile in her poetry, as well as her "eroticization" of exile—including death, the ultimate exile.

Regina Grol, Summer/Autumn 2001

[1] See e.g. the following comments: Jan Kott's remark on the cover of Anna Frajlich, *Between Dawn and the Wind,* Austin (Texas), Host Publications, 1991; Stanislaw Baliński, "Poetka odjeżdżająca w swiat. . . ," *Dziennik Polski* (London), 23 March 1977, p. 4; Maja Elżbieta Cybulska, "W moich oczach," *Dziennik Polski,* 9 April 1994, p. 9; Joanna Rostropowicz, "Poezja nie straconego czasu," *Ex Libris* (supplement to the Warsaw daily *Życie Warszawy*), no. 65, December 1994; and Maya Peretz's review of Frajlich's *Ogrodem i ogrodzeniem* in the *Polish Review,* 40:1 (1995), pp. 111–12. Among other writers and critics who have offered very complimentary commentary on Frajlich's poetry are Renata Gorczyńska, Florian Smieja, M. Broński, and Witold Wirpsza.

[2] Among the younger Polish critics who have heaped praise on Frajlich's poetry are Wojciech Ligeza (*Tygiel Kultury* [Lódź], 27:3, 1998), Anna Wegrzyniakowa (in her volume *Ktokolwiek jesteś bez ojczyzny* (Lódź, 1995), and Stanislaw Podkowiński (in his book *Kocham więc jestem.* Moreover, Wlodzimierz Bolecki included some of Frajlich's poetry in his anthology *Snuć milość: Polska poezja milosna XV-XX wieku.*

[3] Stanislaw Wygodzki, "Listy do Anny Frajlich," *Kontury* (Tel Aviv), 1988, no. 9, p. 55. This and all subsequent translations of both poetry and prose in this paper are mine [RG].

[4] Anna Frajlich, *Between Dawn and the Wind: Select Poetry,* tr. & ed. Regina Grol, Austin (Texas), Host, 1991, pp. 12–13.

[5] Ibid., pp. 14–15.

[6] Ibid., pp. 78–79.

[7] Ibid., pp. 90–91.

[8] Ibid., pp. 16–17.

[9] I am indebted to Alexander Fiut, particularly his essay "In the Grip of Eros" (on Czesław Miłosz's poetry) in *The Eternal Moment* (University of California Press, 1990), for his discussion of the power of Eros.

[10] See Anna Frajlich, "Kobiety Renoira," in her *Ogrodem i ogrodzeniem,* Warsaw, Czytelnik, 1993, p. 35; "New York, November and Rose," in her *Between Dawn and the Wind,* pp. 72–73; and "The Ocean Divides Us," ibid., pp. 64–65.

[11] Frajlich, *Between Dawn and the Wind,* pp. 56–57.

[12] Anna Frajlich, "Prognoza kosmiczna na 29 lutego," *Tygodnik Powszechny,* 8 March 1992, p. 7.

[13] From an unpublished poem provided to me by the author.

[14] The title poem of the volume *Indian Summer,* Albany (N.Y.), Sigma, 1982, p. 32.

[15] Ibid., p. 42.

[16] Frajlich, *Between Dawn and the Wind,* pp. 18–19.

[17] Anna Frajlich, "Bez adresu," in her *Ogrodem i ogrodzeniem,* p. 64.

[18] Anna Frajlich, untitled poem in her *Który las,* London, Oficyna Poetów i Malarzy, 1986, p. 32.

[19] Anna Frajlich, "Taniec-Miasto," *Przegląd Polski* (New York), 29 May 1997, p. 8.

[20] Anna Frajlich, "Wiersz noworoczny," a recent unpublished poem. The untitled poem is included in her *Znów szuka mnie wiatr,* Warsaw, Czytelnik, 2001, p. 19.

[21] Anna Frajlich, "Tanatos i Eros," in her *Znów szuka mnie wiatr,* p. 23.

The Captive Mind Revisited

In the first book-length interview given to a Polish journalist (Ewa Czarnecka), Czesław Miłosz, when asked about the fame brought about by the publication of his *Zniewolony umysl* (Eng. *The Captive Mind*) in 1953, responded with a shrug: "What sort of fame?" (*CCM,* 145). In the original Polish version that statement comes across even stronger, with an almost sardonic dismissal of the issue: "Taka to i slawa" (Some fame, indeed). And yet it cannot be denied that this happened to be a book that launched a little-known Polish poet into the orbit of international reputation, the Neustadt Prize in 1978, and eventually the Nobel Prize in Literature in 1980: "When I found myself an émigré and wrote *The Captive Mind,* my poetry was completely unknown; no one knew that I was a poet, but I became known to many readers as the author of *The Captive Mind*" (321–22). Thus, in spite of his own reservations ("I prefer a different sort of fame"), the book deserves a new, close look, particularly since the literary situation in that part of the world has changed dramatically in the last ten years, ever since communism was abolished and democracy restored there in 1989.

Miłosz's poetic venture into politics had begun earlier, when the leading Polish literary monthly *Twórczość* published his long poem *Traktat moralny* (Moral Treatise) in 1948. Written in the tradition of the eighteenth-century didactic poem, it projects the image of the Polish literary scene on the eve of an unavoidable change: the introduction of the Soviet-type model of socialist realism, which meant a totalitarian control over the entire country, including its intellectual manifestations such as philosophy, literature, arts, and cultural life in general. The poem had been written in Washington, D.C., where Miłosz resided as a Polish diplomat after the war, and from that comfortable vantage point he could see the forthcoming events much more clearly than could his friends confined within the limited perspective of postwar Poland dominated by the Soviets. Trying to assess the moral rather than political aspects of the present situation, Miłosz ended his poem on an almost eschatological note:

There is no hope for you today,
Don't wait for any Treuga Dei,
That life of yours has no escape
Through any major magic gate.
You go ahead in daily harness.
In front of us there's
"Heart of Darkness."

That disturbing image sounded a familiar note to Polish readers, at least to those intellectuals familiar with their compatriot Joseph Conrad's dark vision of ruthless supremacy presented in his novella under the same title. Miłosz, who had seen both the Soviet and the German occupation of Poland during World War II, did not have any illusions about the bright future projected by the advocates of the Soviet system, and he gradually became more and more aware of the dangers inherent in it. When his vision materialized in 1949, with the official proclamation of socialist realism as the only acceptable method in contemporary Polish literature, Miłosz, in spite of his relatively safe position as a diplomat working abroad, realized that as soon as he returned home a trap would be set for him too, and he decided to break with the communist regime. On 1 February 1951 he asked for political asylum in France. At about the same time he started working on *The Captive Mind,* which was completed after a few months and was issued two years later by a leading Polish publisher, the Institut Littéraire in France, becoming an instant success and the harbinger of the international fame mentioned earlier.

The book was, as it were, a continuation of Miłosz's "Moral Treatise," this time describing not only the perils of the communist system but also giving examples of how it worked in reality. In some respects it has been compared to the two most revealing and penetrating works on the same subject previously published—Arthur Koestler's *Darkness at Noon* (1940) and George Orwell's *Nineteen Eighty-Four* (1949)—as studies written by people in the know, insiders of the system who had analyzed its ways and byways in and out. The difference, of course, was in the genre: while those two books were works of fiction, Miłosz had written a penetrating document on the literary scene, illustrating it with portraits of four major writers who in his opinion represented four telltale cases.

In Miłosz's theory, Marxist indoctrination worked like a slow, mind-altering drug envisaged in the novel

Nienasycenie (1932; Eng. *Insatiability*) by Stanislaw Ignacy Witkiewicz. The pill, allegedly invented by "Murti-Bing, a Mongolian philosopher," worked wonders: "A man who used these pills changed completely. He became serene and happy" (*CM,* 4). "Today," writes Miłosz, "Witkiewicz's vision is being fulfilled in the minutest detail throughout a large part of the European continent" (5). Calling Marxism "the New Faith," he develops his comparison even further, and in the next chapter adds another dimension of the indoctrination process, something he calls "Ketman," after a Muslim custom observed by the French writer Gobineau in nineteenth-century Persia: "He who is in possession of truth must not expose his person, his relatives or his reputation to the blindness, the folly, the perversity of those whom it has pleased God to place and to maintain in error." "One must therefore," adds Miłosz, "keep silent about one's true convictions if possible" (57). He goes on to explain various sorts of Ketman—a national one, the Ketman of Revolutionary Purity, Aesthetic Ketman, a professional variety, et cetera—concluding: "He who practices Ketman lies" (80).

Having established those two major premises, the mind-controlling system and the fine art of deception (often turning into self-deception), Miłosz could now proceed to the main body of his study, the presentation of the four contemporary Polish writers he wished to single out, called simply Alpha, Beta, Delta, and Gamma. In the preface to the original Polish edition, Miłosz explains his decision to use pseudonyms rather than real names: "I did not use names assuming that the foreign reader could not care less about real persons, but using their example he could follow the process of submitting to the philosophy required in Poland today" (10). And indeed, in a conversation with Czarnecka, Miłosz recalls an amusing encounter with a poet from Indonesia, where *The Captive Mind* had been received so enthusiastically that Indonesians considered the author one of their national heroes: "What adventures I've had in my life—a national hero of Indonesia!" (*CCM,* 145). One can safely assume that for Indonesian readers it did not make any difference at all whether Alpha's real name happened to be Andrzejewski or an equally difficult Slavic name they could not pronounce anyway. And since *The Captive Mind* had been written basically for a foreign reader, Miłosz added in the Polish preface, "What I am saying about those persons is well known in the literary circles in Warsaw" (*CM,* 10), while thirty years later, in conversation with Czarnecka in 1983, he explains his decision to use pseudonyms by saying simply: "Because I didn't want to be a gossip-monger. . . . Who knows them outside Poland!" (*CCM,* 147). Now, with the Polish literary scene changed completely, with all four protagonists dead and some of their works available in English, one can speak about their true characters and their identities more openly.

Alpha's real name, Jerzy Andrzejewski (1909–83), has become well known outside Poland through the huge international success of his novel *Popiól i diament* (1948), mutilated almost beyond recognition in the English translation as *Ashes and Diamonds* (1962) but better known in its movie version under the same title, made by Andrzej Wajda in 1958. Miłosz acknowledges Andrzejewski's success by saying: "The novel he wrote was a product of a mature talent. It made a great impression on its readers" (*CM,* 102). At the same time, however, he voices criticisms that are quite different from the almost unanimous chorus of praise (and prizes) bestowed upon both the novelist and the novel, which, impressively, soon appeared in more than twenty foreign translations. Miłosz sees the book's usefulness to the Communist Party in the fact that it "was entirely dominated by a feeling of anger *against the losers*" (104–5)—i.e., the patriotic majority of the Polish people. That notion was rediscovered only in the 1990s, when some Polish critics were able to voice their free opinion on the heavily edited, "ideologically corrected" new version of the novel reprinted in mass editions over the last forty years of communist rule (see Krzyżanowski, 1971).

In *The Captive Mind* Miłosz could clearly foresee the moral decline Andrzejewski experienced in the years to come. Only after the brief revival of freedom in 1956 was he able to free himself from the constraints of socialist realism, but he never fully recovered. His last major novel, *Miazga* (Pulp; 1979), bears testimony to that fact, being a compilation of political, social, and moral conflicts within a group of Polish intellectuals, but artistically a failure, as if confirming Miłosz's opinion of his friend: "Only a passion for truth could have saved Alpha from developing into the person he became" (110).

Beta, Tadeusz Borowski (1922–51), represented a younger generation entering the literary scene only after World War II, with the most horrifying experiences of mass killings, concentration camps, gas chambers, and all the inhuman phenomena he witnessed during that period. "Here indeed was a wall of darkness," writes Miłosz. "No hope of liberation, and no vision of tomorrow" (112–13). Thus, Borowski, upon his return from a world of death camps and postwar chaos to Poland, with a book about his experiences to his credit, decided to pursue a literary career at any cost, which in fact meant submission to the political dictates of the Communist Party. Thanks to his great talent, demonstrated in such prose collections as *This Way to the Gas, Ladies and Gentlemen, and Other Stories* (1967), he was pampered by the official critics and soon entered the slippery path of procommunist journalism which eventually led to his tragic suicidal end. "In spite of his talent and intelligence," remarks Miłosz, "Beta did not perceive the dangers inherent in an exciting march" (133). His cynicism on the one hand, and his will to make a brilliant career on the other, made him an easy victim of the corrupting system.

Gamma was a pseudonym given by Miłosz to Jerzy Putrament (1910–91), his fellow student before the war and, as it turned out, his nemesis in the postwar period. "Gamma became a Stalinist," recalls Miłosz. "I think he felt uneasy writing his passionless poetry. He was not made for literature" (148). And indeed, Putrament made his career on politics alone, although he had produced innumerable volumes of poetry, prose, reminiscences, essays, and the like—today, only a few years after his death, all forgotten, and totally unknown in the West. Using Putrament's biography as a perfect example of a person whose collaboration with the system made him a prominent figure in postwar Poland, Miłosz has no illusions as to Putrament's political convictions: "Loyal to the Center, he voiced official optimism, while in reality, after the years he had spent in Russia, he was convinced that History is the private preserve of the devil, and that whoever serves History signs a satanic pact" (168). It was that "satanic pact" that prompted Putrament to try to lure Miłosz back from Paris to Poland, and eventually resulted in the poet's defection.

Finally, there was Delta, Konstanty Ildefons Galczyński (1905–53), one of Poland's most popular and favored poets, who "probably would have been happiest in the days when kings and nobles assured the poet a place at their table in exchange for a song or a jest" (175). Returning from a POW camp to Poland, he knew "he always needed a patron; now he found one who was really munificent, the state" (186). "Delta wanted to serve his lord," Miłosz continues his metaphor: "In order to exist as a poet he needed a genial, amused *seigneur* who believed that neither his government nor anything in heaven or earth deserves to be taken too seriously, that song—half serious, half scoffing—matters more" (189). One should add that Galczyński shortly afterward fell out of grace with the Communist Party, and only recently has his position as an original poet been receiving due appreciation.

The choice of those four cases was not made haphazardly. With each of those writers Miłosz had established a special kind of relationship, thus being able to develop either an analytic or a more personal presentation to use as an eloquent illustration of his thesis. "The man I call Alpha," he wrote, "is one of the best-known prose writers east of the Elbe. He was a close friend of mine, and memories of many difficult moments that we went through together tie us to each other" (82). Recalling many of those moments, he did not mention one instance in particular, artistically perhaps the most stimulating for both friends: their witnessing of the Warsaw Ghetto Uprising in April 1943, when they observed a carefree merry-go-round turning happily in front of the burning walls of the ghetto. Each of them used that memorable image in his own way. As a result, Andrzejewski wrote one of his best novellas, *Wielki Tydzień* (Passion Week; 1945), while the same image inspired Miłosz's famous poem "Campo dei Fiori" (1945), one of the most moving tributes to the Holocaust victims ever written.

There was an eleven-year age gap between Miłosz and Borowski; either as poets or as writers they could not have had less in common, and yet they shared the same critical attitude toward the standard, patriotic vision of the war. Thus, Miłosz quotes with appreciation a fragment from one of Borowski's most famous poems: "There will remain after us only scrap-iron and the hollow, jeering laughter of generations" (113). Calling him "the disappointed lover," Miłosz equates Borowski's yearning for order as a communist with the obsession for *Ordnung* on the part of the Nazis who had incarcerated him in Auschwitz, hence making one of the bitterest comparisons ever between the two totalitarian systems, reflected in one man's biography.

Such a comparison is out of the question when one speaks of Jerzy Putrament, a man already possessing leftist sympathies in the 1930s and a cynical career-seeker during and after World War II. Having known him from the time they were schoolmates down to his recent appointment as ambassador of Communist Poland in the 1950s, Miłosz was able to project many close, personal observations of the process that resulted in Putrament's securing of a high professional position despite his zero-value credit on the literary balance sheet. Today, such an assessment turns out to be quite correct: no one remembers Putrament's works any longer.

And finally there was the case of Gałczyński, perhaps the most popular and beloved poet of postwar Poland, a man whose poetry represented everything Miłosz's did not: captivating charm and serene beauty, humor and wit, imagination and fantasy, easy, down-to-earth poetic form appealing to the masses of readers. "Delta's poetry," remarks Miłosz, "was an added source of legend. It was unlike anything written in Europe in the first half of the twentieth century" (177). And indeed, compared with the avant-garde, cerebral rather than emotional poetry created by Miłosz, that mass ap-

peal made Gałczyński a favorite with readers who had scarcely heard of Miłosz and his kind at all. Isn't there just a little bit of envy when Miłosz writes about Gałczyński's popularity and success?

The Captive Mind evoked a wide variety of opinions. Although originally written and published in Polish, it was, as Miłosz indicated, intended for foreign reception, and as soon as translations into various European languages were available, "it created some opportunities for me at universities, but in sociology or political science," the author told Czarnecka (*CCM*, 144). In fact, its publication must have contributed to his obtaining an offer from the Slavics Department at the University of California at Berkeley, which he accepted in 1960, receiving an appointment at the professorial rank. The book's reception by Polish readers was much less favorable, in the émigré community as well as in Poland proper, and the matter deserves close examination as an example of Polish literary opinion highly motivated by political issues dominating not only the captive but also the free minds of that time.

The hostility of writers living and working under the communist system, partly sincere, partly dictated by the party authorities, was demonstrated in many ways. Among the best known was the publication of a story, "Nim będzie zapomniany" (Before He Will Be Forgotten), by Kazimierz Brandys, in the 1950s the leading writer of socialist realism in Poland and thus virtually an official spokesman of the establishment. In the original Polish text, Miłosz remarks, "The title of Brandys's story is very strange indeed. 'May you be forgotten' happens to be a Jewish curse" (*CM*, 83). It was not a separate opinion, and quite a few prominent writers in Poland shared it. Much more interesting though was the reaction of Polish writers abroad, who represented the free voice of public opinion and were able to speak up with no restrictions. Czarnecka describes that reaction as "a real fury" (*CCM*, 82), trying to make Miłosz respond to those attacks aimed at him quite vehemently.

In that respect, one must remember that the Polish émigré community happened to be deeply divided between the conservative "old guard" gathered around the London-based weekly *Wiadomości* and the adherents of the much more liberal monthly *Kultura*, published by the Institut Littéraire in Paris, with which Miłosz associated himself from the time he decided to stay in the West. Thus, the polemics over *The Captive Mind* disclosed some basic political differences, once more coloring the book's reception. "Converted but Not Entirely?," "A Former Fellow-Traveler Miłosz," "A Stakhanovite in Exile," "The Captive Mind or a Knocked-Around Character"—these were typical titles of the articles on Miłosz published in the London-based émigré press. The *Kultura* writers Jerzy Giedroyc, Józef Czapski, Konstanty Jeleński, and others came forward defending Miłosz and his position.

Discussion of Miłosz both as an individual and as a writer continued over the years, with each new publication adding some fresh arguments for the author's opponents as well as for his defenders. "I used to collect all those most horrible clippings," Miłosz told Czarnecka (82). One of the key issues in that controversy was his admitted adherence to Hegelian philosophy as a basis for Marxism, particularly evident in Miłosz's open admiration of his friend and mentor Tadeusz Kroński (1907–58), who actively promoted Marxism in Poland and thus became largely responsible for the predominance of that ideology over any other system of philosophical thought in the 1950s. Writing on Kroński in his autobiographical work *Native Realm* (1958), Miłosz thinly disguised his friend under the code name "Tiger," openly admitting to Kroński's influence over his writing and calling it euphemistically "the Hegelian bug." Such an admission created a furor, and not only among the émigré writers. Zbigniew Herbert (1924–98), perhaps the most independent and incorruptible among Polish poets at home, exclaimed with disgust: "They say it was a Hegelian bug. Sorry, but Hegel had been resting under the turf for a century, while the bugging was done by Berman [the Communist Party official in charge of cultural affairs], Sokorski [Minister of Culture], Kroński [professor of philosophy at the University of Warsaw]" (JT, 192). Most of these and similar opinions were recalled at a Miłosz session titled "Thirty Years Ago and After," organized at the Institute of Literary Research of the Polish Academy of Sciences (IBL PAN) by Roman Zimand on 31 December 1980, and were later discussed by Kroński's younger colleague Andrzej Walicki in his reminiscences, *Zniewolony umysl po latach* (The Captive Mind Years After; 1993).

Miłosz's personal and political situation has changed dramatically since the collapse of the communist regime. He has been totally reaccepted in Poland, has made Cracow his place of residence for half of each year, and enjoys great popularity, even as Polish émigré circles have ceased to play any significant role in shaping public opinion. One can quote here Maria Danilewicz Zielińska, a prominent historian of Polish émigré literature, who voiced her opinion long before those events took place: "The time flows by quickly. Miłosz has become a winner of prizes, the author of 'books of the year published in exile,' and finally was nominated by the readers to be a jury member of the *Wiadomości* prizes." Quoting a declaration of émigré writers concerning the freedom of opinion, published in *Kultura* in 1951, she concludes: "The declaration

closed 'the Miłosz case.' Recalling it after twenty-five years is only a constructive history lesson" (MDZ, 194–95).

Almost half a century has passed since the publication of *The Captive Mind,* and the international situation has changed completely. Thus it is quite natural that a question emerges: is the book still relevant today? The answer can be only in the affirmative. When one recalls Miłosz's Indonesian incident, one can well understand why his book enjoyed such a huge success even in a country dominated by a rightist regime: "Your book is against absolutism," as his Indonesian admirer told him (*CCM,* 145), and as long as totalitarian regimes exist anywhere, relevant it will remain.

Jerzy R. Krzyżanowski, Autumn 1999

▪ WORKS CITED

Czarnecka, Ewa, and Aleksander Fiut. *Conversations with Czesław Miłosz.* San Diego, Ca. Harcourt Brace Jovanovich. 1987. (CCM)

Krzyżanowski, Jerzy R. "On the History of 'Ashes and Diamonds.'" *Slavic and East European Journal,* 15:3 (1971).

Miłosz, Czesław. *The Captive Mind.* New York. Knopf. 1953. (CM)

———. *Zniewolony umysl* [The Captive Mind]. Paris. Instytut Literacki. 1953.

Trznadel, Jacek. *Hańba domowa* [Domestic Disgrace]. Warsaw. Niezalezna Oficyna Wydawnicza. 1986. (JT)

Walicki, Andrzej. *Zniewolony umysl po latach* [The Captive Mind Years After]. Warsaw. Czytelnik. 1993.

Zielińska, Maria Danilewicz. *Szkice o literaturze emigracyjnej* [Sketches on Emigré Literature]. Paris. Instytut Literacki. 1978. (MDZ)

Czesław Miłosz: Despair and Grace

The reader will forgive me if I begin a discussion of Czesław Miłosz with some personal recollections. I happened to live almost my entire conscious life in the same town in which Miłosz spent his youth and became a poet. We even graduated from the same university (separated by a quarter-century): it was Polish, and later Lithuanian, and then Sovietized; but its buildings were preserved, and along with them that smell of tradition which in a queer way sometimes outlives all historical catastrophes. The city itself is one of the most beautiful, perhaps the most beautiful in Eastern Europe. Miłosz called it "a city of clouds resembling baroque architecture and of baroque architecture like coagulated clouds."[1] The hills there are much like those in Berkeley, where Miłosz now lives and works, but they are greener and more moist. The town has three names: the

Lithuanians call it Vilnius; the Poles, Wilno; and earlier the Russians called it Vilna. In Vilnius there are people who remember the poet well.

It was precisely there that I had occasion to read Miłosz's work for the first time. The book was *Native Realm,* which made its way into Vilnius in a most remarkable way. It was sent in page by page in letters from the West. The process of sending it lasted a year and a half. Nowadays books which are objectionable to the censor make their way into Lithuania in a simpler fashion; at any rate, I am now justified in exposing this "conspiratorial" secret. I do not know how to combine this fact with a notion that all letters sent to the Soviet Union are checked by the authorities; nevertheless it remains a fact. By the way, two pages were missing. I read the book in one sitting, for it was not only well written; it dealt with Lithuania and our epoch and said the most important things about both. Shielding the book from the glances of strangers, I read and reread the lines about the year 1940 when the Soviet troops entered Vilnius.

> I went down to the river, sat on a bench, and watched the suntanned boys in their kayaks, the revolving rod of a tiny steamboat's engine, the colored boats which you rowed standing at the back, using one long oar. I was sorry for my city because I knew every stone of it; I knew the roads, forests, lakes, and villages of this country whose people and whose landscapes had been thrown like grist into a mill. . . . The sandbars in front of the electric-power station where children were standing with fishing poles, the river current, the sky, all spoke to me of an irrevocable sentence. (*NR,* 211–12)

I raised my eyes: in front of me was the same electric-power plant, the sandbar, other children with other fishing poles and other but similar boats. And although much has changed in the people and the languages, and although the standard Soviet Hall of Sports stood alongside the electric-power plant, a vague light of hope struck from the river and the sky. The hope was also in the book, and in the fact that it had returned to its own town.

Later in Poland I read other books by Miłosz. There almost everyone read and reads them, and citations from Miłosz have become a code which many people use in conversing among themselves. Mandelstam became such a secret code in Russia; in Lithuania, perhaps, it is sometimes Brazdžionis, sometimes Radauskas. In exile Miłosz remained the most vital and the most important poet of his motherland. If one considers exile to be not a misfortune but a destiny and a problem, then Miłosz solved this problem at least as well as

the nineteenth-century Polish poets Norwid and Mickiewicz.

Incidentally, Lithuania links these three names. The Lithuanians love to explain, but are not always able to explain to foreigners, that most complex amalgam of cultures which has existed in the so-called historical Lithuania and the Vilnius territory. Miłosz explains this better than others: as a matter of fact, he dedicates the entire above mentioned book and many pages in his other books to this very question. It is not every resident of an area who understands this fine mixture, this aggregate of languages, traditions, behavioral aspects and even the genetic conglomeration which gives birth to great poets and for which it is difficult to find an analogy in the West. The analogy to Ireland is by no means complete; it may be that the analogy to Alexandria is more accurate. Here cultures came in contact, projected onto each other, at times destroyed each other, but they also fostered each other. The most ancient, substratal and, at the same time, the youngest culture is the Lithuanian, which was finally formed only in the twentieth century; the most powerful over several centuries is the Polish. For a certain time they existed in an absurd antagonism which has by now been almost entirely overcome, and this rather complex situation was made even more complex by the cultures of immigrants, conquerors and neighbors from near and far. Oscar Miłosz, Czesław's elder relative and his poetic teacher, is, as it were, a symbol of this complexity. He was a Lusatian Sorb through distant ancestors, Jewish (on his mother's side), Belorussian by place of birth, Polish by his upbringing, Lithuanian by choice, and a great French poet. Not only languages but epochs coexisted within this world. "One lived in the twentieth century, another in the nineteenth, a third in the fourteenth" (*NR,* p. 68). I will add that later on people of this region experienced that "real twentieth century" about which Akhmatova speaks, and the complete absence of time.

The overlapping of cultures, their intersection and coalescence, their impermeability, their dissimilar rhythms teach many things. First of all, they gave Miłosz the sense of distance which is so necessary for a poet in our day. The spatial juxtaposition of the civilizations permitted him to sense keenly their relativity in time. As is known, civilizations know that they are mortal. For a resident of Eastern Europe, this phrase of Valéry is far from being an idle one. Simultaneously, however, civilizations (or more accurately, cultures) possess a power for survival and rebirth about which they themselves seldom know. The attentive observer will note the indestructibility of several cultural arche-types conjoined with the very existence of mankind. They repeat themselves as the appearance of the river and the sky is repeated. The task is to write poetry that is adequate both for the disasters which are destroying cultures and for that striking strength of cultures to survive. It can be written only with a living sympathy for the cultures, and it is inseparable from a living sympathy for people. In the epoch of the Gulag, Miłosz expressed this sympathy perhaps more strongly than anyone else. It is worth recalling his beautiful pages on the Balts in *The Captive Mind,* where this question is directly addressed: "The problem of the Baltics is much more important for every contemporary poet than are questions of style, metrics, and metaphor."[2] Reflection on the fate of the Balts, on the milling of persons and peoples in the totalitarian machine, leads to the only possible and true words.

> There must be, after all, some standard one dare not destroy lest the fruits of tomorrow prove to be rotten. If I think thus it is because for the last two thousand years or more there have been not only brigands, conquistadors and hangmen, but also people for whom evil was evil and had to be called evil. (*CM,* p. 225)

Having imagined the totality of evil throughout history, a man may "either turn gray with horror—or become completely indifferent" (*CM,* p. 223). It would seem that there is no third option. Yet Miłosz gives us this third choice: how to live with the consciousness of the mortality of cultures, of the irreversible suffering of peoples, of the immensity of evil, and nevertheless live and overcome the evil automatism of history.

It is hardly necessary to cite Miłosz's poetry here. If a thinker and cultural historian at times provides formulae which concisely express the thoughts of many pages (and Miłosz possesses this skill to a high degree), one should probably just read the poetry in its entirety or copy it. It is a question of the poetry's substance, of the correlation of the parts, of the change in intonation, of the glitter and darkness of the language. In addition, it is necessary to read and copy the poetry in the original; a good translation is also a poem, but a different poem. Furthermore, each reader has *his own* poems which are important for him but which are not necessarily noted by consensus. (For me, for example, it is Miłosz's "Mittelbergheim," the amazing coda of the collection *Šwiatlo dzienne* [Daylight].) But it is still possible to say a few words about the construction of this poetry, about its course and flow.

It is known that Miłosz had to find his own way among several strong traditions. One usually speaks of Skamandarites and Avant-gardists. The former created poetry which was vital but which suffered from a certain lack of tempo and therefore aged quickly, whereas the latter, as it soon became apparent, caught only the superficial and not the deep structures of the age. But

Tomas Venclova (*Courtesy: Tomas Venclova*)

apparently the magical names of the Polish past are more important: Miłosz, who grew up in Vilnius, had particular ties with them as well as particular accounts to settle. He found his own voice early. Almost from the beginning, a solemn incandescence was heard in it, as well as that surprise from which, it is said, philosophy begins. An irregular rhythm, elliptical images, a peculiar visionary stance were a means for conversing with the age. What always distinguished Miłosz were a penetrating sympathy for people and an awareness of the "clamor of the times" (and almost everything which later happened could be heard in it). He was always an antiformalist and a moralist. Formalism, the creation of a special language for the initiated (which upon examination often turns out to be the simplest Esperanto), is almost the primary temptation of contemporary poetry. In Miłosz's own words, totalitarianism is ready to permit avant-garde eccentricities so that the poet will be occupied with something and will not attempt to influence reality; it is true that in Russia (and, in its own time, in Germany) totalitarianism still did not understand this, but it did understand it in many East European countries, and even perhaps in contemporary Lithuania.

Still, Miłosz has always wanted (as he does even now) to influence reality with verse, to find his place in time, by no means becoming its servant. The poet is the instrument of the epoch (just as he is the instrument of the language); the epoch and the language "think through the poet"; however, this thought should influence the epoch and the language by itself; and here a particular sobriety of view, integrity and self-control are necessary. At first Miłosz experienced an interest in the ideology of the left, in the Marxist "alteration of the world." It may be that such a period is useful in our times for the maturation of the personality: many have passed through it, and some traces of it, remaining behind in the subconscious, give it an additional dimension of not little importance. But he who remains "left" forever obviously did not understand something significant. Miłosz understood the most significant thing: the poet is not so much the reformer as he is the conscience of the world.

Besides, the poet is the keeper of tradition, the keeper of the word. This interest in tradition and in the word distinguished Miłosz from the earliest years on, but it became unusually strong when the poet acquired the experience of war, of the Occupation and of the first years after the war. Totalitarianism, as well as all the chaos of history, threatens the temporal dimensions of humanity first of all; if we wish to have a future, we must have a past. A destroying (and destroyed) world should find a new integrity in consciousness and in verse. It is from here that Miłosz takes his interest in man's attachment in time and space, and from here also derives his love for "persisting matter," his rare understanding and ability to transmit its paradoxicality with a few words. From here comes his love of culture; Miłosz perceives it as a living whole, as the "realia" of the Middle Ages (in general, he is most likely a realist in the medieval sense, in opposition to the nominalist). In this regard he knows and values those areas of European culture which are now known only to a few but which are significantly important; he knows that Swedenborg or the arguments of the Trinitarians and the anti-Trinitarians of the seventeenth century have a direct relationship to our problems.

Miłosz, along with a majority of East European writers, was fated to see history where it actually occurred and assumed eschatological import. Neither political nor poetic doctrines remained intact, nor could they remain intact in this cataclysm; but poetry itself remained, proving to be a higher, unpolitical politics (NR, p. 247). Miłosz formulated this in his philosophical treatise, The Captive Mind:

> The war years taught me that a man should not take a pen in his hands merely to communicate to others his own despair and defeat. . . . Today the only poetry worthy of the name is eschatological, that is, poetry which rejects the present in-

human world in the name of a great change. (CM, pp. 206, 237)

In all probability, it is necessary to understand the term *eschatology* here not in the figurative sense, but in the direct, biblical sense. During his time Oscar Miłosz instilled in the young Czesław a skeptical attitude toward the poetic experiments of the age and explained to him that poetry is, in general, a rarity: it was revealed to people in full only in the Bible, and from that time hence it is given to them only as an exception.

Now the poetry of Miłosz has actually proven to be such an exception. It was necessary to respond to questions for which man has no answer, to write when it seemed senseless and intolerable to write, yet also an unavoidable task. In such a situation a poet is justified in using anything which happens to fall into his hands—ancient and antiquated forms, echoes from folklore, from the Baroque and romanticism, from primitive syllabic verse, from treatises of the Enlightenment and Greek tragedy. The poetic world is created from fragments of culture. It is structurally similar to *bricolage,* the process of creating a myth, as described by Lévi-Strauss; in an émigré period the tendencies toward *bricolage* are likely to be strongly intensified. Miłosz attains the heights and suggestiveness characteristic of myth. His poetry is precise, condensed, filled with the knowledge of man and stripped of any sentimentality, exaltation or unworthy tendency toward irony. At times it is simply a shining, restrained despair, a despair brightened by sense, having measure and rhythm. The measure of thought and vision is the only form of verse and is the sole grace of the poet.

The primary purpose of verse is to overcome despair, to be victorious over entropy; the degree to which this goal is attainable is a secondary question. It arises before the poet at any point on the globe. The space of poetry changes as experience is acquired: it changed sharply and significantly for Miłosz. He was compelled to choose emigration, since he was and still remains an enemy of any kind of totalitarianism. The success of the social experiment never justifies the means (even if there were that success). Whether to remain in a country where similar experiments are being conducted or to abandon it is a complex problem which is resolved in its own way every time. During the time that Miłosz was resolving it, to remain behind meant to condemn oneself to asphyxia and physical destruction, or to something worse—*ketman.* This Arabic word, to the interpretation of which an entire chapter of The Captive Mind is devoted, may be very roughly rendered in English as "conformity" or "hypocrisy." Today many East European artists are abandoning their native countries, sometimes by their own will, at other times against it.

Miłosz passed that way twenty years earlier. At that time he already knew and spoke of the Gulag civilization in both its variants, the German and the Russian; he spoke and shouted about the rights of man, and in that day there did not exist even the slightest "vogue for dissent" which nowadays, preserving all the unpleasant properties of fashion, nevertheless supports new exiles; and even then he had to confront the so-called leftist intellectuals, the provincial, narrowly nationalistic emigration, as well as the simple incomprehension, which he overcame to a great extent.

Miłosz says that at a distance from one's own country, knowledge of it gradually becomes theoretical. His own particular example refutes his words. I have not seen many people who could sense contemporary Poland as well, and not just Poland. He senses the vital rhythm of all of Eastern Europe and speaks for us all— and by no means last of all, for the Lithuanians. Eastern Europe, with its conglomeration of impenetrable cultures which nevertheless illuminate each other, became a model of the entire contemporary world for him. That which happened there could, alas, turn out to be the fate of the entire world. Miłosz also understood this earlier than many, many people.

His poems have remained on the same lofty plane for several decades. One cannot say which are better and which are worse. Rare poets attain this level where, for practical purposes, there is no hierarchy of values. But the poetry has changed. It may be that the tendency toward a symbolic and mystical vision of the world has been strengthened. Without doubt, the lexicon has been refined, strengthened, has become more archaic. Space, as Miłosz himself has noted, became dual, and the poet's vision acquired a profound stereoscopic quality. The sacral center of the world, the Lithuania of genealogy and childhood, is seen in a California perspective, and the whole contemporary world in the perspective of Lithuania. Vilnius and the Lithuanian provinces arise in the poetry with an evocative power like that of Martinville and Combray in Proust. This had already appeared in Miłosz's prose, in *Dolina Issy* (The Valley of Issa). It always seems to me that this novel belongs to a certain conceivable, ideal Lithuanian literature: we have these types and motifs, there are these landscapes and seasons (in Donelaitis), but alas, we have no novel in which everything could be united into such an integral and beautiful entity. The novel belongs to Polish literature. However, from a certain point of view, this is ultimately unimportant.

There is, however, one thing which has changed in Miłosz's poetics; I have already spoken of how he has more and more of a tendency for creating a poetic world from fragments, from "the material at hand." The best

example of this is the poem "Gdzie wschodzi słońce i kędy zapada" (From Where the Sun Rises to Where It Sets), which is perhaps Miłosz's magnum opus. This is a reflection on time, on the responsibility of contemporary man, but probably, above all, on the existence of language and its frailty. The registers of language, or simply the languages—Polish, Lithuanian, Old Russian, English, Greek and Latin—emerge here in a type of medieval debate. Verse and prose collide, as do the naive epigram and the psalm, folklore and the historical essay of the nineteenth century, an ancient testament and a contemporary encyclopedia, a quote from a great poet and a semi-parody of a scientific text. In a polylogue not deprived of carnival spirit echo cultures, landscapes, people, truths and untruths. "The creative conscience stands, as it were, on the border line between languages and styles."[3] As in Borges's *El aleph,* everything closes in on one point. Thus Miłosz returns to the Lithuanian-Polish amalgam of traditions in order to reevaluate it constantly for future resurrection; thus he speaks, seemingly beyond time, of the "zaprzeszły czas krajów niedokonanych" (plusquamperfectum of imperfect countries) so that he, with great courage, might accept his fate, the entire measure of despair, and the entire boundlessness of grace.

The example of Czesław Miłosz inspires hope. He did that which it is now imperative for people leaving the countries of Eastern Europe to do: he preserved his spiritual integrity and made his way back to the motherland. And what was done once may be done in general.

Tomas Venclova, Summer 1978, translated by
Alexandra Karriker

[1] Czesław Miłosz, *Native Realm: A Search for Self-Definition,* Catherine S. Leach, tr., New York, Doubleday, 1968, p. 185. Subsequent references carry the abbreviation *NR.*

[2] Czesław Miłosz, *The Captive Mind,* Jane Zielonko, tr., New York, Knopf, 1953, pp. 236–37. Subsequent references carry the abbreviation *CM.*

[3] M. Baxtin, *Voprosy literatury i èstetiki,* Moscow, 1975, p. 426.

Stanislaw Lem's Fiction and the Cosmic Absurd

Stanislaw Lem was born in Lvov, Poland (now part of the Soviet Union) in 1921. Because of his unique achievements in the field of science fiction, Lem[1] has become, over the last twenty years, Poland's most widely read author abroad. A doctor by training (like Chekhov, Lem puts his medical knowledge to good use in his fiction), he has acquired expertise in cybernetics and other branches of modern scientific endeavor. Endowed with an unflagging energy and a resourceful imagination, Lem writes prolifically. To date he has published well over twenty titles, by no means all of which are science fiction. He has also written, for example, an autobiographical memoir about his childhood and youth, a long contemporary novel, as well as several weighty books and many essays on literary theory, information theory and futurology (i.e., the philosophical implications of our ever-advancing technology). Two of his recent books defy genre classification: *A Perfect Void,* "collected reviews" of imaginary works by fictitious authors (shades of Borges!), and *Imaginary Magnitude,* consisting of prefaces to nonexistent books.

In his well-constructed novels and stories Lem transcends the hackneyed conventions of sf. He felicitously combines erudition with suspense, verbal inventiveness with narrative skill, social conscience with a satiric wit and a marvelous gift for grotesque parody. His best fiction, much of which has now been translated into English, has earned Lem the reputation of a serious creative writer. In this essay I propose to examine those elements of his work that make him an original artist as well as a timely social critic.

When reading Lem one quickly notices two opposite though not mutually exclusive tendencies in his thought. On the one hand, his weltanschauung is scientific; he believes that modern technology is important and necessary. On the other hand, he manifests a humanist's preoccupation with ethical questions. He portrays with irony man's stubborn and arrogant compulsion to subjugate his fellows and the infinite universe around him, yet he clearly admires the very qualities— inventiveness, will and determination—which impel men to compete with each other and with the forces of nature. Lem attacks the absurd excesses of modern civilization from many angles, and his imagination never ceases to amaze readers with its sly and timely resourcefulness. Although diverse literary influences are perceptible—Swift, Jules Verne, H. G. Wells, George Orwell, Kafka, Gombrowicz, Dostoevsky, Sienkiewicz, folktales, popular mysteries and sf (to name only a few)— the narrative style and satiric tone remain uniquely Lem's.

By confronting his heroes with the absurd, the grotesque, and the unknown, he stresses human limitations and fallibility. The novel *The Investigation* (New York, Seabury, 1974, Adele Milch, tr.) uses the detective story format in order to show the inadequacies of scientific rationalism. The action is set in contemporary England, where Scotland Yard is baffled by an apparently inexplicable phenomenon: a series of cadavers (in totally different geographical locations) awaiting final interment, are removed from their temporary resting places (near which they are later recovered). During the course of the subsequent investigation, the likely suspects are one by one eliminated. Gregory, a young detective who has been put in charge of the case, finds himself unable to explain the strange force that has displaced the corpses so violently. He concludes, on the basis of the evidence, that no human being could have been responsible for the crimes, but he knows that such a conclusion will be unacceptable to his superiors. Despite a few striking incongruities (British policemen race about in Buicks and Cadillacs) and a lack of character development, the novel does "work" if it is read as a paranoid nightmare, dreamt rather than lived by Gregory, a lonely and introverted individual who is desperate to succeed.

The dream situation has deeper implications in *Solaris* (New York, Berkeley, 1970, J. Kilmartin and S. Cox, trs.) a compelling novel about a planet endowed with a sentient ocean. This "ocean" (made up of a kind of matter hitherto unknown to man) has remarkable mimetic powers. Capable of learning from its experiences with human beings, the sea dispatches to each of the three scientist-protagonists the simulacrum of a woman whose image has been present in his innermost thoughts. Unaware of their origin and deprived of memories, the female "visitors" are endowed with superhuman strength when threatened with physical separation from the men whom they are impelled to accompany. They cannot be killed, nor do they require food, but they are capable of feeling and suffering. In the case of the hero, Kelvin, the figure of his dead wife (who committed suicide at nineteen, partly as a result of his indifference toward her) resuscitates the guilt he has never forgotten. He realizes that he still loves her; the past, however, remains irrevocably lost, and their reunion has no future. After all, she is the creation of the inscrutable planet which has so successfully resisted all efforts to fathom its workings. Ironically enough, Kelvin, whose colleagues have beamed a transcription of his brain waves into the ocean, never stops to consider that his recurring nightmares may well be an attempt on Solaris's part to communicate with *him.* And so, faced with the majestic indifference and utter silence of an alien planet, the human protagonists despair of being able to establish the "Contact" which has been the object of their mission. (One of them has already committed suicide when the novel begins; another has gone so far as to bombard the ocean with nuclear radiation in defiance of ethics and international conventions.) Suspended in the artificial environment of a mobile observation station, they become increasingly dominated by paranoid anxieties and fear of the unknown.

Descriptions of a surreal landscape play a decisive role in the novel. The planet's red and blue suns alternately set over a sea of matter which constantly spawns baroque formations that grow, flourish, metamorphose, only to subside quickly and disappear. Lem invents a whole terminology to describe these stately configurations of matter: "mimoid," "agilus," "symmetriad," each of which has defined and specific characteristics and a predictable mode of development. The passages depicting such bizarre excrescences that apparently serve no utilitarian goal reflect the author's preoccupation with an esthetic ideal of pure creativity. Like the creative process, whether in the universe or in the artist's imagination, Solaris resists scientific dissection. Lem also "invents" a complete history of "saints, heretics, and buffoons"[2] in connection with the evolution of Solaristic scholarship over the hundreds of years which have elapsed since the planet's first discovery.

In the final analysis, the Solaris controversy, with all its ingenious hypotheses and counter-hypotheses, has never succeeded in explaining the workings or raison d'être of the mysterious ocean. Kelvin ends up by advancing the notion of a "flawed God," a being who creates in total isolation and freedom "without foreseeing the consequences of his acts." Because such a being is not omniscient and exists only in matter, it is doomed constantly to evolve (but without purpose), to create an infinity which is a measure not of its power but of "unending defeat." Kelvin says:

> Solaris could be the first phase of the despairing God. Perhaps its vital childhood still by far exceeds its capacity to reason, and all the contents of our Solarist libraries are merely the great catalogue of its childish impulses. . . . That is the only God I could imagine believing in, one whose suffering is not a redemption, who saves nothing, fulfills no purpose—but simply is.

As one critic has noted: "Since the world is perceived as ugly and existence in it inevitably painful, any creation of a sentient being means to make it suffer, therefore the creative act is reprehensible. Hence the guilt felt by Lem's creators. . . . But the greatest guilt—for the greatest responsibility—belongs to the First Creator. Lem's mockery of God [is accomplished] through the presentation of flawed deities."[3]

The atmosphere of tension dissolves at the end, after Kelvin's wife has been dematerialized by his colleagues. She has realized her "differentness" and has voluntarily agreed (unbeknownst to Kelvin) to undergo an innovative procedure which will end her existence as a human. When Kelvin sits down to write his official report of what has transpired, he is well aware that nothing has really been solved. The "Contact" (if it can be called that) has had only tragic human implications, for the planet's intention in sending them such "gifts" remains unclear. Saddened, he persists nonetheless "in an unshakeable faith that the time of cruel miracles has not yet passed." Indeed, there has been something both cruel and miraculous in the Solarian landscape, which has in the past claimed the lives of so many intrepid explorers, and in its creations, which in human incarnation have so tormented the narrator and his companions. Cruel and miraculous too is the anxious, somnambulent drama played out between the principals. An atmosphere of almost Gothic horror reflects their fears of the unknown and unknowable. Human behavior patterns are dramatized with authenticity, but the underlying motivations remain obscure and lacking in "rationality." Because of its psychological probing, tight narrative structure and grotesquely refined imagery, *Solaris* must remain Lem's most original and complete contribution to the novel.

Social and especially political satire predominates in much of Lem's best work. *Memoirs Found in a Bathtub* (Seabury, 1973, C. Rose & M. Kandel, trs.) delineates the Kafkaesque plight of an unnamed narrator who finds himself entrusted with an unspecified security mission in "The Building," an enclave of paranoid spies and bureaucrats who have isolated themselves from the outside world in order to maintain their ideological purity. The inhabitants of this sinister and ambiguous environment—grotesque caricatures of academics, military officers, petty functionaries, a priest, a doctor, et cetera—constantly undergo Protean metamorphoses, as they peel away false ears and noses, only to reveal new disguises. (At a given moment the priest turns into a military officer, thereby becoming an "abbé provocateur.") The plot's circular movement inexorably leads the narrator to a tragic end, the inevitable result of a hopeless struggle for recognition within a self-perpetuating "system" that, having long ago forgotten its raison d'être, arrogantly defies all ethical principles. Among other things, this absurdist tragicomedy presents a timely satire on militarism.

Often in Lem's work the effects of a dream are humorous: viz., "The Tale of the Three Storytelling Machines," which details the plight of a crass, dull-witted monarch called Zipperupus who gets lost and then permanently immured in a box of dreams constructed by his archenemy Subtillion. This story occurs in *The Cyberiad* (Seabury, 1974, M. Kandel, tr.), the only mock epic of note in Polish literature since Adam Mickiewicz's celebrated *Pan Tadeusz*. These fairy tales of the cybernetic age (which are linked by the figures of their robot heroes, Trurl and Klapaucius) reveal the author's capacity for linguistic invention and improvisation. He coins hundreds of grotesque neologisms and nonsense words (reminiscent of Edward Lear, whose influence is also apparent in Lem's own illustrations to *The Star Diaries*). The stories' fantastic wit depends to a large extent on the combination of diverse linguistic and stylistic levels. Archaic and dialectal language occurs cheek by jowl with scientific jargon, occasionally presented in Latin (the legacy of the Polish Baroque) and officialese (the unhappy influence of modern bureaucratic stultification); poetic diction merges with prosaic colloquialisms. As Lem's principal English translator, Michael Kandel, points out: "A thorough study of Lem's wordplay could easily provide material enough for a dissertation or full-length book. Macaronisms, archaisms, alliteration, rhythm, and stylizations—including scientific lingo, legal jargon, philosophical terminology, bureaucratese, Biblical prose, nursery rhymes and Slavic fairy-tales, underworld slang and dialects, and proper names, and the subtle degrees of nonsense—these might be some of the topics."[4]

Lem excels at depicting imaginary societies that have fallen under the sway of cruel, militaristic despots. The narrator of *The Star Diaries* (Seabury, 1976, M. Kandel, tr.), an *ingenu* by the name of Ijon Tichy, encounters (in "The Thirteenth Voyage," which is partly a satire on the Cold War) a regimented society of humanoids ruled by "The Mighty Hydrant Hermezinius The Fish-Eyed." The populace is obliged to emulate fish by living half-submerged in water; they are only allowed to surface for hurried gasps of air. In "The Eleventh Journey" Tichy meets a society of robots that have supposedly been created by a mutinous computer programmed for expertise in sadomasochism and medieval linguistics. This chauvinistic police state ferrets out and apprehends any human who attempts to infiltrate by disguising himself as a robot. It turns out, however, that the "robots" are actually humans whom an earthling petty official impersonating the tyrannical computer-sovereign (shades of the Wizard of Oz!) has tricked into cooperating with an enemy (the robots) which does not exist.

In one of the *Cyberiad* stories Trurl and Klapaucius encounter an evil dragon, Pugg, a "Pirate with a PhD." This creature inhabits an immense cosmic junkpile and is greedy for knowledge that will lead him to the "Ultimate Mystery of Being." He therefore waylays unwary travelers, demanding that they ransom their freedom, not with material wealth but with information. The heroes summon up a "Demon of the Second Kind" which extracts bits of irrelevant data from a barrel of air (polluted, of course) supplied by the dragon. The demon transcribes with a diamond-tipped pen such pearls of wisdom as:

. . .how exactly Harlebardonian wrigglers wriggle, and that the daughter of King Petrolius of Labondia is named Humpinella, and what Frederick the Second, one of the paleman's kings, had for lunch before he declared war against the Gwendoliths and how many electron shells an atom of thermionolium would have, if such an element existed, and what is the clocal diameter of a small bird called the tufted twit, which is painted by Wabian Marchpanes on their sacrificial urns. . . .[5]

Lem is making the point that modern man is confronted with an information crisis: i.e., our intellectual environment is menaced by pollution from unnecessary and indiscriminate data produced by machines often at the instance of arrogant and stupid despots.

One of Lem's most consistent themes has been the absurdity of utopian dreams about the future. In a society deprived of conflict, stress and danger man loses his capacity for moral commitment and self-assertion. The ingenious and well-intentioned robots Trurl and Klapaucius often try to assert their miraculous powers of scientific invention and improvisation upon an unenlightened universe of men and other robots. The results are usually farcical, if not downright tragic.

Another *Cyberiad* story, "Altruizine," well illustrates the evils of too much affluence and technology. On a rectangular planet Klapaucius discovers a society that seems to have reached the ultimate in freedom and advanced civilization, i.e., the "Highest Possible Level of Development (HPLD)." In Polish their name "Enerefcy" suggests the initials of the German Federal Republic (NRF). The members of "the Most Advanced Civilization of the Entire Universe" resemble dehumanized figures in surrealist paintings. The HPLD's spend their time lounging about on a kind of magic sand littered with refuse; reclining on jeweled cushions, they scratch themselves and idly contemplate the detachable limbs of their incongruous bodies, which are constructed of brightly colored fabrics and garden vegetables. Long ago this race has come to the conclusion that philanthropically motivated intervention in the affairs of other, less fortunate civilizations can only bring grief to the recipients.

There is a good deal of truth in this cynical attitude: Klapaucius learns this when one of these solipsistic beings reluctantly gives him the formula for Altruizine, an untried drug designed to arouse through "meta-psychotropic transmission" feelings of empathy and compassion for one's fellow man. (Dialogue with the HPLD's is effected only by means of an "ontologue computer" which evokes the voice of "a single inhabitant of that square planet"; the actual inhabitants have totally ignored their inquisitive visitors' questions.) Klapaucius then deposits the drug in the water supply of a town on a "geomorphic" planet. Havoc and widespread destruction ensue: Klapaucius sees a gang of ruffians tearing out an old man's teeth in an effort to remove the single rotten molar that has been causing the sufferer so much pain; a belligerent individual in a tavern strikes another, thereby causing a chain reaction of pain that affects all those present and leads the crazed patrons to start a fire; elsewhere a house occupied by newlyweds is besieged by a mob of prurient onlookers, some of these ecstatically blowing bubbles through their noses while the husband's great-grandfather attempts to batter the door down with his wheelchair. Klapaucius ends up in jail for his philanthropic efforts.

The way of the future does not lie in tampering with human nature; Lem's comedy implies a stern warning. *A Futurological Congress* (Seabury, 1974, M. Kandel, tr.) eloquently reveals the author's trepidations about future generations' capacity to deal with the problems of an even more distant future. The notion of an academic reunion—like the annual MLA meeting—here initiates a grotesque farce with serious overtones. Initially Lem satirizes the pompousness and sterility of academic gamesmanship. The congress has convened at the Hilton Hotel of Costaricana (a fictitious Central American republic) in order to discuss the pressing question of overpopulation. The debate has little chance to begin, however, for a revolution, Latin American style, causes the delegates to take flight. The novel's structure—based on a series of drug-inspired dreams—recalls *Memoirs Found in a Bathtub* with its circular development. The satire ridicules movements that advocate "liberation" through drugs and sex; academia, luxury hotels, the military and the medical profession also get some hard knocks in this very funny novel. *Brave New World* motifs dominate the most didactic section of the book (which also happens to be esthetically the least satisfactory). Miraculously transported into a future epoch, the narrator Ijon Tichy awakens in what appears to be an affluent, highly developed civilization. The population is living under an illusion: a small elite group has palliated the reality of miserable and sordid living conditions by placing hallucinogens in the water supply.

The implications of Lem's cosmology are clearly pessimistic. Man, despite, or perhaps because of, his technological achievements, remains an easy prey to his tyrannically inclined fellows. Machines tend, logically enough, to reflect the defects (or longings) of their inventors, while cosmic phenomena can only be perceived from the limited viewpoint of human understanding. Despite his belief in science (whose

terminology, in both serious and parodic form, comprises an integral part of his literary and philosophical idiom), and despite his fascination with the infinite possibilities for expanding our knowledge through space exploration, Lem anticipates that future generations may be deprived of freedom through the very offices of a technology that was supposed to liberate them. By dramatizing the tragic consequences of despotism *cum* science in the future, he stresses man's ultimate responsibility for his own destiny. In fact, if Lem's space travelers (the subjects of the brilliant Pilot Pirx stories, unfortunately not yet translated into English) find adversity and even death during their journeys of exploration, the determining factor is usually human error, not the intervention of alien forces or creatures. In the last analysis, Lem is confronting us with a grotesque but truthful image of ourselves; after all, human nature remains eternally the same.

A final word on Lem's narrative technique: his humorous writing with its surreal guignol effects, should be distinguished from the "straight" fiction,[6] where the emphasis is on plot development. The latter belongs to the same tradition as the historical adventure yarns of Henryk Sienkiewicz (who won the Nobel Prize for literature in 1905). Sienkiewicz looked to Poland's colorful past for inspiration; Lem looks to an equally exotic space-age future. Sienkiewicz enriched his literary idiom by drawing upon seventeenth-century authors (whose language abounds in Latin borrowings); Lem, as mentioned above, borrows from these as well as many other linguistic sources, but the predominating element tends to be modern technical jargon (often heavily influenced by English). Both writers are consummate storytellers; by stimulating the reader's curiosity, they induce him to suspend disbelief. Their serious dialogue, however, tends to sound stilted, and their characterizations are for the most part one-dimensional and lacking in psychological depth. (An exception in Lem's case is *Solaris* with its guilt-ridden narrator and its ambivalent human relationships.)

Because it emphasizes narrative and description rather than character development, "serious" science fiction may be viewed as a quasi-traditional, even retrograde literary genre (while satiric sf clearly derives from the flawed utopias of Cervantes, Voltaire and others in the same tradition). Lem, moreover, betrays an old-fashioned predilection for verbal landscape painting. Whether barren or fertile, Lem's moon- or planetscapes are painted in vivid, graphic colors. Nature in the Cosmos alternately repels and fascinates his prosaic heroes. They record faithfully what they see—they either conquer or are defeated—but there is no time for introspection. Recently Lem has turned away from fiction and devoted his untiring intellectual energy to literary criticism and philosophy, thereby disappointing numerous admirers of his "creative" nonanalytic writing.[7] Those elements of parody that continue now merge with the philosophical essay as Lem "continues to follow his own difficult drummer."[8]

Reuel K. Wilson, Autumn 1977

[1] The author's very name would seem to have futuristic overtones, being identical with the English acronym LEM, the designation of the Lunar Excursion Module used in the Apollo Project, as translator Michael Kandel facetiously points out in his introduction to *The Star Diaries,* New York, Seabury, 1976, p. viii.

[2] Darko Suvin, "The Open-Ended Parables of S. Lem and Solaris," Afterword to *Solaris,* New York, Berkeley, 1970, p. 221.

[3] Michael Kandel, "Lem in Review," *Science-Fiction Studies,* 4:11, pt. 1 (March 1977), p. 66. The article is a tongue-in-cheek review of an imaginary critical monograph on Lem.

[4] "On Translating the Grammatical Wit of S. Lem into English," paper given at the 1974 annual meeting of the American Association of Teachers of Slavic and East European Languages. Kandel's own translations of Lem are impressive; he brilliantly re-creates English equivalents for Lem's neologisms and the other diverse manifestations of verbal and stylistic legerdemain.

[5] *The Cyberiad,* M. Kandel, tr., New York, Seabury, 1974, p. 157. The enumeration from which I quote lasts almost three pages, during which the author masterfully amuses (*without* instructing) the reader.

[6] So far only one "straight" novel has been translated into English: *The Invincible,* translated from the German by W. Ackerman, New York, Seabury, 1973.

[7] Cf. T. H. Hoisington, reviewing *The Star Diaries* in *The Polish Review,* 22:1 (1977), p. 116: "In his early science fiction [Lem] is a social and political satirist, later he is a proponent of moderation in an era of runaway technology, and, more recently, a debunker of those two earlier selves. In this last stage he indulges in an odd kind of epigonism."

[8] Kandel, "Translator's Note" to the *Star Diaries,* p. 275.

ROMANIA

Romanian Literature: Dealing with the Totalitarian Legacy

A full year has passed since the bloody uprising in Romania which led to the downfall of Nicolae Ceauşescu's hated regime in December 1989, and many Romanian intellectuals speak, with increasing concern, of a cultural crisis. Its most obvious sign would be that few new books have appeared in the meantime, and apparently fewer have been, or are being, written. "People don't read books any more," a Romanian friend, a distin-

guished scholar, told me last spring; "the only things that attract them are newspapers and magazines." Since then I have seen this statement reiterated over and over, almost obsessively, in the Romanian press. Significantly, some prominent writers and critics have taken up new roles as journalists. The novelist Gabriela Adameşteanu has published a series of remarkable interviews in the fiercely independent magazine 22, issued by the Group for Social Dialogue (a nonpolitical organization that has consistently criticized the present government of former communists who suddenly became proponents of democracy and a market economy). Romania's most highly regarded literary critic, Nicolae Manolescu, has become one of the sharpest political analysts of his country's difficult exit from totalitarianism. (I myself have followed his "Ochiul magic" or "Magic Eye" columns in *România Literară* with unflagging interest, but I have skipped some of his always well-written and thoughtful articles of literary criticism.)

The most flourishing genre has been the interview, with its ability to capture the immediate reaction to events or probing questions, with its quick, informal, oral-colloquial rhetoric. By comparison with the crisp directness of the interview (albeit simulated), Romanian journalism typically tends, with few exceptions, toward overwriting and frustrating indirectness—an unfortunate legacy of the empty rituals of encomium or, at the other end of the spectrum, of the obloquies to which it was forced by the old regime. Even so, stylistically uneven and not infrequently bombastic as they are, Romanian newspapers and magazines of diverse orientations have been in tremendous demand. Why? Simply because they have told, from different and sometimes conflicting angles, powerful stories: from that of the flight, capture, and secret trial of the former dictator and his wife (the initial secrecy and the apparent doctoring of the videotape of the trial have fueled endless speculations and rumors) to that of the barbaric mid-June episode of vigilante anti-intellectual violence and vandalism sponsored, incredibly, by the newly elected president and his government.

Reading the news and trying to figure out its significance in a political situation that has been in permanent flux has given many readers a sense of participating in the events, a sense which, however illusory, could only be exhilarating after decades of exposure to a wooden language that, among other things, made everyone feel humiliatingly impotent and irrelevant. Under the circumstances, few people are ready to make the commitment of time, attention, and disinterested imagination that goes into the act of reading a book—say, a novel—and making oneself at home in its fictional world. Even art forms that demand a more modest investment of time, such as theatrical performances, have suffered. Why go to the theater when the theater—political theater of the greatest power—has come to the street, and has done so in a breathtaking variety of forms, from that of uplifting revolutionary drama (such as the student-led anticommunist demonstration in Bucharest's University Square in April-June 1990) to revolting, unimaginable examples of the theater of cruelty (such as the club-wielding miners and former secret-police agents disguised as miners beating up students and intellectuals and chanting slogans such as "We work, we don't think!" in Bucharest in mid-June)?

■ ■ ■

To understand what is going on today in Romanian literature—including its possible sources of strength, areas of weakness, and prospects—we cannot avoid considering briefly its history over the postwar communist decades, with a natural emphasis on the more recent past. Between roughly 1945 and 1948 a sizable number of Romanian intellectuals took the decision to leave the country, or not to return if they happened to be in the West at the time. Among the latter the best-known are Eugen Ionescu (the future great French playwright Eugène Ionesco), the historian of religions Mircea Eliade, and the philosopher E. M. Cioran. Those who left Romania during the first years of communist power as best they could—sometimes taking the risk of crossing the frontiers illegally, like the future great German poet Paul Celan[1]—included writers of the most diverse backgrounds: from surrealists such as Ghérasim Luca,[2] who was often writing in French even before emigrating, to literary critics and essayists such as Monica Lovinescu and Virgil Ierunca, who continued to write and publish in Romanian (Ierunca was for years the editor of the émigré journal Limite). The last two were first published in Romania by the newly created publishing house Humanitas in 1990, Lovinescu with a collection of literary reviews broadcast over the years by Radio Free Europe (Unde scurte or "Short Waves"), and Ierunca with a historical essay on the horrendously innovative camp for political prisoners at Pitești in the 1950s. (The Pitești concentration-camp experiment was probably the cruelest in the vast geography of communist gulags: the idea was to create the "perfect" political prison system, one in which each prisoner, forced to confess falsely to the most extravagant crimes, had to become at once an informer, a guard, and an actual torturer of other inmates in order to extract from them false confessions of extravagant crimes and transform them into informers, guards, and torturers of other inmates, and so on.)

In Romania, in the meantime, an extraordinarily harsh version of Stalinism was imposed, for which the country's intellectuals were little prepared. Some of the established as well as younger writers collaborated with the new regime from early on and adopted "socialist realism" as a "method of creation," but many were reluctant and immediately became the object of various kinds of persecution, including imprisonment. Initially the cultural policy of the Romanian Communist Party was one of massive Russification, but little by little, as the Soviet Union itself was de-Stalinizing in the mid-1950s, the Romanian party chief Gheorghiu-Dej instituted a policy of secret re-Stalinization along (pseudo)nationalist lines, which was to be continued by Ceaușescu in the form of an increasingly strident (pseudo)national communism combined with a primitive, grotesque cult of personality.

Even though in the late 1950s Gheorghiu-Dej's re-Stalinization led to anti-intellectual campaigns and witch hunts (there were public unmaskings of intellectuals accused of secret bourgeois leanings or esthetic tastes; there were trials, such as that of the philosopher Constantin Noica and some of his friends, or later that of the critic Ion Negoițescu, on such absurd charges as merely having read certain ideologically illicit books!), the national literary traditions were slowly being rediscovered, the nineteenth- and twentieth-century classics were being reprinted (albeit in censored editions), and "socialist realism" (identified with the Russian model) was being less strictly observed. In the early 1960s the fundamental duplicity of the party toward the Soviet Union became the basis for a variety of forms of cultural duplicity, some encouraged by the party, some merely tolerated. In this general climate of duplicity and hypocrisy a narrow region of intellectual freedom (a freedom whose price, in moral terms, was not negligible, however) became accessible, particularly between 1964 and 1971 but in certain significant cases even after the so-called minicultural revolution launched by Ceaușescu in July 1971.

Between 1964 and 1971, during a period of quasi-liberalization (modifiers such as quasi or pseudo are unfortunately unavoidable when writing about the history of communism in Romania), two new generations of writers asserted themselves. The first was made up of people already in their forties and even older, who had been silent, or silenced, or imprisoned during the Zhdanovist years or during the re-Stalinization of the late 1950s. Some of these had published briefly in the agitated 1940s—I am thinking, for example, of the Sibiu Group (Ion Negoițescu, the poet Ștefan Aug. Doinaș, the critic Ovidiu Cotruș, and others) and also of essayists and scholars such as Alexandru Paleologu or Adrian

Marino—but had been prevented from publishing for over fifteen years. Some younger members of this same first generation had not published before, as in the case of the poet Leonid Dimov, a fascinating early postmodern visionary and ironist who was to become the main inspirer of the "oneiric group," or in the cases of such fine essayists and prose writers as Alexandru George, Radu Petrescu, and others.

The "oneiric group" itself, established by D. Tsepeneag, belonged to the second, younger generation of writers then in their twenties and thirties (among its most prominent, members were Sorin Titel, Virgil Mazilescu, and Daniel Turcea). This second generation of the mid-1960s displayed a great diversity of talent, going in poetry, for instance, from the metaphysical and ludic lyricism of Nichita Stanescu to the bookish-ironic refinements of Mircea Ivanescu to the profound ethical resonance in the verse of Ana Blandiana. In fiction this generation produced several interesting if rather uneven novelists—Al. Ivasiuc, N. Breban, A. Buzura—and some remarkable critics, such as N. Manolescu, Mircea Martin, Lucian Raicu, and Eugen Simion.

To this latter generation also belongs the first important dissident Romanian writer, Paul Goma. Not even during the quasi-liberal late 1960s could Goma get his works published in Romania. His first novel, an account of his experiences as a political prisoner in Gheorghiu-Dej's Romania, was turned down by the censor and had to be smuggled out of the country (it was brought out as *La cellule des libérables* by Gallimard in 1971). In 1977 Goma started a rapidly and brutally suppressed human-rights movement. He himself was arrested, held for a month, then expelled from the country. (He has since been living in Paris, where he has published several novels and an impressive memoir, *Le tremblement des hommes*, 1979). There were other dissident writers—the poet Dorin Tudoran in the mid-1980s, Ana Blandiana, the poet Mircea Dinescu (now president of the Writers Union)—but on the whole literary dissent was very sporadic in Romania. I see three reasons for this: 1) the fear of repression; 2) the pressure on dissidents and potential dissidents to leave the country; and 3), the continued possibility, even when the cult of Ceauşescu was at its most delirious, to publish good, apolitical, and sometimes even obliquely critical books.

Each of these reasons needs to be qualified to make the situation of the Romanian writer comprehensible in its specificity. The fear of repression, in a system of total censorship and total control of everyday life by an all-powerful secret police, can hardly be understood in abstract terms. One must try to imagine the utter lack of scruples of the secret police, the absolute hypocrisy and cynicism, and the communists' inexhaustible store of techniques for smearing and degrading ideological opponents. First and foremost, however, one must understand that dissent was *not* treated as dissent—or, say, as slandering the regime, a punishable offense but one that was rarely invoked under Ceauşescu, who was supposed to have made everybody happy. Dissenting intellectuals were therefore tried, or threatened with arrest, for such crimes as sexual deviance (homosexuality was punished with up to five years in jail), trumped-up charges of rape, drug possession, or other morally disqualifying deeds; they were interned in psychiatric institutions; they were subjected to all kinds of blackmail. (I know, for example, of cases in which the school-age children of dissident intellectuals were severely beaten in the street by unidentified "tramps"; the secret police relished such indirect, mysterious means of persuasion.)

On top of that, dissident writers were treated as lepers by many of their own colleagues in the Stalinistically centralized form of literary life created by the existence of the Writers Union. (That the same organization could also pose a danger to the regime—as was demonstrated in Hungary and Poland in 1956, in Czechoslovakia in 1968, and even in Romania, in a milder form, in the 1980s—is true, but this fact cannot change the Stalinist nature of the way the institution was conceived.) The tacit if not aggressively outspoken ostracism of dissenting writers by some of their colleagues (as Paul Goma has testified) took on a particularly intense and poignant quality in Romania, due to the care with which the party and its secret police had created what I would call a "hostage mentality" within the population at large and within specific professional groups. The principle is simple (as illustrated in terrorist episodes): all are punished, or threatened with punishment, for the insubordination of one; all will, in their own interest, try to stop the odd individual who might wish to challenge the discipline established by the captors; all will, once something damaging has been said or done, try to isolate and punish the rebel who is rocking the boat irresponsibly.

The second reason for the rarity of literary dissent in Romania was the possibility of exile or self-exile, and this was also skillfully manipulated by the Ceauşescu regime. The number of distinguished Romanian authors who have left their country is quite impressive. I have already mentioned the emigration that took place in the immediate aftermath of World War II; the new wave of intellectual emigration, starting in the mid-1960s but becoming stronger in the late 1970s and 1980s, included such poets, novelists, and critics as Paul Goma, D. Tsepeneag, Gabriela Melinescu, Ion Negoiţescu, Mihai

Spăriosu, Virgil Tănase, Dorin Tudoran, Gelu Ionescu, Lucian Raicu, Nina Cassian, Norman Manea, Thomas Pavel, Virgil Nemoianu, and myself, to mention only a few. Exile in the West had, in spite of its difficulties (primarily linguistic), certain undeniable advantages: even the poorest émigré lived a better life, in material terms, than he or she would have in Ceaușescu's Romania, transformed into an impoverished concentration camp where everyone was supposed to simulate happiness. More important, a sense of elementary dignity or self-respect was infinitely easier to attain in the West, even from the bottom of the social scale, than in the home country, where very few could afford to pay the extraordinary price for it: internal exile in a country with a long-standing tradition of submission to the powers that be, strengthened by the communist-induced "hostage mentality" noted earlier. Few literary intellectuals had the fearlessness to sustain internal exile for a longer period of time. One of them was the essayist Dan Petrescu.

The third reason for the low number of openly dissenting writers in Romania was the continued possibility, even through the worst Ceaușescu years, of publishing good books, books that did not make any visible concessions to the political requirements of the moment, books that, in certain cases, were not only apolitical but somehow—and quite strangely for an observer from the outside—*ahistorical,* as if they had been conceived and written at an indeterminate and indeterminable time, or perhaps in a parallel cultural world that had nothing to do with Ceaușescu's absurd Romania. Was this possibility—tiny, remote, and extremely difficult to gain access to—consciously maintained by the regime as a sort of intellectual safety valve? Was it granted, perhaps halfheartedly, for purposes of cultural prestige, which even party functionaries—or at least the more sophisticated among them—could distinguish from the emptiness of party propaganda? Was it the result of pressures from the intellectual community, a minor and insignificant concession, or just an oversight? Was it a perverse innovation of neo-Stalinism, meant to produce a sort of cultural schizophrenia that the party could exploit to its own ultimate advantage? Be that as it may, a number of works untainted by any ideological servility appeared in the 1970s and 1980s. These included literary-philosophical essays by Mihai Șora (*A fi, a face, a avea* [To Be, To Do, To Have]) and by Gabriel Liiceanu (*Jurnalul de la Păltiniș* [Diary from Păltiniș], a fascinating portrait of Constantin Noica as a Socratic teacher; and *Epistolar,* its sequel, actually a collection of letters about the Păltiniș journal edited by their recipient, Liiceanu, as *Epistolarium*); essays in the philosophy of art by Andrei Pleșu; literary essays and

prose by Alexandru George, Radu Petrescu, Tudor Țopa, and others; volumes of literary criticism by N. Manolescu, Mircea Martin, Lucian Raicu (*Gogol și fantasticul banalității* [Gogol and the Fantastic of Banality]), and Eugen Simion; poetry and drama by Marin Sorescu; and a stream of superb volumes of poetry by Ștefan Aug. Doinaș, Leonid Dimov, Ana Blandiana, Ileana Mălăncioiu, Nina Cassian, Mircea Ivănescu, Cezar Baltag, and several extremely talented younger poets, among whom Mircea Cărtărescu stands out.

Saying that the publication of such books was the rare exception rather than the rule does not convey the enormous difficulties which their authors confronted, the pressures they had to withstand, the Kafkaesque censorship they had to endure in order to see their manuscripts through. With regard to the latter, it will suffice to point out that (officially, but under communism reality itself depends on its official recognition) censorship did not even exist. Since it did not exist, it could not have principles or rules; and when (in spite of its nonexistence) it did reject a manuscript or parts of it, it could not explain why. Its verdicts were incomprehensible, mysterious, unappealable. Editors and authors had to guess the reasons of the invisible, nonexistent censor, make the corresponding changes, and try again. Once in a while a lucky author could get hold of what he or she believed to be a copy of a censor's report. In any event, however, a work written in anticipation of censorship and then modified, truncated, and made finally palatable to the censor, even if it escaped the danger of being "co-opted by the system," was likely to displease its own author on rereading. Speaking of his novel *The Black Envelope* (published in 1986), Norman Manea confessed that no words of praise for it could "counteract the irritation I felt when I reread the book. It was not the disappearance from the edited version of various dark details of daily life that upset me, nor the 'softening' of many passages. It was really the warping effect of all that encoding. Obfuscation. Stylistic excess and opacity. Devitalization, circuitousness, waste."[3] In light of such feelings, the question put to the author, now an émigré, by a friend from Romania (Alexandru George), acquires a special poignancy: "What will last, of all. . .that was written in the last forty years?. . . It could be that it will all form a 'parenthesis' in history, meaningless in the future and unintelligible to anyone who did not live it."

What will last, indeed, of so many works written precisely to last, to bypass the misery and shame of an immediate nightmarish history, in order to capture some precious timeless esthetic quality, some elusive element of golden permanence? Of course only time can answer such a question fully. But even unanswered, the question remains interesting for what it reveals by the very way it is posed. It reveals, I would argue, the *esthetic temptation* to which, unlike old Stalinism, the neo-Stalinism of Ceauşescu exposed the Romanian literary intelligentsia, a temptation by which it was able to make many honest writers repress or displace their natural dissenting impulses. In a country brought to physical and spiritual ruin by a ruthless and primitive regime, some of the best literary and philosophical minds developed an almost exclusive interest in the transhistorical and the eternal.

■ ■ ■

I have left out of my account the writers, and they were not few, who supported the Ceauşescu regime *actively* for the various kinds of advantages or privileges (increasingly shabby as these became over time) with which it rewarded them: court poets and propaganda hacks, sycophants and master flatterers, as well as professional mudslingers and slanderers of the enemies of the regime. Their presence in the newly liberated press has made itself felt sooner than one would have thought, and their destructive role has become increasingly obvious, particularly after the episode of Hungarian-Romanian ethnic violence, probably provoked by elements of the former secret police, which took place in Tirgu Mures in March 1990. These writers—Eugen Barbu, C. V. Tudor, Ion Lancranjan, Adrian Păunescu are among its leading figures—have adopted a populist-nationalist, viciously xenophobic program, anti-Hungarian, anti-Semitic, anit-Gypsy, and broadly anti-intellectual. What is more, they have managed to attract a fairly wide following among a disoriented, frustrated, politically illiterate populace; they have even managed to obtain the partial, tacit approval of certain elements of the essentially neocommunist entourage of President Ion Iliescu. That is why the offical publications of the ruling National Salvation Front rarely if ever carry criticism of such extremist, fascist-communist, racist newspapers as *România Mare* (Greater Romania), led by E. Barbu and C. V. Tudor, although they systematically abuse such consistently democratic reviews as 22, *România Literară,* and *Contrapunct* or the major opposition daily, *România Liberă.* It is in such fascist-communist publications as *România Mare,* but also in certain official or semiofficial dailies of the Front (*Azi* [Today] or *Adevarul* [The Truth]), that, incredibly, a campaign of monstrous slanders against the rare former anti-Ceauşescu dissidents is being led; its victims, among the writers, are people like Ana Blandiana, Nicolae Manolescu, Dan Petrescu, and of course the most prominent of the émigrés, Monica Lovinescu, Virgil Ierunca, Paul Goma, and so on.

What does all this tell us about the present crisis of Romanian literature? The crisis of books and readers to which I referred at the beginning of this essay is natural (revolutions do not have much time for culture), temporary, and, I believe, superficial. Much more serious is the moral-political polarization of the literary intelligentsia, some of whose symptoms I have just described. This latter crisis is itself nothing but a microcosmic image of the larger crisis in which the country as a whole finds itself, after the demise of communism, as it tries to come to terms with communism's disastrous moral-political legacy: a legacy of duplicity, lying, and megalomania (both national and personal); a legacy of brutality, abuse, and lawlessness; and, finally, a legacy of fear (including fear of freedom), hatred, and envy. This legacy, once institutional communism has disintegrated, can easily give rise to a variety of new/old forms of totalitarian mentality, but it will be almost instinctively hostile to democratic values and ways of thinking. In Romania, perhaps even more than in other formerly communist East European countries, this can lead to a revival of a narrow-minded populism or nationalism, intolerant, confused, potentially violent, potentially mystical (in terms of rhetoric). A popular triumph, even temporary, of such a mentality would be culturally disastrous.

On the other hand, there are signs that the young generation of Romanians, less affected by the Ceauşescu legacy than their parents, are spontaneously inclined toward Europe, democracy, and pluralism. So are the younger writers who call themselves "postmodern." Consider Mircea Cărtărescu and his delightful recent long (two-hundred-plus pages) poem entitled *Levantul* (The Levant; 1990). An unlikely epic that is at once a series of sophisticated parodies of Romanian poetic styles since the late eighteenth century, a playfully romantic story (with lovers, Byronic rebels, pirates in picturesque Oriental settings, and many enchanting anachronisms), and a Borgesian self-reflexive succession of *mises en abîme* of the figure of the poet and the act of writing, the work seems to capture the spirit of open-minded, good-humored, experimental, sincerely ironic, intelligent, and inventively erudite search that is characteristic of the postmodern literary imagination in Eastern Europe, particularly in the Balkan region (Cărtărescu's poetry has affinities with the intricate dream world of Milorad Pavić's *Dictionary of the Khazars,* for instance). It is on such trends—which might well coalesce into a major new style equaling in importance the phenomenon of magic realism of the last forty years or so—that one could base one's fondest hopes for the cultural future of Romania and of the newly liberated Eastern Europe as a whole.

Matei Calinescu, Spring 1991

[1] A recent book of reminiscences and documents about Celan's relationship to Romania is Petre Solomon's *Paul Celan: Dimensiunea românească* (Paul Celan: The Romanian Dimension), already available in French and now being translated into English.

[2] On Ghérasim Luca, see *WLT* 62:1 (Winter 1988), p. 67.

[3] Norman Manea, "Censor's Report," *Formations*, 5:3 (Winter-Spring 1990), p. 105.

[4] Ibid., p. 106. See also Alexandru George, "Scrisoare deschisă lui Norman Manea," *România Literară*, September 1990.

RUSSIA

The Intellectual Crisis, the Demise of Totalitarianism, and the Fate of Literature

Today, in the post-communist world, we are experiencing a phenomenal moment of truth, and in order to understand much of what is happening in our current literary process, it is necessary to relate what we experienced in our social consciousness when *perestroika* began to what is happening today. *Perestroika* did not occur behind the closed doors of a labor camp, but rather emerged from under totalitarian control and proceeded to develop before the eyes of the whole world. Yes, it seems all the more apparent now that *perestroika* was a great act of historical insight which was achieved by much suffering. It freed the former Soviet society from the illusions and dogma of socialism. Alienated and self-satisfied with personal, unrealizable ideas, we embarked upon the wave of the new historical thinking toward deep-seated inner transformation, toward political and social reforms enticing us to the limits of a civilization common to all.

The freedom of the word and of the spirit, of which we, as a mighty world power, had been deprived during the so-called class struggle and the era of communist demagoguery, became for us not simply the freedom to congregate and to think in a mundane fashion. For us, this freedom became tantamount to a re-creation of the world in which we lived, to a reinterpretation of destinations. It meant a breach through the fabric of the social illusions and unrealizable Utopias which fruitlessly devoured the strength and labor of millions of people and of many generations; a breach through the legalized forms of state and ideological rape as an instrument of authoritarian supremacy. It meant a breach through the fabric of general hypocrisy that dwelled unmistakably in the particular aspect of justifying amorality as the ruling and propagating form of social and private life in the service of literature. Most important of all, we broke through into a new way of life that allows us to recog-

Chingiz Aitmatov (*N. Kochneva*)

nize one priority over all others: the rights and freedoms of the individual in a democratic society, where the state serves the interests of the individual. All this portended a chance for a new existence; all this demanded the indefatigable struggle of the spirit in the process of reconstruction.

Little time passed, however, before the extra-reformist romanticism and euphoria evaporated, unfortunately, like youthful dreams, a process which occurred before our very eyes and was visible to the whole world. On the road to *perestroika* we were beset by perplexing difficulties whose characteristics and possibilities none of our contemporaries anywhere in the world could fathom. I think that neither gods nor prophets nor other political prognosticators suggested that the reorganization was fated to become burdened by such internal conflicts, such unprecedented contradictory developments, which are the essence of the new discoveries in the natural laws of social dialectics, even perhaps in the laws of the general nature of history. And really, *perestroika* has enabled us to fathom such infinite aspects of people's lives: the depths of disaster at the disintegration of totalitarian regimes and all sorts of perspectives which elevate humanity, presenting the right of freedom to the individual as a subject of the universe. The right to dare to take risks, the right to act on one's own fear and peril—these were half opened to us on our way to radical democracy.

Yes, the cost of *perestroika* has turned out to be bitter and severe. Now there are many people who furiously condemn *perestroika* because it did not live up to their hopes. But these are people who do not comprehend the global significance of *perestroika* in the context of the twentieth century. Only our successors will evaluate this phenomenon completely over time.

The events of the past years have also affected to a radical degree the literary process of that ideological configuration and creative technology called socialist realism. Heralded in its day by committed revolutionaries of culture, socialist realism posited as a distinct ideological precept the depiction of reality in its revolutionary development, which in practice meant taboos in the search for the means of expression and definition of themes, with sanctioned topics treated only in a strictly decreed way. At times formulas for writing literary works were openly proposed by the "party clergy," with only works by persons truly dedicated to the party put forth.

It must be noted in passing that Marxism-Leninism was tending more and more toward the canons of some kind of religion, an irrefutable "class" teaching for all of life's situations, particularly as it concerned spiritual culture, art, and philosophy. The reader was trained to believe that, first and foremost, literature exists to serve the interests of the idea, that it is not obliged to reflect his individual life, interests, cares, and experiences, but instead will constantly instill in him how he should live, how he should exist according to communist directives. As a result of the thoroughness and the duration of this process, a totally unique mentality developed which made the inhabitants of the former Soviet Union almost seem to be people selected for a special mission. This fact is important for our discussion, for it now affects rather strongly the situation of the writer seeking his new place under conditions which have changed fundamentally.

What Solzhenitsyn called "double thought" was created not so much by official propaganda as by literature and art. Today a people that had become accustomed to looking to literature for, if not a guidebook to living, at least a didactic premise, still looks for it out of inertia but does not find it, thus heaping blame on the writer both for his past lies and for the fact that he

neither says anything comforting nor calls his people to go anywhere. Meanwhile the writer is in the same quandary as everyone else, because it is not within anyone's power to give sense to the magnitude of changes still taking place so precipitously.

Moreover, the writer was confronted with a problem simply unknown to him before he had to act in accordance with the laws of the market, for the publishing industry and means of mass communication first entered into business based on the market. Today the writer has complete freedom to choose his topics and the means for developing the theme, but he is totally dependent on the tyranny of mass tastes, which, willingly or not, he fostered. The writer can satisfy this taste, but then he enters the embrace of cultural consumer goods, where a book bears an imprint dictated by the will of the marketplace. Even so, after what people in the arts experienced in the Procrustean bed of socialist realism, the market opens to literature a new phase in democratic freedoms and in artistic perspectives.

It seems to me that the problem of the conflict between the spirit and power is the most critical theme taken from our experience of the recent past, one which has universal significance for the creative world. One may say that during the Soviet epoch this problem reached its apogee, having given birth to the phenomenon of conformity as a means of survival.

"The artist and power" is a fundamental problem in intellectual culture. In order to imagine, figuratively speaking, the "environment" of the problem, let us turn our attention to what we have inherited from the present century, which is already coming to an end, keeping in mind the global consortium. In the nineteenth century only 10 percent of the planet's population lived in countries with a democratic social structure; 20 percent lived under monarchies, 70 percent in colonies. Now 50 percent of the earth's people live under stable democratic conditions, 35 percent of them in totally new and developing social structures, formerly nonexistent, which are growing out of the ruins of totalitarianism. (I have in mind here the countries of the former USSR and the countries of Eastern Europe.) The other 50 percent of mankind lives in countries which we call the Third World. This is the geopolitical distribution we now have. Under these conditions, naturally, the artist is in one kind of political situation or another and in one way or another comes in contact with what we call the ruling element—that is, with the problem of "the artist and power."

It is difficult to imagine that there were times when the artist was left entirely free and independent in his creativity, independent of his surroundings, first and foremost independent of those who held power. It is doubtful whether such times could have occurred. Such a state of affairs naturally left a deep impression on the interrelationships between the artist and power, seemingly confirming some kind of systemic order. On the basis of personal experience I can say that I too was included in this order of things. I will choose the case of the artist who, be he a singer, poet, or painter, upon coming in contact with power, found himself, gently speaking, in the role of a courtier. In our time, a time which expired with the advent of *perestroika*, he played the role of a servant of the party. To varying degrees, many exceptional figures of world culture in various countries suffered similar fates. The court poet, the court painter, the court singer, the court dancer, and so on, was the defined status of the artist in various epochs.

The dependency of the artist on those in power was always obvious in our time, but especially after the October Revolution it took on an extremely peculiar character: a dictator appeared not as a dictator per se but in the name of the people, announcing himself to be ruling in their name and in their interests. It seems to me—and this deals primarily with the countries of the former socialist bloc—that many were touched by this phenomenon in their own time. Of course, other people thought about it before we did; there have been legends preserved about it. I would like to relate, very briefly, one legend from the steppes which I keep in my heart. It is about that ultimate power upon which an artist may find himself dependent. A singer who was known in those parts, while serving at the court of his ruler, was forced to accompany his lord as matchmaker to his very own bride and to extol the merits of the khan. He was forced to congratulate the one with whom he lived on his great good fortune.

There are many similar examples from both the past and the present, because serving power is one of the most dramatic and tragic situations in the life of an artist. However, there are, of course, examples of another kind, from Solzhenitsyn to Maximov. The names of such major but contradictory figures as Gorky and Mayakovsky, on the one hand, and Mandelstam, Platonov, Bulgakov, and Pasternak on the other, and how they interacted with power, come to mind from our most recent history. In their time such prominent figures in the West as Romain Rolland, Henri Barbusse, Lion Feuchtwanger, André Gide, and other personalities of art and literature who were attracted by the idea of socialism, having been hypnotized by Stalin and his fateful propaganda, facilitated the phenomenon of conformity in Soviet culture to no small degree.

I would like to call attention to the fact that the concept of socialist realism in such a context may be considered as one of the manifestations of the problem of "the artist and power," for the party spirit and the natural character of literature—the two components of the concept—served as political guidelines, as it were. Having been drawn into literature individually and creating it each in his or her own way, we behaved like conformists under these circumstances, and soon this seemed to be the normal state of affairs; we subjugated ourselves to the great idea, to its political strength. What compels us now, however, at a time which is very unstable, very complicated for our society, is the attempt to impart sense to the eternal riddle of the interrelationship of the artist and power.

It seems to me that there is a guiding star which attracts us all. I have in mind the idea of freedom; the human spirit has been striving for it ever since it became aware of itself. This idea is eternal, because it is unattainable to the extent we all would like to have it. The two principles, power and the artist, unavoidably collide en route toward the acquisition of freedom. Ever since the word acquired the power to inspire, the power of an act of will, the word and everything associated with it—the art of comprehending peace and the internal spirit of man—it has been in a direct opposition to what power stands for, from the beginning of human society. It is not at all coincidental, moreover, that power has an interest in attracting the artist to its side, be he great or small; as our life has shown, power is not particularly discriminating in that respect. It tries to exploit art in any way it can for egotistical, political, or governmental interests. On the other hand, the artist is constantly preoccupied with his position relative to those who hold power. Of course, we are not speaking about personal relations, although there are various kinds, some of which can even be friendly. The position of the artist nevertheless becomes more complicated if he tries to include himself in the governing system, if he tries to define his positions through creativity. As a rule, this results in a drama of the soul. I would like to draw attention precisely to this resistance, which is primal, historical, and in some respects predestined. An artist's striving for freedom and its acknowledged self-limitation lingers both on the conscience of personality and on the conscience of the epoch.

I remember Bertolucci's film *The Conformist*. I could not get this picture out of my mind for a long time. I did not immediately understand it. I was constantly reflecting on what in fact was happening. What was it that hypnotically bound me to that film? What was the tragedy? What was the hero's drama? Only in recent years, when, thanks to *perestroika* and *glasnost',* our thinking had been elevated to a new level, when had begun trying to see our history in a new way and to present ourselves in a new way, did it dawn on me that I understood what was going on in the film. It is as if that film were one of our fates. For me *The Conformist* is an example of the theme of "the artist and power." The artist opts to compromise with power because of the force of circumstances and becomes a conformist figure. This state of affairs is wrapped in tragedy for the artist; he is a sacrifice, whereas the acquisitive or conquering side is power.

On one hand, we cannot avoid power in one form or another, but on the other hand, we cannot subjugate ourselves completely to it, as those who hold power would desire. It seems to me that, in this conflict, particularly bitter experience and great dramas have been the lot of artists of the twentieth century. Fascism and Stalinism had remarkably similar effects. An objectionable thinker, an objectionable artist, an objectionable poet, an objectionable philosopher was not only censured but was also declared a phenomenon hostile and foreign to the people. The bearers of noncanonical ideas were inevitably subjected to persecution and even destruction.

The rhetoric and demagoguery of fascism and Stalinism are strikingly similar; there was constant speculation on the concepts of nationality and the instructive, didactic role of art and how it should serve some kind of social ideals. Moreover, the other qualities of literature and art which are capable of awakening the spirit of quest or of introducing an imbalance into official ideology were "forgotten." Looking back over the course we have taken, we see that the artist stood before a great temptation. Totalitarian regimes could seduce and entice the artist, encourage him and reward him with all manner of titles with the aim of completely "assimilating" him, of drawing him into the ideological orbit. And, though it was possible to object to a king, a prince, or an autocrat, even if only as a jester, during the epoch of fascism and Stalinism even such a pitiful protest by an artist was completely excluded.

The existence of totalitarian regimes was an instructive lesson for history overall, and for us as figures of literature and the arts. The regimes of Hitler, Stalin, and Mao Zedong left their mark on us, a deep impression. We still bear within ourselves what was inculcated in us during those years, and if today we speak of a post-communist revolution, the revolutionary nature of these processes liberates us from the fetters and chains of the past. We are only now extricating ourselves from the totalitarian trap to the extent that we are overcoming the fear which had fatally shackled a culture, an art, a nation, man himself, his thought, his milieu, and the

light in his eyes; we begin to be aware of why man lives on this frail earth.

In my opinion, the ruinous and erroneous nature of our ideologies lay in the fact that we assured ourselves and others that such categories as truth and fairness, after we get to know them once and for all, are defined forever. However, the level of truth and fairness we have achieved today will tomorrow become a phase of the past. They tried to convince us that we already serve a certain absolute truth; this was our misfortune. Many tried to distance themselves as artists, but artists can also be weak, as people. Still, the artist's works, and those of others like him, express the age-old urge of the human spirit toward freedom and beauty. It now finds a concrete expression in repealing the delusions of socialist realism, in the struggle for democracy, for freedom of thought and for personal rights. Even in this arena, however, the artist is confronted with what this or that power purports to be. This power is not always personified in a certain single name or person. It is the system of contemporary governmental structures, of contemporary political organizations.

Of course, freedom from external factors created by any power would be the most ideal situation for an artist, but this is probably an unrealizable dream of mine. It is scarcely possible. The artist is included in real life in one way or another. It is important that each of us answer to himself how much he, as an artist, is at ease with his conscience; is he in harmony with his time, and is this harmony possible? Other thinkers affirm that the artist must be without fail a creature of suffering, a subject not of this world, and if not an exile, then surely possessed of a wounded, tormented soul. I do not know. I am not sure. I dare not think that a wounded bird with an injured wing is the best variant for flight on high; it is the same with a man of the arts. And whatever fate has in store often depends on Providence.

We are already in the post-Soviet era. The dawn of a new history is glowing over Eurasia. The volcano of events continues to erupt.

Many years ago there was a paradoxical event I often recall now. I got into a conversation in the United States with a certain American writer, who said, "How I envy you Soviet writers; they send you to prison, exile you, criticize you in the newspapers and at party meetings, denounce the slanderers of Soviet society," and so on in this vein. "You have the respect and authority of the people. The people see the writer as a defender. But here in America no one considers us as people, write what you will, do what you want; if only a single soul paid attention to your work, if only they would accuse you of something, demand your expulsion, or even got upset. . . . I would be glad to go to prison, any day. But no, there is no reaction; they, the Americans, are indifferent to us. In America we are, in this sense, no one and nothing. At home, you are exalted people; the pages of history await you." I wondered then about the improbable absurdity of his judgments. Now it turns out he was right on several counts.

Within the bounds of the former imperial state the writer and belles lettres have lost their formerly sacrosanct status, that certain halo of the righteous. Times have changed markedly. The need to read troubling, forbidden thoughts into a subtext has disappeared; there is no need to retype in *samizdat* the epistles of the exiled apostles and prophets. These compositions are now available in abundance on the literary market. No one writes "for the desk drawer" any more. The "early Christian" situation of the pre-*perestroika* martyrs and just individuals is over in this sense, having left behind a nostalgic trace in our souls. "What goes around, comes around."

There is, however, one sphere in which the writer can possibly be returned to his pedestal and, to a degree, move beyond competition in the marketplace: namely, the realm of a national culture, serving national interests such as the problem of nationalism. Of course the theme of a national renaissance, of the suffering of the national soul, which, given the increased intensity of the ethnic factor in politics, bewitches and charges the reader with a particularly intensified sensitivity to idea of a nation, becomes a new America, a new devotion. This factor, if it is deemed to become a long-term factor, is fraught with risks of the restoration of totalitarianism, though on a smaller scale than the former totalitarianism of the Soviets, and it bears the same birthmarks and carries with it the self-isolation of nations which have just received the opportunity to emerge into the worldwide cultural space. An example of this is the long-suffering Georgian nation of today.

It is possible to look at what happened from another point of view. During the course of half a century the world was precisely organized on a binary principle: two superpowers determined the earth's counterpoints, and this bipolar system incorporated without exception all manifestations of historical existence. Enemies locked in close combat form a stronger bond between themselves than friendship could ever forge; any movement from one dictates an adequate response from the other. This has doubtless happened in the area of culture: the ideologization on one side prompted a spiritual opposition on the other, albeit less apparent. The ideological binarism has now collapsed. What follows? Should its multiplicity of national oppositions not be replaced as well? Modern communications have com-

pelled the physical interaction of ethnic groups which had formerly been removed from one another. There arises not so much a force of unification, of the search for points of mutual understanding, as a sense that each national culture is being threatened. Paradoxically, it is precisely now, when civilization's achievements are making possible the creation of a rational worldwide order, one within our strength and understanding, that the psychology of the besieged fortress is gaining strength; this is burdensome if not suicidal for any culture. The Western world has great apprehensions about the growth of Islamic fundamentalism and its possible consolidation because of the exaggerated potential of the Moslem republics of the former Soviet Union. The Third World—which no longer deserves this numeric designation in light of the changed conditions—is horrified by the collapse of the USSR and by its now virtually total dependence on the West, particularly on American mass culture. Europe, uniting economically and politically, is guardedly debating the future of its national cultures.

Here I must note that it seems as though certain features of the communist ghost, attracting the popular masses with its collectivist ideals of general fairness and equality, once again are being manifested in the form of contemporary fundamentalism. The similarity is caused primarily by the ideology of totalitarianism. The theosophy of Islam and the "theosophy" of communism are closely related. It may be, however, that the differences between them are more substantial. Although both thrust happiness on mankind according to a strictly defined recipe, communism proceeds from constructs, no matter how speculative they may be, whereas fundamentalism leans on the powerful support of divine revelation. Communism saw the basis for future happiness in the dominant role of the world proletariat; it made internationalism its banner, discarding and trampling the deeply ingrained emotions of a specific national character. In contrast, Islamic fundamentalism calls strongly upon the national and religious feelings of Moslems, bringing to mind thereby the infringements on Moslem worthiness during the period of colonialism. Simply stated, fundamentalists remind Moslems of their former grandeur, of the Shining Port, of victories in battle which caused all Europe to tremble before the green banner, indicating that returning Islam to its fundamental values, to its initial purity, will again place Islam at the head of the world.

Islam's theocratic totalitarianism is also attractive, among other reasons, because in place of the torments of individual selection and conscious individual responsibility for the consequences of this moral choice, it offers the psychological comfort of the collective conscience, one dedicated, moreover, to a religious tradition of many centuries. Today Moslem fundamentalism is a political phenomenon. It plays an isolationist role in culture, negating even the Moslem culture of the past, such as the illustrious phenomenon of Sufism.

Hence a conclusion comes to mind. The question of the relationship of the general with the particular, of the universal with the peculiar, the national with the universal is no longer a topic of academic discussion but rather a factor which plays a role in determining a culture's course of development. Based on the experience of our own country, we know well that it is harmful to impose on a culture functions which are not inherent to it or to demand of literature that which it cannot do by nature. Therefore all discussions of the unifying function—or problem—of literature are simply untenable. Moreover, literature certainly possesses a social function, and it is very important to understand what this is. Apparently, we have to put in first place a spiritual understanding of life in all its manifestations, an understanding which cannot help but be nationally conditioned, because literature does not exist outside language, whereas language bears within itself all the traits of a people, everything that distinguishes one people from all others. However, if the idea of a common meaning is expressed through this particularity, then what we call "great literature" is born. It is not necessary to talk about how literature of this magnitude possesses an immense unifying force; everyone knows this from his or her own experience. The striving toward freedom of the spirit has always been and will be the central idea of great literature.

We have become witnesses to and participants in unique feats in the history of the global social mind, an explosion from within an ideologized totalitarian structure and, along with this, a conscious, voluntary union of the peoples and governments of Europe into an entirely different structure, for which the sole common ideology lies in achieving a common good based on coordinated integration. One may debate what role literature played in the disintegration of the socialist camp, but there is no argument that it has not yet taken part in the creation of a European community.

Does this mean that literature, which includes the eternal spirit of search and protest, is more rapidly and more easily becoming a weapon in the struggle against oppression rather than an instrument of the union which is being created? One wants to see European unification as a model for a future world structure, as the prototype of a possible rational search for the coexistence and interaction of nations. But can it be coincidental that among the multiplicity of the associations coordinating services, those intended for cultural unification are totally lacking?

On the contrary, within the community there is alarm concerning its future national cultures. Inasmuch as literature does not exist outside language, it turns out to be in an extremely unfavorable position compared to music, art, ballet, cinematography, and so on. Of course, one may presume that a certain translation and editing infrastructure will be created, one which will expand the free circulation of literature. This is within human capabilities. Meanwhile, however, the European author is confronting another matter: the dominance of a standardized American mass culture, a danger he acknowledges but cannot oppose. Desirous of defending and preserving his own national culture, will he not proceed on the path of nationalism, on the path which is, in the final analysis, in opposition to the integration processes? Racist tendencies are intensifying on fertile ground in Europe, in a wealthy and sated Europe and not in the overpopulated countries of the Third World or here, where all this is temptingly easy to explain by economic competition, the struggle for a place in the sun. The dialectical contradiction between nationalism and universalism, in all its aspects, requires the deepest and most serious formulation by everyone who writes.

Speaking of contradictions, there is a presage that what is happening in our country now, that self-conflicting spirit which is now shaking Russia, cannot but spill over into art and cannot help but finally produce a great literature. It seemed that such a literature of "universal revelation" could have been spawned, for example, by the great shock we all experienced in 1917, which accompanied the civil war, but the onset of totalitarianism trampled this literature under from its very inception. I pray to God that no such occurrence is repeated in the history and cultures of the nations of the Commonwealth of Independent States.

In the last decade of the twentieth century the world has suddenly collided with changes which no one foresaw or could have foreseen; the disintegration of the Soviet Union is not the end of such changes but merely a beginning, for in place of an ideological monolith, a superpower which determined the world's climate by the very fact of its existence, something different will surely arise. What will this be? Only God Almighty could answer that question. However, it is not predicting all the consequences of what has already happened which occupies us at this precise moment, but rather the effect of the changes on cultural processes, primarily literature. Moreover, given all the grandiosity of what has happened, this is not the only change. Literature is now truly at a turning point, but mankind is at a crossroads. Who knows which path it should follow?

Behind these events, which precipitated a deep intellectual crisis, a shift is occurring in the creative tendencies in art and literature. In particular, postmodernist literature, especially its underground phase, is making itself more and more widely known. It is acceptable to think that in art modernism and postmodernism are related in the following manner: if the search for an internal, unapparent sense and internal form hidden behind external phenomena characterizes modernism, postmodernism perceives and reflects a world in which coincidence and anarchy dominate. The sense of deconstructivism consists, as far as one can judge, in the fundamental lack of a unified approach and fixed point of view, in fundamentally infinite approaches and combinations, which of necessity result in the disappearance of the primary subject, the main hero, and the main idea from works of art, especially literature.

The linear and one-dimensional rationalism which ruled in the minds of the post-Enlightenment era was wrecked by the near-contemporaneity of World War I and Einstein's development of the theory of relativity; that is, the structured and accessible Newtonian universe came tumbling down along with concepts of a rational world order. However, if the subsequent headspinning scientific discoveries made the Newtonian universe or Euclidian geometry part of a general and extremely more complicated picture without changing either of them, social processes seemingly confirmed the irrationality, the anarchy, and the unpredictability of human social behavior. The shredding of conscience and the confusion of living in this world are the bases of postmodernism, deconstructivism, and everything else which will unavoidably arise during the search process.

I would like to note that, given the degree of interest in this search and given all its irrefutable findings, it nevertheless remains the property of a significantly narrow circle of intellectuals, persons who have been prepared to perceive it. Paradoxically, postmodernism is clearing the way for a still broader dissemination of mass culture, which, while preserving the narrative fabric in art, is capable, where required to do so, of camouflaging itself with intellectual respectability. As for the philosophical aspect of postmodernism, it will appear before us as a paradigm of social and cultural consciousness which is limited in time and space by the West at the end of the twentieth century.

Having looked at these problems from the angle of vision of the East, whose philosophical and esthetic thought will enter its sixth millennium in eight years, the picture will appear before us as being of somewhat greater volume, and it will take on a certain stereoscopic nature. Eastern thought defines the task of art as that of an instrument for drawing nearer to that higher reality, to a higher harmony, forcing man to search for and discover it within himself and his environment. During the Renaissance, Western artistic thought elevated man to the throne of the universe, after having deposed God. Today man has fallen from the throne—which, it turned out, was not his size—and abides in confusion. Eastern thought has always seen man as a cosmic being who must realize, for harmonious existence in the cosmos, his place within it and subordinate himself to its laws.

We are faced with seeing what it is that will bring about the interpenetration of Western and Eastern thought for mankind. There can be no doubt that this interpenetration will be beneficial. This is, however, a question for the future. I would like to turn to an analysis of just what postmodernism is amid the ruins of the Soviet empire. In its formal traits, post-communist postmodernism is fundamentally no different from its counterpart in the West: the same shattered conscience, the same rapid succession of thematic developments, or the general absence of a theme as it is usually understood, the same fabricated reality which is capable at any time of transforming itself into whatever one may desire. However, the origin of this phenomenon within the former Soviet Union has nothing in common with its origin in the West. Under the conditions in the former Soviet Union, postmodernism, the literature of yesterday's underground, stands opposed not to modernism but to yesterday's socialist realism. Soviet postmodernism is being created by those who formulated life in a paradoxical world, a fairy-tale world forcibly concocted by real life, in a reality which contradicts normal moral instincts.

Today's creators of postmodernist literature are yesterday's Soviet underground, writers who were driven into clandestine activity. It seemed to them as though while underground they were composing a literature of truth to offset the programmed official lie; and in fact, one may say that much of what was created underground in the pre-*perestroika* era, which reflected the Soviet way of life inside out, was in essence closer than the official version to the most ordinary realism—though with a hint of a surprise, it is true.

However, the underground, which has now surfaced, has collided with a reality which is so complex and contradictory and, moreover, changing with such speed, that its constant battle with socialist realism has turned out to be simply absurd. Furthermore, the literature of fact, of the documentary, which has burst forth on the pages of the periodical press, affects the reading masses in the most direct manner, thereby retarding the search for innovative expressiveness on a mundane level.

It cannot be said that an ideological and totalitarian course of development is no longer possible; alas, such a course conceals within itself a multiplicity of temptations, just as the democratic course of development still conceals an enormous potential. Today we note the opposition of two tendencies: integration and nationalistic factionalism. I will not talk about the entire set of factors prodding mankind in one direction or the other. I am speaking about a literature in which both a certain standardization (invariably accompanied by integration processes in other spheres) and a departure into chauvinistic self-isolation (which is suicidal for it) are equally contra-indicated. The atmosphere of free inquiry, a situation in which the writer, in the words of Molière, takes the good where he sees it, is the most fruitful for literature. Wherever this good may be found, the writer—if he is no epigone, of course—passes it through the filter of his national consciousness and artistic vision.

Literature can plant its roots in a national soil; it can be nurtured by multicultural roots. Such a literature has sprung up right before our eyes and is successfully developing. This is not what we are talking about. Picasso once said that in art it is not the quest but the result which is important. Literature cannot be prescribed or programmed; then it is called propaganda, regardless of its form. Nevertheless, the writer cannot help but get caught up in the question of why he writes. Of course, each has his or her own answer to this question; but the whole experience of world literature, its entire history, demonstrates that art which carries immutable values while reflecting the disharmony of the human soul recalls stable aspirations for harmony.

Chingiz Aitmatov, Winter 1993, translated by
Alexandra Heidi Karriker

"In the Middle of the Contrast": Andrei Bitov and the Act of Writing in the Contemporary World

The evaluation of writers can take many shapes. For an assessment of the contemporary Russian writer Andrei Bitov,[1] say, one could, for example, place him in his historical and cultural context—that is, one could place him within the context of Soviet culture, society, and history. One could discuss the way in which he, like others of his generation, came to maturity at the time of the loosening up of society that came with the death of Stalin and the proclamation by Khrushchev, in 1956,

of the de-Stalinization of Soviet society. This generation, the so-called children of the Twentieth Party Congress, learned to be freer than the generation of its parents had been.

In literature the post-Stalin "thaw" era saw, among other tendencies, the emergence of "youth prose," writing that was centered in the literary journal *Iunost'* (Youth). Youth prose featured urban, rebellious youth enamored of Western culture, style, and music (often jazz). Vassily Aksyonov's novel *Zvezdnyi bilet* (1961; Eng. *A Ticket to the Stars*)[2] contained youthful protagonists whose attitudes and actions linked them to their distant American brother Holden Caulfield, the major character in J. D. Salinger's influential novel *The Catcher in the Rye*.[3] Youth prose, including some of Bitov's earliest stories of the 1950s and early 1960s, often portrayed less-than-perfect "heroes" whose individual subjective realities and less-than-perfect lives were a far cry from the objective depictions of reality and the positive heroes required in socialist-realist literature, the type of literature that had been prescribed in the Soviet Union since the early years of the Stalin era. Many of the youth-prose writers, like Bitov and Aksyonov, later went on to develop their own unique literary voices.

In assessing the writings of Bitov, one could also investigate the way in which he belongs to a particular piece of the history of Russian literature—that is, to the so-called Petersburg tradition. The Petersburg writers, from Alexander Pushkin and Fyodor Dostoevsky in the nineteenth century, to the poets Osip Mandelstam and Anna Akhmatova in the earlier part of the twentieth century, to Bitov, Joseph Brodsky, Yevgeny Rein, and Alexander Kushner among living Russian writers, have always felt that they are self-conscious preservers and continuators of the cultural traditions of Petersburg. In fact, Bitov's major novel is called *Pushkinskii dom* (1978; Eng. *Pushkin House*),[4] named after the nineteenth-century writer as well as after the Soviet Academy of Sciences Literary Institute in Leningrad. Pushkin's famous poem "Mednyi vsadnik" (Eng. "The Bronze Horseman") had been dubbed by its author a "Petersburg tale." Bitov calls his novel a "Leningrad novel."

In analyzing Bitov's works, one could also examine features of his individual creative biography. We could study his writings to date and describe his evolution: from his earliest playful ministries, to his travelogues about distant parts of the Soviet Union, to his short stories and novels documenting the psychological adventures of young men, contemporaries of the author, over a period of some twenty years. One could point to Bitov's varied creative output, to his essays on literature and on the cinema, and to the role he has played in the years since the beginning of *glasnost'*. One could discuss his presentations on television and his contributions to round tables on previously banned Russian literature. One could discuss his role as president of Russia's newly formed PEN Writers Club, as he has sought funding in the West to support Russian writers at this crucial, precarious time in the history of post-Soviet Russia.

In talking about Bitov's oeuvre, one could offer thematic overviews of his works. One could talk about the importance, for Bitov, of the themes of self-deception, of lies that people tell themselves. One could concentrate on Bitov's highlighting, in his writings, the gap between reality and illusion. One could focus on his powerful fictional documentation of the effects of Stalin on his generation. One could emphasize his attention to the cultural ties that he believes bind all people, works of art, and cultural phenomena that are authentic.

For an assessment of Andrei Bitov's writings in relation to contemporary Russian life of the early 1990s, I prefer to take a more unorthodox approach, an approach that asks the reader to stretch and bend his or her imagination. After the death, in 1980, of one of the Soviet Union's most beloved and highly respected "unofficial" cultural figures, the actor and "poet-balladeer" Vladimir Vysotsky, another poet-balladeer and fiction writer, Bulat Okudzhava,[5] was asked about the significance of Vysotsky's life and art. Okudzhava explained that an artist has thinner skin than do other people. It is therefore, according to Okudzhava, the artist who is the first to cry out about society's and the world's problems.

In fact, from our own knowledge of history and culture, we know that writers can sometimes have an uncanny sense of social forces that are only much later documented by historians and social scientists. Dostoevsky, for instance, wrote *The Possessed,* his scathing attack on nineteenth-century Russian terrorists and revolutionaries, in 1871. The Bolshevik Revolution took place decades later, in 1917, yet over the years readers and commentators have noted Dostoevsky's seeming prescience. In his commentary to *Pushkin House*[6] Bitov states that artistic influence can be an extraordinarily complicated process. He explains, for example, that Dostoevsky has had a marked influence on actual life in the Soviet Union. Therefore, Bitov continues, when a contemporary author describes life and it seems as if he is writing under the influence of Dostoevsky, it is important to recall that life itself has begun to imitate Dostoevsky.

Now, how does all of this relate to Bitov as a writer? He often writes about the dissolution of boundaries between and among seemingly disparate realms of life. He writes about the melting of boundaries between life and literature, between art and life, between one literary work and another, between one culture and another culture, between past and present, between one individual human being and another individual human being, between one biological species and another. He has also written about having written something and about then having that thing happen in life. He has joked about the fact that he therefore never writes about death.

Much of Bitov's published work was written between the 1960s and the late 1970s. Let us examine some of these writings, fictional and nonfictional, in the curious context of events that *later* happened in Soviet and Russian history and culture.

Over the years, Bitov has written travelogues about his experiences in different republics of the Soviet Union. Two of his most powerful works, *Uroki Armenii* (Eng. "Armenia Lessons") and *Gruzinskii al'bom* (Eng. "Georgian Album"), single out the cultures of Armenia and Georgia respectively.[7] Given the recent breakup of the Soviet Union, it seems in hindsight as though Bitov were writing as a kind of "response" to the existence of brutal, intolerant ethnic strife. What Bitov does in "Armenia Lessons," for example, is sing the praises of acknowledging the qualities that are unique to Armenian culture *and,* concomitantly, insist that any culture, in its specific, unique reflections, is thereby inextricably bound to any and all other cultures in *their* specific, unique reflections. For Bitov, the quality that serves as a transcendental link between one unique culture and another is "authenticity" (*podlinnost'*).

In "Georgian Album" too, Bitov describes his experiences in that Soviet republic and points to the ways in which he senses strong ties of commonality between himself, a Russian, and Georgians whom he meets. One Georgian reminds him of a member of his family. During another episode recounted in "Georgian Album" he suddenly feels that, although he does not know the Georgian language, so different from Russian, he nevertheless understands it. Thus, even before the end of communist rule hastened the flare-up of nationalist and ethnic friction, Bitov was speaking in the name of tolerance and the commonalities that bind seemingly disparate cultures.

There are other ways in which Bitov's works, written over twenty years ago, speak directly to some of the major concerns of Russia today. Some of the issues surface in his masterpiece, *Pushkin House.* In an interview in 1989 Bitov himself even alluded to some of the contemporary resonances of the novel that he finished writing in 1971. He stated, "Mitishatiev is a potential leader of a nationalist party, of Pamyat, for example."[8] Mitishatiev, one of the major characters in *Pushkin House,* is an old school buddy of Leva Odoevtsev, the novel's main protagonist. In certain key scenes of the novel Mitisha-tiev makes ugly, anti-Semitic remarks. In his 1989 references to Pamyat (Memory) Bitov is of course referring to the ultranationalist, anti-Semitic group that has been active in the Soviet Union and now, in the post-Soviet Union, since the *glasnost'* era of the 1980s.

There are still other ways in which *Pushkin House* is relevant to some of the issues of contemporary Russia. One of these has to do, significantly, with culture itself, with the role that culture has played in the past and will now play in post-Soviet society. It is no secret that high culture has not fared well in post-coup Russia with its "free-market economy." Without government subsidies, publishing houses, journals, and newspapers have folded. Writers and scholars accustomed to circulation figures of 100,000 for their books of poetry, prose, and literary analysis are lucky now to get their books published at all in Russia. A typical scenario is for the publisher to demand a hefty subsidy, in dollars, from the author, and only then to publish the book if the author agrees to distribute the book himself or herself.

These days, if one looks through the Russian weekly newspaper *Knizhnoe Obozrenie* (Book Survey), the lists of books published for the week contain few works of Russian literature, few works of literature at all, and many works dealing with subjects such as how to be a manager. A decade ago a thriving black market in books sold, often for the equivalent of an average Soviet citizen's monthly salary, literary masterpieces that had been banned by the political authorities. Now those same works, no longer prohibited, hardly appear at all on the tables of books for sale that are on display on Moscow streets and near subway stops throughout the city. One might see one lone book by Vladimir Nabokov or Osip Mandelstam or the Soviet absurdist Daniil Kharms, almost lost among pornographic works, detective novels, books about dog breeding, Dale Carnegie's *How to Win Friends and Influence People* (in Russian translation), nude calendars, books on mysticism, a volume on weapons, and pictures of the last czar. Very often the books of literature are much cheaper than those about how to start your own business, how to have enjoyable sex, and how to tap into your mystical powers. Cassettes of Madonna fetch much higher prices than do those of classical pianists or violinists.

When we examine some of the key ideas in *Pushkin House,* we see that Bitov, years ago, had referred to some of the cultural tendencies that are prevalent in Moscow or Petersburg today. One of the paradoxes with which Bitov deals in *Pushkin House* is the result of the traumatic rupture of life brought about by Stalin. The novel as a whole tells the story of a young man, Leva, who was born in 1937, at the height of the purges, and who grew up in a Soviet society whose every niche was stuffed with the lies Stalin forced upon that society. Over and over again, Bitov points out the tragedies that befell the tainted society whose legacy was Stalin.

A major character in the novel is Leva's grandfather, Modest Platonovich Odoevtsev, whose own life had been ruined by Stalin: he had been arrested and had spent many years in Stalin's concentration camps. Modest Platonovich cries out about some of the paradoxes that characterize Soviet society in the face of the dislocations caused by Stalin. In a long speech to his grandson he refers to a paradoxical piece of the Stalinist legacy: namely, that Russian literature, from the eighteenth century to the 1920s, is, like a wildlife preserve, safe. Thus, what we come to understand from Modest Platonovich's words is the fact that precisely because of the lack of continuity in culture caused by the tragedy of Soviet history, Russian literature of the past could not be deformed. He also goes on to attack a consumer attitude toward culture, saying that that is what will destroy culture. And of course, this is what we see happening now in Russia.

The very fate of the elder Odoevtsev is one which is all too familiar to many of the intelligentsia in present-day Russia. Modest Platonovich explains, again paradoxically, that he had not become a broken man when he was arrested and when he spent time in the camps. He earnestly admits that had he been the regime, he would have arrested someone like himself. He says that he fell apart only after he was rehabilitated, for that meant, he argues, that he had spent all those years in Siberia for nothing. After thirty years, he, a noted scholar whose works had been banned under Stalin, returns to Leningrad a broken man who feels that he has no place in society. (In fact, in one scene he literally cannot find his own apartment building among all the identical-looking apartment buildings on the outskirts of Leningrad.)

What Bitov describes in connection with the fate of Modest Platonovich is surprisingly similar to the situation of the intelligentsia in contemporary Russian society. In years past, prose writers and theater directors, actors and poets, scholars and artists whose views opposed the Soviet regime's were prohibited from publishing, were arrested, were harassed by the KGB. These people had great struggles in Soviet society (think, for instance, of the sufferings of Andrei Sakharov), yet, paradoxically, these same people felt that they played an important role in society. Society needed them.

Now, in a new Russian society that has freedom of speech and that preaches "free-market economy," the cultural figures who struggled for so many years for freedom of artistic expression find themselves irrelevant. The economy is in such a crisis that no one can afford to go to plays, no matter how avant-garde a particular theater might have been considered under Brezhnev. Film directors can make films only by obtaining financial sponsorship from the West. Highly respected writers spend more and more time in the West, for they can barely make ends meet if they rely solely on the home-grown economy. Russian writers, who had always understood that they had the special role of being the conscience of society, now find themselves, like Bitov's Modest Platonovich, being all but ignored in the new society.

These, then, are only a few of the ways in which Bitov's pre-1980s works are particularly relevant as we explore the problems of Russian culture today. But how are we to explain Bitov's apparent prescience? We must, I believe, return to Bulat Okudzhava's statement about artists crying out before anyone else does because their skin is thinner than others'. A writer is doing his or her job well if he or she explores and experiences the world and then records the distant sound waves that reverberate—from the past, the present, and perhaps . . . even from the future? . . .

The narrator in *Pushkin House* remarks that a writer lives in a mysterious realm between life and literature. The writer does not live wholly in life, he goes on, for the writer must spend time writing. Yet the writer, who has not been living life fully, is the source for future generations of what life was like (for people who were living life fully did not have time to record their experiences and observations). The writer lives, says Bitov's narrator, in a special space that he calls "the middle of the contrast." We have just observed some of the activities that take place in "the middle of the contrast."

Ellen Chances, Winter 1993

1 For a comprehensive examination of Bitov's oeuvre, see Ellen Chances, *Andrei Bitov: The Ecology of Inspiration*, New York, Cambridge University Press, forthcoming (fall 1993).

2 Aksyonov's novel first appeared in the journal *Iunost'* (Youth) in June and July 1961.

3 Some Russians had, of course, read Salinger's novel in the original. A translation by R. Rait-Lovaleva was published in the prestigious journal *Inostrannaia Literatura* (Foreign Literature) as "Nad propast'iu vo rzhi," 1960, no. 11, pp. 28–137.

4 The novel first came out in the United States: Andrei Bitov, *Pushkinskii dom*, Ann Arbor, Mi., Ardis, 1978. Its first English edition was published nine years later as *Pushkin House*, Susan Brownsberger, tr., New York, Farrar, Straus & Giroux, 1987. The novel came out in the Soviet Union (bland excerpts had appeared in various journals before the Gorbachev era of *glasnost'*) in complete form in 1989.

5 For an excellent analysis of the significance of Okudzhava and Vysotsky to Soviet culture, see the book by Gerald Stanton Smith, *Songs to Seven Strings: Russian Guitar Poetry and Soviet "Mass Song"*, Bloomington, Indiana University Press, 1984.

6 Bitov's commentary to the novel appears, in Russian, in the 1989 Moscow edition but not in the 1978 Ardis edition. The first edition of the 1987 English translation does not include the commentary, but the 1990 paperback edition (also from Ardis) does.

7 Andrei Bitov, *Uroki Armenii*, Yerevan, 1978; Andrei Bitov, *Gruzinskii al'bom*, Tbilisi, 1985. English translations (as "Armenia Lessons" and "Georgian Album") can be found in Andrei Bitov, *A Captive of the Caucasus*, New York, Farrar, Straus & Giroux, 1992.

8 "Andrei Bitov: 'Ne pas marcher au même pas que l'Histoire, mais rester soi-même'" (interview), *La Quinzaine Littéraire*, no. 525 (1–15 February 1989), p. 7.

Russian Writers Confront the Past: History, Memory, and Literature, 1953–1991

A country in which people have been engaged in mutual destruction for half a century does not like to recall the past. What can we expect to happen in a country with a disordered memory? What is a man worth if he has lost his memory?

▪ NADEZHDA MANDELSTAM, *HOPE ABANDONED*[1]

The Soviet author Yuri Trifonov (1925–81) wrote that "to make sense of the present, one must understand the past."[2] A straight-forward sentiment perhaps, but under the conditions existing in the Soviet Union from Stalin's death until Gorbachev's *perestroika* it was not easy even to learn about the past, let alone understand it. This was especially true of the Brezhnev era, when the crimes and injustices visited upon the populace were only superficially countenanced by the regime. From the outset, however, writers were in the forefront of efforts to rediscover the past, not only to paint an accurate picture of past events but also to examine their consequences several decades on, "in order to make sense of the present."

Since 1985, when Mikhail Gorbachev came to power, and in particular since 1986, when his policy of *glasnost'* in the arts and media was first encouraged, we have seen an unprecedented information explosion in the Soviet Union (as it then was). Gorbachev intended that the Communist Party would be the instrument for reform with his program of *perestroika* from above, and that the freedom to publish criticisms and abuses under *glasnost'* would only enhance the esteem of the party. However, we can now see that, even before the party's last stand against the people in August 1991, its authority and legitimacy to rule had been fatally undermined. The intensive and unprecedented investigation into the "blank spots" of history—those areas previously put out of bounds because of their historical or ideological sensitivity—not only did not enhance the party's reputation, but besmirched and destroyed it irredeemably.

For some people living in the USSR, the Revolution itself was still within living memory, and certainly many, many more could remember the Stalin years. Many thousands of people still had personal and often painful experience of the party's rule from the late 1920s, some of the catastrophic collectivization of agriculture from 1928 to 1930, and the ensuing famine of 1933, others of the Great Purge of the mid-1930s. During the Stalin years, it is estimated, some fifteen to twenty million people died in the Gulag.[3] A further twenty million casualties were claimed in four years of war with Nazi Germany, not all of them the result of enemy action. In the course of the war and afterward, Stalin exiled whole peoples, including some Caucasian peoples, the Volga Germans and the Crimean Tatars, to the inhospitable Kazakh steppes and Central Asia, for alleged collaboration. If we also bear in mind the postwar repressions, arrests, and executions (especially in the arts and higher education), then it would be no exaggeration to say that no Soviet family was left untouched by the effects of Stalin's rule.

In the post-Stalin period, although political arrests and incarcerations were fewer and the Soviet state achieved some degree of prestige in the international arena (especially in the military and technological spheres), ordinary Soviet citizens had little cheer as living standards, especially from the 1970s onward, began to decline. As the years went by, expectations could barely rise above the banal, as energies were taken up increasingly by chores such as shopping, housework, and looking after the family—all things which in the West are much less time-consuming. Indeed, it is little wonder that it took only five years for the party's control to collapse, for its moral authority was already close to zero. *Glasnost'* removed the fear.

Still, it would be wrong to think that the opening up of previously inaccessible areas of history began with Gorbachev. To be sure, one of the first consequences of the Soviet Writers Congress in July 1986 was the severe curtailment—amounting to abolition—of the powers of Glavlit, the official censorship body, and greater initiative afforded to the editors of "thick" journals, traditionally the first place of publication for serious literary works. Editors such as Sergei Zalygin and Grigori Baklanov, both appointed in 1986, immediately began publishing works and writers such as Nikolai Gumilev,

Vladislav Khodasevich, and Vladimir Nabokov, previously unavailable in official editions; but these "rehabilitations" were building on others that had begun earlier, even in the immediate post-Stalin years.

Stalin's death in 1953 was followed by "thaws" in the country's political climate which enabled, through the rest of the decade, the release and rehabilitation of tens of thousands of citizens from the Gulag. In addition, selected works of some previously repressed or forbidden writers were published in the wake of the Second Writers Congress in 1954, most notably the recently deceased émigré Ivan Bunin and erstwhile Soviet writers who had fallen foul of the party's scorn, such as Mikhail Bulgakov, Anna Akhmatova, Andrei Platonov, and Mikhail Zoshchenko. The party was still very much in control of de-Stalinization, and the boundaries of permissible debate were clearly set. Writers were at the forefront of the albeit cautious investigation into Stalinism. Works by Vera Panova (*Vremena goda* [Eng. *Spans of the Year*]), Leonid Zorin (*Gosti* [The Guests]), and Vladimir Dudintsev (*Ne khlebom edinym* [Eng. *Not by Bread Alone*]), all published between 1954 and 1956, touched on the issues of the day: Stalinism, its victims, and the implications for the present. Critical articles by Fyodor Abramov and Vladimir Pomerantsev attacked some well-regarded literary works of the later Stalin period and the socialist-realist ethos that brought them about.

It was inevitable that, as the party allowed a tiny glimpse of freedom, writers tried to grab more, with the result that the minithaws of the 1950s were followed by "freezes" and clampdowns, as the party took fright at the criticisms that were threatening to go beyond the bounds prescribed. Writers in Russia have always been at the forefront of public debate and have perceived themselves as fulfilling a solemn duty of moral or spiritual guide to the people. Writers in the post-Stalin period were no different, and the term *literary opposition* came to be applied to those who, in the eyes of the party, were taking de-Stalinization too far. Perhaps the most significant publication of the decade was volume 2 of the almanac *Literaturnaia Moskva* (Literary Moscow), which came out in the troubled year of 1956, the year of Khrushchev's "secret speech" denouncing Stalin and also the year of the Hungarian uprising and its brutal suppression. *Literaturnaia Moskva* contained works critical of Stalinism, such as Nikolai Zhdanov's story "The Return Home," Yuri Nagibin's "Light in the Window," and Alexander Yashin's "Levers," plus works by writers such as Marina Tsvetaeva and Ivan Kataev, who had suffered terribly under Stalin and whose works had since been proscribed. The volume was attacked and its contributors reprimanded, but the whole affair demonstrated liberal writers' desire for independence from rigid political control.[4]

De-Stalinization received a new impetus following the Twenty-Second Party Congress in 1961, when Stalin's body was removed from the Mausoleum. The relaxation in cultural policy reached its apogee with the November 1962 publication of Alexander Solzhenitsyn's short novel *Odin den' Ivana Denisovicha* (Eng. *One Day in the Life of Ivan Denisovich*), a shattering exposé of daily life in the camps, the first such account to be published in the Soviet Union. This and subsequent works by Solzhenitsyn were published until 1966 in *Novyi Mir* (New World), the country's leading journal, once more with Tvardovsky as editor-in-chief (he had been relieved of the post in 1954 during the "freeze" following the first brief post-Stalin thaw; he was reinstated in 1958). Under Tvardovsky's leadership the journal became the flagship of the liberal intelligentsia throughout the 1960s, a symbol for the democratic strivings against a revitalized totalitarian regime. Most of the major literary works of the 1960s made their initial appearance in *Novyi Mir*.

The reassertion of broadly human values and the accompanying depoliticization of literature that began with Stalin's death grew and developed in the 1960s into several differing forms, among which the most important was undoubtedly "village prose." Village prose had its roots in the documentary sketch (*ocherk*) of the preceding decade, a genre employed by writers such as Valentin Ovechkin, Sergei Zalygin, Vladimir Tendryakov, Efim Dorosh, and others to expose and criticize the harsh conditions of life in the collectivized village.[5] This nonfictional, semijournalistic prose drew attention to the low standard of living in the countryside, the lack of facilities such as roads and consumer goods, and the baleful influence of bureaucracy. By the early 1960s writers including Vassily Belov, Vassily Shukshin, Viktor Astafiev, and Abramov joined forces with the likes of Tendryakov and Zalygin in refashioning this documentary writing into fiction, embracing lyric nature description, historical inquiry, and contemplation of man's place in the natural cycle.[6] The significance of village prose is perhaps best expressed by Kathleen Parthé:

> The sense of time in Village Prose is slow, cyclic, focused mostly on everyday life, and often directed toward the past. Even when the setting is the present, it is in the past that the narrator and characters look for roots, beauty, traditions, and values; the fear is that in losing the rural past, Russians will also lose their future. The frequent older characters and their recollections provide a natural access to the past, as do the authors'

personal memories of a rural childhood. Individual memories blend with a national memory of the rapidly vanishing peasant way of life to create works of great intensity.[7]

The legacy of collectivization could only be addressed within the framework of de-Stalinization, and indeed, such an early though important work as Zalygin's *Na Irtyshe* (On the Irtysh), published in 1964, although it could not explicitly condemn collectivization as a policy, showed in stark terms its excesses and inhuman cruelty. This reflected accurately the party line at the time. It was the first literary work to depict the process of collectivization accompanied by brutality and terror, a partial glimpse of the truth behind the party's ideological bombast. Further works in the 1960s pursued the theme of collectivization and the misery it brought about, Belov's *Plotnitskie rasskazy* (Eng. "Carpenter Yarns") of 1968 being the most outstanding (another work of 1968 that can be mentioned in this vein is Tendriakov's *Konchina* [The End]). There was at the same time an increasing body of work depicting the contemporary peasant's living and working conditions as nothing short of miserable, conveying the unmistakable impression that, apart from the consideration of the political legitimacy of collectivization, its effect on the day-to-day lives of succeeding generations has been devastating. Readers of such works as Solzhenitsyn's *Matrënin dvor* (1963; Eng. "Matryona's Home"), Boris Mozhaev's *Iz zhizni Fëdora Kuz'kina* (From the Life of Fyodor Kuzkin; 1966)—both published in Tvardovsky's *Novyi Mir*—Abramov's *Vokrug da okolo* (Round and About; 1963), and many others of this time learned, if they did not know it already, that collectivization had been an unmitigated disaster for the man of the soil.

Under Brezhnev, investigation of the past was not encouraged, and both writers and editors of journals had to tread a fine line between true history and the party's version of it. The fifth edition of the Communist Party history, published in 1980, states the following: "Stalin's cult of personality, especially in the last years of his life, did serious damage to the party and state leadership and the construction of socialism. . . . The party, overcoming the consequences of the cult of personality, gave free scope for the active involvement and creative initiative of the masses, for the development of socialist democracy."[8] In other words, as far as the party was concerned, the past had been overcome, and the tasks of the present now had to be addressed. Writers thought otherwise. It was during the Brezhnev years that Belov and Mozhaev began writing their long, detailed novels on collectivization, with their glowing pictures of village life before the cataclysm, and even managed to publish parts. These novels not only condemn collectivization as a policy and the methods used to achieve it, but also re-create Russian village life in the NEP period in admiring terms.[9] We now know, courtesy of *glasnost'*, that it was also in these years that Tendryakov, Abramov, and Sergei Antonov were writing their devastating and uncompromising critiques of the ethos and methods of collectivization, works that could only see the light of day under Gorbachev.

Collectivization forms the single most important and recurring theme of village prose, as it comprised the factual background to any discussion of modern problems. It was, though, only one historical area under investigation by writers during those years. Another area of intense public interest, naturally enough in the context of the thaw, was the Gulag. Viktor Nekrasov's *Kira Georgievna* (1961) portrayed an innocent man returning from the Gulag. *One Day in the Life of Ivan Denisovich* created a literary sensation that caused its author to wonder, "If the first tiny droplet of truth has exploded like a psychological bomb, what then will happen in our country when whole waterfalls of Truth burst forth?"[10] We now know that the party that had lived by the lie would be destroyed by the "waterfalls of Truth." Still, at the time the story's publication was a shattering experience for those people—and there were many millions of them—unaware of the horrors of the Gulag. However, the Brezhnev regime that took over in 1964 prohibited any further revelations. The Soviet public had to wait until the late 1980s for more information on the camps.

The 1960s and 1970s were difficult years for writers trying to extend the bounds of the permissible, especially with regard to the past. The end of the 1960s saw Tvardovsky lose control of *Novyi Mir,* its editorial board changed, and Solzhenitsyn expelled from the Writers Union. Solzhenitsyn was deported to the West in 1974, following the publication there of *Arkhipelag GULag* (Eng. *The Gulag Archipelago*). Throughout the 1970s many other major writers headed west as well, following problems with censors, bureaucrats, and the KGB: Vladimir Voinovich, Georgi Vladimov, Vassily Aksyonov, Viktor Nekrasov, Alexander Galich. It seemed that the heart had been ripped out of Soviet literature.

Others, however, chose to remain in the Soviet Union, and even in those difficult times the exploration of the past, in particular the legacy of Stalinism, was carried on. Yuri Trifonov began his career with a novel, *Studenty* (The Students), published in 1950, that won a Stalin Prize. Subsequently his works reflected the prevailing political ethos, until the 1960s. In 1964 he published a short historical study of the career and fate of his father, Valentin Trifonov, a prominent Bolshevik ac-

tive during the Revolution and civil war and one of thousands like him to perish during Stalin's purges (Yuri was eleven years old when he last saw his father in 1937). This study was expanded and published in book form in 1966. *Otblesk kostra* (Fireglow) is about not only Valentin Trifonov, but others as well, like the charismatic Don Cossack leader Filipp Mironov, another committed Bolshevik. Mironov was shot under mysterious circumstances by the Cheka in 1921. The book begs questions about the fate of those whose idealism fueled the Revolution, for Trifonov does not doubt the genuine devotion of his heroes; neither does he doubt that this idealism was a fundamental contribution to the October Revolution. What he deplores is its subsequent cynical manipulation and destruction.

The loss of idealism is a theme Trifonov returns to in his subsequent works, such as the Moscow cycle published between 1969 and 1975. In these short novellas he pinpoints the loss of values and triumph of consumer-minded materialism in the Moscow intelligentsia, supposedly the custodian of the nation's spiritual and moral values. In *Dom na naberezhnoi* (Eng. *The House on the Embankment*), published in 1976, he shows how a very ordinary individual is manipulated by higher forces and himself becomes a prime mover of Stalinism. In *Starik* (The Old Man; 1978) Trifonov returns to the civil-war period to examine the murderous methods employed by the Reds to ensure victory, and how the triumph of these methods has led to moral atrophy in the present. Trifonov was published because he created a language and a narrative style consisting of allusions, juxtapositions, and half-truths, but nothing explicitly anti-Soviet. He created a form of Aesopian speech that could be deciphered by Soviet readers accustomed to reading between the lines. Throughout his work he juxtaposes past and present, tracing the roots of the present in the past. In "The Old Man" he goes beyond Stalinism as an explanation for the terror and points to the methods used in the civil war itself. His whole oeuvre can be read as a social history of the Soviet Union from the 1930s to the 1970s. His novel *Ischeznovenie* (Eng. *Disappearance*), set in 1937 and focusing on the fear and terror among the political elite as the arrests escalate, was not published until 1987.

To sum up: Soviet writers before 1986 were intensely keen to investigate their country's recent past, in particular the crimes of Stalin. Furthermore, despite increased repression from the mid-1960s, a substantial body of work was published that informed the Soviet public of the greatest tragedies, if not their actual extent in terms of human lives lost. Yuri Trifonov stands alone among writers published in the 1970s in seeking to establish the root of the present malaise not in Stalinism but in the Red terror of the civil war. The village writers saw the village as the repository of the spiritual and moral values that formed the Russian national character and feared that collectivization had torn the soul out of the village.[11] Still, 1986 proved to be a watershed, and what was officially published before then was only the tip of the iceberg. We can now see that many other works were being written "for the drawer" during those years and came to light only under *glasnost'*.

Of writers active in the 1960s but whose work was published only in the late 1980s, special mention must be reserved for Vassily Grossman. Originally regarded from the 1930s as an orthodox socialist realist, Grossman produced in his last two novels two of Russian literature's greatest contributions to our understanding of the twentieth-century experience. *Zhizn' i sud'ba* (Eng. *Life and Fate*), published in 1988, uses the background of the Battle of Stalingrad to analyze the essential similarity of Soviet-style tyranny and Nazism. *Vse techet* (Forever Flowing), published in 1989, looks for the root of evil beyond Stalinism and is a powerful indictment of Marxism-Leninism as a system of belief. When the manuscript of *Life and Fate* was seized by the KGB in 1961, Grossman was told by the Politburo's ideological watchdog Suslov that the novel would not see the light of day for two to three hundred years. Frank Ellis calls the novel "one of the most damning indictments of Stalinism, and arguably the most subversive piece of literature ever to have been penned by a Soviet writer."[12] Rather than centuries, it was only a few decades before the novel made its own contribution to the demise of the system its author so vehemently came to hate.

In the post-Stalin years writers such as Solzhenitsyn and Anatoli Rybakov were attempting literary portraits of Stalin himself. Both *V pervom kruge* (Eng. *The First Circle*) and *Deti Arbata* (Eng. *Children of the Arbat*) contain long chapters with detailed analysis of the tyrant's way of thinking and his view of the world, but they were published in the USSR only under Gorbachev.[13] Alexander Bek's novel *Novoe naznachenie* (A New Appointment), focusing on Stalin's Minister of Metallurgy Tevosian and also containing a portrait of Stalin, was completed in 1964 and announced for publication in *Novyi Mir* in 1965; it was finally published in 1986. Jenny Woodhouse has recently reflected on the reasons why the work was deemed unacceptable.

> Bek was working on the boundaries of the permissible, and it may well be that the greatest virtue of the novel, as a work of social criticism, led to its suppression: it acknowledges that Stalin was not solely responsible for his "crimes"; that he was aided and supported by a system, resting

on the work of many individuals; that more was at stake than a cult of personality.[14]

Gorbachev intended that his liberalization of the arts would help his own policy of *perestroika*. He stated at the Eighth Writers Congress in 1986 that his reform program would enlist writers to effect the "psychological and moral restructuring" of the population, but that the party's goals remained sacrosanct.[15] Gorbachev is not the first Soviet leader to use literature and writers to further his own program: Stalin, Khrushchev, Brezhnev, and even Chernenko had attempted the same. What Gorbachev did that others before him failed to do, however, was to untie the hands of writers and, more important, editors, to publish works critical not only of past policies but even of the party itself.

The first three years following Gorbachev's accession were characterized by the publication of works by writers long dead, or by writers still alive and residing in the Soviet Union, works which had been refused publication by an earlier regime: previously mentioned novels by Mozhaev, Belov, Rybakov, Trifonov, and Bek; Anna Akhmatova's long poem of the purges, *Rekviem* (Eng. "Requiem"), Andrei Platonov's novel of collectivization and industrial construction, *Kotlovan* (Eng. *The Foundation Pit*); Nikolai Klyuev's poem about collectivization, "Pogorel'shchina" (The Burnt Land); Vladimir Dudintsev's *Belye odezhdy* (White Robes), a novel about the damage done to genetics in the 1950s by the pseudoscientist Trofim Lysenko;[16] novels and poems by Nabokov, Khodasevich, Gumilev. To these can be added the novels *Pushkinskii dom* (Eng. *Pushkin House*) by Andrei Bitov, *Kroliki i udavy* (Eng. *Rabbits and Boa Constrictors*) by Fazil Iskander, *Sofia Petrovna* by Lidia Chukovskaya, and short stories by Yevgeny Popov—all works which had previously been published in the West. This last circumstance was indeed a departure, for under previous Soviet rulers, works printed in the West and not in the Soviet Union were deemed anti-Soviet, their authors often persecuted.[17]

These were all important publications, for they testified not only to the wealth of Russian literature still officially unknown in the USSR, but also to the fundamental reappraisal of the past going beyond the party's purview. The years 1988–89 were to prove fateful for the party and Soviet literature, as the publication of the aforementioned novels by Grossman, Pasternak's *Doctor Zhivago,* and works by Solzhenitsyn, Varlam Shalamov, and other erstwhile "dissidents" formed a different agenda. It was now clear that editors were not so much helping Gorbachev and *perestroika* as seeking to restore the lost works of Russian literature and erase the distinction between "Soviet" and émigré or "dissident" literature. Furthermore, the publication of works such as

The Gulag Archipelago in 1989 not only set out to restore the national memory on the crimes of Stalin but, in addition, subverted any efforts the party may have been making to create its own version of history. Gorbachev could never have been as outspoken as Solzhenitsyn, but more crucially, Solzhenitsyn was damning not only Stalin but also Lenin, the Revolution, and the whole Marxist-Leninist edifice. The year 1989 was the point of no return for the party, for it was then that it became clear that Gorbachev and writers/editors such as Vitali Korotich (of *Ogonĕk*), Zalygin, and Baklanov were moving in different directions. *Glasnost'* had by now been overtaken by a desire for the truth. Writers had written works which were once banned; writers as editors were now giving these works back to the people. History was returned to the people, a history of pain, suffering, tragedy. The party was to blame for this history.

Now not only the more famous émigrés have been published. Lesser-known figures have been introduced to the Soviet reader as well, figures such as Gaito Gazdanov, Mikhail Osorgin, Mark Aldanov, Sasha Cherny, Sofia Parnok, Ivan Shmelev, Vyacheslav Ivanov, Nikolai Erdman, and Ivan Elagin. Other names include Nikolai Turoverov, Boris Poplavsky, and Yevgeny Chirikov.

Neglected or repressed writers from the early years of Soviet power have had important but controversial works published, sometimes for the first time: Leonid Dobychin, Daniil Andreev, Panteleimon Romanov, Yevgeny Zamyatin. Among the lesser names restored to the pantheon are the poets Georgi Obolduev, Andrei Nikolev, Nikolai Oleinikov, Elizaveta Kuzmina-Karavaeva, and Pavel Vasiliev. Seemingly lost works such as Platonov's novel *Schastlivaia Moskva* (Happy Moscow) have been recovered from KGB archives and published. An important feature of the *glasnost'* years has been the publication of documentary materials such as correspondence, diaries, and memoirs relating to major writers and adding to our knowledge and understanding of the life and work of such important figures as Yevgeny Shvarts, Artem Vesely, Daniil Kharms, Marina Tsvetaeva, Boris Pasternak, Mikhail Bulgakov, and Mikhail Prishvin. Ivan Bunin's diaries of the civil-war period, demonstrating his total antipathy toward the Bolsheviks, have also been published in the USSR, having already appeared in the West. The full complexion of Russian literature in the twentieth century is now being restored.

The rediscovery of this treasure trove of Russian literature has made it possible now to rewrite Russian literary history, a task currently being taken up by Russian critics and scholars.[18] An important by-product of this reassessment is the controversy raging around a novel hitherto regarded as a classic: *Tikhii Don* (Eng. *And Quiet Flows the Don*). Since the late 1920s there had been persistent allegations in the West, based on both rumor and textual analysis, that Mikhail Sholokhov did not write the novel but instead either stole or plagiarized at least parts of it. Solzhenitsyn revived the charge in 1974. The debate continues, but now in Russia as well as in the West.

Literature was the first to benefit from the liberalization initiated by Gorbachev, and it is fitting that literature has seen the most profound changes. Editors of journals were quick to obtain and then publish "lost" or forbidden works; writers (even those long dead) were the first to reveal the terrible human cost of Russia's recent history. Fittingly, the literature of the lie, socialist realism, is dead; Soviet literature too died in 1991, when Russian literature was reborn.

The task of properly reappraising the past will in time fall to historians, economists, political scientists, and anthropologists, but Russia's writers, both before and since *glasnost',* have done their part. It is important to realize that writers such as Trifonov, Mozhaev, Belov, and others, by portraying the past and its injustices and cruelties, have been content not only to set the historical record straight. They have also set out to reinterpret the course of Russian history, to search for the laws of cause and effect. For these and others, not only the past is at stake, but the present too.

It is no exaggeration to say that since 1986 we have seen a national cultural rebirth in Russia. With hindsight we can see that socialist realism, the artistic method inaugurated during Stalin's reign, fell into terminal decline when the tyrant died in 1953, although its death throes have been long and painful. Only in 1989 can we really say that the party and literature became totally and irreconcilably separated. Truth has been restored to literature, and writers have achieved this by expressing the people's truth, and its longing for freedom.[19]

David Gillespie, Winter 1993

1   Nadezhda Mandelstam, *Hope Abandoned: A Memoir,* Max Hayward, tr., Harmondsworth, Eng., Penguin, 1976, p. 191.

2   Iurii Trifonov, "Geroi 'Narodnoi Voli'" (The Hero of "The People's Will"), *Literaturnaia Gazeta,* 25 August 1971, p. 3.

3   Geoffrey Hosking, *A History of the Soviet Union,* London, Fontana/Collins, 1985, p. 203. This may yet be a conservative figure, as Robert Conquest estimates that over fourteen million peasants died during and as a result of collectivization. See his *Harvest of Sorrow: Soviet Collectivization and the Terror-Famine,* London, Hutchinson, 1986, p. 306.

4   For detailed analysis of the 1950s thaw, see George Gibian, "The Literary 'Front,'" *Problems of Communism,* 1958, no. 1, pp. 21–27; Tom Scriven, "The 'Literary Opposition,'" ibid., pp. 28–34; and George Gibian, *Interval of Freedom: Soviet Literature during the Thaw, 1954–1957,* Minneapolis, University of Minnesota Press, 1960.

[5] To be exact, Ovechkin's sketches began appearing before Stalin's death, in 1952.

[6] It should be noted that during the Stalin years Mikhail Prishvin wrote many works devoted to the countryside, its peace and natural rhythms, maintaining singlehandedly a tradition that had existed in Russian literature for over a century.

[7] Kathleen Parthé, *Russian Village Prose: The Radiant Past,* Princeton, N.J., Princeton University Press, 1992, p. 9.

[8] *Istoriia Kommunisticheskoi Partii Sovetskogo Soiuza* (History of the Communist Party of the Soviet Union), 5th rev. ed., Moscow, Izdatel'stvo Politicheskoi Literatury, 1980, p. 568.

[9] I have written elsewhere on these novels: David Gillespie, "Ironies and Legacies: Village Prose and *Glasnost',*" *Forum for Modern Language Studies,* 27:1 (January 1991), pp. 70–84.

[10] Alexander Solzhenitsyn, *The Gulag Archipelago* 1918–1956, vol. I, London, Collins/Fontana. 1974, p. 298.

[11] For further discussion of the literary treatment of the past in the 1950s and 1960s, see Deming Brown, *Soviet Russian Literature since Stalin,* Cambridge, Eng., Cambridge University Press, 1978, esp. pp. 253–84.

[12] N.J. Ellis, "Vasiliy Grossman: The Challenge to Ideology," in *Perestrojka und Literatur,* E. Reissner, ed., Berlin, Spitz, 1990, p. 25.

[13] Both Rybakov's and Solzhenitsyn's portraits of Stalin have been examined in detail by Rosalind Marsh in her book *Images of Dictatorship: Portraits of Stalin in Literature,* London, Routledge, 1989, esp. pp. 80–97 and 135–97.

[14] Jenny Woodhouse, "Stalin's Soldier: Aleksandr Bek's *Novoe naznachenie,*" *Slavonic and East European Review,* 69:4 (October 1991), p. 618.

[15] *Literaturnaia Gazeta,* 25 June 1986, p. 1. See also the text of a meeting with the Writers Union that Gorbachev allegedly held in July 1986: "Mr Gorbachev Meets the Writers," *Detente,* no. 8 (Winter 1987), pp. 11–12.

[16] It should be noted that this was not the first time Lysenko had been attacked in Soviet literature. Boris Mozhaev had published in 1973 a bitterly satiric caricature in his short piece "Den' bez kontsa i bez kraia" (A Day Without End), *Novyi Mir,* 1973, no. 9, pp. 19–66.

[17] There have been many surveys and analyses of the literary thaw in the years 1986–89. For the political context, as well as an authoritative overview, see Alec Nove, *Glasnost' in Action: Cultural Renaissance in Russia,* Boston, Unwin Hyman, 1989, pp. 127–55.

[18] Most notably by Evgenii Dobrenko and Galina Belaia. See Dobrenko's articles in *Novyi Mir,* 1990, no. 2, pp. 237–50, and 1992, no. 3, pp. 228–40; see Belaia's *Don Kikhoty dvadtsatykh godov: "Pereval" i sud'ba ego idei* (Don Quixotes of the 1920s: "Pereval" and the Fate of Its Ideas), Moscow, Sovetskii Pisatel', 1989. See also the recent article by V. Pertsovskii, "Skvoz' revoliutsiiu kak sostoianie dushi" (Through the Revolution as a State of the Soul), *Novyi Mir,* 1992, no. 3, pp. 216–27.

[19] One major aspect of the rediscovery of past culture beyond the scope of this essay is the republication in Russia of the remarkable religious philosophers of the early years of this century: Vladimir Soloviev, Semyon Frank, Father Sergei Bulgakov, Father Pavel Florensky, Nikolai Berdyaev. The impact of their writings on the sense of Russian national identity in the 1990s is yet to be assessed.

Solzhenitsyn and Western Freedom

Rarely in modern times—especially in times of relative peace—have one man's voice and words provoked the Western world to an experience of profound soul searching. What Aleksandr Solzhenitsyn said, not only at Harvard last June, but also earlier at the welcoming convention of the AFL-CIO which provided him a platform when the President of the United States, at the urging of his Metternichian Secretary of State, refused to receive him, has stirred the reflective conscience of the Western world more profoundly than the eloquent discourses of Franklin Roosevelt and Winston Churchill. This all the more unprecedented because Solzhenitsyn is using a foreign tongue and expressions and idioms that remain opaque in translation. Nonetheless, the existence of this Conference as well as the continuing comments of leading publicists on his speech testifies to the power of his words, to the fundamental character of his challenge to our mode of life, its basic values, its fears and illusions, and to a philosophy of civilization concealed by the apparent absence of any philosophy.

For purposes of exposition and discussion, I shall classify what I have to say in four rubrics and a final restatement of what I regard as the morally valid challenge of Solzhenitsyn to the West, despite the multitude of defects and inaccuracies in his analysis concerning the nature of freedom, democracy and the causes of decline of the West. First, I shall deal with Solzhenitsyn's indictment of the West. Second, I shall consider some of his specifications of its decline, its dangers and its irrelevancies. Third, I shall discuss his peculiar conception of democracy, his failure to appreciate the distinction between legality and morality, even granting the large measure of truth in his observation about the excesses of a freedom conceived only as absence of restraint or rejection of rational regulation. Fourth, I shall consider his causal analysis of our predicament, his central contention according to which all of our evils can be attributed to the rise of secular, rational humanism, and its belief that an acceptable human morality is intrinsically related to the consequences of our actions on human weal and woe. For according to him, such beliefs generate the heresy that morality is logically independent of religion and theology, especially of the existence of God as "the Supreme Complete Entity." It is here that Solzhenitsyn reveals not only his literary but his spiritual kinship to his great countrymen, Dostoevsky and Tolstoy. Finally, even giving full measure to all of Solzhenitsyn's misunderstandings and errors about Western culture, I should like to restate what I take to be his crucial, abiding and valid messages to the partisans of human freedom for our time. On the basis of his central insight I am confident that those who are opposed to *all* varieties of totalitarianism can work out a unifying moral program which is independent of all our theological and religious differences. Such a program, or rather approach, can serve as a common rallying point for those who still believe that in the current conflict between free and unfree societies, there are other alternatives to war and surrender. It makes possible a strategy for freedom that still holds out promises of a survival worthy of human beings.

■ I

The Indictment. The central point in Solzhenitsyn's indictment of the West is that it has suffered a colossal failure of nerve with respect to its own animating philosophy of freedom, as expressed in its basic documentary ideals and in the slow march of human progress in bringing those ideals closer to implementation. According to him, the map of political freedom in the world is shrinking; the ideals of the Western world are in eclipse even in those areas of the world which its ideals helped to liberate. The vast gains in all forms of human freedom that have been made in all domains of social and political life are either denied or downgraded in virtue of the still limited shortcomings that are always apparent when we appraise, as we should, the status quo with what ideally should be.

With respect to the Communist world, Solzhenitsyn charges that there is no genuine reciprocity either in cultural exchanges or in living up to pledges and agreements. The Helsinki Accords in which the West formally acknowledged the de facto suzerainty of the Soviet Empire in Eastern Europe have been violated by the failure of the Soviet Union and most of its satellites to live up to the elementary provisions of human rights to which they have pledged allegiance. The degrading treatment of the Shcharanskys, the Ginzburgs, the Grigorenkos, and the enforced incarceration of dissidents into psychiatric torture chambers still continue. The failure of the Soviet Union to comply with the Belgrade agreement to investigate the compliance with human rights brought no remonstrance from the United States.

With respect to the so-called Third World, we have witnessed a strange transformation of colonially liberated countries, whose ideals were related to, if not rooted in, the American Declaration of Independence, into one-party dictatorships operating with a cruelty to local population and dissidents almost on par with and, in some cases, worse than the oppression from which they were liberated. The United Nations has in effect become an association of a majority of anti-American nations more intent upon transforming Israel, the victim of a systematic terror campaign, into a pariah state than coping with the genocidal practices of Cambodia or Amin's Uganda.

But the main point in the indictment of the Western world lies, according to Solzhenitsyn, in its very conception of freedom and its material expansion. He believes that the West is so obsessed with its notion of freedom that it cannot distinguish between the freedom or right to pursue and achieve what is desirable and what is undesirable. This results from an emphasis upon and defense of individual rights to a point which makes them almost absolute, to a refusal to understand that essential freedoms cannot function properly without a recognition that there are human obligations just as binding upon us. "The defense of individual rights," he says, "has reached such extremes as to make society as a whole defenseless against certain individuals. Culprits can go unpunished or obtain undeserved leniency with the support of thousands of public defenders. When a government starts an earnest fight against terrorism, public opinion immediately accuses it of violating the terrorists' civil rights."

Many of Solzhenitsyn's formulations are inexact or exaggerated, but I think it is fair to restate his main philosophical points in the following assertions: first, that freedom is misconceived if it is defined as the right to do anything one pleases; that no freedom can be unqualified; that every specific freedom we can reasonably defend must be one that is desirable or normative. Second, that no desirable freedom can be unqualified; that every right, whether moral or legal, carries with it a restriction or a prohibition of the correlative right to interfere with it or violate it. If you sincerely believe that a person has a right to speak, write, assemble or worship according to his conscience, then you must believe that no one has the right or freedom to prevent him from exercising that right, that the freedom to disrupt or interfere with this right must be restrained. If you believe in tolerance, then you cannot believe in tolerating those who are *actively intolerant* of others. Otherwise you do not understand the meaning of tolerance or are insincere in professing belief in it.

Third, Solzhenitsyn is convinced that no matter what schedule of desirable rights or freedoms you draw up, none is absolute because in every moral situation, rights conflict. In his own way he realizes what philosophers like John Dewey and others have expressed more precisely: that the moral situation is not one in which a person is confronted by a conflict between good and bad, right and wrong, but between the good and the good, the right and the right. Kindness and truth are not always compatible. You cannot always give a man a right to a fair trial and permit complete freedom of the press, et cetera. Indeed, if one believes that there exists more than one good or right, one cannot contend that they are all absolute because they may in some situation conflict. Lying is wrong, but so is murder—and sometimes you may have to choose between telling the truth or saving a life!

■ II

Yet the biting impact of Solzhenitsyn's speeches is not his recognition of these truths but rather the dramatic illustrations he cites of what he regards as improper choices and emphases when values conflict. Two illustrations, which I mention briefly, will suffice because other sessions will be devoted to them.

Of course, Solzhenitsyn believes in freedom of the press—since he has been imprisoned and exiled because of it. But in the West he sees a press "more powerful than the legislature, the executive, and the judiciary," and a claim for its freedom regardless of its consequences for the weal, and woe, and security of the nation. And, he asks, if everyone is to be held morally responsible and legally accountable in a just and democratic society, who holds the press responsible and accountable, especially if it enjoys a practical monopoly? He notices that reporters steal government secrets, the press publishes them under the claim "the public has a right to know"; yet when legal inquiries are made into the secret sources of a reporter's news—even if a man's life or freedom is at stake—the press unanimously denies that the public has a right to know—in the interests of freedom of the press. But if that is true, then may it not also be true that in the interests of the preservation of a free society—without which there could be no freedom of the press—the government may also claim that there are some secrets which the public does not, at least for a limited period, have a right to know?

A second illustration. Coming from a country in which people are often severely punished for living up to the laws of their own land, as the Soviet dissidents claim, Solzhenitsyn is taken aback by what he finds in this country, something he characterizes as an excess of legalism over morality in the judicial system of the United States. This is related to what others have recently referred to as our imperial judiciary. At a time when there is a sharply rising incidence in major crimes of violence, he finds increasing concern with protecting the rights not of the victims and potential victims of crime but with the rights and immunities of those guilty or accused of crimes. He claims to find a jurisprudential theory according to which the criminals are basically the victims of society and therefore not really responsible for their evil deeds and a subsequent legally countenanced resort to technical procedures and prolonged delays that defeat the ends of justice. If he had mentioned the absurdity of the exclusionary rule in the area of evidence, he would have been much more eloquent and morally indignant. Rightly or wrongly, he associates these phenomena with the decline in private and public morality, with an increase in selfishness, with the philosophy of grab and run if you safely can. There is something wrong with a society, he says, when "the center of your democracy is left without electric power for a few hours only and all of a sudden crowds of American citizens start looting and creating havoc."

■ III

Let us now turn to a more central point. Even if we grant the validity of many of the *specific* criticisms in Solzhenitsyn's indictment, and with respect to the law and the abuses of the press the picture seems to me to be very grim indeed (the details of which I shall expatiate on in discussion), what does Solzhenitsyn suggest as a political cure or alternative? Here there is a fatal unclarity and ambiguity in his conception of democracy, which I shall relate to his fundamental theology. First of all, many of the defects in current American legal process are not rooted in the democratic system, because in democratic countries like England and Canada, and even in some less democratic jurisdictions, without the slightest abridgement of justice, the courts work much more effectively, and the law is by far less egregiously an ass than it is in so many of our state and federal jurisdictions.

This is even more obvious with respect to the press. In the present state of investigative reporting, the growth in some quarters of advocacy reporting, and the view that because complete objectivity is impossible therefore the whole concept of objectivity is a myth, no man or woman's reputation is safe from careless and irresponsible misrepresentation. Even in this respect, professional standards of media reporting in England are superior to those in the United States, although even there they leave something to be desired. Even without recourse to the English laws of libel and the Official Secrets Act, there is a Press Council to which one can repair if one has been victimized by a false or malicious press story. It is very significant that "when the Twentieth Century Fund, on the advice of some leading figures in American journalism and based on the success of the British example, established a Press Council, such leading papers as *The New York Times* and *The Washington Post* refused to cooperate with that council. Indeed, the American Society of Newspaper Editors a few years ago voted three to one against the establishment of even its internal grievance committee" (Max Kampelman, "The Power of the Press," *Policy Review,* Fall 1978). Lester Markel, a few years ago, wrote:

The press, pretending to believe that there is no credibility gap and asserting its near-infallibility, countenances no effective supervision of its operation; it has adopted a holier-than-thou attitude, citing the First Amendment and in addition the Ten Commandments and other less holy scripture. (*New York Times*, 2 February 1973)

John B. Oakes, Emeritus Editorial Page Editor of *The New York Times,* less than a year ago in discussing the "Dwindling Faith in the Press," pointed the necessity of making the press "voluntarily more accountable as well as more accessible to the public" (24 May 1978). The more powerful it is, the more accountable it should be. Sometimes its power is beneficent, as in Watergate. Sometimes it abuses its power, as when it transformed the military disaster the Viet Cong suffered in its Tet Offensive into a military victory, by false reporting. The effect in this country was to give a political victory to Vietnam, force a President out of office and profoundly affect the untimely outcome.

These are some of the evils of democracy. But the cure of the evils of a democracy is not *no* democracy without relying on the famous trinity of the Dostoevskian tradition: mystery, authority and miracle. What Solzhenitsyn fails to appreciate about Western democracy is the nature of its political faith. There is nothing sanctified about the will of a majority even when it recognizes the civil and human rights of its minorities. It is not infallible. The majority may be unenlightened, but as Felix Frankfurter put it: "The appeal from an unenlightened majority in a democracy is to an enlightened majority," and so long as the political process registering freely-given consent exists, the evils are remediable. The real question we must ask Solzhenitsyn is whether he is prepared to accept the risks of a democracy, and its right to be wrong, provided it has a chance to correct that wrong; or does he believe, as do all totalitarians from Plato to the present day, that most human beings in the community are either too stupid or too vicious to be entrusted with self-government? I, for one, believe that despite some ambiguous expressions, Solzhenitsyn, like his great compatriot Andrei Sakharov, is on the side of democracy. The fundamental argument for democracy against those who are convinced that they know the true interests of the people better than the people itself is that those who wear the shoes know best where they pinch, and therefore have the right to change their political shoes in the light of their experience.

■ **IV**

I come now to Solzhenitsyn's analysis of the causes of the failure of Western courage, the inadequacies of its democracy and the weakness of its morality. And here I find him, together with a long line of distinguished predecessors and successors, profoundly, demonstrably and tragically wrong. To Solzhenitsyn, the cause of Western democratic decline and the collapse of its morality is the rise of secular humanism and rationalism, which began with the breakdown of the medieval synthesis, and the emergence of the scientific world-outlook. Put in its simplest terms, what Solzhenitsyn is saying is that the basic cause of our world in crisis is the erosion of religion, the decline in the belief in the existence of a Supreme Power or Entity, and the reliance not on transcendental faith but upon human intelligence as a guide to human nature and conduct.

I cannot accept Solzhenitsyn's causal analysis for many reasons. Historically, neither Judaism, Christianity nor Islam is responsible for the emergence of democracy as a system of community self-government resting upon the freely-given consent of the governed. In principle they never condemned slavery or feudalism and often offered apologetic justifications for them. Logically, from the proposition that all men are equal in the sight of the Lord, it does not follow in the least that they are or should be equal in the sight of the Law. The belief in the divine right of kings is older than the equally foolish view *vox populi vox Dei.* The existence or nonexistence of God is equally compatible with the existence of any social system whatsoever, except when God is so defined that his moral attributes require the existence of a democratic system.

My criticism goes even further. Not only is theology irrelevant to democracy, to capitalism or to socialism as social systems, but to the validity of morality itself. Solzhenitsyn echoes in his own idiom Smerdyakov's dictum that "if God does not exist everything is [morally] permissible." But this is a non sequitur. Men build their gods in their own moral image. When we profess to derive a moral command from a religious revelation, it is only because we have smuggled into our conception of Divinity our own moral judgments. By definition, God cannot do evil, but we ourselves are responsible for the distinction between good and evil. What makes an action morally valid is not a command from on high or from anywhere else, but the intrinsic character of the action and its consequences for human weal and woe.

Some of the most profound theologians of the West, from the author of the original version of the Book of Job to Augustine and Kierkegaard, have maintained that the religious dimension of human experience transcends the moral experience. The piercing bone in the throat of Western theology on which its apologists have continually choked is the problem of evil—the ever-recurrent question of why an allegedly all-powerful and all-benevolent Supreme Being permits in every age the infinite torture of innocent multitudes. (Kierkegaard in his *Fear and Trembling* portrays Abraham, because of his willingness to sacrifice his son Isaac on divine command, not as a great *moral* figure, comparable to Agamemnon or Brutus the Younger, who also were willing to sacrifice their offspring, but as a divinely inspired religious figure. It would not be difficult to show that Kierkegaard's reading is quite arbitrary and that in the end Abraham's action in sacrificing an animal instead of a human being testifies to the supremacy of morality, the birth of a new moral insight or judgment for which he and we as individual human beings must take responsibility, and not to the acceptance of piety to an established Power.)

But the argument and dialectic are unnecessary. For it should be clear that, if like Solzhenitsyn we wish to unite mankind in the defense of rational freedom and in the preservation of a free society, it is not necessary to agree on first and last things about God, immortality or any other transcendental dogma. Actually the majority of mankind subscribes to other than the Judeo-Christian faith—Hindus, Buddhists, Confucians, Shintoists, naturalists and animists constitute most of mankind. Religion is a private matter, and religious freedom means the right to believe or disbelieve in one, many or no gods. If we wish to unify, if not to universalize, the struggle for freedom, I propose that we find a set of ethical principles on which human beings can agree, regardless of their differing presuppositions, a set of common human needs and human rights that will permit human beings of different cultures, if not to live and help each other, at least to live and let each other live. What unites Solzhenitsyn and Sakharov, and us with them—our love of human freedom and our desire to preserve a free society—is more important than any of our other differences. Solzhenitsyn's strategy divides the common struggle particularly by his criticism of secular rational humanism.

■ V

Despite everything I have said and despite my differences with Solzhenitsyn on matters I have mentioned, and on others that I have left unmentioned, in this final section I wish to indicate why I regard him as one of the great moral prophets of our time. After all, what is it that has moved him to his thunderous evocations of despair with the values and absence of values in the West? It is his observation, repeated in various ways, that the relatively free and imperfect areas of the world are becoming progressively weaker vis-à-vis the totalitarian powers and their assorted varieties of Gulag Archipelagos. And he has been struck to the very heart of his being by the growing feeling among some of the

leading intellectual figures of the West, like George Kennan, that "we cannot apply moral criteria to politics," and that since resistance may lead to a universal conflict in which the survivors will envy the dead, the West, starting with the United States, must "begin unilateral disarmament." And what if the enemies of a free society are not inspired by this spirit of Christian submission and, interpreting in good Leninist fashion pacifism and appeasement as an expression of cultural decadence, move to take over the remaining center of freedom? Better that than the consequences of resistance, says George Kennan. Echoing Bertrand Russell in his last years, Kennan has proclaimed in his famous interview in *The New York Times,* "Rather Red, than Dead." Solzhenitsyn finds that this is a mood not far below the surface in Western Europe and other areas. In moments of crisis we find it expressed in many ways: "It is better to live on your knees than die on your feet," or "It is better to be a live jackal than a dead lion."

Now for one thing—although Solzhenitsyn does not say this—Kennan's and Russell's strategy of ultimate surrender may not work in a world where two super-communist powers possess nuclear weapons with which they threaten each other. We may first become Red and still end up Dead! As I read him, Solzhenitsyn is saying something different. He claims that the greatest danger of war—and he is *against* war—is the loss of moral nerve, the loss of will power, the loss of belief that some things are morally more important than mere life itself, and that without such belief, "weapons no matter how powerful" cannot help overcome "the loss of will power" to defend free institutions. In one of the memorable sentences in his Harvard address he quietly says, "To defend oneself, one must also be ready to die," and the context shows that by this he means the defense of our free institutions as our ultimate concern. There is a profound historical and psychological truth here. The lean and hungry hordes ready to die have always triumphed when confronted by those who sought primarily to save their goods or to save their necks. Not infrequently they lost both. Deny Solzhenitsyn's proposition, and what is the conclusion one must draw in consequence? That survival is the be-all and end-all of life, the ultimate value. But if we are prepared to sacrifice all our basic values for survival, there is no infamy we will not commit. The result would be a life morally unworthy of survival for man.

Solzhenitsyn's abiding message is that if we renew our moral courage, our dedication to freedom, we can avoid *both* war and capitulation in the grim days ahead. Our choice is not between being "dead or red," provided we are prepared to stake our lives if necessary on freedom. For we are not dealing with totalitarian madmen, but with Leninists who worship at the altar of history, who believe their triumph is inevitable without war, and who in virtue of every principle of their ideology will never initiate a world war unless they are certain they will win it. Our task is to be strong enough to prevent such certainty. Indeed, why should the leaders in the Kremlin risk a war when they are gaining power and growing stronger without war, by using other nations as mercenaries in local engagements?

One need not endorse Solzhenitsyn's specific political judgments to agree with him that so long as the West remains strong enough so that there can be no guarantee of totalitarian victory, and so long as it recognizes that the essential moral element in that strength is the willingness to risk one's life in the defense of freedom, there will be no world war. World peace, which has existed under the balance of terror, will be preserved as we rely on multilateral disarmament and the hopes of evolutionary peaceful changes in totalitarian societies. So far we have seen fascist countries become transformed into imperfect democracies without war. So long as we keep our guard up and do not capitulate à la Kennan or Russell, perhaps some day totalitarian communist countries may in virtue of their internal development democratize themselves without war.

Differing as profoundly as I do with Solzhenitsyn about so much, I am confident that he will agree with me in a short answer that I made to the Kennans and Russells of this world in the form of a thumbnail credo:

> It is better to be a live jackal than a dead lion—for jackals, not men. Men who have the moral courage to fight intelligently for freedom have the best prospects of avoiding the fate both of live jackals and dead lions. Survival is not the be-all and end-all of a life worthy of man. Sometimes the worst thing we can know about a man is that he has survived. Those who say life is worth living at any cost have already written for themselves an epitaph of infamy, for there is no cause and no person they will not betray to stay alive. Man's vocation should be the use of the arts of intelligence in behalf of human freedom.

> ***Sidney Hook, Autumn 1979***

Words Devouring Things: The Poetry of Joseph Brodsky

Joseph Brodsky was born in 1940 and until his exile from the USSR in 1972 lived most of his life in the city of Leningrad. The spelling his parents gave the name is not without interest: Iosif. (The normal Russian would be Osip.) Yiddish, perhaps? That is unlikely, in Leningrad, in 1940. It is more likely of Georgian provenance. There was, after all, a powerful Georgian after whom many babies born in that year were named. For about thirty years (given some absences) Iosif lived in the same tight little flat with the parents who had given him that name. If there is a certain prevailing and pervasive bleakness to his poetry, a sense of solitude and desolation yet at the same time a power of detachment and observation, a perspective from which he sees things in their minute particulars and at the same time *through* them to a beyond of which he intimates that the things are sacramental signs, then that curiously spelled first name may have had its part as explanation. In any case, I have the sense in reading even his early poetry that exile was intrinsic to it, that long before a tyrannical and repressive regime forced him into separation from his nourishing mother tongue and immediate cultural milieu, and that although poetry has in general been alien to the contemporary world, he more than most poets was born into exile.

He was born into exile, but at a particular time and in a special place. In Leningrad a generation of poets came of age in the postwar years as hardship and terror relaxed, if they did not entirely subside. Some of the poets later published and even, like Alexander Kushner, joined the Writers Union. But most retreated into what Anna Akhmatova ironically called "a new pre-Gutenberg era," relying on manuscripts, typed or hectographed copies and poetry readings in friends' apartments for whatever publicity they acquired. Any foreigner who attended such gatherings in the quarter-century following 1956 would remember vividly both their seriousness and their élan, the extraordinarily intense atmosphere with which they were charged. Suzanne Massie's anthology *The Living Mirror: Five Young Poets from Leningrad* (Doubleday, 1972), which contains eight splendid poems by Brodsky, was a memento of such visits. What they lacked in terms of broad readership and extensive publicity (often prerogatives of poets in Russia, if not in the United States) they were recompensed in terms of the seriousness and intensity of their limited audience. Certainly the fact that this poetry was largely repressed does not mean that it lacked public stature—quite the contrary.

Broadly speaking, the young Leningrad poets could be divided into two groups, both of which attempted to identify and link themselves to two literary movements extinguished in the 1920s—the Acmeists and the Futurists. Brodsky, for all his striking originality, his occasional love of the grotesque and constant verbal play as well as his links to the young Mayakovsky, considers himself (and rightly so) a traditionalist and a classicist, and therefore an adherent of Acmeism—a movement, moreover, native to Leningrad, whose two greatest poets, Osip Mandelstam and Anna Akhmatova, were Brodsky's cultural lodestars.

Mandelstam had called Acmeism "a longing for world culture." In Petrograd-Leningrad, once "a window onto Europe," that longing had a special poignancy. Brodsky steeped himself in the entire Petersburg tradition, from eighteenth-century poets like Kantemir and Derzhavin, through the great, cerebral nineteenth-century poet Baratinsky (little known outside Russia and a Muscovite by residence, but in his late poems a Petersburger in spirit), to Gumilev, Mandelstam and Akhmatova in the twentieth century. Of Petersburg, Brodsky himself has written, "Nowhere else did classicism have so much space." That there is something paradoxical about a classicism with "so much space"—since classicism is normally thought of as an art of distinct limits and clear definitions, of narrow if lucid horizons—Brodsky no doubt knows. He is a classicist of the age of irony, and paradox is his birthright. In Mandelstam he had an exemplar of a poet's confidence in his own rightness in the face of a regime that destroyed him, and also of world culture as both Mandelstam and Brodsky conceived it. What they meant was whatever had its roots in the pagan cultures of Greece and Rome, and later in Judaism and Christianity. Mandelstam assiduously excluded other religions. Brodsky seems to have been at least somewhat broader and briefly took in some elements of Yoga. Neither made a distinction between religion and culture; whatever remains of culture in the desolate modern world, for them, has its roots in the four main religious streams that nourished Europe. Mandelstam was at the same time pagan and Jew and Christian—Catholic in spirit, but never in any sense sectarian. Brodsky's unquestionable religious feeling is at the same time a feeling for culture. He is remote not only from sectarianism but from any kind of specific religious commitment. Religious feeling, however, the remote, metaphysical stretch of time and space to eternity and infinity, is very strong in him.

A longing for world culture was what plunged Brodsky (a dropout at an early age from formal education) into study and mastery of English and Polish.[1] He claims to have first read the English metaphysical poets—to whom perhaps he came by way of Akhmatova and T. S. Eliot—word by word, with a dictionary. The boldness and directness of the metaphysical conceits, and even those tropes that were far from "conceits," he learned to handle as they had never before been handled in Russian poetry. He translated Donne,

Joseph Brodsky (*Robert H. Taylor*)

imitated Blake, parodied Pushkin. In addition to his mastery of English and Polish, he apparently at some point learned to read some Spanish and Italian: Spanish poetry from Góngora to Lorca has had an impact on him. Among the Italians, those who took up a stance similar to that of the Acmeists against the Symbolists in Russia, against the overblown, overinflated rhetoric of D'Annunzio—Montale and Ungaretti—he made his own. Where or when he came by Beckett and Frost, I do not know, but they are very much there in his poems in that metaphysical dialogue between characters with particular voices and intonations in very particular situations yet carrying the whole weight and stretch of the cosmos as pressure on their talk. One must also add Cavafy: Cavafy's demystifying, demythologizing yet "classicizing" of Alexandria, seen as a model for Petersburg-Leningrad; that unmistakably Byzantine flavor introduced into the poems about Greece and Rome; and the example of another poet born into exile, who made a sufficient world of that exile.

However homespun and self-taught, Brodsky's world culture is, if not complete, large-scale and impressive. It is not limited to poetry alone. Yet there are two great prose writers whose presence (for personal reasons perhaps) I miss in his oeuvre: Tolstoy and Joyce. The qualities I associate with them are not in Brodsky: body-consciousness, joy in the physical, the epic sense in which particulars are not diminished by their link to the cosmic. For instance, Brodsky has a long poem about a butterfly. It is a remarkable poem, and even shaped on the page like a butterfly, in the occasional manner of Herbert and Vaughan. The poet senses the butterfly, a small fluttering thing caught in his hand, as a "something," an affirmation of life, between himself and nothingness. The poem is praise for that slight, fluttering, subsistent "something" brushing against the palm like a lover's eyelids, something so briefly and slenderly alive, yet *there* as a kind of a transition from and buffer against nothingness. But the reader is hard put to guess, for instance, what kind of butterfly it was.

The stance of the lyrical persona in Brodsky's poems is solitary: watching, waiting, looking out a window, gazing at stars or at a landscape. The solitude in these poems is immense. Sometimes it is bracing and strong, the stance of independence and originality, as when, in an early poem, he addresses his own verses: "And must you live in nests of latest style / And sing in concert with the latest lyre?"[2] It is of course a rhetorical question, and for him even at twenty the answer is obvious. Ten years later, steeped in self-irony, he writes: "My song was out of tune, my voice was cracked, / but at least no chorus can ever sing it back."[3] This is stubborn, stalwart Brodsky, who at twenty-four faced judge and prosecutor in a Leningrad court, accused of "parasitism," and proclaimed his commitment to the craft of making poems; who faced unfazed two years of work on a collective farm in the Archangel district and made poems out of it. Yet reading Brodsky, the solitude becomes all-pervasive and begins to weigh heavily. Even the love poems—to "M.B.," to "Mademoiselle Veronique" and others—are poems of solitude and separation. The pieces dedicated to friends (those to Evgeny Rein are especially delicate in the tone and feeling of address) express separation and apartness. Elegies to the admired dead (T. S. Eliot, Robert Lowell, Auden) are poems of solitude and separation. There is an occasional note of solidarity, as in the fleeting, almost shy, occasional references to his mentor Anna Akhmatova, or the remarkable prose obituary he wrote for Nadezhda Mandelstam. But for the most part, the lyrical persona of the poems stands so bleakly alone in such a vastly alienated world that the reader, gripped by the power of the verse, nevertheless begins to long for his own "halt in the desert."

For Brodsky, even the return of the prodigal strikes up a theme of separation.

It's fine that there is no one else to blame,
it's fine that you are free of all connections,
it's fine that in this world there is no one
who feels obliged to love you to distraction.
. . . .
it's fine to walk, alone, in this vast world
toward home from the tumultuous railroad station.
It's fine to catch yourself, while rushing home,
mouthing a phrase that's something less than candid;
you're suddenly aware that your own soul
is very slow to take in what has happened.
(*SP*, 33)

Even a certain solidarity with the past—the normal orientation of a traditionalist-classicist—is generally seen as a distinction and separation from the present: "In recent years whatever stands alone / stands as a symbol of another time" (*SP*, 89). There is a beautiful poem to Dante's Florence, a place to which that poet never returned, although it was he who created the language that is now spoken there. There are poems in which the poet ironically separates himself not only from the world, but from his own soul: "Now that I've walled myself off from the world, / I'd like to wall myself off from myself" (*SP*, 84). And this is done by staring at his now alienated image in the mirror! Or earlier, in a poem in which he cries for reconciliation with his soul, seen as a bird in flight as he walks down a public thoroughfare that takes on the shape of death.

o street, draw me the silhouette of death,
and you, o bird, shriek out the shape of life.
For here I walk, and somewhere there you fly
no longer heedful of our mutterings;
for here I live, and somewhere there you cry,
beating your tremulous, translucent wings.
(*SP*, 32)

In one of his longest and most impressive poems, "Gorbunov and Gorchakov" (*SP*. 143–48), one of Brodsky's Beckettlike characters, Gorchakov, asks the other what he means by love; Gorbunov answers, "Separation, and the solitude that goes with it." Against the weight of the themes of separation and solitude, Brodsky's counterweight of a theme of Christmas and homecoming seems feather-light and fleeting. Yet it is also true that in one of his best-known poems, the long "Elegy for John Donne," he sustains the trope of reunion, of rejoining, as the slow-falling snow, like needles across the night sky, sews body and soul, life and death together (*SP*, 39–45).

The constellation Pisces, seen in the winter sky from the lavatory window of the prison psychiatric hospital where he was briefly confined in 1964 prior to his trial, becomes for Brodsky a trope for the visibility yet utter unreachability and unavailability of the infinite.

Thus, mouths agape and goggle-eyed, we stared
through winter windows at the starry Fish
and wagged our shaven heads, in that place where
men spit on floors—

where sometimes we are given fish to eat,
but never knife or fork to eat it with.
(*SP,* 77)

The poem is dedicated to A. Gorbunov, who lends his name also to the long poem mentioned earlier. In Brodsky's work, madness is yet another form of separation, as lover from lover, soul from body, earth from cosmos. In the madhouse, reason and unreason, activity and passivity, dream and waking, martyrdom and betrayal, words and things are unjoined.

With regard to "words and things" in "Gorbunov and Gorchakov," the case is more complicated. Words become things and things become words. There is an hallucinated, surrealist sequence in which the phrase "he said" becomes a Tatar overlord, wears a turban, takes a stance on top of the table and demands tribute. For an anonymous character, the snowdrifts and piles of firewood in the courtyard are "a conversation." For Gorchakov, dreams are the shadows or projections of the day's events, or selected memories of his Leningrad past. From these selected memories, he says he dreams abstractions like "old age" or "childhood." His counterpart, Gorbunov, dreams only of two things (in his dreams, as opposed to those of Gorchakov, abstractions become concrete images)—mushrooms and the sea. When asked what the mushrooms mean to him, Gorbunov replies: "Always when I look at mushrooms, / I think habitually about love. / I don't know whether in the mind or in the blood, / but I feel the likeness of their interchange."[4] An anonymous pair, doctors perhaps, conversing on the madhouse porch, have this to say about the Gorbunov-Gorchakov exchange of dreams:

"The names of things are sinister and threatening."
"One's head is soon stuffed with these hungry words
which turn upon their things and quite devour
  them!"

. . . .

"Such things for Gorbunov—as the sea—aren't
  healthy."
"It's not the sea racing upon the shore;
it's only words that hard on words are crowding."
"Words seem almost to image the power of relics!"
"If these things could be hung somewhere. . .
These names, as a talisman against things."
"Against the meaning of life." "In a certain sense."

"Against the suffering of Christ?"
"Against all suffering."
(*SP,* 145–46)[5]

Some time before, Gorchakov has gone to the doctors with an account of Gorbunov's dream of the mushrooms. "Unhealthy," he says, because it is "without guidance from the party line." The doctors thank him and promise him release by Easter. Gorbunov knows he has been betrayed by Gorchakov, yet needs him. Christlike and Judaslike, they are nevertheless bound to each other and even cling. Gorbunov prays to God for an angel in Gorchakov's place and proposes to solve the problem of solitude by being split in two, offering his "self" to God as the incommensurable remainder that belongs to neither "half." Gorchakov, bereft and guiltstricken, watches in the end over the sleeping Gorbunov and reflects, "Most of all, I was simply wild about our conversation."

The theme of words usurping or devouring things is a trope that appears elsewhere in Brodsky, in close conjunction with that of words becoming things and that of death (as the anonymous speaker puts it in "Gorbunov and Gorchakov") as "the *only* double-meaninged *thing*"—in "A Song to No Music" (*PS,* 26–33), for instance, and in "Nature Morte," where not only an epigraph from Pavese, but also a theme from Dostoevsky's *Idiot* plays a certain role. One cannot help remembering Myshkin's comments on seeing the reproduction of a Holbein painting in Rogozhin's apartment in which Christ's body, only recently deposed, looks dead beyond all hope of resurrection. That picture, Myshkin notes, could make anyone lose his faith. In Brodsky's poem Mary asks:

"How can I close my eyes,
uncertain and afraid?
Are you dead?—or alive?
Are you my son?—or God?"

Christ speaks to her in turn:
"Whether dead or alive,
woman, it's all the same—
son or God, I am thine."
(*SP,* 164)

Words are at least man's addition to creation—or at least that *with* which man is no mere thing, empowering him

to see that flesh that nature hasn't,
and where the vacuum is, scout
for treasures and for omnipresent

winged female-breasted lions or
dark idols, rather small but able,
great eagles that foretell the score.

. . . .

What matters is not what life has,
but just one's faith in what should be there.[6]

In the warmest and most personal of his elegies, "York. In Memoriam W. H. Auden," Brodsky writes: "Subtracting the greater from the lesser—time from man— / you get words, the remainder, standing out against their / white background more clearly than the body / ever manages to while it lives, though it cry 'Catch me!'— // thus the source of love turns into the object of love."[7]

Although Brodsky's attitude to monuments is always suffused with irony—the public monument acceptable to everyone, the children playing in front of it, the foreign tourist taking its picture, yet seen as "monument to the lie"—he is by no means unresponsive to them, especially to verbal monuments, but, for all the irony, also to memorials of all kinds. There is a wonderful trope in the "Mexican Divertimento" in which the poet looks out at the monuments lining the Paseo de la Reforma and imagines a future monuments to the stolid woman squatting under one of the monuments with her child, hand outstretched for alms; and in the shade of that monument he imagines a woman with child, squatting, hand outstretched for alms (PS, 83).

Brodsky has refused to be co-opted into "public poetry" of any kind. In Leningrad he wrote: "For the innocent head there is nothing in store but an ax and the evergreen laurel."[8] Later he refers to his "change of Empires" and to Cape Cod as the "eastern tip of the Empire" (PS, 107). From Mexico, after a series of brilliant and witty verses, he writes in a poem addressed to his friend Evgeny Rein:

. . . talk of triumphs snatched
over some adjoining tribe of men, smashed
skulls. Or how pouring blood into bowls
sacred to the Sun God strengthens the latter's bowels:
how sacrifice of eight young and strong men before
  dark
guarantees a sunrise more surely than the lark.

Better syphilis after all, better the orifice
of Cortés' unicorns, than sacrifice like this.
If fate assigns your carcass to the vultures' rage
let the murderer be a murderer, not a sage.

. . . .

Life is a drag, Evgeny mine. Wherever you go,
everywhere dumbness and cruelty come up and say,
  "Hello,
here we are!" And they creep into verse, as it were.
"In all the elements . . ." as the poet has said
  elsewhere.
Didn't he see quite far, stuck in the northern mud?
In every latitude, let me add.[9]

One cannot but applaud such firm, stalwart uncooptableness in our too-public time. And yet that "evergreen laurel" is something of a public monument in itself. And there is something of the urge to memorialize in the manner in which Brodsky has chosen to read his poems aloud—a manner which he began somewhat hesitantly but of which he has by now become a master. It is the manner of a liturgical chant, somewhat nasal but powerfully impersonal, commanded with the force of an organ bellows. To an audience that understands Russian, if at all, rather poorly, it sounds mighty and impressive. But it tends to make his poems sound alike. Indeed, it *masks* the great tonal, thematic, dramatic and lexical range and variety of his poems. There is much to be said for an undramatic, even an antidramatic reading of poetry, especially in Russian, where the impact of the Moscow Art Theatre has been too much felt. It strikes me that Brodsky's reading, for so antimonumental a poet, has a strangely monumentalizing effect.

His has been a powerful voice too in recent controversies over poetic translation.[10] He has seen a certain correspondence between the inflated vagueness of the Symbolist rhetoric (against which his most admired poets of a previous generation rebelled) and the loose and flaccid nature of some contemporary free verse. He has protested particularly against the practice of translating his most craftsmanlike and "classical" Russian poets, whose formal, intricate elaborations were of the essence of their poetic personality, into the free verse of looser contemporary Anglo-American style. He has himself been fortunate in gathering to his service a range of devoted and highly skilled poets, with whom, given his own mastery of English, he has been able to work closely: Richard Wilbur, Anthony Hecht, Alan Myers and others (A Part of Speech is surely an exemplary volume); and George Kline has been a highly skilled, sensitive and knowledgeable scholar-translator, almost a poet. Yet the one important poem Brodsky has himself written in English—partly, I suspect, to show how it should be done—did not turn out well. The elegy to Robert Lowell (PS, 135–37), modeled in part on Lowell's own "For the Union Dead" (echoing in turn Allen Tate's "Ode to the Confederate Dead"), for all its intricate, assonantal rhymes and other formal arrangements, strikes me as a dead poem. Brodsky's own much freer practice of translating some of his own poems (especially the sequence from which A Part of Speech takes its title) seems to me more alive and to the point as an exemplar for contemporary practice.

Brodsky ranges from the marvelously humorous poem in the Mexican cycle about Mérida at sunset, to the religious invocation of the last of the Roman Elegies, to the grim despair of "I Sit by the Window": "I Sit in the dark. And it would hard to figure out / which is worse: the dark inside, or the darkness out."[11] He commands a wide range of meters, forms and rhythms. His control over the movement of the verse line is phenomenal. His poetic lexicon is vast. In my opinion he is one of the most interesting and most important poets writing today, not only in Russian but in any tongue.

Sidney Monas, Spring 1983

[1] In February 1978, as a member of the Neustadt International Prize jury, Brodsky nominated and successfully championed Polish poet and essayist Czesław Miłosz over a field of candidates that also included Nadezhda Mandelstam. His friendship and professionalties with West Indian poet and dramatist Derek Walcott also date to that jury meeting on the University of Oklahoma campus. See *WLT* 51:4 (Autumn 1977), pp. 567–81, 52:2 (Spring 1978), pp. 197–202 and 52:3 (Summer 1978), p. 364.—*Ed.*

[2] Joseph Brodsky, "Exhaustion now is a more frequent guest," in his *Selected Poems,* George Kline, ed. & tr., New York, Harper & Row, 1973, p. 32. Subsequent references to this volume are abbreviated *SP.* All translations are by Kline unless otherwise noted.

[3] Joseph Brodsky, "I Sit by the Window," Howard Moss, tr., in Brodsky's *A Part of Speech,* New York, Farrar, Straus & Giroux, 1980, p. 41. Subsequent references in the text to this collection are abbreviated *PS.*

[4] This passage from "Gorbunov and Gorchakov" is in my own translation.

[5] I have slightly altered several lines here from Kline's translation.

[6] Joseph Brodsky, "A Song to No Music," David Rigsbee with the author, tr., in *A Part of Speech,* p. 33.

[7] Joseph Brodsky, "York: In Memoriam W. H. Auden," from the cycle "In England," Alan Myers, tr., in *A Part of Speech,* p. 127.

[8] Joseph Brodsky, "The End of a Beautiful Era," David Rigsbee, tr., in *A Part of Speech,* p. 36.

[9] Joseph Brodsky, "To Evgeny," from the cycle "Mexican Divertimento," Alan Myers with the author, tr., in *A Part of Speech,* p. 86.

[10] See especially Brodsky's essay on the translation of poetry in *The New York Review of Books,* 7 February 1974. For one rejoinder, see Yves Bonnefoy, "On the Translation of Form in Poetry," *WLT* 53:3 (Summer 1979), pp. 374–79.

[11] Brodsky, "I Sit by the Window," p. 42.

Chingiz Aitmatov: Transforming the Esthetics of Socialist Realism

"The mission of literature is to express the essence of the human spirit, of man's spiritual quest," remarked Chingiz Aitmatov in an interview several years ago.[1] Aitmatov's deep concern for man's spirituality in Soviet so-

ciety brings his art into close association with that of Valentin Rasputin and the late Yuri Trifonov, whose works transcend the problems of the Siberian village and the *byt* (manners and milieu) of the Soviet metropolis respectively, to confront the reader with profound ethical questions concerning one's relationship to one's fellow man. Most of Aitmatov's work is set in Soviet Middle Asia, in his native Kirghizia, yet his treatment of eternal questions and his innovative spirit have combined to make him one of the most popular writers in the Soviet Union today. Aitmatov's works have been published in the leading Soviet literary journals, and their subsequent appearances in book form enjoy large editions. A graduate of the Gorky Literary Institute in Moscow, Aitmatov has been active on the editorial board of *Novyj Mir* since March 1967, and his publicistic articles on topical issues, which appear from time to time in *Literaturnaja Gazeta,* are read with interest. Not a very prolific writer, Aitmatov is very serious about his art, and, motivated by a Tolstoyan sense of duty to man and society, he does not shy away from controversial issues. Thus the appearance of each new work by the author has been a literary event, often provoking intense discussion in the Soviet press concerning his fresh approach to socialist realism.

The combination of Aitmatov's Kirghiz heritage and his assimilation of the wealth of classical Russian literature make his art truly unique. The folklore and rich epic tradition of his people have made him keenly sensitive to esthetic problems in literature. His prose is highly lyrical, and at times its style is clearly reminiscent of the Kirghiz national epos *Manas.* Yet the symbols and recurring motifs in Aitmatov's prose do not have merely ornamental function, as is the case in many inferior literary works from Soviet Middle Asia, but serve to give each work its peculiar structure and to dramatize dilemmas and conflicts common to all of mankind.

Thanks to his parents, both of whom had studied in Russian schools, Aitmatov was introduced at an early age to Russian language, literature and culture. He grew up to be bilingual—in a short autobiographical sketch he writes humorously about his first experience at interpreting at age five—and today he writes and translates freely in both Kirghiz and Russian. Although he tends to avoid direct answers to questions concerning the language in which his later works are written (his early works of the 1950s and 60s—"Dzhamilia," "The First Teacher," "Mother Earth"—were written in Kirghiz), it is a fact that beginning in 1966 with *Proščaj Gul'sary!* (Farewell, Gulsary!) his works have appeared first in Russian.

Although Aitmatov's early work was written in Kirghiz, the folklore of his native country played only a modest role in its esthetic conception. Beginning with *Belyj paroxod* (The White Steamer; 1970),[2] however, a much more conscious effort to present human situations and conflicts on both a realistic and a mythical level is evident, with the latter structuring and interpreting the action on the realistic plane. The appearance of *Belyj paroxod* in *Novyj Mir* during the last month of Tvardovsky's editorship of the journal can be considered a turning point in Aitmatov's career in another way as well. In the novella an unnamed boy drowns when he "flees" the real world of brute force created by his sadistic uncle, an embodiment of cynical tyranny, and attempts to reach his own dreamworld of love and beauty embodied in the symbol of the white steamship. Aitmatov's portrayal of the triumph of evil over good was so powerful that an intense controversy concerning the possibility of the tragic under socialist conditions arose in *Literaturnaja Gazeta*. The author successfully defended his work against accusations of pessimism and lack of justice to socialist reality, and his victory has proved to be not insignificant for the course of Soviet letters. One must note, however, that Aitmatov later weakened his position somewhat by altering the conclusion of *Belyj paroxod* in its first edition in book form (*Čingiz Ajtmatov: Povesti i rasskazy,* Moscow, 1970) to introduce a ray of light in the novella's dark world. The role of a minor character, Kulubek, is stressed by the narrator as having offered a possible unrealized alternative for the doomed boy.

Aitmatov has continued to write in the spirit of *Belyj paroxod.* His last three works—*Rannie žuravli* (Early Cranes; 1975), *Pegij pës, beguščij kraem morja* (A Spotted Dog by the Seashore; 1977) and *I dol'še veka dlitsja den'* (And the Day Lasts Longer Than a Century; 1980)—all combine myth and legend with everyday reality to accentuate man's precarious situation in the world. Likewise his belief that man is essentially a tragic creature is maintained in his latest work.

Rannie žuravli is set in a small Kirghiz village during World War II. The novella is based on Aitmatov's boyhood experiences in his native *ail,* Sheker, and reflects the hardship his village suffered during the war when women and children were called upon to do the labor of men in the fields. The author portrays the struggle of five Kirghiz youths in an isolated *ail* to do the work of their fathers, who are away at the front. The boys are requested by the kolkhoz chairman to drop out of school in the winter to prepare the kolkhoz's neglected plows, the few half-starved horses and themselves to do the spring plowing and sowing on the vast Aksai steppe situated in the foothills of the Manas mountain range. The theme of the work itself can hardly be considered very original for postwar Soviet literature, yet Aitmatov

modifies it significantly. The mountain, for example, is a constant reminder of the Kirghiz epic poem *Manas,* in whose images of bravery and grandeur the author casts the boys and their "mission." Even the rhythm of the narration is in a number of passages clearly reminiscent of epic solemnity.

As winter turns to spring the boys become men, and the main character, Sultanmurat, manages to whip his companions into a disciplined *kollektiv.* Uniting the boys is their intense yearning for their fathers and their desire to live up to their idealized conceptions of them. But Aitmatov was not intent on applauding the boys' patriotism or crowning their efforts with well-deserved success. In the final pages of the novella the reader is jolted from his position of serene observer when tragedy suddenly befalls the boys almost immediately after they have finally begun their "mission" in the Aksai steppe. After four days' labor the boys find themselves entirely alone and exhausted, yet encouraged by the hope that the harvest will be bountiful. Their dreams are dashed, however, when horse thieves attack and rob them of their plowhorses, an act which also threatens to deprive the village of sorely needed grain. Sultanmurat pursues the armed men on the one remaining horse (his father's). But the horse is shot from under him, and the story ends with Sultanmurat left alone at the mercy of a wolf that has scented the blood of the dying horse.

The abrupt change of fate in *Rannie žuravli* is typical of Aitmatov's later prose. His works are characterized by long expositions and a deliberate narrative pace, both of which are dramatically brought to an end by a sudden crisis. The novella, however, is an uneven work. The epic background does not adequately compensate for the lack of depth of the characters, nor is it as successfully integrated into the structure of the novella as was the case of myth and legend in *Belyj paroxod.*

These inadequacies are fully overcome in Aitmatov's next novella, *Pegij pës, beguščij kraem morja,* the first of Aitmatov's major works to be set outside his native Kirghizia. *Pegij pës* can best be described as a lyrical and philosophical story of life and death in mythic form. The novella relates the sea journey and fate of three Nivkh fishermen-hunters and the boy they take along to initiate in the hunt and in life at sea. As in all of Aitmatov's later works, the action takes place in a highly isolated area—this time on the sparsely inhabited coast of the Sea of Okhotsk among the Nivkh people in far northeastern Siberia. As in his earlier works, Aitmatov chooses a very dramatic situation to test man's humanity under extreme conditions. The three hunters and their boy initiate, Kirisk, paddle out into the open sea beyond sight of land in order to reach three rocky islands where the hunt is to take place. The men's losing sight of land is marked by the disappearance from view of their orientation point on land, a rocky knoll with spots of trees and snow, which from the distance has the appearance of a piebald dog. The moment is an important one for Kirisk, for he now enters the world of men, who in order to provide for their wives and children must venture out to sea.

Accompanying the boy are his father, his uncle and the elder, Organ, the most experienced fisherman-hunter in the hamlet, whose primitive, animistic understanding of the world is shared by all in the boat. Organ's thoughts and daydreaming during the course of the journey transport the reader into a mythical world. One dream that never leaves the elder is his dream of the great Fish-Woman, the mythological mother of the Nivkh tribe, with whom he yearns to unite. This longing finds expression in a number of erotic images. In his dreams Organ follows her into the sea, swimming along with her until they reach a haven on land where, "overcome by passion, they were to be one at last to experience in one lightning-like instant all the pleasure and bitterness of the beginning and end of life."[3] Yet when they finally reach the haven, their unification cannot be consummated, for the Fish-Woman cannot leave her element and must return to the sea, where Organ can never reach her. The dream is important for the structure of Aitmatov's novella, for it emphasizes the eternal opposition of the sea and the land as expressed in the opening and closing paragraphs: "Along the shoreline of the Sea of Okhotsk, along the whole front between the land and the sea, the fierce battle of the two elements raged—the land impeded the movement of the sea, the sea tirelessly besieged the land" (4). Also, the dream is in a sense a death wish, and as such it foreshadows the catastrophe that will befall the four men in the kayak.

After reaching the first island, where Kirisk's incautious actions spoil the hunt, the men set off for the second island. Immediately upon losing sight of land again they become engulfed by dense fog and must wrestle with a terrifying storm. They survive the storm yet lose their way in the fog. The fog settles down motionless over the sea, and the little drinking water the men have brought with them is soon to run out. Realizing their plight might last for days, Organ steps into the icy water to his death in order to save drinking water for the others in the boat. As time goes on and the fog continues to hang low over the sea, the boy's uncle and then father imitate the elder's act of self-sacrifice, leaving Kirisk the last remaining drops of water. Yet for Kirisk the men never die; they live on in his animistic world—Organ as the wind, his uncle as the waves, his father as the guiding star that the boy, alone and exhausted, sees

when the fog finally lifts. Kirisk is saved on the seventh day as the winds drive the fragile kayak within sight of the "spotted dog" again.

Aitmatov's novella deliberately gives no clear indication of the time when the story takes place. This vagueness of time, of course, gives the story its mythological context. The self-sacrifice of the men is not military or revolutionary heroism, which has often been the theme of socialist-realist works. The sacrifice, although not easy, is still a natural act determined by a harmonious pagan view of the world that, odd as it may seem, has Christian undertones as well. The image of Christ walking on water, for example, is evoked prior to Organ's stepping into the sea.

"A Spotted Dog" can be compared to Hemingway's *The Old Man and the Sea*. In both works individual men stand for mankind, and the external action can take on mythological interpretation. If the creed of Hemingway's Santiago in essence calls upon men to preserve their dignity in defeat, then for Aitmatov's Nivkh fishermen the call is to "remain true to one's humanity"; and in the final analysis the three men's choice is not a choice at all, for it is their only way to live as men in their understanding of the world. Another interesting parallel can be drawn between *Pegij pës* and Stephen Crane's "The Open Boat." Yet in Crane's story blind fate determines which of the five shipwrecked men makes it alive to the shore, whereas in Aitmatov's novella the men themselves actively create their fate.

The publication of *Pegij pës* with its heavy reliance on myth and symbolism quickly brought forth voices of strong criticism. In a brief survey of mythological and allegorical currents in recent Soviet literature, for example, L. Anninsky criticized the use of myth and legend by writers because in his view it distracts them from their chief goal—the realistic portrayal of reality (*Literaturnaja Gazeta*, 1 March 1978, p. 5). Another critic asserted that to resort to myth in literature is far easier than to write "honest straightforward prose" (*Literaturnaja Gazeta*, 12 April 1978, p. 5). Aitmatov countered by reaffirming his staunch loyalty to socialist realism, yet pointing out that his detractors have an oversimplified, naïve understanding of realism (*Literaturnaja Gazeta*, 29 March 1978, p. 5). In an interview with Larissa Lebedeva he expressed the view that literature should break with obsolete one-dimensionality by using legend and myth, thus making the reader's experience of reality a deeper one (*Družba Narodov,* 1977, no. 10, pp. 241–42).

Indeed, in his most recent work, *I dol'še veka dlitsja den',* Aitmatov continues to move away from one-dimensionality by creating a remarkable "symphonic" novel based on the counterpoint of several motifs and temporal planes.[4] The central motif that determines the novel's structure and meaning is Aitmatov's peculiar interpretation of the Kirghiz legend of the Zhuan-zhuany, a cruel nomadic tribe that tortured its prisoners by pulling taut leather skullcaps over their heads, thus depriving those that survived of their memory. The survivors, called "mankurt" by the tribe, thereafter became submissive slaves, obediently fulfilling their masters' most whimsical desires. According to the legend as presented in the novel, one such *mankurt* even kills his own mother, Naiman-Ana, at the behest of his captors, when she desperately seeks to revive her son's memory by repeating his name to him and by constantly asking him to tell her his father's name—Donenbai. According to the legend, as Naiman-Ana fell, pierced by her son's arrow, her scarf turned into a white bird that even today flies over the steppe crying, "Donenbai, whose son are you? Donenbai, Donenbai." The place where she was buried became known to the inhabitants of the Sarozek steppes of Kazakhstan—where the novel is set—as Ana-Beiit (Mother's Repose). Through the centuries Ana-Beiit became the sacred burial ground of the nomadic peoples populating the vast steppes.

The burial ground and the legend associated with it tie together three temporal planes: the legendary past, the recent past and the present, and the near yet hypothetical future. The main character, Edigei Zhangildin, a railwayman at an isolated hamlet in the steppe, represents Aitmatov's conception of the positive hero—a simple man devoted to his labor. Edigei is a *malen'kij čelovek* (little man), similar to the many variations of the type known to us from classical Russian literature. Like them he strives to live with dignity and conscience in a world in which forces are active that he can neither control nor fully comprehend. In the early 1950s Edigei tries to preserve his personality and humanity in the face of Stalinist henchmen, who even in the isolated Sarozeks manage to destroy an innocent family dear to him. Likewise in the present era he is confronted with another type of *mankurt* when he decides to honor a deceased friend's last wish to be buried at legendary Ana-Beiit. The funeral is to take place according to Moslem ritual, but Edigei soon discovers that his deceased friend's son, who arrives from the city, cares little for his father's heritage or Edigei's world view, which encompasses both life and death. The son, Sabitzhan, reveals himself to be a petty party careerist whose unlimited faith in technological progress envisions a world of human robots subserviently following orders from above.

After quarreling with Edigei, however, Sabitzhan grudgingly agrees to join the funeral procession, which

is to go deep into the steppe. Yet the procession never reaches the burial ground. Unknown to Edigei, Ana-Beiit has been incorporated into the off-limits zone of the top-secret Sary-Ozek space center. The officers at the gate show little concern for Edigei's plight, and a Kazakh lieutenant, refusing to speak to him in his native Kazakh, tells him brusquely in Russian that Ana-Beiit will soon be liquidated to make room for a new housing project for the personnel of the space center. Edigei has no choice but to leave, and with deep sorrow and anger he solemnly buries his friend in a ravine within sight of the barbed-wire fence that has separated him from Ana-Beiit.

Paralleling the drama at the funeral procession is an unprecedented crisis, one which Edigei knows nothing about, that unfolds on the third narrative plane. For the first time Aitmatov introduces the fantastic into his prose. An American and a Soviet astronaut, as part of a joint USA-USSR mission, have discovered intelligent life on another planet. Choosing not to inform their superiors on Earth, they visit the planet on their own initiative before deciding to break the news to mankind, which, given its political and ideological differences, they doubt will be inclined to embrace a more advanced civilization. When Mission Control is finally contacted by the insubordinate astronauts, it learns that the "new world" is a virtual utopia, free of disease, civil strife and war. Yet the discovery threatens to throw the world into a dangerous crisis. When the U.S.-Soviet crisis commission is requested to allow representatives from the other planet to visit Earth, it rejects the offer; and to ensure the Earth's inviolability, the commission initiates "Project Hoop," which is to blot the discovery of a better way of life from the Earth's memory by cutting off all contact with the two astronauts, by casting a cloak of secrecy over all aspects of the mission and by setting up an impenetrable ring of explosive orbiters around the Earth to ward off any attempted interference from outer space.

Yet before Project Hoop is put into action, the narrative returns to Edigei, who now stands alone at the barbed-wire fence of the space center. He has vowed to himself not to give up the fight for Ana-Beiit. Deserted by all who had accompanied him in the procession, Edigei decides to go back to the gate, only to turn and flee in terror in the closing apocalyptic scene of the novel, as the Soviet Union commences its part of the project and rocket after rocket thunders from the nearby launch site. Amidst the fire and roar of the rockets the cry of the white bird Donenbai is heard, symbolically warning man to remember his heritage.

Thus in the closing lines of *I dol'še veka dlitsja den'*, a work considered to be Aitmatov's first full-length novel, the author brings all the mythic currents and temporal planes together. The "cosmic myth" created by Aitmatov contains a number of contradictions, but it essentially parallels the myth of Naiman-Ana. The Earth dons a *mankurt's* cap when it tries to cut itself off from all external influence. The cries of the stranded astronauts are clearly reminiscent of the call of the bird Donenbai.

Taken in its entirety, the novel enunciates a powerful plea for freedom of conscience. It condemns the psychology of obsequious careerism and mutual mistrust that characterized the Stalin years and, as the author implies, finds expression in Soviet society today. Similar to Czesław Miłosz, who in his Nobel Prize address warns Western man of the consequences of a "refusal to remember," Aitmatov urges his readers to resist becoming a *mankurt*, without memory, personality or conscience, and as such a pliable tool in the hands of those who have little respect for human dignity. This is the meaning of Edigei's simple life, the courageous act of the astronauts and the legend of Naiman-Ana.

I dol'še veka dlitsja den' is a complicated novel and, as such, not without deficiencies. Aitmatov has received justifiable criticism for his occasional in-appropriate use of archaisms and neologisms in the narration. Furthermore, a number of important characters are sketchily portrayed—in particular, Edigei's wife and the Russian geologist Elizarov. Several sections in the exposition might seem to Western readers unduly sentimental and drawn-out.

Soviet criticism speaks with one voice in lauding Aitmatov's success at creating a believable positive character. Edigei's simple life takes on epic proportions, reaching deep into the heritage of his ancestors and at the same time calling upon modern man to remember whence he has come before rushing blindly into the future. The cosmic myth, however, has become the object of diverging opinions. Some reviewers do not question the justification of the Earth's decision to sequester itself from any contact with the "new world," considering its inhabitants no more than "highly humanistic Zhuanzhuany" (*Oktjabr'*, 1981, no. 5, p. 208) or looking upon the planet as a dangerous Trojan horse (*Oktjabr'*, 1981, no. 9, p. 213). Others admonish Aitmatov for not being more specific as to which of the two partners on the U.S.-Soviet space commission bears responsibility for the Earth's unwillingness to embrace a more advanced form of life (for example, *Voprosy Literatury*, 1981, no. 9, p. 26, and *Pravda*, 16 February 1981, p. 7). Significantly, the novel leaves such questions open, for in Aitmatov's prose all men bear responsibility for life on this planet. Moreover, a number of other burning questions are left unanswered as well. Thus, *I dol'ševeka dlitsja den'*

will certainly continue to be mentioned in literary discussion in the USSR for some time yet.

Aitmatov's official status in the Soviet Union—in addition to editorial responsibilities at *Novyj Mir* and *Literaturnaja Gazeta*, he represents Kirghizia in the Supreme Soviet and is chairman of the Kirghiz Union of Cinematographers—no doubt enables him to write with more artistic freedom than other Soviet writers. He has consistently criticized primitive didacticism and cliché-ridden style in Soviet letters and has become very vocal in recent years in advocating a more imaginative approach to socialist realism, one in which myth, legends and the fantastic are all to be granted a place (see, for example, his interview in *Družba Narodov*, 1977, no. 10, pp. 239–42). If in the past Soviet literature has been straitjacketed by theorists trying to direct the way its development is to go, today there are signs that literary practice in the Soviet Union is beginning to relegate literary theory to an ever-increasing interpretive role. In an interview with N. N. Shneidman Aitmatov sums up this complicated evolution:

> The literary output of contemporary writers is ahead of the theoretical premises for contemporary literature. Theorists of literature, in turn, endeavor to adapt the new theoretical premises to the needs of literary practice. The interaction of theory and practice of Soviet literature in contemporary conditions is often complicated because certain representatives of the past in our literature endeavor to hold back its development.[5]

Chingiz Aitmatov's role in this evolution should not be underestimated. And there is good reason to believe that his art will continue to challenge Soviet literary conservatives in the future.

Joseph P. Mozur, Summer 1982

1 N. N. Shneidman, personal interview with Chingiz Aitmatov from 7 April 1976, printed in *Russian Literature Triquarterly*, 16 (1979), p. 268.

2 For a discussion of *Belyj paroxod* and Aitmatov's early work see Rosemarie Kieffer, "Chingiz Aitmatov: Epic Chronicler of Tradition and Change in Soviet Kirghizia," BA 49:3 (1975), pp. 459–64.

3 Čingiz Ajmatov, "Pegij pës, beguščij kraem morja," *Znamja* (Moscow), 1977, no. 4, p. 17. Subsequent references are by page number in parentheses. All translations are my own.

4 For a detailed discussion of this aspect of the novel see Jurij Surovtsev, "Mnogozvučnyj roman-kontrapunkt," *Družba Narodov*, 1981, no. 5, pp. 246–55.

5 Shneidman, p. 267.

SLOVENIA

Out of the Shadows: Slovene Writing after Independence

At the Turn of the millennium, Slovenia appears to have an enviable position among the newly independent states of Southern and Central Europe. The grip of the Yugoslav Communist Party was somewhat looser than that of comparable parties in the Soviet Bloc, and the transition to capitalism and democracy went more smoothly than in other Slavic states. Slovenia was the most modern and most prosperous of the former Yugoslav republics (8 percent of the population produced 20 percent of the GNP); and, in comparison with its neighbors to the south, it suffered very little from the disintegration of Yugoslavia which it initiated in 1991. Now, according to Euromoney's ranking for country risk, Slovenia places ahead of Hungary, Poland, and the Czech Republic, thirty-third to Austria's ninth ("Facts," 4). It is on the fast track for NATO and EU membership and is systematically shifting its orientation and its public image from the Balkans to Central Europe. Better still, except for the Serbs, who call the Slovenes Western lackeys, there seems to be no governmental animosity toward Slovenians, even those who constitute minorities in the Trieste region in Austria and Italy, though Slovenians think that Italians take every opportunity to remind them of their occupation of the Littoral. Some border problems with Italy and Croatia remain to be worked out, but these disputes do not appear to be heated. On the streets, there are numerous signs of individual prosperity. As Iztok Osojnik says, the country may be poor, but the people are not.

Even the writers do not complain as much as their colleagues in Slovakia and Hungary, though when told this they seem disconcerted and perhaps a little offended. But their situation is different. From the eighth century until 1991, Slovenes were a nation rather than a state, held together by language and culture rather than by self-generated political structures. This feeling is so strong that, in a country perhaps 80 percent Catholic, the door of Ljubljana's cathedral features the first three books printed in Slovene about five centuries ago — all Protestant. From the nineteenth century on, writers like France Prešeren, Ivan Cankar, and Edvard Kocbek served as creators, conservators, and transmitters of Slovene identity, and their names and likenesses are prominent on street signs, public monuments, and currency. Slovenia not only has a high literacy rate, but the people actually read: in 1999, libraries circulated eight to ten million books to a total population of two million, and

a person who reads fewer than ten books a year is not regarded as a serious reader.

Moreover, since 1945, and especially in the decade before independence, writers continued to serve as the conscience of the Slovene people: they were in the forefront of movements for a free and democratic Slovenia, like the founders of the soon-suppressed magazine *Revija 57*; in 1998 the Committee for Freedom of Speech and Writing, associated with the Slovenian Writers Association, sponsored a group whose members wrote a draft that was the basis of the present Slovenian constitution; and a number of writers served in the first democratic government. Also, *Nova Revija* (New Review; founded 1982) was enormously influential. Aleš Debeljak has noted that the organizations and initiatives "represented a kind of *umbrella institution*. Under its precarious protection sought and found refuge astoundingly varied ideological groups, individuals, tendencies, programs, and agendas. Because of its *licentia poetica,* the cultural sphere, vaguely defined as it always was, more or less successfully bypassed the communist control" (Debeljak, "Haven").

This activity was perhaps less dangerous than it would have been in the Soviet Bloc, for repression under Tito and his successors, though not to be minimized, was less severe. True, several collections of poems and rather more fiction and nonfiction had to appear in samizdat, and many writers were arrested and tried and some convicted or, like Edvard Kocbek, officially silenced. This side of the communist era was memorialized in the exhibition and book *Temna stran meseca* (The Dark Side of the Moon), organized by Vasko Simoniti and Drago Jančar, which has not been translated. However, according to a writer who refused to participate in the project, many authors managed to survive official disapproval and even to become part of the nomenklatura. Now it is a mark of distinction to have been jailed. The fact that the sentence might have been for drunkenness is delicately avoided. Writers whose sole theme was dissidence now have difficulty coming up with new subjects.

For a variety of reasons, the government, whether liberal or conservative, is inclined to foster what Iztok Osojnik terms genuine creativity in language and culture. It does so to a far greater extent than in the former Soviet satellites and in greater numbers than it did before 1991. For example, one survival from the Tito era, on a Scandinavian model, is the program of the free artist, which provides to about a thousand artists in all media minimal social and medical benefits and an automatic deduction of 40 percent of income as costs of production. (There is discussion of abolishing the last benefit, and the liberals are regarded as most likely to push for that.) The government gives some support to the Slovenian Writers Association, founded under the Habsburgs, with three hundred members and a very active program. Unlike its counterpart in Slovakia, the Association is unified (though in late 1999 there was an attempted coup by younger writers, which was beaten back by the older members), with one rather than six organizations seeking funds. And unlike its counterpart in Hungary, the Association seems to be in fairly healthy condition.

Moreover, the Ministry of Culture subsidizes publication of books in many genres, totaling about 200 original works a year, including forty to fifty literary works, about twenty translations of Slovene writers into other languages, seventy or so technical and cultural publications, and some translations — including William S. Burroughs's *Naked Lunch*— of foreign works into Slovenian. It also supports magazines like *Literatura* and nine theaters, three of them in Ljubljana, though some dramatists complain that translated popular work has all but driven out new Slovenian drama.

In fact, the number of books published each year has increased markedly since independence. To some extent, this is a result of independence: the need to catch up with the basic Western canon and also to publish in Slovene reference books that had, in Yugoslavia, appeared in Serbo-Croatian. But more original works are also being published.

Given a population of two million, editions tended to be small even under communist rule. As a result, Slovenia did not experience as precipitous a drop in edition sizes as did Hungary and Slovakia. With rare exceptions, 3,000 copies was a standard edition for a first novel before independence, and it sold out in six months. Now, even for books likely to be popular, 2,000 is a high number, with perhaps 500 for poetry. Andrej Blatnik, author of *Skinswaps* (Northwestern University Press, 1998) and other fiction and an editor at Cankarjeva Publishers, says that anything selling over five to seven hundred copies is regarded as a best seller. Their biggest hit was a travel book about Burkina Faso which sold 2,200 copies — why, he is not sure. Cankarjeva is a general publishing house, using cookbooks and other popular titles to finance creative work.

Financial arrangements for writers are simple if not very remunerative. Instead of royalties, they receive a flat fee, usually ranging from $1,000 to $4,000, and magazines still pay for contributions. *Nova Revija* continues to be very important; *Literatura* and *Apokalipsa* (both including some foreign writers in translation) are influential; and many other newspapers and magazines serve as outlets. However, in order to survive, writers must be willing to write in all genres of journalism as well as to produce literature, to teach, to translate, to edit, and to work as cultural managers of associations and institutions. But as Aleš Debeljak says, he and others write in nonliterary genres not so much for money as to maintain their positions as public intellectuals.

However, finding someone to listen is becoming more difficult. Debeljak says: "As individuals who struggled for freedom and against totalitarian limits to the human spirit, [writers] were defeated by their own success. Freedom of choice also implies a freedom not to choose to listen to the writers' voices any longer" (Debeljak, "Ethics"). Perhaps more important, nascent capitalism, farther advanced in Slovenia at the beginning of independence than elsewhere in the Soviet Bloc, has given the potential audience a wider range of positive choice. Evald Flisar, president of the Writers Association, notes that in the free market the number of publishers mushroomed. Matej Bogataj counted 150 in 1999, with 2,500 titles per year (*Mosaic, 7*). Moreover, translations of popular psychology and New Age books, never before available, are bought by the kilo. (However, one does not see on the streets of Ljubljana, as in Budapest, the stalls lined with Harold Robbins, Barbara Cartland, and other writers of disposable books. Iztok Osojnik attributes the difference not to the superiority of Slovene taste but to the fact that other merchandise is much more profitable.)

As a result, average book buyers — lower-middle-class youth and students — not only have more choice but have trouble paying the new prices. Besides, newly available consumer goods, the Internet, and other options have cut into the book market. And books are expensive. The paperback edition of *Naked Lunch* was priced at just over $18, and a bookstore clerk was appalled at how much she had to charge — about $20 — for a very slim volume. One editor speculates that publishers know that a core audience of perhaps 500 will continue to buy books and do not think it worthwhile to lower prices to attract another hundred or so readers.

Nevertheless, a good deal of writing continues to be done by writers of all generations, though the subject matter and sense of mission have gone through obvious changes.[1] Historically, major Slovene writers were acutely conscious of their importance to Slovene identity, and this sense of mission required a language, especially in poetry, that was sometimes more distinguished for exhortation than for lyricism. France Prešeren (1800–49) is Slovenia's universally honored poet; his "Toast to Freedom," which became the Slovenian national anthem, has lines like "Let thunder out of heaven / Strike down and smite our wanton foe!" A century later, Edvard Kocbek (1904–81) wrote "The Lippizaners," which can be seen as an ironic complement to "Toast." His "Slovenian Hymn" has imagery that is more concrete, but it also contains lines like "Disowned, you endure, great mother, quietly calling us, you have been ravaged, fertile body, and your children put to shame." And Kocbek's essay "On Poetry" (*Afterwards,* 45–52) is full of vatic utterances like "Poetry is divination on the border of the world of dreams and the world of reality."[2]

Of course, Prešeren and Kocbek wrote poetry that is lyric rather than rhetorical, but even in poems like "In a Torched Village" (*Embers*), Kocbek is forced to deal with political and historical conditions not only as poet but as partisan and politician. To a less dramatic degree, this is true of writers like Dane Zajc (b. 1929; referred to as "the Nestor of Slovene poets"), Kajetan Kovič (b. 1931), Niko Grafenauer (b. 1940), Svetlana Marakovič (b. 1939), Tomaž Šalamun (b. 1941; probably the Slovenian writer best known in the United States), and Veno Taufer (b. 1933). Taufer is a member of what he calls the Critical Generation, whose ideas were formulated in the late 1940s and early 1950s.[3] His father was killed in 1943, and he sees himself as an heir to the resistance ideas. For readers of English, this is most clearly evident in his sequence "Melancholy of the Second Echelon: In memory of my father, killed in 1943." Though it seems innocent enough of ideology, it was rejected on the grounds that it was "ideologically problematic." It was then published in samizdat. Taufer was also translating — Eliot, Yeats, Hughes, Pound, and currently Wallace Stevens, as well as French, Russian, Macedonian, Serbian, and Croatian poets of his generation and younger — and, like Grafenauer, Šalamun, and others, writing modernist poems when, at least until the early 1960s, modernism was a political statement.

Taufer was also making more overt statements. As one of the founders of *Oder 57,* banned after a year and a half, and a theatrical group which lasted for eight years, he was imprisoned and interrogated for eighteen hours a day. In 1985, he was one of the architects and first chair of the Committee for Freedom of Speech and Writing; a year later, he converted the Vilenica conference into an international literary and cultural forum; and he was one of the authors of the draft constitution and a founder of the opposition party Slovenian Democratic Union and stood for election to the first freely elected parliament. Since then, he has given up politics — which, he said, played no part in his poetry except as a feeling and a general source of experience, largely rage and disillusionment — though he is now president of Slovenian PEN.

The contrast between the modernist generation, who grew up under communism, and their successors, who never knew any other system, is exemplified by the novelist-playwright Drago Jančar (b. 1948),[4] the novelist-travel writer-dramatist Evald Flisar (b. 1945), the scarifying poet Ifegenija Zagornick (b. 1953), and the novelist-poet Iztok Osojnik (b. 1951). Some believe that the generation born between 1945 and 1960 has been ignored, but there are signs that it is gaining recognition. Flisar is now president of the Slovenian Writers Association, and Osojnik is director of the Vilenica festival. They grew up in the hippie generation, and during the 1980s, when the struggles for democracy and independence (not, in the early stages, the same thing) were greatest, Flisar was living in London when he was not traveling to seventy other countries. Osojnik did not equal that range, but he did travel a great deal and recalls the sixties and seventies as an ideal time to be a Yugoslav, because one could travel both east and west. Perhaps in consequence, they shared the political sentiments of their elders without their degree of engagement. But things changed. In the early days, he has noted, someone would say, "Let's go to India," and in ten days they would be there. Later it took twenty days because of complications. Still later they couldn't go at all because of wars in the region. And then they couldn't even go to Zagreb. . . .

In his youth, Osojnik was perhaps the closest a Slav could come to being a Dadaist. He and two friends conducted a series of hoaxes, dumbfounding not the bourgeoisie, which is too easy, but those who wanted to be in on the latest thing. For example, they applied for and got government funding for a philosophical conference at which the speakers spouted gibberish, and at the end let the audience in on the joke. The latter were not amused. Nor were those who attended a so-called experimental rock concert at which Osojnik appeared in drag. Now, he says, he doesn't have to do anything outrageous; he simply has to appear at a cultural gathering to make people nervous.

Perhaps as a result, he is only now able to publish manuscripts that he wrote sixteen to eighteen years ago and that were paid for and then refused, not — or not so much — because of ideological reasons but because the audience, including editors who had themselves been censored, were not ready for his tone and subject matter. His fiction has not been translated, but his poems in translation are, rather surprisingly, as measured and somber as those by many of his elders.

The next generation of writers was born between 1955 and 1965, according to Aleš Debeljak (b. 1961; see "Visions," 428), and never experienced Stalinist-style repression. Therefore, he says, "the external need to write Aesopian tales and in coded metaphors vanished" (*Twilight,* 66), as did the tendency to see good and evil as merely a matter of communist/ noncommunist. "In this way," he adds, "Central and Eastern Europe witnessed a shift in the use of poetry, which too often had been fraught with an exalted political or moral 'noble mind' which has, as Czesław Miłosz once shrewdly observed, no place in poems" (69). Therefore, this generation was even less involved with politics than was that of 1945–60, and more inclined to write about ordinary people and events. Debeljak mentions Jure Potokar, Maja Haderlap, and Alojz Ihan among the poets of his generation — writers he included in the Slovenian section of *Shifting Borders* (Fairleigh Dickinson University Press, 1993) — and Andrej Blatnik (b. 1963) can be mentioned as a fiction writer allied with this generation. He and Debeljak were editors of Aleph, a small independent press, and Blatnik edits *Literatura,* one of the important literary magazines.

This post-hippie generation is characterized by some as being much more interested in organizations and institutions than were its predecessors, and in fact Debeljak began his career as editor of *Tribune,* a fortnightly student newspaper (not, he hastens to add, like American student papers) that was suppressed because of politically provocative texts such as a letter to the president of Yugoslavia, before Debeljak was forced to resign. To the question, which he raised himself, of why he did not become a politician, Debeljak says that his first book of poems came out and that he became interested in pan-Yugoslav culture, partly because he competed with the Yugoslav judo team. These contacts were, of course, interrupted and in many cases destroyed by the war.

The war may also have put an end to nascent interest in postmodernism, which never gained a significant foothold in Slovenia and is now disparaged by every writer I spoke to. Blatnik's generation was — falsely, he thinks — identified with Western postmodernism, and though he tries to develop unusual formal and narrative patterns in his fiction, he claims little influence from Robert Coover and Thomas Pynchon. Lela B. Njatin (b. 1963) another fiction writer, moves from fairy tale to excruciating and oppressive detail in *Intolerance* (1987), and at times finds common ground with "the retroavantgarde Neue Slowenische Kunst movement, which includes the music group Laibach and the art group Irwin" (*Mosaic,* 74; see also *Veiled*).

In the late 1980s, Debeljak edited collected translations of John Barth, Donald Barthelme, Coover, and Pynchon.[5] In the early 1990s, he seemed to value some of his contemporaries' attempts "to seize another [than sociopolitical] reality, that of mental homelessness and human indifference" ("Visions," 429). Now he realizes that what he had in common with other so-called post-

modernists was negative: none wanted explicitly political engagement. He has since argued in *Reluctant Modernity: The Institution of Art and Its Historical Forms* (Rowman & Littlefield, 1989) that unfettered subjectivity failed to account for the Balkan wars and that esthetic standards are impossible without ethics. Therefore, he has addressed the issue of the war in various genres.

Some of the youngest generation of writers, born about 1970, are associated with the Student Publishing House, sponsored in part by the student organizations of the University of Ljubljana and the University of Maribor, about 60,000 in all. The umbrella organization has existed for twenty-five years, but in the last four it has attracted ever greater numbers of people more interested in literature than in money (though some are paid); for the past five or six years, these people have formed a stable group. This organization sponsors various series which publish forty to fifty books a year, including a series in literary theory, one of critiques of media culture, and one in classics of philosophy. It also publishes translations, mostly of living authors, and, in the Beletrina series, eight to ten books by some of the best younger Slovenian writers. It also issues recordings of authors reading from their own work, from Dane Zajc, one of the best performers of his own and others' texts, to the newest writers.

In 1999, Beletrina authors won most of the literary prizes, and the editors try to keep writers on their list to reinforce name recognition of publisher and author. According to Aleš Šteger (b. 1973), one of the editors, this is not the usual practice; authors tend to move to different houses from one book to another. A nonprofit organization — and the only one, according to some older writers, subsidized by the government — Beletrina has to spend everything it earns on publishing and other projects like readings and discussions in order to foster a literary atmosphere throughout Slovenia.

In Šteger's view, many writers of this generation feel free from the earlier necessity to create and further Slovene identity and ideology and from the role of the poet as seer. They are also less hermetic than older writers — perhaps Šalamun is an example, though his name was not mentioned — and more interested in making contact with the reader. While not discounting form, in other words, they want to say something. Jani Virk (b. 1962) takes perhaps an extreme position, claiming not to be "a true Slovene writer" — he claims not to be interested in writers at all — because he has neither writer's block nor "the tangled erotic commitment to literature and similar fashionable ailments." Nor does he regard himself as "a poet seer amongst the mass of pitiful worms" or say to his mother, *"you have born a poet"* (*View of Tycho Brahe,* 6).

A contrast can be drawn — cautiously, because only fragments are available in English — between a midgeneration novelist like Berta Bojetu-Boeta (1946–97) in *Filio Is Not at Home* (1990; see *Afterwards* and *Veiled*) and Dušan Šarotar (b. 1968) in *Island of the Dead* (1999; see the translation in a chapbook of that title published by Beletrina). Both have an air of hallucination, but *Filio,* in what seem to be fragments from a fictional journal, has clear allegorical references to the island prisons under the communist regime. The second, visionary rather than allegorical, relies on closely observed detail that wavers between dream and reality. In an introduction to the chapbook, Šarotar says that he is "writing now that the urgent tasks every individual faces [as opposed to political struggles?] have finally got underway again. Naturally, we should always ask ourselves what these urgent tasks are and what time is right for them but we are probably unlikely to ever get an answer" (4).

As writers, Šarotar and Virk seem to have little in common besides their age, and Šteger's only poem available in English is not clearly popular in its thrust. Of course, these and other writers like the novelists Aleš Čar (b. 1971) and Nina Kokelj (b. 1972) and the poets Peter Semolič (b. 1967), Primož Čučnik (b. 1971), and Esad Babačič (b. 1965) are difficult to assess for non-Slovenes because little of their work has been translated; but clearly there is a good deal of energy in this literary generation, and just as clearly they are still formulating an esthetic or rather a series of individual esthetics.

All of these generations seem to take for granted the inevitability of interacting with the literatures of other countries. Before independence, the most important literary as well as commercial and political contacts were with the other republics of Yugoslavia. In fact, Boris A. Novak (b. 1953), poet, playwright, and activist for peace, was born in Belgrade; Šalamun was born in Zagreb; Debeljak speaks Serbian without an accent. The generations seem to differ on the question of the former Yugoslavia. Andrej Blatnik thinks that the older generation welcomes the split but that the Slovenes in their twenties, who remember Yugoslavia dimly if at all, have a kind of popcult nostalgia for Balkan food and music. Debeljak regrets the loss of the time when Yugoslav "linguistic, artistic, national, and religious differences converged in productive synthesis" (*Twilight,* 35). Now, he feels, he has lost one of the three forces — "Slovenian tradition, the tradition of worldwide mass culture, and finally the unique experience of Yugoslavia's cultural weaving" (*Twilight,* 41) — that formed his cultural and artistic identity.

Most current effort, however, concentrates on creating the sense that Slovenia is a free-standing country and not terra incognita for the rest of the world.[6] One of the problems with sudden independence, according to Iztok Osojnik, is the lack of a tradition in international relations, diplomacy, and cultural ties. And it is clear that in all areas Slovenes are working hard to escape being labeled Balkan and emphasizing their ties with Central Europe and the West.

One initiative tries to bring the rest of the world to Slovenia. A young vineyard owner, Aleks Klinec, wanted to do something for culture, and he and others, with the help of the Student Publishing House, began a wine and poetry festival to bring together from nineteen to twenty-nine younger poets from various countries. The publishing house used its contacts and issued anthologies of work by the participants. Poets could come only once to read, though some returned to listen, and participants stayed in the houses of local people. Readings which drew as many as 400 people from Venice and Austria as well as Slovenia were held each evening under a mulberry tree that was the subject of a poem by a local writer. Work by all participants was published in an annual volume, but the series ended in 1999.

Longer running is the annual Vilenica conference, which began in 1986 and which Veno Taufer developed from a poetry festival into a venue for reestablishing Central European identity. In some ways, this is parallel to the Visegradi political organization, but it is spiritual and cultural rather than political and commercial, and it includes Germany and northern Italy in the unique culture that differs from West, East, and Mediterranean. In recent years, the conference, held each September in the Vilenica cave, has extended its range and purpose to include writers — twenty-eight in 1999 — from the Far East and from North and South America in order to make the world aware of the Central European idea. The Council of Admissions, composed of writers from the Central European countries, proposes a list of future guests and nominates writers for an award of $10,000, which cannot go to a Slovene writer, to be given to a Central European writer for a life's work. The Slovenian jury cuts the list to five people, reads their work, and votes. There is also a crystal prize — a trophy, no money — awarded to one of their number by each year's participants, and work by the participants is published, translated into several languages, in the annual volume.

A complementary effort is being made to bring Slovene writing to the rest of the world. The Ministry of Culture subsidizes translations into other languages, and the Center for Slovenian Literature and other sponsors send writers on reading tours to Scandinavia, Frankfurt, Brazil, and other areas.[7] In recent years, small American publishing houses like Lumen Books, White Pine Press, and Richard Jackson's Poetry Miscellany chapbook series[8] have issued more and more anthologies of Slovene literature and volumes by individual authors like Kocbek, Šalamun, and Debeljak. Slovene writing is increasingly available in French,[9] Spanish, Portuguese, Russian, and several Central European languages.[10] Debeljak, who received a Ph.D. from Syracuse University, has been very active in collecting, editing, and promoting Slovene writing abroad, especially in America. Translators based in the States, like Sonja Kravanja and Michael Biggins, have the linguistic expertise to make still more work available.

Therefore, the concern of a German-speaking writer, voiced at the 2000 Pen conference, that small literatures like Slovenian might not survive in the multinational culture seems misplaced. True, Aleš Debeljak worries about Slovene writers being merely European, "in a direct, unmediated sense," he adds, though he by no means advocates ostrich-nationalism. Rather, he insists on the preservation of "a cultural narrative about the symbolic and material value of the language, ethical values, the fateful burden of history and the mythic tradition" in order to make Slovenes "see our lives against the broader background of the national condition" and "preserve our national culture and language in the era of the current European integration that, openly or not, considers smaller nations an unnecessary inconvenience" (Debeljak, "The Pursuit of Unhappiness").

Older writers like Iztok Osojnik are more hopeful than defiant. He sees Slovenia as the new geographic center of Europe and implies that, through the Vilenica conference and other cultural means, it can be as important culturally as it is geographically. This seems very ambitious prophecy, but for a country and a language that have survived against the odds of Austrian, Italian, and Serbian domination, perhaps it is not impossible.

Robert Murray Davis, Winter 2001

▪ WORKS CITED

Afterwards: Slovenian Writing 1945–1995. Andrew Zawacki, ed. Buffalo, N.Y. White Pine. 1999.

Debeljak, Aleš. "Expulsion from the Paradise of Dissent: Have Changes in Slovenia Altered the Writer's Vocation?" *International Quarterly,* 1:1 (1993), pp. 58–95.

———. "A Haven of Free Speech: The Story of *Nova Revija* in Slovenia." *Budapest Review of Books,* 6:3 (Fall 1996), pp. 149–52.

———. "The Pursuit of Unhappiness: Globalization, Citizenship, and National Identity." Unpublished manuscript, to be published in *Individualism and the Metaphors of Nation* by Rowman & Littlefield in 2002.

———. *Twilight of the Idols: Recollections of a Lost Yugoslavia.* Fredonia, N.Y. White Pine. 1994. (The book has also been published in German, Croatian, Hungarian, Polish, and Czech.)

———. "Visions of Despair and Hope Against Hope: Poetry in Yugoslavia in the Eighties." *World Literature Today,* 66:3 (Summer 1992), pp. 427–31.

"Facts About Slovenia: International Relations." Ljubljana. Slovenian Public Relations & Media Office. October 1999.

The Fire Under the Moon: Contemporary Slovene Poetry, 2d rev. ed. Richard Jackson and Rachel Morgan, eds. Chattanooga, Tennessee / Elgin, Illinois. PM Books / Black Dirt. 1999.

Mosaic of Seven Pebbles: Insight into Contemporary Slovenian Literature. Lela B. Njatin, ed. Ljubljana. Center for Slovenian Literature. 1999. (Includes work by and brief biographical notes about Svetlana Marakovič, Toma6 Šalamun, Aleš Debeljak, Brane Mozetič, Evald Flisar, Lela B. Njatin, and Maja Novak.

Prisoners of Freedom: Contemporary Slovenian Poetry. Aleš Debeljak, ed. Santa Fe, N.M. Pedernal. 1994.

Šarotar, Dušan. *Island of the Dead.* Ljubljana. Beletrina. 1999.

The Veiled Landscape: Slovenian Women Writing. Zdravko Dusa, ed. Sonja Kravanja, tr. Ljubljana. Slovenian Office for Women's Policy. 1995.

Virk, Jani. *A View of Tycho Brahe.* Ljubljana. Beletrina. 1998.

[1] See Aleš Debeljak, "Slovenia: A Brief Literary History," in *Afterwards: Slovenian Writing 1945–1995,* ed. Andrew Zawacki, Buffalo (N.Y.), White Pine, 1999.

[2] Jože Udovič (1912–86) is another important poet of this generation. His "Leaden, Slanting Rain" (*Prisoners,* 45) is particularly striking even in translation.

[3] Here and throughout, I am conscious of being selective rather than inclusive in discussing Slovene writers. For one thing, poets predominate because their work is more readily available in English.

[4] Jančar's *Mocking Desire* (Evanston [Illinois], Northwestern University Press, 1998; Slovene publication, 1993) is, with Boris Pahor's *Pilgrim Among the Shadows* (New York, Harcourt Brace, 1995), one of the few contemporary Slovenian novels available in English. A second Jančar novel is forthcoming from Northwestern.

[5] *Ameriška metafiksija,* Ljubljana, Mladinska Knjiga, 1988.

[6] The phrase is used in *The Imagination of Terra Incognita: Slovenian Writing 1945–1995,* ed. Aleš Debeljak, Fredonia (N.Y.), White Pine, 1997. The collection was published only in Europe.

[7] For a website giving brief biographies, photos, bibliographies, and brief selections from the work of writers on the Brazilian and Frankfurt tours, see www.ljudmila.org/litcenter.

[8] For a list of Slovene writing available in English, see Miran Hladnik's website, www.ijs.si/lit/slov_lit.html. Hladnik notes that Slovene books may be ordered by e-mail from Slovenska Knjiga (http://www.slo-knjiga.si/knjigarna/). For the books published in the USA, check http://www.utc.edu/üengldept/pm/pmhp.html or *Poetry Miscellany Chapbooks* ($3 each), ed. Richard Jackson, richard-jackson@utc.edu. See also "Contemporary Slovenian Literature in Translation," *Litterae Slovenicae/Slovenian Literary Magazine,* 2 (1993) [31:82]. This indicates translations available for publication as well as those in print. For White Pine, see http://www.whitepine.org/.

[9] Meta Klinar (meta.k@usa.net) has done work on Slovene prose in French translation.

[10] Earlier bibliographies of Slovene works translated into other languages were reportedly published in 1975 and 1984 in *Le livre Slovene,* which I have not seen.

UKRAINE

Ukrainian Literature for the American Reader

On a hot day in June 1964 one hundred thousand Ukrainians descended on the city of Washington. It was not a civil rights demonstration. It was not a March on Washington with a list of demands and grievances for the government. The occasion was simply the unveiling and dedication of a monument to the great poet of the Ukraine, Taras Shevchenko. Such crowds at a poet's monument would have been unusual in any land. If you consider that Ukrainians are but a tiny minority in America, less than two million strong, such a crowd on such an occasion is not only remarkable; it is a phenomenon that requires some explanation.

Shevchenko, one of the great romantic poets of nineteenth-century Slavic Europe, is revered by his countrymen as a national prophet. Ukrainians of all religious denominations, of all political persuasions, Communists and Nationalists alike, are united in their homage to Shevchenko. Enemies of the Ukraine realize this great power of the national poet. Hostile regimes have sometimes banned Shevchenko celebrations, regarding them—with good reason—as public manifestations of the Ukrainian yearning for political freedom.

Shevchenko's role in Ukrainian history illustrates vividly the basic predicament of Ukrainian literature. On the one hand, writers are placed on a pedestal and regarded as national leaders above and beyond their purely literary mission. On the other hand, there is a tremendous pressure of public expectations for the literature to be national in both form and content, patriotic and imbued with social significance. This of course is not a new predicament, nor is it uniquely Ukrainian. It is typical for literatures of subjugated nations struggling to gain or regain their political independence.

Great writers—if they are to write for all humanity and if their work is to survive the test of time—must be able to transcend the narrow boundaries placed upon them by their time and place. This does not mean that they must give up their roots in their national traditions, in their people's history. Man is not an abstract concept, but a live individual tied to his historic time and place. But the greatness of a writer depends on his ability to raise his theme to the level of the universal and the timeless. Ukrainian literature, in spite of its tragic history and in spite of its difficult and uneven development, can boast of a number of such great writers.

Written literature in the Ukraine dates back to the eleventh century and to such treasures as the great medieval epic *Slovo o polku Ihorevi* (*The Lay of Igor's Campaign;* ca. 1185). Modern Ukrainian literature written in the living language of the people, however, began in 1798 with the publication of Ivan Kotliarevsky's *Eneida* (The Aeneid). From that time on Ukrainian literature has developed continuously and has produced a body of important writers of universal significance. The three outstanding names of Ukrainian literature are Taras Shevchenko (1814–61), Ivan Franko (1856–1916) and Lesia Ukrainka (1871–1913).

Shevchenko was born a serf, but his great talent for painting made it possible for him to gain his freedom and to complete his studies at the Petersburg Academy of Art. He made his living as an artist, but it was his poetry which earned him both fame and martyrdom. His legacy consists of lyrical poetry, of romantic balads, of numerous long Byronic poems and poetic mystery plays. Shevchenko glorified the Cossack past and attacked the feudal system and Russian domination of the Ukraine. He openly expressed his hatred of tyranny and slavery and his belief in the ultimate victory of right and justice. For his political poetry Shevchenko was imprisoned and punished with ten years of military service along with a prohibition of painting and of writing. This was not the only time that the Russian government attempted to kill off Ukrainian literature by imperial decree. Fifteen years after Shevchenko's death, in 1876, Tsar Alexander II issued a decree which prohibited the printing of books in the Ukrainian language. But Ukrainian literature nonetheless has survived and developed.

Ivan Franko lived and wrote in the Western areas of the Ukraine, which were under the rule of the Austro-Hungarian empire. As a socialist and a Ukrainian patriot, he too had his political differences with the government and spent some brief periods of his life in prison. But in the Western Ukraine literature could develop more freely. Franko was a Vienna-educated encyclopedic scholar and a prolific writer. He left an extensive literary output of the highest quality: poetry (both lyrical and epic), novels and short stories, dramas, scholarly writings, translations from foreign languages. Franko espoused the ideals of the "old humanitarian socialism based on the ethical and broad humanistic enlightenment of the masses . . . , on human and national freedom."[1]

Lesia Ukrainka, the third bright star of Ukrainian literature, was described by her American translator as a "poetess of rare scholarship . . . with . . . a power and vigor of expression not surpassed by any woman writer . . . in Western literatures."[2] Lesia Ukrainka wrote lyric and dramatic poetry as well as dramas in verse. The struggle for liberty, both individual and national, is the chief theme of her writings. She was a modern poet who used subtle symbolic forms of expression. She placed her themes in the setting of ancient or biblical history, in strange lands and distant epochs.

There is considerable literature in English on these three classics of Ukrainian literature. A number of critical studies of Shevchenko and several books of translations of his poetry have been published, including a complete edition of his poetical works. Franko's books likewise have appeared both in Western and in Soviet English-language editions. A selection of his poetry and short stories, as well as two of his novels are available for the English reader. Lesia Ukrainka is well represented by two collections published in North America and by a slim volume of lyrical poetry published in Kiev. (A selected bibliography listing the most important titles available in English follows this essay.)

Not all the other classics of Ukrainian literature can be read in English translation. Panko Kulish, poet, novelist, playwright, translator and a contemporary of Shevchenko, is represented by one novel; such prolific short story writers or novelists as Marko Vovchok, Ivan Nechui-Levytsky or Panas Myrny, who introduced realism into Ukrainian prose, have never been translated into English. Ukrainian modernistic prose is represented in English by two books of short stories of Mykhailo Kotsiubynsky, both published in the Soviet Union, and by two volumes of short stories of Vasyl Stefanyk published in Canada and in the United States. There are, however, no separate English-language editions of Volodymyr Vynnychenko, a most prolific modern Ukrainian novelist and playwright who has had a considerable reputation during his lifetime in both France and Germany.

After a short-lived independence in 1917–21 the Ukraine became a Soviet republic and came once more under the domination of Russia. The first decade after the Revolution, however, was a period of somewhat relaxed political pressures. It produced a cultural revival with a number of interesting and original talents. New writers and new literary movements appeared on the scene. The symbolist Pavlo Tychyna and the neoclassicist Maxim Rylsky were the two towering figures in poetry; Iuri Ianovsky, Valerian Pidmohylny, Mykola Khvylovy were outstanding among the prose writers; Mykola Kulish became the foremost dramatist of Ukrainian literature; Alexander Dovzhenko, the world-famous filmmaker, left a legacy of original scenarios,

notebooks and short stories. The renaissance was as brief as it was brilliant: many of the bright young talents ended up in prison, were executed or driven to suicide; others had to submit to the official literary style of socialist realism superimposed by the ruling Communist Party. Some of the works of this period are available also in English. Khvylovy, Pidmohylny, Kulish and Dovzhenko are represented by one book each; translations from the other writers can only be found in anthologies.

Contemporary Ukrainian literature continues both in the Ukraine and in exile. In the Ukraine the constant pressures of Russification and the imposed ideology and style of socialist realism combine to make literature narrowly utilitarian, ethnographic, propagandistic. Even great talents have difficulty in raising themselves above this general stagnation. The foremost writers in the Ukraine in the last couple of decades have been the poet Mykola Bazhan, the playwright Oleksandr Korniichuk, the poet and novelist Leonid Pervomaisky and the two prolific novelists Oles Honchar and Pavlo Zahrebelny. Samples of Korniichuk's work and a couple of Honchar books are available in English editions. Now and then new promising writers appear on the scene, but too frequently the promises end in disappointment and tragedy. Translations from the younger generation of writers include the short stories of Ievhen Hutsalo, the prison memoirs of Mykhailo Osadchy, the literary essays of Ievhen Sverstiuk and some poetry and short story selections in anthologies. The fact that a number of the young writers, including Sverstiuk and Osadchy, are now in Soviet prisons is another sad commentary on the tragic development of Ukrainian literature.

Ukrainian writers first went into exile after the war for independence was lost in 1921–22. Ukrainian literary centers came into being in Poland and Czechoslovakia. After World War II the center of Ukrainian émigré literary life shifted to the United States and to Canada. At the present time "Slovo," the worldwide Association of Ukrainian Writers in Exile (with headquarters in New York), has over 180 members. There have been a few writers of universal significance among the Ukrainian exiles in the last several decades. One need only mention such prominent poets as Ievhen Malaniuk, Iuri Klen and Todos Osmachka and novelists of such stature as Leonid Mosendz, Ulas Samchuk, Iuri Kosach, Victor Domontovych, Ivan Bahriany. Unfortunately, very little of their work is available in English. There is but one novel each of Bahriany and of Osmachka, and some poetry and short story selections in anthologies. Among the most prominent Ukrainian writers now living in the United States are the novelists Halyna Zhurba of Philadelphia, Iuri Kosach and Dokia Humenna of New York, Oleksa Izarsky of Ohio and the poets Sviatoslav Hordynsky, Vasyl Barka and Vadym Lesych of New York, the satirical poet and novelist Bohdan Nyzhankivsky of Detroit.

In the 1950s and 1960s a younger generation of writers began a modernistic movement, calling themselves "the New York Group" and publishing a regular year-book of modern poetry. The most prominent members of this group are Emma Andievska, Vira Vovk, Bohdan Rubchak, Bohdan Boychuk, Patricia Kylyna and Iuri Tarnavsky. With the exception of the first two, they all live in the United States, and one of them, Patricia Kylyna, is an unusual example of "assimilation in reverse": an American, born of non-Ukrainian ancestry, she married a Ukrainian writer and herself began to write poetry in Ukrainian. Each of these younger writers has had a number of published collections of poetry or prose in Ukrainian. None of their work has been issued separately in English translation.

The Ukrainian writers in exile have no constraints of censorship or superimposed socialist realism. They represent many genres and many ideologies. But the reality of exile literature presents its own limitations and hardships. (See *BA* 50:2, pp.271–328 for a series of articles on "The Writer in Exile," including Wolodymyr T. Zyla's "Manifestations of Ukrainian Poetry and Prose in Exile," pp.318–25—Ed.) The circle of Ukrainian readers in America is small, and the book market in the Ukraine is closed to all émigré writers. As a consequence, book publishing is not profitable; it can continue only at the price of tremendous personal sacrifices. Ukrainian writers in America must publish their books at their own expense or be subsidized by some society or organization.

There used to be a number of periodical literary publications in Ukrainian: for fifteen years a Ukrainian literary monthly called *Kyiv* (Kiev) was published in Philadelphia; there used to be a special literary supplement published by the Ukrainian daily *Svoboda* (Liberty) in Jersey City; there was also the yearbook of modern poetry of the New York Group. None of these are in existence now. Ukrainian writers in America today publish their works in the periodic almanacs of the writers' association Slovo, in the monthly journal *Suchasnist,* in Ukrainian magazines of a general character, as well as in the weekly and daily press. Every two or three years the Ukrainian Literary Fund sponsored by the Ukrainian community of Chicago provides prizes and awards for the most highly acclaimed Ukrainian literary publications.

Does Ukrainian literature have any future in America? Can it survive? The odds are against it. But Ukrainian literature has fought a battle for survival throughout

its tragic history and has prevailed. The vitality of the Ukrainian national spirit is a fountain of never-ending surprises. Ukrainian literature in America today is the product of several generations. Many of the younger writers were born and educated in the West and yet they continue to write in Ukrainian. The precarious political situation and constant pressures of censorship and Russification in the Ukraine give the Ukrainian writers in the West a heightened sense of mission and responsibility to preserve and continue the literary process.

There is a growing interest in Ukrainian literature among American scholars. Harvard and a number of other American universities offer courses in Ukrainian literature. Serious scholarly journals, such as the *Slavonic and East European Review,* the *Slavic Review* and *World Literature Today* publish studies of Ukrainian literature and book reviews of Ukrainian publications. More English-language studies and translations from Ukrainian literature have been published in the last two decades than in the preceding 150 years. The survival of the exile literature may be open to question. But the future of Ukrainian literature as a scholarly discipline, as an area for specialized research and as a promising, newly discovered field for American literary scholars seems quite secure.

Marta Tarnawsky, Spring 1978

Author's Note: This essay is a slightly expanded version of a talk presented at the Temple University Ethnic Festival Act II on 12 April 1977.

▪ UKRAINIAN LITERATURE IN ENGLISH: RECOMMENDED TITLES

encylopedic surveys:

Concise information on Ukrainian literature can be found in most leading encyclopedias. The best comprehensive introductory survey in encyclopedic form is in the two-volume *Ukraine: A Concise Encyclopædia* (Volodymyr Kubijovych, ed., Toronto, University of Toronto Press, 1963), vol. 1, pp. 960–1097.

literary histories:

Čyževs'kyj, Dmytro. *A History of Ukrainian Literature (From the 11th to the End of the 19th Century).* Littleton, Co. Ukrainian Academic Press. 1975. 681 pages.

Manning, Clarence A. *Ukrainian Literature: Studies of the Leading Authors.* Jersey City, N.J. Ukrainian National Association. 1944. (Reprinted by Books for Libraries, Freeport, N.Y., 1971.) 126 pages.

Shabliovs'kyj, Ievhen. *Ukrainian Literature through the Ages.* Kiev. Mystetstvo. 1970. 241 pages.

literary anthologies:

Andrusyshen, Constantine H., and Watson Kirkconnell, eds. & trs. *The Ukrainian Poets, 1189–1962: Selected and Translated into English Verse.* Toronto. University of Toronto Press. 1963. xxx + 500 pages.

Luchkovich, Michael, ed. *Their Land: An Anthology of Ukrainian Short Stories.* Jersey City, N.J. Svoboda. 1964. 325 pages.

Luckyj, George S. N., ed. *Modern Ukrainian Short Stories.* Littleton, Co. Ukrainian Academic Press. 1973. 228 pages.

Stories of the Soviet Ukraine. Moscow. Progress. 1970. 303 pages.

taras shevchenko:

Mijakovs'kyj, Volodymyr, and George Shevelov, eds. *Taras Ševčenko, 1814–1861: A Symposium.* The Hague. Mouton. 1962. 302 pages.

Shevchenko, Taras. *The Poetical Works of Taras Shevchenko, the Kobzar.* C. H. Andrusyshen and Watson Kirkconnell, trs. Toronto. University of Toronto Press. 1964.563 pages.

———. *Selected Works: Poetry and Prose.* With reproductions of paintings by the author. John Weir, ed. Moscow. Progress. 1964.468 pages.

———. *Song out of Darkness: Selected Poems.* Vera Rich, tr. London. Mitre. 1961. xxxii + 128 pages.

———. *Taras Shevchenko, the Poet of Ukraine: Selected Poems.* Clarence A. Manning, tr. & intro. Jersey City, N.J. Ukrainian National Association. 1945. 217 pages.

ivan franko:

Franko, Ivan. *Ivan Franko, the Poet of Western Ukraine: Selected Poems.* Percival Cundy, tr. & intro. New York. Greenwood. 1968 (© 1948). 265 pages.

———. *Boa Constrictor and Other Stories.* Moscow. Foreign Languages Publishing House. 1957. 293 pages.

———. *Moses and Other Poems.* Vera Rich and Percival Cundy, trs. New York. Shevchenko Scientific Society. 1973.163 pages.

———. *Poems and Stories.* John Weir, tr. Toronto. Ukrainska knyha. 1956. 341 pages.

lesia ukrainka:

Bida, Constantine. *Lesya Ukrainka: Life and Work.* Selected works translated by Vera Rich. Toronto. University of Toronto Press. 1968. 259 pages.

Ukrainka, Lesia. *Hope: Selected Poetry.* Gladys Evans, tr. Kiev. Dnipro. 1975. 141 pages (parallel text).

———. *Spirit of Flame.* Percival Cundy, tr. Westport, Cn. Greenwood. 1971 (© 1950). 320 pages.

other major writers:

Kulish, Pantelejmon. *The Black Council.* George S. N. Luckyj and Moira Luckyj, eds. & trs. Littleton, Co. Ukrainian Academic Press. 1973. 125 pages.

Kotsiubyns'kyj, Mykhajlo. *The Birthday Present and Other Stories.* Kiev. Dnipro. 1973. 225 pages.

———. *Chrysalis and Other Stories.* Moscow. Foreign Languages Publishing House. 1958. 257 pages.

Stefanyk, Vasyl'. *The Stone Cross.* Joseph Wiznuk with C. H. Andrusyshen, trs. Toronto. McClelland & Stewart. 1971. 164 pages.

Struk, Danylo S. *A Study of Vasyl Stefanyk: The Pain at the Heart of Existence.* Littleton, Co. Ukrainian Academic Press. 1973. 200 pages.

literary renaissance of the 1920s:

Dovzhenko, Alexander. *The Poet as Filmmaker: Selected Writings.* Marco Carynnyk, ed. Cambridge, Ma. MIT Press. 1973. lv + 323 pages.

Khvylovyj, Mykola. *Stories from the Ukraine.* New York. Philosophical Library. 1960. 234 pages.

Kulish, Mykola. *Sonata Pathetique.* George S. N. Luckyj and Moira Luckyj, trs. Littleton, Co. Ukrainian Academic Press. 1975. 110 pages.

Luckyj, George S. N. *Literary Politics in the Soviet Ukraine, 1917–1934.* New York. Columbia University Press. 1956. x + 323 pages.

Pidmohylnyj, Valerian. *A Little Touch of Drama.* Littleton, Co. Ukrainian Academic Press. 1972. 191 pages.

Slavutych, Yar. *The Muse in Prison.* Jersey City, N.J. Svoboda. 1956. 63 pages. (Eleven sketches of Ukrainian poets killed by Communists and twenty-two translations of their poems.)

contemporary soviet ukrainian literature:

Honchar, Oles'. *The Cyclone.* Moscow. Progress. 1972. 321 pages.

———. *Short Stories.* Moscow. Foreign Languages Publishing House. 1955. 268 pages.

Hutsalo, Ievhen. *A Prevision of Happiness and Other Stories.* Moscow. Progress. 1974. 205 pages.

Kornijchuk, Oleksandr. *Wings: A Play.* Moscow. Foreign Languages Publishing House. 1956. 132 pages.

Luckyj, George S. N., ed. *Four Ukrainian Poets: Drach, Korotych, Kostenko, Symonenko.* Martha Bohachevsky-Chomiak and Danylo S. Struk, trs. New York. Quixote. 1969. 83 pages.

Osadchyj, Mykhajlo. *Cataract.* Marco Carynnyk, ed. & tr. New York. Harcourt Brace Jovanovich. 1976. xxiii + 240 pages.

Sverstiuk, Ievhen. *Clandestine Essays.* George S. N. Luckyj, ed. & tr. Littleton, Co. Ukrainian Academic Press. 1976. 100 pages.

ukrainian literature in exile:

Bahrianyj, Ivan. *The Hunters and the Hunted.* London/New York. Macmillan/St. Martin's. 1956. 244 pages.

Os'machka, Todos'. *Red Assassins.* Minneapolis. Denison. 1959.375 pages.

---

[1] Ivan Franko, *Tvory,* New York, Knyhospilka, 1958, vol. 16, pp. 9–10.

[2] Percival Cundy, "Introduction," in Lesia Ukrainka, *Spirit of Flame,* New York, Bookman Associates, 1950, p. 18.

YUGOSLAVIA

A Comparative Study of Basque and Yugoslav Troubadourism

The Basques were the only people in Western Europe who survived the invasion of the Indo-Europeans. Their language, still spoken by thousands, is a relic of the past, having never been swallowed up by the Indo-European languages. As a result, it has inspired great interest among linguists and ethnologists. As a prehistoric people, the Basques have a predominantly oral character. Basques in general are reluctant to commit events to paper. Their written literature, the first example of which appeared in 1545, was somewhat limited and generally dominated by religious authors and themes. Until the end of the nineteenth century, few Basque books could be considered "literary." In contrast, Basque oral literature is very rich, and its quality compares favorably with the oral literature of the neighboring nations, Spain and France. Especially noteworthy within this oral literature are the old plays (pastorales from Zubero) and Basque troubadourism.

Reading the accounts by Milman Parry and Albert Lord of studies made in Yugoslavia has moved me to undertake a comparative investigation of their "oral-formulaic" theory and Basque troubadourism. I will limit myself to pointing out some similarities and differences between the two phenomena, with special emphasis on the techniques, rhymes, rhythms, themes, and music.

Basque troubadourism can be defined as *herriaren kantuzko hitza* (the sung word of the people), in which improvisation, above all, is the essential quality. The task requires a rapid, threefold action: search, organization, and performance. In a matter of seconds, the Basque troubadour must search for the subject matter of his song, then organize his ideas and images into the best possible mode of expression, and finally express them by performing them in song. In order to do this, the *bertsolari* or Basque bard constructs a phrase in the reverse order of its logical formation. As the Basque saying goes, "Amaia da hasiera" (the end is the beginning). That is, the end is the beginning in the planning stage, although it is the last to come in the execution. Thus the Basque bard searches rapidly for the rhyme of the last line of the verse. This rhyme will be the axis for the entire strophe and the foundation stone of the artistic edifice. Keeping this rhyme in mind, he will begin to sing the first verse.

In Basque troubadourism, composition and execution are simultaneous, with no preparation or pre-established formula intervening. Music is very important in the artistic expression of oral literature, but the Basque bard is no simple singer or minstrel who performs another's composition. On the contrary, he is poet, singer, and speaker combined. Written poetry and Basque troubadourism have something in common in that they both use words, rhyme, and rhythm, but the techniques and the language used are very different. There are consonant and assonant rhymes, both rich and poor, the former being preferred because they are more difficult. The rhythms are quite varied: more than twenty different rhythms can be used. The most common strophes are the *zortziko* and *hamarreko nagusiak*,

the first (as the word suggests) containing eight lines and the second containing ten. In the *zortziko* as well as the *hamarreko nagusiak,* the odd lines are composed of ten syllables and the even lines of eight. Also commonly used are the *zortziko* and *hamarreko txikiak*. As in the previous strophes, the first contains eight lines and the second contains ten, but in the *txikiak* (short ones) the odd lines have seven syllables and the even have six. Finally, there exists a more difficult rhythm called *bederatzi puntuko bertsoa* (a strophe of nine rhymes). This verse is composed of fourteen lines, nine of which carry the rhyme (lines 2, 4, 6, 8, 9, 10, 11, 12, and 14). The odd lines are seven syllables long and the even lines are six syllables long, except for lines 4 and 14, which contain only five syllables.[1]

As an example of this difficult verse, I cite one of three that the current champion Xabier Amuriza had to improvise during the National Championship in 1982 on the required theme of "Woman."

1 Emakumea esan da
2 esana da d*ana*
3 emakumetan bada
4 bat txit bak*ana*
5 irratian han dago
6 Sortu nindu*ana*
7 Baldatikan orantxe
8 noa berag*ana*
9 aita dut jo*ana*
10 hau pena dud*ana*
11 baina haren d*ama*
12 bizirik dut *ama*
13 hauxe da poza bersoz
14 ezin em*ana.*

(Having said the word *woman*
everything is said.
There is one very special woman
among women.
She is listening to me on the radio
the one who gave me life.
From the Balda fronton now
I address myself to her.
My father has died.
What pain I feel.
But his wife
my mother still lives.
This is the joy that
I cannot express in this verse.)[2]

This difficult rhythm is not imposed on Basque bards except on special occasions such as the *txapelketak* or championships, where the winner is crowned with the *txapela* (the Basque beret).

Historically these competitions have been held on various occasions, but the greatest test is the *txapelketa.* The types of competitions are: 1) the *txapelketa,* which lasts six hours a day. The majority of themes, rhythms, et cetera are imposed on the participants. A great deal of concentration is required of the *bertsolari,* and as a result the performer's rapport with the audience is not as close as it is at popular festivals. The audience is large (5,000 persons) and well informed. About eight bards make the finals after surviving three or four elimination rounds involving sixty or more competitors. There is a moderator and a jury of about ten members. 2) *Challenges* between two bards or between two pairs or teams. These took place during the nineteenth century but today have disappeared. Rhymes and themes were not imposed upon contestants, and the challenges lasted only a couple of hours. Public attendance was large; a great quantity was wagered. There was no moderator, but a three-member jury was present. 3) *Popular festivals,* the most common form of Basque troubadourism. Such a festival does not last all day but is a complementary part of a general celebration. Generally the theme is open. There is no jury, but there is a moderator. Not as much technique is required of the *bertsolari* here as in a *txapelketa;* however, the rapport with the audience is greater. The important thing is to create an atmosphere of fun rather than of challenge. There is no set time limit. The performance ends when the audience is satisfied. 4) *Juegos florales* (Floral Games), sessions of oral literature or troubadourism which used to take place on the occasion of literary contests, especially for poetry. They were very famous in the first half of this century, but today they have disappeared.

The central character in Basque troubadourism is the *bertsolari;* the second most important entity is the audience. The jury and the *gai-jartzaile* or moderator also play important roles, especially in competitions such as the *txapelketa.* The *bertsolari* must possess many qualities. Education is beginning to be important but is not absolutely necessary. In fact, there were several illiterates among the best Basque bards of the nineteenth century. Voice and physical presence also play a role, albeit not as large a one as other qualities. A few of the most important attributes are: mental agility, a quick tongue, memory, a knack for captivating the audience, imagination, sensitivity, and communication with the public.

The audience is an absolutely necessary ingredient, since without it there would be no competitions. This artistic expression of oral literature is a kind of intellectual group sport combining diversion and competition. The public takes an active part, applauding the *bertsolari's* best moments and often repeating the last two lines with him. On occasion the audience even guesses the end of the line and sings it with the bard. The lone *bertsolari,* without an opponent and especially without an audience, either refuses to perform or ends the performance very quickly. No *bertsolari* begins singing in his own family; he needs more people, as a fish needs water or a plant needs earth in which to take root.

The contests are difficult and assume a great gift for improvisation. Especially in the *txapelketa* the moderator imposes a complete set of requirements (theme, rhyme, rhythm, and music) on the *bertsolari.* Occasionally the first or last two lines of the strophe are sung for the *bertsolari,* who must quickly finish them. Given the complexity of improvisation, it is no surprise that errors are sometimes made by even the best bards, as we shall see.

◼ ◼ ◼

Troubadourism as encountered within the Yugoslav context, by comparison, is clearly outlined in the book *The Singer of Tales* by Albert Lord.[3] This famous American scholar used as a point of departure the studies made by his professor, Milman Parry, on Homer's *Iliad* and *Odyssey.* Applying Parry's findings and his own "oral-formulaic" theory to the practice of the Yugoslav bards, Lord arrived at a series of conclusions which appear to be quite valuable to the study of oral literature. In spite of the fact that some of these conclusions are today very controversial (e.g., the incompatibility of written and oral literatures), his theory is extremely interesting for the comparative study of other artistic expressions of oral literature.[4] The fact that an illiterate Yugoslav bard was capable of singing thousands of lines of verse about epic themes, accompanied by a musical instrument and using a few formulas, is an extraordinary phenomenon worthy of attention (*ST,* 78).

Bertsolarism and the Yugoslav phenomenon have one element in common, which in turn differentiates them from other similar artistic expressions such as that of the Gaelic bards: in both, the composition and performance coincide, and the creator and the performer are one and the same. The bard is poet, singer, and speaker simultaneously—three facets within a single entity. Lord's words concerning the Yugoslav bard can be applied to the Basque troubadour: "Singer, performer, composer and poet are one under different aspects but at the same time" (13).

In Basque troubadourism improvisation is everything, encompassing even the subject matter. There is no room here for any prepared topic or for any theme known beforehand, as in Yugoslav practice: "Sometimes singers prefer to have a day or so to think the song over, to put it in order, and to practice it to themselves" (26). The Yugoslav bard concentrates exclusively on events that occurred during the time of the Turkish Empire (wars, death, weapons, rescues, castles, victories, et cetera). One could say that, instead of different subjects, these are all variations on the same theme. In contrast, the themes of the Basque troubadour are quite varied and reflect modern life. Epic poetry and the battles waged by the Basques against Poland's and Charlemagne's troops, even though the Basques emerged victorious, are not the main objective of the *bertsolari*. His themes are generally selected from everyday life, from the most serious to the most humorous, from the predictable to the unpredictable. Social, economic, and political themes, sports themes, and especially themes dealing with the language and life of the Basque Country are currently the most often used.

One of the most surprising aspects of both artistic phenomena is the speed of the elaboration of verses. As soon as one Basque bard ends his last line, his opponent must respond without hesitation. To do otherwise would reveal his lack of skill. This speed is such that at times not even two seconds pass between the last lines of one bard and the first lines of another. There is no time to correct the errors one commits, as is done in written literature. The dialectics of Basque troubadourism require very fast reflexes to capture life, like the current of a river which passes swiftly and never returns to its point of origin. This stipulation is indispensable for both experiences: "The singer's problem is to construct one line after another very rapidly. . . . There is urgency" (54).

Given, moreover, that the Yugoslav bard employs lines of ten syllables and must include a short pause in each one, the number of lines he composes is amazing: "It is not unusual for a Yugoslav bard to sing at the rate of from ten to twenty ten-syllable lines a minute" (17). Such syntactic pauses as occur in Yugoslav practice at the end of each line (periods, semicolons, et cetera) do not exist in the Basque counterpart. Even in the longest strophe of fourteen lines, described previously, there is one single period at the end of each line to breathe and, at the same time, to work on the structure of the rest of the verse. In order to calculate the average number of lines a Basque troubadour can perform in a minute's time, I have analyzed the *zortziko* and *hamarreko nagusiak* verses in the music from the "Txapelketa 1982," these lines being the closest in number of syllables to the standard Yugoslav lines of verse. This analysis shows that a Basque bard is capable of singing an average of ten lines per minute. Although the quantity is less than that achieved by the Yugoslavs, it is still amazing, considering that the Basques do not use any preestabli-

shed formula. In both cases, enjambment is rare, since it would interfere with the pause at the end of each line. In bertsolarism, enjambment is practically nonexistent.

Due to the speed with which the Yugoslav constructs verses, errors are not unusual: "His text line may be a syllable too long or a syllable too short" (38). Among Basque troubadours this type of error is rarely committed. The rhythm and number of syllables are not serious preoccupations for the *bertsolari*. He never stops to count syllables; he carries a feel for the meter within him and performs like a dancer who dances without counting the number of steps he must take. On the other hand, the rhyme creates great difficulties for the *bertsolari*. The fact that the structure of the Basque language is postpositive, with a large number of suffixes, solves most of these problems for him, but there are other obstacles as well that do not exist in other languages. For example, the English article the has four counterparts in Basque: the suffixes -*a*, -*ak*, -*ek*, and -*ok*. The choice of suffix depends on the nature of the verb, whether it is plural or singular, and whether or not the speaker is involved in the action. The error that most concerns the *bertsolari* is called *poto egin*, or the repetition of the same word as a rhyme in a verse. However, contractions, omissions of auxiliary verbs, and other devices are not considered errors but rather "poetic license." A similar situation occurs in the judging of the merits of the Yugoslav bards: "Verbs may be placed in unusual positions, auxiliaries may be omitted, cases may be used strangely" (32).

Since the means of transmitting verses is oral and accomplished by singing, music is another element common to both Basque and Yugoslav artistic expression. Unlike the Basque bard who uses only his voice as an instrument, however, the Yugoslav accompanies himself on the *gusle* (a kind of mandolin which plays a single chord). None of the native Basque instruments (*txistu, txirula, txalaparta, alboka, trikitixa*, et cetera) is used in Basque troubadourism. Basque melodies are generally quite varied, popular, and rather slow,[5] and although Basque music is often very rhythmic, in this context it is slow and syllabic—that is, every musical note represents a syllable.

Another poetic expression exists called *kopla zaharra* (the old couplet) in which the music is more rhythmic, but this is different from improvised troubadourism. In *kopla zaharra* the strophes are usually short, consisting of two or three rhymes. This is a very old form and probably gave birth to improvisational practice. It is rather similar to the old songs of the Middle Ages which were sung by women with musical accompaniment. In contrast, women have traditionally been excluded from both Basque and Yugoslav troubadourism. Women have customarily taken no active part in the public life of the Basque Country. As a result, they have been left out of artistic competitions of this type. Basque troubadourism was born in the taverns and cider shops of rural villages, where the presence of a woman was frowned upon. In both the Basque Country and Yugoslavia this spectacle was an exclusively male domain. As Lord says, "It forms, at the present time, or until very recently, the chief entertainment of the adult male population in the villages and small towns (*ST* 14).

The abrupt social changes of the last fifteen years have affected Basque troubadourism in this regard. Currently, women attend these events just as men do; however, the masculine element still predominates. Historically there have been some women who have known how to improvise this type of verse, but the atmosphere in the Basque Country was so restrictive that they were not allowed to perform publicly; women who were capable of such improvisation therefore always remained in the shadow of some great troubadour such as Pello "Errota" or Pello Otaño, who happened to be their brother or their father.[6] In this respect, great progress has been made, and for the first time in the known history of the Basque Country a competition including women has been held in the village of Usurbil (Guipuzcoa).[7] Five female *bertsolariak* took part in this event, and the moderator or *gai-jartzaile* in charge of assigning themes was also a woman. The competition was the fruit of a harvest made possible by the new schools for *bertsolariak,* where women make up a large proportion of the student body. As a general rule the women are young and educated, from industrialized areas and *euskaldunberriak* (new speakers of Basque).[8]

Basque troubadourism is changing radically. In the nineteenth and early twentieth century the *bertsolari* was a kind of clown who enlivened popular festivals but whom no one wanted as a member of the family. For the Basque writer Carmelo Etxegaray (1865–1925), the art of the Basque troubadour was "an enormous collection of simplicities and crudities related in an eminently prosaic manner, and in a language both incorrect and plagued with Castilianisms."[9] The compensation paid to the bards for performing at festivals and in competitions was ridiculously low. In the *II Txapelketa Nagusia* (Second National Championship) in 1936, the champion, "Txirrita" (1860–1936), was awarded the meager quantity of 150 pesetas, not quite the current equivalent of $1.[10] The same thing occurred with the Yugoslav bard, who naturally could not live by his profession: "He is not really a professional, but his audience does buy him drinks, and if he is good they will give him a little money for the entertainment he has given them" (*ST,*

15). Fortunately all this is changing, but even today no *bertsolari* makes a living from his art.

After this brief study of some of the similarities and differences between Basque and Yugoslav bards, one can say that improvisation is more complete among the former, since they did not deal with any type of pre-established formula. In spite of Lord's insistent affirmations to the effect that the surprising results of the bards' efforts are due to creativity and not memory or formulas, the issue is not entirely clear: "It is this faculty rather than his memory of relatively fixed formulas that marks him as a skillful singer in performance" (*ST,* 43). I have stated that memory is an important quality for the Basque troubadour. There have been some exceptional examples of memory in the history of the Basque artistic phenomenon, but it is not the most important quality here. The capacity for improvisation is.[11] Memory is necesary simply to remember the verse of one's adversary and to call forth one's own response prepared during that recitation. I agree with Finnegan that the facility of the Yugoslav bards is basically founded on memory and preestablished formulas, which is not the case with the Basque troubadours: "Contrary to the impression in *The Singer of Tales* and elsewhere that oral poetry is always composed-in-performance, this is not true empirically. . . . Memorization rather than improvisation is in fact involved."[12]

Gorka Aulestia, Summer 1985

[1] J. M. Lekuona, *Ahozko Euskal Literatura,* Donostia, Erein, 1982.

[2] *Bertsolari Txapelketa 1982,* Bilbao, Euskaltzaindia, 1983, p. 291. For a review, see *WLT* 59:1 (Winter 1985), p. 140.

[3] Albert Lord, *The Singer of Tales,* Cambridge, Ma., Harvard University Press, 1960. Subsequent references use the abbreviation *ST*.

[4] R. Finnegan, *Oral Poetry,* Cambridge, Eng., Cambridge University Press, 1977.

[5] In the *"Txapelketa 1982"* eighty different melodies were used. At times, bards create their own melodies. In these competitions there is an additional prize for the entrant who uses the greatest number of melodies.

[6] Pello "Errota" (1840–1919) and Pello Otaño (1857–1910) were two of the best *bertsolariak* in the history of the phenomenon.

[7] *Argia,* no. 1009 (March 1984), p. 30.

[8] Euskaldunberri is a term applied to those born in the Basque Country but who did not learn Basque as their first language.

[9] C. Etxegaray, *Noticia de las cosas memorables de Guipúzcoa,* Tolosa, 1901, pp. 34–36.

[10] *"Yakintza:* Revista de Cultura Vasca 1933–1936," *La Gran Enciclopedia Vasca,* vol. 4, p. 157.

[11] The shepherd Izuela (1780–1837) was an extraordinary case in point. When a tiebreaker was needed in one competition, he was able to repeat fifty verses which he had just sung. This feat broke the tie in his favor. See A. Zavala, *Pator Izuela (1780–1837): Ezkioko eta Segurako itxuak,* Donostia, 1971, pp. 22–23.

[12] R. Finnegan, "What Is Oral Literature Anyway?" in *Oral Literature and the Formula,* Ann Arbor, University of Michigan Press, 1976, pp. 143–44.

The Karamazov Syndrome in Recent Yugoslav Literature

Recent political changes in Eastern Europe have affected the literatures in those countries as well. The Yugoslav literatures are no exception. For decades somewhat freer than their East European colleagues, Yugoslav writers were able to escape the clutches of literary dictates and write as they pleased, except for a few restrictions such as the right of the communists to rule and the sanctity of the revolution in World War II that brought the communists to power. That too has begun to change lately. Since the death of Tito in 1980, writers have been increasingly questioning the basic premises of communist rule and attacking taboos that previously were only hinted at or not mentioned at all.

One of those taboos is an episode in the country's political life that took place in the late 1940s and lasted through the following decade and a half. The conflict arose when Yugoslavia was expelled from the communist family of nations by Stalin and forced to go it alone in building its own brand of communism. In addition to the dangers from abroad, the government perceived one particular danger within its borders: namely, the presence among its own followers of a large number of political opposition members who, until the break with the Soviet Union, were taught to believe in the Soviet Union and Stalin as unquestionable gods but now were to denounce them as enemies. Some of these real or imagined opponents sided with their former idols, whereas others, caught off guard and confused, voiced an opinion that some accommodation with the Soviet Union should be found. All of them were declared "enemies of the people," arrested, and sent to concentration camps, where from 1949 to 1963 they spent several years, depending on the "admission of their mistake." About fifty thousand men and women, 90 percent of them communists, were "processed," and one fourth of them perished either in the camps or from the aftereffects of their incarceration. They were subjected to a process of "reeducation," consisting mostly of unspeakable tortures, the likes of which were not seen even in the most notorious of Stalin's camps. Of the several camps used for such "rehabilitation," one stands out: Goli Otok (Bare Island) in the Adriatic Sea. That camp has given its name to the entire sorry spectacle, and the inmates of these torture chambers are referred to summarily as *golootočani* (Bare Islanders). It may not have

been the worst of the camps (but then, how does one measure scientifically the degree and severity of torture?), yet the name stuck; the episode will most likely be treated under that name by future historians. It is drawing increasing attention abroad.[1]

One must keep constantly in mind that both sides involved in this conflict were, or had been, communists. It is true that some inmates were innocent victims implicated either by mistake or by denunciation, but by far the vast majority were of the same political persuasion.

As in all totalitarian states, writers were the first to draw attention to this injustice, long before journalists, historians, sociologists, and others did. At first only hinting at it, but more and more boldly with time, they attacked the taboo directly after Tito's death. Since then a steady stream of novels, stories, plays (but strangely, relatively little poetry), and especially documentary literature has been flooding the print media, showing no signs of abating. Documentary and historical literature lies outside the scope of this article.

Of the many works on this theme, eleven are singled out here for their artistic quality, forcefulness, and openness, or for the importance of their authors: *Noč do jutra* (Night till Morning; 1981) by Branko Hofman; *Karamazovi* (1981; Eng. *Karamazovs,* translated by George Mitrevski) by Dušan Jovanovič; *Tren 2* (Moment 2; 1982) by Antonije Isaković; *Pismo glava* (Heads or Tails; 1982) by Slobodan Selenić; *Prestupna godina* (A Leap Year; 1982) by Žarko Komanin; *Levitan* (Leviathan; 1983) by Vitomil Zupan; *Ispljuvak pun krvi* (Spittle Full of Blood; 1984) by Živojin Pavlović; *Udri bandu* (Strike the Bandits; 1988) by Miroslav Popović; *Djavolji trougao* (The Devil's Triangle; 1988) by Miodrag Čupić; *Goli Otok* (Bare Island; 1990) by Dragoslav Mihailović; and *Odlučan čovek* (A Resolute Man; 1990) by Mihailo Lalić.

Several predominant themes emerge from these works. Perhaps the most striking is the depiction of torture meted out to the inmates of these concentration camps. Time and again the authors emphasize the amazing brutality that went on unabated throughout the existence of the camps. The tortures took both physical and psychological forms, and it is difficult to judge which was more abundant or more effective. The physical tortures were especially brutal. The prisoners were beaten mercilessly during interrogations in the local prisons, but that was only a prelude. As soon as they landed on the island, they were greeted by a mile-long "cordon of death" made up of inmates, who proceeded to beat the newcomers savagely as they passed through the gauntlet. As one of the victims describes it:

"Suddenly three tiny stars flashed in my head, then many. A starry night spread before me, my mouth full of blood. I recoiled: am I to choke on my own teeth? . . . I fell, unafraid of anything any more. I have been scalded and skinned in a hot tub. . . . I am guarding my eyes, but what is there for them to look at?"[2] When the ordeal finally ends, he is holding one of his eyes in the palm of his hand. This punitive method resembles a similar one in Ernest Hemingway's *For Whom the Bell Tolls,* with one exception: the Spanish communists were beaten by the enemy, whereas the Yugoslavs were savaged by their own. Another torture method was "the boycott," during which everyone had the right to strike the boycotted inmate, spit at him, do with him whatever he wanted, while the victim had no right even to speak with anybody. The inmates were called bandits, and the familiar cry in the camp was "Udri bandu!" (hit the bandit).

One particular form of torture was the coerced performance of meaningless work, usually consisting of crushing rocks or carrying them up and down a hill for no apparent purpose, or carrying a heavy load of rocks on a platform whose front handles, held by the "boycotted" inmate, were shorter and therefore bore a heavier load, which sometimes landed on top of him; inmates were also forced to dredge sand from the sea with a shovel while standing in water up to their chest, or a victim might have his head held in a toilet bowl for hours on end, sometimes a whole night, while other prisoners were relieving themselves. Most of these inhumane acts were perpetrated by inmates who had already admitted to their "errors" and had promised to atone for them, usually at the expense of the defiant ones. To make matters worse, the inmates suffered from various diseases brought on by poor nutrition, lack of adequate sleep, and exhausting work from sunrise to sunset. The available medical help was woefully inadequate, resulting in hundreds, even thousands of deaths. No wonder most of the prisoners perceived Bare Island as a living hell.

The psychological tortures were equally cruel. Not only did the victims have no legal rights from the outset; they were never told why they had been arrested and sent to prison camps, and no sentence or rehabilitation decree was ever issued to them upon their release. Needless to say, the prisoners lived in constant fear of beatings, illness, and deprivation. They had no contact with their relatives or friends on the outside. Escape was literally impossible, and isolated attempts invariably ended in failure or tragedy. Inmates were pressured to complete a process of self-examination, including an admission of guilt. This process consisted of written statements in which the detainees were required to list every person with whom they had had any dealings and who could be considered subversive. Since no confession was ever deemed adequate, the detainees usually wrote down the names of many innocent people, who would then be arrested and brought to camp, thus assuring an endless procession of new prisoners. Sometimes prisoners would list the names of known communists as subversives, but when the ruse was discovered these inmates were subjected to even greater torture or were brought back to the camp, if they had been released. They also had to fear denunciation for every conversation with fellow inmates, no matter how innocuous. Finally, they were released after two to eight years only if they agreed in writing to work for the secret police upon their discharge. Many honorable prisoners considered this to be their worst moral defeat, one they would regret all their life, even if they managed to renege on their enforced obligation. No wonder some inmates saw Bare Island as a massive insane asylum.

The net result of this reign of terror was not only that thousands of men and women were subjected to inhumane treatment, but also that they were maimed for life: "Half the people left the camp without their personality, name, ego . . . totally destroyed; if they still have any sense of life, it's worth nothing. . . . There were times when I ceased to be a man and became an animal. But that was the whole purpose!"[3] The rate of success in breaking these people was phenomenal: 80 percent.

An outsider finds it difficult to comprehend the rationale behind all this. It is not too hard to understand where the authorities learned their trade: from all the masters of terror, the Nazis, the Ustashi (Croatian Nazis), and, most revealingly, Stalin's agents (some of the investigators and guards in the camps were trained in the Soviet Union prior to the split). Many inmates consider Bare Island to be worse than Dachau, Jasenovac, or the Soviet gulag, because it had something those infamous chambers of death did not: a structured regimen of physical torture. It was also immeasurably worse than the prewar prisons for the communists. Speaking of the Yugoslav camps, Dragoslav Mihailović, a former inmate, says, "What Solzhenitsyn describes in *One Day in the Life of Ivan Denisovich* was a picnic, brother, in comparison to what happened here."[4]

As for the frame of mind of both torturers and victims, it can be best explained by the specific circumstances. The authorities, from top to bottom, were convinced that they were protecting themselves from the impending Soviet attack. In their totalitarian mind, trained to disregard human life in the struggle to gain power and keep it, they easily dispensed with a few thousand people. That practically all the victims were their own followers made the authorities feel they held proprietary rights over them. This still does not explain or justify the excessive brutality. Time and again the former prisoners say that they could understand their removal from society as perceived opponents of the regime; what they could not understand or accept was the bestial way they were treated.[5]

The alleged reasons for such treatment are manifold. The communists were eager to preserve their hardearned victory and power. They perceived the danger of the Soviet invasion to be real; in that case, they said to the inmates, "you would have sent us to Siberia."[6] Apparently this is the only way the communists knew how to deal with opponents. They surreptitiously placed many of their agents, notably the apprentice members of the secret-police academy, into the camp as inmates, to provoke and control "the enemy." They also had ample help from the inmates themselves, both those who claimed to have confessed their "crimes" and those who refused to do so. In the first group there were two general types: former war opponents of the communists, such as Chetniks and Ustashi, who saw their chance to redeem themselves or to inflict punishment upon the communists again, or both; and those who either readily believed the authorities' promises of better treatment and early release if they cooperated, or who simply could not take it any longer. That is why many of them were eager to strike a harder blow on the newcomers in the cordon, to denounce every word spoken by a fellow inmate, to involve those outside the camp. The second group was composed of the defiant ones, but those were the exceptions. Most of them did not leave the camp alive. They are remembered by the survivors with awe and respect for their courage.

The fact that almost all the players in this human tragedy were communists recalls the "Karamazov syndrome," evoked by the Slovene playwright Dušan Jovanovič in his play *Karamazovi*. He was one of the first writers to broach the conflict between the old and the new allegiances among the Yugoslav communists after 1948. The hero of his play is bewildered by the sudden change: "Something that was white all the time didn't become black all of a sudden. . . . This earth is a planet and it turns around its axis and around the sun. That's what they taught us. We believed that. . . . I need an explanation. I don't understand this."[7] After the painful "reeducation," however, he is forced to repeat time and again that he is an enemy: "I am a bandit, a deserter, a scoundrel, a degenerate, without dignity and without honor, without pride, a chameleon, a sectarian, a provoker, and a blind passenger on the ship of history of the Yugoslav nation" (8). Perhaps the very fact that those who were perceived as enemies were communists themselves stirred resentment on the part of the defend-

ers of the system to a fever pitch. Although the authorities were no less determined and systematic in eradicating ideological opponents, they were not as cruel in doing so. It was a different matter with their own followers.

The Karamazov metaphor works here on several levels. There is a clash here not only between the father (the Soviet Union) and the sons (Tito and his communists), but also among the Yugoslav communists themselves; the roles are simply reversed. Some of the Yugoslavs (Tito and his regime) now play the role of the father, with those who are ruled by him as the sons. Those considered to have transgressed against the father and what he stands for are the inmates, and they in turn are paying the price for the sins of their fathers. It is ironic that the latter are forced to play the role of the prodigal sons, while the father goes scot-free, unlike Fyodor Karamazov. The consequences, however, are the same for all the sons: they all pay the price, as is now becoming all too obvious.

If we extend the metaphor, the wives, children, and other relatives of the Bare Islanders are also paying the price for the "sins" of *their* husbands and fathers. However, we have here the other side of the Karamazov syndrome at play, the internecine struggle between brothers, as it were. This is illustrated by the fact that many wives rejected their husbands and even turned against them; and although there are some mitigating circumstances in their betrayal (the long wait, the total uncertainty, the loss of jobs and apartments, the loss of a breadwinner, the stigma in the society), the two sides have become mortal enemies. In many cases it has made life bitter and much more difficult for the freed inmates after years of undeserved punishment. Their children, however, are assuming the role of the Karamazov brothers either by turning against their fathers (or mothers) or by ignoring them altogether. In Jovanovič's play the children become estranged, having studied in London, acquired occupations contrary to their fathers' beliefs, and totally abandoned the path of communism. The fathers suffer from double jeopardy many times over.

The theme of right and wrong enters the scene in a significant yet perverse way. It is difficult to say who is right and who is wrong in this situation. After all, had not the wielders of power feared that the accused would have done exactly the same to them, or even worse, had they prevailed? The question of guilt and retribution is at the core of Branko Hofman's novel *Noč do jutra,* wherein a former inmate confronts his torturer from the camp days, an official who is now investigating the case of a young girl's murder or suicide. Peter, a veteran of Bare Island, grapples with the basic question of his existence: was he right or were they? More specifically, were his eight years on Bare Island a mistake and in vain? He feels that he had to go through this experience, because "to be a thing among things is the negation of man's existence, as are the acceptance of death and the right of the stronger. In nature that is the most natural law, but if you agree to that, you admit that your torturers . . . were justified and were doing the most natural thing in harmony with the biological equilibrium."[8] Peter recalls his early idealism, which eventually brought the calamity upon him: "What inspired him was the Gorkyesque ecstasy that 'it is a powerful thing on earth to be a man.' Because of that he imagined that he could change the world with the help of love, reason, and honesty" (19). Now, however, comes a bewildering turnaround at a meeting to discuss the Soviet-Yugoslav relationship: "That which the party taught him was not the simple truth, it was faith which did not tolerate doubt. For years it taught him that one should love the country of socialism and the greatest genius of all, and when they spoke his name the tears rushed to their eyes. . . . He had friends who stood before the firing squad, sang 'The International,' and died with his name on their lips. And what he now heard at the meeting was like thunder from a blue sky. His world had crashed" (125).

Peter sees in the investigator Kovač, his camp tormentor, the embodiment of the evil that has befallen him and other victims, a man who has robbed him of his humanity, of his past and future. Kovač, on the other hand, has his own justification: "I know only that I carried out my duty. No one asked me whether it was pleasant or not. It was necessary. Inevitable. Proven by history. . . . We were forced to do evil in order to prevent a greater evil. Political strategy is not determined by moral ideals but by purpose and efficiency" (167). Peter does not know whom to hate now. The executioners? They were following orders. The state? An abstract notion. The party? "Political *l'art pour l'art* is like masturbation in a harem" (218). On the verge of attacking Kovač physically, Peter understands that Kovač, although a symbol of the system, is but a cog in the machine and that the only way to defeat him and the system is through a realization that "violence will rule the world until we open wide to doubt all spiritual and social life and understand that the goal is not in standing pat but in overcoming the present, and that therefore every power which does not nurture and stimulate the heresy of the spirit is only one of many forms of dictatorship" (153). The murder case under investigation remains inconclusive, just as many questions concerning the suffering endured by Peter and other inmates remain unanswered. Still, Peter has undergone a catharsis that enables him to abandon his self-imposed isolation and perhaps start a new, if uncertain, life.

Aside from Hofman and, to a degree, Isaković, few writers have attacked the dilemma frontally by naming openly the real culprit in this tragedy, the communist system. It may be that, having been related to the system in one way or another, they are reluctant to cover themselves with ashes and accuse their former idol; or it may be that almost all these works were published while censorship was still in operation; or perhaps the magnitude of the crime has numbed them to a point that they are still unable to believe how it was all possible; or perhaps it is because only the communists were "privileged" to go through this unique ordeal and are able to write about it, whereas others lack the firsthand experience necessary for an adequate artistic creation. Whatever the reason, the Bare Island chroniclers are yet to come out totally convinced against the real culprit.

Nevertheless, if they have not done so openly, the undercurrents of an ongoing political discussion are moving in this direction. The best example of this is provided by the venerable Serbian writer Mihailo Lalić, who has just published a short novel, *Odlučan čovek* (A Resolute Man),[9] that epitomizes the whole syndrome surrounding the Bare Island episode. In his earlier works, which made him a leading fiction writer in Yugoslav literature, Lalić steadfastly defended the communist revolution, even though he never stooped to the low level of socialist realism. In his new novel he questions for the first time such basic premises of the revolution as the sacred right of the communists to rule and their infallibility from top to bottom. The eponymous "resolute man" is a retired army general seeking help for troubles—predominantly of a psychological nature—that are besetting him at a time when he should be enjoying the fruits of his lifelong engagement. He still insists that what he and others did in the revolution and afterward was right and justified and that he would do it all again. Moreover, he declares gleefully that he enjoyed persecuting, arresting, and even killing the enemies of the regime. In sessions with a pretty young psychiatrist, however, he reveals a gaping void in his life that only love, like that of the young psychiatrist, could fill and perhaps alleviate the pangs of conscience that have been bothering him of late. When the doctor points out that he killed her only uncle and that he must pay for his crimes, he deliberately drives his car over a cliff, finding deliverance in a fiery death.

Only a writer of Lalić's caliber can encapsulate the entire history of the rulers of his country over the last four-and-a-half decades. He sees that history basically as a moral issue, as a kind of morality play. (The morality-play aspect is underscored by the coincidental fact that several notorious camps of the Yugoslav gulag are situated on islands resembling the famous Devil's Island

and Alcatraz as the epitome of the hell on earth from which there is no escape.)[10] Lalić's protagonist finds escape in death as his only just reward, without waiting for human justice or retribution to run its course.

In Slobodan Selenić's novel *Pismo glava* (Heads or Tails)[11] a character with a similar past becomes a religious fanatic and a social outcast bordering on madness. Other writers have hinted at a similar outcome. It seems as if the Bare Island episode has come full circle by becoming, deliberately or not, the symbol of all the injustice underlying the communist rule in Yugoslavia and, by extension, in all of Eastern Europe. Whether the victims of this injustice find solace in knowing that they were unjustly persecuted, whether the damage done to them can ever be repaired, and whether the enormous human potential that has been wantonly wasted can ever be restored—all that remains to be seen. As one character in Mihailović's *Goli Otok* says about the Bare Islanders: "All who survived will need years and decades for a slow recuperation. After they've recovered—if they have, and even then not fully—only then can they begin to tell somewhat of what they experienced" (227). Perhaps they do not have to; their writers, the conscience of every nation in distress, are doing it for them.

Vasa D. Mihailovich, Spring 1991

[1] Other authors who have examined this theme in literature are Leonore Scheffer, "Goli Otok: Das Jahr 1948 in den jugoslawischen Gegenwartsliteraturen," *Südosteuropa,* 33:6 (1984), pp. 352–77; Oskar Gruenwald, "Yugoslav Camp Literature: Rediscovering the Ghost of a Nation's Past-Present-Future," *Slavic Review,* 46:3–4 (1987), pp. 513–28; and Ante Kadić, "The Yugoslav Gulag," in *Essays in South Slavic Literature,* New Haven, Ct., Yale Russian and East European Publications, 1989, pp. 238–54.

[2] Antonije Isaković, *Tren* 2, Belgrade, Prosveta, 1982, pp. 67–68.

[3] Dragoslav Mihailović, *Goli Otok,* Belgrade, Politika, 1990, pp. 108–9. For a review, see p. 330 of this issue.

[4] Cited in Živojin Pavlović, *Ispljuvak pun krvi,* Belgrade, Dereta, 1984, p. 128.

[5] Mihailović, p. 194.

[6] Pavlović, p. 152.

[7] Dušan Jovanovič, *Karamazovi,* Zagreb, Globus, 1981, p. 6.

[8] Branko Hofman, *Noč do jutra,* Ljubljana, Slovenska Matica, 1981. The quotation is taken from the 1982 edition, published in Zagreb by Znanje.

[9] Mihailo Lalić, *Odlučan čovek,* Belgrade, Rad, 1990. For a review, see p. 329 of this issue.

[10] See Miroslav Popović, *Djavoli trougao,* Belgrade, Višnjić, 1988; reviewed in *WLT* 64:1 (Winter 1990), p. 154.

[11] Slobodan Selenić, *Pismo glava,* Belgrade, Prosveta, 1982.

Northern Europe

Sámi Literature in the Twentieth Century

Samekiella, kooekiella,
manne oakak slundadak?
Ale jaskod eadnikiella,
tastgo vieris kielak, mielak tudnje
juo havddi koivvokik,
vaihkke ik leak vela liddom,
eaige urbbik rahpasam.

▓ H. A. GUTTORM, 1934

Saame speech, golden speech —
O, why did you joyless sleep?
Die not, mother tongue of ours,
e'en if foreign words and foreign will
dug their grave for you
ere you ever came to bloom,
ere your bud had opened wide.

▓ (FROM *MODERN SCANDINAVIAN POETRY*)

In June 1995 I visited Guovdagaeidnu, Sapmi. The river was covered with ice, the fells were snow-covered. In little hollows protected by dwarf birch, the greens and grays of lichen hovered under the rough spring snow. Yet at 10:00 in the evening, when we gathered in a herder's *kota* (tent) for a feast of reindeer stew, the sun was still high and its strength spoke of enormous changes in the days to come.

After a second cup of broth, we stretched out on the skins around the central fire, and talk turned philosophical. My colleague in conversation was a young Sámi woman. With their children, she and her husband tended their combined herds of reindeer; but she was also a publisher, a textbook writer, a poet, a teacher, and an accomplished crafts-woman. In a place about the population of my small Vermont college town, I was hearing deep, thoughtful discussions on every side in Sámi, English, German, French, Swedish, Norwegian,

and Russian. Part of the company was academic, but most were working Sámi, passionately involved with Sámi culture and its revival.

If you look north of the Arctic Circle on a map of Scandinavia, you may not be able to find this place where I ate and talked with the Sámi herders. Your map probably reads Kautokeino, Norway, and it probably says nothing about this arc of the Scandinavian Arctic being Sapmi, the homeland of the Sámi people, stretching from Norway through Sweden across Finland and on to the Kola Peninsula of Russia.

Since the early 1970s, when Sámi banded together to protest the damming of the Alta River in Norway, there has been a flowering of Sámi political and creative energy. Sámi literature is no longer just the *yoik* (songs) and *muitalandáidu* (tales) archived by Western ethnologists and anthropologists, but a thriving, exciting, contemporary literature of its own.

My first experience of the Sámi came in the summer of 1971, when I worked in a tourist hostel in Kilpisjärvi, in Finnish Lapland, right where the boundaries of Norway, Sweden, and Finland come together in the high fells. Tourists from the European South, en route to North Cape, were as thick as mosquitoes all along the E4, the Road of the Four Winds. Sámi occasionally came by the hostel to sell their hand-carved cups and bone tools, but they quickly and quietly vanished, only to be met when I too hiked back into the fells.

It was as if I could not really see the Sámi, as if I were blind, their presence was so fleeting. But not for long; they were just starting to reclaim their culture and their identity. A Sámi poet/artist named Nils-Aslak Valkeapää had just written a polemic entitled *Terveisiä Lapista* (1970; Eng. *Greetings from Lapland*), speaking out for the Sámi. In a very straightforward, unflinching, and charismatic way, Valkeapää talks directly to his reader about the problems confronting the Sámi people in Finland. He expands on his purpose for writing the

Áilu, Nils-Aslak Valkeapää (© *Per-Ola Utsi*)

book in his foreword to the English translation (London, Zed, 1983):

> In your hands you have a book that was originally meant to be an exclamation mark, punctuating a certain moment in time. I wrote *Greetings from Lappland* in Finnish, for the Finns. . . . This little book, which was only meant to be a spontaneous cry of protest, is still fully relevant. And perhaps even relevant in a global perspective, now just as before.

Valkeapää's book had a significant impact in revitalizing the Sámi language and identity movement of the 1970s. Kirsti Paltto, another Sámi, was to write a similar tract, *Saamelaiset* (The Sámi), in 1973, reinforcing the growing Sámi wish to have their own history, language, culture, livelihoods, way of life, identity, and worldviews.

Western and Natural Worldviews

The plants of the earth The animals of the forest The fishes of the sea.	Animals and birds and plants, my sisters and brothers.
Lord of nature. Others. Pagans. Primitives.	I am nature. Nature teaches, reindeer lead.
Earn your bread by the sweat of your brow.	I follow, joyfully.
One god, the Father almighty.	Sun, moon, wind, stars.

Go, do. Into outer space.	Space is within, power internal.
The truth must be felt. Touched. Seen. Proven.	Life is a dream, the dream real, and experience is truth.
Compete. Nations. States. Cities. Collect. Concentrate.	Adapt, move, disperse. Families and clans.
Order. Borders. Streets. Buildings. Power.	Moving protects, borders obstruct.
Subdivide. Make foundations. Make fences. Red cabin. Potato patch. Permanence.	Home knows no walls, fells are home. Winter place, summer place. The wind brings, the wind removes.
Forever. Windows. Stairs. Floor. Roof. Address. Nameplate by the door.	*Laavu, kota, tipi, yurt, iglu.* Set up, take down, move.
Rigid forms. Geometry. Corners. Angles.	Fluid forms. Fell, wind, wave, fire.
Time. Year. Month. Week. Day. Hour. Minute. Second. Nanosecond.	Seasons. Mating. Migrating. Hibernating.

(Adapted from Nils-Aslak Valkeapää, "The Sun, the Thunder, the Fires of Heaven")

My father, Bill Osgood, with his lifelong interest in the North, originally led me to the summer in Kilpisjärvi. That, in turn, led to a scholarship to study at the University of Helsinki, where Valkeapää's traditional music was part of the general voice of protest in the early 1970s. Over the years my interest in the Sámi has been informed and animated by long talks with Ludger and Linna Müller-Wille, whose research in Ohcejohka in the late 1960s documented the passing of much traditional Sámi culture. And most recently, the Arctic Centre of the University of Lapland in Rovaniemi has supported my interest in Sámi literature with research and lecture opportunities, enabling me to meet Sámi scholars and authors and to use the excellent resources of the Library of Lapland.

I do not read Sámi yet, so the material for this article comes mostly from Finnish and English sources. In distinct contrast to literature written in "large" languages which have large readerships, minority languages such as Sámi or Finnish, with their limited audience, are much more sensitive to cultural distortion, especially in translation and criticism. Veli-Pekka Lehtola writes:

> The language of millions is not like a single language; it is like a school of herring all swimming in the same direction. The language of a small

people is like a small fox, unprotected by the pack. It has to look out for itself and hear danger in order to avoid it, it looks about and sees the others. Majority peoples, who are losing their grip on how to stay alive, have much to learn from a small fox. ("Saamelainen kirjallisuus" [Sami Literature], 49)

The Sámi have done significant work reclaiming their history and identities in the last quarter-century through the arts, politics, and scholarship, and I have used those sources, where available. Both Valkeapää and Paltto have been generous correspondents, and I am deeply grateful to the Sámi scholars Vuokko Hirvonen, Veli-Pekka Lehtola, and Rauna Kuokkanen for their time, help, ideas, and interpretations.

In their declarations in the early 1970s, Valkeapää and Paltto had chosen to write their stories in Finnish not only to express their views to a larger audience, but also to communicate with their fellow Sámi. Unlike now, with partial protection by Sámi language laws in Scandinavia authorizing Sámi as a language of instruction and governance, very few Sámi were literate in their mother tongue. Living a largely nomadic life until World War II, most Sámi had been educated at boarding schools, being forcibly acculturated into the dominant culture of the political state where they happened to live. Valkeapää has even written a poem on the subject.

He happily travelled
to school

He came to regret that
a foreign language was spoken
and there was no trout lake
If he felt like fishing
he had to sneak away to the tarn
and catch small red-eyed fish

He longed for the tundra
he felt suffocated among the pines
Became more and more different

At night he wet his bed
Secretly
cried under the hay in a barn
(from *Trekways of the Winds*)

Such grim experiences are typical of postwar acculturation policies around the entire circumpolar North. Drastic changes in livelihood and social structure after the war caused deep rifts in Sámi life, precipitating both social crisis and cultural renaissance, themes highly visible in Sámi writing and art.

This last half-century has seen wrenching conflicts between traditional and modern culture for the Sámi.

On the other hand, nearly a third of the 900-odd titles extant in Sámi have been published in just the last quarter-century, reclaiming language and identity and bridging not only the gap between Western and natural worldviews, but also the gap between a tribal, preliterate tradition and a global, postliterate tradition. Davvi Girjii, the official Sámi publishing house in Kárášjohka, Norway, describes the resulting publishing dilemma:

The market for Sámi books is a relatively small one. The market for Sámi literature is also limited, since the total number of Sámi is not very large. A further limitation is imposed by the fact that many Sámi have lost their mother tongue, while others are illiterate in their mother tongue. This reduces the number of potential buyers and readers so much that no publishing house today can count on covering the production costs of publishing Sámi-language books through sales. Sámi book production is therefore dependent on subsidies.

Other problems of the Sámi as a small, indigenous people have been apparent throughout history on the Scandinavian peninsula, as most Sámi were forced ever farther north, adapting adroitly to Arctic life. Other Sámi migrated southward or westward, blending in with the dominant populations. So, the Sámi people may number as many as 100,000 or as few as 35,000, depending on how they are counted. If language is the criterion, the Sámi population will be quite small, as Sámi is spoken only among the northernmost populations.

The Sámi language is a member of the Finno-Ugric language family, a near cousin to Finnish. There are written documents in Sámi dating from as early as the seventeenth century; however, until the present century the writing has been primarily for religious and didactic purposes, spawning a range of orthographies, including Cyrillic among the Orthodox Skolt Sámi. In fact, a unified orthography dates only from 1979, and the very word *Sámi* has only recently been authorized as the official English spelling for the language and the people by Sámi Instituhtta (the Nordic Sámi Institute).

On the other hand, the oral tradition among the Sámi has been and continues to be a rich and creative one, in practice and in literature. The *yoik* is the distinctive Sámi musical and poetic tradition. Paulus Utsi describes it poetically as follows:

The Yoik
The yoik is the home of the thoughts
where you bring your thoughts.
That's why it doesn't have so many words
to give out —
free sounds fare
farther than words.

The yoik elevates the mind of man
flies with his thoughts
above the clouds,
has his thoughts
as his friend
in the beauty of nature.
(*MSP*, 154)

Originally the mystical domain of the *noaidi* or shamans, yoiks were expressly forbidden by a Danish king
on pain of death. Like the blues, the yoik went underground, becoming an individual, Aesopian, improvisational expression of self and nature—to sing a mood,
to keep wolves from the herd, to lull a baby to sleep.
Forbidden both by law and by society, yoiking became
a very subtle act of self-identification and rebellion.
Sámi tales, like yoiks, also function on several levels, explaining mysterious phenomena through *stálu* (giants)
or *gufihtar* (trolls) but also embodying elements of the
pre-Christian past.

Such subtleties of traditional expression are quite
accessible in more sensory media, such as Sámi children's literature, theater, and film; in contemporary literature the yoik-muitalandáidu tradition is still visible
but much less accessible to a Western reader. A fine introduction to Sámi culture and literature might be
Ofelaš (1987; Eng. *Pathfinder*), a film directed by the
Sámi Nils Gaup. The film vividly retells a traditional
story of a Sámi who knows the richness and deception
of his landscape and who is pitted against covetous
Chud invaders.

Until this century, Sámi literature has been largely
incidental rather than intentional. In the seventeenth
century Olaus Sirma, a Sámi sent to study for the ministry in Uppsala, collected yoiks, two of which were translated into Latin (Schefferus's *Lapponia*, 1673) for an appreciative European audience. Later, Anders Fjellner
collected more Sámi folk poetry, intending to create an
epic like the *Kalevala*, which had helped to spark the
Finnish nationalist movement. Although he never finished the work, Sámi still think of themselves as "the
sons of the sun," as they are described in the epic's creation cycle.

Drawing on this same folk heritage, Isak Saba
(1872–1921) wrote the Sámi anthem "The Song of the
Sámi People," which ends with a powerful cry for language, land, and identity: "Oh, tough kin of the sun's
sons, / Never shall you be subdued / If you heed your
golden Sámi tongue, / Remember the ancestors' word.
/ Sámiland for Sámi!" (translated from the Sámi by Ragnar Müller-Wille and Rauna Kuokkanen).

However, Johan Turi (1854–1936) is really the pioneer of modern Sámi literature. His book *Muittalus sami-*

id birra: En bog om lappernes live af den svenske Lap (literally "A Tale of Sami Life: A Book of Lapp Life by a
Swedish Lapp"; 1910) was written as a corrective for
Swedish bureaucrats who were apt to cultivate false impressions in their ignorance about Sámi life. The original Sámi text flows in long, Joycean sentences, unencumbered by much punctuation, but subsequent
translations such as that by E. Gee Nash in 1966 (*Turi's
Book of Lappland*) were edited for Western readers as an
anthropological text. Vuokko Hirvonen, a Sámi scholar
at Sámi Instituhtta, considers Turi's work to be a narrative, a necessary transitional genre which bridges the
distance between the Sámi oral tradition and contemporary Sámi literature.

Turi's task is well described by Emilie Demant-
Hatt, his mentor and editor, in her introduction to his
book:

> Turi wished to write down what he thought; he
> wished to tell of the nomads' life, but it was not
> easy. The work was strange to him, and the ob-
> stacles were many. He can write and read his own
> language . . . both reading and writing he has
> learnt since he grew up. Turi has never had any
> schooling. Also there were other hindrances. At
> first he wrote in Finnish—he was used to looking
> upon his own language as all too poor for a book
> written in it to have any possibilities—and he can
> talk Finnish quite well, yet his thoughts flow
> more easily in his mother tongue. Then too, both
> Finns and Lapps mocked at him for working at
> anything so useless as writing—they looked
> upon it as a waste of time—as a thing that could
> produce no daily bread; and Turi often thought
> that they were probably right; luckily he had no
> family to whom he was responsible for the way
> he spent his time. (*Turi's Book of Lappland*, 11–
> 12)

Turi sets out his own purpose in writing even more
clearly on his first page:

> I am a Lapp who, throughout my life, have bus-
> ied myself with all manner of Lapp work, and I
> know all about Lapp life. I have heard tell that the
> Swedish Government will help us all they can,
> but they don't really understand our life and cir-
> cumstances, because no Lapp can explain it to
> them. The reason for this is that when a Lapp gets
> into a room his brains go round . . . they're no
> good unless the wind's blowing in his nose. He
> can't think quickly between four walls. Nor is it
> good for him to be among the thick forest when
> it is warm. But when a Lapp is out on the high
> fells, then his brain is quite clear, and if there was
> a meeting-place on some fell or other, then a
> Lapp could state his case quite well.

Turi had little concept of his audience and little control over the design of the book itself. Despite the distortion of the European editions, however, that book has helped many people understand Sámi life with its lively stories and detailed illustrations.

Invigorated by the nationalist spirit at the teachers' college in Jyväskylä, Finland, Pedar Jalvi (1888–1916) looked homeward to collect Sámi stories and poems (*Sabmelažžai maidnasak ja muihtalusak,* 1966). Jalvi was among the first to use Sámi as a literary language, publishing at his own expense *Muohtačalmmit* (The Snowflakes; 1910). This uneven collection of a few poems and stories nevertheless shows great literary potential, snuffed out by his early death from tuberculosis. In the title poem, single fragile snowflakes melt in the spring to become a river, thus gaining in strength. In "I Run in the Mountains" the impressionist quality of a yoik is apparent in the few lines evoking the poet's loss of his childhood: "I run in the mountains, wander on the bare ridges, / I climb the high mountain peak, / I stroll in the forest looking at the rocks, / I sit there pondering things, and remember / my wonderful childhood days" (*MSP*).

Paulus Utsi (1918–75) also has a distinctively quiet voice. His first book of poetry, playfully entitled *Giela Giela* (Snaring the Language; 1974), starts with "The Word," a poem about the intimate connection between nature and experience: "Whisper into the rock / someone is listening in a hidden place / receives the word / carries it forward / and makes it come true" (*MSP*). Utsi's second, posthumous book of poetry, *Giela Gielain* (Snaring with Language; 1980), emphasizes his support of the emerging Sámi nation and its landscape, protesting more loudly the intrusion of modern technology in nature, as in "The New Mountain Waters."

Human hands dam up the waters —
the water rises, pushes the Sámi out,
reindeer food washed by the water,
cloudberry moors, haying meadows.
The fish has lost its path.

The lake was forced by human hands,
rises under weight and pressure.
Promontories, beaches become islets.
The water washes rock and strand,
the waves wash birch and bushes.
(*MSP*)

Hans-Aslak Guttorm (1907–92) deliberately tried to develop Sámi as a valid literary language (see the epigraph to my essay) and Sámi experience as a valid literary experience. His first work, *Čierru jietna meahcis* (A Voice Crying in the Wilderness), written in 1932–33, is an epic poem about searching for a mother tongue; but this work was published only in 1983, near the end of his life. In the collection *Koccam spalli* (Aroused Like the Wind; 1940) Guttorm praised the Sámi language as a new creative tool, honing his ability with everyday realism to paint powerful, if fleeting, visual images.

The work of early Sámi writers validated Sámi as an effective literary language and expanded the Sámi literary genres to include lyric poetry, short stories, novels, and vigorous new forms like photo essays or music/poetry collages. Sámi literature is flourishing, as in the poetry of Inger-Mari Aikio (b. 1961), a new, strong-voiced Sámi poet. Rauna Kuokkanen, a young Sámi scholar, says that Aikio's poetry blurs the lines between humankind and nature (personal communication, spring 1996): "She does not have to step into nature from the outside; she is already there. Closeness to nature and Sámi-ness intertwine; nature is the everyday life she lives." This connectedness is visible in the following lyric from *Gollebiekkat almmi dievva* (Skyful of Golden Clouds; 1989), where a human deliberately violates nature. The pain caused by this act is like a red wave, like blood from a wound. This visceral pain of nature is something we can ignore, although we cannot help but sense it.

juddasmeahttun giehta
gaikkoda soahkelastta.
rukses barrun.
oasazat gahccet eatnamii
isket najmmat goiki suonaide
beaivvasa dalkkodan suolnni.

(thoughtless hand
rips off a birch leaf.
like a red wave.
little shreds fall to the earth
trying to suck into their drying veins
nature's healing dew.)
(tr. Rauna Kuokkanen with K. O. Dana)

Only nature can cure—or try to cure—nature. Aikio's nature imagery and her subdued lyric voice can be traced to the yoik tradition.

Olavi Paltto, a journalist in the Finnish and Sámi press, has just published his first book of short stories, *Juohkásan várri* (Divided Fells; 1995), focusing on issues of immigration, rootlessless, and recovering identities that are central to contemporary Sámi experience. Päivi Alanen, in her review of 2 June 1995 for the northern Finland newspaper *Lapin Kansa* (The People of Lapland), admires Paltto's ability to examine conflicts between old and new with cynical exactitude and pyschological precision, often through human interaction with nature—another theme prevalent in Sámi literature.

Kirsti Paltto (b. 1947) is a prolific writer with a re-markable range of genres, her production extending from stories to political tracts to radio dramas to poetry to children's stories. Perhaps her most important work is what may be the Sámi epic novel, including *Guhtoset dearvan min bohccot* (Let Our Reindeer Graze Free; 1987) and its sequel *Guržo luottat* (Run Now, Son of Njalla; 1991), an intended trilogy describing Sámi life in Finnish Lapland from before World War II. The books follow *siida* (village) life, focusing mostly on the family of eight-year-old Johanas, who is being sent off to school when the story starts and who is fourteen when the war ends and Lapland is being evacuated. These are old-fashioned novels, not of the individual but of a Sámi community in particular, and even the Sámi nation. Paltto's novels have been compared, with cause, to Väinö Linna's epic trilogy about Finland's emergence as a nation, *Täällä pohjantähden alla* (Here Under the North Star; 1959–62).

Paltto is very skilled at detailed descriptions of do-mestic and social life and of reindeer herding, and she provides a convincing portrait of the period when Sámi culture underwent its most significant changes. The conversational tone of the book and the excellent dia-logue between the various characters enlarge on the Turi narrative tradition.

Áilu, Nils-Aslak Valkeapää, is the undisputed mas-ter of many crafts—yoiks and jazz, poetry and photog-raphy, book design and cultural organization—with a master storyteller's fine sense of audience, able to em-brace his own people while simultaneously universaliz-ing the expression of their experience. Valkeapää calls his photo essay *Beaivi, áhčažan* (The Sun, My Father), winner of the Scandinavian Council Literary Prize, a *govadas* or ceremonial drum, intertextualizing meaning and the-matic unity in the poem/picture design. Harald Gaski, an emerging scholar of Sámi literature at the Uni-versity of Tromsø, describes Áilu (in his introduction to *Trekways of the Winds*) as being uniquely qualified to bridge preliterate and postliterate identities in the arts.

> In Valkeapää's view, the time has come to renew tradition, through innovation in traditional artis-tic forms and genres. To challenge the reading, listening and feeling minds of his Sámi audience, he is creating books for people who never had the opportunity to learn to read in their mother-tongue. He makes music it is possible to dance to, but music which is still a yoik. He paints pic-tures expressing the rich history of the Sámi peo-ple. Valkeapää is an artistic polymath who unites words, images, and music in a modern project, aimed at the future and powered by the past. Just as the old Sámi mastered a range of hunting tech-niques to survive in a harsh climate, Valkeapää

has mastered several artistic techniques. In the old society, a hunter could make a good knife and decorate it beautifully, but, most important-ly, he could use it. Similarly Valkeapää creates the words and music of a yoik to be performed. The performance conjures up images that either illustrate what the yoik is describing or become a digression based on the associations produced by the yoik. Valkeapää is a hunting Sámi shaman in our modern media age, and he demonstrates the importance of belonging to location, environ-ment and people.

Sámi literature deserves our ongoing attention as Sámi authors claim their culture and construct Sapmi, their homeland without borders. We can learn a great deal from this small fox which knows how to embody nature, incorporate traditional knowledge, and span genres and eras. Kuokkanen, who has studied culture in Canada with feminists and postmodernists, says that now Sámi literature needs its own critical constructs. Stimulating and illuminating as modern critical theories are for minority literatures, she is nevertheless remind-ed of an asphalt jungle. In her mind, Sámi literature needs its own criticism as well as its own literature, one which is reminiscent of the winds on the high fells, or-ganic and unstructured, a literature recognizing the might of nature and human connectedness to nature. Like Johan Turi, we may need to go high up in the fells to truly appreciate the beauty of Sámi literature.

Kathleen Osgood Dana, Winter 1997

■ **WORKS CITED**

Aikio, Samuli, Ulla Aikio-Puoskari, Johannes Helander. *The Sami Culture in Finland*. Helsinki. Lapin Sivistysseura. 1994.

Hirvonen, Vuokko. "Saamelaisten kirjallisuus ja taide." In *Johda-tus saamentutkimukseen*. Ulla-Maija Kulonen, Juha Pentikäinen, Irja Seurujärvi-Kari, eds. Helsinki. Finnish Literature Society (SKS). 1994.

The Great Bear: A Thematic Anthology of Oral Poetry in the Finno-Ugrian Languages. Lauri Honko, Senni Timonen, Michael Branch, eds. Keith Bosley, tr. Helsinki. Finnish Literature Soci-ety (SKS). 1993.

Lehtola, Veli-Pekka. "Saamelaisen kirjallisuuden vaiheet." In *Lappi 2: Elävä, toimiva maakunta*. Hämeenlinna, Finland. Karis-to. 1984.

———. "Saamelaiskirjallisuus vanhan ja uuden risteyksessä." In *Marginalia ja kirjallisuus*. Matti Savolainen, ed. Helsinki. Finn-ish Literature Society (SKS). 1995.

Modern Scandinavian Poetry: The Panorama of Poetry 1900–1975. Martin Allwood, ed. Mullsjö, Sweden. Anglo-American Center. 1982.

Pathfinder (Norwegian, 1988). Original Sami title: *Ofelaš*. Nils Gaup, writer & director. Copyright 1988 International Film Exchange Ltd. U.S. distribution by New Video Group, New York. In Sami, with English subtitles.

The Sámi Association of North America (SANA) website: http://www.quest-dynamics.com/sana/.

The Sami People. Karasjok, Norway. Sámi Instituhtta / Davvi Girjii. 1990.

Turi, Johan. *Turi's Book of Lappland.* Emilie Demant Hatt, ed. & tr. (into Danish). E. Gee Nash, tr. from Danish. Oosterhout, Neth. Anthropological Publications. 1966.

Valkeapää, Nils-Aslak. "A Way of Calming Reindeer." *Scandinavian Review,* 71:2 (June 1983), pp. 43–48.

———. "The Sun, the Thunder, the Fires of Heaven." Unpublished manuscript. Liisa Ojala, Ernest H. Kanning III, trs. Copyright 1995.

———. *Terveisiä Lapista.* Helsinki. Otava. 1971.

———. *Trekways of the Wind.* Ralph Salisbury, Lars Nordström, Harald Gaski, trs. Guovdageaidnu, Norway. DAT. 1985. Distributed in the Usa by the University of Arizona Press.

Naïve, Naïvistic, Artistic: Some Thoughts on Danish and Swedish Diaries

The range of diaries published in Denmark and Sweden in the twentieth century, whether they were actually written in the twentieth century or merely not published until then, is vast and even somewhat confusing. How can one really compare Kierkegaard's *Journals* with Thomas Frederiksen's *Grønlandske dagbogsblade* (Greenland Diaries)? How can one relate the diaries of twentieth-century politicians to those of a Danish-speaking woman from Schleswig viewing World War I from the German side of the border, both concerned with a world situation but having totally different aims in writing? Can one really consider Paul la Cour's *Fragmenter af en dagbog* (Fragments of a Diary) a diary at all? Or Dag Hammarskjöld's *Vägmärken* (1963; Eng. *Markings*)? Must a diary be seen in its totality, or ought one rather to prefer an edited version? Then there are several nineteenth-century diaries from outlying parts of Danish territory which were intended to give a day-by-day account of life in those distant places and, when transport was available, to be sent to the diarists' relatives. Are they diaries or are they protracted letters? Does it really matter? Perhaps it *does* matter when the concern of the present study is the diary and *not* the letter, much less the autobiography, however closely related the three genres are. Some diaries were, of course, written in the knowledge that they might one day be published— which must itself color their contents—whereas others are purely private jottings never intended for publication.

In considering the esthetic qualities of this motley array, it is clearly necessary to distinguish between diaries of varying scope and size. Those of Kierkegaard or Hans Christian Andersen and, when they become available, the eight hundred small volumes filled by Johannes Jørgensen are so huge and diversified that there can scarcely be any question of considering them as rounded works. Rather, the interest centers on the light they throw on the writers themselves or the surroundings in which they live. There may be, and often is, an esthetic charm in individual passages in these diaries. Then again, there may not. The diaries stand as social and biographical documents. At the other end of the scale are diaries such as that by Olof Lagercrantz, published by the diarist himself in edited form as a unity. In these cases the publication can and must be viewed as a whole. There are also diaries such as Thomas Frederiksen's, which are apparently complete and which possess some quality appealing to the imagination of an international audience.

Frederiksen's are only the latest in a series of diaries concerned with Denmark's former colonies. As early as 1913 there came Carl Emil Janssen's book *En Grønlandspræsts optegnelser* 1844–1849 (Memoirs of a Greenland Priest), which was reissued in 1961, and 1979 brought Viggo Møller's *Dagbøger fra Godthåb* 1871–1872 (Godthåb Diaries). Neither offers much in the way of esthetic enjoyment, but both provide insights into the workings of a now-defunct Greenlandic culture. There is also a very slight connection between the two works, as the then four-month-old Møller is briefly mentioned in Janssen's diary. The writings of educated men, both accounts provide a factual portrait of life in Greenland as seen through the eyes of emigrant Danes in the midnineteenth century. The impression Janssen unwittingly conveys of himself is that of a kindly yet somewhat humorless, colorless man dutifully recording his experiences in alien surroundings. He starts with a description of his actual journey to Greenland, his first encounter with icebergs, and the initial tasks awaiting him on his arrival. He has to examine six confirmation candidates—he fails one of them—and must marry a young Greenlandic couple in rather primitive surroundings: "Then a church was arranged in a half-finished house which Kreutzman was building and which offered a room of some dimensions; a bureau with a writing flap draped with white cloth formed the altar, on which burned quite ordinary candles." This kind of detailed account typifies Janssen's work, which thus stands as a social, ethnological document of some value, but one possessing few literary attributes.

The same is true of Viggo Møller's diaries, published by the Institute of Eskimology at the University of Copenhagen. Indeed, the introduction itself says that the diaries are "not all that exciting" but adds that they are of interest if seen in a general cultural context. They again contain a good deal of concrete information but few personal reflections, and they tell less of the person behind the writing than do Janssen's. On the other hand, they do provide cultural perspectives: Møller was the brother-in-law of the high-ranking administrator H. J. Rink and knew well both Rasmus Berthelsen, an early translator of Greenlandic legends into Danish, and the printer and illustrator Lars Møller.

Neither of these diarists appears as a great personality, and neither projects himself into the work in the sense of making the actual diary come to life. The same cannot be said of William E. Wiinstedt, whose book *En-marinelæges dagbog i Vestindien og ved østersøescadren* (A Maritime Diary in the West Indies, and With the Baltic Fleet) was published in 1983. In its own way this is a more immediately attractive work, a journal kept by an educated though perhaps slightly naïve man, a young doctor who, apparently for his own amusement, committed to paper his experiences in distant parts. Again there is the cultural-historical aspect: an impression of the primitive medical knowledge and medical treatment available on the island of St. Thomas, life among emigrant Danes on the same island, a visit to Santo Domingo and to a primitive Haiti, even a brief glimpse of nineteenth-century Ireland as Wiinstedt returns home. The second section reflects the tedium of duty in the Baltic Sea area during the 1864 war. However, the diary is written in a lively style and is characterized by a good deal of ironic humor: "The daughter Jette was a small, rather heliophobic being who seemed destined to be tormented into her mother's ways; she sang Weyse's songs in a falsetto voice which brought involuntary tears to one's eyes." The diarist himself, moreover, is a living person who emerges, sometimes also involuntarily, from the pages. He tells, for example, of a ball at which he pursues a married woman—at twenty-six a little old-who would clearly prefer not to be with him. When she finally asks his permission to dance with another, he throws himself back into a rocking chair with such force that it overturns: "But I do not think she noticed," is the concluding comment. A reader might wonder how much of this is deliberate self-irony, but the signs are that it is innocent self-revelation.

Equally innocent and genuinely naïve is Thomas Frederiksen, whose diaries created something of a sensation when published in 1980. Accompanied by the author's own illustrations, they depict the life of a Greenland hunter-fisher in relatively recent years, the first entry dating from 1957. Here there is no irony, but a curiously intense portrait of Greenland before the twentieth-century transformation really took hold, a moving account of often overwhelming experiences in daily life. On one occasion the boat in which Frederiksen is sealing strikes a rock and begins to sink. He is the first member of the crew to be taken off the boat and put ashore on a small island, where he is left while attempts are made to rescue the others: "Alone on this tiny islet I suddenly felt helpless. My legs felt heavy and my clothes began to turn to ice. At the thought of perhaps being the only one to be saved, I knelt down and raised my folded hands to heaven in despair. When the others reached the shore in safety I felt strengthened."

The mixture of ethnology and self-revelation found in these various diaries from distant parts has its parallel in others reflecting unusual aspects of Denmark proper. Among the latter is Otto Jonasen's *Pjentemølleren og hans dagbog* (The Good Miller and His Diary), published by Svendborg & Omegns Museum in 1978 and concerned with the diaries of a Svendborg miller named Morten Jørgensen (1772–1845). The book is an edited version of Jørgensen's text, perhaps best described as commentary cum dated questions from the diaries themselves. The work of an intelligent yet unschooled autodidact, the diary gives a lively picture of family life, customs, and habits in a large Danish provincial town in the late eighteenth and early nineteenth centuries: for example, the organization of a funeral, including the cost of mourning clothes, the coffin, the food and drink afterward, et cetera; a consideration of the fear of thunderstorms at a time when houses were built of wood and prone to burn down as a result of lightning; and a description of the effects of a fire near the mill as well as the process and cost of reconstruction. Jørgensen's diary is a gold mine of fact and detailed description and thus provides a valuable social document. Potentially of interest solely to local historians, it is brought to a wider audience by the judicious editing to which it has been subjected.

Closely linked to the local historian's approach is Alexander Linde's diary from Horsens in 1864, with its description of the way in which the 1864 war (the same one reflected in Wiinstedt's diary) is experienced by the Danes in an area overrun by the enemy. The book is written by a seventeen-year-old, and, in curious fashion, the presentation of everyday life in Horsens during a time of war and foreign occupation is accompanied by vignettes of school life.

A much more personal glimpse of war-ridden Denmark is found in Knud Schmidt Petersen's *Optegnelser fra en bevæget tid* (Memoirs from an Agitated Era), published in Vojens in 1983 and containing extracts from the diaries which the editor's grandmother Catherine Schmidt kept from 1914 until her death in 1916. She was one of the Danish majority living in German Schleswig at the time. "I have neither the understanding nor the ability to comprehend all the machinery that is to be set in motion, or all the cruelty that is breathed by the word *war*. I just want to keep a record of what we experience in our home at this time." So runs the entry for 2 August 1914, and Schmidt's factual account becomes the more moving through the presentation of people well known to her who are called up, killed, or maimed, or who flee across the border to Denmark. There are rumors, uncertainties, food shortages; but because the diarist can read both German and Danish newspapers (when they arrive), she is able to confront with each other two conflicting accounts of the war. Perhaps because it is closer to our own times, this work stands as one of the most moving of the "naïve" diaries, written with no intention other than to preserve a record and found in a desk after the writer's death.

There has clearly been an upsurge of this kind of diary in Denmark in recent years, possibly resulting from the modern interest in ordinary people and possibly from an equally modern interest in an ideological presentation of how those people lived. In 1982 Martin Zerland, Lis Toft Andersen, and Bjarne Thorup Thomsen published a book under the title *En selvskreven historie* (A Self-Written History), an analysis of memoirs and diaries written by farmers, artisans, and workers in Denmark. In their introduction the authors make it quite clear that they reject traditional esthetic norms in assessing the value of the memoirs considered, which they see as being products of "the people." The books concerned are, ideologically, seen as placing central figures in a social context, and the trio responsible for the book consciously seek to discover a "collective" tendency in the memoirs resulting from "the ancient sense of community vis-à-vis the landowners." This is not the place to consider their thesis, but rather merely to point out what at the moment is a widespread Danish interest in the lives of ordinary people and the role they have played in the society in which they have lived. The obvious interest in "ethnographic" diaries can perhaps be seen in a similar context, even if the publication of some of them by museums and institutes of Eskimology suggests a different emphasis.

At the other end of the scale come diaries direct from the pens of the authors themselves and clearly published with a specific purpose in mind. In Denmark the obvious representative of this approach is the author Thorkild Hansen, who has turned the diary almost into a literary genre of its own. He writes with an admittedly literary, esthetic intent, as he makes plain in the foreword to his *Rejsedagbøger* (1970), itself a collection of previously published travel diaries, as the title indicates. Hansen explains: "All the pieces in this volume were originally written down in the places they are concerned with and *later adapted*. The main emphasis is on the experiences to which the journeys give rise. They are diary

jottings; if there is a geographic distance between the individual sections, sometimes of several thousand kilometers, the point of view does not stray far from the first-person singular" (my italics). Two main points arise from this foreword: on the one hand Hansen is trying somehow to project himself, his subjective view, through these diaries; on the other he has done so not by publishing them in their raw state but by editing, selecting, and, presumably, rewriting them with an artistic purpose in mind. All of them, including the later ones, are based on real diaries written during his travels and are fashioned with a skilled hand. The balance maintained between the Danish island of Saltholm and Failaka in the Persian Gulf is a clear indication of the artistic awareness that has gone into the work: "In Saltholm history was never allowed to gain a foothold. In Failaka it lies buried beneath ten meters of sand." This comment comes well into the book, after Hansen had spoken at the very outset about a plan to build a new airport on Saltholm, the result of which would be to bury the island beneath concrete. The parallels drawn are clear and consistent, scarcely the sudden inspiration of a diarist.

All in all, Hansen has a tendency throughout his work to derive inspiration from epic failure; this applies to *Vinterhavn* (1972), the "diary" of the author's search for the winter quarters of the unfortunate Danish explorer Jens Munk, and it seems also to be latent in the confrontation often present in his work between the old and the new. Some would naturally say that Hansen romanticizes older cultures, others merely that he is questioning the modern world. Irrespective of this, however, his "diaries" do betray a wholly conscious molding of the raw material of a diary into a finished work of art. The principle is perhaps not so very different from that applied by some of the editors who have selected extracts from the "naïve" diaries to which reference has already been made; the difference is that this is the work of a conscious artist who has a message and is not content merely to provide a series of esthetically pleasing extracts.

The principle adopted by Thorkild Hansen is related to that employed somewhat earlier by the Swede Ivar Lo-Johanssen in his *Dagbok från 20-talet* (Diary from the Twenties), though the actual aim of the two writers is completely different. Lo-Johanssen, like Hansen, incorporated four travel accounts into his book, and they are likewise developments of diaries rather than copies of them. However, his aim is not so much to project himself as to portray the way of life of the working people whom he met. "I had had the idea of writing a book on the workers in each of the countries I visited and worked in," he says in the postscript to the collected version, implying that his writing is in a way more extroverted and less reflective that that of Hansen, as seen in the attempt to give, through brief glimpses, an overall impression of workers fleetingly encountered, their way of life, the atmosphere in the cities, and the warmth and kindness exuding from ordinary men and women. When visiting Northumberland, for instance, he asks an old man to direct him to the post office and is overwhelmed when he is not told how to get there but is actually taken there, over a long distance. He is indeed so overwhelmed that when the old man finally leaves him, he forgets to go into the post office to which he has been taken—and is sure the old man must have noticed this.

In 1954 another Swede, Olof Lagercrantz, published yet another form of artistic diary, under the simple title of *Dagbok*. Unlike the diaries of both Hansen and Lo-Johanssen, this work gives the reader scant information on the author's movements but all the more on his thoughts. Divided into two titled sections, the book consists (apparently) of selections from Lagercrantz's diary from 9 January to 5 February of one year and then from 31 December to 3 May of the following year. No specific year is given in the diary entries, but as one of them is stated to be a hundred years after the birth of Strindberg, it is clear we are talking about 1949–50, though this is not particularly important. There are reflections on many subjects, from music to sex education, and there are thumbnail sketches of people whom Lagercrantz has met. Occasionally, when at their best, the diaries have some of the concentration of Johannes V. Jensen in his *Myter* (Myths), as when Lagercrantz briefly sketches his mother and her stoic reaction to the suicide of his sister. His experience of the ceremonies at Strindberg's graveside on the centenary of the author's birth provides another example of this. There is also humor—sometimes at Lagercrantz's own expense, sometimes at the expense of social mores, as when he recapitulates in his diary that of one Elsa Kniberg, the daughter of a Swedish officer, who died in 1907 and whose diary was published in 1954 as a social document of its day.

In between these two groups of diaries, the one artistic and intended for publication, the other naïve but charming (often) in its naïveté and scarcely intended for publication, there is a third group more difficult to define. It is scarcely possible that the former Danish prime minister C. Th. Zahle or his minister for home affairs Ove Rode never gave a thought to the possibility that their diaries might, in their entirety or in part, be published. Neither, according to the editor Tage Kaarsted, was in the regular habit of keeping a diary, but during World War I both did precisely this under the impres-

sion of events of historical significance. In the case of Zahle, Kaarsted adds that he had "neither the time nor the strength to do so systematically, and the outcome is thus a series of entries of varying interest." It is clear from Kaarsted's introductions that he finds no real literary qualities in either of these diaries and that indeed he does not even look for any, but that they are both of value as *historical* documents. He even goes so far in the case of Zahle as to complain that the diarist does not always distinguish between essentials and inessentials, though from the layman's point of view it is sometimes the inessentials that add life to what is otherwise a pedestrian publication: the recapitulation of rumor, the hasty asides (the head of the general staff is described as "the worst twaddler imaginable"), the odd glimpse of humor ("If Eggers gets a move on, he can travel home in a manner befitting his position; if not, he will have to go on a freighter"). Rode's diaries are even more detailed, perhaps rather more systematic, but certainly also less lively. They will be read by few but the specialist.

A diary of a similar nature, this time published by the diarist himself, is that of a more recent prime minister, Jens Otto Kragh, for the years 1971–72, concentrating in particular on the negotiations surrounding Denmark's entry into the EEC and ending with Kragh's dramatic decision to resign once he knows the result of the referendum to be positive. Kragh kept a remarkably detailed account of these events, sometimes even by the hour, and it is his opinion that they give, as he says, "firsthand source material rather than a piece of history." They appear to have few literary pretensions despite their dramatic finish, but they are surely more than history. Kragh was a politician, and so the possibility of a political purpose behind the presentation of events cannot be discounted. Historical they may be, like those of Zahle and Rode, but they are scarcely entirely objective. A sifting process has been at work, the sifting of a politician, of an intelligent man aware that his words might one day form the basis for a historical judgment both of his time and of himself. Thus, despite the air of immediacy, they are not diaries in the naïve category with which this study began. Instead, they are given the appearance of immediacy. They are naïvistic, not naïve. From a literary point of view they are the least interesting.

Few of the diaries discussed thus far have been published in an unedited form, whether edited by the diarist in person—with or without a conscious objective—or by someone else who has felt able, or compelled, to cut and to organize. Some diaries, as indicated at the beginning, are so vast in scope as almost to defy efforts to produce such an organized whole. Nevertheless, there are some complex diaries where an attempt to produce an esthetically acceptable version has been successfully undertaken.

The first instance results from the diaries of August Strindberg, kept from 1896 until 1908 and subsequently called the *Occult Diary* by Strindberg himself. In 1963 Torsten Eklund published an edited and, in certain respects, expanded version under the title *From an Occult Diary*. This new version concentrates exclusively on the strangely intense yet tragic relationship between Strindberg and his third wife Harriet Bosse, supplementing the original diary entries—those, that is, relevant to this episode—with extracts from the correspondence between the two and with some of Harriet Bosse's own subsequent comments. The result is not the all-round insight into a writer's personality that a diarist might be expected to give, but, as it were, a gripping firsthand account of a remarkable relationship between two people. By his careful choice of texts, Eklund has given to the original a life and a dramatic impact which it scarcely possessed in itself.

A similar achievement, though reflecting a very different relationship, is found in Torben Schousboe's 1983 version of Carl Nielsen's diaries and correspondence with Anne Marie Carl Nielsen. The extracts from Nielsen's diaries are again supplemented by relevant letters exchanged between the composer and his wife. Once more the result is not only an insight into the composer's artistic development, his musical sensitivity, but also a charting of the profound, though at times very uneasy relationship between him and his wife, providing more than the bare bones for an understanding of artistic genius. Thanks to the editing, what we have is both a work of scholarship and, at the same time, a human portrait with distinct esthetic qualities.

■ ■ ■

The examination of a large number of diaries published in one form or another leaves the impression that diaries, the products of occasional impulses, odd moments of personal confession or reflection, uncoordinated observations, often contain the stuff of literature but, like the seed of literary invention in an author's mind, need to be tended and organized before they can acquire esthetic form. In other words, they must, except on the very rare occasion, be edited and fashioned with artistic intent. On that rare occasion, as with the brief diaries of a Thomas Frederiksen, they may unexpectedly reveal a naïve charm of their own. Elsewhere, as is often made plain in forewords to published versions, the intention is not at all an artistic one but instead solely to provide source material for the researcher. Even the Carl Nielsen papers are published as source material, and their es-

thetic effectiveness is probably coincidental. Indeed, one easily reaches the conclusion that except in the conscious products of creative writers like Thorkild Hansen or Olof Lagercrantz, the esthetic potential in a diary needs the careful hand of an editor if it is to be extracted from the innately different qualities which those diaries otherwise exhibit.

W. Glyn Jones, Spring 1987

Might-Have-Beens: The North and the Nobel Prize, 1967–1987

My name is Might-Have-Been: I am also called No-More, Too-Late, Farewell.

▨ **D. G. ROSSETTI,** *THE HOUSE OF LIFE*

In his contribution to *Books Abroad*'s Nobel Prize symposium of twenty years ago,[1] Richard B. Vowles reflected on the twelve awards that had been made to authors from the North since the establishment of the prize: Bjørnstjerne Bjørnson (1903), Selma Lagerlöf (1909), Verner von Heidenstam (1916), Karl Gjellerup and Henrik Pontoppidan (1917, a shared prize whose genesis Knut Ahnlund has analyzed in a brilliant essay),[2] Knut Hamsun (1920), Sigrid Undset (1928), Erik Axel Karlfeldt (1931, the single instance of a posthumous award), Frans Eemil Sillanpää (1939, with the award's air of being a gesture of support to Finland, about to be attacked by Russia in the Winter War), Johannes V. Jensen (1944, a belated sign of recognition to the Danish author, born in 1873 and very near the end of his career), Pär Lagerkvist (1951), and Halldór Kiljan Laxness (1955). There is no need to mention the vagaries, real and apparent, of these prize-givings once more; the omission of Ibsen and Strindberg has been subjected to more than sufficient comment, while the case of Georg Brandes—often a bridesmaid with an immoral reputation but never a bride—has been treated, at last, by Carl Fehrman;[3] concluding his essay, Fehrman notes that, in Brandes's instance, the absence of both a regular professorship in Denmark and the Nobel Prize constitutes "perhaps the highest distinction"—Brandes was too great a man for such honors, which had often gone to mediocrities.

Viewed by our contemporary eyes, the record of the Scandinavian prizes is in truth not particularly impressive: we should agree that Hamsun certainly was deserving (if not necessarily for *Markens grøde* (1917; Eng. *Growth of the Soil*), but in every other case, opinions might be mixed. Lagerlöf, Undset, Pontoppidan,

Jensen, and Laxness still have their special pleaders, and Americans in particular have been hypnotized by Lager-kvist's mysteries, or mystifications, although some perspicacious readers remain skeptical. The awards to Heidenstam and Karlfeldt smack a little of Swedish local patriotism, and the latter gift as well might have been made by the Swedish Academy—to a degree—for good and faithful service. All the winners, to be sure, even the unreadable Gjellerup, appeared to meet at the second, "idealistic" part of Alfred Nobel's much-debated and murky requirement of finding the author who has produced "the most distinguished work of an ideal tendency."[4] The national distribution of the prizes during the years from 1901 to 1967 merits some passing attention: Sweden got four, Norway three, Denmark two shared awards and one full, Iceland one, and Finland one—a probably unintentional symmetry which reflected the literary centrality of the three "core" Nordic countries and the peripheralism of the two new republics, the Atlantic saga island and the sometime czarist Grand Duchy. (A kind of addendum can be made to the totting-up: Nelly Sachs, writing in German but resident in Sweden, shared the 1966 prize with Samuel Agnon.)

The absence of Scandinavian (or Nordic) names from the Nobel table of honor during the last two decades does elicit concerned thoughts. The sole Scandinavian appearance, the exception proving the non-Nordic rule, has been—as everyone knows—the shared prize of 1974 to Sweden's Eyvind Johnson and Harry Martinson. The award had something of the air of the Jensen prize (of just thirty years before) about it, a farewell salute to two literary careers winding down: Johnson was born in 1900 and survived until 1976; Martinson was born in 1904, dying in 1978. The works of both surely have an ideal tendency: the novels of Johnson pondering the fate (not least the political fate) of man, Martinson incorporating the ambiguities of man's freedom in his feckless tramps and also penning the excruciatingly germane epic *Aniara* (1956) about a spaceship that leaves a doomed earth, itself doomed to wander until its own death in space. The double award was thus as readily defensible as those made to such more obvious idealists as Bjørnson and Lagerlöf and Undset, although the idealism of the 1974 winners had a darker hue, with good cause: Johnson had seen the depredations of totalitarianism close up; Martinson rightly and frighteningly predicted horrors to be wrought by technology. It is interesting to wonder too how much the award to Johnson and Martinson was a bow in the direction of the "democratization" of Swedish life—not least intellectual life—in the 1960s, when a proletarian background became, more than ever before, a literary merit. In his presentation speech Karl Ragnar Gierow made a great deal

of the extremely simple beginnings of both authors, reaching a rhetorical climax with a special claim: "Both Eyvind Johnson and still more Harry Martinson have a lot in common with the oldest and perhaps greatest of all proletarian writers . . . Aesop."[5]

Sadly, the award did little for the international (or, at any rate, the English-language) reputation of the two septuagenarians: in the thirteen years since 1974 the works of Johnson translated into English have been allowed to go out of print and only one new translation has appeared; a new English rendering of Martinson's *Aniara* by Stephen I. Klass and Leif Sjöberg, given the annual translation prize of the American-Scandinavian Foundation in 1986, has searched thus far in vain for a publisher.[6] So much for the practical benefits of a Nobel Prize to Scandinavian authors in the American and British publishing world. Earlier, when Nordic letters seemed much more vital and essential to what was then called the "Anglo-Saxon" literary mind, the prizes to Lagerlöf, Heidenstam, Undset, and even Karlfeldt did manage to call forth publishers' interest.[7]

Not being privy, of course, to the proceedings of the Swedish Academy, I can only conjecture, very wildly, at what authors from the North may have been considered for the prize during the two decades just past; in this quest I feel like the dandified detective Gabriel Syme in G. K. Chesterton's novel *The Man Who Was Thursday*. Syme learns that his crusade against the all-powerful and apparently all-destructive Supreme Council of Anarchy has been in vain: the council does not in fact exist, and the whole adventure has been a nightmare. However duped, Syme still keeps his knightly self-respect; a conjecturer on Nobel Prizes that were not given—a theme that has something of the wistfulness of the title of that old German tearjerker, Elisabeth von Heyking's *Briefe, die ihn nicht erreichten*—cannot make the same claim. Going from Nordic country to Nordic country, in alphabetical order, the wretched searcher-and-guesser can only make his surmises, thereby revealing himself, no doubt, as *asinus in cathedra*.

Nonetheless, a valiant beginning will be attempted with a mildly fantastic scenario. What would have happened if Denmark's Karen Blixen had lived longer than September 1962—lived, say, until the end of the decade? Would Blixen, because of the subtlety of her writing, the theological-philosophical hints it drops, and its special duo-lingual status (the twin product, in Danish and English), have got the supreme literary accolade? My own sole contribution to the secret history of the Nobel Prize can be made in connection with her. In the summer of 1960 Fredrik Böök, the man whom Thomas Mann once called the kingmaker of the Academy, emerged privately as a queen-breaker. Generous with words as always, Böök expatiated on the prize as he conducted a monologue for the dazzled translator of his book on Hans Christian Andersen. Quite flatly, he said that Blixen, "that old witch," would never receive the prize; instead, he proposed that Sweden's Olle Hedberg, a fecund novelist in the readily accessible fashion Böök favored, would be the candidate to watch. Böök died in December 1961, Blixen nine months later; what would have occurred if the Böökian barrier (if it in fact existed) had been removed and Blixen's health had improved? Since then, it is hard to see what Danish candidate would have a chance: Blixen's adept, the elegant lyricist Thorkild Bjørnvig? The preternaturally productive Klaus Rifbjerg? The satirist-novelist Hans Scherfig? None of these possibilities rings true. (Were the prize still given, as once upon a time, to authors who are primarily "interpretive" rather than "creative," would Willy Sørensen be considered? But this is clutching at straws.)[8]

Finland offers a particularly delicate constellation. For all its bravado as an inexpensive Swedish coming-to-the-succor of plucky little Finland, the prize to Sillanpää in 1939 remains an embarrassment ranking with such other stumbles of the irregular 1930s as the awards to Ivan Bunin and Pearl Buck. (The decade had its semigrandeurs as well: Pirandello, O'Neill, Martin du Gard.) The case would have been more painful still if, for parity's sake, the thought of a prize shared between Finland's language groups had been realized. In 1917 (then too on the eve of a major upheaval in Finland's national life, the declaration of independence of December 1917 and the civil war of 1918) the suggestion had been made of a prize divided between the Finnish-language prose writer Juhani Aho and the Swedish-language poet-cum-patrioteer Bertel Gripenberg; in the 1930s, in connection with the Academicians' evidently repeated discussion of Sillanpää (who *did*—it should be remembered for fairness's sake—possess a considerable international public just then, in the rest of the North and in Germany), the thought of the divided prize returned, again shared with Gripenberg (the quality of whose verse had not improved over the years) or with Jarl Hemmer, whose lyrics were mellifluous and whose novel *En man och hans samvete* (1931; Eng. *A Fool of Faith,* 1935) bore a laudable message of brotherly love and sacrifice. It would have been wholly out of the question that the conservative Academy of the time could imagine Sillanpää's sharing the prize with one of the Finland-Swedish modernists, who had begun a revolution destined to change the whole shape of poetry in the North: modernism's prophetess, Edith Södergran, had passed away in 1923; her friend Elmer Diktonius was a notorious socialist (or worse) who did not use rhyme, and Gunnar Björling was an equally notori-

ous dadaist (or worse) whose poems could not be understood with the best will in the world (and such a will would scarcely have been found in the Academy of those days). Some thirty years later the Academy could at last have recognized the vast importance of Finland-Swedish modernism by making an award to the youngest of the group, Rabbe Enckell (1903–74), who was, as well, respectable in a way that Björling (1888–1960) and Diktonius (1896–1961) were not, a poet and critic of magisterial quality, reminiscent of T. S. Eliot, and a writer to whom nothing disturbingly Finnish (as in Diktonius's case) attached. After Enckell succumbed to cancer, the propagandist and persistent novelist among the modernists, Hagar Olsson, lived on for another four years; but did her creative work, truth to tell, come anywhere near the literary quality that, since the improved days of the 1940s and 1950s, the world had come to expect of Nobel Prize winners?

On the Finnish-language side, the viable candidates between the 1960s and the 1980s have been two, of radically disparate natures. Väinö Linna's novel about the "Continuation War" of 1941–44 with the Soviet Union, *Tuntematon sotilas* (1954; Eng. *The Unknown Soldier,* 1957), was a Scandinavian best seller, thanks in some part to a film based on it; its apparently pacifistic message was interwoven with a good dose of old-fashioned Finnish patriotism and even a glorification of the Finnish fighting man. Linna's *Täällä Pohjantähden alla* (1959–62; Eng. *Here under the North Star,* forthcoming), a trilogy about the vicissitudes of a simple Finnish family from the century's beginning to its middle and about the triumph of Finnish socialism, repeated the success of the war novel. Linna's straightforward narration, his human sympathies, his own humble start, and the still more humble starts of his characters made him a candidate to be reckoned with in the sixties and even early seventies—after all, the prize (should it have been Linna's?) went to Mikhail Sholokhov in 1965 and to Heinrich Böll in 1972. Despite repeated predictions in Finland, Linna was never tapped; after the trilogy, he fell silent; and in consideration of the sophisticated—if not sometimes esoteric—turn the Academy's taste has taken in the last decade, it has become painfully clear that Linna's time has long passed.

The new sophistication, however (as indicated in the choices of Czesław Miłosz and Jaroslav Seifert), might work in favor of Paavo Haavikko, the irony or ambivalence of whose historical-political vision has been much admired (and sometimes attacked) in Finland as well as abroad. Haavikko has become one of his literature's truly major figures, has been fairly widely translated, and was awarded the Neustadt International Prize for Literature in 1984—and how often jurors or candidates or winners of the Neustadt have found their way to the Academy's final approval, from Solzhenitsyn in 1970 to Brodsky in 1987. The dossier on Haavikko has not yet been closed; like the late Pentti Saarikoski (1937–83), he must attract the attention of the Academy in recent years, inclined as it has often been toward difficult poetry. In consideration of the undoubted vigor of Finland's contemporary letters, a Nobel Prize to that country is not unthinkable—but never again as a by-blow of tensions between Finland and its eastern neighbor.[9]

How Iceland could return to the Nobel lists, it is impossible to see; yet another little far-western community, the Faroe Islands, has done so. If Laxness was deemed worthy in 1955, then William Heinesen would seem equally worthy two decades or so later. Indeed, Heinesen has been not only among the called but almost among the chosen; we have his own word for it. According to an interview given Ole Schierbeck of the Copenhagen newspaper *Politiken* and published there on 27 January 1981, Heinesen wrote to Artur Lundkvist of the Swedish Academy asking that his name be withdrawn from candidacy; with dismay, he had heard that his stock was very much on the rise. The reason he gave was that he was not, after all, an author who wrote in Faroese but in Danish: "The Faroese language has created a great literature, and it would have been reasonable to choose someone who writes in Faroese. [Was Heinesen thinking of his contemporary, the prose writer Hedin Brú?] If [the prize] had been given to me, it would have gone to an author who writes in Danish, and the result would have been that Faroese efforts to create an independent Faroese culture would be dealt a mean blow."[10] There is no cause to doubt Heinesen's veracity in this matter; a prize given to him for his life's accomplishments as a novelist (one of the most vital Danish-language novelists of his time) would have been particularly appropriate in 1980, the year of his eightieth birthday. However, the possibility exists that he may have been counting his chickens, and rejecting them, before they were hatched. The prize for 1980 went to Miłosz, at a period when, in the perceptive analysis of the Academician Kjell Espmark (who quotes an article by Lundkvist from 1977 in support of his argument), the prizes were given in order to "direct attention" to "writers unknown to the majority of readers."[11] The choices of Isaac Bashevis Singer in 1978, Odysseus Elytis in 1979, Miłosz in 1980, and Elias Canetti in 1981 "form a pattern," in Espmark's words, and from the Scandinavian perspective Heinesen could scarcely fall into the category of the obscure. A rough-and-ready headline Espmark quotes from the Swedish newspaper *Expressen,* "Elytis—who the hell is that?," could surely

not have been written in the North about Heinesen. (Nor would it have been altogether apt if it had appeared in the Anglophone or German press; Heinesen's novel *Noatun* had come out in English as *Niels Peter* in 1936 and in German in 1939, and a number of translations, English and German, appeared in the 1970s, as did a monograph by W. Glyn Jones.) Furthermore, Heinesen's reliably lucid and "old-fashioned" narrative art did not quite fit with the pattern of obscurity or obliquity of expression often favored by the Academy in its choices from the late 1970s onward.

Norway had a contender whose qualifications to some extent resembled those of Heinesen: Tarjei Vesaas (1897–1970). Vesaas's long and distinguished production, and his concern with essential problems of mankind, must have brought him to the serious attention of the Academy. That Vesaas wrote not in *bokmål* but in *nynorsk,* Norway's second and, it is sometimes argued, more authentic language, should have made him attractive too as an instrument for saluting that other aspect of Norway's linguistic culture. (Bjørnson, Hamsun, and Undset all had written in *bokmål*—or *dansknorsk* or *riksmål,* as they would have described it. Arne Garborg, the first major author in New Norwegian—called *landsmål* or "country language" in his day—had been a candidate as early as 1902 and during World War I had had his name coupled with that of the dramatist Gunnar Heiberg for a shared prize; in 1920, although his glory days were long behind him, he had been a rival to the great Hamsun himself.) In addition, Vesaas owned an international *rénommée,* thanks to wide translation, beginning in the 1960s; the Academy of that decade and a little beyond was not disinclined to favor figures of already large reputation—witness Steinbeck in 1962, Sartre in 1964 (though he refused the prize), and Neruda in 1971. However, death (or, before it, whatever objections or considerations may have swayed the Academy) got in Vesaas's way. For the rest, it is difficult to see what other figure in Norway's literature during the last twenty years could have been an altogether serious contender: Jens Bjørneboe (1920–76) perhaps, with his explorations of the causes of human cruelty, a plumbing of inhumanity made in humanity's ultimate service (recalling Ivo Andrić and his *Bridge on the River Drina* in 1961)? Johan Borgen (1902–79), with his exploration of the fascist mentality in the trilogy *Lillelord* (1955–57)? Finn Carling, with his concern for the isolated and the handicapped? Rolf Jacobsen, with his lyric glosses on the endangered species of man? Stein Mehren, with his extensive cultural criticism, in prose and essays and novels? These are guesses, shots in the dark.

Finally, there remains the Swedish homeland of the prize: Gunnar Ekelöf (1907–68), by virtue of the intellectual distinction and stylistic refinement of his verse, would have been a natural candidate, and a choice the outside world would not have called narrowly selfish.[12] To be sure, he would have been a novelty among Scandinavian recipients, with his learned and allusive poetry; the Scandinavians have previously been easy of access, not "poets of the difficult school," in Rabbe Enckell's famous phrase, although the problems they posed may have been difficult. Conversely, Vilhelm Moberg (1898–1972) would have been in the tried-and-true line of Lagerlöf and Undset and Laxness; and Americans, at any rate, would not have been surprised if the magic name sent out by Stockholm had been that of the immigrant-tetralogy's author. The much denser narrative art of Lars Ahlin cannot have been ignored by the Academy, and it is possible that, even today, Ahlin or Sven Delblanc or Lars Gustafsson or P. C. Jersild can dream, or be dreamt of, as frontrunners for their novels. Likewise, in Sweden's very fecund literary culture, Werner Aspenström and Tomas Tranströmer are lyricists whose election would not be embarrassing to the Academy—and would certainly not need the sort of apologetics engaged in at the ceremonies for the late Karlfeldt, where the speakers Anders Österling and Sven Söderman harped on the quintessential Swedishness of Karlfeldt's poetry, so impenetrable for foreigners. A frightening postscript: can the screenplays of Ingmar Bergman be taken seriously enough as literature (by himself or by others) that he might contend? (But Bergman's is not an unsung talent that needs to be brought to the world's attention.)

In these days the Academy must have thought of a prize for a woman writer; a woman has not been honored by the Nobel since Nelly Sachs shared the 1966 award, and Gabriela Mistral's lackluster victory in 1945 was the last time a woman won outright. Kerstin Ekman is a member of the Eighteen; has she chivied her male colleagues into consideration of, say, the lachrymose Sara Lidman from Sweden, or Suzanne Brøgger from Denmark, or Märta Tikkanen (writing in Swedish, about a distressing husband) from Finland, or—the possibilities (and nominations) are legion, however doubtful at times the quality as literature.

Nevertheless, a good many factors militate against the choice of a prizewinner from the North. The Academy has made a laudable effort, over the years, not to be content with the products of European culture and its children (in North and South America and Australia) but to look to other cultural realms: witness Yasunari Kawabata in 1968 and Wole Soyinka in 1986. The slot that once might have gone to the North may now be filled by a representative of a new and exotic realm. Also, a fear of the charge of parochialism may be to the disadvantage of Scandinavian authors: a prizewinner from abroad, unknown or not, is more easily explained to the world at large than is a prizewinner from the home front. Finally, it should be admitted that the Nordic literary realm presently teems with busy talents but lacks the overriding geniuses that attracted attention to it almost a hundred years ago, geniuses themselves unrewarded by the Academy but whose richness then seemed to excuse the rash of Scandinavian winners in the prize's first sixty-six years—a dozen among sixty-three, nearly one-fifth the total.

George C. Schoolfield, Spring 1988

[1] Richard B. Vowles, "Twelve Northern Authors," *Books Abroad* 41:1 (Winter 1967), pp. 17–23.

[2] Knut Ahnlund, "Ett delat Nobelpris," in his *Diktarliv i Norden: Litterära essäer,* Stockholm, Brombergs, 1981, pp. 248–79.

[3] Carl Fehrman, "Georg Brandes och det uteblivna Nobelpriset," *Nordisk Tidskrift,* 60 (1984), pp. 320–38, esp. 337.

[4] The question of what Nobel really meant has been repeatedly discussed. See, for example, Elias Bredsdorff, "Vad menade Alfred Nobel med uttrycket 'i idealisk rigtning'?," *Bonniers Litterära Magasin,* 33 (1964), pp. 352–54, and, much more recently, the Swedish Academy member Kjell Espmark in the first chapter of his book *Det litterära Nobelpriset: Principer och värderingar bakom besluten,* Stockholm, Norstedt, 1986. Espmark offers an extraordinary elucidation of the varying principles that have guided (or misguided) the Academy in its selections since 1901. A French version exists: *Le Prix Nobel: Histoire intérieure d'une consécration littéraire,* Paris, Balland, 1986. An English translation should be made available. The book has been of great value in the writing of the present essay.

[5] "Eyvind Johnson's education . . . ended when he was thirteen and was as imparted at a little village school north of the Arctic Circle. The future awaiting the young Harry Martinson opened up to him when, at the age of six, as a so-called child of the parish, he was sold at auction to the lowest bidder. . . . The fact that, with such a start in life, both of them have their places on this platform today, is the visible testimony to a transformation of society which, step by step, is still going on all over the world. With us it came unusually early; it is perhaps our country's biggest blessing, perhaps also its most remarkable achievement during the last thousand years." Quoted from the English translation (which seems, in its inelegance, to be very proletarian indeed) in *Les Prix Nobel en 1974,* Stockholm, Norstedt, 1975, pp. 26–27. On Johnson and Martinson's receipt of the Nobel, see BA 49:3 (Summer 1975), pp. 407–21.

[6] The translation by Erik Friis of *Drömmar om rosor och eld* appeared as *Dreams of Roses and Fire* in 1984 from the Hippocrene Press. Martinson has fared slightly better: Robert Bly included some of his poetry in *Friends, You Drank Some Darkness: Three Swedish Poets,* Boston, Beacon, 1975; and William Jay Smith and Leif Sjöberg offered a selection of Martinson's nature poems in *Wild Bouquet,* Kansas City, University of Missouri, 1985.

[7] For example, the Yale University Press brought out a selection from Heidenstam's poems in 1919, the American-Scandinavian Foundation published a new translation of *The Charles Men* in 1920 and a translation of *The Swedes and Their Chieftains* in

1925, while a translation of *The Tree of the Folkungs* was issued by Alfred Knopf's publishing house the same year.

[8] On Bjørnvig, see *WLT* 51:4 (Autumn 1977), pp. 568–69. On Rifbjerg, see *BA* 49:1 (Winter 1975), pp. 25–28.

[9] On Haavikko, see *WLT* 58:1 (Winter 1984), p. 48, and 58:4 (Autumn 1984), pp. 493–562.

[10] Quoted, in translation, by Hedin Bronner in the introduction to his translation of Heinesen's short stories, *The Winged Darkness and Other Stories,* New York, Irvington, 1983, p. 12. Bronner thinks that the story has to do with the prize for 1981, but 1980 must have been the year in question, not only because of Heinesen's new octogenarian status but because his letter—sent to Lundkvist, according to Bronner, "in the eleventh hour"—must have been composed in the late summer or early autumn of 1980. On Heinesen, see also WLT 62:1 (Winter 1988), pp. 79–82.

[11] Espmark, pp. 108–9.

[12] On Ekelöf, see *WLT* 51:4 (Autumn 1977), pp. 530–34.

BALTIC STATES

Carnival of Death: Writing in Latvia Since Independence

This article surveys the condition of Latvian writing during the past decade and briefly discusses several contemporary authors, including Māra Zālīte, Modris Zihmanis, and Andra Nieburga, among others. The article then enters into greater detail with the writing of Aleksandrs Pelēcis. Pelēcis's most recent writing emerged during a crucial phase in Latvian history just prior to and immediately following the declaration of independence (1990). In particular, his *Sibirijas grāmata* (Siberia Book) is emblematic of the Latvian struggle against overwhelming cultural, political, and military oppression. Pelēcis offers a fragmented, kaleidoscopic vision that is rich in wry humor and conveyed through a sophisticated, post-modern structure.

This paper formulates and applies a hybrid theoretical perspective that posits Baltic and Latvian literature in reference to the Soviet Union as "Other" (i.e., in the sense forwarded by thinkers such as Lacan and Kristeva). I address a clash of worldviews as it manifests itself in language. In my reading of the period of occupation and the period of independence that follows, censorship and self-censorship are practiced as a kind of linguistic amputation. Under the authority of the Soviet Union as dominant Other, Latvian native daughters and sons experienced the severing of the mother tongue (in the Kristevan sense) or removal of language-as-phallus (in the Lacanian sense). After independence, censorship continued to be inflicted sometimes, paradoxically, by Latvians against themselves. The oppression of free expression through censorship and propaganda results in a double-edged pattern. The oppression *of* discourse *by* discourse is related to a Foucauldian sense of language as it is related to power. During the period of occupation, the Soviets tried to alter the Latvian identity through a "renaming" of Latvia and the Latvian culture. The contemporary term "ethnic cleansing" carries much the same ironic meaning as the Soviet notion of "betterment of the state," a term which was used to justify mass deportations and killings. In some cases, resistance to the oppression of language by language arose in the form of literary irony, which sometimes adopted what Bakhtin has identified as the "carnivalesque" mode. The double blade of discourse comes to its sharpest point with the double edge of irony.

Fundamental to this ironic mode is a subversion and inversion of the hegemonic Soviet worldview. The heart of the struggle in discourse involves a violent clash between Latvian and Soviet worldviews. For Foucault, knowledge and the capability of expression through language constitute a form of power. For Lacan, language as phallus represents a universal signifier (not the sexual organ) and evokes metonymically the *manque à être* (or fundamental *lack* at the core of being). Kristeva suggests that the link to the mother tongue is marked by an intimate and even unconscious self-awareness. Censorship, or the attack against language within this context, can be understood as a form of psychic castration. Whether we think of language as phallus or as mother tongue, such an attack is a silencing, an exile, and an act of violence against the collective mind. It is also symptomatic of a colonization of the mind, which, in spite of Latvia's recent political independence, has proven to be resistant to change and causes a separation between what is believed and what is done. This gap between belief and action results in an existential crisis. Many native Latvians find themselves in a kind of psychic exile. The condition of the collective psyche is evident in the comments of the Latvian author Māra Zālīte (editor and publisher of *Karogs* magazine and Karogs Books) at the Rīga Philharmonic Auditorium on 14 June 1989, during a gathering held in commemoration of those who died during the Stalinist purges:

> We have been made to feel like exiles in our homeland. We have been expelled from our spiritual birthplace. Banished from our way of life, driven from our farm-lands. Torn away from our culture—severed from our folklore! Separated from our songs—cast out of our language! Driven from Europe—exiled from civilization! A banished nation! And attempts are being made to remove us still farther. To remove us from our very lives. To remove us from humanity. (160)

Zālīte's comments are, sadly, representative of the Latvian mind-state at the turn of this decade. In the years immediately prior to Latvia's recent declaration of independence, there is a common sense of being banished, of being in exile in one's own homeland. One year later, Latvia regained independence for the second time in this century (the first declaration of independence occurred in 1918). But the psychic trauma indicated in Zālīte's address remains largely intact to this day. I contend that the long-term persecution of Latvia throughout history, and particularly in this century, is fundamental to an understanding of the emergent and uniquely ironic Latvian worldview which manifests itself in the form of irony and satire in recent Latvian literature. The ironic mode is often augmented with a disjointed narrative form, which serves to emphasize a sense of psychic disruption or trauma.

Like the Lithuanians and Estonians, Letts have inhabited the region adjacent to the Baltic Sea for some four thousand years. During the second half of this century, the struggle to retain what might be identified as a "Latvian" worldview has been linked to the question of language itself. I am not speaking here of such minor changes in language as occur in the natural course of events. Like other languages of the world, Latvian has had its share of cross-cultural influences and has adopted its share of neologisms and linguistic pattern changes. Nor am I arguing in favor of any so-called ethnic or cultural "purity." Latvia has had a history of being occupied by other nations, including Russia, Germany, Sweden, Poland, and Lithuania, and consequently has become populated by what one might call "the bastards of the world," to borrow a phrase from author Michael Ondaatje. Rather, I am speaking here of a systematic effort to eradicate the Latvian culture during the Soviet occupation. Only under the German Teutonic Order or Knights Templar (approximately A.D. 1200) was Latvia forced to abandon its religion, although it was permitted to adhere to its language. No invading culture except the Soviet Union has ever insisted on a complete agenda of cultural genocide that included the suppression of local customs, education, religion, and, most important, language.

Akin to Sanskrit, Latvian and Lithuanian, like Celtic, are among the most ancient living Indo-European languages, and therefore not only constitute exceptional subjects of study for linguists and philologists but also incorporate unique worldviews. In this century, the Soviet Union situated itself in a dominant noncooperative position and established a Manichean master/slave model of governance in the Baltic states (Estonia, Latvia, Lithuania) and in the other "satellite" nations. Rather than integrate, the Soviets chose to isolate, alienate, and exterminate Balts and the Baltic worldview. This mode of subjugation was accompanied by an extensive agenda of russification. The Manichean Soviet model generated a sense of alterity and inspired a cultural self-awareness in Latvia in terms of what I call the "Other." The Soviet presence resulted in a resituation of Latvian identity from one that was relatively independent to one that was increasingly dependent upon the imperial Other. I suggest that the sense of detachment and alienation that Latvians now feel in their homeland has led to a profound and collective sense of irony, which has become one of the significant literary modes in recent Latvian literature. Furthermore, a tendency toward a disrupted narrative flow in recent Latvian writing (including that of Pelēcis) serves to evoke the sense of psychic dislocation characteristic of the Latvian experience.

During the Soviet occupation, a process of what Roland Barthes has termed "naming," "renaming," and "unnaming" took place. The Latvian culture and worldview was in a sense "renamed" in order to change what was/is Latvian to what was Soviet. In August of 1939, the Molotov-Ribbentrop Pact was signed. This was a nonaggression treaty between Hitler and Stalin in which both parties agreed to a noninterference posture should either nation choose to invade its neighbors. Shortly thereafter, on 17 June 1940, Soviet tank divisions launched a full offensive and occupied Latvia under military rule. This invasion occurred in spite of the Latvian-Soviet Peace Treaty of 11 August 1920. On 20 June the occupying Soviet forces formed the ironically named "Latvian People's Government," a pro-Soviet body which attempted to legitimize the annexation of Latvia into the USSR. On 14–15 July 1940 the Soviets sponsored a one-party parliamentary election which brought to power the Soviet-controlled "Latvian Workers' Bloc." Following the sham election, the puppet government insisted on a close alliance with the USSR and "renamed" Latvia as the "Latvian Soviet Socialist Republic." This pattern was repeated at the end of World War II, when the USSR set up mock one-party elections in Latvia to install a Soviet-backed puppet government.

The USSR flouted agreements made at the Potsdam, Tehran, and Yalta peace conferences. A process of "unnaming" ensued and was initiated through the systematic genocide of the Latvian people and the cultural genocide of the Latvian world-view. In 1941 (known to Latvians as the "Year of Horror"), a series of atrocities, including mass murders and mass deportations, took place. During the second half of this century nearly 50 percent of the population of Latvia was evacuated, deported, or killed. Hundreds of thousands of Latvians were either murdered outright, imprisoned, or shipped to slow deaths in the Siberian gulag. Out of a population of two million, only one million remained. In the meantime, the nation was russified to the extent that now the population has been restored to two million, though only half of those are of Latvian origin. The world's general ignorance of these atrocities and the appalling nature of the events themselves constitute, for Latvians, one of this century's darker ironies. This litany of aggressions by the Soviets constitutes an act of violence not unlike that practiced by imperial powers against the Chiapas Indians in Mexico, the East Timorese in Indonesia, the native blacks in South Africa, the Aboriginals in Australia and New Zealand, the Asian Indians under British rule, the Tibetans under China, and the First Nations people in North America, among others.

Under the Soviets, Latvians were granted few opportunities to "name" or assert their cultural perspective; neither were they permitted to retain their cultural identity. The Latvian language was attacked from a variety of fronts, including education and publishing. It is common knowledge that during the Soviet occupation students could attend either Russian- or Latvian-speaking schools. However, only those who attended Russian-speaking schools could continue with a postsecondary education. Similarly, in publishing, texts that overtly identified a Latvian sociopolitical or cultural position were often either openly censored or surreptitiously suppressed. To a considerable extent, the oppression encouraged what Umberto Eco has called "open" modes and techniques of writing that convey double or polysemous meanings (e.g., irony, satire, allegory, science fiction, surrealism, absurdism, defamiliarization). Furthermore, a subversive underground culture began to develop, and a *samizdat* or counterculture mindset emerged. Conditional to this mindset was a view of writing and, more important, of reading as an act of resistance or even defiance. In spite of the renewed political independence in the 1990s, Latvians, after being decimated and Russified for half a century, find that their sense of language and their sense of self have been diluted and mixed with an infusion of the nonindigenous culture of the Other.

In his study on linguistic patterns in *Language, Thought, and Reality* the noted linguist Benjamin Lee Whorf discusses early conceptions of language. He explains that for centuries academics believed that thought was translatable from one language to another without loss of meaning. But, Whorf contends, this view of translation is flawed. He explains that a language actually shapes the worldview of a people. There is more to translation than simply finding corresponding words. One must also recognize cultural differences and differences in world-view that accompany each lan-

guage. The conception of time, for example, can be radically different in various cultures. Whorf has used the Hopi as an example of a culture whose language has no past or present tense. The Hopi view of space-time is radically different from most Eurocentric cultures and perhaps finds its closest conceptual counterpart in the worldview of nuclear physicists. Whorf has argued that any change in language will transform one's appreciation of the cosmos.

If one accepts the Whorfian link between worldview and language, and if one considers the imposition of the language and worldview of the Soviet Union as Other during its extended period of occupation, then this imposition can be recognized as a form of cultural genocide. Subsequent to this imposition is a collective culture shock. Through the very act of writing his "Siberia Book," Aleksandrs Pelēcis, in an existential act, closes the abovementioned gap between belief and action. He speaks of a shock of the mind that occurs and reoccurs during and after an oppressive occupation. In his introduction he asks, "Ko darīt ar murgiem, kas atkārtojas?" (What is to be done with the recurring nightmares? 7). One answer is to deconstruct the worldview that caused those nightmares. Pelēcis's question regarding the psychic shock experienced by the colonized echoes the thoughts of Ngũgĩ wa Thiong'o, who in his study *Decolonising the Mind* has noted a recurring pattern in colonial oppression.

> The oppressed and the exploited of the earth maintain their defiance: liberty from theft. But the biggest weapon wielded and actually daily unleashed by imperialism against the collective defiance is the cultural bomb. The effect of the cultural bomb is to annihilate people's belief in their names, in their languages, in their environment, in their heritage of struggle, in their unity, in their capacities and ultimately in themselves. It makes them see their past as one wasteland of non-achievement and it makes them want to distance themselves from the wasteland. It makes them want to identify with that which is further removed from themselves; for instance, with other peoples' languages rather than their own. It makes them identify with that which is decadent and reactionary, all those forces which would stop their own springs of life. It even plants serious doubts about the moral rightness of struggle. (3)

For over sixty years, natives of Latvia have endured the effects of this "cultural bomb" as an attack against the Latvian worldview calculated to "shock the mind" into submission. The ground on which this war was waged was in the arena of language. In the broadest and narrowest terms, language serves as a key to both imprisonment and liberty. Consequently, literature plays a fundamental role in resisting psychic colonization and in reasserting the Latvian identity and worldview. At times, even the language used to describe this cultural genocide inadvertently perpetuates the condition. The Soviets' use of euphemism to describe massive agendas of genocide was received with ironic derision from the victims. Terms such as "for the betterment of the state" (used to describe the purges) and "rehabilitation" (describing the gulag experience) carried roughly the same significance as the term "ethnic cleansing" does today. The word *postcolonial* is another signifier that is indicative of the perspective of the colonist, not the colonized.

The word *postcolonial* illustrates the potency of language in maintaining a reactionary worldview. The designation *postcolonial* implies a definition of the occupied nation in terms of the imperial Other; even with the withdrawal of the empire, the newly independent nation continues to be identified with the violence of colonization. Neither does the word consider the condition of the original inhabitants in the formerly occupied territory *prior* to invasion. A term that connects the period of liberty prior to and following occupation would be more representative and appropriate. For example, to think of a nation with a history as ancient as India's in terms of a relatively brief period of British occupation, and then to label India forever as existing in a "postcolonial" state, is to stigmatize and brand that nation with the mark of imperialism. Such a "naming" implicitly denies self-assertion and psychic liberation. The term *postcolonial* constitutes a form of arrogance that insists on viewing the occupied territory from the point of view of the aggressor or colonist, not from the point of view of the indigene. I recommend that this figure of speech be permanently placed under erasure, and that the conditions of colonization be addressed in terms such as *occupation* or *liberation*.

If one considers the importance of language and the implications of Whorf's theory within the context of Ngũgĩ's statement regarding psychic colonization, then the Russo-Soviet agenda of eroding the Latvian language can be read as an act of aggression against a particular worldview. I contend that it is the undermining of this worldview that has led to the psychic and existential malaise presently evident in Latvia. The prevalence of the literary form of irony is inspired by recent Latvian history and is endemic to this psychic condition, characterized by a spectrum of outlooks ranging from Horatian lighthearted skepticism to Juvenalian apocalyptic cynicism.

There are numerous contemporary authors and artists who, since independence, have written texts that celebrate the new phase of freedom in Latvia. Some of

these writers draw with a palette of lighter hues than others. The Latvian tendencies toward wit, absurdism, language play, humor, and magic realism are well known and perhaps partly explain the endurance of the Latvian spirit. As Freud and others have suggested, every joke has its dark side, and a good deal of Latvian humor alludes to this darkness. In particular, irony has come to represent one aspect of the Latvian worldview. During some of the more virulent battles of World War II, Latvians were known to "encourage" one another by saying, "Enjoy the war while you can, the peace will be horrendous." Those words were all too prophetic. With reference to the numerous occupations that Latvia has endured, a standard quip remains: "We Latvians know a good deal about freedom, we have been 'liberated' many times."

The critic Linda Hutcheon has commented on the use of irony for political purposes in her study *Irony's Edge*. She speaks of irony used for purposes of satiric attack and explains that it may be employed either to defuse or to engage anger. Further, irony may have a "charged" or loaded message which is interpretable only by those familiar with a given sociopolitical condition: "In other words, this study argues that there is an affective 'charge' to irony that cannot be ignored and that cannot be separated from its politics of use if it is to account for the range of emotional response (from anger to delight) and the various degrees of motivation and proximity (from distanced detachment to passionate engagement)" (15). Postindependence writing is more aligned with anger than with delight, but it is worth noting that this anger is characterized by a peculiar detachment. A number of Latvian authors have developed a style that seizes the reader emotionally while maintaining a sense of distance. Henri Bergson in *Laughter* argues that humor and irony should be detached and should appeal to one's sense of reason. Most would agree. However, Latvian irony develops a unique flavor because, while it appeals to *logos,* it still skirts the fringes of *pathos.* Perhaps this dualistic and almost paradoxical ironic tendency is the result of a binocular vision, which looks both to victim and victimizer.

Hutcheon continues as follows: "Unlike synecdoche, say, irony always has a 'target'; it sometimes also has what some want to call a 'victim.' As the connotations of these two terms imply, irony's edge is a cutting one. Those who might not attribute irony where it was intended (or where others did) risk exclusion and embarrassment" (15). Arguably, in Latvia, one of the reasons for a prevalence of irony—apart from the more obvious purpose of social critique—relates to what Hutcheon has identified as the sense of exclusionism. During the Soviet occupation, particularly under Stalin,

Latvian nationalists were excluded from positions of power and influence. I will add to Hutcheon's definition of irony by stating here that irony (whether rhetorical, situational, or structural) is predicated on the principle of a privileged awareness. In any irony, there must be at least an implied if not actual "insider's" or privileged view in juxtaposition with an "outsider's" uninformed view. Because of the binary relationship of privileged and uninformed perspectives, any ironic expression can potentially *reverse* the sense of exclusion. The so-called "cutting edge" of irony cuts both ways and in recent times has permitted Latvians to espouse their own worldview while simultaneously isolating and denigrating the worldview of the Soviet Other. As history teaches, the political occupation of Latvia was based on propaganda that forwarded an authoritarian or hegemonic worldview. Irony served to undermine this authority and to displace the hegemonic with a heterogenous worldview. In this light, I will consider the works of several Latvian authors published during the last decade.

I have noted not only an ironic tone in writers of the past decade or so, but also a tendency toward narrative disjunction. Numerous contemporary Latvian authors have adopted ironic literary modes that interweave myth, fantasy, science fiction, magic realism, and actual history. These works also make use of disjunctive narrative strategies. Such narrative forms blur the actual and fictional and, in so doing, transcend matters of forensic "truth" and instead pursue a higher "mythic" truth. This mythic truth is one that embraces the Latvian worldview and overcomes the problematics of the distortions that result from years of censorship and propaganda. Irony and narrative disruption work well together as a stylistic strategy. *Odu laiks* (Time of the Mosquito Ode; 1989), co-written by Lienīte Medne, Vladis Spāre, and Juris Zvirgzdiņš, bills itself on the title page as a true life story that includes the authors' fantasies as well as lies and distortions which ultimately make the truth unrecognizable. The novel is a carnival of death and in one or two pages can feature jumps from the narrator's childhood thoughts to his adult ruminations and through time and space from the Siberian wasteland, to Rīga, to the prison workshop of a coffin-maker who helps inmates escape by smuggling them out in his caskets (165–66). Alberts Bels's novels frequently combine historical fact with myth, folklore, narrative rumination, and a nonsequential ordering of time and space. His most recent novel, *Saulē mērktie* (The Sun-Drenched; 1996), a chronicle of war and death, continues this pattern (see Juris Silenieks's review in *WLT* 71:1 [Winter 1997], p. 194). Egils Ermansons's *Cilvēks are bērnu ratiņiem* (A Man with a Baby Carriage; 1994; see *WLT*

69:1 [Winter 1995], p. 193) is aptly described by Silenieks as a "fantasy cum science fiction, slouching slightly toward morality tale, perhaps of virtual reality." In this novel, the postapocalyptic condition is depicted allegorically and features significant degrees of narrative disjunction. The fragmented patterns of narration are structurally appropriate in that they successfully convey a sense of trauma and psychic fragmentation. A carnivalesque and darkly satiric portrayal of the macabre carnival of death typifies the writing of these and other contemporary authors, including Modris Zihmanis, Andra Nieburga and Aleksandrs Pelēcis.

In his 1990 poem "Šai neredzamajā" (In This Unseen), published in *Atmiņu lauskas* (Memory Fragments), Modris Zihmanis writes of an "invisible war" that is being waged and that has taken its toll on the collective Latvian psyche in what he terms a "carnival of buttons" that symbolizes death (131). The reference may well be to the numerous buttons found on Soviet military uniforms, but may also be a more subtle one to the Soviets' demoralizing practice of removing all fasteners, including zippers and buttons, from prisoner's uniforms. In "Šai neredzamajā" Zihmanis gestures to an invisible war which is being waged physically, psychologically, spiritually, politically, economically, and, what is perhaps most important, linguistically against a Latvian world-view. In his poem "Krāsas" (Colors) he writes of the general trauma that arose from the deportations in an elegy to the tens of thousands of Latvians who died in the gulag and more specifically at Vorkuta. To translate texts by Zihmanis or Nieburga or Pelēcis is no simple task, for the translator must identify with both *logos* and *pathos* in an effort to "inhabit" the mindset of the author and the extremity of the difficult conditions experienced. Nevertheless, in the following translation and others in this article, I try to capture the spirit of the writing:

So it once was my child
that the winged serpent flew
and blew from your grandfather's mind
at least three senses
   the sense of sight
   the sense of hearing
   the sense of speech
but in some crook of the mind
two remained hooked,
the sense of thought and
the sense of feeling,
until finally my pillow
threw a wheel
and in nightmare confusion
I mistook the wheel for the serpent's head
   as soaring over the sleepers

it clattered
vor-kut-ta-vor-ku-ta-vor-ku-ta
vor-kut-ta-vor-ku-ta-vor-ku-ta (132)

This poem features an apocalyptic vision. What I translate here as the "winged serpent" appears in the original poem as "pūķis," which can variously be understood as a kite, a winged serpent, or a dragon (including an allusion to the beast in the Book of Revelations). Also, "pillow" is a complex signifier referring to dreams and the unconscious while alluding as well to eternal rest. The idea of a "thrown wheel" implies both a psychic breakdown and a mechanistic loss of control which alludes to the serpent's head as metonym for the train wheels that carried the condemned to the concentration camps of Vorkuta. The litotic and onomatopoeic allusion to the sound of the train wheels passing "over" the sleepers (i.e., those already buried) is an ironic evocation of the apocalyptic gulag experience. This sense of the ironic and the apocalyptic enters the works of a significant number of other contemporary writers in Latvia.

The author Andra Nieburga, a resident of Rīga, writes of the annihilation of the human ego felt during the collapse of the Soviet empire and in the early years of independence. She weaves her poem with intertextual references to the writings of Huizinga as well as to biblical and Egyptian myth: "AND THE EARTH WAS WITHOUT FORM, AND VOID / A stone thrown to heaven always returns to earth, a dying man—a child's mind. Tears and blood are physiological fluids. Thousands of troops march in ant tracks, crossing the earth in imagined order. A hydrocephalic homunculus fingers holes in the sky, and, with idiot giggling, toys with rockets. *Homo ludens*—imbecile civilized senility" (44). The text refers to Huizinga's view that war can be thought of as an elaborate but insane "game." Nieburga's parodic deconstruction leaps from the Book of Genesis directly to the Book of Revelations and moves with the toss of a single stone from creation to apocalypse. This satiric portrayal is disturbing for its detached, matter-of-fact tone. Nieburga continues, and not unlike Zihmanis, she portrays an insane carnival of death that speaks of social expulsion and abandonment while inverting what one might call the "normal" ethos.

DUST STORMS, ASH STORMS, SOUL STORMS

The last Chinese emperor weeps in Stalin's death camp, neither Allah nor Mohammed came to aid the Kurds. Fortune [Laima] wanders Latvia empty-handed. The sky, an oil-stained rag, and in flight there, the souls of dead birds. Wells burn, Wormwood falls, and the third part of the waters are made bitter, the sun a sackcloth of hair (ashes permeate your eyes, your mouth—inferno: the mother of order—in moonlight

bounds Anubis, the hound of darkness, over fields of white ash, this symphony of silence). (44)

This bleak Juvenalian satire includes a reference to "Wormwood"—known as La-anah in Hebrew, Absinthos in Greek, and Chernobyl in Russian—and relates to a biblical prophecy from the Book of Revelations (8:11) which states that the poisoning of one-third of the earth's waters will occur upon the opening of the seventh seal and following the trumpeting of the four angels. The Chernobyl nuclear disaster is portrayed here as an indication that we have entered the apocalypse. In spite of Latvian independence, under such circumstances life remains meaningless and all human action is ironic and pointless. The "psychic shock" that I spoke of earlier in this paper is evident here as in other postindependence Latvian authors. Although it too is cynical, Aleksandrs Pelēcis's writing evinces some wry humor and a ray of optimism when he argues that we must face and exorcise the past in order to ensure a more desirable future.

Pelēcis was a noted poet and a recognized author prior to his imprisonment in Siberia. His "Siberia Book" is comparable to Solzhenitsyn's *One Day in the Life of Ivan Denisovich*. Pelēcis's use of reflecting imagery, shifting perspectives, spatio-temporal leaps, polyglossic linguistic innovations, and dead-pan irony invites comparisons to works such as Ben Okri's *Stars of the New Curfew* and Jerzy Kosinski's *Painted Bird*. Pelēcis was arrested in 1946. He was tried and sentenced for belonging to political parties to which he had no connection and was accused of saying things he never uttered. While being held in a Rīga prison prior to deportation, he was stripped of everything of value, including the buttons on his clothing, save one on his trousers which was spared in a capricious moment by a friendly guard. He was then shipped to the gulag, where he endured for twenty-three years. Following the publication of the uncensored version of his Siberian experience, I wrote to Pelēcis and asked permission to translate his writing. He responded asking only that his words be disseminated, so that his acknowledgment of the dead could be partly fulfilled. In 1994 he won the General Gopera Foundation Literary Prize for "The Siberia Book," one of the highest literary honors available to authors writing in Latvian. He died shortly thereafter, in October of 1995. Pelēcis's concern over his acknowledgment of the dead arises partly from his encounters with censors.

Michael Holquist, who is noted, among other things, as the translator of Bakhtin, writes in the January 1994 issue of the *PMLA* (109:1) that censorship can be viewed as a complex phenomenon resulting in a dynamic and multidirectional relationship between the censor and the censored.

> Work in this area seeks unsentimentally to understand why censors never succeed (or at least never succeed for long), in totally instrumenting their desire to purge. The assumption increasingly is made that they cannot do so because they are locked into a *negotiation,* an exchange with the works they seek to bridge. Although censors may see themselves as the authors of prohibitions, they are subject to environmental restraints: censors too are always censored. Together with their victims they are constrained by what is possible amid social forces whose lines of influence bound—while extending beyond—the ecosystem in which censorship seeks to exercise discursive hegemony. (17)

Holquist goes on to explain that the censor's actions draw a number of reactions and that unpredictable side effects result from attempts to inflict a hegemonic worldview. It is worth noting that during periods of extensive censorship, Latvians learned to work with ideological "loopholes" and began to write in ironic modes that shared an "insider's" vision but excluded and attacked the "discursive hegemony" of the Soviet Union as imperial "Other."

Aleksandrs Pelēcis's release from the gulag system in 1969 did not end his victimization, nor did it guarantee him freedom of expression. He explains that upon his return to Latvia his writing was censored. Pelēcis's "Siberia Book" is a wide-ranging documentation of what Lacan terms the "Innen-welt" (psyche) and "Umwelt" (environment) of the author. "The Siberia Book" compresses twenty-three years of subsistence within the gulag archipelago into a mere 246 pages. In his foreword to the book he mentions that another five hundred pages of manuscript chronicling his Siberian experience remain unpublished (9). Many of the events are so bizarre that the text takes on a surreal, even carnivalesque quality. This macabre panorama through time and space is not only a documentary text, but also a self-portrait. The narrative finds its principal motif in the recurring image of a broken kaleidoscope, which becomes symbolic of the dismemberment of the body, the fragmentation of the psyche, and the slaughter of an international cadre of prisoners (some thirty-seven nationalities). The leitmotiv of the shattered kaleidoscope also gestures to the chronicle's disjointed narration, which serves well in presenting the psychic fragmentation or trauma of the gulag experience.

There are two versions of Pelēcis's book. The first was issued in Latvia by the publisher Avots under the title *Ar melno veju* (With the Black Wind) in 1991. A second, uncensored version was published in the United States under the title *Sibirijas grāmata* (The Siberia Book) by the Latvian Press Group out of Ithaca, New York, in 1993. Pelēcis explains in his foreword to "The Siberia Book" that the first published version is problematic, because the Latvian editors censored and watered down the text until it was almost unrecognizable. This purging of the text was peculiar considering the fact that Latvia had already gained independence, but the editors feared reprisals from Soviet authorities, who still held a majority of the positions of power in Latvia. Among the many passages that were omitted from the first version were those which described the prison guards' complete lack of emotion in carrying out tortures and executions (9).

The notion that subjects are constituted by power and that an internalized moral code of behavior can only be inculcated through threats and violence has roots in Nietzsche. The Soviet system of oppression was based on both threat and violent action. However, after the collapse of the Soviet empire, Latvians continued to practice forms of *self*-restriction or *self*-censorship. A new horror confronted Latvians: the realization of their self-enslavement in bending to the oppressor's rule in order to stay alive. This horror is examined by Foucault in his "Discourse on Power," where he speaks on the degree to which attempts at indoctrination can alter group behavior. For Foucault, "power" has the characteristics of a network and can be measured in terms of its application. This marks a shift from the question of "Who has power?" to that of "What intentions or aims do holders of power have?" The shift marks the way in which subjects or citizens are constituted as *effects* of power. However, the blade of irony cuts in two directions. If Holquist is correct in his assessment of censorship, then the censorship of Pelēcis's writing inadvertently served to signify Pelēcis's as an agent of power. The purpose of censoring Pelēcis's writing was to decrease his "effects of power." However, the attempt to suppress him brought about the opposite result. Partly because of the efforts at censoring him, his writing began to attract attention. Nieburga, Pelēcis, and numerous other writers in the past decade have, in their different ways, become agents of an alternative ethos through the exercise of power *via* language and literature.

In "The Siberia Book" Pelēcis reminds the reader that the second holocaust under Stalin is a phenomenon that must be spoken of now, so that it may never happen again. He numbers the dead in the gulag death camps of Kolyma, Vorkuta, Taišeta, Inta, and Komsomoļska among other places, and explains that the prisoners constituted not just a Latvian but an *inter-*

national body of intellects. If we now acknowledge that those destroyed under Hitler may have totaled as many as six to eight million, Pelēcis continues, then how can we ignore what happened to the estimated ten million dead in Siberia? He adds that, although there were casualties in the millions as a result of the deportations, there remains a psychic trauma resulting not only from the Siberian experience but also from the social atmosphere of cultural annihilation that existed in Latvia during this period (5–6). This holocaust vision is what underlies the "identity" of a nation now in exile in its own land. Exile and dislocation are not confined to physical removal but can also involve a psychic dislocation.

In Siberia, Pelēcis maintained his writing by trading local black marketeers some of his rations for the stub of a pencil and a Portland cement bag made of many layers of paper. He found that the layered bag served well, but the pencil constantly required sharpening, and each sharpening required payment, in the form of rations. Eventually the pencil was used up, and, lacking writing instruments, Pelēcis was reduced to recording his writing in the Siberian permafrost, using only his finger. I translate the passage in which he describes writing his poems in the ice:

> Sometimes, while a fragile bird gives voice to song—a thousand years pass by. Sometimes, while you are taken ten thousand miles away, three lifetimes pass, each better than your own.

> Still, I keep writing in the snow, although I never have a chance to read my words. Mornings I write sonnets, but by evening sheets of snow are drawn over them. Somewhere below the drifts, my words no doubt remain. Here, in the permafrost, they gather, and gather. Here, snow-besieged woolly mammoths lie suspended a million years after grazing, tufts of grass still delicately gripped by curled trunks. And am I then the only poet of snow? This gulag is broad. Perhaps in the desert of Karaganda there is a poet of sand? Perhaps in Vorkuta, on the coaldust-blackened snow, there is a requiem longing for home. And where rests the epic of Kolyma? And who is to say that only words are recorded? Perhaps some Siberian Beethoven records a symphony beneath the drifts. An *Ode to Joy*. Humans are a divine breed—dying a death of hunger, hoping beyond hope to overcome their fate. And beneath which drifts are the blood-words written where mortars reaped and lives fell, like so much clover, or grass? (46)

Pelēcis's book presents a compelling sense of time and space. He asks that those who read his "Siberia Book" return both literally and figuratively to with the snows of Siberia to seek the words that lie beneath the frost. In essence, he is speaking of a resurrection of the dead in the form of an acknowledgment and a memory. As Zālīte's comments above suggest, to be completely forgotten, to be erased forever, is perhaps the greatest horror of all. And so, Pelēcis writes about writing, and this self-reflexivity reveals an anxiety that the Siberian annihilation will be overlooked and the dead forgotten.

Pelēcis shows masterful control of language and imagery. My translation does small justice to the original Latvian. Even so, the recurring images of grass and greenery frozen in time are collocated with the frozen mammoth from another age and with the notion of language itself which lies in suspended animation awaiting the presence of a future audience that might recognize the dead buried beneath the ice, amid the songbird's trill. The image of trunks still gripping grass under the permafrost echoes attempts by the Siberian prisoners to maintain their tenuous grip on life. Pelēcis's ironic reference to Beethoven's *Ode to Joy* recurs throughout the book and is emblematic of his dialogic perspective. This irony cuts both ways and simultaneously recognizes the joy and horror of existence. Underlying the passage is an allusion to censorship. The "sheets of snow" drawn over the words written in ice reflect the image of a sheet drawn over a corpse. Silence, whether it results from removing one's life or removing one's tongue, inspires the fear that those ten million who died will be overlooked after they are covered by the drifts of time.

Pelēcis was imprisoned for purportedly writing anti-Stalinist poetry. A majority of those in the gulag were there for purported crimes against the state. In other words, they were political prisoners who were silenced through isolation and extermination. With the death of Stalin, the gulag archipelago was gradually abandoned, and those few who survived at last had an opportunity to make their experience known to the world. However, freedom did not guarantee freedom of expression. Furthermore, this passage is typical of Pelēcis's use of what Kristeva has called "intertextual" references and serves to expand or open the dimensions of this text. Apart from the recurring and frequently ironic references to Beethoven's *Ode to Joy*, "The Siberia Book" contains allusions to other writers and artists including Leonardo da Vinci and several Latvian authors, as well as to biblical passages such as the account of the Seven Plagues of Egypt, which are parodied in this depiction with alternate plagues, including starvation, betrayal, corruption, cruelty, ice storms, predatory animals, and madness, thereby establishing Siberia and, by extension, the Soviet Union as a kind of neo-Egypt (78). In Pelēcis's hands, parody and irony serve artfully as weapons of resistance.

Although "The Siberia Book" is nonfiction, it assumes many of the features of what Bakhtin has called the "dialogic" novel or what Eco has dubbed the "open" form. This writing style is postmodern in its fragmented evocation of a world of sensory breakdown in which time and space seem suspended. Pelēcis's recurring image of the shattered kaleidoscope with its broken shards of glass and disrupted sense of vision serves as a worthy illustration.

> The winter wind is death. Nightmare visions keep repeating. Tanks approach the barracks locked from outside after curfew. Mortars open fire, screams from within are soon crushed beneath the treads: Screaming voices in the night. Exterminations. This broken kaleidoscope. A broken symmetry, the spirit torn on multicolored shards of glass. On the day of the Constitutional Celebration, amazement at music being played. Amid the "festivities," unexpectedly, a door crashes open, a young woman bursts out of the guardroom, a scream on her lips, hair disheveled, clothes torn, half-naked, throws herself onto the high-voltage barbed wire, hangs there, body trembling under the charge long after, both hands frozen in a death grip, the smell of searing flesh. She hangs until daybreak. Cutting off the voltage also means shutting off the searchlights and electricity to the fence. This can't be done. The fence is several kilometers long, there might be an opening. Tonight she hangs, electric Fatima waiting for day, waiting for the sun, the glass of the broken kaleidoscope. (70)

Long after the conscious awareness of the experience has elapsed, the unconscious generates an ineradicable and involuntary recollection of the event that haunts the narrator indefinitely. The abuse of women in the gulag was both horrific and tragic. Nothing could be done to escape, except to die. Here we witness an irony of *logos* and *pathos*. Pelēcis's personal ex libris features the image of this woman, who, in a final gesture of revulsion and defiance, flings herself at the electrified barbed-wire fence rather than endure further abuse. The ex libris also includes three stars, which, among other things, represent the liberty of the Latvian state. This feminine image personifies the nation of Latvia and is a parody of the Fatima figure, the giver of life. However, within this context the life-giving and life-taking values are inverted, and the image carries a disturbing suicidal signification.

Other nightmare scenarios recur regularly in the book. When "The Siberia Book" finally came out in 1993, Māris Çaklais commented in a review that it served both as an "unmasking" of the original censored version of the book ("With the Black Wind") and as an unmasking or "renaming" of the political regime that led to the mass annihilations. Çaklais noted as well Pelēcis's notoriety and excellence as an author and compared his writing to the works of several other contemporary writers, including Ojāra Mednis's *Tris burtnīcām* (For Three Journals) and Melānijas Vanaga's *Velupes krastā* (Banks of the Vel River). Çaklais's review appeared shortly after the uncensored version of the book had won the General Gopera Literary Award (1994) and was published in *Diena,* a major Latvian-language newspaper in Rīga, indicating that by 1994 it was safe to comment on censorship and the atrocities committed under Stalin, even though as recently as 1991 the self-same book could only be published in censored form.

In Pelēcis's writing, one of the most heavily censored topics was the experience of psychic trauma. Contrasts between the censored and uncensored versions of Pelēcis's book are revealing. For example, the chapter titled "The Death of Anatol Korolov's State" in the uncensored version features Korolov, a handsome man who served as the dentist for the prison keepers. He had gained influence and respect, and other prison keepers would come from hundreds of miles away for his dental services. After being caught in a love affair with one of the commandant's concubines, however, he is removed from his position of privilege, brought before the assembled prisoners, and warned not to try to escape. While he stands in puzzlement at this odd request, three shots are fired into the air. The weapons are fired in order to comply with the Hague convention regarding "three warning shots" to deter so-called "escaping" prisoners. After that, thirty-two rounds from the guard's machine gun are pumped into his body. Pelēcis ironically reports that "fewer bullets would have done the job as well, but with a person of Korolov's high standing there was no skimping on the bullets." The concubine is then ordered to cut Korolov's penis from his body and place it in a jar of alcohol to be kept as a reminder of her encounter. A dispatch is sent to the dentist's family euphemistically stating that he has passed away as a result of "perturbations of the heart" (131).

In a later passage, a bored guard tosses the embalmed penis onto a dung heap and then drinks the remaining fluid in an effort to get drunk. This passage constitutes what can be termed as an "embedded text"—that is, one of a series of stories within stories, or narrative digressions. The structure of this subsection as it is juxtaposed with the larger text serves to establish one of the many kaleidoscopic shards in Pelēcis's ironic vision. The passage follows a section which describes a visitation by delegates from the United Nations. Immediately prior to that visit, the machine-gun towers are lowered, work details are reduced, shabby mattresses are placed temporarily on prisoners' beds, and food rations are raised to a subsistence level. All this is carried out in an effort to indicate that many in the gulag system are there willingly, serving time in order to become "socially rehabilitated" so that they can return to society as good citizens. The delegates come and go, satisfied with the "fair" treatment of the prisoners (130). Pelēcis avoids the didacticism of lesser writers. Through his juxtaposition of passages, he generates an understated irony. With a remarkable economy of language, he offers a privileged perspective which shares with the reader the "insider's" litotic point of view. Litotes is an ideal figure of speech for those who are censored, because it is the "not said" that sometimes speaks most eloquently. Furthermore, Pelēcis's structural innovations are well integrated with the semiotics of his image network, which includes various forms of physical dismemberment.

The act of discarding Korolov's phallus is rife with symbolic signification, and refers not only to a loss of life and dignity but also to a loss of meaning in expression. Korolov's sense of the situation is beyond words. He is met with an incomprehensible accusation, and his language is impotent in his defense. He meets his death in silence. The irony of the line "perturbations of the heart" indicates not only an inversion of social values, but a skewing of meaning to the point where a broad gap opens between signifier and signified. That gap or fissure in meaning is indicative of the violence done to language itself, a kind of linguistic rupture or "dismemberment." The literal and symbolic attempts to castrate phallus and language can be read as forms of censorship. Yet these attempts inadvertently gesture back to the *aggressor's vulnerability* in terms of power and discourse.

I believe that the inversion Holquist speaks of in regard to censorship applies here, and that in writing "The Siberia Book" Pelēcis was not only commemorating the dead but also identifying a mode of resistance through language. In true ironic fashion, the blade of words cuts both ways; the opening between signifier and signified permits polysemy. The multiple meanings in language that result from Pelēcis's linguistic free play slice an opening or gap in the linguistic fence of propaganda through which the imprisoned mind can escape. The *subject matter* and *open form* of Pelēcis's account both defy the hegemony of the Soviet worldview. Consequently, the "gap" between signifier and signified, between what is said and what is meant, opens into a broad field of possibilities that uphold the polysemous, dialogic, and heterogenous worldview in defiance of the

thetic, monologic, and hegemonic worldview of the Soviets.

A notable and related element in Pelēcis's open text is his heteroglossic use of voices. Bakhtin defines *heteroglossia* as the wide range of socioideological sublanguages that enter either common or literary discourse. Throughout "The Siberia Book" Pelēcis introduces a variety of voices coming from what he calls the "international" cultural group that was detained in Siberia. Oppression on this level takes on universal significance, but it also reflects the heterogeneity and diversity of world culture. Furthermore, the polyphonic element of Pelēcis's book indicates the overall social structure both within and outside the Siberian environment. Figures such as the dentist Korolov, the black-market thieves, the prison guards, and the writer himself help establish not only the social hierarchy found within the prison system, but also the range of social groups within any society. Bakhtin has maintained that the tendency toward the polyphonic and the heteroglossic can be understood in reference to the text's larger structural innovations. This innovative form also marks a shift away from the monologic to the dialogic. The dialogism of Pelēcis's book is evident in the multiple perspectives he offers, as suggested by his recurring image of the *sasistais kaleidoskops* or "broken kaleidoscope" which serves as a motif establishing the sense of psychic fragmentation. Pelēcis explains: "If you look through a kaleidoscope, you can see wonderful abstract scenery. Like a geometrical martian illustration. But if you break the kaleidoscope, the symmetry collapses. Instead, the soul is pricked by multicolored shards of glass" (69).

Pelēcis's testimony can be understood as a deconstruction not only of a political regime, but also of formal conventions of literature, including unities of time, place, action, narrative viewpoint, and even conceptual flow. Such "open" texts tend to be associational rather than linear, absurd rather than rational, disjunctive rather than unified, dialogic rather than monologic. Through these structural forms, the worldview of the imperialists and the worldview of those in resistance come into stark contrast. One section which serves to illustrate the confrontation of worldviews involves a certain creative expression by the prisoners.

> For the past month I have been on latrine duty. The icy winter prohibits the usual venue. Outhouses with pits beneath them are useless. They are impossible to empty. Instead, the guards had us build privies some ten feet above ground. Mounds of layered and multicolored excrement collect and freeze solid. After a while the snow and ice polish them. We affectionately dubbed these frozen monoliths "The Marbles of Bolshe-

vism." It is our job to use the "pencils," the two-meter crowbars, to remove these columns. This evening we are dragged from our barracks. The wind is high, howling. Guards shove us rudely. Something is up. They assemble us in the compound, some are near collapse. We stand for an interminable time, the wind rips through us, our clothing flapping like the feathers of crows caught in a storm. The temperature is minus 38°. There is an international regulation that if it drops to minus 40°, then we are permitted to return indoors. Our feet paw the earth. The standard-issue black canvas-top basketball shoes from America could never have been meant for this. After a while the commissar addresses us with ambiguous questions, accusations. "Who has done this deed?" His anger ignites. "I will teach you to love your motherland! Here, I am your Czar and God! You will remain standing all night until someone confesses!" The crime remains unnamed. We stand, unknowing. Some grin, some have trouble breathing, standing, lean against others. Finally, the guards haul forth a frozen figure under burlap. It is human. Another stiff. So what. But perhaps a murdered guard? Unthinkable. No point, only punishment for such things. They place it in front of us. Oddly it stands by itself. They pull the burlap off. A marble monolith, but reshaped into a statue of the commissar, uniformed, complete with scar, patch over the eye, war medals on the chest. Superb. In the heroic Soviet Realist style. One arm akimbo, looking slightly upward. It looks like marble. Some begin to chuckle knowingly. Others catch on. The commissar starts swearing a blue streak, a machine-gun volley passes over our heads, but we can't stop laughing, our group is in disarray, several bending over splitting their guts. Some artist has expressed himself. We'll pay for this. But for now, we laugh. After several frozen hours, we are rudely returned to our barracks. Several have died waiting. (*Rampike*, 51).

Earlier, I spoke of the act of "naming, renaming, and unnaming" a culture. In this section a reversal of that process occurs. True to the Bakhtinian form, in a morbid but carnivalesque fashion, Pelēcis presents a play of language typical of satire and executed according to an excremental vision that situates human feces above human life. Several die during the interrogation, but, more important, a symbolic "renaming" of the prison commander has occurred. The initial signification of this action is as a practical joke. However, a second layering or perhaps marbling of meaning involves the excrement itself. Here, resistance is offered through the only creative medium available to the prisoners. The parodic form of the commander, complete with eyepatch and medals marks an ironic inversion of values and, not

surprisingly, is met once again with the customary censure by the authority figure. The "name of the father" ("I am your Czar and God") is evoked, and we see the castration or censure of language even in its excremental form. Nevertheless, using the symbolic "pencils" or body-length crowbars to collect their chosen medium, the prisoners then invert or deconstruct the "Marvels of Socialism" and reply with the excremental "Marbles of Socialism." The commandant's attempt at psychic castration fails this time, and instead the tables are turned. Satire, irony, and parody all share the weapon of derision or laughter, before which even the totalitarian is rendered impotent. However, the victory is shortlived. The equation of human life with dung is restated through the death of those who could not survive the interrogation. The equation is emphasized through the juxtaposition of this chapter with the following one, which features Pelēcis's second-to-last year in the prison and a commemoration at Christmas (1968) for the children who had died of starvation and were buried beneath the trees. As with the aforementioned images of grass, here vegetation serves as a life-in-death signifier. The children's presence is marked by arctic rhododendrons that emerge in the spring. Through these understated but recurring juxtapositions and digressions, Pelēcis unfolds his ironic kaleidoscopic vision and intersects *logos* with *pathos*.

A passage in the chapter "Dārziņš" (The Garden) illustrates the power of voice. Here what we have is a parody of a garden. This ironically named Siberian "garden" is surrounded with pointed stakes and barbed wire, with guards armed with automatic weapons in the towers, and with bloodhounds patrolling outside. But a man in rags and with four numbers on his clothing (signifying that he is to be shot if attempting to escape) hums a song without words. The importance of voice is established here. Earlier in this section, the protagonist escapes difficulties by feigning deafness. But in regard to his fellow prisoner's song, he has no problem listening and hearing. There is some anxiety concerning the danger of vocalization because of the intense awareness of the power of song or voice. The significance of the song is both literal and symbolic and becomes clear with the prisoner's words, "I know that one day I will have a garden" (41). This simple statement, with its reference to the double meaning of *garden* juxtaposed with the song's transcendental significance, helps establish the mutual interdependence of language and worldview. The tacit silence of the narrator-as-listener indicates the act of choosing to listen to one voice and choosing to ignore another. This apparently passive action is nevertheless an act of resistance. Furthermore, the narrator's position as listener gestures to the situation of the broader reading or listening audience and by extension suggests that a similar "choice" can be made by the reader. We may listen to many voices, but we need accept only some. The implied self-reflexivity here (artist/writer depicting artist/singer) is dependent upon the multivoicedness or heteroglossia of the narration.

Yet, while bodies and psyches experience a rupture or disjunction, a certain unity remains in this text. There are continuities in language and song. Pelēcis reports that he lost track of the fellow prisoner who used to hum that particular song about a garden. After his release from Siberia, however, as he walks with a companion in a sunny wooded area back in Latvia, Pelēcis catches himself humming the same song (43). The struggle to maintain identity is related to the struggle to assert one's own voice. The following passage documents his arrest, and the removal of zippers and buttons emphasizes the severing of connections with the past as well as with his former self.

> Upon departure I am stripped of all save the clothes I wear, and even these are stripped of zippers, buttons. Save one. The fellow working at the prison in Rīga chose to be generous that day and left one button on the trouser front, a small act of kindness that freed both of my hands and so perhaps spared my life. A week on the train amid piss and shit and others that stink and fear as much as I. The first time behind the wire barbs is instructive. I am asked to fetch some wood that has been pre-cut. It seems simple, almost thoughtful, until my little crew is taken to a pile of timbers in the black-fly woods. Each log is just heavy enough to require the full strength of three men, the timbers to be carried on shoulder across a mile or two of tundra and muskeg, an imbalance or stumble causes the log to fall, and precious calories are spent upon raising it again to shoulder height. I notice that some men must hold their trousers up with their hands, their buttons, zippers, belts have all been removed. The value of a belt is beyond comprehension. Strings or safety pins are highly marketable items. I watch the others struggle. I feel an idiotic joy for my single button. Food is offered at less than subsistence level, and eventually all will die from malnutrition, unless they learn to adapt quickly. Gruel the daily food. "Sundays," I ask, "what happens on Sundays? Do we have a day of rest?" The guard laughs, "Of course, on Sundays, the task is much lighter, no logs to carry then." I endure until the end of the week, when I learn the task is now to bury bodies. Three stiffs to a grave, "to save time" in digging and wood in the making of markers, they say. The earth is rock hard, the shovel ineffectual. The guard is heavy and armed with a submachine gun and metal teeth. He

laughingly gives me what they call a "pencil," a steel rod with a sharpened point for hacking the permafrost. This work turns out to be harder and more melancholy than the daily routine, by Sunday noon we look forward to hauling timbers. (*Rampike*, 50)

In Pelēcis's account, the balance between life and death is so fine that a single button can tip the scale. In counterpoint to his recurring image of the smashed kaleidoscope, he keeps returning to the image of the "pencil." This double signifier simultaneously refers to both his imprisonment in the gulag and his freedom as an artist. The "pencil" as metonym refers to the manner in which language can confine or liberate through censorship or freedom of expression. It underlines the clash between worldviews. The double blade of irony cuts through this text to the final pages. With Stalin dead, the gulag becomes more or less irrelevant. But Pelēcis is not informed of the prisoners' imminent release. To the last day, prior to his freedom, the authorities pressure him to sign a document pleading guilty to "political dissidence" and "crimes against the state." He refuses on the grounds that his only crime was to tell the truth through poetry. The next day Pelēcis is surprised to receive his release papers. He learns shortly thereafter that all the prisoners are to be set free, whether they signed a prewritten "confession" or not. This conclusion serves to emphasize the relentless use of language as a weapon in the contest between worldviews.

Finally, after twenty-three years, Pelēcis was released. He was issued some secondhand items of clothing and put on the train back to Rīga. Little remained of his original garments, save the single button that had been spared in a capricious moment.

Karl E. Jirgens, Spring 1998

■ WORKS CITED

Andrups, Jānis, and Vitauts Kalve. *Latvian Literature*. Stockholm. Goppers. 1954.

Austrina, Ina, with Indra Sildega and Modris Zihmanis. *Atmiņu lauskas* (Memory Fragments). Rīga. Latvijas Rakstnieku Savienibas. 1991.

Bakhtin, Mikhail M. *The Dialogic Imagination*. Michael Holquist, ed. C. Emerson and H. Holquist, trs. Austin. University of Texas Press. 1990.

Baltic States. Tallinn/Rīga/Vilnius. Estonian/Latvian/Lithuanian Encylopaedia Publishers. 1991.

Bels, Alberts. *Saulē mērktie* (The Sun-Drenched). Rīga. Preses Nams. 1995.

Bergmane, Anna. *Latviešu rakstības attistības* (Developments in Latvian Writing). Rīga. Zinatne. 1986.

Bergson, Henri. "Le Rire: Essai sur la signification du comique." In his *Œuvres*. Paris. PUF. 1959.

Berzins, Alfreds. *The Unpunished Crime*. Senator Thomas J. Dodd, intro. New York. Speller. 1963.

Bilzens, Indulis, ed. *Rīga: Lettische Avantgarde* (Rīga: Latvian Avant-Garde). Berlin. Elefanten. 1988.

Blanks, Ernests. *Latvijas atdzimšana* (Latvia's Rebirth). Stockholm. Latviešu Nacionalais Fonds. 1989. [Reprint of a 1928 document.]

Čaklais, Māris. "Atdzimušajai Grāmatai—Gopera Balva" (Reborn Book Wins Gopera Prize). *Diena* (Rīga), 1994.

Cedrins, Inara, ed. *Contemporary Latvian Poetry*. Iowa City. University of Iowa Press. 1984.

Dunsdorfs, Edgars. *The Baltic Dilemma, Part II*. Melbourne. Baltic Council of Australia. 1982.

————. *Latvijas vēstures atlants* (Latvian Historical Survey). Melbourne. General Gopera Fund. 1976.

Dzillēja, Kārlis. *Poetika* (Poetics). East Lansing, Mi. Gauja. 1985. [Reprint of a 1949 book.]

Eglitis, Anslavs. *Esejas: Par raksniekiem un grāmatām 1973–1991* (Essays on Authors and Books 1973–1991). Newton, Ma. Latviešu Rakstnieku Apvienibas. 1991.

Ermansons, Egīls. *Cilvēks ar bērnu ratiņiem* (A Man with a Baby Carriage). Rīga. Karogs. 1994.

Ezergailis, Andrew. *The Holocaust in Latvia*. Rīga. Historical Institute of Latvia. 1996.

Foucault, Michel. *The Archaeology of Knowledge and the Discourse on Language*. A. M. Sheridan, tr. New York. Pantheon. 1972.

————. *Knowledge and Power*. C. Gordon, ed. New York. Pantheon. 1980.

Gimbutas, Marija. *The Language of the Goddess*. San Francisco. HarperCollins. 1991.

Hausmanis, Viktors, ed. *Musdienu latviešu padomju literatūra, 1960–1980* (Contemporary Latvian Literature, 1960–1980). Rīga. Zinatne. 1985.

Hayes, Carlton J. H. *Contemporary Europe Since* 1870. New York. Macmillan. 1959.

Holquist, Michael. "Introduction. Corrupt Originals: The Paradox of Censorship." *PMLA*, 109:1 (January 1994), pp. 14–25.

Hutcheon, Linda. *Irony's Edge: The Theory and Politics of Irony*. New York. Routledge. 1994.

Jegers, Benjamins, ed. *Latviešu trimdas izdevumu bibliografija* (Bibliography of Latvian Publications in Exile). Stockholm. Daugava. 1988. [Volume for the years 1971–80.]

Karogs (Flag: A Literary Monthly). Rīga. 1996.

King, Thomas. "Godzilla vs Post-Colonial." *World Literature Written in English,* 30 (1990), pp. 10–16.

Kosinski, Jerzy. *The Painted Bird*. New York. Bantam. 1965.

Kristeva, Julia. *Desire in Language: A Semiotic Approach to Literature and Art*. Leon S. Roudiez, ed. Thomas Roga, Alice Jardine, and Leon Roudiez, trs. New York. Columbia University Press. 1980.

Labsvirs, Janis. *The Sovietization of the Baltic States: Collectivization of Latvian Agriculture*. Indianapolis, In. Taurus. 1988.

Lacan, Jacques. *Ecrits*. A. Sheridan, tr. New York. Norton. 1977.

Landsmanis, Arturs. *Persist or Perish*. Stockholm. Latvian National Foundation. 1976.

Latvia and Latvians. London. Daugavas Vanagi. 1978.

Mangulis, Visvaldis. *Latvia in the Wars of the 20th Century*. Princeton Junction, N.J. Cognition Books. 1983.

Medne, Lienīte, with Vladis Spāre and Juris Zvirgzdiņš. *Odu laiks* (Time of the Mosquito-Ode). Rīga. Artava. 1989.

New, W. H., ed. *Native Writers and Canadian Writing*. University of British Columbia Press. 1990.

Ngũgĩ wa Thiong'o. *Decolonising the Mind: The Politics of Language in African Literature*. London. James Currey. 1991.

Nieburga, Andra. "From XXX." Banuta Rubess, tr. *Rampike,* 8:1 (1995), p. 44.

Okri, Ben. *Stars of the New Curfew*. New York. Penguin. 1988.

Ong, Walter J. *Orality and Literacy: The Technologizing of the Word*. New York. Routledge. 1989.

Osa, Aija. *Sarunas ar maksliniekiem* (Interviews with Artists). Rīga. Liesma. 1987.

Parolek, Radegast. *Baltijas literatūres slidzinora apcere* (Survey and Overview of Baltic Literature). Rīga. Liesma. 1985.

Pasaules spogulī: Prozas antologija (Prose Anthology). Rīga. Liesma. 1990.

Pelēcis, Aleksandrs. *Lapegle* (The Larch). Rīga. Liesma. 1977.

————. *Spītīgais osis* (The Stubborn Ash). Rīga. Liesma. 1987.

————. *Dzintara rasa* (The Amber Dew). Los Angeles. Ramave. 1989.

————. *Ar melno vēju* (With the Black Wind). Rīga. Avots. 1991.

————. *Puisiska dvēsele* (The Boyish Soul). Rīga. Liesma. 1990.

————. *Sibirijas grāmata* (The Siberia Book). Ithaca, N.Y. Latvian Press Group. 1993.

————. "Excerpt from *The Siberia Book*." Karl Jirgens, tr. *Rampike,* 8:1 (1995), pp. 50–51.

Puisāns, Tadeušs. *The Emerging Nation*. Rīga. Centre for Baltic-Nordic History and Political Studies. 1995.

Resolution with Appended Documents Concerning the Decolonization of the Union of Soviet Socialist Republics to the United Nations General Assembly. New York. The Conference of Free Byelorussians, The Estonian World Council, The Lithuanian World Community, The World Congress of Free Ukrainians, The World Federation of Free Latvians. 1977.

Rubulis, Aleksis. *Baltic Literature: A Survey of Finnish, Estonian, Latvian and Lithuanian Literatures*. Notre Dame, In. University of Notre Dame Press. 1970.

———— and Marvin J. Hood, eds. *Latvian Literature*. Toronto. Daugavas Vanagi. 1964.

Said, Edward W. *Orientalism*. New York. Vintage. 1979.

Šilde, Ādolfs. *Trimdinieka raksti, 1944–1990* (Writing in Exile, 1944–1990). Münster, Ger. Latvija. 1991.

Silenieks, Juris. Reviews of Egīls Ermansons and Alberts Bels. *World Literature Today* 69:1 (Winter 1995), p. 193, and 71:1 (Winter 1997), p. 194.

Silkalns, Eduards. *Kritikas krāja: Grāmatu vērtējumi 1957–1994* (Anthology of Critiques and Reviews 1957–1994). Sydney. Latviešu Preses Biedrības. 1994.

Skalbe, Kārlis. *Daugavas vilņi* (Waves of the Daugava). Rīga. Zinatne. 1989.

Solzhenitsyn, Aleksandr. *One Day in the Life of Ivan Denisovich*. New York. Bantam. 1966.

————. *The First Circle*. New York. Bantam., 1968.

Spivak, Gayatri Chakravorty. *The Post-Colonial Critic*. New York. Routledge. 1990.

Trinh T. Minh-ha. *Woman Native Other.* Bloomington. Indiana University Press. 1991.

Whorf, Benjamin Lee. *Language, Thought, and Reality: Selected Writings.* Cambridge, Ma. MIT Press. 1966.

Valgemäe, Mardi, with William L. Winter and Arvids Ziedonis Jr., eds. *Baltic History.* Columbus, Oh. AABS. 1974.

Vardys, V. Stanley, ed. *Regional Identity Under Soviet Rule: The Case of the Baltic States.* Kiel, Ger. Institute for the Study of Law, Politics, and Society of Socialist States. 1990.

Zālīte, Māra. *Kas ticībā sēts: Runas un raksti Latvijas atmodai 1979–1997* (What Is Believed: Lectures and Articles on Latvia's Awakening 1979–1997). Rīga. Karogs. 1997.

Ziedonis, Imants. *Flowers of Ice.* Toronto. Exile Editions. 1987.

Post-Soviet Literature in Lithuania: An Overview

After Thomas Jefferson's immortal words opening the Declaration of Independence, the birth, or rebirth, of a nation may be regarded in some measure as a matter of style, of the written word. From this perspective, Lithuanian letters after the reestablishment of independence in 1991 appear to reflect the nation's search for its own Word—that is to say, for itself. The quest began soon after Khrushchev's "thaw" around 1956. With the melting outlines of socialist realism, the established Moscow-made image of Lithuania also started to dissolve, and one could begin to trace the reemerging dim features of the nation's true face, its historical and cultural identity.

The deepest well the nation could look into in the hopes of seeing its own face was the ambience of ancient myth. The notion of myth in Lithuania is not primarily narrative, for there are not many stories told. It is instead poetic, for it conveys a certain wordless experience of being a part of some timeless mystery that includes an ancient, secure belonging to every thing that grows and dies in the world of nature. For the writers, the contemplation of this mythic ambience was in essence an effort to regain a pre-Christian and "purely" Lithuanian world, because after the arrival of Christianity and letters—that is, after the country stepped into the "stream of history"—Lithuania as a nation was most easily described in terms of the effects that other cultures—Polish, German, Russian, and, most importantly, Soviet—have had upon it.

The motif of rural, pre-Christian consciousness is strong in the poetry of Marcelijus Martinaitis (b. 1936), particularly his famous *Kukučio baladės* (Ballads of Kukutis; 1977), depicting a symbolic Lithuanian figure moving across history and time to become a transforming presence in the creation of the nation's unique identity. Judita Vaičiūnaitė (b. 1937) combined the emblems of this lost pagan world—stone markings, amber carvings of longdead gods—with urban images of old city squares, antique shops, or fountains, all suffused with sacred and profane love, to create a nostalgia for things that had become irrelevant to Soviet Lithuania but nevertheless constitute a poetic sign of the nation's true essence. Sigitas Geda (b. 1943) cast a spell of myth upon the country's landscapes to create a magical present that somehow contains in it mystical memories from time out of mind.

In prose, Romualdas Granauskas (b. 1939) brought the aura of myth to the Old Prussians and Lithuanians in recorded medieval history. His story "Jaučio aukojimas" (The Sacrifice of the Ox; 1975) depicts a time when the ancient pagan beliefs and rituals, in which all life was a magical presence, came to a fatal confrontation with the advancing, urbanized Christianity of the Teutonic Order. The destruction of the old way of life brought about by this new armor-clad and bloody faith suggests similar tragic encounters between the rural, small-town Lithuania and the new era of the Soviet juggernaut. Life under the Soviets is depicted in such stories as "Duonos valgytojai" (The Bread Eaters; 1975) and "Gyvenimas po klevu" (A Homestead Under the Maple Tree; 1988). There we witness the slow decay and dissolution of all human dignity and hope in the Lithuanian countryside under the grindstone of the alien Soviet ideology that spoke all the while of the happy new life it was bringing.

The changes which this new faith wrought in the Lithuanian countryside were described with an epic sweep by Jonas Avyžius (b. 1922) in his trilogy *Kaimas kryžkelėj* (Village at the Crossroads; 1964), *Sodybų tuštėjimo metas* (The Time of Emptying Settlements; 1970), and *Degimai* (Scorched Land; 1982). These three works all deal with the forced transformation of single Lithuanian settlements into collective farms, even agro-cities, during the Soviet rule.

Historical drama was the strongest genre in Lithuanian theater before the war, and this trend continued during the Soviet occupation. One of the main figures was the dramatist and prose writer Juozas Grušas (1901–86), whose historical plays explored several moments in Lithuanian history where the idea of nationhood underwent a trial of fire by force of arms or political circumstance that put to question its very existence. The poet Justinas Marcinkevičius (b. 1930) achieved fame with his verse dramas revolving around outstanding Lithuanian historical personages whose accomplishments contributed toward the substance of national, political, and cultural identity.

We may note that in all genres of this period, especially poetry and prose, the identity of Lithuania is conveyed primarily in terms of what the nation has lost, not what it has built or acquired. This produced a conservative, defensive literature in which, as often as not, homage to the land came to resemble a funeral rite in its remembrance.

The "singing revolution" of 1991, with its explosive outburst of national pride and determination, brought with it a brief euphoria of freedom, including the freedom of the written word. Under the Soviets, one had to submit to the often quite prudish demands of the ruling party that literature should present a bright, beautiful, happy image of life, of which the dark side could only be referred to as "relics of the past." Everyone knew, of course, that the evils of the dictatorship were not "relics" of anything but, on the contrary, the dreadful reality of the present. With independence, the dark abyss of the past opened up like a huge wound, and the pendulum swung so far back that writers began to feel that telling the truth meant saying nothing but terrible things about the country and the human souls in it. After all the beautiful official lies, this seemed the only way to regain a sense of personal integrity. Thus came the period of a literature of exorcism, of exposing, exploring, resuffering the unspeakable horrors of its recent past, of cleansing its wounds, as it were, with the white-hot iron of memory.

Much of this literature was not actually fiction, but belonged to the in-between genres of straightforward or embellished memoirs of exiles to Siberia and of guerrillas who fought on in the forests for eight or nine years after the Soviet armies came back in 1944. The flood of such tales is still continuing today, and many of them are heartbreaking enough; but for the most part they lack the hot stench of hatred or of perverse, even sadistic, imagination that some fiction writers have brought to the topic. Notorious among them is Ričardas Gavelis (b. 1950), who seems to work on the premise that the face of real life in the Soviet Union has been so disfigured that looking at it as if it were some sort of fantastic nightmare was the only way to recognize its true nature. In his novel *Vilniaus pokeris* (The Vilnius Poker Game; 1989) Gavelis presents a grotesque and tortured city, Vilnius, the Lithuanian capital, ruled by an abominable secret society he refers to as They, the very incarnation of worldwide, eternal, and ultimate evil that looks over the city with the dead eyes of a basilisk. Under its glance everything turns to ashes, stinking mud, unspeakable figures in murky, twisted streets, and the very air itself becomes transformed to ghoulish fear that seeps into the blood with every breath. In such a world, reality itself becomes repulsively mythical, and the city becomes

disfigured into shapes of a surrealistic terror, not unlike the nightmarish Prague of Franz Kafka's classic, *The Trial*. Indeed, there is a sculptor in the novel who creates a figure much like Kafka's giant cockroach in "The Metamorphosis" that represents the process of a woman becoming a spider, and the horrible thing is precisely this becoming, this sculpture changing before the viewer's eyes from a woman to a monster with a spider's mind. The novel contains something like a love story, but in the hero's mutilated mind, love itself becomes a nightmare experience, haunted by the ghouls of paranoia, sadism, and sexual impotence. In the end, Vargalys, the hero, kills his beloved (better: object of helpless desire) by cutting her to pieces, as if looking for something in her, possibly a soul.

By some assessments, Gavelis's best work is *Jauno žmogaus memuarai* (The Memoirs of a Young Man; 1991). It could belong to the genre of a "posthumous confession" or diary. It too has horrors similar to those in *Vilniaus pokeris,* and several major characters also seem to wield an incomprehensible semimystical evil power, slithering their slimy tentacles all over other peoples' lives. But the text has other dimensions as well, in particular that of the dichotomy between true creativity and mere mechanical skill which troubles the young hero as he tries to become a master physicist but can only reach the stage of a competent juggler of equations, a kind of Wagner (Faust's assistant) or Salieri in the realm of physics. This tension plays itself out in the context of confrontation between free will and tyranny that encompasses the entire society of what now is openly presented as Lithuania under Soviet rule. It also takes the shape of the young man's letters to high communist officials in Moscow, or to other ruling figures in the world, letters that are full of holy fury and, in that anger, somehow also euphoric in their cry for freedom and for the dignity of being human.

The genre of pretended personal memoirs, which to some extent is also a pretense of avoiding "literature," seems based on the notion that in the horrid world of Soviet rule art itself becomes almost an irrelevance with respect to the reality which it portrays. Such a stance is taken by Leonardas Gutauskas (b. 1938), who writes prose and poetry and also paints. In his series of volumes under the general title *Vilko dantų karoliai* (A Wolf-Teeth Necklace; books 1–2, 1990/1994; others still coming) he tries to imitate the authentic flow of life in that he neither structures his texts like a novel nor organizes his memory in some selective fashion. Instead he claims that the Memory (*sic!*) of things he went through in the past simply dictates to him, and he cannot stop until it fades, almost as if an alien presence, from his mind. Anything that can dictate a text becomes thereby personalized, and if it is an abstraction, it becomes symbolic—that is, an artifact. Thus, paradoxically, Gutauskas's authentic memoirs read like intense fiction. Disparate events seem automatically organized by Memory to create symbolic linkages of image among them and produce a flowing, even meandering, yet firmly guided line of text. For example, an exile from Siberia returns with his limbs frozen in the arctic cold, the flesh already rotting and falling off of him. He recalls the big piles of dead and rotting rats in their Siberian barracks which they would sweep into a corner and set on fire. At this point, another reminiscence crawls out of this remembered flame—about the Lithuanian Jews under German occupation: "There in Kaunas's suburbs, they gathered the Jews and locked them in, and set them on fire, and their ghetto burned like the last picture from St. John's Apocalypse will burn, or like the living word imprisoned in your aching head."

From these rotting limbs, and burning rats, and from the apocalyptic agony of the Jews, another image-memory arises: bones. These are the bones of Lithuanian anti-Soviet guerrillas. They are now in a swamp, thrown in together with the bones of dead horses and cows, but their journey there began from the town's marketplace. One of them, now a skeleton, leaning, as Dylan Thomas once said, on his elbow, tells his story to the narrator: "There were six men of us lying dead in the market square. A guard had defecated on one man's face, others had their arms chopped off, and I lay on my back with the holy rosary wound around my . . . male thing." The narrator, a young boy, goes to the swamp at night and extracts these bones—of the animals as well as of the guerrillas—and sells them to the lone remaining Jew in town, a sort of "recycling person" who, in return, gives the boy stamps postmarked in Tula, a distant Siberian place where the boy's father has perished.

Another image series leads from matter-of-fact activities in a "castration combine for horses," as it is called, one of the "building projects of socialism," to sadistic boys' games, also vaguely having to do with sex, to the thoughtless and casual raping of girls by their high-school classmates. First, the horses. Having just been castrated, they now run around and around in a circle as if gone totally berserk.

> Now only work horses, only the slaves of man, they dash and dash in a circle, and they trample and trample underfoot those powerful, bloody balls of theirs; around and around like maddened animals from a burning barn, or like beasts stung by a scorpion—this was a sight the like of which you shall find nowhere else on earth, or maybe even under the earth, in hell.

Now the children and the rapists: "They catch three or four frogs, knock them half unconscious with a little stick, or a fillip, then they peel their skins off and fold these 'shirts' of theirs over the frogs' heads, just like Jonas did to Magdutė down by the river, and then they place the frogs in a row and . . . the race begins." In their insane agony, some of these frogs fall into the boys' campfire and burn there, thus closing the ring of images of burning flesh. The painful point to make is that these events are not the fruits of some madman's fancy; they all actually happened in Gutauskas's life, and the lives of others.

All these horrors might seem to suggest that the written word in post-Soviet Lithuania signals not so much a rebirth as the demise of the nation. In actuality, something else was going on: a slow and painful ordeal or trial by fire, a gradual thinking and feeling one's way through the debris left in the mind by the monstrosities of the Soviet state toward what actually could be a new Word, a discourse significant as art and not merely as a cry of the soul. Whatever his stance, Gutauskas does not really write like a chronicler, or a journalist, and he cannot escape from literariness as long as the esthetic function in his work remains dominant. In this respect, both Gavelis and Gutauskas do transcend their depressing subject matter and develop subtle, sophisticated stylistic and structural devices. Aside from painting, Gutauskas has also experimented with verse and children's literature. One of his best books in the latter genre is *Kam katinui ūsai* (What Are Cat's Whiskers For; 1996), a dialogue between grandfather and grandson, full of vaguely folkloric fancy and puckish humor arising from skewed logic.

There is also humor in the novels of Jurgis Kunčinas (b. 1947), even if it takes a while to recognize it amid the putrid rot in city slums and the hopeless drunkards (particularly the authorial "I") who seem to seek the full and truthful experience of being human in the very depths of alcoholic degeneration and abandoned love. The humor comes from flights of grotesque fancy and social satire in the often hilarious portrayals of what passed for culture in the life of Soviet Lithuanian academe. Yet, as in Kunčinas's novel *Tūla* (Tūla; 1993), the entire decaying world around the narrator is so replete with desperate love, love into which one sinks with total abandonment to a far lower level than in any twilight of the soul, that the world becomes twisted out of all logic, and the emotion is carried in images of fairy-tale fancy, as when the lover, in a distant detention place for alcoholics, becomes a bat out of sheer longing for his beloved, flies over to her, and strews white lilies on her sleeping form. The book is not so much a novel as a long love letter by its hero to his beloved, Tūla. In the force field of this love, all the grimy and cruel reality seems somehow to transcend itself; all the horrible details of suffering, filth, alcoholism, neglect, oppression, hopelessness seem to acquire a metaphorical quality, to become a mode of signifying love. A similar blend of heavy sorrow, reckless humor, and complete fantasy exists also in Kunčinas's *Glisono kilpa* (Glison's Noose; 1992), and particularly in his latest novel, *Blanchisserie-Žvėrynas-Užupis* (1997; Žvėrynas and Užupis are two decrepitly picturesque suburbs of Vilnius), where it really feels like downright fun to be a total degenerate as long as love walks patiently by your side.

Kunčinas sometimes reads like a peculiar blend of Knut Hamsun, the Three Stooges, and Franz Kafka. He and Gavelis, in a way Gutauskas, and also Saulius Tomas Kondrotas (b. 1953), and several others, could be called "deconstructionists" because of their systematic dismantling of the entire structure of values upheld by the former Soviet society. As Roland Barthes said of the bourgeoisie, so also are the Soviets presented as entirely natural and rational their particular twisted sets of beliefs, coopting the ancient notions of morality and human dignity to make their own asserted power seem like the inevitable truth. In order to sweep away all aspects of this tyranny, it was necessary to undermine and destroy that which morality and human dignity had become in its grasp. Inevitably, much healthy tissue of the soul had to be cut out together with this cancer. In that sense, their work was a radical operation, and this explains the aftermath of devastation in all spheres of present-day Lithuanian culture as well as ordinary life that we feel in reading these authors. The Lithuanian landscape looks especially bleak and moribund in the novel *Šermenys* (The Wake; 1990) by Vanda Juknaitė (b. 1949), a person of middle years who had seen and known well all the agonies the country went through under the Soviets and by this experience had gained a calm, deadly maturity of spirit that permits her to speak without rhetoric and with a stoic simplicity. The novel does not so much present a plot as chronicle an inexorable process of dying in the countryside, with homesteads standing empty because most of the villagers have settled permanently in the village cemetery, with new ones coming in steadily. The entire land, it seems, is quietly sinking into death, in the wake of mass deportations to Siberia and the bloody agony of the long guerrilla war, in the midst of abandoned fields, from disease, old age, alcohol, despair. The work is a tragedy without a tragic hero. From a less depressed perspective, one could speak of historical changes in the countryside, changes that will transform this basically agricultural land into a modern urban society, even at this high

human cost. From what the writers say, however, it is not clear what that new life might be like and if it will come.

Jurga Ivanauskaitė (b. 1961), a playwright and prose writer, entertains a vision that has nothing to do with urbanization. Her best novel, *Ragana ir lietus* (The Witch and the Rain; 1993), can be regarded in some ways as a parallel to the literature of ancient mythical world-perception in which writers sought the ultimate roots of the nation's identity. Ivanauskaitė, however, looks at time and myth through a different prism, that of eternally recurrent erotic encounters between a man and a woman on the dreadful edge of the fear and love of God. The novel consists of three thematically interlinked episodes widely spaced in time, with Mary Magdalene as the main figure in three different incarnations: as the biblical sinner fiercely hungry for the love of Christ, as a medieval witch spellbound by a forest prophet who speaks with the kingdom of birds, and as a contemporary Lithuanian woman passionately in love with a priest. The men of God and the woman of the earth, love sacred and profane, hope and agony consume Mary's body and her soul. Christ is the only one whom she cannot touch, and also the only one who does not betray her or defile her love. *Ragana ir lietus* is, again, not a novel of action, but rather of some ill-defined inner quest for both the fulfillment of bodily passion and the salvation of the soul. Lately, Ivanauskaitė has moved from fiction to stories of travel, of pilgrimage, spiritual accounts of her quest, seeking enlightenment among the snowbound monasteries of Tibet.

The process of transforming a cry of pain into art is still taking place in post-Soviet Lithuanian poetry as well. The distinction between older, established poets and the younger, contemporary generation is to some extent blurred because the older authors, such as Justinas Marcinkevičius, Judita Vaičiūnaitė, or Eduardas Mieželaitis (1919–97), are continuing to write, adjusting their themes and often their style to run along with the evolutionary process of contemporary verse in Lithuania. In addition, the generation that has followed them is often itself not much younger, if at all, and it cannot always justify its claim of spearheading the search for the new Word. Among these poets—all of them highly talented and often quite prodigious—one could count such major figures as Sigitas Geda and Vytautas Bložė (b. 1930), or Donaldas Kajokas (b. 1953) and Gintaras Patackas (b. 1931), or even Sigitas Parulskis (b. 1965), who, at thirty-two, has just stepped over the line of credibility in some people's eyes. This particular generation cuts a wide swath in contemporary Lithuanian poetry and remains the dominant presence, in the light of which some (not all) of the youngest talents are but dimly visible.

In the period of transition since independence, one can see a development from the dominant nightmares of pain and horror in the Soviet past toward a considerably wider thematic spectrum, including issues of universal human interest, some philosophical verse, and, in particular, the continuance of the "mythological" strain in which the natural world presents itself as a thing of beauty, a puzzle, a teacher, a subject for meditation, a path to the nation's soul, and sometimes, particularly in the verse of Sigitas Geda, even as a wellspring of sheer poetic joy.

Julius Keleras (b. 1961) is one of the "angry young men" in Lithuanian poetry whose anger is becoming only one among a number of other facets of his work. Thinking of the nightmarish Soviet rule, Keleras depicts the Lithuanian nation as looking at itself in the mirror and seeing there a revolting submissiveness and treason: "The mirrors full of corpses: wherever you look, dogs are singing to the moon about their submissiveness and their treason; women are lulling fear to sleep in their cradles and listening to the key being turned in the door as if in acceptance of someone else's guilt: an alien love to an alien master."

Sigitas Parulskis did his obligatory military service in the Soviet elite shock troops. The Soviet army inherited and continued the old Russian army tradition of intimidation and inhuman treatment of its recruits in order to, as the Marines here sometimes say, "break a man down and build him up again." Most of the cruelties were perpetrated by soldiers of senior standing, those who were serving their third or fourth year. Having survived this sort of hell, Parulskis wrote down his experiences in lines like these:

> You will remember one night. Drunken "seniors" were trying to force your neighbor, a Ukrainian, to sew a button on one of their overcoats. When he demurred, they started kicking him with their heavy boots, and kept on doing this for a long time. You were listening to all this full of fear, from fear dust fell down upon your ears, upon your bare head, from the upper bunk over you. In fear you closed your eyes, in fear you swallowed a cry, just hoping that they would not notice you, that only . . . The Ukrainian was then brought to the hospital, where he groaned all day and night, and the next morning his blue face offered its dead smile to you. But you closed your eyes once more.

Then Parulskis makes his main point: this dehumanization will not defeat you until the time when, having become a "senior" yourself, you raise your hand against a frightened new recruit and thus become the heir and carrier of the tradition.

The verse of Parulskis and Keleras and several other similar poets has been remarkable for its paucity of conventional literary devices. Such literary paraphernalia as were present in their poetry did not figure as its defining factor, as if the poets were deliberately trying to diminish the esthetic function of their texts and to push beyond literature into the raw nerve of the revealed gruesome reality. In later works, however, they are becoming more and more "literary," allowing the esthetic function *per se* to regain its primary role. In his later collections, such as *Baltas kalėdaitis* (The White Christmas Wafer; 1988) and particularly *Sauja medaus* (A Handful of Honey; 1995), Keleras is developing an intensely metaphorical style in which the complex process of renaming things serves as a sort of guide to the labyrinth of thought toward feeling and perceptions about one's own self that were hidden or only half understood heretofore. Parulskis, on the other hand, in one of his latest collections, *Mirusiųjų* (Of the Dead; 1994), aims for the maximum density and at the same time the stoic simplicity of utterance that would serve as a sort of "matrix" (to use Michel Riffaterre's term), a sign, of a myriad unspoken images in the mind. Here is an example from this new collection:

cleaning out the ashes from the hearth
those congealed lumps of slag
I found a bloody nail

so many centuries I've been warming myself
by your agony

I'm cold
("A Transfixed Morning," 49)

Donaldas Kajokas has also written about the abysmal deserts in the post-Soviet Lithuanian soul. He sometimes exploits the traditional strong presence of nature themes to reveal with a sudden and revolting clarity the ugly mutilation of that very countryside. One poem, "Springtime IV," begins charmingly enough with violets on the snow-covered slopes and a little girl straining upward to look at the catkins, only to continue without even a change of pace or tone, "lean rats enjoyed the warm, dear sun, / their flanks, consumed by some disease / were steaming horribly," and so on, in a sweeping view of the now empty guard towers rattling in the wind and the entire desolate landscape where humans so recently plied their murderous trade. In other poems, Kajokas raises the dysphoric plain of his landscapes to what might be called an "esthetic" experience. His poem "J. S. Bachas, Mišios si minor" (J. S. Bach, Mass in C Minor), an apocalyptic fantasy, abstracts depicted human agony above all plausibility and elevates it to the highest pitch of horror at the point where it meets the glory of one of the most beautiful human creations, Bach's *St. Matthew Passion,* to create an experience of searing pain and beauty as a metaphor for the tragedy of his nation.

When not in this catastrophic mode, Kajokas likes to focus upon the slightest nuances of perception and to nurse from them an awareness of the inner core of being. There is also a great deal of tender love in him, sometimes just touched with a puckish sense of humor, as in this poem about his own little daughter: "Moon from a dream. A crib. / The wing of a wooden horse. / A warm, sleepy angel / Sitting on the night-pot."

Much more serious than that is Gražina Cieškaitė (b. 1951), a poet of philosophical and even mystical bent who does not in her work seem to relate directly to any of the convolutions in recent Lithuanian history. Hers is an inner world as large as the entire universe of human self-awareness, a philosophical world that, as she puts it, "cannot be thought through to the end." As such, it is also a ponderous world of pained concentration in which the poetic language itself, at first glance, seems to labor heavily at the very edge of incoherence. As we keep looking, however, patterns of images, intertextual allusions to various aspects of world culture, and metaphorical constructs emerge gradually to form a well-wrought artistic discourse that powerfully enhances our awareness of what we are as human beings as we stand at the crossroads of cosmic mysteries stretching out beyond the horizons of thought. The coherence among these various elements is strengthened also by sets of constant recurrences, allusions within a poem to its own images as well as outside, to her other poems. Indeed, one could speak of Cieškaitė's entire poetry as one continuous meditation on the meaning of all things in terms of philosophy, religion, and art. In this meditation, time, space, and material objects all carry the semantic load of thought. The poetic persona in her verse is not really an observer of a scene, nor primarily the topic of a poem, but rather an *actant,* together with its objects, metaphors, images, and allusions, so that there is direct, as it were "physical" interaction between the persona and objects, events, and time within the sphere of its perceptions, as in these lines from *Auka žvaigždžiu vainikui* (An Offering to the Wreath of Stars; 1991): "I lived by art — in it there was repeated / The life of harmony inspired, / accords of universal forms, as if / I were creating future from my soul; and books, / moss-covered, sprouted from my palms." Lines such as these can, in a sense, be perceived as modern variations on the mythological themes of Ovid's *Metamorphoses,* where the poet herself, within her text, becomes a myth.

Cieškaitė's work is a strong departure from the nightmare visions that to some extent still continue as a trend. As a philosophizing poet in her particular style, she is unique in Lithuanian poetry and has no imitators. On the other hand, thematic horizons have indeed widened in the last few years, and the poets again seem curious about regaining touch with the ordinary flow of life as it becomes transformed into esthetic experience. Sigitas Geda has written some wonderfully enthusiastic verses full of delighted astonishment at the beauty of God's creation as it manifests in the smallest stems of grass, the colors of a butterfly, and the entire fairy-tale presence of nature that seems to grow out of some ancient mythological consciousness.

Aidas Marčėnas (b. 1960) tends to focus upon the poetic "I" as a form of unique and transitory consciousness in relation to nuances of existential experience between reality and word, existence and meaning, as in the line "young death, entangled in my words, was resting in the lilies, beautiful like a bride." He also likes classical themes, to which he turns as if to some peaceful harbor for the mind. A central metaphor in his verse is the figure of an "angel," touching things and people lightly as it passes by and suddenly turning into something unknown, terrifying, and wonderful—in other words, into poetry, or, which is the same, truth.

As the sun
appearing suddenly from behind the cloud
startled the magpie from the evergreen
the thought came to me how
awe full the truth would be if we
could ever know it

Lord
let me
die from the glance
of Thy angel

Kęstutis Navakas (b. 1964), a student of German expressionism, is similarly concerned with the historical landscape of culture which he often perceives as a relationship between open and enclosed inner spaces, a "prison house of language" and a larger one of feeling. His poetry is in a sense an intense effort at liberation from enclosure, marginality, solitude of the spirit, from a sort of room full of insects of the mind (to follow the image of one of his poems). Multiple references to Western culture and literature seem like so many guideposts on the way to belonging to the entire world, not just a small and tortured corner of it where he was born.

A much broader view is taken by Vytautas Bložė. In prefacing his collection *Polyphonies* (1981), Bložė declared that he seeks "to give meaning to the universality of human existence in various planes of space and time." He tries to accomplish this by structuring our sometimes murky consciousness of the flow of life into a poetic text. For this purpose, he not only creates a particular perspective, a place in the mind and outside of history, but also develops a statement about history as it flows through us by taking separate complexes of time, space, and events, discrete worlds of little inherent relevance to one another, and bringing them by poetic association into relationships that can speak to our understanding.

Tautvyda Marcinkevičiūtė (b. 1955) is also interested in the flow of time across memory and experience, and, at least in her book *Tauridė* (Tauris; 1990), she is one representative of the recent tendency toward a sort of nostalgia for classical antiquity, the golden myth of Greece, and the Greco-Judeo-Egyptian cradle of Western civilization. Those distant, sunny shores seem to provide some Lithuanian poets with a counterweight in the mind to the dimly lit, cold, and sorrowful landscapes of recent East European history. In this and other books, Marcinkevičiūtė is, by turns, an affectionate mother, a curious and even puckish observer of new and strange places, and a sardonic, sometimes quite shocking satirist of contemporary life. Throughout all this, she keeps her wit and carries lightly the sometimes considerable complexities of her poetic language.

Among other interesting poets, one could mention Antanas Jonynas (b. 1953), who seems to be writing in a language in which only a part of what is being said is actually articulated; the rest remains inside the mind but acts upon it and fills in the empty spaces to create a meaning, even though the realized words upon the surface may seem ungrammatical or even inarticulate. Nijolė Miliauskaitė (b. 1950) has the gift of sustaining the simplicity of reality, and its ordinariness, while yet informing it with an open and naïve and at the same time profound and touching poetic ambience. Kornelijus Platelis (b. 1951) is a poet of classical, philosophical bent, erudite, calm, and confidently in touch with the sources of his own talent.

Artūras Tereškinas (b. 1965) returns to the dark, contemplative mode of the earlier poetry of pain and scans the horizons of Western civilization as a panorama of ruin in body and spirit, particularly in his own little corner of this world, Lithuania. His verse is heavy with symbols and images of decay, abandonment, solitude, and death, all articulated with a bitter eloquence.

Quite a few young people are appearing on the scene, but at this date it is a little early to sort them out in some coherent fashion. On the whole, it seems that the gaping wound of horror is healing and the world is again presenting itself to the young poets as a place of welcome to their creative imagination.

There have not been any remarkable developments in recent Lithuanian drama. Many Western plays are presented on the stage, but the truly important original works belong to the somewhat older generation of Juozas Grušas or the later one of Justinas Marcinkevičius, Kazys Saja (b. 1932), and Juozas Glinskis (b. 1933). Most of the major playwrights in Lithuania between the two world wars wrote on historical themes, perhaps for the simple reason that contemporary life in this small republic was not particularly interesting whereas the consciousness of the nation's grand history was much needed to help establish a sense of meaningful identity. It is also true that Lithuania's heroic vision was a popular subject among the Polish Romantics, especially the poet and playwright Adam Mickiewicz (1798-1855), whose tales in verse *Grażyna* (1823) and *Konrad Wallenrod* (1828) spoke of legendary events in medieval Lithuanian past in an intense romantic spirit, while the verse drama *Dziady* (Forefathers' Eve; 1823) portrayed a much later time when both Poland and Lithuania were under Russian oppression. Mickiewicz could have inspired a number of Lithuanian authors, among them Vincas Krėvė-Mickevičius (1882–1954), also a major prose writer, who was especially interested in the formation of the medieval Lithuanian state in the play *Šarūnas* (1911), depicting the semilegendary ruler who first tried to unify the country. In his later play, *Skirgaila* (1925), Krėvė focused on another turbulent period in Lithuanian history, the fourteenth century, when Skirgaila, the son of Grand Duke Algirdas, played a major part in the internecine power struggles among Lithuanian rulers that were eventually resolved by the establishment of the Lithuanian-Polish commonwealth. The poet and playwright Balys Sruoga (1896–1947) wrote a series of plays on historical themes, the most famous of which is *Milžino paunksmė* (A Place Under the Shadow of the Giant; 1929–30). The giant is the Lithuanian Grand Duke Vytautas the Great (circa 1350–1430), under whose rule Lithuania reached the apex of its power, and the place under his shadow is Poland ruled by King Jogaila, who, under the influence of Polish nobles, tried successfully to prevent Vytautas from being crowned the king of Lithuania in his old age.

Juozas Grušas, the major postwar Lithuanian playwright in prose, followed in the tradition of Krėvė and Sruoga with *Barbora Radvilaitė* (Barbora of the Radziwills; 1971) and *Švitrigaila* (1976). The first play deals with a romantic and dramatic love story between the Polish-Lithuanian king Žygimantas Augustas (Sigismund Augustus, 1520–72) and Barbora, a member of the Radvila family, major Lithuanian magnates. After a long and painful politically motivated struggle against the Polish and Lithuanian nobility, Žygimantas finally succeeds in marrying Barbora and having her crowned queen. The second play treats the troubled time of struggle for succession to the leadership of Lithuania after the death of Vytautas. Grušas's most important historical play is *Herkus Mantas* (1957), about the powerful and devastating uprising in the thirteenth century by Herkus Mantas, a leader of the now-extinct Old Prussians, against the Teutonic conquerors of his land.

Grušas was also much concerned with changing value systems in Lithuania that were creating painful conflicts between generations even under the firmly autocratic Soviet rule. He expressed his concerns in the play *Meilė, džiazas ir velnias* (Love, Jazz, and the Devil; 1967). Rebellious youths in the city, children of the high Soviet bourgeoisie as well as of the poorest strata of the population, band together in direct confrontations with their parents, people who still believe, or pretend to believe, in old-fashioned principles of honesty, decency, and decorum. Grušas had to tread very carefully between his desire to bring into the open the problems of the changing society and his fear of Soviet censorship, or even punishment, for "slandering Soviet reality."

Justinas Marcinkevičius has walked this tightwire himself in much of his poetry as well as in his drama. The core of his contributions to the theater consists of three historical verse plays: *Mindaugas* (1968), *Katedra* (The Cathedral; 1971), and *Mažvydas* (1977). Unlike Adam Mickiewicz, the Lithuanian playwrights, including Marcinkevičius, did not so much celebrate the past as a romantic vision as ponder it, analyze it with the anxiety of heirs to a kingdom which fell apart for reasons that needed to be understood. This made *Mindaugas* a psychological play, a study of the strengths and weaknesses of this first Lithuanian king, who united the country in the thirteenth century by means of ruthless force and treachery that also sowed the seeds of his own violent death as well as the destruction of the kingdom in centuries to come. The very framework of the play is dialectical in that historical truth is shown to be a matter of debate between two chroniclers with opposite readings of events. Between them, Mindaugas appears as a tortured yet strong individual, eloquent to the point of irony and humor, and tragic in his inability to keep together the pieces of the world he has forced into being.

In *Katedra* the floodlights are on Laurynas Stuoka, an architect who rebuilt the Cathedral of Vilnius in the years 1782–94, when the Polish-Lithuanian commonwealth was on the threshold of total collapse after its third and last partition between Russia, Prussia, and Austria a year later. The central issue is the struggle of a talented and dedicated hero against the corruption of power-hungry high church and government officials who try to exploit him to increase their own power and glory. In both *Mindaugas* and *Katedra* one can trace a hidden thread of condemnation directed at the corrupt Soviet power that maintains itself by means of violence and exploits the people for self-aggrandizement. Yet, by attacking kings and feudal powers, Marcinkevičius could claim to be doing a proper Marxist reading of history. The third play, *Mažvydas,* describes the tribulations of Martynas Mažvydas, a Protestant pastor in Lithuania Minor (East Prussia) and the publisher of the first printed book in the Lithuanian language (1547), as he struggles with his recalcitrant parishioners who seem to him still beset by pagan beliefs and rituals, opposes the oppressive German power, and challenges the Catholic hierarchy in Russian-ruled Lithuania.

Juozas Glinskis (b. 1933) made his mark with the play *Grąsos namai* (The House of Dread; 1971). It is a piece akin to the West European "theater of cruelty," set in an insane asylum into which the powers that be have thrust Antanas Strazdas (1760–1833), a priest of maverick behavior but a brightly shining, cheerful poet to the simple people of his land, full of sunny love for nature and humanity. The madhouse he is in becomes a metaphor for our time, by implication especially in the Soviet domain, and it is a chaotic, dreadful place where all sense and nonsense blends into one foul brew of insanity.

One of the most interesting and prolific playwrights in Lithuania is Kazys Saja. Although his numerous, rather short plays are in essence dramas of social satire, he does enjoy spicing them up with humor based mostly on various grotesque inconsistencies in so-called ordinary life that his sharp eye is quick to catch. One of his best plays is *Pranašas Jona* (Jonah the Prophet; 1967), a "tragicomedy on biblical motifs," as the author calls it. In spite of a merciless storm tossing the boat and a huge leviathan of a whale threatening to swallow everyone, there is not much action in the play. Mostly we have oratory, elevated speeches by the helpless and angry prophet Jonah railing against the evils of this world. The particular evils quite clearly depict an oppressed society under a tyrant's thumb, making it easy to guess who the tyrant may be. However, it is not Jonah who gets swallowed by the whale, but Paschor, a biblical scholar. Paschor's head is so full of wisdom that even the whale cannot digest it, and he comes out in the end blind and deaf, enriched by a sad mock-wisdom of surrender to overwhelming power. This is that wisdom: "Perhaps it is a great honor for a weak creature, a bug, to blend with a large fish. You see, it's like this: the whale will squeeze you hard inside its stomach and let go, squeeze again and again let go—as long as you stay submissive and quiet."

With the coming of independence in 1991, when Lithuanian literature was finally freed from the belly of the whale, it was not in a submissive mood. A number of writers cried out fiercely, pointing to the wounds inflicted upon the nation, sometimes in a language as ugly as the evils they were protesting against. Some, like Gutauskas, remain obsessed with the memory of that terrible time, at least in part because in effect they are their own past, unlike someone who might have merely walked through it as a detached observer. As the first decade of freedom comes to its close, quite a few writers seem somewhat lost in the wide spaces newly opened for their creative imagination, casting about for some guideposts, a sense of direction, some notion of a purpose. A new word needs to be said, but it seems hard to know where to look for it. In a way, it was easier to write before, when there was oppression to be fought and censorship to be evaded with the help of the subtle literary devices of Aesopic language that brought the written text to a level of great complexity and at times great depth. Today, the daily run of life does not offer much of substance for the imagination; the country's achievements so far seem somewhat less than inspiring, and the evils it suffers are for the most part mere banalities—corruption, thievery, low standard of living, and the like. Neither the Lord's Angel nor the Prince of Evil seems very interested in this weary land.

On the other hand, this twilight of the soul may be exactly what the writers need to work things out deep within themselves, so they will be ready to meet the Word when it speaks to them again. Many of the writers may not even know that as they cast about for a topic, a feeling, a style, they are not really helpless or lost; rather, they are actually undergoing a process of healing and regeneration. Not everything is bleak even now—there are some very good things being written, in both poetry and prose. This gives one reason to think that the next literary decade in Lithuania will surely be much more interesting.

Rimvydas Šilbajoris, Spring 1998

The State of Estonian Literature Following the Reestablishment of Independence

Literature's emergence (in world culture) is a relative process wherein the logical and the predictable does not always function. This is even more so in the case of a "minor" literature, because the language itself erects an almost insuperable barrier. In the case of "major" literatures, not only do commercial and ideological mechanisms lend powerful support to literature's crossing of national frontiers via translation, but the effect of the latter is immeasurably broadened by the direct access to literature written in major international languages (English, Spanish, French, and, to a lesser extent, German, Russian, Italian, et cetera), as these are extensively taught and studied in all parts of the world. And yet, "minor" literatures are the overwhelming "silent majority" of world literature. From time to time—as in late 1996, when the Nobel Prize in Literature, in an almost total surprise, went to the Polish poet Wislawa Szymborska—the world realizes how little it really knows of its own literature.

Language barriers are seldom the only "walls" that separate cultures and people. They are strongly fortified by ideology and politics. Thus, in the former Soviet Union, all writers, regardless of their nationality and language, were labeled as "Soviet writers." As Russia was the dominant center of the "Soviet essence," any view from outside identified virtually everything coming from the big communist country with Russian values. I remember how, during my stay in Cuba in 1979–80, it was extremely difficult to explain to Cubans that, despite my being inevitably a *soviético,* I was not yet a *ruso* but rather an *estonio.*

Until the recent fall of the Soviet empire, few younger people in the West—not to speak of those in other parts of the world-knew that Estonia and Latvia were located not in Siberia but in Europe, in fact much nearer to Stockholm and Copenhagen than to Moscow. In other words, the imperial framework was largely successful in suppressing ethnic identifications. Therefore, the word *emerging,* as applied nowadays to smaller literatures of the former Soviet Union, is very fitting. But it also alludes to the fact that the "body" of these literatures, however hidden or "submerged," has always existed; it is only now that a part of that body is becoming visible in the eyes of the world.

All "borders," as the great Tartu-based patriarch of semiotics, the late Yuri Lotman, has taught, are dialogic in their essence. However, under a forcefully imposed ideological monologue such as that of the former Soviet regime, borders become especially ambivalent. They accumulate tensions and polysemies. Then, under certain favorable historical conditions—say, the spectacular fall of the Soviet Union—they can produce surprising "leaps." Because the Baltic countries constitute one of Europe's most significant border zones, it is no wonder that until recently many people in Estonia still believed in the miracle of Estonia's becoming the first among the former Soviet republics to make the leap to membership in the European Union and even in NATO by the end of this century.

I myself have always felt somewhat more skeptical than our politicians as regards economic developments. The geographic distance between the Finnish capital of Helsinki and the Estonian capital of Tallinn is only eighty kilometers, but the difference between average salaries in Finland and Estonia is still about seven times, to our disadvantage. One need not be a specialist in economic matters to surmise that such a gap cannot be easily "overleaped" by an annual growth of the national economy scarcely amounting to 3 or 4 percent.

In the cultural sphere, however, Lotman's theories do seem to work. As the Iron Curtain separating the West and the East has fallen, many of us, both in the West and in the East, have discovered with surprise that among the main candidates for the Nobel Prize in recent years, for instance, writers from Eastern Europe and former "socialist" countries like our Estonian novelist Jaan Kross, the Latvian poet Vizma Belševica, and the Albanian author Ismail Kadare have been frequently mentioned. And in 1996 the Polish poet Szymborska won the prize. In contrast, many of the acknowledged "giants" of Western literature—I am thinking, for instance, of the novelists Günter Grass, Carlos Fuentes, and Mario Vargas Llosa, among numerous others—at least for the time being, seem to have withdrawn modestly to the back rows of the Nobel "waiting room."

Thus, the wall has been dragged down, and literature too seems to be experiencing a kind of leveling. From Estonia, not only Jaan Kross (b. 1920) has stood out in recent years. In 1996 the poet and essayist Jaan Kaplinski (b. 1941) was also mentioned among the official candidates for the Nobel Prize, while the much younger Estonian writer Tõnu Õnnepalu (alias Emil Tode, b. 1962) has recently produced two highly successful novels, *Piiririik* (Border State; 1993) and *Hind* (The Price; 1995), which, under the postmodernsm label, have been and are being translated into several European languages. However, it would be totally wrong to imagine, as people in West sometimes still do, that the leveling "leap" has been achieved first and foremost thanks to the new liberties the writers of Eastern Europe now at last can enjoy. In fact, the leap, like any radical, dynamic development in literature, is the result of a cumulative creative process. No major literary work can be produced overnight, or in a cultural vacuum.

Let us first take the language, which is the most important tool of any writer and, basically, the identifying sign of most cultures. When the Soviet Union collapsed and massive Western tourism started to pour into the Baltic countries, one of the biggest surprises for visitors was the discovery that the Cyrillic alphabet was not used in these areas and that, besides, Estonians, Latvians, and Lithuanians could not understand one another's languages. (The language difference is especially exclusive in the case of the Estonians, who, unlike the Latvians and the Lithuanians, are ethnically not even Indo-Europeans, but instead, together with Finns, Hungarians, and other minorities, belong to the Finno-Ugric family of peoples and languages.) This has seriously disturbed the idea of a united Baltic state or federation, an illusion which, after our regaining of independence, was cherished by many Western politicians.

The next surprise was to discover that the local languages were widely used in all social spheres: schools, universities, newspapers, offices, radio and television, et cetera. In 1994, while speaking in Arenys del Mar near Barcelona—a small town where the Catalan poet Salvador Espriu spent his younger days-about parallels and differences in Catalan and Estonian literature, I felt pained when answering the question one of my listeners asked me: "What about the normalization of the Estonian language in Estonia?" The differences are great, indeed. Whereas in the first decades of Franco's Spain the Catalan language was suppressed by all available means, and even now, under democracy, the "normalization" of the Catalan language situation is a hot subject, sparking much controversy and polemical debate in Spanish society as a whole, in Estonia and the other Baltic states we could use our mother tongue even during the harshest years of Stalinist repression.

Preceding the Stalinist era, of course, were the twenty years of the Baltic states' first period of independence, between the two world wars (1919–39), when the Estonian language became deeply rooted in society. In the 1930s, for instance, about 100 newspapers and 200 magazines in the vernacular appeared. Above all, the written language seemed, and seems, to be important. Even nowadays, radio, television, and the electronic media alone can hardly hope to fulfill the function that newspapers, magazines, and books have served in the maintenance and development of the literary culture of a given nationality. In present-day Catalonia, for instance, only one major newspaper in Catalan appears (*Avui*, in Barcelona), and even that can scarcely compete with the major dailies in Spanish. In Estonia, by contrast, during the whole Soviet era three major Estonian daily newspapers appeared in Tallinn and one in Tartu.

Although there were setbacks in editing cultural magazines, compared with the first Estonian Republic, the main Estonian literary monthly magazine, *Looming* (Creation; founded 1923), has continued to appear almost without interruption down to the present day, while in 1958 another important monthly magazine, the decidedly more academic *Keel ja Kirjandus* (Language and Literature), was established in Tallinn. Especially since the 1970s, several other Estonian monthly cultural journals, like *Noorus* (Youth) and *Kultuur ja Elu* (Culture and Life), all published in Tallinn, have likewise contributed to the Estonian literary process by publishing translations of poetry and prose by both Estonian and international authors. In the years of Gorbachev's *perestroika,* the journal *Vikerkaar* (Rainbow; founded 1986) became an important addition to the abovementioned monthlies. *Vikerkaar's* aim has been to convey to the reader the aspirations of the younger generation, and it is at present the main channel for the dissemination of postmodernist and deconstructionist trends in world literature and philosophy.

Finally, on the eve of Estonia's new independence, Tartu, the second-largest Estonian city and the traditional center of Estonian culture, gradually began to recover its postwar role. The 1989 founding, in Tartu, of *Akadeemia,* a monthly journal of philosophy and literature, has had special significance. With its aim of publishing mainly philosophical essays translated from Western languages, it marked an energetic determination to fill the huge gap the Soviet era had left—because of its ideological taboos—in the reception of world philosophy. In the intervening eight years, *Akadeemia,* headed by one of the leading intellectuals in postwar Estonia, the poet and essayist Ain Kaalep (b. 1926), has published a long series of essays reflecting a broad spectrum of modern philosophy. (It is enough to mention such names as Heidegger, Ortega y Gasset, Russell, Berdyaev, Cioran, Popper, Dilthey, Huizinga, de Man, and Derrida, whose texts had previously been inaccessible in Estonian.) Along with modern philosophers from throughout the world, *Akadeemia* has never forgotten to offer its pages to a great intellectual whose home for more than forty years, until his recent death, was located only a few steps from the main building of Tartu University and *Akadeemia's* own office: Yuri M. Lotman (1922–93). The journal has thus provided a highly stimulating intellectual environment for the debuts of Estonia's own young thinkers and scholars.

In times of transition, literary magazines and cultural weeklies may serve a special function. When, in the initial chaos of Estonia's transition to independence—above all, between 1991 and 1994—all the former monopolist state-subsidized publishing houses underwent a profound crisis, reviews and magazines provided an invaluable channel for keeping literary spirit alive. Now, as the crisis in book publishing has been gradually overcome, literary magazines still play an important role in conveying to readers some aspects of literary creation—for instance, both Estonian verse and translated poetry—which otherwise could face the danger of extinction.

Luckily, the young Estonian state has until now understood the importance of cultural periodicals and has supported them financially. Therefore, all the abovementioned magazines have continued publication without interruption and with a regularity that almost certainly would be envied by editors of many Western literary reviews. If I add that our traditional cultural weekly *Kultuurileht* (Cultural Paper) has recently been rivaled by another privately financed cultural weekly, *Kultuurimaa* (Culture's Country), the reader may ask if the tiny nation of Estonia—with only a little more than one million inhabitants—does anything other than write and read literature. Well, yes, we do other things too, but it seems to be true that Estonian writers have at present more available space and opportunity for publishing their work than do most of their Western colleagues. All these periodicals also pay honoraria, which, however tiny they may be, nevertheless help Estonian writers survive.

Since I have mentioned my older university colleague Yuri Lotman, the man who above all has brought universal glory to venerable Tartu University in the postwar years of Brezhnevist stagnation, a few more words about him might be in order. He too was a potent factor in the silent preparation for the "leap" or "explosion" that, at least in the intellectual sense, followed the collapse of the USSR. In fact, the semiotic philosophy he gradually developed in Tartu was in radical opposition to the dogmatic preachings of communist ideology that for several decades reached us from Moscow. Tartu (like Estonia as a whole) was also a perfectly ambiguous "periphery"—to stay with Lotman's terminology—where such heretical teachings as his could survive.

A Russian Jew who had come to Tartu in 1950, Lotman was always highly respected in Estonia and, unlike Jewish intellectuals living in Russia, could enjoy at Tartu University a friendly atmosphere which, no doubt, aided his research work. Not long before his death, he confessed in an interview that Tartu had been for him the only place where he could imagine himself living and working. He became rooted in Estonian soil, his grandchildren are Estonians, and on the eve of Estonia's independence he publicly defended the Estonian cause against the accusations of "separatism" launched by Moscow's academicians—"mistaken friends," Lotman called them. However, the official grip could always be felt, even in peripheral Tartu. At the end of the 1960s, the KGB searched Lotman's home, and until the early 1980s, despite his worldwide fame, he was never allowed to travel abroad.

Lotman's closest followers, several of whom later formed the Tartu branch of the Tartu-Moscow school of semiotics, were almost exclusively his former students in the department of Russian philology (Igor Chernov, Peeter Torop, and Lotman's own eldest son Mikhail). The series of semiotic studies Lotman led, *Semiotika,* was published in Russian (the compulsory lingua franca of science in the former Soviet Union). Lotman could not write directly in Estonian, though he understood it. His first book to be translated into Estonian was his monographic study of Pushkin (1986), followed in 1990 by a selection of his writings already published in Russian and other languages.

Though Lotman was generally admired among Estonians, the language difference, one must admit, somewhat curbed local enthusiasm. It remains a fact that, coinciding with the apogee of Lotman's international recognition in the second half of the 1980s, the philosophers of Tartu University were rather more absorbed in Heidegger than in Lotman. Indirectly, of course, Lotman influenced a whole generation of Estonian intellectuals. Above all, he established a program of academic seriousness and openness that could not be overlooked by anyone. At his death, since he himself had been the inimitable quintessence of his program of study, Lotman left behind a "diaspora" rather than a "school" as his living heritage in Estonia's intellectual life.

In the basement of the "emerging" Estonian literature there is one more asset that has often been overlooked: namely, the translation of literary works. In his *Literatura catalana contemporània* the outstanding Catalan critic Joan Fuster makes a significant observation: in the first decades of Franco's dictatorship, translations from other Western languages were allowed considerably later than were publications of works by Catalonia's own classical authors. In other words, totalitarian regimes are especially vulnerable to works conveying a different ideology.

In Estonia too, until the 1960s, literary translations from modern Western literature were almost nonexistent. However, this gap was partly compensated by translations of classical authors of world literature whose humanism the official Marxist ideology liked to contrast with the decadence of Western modernism. Thus, Georg Meri—the father of the current president of Estonia, the writer Lennart Meri—undertook the translation of Shakespeare's complete works, a huge task that was successfully concluded in 1975. At that time, bulky anthologies of ancient Greek, Roman, medieval, and Renaissance literature were planned (published respectively in 1964, 1971, 1962 and 1984). The great advantage was that state publishing houses—in fact, there was only one publishing house issuing translations in Estonia—could afford to remunerate even verse translations well. The "golden age" in this respect was the 1980s, for on the one hand the ideological censorship had loosened its grasp and, on the other, state subsidies still strongly supported book publishing, including poetry. Among classical works of verse, Wolfram von Eschenbach's *Parzival* (1989), the Anglo-Saxon epic *Beowulf* (1990), Marlowe's *Tragedies* (1983), Quevedo's *Poems* (1987), and several fundamental works from the classical Oriental treasury (Lao-Tse, Confucius, the *Bhagavadgita,* et cetera) were all rendered into Estonian.

As for modern world literature, a real awakening began in the 1960s. Along with the hitherto monopolist publishing house Eesti Raamat (Estonian Book), the firm Loomingu Raamatukogu (Looming's Library) was founded. Formally it functioned—and has continued to do so until the present day—as a periodical magazine. In fact, what it published were books, though in paperback and of limited size. However, by using small fonts, it managed to squeeze between its covers such works as, for instance, Joyce's *Dubliners,* Bellow's *Mr. Sammler's Planet,* Faulkner's *As I Lay Dying,* Hesse's *Steppenwolf,* Woolf's *To the Lighthouse,* and Rulfo's *Pedro Páramo.* The new house's advantage, compared with Eesti Raamat, was the speed at which these books were issued.

Therefore, at some happy moments when the censors were taking a nap, Loomingu Raamatukogu managed to bring out books that otherwise, under longer preparation, would no doubt have been banned. Among these were, for instance, Camus's *Mythe de Sisyphe* (1972) and Kafka's *Prozeß* (1966) and short stories (1962). (It might sound amazing, but it is true: in 1986 a complete edition of Kafka's novels was banned; after angry protests by Estonian writers, the volume appeared a year later). Under the label of "Third World Literature"—which, along with classical works, were favored by the official ideology—Loomingu Raamatukogu published Jorge Luis Borge's intellectual prose much earlier than it appeared in Russian translation.

There was one more factor strongly enhancing the reception of high-level world literature in Estonia: the absence of mass literature. It is true that Russian authors, like their Western counterparts, produced police and spy novels in great quantities, but these had relatively limited circulation among Estonian readers. Western mass literature, on the other hand, was happily despised by the official ideological establishment. Following the reinstitution of our independence, these defense mechanisms have ceased to function. The only remaining comfort is that we Estonians, as a nation, are too tiny to produce our own mass literature.

I could list a large number of leading twentieth-century Western writers whose work until 1990 was known in book translations published in Soviet Estonia: T. S. Eliot, García Lorca, Proust, Joyce, Kafka, Woolf, Hesse, Pirandello, Cavafy, Pessoa, Artaud, Eluard, Camus, Sartre, Beckett, Aleixandre, Espriu, Faulkner, Borges, Elytis, Dylan Thomas, Canetti, Kawabata, Bellow, Golding, Singer, Paz, Cela, García Márquez, Vargas Llosa, Fuentes—and so on. Minor samples from and selections of many others could be found in literary magazines and anthologies. My firm opinion is that translated literature becomes a part of one's "own" literature. It is quite possible that major twentieth-century works of world literature in some of our best translations (e.g., the novels of Faulkner or *Cien años de soledad* by García Márquez) may have enriched our literary language to a greater extent than has any average Estonian novel.

To this one could add that the main epochs and phenomena of Western literary history have always been taught at Estonian universities, while at least for the last two decades of the Soviet era there were only very lax controls on what these programs comprised. In fact, in my own university lectures on twentieth-century literature, Joyce, Proust, Kafka, Camus, and Sartre have always been present, and I do not remember any pressure from above to exclude them. All our Estonian high-school students are given at least one course in world literature, which should make them aware of the ancient epics, Dante, Shakespeare, Cervantes, Molière, and Goethe, as well as a selection of modern authors.

Over two decades, other fertile impulses reached Estonia from outside. For example, Ivar Ivask (1927–92), the émigré Estonian-Latvian poet and longtime editor of *Books Abroad / World Literature Today,* generously provided us with books by modern world authors and, on the other hand, had the works of Baltic writers, both in the occupied home countries and in exile, regularly reviewed in this prestigious magazine.

All the above should prove that the "wall" between the West and the Baltic countries, intellectually, was not so high as it has sometimes been imagined. We may even ask if, following the reestablishment of Baltic independence, any "leaps" have really taken place, or whether we have simply stepped into the European cultural context with the naturalness of old Europeans who for some reason have been kept behind a locked ideological door for nearly half a century. However, I, for one, believe there is room for "leaps" in Estonian literature following the reintroduction of independence, though not in the sense of leaping to what has already been done in Western literature. The leap, supported both by our own recent cultural and social experience and by the new philosophical openness, should rather conduce to creating a new Estonian literature. There are signs that this may happen. A certain dynamic state in philosophy has often been a precondition for an "explosion" in literature. And as I have tried to show, there is a notably expanding philosophic and esthetic horizon in current Estonian letters.

It is true that a writer's life is not easy these days. However, by 1995, the initial chaos of the transition had been gradually replaced by a situation in which our bookshops had once again become filled with books and people. Though book prices are high and both editors and consumers grumble, it is almost certain that no book of value remains unpublished in today's Estonia.

Much relief has been provided by a cultural foundation which has its predecessor in the first Estonian Republic and is called Eesti Kultuurkapital (Estonian Cultural Capital). This firm obtains through state appropriations its financial share of taxes on several human vices: alcohol 3 percent, tobacco 3 percent, and gambling 30 percent. The fund is designed first and foremost to help writers and artists and to stimulate cultural life as a whole. Thus, the literary council of Estonian Cultural Capital has restored the Annual Prizes in Estonian Literature, which, due to money shortages, disappeared during the first years of the transition. Estonian Cultural Capital strongly backs book publishing (and almost every Estonian book, especially poetry, needs support nowadays). It awards writers individual "creative grants" to enable them to pay their rent and for the heating of their homes and generally to reduce their depression. It gives writers travel money so that they may see other parts of the world and become inspired. It provides some additional funding to cultural and literary magazines and weeklies so that they may pay their authors. Periodically, the literary council of the foundation selects a limited number of talented and promising writers to receive more substantial grants of one or two full years' duration—at a level somewhat more than the average monthly salary of their fellow citizens. All literary events, conferences, colloquiua, and the like are subsidized by the foundation as well.

Besides Estonian Cultural Capital, several other foundations have also been useful in the encouragement and promotion of Estonian literature. The Open Estonia Foundation, generously financed by the American-Hungarian philanthropist George Soros, is at present supporting a larger project of publishing translations of significant works of philosophy. The first authors represented in this series have been Seneca, Aristotle, Derrida, Nietzsche, Russell, Camus, and Heidegger. Unamuno's principal essay, *Del sentimiento trágico,* is the most recent addition.

In Tartu's cultural renaissance, besides the powerful activity of the magazine *Akadeemia,* the founding of the publishing house Ilmamaa and especially its majestic project "The History of Estonian Thought" deserves mention. With the support of several foundations and also of Estonian municipal governments, it aims at gathering and editing, in more than a hundred volumes, everything of value that Estonian essayists, thinkers, and scholars, both in the past and in more recent times, have produced (a dozen bulky volumes have already been published in the first three years, 1995–97).

On the other hand, as regards contacts with the world, the recently founded Estonian Association of Comparative Literature, with its center at Tartu University, has begun publishing a tetralingual annual magazine, *Interlitteraria,* and in 1996 organized in Tartu its first international conference (on the language of the grotesque). In Tallinn, the Estonian Institute (founded by the current president of Estonia, the writer and anthropologist Lennart Meri) has published since 1995, twice a year, the *Estonian Literary Magazine,* a paper in English that intends to outline regularly the main features in contemporary Estonian literature. (By the way, it can also be read on the Internet at www.ee.einst/literary/.)

What about Estonian writers themselves in this age of new liberties? As Estonian intellectuals had been the nucleus of the silent opposition to Moscow's totalitarian rule in the Soviet years, so do many now find themselves actively involved in politics. Lennart Meri (b. 1929) was Estonia's first ambassador to Finland, then foreign minister, and two years ago was elected to his second term as the country's president. Several leading writers, including Jaan Kross, Jaan Kaplinski, Arvo Valton (b. 1935), and Paul-Eerik Rummo (b. 1942), have been members of parliament. The poet Rummo even led for a while the small Liberal-Democratic Party and served as the country's minister of culture.

Some have been state functionaries. Tõnu Õnnepalu worked at the Estonian Foreign Ministry, later describing his bureaucratic job with sarcasm and irony in his second successful novel, *Hind* (The Price; 1995). Mihkel Mutt (b. 1953) too has been inspired by his position as chief of the information bureau of the Foreign Ministry. In his *Rahvusvaheline mees* (The International Man; 1994) he amicably parodies his former chief, Lennart Meri, and at the same time offers a wittily grotesque depiction of the building of the new Estonian Republic amid the social chaos of the transition years and the threats of being dragged anew into the lap of the giant neighbor to the east.

By the fifth year of independence, however, nearly everybody had returned from politics and taken up the pen again. To maintain themselves (or their families), many have had to work for newspapers. But despite everything, three generations of Estonian writers—the Estonian Writers Union, by the way, has about two hundred members—go on toiling hard, both to create and to survive. The best known internationally, from these three generations, are respectively Jaan Kross (whose most important historical novels have been translated into nearly all the major Western languages), Jaan Kaplinski (an outspoken critic of antidemocratic tendencies in the new society, who has recently had his fourth book of poems published in English), and the "postmodern" Tõnu Õnnepalu. The rest have been less fortunate in finding publishers abroad, though there is at present some notable international activity around Estonian literature, as many younger literary people in the West have shown an interest in our language and literature and are willing to take up the job of translation.

Recently there has been some friction between the younger and the older generation of Estonian writers. To wit, an extrovert "ethnofuturist" poet has disseminated over the Internet a list of "Soviet Estonian writers"—in his own definition, a poem—in which, introducing camp attitudes, he mockingly indulges in calling his older colleagues names, including many whose participation in the oppositional culture during the Soviet era was highly meritorious. Unfortunately, not everyone interpreted the gesture as merely a childish whim.

Despite these controversies, my guess is that Estonian literature, whether by a "leap" or by a natural "walk" over ever firmer philosophical soil, will meet the twenty-first century in a condition of openness, capable of carrying forward both historical awareness and a strong spirit of renovation.

Jüri Talvet, Spring 1998

DENMARK

Ole Hyltoft and the Neorealistic Trends in Contemporary Danish Literature

Life is so many-sided: poetic, criminal, full of love, taunting.

■ OLE HYLTOFT

When Klaus Rifbjerg (see BA 49:1, pp. 25–28), the writer largely responsible for the growth of modernist poetry in Danish literature during the 1960s, published his collection *Amagerdigte* (Amager Poems) in 1965, it became evident that a reaction against this experimental and hermetic mode of writing—a mode actually introduced by Rifbjerg himself—had begun. In 1961 his controversial poem *Camouflage* had caused bewilderment and indignation. The public had fastened upon the complete lack of punctuation and overlooked the fact that the work was a grandiose, almost ecstatic yet artistically structured attempt to conquer reality through a voyage into the realm of the subconscious. Rifbjerg used an associative technique, playing with words and putting them into unexpected combinations in a fragmented syntax. With *Amagerdigte* reality, the banal monotony of the author's childhood in a suburb of Copenhagen, is rendered in a reportorial and matter-of-fact style. The critics correctly labeled the volume an example of a neorealistic or neo-simplistic trend in Danish literature.

Other lyrical poets followed suit, but it was particularly in prose writing that the reaction against exclusive modernism manifested itself. The major representatives of modernism during the late 1950s had been Villy Sørensen and Peter Seeberg. Sørensen's writings consisted of philosophical analyses of modern man's alienation and isolation. He used the form of allegorical tales inspired by Kafka and Isak Dinesen. Seeberg dealt with the same theme but employed a more absurdist and symbolic approach in the tradition of Beckett and Ionesco. During the early 1960s the French *nouveau roman,* characterized by both an absence of the traditional plot and a sharply defined distinction between the narrator and the protagonists of the text, found two major Danish representatives: Ulla Ryum and especially Svend Åge Madsen. One of the dominant themes in Ryum's writing is the unbridgeable gap between human beings, described in a language full of ambiguity and reminiscent of the mood and method found in the works of Djuna Barnes. Madsen, on the other hand, employs a deliberately monotonous and image-free language in order to explain his relativistic view of reality as a fictional creation completely dependent upon the ideas of a given author.

As had been the case with the lyrical poetry, this experimental, partly abstract prose was succeeded by a much more factual and more easily accessible style of writing after 1965. The forerunner had been Thorkild Hansen, whose first published documentaries, *Det lykkelige Arabien* (1962; translated as *Arabia Felix,* 1964) and *Jens Munk* (1965; translated as *The Way to Hudson Bay,* 1970), were based on historical material. *Arabia Felix* tells of an eighteenth-century Danish expedition to the Arabian peninsula and has as its theme the estrangement of human beings who have been torn away from their cultural milieu. *The Way to Hudson Bay* deals

with a seaman and his bold but unsuccessful attempt to find the Northwest Passage to India and China. Time and again, however, Hansen oversteps the bounds of objective reporting, particularly in his subjective style and his use of inner monologue and literary leitmotivs. It is these features that raise his writing to the level of brilliant realistic fiction.

This neorealism with its more traditional narrative technique, based on Thorkild Hansen, on various Swedish models and on Mary McCarthy's novel *The Group,* not only influenced a number of already established modernist writers such as Rifbjerg, but also created a new literary school. The complete break-through took place with the works of Anders Bodelsen, Christian Kampmann and Henrik Stangerup. Bodelsen became the most popular and productive of the neorealist generation. His books are characterized by a detached narrative tone and considerable formal skill. These features emerge clearly in *Drivhuset* (The Greenhouse; 1965), whose fourteen mystery stories and detailed portrayals of the Danish welfare state announce the two essential elements of his subsequent works. The writings of Kampmann and Stangerup are likewise composed of critical studies of the middle-class way of life, but their psychological analyses are more acute. Stangerup, in particular, focuses on the social and political problems caused by a welfare society, in which he sees threatening tendencies of guardianship and totalitarianism.

What these three authors lack, especially Bodelsen and Kampmann, is the sharp political satire which can be found in the works of a fourth and somewhat younger writer, Ole Hyltoft (b. 1940). Prior to his first novel in 1970 he had already established prominence in the public debate as a critic and journalist, the secretary to various ministers of cultural affairs and, above all, since 1970 as the influential head of the Cultural Commission of the Danish Social Democratic Party. The view of man and society which underlies Hyltoft's fictional writing was formed precisely during these years and received its initial treatment in the essay collection *Tør du være fri?* (Do You Dare to Be Free; 1968) and the pamphlet *Good Day Sunshine* (1969), a view further expanded in the volume *Tør du være med?* (Do You Dare to Come Along; 1974).

Against the backdrop of the Vietnam War, the Soviet occupation of Czechoslovakia and the international student rebellion Hyltoft analyzes the two major ideologies, Marxism and capitalism. Both are rejected as social systems which place human well-being and growth second to a constant expansion of production. Lenin and Marcuse are attacked because of their endorsement of political violence, and capitalist society is criticized for its commercialism and cutthroat competitive spirit:

"Achievements give external power. Fine exams, successful businesses and a great output of work give us external status which can soothe our fear of our own inadequacy. In societies based on achievement you can buy personal security through power. But at the same time the lack of power inspires us with dread." This dread and its causes can only be eliminated in a future society, a "deeply democratic society of people with a social conscience. That is to say people who feel uncomfortable when others suffer and who do not accept inequalities which grow in a class system."[1]

An episode in Hyltoft's novel "The Vanquished" (see below) describes the Danish counterpart to the student rebellions of the late 1960s with a mixture of sarcasm and sympathy—sarcasm because the rebellion gets out of touch with reality, sympathy because here Hyltoft finds the beginnings to that peaceful revolution which eventually can bring about his own social utopia. The process which leads to a human, undogmatic socialism rests on a realization that we are all different. A common fundamental feature, however, is our need for love and affection. This trait lies at the base of Hyltoft's view of man, his emphasis upon love as a transforming and liberating force which creates a human fellowship: "To love is to give yourself to another person. And in the beloved person you include everybody else. To love is the greatest openness a human being can attain, and it constitutes the most intensive experience of man's collective situation."[2]

The artistic experience, specifically, is able to release as well as express this altruistic urge: "In modern-day life, which threatens to become monotonous, people occasionally need to move in leaps, to change dramatically. In art we find a dramatic change which can help many attain psychological balance in an everyday life which is much too trite" (*TD*, 116). A logical extension of this view is Hyltoft's attack on the overcrowded and polluted metropolis, which in spite of its crowd of people only furthers anonymity and isolation. Anticipating today's ecological movements, he conjures up a vision of a livable city which incorporates nature and is built around our need for fellowship.

> We could give our cities colorful squares, imaginative playgrounds, botanical gardens. We could turn the coastlines near our cities into green recreational areas with marinas and woods stretching down to the beach. Here we could stroll without being hindered by signs reading Private and No Admittance, without being chased by cars and engines. Here we could make love, here we could experience the changing of the seasons, the stormy waves during the fall, the ice of the winter, and here we could swim during the summer in an ocean which is clean.

Is this vision, which emerges again in "The Vanquished," an impractical and naïve utopia when measured with the yardstick of today's reality? It is, after all, consistent with that humanist view of society which Hyltoft defends publicly both as a debater and writer. He believes that the role of the artist is to point ahead toward new possibilities. His essays—which were instrumental in bringing the social and political debate of the 1970s beyond its narrow, dogmatic Marxist orientation—not only form the necessary theoretical basis for his fictional works, but anticipate them thematically as well. Through his fiction Hyltoft's ideas take on a more tangible form, gaining the necessary credibility and cogency as they are measured against the present state of egotism, corruption and violence.

Hyltoft's first novel *Hvis lille pige er du?* (Whose Little Girl Are You; 1970), contains an extraordinarily stringent depiction of contemporary life in milieus ranging from the Danish State Department to embassy and architecture circles in New York. The satire thus is aimed both at segments of the American way of life, exemplified by brilliant snapshots from New York that are based on the author's observations during a study trip in 1962, and at the bourgeois milieu of government officials in Copenhagen. At times the book can be read as a roman à clef with some indiscreet portraits of easily identifiable cabinet ministers; but basically it is a crime novel, a genre to which Hyltoft returns in later works, often in combination with elements from the international hard-boiled-spy story. An official at the State Department, Anker Karlsen, is suddenly torn from a quiet daily routine into a world of hot pursuits, assaults and attempted murder. The action starts with the theft of Karlsen's dissertation manuscript, which was to have aided his advancement in the Foreign Service. The suspect is a conceited and ambitious colleague who, like Karlsen, lives under constant pressure to advance in his career; both are victims of social constraint. This message takes priority over the development of the rather simple plot, which reaches an acceptable if not quite unexpected solution.

Hyltoft's next novel, *Hjertet sidder til venstre* (The Heart Is Situated on the Left Side; 1973), is more complex and contains stronger character delineation. The well-established middle-class man with vague revolutionary sympathies and the younger, lower-class girl with whom he falls in love are characters previously sketched in Hyltoft's first novel. Here they are expanded into two brilliantly executed psychological portraits and become an integral part of the book's political plot. Niels Jensen is a deputy principal and moderate left-wing pragmatist who is able to maintain a balance between progressive pedagogues and conservative officials. Ditte, a vocational-college student, on the other hand, is a revolutionary PLO activist whose heart is situated so far to the left that she places her uncompromising political commitment ahead of her love for Niels. She forces him to steal secret documents during a dangerous mission to East Germany, and when in the last chapter she emerges as a skyjacker she is even willing to sacrifice him in her fight against Israel; but she herself is killed instead. Where does Niels stand in this political battle? Is he able to follow Ditte of his own free will? Or has he allowed himself to be totally manipulated? Perhaps even Ditte is only a pawn in a bigger, impenetrable scheme. The author gives no clear answers in this simultaneously ironic and highly serious look at the conflict-filled impact of love, social roles and political activities in our lives.

With pungent wit Hyltoft records the jargon of left-wing pseudo-intellectuals, particularly the self-righteous pedagogues surrounding Niels whose deceptive emancipation only masks intolerance and pharisaism. This exposé of fashionable trends becomes the main purpose of the short-story collection *Revolutionens fortrop* (The Vanguard of Revolution; 1975), one of the most hilarious political satires in modern Danish literature. The volume focuses on corruption and hypocrisy among leftist intellectuals, the opportunistic yes-people as well as the more dogmatic Marxists. Both groups manipulate their surroundings. They make up "the vanguard of revolution," but they are unable to break away from their own bourgeois background, using revolutionary clichés and the working class only as false fronts for their efforts to further their own careers. A young proletarian writer, for example, expresses his—and the author's—disgust: "You probably think that all your double-dealing has a higher meaning. But do you know what that higher meaning is called? Be smart, smart, smart—and give the lower classes the shaft. That is precisely what it is called! You may be the vanguard of revolution, but I prefer to belong to the rear guard."[3]

It is crucial to be up-to-date not only in politics but also in the realm of sexuality. Hyltoft illustrates this in two subdued, semi-tragic stories dealing with the generation gap and involving the futile attempt of a middle-aged couple to live up to the sexual emancipation of their daughter. We meet these characters and others in various combinations throughout the seven texts contained in the volume. In this way Hyltoft succeeds in creating a coherent and universal picture of his own time, an age that is permeated with self-delusion and superficiality and, as a consequence, with insecurity and dread.

Insecurity—a prominent feature of Hyltoft's protagonists—also characterizes Henning in the novel *Hvem er angst for den stygge ulv?* (Who's Afraid of the Bad Wolf; 1976). He too comes from a middle-class milieu. Once a successful Volkswagen salesman, he now sees his position threatened by the more popular Japanese cars. However, Henning's fight for his professional career only constitutes the background for his numerous attempts at liberating himself, which is the true subject of Hyltoft's book: a liberation from his own milieu, from the conventions of society and, finally, from the great multinational firms. All these opponents are symbolized in the "bad wolf" of the title. But whereas Henning's first rebellion—an affair with a militant feminist—succeeds, his role slowly changes through a number of confrontations with the "wolves." He evolves almost imperceptibly from manipulator to manipulated in a manner similar to that seen in "The Heart Is Situated on the Left Side."

In his writings Hyltoft frequently shifts in the same volume from a local, provincial milieu—residential areas north of Copenhagen—to more cosmopolitan surroundings. The two-volume novel *De befriede* and *De besejrede* (The Liberated; The Vanquished; both 1979), on the other hand, is a poetic declaration of love for Copenhagen and constitutes a move away from pure realism toward a more visionary outlook. The city not only provides the setting of the work, but even symbolizes the mental state and spiritual development of the principal character, Kim. "The Liberated" begins in 1945 and describes the expectations of the postwar generation, its dreams and hopes for a new, changed society. However, through Kim's eyes we see how envy and the quest for power lurk behind the optimistic surface. The idealistic plans for a "new and purified Denmark" shared by a group of young artists, upper-class business students and members of the working class turn out to be illusory. This revelation is symbolized in a subplot involving the murder of one member of the group, the poet Ib, who has preached the gospel of all-encompassing love—a demand which none of the characters can live up to. Was this why Ib had to die?

The answer is in the affirmative and is demonstrated in the second part, which takes place between 1968 and 1979, the period of the Vietnam War, the student rebellion and budding feminism. Here Hyltoft once again draws on his extensive knowledge of contemporary Danish society and his impressive insight into the most typical trends. His narrative talent unfolds in both a satirical and—a new development in his writing—a highly imaginative direction. He depicts the professional success which the artists and academics of the group have now achieved, often through corruption and compromise. But true success as a human being is reached only by the outsider Kim, who abandons a promising career as a business executive in order to become a street musician. Hyltoft's entire sympathy is focused on Kim's growing doubts about the economic boom of the 1960s and his longing "to realize himself." The children of Kim and his friends have now become young revolutionaries. To some extent Kim (and therefore Hyltoft) feels solidarity with their goal of changing society, but at the same time he must warn them sternly against the same egotism and narrow-mindedness which turned their parents into "the vanquished."

Neither generation, therefore, has been able to bring about the revolution of love which is Ib's (and Hyltoft's) message. Neither economic nor political means and solutions suffice, but this revolution is nevertheless possible, as is demonstrated in one crucial scene: a festival which, characteristically enough, takes place at the Academy of Arts. Kim participates in this fantasy, an experience of love and an almost surrealistic orgy of color, sound and form which furthers his growing self-realization and his final liberation from any social attachments. Thus art and love alone comprise the forces which are able to change and ennoble man, a step toward that universal sense of humanity which was suggested in Hyltoft's previous books and here is realized not only in Kim but also in the author's vision of a new Copenhagen, a city in which all are allowed to unfold and fulfill their creative talents. Significantly, this vision, described on the final pages of the novel, will become a reality through Kim's son, who has been elected Commissioner of City Planning.

Whereas Hyltoft's two-volume 1979 novel is simultaneously an *Entwicklungsroman,* an exquisite prose hymn to Copenhagen and a glorification of art and love, his next novel, *Byggekongen* (The Construction King; 1981), resumes the unveiling of human corruption and hypocrisy. Although Hyltoft returns to a basically realistic technique, he also blends lyrical elements into his narration, as in his previous work. Moreover, the tenor of these passages is the same as before: reflections about art and love as life-renewing forces, symbolized by seasonal changes in a number of exquisite nature scenes. Hyltoft thereby adds a spiritual and philosophical dimension to his novel. Combining satire, character portraits and milieu descriptions, the work emerges not as a roman à clef, as suggested by most critics, but as a timeless epic about the rise and fall of human pride and vanity.

The milieu is that of wealth and big business. Frans, a social upstart, attempts through various risky transactions to rise from local contractor to head of a multinational computer empire. His success seems due in part to his wife's family connections with the world of high finance and with the Danish royal house. This ascent, however, is accompanied by an inner decline, as Frans increasingly becomes the victim of his own ruthless manipulations—a favorite theme in Hyltoft's writings. The protagonists's misanthropy peaks when finally, driven by his ambitions, he sacrifices his loyal secretary Annemette and thereby isolates himself completely. The novel is permeated with death symbols, and Hyltoft's outlook is indeed pessimistic. Yet his confidence in the positive prevails. Love, represented by Annemette, as well as art, represented by the painter Tonni, the enfant terrible of the book and a counterpart to the artists in Hyltoft's 1979 novel, are victorious.

Hyltoft's latest work, the short-story collection *Tante Isidora* (Aunt Isidora; 1982), again focuses on human compassion. With subtle irony a number of human follies—snobbishness, vanity and haughtiness—are unveiled, but without the satirical attacks which frequently characterize the earlier writings. Some of the texts are permeated with pure slapstick effects, but on the whole Hyltoft emerges as a master of suggestion. Together with a delicately sustained balance between the comic and the tragic, this significant feature makes several of the short stories here obvious choices for any anthology of modern Danish prose. A common trait in Hyltoft's protagonists is the fact that they have all passed the middle stage of life and are either seeking a place in today's world or attempting to live in the past. But—and this is one of the book's points—more or less visible threads connect their childhood with the present. Life cannot be split up in isolated parts but must be accepted as an entity.

In spite of their oddities and flaws Hyltoft embraces his characters with love and compassion. In its subtlety his humanism emerges more strongly than ever before. Critical yet always with positive solutions and without any kind of ideological or moral self-righteousness, Ole Hyltoft has carved out a unique position in contemporary Danish literature.

Sven H. Rossel, Winter 1983

[1] Ole Hyltoft, *Good Day Sunshine,* Copenhagen, 1969, pp. 16, 18. All translations are my own.

[2] Ole Hyltoft, *Tør du være fri?,* Copenhagen, 1968, p. 43. Subsequent citations use the abbreviations *TD.*

[3] Ole Hyltoft, *Revolutionens fortrop,* Copenhagen, Fremad, 1975, p. 108.

FINLAND

Finland and World Literature

When we speak of Finland and world literature, we must remember certain general background factors.

The first of these is geographical and historical. Finland is one of the Scandinavian countries, the easternmost one, and her culture and social system reflect her Western heritage. To start with, she was for over 600 years a part of Sweden. Then in 1809 Finland became a part of the Russian empire—a surprisingly autonomous part, with many privileges. In 1917 she broke off from Russia and has since been an independent state. Her position has not been without its problems, especially during World War II and the immediate postwar years, but the fact remains that Finland is the only country among those that became independent after World War I to preserve its democratic social system.

The second factor is linguistic. Finland has two official languages: Finnish and Swedish. For a long time Swedish was the language of the cultured classes and the language of officialdom; today it is the first language of about 7 percent of the population, whose rights are guaranteed by very liberal legislation. A considerable volume of Swedish-language literature is still published in Finland (see *WLT* 54:1, pp. 15–20, 47–50 and 66); there are also a good number of well-edited Swedish-language newspapers, one Swedish-language university and many Swedish-language theatres. In structure, vocabulary and syntax the Finnish language is completely different from Swedish or Russian; it is remotely related to Hungarian, but no Finn can understand Hungarian without learning it properly. The only really close language is Estonian, which is spoken in Soviet Estonia (official name: the Estonian Soviet Socialist Republic), located on the southern shore of the Gulf of Finland.

The third factor is cultural. Although the first Finnish-language books were published as early as the mid-sixteenth century, and although a university was founded in Turku (Åbo in Swedish) back in 1640, literature proper—in the sense of belles lettres—did not begin to flourish until the end of the eighteenth century and the beginning of the nineteenth. Literature, especially poetry, did appear in Finland before that, even in many languages—not only in Swedish and Finnish, but also in Latin, Greek and even Hebrew—along with religious texts. But the volume was small and the scope of the subject matter narrow. For this reason I shall speak only very briefly about the oldest phase of our literature, which arouses more historical and philological than esthetic interest.

■ ■ ■

Medieval Finland was a Catholic country. This meant that the leading language of culture was Latin. The bishops in the country—who were, almost without exception, of Finnish birth—received their theological training in the great European universities, chiefly in France,

Italy and Germany. With the Reformation at the beginning of the sixteenth century, Germany became established as the place of learning for many, and the first Lutheran bishop of Finland (and translator of the New Testament into Finnish, in 1548), Mikael Agricola, studied under Melanchton and was probably also acquainted with Martin Luther. Most of Agricola's work is in the form of translations into Finnish, but the handful of texts that he himself wrote show that he knew the leading authors of his time. The same can be said of Bishop Ericus Erici (Sorolainen), a learned writer of sermons at the beginning of the seventeenth century: he cites some eighty philosophers and writers, most of them from ancient times.

In the following century, the eighteenth, French influence can also be seen; many of the libraries in country manors contained the works of French philosophers of the Enlightenment. At the end of the century Turku University flourished anew, thanks in particular to one of its professors, Henrik Gabriel Porthan. Porthan, who wrote mostly in Latin, was a learned man: he knew the German science of the time, and he was interested in English poetry: Edward Young's "Night Thoughts" and Macpherson's "Songs of Ossian," for example, were familiar in Turku.

Porthan was thus the most important representative of the Age of Enlightenment in Finland, but he is also connected with the early romantics. Between 1766 and 1778 he published a general introduction in Latin to Finnish folk poetry, *Dissertatio de poësi Fennica*. He found the subject independently, but at the same time the mainstream of interest in folk poetry was appearing elsewhere in Europe, with Johann Gottfried von Herder as its chief representative. Porthan was acquainted with Herder's ideas, and to some extent adopted them in his later work. The influence of these two scholars continued to be felt in the next century, leading to a broad interest in Finnish folk poetry and indirectly to the birth of a national epic, Elias Lönnrot's *Kalevala*. At this stage the relation between Finnish literature and world literature becomes, for the first time, really interesting.

Porthan died in 1804, three months later than Herder and four years before the outbreak of war between Sweden and Russia, the war which led to Finland's coming under Russian rule. The death of Porthan and, even more, the political upheaval changed the cultural atmosphere in Finland. A little group of scholars in Turku, known as the Turku or Åbo Romantics, drew their own conclusions from what had happened, and in their newspaper and albums they expressed their stand cautiously but clearly: Finland must now find her own way. This meant exploring the Finnish indigenous culture and consciously developing it—in other words, consolidating Finland's own cultural identity.

A little before the Turku Romantics began to proclaim their program, two young students had been attracted by Herder's ideas. These schoolmates, Abraham Poppius and Anders Johan Sjögren, had studied Herder's periodical, *Adrastea,* and solemnly agreed in 1812 to begin to collect old Finnish poetry. Poppius became a poet writing in Finnish, and Sjögren a learned folklorist and academician in St. Petersburg; but neither of them was yet the man who would carry the work begun to its conclusion. I mention them only to indicate how stimulating Herder's direct influence could be at that time.

Others had been interested in and had collected Finnish folk poetry too: for example, the German Hans Rudolf von Schröter, who published a bilingual anthology of Finnish folk poems, *Finnische Runen,* in Uppsala in 1819. Other publications of Finnish folk poetry also appeared around the same time. These would have remained disconnected efforts, however, had there not appeared a man who devoted all his energies to collecting folk poetry: Elias Lönnrot, the compiler of the *Kalevala.*

Concerning the *Kalevala*—which appeared for the first time in 1835–36, the final version in 1849—there exist many misconceptions. Romantic fancy brands it as a national epic given anonymous birth in the depths of the forest and there preserved in separate fragments until Lönnrot discovered and reconstructed it. This fancy is based on two fundamental errors. In the first place, no extensive, coherent epic ever existed, in all likelihood; there were only separate clusters of poems— connected with each other, it is true. Second, Lönnrot did not reconstruct the epic; he *constructed* it, using material he obtained from rune singers. In short, one might say that the material of the *Kalevala* is authentic folk poetry; but as an epic, a work of art, it was composed and executed by Lönnrot. The coherent plot, the order of events, the figures characterized, the national symbolism embodied in the text—all this is Lönnrot's work. The final form of the *Kalevala* was also influenced by international models: the epics of ancient times, European narrative poems and the epic theories of the day, and especially the ideas of the German Fr. A. Wolff at the end of the eighteenth century.

The *Kalevala* is one example of how a literary work can continue its life and its impact far into the future. It is one of the few Finnish books that has managed to produce international feedback: it has been translated into many languages—the number so far is at least forty to fifty, and there are in addition innumerable adapta-

tions, imitations, abridgments, et cetera—and thus has given stimuli to other literatures. At the moment, Third World nations seeking their cultural identity are especially interested in the *Kalevala,* for this work was one of the creators and keystones of Finnish cultural identity. Its influence in the home country has been enormous. I shall return to its role later, in connection with what came to be known as national neoromanticism.

The *Kalevala* is also a good example of how a theoretical impulse from abroad can be fruitfully modified in the Finnish cultural sphere and produce a completely original result. A similar phenomenon can be observed in other literatures of the time. The production of those Finland-Swedish authors known as the Helsinki Romantics differs clearly from the Swedish romanticism of the same period. The poetry of the national Finnish poet Johan Ludvig Runeberg combines influences from many quarters: from the world of antiquity (Runeberg was a scholar of Greek and Roman literature), from the ideas of European romanticism and from the stimuli of folk poetry. Compared with Swedish romanticism, the poetry of Runeberg contains much more classical substance; but at the same time, in its mode of expression it approached the simplicity and "natural" style of folk poetry.

The same thing can be observed in the work of Zachris Topelius. In his historical novels he adapted Sir Walter Scott's methods to the material of Finnish history, strongly emphasizing the Finnish national element. In his fairy tales he learned from the Danish author Hans Christian Andersen, but combined in them his own folkloric, mythological and historical material.

The influence of the *Kalevala,* Runeberg and Topelius on Finnish culture was long-lasting and important. Characteristic was the crossing of the language barrier: the *Kalevala* was highly regarded in Swedish-speaking circles, while Runeberg and Topelius were translated enthusiastically and widely into Finnish. Lönnrot, Runeberg and Topelius thus created significant models for later Finnish literature. Only one slightly later writer deviated significantly from the line they had marked out: the originator of the Finnish novel and author of *Seven Brothers,* Aleksis Kivi. He of course was familiar with all their works—he even knew two of the three men personally—and his own writings sometimes showed their influence; but his real spiritual forebears came from afar and from much earlier times— Shakespeare, Cervantes, Ludvig Holberg.

■ ■ ■

It took about fifty years from the time of the *Kalevala* and Runeberg before the next great universal literary stream, realism, reached Finland. The heyday of this movement came in the 1880s, and its chief representatives were prose writers: the playwright Minna Canth and the master of the short story, Juhani Aho. Some features established during this period became a vital part of the Finnish prose tradition and are visible to this day, especially a combination of natural realism and humor and the theme of social justice.

Scandinavian realism had its roots in Europe generally. The influence of philosophers and naturalists was powerful, specifically the theories of Charles Darwin, which toppled man from his pedestal as lord of nature and made him just another biological species, revolutionizing former concepts. Those who applied the theories of Darwin to other fields—particularly Spencer, John Stuart Mill and Buckle—also found readers in Finland. Many theories became familiar via other Scandinavian countries. The intermediary was primarily Georg Brandes, who had personal contacts with Finland; he corresponded with Finnish cultural figures, held Juhani Aho in esteem, visited Finland three times and lectured in Helsinki. Brandes's demand (in the introduction to his multivolume history of nineteenth-century literature, *Hovedstrømninger*) that literature should "present problems for discussion" was taken almost literally as a maxim by Finnish realists. There was an attempt to translate this classic work into Finnish, but only one installment was published—at the instigation of Minna Canth—in 1887. Canth's works were the focal point around which all the ideas and issues of the realist period were gathered: women's issues, the seeds of socialism, the labor question, criticism of the Church, the conflict between the different generations.

Brandes was the theoretical godfather of Finnish realism. At the practical level the most powerful influences came from Norway, particularly from Ibsen and Björnson, but also from Jonas Lie, Alexander Kielland and Arne Garborg. The impact of Norwegian literature was so strong that, according to the Finnish literary historian V. Tarkiainen, Finland in those times became "for about a decade a literary domain of Norway." This statement may seem exaggerated, but there is justification for it. I will take a couple of less well-known, concrete examples. In what country did the first academic study of Ibsen appear? The answer is Finland. It was a doctoral dissertation by Valfrid Vasenius on Ibsen's youthful historical dramas, and it appeared as early as 1879. Three years later, in 1882, Vasenius published a popular monograph on Ibsen. These works appeared in Swedish. Ibsen's plays started to be translated into Finnish at an early stage; for example, *A Doll's House,* first performed in Copenhagen at Christmastime in 1879, was already being acted in Finnish in early 1880, two

months later. One of Ibsen's most famous plays of his last period, *John Gabriel Borkman,* was given its world premiere in Helsinki at the beginning of January 1897—and simultaneously in two theatres in two languages, Finnish and Swedish! The Norwegian premiere took place nine days later. "We adopted him at once," wrote Juhani Aho in an article on Ibsen and the Finns, and this was really true.

Brandes, Ibsen and Björnson are not the only Scandinavian writers to influence Finland. With them must be counted August Strindberg, although his time really came a little later. But this was not all. Stimuli also came for perhaps the first time from a new direction: from the East, from Russia. All through the nineteenth century, Finland was strongly oriented toward Western culture. Attitudes toward Russia were polite, but few knew the language and Russian literature was little known. Regarding the language, the same is true today; very few people in Finland speak Russian. I, for example, did not learn it at school; I only know the Russian alphabet and a few words—nothing more.

For a long time Finnish literary scholars believed that, with the exception of Tolstoy, the Russian influence on our literature was also very slight. These ideas changed when Annamari Sarajas published a study in 1968 called *Tunnuskuvia* (Symbols), showing that there were more points of contact than had been believed (see BA 43:2, p. 293).

One cultured Finnish-Russian family, the Järnefelts, occupied a special position: the mother Elisabet, who hailed from the liberal intelligentsia of St. Petersburg, sponsored a literary salon which included Minna Canth and Juhani Aho, among others. One of the sons, Arvid Järnefelt, was a writer, a disciple of Tolstoy. Another, Eero, became an artist, and a third, Armas, a conductor. The daughter of the family, Aino, married the composer Jean Sibelius. What is most important here, however, is not the family history, but Elisabet's salon. There she reported on the new Russian periodicals and books and on Tolstoy, Dostoevsky and many other writers. In this way the idea of character *types* in the sense put forward by the critic Vissarion Belinsky was passed on to Finnish realism. The type was also a central concept in the theory of French realism, but Sarajas shows that through the Järnefelt family it came to Finland a little earlier than did the French theory, which arrived via Scandinavia. It is not possible here to go into Sarajas's interesting study more fully, so I must condense the essential point: for a short time, at an opportune moment, in the right environment, the door to Russian literature was opened to Finland in the 1880s and 90s. The single most important Russian influence was Tolstoy. But with him we have already reached the next period.

The symbolist movement reached Finland immediately after realism and won its supporters from among the former leading proponents of realism. The influx came directly from France this time: first with the artists who had studied in Paris, then with writers, later through elements of Danish "mystical symbolism" (Johannes Jørgensen and the *Taarnet* magazine). In the present century Nietzsche and Art Nouveau also made their own contributions to the movement.

The Finnish version of symbolism has generally been called "national neoromanticism" in Finnish literary history. One might also speak of "national symbolism." The older name has some justification, because several of the representatives of this trend (for example, Juhani Aho) really were romantics of a kind. The additional designation "national" is necessary here, because the esthetic of symbolism produced very original results in Finland, visible equally well in literature and in pictorial art and architecture. What is typical is the "translating" of European influences into a Finnish form, the strong share of national elements—the same feature that could be observed back in the time of the *Kalevala* and the Helsinki Romantics.

The Finnish landscape, especially that of eastern Finland, Karelia, fascinated many artists in the 1890s and took them on long pilgrimages. They sought untouched nature, people unspoiled by civilization; in other words, Finnish artists and writers were driven to the Karelian woods by the same longing for primitive originality that took the painter Paul Gauguin from France to the isles of the Pacific. National ornaments and European Art Nouveau hit it off well together and sustained each other. Symbolist ideas were implemented through Finnish materials and Finnish form, and, conversely, Finnish themes were given symbolist interpretations.

Two important features must still be noted: the rise of the *Kalevala* as a central thematic and artistic source, and the close cooperation between the different arts. Never before or later have art, musical composition, architecture and literature been so close to one another as in the 1890s and at the beginning of this century. "The Finnish Renaissance!" wrote the most important poet of the time, Eino Leino. The same motifs moved from one form of art to another; the representatives of different realms of art inspired one another. To take a single example: the greatest Finnish composer, Sibelius, drew the impulse for his tone poem "Swan of Tuonela" from the *Kalevala*. The greatest Finnish-language poet of the period, Leino, wrote a lyric drama of the same

name, in which the *Kalevala* events and characters were given new features. The painter Akseli Gallen-Kallela, the leading artist of the time, painted the swan of Tuonela in one of his pictures with a *Kalevala* theme. The impulses moved like a tide from one art form to the next, uniting and inspiring. They can been seen in architecture too: Eliel Saarinen, who moved to the United States and did important work here, belonged to the same generation and was the friend of Sibelius, Leino and Gallen-Kallela. Many other important names could be mentioned: the poet and translator Otto Manninen; the prose writers Ilmari Kianto, Volter Kilpi and Joel Lehtonen, who later produced some of the best achievements in the Finnish novel but whose works I can hardly touch upon within the scope of this survey. Strange names without examples are mere abstractions, however. Leino's slogan "the Finnish Renaissance" must suffice to portray this period.

The influence of symbolism was felt for a long time in Finnish literature, especially in poetry. The national ingredients diminished gradually, and instead came Nietzschean tragic optimism or the postsymbolist worship of beauty. These features still appear in the work of poets between the world wars (e.g., Uuno Kailas and Kaarlo Sarkia) and even in poetry written after World War II. The national neoromantic period had by then faded into oblivion. But it had not died, for the art of that day has been rediscovered several times, both in past decades and in our own.

The next new wave in Finnish literature arrived during and immediately after World War I. Its earliest and best representatives were all Swedish Finns, and almost all were poets. Collectively they have been called the Finland-Swedish modernists of the 1920s. This modernism was one of the numerous reform movements that arose at the beginning of the century in various parts of Europe. Parallel occurrences are cubism, futurism, expressionism, imagism, dadaism and surrealism, just to mention the most important movements. At its point of departure this modernism is close to expressionism, but it cannot be wholly placed under this label. If we compare it to the European schools of poetry of the same time, it would perhaps be best to call it avant-gardism. It was in fact an avant-garde phenomenon, a powerful upheaval in poetic style which at first met with strong opposition and criticism. The reforms of Finland-Swedish modernism can be summarized under six headings: 1) free verse, 2) the discarding of rhyme, 3) a new and bolder use of imagery, 4) a change in vocabulary and a breaking of the former boundaries between different stylistic levels, 5) a broadening in the range of themes, 6) a more complex poetic structure. The reforms were similar to those occurring elsewhere in Europe at the same time, and influences came from many quarters—Germany, Russia, Britain, France. But there were two essentials: first, the modernists did not follow any single school but instead freely and personally adapted stimuli from various quarters, each according to his own purpose; second, they carried out their reforms both concurrently and independently, sometimes knowing little of other trends. The result was their own independent school, an avant-garde movement operating on its own terms, the spearhead of all contemporary Scandinavian poetry. As such, it was capable of influencing poetry at least in Sweden and to some extent in other Scandinavian countries. The earliest of its representatives, Edith Södergran, has quite recently won international recognition and found new translators both in the Anglo-Saxon and the Francophone areas. I am convinced that Finland-Swedish modernism is a significant part of the history of European avant-gardism.

The Finland-Swedish modernists did not form a close group, though they were linked by the joint opposition they encountered and by two periodicals of brief duration. Individually they were very different. Södergran, the pioneer, began publishing verse in 1916 and developed a visionary style characterized by powerful images and dynamic expression. Her early poems are colored by Nietzschean defiance, her later work by Christian humility. The most expressionistic of the Finland-Swedish modernist poets was Elmer Diktonius, a powerful genius who used brutal, startling word combinations, sometimes even rough everyday language, and who employed bold acoustic effects and musical structures. The most radical modernist was Gunnar Björling; he created his own syntax and grammar to express the limitlessness of life, espousing a philosophy of constant growth and spontaneity. His poetry can sometimes be remotely compared to that of E. E. Cummings, chiefly in its typography. Björling has not yet found a translator, but some who know his poetry give him a prominent place in their anthologies (e.g., the German Hans Magnus Enzensberger, *Museum der modernen Poesie,* 1960). Rabbe Enckell, also a good painter, began with impressionistic poems full of nuances and ended with verses using the myths of ancient Greece to reflect modern problems. Enckell deserves attention also for some of his long, meditative poems. Henry Parland, who died young, was the wunderkind among the modernists, a sharp observer of his times who used fashionable illustrations of the twenties and wrote of automobiles or bargain sales with both irony and melancholy.

These Finland-Swedish modernists wrote in the Swedish language. A new generation of poets writing in Finnish also appeared; they took the name of *Tulen-*

kantajat (The Torchbearers), wrote free verse and sought sometimes exotic themes, sometimes themes connected with the romance of machinery. Their reforms were not so permanent as those of the Finland-Swedish poets, for many of them eventually returned to a traditional style. Nevertheless there were many among them who became well-known, such as the important lyric poet P. Mustapää (Martti Haavio; see *WLT* 54:1, pp. 38–40) and Mika Waltari, who won international fame as a novelist (*The Egyptian,* 1945). Aaro Hellaakoski, the most interesting Finnish-language innovator and a little older than the others, kept his distance from the group; his poems from the later twenties show signs of contact with cubism and with Apollinaire. Together with P. Mustapää, Hellaakoski prepared the way for the reform of poetry after World War II.

▪ ▪ ▪

From the chaos of World War II there arose the next vanguard of poetry, commonly known as the modernists of the fifties. Their common features were skepticism toward all ideologies—national, political or religious—and a restraint from big words and highsounding phrases. Their style was marked by a lowering of the voice, understatement, reticence and suggestion. Their points of departure were the poetry of T. S. Eliot and Ezra Pound on the one hand, and Swedish poetry from the forties on the other. Eliot's 1948 Nobel Prize made him suddenly famous in Finland (as elsewhere), and the first selection of his poetry in Finnish appeared as early as 1949. This included both *The Waste Land* and all of the *Four Quartets.* This selection opened the way for a new poetic style of a kind that had not been used before in Finland. The background to this reform movement was a liberation from former (especially wartime) ideals, a powerful desire to know what had happened in world literature during the war, and a desire to define the Finnish position in a new and disordered world and in a new situation.

It was not realized until later that our own Finland-Swedish modernists of the twenties were in many respects kindred spirits with the Finnish-language modernists of the fifties. Their technical and stylistic innovations had been more or less the same as were now being put into practice. These stylistic changes of the fifties remained permanent; Finnish poetry today still speaks very much a language whose fundamental characteristics come from the fifties. But it is typical that many Finnish poets of this period translated the Finland-Swedish poets of the twenties: Södergran, Diktonius, Björling, Enckell and Parland.

The modernists of the fifties are the middle generation of Finnish literature today. Some of them have died, like Helvi Juvonen and Lasse Heikkilä. Others are still working with full vigor: Paavo Haavikko, Eeva-Liisa Manner, Eila Kivikkaho, Tuomas Anhava, Aila Meriluoto, Lassi Nummi. The richest, most wide-reaching and unpredictable of them is Paavo Haavikko, to my mind the major poet at the very head of modern Finnish poetry, at the same time an ironist, a skeptic and an extremely realistic writer in his opinions (see e.g. *BA* 50:2, pp. 237–41 and *WLT* 53:2, pp. 244–45). There are many names in the following generation that also deserve mention, especially Pentti Saarikoski (see *WLT* 54:1, pp. 41–46), but also Väinö Kirstinä, Pentti Saaritsa, Caj Westerberg and others. Many of the Finland-Swedish poets of today are relatively close to their Finnish-language colleagues both in style and beliefs—for example, Bo Carpelan (who has been given the highest literary award of the Nordic Council), Lars Huldén (see *WLT* 54:1, pp. 47–50) and Claes Andersson.

The stream of international movements flowing into Finland has been lively in recent years. We have had our own protest songs, our own prophets of social revolution in the sixties and seventies, our own opponents of nuclear weapons and especially our own environmentalists. Many of them are important for their ideas, but they have neither formed a school nor established an unmistakable style of their own; so I will say no more of them.

Thus Finnish literature has had many contacts with world literature, and these international influences have been combined almost regularly with Finnish elements. The result has been best when the two sets of ingredients, that which has come from abroad and that which is our own, have been in balance and in fruitful conflict. Michael Branch, an Englishman who knows Finnish culture well, has spoken of the two traditions of Finnish culture, the "great tradition" is European, opening toward Europe; the "little tradition" is our own, narrowly national. Both have contributed to Finnish letters. Together they have shaped the features of our literature and our whole culture.

Kai Laitinen, Summer 1983, translated by Philip Binham

Ed. Note: Laitinen's paper was presented at the University of Washington on 2 May 1983 in conjunction with one of the several conferences on "Finland in the World Today," part of the "Scandinavia Today" program sponsored 1982–83 by the Scandinavian countries and various allied organizations in the U.S.

Unusual Men: Three Masters of Contemporary Finnish Prose

The Finns love steady narrative. Repetition was a central expressive device in our folk poetry, and perhaps the sober progression of our prose—we do not readily tolerate leaps in time or from theme to theme—stems from the same root; the writer, like a good farmer, prepares the ground for his characters and then draws aside to record what develops. Passionate voices and complicated structures arouse attention against this sober literary background. But the ordinary Finnish epic novel is not at all bad, and when it is concentrated and deepened, the result is excellent.

I shall introduce the work of three writers, all of whom have this kind of craftsman's approach to writing. They have bridged the language gap; works by each of them are at present being translated into various languages. At home their main works, which I shall be discussing in this article, have received critical acclaim and have also been rewarded with more tangible honors: the two novels I consider first received state literature prizes and the third garnered all the other major Finnish literary awards.

■ A EUROPEAN

Markku Lahtela (b. 1936) is far removed from both basic types of Finnish writer. There is nothing in him of the instinctive storyteller who restricts himself to the level of his subject (we have more of this kind of writer in Finland than we care to admit). Neither does he really belong to the type of Finnish artist-writer who is currently more politically aware, for this class of writers is surprisingly romantic and idealistic, even the social epic writers, as Yrjö Varpio has shown in his study of the Tampere group. It is certainly true that Lahtela has pondered the problems of the artist and given vent to his genius complexes in a way suiting our Nordic country, but now he has advanced beyond that. He has somehow found a personal solution to the "messiah complex" problem, that unassuageable desire to free mankind which possesses some of his colleagues. His tone is no longer solemn.

It seems that Lahtela learned a great deal from his experiences during the late sixties when he, together with a great many others, threw himself into political action. After a couple of promising collage-novels, he left writing to put the world to rights as a politician and social prophet. In politics he was not successful either as a Communist or later as a member of the Agrarian Party, and his pronouncements as a family philosopher, a constantly complaining critic of the state and hallower of mothers and children soon took on a hollow ring. His return to literature was not without its difficulties, but the novels *Yksinäinen mies* (The Lonely Man; 1976) and *Sirkus, eli merkillisiä muistiinpanoja* (Circus, or Curious Memoirs; 1978) are already magnificent examples of writing. Lahtela's present literary attitude is refreshingly unromantic. It reminds one of the modernists in Finland before the exciting years of the golden sixties. Lahtela is in many ways a modernist and, as such, the only one of his type in the literary world of the seventies, for our contemporary prose is "national" and "neoromantic" and so on, but hardly "new." The searching and experimental tradition in our literature continues precisely in Lahtela's works.

But the connections with earlier modernists go deeper. Finnish modernism was concerned with the precise and unsullied use of language, with the means of expression; it was a method, not an ideology. Its dominating characteristic was the importance of a critical outlook, and a critical outlook in itself is not a world view. Markku Lahtela has his own experiences of the difficulties a writer encounters in creating a complete world view; he has explored the world of ideologies and systems of learning thoroughly. He has been dogged by bad luck: he spoke of Freud when others spoke of Marx, and vice versa; he was always the one voice speaking in opposition to everyone else, making his solitary attempts to reconcile differing schools of thought. His damning sin was to appear too wise and learned in the exposition of his theories; in this commonsense country this was not popular. His punishment was that his audience misunderstood him, or simply closed its ears.

This punishment was all the harder to bear as Lahtela's crusades in regard to ideologies had been desperate from the beginning. He had perhaps set out with the conviction that this century's European is incapable of creating or holding a harmonious and complete world view, and from then on, his journey was the bitter testing of this hypothesis and the discovery that it was true.

In "The Lonely Man" Lahtela describes his journey, and the book is a powerful experience for the reader too. The writer presents his readers with his former public self and maliciously destroys it. He shows us all his loneliness and isolation, together with their personal and more general causes. The novel describes man's despairing struggle to gain a firm grasp on reality, something the established ideologies do not provide. Although a complete world view helps one to make sense of the world, at the same time it separates one from the world: each abstract statement about the world is a hairsbreadth from the reality it describes. Ideologies cannot

describe reality in all its detail; conceptual frameworks do not function in the same way as reality. This is Lahtela's message, and the message of every work of art. The writer has returned to his work.

Thus Lahtela's newest work, the novel *Sirkus,* is a liberated and joyful work of art. Its style is brilliant; in fact Lahtela employs a dazzling range of styles. The novel plays with detail, with so-called profound thoughts as well as with the most immediate physical impressions. It enjoys itself; it is a game.

The main character of the novel, Xesmer Reodisius, is the child of an extraordinary family. The family runs an industrial firm with contacts throughout Europe; its members have for centuries been bishops and thieves, Russian gypsies, tradesmen and academics. Xesmer is examining his father Theodisius's literary remains, which consist of crate upon crate of material, in large measure painfully detailed descriptions of physical objects such as forks, lamps and house porches. In fact, the father Theo also claims to have visited the moon—nothing can be taken at its face value.

Thus it is evidently not the aim of this novel to provide a convincing illusion of reality. Perhaps this is why the work is so light-hearted as it gambols freely through the whimsical world of fantasy. The work is born of imagination and language; it is both of these, and in them is the basis of its existence. Of course language and mind together inevitably form structure. It is the formal structure of the Reodisius family which keeps this frisky novel in check as it romps through time and space. The work is a complex structure of reflections and implications and contains many clues to its own interpretation. In its 200-odd pages there is ample material for analysis by many a furrowed-brow academic; but before their work is published, I intend to enjoy Lahtela's games freely, to read the book backward and forward and in chunks, and I shan't think yet about just how it is that the work reflects so-called reality. For the moment it is a part of my own reality.

▪ A SCANDINAVIAN

Markku Lahtela, like many writers, has attained maturity through struggle. He describes his own battles, and his search will no doubt continue into the future. Antti Tuuri (b. 1944), on the other hand, has been an astonishingly mature writer from his very first novel onward. In fact, his maturity is almost irritating. Ever since his first work, he has published consistently good, polished, extraordinarily pithy prose. He himself does not make a habit of explaining his work; we friends of literature, who love to think of the suffering involved in creation and the intoxication of the senses, are in for a serious disappointment.

Tuuri's account of the beginning of his career as a writer is almost offensive in its matter-of-factness: "When I had finished my national service, I didn't know what to do next, so I tried my hand at writing a novel. After I had written a couple, a publisher wanted to publish them." At this stage Tuuri was twenty-five years old and had just qualified as an engineer. Since then, throughout the seventies, he has had a so-called "respectable job": he has directed a large printing works and the export operations of a Finnish paper-processing plant. One has the impression that he must have written all his eight books in hotel rooms in the spare moments of his business trips.

Tuuri is an engineer who—as someone to whom technology is a means of earning a living—stands in glaring contrast to the professed values of his own generation of writers. In Finland, as elsewhere, opposition to the system is what makes the intellectual, and economics is a bête noire for everyone. Is Tuuri perhaps a secret agent for the EEC? But joking apart, Tuuri's works are extremely perceptive in a social sense. Often they picture city dwellers unhappy despite their material riches, or country people living through the crumbling decay of their traditional culture. In these works today's Finland, shaped by technology and the ever-increasing influence of diverse institutions, hardly seems the ideal place to live.

But the essential meaning of Tuuri's prose lies a little deeper. The clarity of expression, the precise recording of experience and the uncommenting, neutral narrative lead the reader to look between the lines. There he finds the basic experience of human existence, common to all and private to each; this is central to Tuuri's work, present in all his short works as well as in his single long novel. *Joki virtaa läpi kaupungin* (The River Flows Through the Town; 1977) describes the lives of three people in a largish town in northern Finland during one winter in the 1970s. Ilmari Autio is the young foreman of a printing plant, Ilmari Pihlaja an elderly academic, and his son Seppo an unsuccessful painter. Autio is concerned with the concrete realities of life, as only a man who is nearing his thirtieth year can be: his work, his living and the starting of a family are what fill his mind. Ilmari Pihlaja, on the other hand, is far removed from material things; he doubts the basic premises of our scientific view of the world, reads Steiner and prepares for death. Seppo Pihlaja was supposed to become an artist, but an almost self-destructive weakness of character makes him a drifter who tries to escape from himself by fleeing to Paris.

The novel is in the form of a narrative by Ilmari Autio, interpolated with monologues by Ilmari Pihlaja and his son. These three points of view give the work a spacious dramatic structure which enables Tuuri to pack a great deal into the book. He manages to include almost all the questions, temporal as well as eternal, which have concerned the Finnish nation over the past decades. The novel absorbs into itself many of the customary genres: from the social epic, always popular in Finland, to the artist novel, which comes to the surface from time to time there, and the intellectual and philosophical novel, very rare in Finland.

Despite their rich variety, the many layers of the work successfully form a coherent whole because they all focus on the same point: the characters' basic existential problem of living with their own selves. To the extent that one can transform or, more accurately, reduce the contents of every novel to its concern with that basic question, the important and unique element in any individual novel is simply the particular aspect of the basic problem the work emphasizes. For Antti Tuuri's characters, the answer is "getting through" life; it is as if life is for them a task which they must carry out, a difficult situation from which they must extricate themselves with honor, preserving their own identities. For what? "For death," Ilmari Pihlaja would reply; "for life," would be the answer of his younger namesake.

"The River Flows Through the Town" reminds one of Veijo Meri's novel *Peiliin piirretty nainen* (The Woman in the Mirror; 1963); both novels are ambitious attempts to create complicated structures, "grand novels." Both Tuuri and Meri are masters of style and the small form; the basic element in their writing is the well-turned phrase which draws the reader on. Like Meri in the sixties, Tuuri has now decided that this time he won't give the reader a string of good Tuuri sentences, one after another; he will place them on top of each other, crosswise. He builds a work which stands in relation to its basic elements, sentences, as a house does to the bricks of which it is made: the whole is greater than the sum of its parts.

It is interesting to note that in doing this, neither Tuuri nor Meri has produced his "best" prose. These men are such masters of the sentence that large constructions do not succeed as well as smaller forms. But "The River Flows Through the Town" and "The Woman in the Mirror" are nevertheless good novels; it is extraordinary that although both writers concentrate on the problems of individual existence, they in fact give a picture of society at the time of writing—and a sharper one than in many of the more usual social epics.

■ A FINNO-UGRIAN

Are we not all of the opinion that a Real Writer is a man who has spent a dissolute youth, a globetrotter who has

practiced fifteen different professions, a self-taught
polymath who has visited university lecture halls but
who has never made the mistake of supposing that professors are wiser than himself? We Finns are keen to add
an element of suffering to this recipe, a measure of temporal difficulty and metaphysical pain. The result is
"arctic hysteria," a compôte of shamanistic clairvoyance
plus generous helpings of Western intellectual hyper-
consciousness.

The character of Matti Pulkkinen contains elements
of all this. This man, born in northern Karelia in 1944,
has traveled in Europe in the way American writers find
so congenial; he has lived in Frankfurt, Bern and Athens. He has earned his living at many different trades,
as so many have done (for instance, Samuli Paronen).
Like Timo K. Mukka, he has experienced material hardship and physical pain. The shadow of oppression and
madness which has followed Finnish writers from Aleksis Kivi on is also familiar to Pulkkinen, though in a
slightly unusual way: he is a qualified group therapist
and has worked as a psychiatric aide in Finland and
abroad. He speaks of clinical theology and Arthur
Janov; he claims to have passed beyond his own "primal
scream" through self-analysis.

Pulkkinen's fame as a public figure grew quickly.
His burning gaze, full of past suffering, his way of
speaking, bringing out profound comments in his slow
country dialect, quickly gave him a charismatic appeal.
Romantics may be satisfied with this; I shall nevertheless go on to examine his literary output, which at present consists of just one novel. *Ja pesäpuu itki* (And the
Nesting Tree Wept; 1977) is an extensive epic and dramatic work on three themes: the place of Finland's
younger generation in the world, the development of
Finnish society during the present century and the capacity of people to do good or harm to each other. As
well as being of different degrees of complexity, each
theme "contains" its predecessor, and there are also direct connections between the themes, some of them
surprising.

In handling his first theme, Pulkkinen describes the
isolation and alienation which characterize the young
people of the seventies. Compared to them, the student
revolutionaries of the sixties seem arrogant in their
cheerful assurance that they were in the right; one can
afford to be a radical when the going is good, but times
have no longer been good for young people. The main
character of the book, Paavo Kuittinen, feels his existence to be a heavy load. He walks the streets of a
strange town, searching for his own identity. Pulkkinen
has clearly drawn on personal experience, and occasionally one feels that writing about it has brought a
lump to his throat—the theme itself is full of welt-

schmerz, and in handling it Pulkkinen shows his lack
of experience as a novelist.

But from here on Pulkkinen has a master's touch.
For him, the transformation of Finnish society is not the
old story of "postwar urbanization," the goodbye to the
fields and lakes. He presents his own penetrating interpretation of the confrontation between the traditional
agrarian society and contemporary society, masses yet
fragmented—a process which he sees as having begun
in the nineteenth century. Pulkkinen's historical and social vision finds its expression in an extensive and diverse Karelian saga in which he tells the story of the decline and eventual extinction of the great Suutarinen
family, as well as of the weaker Kareinens and Kuit-
tinens, who are thrown in different ways on the mercy
of the times. The climax of the work is the ballad-like
account of the love between Lahja and Ranssi, members
of two opposing families.

Matti Pulkkinen takes as his third theme the interaction between people. This kind of transaction analysis
is for him not so much a method as a kind of moral
prism. It could be said that "And the Nesting Tree
Wept" is a book about the good or harm people can do
to each other; the theme pervades the work. The book
is full of different kinds of encounters between people—sometimes in the spirit of cooperation, sometimes
of conflict. The shifting of nuances is masterfully portrayed. Pulkkinen's wit is at its most mordant in his descriptions of pseudo-Freudian group sessions; his most
brilliant pages about the way in which the spirits of
older people take the measure of each other are found
in the scene where old Mrs. Kareinen massages the rich
Suutarinen.

As I have already mentioned, there are surprising
interrelations between the themes. When Paavo Kuittinen, searching for his real self, finds in the city mental
asylum an elderly chronic patient who turns out to be
the son of the legendary Lahja and Ranssi and therefore
one of his own relatives, the reader finds himself drawn
along by the plot and the structure of the book is significantly strengthened. The writer ambitiously creates a
number of such connections between the different levels of the work and succeeds in convincing his readers
that an extremely impressive structure may be built
within the scope of the novel. The cathedral stands,
even if the mortar between some of the stones is crumbling. It is this passion for construction which encourages one to believe in Pulkkinen's future as a writer.

Juhani Salokannel, Winter 1980, translated by Hildi
Hawkins

Paavo Haavikko (*Robert H. Taylor*)

The Lyrical Space: On the Poetry of Paavo Haavikko

Poetry is nothing other than an enunciation aiming at expression.

■ ROMAN JAKOBSON

"To rule is to rule over mapped-out lands."[1] Paavo Haavikko is generally regarded as the most important modern Finnish poet of the postwar period. He has been extremely prolific, a master of various styles and genres for more than three decades. In the poetry of Haavikko, language is the space to be constantly reconquered. His poetry explores an empty space that forever seeks to be filled, only to be emptied anew. Several series of negatives, abstractions and ironical statements, as is Haavikko's style, perform this poetic act. It is one of the supreme ironies that the recipient of this year's Neustadt Prize writes in a language inaccessible to virtually anyone but his few compatriots and a small number of intelligent readers: "Poetry oh poetry is my only native land, about it I speak, / it is my beloved that bursts out singing, / but I also long for myself and for where I am, there / is an empty space, / it is a soul amidst flowers."[2]

In this essay I shall focus my interest on Haavikko's lyrical poetry.[3] Despite the many arenas of his poetic influence in Finland, the principal themes of his creative output have not changed essentially. The two related themes of power and impotence have been investigated in the realms of Byzantium and Finland's mythical past, but also in the everyday world of business transaction. Most of Haavikko's lyrical work too emerges directly from dealings in the more dynamic business world, where everything is stated concretely and unequivocally, in terms of buying and selling, of bidding and borrowing, of stocks and real estate: "This is, is the bureaucracy of poetry, fruitless. / I am just as tired of it. / This is, is a swindle, bringing with it / not even promises."[4]

In this world the taste and flavor of power are a topic of conversation, whether that power is "raw" or "very delicate."[5] Haavikko is a master of satire in the tradition of Horace, who in his *Sermones* talks about money while talking about Maecenas, as Alexander Pope well understood. But the lot of the ironist can be to live the ironical truth of his affirmations. The pathos is classical, and the language is sophisticated (sophisticated in the sense that poetic language cannot escape its history and its knowledge). At the same time, the discussion of elemental, primary issues is generally avoided, except in an ironical way. In this respect Haavikko differs from the symbolists, for example. Unlike Mallarmé, whose language is sophisticated in the extreme ("La chair est triste, hélas! et j'ai lu tous les livres," we read in *Le Parnasse contemporain*), and consciously so, but who talks about elemental, primary issues in vividly descriptive, concrete language imitated by the early modernists, Haavikko is skeptical about the vital relationship betwen language and the universe outside it. Language refers to a world that is hermetic, unwilling to communicate: "So many will be sealed in an envelope for good, / and if one set to open them, if someone did it / he would almost have to admit that / it is empty, there is no letter there."[6]

One of the central questions of twentieth-century poetry—namely, whether language is principally creative or principally significatory—is stated in Haavikko's work with the sophisticated awareness of a supreme word architect. In the Finnish poetic tradition the supposed capacity of poetry to generate new meanings has been a fundamental idea. To some extent Haavikko endorses this view, but it has been voiced with much greater force in the work of the late Pentti Saarikoski. Haavikko identifies the development of language with poetic practice, but he is basically antimythical—antimythical in his use of language, not in his choice of topics. Haavikko's poems are antimythical because in them thought precedes the poetic form. Thus his work tends to have a distinctively conceptual character. Language is not constitutive of thought but is instead an extremely supple, responsive and compliant instrument of thought.

Heavy is the wet sky, the earth is light here,
the earth is light, light is the earth wet on top of this
　son
the mere hair is well worth one forest of spruce trees,
the voice is heard from the earth like the voice of the
root that is lifted from the earth.
(B, 66)

Haavikko's poetic language is based on compelling rhythm. It emanates from simple sounds, juxtaposition and frequent repetition. The rhymeless lines create a lyrical space that resounds dryly, a winter palace. For instance, in the poem quoted above, *maa* (meaning "earth") and other words with similar sound values are repeated through the broad, long lines, like a cello sonata, until they expire in a terse Adonic line of a Sapphic stanza, repeated from the middle of the poem, "keskellä kukkain" (amidst the flowers), with its harsh consonants, creating a deep, final silence, whereby death is suggested, as in a partisan song. However, it is controlled, reflected and, in a sense, wholly secular.[7]

Jean Paulhan, in *Les fleurs de Tarbes* (1941), differentiates two distinct categories of poets on the basis of their use of language. These groups he calls the "terrorists" and the "rhetoricians." The "terrorists" would be the romantics, symbolists and surrealists, those who want to eliminate from language completely the commonplace, conventional forms and readymade clichés and who emphasize pure and original inspiration at the expense of language. The "terrorists," according to Paulhan, fight against the consolidation of the living, fluid and intimate life of the mind, against externalization and institutionalization and eventually, if taken to the logical extreme, against all culture. The other group, the "rhetoricians," are those poets who take the view that literature is communication and that the price of mutual understanding is convention and commonplace. The latter group is essentially represented by the classical poets, who emphasize taste and decorum, and by writers within a nationalistic tradition.[8]

Within this frame of reference, Haavikko, in contrast with most modernists in Finland such as Saarikoski and Eeva-Liisa Manner, would be in the category of the "rhetoricians." Haavikko is Finland's classical poet par excellence. The gallant resignation is stated with considerable bonhomie—"These shoulders, breasts, for which I have cried honey and amber"[9]—and the skepticism concerning poetry vis-à-vis the business of living is expressed with elegance: "But in matters of life and death, nearly all is error" (TP, 156).

Should poetry reflect the mind in its state without language? Or should it be concerned with representing the act of representation itself? These questions, central to modern lyrical poetry, need to be examined further. My suggestions are not intended to be conclusive here, but I hope they might illuminate some aspects of Haavikko's work.

▓ ▓ ▓

"Trees in All Their Verdure." In Haavikko's world, trees are trees. The tree is the generic name for a great variety of perennial plants with a single woody, self-supporting stem (*OED*). It is rarely specified but is occasionally called a spruce, a pine. Trees do not stand for something else; they are neither romantic nor allegorical: "There are many wise men, but, on the other hand, not one crazy tree" (TV, 143). In nature, objects do not represent. This is the world for which the poet yearns; it is peaceful, straightforward, a world without human language. But since it is a world without language and without representation, it is also a world without art. Art is artfulness; the forest, even when planted, is natural, without conceit. It is the sacred wood, the only world where the cynical and secular poet (or a poet who has chosen to live thus) can come close to a religious sentiment. Occasionally, though rarely, the poet may experience an epiphany: "A shred of verse came to mind yesterday . . . went by. / The immortals are in a hurry" (TP, 227). But gods, like women, are too complicated, too elusive, not really profitable in the world of investment; the dilemma is therefore left unsolved.

The prominent and important place that trees occupy in Haavikko's poetry is explained not only by pantheistic and Finno-Ugric associations. It also brings us again to the question of poetic language. Whether Haavikko is a nominalist is uncertain: undoubtedly, the tree is more than the name of the tree. In Haavikko's view, language is a set of symbols.[10] He admits, however, that these symbols tend to lead a life of their own. When they are used, they dictate their own terms and conditions and eventually, according to Haavikko, become totally divorced from reality. Thus he contends that the task of the poet is to be constantly on his guard against this process whereby symbols may overtake reality; in short, the poet's job is to shape these symbols into truth.

There is a puzzling dichotomy in Haavikko's notion of poetic language. Poetic language seems to be composed of common symbols that are false and of private language that bears a direct relation to reality. Haavikko claims more explicitly that the symbols are treacherous. The perspective on language is bizarre, perhaps humorous. Perhaps Haavikko has in mind myths that indeed can be false notions; the statement would then be more appropriately given by a politician in a rare moment of honesty. The symbolic in poetry is intricately related to the very nature of language itself, and symbols in poetry may be the vestiges of a collective imagination—as, indeed, it seems to me, the trees in Haavikko's work clearly are. Language may, admittedly, be treacherous, since it is always inadequate. Therefore all art is illusion. But for Haavikko this is not a question of representation but a question of value: art can be futile, vain. The poet has a set of symbols at his disposal, and he manipulates them while preserving their conventional and significatory function. The sentiment is baroque; the idea is part and parcel of the modernist canon.

Two points need to be made. First, it seems to me that Haavikko, thanks to his notion of poetic language, has a place in the mainstream of modernist poetry, which prefers conceptual clarity to rich, profuse imagery. But second, poetic language presents a special case of language, and perhaps is the original language. In modernist poetry it is understood, being in fact the burning focus of interest ever since the symbolist movement, that the significatory aspect of language is extremely complicated. In poetic language the sign assumes an autonomous value by virtue of sound symbolism and becomes an actual factor in the creation of meaning.[11] Has Haavikko distrusted the symbol too far? And does his poetry indeed stand as evidence of an instinctual understanding of the very nature of poetic language?

■ ■ ■

"You want other than you'd like, dream says."[12] Imperfection (fully explored in the Greek myth of Sisyphus) is among the themes discussed in the series of ten lyrics called "Poems from the House of the Novgorod Merchant," included in the collection "Poems from a Voyage across the Sound" (1973). It is a remarkable series, among the best in Haavikko's oeuvre, and its concise clarity compares favorably with the longer poem "The Winter Palace" (1959), which was obscured by sheer linguistic virtuosity. Fate, never fulfilled in the human life of imperfection, is looked at from various angles.

The series belongs to the period during which Haavikko ventured into historiography, stating his pseudohistorical theory of Finland's past. These views were taken in apparent earnest in Finland, probably because the perspective on Byzantium so carefully portrayed the climate of postwar Finland. *Kaksikymmentä ja yksi* (Twenty and One; 1974) showed an amateur historian seeking to explain historical development through parallelism. Archaic poetic language proved the

saving grace of these speculations concerning the epic origins of the Finns, and they may be best regarded as a visionary item in the multifarious Kalevala lore. They offer no coherent interpretation beyond snippets of historical detail and hardly illuminate the nature of the *Kalevala* either. It must be remembered, however, that this period marked a transition when Haavikko's treatment of historical themes became his primary function as a writer, culminating in "The National Line" (1977). The last genuinely lyrical works were "Poems from a Voyage across the Sound" and the more impressionistic *Viiniä, kirjoitusta* (Wine, Writing), from 1973 and 1976 respectively.

"Poems from the House of the Novgorod Merchant" is an exploration of life in the most elemental form to be found in Haavikko's work. A limited life (starting from "Man is in search of himself" and terminating in "How did we come to this") is presented as complete. The exploration is carried out on the threshold of awareness, during moments of falling asleep when suddenly perception becomes sharper. Analyzed by Proust, whose first pages of *À la recherche du temps perdu* are the locus classicus on poetic imagination, this state enables an easy access to layers of consciousness and even to the remotest corners of one's personal past. Stripped of his biological constraints, the human being is ageless.

And man, he is so constructed, an island-dweller,
ageless like sheep, odd nails,
like those of a bird scratching the earth.
That his sex may safely change
even by each generation.
(PS, 195)

Moreover, the short poems explore again the problematics of power. On the one hand there is the personal power of sexuality, which in Haavikko's work is always female. It is significant that this female personal power does not manifest itself in beauty but in sexuality. The woman is "made of a dream," hence her eternal power over the male who is "framed of twigs" (PS, 196). Eventually, therefore, the woman nurses "not the child but fate" (PS, 202). In this series the questions about sexuality acquire more general significance as they become questions about personal identity. Individual freedom does not exist there. Freedom cannot be realized because man is in the prison house of not only his conscious but also his unconscious thoughts. There is no doubt that Haavikko wishes to express his disgust for this human condition.

You want other than you'd like, dream says.
Evil dream. Punish it. Expel it from your house.
Tie it by the horses, run it with the horses.
Hang it. It has deserved it.

Feed it with mushrooms, poisonous.
(PS, 197)

On the other hand there is public power, which is discussed in terms of politics and big money. This is preeminently male power. Occasionally it is identified with the power of wisdom, and of knowledge, but also with evil, corrupt power: the ruler can be transformed into a tyrant in no time. In this series evil power is personified by the wicked merchant who appears in the poet's dream offering forged money; but the poet retaliates by offering "rotten goods" and thus gains his redemption, at least for the time being (PS, 199).

In the tenth and final poem the disillusionment has been made totally explicit and exposed by the various glimpses given by the dream. The woman offers her breast, which is the fruit. The knowledge offered is ambiguously both good and evil; but the lyrical tone suggests a longing for the good, enhanced by the poet's acquiescence to female sexual power. If there is any transcendence, it is in the poet's admission that growth and ripening have taken place unawares despite the central consciousness of perpetual alienation, so crucial to the poet's existence. Haavikko's lyrical space is a chilly, slightly pathetic world where transcendence can be only imagined in irony and in self-contradiction.

Kirsti Simonsuuri, Autumn 1984

1   Paavo Haavikko, *Tiet etäisyyksiin* (The Ways to Far Away; 1951), as reprinted in *Sillat: Valitut runot* (Bridges: Selected Poems), Helsinki, Otava, 1984, p. 10. All page references are to this edition. All translations are my own.

2   Paavo Haavikko, *Synnyinmaa* (Birthplace; 1955), as reprinted in *Sillat,* p. 66. Subsequent references use the abbreviation B.

3   In particular the following collections: *Tiet etäisyyksiin, Tuulöinä* (On Windy Nights; 1953), *Synnyinmaa, Lehdet lehtiä* (Leaves, Pages; 1958), *Talvipalatsi* (The Winter Palace; 1959), *Puut, kaikki heidän vihreytensä* (Trees in All Their Verdure; 1966), *Runoja matkalta salmen ylitse* (Poems from a Voyage across the Sound; 1973) and *Viiniä, kirjoitusta* (Wine, Writing; 1976). The first collected edition of poems, *Runot, 1949–1974,* was published in 1975 by Otava.

4   "A Study of the Realistic Conditions of Living Really Poor and of the World," 1976, p. 274.

5   "In Praise of Investments," 1973, p. 205.

6   "Ten Poems from 1966," 1966, p. 156. Subsequent references use the abbreviation TP.

7   Saarikoski, on the other hand, might be called religious. See also Richard Dauenhauer's essays "Some Notes on Zen Buddhist Tendencies in Modern Finnish Poetry" and "The View from the Aspen Grove: Paavo Haavikko in National and International Context," in *Snow in May: An Anthology of Finnish Writing, 1945–1972* (Cranbury, N.J., Fairleigh Dickinson University Press, 1978), which takes a very different line than does my own essay here. On Saarikoski see my article "Myth and Material in the Poetry of Pentti Saarikoski since 1958," *WLT* 54:1, pp. 41–46.

8   Jean Paulhan, *Les fleurs de Tarbes, ou La terreur dans les lettres,* Paris, 1941. The distinction between "terrorists" and "rhetoricians" constitutes the whole argument of this collection of essays: "C'est parce que l'écrivain ne s'est *pas assez* soucié de mots qu'un lecteur le trouve tout langagier, astucieux, verbal" (117).

9   "Trees in All Their Verdure," 1966, p. 109. Subsequent references use the abbreviation TV.

10   As stated during the course of several interviews and as quoted by Kai Laitinen in *Books from Finland,* 18:1 (1984), p. 1.

11   See e.g. Roman Jakobson, *Six Lectures on Sound and Meaning,* Cambridge, Ma., Harvard University Press, 1978, p. 113; Hazard Adams, *The Philosophy of the Literary Symbolic,* Tallahassee, Florida State University Press, 1983, pp. 20–21; and Eric Gans, *The Origin of Language,* Berkeley, University of California Press, 1981, pp. 2–4.

12   "Poems from a Voyage across the Sound," 1973, p. 197. Subsequent references use the abbreviation PS.

ICELAND

Postwar Literature in Iceland

Until the turn of this century cultural life in Iceland, although vigorous, was highly uniform. It was confined to the literary arts, particularly poetry, with a sprinkling of handicrafts and folk music. Painting, drama and musical composition were almost nonexistent. The novel was resurrected in the middle of the nineteenth century but did not flourish until after 1900.

The nineteenth century saw a great upsurge of romantic and nationalistic poetry, inspired largely by the literary treasures of the "Golden Age," the *Edda* and the *saga* (twelfth and thirteenth centuries). The poets were mainly preoccupied with a new national consciousness, the beauties of the country, the purity of language. They were the heralds of a new age which would bring political independence and cultural revival. That tradition lasted in various forms until World War II.

With World War II Iceland's almost total isolation came to an abrupt and rather uncomfortable end. The nation was thrown, largely unprepared, into the maelstrom of international affairs with all the attendant complications, problems and hazards. In 1944 Iceland gained full independence and became a republic (it had been sovereign since 1918). With the opening of the cultural frontiers, fresh impulses from all directions flooded the country, and all the arts began to flourish.

▪ POETRY

In poetry this meant that modernistic trends replaced the traditional ones, and an entirely new kind of poetry came to the fore, more introspective and complex and less immediately understandable than traditional poetry. The new poets moved away from the outward excellence of meter and high-sounding diction, making less frequent use of stock images and clichés, seeking their own idiom and symbols, often private ones, to capture the more evanescent qualities of intuition, sensibility and feeling. This has in many cases resulted in a loosening of strict metric forms and in freer modes of expression, but at the same time in greater precision of diction and of imagery, which has become more daring, rich and variegated.

There are naturally all kinds of gradations among the postwar poets of Iceland, some being more, some less lucid. The evolution has been slow, and the new trends came much later to Iceland than to most other countries, due no doubt to the ingrained reverence of most Icelanders for the old tradition with its emphasis on lucidity and strict metric rules (alliteration being chief among them). Most significant poetry today has departed, to a greater or lesser extent, from the old traditions, but a number of outstanding poets have managed to amalgamate old forms and new content in a fresh synthesis which stirs modern sensibilities. Two of these are actually the only Icelanders so far to have been awarded the annual Literary Prize of the Nordic Council, instituted in 1962.

Ólafur Jóhann Sigurðsson (b. 1918), who received the Prize in 1976, is mainly a fiction writer, but in 1972 and 1974 he published two volumes of poems which were issued in Swedish translation under the title *Du minns en brunn* (You Remember a Well; 1975). In these highly personal and lyrical poems, at once classical in form and rich in nuances and emotion, he succeeds in communicating a critique of modern times which never quite comes off in his beautifully written stories. In arresting images he plays the bewildered city life of today against memories from his youth in the country, idyllic pastoral scenes against modern alienation. It is not so much a question of nostalgic lyricism or sublimated conservatism as it is a question of consciously trying to overcome an apprehension toward modern culture and to recover the world by reestablishing continuities without which one cannot survive. This theme may be said to be a kind of leitmotiv in postwar literature in Iceland: the transition from the old and stable agrarian society to the modern industrialized welfare society, centered in the city.

Snorri Hjartarson (b. 1906), who received the Nordic Literary Prize in 1981, made his debut in Norway with a novel written in Norwegian, but in 1936 he returned to Iceland, where he was to become a leading and very influential poet, even though he stands apart from his younger colleagues and has published only four collections of poetry. His first two volumes are characterized by exquisite music and a truly fascinating display of color, probably explained by the fact that he started his career in Norway as a painter. The poems are quiet, tender and refined, expressing the poet's deep love of nature and his native land which sometimes attains mythical aspects in his vision. His later collections (1966 and 1979) are more succinct in diction and somber in tone, constantly seeking the simple phrase and the genuine expression. As in much modern Icelandic poetry, nature plays a central part and becomes a kind of reference frame for all those permanent values the poet is trying to establish. It is both a refuge and a source of inspiration.

Although there had already been fruitful innovations and experiments in the modernistic vein by poets like Jóhann Sigurjónsson (1880–1919), who was Iceland's leading dramatist writing in Danish as well as Icelandic, and Jóhann Jónsson (1896–1932), who spent his adult years in Germany and died of tuberculosis, the first spokesman for a conscious modernistic "revolution" in Icelandic poetry was Steinn Steinarr (1908–58), a skillful versemaker in the traditional style, but above all a poet of sensibility, integrity and courage. He established modernistic poetry in Iceland against heavy odds, especially with the last of his five collections of verse, *Tíminn og vatnid* (Time and the Water; 1948), a cycle of twenty-five poems, each reflecting the poet's self, time, the present, the timeless, but above all his despair at unrequited love. In his last three collections the theme of doubt became ever more pervasive and is essentially the keynote of all his poetic production, played with greater consequence and intensity by him than by any other Icelandic poet of this century. In his poems life gradually takes on the appearance of artificiality, illusion, hallucination—a fantastic jugglery beyond the grasp or control of the individual. As his gloom and pessimism intensified, so also did his sarcastic humor, which sometimes verges on cynicism. His poems grew more metaphysical and abstract and his sense of form more secure. Irony and bitter humor mingle with philosophical resignation and an almost religious "mysticism." His images are concise and clear: he had made a close study of modern painting to good effect.

The modernistic poets following Steinn Steinarr are a curiously incoherent group with little in common except their determination to follow their own bent and write significant poetry in a fresh and stimulating way. With one or two exceptions, they have not enjoyed popularity among the common run of readers, but they were the most expressive and articulate interpreters of reality in Icelandic literature during the first two decades after World War II.

The first was Jón úr Vör (b. 1917), who published two traditional volumes of poetry before he broke through in 1946 with *Þorpið* (The Fishing Village), one of the most original contributions to the free-verse tradition. This is a description of the extremely poor and primitive life of fishermen and their families in a small fishing village before and during the Depression, a simple and straightforward account, without bitterness or protest, filled with sympathy and tenderness and showing intimate familiarity with the lot and feelings of the poor and downtrodden. His later poetry is in much the same vein, his range being limited, his voice quiet and genuine.

The most significant foreign impulses during and after the war came from countries like Sweden, Finland, France, Germany, England, Spain, Greece and America. Steinn Steinarr and Jón úr Vör learned much from Swedish and Finland-Swedish poets of the thirties and forties, and so did some of their younger colleagues, while others turned to France and Germany, and still others sought farther afield. There was thus no single influence to dominate the development, which is one reason for the extraordinary variety of postwar poetry in Iceland.

In the years 1946–53 five poets made their debut and formed the group that was later to be labeled "atom poets," though they were quite heterogeneous. The very fact that they never formed any literary school or movement is an indication that their break with old traditions was not an arbitrary decision inspired by foreign fads, as most of their detractors maintained, but a deeply felt personal need to find new poetic means for expressing their visions in a hitherto unknown social context.

The five poets had and still have very distinct profiles, and they entered the arena in the following order: Stefán Hörður Grímsson (b. 1919) has published three slim volumes since 1946. He has a powerful lyrical talent, a vivid imagination and a sure sense of form and rhythm. The fishing village and the seaside are his favorite settings. Some of his poems express a certain tedium of life, but they are usually enlivened by whimsical humor, startling imagery and a language rich in nuances and cadences. Hannes Sigfússon (b. 1922), who has published four volumes of poetry since 1949, is among the most "difficult" and subtle poets, with an apocalyptic vision, wrestling with the great issues of man's future in the atomic age as well as his severed ties with the past. His first two volumes were poetic cycles where the allusive qualities of words and lines are stretched to the utmost, with striking consequences. Einar Bragi (b. 1921), who has brought out nine slim volumes of verse, has in effect been publishing the same book over and over again, constantly polishing older poems and weeding out those he no longer cares to acknowledge. He is a sensitive master of semi-traditional form, also writing prose poems to good effect. Sigfús Daðason (b. 1928) has only published three volumes since 1951, of which the second was a landmark in Icelandic poetry. He studied in France for many years and was strongly influenced by French thinking and poetry. He shares with Hannes Sigfússon a passionate need to penetrate the essence of contemporary reality but is more philosophical than visionary, exhibiting a fine sense of the nuances of language. In his later poetry there is an air of distant lands coupled with intense nostalgia for his native soil. Like most of his colleagues, he has strong political convictions which lend a sharp edge to some of his poems. Jón Óskar (b. 1921), who has published four collections since 1953, has been considerably influenced by French poetry, some of which he has translated, but his best poems have a peculiarly native ring and are highly suggestive in their repetitive and contrapuntal manner.

In 1955 the "prodigy" of postwar Icelandic poetry, Hannes Pétursson (b. 1931), made his debut and has since added seven widely read and discussed volumes to his poetic output. He is by far the most popular poet of his generation, partly because he has never entirely abandoned the formal patterns of traditional verse, preferring to renovate old meters in much the same way as Snorri Hjartarson and others had done, and to mingle old and new motifs to good effect. He has a marked penchant for historical subjects and a rare ability to give these fresh and often startling significance. Although Hannes Pétursson is an introspective and meditative poet, his verse is vivid and arresting, its sense rarely obscure. In his last volume, *Heimkynni við haf* (Abode by the Sea; 1980), his best to date, he exhibits all his finest qualities and confirms once more that the synthesis he has been striving for is both viable and highly productive of outstanding poetry. Hannes Pétursson studied in Germany and has been strongly influenced by such poets as Hölderlin, Rilke and Else Lasker-Schüler.

Two very dissimilar poets made their debut in 1958. Matthías Johannessen (b. 1930) has published ten collections of poetry, including two cycles which center on the poet's identity and orientation in a chaotic and paradoxical world, weaving mythological references into contemporary contexts. He has a talent for unexpected associations, which are often effective, but is at times tempted to outdo himself in eloquence. His later poetry has turned increasingly religious and "open" without gaining in poetic value. All the same, his voice is distinct and his fecundity admirable. Þorsteinn frá Hamri (b. 1938) has published seven volumes of poems and three outstanding novels which have no counterparts in Icelandic fiction. His verse is deeply rooted in old traditions, but he has gradually evolved a highly personal style, combining modern sensibility with rather traditional diction and imagery. Many of his poems express an inner struggle, contrasting his original rural and new urban milieux. He is introspective, his tone questioning, slightly ambiguous, characterized by doubt and circumspection, imbued with quiet irony and satirical comment on the modern predicament.

There are a host of other poets who have made significant contributions to postwar poetry in Iceland. Among them should be mentioned Jóhann Hjálmarsson (b. 1939), Dagur Sigurdarson (b. 1937), Bödvar Gudmundsson (b. 1939) and the women poets Vilborg Dagbjartsdóttir (b. 1930), Nína Björk Árnadóttir (b. 1941) and Steinunn Sigurdardóttir (b. 1950). The early sixties were rather barren as regards new talent, but in the late sixties and early seventies there was again a fresh flowering. Many of the new poets convey a new tone and a fresh way of looking at the world, both at home and abroad. This group is much less concerned with form than were its predecessors. There is a greater variety of tone and treatment, a casual, matter-of-fact, sometimes whimsical approach, even when serious subjects are being dealt with, whereas the older poets were preoccupied with the so-called "formal revolution," cautiously exploring the possibilities of their new medium.

As to themes, Icelandic poetry naturally deals with the perennial subjects of all poetry: life and death, growth and decay, love and grief, nature and the social environment; but there is perhaps a greater attachment to the native soil than is customary in modern poetry elsewhere, and a very strong sense of history. The contrast between rural and urban life is another conspicuous theme, and so is a deeply felt apprehension about the future of the tiny island nation (population 230,000) in an encroaching world, with special emphasis on the American presence through the military base at Keflavík. At the end of the war, after Iceland had been declared a republic, there was a kind of euphoria, and the people felt united as never before. But with the permanent establishment of the American military base in 1951 all illusions about the unity of the nation were shattered once and for all, and the base has been one of the most persistent motifs in Icelandic postwar literature, prose as well as poetry. An overwhelming majority of writers and intellectuals feel it as the most painful thorn in their flesh, irrespective of their political affiliations. This state of affairs has also made them more keenly aware of national problems in other parts of the world, especially Latin America and Africa.

■ FICTION

The variety and vitality of Icelandic poetry were in no small measure due to the coexistence of more than one poetic tradition from the very beginning (Eddic as well as skaldic or court poetry). In the realm of prose this was not the case. Here the epic-realistic style of the sagas reigned supreme and was dominant in Icelandic prose writing until the mid-1960s with surprisingly few deviations.

The modern epic-realistic tradition reached its peak in two writers—in most respects dissimilar—who had a far-reaching influence on all later prose writing in Iceland. The older of the two, þórbergur þórarson (1889–1974), created a sensation with his essays and eccentric memoirs from 1924 onward. They were revolutionary both in style and ideology. His radical socialist outlook was mixed with a curious interest in occultism and supernatural phenomena. His self-mockery gave sparkle as well as weight to his scathing social satires and frontal attacks on the ruling order. Only a portion of one of his books has been translated into English (and several other languages), under the title *In Search of My Beloved* (New York, 1967).

Another revolutionary author of international stature is Halldór Laxness (b. 1902), who was awarded the Nobel Prize in Literature in 1955. With his narrative skill and vivid style he has done more than any modern novelist to renew Icelandic prose. Indeed, he dominated the literary scene in Iceland from the mid-1920s to the mid-1960s. In his heyday he was an odd mixture of a universal creative genius and a partisan essayist propagating radical socialism and revolution. However, he made a point of separating his art and his social and political preaching, with the result that his novels are largely free from those tendencies which often mar the works of socially conscious writers. He has a surprisingly large range of styles and subjects, so that no two of his novels resemble one another in anything but their felicity of expression and power of character portrayal. A large number of his characters have become as much household figures in Iceland as the old saga heroes or, say, Babbitt and Gatsby in America.

After completing four monumental novels between 1931 and 1946 which capture the Icelandic scene more thoroughly than do any works written in Iceland since the thirteenth century, Laxness in 1948 published a brilliantly executed and consciously tendentious satirical fantasy on contemporary Iceland, *Atómstödin* (*The Atom Station*), which prompted some older patriots to demand that its translation into foreign languages be forbidden. In 1952 came *Gerpla* (*The Happy Warriors*), based on certain classical sagas and written with unfaltering skill in the idiom of the thirteenth century, a feat which most experts would have considered impossible. The novel is a thorough deflation of the ancient heroic spirit and understandably upset some classical scholars in Scandinavia. In 1957 Laxness again surprised his compatriots with a finely wrought, almost lyrical novel about life in Reykjavík at the turn of the century, *Brekkukotsannáll* (The Fish Can Sing). This was the least socially critical of his novels and inaugurated a new phase in his writing. The picaresque novel *Paradísarheimt* (*Paradise Reclaimed*; 1960) was a further departure from his earlier works; it is essentially a philosophical fable about man's quest for the infinite, partly set in the Icelandic Mormon settlement in Utah.

At that point Laxness suddenly turned to the theatre and wrote several plays with moderate success. This detour was misguided, since his peculiar talent is above all epic and only dramatic in the non-theatrical sense. The upshot was that he returned to the novel and published in 1969 *Kristnihald undir jökli* (Christianity at the Glacier), a quasi-fable on the theme of the self-effacing, saintly man of inner peace and natural charity pitted against a man of the world with all the trappings of power and financial success. This is also the theme of his best play, *Dúfnaveislan* (The Pigeon Banquet) and of most of his later work, including *Innansveitarkrónika* (A Country Chronicle; 1970), a description of the valley near Reykjavík where he was brought up on a farm called Laxnes (hence his pen name). Since 1975 he has been publishing his memoirs from childhood and adolescence. His earlier book of autobiographical sketches, *Skáldatími* (A Poet's Time; 1963), aroused international attention owing to the author's scathing revelation of his own gullibility while under the spell of Stalin and communism.

The dominant theme of Icelandic fiction after World War I was the rapid emptying of the countryside and the resulting collision between the old rural way of life and the new urban society which was searching for its own identity, style and valid traditions. Icelandic novelists (not Laxness) tended to romanticize the old values, stressing rural idylls and peasant virtues in the face of an amorphous urbanization. This was invariably done in the tested epic style of the sagas. The overwhelming majority of Icelandic novels treated this theme in one way or another, despite the fact that over seventy percent of the population lived in towns and fishing villages. The emphasis on pastoral novels tended to make Icelandic fiction rather uniform, since the same theme was exploited in one novel after another with only slight variations in style and approach. One explanation of this may be that the new society had not yet evolved the patterns of conduct and moral values necessary for significant novels, nor had the novelists developed adequate techniques to deal with a totally new situation.

Ólafur Jóhann Sigurðsson is a case in point. He is a highly sensitive and lyrical novelist, endowed with acute psychological insight and a strong feeling for nature. He is at his best when dealing with pastoral themes—for instance, in *Litbrigði jarðarinnar* (Shades of the Soil; 1947), about a young man's first love and his subsequent departure from home, or in two novels from 1944 and 1951 about the irreconcilable antithesis of the rural population's dreams of a happy life and the harsh everyday reality. But in his later novels about the postwar situation in Reykjavík there is a feeling of inadequacy: somehow his fine and beautifully composed language fails to capture the texture and quality of the new reality. In this respect he fares much better in his finely wrought short stories and in his poetry mentioned above.

Indriði G. Þorsteinsson (b. 1926) also writes in the traditional manner, but with a difference. His best novels expound the inexorable principle which forces the rural population into abandoning their farms and moving to urban districts and deal with their frequently sad fate in a new and unfamiliar environment. His two best novels are *Land og synir* (Soil and Sons; 1963), describing the painful uprooting of a young farmer from his ancestral farm where his father decides to carry on with his hopeless toil, and *Þjófur í paradís* (A Thief in Paradise; 1967), an idyllic fable describing the pastoral serenity of an isolated parish which is suddenly disrupted by the intrusion of a new settler and his family. Some readers have seen in the latter a sly reference to the American military presence in Iceland.

Of the postwar novelists, Thor Vilhjálmsson (b. 1925; see *BA* 46:3, p. 432 and 47:1, pp. 54–59) was the first real avant-garde writer, bringing home from Paris new impulses and stimulating attitudes. His first publications were three collections of original and colorful short stories and sketches, but since 1968 he has published a series of highly intricate and allusive novels, mostly set in southern climes. Three of these, *Fljótt, fljótt, sagði fuglinn* (Quick, Quick, Said the Bird; 1968), *Óp bjöllunnar* (The Cry of the Beetle; 1970) and *Mánasigð* (Moon Sickle; 1976), form a kind of trilogy about an individual searching for his identity in a crumbling world of lost values and faded ideals. In the first two the reader discerns some sort of mythological or ritual pattern beneath the kaleidoscopic surface of the text, but in the last one the structure of allusions and associations is replaced by a subtle system of repetitions and variations on a host of material and metaphorical motifs; structurally the text forms a circle. Everything takes place on the same level, in one dimension; time is an eternal now, one instant. This structure corresponds to the theme of the novel: repetition and renewal, renewal through repetition. Once again a man in flight, seeking his own, his real self—which in the earlier novels might be found in sensual enjoyment or in a loving relationship with another individual—but here the question is left open: the search is described as a permanent state, a way of life. In most of his other novels Vilhjálmsson treats this theme in different keys and always in his characteristically opulent and vivid language, which frequently calls to mind the painter's palette.

Guðbergur Bergsson (b. 1932) produced, with his novel *Tómas Jónsson metsölubók* (Tómas Jónsson Bestseller; 1966), perhaps the most significant literary revolution since Laxness published *Vefarinn mikli frá Kasmír* (*The Great Weaver from Kashmir*) in 1927. It broke away from all the hallowed narrative and compositional norms and opened up entirely new possibilities for Icelandic fiction. The novel has the form of a monologue conducted by a senile old man, Tómas Jónsson, who is in the process of writing his memoirs. The time element is wiped out: everything happens simultaneously, whether memories or the sensations of the moment's needs; there are no absolutes in human existence, everything is relative and illusory, all boundaries between inner and outer reality disappear, the personality is dissolved and objectified, or transformed into other personalities. There is a feeling of physical decay, darkness and death. In the copious and often coarse descriptions of contemporary Icelanders the author draws a terrifying picture of social and political disintegration and sterility.

In his later books Bergsson has continued to explore the various manifestations of the "anti-life," the wretched and pitiful existence we accept. He has, in the manner of Faulkner, created a whole self-contained world which he expands with every new novel (the same characters appear in novel after novel), a kind of microcosm corresponding to Icelandic society. He is quite merciless in his cruel humor and his exposure of the clichés of everyday thinking habits and values, and like Laxness in *The Atom Station,* he has searchingly and wittily demonstrated the demoralizing effect on the nation of the American military base at Keflavík (his microcosm is located in its vicinity).

Even though Vilhjálmsson and Bergsson are both innovators in Icelandic letters, they are in every respect dissimilar. Bergsson is a kind of fantastic epic writer, concentrating on the contemporary scene in Iceland and creating a wealth of memorable characters, while Vilhjálmsson is a lyrical writer dealing with the predica-

ment of "modern man" in no particular locality and creating no round and living characters.

Not until the mid-1960s did women writers enter the front ranks of Icelandic fiction. There were two of them, both skillful and clever satirists, but different in style and approach. In her second novel, *Snaran* (The Snare; 1968), Jakobína Sigurðardóttir (b. 1918) gave a worker's view of the conditions created by the establishment of foreign industrial concerns in the country, leading to the gradual degeneration of all initiative on the part of the Icelanders. The novel is a short masterpiece and created a sensation when it appeared. Her third novel, *Lifandi vatnið* (The Living Water; 1974), tells the story of a laborer, brought up in the countryside, who suddenly revolts against his inextricable involvement in a society he loathes and finally loses his way entirely. These novels by a farmer's wife in the northeast of Iceland certainly testify to a living literary tradition among the ordinary people.

Svava Jakobsdóttir (b. 1930) is an ambivalent author who seldom makes direct statements. Her first novel, *Leigjandinn* (The Lodger; 1969), is superficially a realistic narrative of a young couple's marriage and housing problems, but this conceals a mordant political satire, one of the most remarkable and effective in Icelandic literature. Jakobsdóttir is also a sensitive short-story writer and an adroit playwright, specializing in the predicament of women in modern society.

Many other fine writers have contributed to the development of Icelandic fiction over the past two decades, such as Þorsteinn frá Hamri, Þorgeir Þorgeirsson (b. 1933), Vésteinn Lúðvíksson (b. 1944), Ólafur Haukur Símonarson (b. 1941) and Pétur Gunnarsson (b. 1947), but their contributions have so far been less weighty than the ones discussed above, even though individual works have been fresh and stimulating, particularly those of Þorsteinn frá Hamri.

Sigurður A. Magnússon, Winter 1982

NORWAY

Tor Edvin Dahl and the Poverty of Norwegian Prosperity

Norwegian literary critics have drawn a curious array of metaphorical arrows from their quivers to describe Tor Edvin Dahl, who presently reigns as Norway's most prolific littérateur and is unquestionably one of Scandinavia's most gifted. Having published as many as nine books in a year, the young Osloite has been hailed as "the millipede of the publishing world," "the rally driver of literature," "the DC-9 of Norwegian letters" and, summarily, "Tor Edvin Superstar." Yet such metaphors fail to convey the talent of this writer, who has been nominated for but has never received the Nordic Council's prestigious literary prize. Nor do they do justice to Dahl's unparalleled versatility, for which he may eventually be best remembered in the annals of Scandinavian literature. Since making his literary debut two decades ago, he has written over a dozen novels, scores of short stories, several radio and television plays, curricular materials for the public school system, analyses of popular culture, works about the Lapps and their assimilation in Norwegian society, books about photography and travel, and children's literature. Dahl has also pseudonymously produced seven book-length works of detective fiction during the past decade. When not further augmenting his imposing personal bibliography, the frenetic author serves as a literary consultant, reviews books for the Oslo daily *Aftenposten,* plays an active role in the Norwegian Writers Guild and pursues his personal interests in jazz and photography.

Dahl's prolificacy proceeds form an innate creativity and an insatiable curiosity, which he harnesses in personal discipline and an efficient daily routine more characteristic of journalists than of the sterotypical novelist. After shaving and "cleaning the last drop of water from the vanity," Dahl seats himself at his typewriter and writes for at least two—more usually four or five—intensive hours, emerging with an average of ten to fifteen pages of unrefined manuscript. Following a midday pause that almost invariably includes a period of swimming, cycling or skiing, he returns to the printed word, reviewing books, editing his own work or evaluating manuscripts for publishers. When in Oslo, Dahl shaves minutes from his local itinerary by weaving through the streets astride a small motorcycle. Yet much of the time he spends away from his family and the Norwegian capital, where he finds it difficult to write efficiently. The solitude of an eighteenth-century mansion in Guasdal, some three hours north of Oslo, proves more amenable to his task. At other times Dahl retreats to the Arctic expanses of Finnmark to ply his trade. Few hours of his week are devoted to socializing. Though affable, he concedes that he feels most comfortable when alone. A voracious reader, Dahl caused a minor uproar several years ago by announcing that he rarely touched the newspapers, an oft-cited admission that helped to burden him with an undeserved image of self-imposed cultural isolation. He devours literary, political and cinematic journals, however, but sacrifices little of his time before the television screen.

Dahl's devotion (one is tempted to say obsession) to literature has deep biographical roots. Born in Oslo in 1943, he grew up in one of its undistinguished quarters while Norway experienced unprecedented prosperity. Although his life-style is in some respects almost Spartan, Dahl concedes that the expectations of the 1950s left an indelible impression on his personality and that he derives no little satisfaction from the bundle of royalty checks that fill his mailbox every January and swell his annual tax return to half a kilogram. He recalls, however, that at an early age he became "skeptical and withdrawn," owing partly to his family's affiliation with Norway's largest nonconformist denomination, the Pentecostal Church, in which Dahl remains an active if atypical member. The introspective youth became a regular visitor at Oslo's main public library and began to develop a familiarity with both Norwegian and foreign literature. Reflecting his eclectic interests, he followed the natural-science line at one of the city's most respected preparatory schools, from which he graduated in 1962.[1]

Dahl harvested a cornucopia of experiences from the turbulent 1960s that are reflected in many of his works. After serving a short stint as an uncertified teacher at Børselv, a desolate harbor village confronting the Arctic Sea, he taught briefly at a home for the mentally handicapped in southern Norway. Cementing his ties with Finnmark, Dahl married in 1965 one of that northernmost county's Lapp natives, with whom he has two children. He matriculated at Sagene Teachers College in Oslo that year and graduated in 1967. The following year Dahl received supplementary accreditation in Nordic languages and literatures at the University of Oslo. That institution was then a caldron of political activity which continued to boil for another decade, but without Dahl's participation. Notwithstanding his undeniable brilliance, he enjoyed only moderate success as a student. Nor was Dahl born literarily with the "generation of 1966," the coterie of leftist writers (Dag Solstad, Jan Erik Vold and others) who took impulses from that day's student radicalism and have contributed heavily to the Marxist literary journal *Profil,* for which he recently has written.

Dahl began to contribute short fiction to several Norwegian periodicals during the mid-1960s. In 1968, at the age of twenty-five, he published his first book, a middling volume of a dozen novellas titled *En sommer tung av regn* (A Summer Full of Rain). In the following year came *Ikke om håp, men heller ikke om håpløshet* (Not About Hope, But Neither About Hopelessness), a more substantial collection focusing on forms of love, a recurrent theme in Dahl's work. His third volume of short fiction, bearing the provocative title *Syv noveller om nødvendige mord* (Seven Short Stories About Necessary Murders), was published in 1971. In a quasi-documentary style that in some respects foreshadowed his detective fiction, Dahl analyzed how incest, social clefts between the lovers and other factors had ended several romantic relationships.

Given the heterogeneity of Dahl's fiction, it would be neither enlightening nor fair to seek an overarching motif in his many works. Yet two intertwining threads which loosely unite several of his novels are apparent. The first is the difficulty of finding one's niche in what many contemporary observers perceive as a disintegrating society. Second, he has underscored the impossibility of preserving whatever values and sanity youth may have in a country whose debilitating maladies include a permeating drive for self-seeking, materialistic freedom and happiness without an awareness of the metaphysical in one's life. Since Dahl himself was molded by a lonely childhood in a city lurching through the vicissitudes of postwar prosperity and secularization, it is hardly surprising that many of his characters are young Osloites whose formative years in broken homes and estrangement from parents and peers alike lead to a thicket of emotional crises and social maladjustment. Precisely this emphasis, so recognizable in various forms and degrees to many urban Norwegian readers, goes far to explain the popularity and timeliness of his works.

Nowhere has Dahl's concern about youth in crisis come to more creative expression than in several imaginative Bildungsromane of the past decade. His first novel, *Den andre* (The Other), published in 1972, deals with a Norwegian student who shows neither remorse nor guilt after killing a friend. Handling his antagonist as a social type, Dahl analyzes how society shares culpability for the crime. Its empty myths of worldly happiness have stunted the murderer's emotional and moral growth, leaving him isolated in the student world of the late 1960s, which sought with little success to fill the void left by the abandonment of traditional values as Norway and other lands stumbled over themselves in their spring into modernity.

Yet Dahl is anything but a romantic seeker who would set back the Norwegian clock to the never-never land which many disgruntled Norwegians credulously believe their country to have been. In the 1973 novel that took him six weeks to write and propelled his name to the forefront of Norwegian letters, *Guds tjener* (God's Servant), Dahl dispenses with the recent past as an emotional refuge for the memories of those disillusioned with the present and as a rhetorical foil for middle-aged Norwegians who would contrast their own childhoods with the challenging environment of their offspring, from whom they now feel estranged. Writing in the

first person and marshaling a number of quasi-autobiographical elements, Dahl paints a memoiristic portrait of Anders Renstad, born in Oslo's blighted East End during the German occupation of Norway. Lacking contact with both his emotionally unstable mother and his aloof father, Anders finds companionship in the imagined presence of his deceased twin brother. He feels accepted only in a Pentecostal church where his half-uncle is the pastor. Yet Anders's involvement with that enthusiastic, nonconformist congregation only widens the cleft separating him from his classmates. Moreover, its piety and legalism leave him ill-prepared for confronting worldly challenges. In his adolescence Anders yearns to escape to what he imagines is freedom but actually amounts to little more than unfettering himself from rapidly fading social taboos. Like a greenhouse plant lacking immunity to the diseases of a normal environment, the youth later succumbs to immoderate drinking, and a warped introduction to sexuality leaves him inadequately equipped for what proves to be shaky marriage. He becomes a victim of his misdirected, isolated striving for personal autonomy. Anders ends his tribulation by returning to a spiritual fellowship armed with broadened social and political horizons and an awareness of his psychological needs.

Though Dahl vowed in the mid-1970s never to write another novel, he returned to the genre in 1980 with the first volume of a trilogy whose sequel appeared the following year. While Dahl is concerned primarily with the impact of postwar social and cultural developments on Norwegian behavior, the chronological scope of these works points to his acumen as an analyst of human nature generally. In *Den første sommeren* (The First Summer), a novel set in the 1950s, Siv, a newlywed in her early twenties who has rebelled against a domineering grandmother and has entered an unhappy marriage, flees from her husband during their honeymoon. The product of a politically reactionary home and religiously oriented if spiritually unbalanced, she meets a fourteen-year-old boy who has run away from his communist parents. The woman is obsessed with a craving for freedom, her juvenile companion with thoughts of death. Though both are immature and alienated by a lack of normal contact with emotionally sound peers, these two polar types eventually contribute to each other's readjustment.

Dahl steps two generations backward in *Renate* to focus on the grandmother, showing how a will to power lurked behind and even prompted many of her ostensibly charitable deeds beginning in the 1920s. Like many of Dahl's other characters, Renate has a personality that can be traced in part to a woefully deficient childhood. Born out of wedlock around the turn of the century, she is raised in an orphange and in 1924 becomes a young widow with a son to care for. Wandering through Norway during the lean interwar years, Renate conducts herself outwardly in accord with the prescriptions of petit-bourgeois ethics; she even initiates a self-help program to aid unemployed fish-cannery workers in Oslo but nevertheless manipulates people in her struggle for survival. Moreover, the increasingly jaded woman develops an emotional shell of defensive armor that leaves her socially impregnable. Her chief, unintentional victim is her cowering son, whose insecurity leads him into the Norwegian Nazi Party and gives rise to an authoritarian personality against which Siv reacts by seeking freedom from familial contact. Once again the iniquities of the fathers—and mothers—are visited upon subsequent generations and, in Dahl's perception, have allied with rapid social change to mold the personalities of many postwar Norwegians.

Dahl completed the trilogy in 1982 with *Abrahams barn* (Abraham's Children), which chronologically follows *Den første sommeren*. Geir Amundsen, the teenage lad of that novel, yields center stage to his older brother Walter, a reformed alcoholic who leaves his career as a seaman to become a (masterfully portrayed) revivalist in Oslo. After the enthusiastic preacher is murdered, Dahl shifts gears and writes what at first glance appears to be a work of detective fiction. The sleuth plays a secondary role, however, as he delves into Walter's life and discovers authoritarian traits that served neither good nor evil exclusively. Moreover, the behavior of the victim's friends and relatives includes homosexuality, dishonesty, marital infidelity, incest and—Dahl implies—murder. In short, *Abrahams barn* encompasses more socially unacceptable acts than most Norwegian readers will admit to confronting in the course of several years. Dahl's simultaneous coauthoring of another 1982 publication, *Den store kriminalboka* (The Great Criminal Book), may help to explain what seems to be an obsession with deviant conduct in this otherwise impressive novel.

The glib Dahl offers no apologies for his pessimistic anthropology. "I have no answer to what is called the murky side of personal love," he concedes. "Perhaps we are closer to love when we relate to one another cautiously than when we strive for something intensely personal and intimate." Yet Dahl prescribes no detailed solutions to the plight of humanity or the pervasiveness of evil. "My task," he declares, "is merely to describe the situation as accurately and in as much detail as I can." Nor does Dahl see his Christian faith as a nostrum for the fundamental problem of evil, partly because he is not convinced that it infuses the believer with a surplus

of charity. Nothing could be more foreign than supererogation in Dahl's fiction.[2]

In harmony with his perception of both postwar Norway and human nature, Dahl has written detective fiction under the pseudonym David Torjussen for over a decade, turning out book manuscripts in as few as eight days. The first, *Etterforskning pågår* (Investigation Under Way), came in 1973 and received the Riverton Prize as the best Norwegian book in the genre that year. Several of his ventures in this field have reflected Dahl's related concerns about modern society and the individual's relationship to it. "Detective novels are by nature politically conservative," he generalizes. "In my opinion, their function is to confirm the reader's hope that this is the best of all worlds—that everything is under control, and that he himself is a good person."[3] Yet Dahl, a political independent who deplores the conservative trend in Norway that swept the Labor Party from power in 1981, refuses to cast his own works in this mold. His willingness nevertheless to write detective fiction is explained in part by the stark opportunity the genre provides "to show that to live in a nonmetaphysical world makes people lonely and abandoned."[4] Moreover, Dahl has utilized detective fiction as a vehicle for keen-eyed social analysis, an international trend manifested in the works of several other Scandinavian writers who have, literarily, turned to crime. Indeed, in Scandinavia this can be traced back at least as far as Carl Hansen's watershed novel *Spild* (Waste), published in Copenhagen in 1905.

Dahl launched his intertwining career in nonfiction in 1970 with a book titled *Samene i dag—og i morgen* (The Lapps Today—and Tomorrow). This timely volume, in which he excercised the pens of a social scientist, journalist and social philosopher, acquired even greater relevance later in the decade when the national government became embroiled in a protracted struggle with representatives of Norway's indigenous minority over the harnessing of the Alta River north of the Arctic Circle. Lamenting that most previous studies of the Lapps had stemmed from outsiders whose view had seldom extended beyond the relatively large towns of Kautokeino and Karasjok, he based much of his own analysis on interviews gleaned in the remote Tana Valley. This approach revealed tensions in what is too loosely thought of as the Lapp "community," especially juxtaposed attitudes toward assimilation and cultural retention as well as the contempt with which sedentary Lapps regard the dwindling number who still follow reindeer herds. Dahl's analysis also sheds light on his perception of Norwegian society generally. Along with many other observers, he finds the homogenizing tendencies of the centralized Norwegian bureaucracy inimical to social pluralism and the commitment to a growth economy destructive, especially to the Lapp way of life. Most well-intended governmental efforts to assist the group, Dahl complains, have in effect strapped them more tightly into a union with anti-pluralistic Germanic Norwegians at the expense of their own culture. Given the present structure of Norwegian society, he sees no via media between the Scylla of Lapp separatism—which he and most Lapps reject as unrealistic—and the Charybdis of assimilation on the majority's premises. Finding little ground for smug satisfaction with the status quo in Norway, Dahl calls for a pluralistic populism to replace the long-standing path of centralized growth capitalism. In terms echoing social philosopher Ernst Schumacher's "Small is beautiful" dictum, he advocates a return to a more diversified economy geared to local resources and cultural interests. Only such an overhauling of Norwegian society, including a resumption of cottage industry, can free Norway from a system to which it is captive and ill-suited.

Since Dahl has long maintained a keen interest in the interplay of literature and society, it was natural for him in the mid-1970s to begin to write about those aspects of popular culture that in Norway fall under the rubric *underholdningslitteratur,* or entertainment literature. By doing so he has cast considerable light on the shaping of the contemporary Norwegian mind. In the first of several books about the subject, *Tegneseriene: Verdens mest populære lesestoff* (The Comics: The World's Most Popular Reading Material), Dahl rejects categorical attitudes that either laud this form as "the most interesting and meaningful means of expression of our time" or damn it as "garbage, pollution of both the environment and children's minds, et cetera." He admits that he personally finds the comics "exciting as a means of expression," one which gives him "joy and satisfaction." But this, adds Dahl, is largely because he reads specialized, imported material within the genre. The indigenous Norwegian entries in the market have little artistic value in his estimation. Owing to a dearth of constructive criticism and to the fact that only those with a circulation of over 8,000 copies can survive, "the comics in Norway today are of thoroughly low quality, characterized by commercialism, repetitiveness and a lack of imagination."[5]

In a tetralogy of analyses written in part for use in the public schools, Dahl then sought to instruct consumers about the impact on them of what in Norwegian is called *kiosklitteratur*—the immensely popular paperbacks that chronicle the heroics of frontier gunslingers and the wartime valor of Allied commandos, trace romantic intrigues through the corridors of Norwegian hospitals and mansions and expose the foibles of con-

temporary celebrities. In the concluding volume of this series Dahl dissects the *underholdningslitteratur* industry itself, posting many a caveat in his campaign to warn readers about its influence, which he believes is essentially negative.

Dahl is especially penetrating in analyzing the popularity of Kjell Hallbing (b. 1934), whose scores of books about U.S. Marshal Morgan Kane have sold over 8,000,000 copies in Norway and have been translated into several other languages, including English.[6] Dahl gives tongue-in-cheek credit to this singular achievement in Norwegian letters and admits that Hallbing writes well at times. Yet his reformer's view of *underholdningslitteratur* in general remains firm: "A serious indictment of much of this literature is that it fails to give any insight into problems, only momentary relief. Instead of investigating crime as a social ill, one simply waits for Sherlock Holmes."[7]

Dahl's first love remains fiction, however, through which he believes he can best depict the ever-present tensions of modern life. "Nonfiction places reality into a system, but belles lettres reveal that it is more complicated," he explains. "In real life, the calculations don't always balance so nicely."[8]

Dahl admitted in 1981 that his worst "nightmare" as a writer whose productivity exceeds mere prolificacy is that someday his seemingly bottomless well of ideas will run dry.[9] Presumably few observers of contemporary letters expect such a drought ever to lay waste to all of this writer's diverse fields. Though his familiar chipmunk smile is beginning to sag and his boyish image is receding along with his hairline, Dahl will likely remain at least as perspicacious and prominent a critic of Norwegian society and culture for the rest of the twentieth century as he now has been for a decade.

Frederick Hale, Winter 1983

[1] Bjarne Lindbekk, "Romanforfattaren Tor Edvin Dahl," *Norsk litterær årbok,* Oslo, 1974, pp. 154–66; "Denne Dahl," *Boktips fra Sentralbokhandelen,* 2 (September 1981), p. 13; *Arbeiderbladet* (Oslo), 14 November 1981.

[2] Lise Vislie Jor, "Røyken som farer langs bakken," *Vår Kirke,* 95 (17 October 1981), p. 10.

[3] Tor Edvin Dahl, "Kriminalromanen," *Vinduet,* 26:3 (1972), p. 30.

[4] *Vårt Land* (Oslo), 26 January 1974.

[5] Tor Edvin Dahl, *Tegneseriene,* Oslo, 1977, pp. 7, 125–27.

[6] Tor Edvin Dahl, *Helter og mordere,* Oslo, 1978, pp. 18–31.

[7] *Aftenposten* (Oslo), supplement, 20 November 1981.

[8] Ibid.

[9] *Arbeiderbladet,* 14 November 1981.

Alfred Hauge's Utstein Monastery Cycle

Norwegian fiction in the 1970s has been dominated by a group of young authors who together have attempted to create an ideologically-based literature. The avowed purpose of such writers as Dag Solstad, Tor Obrestad and Edvard Hoem has been to use their art as a weapon in the class struggle. As their subject matter they have generally taken the life of the common man and his position in society past and present, emphasizing groups of people rather than individual human beings. This is a familiar theme in Norwegian literature, and the narratological devices used by these writers also seem slightly less than innovative.

In contrast with the somewhat traditional works of these radical writers, however, the student of modern Norwegian literature also finds the technically and thematically innovative work of the ideologically less flamboyant novelist and critic Alfred Hauge. This is particularly remarkable because the author has reached his level of narratological sophistication relatively late in his career. This article will examine his most recent work, the five-volume Utstein Monastery cycle (1967–79).

Born in Stjernarøy in Western Norway in 1915, Hauge grew up in a rural area which has been one of the strongholds of popular pietistic religiosity in Norway. He early accepted the religious ideas present in his surroundings, and he has maintained his religious interest throughout his life. Hauge is, however, also a humanist who repeatedly returns to questions of the individual's situation in life and the choices with which he is confronted. His literary debut took place in 1941, when he published *Septemberfrost* (The Frost of September), a historical novel with a message of encouragement to people in occupied Norway. Then came several novels in which the author drew on his intimate knowledge of life in Western Norway; their main value lies in their faithful portrayal of a local community at a time of transition from the old agrarian social order to a twentieth-century reality. Two novels from this period, namely *Ropet* (The Cry; 1946) and *Ingen kjenner dagen* (Nobody Knows the Day; 1955), also treat the conflict between religious and artistic demands so keenly felt by the author.

Hauge became internationally known for his *Cleng Peerson* (1961–65; the English translation was published by Twayne in 1975), a trilogy based on the life of the man who has been called the father of Norwegian emigration to America. In addition to portraying the phenomenon of emigration itself, however, Hauge has also succeeded in fictionally recreating a personality

which from the historical sources emerges as no less than enigmatic: the historical Cleng can be viewed as a hero and even a saint, or as a cheat and a liar. In his trilogy Hauge solves the problem of how to bring the many conflicting aspects of Cleng's character together into one whole by having the aged Cleng tell the story of his life in a series of letters to his foster daughter Anne.

Alfred Hauge's major work is his Utstein Monastery cycle, which consists of the novels *Mysterium* (Mystery; 1967) and *Legenden om Svein og Maria* (The Legend of Svein and Maria; 1968), a collection of poetry titled *Det evige sekund* (The Eternal Second; 1970) and an intended series of novels under the common title *Århundre* (Century). Two of these have so far appeared, namely *Perlemorstrand* (A Shore Made of Mother-of-Pearl; 1974) and *Leviathan* (1979). What connects these works is their central idea, namely the question of how it is possible for human beings to endure suffering in such a manner that their humanity is preserved or even enhanced, and how people can be aided by others in enduring suffering. Hauge has posed this question both poignantly and without sentimentality.

When *Mysterium* was first published, it was particularly the narrative technique which surprised the reviewers. The narrator repeatedly addresses the reader, discusses the novel's characters and their actions with him and even invites him to finish the work: the last sentence in the book ends with a colon, and the reader is asked to fill in two names. The novel also has little action in the traditional sense. A victim of amnesia named Victor arrives at a place which can be identified as Utstein Monastery, where he meets a Greek professor of archeology named Hermes Oneiropompos. Victor is searching for his lost memory in order that he might know where to find his wife and daughter.

The illusion of reality is completely shattered, however, when Victor and the professor begin exploring some tunnels and caverns under the monastery. It soon becomes apparent that their wanderings are actually taking place in the hidden recesses of Victor's unconscious. These experiences are also supplemented by reports of dreams which Victor has between his trips with Oneiropompos. The text thus takes on the appearance of a psychiatrist's journal. Victor finally comes out of his amnesia, and he remembers that he left his wife and lost his memory at a time when she was in the midst of a sudden attack of pain caused by a malignant brain tumor. He is now ready to return to her and to face the effects her illness will have on their life together.

What, then, is the mystery referred to in the novel's title? I would suggest that it is the question of the author's message to the reader, or the meaning of the book. In his final section the narrator, who is Hauge's alter ego, explicitly refuses to illuminate the question of meaning: "No matter how willing the narrator is to assist the reader, it would still be impossible to answer all questions which might be asked. A book is its own interpreter. Or the reader is its interpreter."[1] In an essay which Hauge was asked to write for *Norsk litterær årbok* (Yearbook of Norwegian Literature), however, he states that *Mysterium* can only be understood correctly to the extent that the archetypal language of the dreams in the novel is understood.[2] An ironic reference to C. G. Jung toward the end of *Mysterium* also indicates that Jungian thought might possibly illuminate the novel (see p. 210). The ironic quality of the remark shows, however, that *Mysterium* should not be treated simply as a Jungian case study.

Alfred Hauge's friend, the psychiatrist Gordon Johnsen, wrote in an article included in a volume published to honor Hauge that "a book like *Mysterium* can tell us more about how it is to pass through an analysis together with a human being than any textbook in analysis."[3] The character Victor can well be regarded as a patient, and Hermes Oneiropompos as a fellow human being or even analyst who accompanies him on his journey into the depths of his inner being. (Hermes is god of the underworld as well as protector of travelers, and Oneiropompos means "he who guides through dreams.") Victor is approximately fifty years old at the time of this experience, and his process of individuation has come to a halt. He has not been able to reach a state of integration and wholeness, "an attitude, . . . a consciousness detached from the world" which would have prepared him for death.[4] When his wife has a melanoma removed from her cheek a few years after their marriage, he has a nervous breakdown. When her malignant brain tumor is discovered shortly before their twenty-fifth wedding anniversary, husband and wife take a vacation during which her attack and his second breakdown occur.

Victor flees into the nervous breakdown with its accompanying amnesia not only because he cannot tolerate the sight of his wife's suffering, but also because her impending death forcefully reminds him of the fact that he too must die. His awareness of this concern for self in the face of his wife's misery causes him to feel deeply ashamed. This feeling manifests itself in a series of three dreams which emphasize the tension between appearance and reality, as well as in a scene during the first journey through the subterranean vaults. Here Victor sees himself sitting on a throne as a god, and a figure which is half himself and half turkey is dancing around the throne.

Hauge encourages the reader to compare himself to Victor and to search his soul in order to determine if he possesses the human qualities of empathy, tenderness and the ability to sustain others through suffering which Victor is in part lacking. Victor's process of individuation advances in the course of the novel, and through the archetypal symbolism Hauge hopes to engage not only the reader's intellect, but also his unconscious. *Mysterium* thus becomes a kind of Jungian Bildungsroman in that it attempts to further the reader's process of individuation by portraying that of its main character.

Hauge's question of how to achieve an integrated self is one which is typical of existential humanism. The answer is to be found in *Mysterium's* most important symbol, a rotating cross to which human beings have been fastened. The cross is a symbol of suffering, but through its rotation it takes on the appearance of a sun, the Jungian symbol of both the unity of the self and the divine.[5] Man can achieve unity of the self by passing through suffering and by actively identifying with the suffering of others, thus helping them to bear their burdens. Since Hauge is a committed Christian, however, he has also pointed out how, to him, religion makes suffering more bearable. He quotes the prophet Isaiah, whose statement he reads as referring to Christ: "Surely he hath borne our griefs, and carried our sorrows" (53:4, King James version; *Mysterium,* p. 214). He then bears personal testimony to the effect which a religious stance has on the human perception of suffering: "This certainly means that through Christ there are ways out of suffering. But it also means that through him, the blessed one, there are ways which lead into suffering, for the ways of suffering are the ways of love" (214).

Such homilies are few and far between in Hauge's mature authorship, and most readers are probably appreciative of that. It should be noted, however, that Hauge views religion neither as a substitute for genuine personal development nor as an agent which will magically transform suffering into felicity. It is Christ the man who has both suffered himself and aided others in passing through their tribulations. This view of Christ is both a genuinely religious one and one which is compatible with Hauge's general humanism.

The use of archetypal symbols is continued in *Legenden om Svein og Maria,* where Hauge has created an elaborate myth which portrays the struggle between good and evil. A brother and a sister have been charged with bringing a bag of straw from the manger in which Christ was born to a place called The Dead Paradise, or the Garden of Eden in its fallen condition. They are to be met there by the Prince, whose receipt of the straw will ensure the inability of the powers of evil, embodied in the bird Tubal, to conquer and bring death to all the world. Maria, an anima figure, is given a mirror in which she will be able to see the Prince's face, and a conch shell which will enable her to hear his voice. She is particularly warned not to lose her magical objects through trickery which plays on her noble sentiments. Svein, who represents the young hero, is given a double-edged sword with which to defend his sister. Maria, the more important of the two, will be married to the Prince upon the successful completion of her task.

The Prince is to be identified with Christ. At the end of the myth, he becomes the dying hero and is fastened to the now dead Tree of Life as if to a cross. Tubal, who throughout the story uses those who follow him to frustrate Maria's purpose and who in the end appears to be victorious, corresponds to the Jungian shadow archetype, or the evil which is to be found in all human beings. This is borne out by the fact that he, flying through the air, brings a deadly plague to those on whom his shadow falls.

Hauge's myth thus deals with man's situation in a world where good and evil are not easily distinguished. The author makes extensive use of motifs from legend and folktale, but the basic structure of his myth is a biblical one. In myth the death of the hero demands a regeneration, be the hero's name Balder, Osiris or Christ. The symbolic death of Hauge's Prince implies a restitution, in this case the return of the paradisiacal condition of the world.

At least as important as the legend itself, however, is the frame in which Hauge has placed it. The story is told by the monk Mortem Portendo (the name signifies "I foretell death"), who comes to Utstein Monastery on the evening of 31 October 1517. The time is a turbulent one; the monastery has recently been attacked by a rival of its abbot, and only seven monks are left. Over a period of three weeks they listen attentively to Mortem's story, but they do not like the apparent victory of evil in the tale and do not perceive its true significance. Then several of them become ill with the plague which, in the legend, Tubal brings upon the world. When the dying monks are brought into the church and are placed before the altar, the image of Christ which hangs there suddenly breaks out with the draining abscesses which are characteristic of the plague. The remaining monks expect those who have fallen ill to be miraculously healed. They do not understand that a miracle has actually taken place: Christ has shown them that he bears their illness and their affliction and that through him they can find a way out of their suffering. The myth in *Legenden om Svein og Maria* thus becomes an elaborate illustration of the Isaiah passage which is quoted at the end of *Mysterium*.

Del evige sekund is not so much a collection of individual poems as a poetic cycle; the author has stated that the order in which the poems appear is of primary importance. Hauge has also pointed out that Jungian thought has influenced the book greatly: "When I started reading Jung, it was as if shock after shock of recognition went through me. I was at home in his world."[6] *Det evige sekund* shows that Jung has both given Hauge added understanding of his own internal life and influenced his imagery. A good example of this is the poem "Mytisk biletbok" (Mythical Picturebook), which Hauge in an article has characterized as a myth about the encounter of animus and anima, or the masculine and feminine elements of existence.[7]

In the volume's introductory poem Hauge indicates that an unusual kind of experience has given rise to his poetry: "I have not sought out the unusual. / But the unusual / has sought me out" (16). It appears that this experience underlies the whole of the Utstein Monastery cycle, for in the same article Hauge quotes the above three lines as an answer to the question of why he, starting with *Mysterium,* writes in such a different manner. It should therefore not be surprising that *Det evige sekund* contains thematic elements which connect it with the two previous novels, but there are also aspects which point forward to *Århundre.*

One of Hauge's most significant achievements in *Det evige sekund* is the formulation of a philosophy of history which informs his choice of narrative technique in his later books. This philosophy is expressed mythically in the prose poem "Forvandling" (Metamorphosis). A young nobleman and a woman of the people have a beautiful daughter named Iselin. At the age of five, however, she is suddenly changed into an ugly monster. The parents seek for means by which the process can be reversed, but Iselin becomes more monstrous each time another remedy is employed. She finally returns to normal, however, and a suitor comes. In the marriage ceremony, which takes place in church, the groom is referred to as Isidor Saeculum XX, and the bride is called Iselin Saeculum XV. The two are wed but immediately disappear. At the same time the life processes of their parents are reversed, and they gradually become two newborn infants. The priest then christens the father Isidor Saeculum XXI and the mother Iselin Saeculum XVI.

On one level this prose poem deals with parenthood and the commitment of parents to a child who has to pass through much mental or physical suffering. On the historical-philosophical level, however, Hauge expresses his view that the fifteenth century and the twentieth century are basically similar. Elsewhere he has said that this similarity consists in a fundamental change in people's situation in life.[8] The fifteenth century brought about the historical situation in which the Reformation later took place, and the religious and political upheavals caused people to lose their spiritual bearings. The result was growing fear, superstition and such atrocities as the witch burnings. Saeculum XVI was the result of Saeculum XV, and the events of Saeculum XXI will be the result of the actions of Saeculum XX, which have caused the present generation to lose the firmer spiritual foundation of the past.

In *Perlemorstrand* and *Leviathan* Hauge continues his inquiry into the question of how human beings can experience growth through suffering. Whereas *Mysterium* and *Legenden om Svein og Maria* dealt with the theme from an individualistic and mythical perspective, however, Hauge now places his figures squarely in a twentieth-century sociological reality. Both novels are set on a small island which appears to be modeled on the one where Hauge grew up, and the author's intimate knowledge of life there enables him to create a strong aura of reality. In addition to the historical perspective, the two books also express the philosophy of history which Hauge imbedded in his myth "Forvandling."

The main character in *Århundre* is Bodvar Staup, "en mann som har sin levetid i vårt århundre" (a man who has his life-span in our century; *Leviathan*, p. 9). The first-person narrator of both books, who is virtually identical to Hauge, is one of Bodvar's childhood friends. In *Perlemorstrand*, which the author/narrator says is written down at his cabin Sjoarbu during the months of September and October 1973, the narrator primarily tells the story of Bodvar's childhood during the decade 1920–30. The events of this period are thus seen from the perspective of a contemporary observer who was then a child and who is now a man well past the middle of his life. There is an additional temporal level, however, for the narrator also tells about a period of time which he and Bodvar spent together at Utstein Monastery during the month of June 1973. At this time they often talked about the events of their common childhood. The narrator is thus enabled to give the reader access to Bodvar's own childhood memories.

The story of Bodvar Staup is brief. He grows up together with his first cousin and foster brother Mons, and the two are rivals for the love of their common aunt and stepmother. Bodvar, who before his father's remarriage has had the upper hand in his relationship with Mons, sees that he is no longer favored and becomes intensely jealous. The narration on the first temporal level ends when Bodvar brings Mons and another of their aunts, Tina, to a drinking bout at the home of a questionable character named Kid Skarvaskjer. The two boys and Tina get drunk, but Bodvar leaves before completely losing control. While both Mons and Tina are in a stupor, Tina is raped by Kid, who then leaves the island. Mons awakens, sees the bloody Tina, believes that he has committed the crime and takes his own life.

Bodvar, who feels that he is responsible for his brother's death, has a nervous breakdown. He spends some time in a mental institution but continues to feel a desperate need to atone by taking upon himself the suffering of others. The narration on the second temporal level, or the month of June 1973, ends with one of Bodvar's numerous failures to remove suffering from other people.

In *Leviathan* the story of Bodvar Staup is continued on three temporal levels corresponding to those of *Perlemorstrand,* namely a level of remembered experience spanning the years 1930–70, a second level when Bodvar and the narrator are together at Utstein Monastery in the summer of 1981, as well as the time when the story is being written down by the author/narrator in January 1979. The burden of the story is Bodvar's continued search for atonement and his repeated failures, until he recognizes his fundamental megalomania and understands that he cannot free others from suffering, but only assist them in enduring it. Bodvar's path therefore leads from a state of wholeness felt in his earliest childhood, through his fratricidal experience and its attendant schizoid state, then back to a state of inner unity and peace. The mother-of-pearl image, which also refers to the womb, serves as the most important image of wholeness, and the shore made of mother-of-pearl becomes symbolic of the goal of the process of individuation. The sea monster Leviathan stands for those forces which prevent man from reaching his spiritual destination. In *Leviathan* the monster appears in the shape of a sea serpent, a giant whale which is being trapped and killed, and a shipwrecked oil tanker. The forces which inhibit man's spiritual progress can thus be identified as primarily fear and greed. The twentieth century is dominated by the latter.

The theme of growth through suffering is reinforced by the examples of several secondary characters. The most important one is *Leviathan*'s Barbro Bjelland, who in 1622 was accused of witchcraft and burned. Her story is used to convey to the reader what to Hauge is the essence of the sixteenth century, namely fear. In his myth "Forvandling" Hauge links the sixteenth and the twenty-first centuries, and he thus shows that he expects the present century of greed to be followed by another century of fear. Barbro Bjelland's story indicates, however, that such qualities as tenderness, empathy and the ability to sustain others through suffering can flourish in select individuals even under conditions of mass hysteria.

Both *Perlemorstrand* and *Leviathan* are similar to *Mysterium* in that Hauge frequently addresses the reader directly, thus breaking down the illusion of reality which he so skillfully creates. By alternating between illusion and reality, Hauge is able to communicate directly with his readers both through their reason and their emotions. By means of his archetypal imagery, he also attempts to reach the reader's unconscious. His sophisticated narrative technique serves as the vehicle for a simple yet important message: even though he finds himself in an often hostile world, man must not neglect the cultivation of some quintessentially human qualities.

Jan Sjåvik, Winter 1982

¹ Alfred Hauge, *Mysterium*, Oslo, Gyldendal, 1967, p. 212. All of Hauge's Utstein Monastery books have been published by Gyldendal. Translations are my own unless otherwise indicated.

² Alfred Hauge, "Røynsler og refleksjonar kring romandiktinga," *Norsk litterær årbok*, 1968, p. 180.

³ Gordon Johnsen, "Innsyn," in Odd Kvaal Pederson, ed., *Alfred Hauges landskap*, Stavanger, Lu-Mi, 1975, p. 103.

⁴ Anthony Storr, *C.G. Jung*, New York, Viking, 1973, pp. 81–82. Storr quotes Jung's "Commentary on 'The Secret of the Golden Flower,'" in *Alchemical Studies, Collected Works*, 13, 46.

⁵ Kjetil Flatin, "Fra *Septemberfrost* til *Leviathan*: En studie i tematisk utvikling i Alfred Hauges romaner" (forthcoming).

⁶ Alfred Hauge, "Om 'Det evige sekund' og kritikken av boka," *Syn og segn*, 77 (1971), p. 393.

⁷ Ibid., p. 394.

⁸ Ibid.

SWEDEN

Karl Ragnar Gierow: A Skeptic's Way

Karl Ragnar Knut Gierow was born in the southwestern port city of Hälsingborg on 2 April 1904. His poetry first appeared in a school publication when he was seventeen. At the University of Lund Gierow belonged to the circle around the student paper *Lundagård,* in which he published numerous poems. He attracted critical attention first with *Solen lyser* (The Sun Is Shining; 1925), a collection of pallid but graceful and melodious verse. In general these poems reveal more youthful self-consciousness and posing than deep thought or experience, but they do show a considerable formal talent. Some progress is made in the 1928 volume *Den gyllene ungdomen* (The Golden Youth). The majority of the poems are still vague and impressionistic, but in the last

section of the book, "Vandrare pa vägen" (Wanderer[s] on the Journey), something of the mature Gierow is visible. The image of the wanderer, unsure of the goal but committed to the journey, became one of Gierow's most pregnant metaphors for the enigma of human existence.

The somber tone of *Den gyllene ungdomen,* a radical shift from the carefree optimism of Gierow's first volume, reflects the skepticism and relativism that pervaded post-World War I Europe. Gierow, whose major subject was philosophy, was deeply affected by the speculation over the validity of existing notions of ethics and metaphysics which flourished especially during his university years. He found a counterinfluence to attacks on the very notion of values in Nicolai Hartmann's theories of philosophical ethics.¹ To a large extent Gierow's oeuvre can be understood as an ongoing attempt to gain insight into the nature of morality. He never quite got over the sense of ideational rootlessness and consequent uncertainty of purpose articulated in *Den gyllene ungdomen.* The wisdom that "our life has a finish, but no goal," which concludes the title poem of the volume, is the only wisdom that poet Gierow ever feels safe in expressing.

In 1930 the noted literary historian Fredrik Böök recommended Gierow for an advisory position with the prestigious Stockholm publishing house Norstedts & Sons, where he remained until 1937. During the years at Norstedts Gierow managed to produce a steady output of reviews, poems, translations and several feature programs for radio. Gierow joined the staff of the Swedish Radio Service, Radiotjänst, in 1937. During his nine-year stay he made a truly innovative contribution to Swedish radio programming. Sweden in the 1930s and 1940s was predominantly rural, with its sparse population scattered over a wide area. Radio was an effective and important medium for disseminating educational and cultural information. Demographic circumstances, combined with Swedish Radio's close ties in personnel and repertoire to Swedish theatre and film, gave rise to the notion of radio as a kind of broad-based popular theatre. A similar development took place in England.

In keeping with the notion of radio as a folk theatre, Gierow translated and adapted dramas from classical and contemporary theatre repertoire for radio. He wrote introductions for these dramas as well as for various recital series. In addition he wrote radio dramas, travelogues and even a libretto for a radio operetta. A popular form developed by Gierow was the witty and humorous debate on unexpected issues. His most valuable contribution to radio, though, was the feature program. Gierow wrote features on a wide variety of topics from geography to ballads. His historical chronicles were particularly popular, blending factual reportage and historical documents such as letters or newspaper accounts with poetry, music, acoustical effects and bits of dramatic dialogue.

These chronicles and features were invaluable not only for their entertainment and pedagogical content, but also for their propagandistic effect during the war years. In drawing attention to Swedish history, literature, music and national heritage, Gierow's programs could not help but bolster public morale. His radio features are the direct counterpart of American and British wartime radio drama. For example, Gierow's "1914—In Memoriam" and subsequent documentaries of specific years are the Swedish equivalents of the popular British series, the "BBC Scrapbooks." Gierow stood in close personal and professional contact with Laurence Gilliam, head of the BBC's feature department, and the two cooperated on a number of programs. The feature and the historical chronicle as developed by Gierow had their peak of popularity in the 1930s and 1940s. With the end of the war and the accompanying demographic and social changes, the pedagogic and propagandistic feature program lost its primacy. Gradually, a more esthetically oriented literary radio play began to gain in importance.[2]

Gierow muses retrospectively that radio may have had a deleterious effect on his writing. In his nearly ten years of steady, hasty activity there had been no time for revision. Many of his features were written for one occasion only, and often were composed to fit a specific cast. At times Gierow dictated lines to the cast as he wrote them.[3] Nonetheless, Gierow's years with radio coincided with his most active creative period. During this time he collaborated on a number of films, some of which were quite successful. From 1937 through 1946 Gierow remained active as a critic and essayist, published two volumes of poetry and saw five dramas produced.

Gierow captured the imagination of his contemporaries with the 1937 volume of poetry *Ödletid* (Dinosaur Age). Foreboding of war is combined with a general criticism of civilization in the title poem, which takes its images from the prehistoric reptilian era. Gierow condenses geologic time in depicting the emergence of man as coeval with the decline of the great reptiles, but this enables him to draw a parallel between human arrogance and primordial, unabashed primitiveness. Despite Gierow's critical attitude, his depiction of the monstrous reptiles and man's monstrous presumption has a vitality that threatens to celebrate the regression he condemns.

Herd by herd
Wandering monsters excreted
Droppings like massive stones.

Breath by breath
Up from gorges and jungle-marsh floated
King Pythons death-dealing exhalation.[4]

Civilization's unreflecting progress and progression toward war appear as a monumental regression. Gierow's reference to modern man as the "monster-superman" (*vidunderövermannen*) in the sixth stanza might well be an allusion to the Nietzschean concept of the *Übermensch,* vulgarized by the Nazis. This perverse and presumptuous "superman" has created a new "age of reptiles."

Once more the earth
Witnesses lumbering hulks in armor.
Once more sea spray
Dances round gray leviathans' snouts.

Once more deadly
Dragons attack from the skies.
Once more from gorges and gloomy marsh
Death-dealing vapors stream.

The poem concludes with a grim prediction that surfeited mankind will perish through its experiments with microbes, a fate that still looms very possible. Just as the dinosaurs literally outgrew their biological limits, mankind will destroy itself through hyperdeveloped cunning. Gierow's vision of a writhing, monstrous new primitivity in the title poem is complemented by other texts which protest against war in general, and a rather sentimental tribute to those who suffered in World War I. Other poems are completely nonpolitical. "Näktergalen" (The Nightingale) depicts the quest for poetry itself in its description of the search for an elusive melody of the songster "heard midst the shadows, and seen by none." The delicately understated lullaby "Natten sjunger själv" (The Night Herself Sings) has been called one of Gierow's most successful poems.

Mother who bore you
knows what she bore.
Still I can hold you,
form of my form
—glance which you learn with,
knee which you grieve with,
arms which embrace you
when you are worn.

Days which you run through,
give out at last.
Your self-delusions
loosen their grasp.
Legends I tell to you.
Shrouding I spread for you.
One day your pupils,
I will blow out.

Although Sweden was officially neutral during World War II, there was no certainty that that status would be honored. In fact, Sweden's ability to remain at least theoretically neutral depended to a large extent on the concessions the government made to Germany. The country was mobilized without much conviction that it could successfully defend itself. Public opinion with regard to neutrality was divided, especially after the Soviet invasion of Finland. The literary response to Sweden's precarious situation was largely traditional, patriotic and inspirational in form and tone. The emphasis of this production ranged from impassioned campaigns against the policy of neutrality to a general rallying around the notions of homeland and humanistic values.[5] Gierow's historical chronicles are one example of his contribution to the literature of mobilization, or *beredskapslitteraturen*. *Ödletid* tended in this direction, but *Vid askens rötter* (At the Roots of the Ash; 1940) openly reflects the spirit of mobilization.

This sentiment is highly ambivalent in Gierow's poems, for it is qualified by abstraction, fatalism and a criticism of violence, even in self-defense. The first cycle in the volume, "Väktarsånger" (Watchman's Songs), interprets the war on an abstract level. Both the title of the cycle and that of the volume are taken from Nordic mythology. The ash is Ygdrasil, the mighty tree whose roots and branches support and unite the parts of the universe, and the watchman is Heimdal, the guardian of the bridge leading to Asgard, the abode of the gods. It is Heimdal who will give the signal to begin Ragnarök, the final battle between good and evil in which all creation will be destroyed. The poems in "Väktarsånger" are Heimdal's observations of events leading up to the final destruction and the rejuvenation that will follow it. Apocalyptic imagery was common in Swedish poetry of the time, and although other writers alluded to Nordic myth, Gierow was the only poet to exploit it consistently.[6]

The fifth poem in the cycle, which focuses on the tense moment before the outbreak of Ragnarök, illustrates the fatalistic, somber tone of the cycle. Pronounced rhythmic accents and absence of rhyme have an austerity reminiscent of Old Germanic verse.

Asgard's
hero and hope,
dread of all life in Utgard!
Sleep-weighted, weaponless
you slept in impotent peace.
Evil thrives,
swells in the bud.
The trolls raise their battleground,
Madness breaks loose,
The time of the vultures has come.

Gierow's critical attitude toward his own time is evident in Heimdal's reproachful tone. The poem closes on a note of fatalism and foreboding.

Bare
Seeking the weapon's shaft
I see your fingers groping.
Torpor has plundered calmly
him who in torpor trusts.
Valhalla
has lost its might.
The gods are getting older.
Sleep-drugged, blissful, inert
slept the powerful Thor.

The pessimism of this text and others in the cycle is qualified by the last poem of the cycle, which affirms a recurring pattern of genesis and destruction.

"Väktarsånger" was conceived as a personal vision of world events, but Heimdal-Gierow's sub specie aeternitatis perspective counteracts the actuality of the subject. Nazism is never named specifically. Instead, Gierow depicts a kind of collective masochism. Humanity tortures and deforms itself. Such abstraction was by no means unique to Gierow. Of his contemporaries in Sweden only Gullberg and Lagerkvist referred explicitly to Nazism in poetic works.[7] Abstraction is found in the works of the German exiled writers and is the most salient feature of the literature of the so-called "inner emigration" in Nazi Germany. The ambivalence of Sweden's role in the war combined with Gierow's tendency toward speculation may explain the abstraction in his wartime verse.

The poems in the section "Nordisk vinter" (Nordic Winter) are overtly political, but even they are ambivalent. On the one hand Gierow portrays Scandinavia's neutrality as self-satisfied passivity that will not preclude its demise. In "Nordic Winter" he writes:

We huddle inside Europe's frozen nook,
five aging folks, in winter's dusky night,
with wind and darkness waiting at the door,
we fluff our feathers out, and pass the time.

. . . .

We sit, each for himself, in firelight glow.
We hear the fingers fumbling at the catch,
and we shall one by one go toward the door,
with very little hope of coming back.
(1936)

On the other hand, in texts such as "Ett land" (A Land), "Övervintring" (Wintering), "De stora orden" (The Great Words) and "Folksaga" (Folk Saga) Gierow appeals unabashedly to a simple patriotism. Ultimately, however, the "mobilization" which he supports is an inner preparedness rather than military defense: "You'll find that border on map nor chart / That border runs right through my heart," he writes in "Försvars-förbund" (Defense Pact).

■ ■ ■

The spirit of mobilized Sweden does not emanate from Gierow's dramas as it does from his poetry, but there can be little doubt that the war had a formative impact on them. The plays are dominated by Gierow's concern with ethical and metaphysical issues. The existence of evil, the problem of power and human free will and individual responsibility are Gierow's themes. The phenomenon of Hitler may well be reflected in Gierow's fascination with cruel, amoral tyrannical figures. Apart from his one comedy, *Av hjärtans lust* (To One's Heart's Content), each of the dramas contains at least one such figure.

Evil appears basically in two guises in the plays. It is either a radical, incomprehensible force that intrudes into the human sphere at the slightest opportunity, or it is the product of human arrogance and egocentricity. Gierow equates the two in the allegorical *Domkyrkospel* (Cathedral Play; 1946), in which the protagonist breaks evil's spell by guessing its name: "The Evil One's name is I." Egocentricity in Gierow's dramas is inimical to humanness even if it does not actually unleash evil. This is the lesson of *Färjestället* (The Ferry Landing; 1946), in which the young lovers Olof and Ingrid learn that life without pain, suffering, sacrifice, and anxiety is a living death.

Paradoxically, Gierow's attempts to examine the nature and origin of evil lead him first to make it understandable, and consequently to make it human. The werewolf in *Rovdjuret* (The Beast of Prey; 1941) is both Satan's agent and victim. He embodies the evil, guilt and self-destructive drives of the human race. He is a scapegoat, and his symbolic function is underscored by the fact that he has no name. He is simply "the man." The amoral, egocentric jarl Magnus in *Helgonsaga* (Saint's Legend; 1943) is a similar villain-protagonist. Magnus is trapped in a pattern of brutality by a murder he committed in a futile attempt to spare his people from war. At the play's conclusion he is transformed into a saint. Even Esbern in *Färjestället*, the most consistently evil figure in Gierow's oeuvre, is given a touch of humanity in the final scenes. Moreover, Esbern is the mouthpiece of a radical materialistic philosophy. He justifies his cruelty on the basis of the dispassionate struggle for survival in nature, and thereby places it beyond the realm of good and evil. Herod in *Den fjärde vise mannen* (The Fourth Wise Man; 1970) is more weak

than evil. He is manipulated by the High Priest, who in turn operates from a merciless political design.

Cembalo (1961) is more subtle than the other dramas. The dilemma is more existential than metaphysical, and its resolution is correspondingly more ambiguous than are those of the other plays. Technically the drama is interesting in that it has two protagonists, each the antagonist of the other. Despite the eloquent defense of human dignity, the integrity of the individual and a purpose in life beyond mere existence made by the young Johannes Gabras, and also the aging Lomellino's personal sacrifice to duty, *Cembalo* is the most somber and problematical of Gierow's dramas. There is no reconciliation, only resignation and a profound sense of the absurdity of human life.[8]

Gierow's plays are often mentioned in connection with the verse dramas of T. S. Eliot and Maxwell Anderson. All three playwrights sought to inject a new note into theatre by reviving the verse drama. Yet although there are pronounced similarities in their search for valid esthetic and ethical standards through the medium of drama, the question of influence is moot. Gierow experimented with the verse drama as early as the 1920s, albeit unsuccessfully. He was greatly impressed by the verse and strong moral thrust of Bidermann's *Cenodoxus* and Marlowe's *Dr. Faustus,* both of which he translated in the 1930s. Possibly as a result, an esthetically dubious attraction to the morality play is characteristic of Gierow's dramas. In his view "plot" and "moral" are virtually synonymous, and drama is the genre most suited to the examination of metaphysical and existential issues. As such it is imbued with the solemnity of religious ritual. Blank verse is the most natural dramatic language for such a serious undertaking.[9] Of Gierow's seven dramas, only his comedy is not written in blank verse. Above all, the influence of Shakespeare should not be overlooked in Gierow's work for the stage. His characters, language and even the structure of his plays have a distinctively Shakespearean aura.

While the dramas are most often discussed in terms of ideas and form, Gierow is skilled in creating atmosphere and character. The gloomy medieval castle in *Rovdjuret,* the semi-pagan Viking world of *Helgonsaga,* the fantastic folkloristic setting of *Färjestället* and the power-hungry, amoral air of the Renaissance in *Cembalo* are all vital to the dramas' action. Gierow is capable of sketching believable characters with only a few deft strokes. Especially the minor figures enliven and enrich the scenes. Unfortunately, Gierow's astute sketches remain just that, for he subordinates character to the abstract superstructure of the plays. Too often the action is propelled by the ideas the characters represent rather than by interaction of the characters themselves. The fact that Gierow's characters do stand out as credible individuals attests to their vigor.

Reaction to Gierow's dramas has always been mixed. His formal dexterity is unquestionable, and his blank verse can be both sonorous and graceful. The question arises whether he does not overburden it with involuted, abstract rhetoric. The theatricality of the plays has been called into question. More recent criticism of Gierow's drama reflects in part the politicization of Swedish literature which occurred in the 1960s and 1970s. Critics have lost patience with abstract issues and demand concrete depictions of actual historical and social phenomena. That *Den fjärde vise mannen* received predominantly negative reviews and was judged incomprehensible and indistinct may reflect a change in general attitudes as much as the merits or demerits of the play itself.

■ ■ ■

A side of Gierow which is not readily apparent in his poetry and drama is a ready wit and urbanity. These traits are the hallmark of his essays. Gierow has published two volumes of essays, *Mina utflykter* (My Excursions) in 1951 and *Europa och tjuren* (Europa and the Bull) in 1972. He is a peculiarly competent prose writer. His essays are highly readable, not only because of his proclivity toward unexpected aspects of uncommon topics, but also for their structure. Typically, Gierow starts the essay in one direction, only to maneuver the discussion elsewhere. At the end of the essay he arrives at the initial idea. This technique gives the essay a final, often novel point, which is not to say that Gierow presumes to answer all the questions he raises.

Gierow was head of the literary department of the newspaper *Svenska Dagbladet* from 1946 through 1951, during which time he enhanced the prestige of the paper considerably.[10] In 1951 he was appointed Director of the Royal Dramatic Theatre, or Dramaten, in Stockholm, and held the post into 1963. He quickly gained a reputation for his aptitude for dealing with actors, of whom he once remarked, "Ninety percent are hysterics, and I have no use for the rest."[11] Risking negative reactions from critics and public alike, Gierow tried to give promising Swedish playwrights access to the resources of the Dramaten. Nor was he afraid to produce dramas by writers virtually unknown outside their own countries at the time, such as Iones-co's *La leçon* in 1954 and Djuna Barnes's *The Antiphon* in 1961. In 1953 he oversaw a successful production of O'Neill's *Moon for the Misbegotten,* which had been a dismal failure in the U.S. During Gierow's tenure as Director he sent his ensemble to Vienna and Paris, where it received very favorable reviews. Above all, the Swedish stage gained international recognition for its world premiere of O'Neill's *Long Day's Journey Into Night* in 1956. The Dramaten's stunning production of O'Neill's masterpiece sparked a revival of interest in the playwright, who had died virtually forgotten three years previously. O'Neill's *Hughie* and *A Touch of the Poet* also had their world premieres on the Stockholm stage. Working from O'Neill's partially revised manuscript, Gierow produced a stage version of the incomplete *More Stately Mansions,* which was performed in 1962.

In 1961 Gierow was elected to the Swedish Academy, and served as its Permanent Secretary from 1964 to 1974. Gierow has always taken great interest in international literary understanding. He has furthered an international dimension in Swedish letters not only with his numerous articles and reviews, but also with his fine translations. These include Hebbel's *Der Diamant,* Ibsen's *Brand* and *Peer Gynt,* Shakespeare's *Macbeth* and *King John* and Barnes's *The Antiphon,* the latter in collaboration with Dag Hammarskjöld.

Gierow's poetry of the 1960s and 1970s has drawn mixed reviews. Ironically, as Gierow perfected his poetic style, it became less and less fashionable. On the surface there is not a great deal of difference between Gierow's early and late poetry. The themes are essentially the same, and form and language become no less traditional in time. The differences lie in a greater simplicity of expression and a move from a rather egocentric lyric perspective to a more universal point of view.

Om livet är dig kärt (If You Value Your Life), which appeared in 1963, contains some of Gierow's most mature verse. Its best poems are marked by a laconic style and subtle use of sound and rhythm. The expression seems more personal than in the preceding volumes, yet more sublimated. A sense of quiet desperation in the face of life as well as death runs through the collection. The familiar figure of the wanderer makes his way toward a final oblivion in "Ut mot udden" (Toward the Headland), one of Gierow's finest poems. Sound and imagery are so compressed in this text that a translation gives only an approximation of it.

Sand erases
all the tracks
toward the headland, where I pass.
Wind effaces all.
The seagull calls
in my tracks,
the ocean crashes.
Singly o'er the ocean crashes
billow after billow.
The seagull calls
without reply,

no one left?
No one left to follow.

A contrasting but complementary perspective is presented in "Flyttfåglar" (Birds of Passage), in which earthbound figures watch migratory birds disappear like the years that have gone by.

Yes now they leave us, and the sky fills up with tears
just like a farewell gaze at their clear cry.
We follow with our gaze as in past years,
when we were young still, and they hastened by.

Skall jag taga vara på min broder? (Am I My Brother's Keeper?) of 1968 is Gierow's most problematical volume of poetry. It is the one collection that has none of his typical lightness and grace. The strictness of the form, rigorous even for Gierow, underscores the tense, serious impulse of the work. Not only are the individual poems stylized, but the entire volume is arranged as a three-part musical composition with a postlude. The first section, "Fugato," is marked by a social-critical impulse, while the middle part, "Modulationer" (Modulations), is mystical and aphoristic. The last division, "Fuga" (Fugue), is composed in the extremely difficult form of the "sonnet wreath," a cycle of fifteen sonnets. Each sonnet begins with the last line of the preceding text, and the final sonnet is made up of all the first lines in the order of occurrence. This cycle, like the dramas, concentrates on questions of guilt, responsibility and the source of evil. Its anti-hero is Cain, who paradoxically assumes a kind of redeeming role.

This book raised the ire of certain critics who viewed Gierow's concentration on guilt and, more concretely, human misery in the Third World as defeatist and hopeless. For the critic committed to the idea of a changeable society, Gierow's depiction of life's cruelty and inequity without any real note of hope was unpardonable. To add insult to injury, Gierow satirized the protest-and-placard mentality and pointed out the futility and self-righteousness of such agitation. In addition to the social-critical impulse, "Fugato" is marked by an intense skepticism. In "Epitafiskt" (Epi-taphic) Gierow writes, "You raise the tombstone when the earth has sunk together / For then arises that small vacuum, which was I." "All Skapelses Bön" (The Prayer of All Creation) is a merciless depiction of life as "a crawling swarm, which tramples to death all the surplus life that sees daylight." The poet, who affirms that "the coarsely grotesque takes place in love's most heavenly home," hears in the shrill din of mating frogs the breathing of the Godhead. "Fugato" also contains a passionate defense of the individual. Gierow may be referring to himself when he writes in the second "Eremite Song," "I go my way, my own way / my own."

Gierow returned to simplicity of expression in *Innan Klockan slagit noll* (Before the Clock Has Struck Zero; 1978). These poems have an aura of gentle melancholy. Images of old age, impending winter, cold and shorter days suggest an anticipation of death. Gierow's wanderer, "astray in the valley's darkness," has reached no more certainty than the questions "And if you had not been born? / What difference? / If you shall not go away, where shall you go?" ("Vilse i dalens mörker" [Astray in the Valley's Darkness]). Nonetheless, he is comforted by the certainty that he will reach "home."

Karl Ragnar Gierow has contributed to virtually every sphere of Swedish literary life, both as creative artist and as influential critic and essayist. He has participated actively in Swedish cultural life through his translations and through his innovative work with radio, film and theatre. In turn he has contributed to international literary understanding through his activities with the Swedish Academy. He was instrumental in adding O'Neill's *Long Day's Journey into Night, Hughie* and *A Touch of the Poet* to the world dramatic repertoire.

Gierow's literary production not only casts light on developments in Swedish letters but also places him in a global context. His unrelenting attempt to find a place for value in a world of skepticism and facts combined with his formal traditionalism relates his work to the endeavors of T. S. Eliot, Maxwell Anderson and the New Humanist movement in the U.S. His poetry in *Ödletid* and *Vid askens rötter* along with his wartime dramas provides insight into Swedish *beredskapslitteratur* and a point of comparison and contrast with both the production of the "inner emigration" in Nazi Germany and that of the exiled German writers.

Recent criticism of Gierow's traditional form and choice of themes raises pertinent esthetic issues. The relevance and resonance of outwardly conventional, broadly humanistic writing in a time when political engagement and formal experimentation are the norm are not easily determined. Gierow, who composes his poems according to his own sense of melody, might well answer, "I go my way, my own way, my own."

Jeanette Lee Atkinson, Spring 1981

[1] Personal interview with Karl Ragnar Gierow, 10 October 1980.

[2] Information concerning Swedish radio and Gierow's contribution to it is taken from Gunnar Hallingberg, *Radioteater i 40 år: Den svenska repertoaren belyst,* Stockholm, Sveriges Radio, 1965, and *Radiodramat: Svensk hörspelsdiktning—bakgrund, utveckling och formvärld,* Stockholm, Sveriges Radio, 1967.

[3] Personal interview with Gierow.

[4] Karl Ragnar Gierow's works were published by Norstedts in Stockholm. Translations are my own.

[5] See Bengt Landgren, *Hjalmar Gullberg och beredskaps-litteraturen: Studier i svensk dikt och politisk debatt 1933–1942,* Stockholm, Almqvist & Wiksell, 1975.

[6] Carl Fehrman, "De fyra ryttarna: Apokalyptiska motiv i svensk 30- och 40-talsdikt," in his *Poesi och parodi,* Stockholm, Norstedts, p. 269.

[7] Jöran Mjöberg, *Dikt och diktatur,* Stockholm, Natur & Kultur, 1944, p. 20.

[8] Gunnar Brandell and Jan Stenkvist, *Från första världskriget till 1950,* vol. 2 of *Svensk litteratur 1870–1970,* Stockholm, Aldus, 1975, p. 291.

[9] Ingvar Holm, ed., "Karl Ragnar Gierow—Ake Janzon: Intervju," in *Vänkritik: 22 samtal om dikt tillägnade Olle Holmberg,* Stockholm, Bonniers, 1959, pp. 205–209.

[10] Sven Stolpe, "Karl Ragnar Gierow," in his *Svenska humanister,* Stockholm, Bokvännerna, 1962, p. 61.

[11] Jarl W. Donner, "Uppbrott från Dramaten—Intervju med Karl Ragnar Gierow," *Sydsvenska Dagbladet Snällposten,* 16 June 1963, p. 6.

Tomas Tranströmer (*Gil Jain*)

Tomas Tranströmer and "The Memory"

1. Tomas Tranströmer seems to me the best poet to appear in Sweden for some years. He comes from a long line of ship pilots who worked in and around the Stockholm Archipelago. He is at home on islands. His face is thin and angular, and the swift, spare countenance reminds one of Hans Christian Andersen's or the young Kierkegaard's. He has a strange genius for the image—images come up almost effortlessly. The images flow upward like water rising in some lonely place, in the swamps, or deep fir woods.

Tranströmer's poems, so vivid in English, show the ability of certain poetry to travel to another culture and actually arrive there. As Tranströmer said in a letter to the Hungarian poets, published in the magazine *Új Írás* in 1977: "Poetry has an advantage from the start. . . . Poetry requires no heavy, vulnerable apparatus that has to be lugged around; it isn't dependent on temperamental performers, dictatorial directors, bright producers with irresistible ideas." He also remarked, "Poems are active meditations; they want to wake us up, not put us to sleep." At many places I go in this country, I meet people for whom Tranströmer is an awakener. They receive the fragrance of the depth from him; they see the light suddenly released by one of his brief quatrains. His work has become a strong influence now on many younger American poets.

Swedish society is most famously a welfare society, *the* welfare society; it is perhaps the first society in history that has had the means to adopt as an ideal the aboli-

tion of poverty. But it is also a technological society like ours, and one given to secular solutions. Tranströmer reports how difficult it is in such a society to keep in touch with inner richness. What happens to the "vertical" longings, the longings for the divine? A poem called "Below Freezing" brings up this issue.

> We are at a party that doesn't love us. Finally the party lets its mask fall and shows what it is: a shunting station for freight cars. In the fog cold giants stand on their tracks. A scribble of chalk on cardoors.

> One can't say it aloud, but there is a lot of repressed violence here. That is why the furnishings seem so heavy. And why is it so difficult to see the other thing present: a spot of sun that moves over the house walls and slips over the unaware forest of flickering faces, a biblical saying never set down: "Come unto me, for I am as full of contradictions as you."

> I work the next morning somewhere else. I drive there in a hum through the dawning hour which resembles a dark blue cylinder. Orion hangs over the frost. Children stand in a silent clump, waiting for the school-bus, the children no one prays for. The light grows as gradually as our hair.*

"The children no one prays for" is a painful line. Tranströmer is not coming down on the side of orthodox Christianity, yet a part of him is aware that children are deprived, even endangered, by not being prayed for. There is more light now than in primitive times, but it moves over "an unaware forest of flickering faces."

2. Tomas Tranströmer was born in Stockholm on 15 April 1931. He is an only child. His father and mother divorced when he was three; he and his mother lived after that in an apartment in the working-class district of Stockholm. He studied music and psychology and still plays the piano enthusiastically, as his recent poem on Schubert makes clear.

The early fifties were a rather formal time, both here and in Sweden, and Tranströmer began by writing highly formal poems, all elements measured. His first book, *17 dikter* (17 Poems), published in 1954, contains several poems written in classical meters adapted from the Latin. That collection includes many baroque elements in its language. Tranströmer's language has gradually evolved into a more spoken Swedish, and he has written both prose poetry and free verse; but, as he remarked during a recent interview published in *Poetry East:* "Often there is a skeleton somewhere in the poem with a regular number of beats and so on in each line. You don't have to know that, but for me it's important."

Tranströmer's second book, *Hemligheter på vägen* (Secrets on the Road), contained fourteen poems and appeared four years later. In 1962, after another gap of four years, he published *Den halvfärdiga himlen* (Half-Finished Heaven), with twenty-one poems—fifty-two poems in all in about ten years. In 1966 came *Klanger och spår* (Resonance and Foot-Tracks) and in 1970 *Mörkerseende* (Eng. *Night Vision*). Three years later he published *Stigar* (Paths) and in 1974 a long poem, *Östersjöar* (Eng. *Baltics*), describing the island where his family on his father's side have lived for generations.

Tranströmer's early poetry could be described as baroque romantic, with elements visible from both the eighteenth and the nineteenth century. Like the romantics, Tranströmer loves to travel, and a chance encounter may evolve into a poem; but Göran Printz-Påhlson notes a crucial difference between Tranströmer's work and that of the romantics: "The traveler is brought to a halt, and the experience is imprinted with ferocious energy, but not interpreted." Tranströmer works slowly and steadily on poems and often writes only seven or eight a year. That may be one reason why his poems have so much weight.

Tranströmer worked for some years as a psychologist at the boys' prison in Linköping and then moved with his family to Västerås, about sixty miles west of Stockholm. There he works as a psychologist for a labor organization funded by the state. His responsibilities involve helping juvenile delinquents reenter society, assisting persons with physical disabilities in choosing a career, and work with parole offenders and drug rehabilitation. His family consists of two daughters, Paula and Emma, and his wife Monica, who finished her training as a nurse a few years ago and has worked from time to time with refugees who are resettling in Sweden.

Tranströmer's three most recent books have been *Sanningsbarriären* (Eng. *Truth Barriers*) in 1978, *Det vilda torget* (Eng. *The Wild Marketplace*) in 1983, and last year a fine new collection, including some of his strongest poems, *För levande och döda* (Eng. "For Living and Dead").

3. Tranströmer values his poems not so much as artifacts but rather as meeting places. Images from widely separated worlds meet in his verse. In the letter to the Hungarian poets he said, "My poems are meeting places. . . . What looks at first like a confrontation turns out to be connection." The poem "Street Crossing" describes an encounter between the ancient Swedish earth and a Stockholm street.

The street's massive life swirls around me;
it remembers nothing and desires nothing.
Far under the traffic, deep in earth,
the unborn forest awaits, still, for a thousand years.

He remains "suspended" so as to hear things.

one evening in June: the transistor told me the latest
on the Extra Session: Kosygin, Eban.
One or two thoughts bored their way in despairingly
    . . .
    I saw heard it from a suspension bridge
together with a few boys. Their bicycles
buried in the bushes—only the horns
stood up.

("Going with the Current")

He likes this "suspension," where objects float in a point of view that cannot be identified as "Marxist" or "conservative," right or left. During the sixties many critics in Sweden demanded that each poet commit himself or herself to a Marxist view, or at least concede that documentaries are the only socially useful form of art. Tranströmer has received several attacks for resisting that doctrine. Art still needs the unconscious, he believes; that has not changed. He also believes that a poem needs a place for the private, the quirky, the religious, the unexplainable, the human detail that the collective cannot classify. "Out in the Open," for example, is neither a nature poem, nor a political poem, nor a religious poem. One of its purposes evidently is to draw from all these sections of psychic experience without choosing among them.

Sun burning. The plane comes in low
throwing a shadow shaped like a giant cross that
   rushes over the ground.
A man is sitting in the field poking at something. The
shadow arrives.
For a fraction of a second he is right in the centre of
   the cross.
I have seen the cross hanging in the cool church
vaults. At times it resembles a split-second shot
of something moving at tremendous speed.

One of the most beautiful qualities in Tranströmer's poems is the space we feel in them. I think one reason for this is that the four or five main images which appear in each of his poems come from widely separated sources in the psyche. His poems are a sort of railway station where trains that have come enormous distances stand briefly in the same building. One train may have some Russian snow still lying on the undercarriage, and another may have Mediterranean flowers still fresh in the compartments and Ruhr soot on the roofs.

The poems are mysterious because of the distance the images have come to get there. Mallarmé believed there should be mystery in poetry, and he urged poets to get it by removing the links that tie the poem to its occasion in the real world. In Tranströmer's poems the link to the worldly occasion is stubbornly kept, yet the poems have a mystery and surprise that never fade, even on many readings.

4. Tranströmer has said that when he first began to write, in the early fifties, it still seemed possible to compose a nature poem into which nothing technological entered. Now, he says, he feels that many objects created by technology have become almost parts of nature, and he makes sure in his poetry that technology and its products appear. Some sights brought about by technology help him see more vividly a countryside scene: "All at once I notice the hills on the other side of the lake: / their pine has been clear-cut. They resemble the shaved / skull-sections of a patient about to have a brain operation." Perhaps nature can help you see a semi: "The semitrailer crawls through the fog. / It is the lengthened shadow of a dragonfly larva / crawling over the murky lakebottom." Man-made objects are not necessarily without life.

I drive through a village at night, the houses step out
into the headlights—they are awake now, they want
   a drink.
Houses, barns, nameposts, deserted trailers—now
they take on life. Human beings sleep:

some can sleep peacefully, others have tense faces
as though in hard training for eternity.
They don't dare to let go even in deep sleep.
They wait like lowered gates while the mystery rolls
past.

5. Recent poems bring forward a fresh emphasis: the poems circle in an intense way around the experience of borders, boundaries of nations, the passage from one world to the next, the weighty instant as we wake up and step from the world of dream to this world, the corridors through which the dead invade our world, the intermediate place between life and art, the contrast between Schubert's music and Schubert, "a plump young man from Vienna" who sometimes "slept with his glasses on."

The title of a recent collection, *Sanningsbarriären*, translated as both *Truth Barriers* and *The Truth Barrier*, suggests a customs gate. Tranströmer remarked that truth exists only at the border between worlds. On this side of the border there is doctrine, and on the other side infinity, so that we experience truth only at the moment of crossing. But, alas, there are guards who do not want us to cross.

In "Start of a Late Autumn Novel" Tranströmer, inside an uninhabited island house, finds himself neither asleep nor awake: "A few books I've just read sail by like schooners on the way to the Bermuda Triangle, where they will disappear without a trace." This description is rueful and funny. He's right: sometimes we finish a book and can't remember a word. As the poem continues, he lies half asleep and hears a thumping sound outside. He listens to it—it is something being held down by earth. It beats like a heart under a stethoscope; it seems to vanish and return. Or perhaps there is some being inside the wall who is knocking, "someone who belongs to the other world, but got left here anyway, he thumps, wants to go back. Too late. Wasn't on time down here, wasn't on time up there, didn't make it on board in time." So apparently a successful passage to the other world and back has to do with timing: the Celtic fairy tales also emphasize that. The poem ends with his amazement the next morning when he sees an oak branch, a torn-up tree root, and a boulder. When, in solitude, we see certain objects, they seem to be "left behind when the ship sailed"; Tranströmer says they are monsters from the other world "whom I love."

A poem called "December Evening '72" begins: "Here I come the invisible man, perhaps in the employ / of some huge Memory that wants to live at this moment. And I drive by / the white church that's locked up. A saint made of wood is inside, / smiling helplessly, as if someone had taken his glasses." The first two lines suggest that Tranströmer as an artist believes himself to be a servant of the Memory. He writes a poem when some huge Memory wants to cross over into this world; and this view of art seems more European than American. Often in America the artist believes his or her job is to tell the truth about one's own life: confessional poetry certainly implies that. Following that concept of art, many workshop poets comb their personal memory and write poems about their childhood, filling the poems with a clutter of detail. This clutter sometimes ensures that the piece will remain "a piece of writing" and will not become "a work of art."

Tranströmer has the odd sense that the Great Memory can only come in when the artist is alert to it. While on guard duty in a defense unit a few years ago, he wrote:

Task: to be where I am.
Even when I'm in this solemn and absurd
role: I am still the place
where creation does some work on itself.

Dawn comes, the sparse tree trunks
take on color now, the frostbitten
forest flowers form a silent search party
after something that has disappeared in the dark.

But to be where I am . . . and to wait:
I am full of anxiety, obstinate, confused.
Things not yet happened are already here!
I feel that. They're just out there:

a murmuring mass outside the barrier.
They can only slip in one by one.
They want to slip in. Why? They do
one by one. I am the turnstile.
("Sentry Duty")

He experiences the Great Memory as "somebody who keeps pulling on my arm each time I try to write." Again we feel ourselves at a boundary, being influenced by something on the other side. In "From the Winter of 1947" the dead press through into our world, as the stains in wallpaper: "They want to have their portraits painted." And in "Street Crossing," for one second as he crosses a busy Stockholm street, the poet has the sensation that the street and the earth below it have eyes and can see him.

Tranströmer begins his Schubert poem by describing New York from an overlook, "where with one glance you take in the houses where eight million human beings live." He mentions subway cars, coffee cups, desks, elevator doors. Still, "I know also—statistics to the side—that at this moment in some room down there Schubert is being played, and for that person the notes are more real than all the rest." And what are notes?

When sounds are absorbed and shaped by and inside, say, a string quartet, they contain vibrations that resonate somewhere inside us and awaken "feelings" that we seem not to have felt in daily life. There is evidently a layer of consciousness that runs alongside our life, above or below, but is not it. Perhaps it is older. Certain works of art make it their aim to rise up and pierce this layer, or layers. Or they open to allow in "memories" from this layer. Some artists—Tranströmer, Pasternak, and Akhmatova come especially to mind—keep the poem spare and clear so it can pierce the layers, or leave room for the Memory.

The art of Schubert puts Tranströmer at a boundary between worlds, and at such a boundary he sees astonishing truths.

The five instruments play. I go home through warm woods
where the earth is springy under my feet
curl up like someone still unborn, sleep, roll on so weightlessly
into the future, suddenly understand that plants are thinking.

Art helps us, he says, as a banister helps the climber on a dark stairwell. The banister finds its own way in the dark. In certain pieces of music happiness and suffering weigh exactly the same. The depths are above us and below us at the same instant. The melody line is a stubborn "humming sound that this instant is with us / upward into / the depths."

Swedish magazines often fill themselves with abstract hallucinatory poetry, typewriter poetry, alphabet poetry—poems that are really the nightmares of overfed linguists, of logical positivists with a high fever. Tranströmer, simply by publishing his books, leads a movement of poetry in the opposite direction, toward a poetry of silence and depths.

Robert Bly, Autumn 1990

*All translations are my own.

In Defense of People and Forests: Sara Lidman's Recent Novels

The novel with which the Swedish author Sara Lidman made her debut in 1953, *Tjärdalen* (The Tar Pit), is a neat and reassuring moral tale. Set in a tiny village in the far north of the country, it describes how a man known as The Fox wrecks the elaborate structure from which one of the village men is just about to start extracting many barrels of precious tar, breaks his leg in the process and is left to die as punishment for his sin. The novel's critique of the Lutheran concept of man as guilt-ridden and deserving of judgment points ahead to Lidman's more recent works, as does the highlighting of the corruptive powers of capitalism: the only man to speak out against the murder of The Fox turns out to be wholly in the hands of that far-sighted neighbor who exploits the tragedy for the sake of money. Significantly, however, the plot runs full circle, with the life of the community returning to normal once the death of The Fox has produced a spate of purely personal reckonings; and any potentially far-reaching criticisms are rendered harmless by the confines of the setting, the highly polished plot and the sheer verbal brilliance demonstrated by the author.

In many respects, *Tjärdalen* is a typical example of Swedish writing of the 1950s; and Lidman's entire output can be seen as adding up to a paradigm of the changing preoccupations of Swedish authors over the past three decades. Having attempted a collective approach in *Hjortronlandet* (Cloudberry Country; 1955) and delved further into the psychology and morality of individual characters in *Regnspiran* (The Rain Bird; 1958) and *Bära mistel* (Carrying the Mistletoe; 1960), Lidman abandoned her native Norrland as a setting for her novels. In the early 1960s she had gone to live in Africa, where she spent several years, first in South Africa, then in Kenya and Tanzania. The experience of South Africa, she has testified, became a watershed in her development. Her two African novels, *Jag och min son* (I and My Son; 1961) and *Med fem diamanter* (With Five Diamonds; 1964), contributed to that process of national consciousness-raising which, during the 1960s, transformed the isolated Swedish idyll into part of the contemporary, conflict-ridden world. In the middle of the decade, Lidman emerged as a leading figure in the influential Swedish movement against the Vietnam War, and the urgency of the issues with which she found herself involved was such that she ceased to write novels, preferring instead the direct line of communication provided by journalism. This change was symptomatic, with reports and documentary novels dominating Swedish writing during the second half of the 1960s. Lidman has spoken of the impact made on her by Jan Myrdal's *Rapport från kinesisk by* (Report from a Chinese Village; 1962); and in articles about North Vietnam, which she visited during the war, she depicted the tenacious efforts of its people to maintain a functioning society in the face of systematic devastation. *Samtal i Hanoi* (Conversations in Hanoi; 1966) has been followed by *Vänner och u-vänner* (Friends and Emerging Friends; 1969) and *Varje löv är ett öga* (Every Leaf Is an Eye; 1980), the title of the last book paying tribute to that respectful interrelationship between man and his environment which Lidman had encountered in North Vietnam. When, in *Varje löv är ett öga*, articles about Vietnam and Sweden appear side by side, the author is drawing our attention not only to the universality of the patterns of exploitation, but also to mankind's total dependence on a delicately balanced and increasingly threatened environment.

The 1970s saw a return to the conventional novel in Sweden, with many authors bringing with them a sharpened political awareness and an eye for the significance of documentary material. Conspicuous among the novels of the 1970s and early 1980s are multivolume historical works tracing aspects of the development of Swedish society in vivid and often carefully researched detail. Sven Delblanc, Lars Ardelius and Kerstin Ekman (see WLT 55:2, pp. 204–209) have all written series of this type; and to this category also belong Lidman's more recent novels: *Din tjänare hör* (Thy Obedient Servant; 1977), *Vredens barn* (The Children of Wrath; 1979) and *Nabots sten* (Nabot's Stone; 1981).[1]

In these three works we are again in the far north of Sweden, in an inland area known on the map as Jörn and in the novels as Lillvattnet. While Lidman had paid minimal attention to this northern setting in *Tjärdalen*, she had succeeded in conveying something of its harsh demands and rare moments of generosity in *Hjortronlandet*; but perhaps it took the experience of other countries—and of her return to her native Missenträsk in the mid-1970s—to alert her to the uniqueness of this part of Sweden and to inspire her into finding the language and diction that can bring out the universal significance of this land of bogs and primeval forests, of snow and darkness and isolated human habitations.

Six miles up country, without a cottage, without an encounter, without sun or moon, without a road to be seen.
All that can be seen is snow-covered spruce and fir, moving toward you unendingly
until you are seized with fear and with mounting respect for the Horse who manages to veer
just in time to prevent you from being buried under snow and pine needles
how the Horse finds the road and keeps to it
it is a miracle
and the most insignificant fellow traveler becomes valuable
his voice, his breath, his movements
and all the memories that go with him
compressed in one tenacious being

maintaining the difference between itself
and these monotonous omnipotent straggling trees.
(*Nabots sten,* 59–60)[2]

Lidman's intimate knowledge of this environment
and her affection for its people combine with her historical perspective to make the humble community of Lillvattnet emerge as a metaphor for our fragile and precious civilization. In the context of a setting which
persistently conjures up the Norsemen's Nifelheim, that
realm of perpetual darkness and cold, Lidman is able
to remind us, again and again, of the miracle of life and
of the respect due to each human being who is struggling to maintain his or her existence against all odds.
And every survivor assists in imposing a measure of culture on this wilderness. The man who fells trees, builds
a hut and clears patches for growing potatoes and barley
harnesses a fragment of it into mankind's rhythms of
hours, weeks and months, the patterns established by
him sustaining others long after he has gone. "When the
clock is going, you don't think about it," says someone
on an isolated homestead in the depths of the forest;
"But when it has stopped, you cannot think," adds another (*Nabots sten,* 142), thus defining that fear of being
swallowed up in an inhuman limbo which haunts many
of Lidman's early settlers. And this fear is not merely
metaphysical: when the narrative begins, in 1878, the
Great Famine Years (which occurred ten years earlier)
are still fresh in the memories of the survivors. Moving
around in a haze of starvation, the living during those
years mingled with the dying and the dead, their suffering blotting out all individuality and undermining the
distinctions between the straggling trees and the stumbling skeletons. Ultimately the great miracle in this
harsh environment is that children continue to be born,
that the breasts of mothers fill with milk for them and
that there is enough food for at least some of them to
survive and become fully grown women and men.

A focal point of Lidman's narrative is the homestead of Månliden, inhabited by Mårten and Lena and
their seven surviving children, including their son Didrik, who is twenty-one years old in 1878. Mårten had
arrived there in 1848, after a long journey on skis from
the coast, and but for chancing upon an empty cottage,
he would have perished in the snow. Mårten knows
only that his predecessor was called Isak, his name
being carved near the single window; but out of respect,
he leaves his cottage intact among the bigger, better
buildings that gradually spring up at Månliden.

Six miles away there is an older settlement, the
more prosperous of its two homesteads belonging to
Moses, who is famous for his drainage schemes. By digging long and deep ditches through the wet, root-
infested soil, using no other tool than a spade, it is pos-

sible to improve the land, making the newly created
fields yield much-needed winter fodder for the cattle,
which in turn provide milk, butter and even meat for
the people. So successful has Moses been that he is
awarded a government grant for his land reclamation;
and even Mårten, who can merely boast that his ditches
have checked the mists bringing the early frosts, remains convinced that only more and longer ditches can
secure the future of Månlinden. The relentless toil of
draining the land, which demands the energies of all
available male labor, fills any gaps in the farmer's year
of given tasks, leaving no glimpse of frivolous leisure.

Lidman's small farmers have their contrast in
Nicke, who lives with his sprawling family in a cottage
that he has found in the forest. Nicke has never bothered to clear—much less drain—any land to establish
himself as a farmer: instead, he and his family live off
the animals and birds in the forest and the fish in the
rivers and lakes. It is with some envy that Mårten, the
legal owner of the land on which Nicke lives, has to acknowledge the other man's total lack of interest in possessing these natural resources: as long as he can catch
what he needs for the family's survival, he is perfectly
content, living seemingly irresponsibly from one day to
the next. Nicke is famous for his skill in working with
wood, having an unfailing eye for that curving trunk,
forking branch or bulging growth which can provide
the raw material for a tool or vessel; and even a persistent critic like Didrik has to admit that the forest benefits from Nicke's selective use of its assets.

The contrast between characters such as Mårten
and Moses on the one hand and Nicke on the other allows Lidman to highlight a development more commonly extending over millennia: while Nicke is the
primitive hunter-gatherer, Mårten and Moses are early
farmers. In these novels, then, we are made to discern
the actual rise of our civilization and its built-in conflicts as well as its preciousness, for the society that
emerges in the wilderness is not an ideal one. Once the
settlements are established and self-supporting, the
weakest members of the community tend to become increasingly exploited, with orphans being used to dig
ditches for Mårten and Moses and even Nicke finding
his existence circumscribed as the landowners—and
the state—begin to enforce their rights. Those who are
not directly exploited are abandoned to indifference, as
happens to Hans Gretason. His name recalls Hansel and
Gretel in the Grimm fairy tale, with the parallel only
serving to underline the mercilessness of his lot: on his
tiny, isolated settlement, where any drainage schemes
must remain impossible dreams, Gretason and his large
family are left to perish, much as the brother and sister
in the fairy tale were abandoned by their parents in the

forest. And in Lidman's narrative there is no scope for a wicked witch who can initiate a magic rescue: Gretason dies, the children are scattered throughout the parish, and a charitable farmer accepts the widow with the youngest child as a servant. Lidman brings out the community's lack of concern with the fate of the Gretason family by letting it remain little more than a name until Didrik and some of his neighbors, toward the end of *Vredens barn,* arrive to fell timber in the area; but their somewhat shameful exploration of the remains of the family's everyday life can only raise questions that will never be answered.

It is the ambition of Didrik, who emerges as one of the central characters in these novels, to puncture the compact indifference of the state by making its powerful men perceive that the odd drainage grant is not sufficient for the survival of this community: only if the projected railway line is built through the parish of Lillvattnet can the iron grip of the environment be broken and more people be attracted to the area. Coupled with this ambition is his desire to marry Anna-Stava, and although his feelings for her sometimes seem obscured by his mounting preoccupation with personal wealth and status, especially after he has become chairman of the local council, the marriage does take place toward the end of Lidman's second volume. But in the third the railway still has not advanced much beyond the stage of discussion; and Lidman's series about "the cost of populating the Norrland hinterland," to use one of her own definitions, appears to be well on the way toward extending into four or five volumes.

While Didrik is convinced that the railway scheme will be the salvation of the community, the attention of outsiders turns out to have a different effect: Lillvattnet becomes enmeshed in expanding and increasingly pernicious patterns of exploitation. The distant businessmen are capable of a malevolence which, although related to that indifference toward their inferiors displayed by the early farmers, still leaves the victims incredulous; and when Abdon's horse dies because a businessman's clerk has cheated him into overloading his sleigh, he has no doubt that he must unmask the guilty man by writing to the King himself. The person who prevents the draft from being turned into a fair copy is Didrik; and the fraudulence and brutality suffered by Abdon can be seen to crystallize not only the treatment Didrik experiences at the hands of the businessmen, but also the treatment he metes out to others.

Via the local police superintendent, who has effectively distanced Didrik from his peers yet asserted control by means of a mixture of flattery and superiority, Didrik gets to know a businessman in the coastal town who uses similar but far subtler tactics. The business-man assists him in setting up a shop selling American bacon, oats, modern saws and anything else required to exploit the forests of Lillvattnet; so impressed is Didrik by the magnanimity of the businessman's vision and his sympathy for the railway scheme, that he fails to perceive that he is allowing himself to become the linchpin in an elaborate system of exploitation. By the time he overhears an account of the ruthless policy which is forcing family after family away from its homestead and forest, allowing them to return only in a state of perpetual debt, he is too entangled in this policy and too dependent on it for his own survival to act in accordance with his conscience.

The mounting exploitation thus results in deepening social chasms; and Lidman enphasizes the extent to which the social divisions are provided with an ideological framework—and indeed rationale—by Lutheranism. For the early settlers, cooperation—between husband and wife, between neighbor and neighbor—has been a necessity of life, and as a result they have been able to treat Luther's social stratifications with a certain healthy skepticism. But as their society changes, Didrik's wife Anna-Stava becomes increasingly concerned about the influence of Luther's division of mankind into "authority" and "the rabble." Luther's message, she perceives, is a double one, with "grace alone" being reserved for the former category and "law and punishment" for the latter.

▪ ▪ ▪

Writing "in defense of people and forests," as she herself has put it, Lidman in these three novels presents a comprehensive refutation of society's—and Luther's—exploitative stratifications, forcing us to face, ultimately, that indifference to our fellow human beings which is their prerequisite. The language, the treatment of individual characters (especially those who are oppressed), the composition of the narrative and the structuring of the plot are all integral parts of this artistic statement which, in the last instance, turns on precisely those "digressions" to which the author refers, half apologetically, on the back cover of *Vredens barn.*

The language in these three novels can be felt to be wrenched out of the harsh environment in which its users live: a sparse and condensed medium, relying on a range of precise and vivid dialect words and frequently resorting to biblical turns of phrase and nineteenth-century spellings, it palpably carries the sum total of precious human experience and tradition. Lidman places strong emphasis on the sheer pleasure of communicating, depicting Abdon's delight as he observes the words which he has just learned to write—on a piece of birch bark—making sense to others and conveying Didrik's feelings of intoxication as experiences from his everday life fuse with images from the Bible to give him the earthy and powerful language of his first public speech. The rare gatherings of Lidman's settlers and small farmers stand out as celebrations of language: when the horses are let out into the forest in early summer, the occasion is accompanied by a host of tales, jokes and humorous recitations; a visit to the distant church holds the promise not only of a sermon and a range of public announcements, but also of news and gossip, and perhaps even the elaborate ritual of the local council meeting; moreover, the long evenings spent away from home by the men felling timber are taken up with tales, favorites such as the one about Abdon's horse sometimes expanding into dramatic performances.

Asked by the police superintendent to write from dictation, young Didrik is so absorbed by the pleasure of working with pen, ink and paper that he "[forgets] the contents of the texts, their pain" (*Vredens barn,* 26), despite the fact that one of them is concerned with the death of Hans Gretason; but Lidman, for all her obvious pleasure in handling language, never loses sight of the pain inherent in her subject matter. In her explicitness she can be shockingly brutal, as when she describes the dying whore who arrives at Anna-Stava's home on a bed of rotten straw and excreta and who, after a few hours in the warmth of the house, turns out to be covered with a teeming mass of lice. While the first book in the series is comparatively gentle, there are more of these shock effects, of unflinchingly honest truths which stink and make the stomach turn, in *Vredens barn* and *Nabots sten.* But Lidman also has rather more subtle means of conveying the plight of those at the bottom of the social hierarchy. One of these techniques is illustrated by her treatment of Nabot, a boy of uncertain parentage who for many years lives—and, more especially, works—at Månliden. On one occasion he fails to lift a heavy stone from a drainage ditch he is digging, the task instead being accomplished by the stronger and better-fed Didrik. The following morning the stone is back on the bottom of the ditch; but this remains our only proof of Nabot's feelings. While struggling in vain to lift the stone, he inevitably becomes the butt of the guesses and assumptions of those present; Lidman, however, emphatically refuses to confirm or deny any of these possibilities. Instead, she exploits this merciless curiosity, the unanswered questions creating a protective space around Nabot. Its silent mystery communicates the pain suffered by a human being relentlessly exposed to infringements on his dignity and self-respect.

The same kind of silent mystery surrounds Nabot's girlfriend Hagar, at one time a maid at the police superintendent's and, in *Nabots sten,* the woman whose milk saves the life of Anna-Stava's and Didrik's son. Hagar is of course the bondwoman who, with her son, is driven out into the desert by Abraham in Genesis; and Sara Lidman's Hagar, who is accompanied by her son when she turns up at Månliden, is similarly ostracized because of her class and sex. Some of the attitudes she encounters are crystallized in the description of the day when the infant son is christened, the juxtaposition of events at once highlighting and exposing the public degradation of Hagar.

While Anna-Stava and Didrik have traveled with their son to the parish church, the older members of the family have assembled with some of their neighbors in the kitchen at Månliden to read Luther's commentary on one of the Gospels. In an upstairs room Hagar, who has declined to accompany the christening party, is busy with some unknown task, and the intriguing sounds penetrating the kitchen soon have the others paying more attention to the activities of Hagar than to the words of Luther. Again Lidman maintains the distance between her character and the reader by refusing to reveal to us the nature of Hagar's work. But the men in the kitchen are soon lost in lascivious daydreams, all hinging on the fact that the nurse of the infant son is an unmarried mother and thus, by implication, generally available. Not only is the uncharitableness of these listeners brought out by the simultaneous reading of Luther; but by turning these events into a parallel of the churching ceremony of an unmarried mother immediately after the christening, Lidman shows us that this kind of mental rape is publicly endorsed. Eventually Hagar exposes the unspeakable baseness of the treatment she has to suffer merely by her reception of Anna-Stava's and Didrik's son, the mutual love of nurse and child triumphantly transcending all social and sexual boundaries.

> She unswaddled him without sitting down, she peeled him in the air like a head of cabbage and let his swaddling fall to the floor or into the disgraced pot, did it as fast and firmly as if she had had four hands; and at last she took the corner of one of his garments, dipped it into the pot of warm water on the hearth, swung it in the air to cool, and wiped his behind clean; then she sat down in the nursing chair with the head of the naked child in her lap and its feet towards her body and she held the child by the hands and they smiled at one another as if making fun of the day's ceremony and entering a different ritual altogether: she licked his heels all the way round and put his toes into her mouth. Oh, what brilliant impudence! Laurentia, Sophia, and Matilda who had begun to collect the swaddling and separate the christening gown from its innermost,

ochre-yellow, sloppy contents; they were stilled
in wonder

and when at last nurse and child had celebrated
his nakedness—and without a thought for her
own child who stood pressing at her elbow stepping on his own toes—she lifted the corners of
her great apron and swaddled the child lightly in
it, unbuttoned her blouse and began to nurse
him. (Nabots sten, 121–22)

As Didrik advances to become chairman of the
local council, a prosperous shopowner, the father of
three daughters and a son—whose arrival only makes
the railway all the more necessary—Lidman shows his
successes to be underpinned by a network of dependen-
cies: on Nabot and Hagar, on the outcast who is said
to have been Nabot's father, and on Hagar's mother,
who turns out to have been the wife of that unknown
first settler at Månliden, Isak. Significantly, this network
surfaces only gradually, the author handling central elements such as allusions, imagery and the structuring of
the narrative with a sense of refinement that becomes
masterly, notably in Nabots sten. Didrik himself is, or
prefers to be, ignorant of his dependence on those
whom he views with contempt; and to him the outrage
against his horse, which results in its having to put
down, must remain a mystery. Rather more perceptive—and honest—is his wife, who prefers the writings
of Johan Arndt to those of Luther and who listens to her
eldest daughter reading about the entity of God's creation and about the fact that the firmament exists within
the human being as well as in the universe. Anna-Stava's
first, painful encounter with a scornful Hagar is juxtaposed with her thoughts about a farmer whom she has
always included in her prayers because of his savagery
toward his horse; and as we might expect, the composition here turns out not to be accidental. While nursing
Hagar's dying mother, Anna-Stava learns that the old
woman once worked for this farmer and that he has
been guilty of violating her daughter. The act of forcing
an ice-cold sledgehammer into the mouth of a horse so
that the sensitive skin sticks to the metal not only has
sexual overtones; it crystallizes the pain of being alive
in a society where the insensitivity, degradation and oppression emanating from fellow human beings make the
cold perpetual.

In Tjärdalen the man whom the community is killing by ignoring his fractured leg has his hovel decorated
with dandelions; but before taking the flowers indoors,
the woman picking them takes care to shake out any insects, holding the flowers close to the ground as she
does so to prevent the insects from breaking their legs.
Dismissed by the community as a half-wit, this woman
clearly has a truly Arndtian understanding of the inter-

dependence of every element in God's creation. In a
sense, then, Lidman's basic preoccupations have
changed very little since she wrote her first novel. What
has changed are their implications—as the author's
world has grown more complex and divisive—and,
more significantly, their applications; Lidman succeeds,
in these three books, in giving us a novelist's version of
the Arndtian universe and alerting us to the delicate balance of a creation in which everything is dependent
upon everything else. What makes Lidman's achievement so exciting is the fact that hers is, in every sense,
a work in progress, with the author's continuing exploration of her medium becoming bolder, more original
and seemingly more crucial with every volume.

Helena Forsås-Scott, Winter 1984

1 Lidman's *Din tjänare hör, Vredens barn* and *Nabots sten* were all
    published by Bonniers in Stockholm; page references to these
    editions are given parenthetically following citations. Transla-
    tions are my own unless otherwise noted. For *WLT*'s coverage
    of Lidman's recent work, see *WLT* 55:2, p. 263.

2 I would like to thank Linda Schenck for making some helpful
    comments on an early draft of this translation and for permit-
    ting me to use her translation of the passage that appears on
    p. 20.

Gunnar Ekelöf: Poet, Visionary, and Outsider

No discussion of modern Scandinavian literature is possible without reference to the works of the Swedish poet
Gunnar Ekelöf (1907–68). Numerous are the works
and writers who have been influenced by this giant in
twentieth-century poetry: for example, the obscure and
complex poetry of the Icelandic modernist Hannes Sig-
fusson, in particular in his collection *Dymbilvaka* (Vigil
During the Holy Week; 1949); the entire oeuvre of the
contemporary Danish lyricist Jørgen Sonne (b. 1925);
and the Swedish modernist school of the 1940s and its
views of the cognitive task of literature and use of musical structures. Ekelöf's opinion that music is a manifestation of the Absolute is also shared by another Swede,
the religious mystic Östen Sjöstrand (b. 1925).[1]

Likewise, a major study could be written about
Ekelöf and the Fenno-Swedish modernists Rabbe Enckell, Emil Diktonius, and Hagar Olsson. Ekelöf knew all
three of them personally and in July 1935 visited Helsinki and met with Diktonius and another Fenno-
Swedish poet, Gunnar Björling. In 1938, after having
been repeatedly urged by his Finnish friends to revisit
them, he returned to Finland and, together with Diktonius, visited the Karelian home in Raivola of yet an-

other Fenno-Swedish poet, the then-deceased Edith Södergran. Thus it is quite obvious that a sort of congenial spiritual relation existed between Ekelöf and these writers, and in the recently published biography *Gunnar Ekelöf* by Carl Olov Sommer* their close friendship forms one of the most successful sections of the volume. Particularly fascinating is Sommer's inspired, somewhat lyric description of Ekelöf's boundless admiration for Södergran.

In general, Sommer leaves no stone unturned. He has utilized a wealth of material from letters and diaries and information obtained from the poet's closest friends but fortunately avoids the pitfall of losing the narrative flow in an abundance of more or less relevant details. To what degree Ekelöf and the Fenno-Swedish writers appreciated one another and their writings, on which they frequently commented, becomes even clearer when another source is consulted, also published by Sommer, a simultaneously issued edition of selected letters, *Brev 1916–1968*.** Here we can find additional information and enjoy that personal tone which a biography can never convey. Thus, in a letter to Diktonius dated 23 December 1932, Ekelöf still addresses him with "Mr.," and the tone is, in spite of a very candidly expressed contempt of several fellow writers ("I detest the entire Swedish literary mob"), quite formal. In the same year, however, Diktonius reviewed positively Ekelöf's debut collection *Sent på jorden* (Late Arrival on Earth), praising its formal radicalism and thereby distancing himself from the mostly negative reception by the Swedish critics. Consequently, in an undated letter from December 1933 the address is now "Brother": "It is so nice to write to you again without reservation, you are good and wild and you like cats."

Generally, the two volumes brilliantly supplement each other, and at the same time they both give evidence to what degree Ekelöf was a central figure in the literary world of his time. He was a diligent letter writer, and approximately three-fourths of his more than two thousand letters have been preserved in archives or with the individual correspondents. Thus the 141 letters which have now been made available constitute only a sample, but a sample which whets the appetite for more. Nevertheless, Sommer has succeeded in presenting quite a multi-faceted portrait of the poet.

The volume opens with two letters to Ekelöf's mother, which are followed by others to family members. The earliest of these letters, from 1916, are naturally still childishly naïve, but they are surprisingly expressive and sensitive, clearly heralding the budding poet. In subsequent letters to friends, publishers, and critics one can follow the development of an unmistakable satiric undertone. Particularly the letters to various

literary scholars, such as to the prominent Ekelöf expert Leif Sjöberg in New York, reveal cutting viewpoints at the same time as they throw interesting sidelights on the poet and his work. This correspondence began in 1962 and comprises over eighty letters from Ekelöf, of which Sommer regrettably has included only two. These demonstrate Ekelöf's readiness to clarify and interpret problematic passages in his texts down to the smallest detail. Surprisingly strong is Ekelöf's dislike of T. S. Eliot, a writer whose influence on and affinity to Ekelöf is usually stressed in the standard reference works. Ekelöf does acknowledge a certain formal impact, but in the same letter (dated 29 July 1966) James Joyce and Ezra Pound (whom Ekelöf in a letter from 1959 to Pär Lagerkvist suggested for the Nobel Prize) are his heroes, whereas Eliot is characterized thusly: "His entire type, from St. Louis via Boston to London, is deeply repulsive to me" (200). The significance of this correspondence with Sjöberg is evident and calls for a separate publication.

Even though the rather negative reception of Ekelöf's debut collection from 1932 is unjustified, it is nevertheless understandable in the context of the history of Swedish poetry from the early part of the twentieth century. With a few exceptions, it had remained firmly rooted in neoromantic esthetics, dominated by melancholy love poetry and nature descriptions employing classical imagery and quiet rhythms. However, in the works of Vilhelm Ekelund (1880–1949) this subdued approach gave way to ecstatic emotions in a series of rather inaccessible texts increasingly marked by a striving for verbal conciseness and associative links to antiquity as well as Christian mysticism. With Pär Lagerkvist's debut collection from 1916, *Ångest* (Anguish), the originality of which lies neither in formal experimentation nor in new imagery but in the spontaneous outburst of the poet's innermost desperate moods, expressionism finds its earliest Swedish representation. The same anguish permeates the poetry of Birger Sjöberg, who, after having renewed the Swedish song tradition in the path of Bellman and Fröding with the tender love poetry in *Fridas bok* (Frida's Book; 1922), with his next collection, *Kriser och kransar* (Crises and Wreaths; 1926), shocked the public. In order to cope with his feelings of the senselessness of life and the impenetrability of the mystery of death, Sjöberg resorts to a language characterized by broken syntax, abstractions, and cryptic images which were not fully comprehended until the modernist school of the 1940s, heralded by Sjöberg himself. The most radical break with traditional esthetics, however, took place with Ekelöf's Fenno-Swedish friends. They became a major source of inspiration for Ekelöf's own never-ending linguistic experimentation, which found its earliest expression in his debut collection.

"Late Arrival on Earth," which according to Ekelöf's own words was written under strong influence from the music of Igor Stravinsky, was immediately described as "surrealist," a label which Ekelöf himself only reluctantly accepted. Indeed, he always maintained full control of the intellect over his free-flowing associations. In fact—and Sommer seems to overlook this in his biography—Ekelöf is rather rooted in French symbolism, particularly in the poetry of Arthur Rimbaud, who also inspired him in his view of the writer as a seer and redeemer from our chaotic existence. It is undoubtedly this perception which in his next collection, *Dedikation* (Dedication; 1934), helped Ekelöf overcome the suicidal, often nihilistic moods of his first poems, even though he could never quite relieve himself of his perception of being an outsider. The theme of the outsider, of Ekelöf's rootlessness and impatience, constitutes the fundamental approach of Sommer's biography. It follows the poet from a childhood marked by the early death of his father, through his marriages and constant yearning for new impressions. These Ekelöf found either through frequent and spontaneous travels abroad or through extensive readings in world literature and studies of other art forms and foreign cultures, of which the Orient in particular held a strong fascination for him.

Whereas the collection *Strountes* (1955), through a series of fragmentary texts, explores the emptiness of existence, *En natt i Otočac* (A Night in Otočac; 1961) signifies an advance toward a dearly acquired synthesis (the symbolic expressions of which Ekelöf found in the structures of music). The latter volume ends in this tension-laden idyll:

On the blue of the sky
the clouds are colors
for the wind's light brush.
On earth they become shadows
out of which dusk builds
that realm of Hades
where the dark violets grow.

En Mölna-elegi (1960; Eng. *A Mölna Elegy,* 1979) became the most harmonious of Ekelöf's works to that date. The point of departure is that moment of mystery when the individual experiences his existence as a unification of the past and the present, a theme which, as in a piece of music, is introduced, varied, and interwoven throughout the volume. By allowing language to be the primary bearer of cognition, Ekelöf lets his visions of the past be reflected in extensive quotations in Greek and Latin, printed on the left page with the Swedish text on the right.

In the 1950s Ekelöf went on several trips to the Mediterranean countries, which resulted in frequent references to Mediterranean culture in his texts. A charter tour(!) in 1965 to Turkey unleashed an intense period of productivity concluding in Ekelöf's last three collections, in which he consistently transfers his conception of the present into a past Byzantine world. These three volumes—*Dīwān över Fursten av Emgión* (Divan over the Prince of Emgión; 1965), *Sagan om Fatumeh* (The Tale of Fatumeh; 1966), *Vägvisare till underjorden* (1967; Eng. *Guide to the Underworld,* 1980)—unequivocally constitute the consummation of Ekelöf's oeuvre. A blossoming Byzantine culture in transition from antiquity to the Middle Ages forms the backdrop for a series of ecstatic hymns and fantasies about the concept of love, the unifying force of which eventually is the only means of abolishing the tragic contradiction between life and death. The individual steps in the genesis of these texts have been mapped out meticulously by Sommer, as have the poet's consultations during this period with the literary scholar Reidar Ekner, constituting fascinating insights into the creative process itself.

Altogether, Sommer's well-written, at times entertaining, but always well-documented biography offers the best available—and actually the first—introduction to Ekelöf's life and work. Indeed, even though one must agree with Sommer that the poet in many respects was an outsider—both in a social meaning, through the inaccessibility of so much of his verse, and through his continual experimentation with artistic expression[2]—Ekelöf, in his last works, nevertheless managed to establish a coherent poetic universe of a mysterious beauty that is one of the unique achievements in world literature.

Sven Hakon Rossel, Winter 1990

*Carl Olov Sommer, Gunnar Ekelöf: En biografi, Stockholm, Bonniers, 1989, 634 pages, ill.

**Gunnar Ekelöf, Brev 1916–1968, Carl Olov Sommer, ed., Stockholm, Bonniers, 1989, 224 pages.

[1] On Östen Sjöstrand, see *WLT* 55:2 (Spring 1981), pp. 245–50, 55:4 (Autumn 1981), p. 633, and p. 39 of this issue.

[2] On the poetry of Ekelöf and his contemporaries, see Ross Shideler, "'The Glassclear Eye of Dreams' in Twentieth-Century Swedish Poetry," *WLT* 51:4 (Autumn 1977), pp. 530–34.

Western Europe

René Char in Search of the Violet Man

Certain poets moved away from the impertinences of surrealism after what has been called its "exalted years." Although many detached themselves or were expelled from the ranks, the subsequent paths of the defectors were far from being similar. In taking leave of coterie surrealism, René Char, half a generation younger than André Breton, interestingly moved in a direction parallel to that of Breton the poet, if not of Breton the surrealist activist. Both continued in the visionary path of Rimbaud, who had taken a new look at nature and at its dynamics; when he bid the Deluges return so that the sorcerer's knowledge of convulsive natural forces might become the substance of the poet's verbal alchemy,[1] he opened a new chapter in the poet's relation with the cosmos.

Calling upon those forces, Breton and Char (as well as the much less known Jehan Mayoux) developed a new kind of nature poetry which, without assuming any particular classification or new label, is an essential segment of modern poetics—one that is not yet sufficiently recognized. From *Le marteau sans maître* (including poems written from 1927 to 1937) to *Le poème pulvérisé* (1947) we follow Char's movement away from playful mating of objects and images to the mastery of a type of vision (also manifest in Breton's poetry of the 1930s and 40s), which becomes thereafter a fundamental and deeply moving mark of his poetry.

Avowedly, nature could no longer be viewed anthropocentrically, and the complicity suggested by a system of anagogic correspondences was to be replaced by a vision consistent with scientific data. Henceforth the poet had to take the initiative in establishing links between his sensibilities and nature if indeed any rapport was to be preserved. The poetics of Breton, Char, Jehan Mayoux, of the Mexican Octavio Paz, the Argentine Aldo Pellegrini, the Chilean Gómez-Correa and the African Léopold Senghor are based on a *naturism* which duplicates in language the convulsive character of natural forces. Philosophically, it is based on the concept of a golden age, not sponsored by exterior divinities but based on our perception of divine manifestations in nature, forgotten and suppressed; for the development of a rational mentality has produced dichotomies that have gradually separated us from the context of the natural world.

In his prose poem "Jacquemard et Julia" Char expresses the occurrence of this rupture nostalgically. It is a poem that can be read two ways, one with an eye for the contradictions, such as light and darkness, land and sky, water and aridity. But one can also see that the contradictions which are of the present are set against a past when grass "knew a thousand devices which did not contradict each other" ("Jadis l'herbe connaissait mille devises qui ne se contrariaient pas"; *PP*, 59) and which in their conciliation embraced man as well. So, from the angle of the past all the roads are in concordance, animals in enchantment, time annihilated, errors sheltered, human tears wiped away; the bowed grain finds a direct path to the mouth of the bird. Grass was unkind only to those who were not willing to wander and lose their way. Then an abrupt break occurs in the poem, warning us of the passing of the idyllic golden age; the break is manifest in the very contradiction in language: "L'inextinguible sècheresse s'écoule." "Inextinguishable" suggests burning, which proceeds to the next word, "dryness" or absence of water, which is contradicted by the next word, *s'écoule,* i.e., water running. But when the figurative meaning is substituted, the protest of the poet, injected into the language, emerges. The dryness of man's life continues, runs on; for man has made himself "a stranger to the dawn" ("L'homme est un étranger pour l'aurore"; *PP*, 60).

However, the poet ends on a note of hope rather than of dejection, for there are still those who recognize

René Char (*Lütfi Özkök*)

the tremors of the grass: "Cependant à la poursuite de la vie qui ne peut être encore imaginée, il y a des volontés qui frémissent, des murmures qui vont s'affronter et des enfants sains et saufs qui *découvrent*" (In the pursuit of life that cannot yet be imagined, there are free wills that tremble, murmurings that will be assertive, and children safe and sound who will *discover*). We are back to the faith expressed in Breton's First Manifesto: that the eidetic power which was taken away from us will someday be restored. The poetry of Char is full of that tenderness of childhood which must be guarded to rediscover the missing links to the circuit of nature where resides a state of grace.

Breton's theory of convulsive beauty was intricately connected with his concept of a cosmography of nature, of the delirium of interpretation which guides man in a "forest of indices," as he explained in *L'amour fou*. So it was that he linked the flesh of the woman he loved with "the snows on the summits in the rising sun." And in *L'air de l'eau*, love poems of the same period—which also marks Char's brilliant poetic genesis—Breton had traced the rainbow of his erotic embrace: "Ta chair arrosée de l'envol de mille oiseaux de paradis / Est une haute flamme couchée dans la neige." If we let the sense of these two poetic statements invade us with their full impact, we have at the same time the groundwork on which Char was to build the most resplendent levels of his poetic edifice through verbal resources particularly suited to universal coordinations.

The first of Breton's images fuses the human carnal substance with the element of water, combined with the quality of white/purity, and earth in its highest manifestation of summit, together with fire in terms of sun. The feminine elements of earth and water are invaded by the masculine one of fire, creating fusion and consummation on two levels: human love and cosmic concordance. In the second image again the human flesh is the starting point, and again it crosses barriers of nature's kingdoms: birds drenched in water, and flame in snow. The passage from human love to the cosmos is so smooth, like the flight of birds, that the contradictions of hot and cold, of solid and fluid, of visible and invisible are overcome in the conciliation which represents the fusion of the human embrace.

The power to enlarge his universe had seized Breton in a most gripping manner in such dazzling natural landscapes as the grottoes of Vaucluse and of Montpellier. The provocative character of natural phenomena had stirred his imagination. It is interesting to note that the major inspiration of Char's cosmic naturism derives also from a region of the Vaucluse area, that of his parents' property at l'Isle-sur-Sorgue.[2] The sense of Breton's elision of the inanimate and the animate, of the human and the vegetal or animal, is at the same time the basis on which Char was to create the magnetism of his poetry.

The collaborative work of Breton, Éluard and Char called *Ralentir Travaux* (1930) attests to the conjecture that this interweaving of the human with the cosmic must have been reached in consortium by the three poets, who henceforth relinquished overtly or subtly (as in the case of Breton) the more urbane, gratuitous poetry of wordplay and image substitution representative of the earlier surrealist mode (which continued unabated in many of the other erstwhile members of the group). The Second Manifesto (1930) had proclaimed the need for occultation, and indeed henceforth the more profound surrealist manner was to establish a conjunction between the psychic automatism manifest in language and the catalytic movements in nature evidenced in vision ranging from the grain of grass to the remotest constellations.

In a 1931 poem Char declares the love process as the basic poetic process—attraction, gravitation, accolade: "Dans le domaine irréconciliable de la surréalité l'homme privilégié ne pouvant être que la proie gracieuse de sa dévorante raison de vivre: l'amour" ("Poème," *MM*, 27). From gravitation toward the loved one to movement toward nature is the sequential order: "Le visage de la femme que j'aime, chemin des sources, ancien chemin des sables" ("Sommeil fatal," *MM*, 28).

Further in the collection of *Le marteau sans maître* we find a poem called "L'amour":

Tu ouvres les yeux sur la carrière d'ocre inexploitable
Tu bois dans un épieu l'eau souterraine
Tu es pour la feuille hypnotisée dans l'espace
À l'approche de l'invisible serpent
O ma diaphane digitale!
(*MM*, 38)

Man's search, expressed in the metonymy of the hunter's stick, is linked with ochre (earth), subterranean water, leaf in sky (vegetal and air), invisible serpent (fauna) and digital flower (flora); in fact, the flower classified as "digital" resembles the human finger and thus has a built-in linguistic duplication of the connection between the botanical and the human. The love upon which the poet opens his eye in this intricate design of nature, recipient of the human imprint, turns the notion of the *juxtaposition* of distant realities into the *coordination* of realities which lose their distance from each other under the spell that the poet casts upon them. And the adjectives *hypnotisée* and *diaphane* qualify the unimaginable union with an ecstatic purity best defined by the title of the poem, "Love."

René Char's poetry coordinates the universe in emanations and gravitations that synchronize the human heartbeat with the mysterious tremors which pulsate in the natural world. Since so much of the poet's work is the product of unconscious forces, the distance between art and nature is minimized, making way for interweaving and amalgamation. What Mallarmé called the "fiction" of the poet is in the poetry of René Char not the rival of the natural world but very close to nature's own fantasies. Poetry is perceived, then, in Char in "the fusing angle of an encounter" ("l'angle fusant d'une Rencontre"; "Biens égaux," *PRC*, 102/103). Chance meetings create an image of fusion such as this: "La lune du lac prend pied sur la place où le doux feu végétal de l'été descend à la vague qui l'entraîne vers un lit de profondes cendres" ("Donnerbach Mühle," *PP*, 26). Here we see light (*lune*), water (*lac*), earth (*plage*) and fire (*feu*) swept into a bed of cinders. In terms of the alchemical process of reducing to essence, we see, then, the interplay of the sidereal (*lune*), the vegetal (*feu végétal*) and the liquid (*vague*), a concert of forces creating movement, luminosity and darkness as if it were a contemplation in a hot moonlit summer night just before it gives way to the darkness of sleep and oblivion ("un lit de profondes cendres"): we have grasped man's brief moment of illumination before it turns to darkness. In fact, in the throes of such visions the poet becomes "lord of the impossible" ("A Pain I Dwell In," *PRC*, 105).

Had not Rimbaud asserted that if flight is impossible, the poet's sole exit is through the alchemy of the word? René Char is of Rimbaud's heirs, and in *Le poème pulvérisé* he dared describe what does not exist and give presence to the indescribable, calling on all earthly forces to nourish his poetic spirit. The terra firma is a source of the light of diamond and of snow; it brushes his being, kindles his flesh. As the invisible becomes visible, so the visible becomes invisible to intensify perception: "La nuit et la chaleur, le ciel et la verdure se rendent invisibles pour être mieux sentis" ("Le bulletin des baux," *PP*, 64). He arranges tiers of poetic values, oriented toward the core of a pristine natural force:

> Disposer en terrasses successives des valeurs poétiques tenables en rapports prémédités avec la pyramide du chant à l'instant de se révéler, pour obtenir cet absolu inextinguible, ce rameau du premier soleil; le feu non-vu, indécomposable.
> ("Partage formel," *PPC*, 218)

From solid stance he proceeds to fluid passage, whose movements are associated with the dance of butterflies. Thus he gives the reader a sense of passing from one level of motion (water) to another (air). The poet learns to read the microcosm of nature: the storm and garden of its passage are self-contained in the trajectory of the swallow: "Dans la boucle de l'hirondelle un orage s'informe, un jardin se construit." He also knows how to project the microcosm into the macrocosm:

Les eaux parlaient à l'oreille du ciel.
Cerfs, vous avez franchi l'espace millénaire,
Des ténèbres du roc aux caresses de l'air.

(The waters spoke on into the sky's ear.
Stag, you and you and you have crossed millennia,
  the space
From rock darkness to the air's caresses.)
("The Black Stag," *PRC*, 144/45)

His fusion of beings and things sometimes reaches gratuitous proportions: "L'encre du tisonnier et la rougeur du nuage ne font qu'un" ("À la santé du serpent," *PP*, 87).

If such images were simple practices in the juxtaposition of distant realities, we might be tempted to accept them as a game process like those of Raymond Roussel; and indeed even as such, the versatility might be considered poetic virtuosity and a renewal of the system of analogies. However, in Char's poetry that type of expertise is not the seat of greatness in itself. Poetry is lodged in language, but since the poetic revolution of the nineteenth century it is also the substance of a philosophy and the basis of an epistemology. Of this Char is very much aware. Poet and lover are constantly identified: "Tu es dans ton essence constamment poète, constamment au zénith de ton amour" (*PP*, 83). Poetry is the power of the visionary, giving man new qualifications as a human being: "Poésie, la vie future à l'intérieur de l'homme requalifié" (*PP*, 88). Poetry becomes the touchstone of the requalification of the human.

In truth, for René Char poetry is an existential stance. It is a *becoming,* a movement into high gear; it is man's only remaining contact with his revised definition of the eternal: "Si nous habitons un éclair, il est le coeur de l'éternel" (*PP*, 87). It is an invitation to return to the natural insights with which other creatures are endowed, to reenter the universal order: "Pouvoir marcher sans tromper l'oiseau, du coeur de l'arbre à l'extase du fruit" (*PP*, 85). Finally, it is a rejection of the mechanical materialism that places man in a system without conscious design, despairingly automatic: "Néglige ceux aux yeux de qui l'homme passe pour n'être qu'une étape de la couleur sur le dos tourmenté de la terre" (*PP*, 86–87). Char's vast fresco of the natural world is not unlike Paul Claudel's, but without the promises of religious transcendence to the ultimate recognition of meaning. For Char, as for Breton and for a number of other nonreligious mystics, man's creativity has to meet nature's halfway; it is not a question of recognition but of invention of associations, such that each man's universe becomes as complex as his power of cognition, as the elasticity of his sensory tentacles.

Rimbaud, in his poem "Les voyelles," epitomized the spiritual by the color violet, radiant in eyes whose possessor remained ambiguous in the semantic hermeticism of his possessive adjective: "rayon violet de Ses Yeux." Char was to appropriate the color and identify it as the supreme degree of man's manifest divinity. In a very hermetic poem of *Le poème pulvérisé* entitled "Suzerain" he gives us the spiritual autobiography of his childhood: arising to awareness in a crepuscular light, effecting a kind of symbiosis with river, butterfly, weed; and then the death of that world, leaving only a mute Friend. The word "friend" as a luminous phantom plays the role of *Génie* in Rimbaud and *Engel* in Rilke. He teaches the adolescent how "to fly over the night of words" ("Il m'apprit à voler au-dessus de la nuit des mots"), to be free of stationary things like "ships at anchor." At the end he knows that he must leave his hometown to find love and to reach the next stage of his becoming. And strangely, when he attains the next abode, that of *L'Homme Violet* (capitalized by the poet), he is disappointed by what he finds; he observes the same kind of corruption as in "Jacquemard et Julia." He finds a prisoner instead of a fugitive: "Mais il ne disposait là que du morose état-civil de ses prisons, de son expérience muette de persécuté, et nous n'avions, nous, que son signalement d'évadé" (*PP*, 76). So ends the confessional-poem.

But what did the poet want to escape in the guise of the violet man? And where did he want to escape? Certainly not from his corporal existence into an eventual soul-existence! "Tu feras de l'âme qui n'existe pas un homme meilleur qu'elle" ("À la santé du serpent," *PP*, 84). Better than the soul-man is the earth-man whom the poet identifies throughout his work. His escape is from a blind assumption of the human space, and it is a penetration of the subjective and objective worlds simultaneously. The poet comes to grips with the non-anthropocentric universe without damning himself as hapless, for he has learned to become part of the network. And thus he is relieved of his solitude and of any sense of drifting. His is neither the ship at anchor nor the shipwreck of Mallarmé's *Coup de dés.* The vision that links man to bird, plant, stone, sun, moon and to the bowels of the earth also turns his eventual demise into a metamorphosis. Fire and water, in their power of transformation and absorption respectively, promote a kind of serenity in the poet rather than a noble but self-consuming despair such as Pascal's. Reentry into the natural system is at the antipodes of the dichotomous eschatology underlying Pascal's notion of the *roseau pensant.*

Let us not forget that René Char is a poet of the 40s and 50s, of that time when existentialism was highlighting *Dasein* as an act of human salvation; but the existentialist notion of involvement related to political action as the sure solace, whereas the poet's existential stance is of a quite different nature of involvement: it is a cosmic embrace. The poet's sense of personal mortality is assuaged by the comprehension of what solders all into one: "aide à fendre le flot du devenir" ("Rougeur des matinaux," *LM,* 104). It is deemed a privileged destiny to be able to absorb unto oneself the sun and the wind and to contemplate the kind of eternity Char accords to Antonin Artaud in his memorial to the erstwhile companion of his surrealist days:

Puis renaît plus tard dans la douceur du champignon
. . .
Il suffit. Rentre au volcan.
Et nous,
Que nous pleurions, assumions ta relève ou
   demandions:
   "Qui est Artaud?" à cet épi de dynamite dont
   aucun grain ne se détache. . . .
("Un adieu, un salut," *LM,* 68)

All of this explains if not logically, at least poetically, the contradiction of Char's self-assigned epigraph: "vivre, limite immense" (*PP*, 26). Recognizing the limits of the living process, by unfurling the infinite possibilities of the associations of man with his contiguities,

Char has illustrated in his poetry what another companion of his youth, Louis Aragon, had stated in *Le paysan de Paris*: the only inconceivable notion is that of limit ("Il n'y a vraiment d'impensable que l'idée de limite absolue").[3] Indeed, the unconditional possibilities of passage into the variations of nature in the work of Char illustrate the notion that limit is unthinkable. In the vertiginous layers of existence are gateways to insights, what Char calls "la connaissance aux cent passages" (*PP*, 82).

The naturalism of modern poets like Char is not linked to the romantics' love of nature nor to the sensual courtship of physical realities that are manifest in the poetry of Walt Whitman and in his wake in so many modern American poets. The romantics had a mother/child relationship with nature, or when their hostility to life mounted, the relationship would turn into a mother/stepchild rapport. In either case there was on the part of nature a guardianship of man, sometimes effective and protective, other times resulting in a failed relationship. In the case of Whitman, or of more recent and less powerful American poets, the relationship to nature indicates a reduction of the cognitive power in the process of an intensification of the sensuous. For these, nature is a deep well of pleasures; it serves the hedonistic needs of the poet, who is constantly in a position of taking, sucking, appropriating for the self whatever is found to be stimulating to the senses and provocative to his language.

In the case of poets of the category I have called "naturist"—of which René Char is perhaps the most versatile and resourceful living example—nature is a coordinator between the forces in the poet and the forces outside of the poet; whether within or without, they are forces of which the poet is not fully the master. The mystery of those latent powers in him—similar to the blinking of an animal's eye or the burning of a tree or the boiling of a worm in the wood ("Robust Meteors," *PRC*, 4/5)—creates the sense of wonder in him, prepares the dialogue between himself and the mute universe. The reciprocity he has known in love is his sole index to the meaning of the universal reciprocity which he considers to be the primal purpose of existence. In repairing the separateness of man, source of alienation and despair, he is releasing the violet man from his prison house to resume his freedom. When the barriers are let down and the contact becomes communication, it is no longer a question of *taking* from nature or asking nature's protection; it is exchange, it is emergence from the labyrinth, it is that existence which Breton called "elsewhere" in the last sentence of the First Manifesto: "C'est vivre et cesser de vivre qui sont des solutions imaginaires. L'existence est ailleurs." Char challenges his

fellow beings to take stock of the riches within them left inert and in chains: "Les hommes d'aujourd'hui, l'instinct affaibli, perdent, tout en se gardant vivants, jusqu'à la poussière de leur nom," he tells them in the introduction of *Le poème pulvérisé*. He continues:

> Né de l'appel du devenir et de l'angoisse de la rétention, le poème, s'élevant de son puits de boue et d'étoiles, témoignera, presque silencieusement, qu'il n'était rien en lui qui n'existât vraiment ailleurs, dans ce rebelle et solitaire monde des contradictions.

Char's "elsewhere" is immediate, a series of moments that constantly replenish each other, creating ubiquity out of immobility. It absolves the "I" from the particular to enter into the universal. Rarely does Char have to use the personal pronoun, for his sensibility is the radiance with which he endows the world around him.

Anna Balakian, Summer 1977

[1] Rimbaud in "Après le Déluge," from *Les illuminations*: "Waters, griefs, arise and raise the Deluges. For ever since they have been dispelled,—oh the precious stones sinking into the ground, and the flowers opened!—what a shame! and the Queen, the Sorcerer who kindles the coals of her cauldron, will never want to tell us what she knows, and what we do not know."

[2] It can also be observed that Ussel, where Jehan Mayoux lived and wrote most of his poetry, is not far from the inspirational bases of Breton and Char.

[3] Louis Aragon, *Le paysan de Paris*, Paris, Gallimard, 1926, p. 235.

Brassaï, the Writer

A few weeks after the Liberation of Paris, Jean Paulhan, the editor of the prestigious *Nouvelle Revue Française*, took me with him to visit Picasso in his studio on the rue des Grands Augustins. A number of figures of the Rive Gauche artistic colony were gathered there, including the Hungarian-born photographer Brassaï, already known for works such as *Paris de nuit*. I was introduced to him, and we began a conversation about American literature, then all the rage among Paris intellectuals, and especially about his friend Henry Miller. From that time onward we remained in contact—in Paris, in Cannes, in New York, where he had an exposition at the Museum of Modern Art—until his death in 1984. Already in the 1930s, he had an international reputation, with shows in museums throughout Europe as well as in the United States. Currently his photographs are on view at the National Museum of Art in Washington, D.C.

Brassaï had also been very productive, if less well known, as a writer, with a variety of published works such as his biography of Henry Miller, his *Conversations avec Picasso,* and an essay on Marcel Proust "sous l'emprise de la photographie." In addition, he published texts on "Paris at night" accompanied by his photos, a volume titled *Letters to My Parents,* and two collections of poems, *Histoire de Marie* and *Paroles en l'air.* More attention is now being given to his literary activity, notably in Roger Grenier's *Brassaï* and in Marja Warnheim's admirably written and documented *Brassaï* (1996), which contains an excellent chapter on "The Photographer as Writer." Brassaï was fascinated all his life with theoretical questions such as the interrelation of word and image (which he treats at length in his book on Proust) and the connection between the written and the spoken word, between "popular" and "literary" expression.

Brassaï led an existence rich in movement and variety, as a painter, designer, photographer, movie director, and writer. Gyula Hálasz was born in 1899 in Brassó, a town in Transylvania, today part of Romania. ("Brassaï," the pseudonym he adopted in France, means simply "a native of Brassó.") He came from an intellectual, middle-class family. His father, a professor of French, had studied at the Sorbonne. The family spent the year 1903 in Paris, where the father was doing research. The young Gyula, playing in the Luxembourg Gardens, walking along the streets of the Rive Gauche, immediately fell in love with the city which was to play a central role in his career.

In 1920 Brassaï went to Berlin to study painting. But he wanted to return to Paris, and in 1924 he succeeded in obtaining a French visa. He arrived penniless and tried to scrape out a living as a free-lance journalist, but remained dependent on aid from his father. Fascinated by Paris's night-life—and lowlife—he roamed the streets tirelessly, and the spectacle inspired him to take photos, published in his first book, *Paris de nuit* (1933), with a text by Paul Morand. Soon his work was appearing in well-known French and American magazines such as *Harper's Bazaar,* to which he was to be a regular contributor for some thirty years. Through the art critic Tériade, he met Picasso and photographed his sculpture for the first issue of the Surrealist periodical *Le Minotaure,* thus launching a lifelong friendship. Later, he would write his important *Conversations avec Picasso* (1964), translated into five languages. In 1947 he married an attractive young lady, Gilberte Boyer, who to this very day faithfully continues to arrange expositions of his work.

At that time, the young artist became interested in the theater and, using giant photos, designed sets for Raymond Queneau's *En passant* and for the ballet *Phèdre* by Cocteau and Auric, presented at the Paris Opera in

1950. However, he wished to move beyond a career as a professional photographer and to spend more time writing. In 1949 he published *Histoire de Marie,* a collection of "poèmes en prose" with a preface by Henry Miller. In 1961 he brought out another tribute to popular life and art in an album of photos (with his commentary) of the graffiti which covered the walls of the Paris slums. A sequel to *Histoire de Marie* titled *Paroles en l'air* appeared in 1977, with a preface by the author. He was also continuing his exploration of "Paris by night" with a collection of naughtily seductive photos, *Le secret des années '30,* for which he wrote a lively text. In 1982 he produced an album of the work of outstanding modern artists—Picasso, Matisse, Dalí, and Braque, among others. His *Letters to My Parents,* with his touching preface, was published in Hungarian in 1977, but appeared in English translation only in 1997. Shortly before his death in 1984, he had completed *Marcel Proust sous l'emprise de la photographie,* which demonstrated the influence of photography on the composition of *A la recherche du temps perdu.* It was published by Gallimard in 1997.

■ LETTERS TO MY PARENTS

Letters to My Parents, published in English by the University of Chicago Press in 1997, had appeared in Hungarian in 1977, with a preface by Brassaï himself. It covers the period 1920–40. Two-thirds of the letters were written before 1929.

Subsequently Brassaï had a very busy life, and there are considerable lapses in the correspondence. During the years 1920–22 he wrote from Berlin, where he was studying painting, and then from Paris, where he resided for the rest of his life. In the preface he points out, with a certain irony, that "nothing is more disturbing than to read one's writings from long ago . . . much stumbling and straying," and admits that he has "a hundred faces to conceal myself." Penniless in Berlin, as a free-lance journalist he "manufactured interviews with world luminaries." Henry Miller, recalling their tough times in Paris, admitted that they would sometimes "retype old newspaper articles and sell them to editors as original works." Paris had soon become the passion of his creative life.

As "the eye of Paris," Brassaï had his first success with the album *Paris de nuit,* published in 1933, with a preface by Paul Morand, and enjoyed even greater success with *Le Paris secret des années '30.* In his introduction he refers to the diversity of his artistic gifts: "Fate has blessed me—or rather cursed me—with many different competing propensities which have caused me tension and anguish." Picasso and others tried to persuade him "to throw away the camera" and concentrate on painting. But he continued to believe that his work as a photographer "has turned out to be the widest branch of my life's river."

The first letter in the collection of correspondence to his parents describes his stay in Berlin. In order to keep the wolf from the door while studying painting, he began writing articles for Hungarian newspapers. Finally, to his delight, he received a French visa and, in February 1924, arrived in Paris. He felt very much at home: "I come and go in the city like an old Parisian." He laments constantly about his financial difficulties; he can't pay his rent, can't afford a good meal, subsists "on bread and milk." However, he makes the acquaintance of rich ladies who are willing to pay the check when dining with a charming young Hungarian artist. But high society has its servitudes. He has to "shave every morning, dress impeccably, and have his long hair cut." He has the good luck of landing a job as a representative of a German photographic agency, which offers him technical training in the field so that he himself can produce photos for them instead of buying prints from French photographers.

This marked the beginning of Brassaï's career as a professional photographer, but he soon got into trouble with the agency when it was discovered that he conducted an "interview" with an ex-czarist official whom he had never met. Kicked out of his job, he nearly died of hunger and was forced to shave "with soap stolen from a café." But he began to acquire a reputation as a photographer with the publication of *Paris de nuit* and an album on painters in their studios, "The Artists in My Life" (1934). In 1932 he had his first American exposition, in the Julian Levy Gallery in New York. Soon afterward, he received an offer from the film director Alexander Korda to shoot still photos of the latter's next production.

Under pressure, the correspondence slows down. The letter of October 1935 is the first since that of December 1933. He assures his family that he is making money, taking photographs for a number of international publications, including *Harper's Bazaar*. Now, he exults, besides the underworld of nightlife, "I am photographing 'high life'." He is deeply disturbed by the war, but in his last letter (Cannes, 1940) he informs his family that, in spite of the risks involved, he will return to Paris, where he remained throughout the Occupation. He endured material hardships, since he had refused to do photography for the Germans and consequently was cut off from other sources of income. But following the Liberation, he resumed his flourishing international career.

These letters, covering the first twenty years of Brassaï's adult life, provide precious insights into his complex personality and his incredibly varied gifts as a photographer, painter, and writer. And his work as a writer became increasingly significant for him during the later years of his activity, when he produced important volumes on Henry Miller, Picasso, and Proust.

■ BRASSAÏ'S POETRY

Brassaï's first book of poems, *Histoire de Marie* (1949), presents a collection of forty-four brief "poems in prose" with an introduction by Henry Miller, whom Brassaï had met in 1930 through their mutual acquaintance, A. Perlès. Miller immediately admired Brassaï not only as an artist but also as a human being: "He was always ready to talk to people. He was at home with everyone, with workers as well as intellectuals." Miller often accompanied Brassaï on his nocturnal roaming through the popular neighborhoods of Paris. His introduction to *Marie* presented a sketch of Marie that was both more honest and more accurate "than the sociological portraits of Zola." Mlle Malarmé, the cleaning woman in Brassaï's apartment building, insists on being called simply "Marie" since she "is not a demoiselle." She "believes in God" with the simple faith of common people. She works hard, she pays her rent, but the concierge doesn't like her and wants to have her evicted from her apartment. Marie knows how to defend herself, however. She goes to court and wins her case. In her self-esteem, her independence, her refusal to be looked down upon or pitied, Marie resembles many of the marginal figures presented by Brassaï in *Le Paris secret des annés '30*.

Paroles en l'air (1977), written during the Occupation, includes a reprint of *Marie* together with a group of prose poems—"Le Bistrot-tabac," "Le Chauffeur de taxi, 1943," "Soliloque à la fermeture"—preceded by an introduction by Brassaï on "the transmutation of the written and spoken word." During the Occupation he would often go to write in a *bistrot-tabac* near the Luxembourg Gardens. He could not see the people at the bar, but he could hear their voices and, fascinated, would close his notebooks and listen. The noisy chatter suggests to him "a moment in history" during the Occupation, as the cashier of the café reminds a customer, "We're short of everything." In "Soliloque" a poor homeless drunk, even though it's closing time, begs the bartender not to kick him out and to give him another drink. The driver in "Le Chauffeur de taxi" doesn't shut up for a single moment as he races across Paris, and Brassaï is fascinated once more by "the transmutation of the spoken word," a question which "preoccupied Proust and also Joyce and Diderot." The written language runs the risk of becoming "dry and lifeless" unless it is injected with the serum "de la langue parlée et la langue populaire."

In *Paroles en l'air* "the eye has been replaced by the ear." Brassaï also envisages the possibility that in the future "fact will replace fiction" and that lived experience may be a successful rival of the traditional novel.

■ CONVERSATIONS AVEC PICASSO

In *Conversations avec Picasso* Brassaï has not written one of those current thousand-page biographies wherein the footnotes frequently outweigh the text. Instead, he remains faithful to his title, conducting a series of "conversations" with Picasso in which he himself often has more to say than does Picasso, and he also speaks with a good many of their friends. The conversations are delightful to read in spite of being somewhat randomly assembled, but any good conversation defies strict formal discipline. The volume consists of a long series of diary entries dating from September 1943 onward, then "backs up" to 1939. The entries continue from there to January 1947, then are taken up again in May 1960, the first time Brassaï and Picasso have seen each other in thirteen years. They continue until November 1962. Picasso does not take part in the exchanges of October and November 1963.

The largest number of the conversations take place in the feisty 1940s, during the exuberant years of the Liberation period. The first entry in the volume recalls Brassaï's initial meeting with Picasso, arranged by *Minotaure* editor Tériade, who wished to publish photos of Picasso's sculpture and chose Brassaï to take the pictures for the journal. Thanks to his relations with *Le Mino taure,* Brassaï made the acquaintance of "un étrange couple," Salvador and Gala Dalí. Picasso received his fellow Catalan cordially and introduced him to the formidable Gertrude Stein, already well known as a collector of contemporary art. She lent him the money to make his first trip to the United States.

The long entries of 1943 are followed (with little con cern for chronology) by those of 1939, when Brassaï and fellow immigrants were alarmed by the apparent inevitability of war. But it was also a year of professional recognition. Picasso had an exposition at the Moma in New York, and *Life* magazine made a generous offer to Brassaï for photos of modern artists. Picasso, however, was having marital difficulties, which ended in separation from his wife, but simultaneously he also had the good fortune of meeting Dora Maar, who was to play an important role in his life. She was a photographer and wished to become "his camera woman."

Picasso often expressed his admiration for the work of Brassaï. He loved the photos of Paris by night and predicted that photography would "liberate us from literature." Praising Brassaï as "un grand dessinateur," he

encouraged him to devote himself to design rather than to photography: "You have a gold mine and you're exploiting a salt mine." One day, when arriving for a visit with Picasso, Brassaï found the house in an uproar. Picasso was raging: "Someone has stolen my flashlight!" Sabartés, an old friend and the artist's informal business agent, whispered, "He's certainly the one who misplaced it, but he wants to blame everybody." The flashlight was found the next day. Picasso had left it in the bathroom. *Conversations* abounds in such incidents.

But then, without transition, we pass from the trivial to the serious. Once the flashlight was recovered, Picasso plunged into a discussion of the prehistoric paintings on the walls of the caves in the Dordogne. References to the war became more numerous and frequent. Both Picasso and Brassaï, as foreign residents, feared arrest by the Gestapo. Picasso fled to Cannes, in the nonoccupied zone, while Brassaï abandoned his apartment to "hide out" with friends. Nevertheless, the conversations remain largely concerned with "art business"—expositions, museums, publications.

In May 1945, when the victory of the Allies was certain, all of Paris rejoiced. Picasso stepped up his activity, and he invited Brassaï to design the sets for his ballet *Rendez-vous,* in which Roland Petit would star. The first section of *Conversations* concludes in January 1947, with a brief entry on a Picasso exposition that is being planned for New York.

There follows a long silence until May 1960, when the two friends meet in Cannes. Their reunion is celebrated in one of the most touching and personal of the conversations. Picasso had sorely missed his friend, for during the past few years in Cannes he had lived "the life of a prisoner" because of his celebrity. He was always "besieged" by visitors. Brassaï asks himself with emotion how he can ever express in writing all the precious memories flooding back to him. Picasso praises his friend's book on graffiti, pointing out that "abstraction always begins with concrete reality." He asks Brassaï to read to him some of the "conversations" and approves of them as "vrais, authentiques." "They must be published," he adds.

This was the last conversation in which Picasso took part. In the remaining entries, friends—the daughter of Matisse, Sarbatés, Michel Leiris—speak of him. Brassaï's volume stands out as a precious and invaluable contribution to the vast literature devoted to Picasso; few authors had enjoyed such long and intimate contact with the great artist as had he.

■ HENRY MILLER: "GRANDEUR NATURE" AND "ROCHER HEUREUX"

Brassaï published the first volume of his biography of Miller, *Henry Miller: Grandeur nature,* in 1976. The second, *Henry Miller: Rocher heureux,* appeared in 1978. Both, however, illustrated with Brassaï's photos, had been in preparation for many years, going back to Brassaï's first notes on Miller and his letters to the American author in the 1930s. Brassaï remembers Miller's arrival in Paris: "Dead broke, his fortune consisted of a razor, a toothbrush, a fountain pen, a raincoat, and a Mexican cane." They immediately became friends and remained close until Miller's death in 1980.

Like *Conversations avec Picasso,* these two works can not be considered as conventional biography, consisting as they do of a mixed salad of letters, diary entries, reports on conversations, and quotations from literary works. The two friends had almost daily contacts until Miller fled Paris upon the outbreak of war to join Lawrence Durrell on Corfu. Both volumes confirm Brassaï's conception of literature as a "transcription of the spoken word." Thanks to Brassaï, Miller discovered Paris, which became one of the passions of his life. In *Tropic of Capricorn* he writes: "My eyes opened wide and clear only after I had put my feet on the soil of Paris." He often accompanied Brassaï on his nighttime wanderings through lowlife sections of the city, recorded in *Paris de nuit* and *Le Paris secret des années '30.* During these wanderings, Miller "rediscovered himself" and reanimated his literary gifts after a long silence, which he attributed to "the sterility of America."

When Miller could not find an American publisher, the Obelisk Press in Paris brought out *Tropic of Cancer* (1934), *Black Spring* (1936), and *Tropic of Capricorn* (1939). In Paris, Miller finally found, at the age of forty, "my joy in life." Brassaï describes him as passing hours on the *terrasse* of the Deux Magots or the Dôme, writing, chatting, having a drink, and "looking for someone to come by who would pay the check." He was bewitched by the urinals which, in that period, stood on almost every streetcorner. (The city has since replaced them with "comfort stations.") He found it "so charming" to urinate, standing there in a *vespassienne* and watching the pretty girls go by. Miller often reminisced about the days when he had no money, no home, and was as free "as a bum." But he was not only "roaming the streets"; he was also spending his time reading "mountains" of books. Some of his favorite authors surprise us. He loved Saint Francis of Assisi, for example, and praised the virtues of "holy ignorance."

Still, "devouring books" did not interrupt Miller's tireless sex life, as a chapter on the formidable Anaïs Nin

makes clear. The six volumes of Nin's tell-all diary and her autobiographical novels depict her as "the free woman" who has become an icon in the field of gender studies. Immediately upon meeting Miller, she invited him to stay with her. The idyll did not last, and Nin abandoned "her fabulous animal" in favor of Jane, his former wife.

Moreover, the time had come when his friends who had been supporting him decided that he should earn his own living, and so got him a job as an English assistant at the University of Dijon. He put up with the Dijon post for only three weeks before returning to Paris and signing on as a proofreader for the *Chicago Herald-Tribune.* He was soon fired, however, since he did not have the proper work-papers. Because his article "Claude" had been accepted by Samuel Putnam's *New Review* and the important French writer Raymond Queneau had published a flattering review of *Tropic of Cancer* in the *Nouvelle Revue Française,* Miller felt that he might finally "make it." He returned to New York in 1935, but, disappointed, hurried back to Paris within a few months.

Despite his long residence in Paris, Miller never became "Frenchified," and Brassaï describes him as intellectually "a direct descendant of Emerson." When the war broke out, he quickly understood that France, menaced by the Nazi invasion, was no place for an American. He obtained a visa for Greece and went to stay with his friend Lawrence Durrell on the island of Corfu, where he began writing one of his finest works, *The Colossus of Maroussi* (1941), a love song to Greece, where he had found "serenity and joy."

The second volume of the biography, *Henry Miller: Rocher heureux,* posed new problems for Brassaï. His subject was no longer available for long conversations, having returned to the United States in 1941 and, after two unhappy years in New York, fleeing to California, to Big Sur, to a cabin in the mountains. Miller had at last had the good fortune to find American publishers and was producing a new title almost every year: *Sunday After the War* (1944), *The Air-Conditioned Nightmare* (1945), *Remember to Remember* (1947), *The Smile at the Foot of the Ladder* (1948). Norman Mailer wrote a lengthy introduction to an anthology of his work, *Genius and Lust,* that appeared in 1976. The twenty-four chapters of *Rocher heureux* draw largely on Brassaï's correspondence and conversations with Miller and on his own diary. Upon his return to the States, Miller had quickly become a celebrity, the patron saint of the Beats, but it seems clear that, for Brassaï, the celebrity author was less sympathetic than the "bum" he had first known.

Once established in Big Sur, Miller met and swiftly married a young woman, Janina Lepska, by whom he had two children, "Tony" and Barbara. But after seven tumultuous years, the marriage broke up and Lepska abandoned Miller, leaving him to care for the children. However, Eve McClure, the sister of one of his painter friends, came to give him a hand. She "adored" him and soon moved in. Miller's financial situation had been rapidly improving, thanks to royalties received from his publishers. With cash in his pocket, he returned to Europe in December 1953, accompanied by Eve and the children. It was Eve's first trip abroad, and after leading a primitive existence without gas or electricity in Miller's cabin, she was delighted with Paris. She wanted to remain in France, in fact. Miller was less enthusiastic, but they did visit Paris again in the spring of 1959. Miller complained to Brassaï about all the changes which had taken place since he first knew the French capital. He had grown to hate big cities and wanted to remain in Big Sur, where he could still find the peace and tranquillity he had lost since becoming an international celebrity. Discussing with Brassaï his responsibilities as a parent, he pitied the offspring of "men of genius" and often wondered what had become of Paulo, Picasso's son: "What a tragedy for a child to have a famous father."

After a few months, the family returned to California, but not even in Big Sur could Miller now enjoy the solitude he longed for. He and Eve separated, and he returned to France alone in April 1960, as a member of the jury of the Cannes Film Festival. He held forth to Brassaï (who had joined him there) on his newfound passion for Oriental philosophy. He longed to travel to Tibet and, clothed in the robes of a Buddhist monk, make a pilgrimage to the holy city of Lhasa. During the film festival, he and the Belgian-French novelist Georges Simenon were interviewed on television. Miller refused to be considered "a giant of pornography," and Simenon, in the American author's defense, hailed him as "un saint laïque"(!), revered by young people as a "liberator."

Four years later, Brassaï traveled to Pacific Palisades to visit Miller in his "belle maison blanche." The writer now lived alone, since Hoki, his young Japanese wife, had left him. He no longer had any desire to write: "I've said it all." This final encounter of the two friends of forty years was far from heartening. Miller sadly felt the ravages of time: "In December, I'll be 83. . . ." As the volume closes, the light is fading and the night descends.

▪ MARCEL PROUST

Brassaï's posthumous essay *Marcel Proust sous l'emprise de la photographie* appeared only in 1997, although his intense interest in the author of *A la recherche. . .* dated from his early youth and his previous works on Miller and Picasso constantly refer to Proust as someone who was "crazy about photography, which had a lifelong impact on his writing." Photography influenced Proust's narrative techniques, Brassaï claims: the changes in perspective, "the angle from which the light is thrown," and the desire to create "a permanent present." Illustrated with Brassaï's photos, the volume contains three interrelated sections: "La Photographie dans la vie de Proust," "Des Clefs pour *La Recherche*. . . ," and "L'Influence de la photographie sur la pensée de Proust." In the introduction, Brassaï points out that Proust invites the reader to view his novel from several different angles and thereby to propose new interpretations of it.

Brassaï understood early "la place prépondérante" of photography in Proust. He first read *A la recherche*. . . . in 1926, when photography still did not interest him at all. Only later was its significance recognized by thinkers like Walter Benjamin and Roland Barthes. But Proust was far in advance of them. In his struggle with time, in his ambition to create "une sorte d'éternité," he found in photography his best recourse, "sa meilleur alliance." Brassaï made the acquaintance of "another Proust," "un photograph mental," the author of a great novel which was "une photographie gigantesque." In his letters to friends, Proust often included one of his photos, requesting that they send him one of theirs in return. Over the years, he accumulated a vast archive of prints, which he utilized in creating his characters. He considered photography to have a place in the history of art, since it is itself an art which opens up "une nouvelle vision du monde." For Brassaï, Proust transformed the whole world into a photographic studio.

Much has been written, by Painter and others, about Proust's "relativism" and its connection with the theories of Einstein. Brassaï, however, feels that photography also played an important part. All the characters in *A la recherche* . . . have multiple personalities. The narrator, while giving a kiss to Albertine, discovers, in a brief moment, "dix Albertine." Although Proust claims that his concept of "involuntary memory" is completely original, Brassaï points out that he had a number of precursors, among them Chateaubriand, Gérard de Nerval, and Baudelaire. At the end of his career, Brassaï certainly experienced great satisfaction in writing an essay which opened up new perspectives on Proust—and which produced a love match between the two great passions of his own life: word and image, literature and photography.

John L Brown, Winter 2000

J.M.G. Le Clézio (*Jacques Sassier © Gallimard*)

From the Renaudot Prize to the Puterbaugh Conference: The Reception of J. M. G. Le Clézio

The 1997 Puterbaugh Conference on World Literature is one of the very first international colloquia to have been devoted to J. M. G. Le Clézio.[1] Moreover, this is no ordinary colloquium, as it aims to highlight the consecration of a contemporary author, "a living classic." This event has led me to take a step back and to examine the way in which Le Clézio's work has been received and the manner in which he has been canonized. To this end, I will draw on the ever-increasing number of articles which have been written on reception theory.[2] Within this theoretical and methodological framework, the basic premise is that public recognition of a writer is essential in terms of literary value. In other words, it is consensus which turns a writer into a great author.

The first issue I propose to address is that of knowing how the process of canonization occurs. Writers who remain unknown during their lifetime contrast greatly with those who achieve a measure of renown during their productive years. This success is modified by variables, being either immediate or occurring later in an individual's career. The second issue I seek to clarify is that of determining what readership is responsible for the writer's accession to a place in posterity. Is it due to the general public, to a readership of literary reviewers, or rather to literary and scholastic institutions? These different factors need not necessarily concur. Finally, I shall attempt to comprehend why and to what extent Le Clézio has become part of our country's literary heritage.

My analysis will focus on the high points of Le Clézio's career, *Le procès-verbal* in 1963 and *Désert* in 1980. However, this evocation of his moments of greatest glory will be followed by a study of the opinions of his detractors, and I shall attempt to analyze the divergent views of these detractors and his supporters.

▪ I. THE RENAUDOT PRIZE FOR *LE PROCÈS-VERBAL* (1963)

In 1963, when he was twenty-three years old, Jean-Marie Le Clézio was awarded the Théophraste Renaudot Prize for his first novel, *Le procès-verbal;* he also figured

on the short list for the Goncourt Prize, the most prestigious of the hundreds of literary awards presented annually in France. This exceptional literary debut is often recalled at the outset whenever the press presents a new work by Le Clézio. For example, an article by Michèle Gazier which appeared in *Télérama*[3] (a quality cultural magazine) upon the publication of *La quarantaine* in late 1995 alludes to the event: "Has he changed since 1963, when he erupted on the literary scene with his volcanic novel *Le procès-verbal?*" In another example dating from the same period, a television interview Le Clézio gave was reproduced in part in *Paris Match,* a more downmarket magazine.[4] In this instance the reference is more direct: "In his first novel, *Le procès-verbal,* he wrote of a solitary man and won the Renaudot Prize at twenty-three." If one leafs through Le Clézio's press clippings, one is struck by the recurrence of this theme, which goes beyond the purely commercial function: it becomes a leitmotiv, almost a cliché, henceforth linking the author to success, a success which is of both a media-commercial and a literary nature.

A. A Commercial and Media Success. The success linked to the Renaudot Prize is first of a commercial nature, as the function of the prize is neither that of recompensing well-established authors nor that of bringing original work by great writers of the future to the public's attention. The major function of literary prizes in France is one of boosting book sales and also of launching traditional-style books, essentially novels written in an accessible style, regardless of the nature of the author's career. From this perspective Le Clézio is a rather atypical Renaudot winner, for not only was he a complete unknown in the literary and publishing worlds, but his novel hardly conformed to the criteria necessary for commercial success. Le Clézio thus brought off a double coup, that of garnering the Renaudot Prize and that of doing so with an unconventional novel. His book sold a respectable number of copies: some 74,000 by the end of 1963.

The reception accorded to Le procès-verbal was thus also that accorded to a media event which was of course linked to the Renaudot Prize but was also connected to the author's image.[5] Although anecdotal, this aspect is not to be neglected, because it is striking to find that it still is commented upon, even in the most recent press articles, to a greater or lesser degree depending on the target readership of the magazine. This image, to a certain extent, justifies the notoriety of the writer in a society obsessed with physical appearance. Thus, in the Télérama article cited previously, the image of the author is associated with the success of his first book; both elements become defining characteristics: "Still as blond and trim as ever, has he changed since 1963, when he erupted on the literary scene . . . ?" Youth and good looks, which encourage comparisons with film stars, reinforce the spectacular side of things.

The other justification for this media attention is to be found in the personality of the author, or at least in that which we are allowed to see—i.e., great discretion, which endows the author with an aura of secrecy and mystery, a fertile feeding ground for dreams and imagination. Paradoxically, the media success of Le Clézio is based at least in part on the fact that he maintains a certain distance from the literary scene; because of his absence, each appearance constitutes a kind of minor media event. The conjunction of these two factors—appearance and personality—is the source of the author's early acquisition of a mythical side to his character.[6]

B. Literary Success. However, this commercial and media success did not prevent Le Clézio from being perceived immediately by numerous literary critics as having the makings of a great writer. This only increases the spectacular dimension of his literary debut, which, one is forced to admit, occurred on all fronts. Without a doubt, this impression is reinforced by certain comparisons which were made with the works of the *nouveau roman* school, which dominated the literary scene at the

time. Le Clézio has objected to these comparisons, and I do not wish to enter into a discussion on the subject here. The interesting element, from the point of view of reception theory, is that the novel was *perceived* as following this trend.

In the second place, from a thematic perspective, young people found in Le procès-verbal an echo of their existential unease. The hell of urban existence and the limits of consumer society in a search for happiness emerge as special themes. (The latter is examined in a radical fashion in Georges Perec's novel Les choses two years later, in 1965.) Thus, the cultural representativeness of the novel allows for reader identification.

The post-Renaudot period was characterized by a drop in Le Clézio's popularity, as indicated by the failure to publish a paperback edition of the works of fiction which followed Le procès-verbal. This decline was due to the works' disturbing technique and their nonconformist character. However, Le Clézio was not forgotten, for literary researchers, who became interested in him at an early stage in his career, took up the torch, at least in the United States, where the first theses devoted to him were written. As early as 1971, Le Clézio was the subject of a comparative study which examined his work alongside that of the German novelist Uwe Johnson,[7] and seven more theses were written between 1971 and 1978.[8] The publishing world played its own small but determining role in the legitimization of the author from 1977 on. It was during this year that Jennifer Waelti-Walters's general introduction to Le Clézio's work appeared in the Twayne World Authors Series.[9] France's interest in him came later (this phenomenon conforms to the traditions of both nations): the first French book and the first three French theses on the Le Clézio's writings all appeared in the same year, 1983[10]—i.e., during what has come to be known as his second period.

▪ II. MONDO ET AUTRES HISTOIRES (1978) AND DÉSERT (1980): FROM SUCCESS TO CANONIZATION?

In 1978, Mondo et autres histoires, a collection of short stories, introduced a new style of writing, one previously only experimented with in Voyages de l'autre côté (1975). However, it is difficult to disassociate the volume's reception from that accorded to the novel Désert, which followed two years later in 1980. The novel form is far more popular in France than is the short story, which is less deeply rooted in our literary tradition. On the occasion of the publication of Désert, Le Clézio appeared for the first time on "Apostrophes," a literary television program with a wide audience. The novel sold very well, and the process of canonization really began at that point.

A. The Process of Canonization. The signs of popular success are obvious. *Mondo, Désert,* and later writings figure on the best-seller lists.[11] All of Le Clézio's later work has been issued in paperback, beginning with *Mondo* in 1983 and followed by *Désert* in 1985. Moreover, by the age of forty, Le Clézio had been translated into fifteen languages.

Alongside this commercial success and increasing notoriety, a growing interest was being shown in Le Clézio's work within the university sphere as well, with approximately a dozen theses devoted to him in France between 1983 and 1995. The number of critical assessments of his work increased, as did the interest shown by scholastic institutions, which had begun to include the author in its syllabuses. The first visible sign of institutionalization in France came from the nation's most prestigious literary body, the Académie Française, which in 1980 awarded the Paul Morand Prize to Le Clézio for *Désert.*

In the publishing field, critical studies began to multiply at the end of the eighties and especially in the early nineties. The books are of various kinds. Those published by university researchers are sometimes assessments of the author's complete output.[12] On the other hand, Simone Domange's book dealing with *Désert* underlines the fact that this novel attracts special interest.[13] Recently, school-notes publishers became particularly interested in *Désert,* and two manuals were released;[14] two guides to *Mondo* have also been published.[15] These manuals are aimed at a school-going readership. It is also important to note that dictionaries, literary histories, and school manuals include articles on Le Clézio as a matter of course.

The interest shown by educational publishing companies is closely linked to the position occupied by the writer within the school system. Le Clézio figured on official syllabuses quite early in his career. The childlike element in *Mondo* has led to its being studied at the junior-high-school level. In 1986 the pedagogical magazine *L'Ecole des Lettres* published a long study which dealt with this collection of short stories.[16] *Mondo* is also popular abroad; it is used, for instance, as a set text for first-year French-literature students in Japanese universities. Extracts from Le Clézio's works have also discreetly appeared on teacher-recruitment examination papers in France.[17]

The combined impact of publishing policy and educational practice has contributed to the forming of a public opinion which now views Le Clézio as one of the foremost contemporary French writers. In 1994 he was elected "the greatest living French writer" by the readers of *Lire* magazine as well as by French teachers, through a poll organized by that literary review.[18]

B. The Parameters of Recognition. Let us now try to comprehend the reasons for this success and for Le Clézio's canonization.

1. The Autobiographical Dimension. The autobiographical dimension of most of Le Clézio's texts favors their popularity, since the public is always interested in this kind of intrusion into an author's life.[19] The interest displayed is all the more intense because of the fact that Le Clézio continues to maintain his aura of discretion and mystery. The autobiographical element had already been underlined in *Le procès-verbal,* and it is present to varying degrees and varieties in his subsequent works. One distinction can be made between individual memory and family memory: these different facets are illustrated by *Onitsha* on the one hand and *La quarantaine* on the other, to chose the most obvious examples. Another distinction can be made between the foreground and the background—in other words, between anecdotal experience as the object of discourse and a manner of seeing, of feeling, and of being moved that circulates within the texts.

2. A Traditional Novel Form. When one examines the notion of form, one is obliged to underline Le Clézio's return to a more traditional style, often close to that of the adventure novel, which ensures that the novels have become accessible to a wider readership.

3. A Thematic Cluster. A third element which may explain Le Clézio's increased readership is the cluster of themes representative of contemporary values. From *Mondo* onward, the thematic concerns are remodeled. These go through a process of inversion, and the seeds planted in the first texts begin to flower. Initially, the theme of the urban hell almost disappeared, to be replaced by its antithetical counterpart, the paradise of nature; this change occurred at a time when ecological values were becoming widely accepted in the Western world. Second, the exoticism associated with travel marks almost all of Le Clézio's work.[20] This has coincided with a democratization of long-distance travel, which has gradually become a widespread phenomenon within society. Finally, a feeling of individual unease was partly replaced by a concern for the collective suffering of oppressed peoples, as a result of colonialism in particular. This discourse of sympathy for the little people is linked to the humanitarian movement which developed during the eighties and, in more general terms, is connected to the defense of the weaker societal sectors, which became an important issue for the intermediate level of French society, the average "progressive middle-class" person who came to political power through the elections of 1981.[21]

Basically, Le Clézio's books transmit humanist values which date from an earlier time and which underlie present preoccupations. They update the debate between nature and culture, and they achieve a spiritual dimension through a quest for original purity.

4. A Poetic Complexion. Another factor which influences public recognition is the fact that a novel such as *Désert* attracts a lot of attention because of its "poetic" nature. This adjective is useful as a kind of catch-all category. It designates certain themes in Le Clézio's work such as communion with nature and the imaginary world.[22] The notion of poetry also alludes to a certain style of writing, based on repetition and images, which is sometimes close to poetic prose when the sentence develops perceptible rhythms. Aside from its association with escapism, a poetic quality to writing can above all be considered as a characteristic of literary writing.

5. Mythical Echoes. Finally, it should be noted that a rich mythical network runs throughout Le Clézio's work, adding a structuring quality; critics have greatly enjoyed examining this device.[23]

C. Le Clézio's Two Readerships. According to this series of parameters, a twofold explanation for the success of Le Clézio's work can be outlined: one concerns his success with a general readership, whereas the other explains his legitimization by institutions. This process really began to operate simultaneously from *Désert* onward. Alain Viala examines this polysemic occurrence from the inside—that is to say, through a study of Le Clézio's writing strategy and through the consideration of the inscription of the figures of the writer and the reader *in* the text. He comes to the conclusion that Le Clézio's texts appeal to two potential readerships, one being an elite of more learned readers who are cultured without being erudite, capable of deciphering the myths; they are also popular with a wider public who are interested in a good read.[24] This opening is an essential factor in understanding the writer's audience.

▪ III. LE CLÉZIO'S DETRACTORS CLAIM HIS IS A SIMPLISTIC WORK

One is forced to admit, however, that public opinion is divided with regard to Le Clézio. There are two camps: the enthusiasts and the detractors. The latter show up in the press, since that kind of literary critic is basically and openly subjective (and may sometimes involve obscure personal concerns). Although unwritten, similar opinions do exist among university critics. The principal arguments of the detractors are based on the ambiguity of the work, which can be read at two levels.

A. Unreadable Early Texts. One frequent reproach made with regard to Le Clézio's early texts is that they are hermetic. *Le procès-verbal* seems to take the form of a rough draft. The impression of anarchy and obscurity is not, in the detractors' view, the result of subtle and complex writing but instead corresponds to a real fault in the book's makeup. Besides, the unreadability of the early texts comes from an author who is guilty of displaying the extent of his learning in what could be called a philosophical and metaphysical hotchpotch. In short, Le Clézio stands accused in the name of a classical ideal of order and clarity.

B. A Repetitive and Monotonous Body of Work. In general, Le Clézio's work suffers from a lack of innovation—still according to his opponents. In his first novels the scripts and the themes scarcely change at all. The characters are young people who are ill at ease in the city and spend their time walking around the urban center or seeking refuge in the out-skirts. From *Mondo* forward it is a different story, yet still the same: the quest is more positive; characters are looking for their roots. Some people laugh at Le Clézio's telling of his family history, the stories of his paternal grandfather, of his maternal grandfather, or his own story. This permanence is interpreted negatively in terms of poverty.

The repetitive nature of the work also plays a role within the individual texts and is criticized just as vehemently. *Désert* in particular is faulted for its slow progress and its monotony.

C. Simplicity: Ethics and Esthetics. Repetition leads to a feeling of slack effort, to a notion of simplicity, on both an esthetic and an ethical level. Le Clézio is accused of a "lack of psychology," "naïveté," "innocence," "angelism," and even "sentimentality," thus creating "a Manichean vision." A double paradigm opposes the city and modern Western society and economic values, on the one hand, to nature, small human communities, poverty, and sensitive and spiritual values on the other. The characters, who are always young people or children, have a vision of the universe which is full of hope and good intentions. Inevitably, they confront the incarnation of evil in a kind of exotic western. Such a reading of Le Clézio's work seems to have been inspired by Gide's phrase, "Good sentiments make bad literature."

This vision of the world is linked to a supposedly simple style of writing in the works of the author's second period, which serves as a weapon in the hands of Le Clézio's detractors. In the *Paris Match* article quoted at the beginning of this essay we can read, "[Le Clézio's] physique and ideas have remained as otherworldly and simple as they were during the era of the Renaudot Prize

. . . and his work suffers from a poor writing style." The connection is made between the writer's image—which was referred to earlier—and his writing, both its substance and its form. From simplicity and sobriety, it is tempting to infer poverty and so favor a negative connotation produced by the *doxa,* which valorizes intellect and complexity. Le Clézio ends up accused of being simplistic. This interpretive process is capped by the supreme condemnation of being the author of an easily accessible work, or of being the writer of children's literature in the case of certain texts.

With regard to the basis of these arguments, I propose the following counterobjections.

First, there are elements for which Le Clézio claims total responsibility, starting with the "rewriting" of the same story (his novels may be considered different chapters of the same book, he explains in an early interview). The same can be said of his simplicity, as when he commented to *Paris Match:* "I would like people to say that I am close to children, that I am myself simplistic; it doesn't bother me. I don't want to be considered as intelligent; that isn't my aim." The scale of values which his detractors use to judge his work obviously does not coincide with that of the author himself.

Second, simplicity ought not to be confused with a desired *effect* of simplicity. This allows one to say that simplicity of writing is only *apparent* in Le Clézio's works, as certain people have happily underlined and as could easily be proved through close stylistic study.

Finally, certain arguments can be reinterpreted in a positive manner. Simplicity can be seen as a symbolic form, an esthetic sign of a desire for the absolute, the essential, the pure. As for the repetitive character of the work, it is important to remember that rewriting—intertextuality, in other words—based on variation is one of the elements which endows the text with a literary quality.

The reception accorded to Le Clézio's work is an area of study which remains wide open. My presentation here, far from having exhausted the subject, aims only at indicating trends and, without doubt, has failed to pick up on all the nuances. I wish to conclude therefore by underlining both the clarity of the process of canonization and the fact that this process has not yet ended, that Le Clézio is still controversial.

The author's progress is characterized by a spectacular debut with a first novel (*Le procès-verbal,* 1963) which enjoyed both a certain measure of success and simultaneously an initial degree of recognition of the author's literary value as a writer. This first period was followed by an ebb in the novelist's fortunes and a period of relative indifference with regard to institutional rec-

ognition, at least in France. The second important period of Le Clézio's career commenced in 1980, almost twenty years after his debut, with the publication of *Désert.* This marked the beginning of real popular success allied with literary canonization.

However, the notion of the author as great writer was formed on the basis of a twofold selection made among his works. This selection is first of all chronological, with the texts written between 1966 and 1975 left to one side by public and press alike. It is also genre-based, with the traditional novel form attracting the most attention, to the detriment of the short stories and essays. The novel benefits from the prestige generally accorded it today as the major literary form, but also from the vacuum created by the different attempts made from the fifties to the seventies to deconstruct the novel form. *Mondo,* the collection of short stories, is an exception, benefiting from a certain degree of interest because of its child/adolescent-oriented composition, which makes it easily adaptable for school use. University critics display more moderation on the issue of selectivity, but without reversing the trend.

Le Clézio's success can be partly explained in terms of his modernity, which is visible on more than one level and which can be defined in terms of cultural and ideological representativity. His great strength is to be found in his writing strategy, which allows him to reach both a cultured audience and a less-cultured readership. His modernity can also be seen in the formation of a mythical image of the writer which goes beyond the anecdotal level: the mythification which operates within the texts is allied to the image of an "intermediate" writer who is neither an intellectual nor an explorer of language and who remains on the edge of literary life. This indefinable profile which shapes his writings makes him the epitome of a writer, a pure writer.[25] Without doubt, as the present century draws to an end, France's literary landscape favors the development of such a phenomenon. The rarity of great authors, the crisis experienced by the novel as a genre and by literature in general, ensures that there are places going a-begging within the closed circle of those considered to be great writers; critics await the discovery of a popular new great writer. It remains to be seen if Le Clézio's name will one day be as famous as that of Molière or Victor Hugo.

Sophie Jollin, Autumn 1997

---

[1] The only one published is that from the University of Valencia (Spain), by E. Real, French and Italian Philology Department, "Lecció Oberta," 1992.

[2] In particular, those presented in a volume titled "Qu'est-ce qu'un classique?" *Littératures classiques,* special issue, Paris,

1993; and Alain Viala's chapters dealing with *La ronde et autres faits divers* in *Approches de la réception,* Paris, PUF, "Perspectives littéraires," 1993.

3 "L'aventurier de nulle part," no. 2395 (6 December 1995), pp. 76–77.

4 23 November 1995, pp. 8–9.

5 It was the first time that the Gallimard publishing house organized an advertising campaign of this kind.

6 It is represented by the emblematic expression "beau comme un dieu" (literally, "handsome as a god"), which is found in several articles. A whole series of expressions substantiate this: "ideal star," "Prince Charming," "great Viking," "archangel," "Apollo," and even "living myth."

7 H. J. Salij, "Modern Dilemmas and the Technique of Writing in the Novels of Uwe Johnson and J. M. G. Le Clézio: A Comparative Study," University of Washington, 1971.

8 Sister M. Black, "Problems and Techniques of the French Novel, 1950–1970: A Study of the Literary Theory and Practice of Five Novelists," University of Wisconsin, 1972. J. P. de Chezet, "Continuité et discontinuité dans les romans de J. M. G. Le Clézio," University of California at Irvine, 1974. M. Le Clézio, "Mirrors of Disintegration: J. M. G. Le Clézio, from *Le procès-verbal* to *Les géants,*" Columbia University, 1976. L. K. Penrod, "The Rules of the Game: The Novels of J. M. G. Le Clézio (1963–1973)," Ohio University, 1975. K. Reish-White, "The Building of a Fictional World," University of Wisconsin, 1973. G. C. Waterston Jr., "A Suggested Reading of a Puzzle Novel: Oedipal Themes in J. M. G. Le Clézio's First Work, *Le procès-verbal* (1963)," University of Michigan, 1978. J. S. Weiner, "Conceptions of Language in the Works of J. M. G. Le Clézio," University of Pennsylvania, 1978.

9 *J. M. G. Le Clézio,* Boston, Twayne, 1977.

10 T. Di Scanno, "La vision du monde de Le Clézio: Cinq études sur l'œuvre," Paris, Nizet. T. Jappert, "Le thème de l'enfance dans l'œuvre de Le Clézio," University of Aix-Marseille I. H. S. Jung, "Les métamorphoses de la ville dans l'œuvre de J. M. G. Le Clézio," University of Nice. C. Vieuille, "Le féminin dans l'œuvre de J. M. G. Le Clézio," University of Aix-Marseille I.

11 In the case of *Onitsha,* sales were estimated at between 100,000 and 150,000 copies in July 1991.

12 Germaine Brée, *Le monde fabuleux de Le Clézio,* Amsterdam, Rodopi, 1990. J. Onimus, *Pour lire Le Clézio,* Paris, PUF, 1994.

13 *Le Clézio ou la quête du désert,* Paris, Imago, 1993.

14 M. Borgomano, *"Désert,"* J. M. G. Le Clézio, Paris, Bertrand-Lacoste, "Parcours d'une œuvre," 1992. B. Doucey, *"Désert,"* J. M. G. Le Clézio, Paris, Hatier, "Profil d'une œuvre," 1994.

15 F. Evrard, E. Tenet, *"Mondo et autres histoires,"* J. M. G. Le Clézio, Paris, Bertrand-Lacoste, "Parcours d'une œuvre," 1994. F. Marotin *"Mondo et autres histoires,"* J. M. G. Le Clézio, Paris, Gallimard, "Foliothèque," 1995.

16 R. Boudet, P. Pichard, 1–15 September 1986, pp. 37–46; 1 October 1986, pp. 22–32.

17 M. P. Schmitt, "Les cotes aux concours," in *Qu'est-ce qu'un classique?,* pp. 281–91.

18 November 1994, pp. 22–23.

19 Autobiography has also been very much in vogue as a literary genre in France since 1968.

20 From North Africa in *Désert* to sub-Saharan Africa in *Onitsha,* from the islands of the Indian Ocean in *Le chercheur d'or* and *La quarantaine* to the Middle East in *Etoile errante.*

21 See Viala, p. 293.

22 It should be noted that the childlike and poetic registers are united through this category in *Désert* and *Mondo.*

23 For instance, M. Gillier-Pichat, "Image, imaginaire, symbole: La relation mythique dans l'œuvre de J. M. G. Le Clézio (*Les géants, L'inconnu sur la terre, Désert*)," diss., University of Paris III, 1985. Viala, in reference to *La ronde,* shows that the mythical connotations of trivial facts act as "mythifiers of everyday things." This notion offers another more unorthodox manner of looking at reality.

24 See Viala, pp. 239, 283.

25 See Viala, pp. 292, 294.

Le premier homme: Camus's Unfinished Novel

When Albert Camus died in a car crash in January 1960, the manuscript of part of a novel on which he had been working was found in his briefcase. Thirty-four years later his daughter Catherine Camus, the literary executor of her father's estate after the death of her mother Francine in 1979, has edited this uncompleted novel, *Le premier homme,* and allowed it to be published.[1] It became a major publishing event of 1994 in France, with over 100,000 copies sold within the first few months following its release. There were articles, sometimes many pages in length, devoted to discussion of the text in all the major newspapers and weekly magazines

Publication of *Le premier homme* is also an event for the scholarly community. The international Société des Etudes Camusiennes organized its annual meeting in May, only six weeks after the novel was published, as a discussion, "First Impressions of *The First Man.*" Already in France there are Master's theses being written on the novel, which had previously been the subject of an unpublished thesis based on the manuscript. The interest in the general community and among scholars can be partly explained by the continuing reputation of Camus as one of the most widely read novelists of this century (*L'Etranger* is the best selling novel on Gallimard's list and has been for many years). Studies of Camus are numerous. There are also more specific reasons, both in terms of Camus's biography and in terms of politics, for the wide discussion of *Le premier homme* at this time.

Before he died, many felt that Camus's inspiration had dried up. He had not published an original creative work since *L'exil et le royaume* in 1957. After winning the Nobel Prize in Literature in 1957, he had seemed obsessed with the problems raised by the Algerian war of independence. He told Robert Gallimard, for example, that he could no longer write, but would work in the theater. His enemies on the left, and they were numerous following his famous quarrel with Sartre after the publication of *L'homme révolté* in 1952, used his lack of new work as another stick with which to attack him. Even many critics favorable to Camus wondered if he had the creative stamina to continue. Catherine Camus waited to allow publication of *Le premier homme* partly because she felt the style of this first draft might be used to confirm doubts about her father's artistic ability.

For years Camus's refusal to embrace the cause of Algerian independence was considered an act of treason by the French left. The Algerian rebellion was by far the major political event in France during the 1950s, until de Gaulle finally granted the colony independence in 1962. The attitude toward Algeria of Camus, who describes the *pied-noir* culture of his youth with considerable admiration and love in his earlier work, always aroused controversy in France. After Camus's death, for example, some even read *L'Etranger* as a "racist," anti-Arab novel. Catherine Camus waited until the political climate was less hostile toward her father. Undoubtedly as well, she was reluctant to go against the wishes of her mother, who knew that Camus himself would have been unwilling to let an unfinished work be printed. *Le premier homme,* in fact, is not even an unfinished novel, but merely a draft of some chapters, with notes for additional material to be added. Some of the autobiographical material, particularly references to Camus's love affairs, may also have influenced Francine Camus's initial decision.

There were also by the 1990s other reasons to allow publication. In the present political situation, France is trying to maintain contact with the government of Algeria, the successors of the FLN against which France fought, but now the group which France has supported in its decision to annul the elections that gave a majority to the violently anti-French Islamic fundamentalists. With this political situation in the headlines almost every day, Camus's thoughts on Algeria seem of contemporary relevance and not necessarily politically suspect.

Since Camus's death, many critics and scholars have looked for more texts. Scholarly interest in Camus has been intense. Six of the seven volumes in the Cahiers Albert Camus series are previously unpublished or uncollected writings by Camus. The unpublished early novel *La mort heureuse* was printed in the series in 1971. A collection of early, mostly unpublished stories appeared in 1973. Articles from *Combat* were collected. An early version of *Caligula* was published. Catherine

herself became involved in editing the uncollected articles from *Alger-Républicain.*

Considerable work was needed to make this early draft available. Francine Camus had typed the handwritten manuscript, which contains many additions and marginal corrections and which is written in what seems to the reader looking at the sample pages included in this edition a handwriting almost impossible to decipher. In addition to the draft manuscript of thirteen chapters, *Le premier homme* includes loose notes for insertion found in the briefcase, and Camus's plans and general notes for the novel. Catherine also added correspondence between Camus and Louis Germain, his primary-school teacher and first important mentor in Algiers and the model for a central character in the draft chapters that exist.

Le premier homme is closely autobiographical, relating the childhood of a character modeled on Camus himself, though named Jacques Cormery. It was, however, intended as a novel, in fact the first work to which Camus presumably meant to give the label "roman." (*L'Etranger* and *La Chute* are called "récits"; *La Peste* is a "chronique.") In the existing draft, characters are occasionally called by their real names—an indication of how the writer had only begun to fictionalize his material. While Camus himself would have been very reluctant to let this work be published, many today will read it as much for its biographical interest as for its confirmation of Camus's ability as a writer.

Readers of Camus will initially be surprised by the wealth of detail, the capturing of a precise place, the realism of this work, in comparison with everything Camus wrote earlier. (Some of the notes, composed in the epigrammatic style of Camus's notebooks, are closer to what readers of Camus might expect than are the draft chapters themselves.) The Algeria of *L'Etranger* and *La Peste* is a Mediterranean country, but with little description to make it specifically North African. When Camus wrote descriptively, particularly in the early *Noces,* it was with a poetic intensity not suited to his fiction, in which the narrative voice is a principal organizing element. Another stylistic difference from the earlier work is the presence of a number of extended, page-long sentences, often beautifully written, a bit Proustian.

Le premier homme is divided into two sections: "Recherche du père" and "Le fils." Neither, however, is complete. The father for whom the hero searches died, as did Camus's own father, fighting in World War I for a country he had never seen before he was drafted. Jacques's search for some understanding of his father is rendered particularly difficult by the limited ability of his mother to tell him anything. She is illiterate, speaks little, suffers silently in a life of extreme poverty, supporting her children by doing housework, while dominated at home by her equally uncultured but tyrannical mother. As one commentator has noted, however, the very fact that the father chose to marry this woman should be of interest to the son, although he never mentions this.[2]

Apart from a realistic description of the birth of the hero, in which his father is introduced as the new supervisor of a vineyard in Mondovi (Camus's actual birthplace), who arrives with his pregnant wife just prior to the birth of their second son, both sections of the novel are recounted in the third person but from the perspective of the hero. When he is forty, he visits his father's grave in France, only to realize that there is little he can learn about a man who died at the age of only twenty-nine and who, as a poor Algerian, left little trace. Some of those to whom Jacques turns are substitutes for his father: the schoolteacher based on Louis Germain, or the intellectual to whom the adult Cormery speaks and who is clearly based on the philosopher Jean Grenier, Camus's mentor from his lycée days.

In the childhood sections, which are the most complete, the sensual detail, and particularly the descriptions of the odors of poverty, are exceptionally vivid. The characters are to some extent familiar from earlier texts: the silent mother, the domineering grandmother, the deaf uncle. Interestingly, the older brother is almost never mentioned. The poverty of Cormery's childhood (and of Camus's) is more extreme than has usually been realized. While the essays in *L'Envers et L'Endroit,* Camus's first published work, give some indication of his cultural isolation at home, this becomes clear in *Le premier homme's* descriptions of Jacques's mother and grandmother attending school prize days with no understanding of the ceremony. Several French critics have commented on the vast difference between the childhood Sartre described in *Les Mots* and that of Camus. French literary discussion seems never to get beyond contrasting Sartre and Camus.

In the draft chapters relating the adult Cormery's search for his father, Camus sometimes appends marginal notes such as "make Jacques more of a monster," without indicating in what way the character is monstrous. He does comment, however, that he feels himself to be a monster. The bitter self-examination of *La Chute* has not been forgotten.

The title has already been a subject of much discussion. Is either father or son "the first man"? One explanation of the title is Catherine's: the first man is the Algerian, either European or Arab, the poor man without

a past, whose life is completely forgotten on his death: "C'est tous ceux qui passent sur la terre sans apparemment laisser de trace mais qui quand même construisent ce monde dans lequel nous vivons."[3] Like several other commentators, Catherine took pains to stress that, for Camus, both Arabs and *pieds-noirs* are of equal importance in an Algerian culture often at odds with that of the metropolis. There are indications that Camus considered both the Arabs and the *pieds-noirs* as new men, without roots in cultures of the past and sharing a life of poverty, but it is clear from this manuscript that he also considered the Arabs as fundamentally different from himself.

More often the "first man" seems to be Jacques Cormery (or Camus) himself, the son without a father to help him find his way in the world, to transmit a tradition. He describes himself as the "first inhabitant or the first conqueror" (257). A similar theme that recurs is the dual world of Jacques, defined sometimes as the split between this hard, empty, traditionless Algeria and a Europe of measured spaces filled with centuries of culture; at other times the two worlds of Jacques are those of the family without books, where he must read the titles of silent films for his illiterate grandmother, and of the school and lycée, where books are the sustenance of his imaginative life.

The chapter relating a conversation with the (unnamed) Grenier character, stylistically one of the least successful, is labeled by Camus in a marginal note: "To write and then to omit." The notation, illustrating how Camus planned to work through his autobiographical material, should make us wary of thinking that the more realistic and detailed style in *Le premier homme* was necessarily one that Camus intended to keep. In fact, some of the notes suggest what might have been a radical revision of the text: "Alternate chapters would give the voice of the mother. Comments about the same facts but with her vocabulary of 400 words" (312). This possible organization sounds to me much closer to the earlier Camus, finding the tone for his fiction through the voice of an individual character.

Some draft material on the early history of the French colonization in Algeria, based on documentation of, for example, the number of deaths from disease among the first settlers, would presumably have been related to the search for a father who could hardly be known except as an example of this settler community. Other draft material, about terrorism in the 1950s, is not integrated into the story successfully in the existing manuscript. At one point Camus's marginal note suggests he was unsure whether or not to include one long passage about a terrorist attack.

Beyond the impressive description of his poor childhood, Camus was going to evoke a whole life close to his own, including (it appears from the general notes and plans) a passionate love affair, the discontent of a life in Paris, the impossibility of accepting terrorism in support of independence when it might hurt his family, and admiration for many Arabs who are contrasted to those fighting in the revolution. But it is perhaps impossible to speak about the themes of a work which is so incomplete. As it stands, *Le premier homme* is a tribute to Camus's mother (surely one of the few illiterate parents of any Western artist in this century), an impressive evocation of a childhood in Algiers, and a tantalizing glimpse of what Camus might have revealed of his adult life through a fictional form that he did not have time to finish.

Adele King, Winter 1995

[1] Albert Camus, *Le premier homme*, Paris, Gallimard (Schoenhof, distr.), 1994, 331 pages, 110 F.

[2] Michel Cournot, "La confidence inachevée," *Le Nouvel Observateur*, no. 1536 (14–20 April 1994), pp. 48–50.

[3] This comment, from the presentation of the novel in Paris on 6 April 1994, was published in a transcription by Pierre le Baut in the *Bulletin de la Société des Etudes Camusiennes*, 33 (May 1994), pp. 15–19.

Writing Away

For many critics, J. M. G. Le Clézio's principal virtue as a writer is his ability to construct a novelistic landscape that is dramatically different from the real world of his readers, a deeply evocative, seductive "elsewhere" to which we travel on the virtual journey of his fiction.[1] Such a technique is of course one of the privileged gestures of narrative, at least since Homer; yet in Le Clézio's texts it assumes a richly personal specificity which may be read, I think, as his authorial signature. I should like to examine that effect, focusing upon what I consider to be the most exemplary of Le Clézio's recent novels, *Onitsha*.

Like many of Le Clézio's writings, *Onitsha* is a novel of apprenticeship. It tells the story of a young boy named Fintan who leaves France for Africa with his mother in order to join a father whom he has not seen for many years. The very first words of the novel inscribe the theme of the journey and announce that it will occupy the foreground of the tale: "Le *Surabaya,* un navire de cinq mille trois cents tonneaux, déjà vieux, de la Holland Africa Line, venait de quitter les eaux sales de l'estuaire de la Gironde et faisait route vers la côte ouest de l'Afrique, et Fintan regardait sa mère comme

si c'était pour la première fois" (13). Fintan's reluctance to embark upon that journey—"Je ne veux pas partir, je ne veux pas aller là-bas," he protests (16)—may be interpreted as a move in the strategy Le Clézio deploys in order to enlist his reader in the imaginary voyage of the novel. For Fintan's remark is figural of the reader's own natural hesitation to leave the familiar behind and strike out for the unknown. It serves to situate the reader in solidarity with the principal character of the novel and to suggest that, just as Fintan's journey becomes inevitable once he embarks upon the *Surabaya,* so too our journey becomes inevitable once we begin to read.

During the ocean voyage, which occupies the first of the novel's four parts, Fintan will refer to his destination as "là-bas." It is an apparently simple term, and yet the fact that it recurs in Fintan's discourse with such insistence leads one to believe that it is less innocent than it might seem.[2] It is useful to remember too that the term *là-bas* comes equipped with certain literary connotations in the modern French tradition, and a broad allusive field fashioned in the first instance by Baudelaire and Mallarmé. Baudelaire's "Invitation au voyage," much like *Onitsha,* describes an initiatory ocean journey toward a radical "other," a place that is utterly different from the world we know: "Mon enfant, ma sœur / Songe à la douceur / D'aller là-bas vivre ensemble!" And Mallarmé's "Brise marine" likewise prescribes an ocean journey into the unknown as antidote to the mortal ennui which afflicts the poet: "La chair est triste, hélas! et j'ai lu tous les livres. / Fuir! Là-bas fuir!"

Clearly, Le Clézio appeals to that tradition in the first part of *Onitsha.* Under his pen, the term *là-bas* is powerfully intertextual, an overdetermined signifier that serves to designate a place defined, for the moment, only by its alterity. Throughout his novel, Le Clézio will play on the idea of alterity, shaping it and nuancing it within the structure of the text in order to propose it as his principal theme. Gradually elaborating his novelistic vision of Africa, Le Clézio relies on a discourse of opposition: seen through European eyes, Africa is a place where everything, from social conventions to the most trivial protocols of daily life, is *different.* In refining that difference, Le Clézio exploits the notion of the exotic massively,[3] invoking it as both a natural and a cultural term. On the one hand, Africa is vast, tropical, abundant, and opulent, a perfect example of Mallarmé's "exotique nature."[4] As a landscape, it is everything that metropolitan France is not. On the other hand, its cultural conventions, as they are described in *Onitsha,* seem bizarre, "foreign," and strangely encoded to Fintan—and, by extension once again, to Le Clézio's readers.

The most powerful technique that Le Clézio uses to project his vision of the exotic upon the reader is involved with his naming practice. In the economy of fiction, as Roland Barthes has pointed out, the proper name is "the prince of signifiers."[5] Proper names, whether anthroponyms or toponyms, are always semiotically motivated in fiction, unlike in real life; they speak volumes about the people or places they designate. Le Clézio's novel is no exception to this rule, and in fact his onomastic strategy is announced in the very title of the book. For most of Le Clézio's readers, the word "Onitsha" is a floating signifier, waiting to be invested with meaning. As such, it is the first cipher in the hermeneutic code[6] of the text, for it serves to pique the reader's curiosity. Clearly, the word is a "foreign" one whose resonances, to a French ear at least, are exotic. Even if the reader happens to know that "Onitsha" is the name of an actual city in Nigeria, the evocative force of the word is undiminished, within the same connotational field. In other words, the title of the book itself serves to announce the theme of the journey toward the unknown; and it will serve throughout the novel as the principal locus of "otherness." To ensure that his reader will recognize this, Le Clézio stages the word "Onitsha" very deliberately: "C'était un nom magique. Un nom aimanté. On ne pouvait pas résister. . . . C'était un nom très beau et très mystérieux, comme une forêt, comme le méandre d'un fleuve" (46).

The word itself has an incantatory power, Le Clézio suggests; in Fintan's mind it conjures up a world of mystery and strangeness. For Fintan, it is the primary term in a catalogue of other "magical names" that he hears during his voyage.[7] The reader is encouraged to interpret it in the same way. Moreover, granted the elaborate way Le Clézio weaves the word "Onitsha" into the associative texture of the novel, we recall each time we encounter it that it is also the title of the text. That is, it serves as a sort of shifter, urging us to read doubly, not only on the level of the novel's intrigue but also on the metaliterary level, reminding us incessantly that the novel is not only the story but also the *writing* of the story. And if Le Clézio intimates so often that the word "Onitsha" casts a sort of spell upon Fintan, he obviously hopes that the novel of the same name will have an analogous effect upon its reader.

On the ship carrying him to Africa, Fintan succumbs willingly to the power of the place-name: "Il y avait ces noms, qui circulaient de table en table dans la salle à manger: Saint-Louis, Dakar. Fintan aimait entendre ce nom aussi, Langue de Barbarie, et le nom de Gorée, si doux et si terrible à la fois" (31). Indeed, the mere enunciation of those exotic names sends him into a dreamlike state, a kind of trance. Uttered one after an-

other, as in a litany or an incantation, they make Fintan dream of strange worlds: "On allait vers Takoradi, Lomé, Cotonou, on allait vers Conakry, Sherbro, Lavannah, Edina, Manna, Sinou, Accra, Bonny, Calabar. . . ." (36). In short, for Fintan at least, those names are the initiators of fiction, projecting his imagination into realms of rich—and hitherto unsuspected—narrative possibility. In similar fashion, Le Clézio intends that these names should open a narrative vista for his readers, a horizon upon which his novel will take shape.

Just as the toponyms in *Onitsha* evoke the unfamiliar, the "foreign," so too do the anthroponyms. Fintan's own name, for instance, is a very strange one. Indisputably, it is not a French name; and indeed a French reader would find it difficult to identify its origin. Perhaps it sounds Celtic. But in any case, granted its opacity in the referential code of the text, it marks the character who bears it as a strange person. And indeed, all the other major figures in the novel bear the same stamp of alterity, imprinted upon them in the first instance by their names. Fintan's mother, for example, is named Maria Luisa, for she is Italian by birth; his father is an Englishman named Geoffroy Allen, who is marked by the archaic spelling of his first name; the ship's officer who takes Fintan and his mother under his protection during the ocean voyage is a Dutchman named Heylings. When Fintan and his mother arrive in Onitsha, the reader is bombarded with a variety of native names that seem equally strange to a French ear: Marima, who keeps house for Geoffroy Allen (and after whom Fintan's sister, conceived in Onitsha, will be named); Okawho, a servant in another European household; Bony, a fisherman's son who befriends Fintan; Oya, a young woman upon whom Fintan and Bony spy as she bathes in the river. Among the European community, there is Sabine Rodes, a shadowy acquaintance of Geoffroy's. Rodes is marked by the fact that his first name is that of a woman rather than a man. Yet Le Clézio suggests that his alterity is more profound still, and Fintan's father warns him away from Rodes, insisting precisely upon the strangeness of his name, appealing to a logic that the reader understands, even if Fintan himself does not: "Il a dit, Rodes, ça n'est pas un nom très bien, ça n'est pas un nom comme le nôtre. Tu comprends? Fintan n'avait rien compris" (100).

In one way or another, then, all the principal characters in *Onitsha* are designated as "other"—if to varying degree—by virtue of the fact that their names fall outside the referential field of French language and culture. And there is another curious phenomenon at work here, for in fact there is no character who bears an ordinary, easily identifiable French name. It is as if the referential field defined by the language of the novel had no sure guarantor, no center as it were. Personal identity (which the proper name normally serves to reify, after all) is consequently unstable and problematic in *Onitsha*. This is exacerbated by the fact that the central figures of the novel are plurinymous. Heylings calls Fintan "Junge," for instance. Fintan himself refers to his mother not as "Maman" or even "Maria Luisa," but rather as "Maou." Fintan cannot bring himself to call Geoffroy Allen "Father," and his mother refers to her husband sometimes by his first name, sometimes by his family name. Bony's name is likewise unstable: "Il s'appelait de son vrai nom Josip, ou Josef, mais comme il était grand et maigre, on l'avait appelé Bony, c'est-à-dire sac d'os" (69). One suspects early on that this plurinymity is a very deliberate effect, and that it is deeply intricated in the thematics of the novel, a suspicion that is amply confirmed by the final words of *Onitsha,* where Fintan learns of Sabine Rodes's real identity, some twenty years after he first encountered him: "La lettre précisait que, de son vrai nom, il s'appelait Roderick Matthews, et qu'il était officier de l'Ordre de l'Empire Britannique" (251).

Le Clézio's use of onomastics to elaborate a discourse of alterity is part of a broader strategy through which he questions language itself. His novel constantly puts "foreign" languages into play against the backdrop of the referential language, French. When Fintan gets to Onitsha, he is fascinated by the languages he hears there. He listens with delight to the native voices, which suggest vast new linguistic possibilities to him: "Ils criaient le nom de la pluie: Ozoo! Ozoo! . . . Fintan écoutait les voix, les cris des enfants, les appels: 'Aoua! Aoua!'" (62–63). His mother shares his fascination, and in fact sets out to learn Marima's language: "Maou apprenait des mots dans sa langue. *Ulo,* la maison. *Mmiri,* de l'eau. *Umu,* les enfants. *Aja,* chien. *Odeluede,* c'est doux. *Je nuo,* boire. *Ofee,* j'aime ça. *So!* Parle! *Tekateka,* le temps passe . . . Elle écrivait les mots dans son cahier de poésies, puis elle les lisait à voix haute, et Marima éclatait de rire" (149). But there are other new languages too, such as English, the language of the colonial rulers. That is Fintan's father's native tongue, of course; curiously, however, Fintan turns toward Bony rather than Geoffroy Allen for advanced instruction in English—and in another language as well: "Il savait toutes sortes de jurons et de gros mots en anglais, il avait appris à Fintan ce que c'était que 'cunt' et d'autres choses qu'il ne connaissait pas. Il savait aussi parler par gestes. Fintan avait rapidement appris à parler le même langage" (69).

Throughout *Onitsha,* Le Clézio interrogates the notion of the "mother tongue." For the vast majority of his readers, that language is French; yet for Fintan, things are not quite as simple, because his mother's native language is Italian. Maou speaks French with an accent, with "foreign" inflections that appeal strongly to Fintan's ear: "Fintan écoutait la voix chantante de Maou. Il aimait son accent italien, une musique" (21). Often, Fintan asks Maou to speak to him in Italian: "Parle-moi dans ta langue," he says (119). And when she does, the music which Fintan hears in that language becomes literal, for Maou sings to him in Italian: "Maou se balançait dans le fauteuil de rotin, elle chantonnait des filastrocche, des ninnenanne, doucement d'abord, puis plus fort. C'était étrange, ces chansons, et la langue italienne, si douce et qui se mêlait au bruit de l'eau, comme autrefois à Saint-Martin" (155). Whereas for most of us the idea of the "mother tongue" is essential and largely unproblematic, subtending much of the way we view the world of experience, Le Clézio carefully points out how slippery that notion may be. For Fintan, his mother's tongue is *étrange*—that is, "strange" or "foreign"—and yet he takes great joy and comfort in it.

Not everyone in Onitsha shares his linguistic relativism. When Fintan's family attends a party at the home of the British Resident, for instance, Maou happens to call out to Fintan in Italian, with socially catastrophic results.

> Maou avait appelé Fintan en italien. Mme Rally était venue, elle avait dit, de sa petite voix effarouchée: "Excusez-moi, quelle sorte de langue parlez-vous?" Plus tard Geoffroy avait grondé Maou. Il avait dit, en baissant la voix, pour montrer qu'il ne criait pas, peut-être aussi parce qu'il sentait bien qu'il avait tort: "Je ne veux plus que tu parles à Fintan en italien, surtout chez le Résident." Maou avait répondu: "Pourtant tu aimais ça autrefois." C'était peut-être ce jour-là que tout avait changé. (156)

Within the narrative economy of the novel, that event is crucial, because it marks a point where Geoffroy Allen begins to distance himself from his wife and his son. Thematically, it is crucial too, for it is emblematic of the way in which, according to Le Clézio, we are *determined* by language. In the eyes of the British colonial community, Maou is marked as "other" by the fact that she speaks Italian, and the members of that community will shun her because of that. Though other reasons for excluding her are invoked (she is too "familiar" with the natives, she is unwilling to embrace the colonial ethic, she is "unconventional," and so forth), her original sin is linguistic in character: her language is not the language of power. The "ceremony of punishment," as Michel Foucault puts it (49), must be enacted upon Maou; she must be marginalized in order to preserve the disciplined society of Onitsha.

The novel which bears that name, however, takes a rather different stance on the issue of language and power. Just as Le Clézio problematizes the idea of the "mother tongue," so too does he suggest that language's capacity to establish and preserve power is not absolute. *Onitsha* presents its reader with a linguistic polyphony in which a variety of languages—and theories of language—vex one another, question one another. The French of Le Clézio's novel is deliberately unstable, constantly interrupted by other languages: Italian, English, African languages, pidgin. In the place called "Onitsha," Le Clézio asks us, what is a "native language" and what is a "foreign language"? Is autochthony a question of birth or of power? What makes for an exile? When Maou is banished from colonial society, it merely serves to confirm a marginality which marked her from the beginning of the story. Born into an Italian family, uneducated and dirt-poor, Maou was already a marginal figure, even in metro-politan France. The fact that she was an orphan was indeed one of the reasons Geoffroy Allen had been attracted to her: "Peut-être était-ce pour cela que Geoffroy l'avait choisie, parce qu'elle était seule, qu'elle n'avait pas eu, comme lui, une famille à renier" (84). Yet she is not alone in the margins of Onitsha's society, whether "native" or "colonial." Oya, the young woman whose sexuality fascinates Fintan and Bony, is an outcast among the natives: "On disait que c'était une prostituée de Lagos, qu'elle avait été en prison" (93). Sabine Rodes is feared and shunned by the other Europeans: "Il était sans aucun doute l'homme le plus détesté de la petite communauté européenne d'Onitsha" (99). More broadly still, Le Clézio describes the radical alienation of both the native community and the European community, pointing out an essential truth about colonial regimes: in such a society, nobody is truly "at home." Through the evocation of issues such as this, as in his onomastic strategy, the lesson that Le Clézio wishes to convey is that there is no *center* here, no fixed, reliable point from which the question of marginality may be adjudicated.

In that sense, *Onitsha* is a book about exile, in which that condition is taken to be universal. The principal vehicle of that discourse is Fintan himself. Like his mother, he is described from the beginning as a marginal being. He is a male, yet he grew up in a feminine universe, ruled by his grandmother and his aunts as much as by his mother. He is a young boy, and thus he sees the adult world from outside. He is French, but his mother is Italian and his father is English. In Onitsha, he is not enfranchised in European circles; yet neither is he admitted into the society of Bony and the other African boys. When he returns to Europe near the end of the novel, he is sent to an English boarding school.

There too he becomes a pariah, and it is interesting to note that his alienation is linguistic in origin. Quite simply, the English boys exclude Fintan because he doesn't speak their language.

> Quand il était arrivé au collège, Fintan parlait pidgin, par mégarde. Il disait, *He don go nawnaw, he tok say,* il disait *Di book bilong mi.* Ça faisait rire et le surveillant général avait cru qu'il le faisait exprès, pour semer le désordre. Il l'avait condamné à rester debout devant un mur pendant deux heures, les bras écartés. Il fallait oublier cela aussi, ces mots qui sautaient, qui dansaient dans la bouche. . . . Il ne pouvait pas lire dans leur regard, il ne comprenait pas ce qu'ils voulaient. Il était comme un sourd-muet qui guette, toujours sur ses gardes. (234)

Fintan's keenest insight—and the crux of this novel of apprenticeship—comes as he gradually recognizes his existential status as an "outsider" and learns to deal with it productively. It has been pointed out, by critics such as Sander Gilman, Edward Said, and Gayatri Chakravorty Spivak, for example, that the outsider, while painfully excluded from society, nonetheless occupies a position which offers certain real advantages in terms of perspective.[8] Speaking of the alienation of the intellectual in society, Said argues that point eloquently: "So while it is true to say that exile is the condition that characterizes the intellectual as someone who stands as a marginal figure outside the comforts of privilege, power, being-at-homeness (so to speak), it is also very important to stress that that condition carries with it certain rewards and, yes, even privileges" (1994, 53). Fintan's situation in *Onitsha* is a similar one: though he cannot speak the language of power to power, his very exclusion from power, coupled with his sharp recognition that his marginalization emanates from a highly dubious "center," enables him to survive. He will engage in what Ross Chambers has called "oppositional behavior"—that is, he will exploit small faults, or flaws, in the system of power, in order to disturb that system (Chambers, xi).

According to Le Clézio, one of the areas in which power's hegemony may be seen to be less than total is in its cultural practices, and most conspicuously in literature. When all else fails and his marginality threatens to submerge him, Fintan takes refuge in stories. He inherits his taste for literature from his mother. Maou is a reader, Le Clézio tells us; she turns constantly toward literature in order to palliate her solitude and her sadness. Alone with her infant son in France during the war, with Geoffroy in Africa and unable to join them, Maou reads *Gone with the Wind* (82); depressed and ill with fever in Onitsha, she reads Joyce Cary's novel *The Witch* (108). Geoffroy too is a reader, and he sees in literature a radiant image of everything his life might have been, had things turned out differently. His library in Onitsha contains various kinds of books: anthropological studies by Margaret Mead, Sigfried Nadel, and E. A. Wallis Budge; novels by Cary and Rudyard Kipling; travel narratives by Percy Amaury Talbot, C. K. Meek, and Sinclair Gordon (110). As different as they may seem, however, Geoffroy's books share a common theme: like *Onitsha* itself, they are all devoted, in one way or another, to the evocation of an exotic "other." And Geoffroy is powerfully seduced by that "other." He spends days poring over the Egyptian Book of the Dead, for example, losing himself in it, until the world it offers him comes to seem more real than the far less attractive world surrounding him in Onitsha. In a sense, then, Maou and Geoffroy are ideal readers: they enter into the textual contract wholly and unreservedly, fulfilling the role assigned to them as readers to the very letter. Clearly, Le Clézio hopes that we will approach his novel in much the same manner.

Fintan's devotion to literature is still more profound. Like many children, he is introduced to literature by his mother: as far back as he can remember, Maou had told him stories, recited nursery rhymes and poetry to him. During moments of particular stress, he continues to ask her to do that, even now that he knows how to read on his own. During the ocean journey, for instance, he asks Maou to recite some "verses" to him, and she responds with a poem in Italian, which soothes him (29); once they get to Onitsha, he continues to ask her for the same sort of consolation, and she recites Italian nursery rhymes to him (113, 208). In each case, Le Clézio produces these texts in Italian in the pages of his novel, perhaps to suggest that, for Fintan, the "mother tongue" is literature itself. For it is through his mother's voice that Fintan accedes to the world of fiction and dream. Indeed, the text itself is less important to Fintan than the voice that reads it, for the voice has a power to shape the text—any text—to its own ends. As Maou reads aloud to him from a book called *The Child's Guide to Knowledge,* for instance, Fintan perceives a strange and wonderful world *through* the simple, prosaic words of the text: "Fintan aimait rêver à toutes ces choses extraordinaires, ces merveilles, ces peuples fabuleux" (204). Once again, Fintan's experience is staged as emblematic, for Le Clézio intends that we should approach literature in the same way, and that through our reading of *Onitsha* we should be offered a vision of the marvelous "other" similar to Fintan's own.

If Le Clézio proposes reading as a means of ingress into that "other," he also intimates that writing may lead one there. In Fintan's case, just as his mother's example had guided him in his apprenticeship as a reader, so too

does her writerly activity inspire him. For Maou writes incessantly, and writing, like reading, offers her a way of coming to terms with her alienation. Her writing is not sophisticated or polished, but, on the contrary, naïve (in the mathematical sense of that word) and happily unaware of literary convention; it is process rather than product. Moreover, Le Clézio carefully describes Maou as being free of specific linguistic constraints when she writes, as if writing itself, *écriture,* were somehow beyond the various languages that she is obliged to juggle, with more or less success, in her daily life: "C'était des histoires, ou des lettres, elle ne savait pas très bien. Des mots. Elle commençait, elle ne savait pas où ça irait, en français, en italien, parfois même en anglais, ça n'avait pas d'importance" (26). Writing represents for Maou everything that her daily experience refuses her: integration, serenity, expression, and the access, through dream, to a virtual, and better, world: "Ecrire, en écoutant le froissement de l'eau sur la coque, comme si on remontait un fleuve sans fin. . . . Ecrire, c'était rêver. Là-bas, quand on arriverait à Onitsha, tout serait différent, tout serait facile" (26–27).

Her example is a determinative one for Fintan. Watching her write, he is awakened to the possibilities that writing offers a person, even one as besieged as his mother. After returning to Europe, Maou gradually ceases to write. When she moves to the South of France, leaving Fintan in boarding school in England, she gives him her old notebooks. Two decades after the events in Onitsha, Fintan looks back upon Maou's writings from that period, seeing in them a powerful, enduring legacy.

> Elle n'écrit plus l'après-midi dans ses cahiers d'écolière les longs poèmes qui ressemblent à des lettres. Quand Geoffroy et elle sont partis pour le sud de la France avec Marima, il y a plus de quinze ans, Maou a donné tous ses cahiers à Fintan, dans une grande enveloppe. Sur l'enveloppe elle avait écrit les *ninnenanne* que Fintan aimait bien, celle de la Befana et de l'Uomo nero, celle du pont de la Stura. Fintan avait lu tous les cahiers l'un après l'autre, pendant une année. Après tant de temps, il sait encore des pages par cœur. (246–47)

Maou no longer writes now; but Fintan does. Following his mother's example, Fintan had begun to write long ago, during the ocean voyage from France to Africa. Even at that initiatory moment, Fintan senses that writing may provide him with the same kind of solace that Maou finds in it. Troubled by the attentions that an Englishman named Gerald Simpson is paying to Maou on the *Surabaya,* and dreading the encounter with his father which awaits him at the end of his journey, Fintan sits down to write a story: "C'était bien, d'écrire cette histoire, enfermé dans la cabine, sans un bruit, avec la lumière de la veilleuse et la chaleur du soleil qui montait au-dessus de la coque du navire immobile" (49). His story is the tale of a young woman who goes to Africa for the first time and discovers a strange new world. Clearly, he is writing his own story, scripting it as he wishes it to unfold, using fiction—much like the marvelous new African words he hears during the voyage—as incantation. And he will continue to work on his story throughout his time in Onitsha,[9] embroidering upon his fictional world in an effort to come to terms with the experiential world he encounters there.

Fintan entitles his story "Un long voyage." The fact that this is also the title of the first part of Le Clézio's novel, during which we see Fintan begin to write, suggests in a very compelling manner the theory of literature that Onitsha proposes to its reader. For literature is essentially reciprocal, Le Clézio argues: its reciprocities are played out creatively and infinitely in any literary exchange—between writer and writer, for example, or between writer and reader. Fintan's "long voyage" is emblazoned in specular fashion within Le Clézio's "long voyage." Yet from our perspective as readers, the relations of container and contained are not quite that clear, for in fact we read the one as we read the other. Thus do stories speak to each other, Le Clézio implies, easily traversing boundaries that in real life may appear to be hermetic. The uses of literature too are distributed reciprocally among the partners in literary exchange, and they also may be turned toward a questioning of the boundaries that surround us. A character in a novel may choose to write a story in which he invokes an exotic, foreign world as a means of coming to terms with his own sense of being an "outsider." A novelist may offer an imaginary journey to his reader in order to encourage him or her to consider what alterity means and how it works in our lives. A reader may see the literary construction of the "other" for what it is and begin to consider otherness as, precisely, a construct.

That is the range of reflection which Onitsha presents most eloquently, I think. At the end of the novel we once again see Fintan writing, this time as an adult. He is composing a letter to his younger sister Marima, trying to tell her about Onitsha. It is a world that she has never seen, starkly different from her own. Yet Fintan feels that it is crucial that Marima should imagine that world—if only through his description of it, and thus tentatively. For he is deeply persuaded that, however distant and foreign it may be in Marima's eyes, Onitsha is somehow hers too. We leave him there, struggling to build another world from words, much like Le Clézio himself, writing *away*.

Warren Motte, Autumn 1997

■ **WORKS CITED**

Barthes, Roland. "Analyse textuelle d'un conte d'Edgar Poe." In *Sémiotique narrative et textuelle.* Claude Chabrol, ed. Paris. Larousse. 1973. Pp. 29–54.

———. *S/Z.* Paris. Seuil. 1970.

Chambers, Ross. *Room for Maneuver: Reading (the) Oppositional (in) Narrative.* Chicago. University of Chicago Press. 1991.

Foucault, Michel. *Discipline and Punish: The Birth of the Prison.* 1975. Alan Sheridan, tr. New York. Pantheon. 1977.

Gilman, Sander. *Inscribing the Other.* Lincoln. University of Nebraska Press. 1991.

Le Clézio, J. M. G. *Onitsha.* Paris. Gallimard. 1991.

Pobel, Didier. "'Un long voyage' dans l'immobilité du regard: Variations autour d'*Onitsha* et de quelques autres livres de J. M. G. Le Clézio." *Nouvelle Revue Française,* 464 (1991), pp. 76–80.

Said, Edward W. *Culture and Imperialism.* New York. Knopf. 1993.

———. *Representations of the Intellectual.* New York. Pantheon. 1994.

Spivak, Gayatri Chakravorty. *In Other Worlds: Essays in Cultural Politics.* New York / London. Methuen. 1987.

[1] See, for example, Didier Pobel, pp. 79–80: "La force de J. M. G. Le Clézio semble, certes, résider pour bonne part dans son aptitude à faire de nous, sans exotisme, d'indissociables compagnons d'*Un long voyage*. . . . Lire Le Clézio, c'est être protégé et étranglé à la fois, au cours d'*Un long voyage* dans l'immobilité du regard, en quoi nous ne cessons de nous réduire, en quoi nous ne cessons de nous dépasser, en quoi nous ne cessons de nous renouveler."

[2] See also pp. 17, 18, 27.

[3] Here I demur at Didier Pobel's assertion that Le Clézio's manner of enlisting his readers in a "voyage" excludes exoticism. Quite to the contrary, Le Clézio positions his text explicitly in a literary tradition which uses the "exotic" as one of its central terms. That practice distinguishes him, moreover, from many of his contemporaries (Jean Echenoz, Marie Redonnet, Jean-Philippe Toussaint, and Emmanuéle Bernheim come to mind) whose writings evoke ordinary, quotidian, "endotic" worlds.

[4] See "Brise marine": "Steamer balançant ta mâture, / Lève l'ancre pour une exotique nature."

[5] See Barthes, "Analyse," p. 34: "Un nom propre doit être toujours interrogé soigneusement, car le nom propre est, si l'on peut dire, le prince des signifiants; ses connotations sont riches, sociales et symboliques."

[6] In *S/Z* Barthes defines that term in the following manner: "L'inventaire du code herméneutique consistera à distinguer les différents termes (formels), au gré desquels une énigme se centre, se pose, se formule, puis se retarde et enfin se dévoile" (26).

[7] See, for example, p. 20: "Un chapelet d'îles noires était accroché à l'horizon. 'Regarde: Madeira, Funchal.' C'était des noms magiques"; and p. 24: "Il avait dit des noms magiques: 'Tenerife, Gran Canaria, Lanzarote.'"

[8] See Gilman, p. 17: "I am not neutral, I am not distanced, for being an outsider does not mean to be cool and clinical; it must mean to burn with those fires which define you as the outsid-

er"; Said, *Culture and Imperialism,* p. xxvii: "Yet when I say 'exile' I do not mean something sad or deprived. On the contrary belonging, as it were, to both sides of the imperial divide enables you to understand them more easily"; and Spivak's response to the assertion that her critical attitudes reflect the fact that she is an "outsider": "I have thought about that question. Even after nineteen years in this country, fifteen of them spent in full-time teaching, I believe the answer is yes. But then, where is the inside? To define an inside is a decision, I believe I said that night, and the critical method I am describing would question the ethico-political strategic exclusions that would define a certain set of characteristics as an 'inside' at a certain time. 'The text itself,' 'the poem as such,' 'intrinsic criticism,' are such strategic definitions. I have spoken in support of such a way of reading that would continue to break down these distinctions, never once and for all, and *actively* interpret 'inside' and 'outside' as texts for involvement as well as change" (102).

[9] See, for instance, pp. 56, 95, 106.

Marguerite Yourcenar (*Lütfi Özkök*)

Marguerite Yourcenar: Independent, Imaginative, and "Immortal"

Elections to the time-honored French Academy normally turn out to be mundane Parisian events, derided by the young and by most intellectocrats; they stir up scant interest in the country at large and even less outside France. The superannuated army generals, archbishops and retired university professors who, with an occasional sprinkling of dukes and of once authentic writers, make up the body of the would-be Immortals, are seldom eager to cast their vote for any author under seventy who might disturb their slumbering peace of mind. A few who had once held out promises of revitalizing the conservative ideology—Jacques de Lacretelle, Pierre Gaxotte, Thierry Maulnier—appear, once ensconced in one of the forty armchairs, to have taken refuge in the "prudent silence" once mockingly praised by Boileau as the chief claim to fame of Conrart, the originator of Richelieu's original Academy. Gide, Malraux and Sartre all spurned the body which had once closed its doors on Balzac, Baudelaire and Zola. Camus might have agreed to accept election, had he lived; after his 1957 award from the Swedish Academy he was sarcastically accused by some of his former friends of currying bourgeois approval and of adopting the sumptuous manner of Chateaubriand.

It had been taken for granted that women writers were never to be included in a traditional body as jealously male as the conclave of Cardinals, the House of Lords and the German General Staff—the groups once singled out by Academician Paul Bourget as the three other pillars of Western civilization. Anna de Noailles, Colette and one or two other women of letters had, as a compensation, been invited to join the Belgian Academy, as had, in 1971, a French woman born in Belgium in 1903 and naturalized as an American citizen in 1947, Marguerite Yourcenar. Almost exactly ten years later, on 22 January 1981, at the age of wisdom of threescore years and seven, Mme Yourcenar was officially received "under the cupola." She had, by a special decree, been restored to French citizenship; she was spared the ordeal of paying visits of candidacy to the established Academicians; she had kept out of the Paris salons which boast of acting as the antechambers to the Academy. She praised with earnest conviction her predecessor Roger Caillois and, in her turn, was intelligently eulogized by another scion of the École Normale (the nursery of one-fourth of the members), Jean D'Ormesson. He is the one who had engineered and, despite the reluctance of other members of the academic profession hesitant to break with a hallowed tradition, secured her election. The gates seemed now ominously open to other septuagenarian female writers such as Nathalie Sarraute and Simone de Beauvoir, perhaps even one day to a matured Françoise Sagan (b. 1935), once the favorite of the insolent generation!

That revolutionary election could not well be hailed as a victory for feminism. Yourcenar has evinced not a shred of interest in the claims of "the second sex." None of her successful novels and few of her early récits or plays grant much attention to female characters. Hadrian's wife and his occasional mistresses pale beside the emperor's passion for Antinous. Zeno's encounters with women are merely episodic, in contrast to his moving friendship with the Prior, with alchemists and with the very ecclesiastics who sentence him to die. Yourcenar's grandfather and father monopolize her interest, and that of the reader, in her autobiographical volumes; she hardly knew her own mother. Her most touching heroines—the neglected wife of Alexis, and Sophie, hopelessly and vainly in love with another homosexual male—are as forlorn and as dolorously resigned as the female characters in Gide. Electra herself, in the undramatic play named after her, Phaedra and Ariadne in another "mystery" play, even the less meekly obedient Alcestis—these hardly stand as memorable portrayals of femininity. There occur a few touching pages on the American woman poet Hortense Flexner introducing the expert translation of her poetry by Yourcenar. One may regret that the author has not as yet left a sketch of Grace Frick, her companion of many years on her Maine island and her gifted translator.

Nor has Yourcenar ever condescended to yield to the trends which have swept many French and some non-French critics and journalists in the last half-century. There are few words that she despises more than the adjective nouveau, indifferently qualifying cuisine, hairstyles, the novel, criticism or sexual mores. The literary fashions of the thirties and forties (surrealism, the cults of Faulkner and Dos Passos, existentialism, tropisms, the virtuoso acrobatics of Robbe-Grillet, the pronouncements of Lacan and of Barthes, structuralist and deconstructionist experiments) are placidly ignored by her. She has been lured to Greece and to Asia rather than to Paris and New York. Her formidable culture must have struck her contemporaries with awe: classical and medieval Latin had no secrets for her, nor had the language of theology and of medieval alchemy. As a very young woman she published a translation of the most abstruse of Greek poets, Pindar. Later she devoted several years to an expert rendering into French of ancient Greek lyricists, from Tyrtaeus and Sappho to Proclus, covering some twelve centuries. Her notes on those poems and fragments in La couronne et la lyre (1979) display her grammarian's competence and her skill as a metrist. She has translated novels by Henry James and Virginia Woolf, texts from Far Eastern languages and from one of her favorite moderns, the Alexandrian Greek poet Cavafy, who also fascinated E. M.

Forster, W. H. Auden and Lawrence Durrell. In a learned but warm critical presentation of that master of conciseness whose obsessive theme is discreet pederastic love, she defined his originality in felicitous terms.

Marguerite Yourcenar had, in her younger days, been a poet in her own right. Her poems in prose, Feux (written in 1935, translated in 1981 as Fires), are more burningly passionate than anything in Sappho or Louise Labbé. They stemmed from an excruciating love crisis experienced by the author in her early thirties. The remarks added to the prose pieces by the fervent and more than once forsaken woman lover are unashamedly personal. The lyricism of those texts is all the more ardent for being indirect. The monologues in Feux, somewhat reminiscent of Ovid's Heroides, that gallery of loving and suffering mythological heroines deserted by their lovers, transpose the author's complaints into dramatic tirades by Achilles, Patroclus, Phaedra, Sappho and others—even Mary Magdalene. Such blind, unrestrained love is presented by the author as "a form of transcendence."

In contrast, Yourcenar's other early récits and plays are conspicuous for their restraint and their fastidious, grave, at times even stilted manner. She has revealed that her strangely aloof heroes, elaborately and obstinately rejecting the women who implore their love, were modeled after life. But there is little that is concrete or anecdotal in their narratives. The references to their homosexual leanings are solemnly guarded, as if their sexual preferences were a distinction conferring a sacerdotal gravity. The author has more than once confessed her distaste for Gide's writings and treated his Thésée (rightly, in my opinion) as an effete and ponderously ironical tale. Yet the very title of her 1929 récit, Alexis ou Le traité du vain combat (reprinted in 1952), unmistakably recalls Gide's early "treatise," La tentative amoureuse ou Le traité du vain désir. Alexis, the character who is supposed to have written that solemn farewell letter to his wife as an avowal of his guilt and of the "singularity" which prevents him from loving her, is the Vergilian figure of the second Bucolic to whom Corydon, another shepherd, vainly proffers his love. The complacent and cruel explications poured out to Alexis's wife in that "treatise" are reminiscent of Michel's behavior toward Marceline in L'immoraliste. This modern Alexis, raised by women, stricken with respect and awe for the female sex, has married Monique. He hesitates for a long time before finally condescending to "la consommation du mariage." Still, Monique has a child by him. Then, again like Gide's Michel, Alexis undergoes the revelation of love through an adventure which "[teaches] him that we have a body." Divided against himself, moved to compassion for his spouse, the pious, Protestant, resigned and suffering companion whom he uniformly addresses as "mon amie," he justifies himself for abandoning her with a 160-page epistle of feigned humility and hypocritical self-condemnation couched in noble classical language. The author hints in a foreword that the "adventure" of Monique and Alexis occurs more frequently than some of us like to imagine. The abstract remoteness of the tone, however, fails to grip the plain reader.

Le coup de grâce, composed in 1938–39 during a stay in Sorrento, is likewise the confession of a man forced by his nature to spurn a woman's love. The narrative vividly conjures up the scenery of the Baltic Kurland in 1919 and the misty atmosphere of confused fighting between German soldiers of fortune and the Red army. The hero, Erick von Lhomond, is a highly cultured German of French ancestry, passionately devoted to a male friend and fighting companion, Conrad. Conrad's sister Sophie falls in love with him. "Why is it," he ponders, not without naïveté, "that women fall in love with the very men who are destined otherwise and who accordingly must repulse them, or else deny their own nature?" Sophie offers herself to him, pathetically and in vain. Rejected and vexed, she goes over to the enemy and is eventually taken prisoner by Erick's soldiers. Prisoners were not spared in that ferocious war. Her fate is sealed. She insists that Erick himself be her executioner. He fires a shot at her, tears her face open, shoots a second time: that is "le coup de grâce." Sophie's revenge is to leave him beset with remorse. In a final and rather awkward sentence, the narrator Erick (a polished and cultured officer who quotes Retz, alludes to Rembrandt's picture in the Frick collection and to an engraving by Dürer) casually concludes: "I do feel remorse at times. One is always trapped, some-how, in dealings with women."

There is a certain haughty rigidity and some coldness in those brief novels, with only one introspective character, no conflict and practically no dialogue. The esthetic distance contrived by the author keeps the characters, and the women especially, at discreet remove. In two plays composed on Greek themes, however, the author boldly invited comparison with the ancient Greek dramatists and with Cocteau (who, among the moderns, appealed to her more than did the playful Giraudoux) by driving her heroines to the forefront. Neither of the plays was written for the stage, although both may well have been performed by amateurs and students. In *Electre ou La chute des masques* (1954) Electra is courted by Pylades, who plays the shady part of a double agent. She does murder Clytemnestra, who is treated with greater sympathy than her daughter, and she and her brother learn at the critical moment that

Orestes was actually Aegisthus' illegitimate son. That strange, rather tender and loving father, in the presence of Clytemnestra's gory corpse, is duly murdered by his son and nobly forgives him. The effect of surprise at the denouement, as all masks are lifted, smacks of artifice. A long, dissertational preface discussing the various impersonations of Orestes on the Greek stage, in Racine, in O'Neill and even as a half-brother of Hamlet is replete with subtle suggestions and sounds less far-fetched and strained than the paradoxical play itself.

Euripides' Alcestis has more convincing reality in the second work, *Le mystère d'Alceste* (1963), a one-act play. The wife who agreed to die so that her selfish husband might be spared sacrifices herself without any illusions. Her repartees are blunt and crude. She denounces Admetus' placid egoism as would any untamed shrew. Her rescuer Hercules does not balk at vulgar talk any more than he did in Euripides. In another entertaining comedy, published along with *Alcestis,* Theseus is freely ridiculed as a crude male seducer, whom Phaedra and Ariadne both mock. Bluntly, the author upbraids Gide, who in 1946, fresh from the tragedy of World War II, had turned his *Thésée* into the lifeless protagonist of a pseudo-Voltairean conte, devoid of poetry and truth. She wonders, as many of us must have done, what might have become of Alcestis in the play that Racine, before retiring from the stage, had intended to compose on the Euripidean theme. Classically restrained and haughtily impersonal as she likes to appear, Marguerite Yourcenar seems not to have felt many affinities with the French classical age. Her regret that Racine's Orestes, turned into a mere lover and the murderer of Pyrrhus, apparently not once remembered his assassinated parents in Argos is one that not a few devotees of *Andromaque* have shared.

Early in her career Yourcenar was lured away from shorter narratives and sophisticated variations on ancient myths and tried fiction. Her one attempt at a contemporary subject, written in 1934 and expanded and transformed in a later version in 1971, is entitled *Le denier du rêve.* The setting is Rome during the Fascist era. The author, who knows Italy thoroughly and never was partial to Fascism, re-creates the atmosphere of conspiracy, police spying and liberal and anarchist plots that characterized the years preceding the Abyssinian War. The novel is episodic, with seven or eight characters briefly sketched but none of them vivid or deep enough to hold the reader's interest for long. An English girl involved in banal love affairs, a French painter threatened with angina pectoris and trying to relive in Rome the artistic successes of his youth, a Triestine Slav who dies in deportation, a jilted husband and a doctor who observes, talks abundantly and dispenses advice are among the characters who appear fleetingly. The one who is endowed with some consistency and almost rises to tragic stature is Marcella, a single-minded woman who attempts to shoot Mussolini but misses him and is killed. The symbol which provides the title of the novel is a ten-lire coin which is lost, recovered, passes from one of the actors to another and is thrown away again. It is a frail and artificial symbol. The author ambitiously aimed at juxtaposing myth and actual life; but she strained her inventiveness in scattering the reader's attention on too many diverse and pallid figures, most of them merely commenting, in banalities worthy of the choruses of Greek tragedies, on life, on human foolishness and on politics and its woes. The fusion of dream and reality promised by the title is not felicitously achieved.

■ ■ ■

Much later, some ten years after her most successful book, *The Memoirs of Hadrian* (by then a best seller), Yourcenar, relinquishing antiquity and the Mediterranean world, published an even more vast, learned, episodic and unwieldy novel, *L'œuvre au noir* (1968), a colorful and baroque work laid in northern Europe in the sixteenth century. The novel was hailed by some as an ambitious historical and philosophical fresco. It plays with a great many, perhaps too many, ideas; it grips our emotions only passingly. The title is drawn from the *opus nigrum* of the alchemists; Zeno, and presumably his creator, evince some sympathetic curiosity for that art, or science. The title phrase also suggests a symbolic meaning: that a preliminary stage of breaking up our accepted ideas and of shattering our illusions must precede the next phase, "l'œuvre au blanc," and the work of purification.

The multiple intentions injected into the meandering narrative are too numerous. The scene shifts from Flanders to Germany and to Turkey. Women play a restricted part in the picaresque wanderings of the males, whom the author has characterized as bisexual, like Hadrian, rather than homosexual. Zeno (the name of one of the author's ancestors) is baffling in the incredible diversity of his gifts and interests: medicine, magic, hermetic doctrines, metaphysical speculations, saintliness. Above all, he is determined "to be more than a man." His creator has generously lent him features of Erasmus, Paracelsus, Campanella, and of persecuted thinkers like Dolet, Servet, Giordano Bruno. Through many wanderings and changes of profession (as well as of name), after consorting with Indians and Turks, dabbling in Buddhism and encountering a model of holiness in the most touching character in the book, the Prior, Zeno is charged with being an atheist. He could easily justify himself and retract his more imprudent statements, for he has only anticipated Diderot's famous call, "Elargissez Dieu." But he will not condescend to that, convinced as he is of the universal absurdity. Like Petronius, whom a warrior in the novel surprisingly quotes as "one of my intercessors and saints," he opens his veins and forestalls an absurd execution through a voluntary death.

The multiplicity of episodes and of intentions in this vast historical novel, the conflicting directions toward which the author appears to guide us, her enormous knowledge of sixteenth-century thought, religion and science are bewildering even to the serious reader. Such chaotic profusion comes perilously close to confusion. Only here and there does Yourcenar succeed in imparting life and mystery to her creations, even to Zeno, whom she obviously cherishes. Ultimately the critic's verdict must probably be that *L'œuvre au noir* is a failure, but one of those honorable failures which greater creators like Balzac, Dostoevsky and Thomas Mann have more than once experienced.

The form adopted in *The Memoirs of Hadrian,* recalling the less ambitious attempts of her early récits told in the first-person singular, suits her talent better. The artistic unity of the work is more easily preserved through imaginary memoirs in which a single character longingly retraces his struggles and achievements, relives his hours of passion and records his half-resigned wrestlings with age, disease and death. The individual is no more a common man hampered at every stage by sordid practical difficulties than were the tragic heroes of Shakespeare or Racine. A Romanized and, later, Hellenized Spaniard, Hadrian succeeded Trajan as emperor and, more expertly than his predecessor and sponsor, administered the vast Roman territories and led the legions to Britain, Gaul, Germany, along the Danube, to the Black Sea and down the Euphrates. The novelist had pondered long over the histories of the age, distrusting Suetonius and Tacitus, whose concerns and prejudices centered on Rome alone and voiced the bitter hatred of the humiliated aristocracy. Her erudition is faultless; her knowledge of the iconography of Antinous is incomparable. She is never weighted down by her knowledge, as Flaubert had been when he depicted Carthage, St. Anthony and Herod. Her imagination is vivified by the documents she interprets. Since we have, in the case of Hadrian, none of the autobiographical documents which Caesar, Ovid, Marcus Aurelius and even Julian left behind them, ample room is left for the author's recreation of history. The local color of Greece, Asia Minor, the Nile Valley and the Egyptian oases is never obtrusively lavish. The emperor's inner life remains the focus of interest throughout.

Yourcenar admires Hadrian as a statesman, as a superb administrator, a man of action and also a wily and often ruthless politician surrounded by envious rivals. He is nowhere idealized. He can be cruel and unforgiving, brutally scornful of his mistresses, of his wife and of womankind in general. He seeks wisdom but even more avidly seeks beauty. He is detained by no moral scruples. "Every pleasure enjoyed with art seemed to me chaste," he declares. His wisdom is not that of a rationalist obsessed only with efficiency and order. There are scenes of savage hunting for wild beasts, of reckless killing of war captives, of initiation into strange barbaric rites. Like all Yourcenar's characters, Hadrian leaves room for mystery and for some mysticism in his quest for a higher wisdom. Passion rules him in his very pursuit of efficiency, a passion that involves the whole being. "What is the act of love," reasons the emperor and, through him, his biographer, "if not a moment of passionate attention on the part of the body?"

The scenes on which the author poured her most loving care and which rise to a pathetic pitch are those in which the emperor is carried away by his attachment to the Asian shepherd Antinous. He first met the boy at a poetry reading of the most subtle and obscure minor Greek poet Lycophron. He likes to fancy that the youth's family hailed from pastoral Arcadia and that the mysterious ephebe from Bithynia might have something of Hellenic beauty about him. Antinous remains a pale and silent figure thoughout the book, hardly responding at all to the adoration of the older man. He might have realized that he was being transfigured into an objet d'art or, prematurely, into a god. Bewildered, aware perhaps that his youth and beauty could not endure, that he was incurring the hatred of the emperor's entourage and wife, one morning he sought his own death by drowning in the mud of the Nile. The emperor's grief, restrainedly depicted, matches in pathos the most sorrowful scenes in modern literature of revolt against death's dominion. Hadrian wants to believe that the suicide was a sacrifice through which the young lover immolated himself to the emperor's passion. He then madly undertakes to immortalize the dead youth through statues and coins spread all over the Mediterranean world.

In two volumes of conversations with Patrick de Rosbo (1972) and with Matthieu Galey (1980) Yourcenar earnestly insisted that Hadrian was not a mouthpiece for his creator and that the Keatsian "top of sovereignty" to which passion exalted him was in no way a transposed or transvested personal experience. True indeed, and many of us have, like her, blamed Proust's transposition of the sexes in the depiction of Albertine. But Yourcenar identified with the Roman emperor in his villa, his wanderings, his inner solitude, so long and so fully that the creator became one with her creation. The novel is far too discreet and reserved, its writing too faultlessly controlled, for anyone to read it as a confession in disguise, much less as a didactic plea. Yet the lineaments of a vindication of the flesh, in its vibrant and refined sensuousness, appear through the controlled objectivity of the style. Hadrian was hardly aware of the existence of the Christians, whom his predecessor Trajan had persecuted. But Yourcenar clearly evinces scant patience with all asceticism, whether it be religious or, as in Sartre's nauseous revulsion against the flesh, atheistic. She, who has not once set a story in America, where she has resided for half a century, who feels no sympathy with the modern age, chose to live in imagination in the centuries which have attracted other modern writers: those who re-imagined the longings of Ovid among the Scythians, the thoughts of dying Vergil, the enigmatic surliness of Tiberius, the madness of Caligula and the woes of *I, Claudius.* She stated, in her revealing notes to *Hadrian,* how lastingly haunted she had been by a sentence she had read in 1927 in one of Flaubert's letters: "Just when the gods had ceased to be, and Christ had not yet come, there was a unique moment in history, between Cicero and Marcus Aurelius, when man stood alone." Marcus Aurelius, adopted by Hadrian, is the one for whom Hadrian writes these imaginary memoirs. For a few discerning moderns, among them the author herself, the ethics of paganism in its nobler representatives, from the Stoics to Celsus, stand among the noblest ever proposed and lived. Unfortunately, they held too little appeal for the masses.

There is far more revelation on the part of the author in that masterpiece of imaginative erudition and of vindication of intelligent sensuousness than may be found in Yourcenar's recent autobiographical volumes, ambitiously entitled *Le labyrinthe du monde.* Yet, especially in the second volume of her reminiscences, *Archives du Nord* (1977), after having ransacked old papers and private letters written by her grandfather and her father, the septuagenarian writer relives with gusto and humor the picaresque adventures of her male ancestors. She hardly knew her mother, who died young, and she is not partial to the other female individuals with whom her father, twice a deserter from the French army and a notorious womanizer, associated. There are thoughtful digressions here and there on Italian art and on baroque painting, in which (particularly in Rubens) she sees a glorification of the will to power and a devouring hunger for matter. In contrast to the restrained and punctiliously classical style of her early récits, her tone is playful and wistful; she seems to have reached an ironical detachment. Writing on her solitary and

Michel Butor (© *Barbara Klemm, FAZ*)

semi-primitive island off the Maine coast, her friend and expert translator Grace Frick dead, she delights in reimagining the adventures of the not very staid and conformist *grand bourgeois* of Flanders from whom she may have inherited her umbrageous intellectual independence. Academic honors and popularity have not altered her proud aloofness from passing vogues. More securely than nineteen out of twenty acclaimed French writers of the second half of this century, she may rest assured of survival in human memories.

Henri Peyre, Spring 1983

Michel Butor: Past, Present, and Future

During a major symposium on "The Languages of Criticism and the Sciences of Man," which was held at Johns Hopkins University back in 1966, Roland Barthes, responding to Paul de Man, who had challenged his use of the word *romanticism*, said that as far as he was concerned the term stood for everything that had ever been said about romanticism.[1] In like fashion I should like to emphasize that the first two words of my own title here today stand for everything that has been or might be published concerning works that bear the signature of Michel Butor.

Hence, what I have in mind to discuss is the past, present and future of the criticism, analysis and commentary that have taken such works as their object. The present is of course occurring today and tomorrow at the symposium that brings us together under the aegis of the University of Oklahoma and its president, William S. Banowsky, and the dynamic guidance of Ivar Ivask and his review, *World Literature Today*. The seven scholars we are to hear have each chosen a significant topic and in at least one instance a tantalizing title. The program bodes an auspicious present indeed.

As to the past, I have no intention of offering a survey of the numerous studies that have been written on Michel Butor's texts, together with a presumptuous verdict. Rather, I shall examine what I consider to be a fundamental problem. Before I do that, however, I must point to a weakness of the past, in English-speaking countries at least. The weakness I have in mind is due to a dearth of translations. It is a deplorable situation. As far as I know, the most recent book by Michel Butor to have been translated in this country is *6 810 000 litres d'eau par seconde,* which came out as *Niagara* in 1969.* Surely the Germans and the Japanese have done better than that! Since 1965, the date of the French volume, he has published more than twenty books in regular trade editions, to which one must append quite a few items in limited editions, works done with painters or other artists. I must add that he is not the only French writer to have become the victim of the economics of publishing in the United States. The names of first-rate writers come to mind, writers who have been condemned to remain little known or even unknown to an English-speaking audience, writers like Maurice Blanchot, Philippe Sollers or Maurice Roche. And there are others. Small publishers like Red Dust in New York are attempting to do something about this, but they are faced with distribution and reviewing difficulties. Perhaps university presses, with the assistance of foundations, could become more involved in this area.

Now to proceed to an even more serious problem. It is one of which a number of critics have been aware, but on the whole we have been slow in allowing that awareness to register, slow in translating awareness into practice. It involves the separations that have been established within literature on the one hand, between literature and the arts on the other. With respect to the writer we are honoring at this eighth Puterbaugh Conference, the issue was not seriously raised while his reputation was primarily that of a novelist; significantly enough, Michel Butor was known as a novelist long after he stopped writing novels. We should keep in mind that although he has been publishing for more than thirty-six years, the time span during which his four novels appeared is roughly half a dozen years in length. Since then we have had many of what François Aubral, tongue in cheek, with a touch of sarcasm directed at fellow critics, called "those bizarre texts."[2]

As to the novels, it is true that a sensitive writer like Georges Perros had noted that they verged on poetry; but the same thing had been said many years earlier by Valery Larbaud about his own work and by critics about such novelists as François Mauriac.[3] In this country we find Edmund Wilson referring to the "magnificent poetry" of James Joyce's *Ulysses* and calling Flaubert a "great prose poet."[4] It was becoming a commonplace to detect "poetry" in quality writing. And a number of different things, doubtless, were subsumed under the rubric.

In spite of that, and because it was close to being accepted, there was no real problem for critics until the sixties: what Michel Butor published could be classified readily. Whether or not the classifications were accurate is beside the point; the fact is that *Passage de Milan* was received as a novel, *Le génie du lieu* as a book of essays, *Répertoire* as a collection of articles in literary criticism, *Jacques Hérold* as art criticism, and the verse published in several periodicals as poetry. Everything was pigeonholed, properly or not, and persons who disliked this or that item were pleased to condemn it on the basis of laws of the genre to which it had been assigned.

Everything changed, however, after 1962. That was the year of the publication of *Cycle, Rencontre, Mobile, Réseau aérien* and *Votre Faust.* Did we, as critics, examine those works with a view to understanding them, identifying the rhetoric involved, realizing what was going on? Of course not. With a few exceptions, Roland Barthes among them, critics, being creatures of habit, stuck to their conventional, predictable categories.[5] Michel Butor was a novelist who had gone astray, who was guilty of bizarre performances. Since the books did not fit into established categories, they were generally condemned or ignored. *Mobile and Réseau aérien* violated the laws of genre, and *Mobile* was particularly offensive on account of its typography; it displayed something that, even though Mallarmé had introduced it sixty-five years earlier in *Un coup de dés,* critics (as opposed to scholars) were still unable to deal with.

Theoretically, the three other titles I listed should have alerted us to the other facet of the problem: the institutional separation that exists between literature and the other arts. Actually, they did not, and little notice was accorded to them. Perhaps there are good reasons for this: *Mobile and Réseau aérien* were published by a major publishing house and the usual review copies distributed; *Cycle* and *Rencontre,* however, were limited editions, and *Votre Faust* was something like the libretto of an opera yet to be performed. Art critics can visit museums, galleries, artists' studios and occasionally the homes of art collectors. One can also visit the rare-book rooms of libraries, but not quite as easily as a museum; contemporary limited editions also do not find their way into rare-book rooms as easily as one might wish; furthermore, while scholars are used to studying rare books of the past in specialized libraries, critics of contemporary literature are simply not accustomed to it. If, on the other hand, someone really wanted to examine a publication like *Rencontre,* that person could probably locate a copy of the work and do so. It may thus be that the difficulties I have just mentioned are not reasons but merely excuses. Clearly, the root of the problem lies deeper.

A little over eight years ago a seven-day colloquium on the work of Michel Butor was held in France, at Cerisy-la-Salle, and one session was devoted to the relationship of that work with music. During the discussion one of the participants exclaimed, "I am thunderstruck by the way in which the audience has been split. People are absent, people are leaving the room for the first time since the beginning of the colloquium. Music has effected a split."[6] Now I am sure all of you remember the famous, controversial saying by Walter Pater, "All art aspires to the condition of music." More recently, and on a different level of analysis, Julia Kristeva has suggested that, while scientific presentations or demonstrations manifest an almost exclusive working of what she has defined as the symbolic modality and music operates mainly within the semiotic modality, art constitutes the "semiotization of the symbolic."[7]

We apparently have on our hands a contradiction between theory and common practice, and perhaps also some misunderstanding. If, according to both a nineteenth-century esthete and a twentieth-century analyst, art, hence literature, is drawn in the direction of music, why were so many, at Cerisy, turned off by the discussion? I have also overheard musicians complain, at a concert of contemporary music, that literary people, while they pretend to like music, really do not understand it. If that is true, could it be that literary people do not understand what they are doing? Where a number of critics are concerned, I am inclined to answer, "No, they do not." Mind you, I am not saying that we all must have a thorough grounding in the theories of musical composition; I do posit, on the other hand, that if we had a better understanding of the literary process, we would have easier access to music and a better understanding of the relationship between literature and music. Nor am I talking about the better critics, say, Roland Barthes again—who, as it happens, was also knowledgeable in music—and a few others; unfortunately they are not, and this almost by definition, representative critics, nor is their work emblematic of the critical reaction to texts by Michel Butor.

One well-known critic has had at least the honesty to recognize that he lacked the necessary competence to pursue the matter of the writer's relationship with music beyond quoting what Michel Butor had himself told an interviewer or written in an essay. The irony is that this critic is probably better equipped than others to understand what he said he was not professionally competent to discuss. His quotations were intelligent, his article sympathetic. Those who are truly incompetent do not confess their failings.

While there have been attempts to deal with interdisciplinary matters on the part of a few critics and scholars (and some are participating in this symposium), such attempts have been relatively few. What many literary critics and amateurs, professional reviewers and readers as well, are still unwilling to come to terms with, after all these years, is the following. (Let me say in passing that I do not mean to disparage such persons, for they are the unwary victims of prejudices that have come down to us from earlier times.) What they do not fully grasp is yet a very simple thing: that there is a fundamental difference between, at one extreme, the skillful spinning of a yarn, as the phrase goes, and at the other, working in and with language to produce a literary text, performing an act of scription. They understand that there is a difference, but they do not comprehend the nature of that difference. What they also do not fully grasp is the difference between the pleasures given to readers by those two kinds of art: a satiating pleasure, as André Malraux might have put it, for the former; an exhilarating, illuminating, appetizing pleasure in the latter. In more contemporary terms, I would contrast the pleasure caused by the same to the pleasure caused by the other. (I emphasize pleasure with malice aforethought, for it is a quality that tends to be forgotten in some of the literature departments in a number of our graduate schools.)

Allow me now to shift the perspective: what those people do not fully grasp is the difference, say, between drawings of the cathedral of Rouen, in which the object of our pleasure is the cathedral's beauty and in secondary fashion the skill of the draftsman, and Claude Monet's paintings of the same cathedral, paintings that Michel Butor discusses in one of his essays, where the object of our pleasure is the painting and the cathedral is no more than a pretext.[8] They obviously understand and see that there is a difference, but in both instances they focus on the cathedral. If they did fully comprehend that difference, they would realize that contemporary writers, and some earlier ones too, use words the way painters use paint (as William Carlos Williams pointed out when he brought together the names of Gertrude Stein and Georges Braque),[9] and that some writers arrange those words in accordance with principles they have learned from musical composition. If they did comprehend, they would realize that words have material qualities that are related to their meaning in very complex fashion, now in harmony with it, now independent of it, now in contradiction to it; at times they enhance semantic fields, at times they restrain them; on occasion they open up unsuspected connotations and are related to unconscious drives. To quote William Carlos Williams, "But can you not see, can you not taste, can you not smell, can you not hear, can you not touch—words?"[10] Such sensuous attributes may not necessarily be present in the words we read in our daily newspapers, but they are so in the words that have been fashioned into a work of art by a poet—and here, as Edmund Wilson did for Flaubert and Joyce, I would expand the connotations of that word to include what is covered by the German word *Dichter*: in contemporary terminology, one who performs a work of scription. "We find scription wherever words have savor," Roland Barthes said in his inaugural lecture at the Collège de France in January 1977, adding, "It is the flavor of words that constitutes deep, fruitful knowledge." He pointed out that *savor* and *sapience* (i.e., knowledge or wisdom) have the same etymology.

A considerable amount of knowledge has been added, since the latter part of the nineteenth century, to our understanding of language, the psyche and, generally speaking, those disciplines included in what, in France especially, are called the sciences of man. Again, we have not always assimilated what we have learned, nor has the knowledge been adequately disseminated. And on occasion, when it has been widely disseminated, the rage of fashion has taken hold of it and made a mess of things. If literary critics were better to acquaint themselves with those ancillary disciplines that are relevant to our accounting for the work of a poet (the performer of scription), an artist, a musician, they surely would be better equipped to elucidate works that transcend arbitrary categories.

Now it stands to reason that there are differences in working with words, composing music, painting on a canvas and chipping away at a block of stone. The differences pertain to the nature of the materials with which poets, musicians, painters and sculptors work; they also are related to the notions of time and space and how these get involved in the work. Ironically, however, the ideological walls dividing those various arts among one another, the same "fundamental walls" Michel Butor had complained about at the outset of his essay *Les mots dans la peinture*, have been strengthened by the failure to pay greater attention to the very materials being used—ink, typography, paper, the surface of the page, the shape of the book, for instance, where scription is involved. Our minds have been literally imprisoned within such walls, the more so as these have been taken for granted and implanted in our consciousness during our earliest years and ultimately maintained there by the separate and sometimes antagonistic university departments, which strive to maintain a jealous hold over their grand duchies.

I tend to agree with Umberto Eco that "the crisis undergone by our middle-class civilization is due in part to the inability of average persons to extricate themselves from a system of acquired forms that have come to them from without rather than having been conquered through a personal exploration of reality."[11] Artists are conquerors of forms; critics later consecrate such forms after having become inured to them; later still, academics impose them on the multitudes as if they were natural and immutable. Actually, one could well view the entire history of the arts as an unending struggle on the part of artists and poets to wrest form out of formlessness. The struggle is waged, whatever the material one is working with may be; the goal is to come to terms with the the social, historical, spiritual and material challenges of the epoch. For, to paraphrase the French art historian Pierre Francastel, time and space are not entities in themselves, they constitute the experience of mankind; artists do not imitate the world, they elaborate a mental system of representations (and language, I might add, is also a means of organizing whatever is—let me call it the "real"—into a usable "reality"); and finally, "the work of art . . . is an object truly emblematic of the intents and desires" of the artist's time, even though his contemporaries may not always be fully conscious of them, perhaps because they are repressed or denied.[12]

In what I consider to be a collection of generally wrong-headed essays entitled *The Dehumanization of Art,* Ortega y Gasset wrote something analogous: "It is amazing how compact a unity every historical epoch presents throughout its various manifestations. One and the same inspiration, one and the same biological style, are recognizable in the several branches of art." He included music, painting, poetry and the theatre in those several branches. And he further asserted that "All modern art is unpopular, and it is so not accidentally and by chance, but essentially and by fate."[13] That comes

close to what I see as the truth, but I think the reasons are not so much those developed by Ortega y Gasset as they are a failure of criticism—including that of Ortega y Gasset himself. In the final analysis, people do not understand contemporary art because they do not understand the contemporary world. It may be too that they do not understand the contemporary world because they do not understand contemporary art. A dialectical process is involved.

■ ■ ■

Mindful of the stress placed on belles lettres in *World Literature Today,* I assume that the primary concern of those attending this Puterbaugh Conference lies in the study of what one has agreed to call "literature." I shall therefore return to those separations, those walls that have been erected within the existing corpus of written texts and to which I have alluded earlier. Here the separations have a much weaker material basis than the ones separating the various arts. Thus, while no one would deny that valid categories of writing have existed and that some are still valid today (we do need criteria that will enable us to distinguish the writings of Michel Butor from those of, say, a mathematician like Kurt Gödel), we surely need to recognize that the categories with which we are all familiar are both fuzzy and shifting. Perhaps Gertrude Stein was right; perhaps indeed a rose is a rose is a rose. But one could not, in that statement, substitute either *novel or church* for the word *rose.* Think of Gaudi's Sagrada Familia in Barcelona, the church of Assi in the Alps, Saint John the Divine in New York, or Philip Johnson's Glass Cathedral in Garden Grove, California; think of all the different twentieth-century "novels" that you have read—from *L'étranger* to *Finnegans Wake.*

The present cathedral of Notre-Dame, in Paris, was built in response both to a material need and a spiritual desire; those who labored to build the church as well as those who planned and designed it shared the desire and recognized the need, and they were moved by a common faith. During its first several centuries of life, there is no denying that it was integrated with the lives of the people of Paris, the knights and the gowned ladies, and the merchants, harlots, paupers and cripples as well. In his *Description de San Marco* Michel Butor stresses a similar link between what the church in Venice represents today as tourist attraction, architectural landmark and trade promoter on the one hand, and its entire history on the other—the original sin that presided over its foundation, the Venetian struggle for power that it served, the greed that it witnessed. Had he written a "description de Notre-Dame," its format, scription, tone and impact would have been thoroughly different.

Ideologically speaking, each church could be envisaged as a texture composed of many cultural strands; both churches would have a major strand in common, that of the Catholic tradition with its particular view of the divinity, its rituals of Mass and confession; interwoven with that are many strands and threads borrowed from the texture that encloses each church—that is, the culture and civilization of the society it serves. If you will excuse my straining the metaphor to some extent, neither texture is static, unchangeable. The forces of history, the constraints of social change see to it that some threads are removed, others added or the pattern modified. Sometimes the effect of change is so great that there is no real texture left standing, just a few puzzling shreds. We are still trying to figure out what Stonehenge was all about.

Writings likewise form textures that are interlaced with the threads of the culture and civilization of the society in which they have been elaborated. What we call, or used to call, genres are textures that enclose particular texts and are themselves enclosed within specific cultures. And all that too is in a constant state of flux, in spite of the pedants who would like to freeze it for eternity.

In 1970 Julia Kristeva published a study, *Le texte du roman,* in which she proposed to show that the European novel was basically conceived toward the beginning of the fifteenth century as a texture that borrowed its strands from a number of other established textures, under the pressure of societal and historical changes that modified what Michel Foucault would call the *episteme* of the times. A couple of years ago, struck by an analogy between the changes that were taking place, I suggested, during another colloquium, that our own times are witnessing an extraordinary upheaval (and I do not believe you will require me to furnish proof of this), and that, as the texture of our culture changes, equally significant transformations might be taking place in the texture of writing. Perhaps the process that effected the emergence of the texture we call the novel at the close of the Middle Ages is being repeated today —with inevitable differences. New textures may well be taking shape under our very eyes, even though we may not be able to see them clearly. We can detect changes, but we have no idea what the resulting texture will look like. Maybe there will be no texture left, only shreds in the manner of Stonehenge. I hope not.

Be that as it may, I found that set of texts by Michel Butor, the untranslated *Matière de rêves,* "The Stuff of Dreams" (four volumes, 1977–81), to be composed of strands borrowed from a number of different textures— just as a novel by Antoine de la Salle had been, in the fifteenth century, although those textures, of course,

were other. There have been, to be sure, heterogeneous fictions in the past; usually, however, they provided examples of juxtapositions rather than interweavings; they constituted textures interrrupted by inserts: *Moby Dick* is such a heterogeneous text. In "The Stuff of Dreams," on the other hand, the threads from other textures run through the length of whole sections, or volumes, or occasionally the complete set. Among such borrowed threads there are transpositions from dream narratives, as one might have expected from the title, but I do wish to emphasize that they are not complete dream narratives inserted within a fictional context; rather, the fiction exhibits features that are typical of dream narratives. In addition, there are transpositions from standard fiction narratives, from literary commentaries (including quotations and paraphrases), artistic commentaries (including descriptions of paintings), musical composition (including repetitions, now with variations, now *ostinato,* counterpoint and serial procedures), fictional autobiography and poetic prose. What this adds up to is an as yet unidentified texture.

Now this tells us a little about the way in which "The Stuff of Dreams" was composed; it tells us something about the ideologies of language and culture within which Michel Butor is working. But that is not very much. That is only a beginning. It could constitute an important beginning, provided it enabled us to focus on the heterogeneity of the text—not only "The Stuff of Dreams" but other works of scription as well. We probably need to focus on it first, because it goes against the habits that have been imposed on readers by generation upon generation of critics. After some time has passed, after we have cultivated our receptivity, we can start concentrating on the signification that the text conveys, on the process by means of which it signifies.

In other words, I view the past criticism dealing with what Michel Butor has written, valuable and essential as it might have been, as having furnished only a small beginning for the critical analysis that needs to be performed. As I look to the future, I believe such efforts will have to be predicated on a greater awareness of what is involved in the acts of writing (particularly that of scription), painting and composing, about which too much has been taken for granted. Louis Althusser once predicted that our own times would someday be viewed as having been branded by the most dramatic, arduous ordeal one could imagine: "the discovery of and apprenticeship in the 'simplest' acts of our existence—seeing, listening, speaking and reading."[14] He should have added, "writing." As we learn to understand more thoroughly what is involved in writing and reading, we shall better be able to account for the scription of Michel Butor, and that of other writers as well. You have doubtless gathered, in addition, that to my mind such an understanding would benefit from placing the acts of writing and reading within their total context, practicing what I call integral criticism. This implies positing a generalized concept of texture—a texture for which there is no single weaver, no matter what aspect of it you examine. Thus the texts woven by Michel Butor, like the churches mentioned earlier, form a texture that finds its uncertain, shifting place among the textures of Mondrian, Pousseur, Joyce and many others within the intellectual, literary, artistic, political and social textures of contemporary society and enclosing his own familial, biological and psychic textures. Discovering what they signify will not be an easy task; this is where one should seriously consider the possibility of collective, cooperative undertakings, unorthodox as this procedure may seem in the area of the humanities.

Michel Butor himself has said that he expected critics to reveal to him those facets of his work of which he was not aware. So far I do not think we have been able to tell him enough. In the future let us try and surprise him.

Leon S. Roudiez, Spring 1982

*While the Conference was in progress, first copies of the newly released *Letters from the Antipodes* were received at the *WLT* office. The book is an English version of the Australian (red) portions of Butor's *Boomerang,* translated by Michael Spencer and published jointly by the University of Queensland Press and the Ohio University Press.—*Ed.*

1   Richard Macksey and Eugenio Donato, eds., *The Languages of Criticism and the Sciences of Man: The Structuralist Controversy,* Baltimore, Johns Hopkins University Press, 1970, p. 150.

2   François Aubral, *Michel Butor,* Paris, Seghers, 1973, p. 43.

3   Valery Larbaud, *Journal,* in his *Œuvres complètes,* vol. 10, Paris, Gallimard, 1955, p. 162; Kléber Haedens, *Paradoxe sur le roman,* Paris, Sagittaire, 1941, p. 203.

4   Edmund Wilson, *Axel's Castle,* New York, Scribner's, 1931, p. 203.

5   Roland Barthes, "Littérature et discontinu," in his *Essais critiques,* Paris, Seuil, 1964, pp. 175–87.

6   Georges Raillard, ed., *Butor: Colloque de Cerisy,* Paris, Union Générale d'Éditions, 1974, p. 307.

7   Julia Kristeva, *La révolution du langage poétique,* Paris, Seuil, 1974, p. 77.

8   Michel Butor, "Trente-six et dix vues du Fuji," in his *Répertoire III,* Paris, Minuit, 1968, pp. 162–63, and "Claude Monet ou le monde renversé," ibid., pp. 254–56.

9   William Carlos Williams, "French Painting," in *The Embodiment of Knowledge,* Ron Loewinsohn, ed., New York, New Directions, 1974, pp. 21–22.

10 William Carlos Williams, *The Great American Novel,* Paris, Three Mountains, 1923, p. 10.

11 Umberto Eco, *L'œuvre ouverte,* Paris, Seuil, 1965, pp. 107–108.

12 Pierre Francastel, *Peinture et société,* Paris, Gallimard, 1965, pp. 29, 211.

13 José Ortega y Gasset, *The Dehumanization of Art,* New York, Doubleday, 1956, p. 4.

14 Louis Althusser, *Lire le Capital,* Paris, Maspero, 1970, p. 12.

On Yves Bonnefoy: Poetry, Between Two Worlds

"They look'd as they had heard of a world ransom'd, or one destroyed." This sentence from the last act—the recognition scene (5.2)—of *The Winter's Tale* serves as the inscription of *Dans le leurre du seuil,* which constitutes the concluding part of the recent volume of *Poèmes* by Yves Bonnefoy. The preceding collection, *Pierre écrite,* now the third of the four parts brought together in the *Poèmes,* also carried an epigraph taken from the same play (33): "Thou mettest with things dying; I with things new born." Borrowed from a work which Bonnefoy has admirably translated and whose mythic substance is dear to him, these epigraphs do not imply the choice of a landmark in the great poetic tradition of the West; they are the voice of the past as it warns, as it signals what is presently at stake; and they indicate precisely, it seems to me, in an emblematic and seminal manner the double question predominant in Yves Bonnefoy's poetry. The word *monde* first tells us that it is indeed a question of the world, or of a world of a coherent totality, and a set of real relationships. But the very existence of this world is in suspense, in the alternate terms set up in opposition: ransomed and destroyed, things dying and things newborn. The poetic world thus indicates its original concern, the place of its coming forth, which is the instant of peril, where everything is balanced between life and death, "redemption" and perdition. The Shakespearean epigraphs, in the very strength of antithesis, tell of the rending apart, the insecurity, but also the surge of hope: the only springs—apart from any clamor of a "possessed" stance—that Bonnefoy assigns to his poetry. Those are the *constants.*

The epigraph borrowed from Hegel which is found at the beginning of *Du mouvement et de l'immobilité de Douve* already evoked the confrontation of life and death: "But the life of the spirit is not frightened at death and does not keep itself pure of it. It endures death and maintains itself in it."[1] The question of the *world,* in its turn, had been pointed to, but in a critical fashion, as the inscription of the second collection, *Hier régnant désert,* in a sentence borrowed from Hölderlin's *Hyperion:* "'You want a world,' says Diotima. 'That is why you have everything, and you have nothing'" (P, 93).[2] Here again, the idea of the "world" is linked to an alternative, itself established in the major opposition of the "all" with the "nothing." In an artist so enamored of lucidity, the choice of epigraphs is equivalent to a declaration of intent, guiding the reading and the understanding, permitting the new text to be grasped, beginning with the works of the past whose memory it has kept and for which it feels the need of giving an answer. *The Winter's Tale* is a great myth of reconciliation. Behind the quotations from Hegel and Hölderlin, the neo-Platonic themes of the One, of division and reintegration can be detected. Questions whose urgency is renewed for Bonnefoy, beyond any guarantee given at the beginning, are the speech of the past, an encouragement to think of the *present* situation of language as a moment in which human relations must be reborn, beginning by a state of dispersion. The speech quoted is the viaticum—at the threshold of a voyage confronting the earth unexplored, the nocturnal space, the places of disunion.

■ ■ ■

Let us retain the indication: it is a matter of the *world*. And it is certainly important to remember that the expression *world* has taken on in the last two centuries, especially in poetry, a value which it did not formerly have. In its old meaning it first included the set of created things ruled by the natural order; then, in the religious sense, the earth here below in its opposition to the "other world"; finally, in a freer sense still, a large earthly space, a continent, "new" or "old." When Shakespeare speaks of the world "redeemed" or "dead," it is in the religious sense that he uses the term, and, on the side, in the last meaning evoked here, that of continent. But as we know, Shakespeare, as well as Montaigne, is the witness of a crisis in the representation of the cosmos. Soon the Copernican image of the central sun will triumph, mathematical physics, calculating abstraction, doubled by disciplined experience.

This new figure of the physical world was constructed and described at the price of a refusal of sensory appearances. The witness of the senses gave credit to a universe of substantial qualities; now it is revoked in doubt, and from now on the secrets of nature will be revealed only to the "inspection of the mind" (Descartes). The celestial bodies, the strengths which are *usable* on this earth, follow laws which conform to the rule of numbers and thus let themselves be predicted and dominated. And if the witness of the sense is required in the experimental approach, the price is the abandonment of the first region of sensible life. The forward drive of mathematical physics, prolonged by that of technology has at once increased the material security of men and displaced the situation of knowledge: they put the *forces* of nature at the service of men (human

desires, in this world), but they have had, because of that, to renounce the contemplation of natural objects, of singular things—thus leaving without any heritage the whole territory where what surrounds us is perceived in its color, its music, its palpable consistency. Joachim Ritter has shown that the *esthetic* attention to a landscape, at least in the West, was born at the instant when certain men became conscious of the risk implied in renouncing the richness of spontaneous perception.[3] But he also insisted on the fact that the landscape could only be perceived as the object of disinterested pleasure from the moment when scientific techniques permitted men to feel themselves less menaced by nature, less slaves to the tasks of simply subsisting.

Art, poetry, receive thus as their portion this domain deserted by calculating reason, disqualified from the point of view of science which constructs a world of algebraic relations: art has from now on for its task to repopulate it, to distinguish within it the virtualities of happiness, to pursue there even a sort of knowledge, founded on other proofs and taking its being from another legitimacy. Scientific knowledge "takes its instruction from isolated systems" (I am quoting Bachelard) and remains scientific only to the extent that it recognizes itself dependent upon the choice of its parameters; on the other hand, esthetic activity takes up the ancient function of the *theoria tou cosmou,* of the contemplation of the world as totality and as meaning. Poetry, taking the world of appearances as its charge, does not confine itself to gathering up the inheritance of the sensible world from which scientific thought turns away. The triumph of physics and of mathematical cosmology has entailed the disappearance of the religious representations linked to the ancient image of the cosmos: there is no more empyrean, beyond the planetary orbits, no more habitation for the angels or for God. Nothing above, in the universe, differs from what is here below: the profane world which is the sole beneficiary of the application of scientific rationality. The sacred, if it is not to disappear, takes refuge in "interior" experience, is linked to the act of living, of communication, of love shared—and thus takes for its dwelling the sensible, language and art.

Such is, it seems to me, the paradoxical condition in which poetry has found itself for at least two centuries: a precarious condition, because it does not dispose of a system of proofs which might assure the authority of the scientific discourse, but at the same time a privileged condition in which poetry assumes consciously an onto-logical function—I mean, at once, both an experience of being and a reflection upon being—whose burden and whose concern it has never had to bear in preceding centuries. It has behind it a world lost, an order in which it was included and from which, it knows, nothing can return to life. It bears in it the hope for a new order, a new meaning, the establishment of which it must imagine. It uses everything available to hasten the arrival of the world as yet unexpressed, the set of living relations in which we might find the plenitude of a new presence. The world thus taken in tow by poetry is thought of in terms of the future, as the recompense of poetic work. Rimbaud, one of those who have most contributed to imposing this new acceptance of the expression *world,* observes: "We are not in the world," and utters an invocation: "Oh world! and the clear song of new unhappiness."[4] The *Weltinnenraum* designates an analogous space, toward which the thought of Rilke turns, in awaiting the most sensible of worlds.

Bonnefoy's work proposes for us today one of the most committed and thought-out examples of this modern vocation of poetry. His writings as a poet and an essayist, whose personal accent is so marked and in which the "I" of objective assertion is manifested with strength and simplicity, have as their object the self in its relation to the world and not in its internal reflections.[5] This work is one of the least narcissistic possible. It is entirely turned toward the exterior object which matters to it and whose singularity, whose unique character, always implies the possibility of sharing. The subjective assertion is thus only the first term of a relation whose developed form is an interpolation; the "thou" which addresses another (the reality outside myself), but also the "thou" in which the poet transcribes a summons which is addressed to him—both are at least as insistent as the "I" of personal affirmation. The "I," we might say, is kept awake by the concern of the world, for which it is accountable through its use of language. Having recourse to the vocabulary of ethics, Bonnefoy tells us that the stakes are a common *good*—a good which must necessarily be realized and be tested in individual experience, but not for the sole benefit of the separate individual. The subject, the self so strongly present in the act of enunciation, does not remain on the scene of what it is enunciating: it makes a large place for the other, for that which requires compassion, and it accepts that individual consciousness, face to face with the world, bends to the requirements of a *truth* of which it cannot arbitrarily dispose. The solipsism of so many "poetic discourses" of modern times is what Bonnefoy challenges most vigorously. It is not the self but the world which must be "redeemed," or more exactly: the self cannot be "redeemed" unless the world too has been as well. On this point again, the epigraph chosen is perfectly revealing.

Having pursued, for a time during his youth, mathematics, history of science and logic, Bonnefoy knows from experience the attraction of abstract thought, the joy which man can feel in constructing an edifice of concepts and of pure relations. But like Bachelard, whose scientific teaching he has followed, he knows that the rigor of knowledge demands the sacrifice of immediate evidence, of primary images—and he cannot be resigned to that. Bachelard also, after having exalted scientific asceticism, has become enamored of what he had himself rejected: the convictions of dream, the configuration that desire gives to space, the imaginary virtues we lend to matter. In contrast to Bachelard, it is not a dimension of the imaginary of which Bonnefoy felt the need in order to safeguard the fire necessary to life, but rather a simple, full and meaningful *reality*: that of an earth (*terre*), he will say insistently. Not that the imaginary and the dream have not exercised on Bonnefoy's mind a persistent seduction: the few years when he sympathizes with surrealism bear witness to that. But he felt very early what was revealed in the surrealist "marvelous," that it was not the background of sensible experience, with the unperceived richness of ordinary reason, but the "black presence in which what is becomes absent at the moment when it appears before our eyes, closing itself off from our reading."[6] Rereading the text in which Yves Bonnefoy explains his rupture with the surrealists, it is clear that what in his eyes was supposed to prevail against the *image,* in which there shines "the idea of another light," is *reality* ("which is more than the super-real"), "simple things," "the figure of our place" or, finally, the "world."

> There is no real presence unless sympathy, which is knowledge in its act, has been able to pass like a thread not only through a few aspects lending themselves to reveries, but through *all the dimensions of the object, of the world,* assuming them, reintegrating them in a unity which I for my part feel guaranteed to us by the earth, in its evidence, the earth which is life.[7]

The reproach which Bonnefoy addresses to surrealism, symmetrical with but also the reverse of the one he addresses to science, is to have deserted the place, the world to which we are assigned, in the name of *another* order of reality, which is revealed only in a fugitive manner, in privileged beings and instants; the *aura* marking suddenly a certain being or object—according to the surrealist experience—has the effect of persuading us "that a part of our reality, this object, bears . . . in its being the traces, at the very least, of a superior reality, which takes value from *the other things in the world,* and gives the feeling that the *earth* is a prison."[8] That is, for Bonnefoy, the sign of a gnostic attitude: an attitude which, in order to justify its refusal of the appearances of the world, calls upon the notion of the lost unity, of the Fall, of the necessary quest for salvation in another region of the real. But the presence of the world, and the presence *to* the world, whose necessity Bonnefoy feels so intensely, should, he thinks, be maintained against all the dreams and all the summonses which call our mind toward separated kingdoms. Surrealism, with its penchant for astrology, for occultism (accentuated in the postwar writings of André Breton), only proposes a prescientific version, a "magic" one, of the very discourse of deterministic science: its quest for the secret did not remove it any less from the immediate, from the "simple," from concrete existence, and, by this token, was no less separating than was the law of conceits and numbers.

Let us observe here that the *world* whose emergence Bonnefoy tries to assure takes its entire meaning only in the opposition upon which it relies: it is the world reconquered from abstraction, the world disengaged from the nightly waters of dream; but this implies effort, work, travel. The world, even if one must finally say that it was already there, is first of all absent and must be rejoined by gaze and speech, starting with a situation of divergence and of privation. All Bonnefoy's texts— poetry, prose, essays—comprise a suite of moments, comparable to those of a crossing, in which there remains a desire shared between memory and hope, denunciation of the "lure" and the aim for the goal. They are situated, so to speak, between two worlds (in personal history as in collective history): there *was* a world in them, a plenitude of meaning, but they have been lost, broken, dissipated. (This is the affirmation with which gnostic doctrines begin, and sharing those opinions renders Bonnefoy all the more attentive to separating himself from them in later stages.) For the one who lets himself be duped neither by chimeras nor by despair, there *will be* once more a world, a habitable place. And this place is not "elsewhere," nor "over there"; it is "here," in this very place, found once more like a new riverbank, under a new light. But this new riverbank is itself only foreshadowed, prefigured, invented by hope. So that this space, *between two worlds,* can be considered like the field in which Bonnefoy's speech is developed—a field necessarily opening on images of path and of voyage, which sometimes determine the narration, with all the "adventures" which intervene in the tales of quest: wanderings, traps, false roads, the entry into towns or buildings. But this projection into space is only an image, an allegorical virtuality against which Bonnefoy knows that he must just as surely defend himself. Between two worlds: the journey is essentially one of life and thought, is constituted by the changing of the relation of objects and beings through the development of an experience of languages.

Bonnefoy's extreme exigency, as to the *authenticity* of the second world with which he hopes to end, determines a series of warnings and of pleas, concerning anything that runs the risk of turning us away from it or of replacing it too cheaply. Let us go so far as to say that because of its projection into the future, ahead of the point where our research has led us, the second world is defined less by its own character (which could be revealed only by its coming) than by the refusal of illusory or partial worlds which are proposed in its place.

The dimension of the future and of hope is capital. However intense the feeling of a world lost, Bonnefoy does not permit the gaze toward the past, the nostalgic thought to prevail. Many times, to be sure, he lets it be understood that in the past of human cultures there was a sacred alliance with the earth, whose witness has been gathered by mythologies: but the mythic speech, now silent, cannot be born exactly as it was. It only indicates a possibility of "fullness" of which human existence has been capable, in a world anterior to the scission which separates the language of science (of the concept) from that of poetry. From now on poetry, or at least a new practice of speech, must invent a new relationship to the world—a relationship which, as heavy with *memory* as it can be, will not be the *repetition* of the ancient alliance. If in Bonnefoy the light of unity returned seems to shine, in a fleeting fashion, it is never to make way for a restorative (or regressive) day-dreaming, which could accommodate the simulacrum of a return: Bonnefoy limits himself to evoking, strongly but without insistence, a first intimacy with natural innocence. But the rupture, or the "Fall," is for him too evident to permit him to engage in an activity of pure restitution: the day-dreams of the Golden Age, the lyricism of the idyll are strangers to him. Such a "fixation of regret" cannot be imagined except by the person who would want to spare himself difficult confrontations and content himself with an "image" in the place of the missing "real."

No passion, then, although a certain past (difficult to pin down) appears as privileged in relation to our present condition. The first world can no longer serve us as a refuge. If it happens that Bonnefoy uses words (verbs in particular) which are marked by the prefix of repetition—to "re-animate" or "re-center" speech, "to begin an earth again," "to find presence again"—he lets us know that it is never in order to suggest the return to some ancient fullness, or to attribute to it an incontrovertible authority: it is a matter of defining the second world, like the space of a new life, another plenitude, a different unity, by which the loss of the first world can be, as it were, repaired. Marking his distance in relation to Christianity and Hegel, Bonnefoy remains nonetheless attached to a certain figure of transcendence, of the step forward, which hopes to find, *at last,* in a form infinitely enriched thanks to the world of mediation (which is trial and death), what was lost or left behind *in the beginning.* The gaze backward, to be sure, is not denied: works, languages, myths call upon mediation and hearing, but in order to nourish hope and to orient the mind toward what is still the unknown.

To confide this task to language, to poetry, is, for Bonnefoy, to pose as a principle that the second world has its foundation in the act of speech which names things (and which perhaps founds "being"), in living communication with the other, nearby. Bonnefoy defines this task, in his texts on art and poetry, principally by the *via negativa,* denouncing the danger attached to the exercise of language, when breaking with the world, and above all with the other, it pridefully opts for its own autonomous perfection. Bonnefoy has often reminded himself—and his commentators, starting with Maurice Blanchot, have all given it a great deal of attention—of all the arguments to be used against those seductions which might turn us away from the quest for the "real place" in order to "trap" us (an expression vividly indicative of an unhappy final immobilization) in a separate universe. This warning is not just theoretical; it is not an article of esthetic doctrine (or of an antiesthetic) advocating a sort of "death of art" as the condition of access to the second world. Reading *L'arrière-pays,* which bears witness to personal progress, we observe that it is a matter of a peril sensed internally in the gnostic temptation of an "elsewhere," in the fever aroused by the summons, "over there," of a "true place," but which is only in an illusory fashion the real place, because it would require the desertion of the *here,* of the reality in which the poet feels himself to be decentered and exiled. To separate is a fault: and it is the fault which the "sayers of words" commit when they abandon the "real" (or being) for notions; when dream turns away toward the distance; when the image, in all its glory, takes precedence over the humble presence of things; when the book or the work is isolated in its closed perfection, to the side, in the "abstract" purity of its structure.[9]

There is in language a mortal power—when it shows forth reality while hiding it, while substituting for it the image, the unsubstantial reflection. Then it must be brought back to silence. But nothing can arrange for language not to be also the bearer of our "hope of presence." It is thus in writing itself that the peril is lodged which will decide for a "dead world" or a "world redeemed." If there is somewhere a danger menacing "being," Bonnefoy does not claim to be untouched by it himself and does not blame it only on an evil speech which would be strange to him: the epoch, the society, the deceptive ideologies. He accepts the perceiving of it in the signs traced by his own hand, in the objects whose beauty rivets his gaze, in the false "gnostic" road where his own dream of salvation runs the risk of being lost.

For Bonnefoy, there exists not only a first loss of the world, a first scission (in which, as we have seen, the "concept" bears its part of responsibility), but on top of that, a redoubled loss, when deliverance is sought in a "world-image," this time again through what Bonnefoy calls "concept," but in order to designate the purified works, the verbal essences, the forms dreamed. The world-image is the product of a fault, aggravated even if, at its source, one must recognize a real hope of unity, the motion desirous of plenitude: but this movement is fixed like a "mask" and constructs the obstacle which would interpose itself between our desire and its finality—real presence. To be sure, this image-world, this world-mask is the negation of the world impoverished and "disassembled," where we live in a state of waiting; but these words, these essences, which are born out of the sacrifice of the immediate, of the execution of the first givens of existence, do not give birth and life to the second world: they shine with all the brilliance of death. The existence whose *porte-parole* Bonnefoy makes himself (an ethical exigency or rather an ontological one, much more than an esthetic one) reclaims a second negation, a second death, a negation of negation: an "existential" negation of the "intellectual" negation whose product was the work—the closed figure in which "Beauty" used to isolate itself must be broken, consumed and shattered, that system (the verbal world) in which *language* or, better, the work as language was imprisoned—that from this death traversed *speech* should be born, the living act of communication.

Let me add immediately one thing on this point: it is because conceptual organisms in their expansive pride, in their "cold" radiance and also in a power of occultation take on the figure of world, that this term itself in most cases makes way for others, when it is a matter of designating what we have termed the "second world": Bonnefoy prefers to speak of "Second Earth" ("Terre seconde," the title of an essay in *Le nuage rouge*) or of "country" (*pays*); or again he says "true place." For the term *world* (*monde*), heavy with ancient reminiscences, where the cosmos has as one of its attributes the stable character of *harmony,* does not speak sufficiently of finitude, the mortal condition, the time given in passing instants, which are the lot of earthly life, in which we must acquiesce. And we see Bonnefoy taking recourse regularly to the term *world* in order to speak of *intelligible* worlds, of *languages* (e.g., NR, 280).

The earth found once more, thanks to speech (*une parole*) which could reunite, *reassemble*. This verb, often used by Bonnefoy in his essays and appearing at the end of *Dans le leurre du seuil,* belongs to the above-mentioned category of terms which begin with the prefix of repetition yet do not mean a simple return. To reassemble (most often conjugated in the conditional, the mode of hope which does not include certainty) is to realize this "co-presence" which the concept had promised but had not really accomplished. It announces the simultaneous grasp: *con-cipere* or *be-greifen,* which an etymological relation makes almost the equivalents of *reassembling.* Yet if we listen to Bonnefoy, the concept universalizes the thought of the object but misses the object itself in its finite presence. The pride of spiritual *grasp* works against the incarnation: in this regard Bonnefoy insists on the term *excarnation.* On the contrary, reassembling, as it is defined in some of Bonnefoy's most compelling texts, serves to hold together, in the light of the instant, precarious existences sustained by meaning, acceding to being by the grace of speech which has been able to open upon them, to prefer them to itself, in confidence and compassion.

The earth, the place, the simple, has thus no need to deploy before us a world complete: it is enough that through a few necessary words, it has given its proof of truth. The "second earth" is not found in the bustling about of sensory images, in the "bad" infinite of the enumeration of things (unless, according to one of the qualities of Saint-John Perse which Bonnefoy admires, each word, charged with the memory of the real, is capable of awakening instantaneous divinities, sometimes encountered in childhood, in the heart of the natural world). Bonnefoy's fundamental intuition does not take him toward verbal luxury, those great lexical figures of abundance, the polyphony of perception—even if he attributes to regenerated language the raising power of the wave—"the waters which lift" (NR, 343), "the wave without limit or reserve" (P, 328). The ark he builds is not that of exhaustiveness. In poetry only those terms should relive which have traversed (for the consciousness of the poet) the trial of meaning, which have been snatched from the cold and from inertia, in order to unite by a living bond. It is not, for Bonnefoy, the multiplicity of the denoted objects which matters, but the quality of the relation which places them in a reciprocal presence—a relation which we might call syntactical, if syntax did not exhaust itself in the order it institutes: Bonnefoy hopes for a movement which establishes (or *reestablishes*) an order, which traverses and *opens*—the metaphor of openness being from then on apt to reconcile faithfulness (to find the world *again* or at least to *remember* it) and the inchoative function which devolves upon speech (to begin to live according to meaning.)

The project Bonnefoy has expressed many times over is that of "clarifying" some of the words "which help us to live." An apparently limited wish, but one which takes on dominant energy in the image of dawn ("this glimmer appearing in the east, in the thickest of night") or of the flame catching and becoming a fire. The task assigned to poetry is to reanimate "a few great words so that they may together open upon an infinite radiance" (RM, 120). The infinite is in the radiance, no, in the multiplicity of words. Or, as a more recent text puts it:

> Let us not "abolish" chance, as words permit us to do, but on the contrary, assume it, and the presence of the other, to which the infinite is sacrificed and our presence to ourselves, which is the consequence of it, will open a possibility for us. Events, those which punctuate destiny, will detach themselves as significant from the field of mute appearances. Certain words—the bread and the wine, the house, and even the storm or the stone—words of communion, words of meaning, are in like manner about to disengage themselves from the web of concepts. And a link will be made, from these assumptions and these symbols, which, although it is nothing in its last substance, will be our form of completed man, whose unity in the act is the advent of being, in its absolute. The incarnation, that outside the dream, is a nearby good. (NR, 278–79)

Other texts, oriented along these lines, attenuate the aspect of Parousia or of utopia which is, all the same, never completely to be separated from the advent of the "second earth." At the very least they insist upon the idea that it is never attained once and for all. And they affirm the central responsibility of the subject (often promoted to the collective "us") which performs the act of language.

> If one dedicated oneself to the words designating the hearth, the tree, the path, the wandering, the return, it would not be necessarily a deliverance; even in a sacralized world the spirit of possession can be reborn, making of presence an object once more, of a living knowledge a science again, and instantly impoverished: but at least whosoever wants to may work, free of interior contradiction, to *reassemble what avarice disassembles,* and would be reformed in this *co-presence where earth becomes speech* and where the heart is appeased because it can at last listen and even mingle its voice with others. *The world of those few words* has indeed no structure except through *us,* who have built it of the sand and the quicklime taken from outside. (NR, 342–43; my emphasis.)

The evidence of that conviction, carried by a writing which makes itself an ardent voice, does not need confirming by exterior witness. All the same I cannot help mentioning here what I read in one of the best contemporary philosophers. In his *Logique de la philosophie*, which extends and reinterprets Hegelian thought, Eric Weil disposes of the category of "meaning" (*sens*) and insists on "presence" (*présence*).

> Poetry is creative of concrete meaning. Where there is not this creation (which can be, and at certain moments of history can only be, a creation *against* an existing meaning, a destructive creation), poetry is not, and it exists everywhere where a meaning appears, whatever might be its "form.". . . In this widest or deepest meaning . . . poetry is not the business just of gifted and talented people: it is man itself. . . . Poetry is presence. . . . It is immediate Unity, and the poet does not know . . . if he has spoken of himself or of the world.[10]

What a thinker given to conceptual rigor says is inscribed and fixed here once and for all, in a definitive formulation. What characterizes Bonnefoy's approach, in a convergent vision, is the multiplicity of forms and metaphorical figures through which he evokes the possible advent of presence and unity. Only taking into account Bonnefoy's essays and the prose texts, I could cite a dozen more passages analogous to those which have just been partially transcribed, texts where, to be sure, identical words are found, and also the same use of the conditional of hope, but whose rhythm, whose system of images is renewed each time in order to tell of a same transfiguration which is the illumination of the real, once every conceptual form has been set aside. Bonnefoy repeats the promise of this advent in varying it ceaselessly, as if to abolish the figure he had given in a preceding text, and in order to prove it possible by a mobility, by an infinite freedom, by the rupture of form. It is not enough to see in it the witness to a tenacious hope which seizes every occasion to make itself explicit and which does it generously, ardently, in a burst of energy which is never the same although always oriented toward the same goal. Untiring renewal, in the hope enunciated, is required insofar as "presence" aspires to disengage itself and to distinguish itself from everything which is fixed in a *writing*. So that "presence" not be hidden by the images naming it or which quite simply summon it, these images must be fluid, impermanent, able to slide, so to speak, into each other; and the dwelling, the earth, the fire and the moment must be able to exchange their symbolic power.

This aspect of the essays and the texts on art connects them intimately with the *Poèmes* themselves. The critical statement, in these pages, is continuous with the

voice speaking in the poetic works. The poem constitutes the putting to the trial of what, in the essay, is only designated from a distance; the common horizon, seen through Bonnefoy's essays and poems, is (to take up a term which he often uses) one identical *place*. Its approach announces itself in increased luminosity, in the feeling of simplification and reconciliation—in another diction, where the accent of consent succeeds to that of struggle, while even in the syntax the net of formal constraints extends.

But the multiplicity of the impulses which, in Bonnefoy's essays, leads to the boundaries of presence finally held to be possible calls for still another commentary: these impulses must be renewed ceaselessly, because once hope is declared, it is essential to come back to the world—or rather to the absence of the world to which history has destined us; it is essential to return to our place of wandering and waiting, to the space between two worlds. And from there to set out once more. After having saluted the dawn, celebrated even the new day, we are led back to the gray and to the cold—not, of course, without a certain knowledge, not without a warning about the traps to avoid, the illusions in which desire might stray.

Once more, too, there are reborn the temptation of separate worlds, the summons of images, the succour demanded of writing and its captive forms. So that the necessity of pulling oneself away from this "world-image" imposes itself once more, and that of summoning upon it the consuming "lightning"—so that our eyes might open on the "true place." *Beginning over* has become, in Bonnefoy's reflections, an insistent theme.

> A moment of true light upon some rocky path I shall follow one morning, one evening, this will be quite enough to project on the writing this illumination, barely skimming along to reveal the useless reliefs and the abandoned crevices. And this higher truth will help me, then, to correct my desire and to simplify it—for another dream, of course, in still another writing—one cannot unknot the circle—but this writing would be at once more elementary and more enveloping, a place where *another* would already be better received and finitude better understood. To write, certainly—who has ever been able not to do it? But also *to unwrite,* in an experience complementary to the poem, in the maturing which it alone permits, these phantasms and chimeras with which, otherwise, our past would obscure our view. And on the whole, never again some book blindly confirmed two years later by another, but a life where the written being in its very depth of multiple meanings and images no more than a sketch which would be effaced little by little, and would speak as such, is a presence to itself, a des-

tiny: finitude making itself clear and keeping watch thus over meaning. No, this book I am finishing at present is nothing, and precisely because it is everything. A world which my gaze seizes, in this instant of the past is also the step left behind one, the stop which can be further along the way simply through a decision coming in us from something else other than itself—the path, from then on, toward this invisible before us, which is the place. (NR, 76)

Beginning again is assumed here as the very condition of a progress. But two distinct times are affirmed, and we are told that they must repeat themselves: the moment in which hope finds its terms in the world of words it has itself constructed; and the rupture, "further along," which sacrifices words for a future inhabited by a greater truth. To leave the arid world to "write." then to leave writing (that inevitable fault) for the "place." Even that can only write itself, and only escapes danger by writing itself once more in another fashion, in works reexperienced as less opaque.

The progress through fresh beginnings and ruptures is perhaps most evident now that Bonnefoy's four poetic collections are reassembled in a single volume, *Poèmes.* Each of the four constituted parts traces a way, organizes the sequence of its elements, orienting them in the direction of the "true place." Placed side by side, reassembled under one cover, each of the endings loses the absolute quality we would have been tempted to attribute to it, becomes provisional, like the crest of a wave fated to fall once more, to be followed by another. And for the reader of the collection who follows it properly, that is from one end to the other, it is evident that by degrees, the way between two worlds is drawn with more latitude, with a stroke less anxious, in a transparency which accepts in increased number the forms of the visible. The fourth part, *Dans le leurre du seuil,* begins by the observation of the ebb: the reassembling force (which had radiated) has been dissipated; we are once again in the night. To what was once revealed as having been only a dream (where anything "to be celebrated" was lacking), another dream succeeds. Negation is once again present, in the initial position: "No, each time / The wing of the impossible unfolding / You awake with a cry / From that place, which is only a dream" (P, 231).[11] The real is freshly perceived not in its incarnate presence, in its finitude, but only as the reflection of a world situated elsewhere: "The floor which seems painted on air, / The mass of limestone in the ravine, / —They hardly stir, they might be the reflection / Of other trees and other stones, in a river" (P, 232).

To tell oneself that appearance is only reflection is, according to Bonnefoy, the eternal "Platonizing" temp-

tation haunting Western thought. He recalls it in a recent study on the haiku, opposing two attitudes to the real.

> And I who wish to show the gleaming storm cloud, the white cloud where everything is taken in and dissipated, I am in this very instant, by means of my thought, in one of our villages on the mountains, with the heavy houses of limestone, one of those places Japan does not have, made to retain the absolute in our existence as a fire is preserved between the stones of the hearth: and I come forth from one house half in ruins, but holding in it a life, and I look on the horizon, in the West, as a red cloud sets the sky afire with its light, *always wondering if it is not the reflection of another.*[12]

In the future itself, the "impulse toward the impossible" will be repeated, this recent text tells us, whereas at the end of *Dans le leurre du seuil,* answering the second verse of the long poem (where the wing of the impossible was unfolded), unity was declared among the things present—"wing of the impossible folded again" (P, 328). Thus the step forward is never taken. We must set out once more within the dream, and once more deny it.

Deny it? Perhaps, finally, Bonnefoy (author of some admirable dream tales) arrives at a sort of armed truce. Perhaps, without losing his hope of a "true place," he accepts that the space of speech is that between two worlds, caught between this mirage and the "garden of presence." Perhaps we must consent to the image, the form, the structures of "languages" (which are conceptual exile) in order to accede to "speech" (*parole*) and presence, which is not a second transcendence but a consenting return to the precarious truth of appearance. The image can lead us to it, in spite of its "coldness," if we avoid solidifying it, if we know how to make it confess its own precariousness. At the conclusion of *Dans le leurre du seuil* the worlds (where I read "world-images") form once more, after having been dissipated.

Cendre
Des mondes imaginaires dissipés,

Aube, pourtant,
Où des mondes s'attardent près des cimes.
Ils respirent, pressés
L'un contre l'autre, ainsi
Des bêtes silencieuses.
Ils bougent, dans le froid.
(P, 328)

(Ash
Of the imaginary worlds dissolved,
And yet dawn,
When worlds linger near the peaks,

And breathe, pressed
Against each other, like
Silent beasts.
They move, in the cold.)

The two times—of a refusal of the imaginary, then of a return of that imaginary but pluralized and once more "breathing"—are here marked, as I see it, in the clearest way. Everything happens as if the imaginary, accused of having hidden the real, of having calumniated appearances, of having constituted itself a separate world, were finally accepted as a legitimate part of a wider world reconciled. A text on Bashō indicates in a wonderful way the same consenting to what had been denounced as a concealing power (language as a stable structure, formal beauty), on condition that the agent of openness should immediately intervene. Bonnefoy discerns a very delicate separating line which marks, in the interior of a brief poem (the haiku), the split between two worlds.

> On listening more intensely, two sounds are heard under this appearance of fixed stars, two sounds at once distinct and very near, as the cry of the owl, and this union indifferent in its brief duration is the very dialectic of distraction and return. . . . Notions, yes, and first this structure tending to exist as soon as there are words in our mouths, with these lightning exchanges between them in the intelligible. . . . To the moment of this excarnation, always virtual in language like its native fault, succeeds the cry of incarnation. A cry as minimal sometimes as a dry leaf falling, but what more does it take than a few wrinkles on the water for the idea of the instant to trouble the peace of essence? (NR, 344)

The two moments—and the divergence between two worlds—are here extremely close, establishing a "dialectic" condensed in the "brief duration." An attentive examination would show that this "dialectic" is at work, every moment, in the very tissue of *Dans le leurre du seuil,* so that the between-two-worlds should not make itself felt only between the opening and the final lines, but in each moment, up to the conclusion.

Words like the sky
Today,
Something which gathers, disperses.

Words like the sky,
Infinite
And yet contained in this moment within the brief
   pool.
(P, 329)

The *double* element is everywhere: the world-image of words and the open space of the sky; a time of reassem-

bling, immediately followed by dispersion; infinity captured in the "brief pool" (a reflection and an image legitimized, by reason of their very precariousness, their brevity); the space on high, where the storm clouds pass, and the earthly soil, where water dwells simply in the pool. In these simple words the conflict is appeased, but the threshold has not been crossed: the peace established still leaves the divergence between the worlds, the opposition without which the unity would carry no meaning.

Jean Starobinski, Summer 1979, translated by Mary Ann Caws

[1] Yves Bonnefoy, *On the Movement and Immobility of Douve,* Galway Kinnell, tr., Athens, Oh., Ohio University Press, 1968, p.v.

[2] NR = *Le nuage rouge;* P = *Poèmes;* RM = *Un rêve fait à Mantoue.* For full bibliographical information and a complete list of abbreviations used in this issue, see sections 1 and 2 of the Selected Bibliography. All translations are by Mary Ann Caws unless otherwise noted.

[3] Joachim Ritter, *Subjektivität,* Frankfurt a.M., 1974, pp. 141–90. The essay on landscape has appeared in French (Gérard Raulet, tr.) in *Argile* (Paris), 16 (Summer 1978).

[4] See the commentary on "Génie" which Bonnefoy offers in his *Rimbaud par lui-même,* Paris, Seuil, 1961, pp. 147–48.

[5] John E. Jackson, *La question du moi: Un aspect de la modernité poétique européenne—T.S. Eliot, Paul Celan, Yves Bonnefoy,* Neuchâtel, La Baconnière, 1978.

[6] Yves Bonnefoy, "Entretien avec John E. Jackson," *L'Arc,* 66 (October 1976), pp. 85–92.

[7] Ibid., p. 90.

[8] Ibid., p. 89.

[9] "The poet is a teller of words," writes Pierre-Jean Jouve in his *Tombeau de Baudelaire.* Bonnefoy's study on Jouve (in *Le nuage rouge*) dismisses the idea of a salvation through poetry.

[10] Eric Weil, *Logique de la philosophie,* Paris, 1950, pp. 421–22.

[11] Translations from *Dans le leurre de seuil* are taken from an unpublished manuscript, "In the Lure of the Threshold," Susanna Lang, tr. On the wing vibrating in the sky and its value as a sign annunciatory of an "over there," of a "country beyond," see the essay on Morandi in *Le nuage rouge,* p. 112.

[12] Yves Bonnefoy, "Du haïku," in *Haïku,* Roger Munier, ed., Paris, Fayard, 1978, pp. xxxv-xxxvi.

GERMANY

Transgenerational Representations of the Holocaust: From Memory to "Post-Memory"

The Holocaust continues to resurface in the public arena as an unresolved memory, forcing us to confront and work through its legacy. As the fervent and emotional responses to Jonah Goldhagen's book *Hitler's Willing Executioners* (1996) reveals, to cite one recent example, the Holocaust still resides in a liminal zone between history and memory—that is, between the past as object of dispassionate study and the past as an affective part of personal and collective consciousness.[1] Historians have pointed out how the Holocaust's inherently traumatic nature precludes collective resolution or integration into a cohesive historical narrative.[2] Instead, memories of the Holocaust continually return into the present, keeping the event from receding into the "cold storage of history" (Améry, xxi), as one survivor of Auschwitz, the essayist and philosopher Jean Améry, once feared it would. In recent years there has been a noticeable boom in publications about the Holocaust and memory in particular. Interest has shifted away from the recording of historical facts to an exploration of how we remember and make sense of these facts today, several generations later.[3]

The memory of the Holocaust has not faded with the passing of the generation that personally witnessed its atrocities. As the writings of the next generation reveal, these memories have been transmitted, often silently and unconsciously, from the survivors to their children and grandchildren. In this essay, I examine the narrative strategies used by secondhand witnesses to articulate their relationship to an inherited, not personally lived past that has nevertheless become an integral part of their own identity. In my discussion, I borrow Marianne Hirsch's term *post-memory* to describe a hybrid form of memory that distinguishes itself from personal memory by generational distance and from history by a deep personal connection (Hirsch, 8). As we will see in the examples of two contemporary novelists, Henri Raczymow and Esther Dischereit, the relationship of post-genocidal children to these post-memories is often a complex and uneasy one. In an attempt to understand the inherited yet elusive past that resurfaces psychosomatically, Raczymow and Dischereit do not focus on the actual, veridical truth about the past, but rather on "memories" that possess a certain narrative and emotional truth to them—memories that reveal trauma's lingering affect.[4]

Can the second generation justifiably claim any personal connection to and post-memory of the Holocaust? For the French philosopher and cultural critic Alain Finkielkraut, any Jew born in the post-Holocaust era who makes such a claim is highly suspect.[5] In *The Imaginary Jew* (1994; orig. *Le Juif imaginaire,* 1980) Finkielkraut uses his own intellectual evolution as an example to condemn how his generation has disingenuously appropriated the suffering of their parents' gener-

ation in order to give weight and meaning to their own, comparatively privileged lives.[6] He writes: "Cowards in life, martyrs in dream, post-genocidal children love historical self-deception, confusing the sheltered world in which they live with the cataclysm their parents endured. . . . They have chosen to pass their time in novelistic space full of sound and fury that offers them the best role— . . . spellbound, these young people live in borrowed identities. They have taken up residence in fiction."[7]

Finkielkraut coins the term *imaginary Jew* to describe those—himself included—who live fictional, inauthentic lives because they have borrowed their identity from their truly persecuted predecessors. They vicariously live off the Holocaust, identifying themselves with the victims and lamenting their status as orphans of a destroyed culture. To illustrate his point, Finkielkraut traces how he himself once "shamelessly annexed" and "voraciously appropriated" the suffering of his Polish-Jewish extended family.

> Others had suffered and, because I was their descendant, I harvested all the moral advantage. The allotment was inescapable: for them, utter abandonment and anonymous death, and for their spokesperson, sympathy and honor. . . . The effect produced wasn't intentional. I did not set out like a cynical and sordid swindler to embezzle what they possessed. But it isn't only intention that matters. I owed to the bond of blood this intoxicating power to confuse myself with the martyrs.[8]

Finkielkraut epitomizes the complex predicament of those born in the aftermath of the catastrophe. Although this past may haunt their imaginations and inner lives, he feels that they cannot rightfully and authentically speak of a suffering reserved for the actual Holocaust survivors. If the children claim a part in this past, they are being inauthentic, in the Sartrean sense, and self-serving.[9]

In the following passage, the speaker also expresses a deep discomfort with such an identification with the past, yet here Finkielkraut's angry and selfcondemning tone is transformed into one of guilt: "Even now, when I see someone with a number engraved on his arm, what I feel more than anything else is an almost incommunicable feeling, made up for the most part of jealousy. . . . What they lived through was a drama that is not mine. They lived through it, they experienced it, and I have nothing but that absurd, desperate, almost obscene regret for a time in which I cannot have been" (Fresco, 421). The statement clearly reveals how this generation's feelings of regret, jealousy, and longing for a missed past are accompanied by feelings of discomfort and guilt. The speaker's critical self-awareness of "being prey to a nostalgia that has no legitimacy" (ibid.) only underlines the complexities and ambiguities of the post-genocidal child. These feelings of guilt and illegitimacy are reminiscent of survivors themselves, like Primo Levi, who felt that because they had returned alive and had therefore not "fathomed the bottom" (Levi, 17), they could never fully be regarded as true witnesses.

Psychoanalytic research reveals that the vicarious sharing in past traumatic experiences is not, as Finkielkraut would have it, a ploy, albeit unconscious, to validate one's identity in the shadow of catastrophe. Rather, it is quite often a psychological reality for children who inherit the incomplete mourning of their parents and are left to come to terms with this often silenced past that resurfaces as intrusive images, behavioral reenactment, and even physical sensations.

> The children of survivors often show symptoms that would be expected if they had actually lived through the Holocaust. . . . They seem to share an anguished collective memory of the Holocaust in both their dreams and fantasies reflective of recurrent references to their parents' traumatic experiences. The children come to feel that the Holocaust is the single most critical event that has affected their lives although it occurred before they were born. (Barocas, 331)

As far as pathogenic effects are concerned, a definite continuum exists between real and imagined trauma. To those who have not experienced it, the Holocaust may create an "in-between state where the virulence of traumatic fantasy approaches in potency a real event, even though the trauma did not occur to them directly" (Luel, 150). The French psychoanalyst Nadine Fresco describes how children of survivors, like herself, are caught in the grip (l'emprise) of an inherited past. Like survivors, these children return to the past to try to fill in the gaps of what remains unsaid or unresolved. When the parents have transmitted only the wound of the past and not the memory, the children grow up in the "compact void of the unspeakable" (Fresco, 419). From within this void, they must rely on the imagination, which contains the reverberations of these wounds, to reconstruct the memory of the elusive past. As Marianne Hirsch points out, these "postmemories" of a generation once removed from the event come to be "as full and as empty as memory itself" (Hirsch, 9).

The visceral connection a survivor's child might feel with the parents' traumatic past is particularly evident in the following passage from an anthology by and about Jewish-German women, *Nach der Shoa geboren* (Born After the Shoah; 1994): "Again, the past and the present were superimposed. A past I had never experienced myself, but that had reached into my life ever since early childhood. The frozen terror on my father's face every time he entered the room prevented me from growing into a present that was clearly separated from the past."[10] The past resurfaces through the father's nonverbal language of terror and superimposes itself onto the daughter's present, impeding her growth into an unfettered present. Her father's legacy makes it impossible for the narrator to share in Germany's public celebration of the opening of the wall on 9 November 1989. For her, the horror of Kristallnacht fifty-one years earlier overshadows the euphoria of the present moment.[11] The daughter's strong identification with her father translates into a particular sensitivity and perspective—a doubled vision, perhaps—from which she gauges and critiques contemporary Germany. By internalizing her father's unspoken legacy, she becomes the moral guardian of Holocaust memory, hoping to protect it against the onslaught of relativism, denial, and collective amnesia.

The second generation, with its degree of temporal separation from the event, feels that it has been given a particular task: members of this generation are to be the museums that preserve and transmit their parents' legacy for posterity. "We are the museums in which our parents and grandparents have locked away their memories, experiences and nightmares," writes Ilany Kogan. "Like them, we die a thousand deaths" (Kogan, xiv). They are the sites of mediation between the personally lived past and the inherited past that can now be reassembled and remembered only through history and the arts.

The children of survivors were long ignored as "legitimate" survivors until they reached adolescence in the 1960s and psychiatrists began observing deep psychological effects of the Holocaust on the next generation. Although one might share Finkielkraut's moral qualms about expanding the notion of the "Holocaust survivor" to include the postwar generation, there is ample evidence to suggest that the parents' traumatic experience reverberates in the lives of their children in a very tangible way, engendering real wounds. The children often live double realities as they reconstruct and internalize their parents' past, imagining themselves to be actors in it. Just as the Holocaust has an "anachronistic hold" (Fresco, 420) on the post-Holocaust lives of survivors, so too can it intrude upon the lives of their children in unpredictable and disturbing ways. This fusion of past and present identities cannot merely be dismissed as a disingenuous posturing and an appropriation.

The German writer Esther Dischereit explores how doubled or substitute identities manifest themselves in the lives of the children of Holocaust survivors. In her novel *Joemi's Tisch* (Joemi's Table; 1988) she depicts how the boundaries between past and present, self and other, the real and the imagined are blurred in the minds of post-genocidal children. Perceptions of the present and self-identity are overwhelmed by vestigial images and symbols from the past, revealing the extent to which "the event of the Holocaust shapes the next generation's internal representations of reality" (Luel, 153). Both structurally and thematically, *Joemi's Tisch* shows how children of survivors internalize the unresolved traumatic memories of their parents and thus suffer similar anxieties. The novel is a postmodernist collage of over fifty fragmentary scenes which move back and forth between the past and the present, first- and third-person narration, Jewish and German perspectives, as well as individual experience and imagined history. The transition from one scene to the next is sometimes associative, at other times seemingly arbitrary. Some scenes are repeated with slight variations and thus form a web of recurring motifs; others remain isolated with only tenuous links to the rest of the narrative. In its very structure, the novel reflects the fragmentary, elliptical character of post-Holocaust memory and identity for both the surviving parent and for the child who is left to piece together the remnants of what she imagines to have been her mother's past. The reader must follow symptomatic clues and mark narrative gaps in order to draw the meaningful connections between experience and effect that have not yet been made explicit.

What creates a link between the otherwise disparate scenes is the mother/daughter dyad in which the identities of the two women are blurred. Dischereit's novel begins with the daughter speaking as an adult in the first person. She is never mentioned by name, but rather exists merely as "Hannah's daughter." In other words, her identity is inextricably bound to that of her mother, who narrowly escaped deportation and survived the war in hiding. The narrator's reference to the telltale "mark of Cain at birth that resurfaces on her skin" (my translation) describes the visceral, intergenerational link between a mother's burden and its imprint on the daughter's somatized psyche.[12] This inherited mark, whether real or imagined, also explains why the adult daughter shares her mother's anxieties. A perfunctory inspection at the border, for example, becomes ominous, as the narrator imagines herself as a Jew attempting to flee Nazi Germany fifty years earlier. In the following passage, two voices from different time frames are superimposed in the daughter's thoughts: "What if they demanded I undress? *Why would they ask that?* What if I were to undress and they were to see the star

through my clothes? *One can't see the star.* What if they were to see the star through my clothes, burned onto my skin? *It's not burned onto my skin, I've never been there.* What if it were burned onto my skin and the dogs were to come in?"[13] The daughter's doubled reality is reflected in the oscillation between indicative and subjunctive moods, affirmative statements and their negation, outer and inner worlds. In her reality the hypothetical and the real compete equally for meaning. The parenthetic remarks rooted in actuality (they won't ask her to undress, no one can see a star because she has none, she was never there) do not impede the advancing narrative from concluding that, in her imagination, the star has been burned onto her skin and the dogs will soon come in to get her.

This reembodiment and strong identification with the past in post-Holocaust self-consciousness is problematic in the eyes of Alain Finkielkraut, yet it points to the inherent predicament of those living and writing after the catastrophe. For the postwar generation, the Holocaust is simultaneously tangible and abstract, physical and imaginary, "intrinsic and alien" (Adelman, 3). Members of this generation are "entangled with a past which is in their bones, yet which was never a part of their lived experiences at once" (Adelman, 18). Nadine Fresco evokes a powerful metaphor to describe this predicament: they are like "people who have had a hand amputated that they never had" (Fresco, 421). Although they feel the pain, it is a "phantom pain in which amnesia takes the place of memory. . . . One remembers only that one remembers nothing" (ibid.).

Finkielkraut claims that the genocide has no inheritors and that those who were not there cannot speak with authority because they do not know. As the French novelist Henri Raczymow suggests, the question "By what right could I speak, I who was not a victim, survivor, or witness" may not be the appropriate one to ask, since it inevitably implies the answer "I have no right to speak" (Raczymow, 1994, 102). Raczymow's novel *Un cri sans voix* (1985; Eng. *Writing the Book of Esther*, 1995) deals precisely with this question of guilt and legitimacy associated with act of writing about the Holocaust. In order to bring his silenced family history to the surface, the postwar narrator must confront and overcome his own inhibitions about speaking for the dead. As he writes a book about his dead sister Esther, he recognizes how easy it is to coopt her voice, to transform her into the mere fruit of his imagination. Nevertheless, writing remains the only means to localize and contain the ghost of Esther, who functions as a surrogate for those who never returned from the camps. By writing the Book of Esther, the narrator expels her into the external, concrete form of a book. He writes: "Localized.

Esther is no longer in me. I've ejected her" (Raczymow, 1995, 204).[14] This separation is possible because words have usurped her place, erased her memory, blotted her out (ibid.). He justifies the "sin" of having erased Esther's memory by pointing toward the next generation. He has written the book so that there may be closure on the past. In the closing pages, the narrator says: "My child will be spared the past. He won't carry its stigma. He'll really be an *afterward* child. Standing between him and the war will be a new generation. An interval of space will protect him from a horrible taint. Never will I talk to him about Esther. Her name will be dead" (ibid.).[15]

Raczymow's novel presents a complete cycle of delayed mourning: the narrator resurrects the lost object through writing, temporarily merges with it, and then, in the final phase, casts it off as a dead part of himself. According to Freud, this latter phase of mourning makes room again for life. The work of mourning "impels the ego to give up the object by disparaging, denigrating, even, as it were, slaying it, thereby offering the ego an inducement to continue living" (Freud, 139). In order to make room for his son and for life, the narrator "kills" Esther. She is no longer a part of him, but rather an alien and undesirable body, "a foreign body, a tooth, a dead branch, a rotten fruit fallen from a tree" (ibid.).[16] Between guilt and life, the narrator chooses life, because his child "must live, not simply survive."[17] Raczymow argues that although he might find himself caught in a double bind—"in the abyss between [the] imperious need to speak and the prohibition against speaking"—at one point it becomes necessary and inevitable "to speak of what is troubling you" (Raczymow, 1994, 102–3). In other words, Raczymow is less concerned with the moral issue of who is authorized to speak than with the necessity of articulating the "second life of Holocaust imagery" (Rosen, 47) in the post-Holocaust generation. Only by bearing secondhand witness through the imagination can the previous generation's unfinished process of mourning be completed. The children of survivors can only hope to make room for an "afterward child" ("un enfant d'après") by acknowledging and writing about the real, lingering phantom of the past in their lives.

For both Dischereit and Raczymow, identifying with and reenacting their inherited past is an inevitable and necessary part of working through its legacy. In comparing the two, one is compelled to note distinct gender differences in relation to the project of recuperating an absent memory. Dischereit describes how traumatic memory is transmitted from the mother to the daughter through a process of identification. The fusion of identities, evident in the blurring of narrative voices,

assures that a critical sensibility and awareness born from the history of persecution will be passed on from one generation to the next. The final scene in *Joemi's Tisch* anticipates that this legacy, transformed into a ritual of remembrance in the celebration of Purim, will be transmitted from mother to daughter to granddaughter. The mother considers this transmission of memory part of her duty—as a mother and as a Jew. Raczymow presents a notably different trajectory. The narrator sees it as his paternal duty to grant his son the unburdened life to which he is entitled. Therefore, he must sever all ties from the "horrible taint" ("une souillure abominable") of the past, embodied in the form of his sister, in order to make room for the son. The narrator purges the feminized past by killing its pathological memory within himself. On the novel's surface, closure is attained by transforming the past into a book that mediates between the father and the son. The book serves as a transitional object leading toward a more normalized, distanced past. Yet this strong need to deny the past suggests an inability to come to terms with it. What Raczynow seems to be asking is whether, by refusing memory, one can truly purge oneself of its wounds. It is the family's very refusal to confront and mourn the past that made it possible for the phantom of Esther to surface in the first place. If the father obscures the past from his own son, inventing a false history to replace a tragic one, will this erasure not backfire as it did a generation earlier? *Writing the Book of Esther* ultimately remains open-ended and unresolved in terms of how this memory will manifest itself in the next generation.

Alain Finkielkraut, Esther Dischereit, and Henri Raczymow all reveal how their generation grapples with a double bind similar to that of eyewitness survivors: how to speak and how not to speak. For them, this dilemma raises complex questions about their legitimacy and authority as conveyers of the Holocaust's postmemory. In order to articulate the specificity of their generational experience—an absence of real, personal memories coupled with flashbacks, behavioral reenactments, and physical sensations from the past that are psychologically real—they invariably break previously held taboos about who is qualified to speak and how one is to speak. Their transgressions, however, provide points of entry into a past that is at once alien and intrinsic, empty and full, imaginary and real to them.

Karein Goertz, Winter 1998

▪ WORKS CITED

Adelman, Anne. "Representation and Remembrance: On Retelling Inherited Narratives of the Holocaust." Dissertation, City University of New York, 1993.

Améry, Jean. *At the Mind's Limits: Contemplations by a Survivor on Auschwitz and its Realities* [1980]. Sidney Rosenfeld and Stella

P. Rosenfeld, trs. New York. Schocken. 1986. (Translation of *Jenseits von Schuld und Sühne*, Stuttgart, Klett, 1976.)

Barocas, H., and C. Barocas. "Wounds of the Fathers: The Next Generation of Holocaust Victims." *International Review of Psychoanalysis*, 6 (1979), pp. 331–41.

Dischereit, Esther. *Joemi's Tisch: Eine jüdische Geschichte*. Frankfurt a.M. Suhrkamp. 1988.

Finkielkraut, Alain. *The Imaginary Jew*. Kevin O'Neill and David Suchoff, trs. Lincoln. University of Nebraska Press. 1994. (Translation of *Le Juif imaginaire*, Paris, Seuil, 1980.)

Fresco, Nadine. "Remembering the Unknown." *International Review of Psychoanalysis*, 11 (1984), pp. 417–27.

Freud, Sigmund. "Mourning and Melancholia" [1917]. In *A General Selection from the Works of Sigmund Freud*. John Rickman, ed. New York. Doubleday. 1957. Pp. 124–40.

Goldhagen, Daniel Jonah. *Hitler's Willing Executioners*. New York. Random. 1996.

Hirsch, Marianne. "Family Pictures: *Maus*, Mourning, and Post-Memory." *Discourse*, 15:2 (1992), pp. 3–29.

Kogan, Ilany. *The Cry of Mute Children: A Psychoanalytic Perspective of the Second Generation of the Holocaust*. New York. Free Association Books. 1995.

Jacooby, Jessica, Claudia Schoppmann, Wendy Zena, eds. *Nach der Shoa Geboren: Jüdische Frauen in Deutschland*. Berlin. Elefanten. 1994.

Levi, Primo. *The Drowned and the Saved*. Raymond Rosenthal, tr. New York. Summit Books. 1988. (Translation of *I sommersi e i salvati*, Turin, Einaudi, 1986.)

Luel, Steven, and Paul Marcus, eds. *Psychoanalytical Reflections on the Holocaust: Selected Essays*. New York. Holocaust Awareness Institute Center for Judaic Studies and University of Denver / KTAV. 1984.

Raczymow, Henri. "Memory Shot Through with Holes." *Yale French Studies*, 85 (1994), pp. 98–105.

———. *Writing the Book of Esther*. Dori Katz, tr. New York. Holmes & Meier. 1995. (Translation of *Un cri sans voix*, Paris, Gallimard, 1985.)

Rosen, Norma. *Accidents of Influence: Writing as a Woman and a Jew in America*. Saratoga Springs. State University of New York Press. 1992.

[1] For an overview of the transatlantic debates that centered on the appropriateness, originality, and/or accuracy of Goldhagen's revisionist study, see the following essays: Clive James, "Blaming the Germans," *The New Yorker*, 22 April 1996, pp. 44–50; Arthur Allen, "Ordinary People: Scholars Meet to Trammel Younger Colleague," *Village Voice*, 23 April 1996, pp. 65–66; Thomas Disch, "A Nation and People Accursed," *The Nation*, 6 May 1996, pp. 50–54; and Omer Bartov, "Ordinary Monsters," *New Republic*, 29 April 1996, pp. 32–38. In Germany, Goldhagen's book has provoked a veritable "historians' conflict" (*Historikerstreit*) reminiscent of the debate waged a decade ago between the historians Jürgen Habermas, Ernst Nolte, and others about the (in)comparability of the Nazi genocide with other atrocities. For an excellent analysis of this earlier debate, see Charles Maier, *The Unmasterable Past: History, Holocaust, and German National Identity*, Cambridge (Ma.), Harvard University Press, 1988.

[2] For a more detailed discussion of trauma and its disruptive effect on traditional historiography and narration, see Saul Friedländer, *Probing the Limits of Representation: National Socialism and the "Final Solution"*, Cambridge (Ma.), Harvard University Press, 1992, and *Memory, History, and the Extermination of the Jews of Europe*, Bloomington, Indiana University Press, 1993; Dominick LaCapra, *History, Theory, Trauma: Representing the Holocaust*, Ithaca (N.Y.), Cornell University Press, 1994; Cathy Caruth, *Trauma: Explorations in Memory*, Baltimore, Johns Hopkins University Press, 1995; Shoshanna Felman and Dori Laub, *Testimony: Crises of Witnessing in Literature*, New York, Routledge, 1992. For more on the relationship and/or distinction between history and memory, see Pierre Nora, *Rethinking the French Past: Realm of Memory*, New York, Columbia University Press, 1996; and Andreas Huyssen, *Twilight Memories: Marking Time in a Culture of Amnesia*, New York, Routledge, 1995.

[3] Some of the recent titles on the Holocaust and memory, in addition to those mentioned in note 2, include Lawrence Langer, *Holocaust Testimonies: The Ruins of Memory*, New Haven (Ct.), Yale University Press, 1991, and *Admitting the Holocaust: Collected Essays*, New York, Oxford University Press, 1995; James Young, *The Texture of Memory: Holocaust Memorials and Their Meaning*, New Haven (Ct.), Yale University Press, 1993; and Geoffrey Hartman, *Holocaust Remembrance: The Shapes of Memory*, Cambridge (Eng.), Blackwell, 1994.

[4] For further discussion of the distinction between historical and narrative truth, see Donald Spence, *Narrative Truth and Historical Truth*, New York, Norton, 1982. In his defense of the therapeutic value of narrative truth, Spence argues that "making contact with the actual past may be of far less significance than creating a coherent and consistent account of a particular set of events" (28). As both Dori Laub (*Testimony*, 60) and Cathy Caruth (*Trauma: Explorations in Memory*, 153) point out, the truth of a traumatic event resides not merely in the facts of the event but also in the way it defies a logical, causal, cohesive, factually accurate, and historically truthful accounting. Trauma forces us to rethink the traditional parameters whereby we measure truthfulness.

[5] Finkielkraut, born in 1949 to Polish-Jewish Holocaust survivors, has written several other books with Jewish themes. In *L'avenir d'une négation: Reflexion sur la question du génocide* (The Future of a Negation; 1982) he discusses how the Left has embraced some of the rhetoric of Holocaust denial; in *Défaite de la pensée* (Defeat of the Mind; 1987) he examines the relationship between minority groups and society at large; and in *La mémoire vaine: Du crime contre l'humanité* (Remembering in Vain; 1989) he offers a critique of the Klaus Barbie trial.

[6] As Finkielkraut puts it, Jews born after the Holocaust have a privileged life in the "security of anachronism" (12), in the sense that their proximity to the event of the Holocaust protects them from its recurrence: "I was born too close to the Holocaust to be able to keep it from view, and at the same time I was protected by all the horror of this event from a renewal of anti-Semitism, at least in its organized and violent form. In a sense, I was overjoyed: the war's proximity at once magnified and preserved me; it invited me to identify with the victims while giving me the all but certain assurance that I would never be one. I had all the profit but none of the risk" (12). Finkielkraut hastens to add, however, that this does not imply that anti-Semitism has disappeared or that it will never resurface again in its virulent form.

[7] "Trouillards dans la vie, martyrisés en songe—ils aiment se tromper d'époque et confondre le monde ouaté où ils évoluent avec le cataclysme qu'ont subi leur parents. . . . Ils ont choisi

de séjourer dans un espace romanesque plein de bruit et de fureur et qui leur fait part belle. . . . Ces jeunes gens hypnotisés procèdent par identification: ils ont pris pension dans la fable" (22–23).

8 "D'autres avaient souffert, et moi, parceque j'étais leur descendant, j'en recueillais tout le bénéfice moral. Le partage s'imposait de lui-même: aux uns le délaissement absolu et la mort anonyme; à leur porte-parole la commisération et l'hommage. . . . L'effet ainsi produit n'était pas voluntaire. Ce n'est pas délibérément que je faisais servir la catastrophe à des fins mesquines de splendeur personnelle. Je ne procédais pas en escroc cynique et sordide à un détournement d'affects. Mais il n'y a pas que l'intention qui compte . . . je devais au lien du sang ce pouvoir enivrant de me confondre avec les martyrs" (18–19).

9 In *Anti-Semite and Jew* (1948) Sartre argues that anti-Semitism created the Jew and that the Jew's response to anti-Semitism is the sum total of his essence. The "authentic" Jew embraces the externally imposed condition—"The authentic Jew makes himself a Jew in the face of all against all" (137)—while the "inauthentic" Jew seeks to deny this condition: "The inauthentic Jew flees Jewish reality" (137). For Finkielkraut, the post-Holocaust Jew who seeks to define himself according to a past persecution is "inauthentic" because this imagined suffering no longer corresponds to the privilege of his postwar reality.

10 "Wieder einmal waren Vergangenheit und Gegenwart übereinandergerutscht. Eine Vergangenheit, die ich selbst nie erlebt habe, aber die doch seit früher Kindheit in mein Leben hineingereicht hat. Der erstarrte Schrecken auf dem Gesicht meines Vaters, jedes mal, wenn er das Zimmer betrat, lieβ nicht zu, das ich in eine Gegenwart wuchs, die von der Vergangenheit deutlich getrennt gewesen wäre" (12).

11 One of Fresco's interviewees describes a similar inheritance of fear: "Fear . . . that's what I've inherited. I always feel that the fear with which I live almost permanently is the fear of what I have not myself had to face. It's because I haven't had to face it that I'm afraid of it" (420). Fear is thus a sentiment that both connects the parent and the child and underlines their different experiences.

12 "Das Kains-Mal der Geburt . . . schimmert durch auf meiner Haut" (9). In his novella *Vati* (1989) Peter Schneider describes how the son of a Nazi perpetrator bears a similar psychosomatic mark that publicly announces his father's crime and steadfastly confirms his own inherited guilt: "I carried the secret around with me like writing on my forehead, that everyone could decipher except for me. As if I had a fatal illness that one prefers to keep hidden from the patient. Some kind of stigma I couldn't see myself seemed to be sticking to me—how did all of you recognize it?" (12, my translation).

13 "Aber wenn sie verlangten, ich solle mich ausziehen—warum sollen sie das verlangen—wenn sie das verlangten, ich solle mich ausziehen, und ich zöge mich aus. Und man sähe den Stern, durch die Kleider hindurch auf meine Haut gebrannt—ist nicht gebrannt, bin niemals dort gewesen—auf meine Haut gebrannt, und die Hunde kämen heran" (35).

14 "Localisé. Esther n'est plus en moi. Je l'ai expulsée" (214).

15 "Mon enfant, du passé, sera épargné. Il n'en portera nul stigmate. Ce sera vraiment un enfant d'après. Entre la guerre et lui, une génération aura grandi, un espace qui l'aura preservé comme d'une souillure abominable. Jamais je ne lui parlerai d'Esther. Son nom sera tu" (213).

16 "Un corps étranger, une dent, une branche morte, un fruit pourri tombé de l'arbre" (214).

17 "Mon enfant devra vivre et pas seulement survivre" (214).

Arab-German Literature

In the following survey I will introduce several male authors and one female author of Arab descent who live in Germany and write in German.[1] By no means do I wish to claim that I have exhausted their number with this survey. The biographies of the authors covered show that the overwhelming majority come from Asian "Arabia," if I may use this collective term for the time being. Four authors come from Iraq—including the only woman I know of who writes in German—four from Syria, one from Lebanon, two Palestinians from Jordan, and one Bedouin from the Negev Desert. They originate mainly from regions in the Middle East characterized by political instability and considered for decades as trouble spots. The only two authors I know from the North African part of the Arab world come from Morocco and Tunisia.[2] The fact that most French-speaking intellectuals from the Maghreb states—Algeria, Morocco, Tunisia—emigrate to France rather than to Germany may be attributable to postcolonial cultural ties as well as to linguistic reasons.

Most Arab authors in Germany initially came either as students[3] or as political refugees.[4] They all had spent their childhood and youth in their native countries. To date there has emerged in Germany no so-called second or third generation of Arab writers. To my knowledge, there is no Arab author group in Germany, although occasionally two or three individuals will work together temporarily on a certain project, such as the translation and editing of anthologies.[5] Most of the authors write directly in German,[6] several write in both languages, others have translated their own original Arabic texts or have had them translated. Increasingly, especially in poetry, bilingual texts are published in which the poems appear in both German and Arabic.

The beginnings of the presence of an Arab-German literature in the Federal Republic of Germany go back to the Arab "pioneers" Jusuf Naoum, Suleman Taufiq, and Rafik Schami. At the beginning of the 1980s they attracted attention through their publications and readings under—or in spite of—the controversial classification "Gastarbeiterliteratur" (guest-worker literature). In the former German Democratic Republic, the Syrian Adel Karasholi was an "isolated case," as he had already succeeded in the seventies in gaining an audience for himself as a foreign author writing in German.

For the most part the early publications by the Arab authors living in Germany in the early eighties were poems, short stories, satires, fairy and fantasy tales, and realistic narratives, which appeared in anthologies of works by foreign authors. Most often they dealt, in one form or another, with the then still current theme of immigration. Like many other migrant authors from other countries, they examined in their literary texts the conditions of life on foreign soil. It was also a time of sociopolitical engagement for many migrant authors, a time in which the three aforementioned Arab writers, together with their Italian colleague Franco Biondi, founded the book series "Südwind-Gastarbeiterdeutsch" (South Wind Guest-Worker German), later called "Südwind-Literatur" (South Wind Literature), and until 1986 edited various anthologies. During this period of intensive extraliterary work to promote the interests of migrants, the "Polynationaler Literatur- und Kunstverein" (Polynational Literature and Arts Association; 1981–86) or Po-LiKunst was also established under their collaboration. This was the first attempt at a multinational union of foreign artists in the Federal Republic. By means of their essays, these three authors also participated in the debate over the status and the still-disputed definition of literature by foreign authors and, in general, over the recognition of minority arts in the Federal Republic.

Another aspect of their literary work has placed them outside the "Migrations-Gastarbeiter" theme. In my opinion, they turned with more success to other areas, namely those concerning the Arab Orient, or they employed in their works Oriental motifs and narrative traditions. One recalls Naoum's books about Lebanon *Der Rote Hahn, Der Scharfschütze,* and *Kaktusfeigen,*[7] or Schami's novels *Eine Hand voller Sterne, Erzähler der Nacht,* and *Der ehrliche Lügner.*[8] Whether or not Germany appears in the texts as a thematic point of reference, the migrant experience exists subliminally and, to be exact, from the perspective[9] of the foreigner in the host country—i.e., the new homeland. Even when the texts' action does not take place in Germany, the target audience is primarily the German readership.

I would like to describe two features the authors have in common as specifically "Arab." First, they share the Arab cultural heritage in the broadest sense, just as they share Arabic as a mother tongue despite regional dialects. Second, as Arabs living abroad, they are constantly confronted with the stereotypes and clichés so widely held in the West, which they as writers try to dispel through their work. However, it is not the common features, but rather the differences between the writers' personalities that I wish to emphasize in this survey by focusing on the diversity of their literary contributions in form, content, intent, and point of view. I intend to show how the impression of a certain stereo-

typical image—which the common geographic, cultural, and linguistic background of the authors may arouse in the Western reader's perception—can be refuted and corrected through the broad spectrum of their literary products.

There is no doubt that all of them draw, directly or indirectly, consciously or unconsciously, upon the same source: the Arab culture from which they come. The way they handle this cultural heritage in their literature, which elements they select, what they create from it, ultimately remains a matter of the individual writer's personality. In the following section I will outline sketchily, due to space considerations, some of the resulting shades and nuances with regard to the writers' choice of genres. Textual analysis, for the purpose of the survey, will be dispensed with; instead, particular aspects of the literary works of the authors will be highlighted. Authors or references will be cited for the purpose of illustrating my point, without judging or exploring the esthetic quality of individual works.

I will begin with oral narration, which has struck a resonant chord in the last decade with the German audience in both East and West. Three male authors and one female author represent this genre: the Iraqi woman Huda Al-Hilali, the Bedouin Salim Alafenisch, the Lebanese Jusuf Naoum, and the Syrian Rafik Schami. In the German language, they carry on a popular Oriental narrative tradition from their countries of origin. However, it is a tradition that has been increasingly supplanted there by the modern media and, according to Naoum, is also at the point of vanishing in that region.[10]

Due to the special form of presentation, these four storytellers do not deliver readings (*Autorenlesungen*) in the usual sense, but rather performances, more precisely referred to as evenings of storytelling (*Erzählabende*). Rafik Schami, who was known primarily as a teller of fairy tales (*Märchenerzähler*) at the start of his career, has laid claim to the greatest success in this area and currently receives over 120 invitations a year to present his oral art of storytelling, followed by Salim Alafenisch, who gives around 100 performances a year.

At a casual glance, not only the four representatives of oral narration but also other Arab authors as well are regarded in Germany as narrators of fairy tales and as storytellers, although they do not employ this form. However, on closer inspection the reader can recognize distinctive characteristics that differentiate the individual authors from one another and delineate their respective literary contributions. First, I would like to shed some light on the differences and contrasts among the four storytellers (*Geschichtenerzähler*).

The four authors reach back to the oral tradition and, in so doing, draw on the popular narrative roots of Arab culture. The contrasts result from their individual treatments of the common source, since each deals esthetically in a different manner with this shared cultural heritage. In this context, a decisive factor is the selection of themes and artistic means from the popular literature. In addition, it is important to observe how the authors integrate these Arabic elements into their German texts.

Rafik Schami, today a best seller and one of the most widely read immigrant authors in Germany, became well known through the oral narration of fairy tales, fables, and fantasy stories. Schami tells his fabulous tales—as well as satires, realistic stories, and episodes from his novels—extemporaneously. His fairy tales are not necessarily Oriental but rather a fusion of Western and Eastern motifs from tales, sagas, and legends in fairy-tale form, which he calls "the other fairy tale" ("das andere Märchen").[11] He improvises, interjects spontaneous commentary, anecdotes, and jokes, and likes to experiment with puns and punchlines before he writes them down. He converses with the audience and knows, through questions and answers, how to engage the listeners and to encourage them to participate in the creation of the text. Schami attaches importance to lively interaction between the narrator and his circle of listeners. This interaction is also skillfully transferred to the written text. A good example of this narrative technique can be found in his successful novel *Erzähler der Nacht* (Eng. *Damascus Nights*), which appeared in 1989. Schami's respect for Scheherazade's art of narration is evident. He takes the *Thousand and One Nights* as a model and utilizes extensively the technique of the frame tale and the story-within-a-story, into which he weaves, with much wit and irony, numerous fantasy stories without abandoning the realm of reality.

Jusuf Naoum also employs oral storytelling. However, in contrast to Schami, he draws from another Oriental narrative tradition and defines his texts expressly as coffeehouse stories (*Kaffeehausgeschichten*). He is not concerned primarily with the narrative strategies of Scheherazade but rather with those of the coffeehouse storyteller. As the first-person narrator, he slips into the role of the fictional character "Abu al Abed," taking up the narrative threads, interrupting his stories at the climactic moment in order to "wet his throat" with a drink of tea, then continuing the stream of narrative with the recurring rhetorical question "Now, where was I?" With this and other oral-formulaic expressions, he transports his Western listeners to an Eastern story-telling circle. At the beginning of his performances he elucidates this aspect of the Oriental oral tradition for the audience.

Naoum's "coffeehouse stories" have appeared in the same narrative style in two books. He explains in the

introduction to his first volume, *Die Kaffeehausgeschichten des Abu al Abed,* the profession of the coffeehouse storyteller, the *hakawati*.[12] The 1994 volume *Nacht der Phantasie* (Night of Fantasy) continues the stories around and about Abu al Abed as a matter of course.[13] Naoum further delves into the Oriental culture to find the character of the wily Karagöz (or Karakus), a figure from popular Turkish literature whose adventures have spread throughout the Mediterranean region. Karakus, the hero of the collection *Karakus und andere orientalische Märchen* (Karakus and Other Oriental Fairy Tales), is also a part of Jusuf Naoum's repertoire, where one sees much of the adventurous and burlesque, consistent with the popular characters of Abu al Abed and Karakus. Naoum, who as a writer and poet has also worked in other genres, is considered in the area of oral narration as a teller of Oriental fairy tales and coffeehouse stories (*orientalischer Märchen- und Kaffeehausgeschichtenerzähler*).[14] This, despite many parallels, distinguishes his literary contribution—whether oral or written—from Schami's, whose fairy tales cannot be restricted to the category of "Oriental."

Whereas Naoum's and especially Schami's interest in interaction with the audience is striking, we encounter a completely opposite approach in the works of the Iraqi woman writer Huda Al-Hilali, who seeks to eliminate discussions with the audience altogether. Instead, she attempts to confront the audience with "images," and thus her oral narration takes on a unique form. She does not narrate but rather plays out her stories and functions single-handedly as author, director, and actor all rolled into one for the entire evening. In her experience, discussions with her as an Arab female degenerate into repetitive themes of polygamy and the oppression of women. Therefore, she wants to surprise the audience with "images" that they cannot discuss but are expected to reflect upon. She majored in film history and drama at Kassel; after concluding her studies, she wrote stories in order to enact them on stage. In 1984 she began her literary career with performances in Hamburg, where she has lived for the past ten years.

In her performances, which she characterizes as long nights of storytelling (*lange Erzählnächte*), Al-Hilali depicts Iraqi women in their daily life. She wants to show "how they are dressed—one modishly, one traditionally—and to demonstrate realities unknown to the West."[15] For that reason, she appears in the traditional dress of Arab women to show that those who wear this costume are not inanimate creatures but rather women who have a life and feel a love for life. At the end of the evening "the strange clothing no longer plays any role." In an interview with me in the summer of 1994, Al-

Hilali stated: "I do not describe a condition, I let the woman talk. She describes her own condition."[16]

In Salim Alafenisch we are confronted with a further variant of the oral tradition in the Middle East. Whereas Al-Hilali graphically portrays the daily life of women in Iraq, Alafenisch applies himself to Bedouin life in the Negev Desert, where, as the son of a Bedouin sheik, he lived until the age of fourteen. In Heidelberg he studied ethnology and sociology, and in numerous scientific articles he has dealt with the tribal culture and daily life of the Negev Bedouins.

As a writer and narrator, Alafenisch draws from the exclusively orally transmitted narrative tradition of the desert-dwellers—that is, of his tribe. The atmosphere of the *Thousand and One Nights* with Damascus, Baghdad, and Cairo as cultural centers is remote in his work. He characterizes the latter as metropolitan art in contrast to the narrative style of the nomadic peoples, who live in the isolation of the desert.[17] His style also bears the stamp of this desert atmosphere: the narrative rhythm in his stories—whether they are told orally or written down in books—is tranquil, the stream of narration is lineal, the language is straightforward, parataxis predominates. Laconic, direct, without frills or ornamentation, the style here is totally different from Schami's labyrinthine and complex interlocking episodes, Naoum's coffeehouse narrative strategies and rich use of metaphors, and Al-Hilali's lively and varied delivery.

Alafenisch tells stories of desert life in this relaxed, nearly recitative tone. He reports on the lifestyle, customs, and myths of the nomadic tribes in the Middle East, about a subculture within the farflung Arab cultural sphere scarcely known even in the Arab world. To my knowledge, he is the only Bedouin in the West who has consciously made his task the literary documentation of this Negev subculture, whose existence is now threatened by technology, civilization, and politics. Consequently, in the volume of stories *Das Kamel mit dem Nasenring* (The Camel with the Nose Ring) the border problems in the Near East are discussed for the first time from the point of view of the nomads themselves: "Borders are a source of distress for man and animal."[18] Borders signify restrictions on their nomadic life. The first border with which the Bedouins were confronted resulted from the construction of the Suez Canal—a great achievement for the world, a "catastrophe"[19] for the Bedouins. The novel *Das versteinerte Zelt*[20] (The Petrified Tent) depicts the advent of modernization that forced the nomads to settle and turned their tents into stone houses where dreams no longer found entry. In this respect, the narration of Alafenisch occupies a special position and cannot be compared either in respect to its subject matter or as regards its method of delivery

with that of the other representatives of oral narrative art in Germany.

In contrast to storytelling, poetry constitutes a different aspect of Arab-German literature, one which is less known in Germany. Several authors—Jusuf Naoum, for example—have also turned their hand to poetry in addition to other genres. In his volume of poems from three decades entitled *Sand, Steine und Blumen*[21] (Sand, Stones, and Flowers) we find no trace of the style of the coffeehouse storyteller. The Syrian writer and translator Suleman Taufiq, who has lived in Aachen since 1971, published several collections of verse in the eighties, such as *Layali* and *Das Schweigen der Sprache* (The Silence of Language). In 1993 his new volume *Spiegel des Anblicks* (Mirror of the Gaze) appeared, with German poems and a few bilingual ones.[22]

Fouad Awad from Syria, one of the youngest of the Arab authors, who has been in the Federal Republic since 1986, has published two volumes of poetry.[23] In contrast to his Arab colleagues, Awad is not only a poet but also a singer and musician. He writes, composes, and sings German and Arabic songs in live performances and on tapes, of which there are several.[24] Occasionally he accompanies Naoum's coffeehouse stories on the lute; the combination of singing and music lends Awad's work a special character. Other Arab poets have contributed single poems in German to anthologies, have issued their own volumes of poetry or have had them published by small publishing houses, but have not yet gained a foothold as poets in Germany.[25]

With regard to subject matter, there are poems about the world abroad, the homeland, and childhood; there are love poems and poems about nature, as well as philosophical and political poetry. With regard to style, there are poems without exotic elements or Eastern local color. Though far fewer in number, there are also poems "with an Oriental accent"[26]—i.e., poems that employ metaphors and expressions emphasizing cultural difference and point to the foreign origin of the poetic "I." A poem without Eastern images, for example, is Taufiq's "anti zeitgeist" from his *Spiegel des Anblicks*.

the hours become narrow
they revolve
they dance
they whisper
they fly
the time comes
strides ahead
and you sit there
with the books
move
between the letters
and occupy yourself with the words.[27]

As an example of poems with an Oriental accent, here is the first verse of Naoum's "Selbstporträt" (Self-Portrait): "I was born in a land / where orange trees and olive groves / grow under hot sun, / where dates and figs / ripen under hot sun, / where thyme and rosemary bloom."[28] Or, to continue with Taufiq, a few lines from his poem "in deinen augen" (in your eyes): "when you laugh, I hear the laughter of children / when you clap your hands, I hear the rhythm of Arab dances / when you move, caravans move in a desert / when I take your hand, I take the hand of morning."[29]

Taking as an example the two authors Karasholi from Syria and Al-Maaly from Iraq, who are considered exclusively poets, I will try to point out the differences between them. Khalid Al-Maaly comes from a Bedouin family in southern Iraq that gave up the nomadic life at the end of the sixties. During his childhood he was a nonconformist vis-à-vis the tribal system. In Baghdad he was an outsider. Today he is convinced that the poet lives in an "eternal exile." This phenomenon, the status of the outsider, the poet as alien, is also one of his central themes. In a radio broadcast from October 1991, his interest in literary "outsiders and nonconformists," whether from the Orient or the Occident, is described as "a certain type of subculture."[30] In relation to content and form, his interest lies with the European and Arab avant-garde.

Through his reading of existentialists, surrealists, and dadaists, especially the French poets Baudelaire and Rimbaud, as well as the Arab mystics of the ninth to the eleventh centuries, Al-Maaly has been able to detach himself from all that is traditional in literature. He avoids appearing as a cultural mediator in Germany or discussing the condition of foreigners in readings; literature should reflect inner worlds, historical worlds, poetic moments—not social questions.[31] Al-Maaly's prose texts in the volume *Gedanken über das Lauwarme*[32] (Thoughts About the Lukewarm) impress one as lyrical. His poetry is "hermetic."[33] His writing is justly characterized as "delving deep into the inner world of a fully self-absorbed ego."[34] The poems from his 1992 book *Klage eines Kehlkopfes* (A Larynx's Lament), translated by the author himself from the Arabic, show inwardly reflected thoughts: "My constant defeat / its memories on the scale / without water, without wall. / The others knew something about it. / And I knew the meaning of senseless sitting."[35]

Karasholi, the Syrian poet who has lived in Leipzig for thirty years, represents a different attitude as a poet. In his verse collection *Umarmung der Meridiane*[36] (Embrace of the Meridian), published in 1978, he criticizes social conditions in what was at that time the German Democratic Republic. In the seventies he was still in ac-

cord with the societal goals of the East German government. Therefore, in his poems he brought criticism to bear in an attempt to improve society, not to abolish the system as such. In the eighties, however, melancholy and helplessness predominated in his critical examination of the socialist system; he had given up hope that this system could be reformed or that it would develop a more human face. I cite the poem "Zügelung" (Restraint) from the volume *Daheim in der Fremde* (At Home Abroad), published in 1984, as an example of Karasholi's criticism of the system.

The word
flung out in anger
or out of concern
and thus not weighed out
on the scale of caution
will perhaps become the fire
that fills the horizon
with ashes
and wears away the name
slowly
behind closed doors.[37]

Karasholi writes love poems and philosophical poetry in which everyday life and politics play no role. However, it is precisely his socially committed poetry that forms an interesting contrast to Al-Maaly's hermetic verse. Despite the differences between the two poets with regard to the details of their approaches, their poetic contributions are opening up an aspect of Arabic literature in the Federal Republic which has yet to hold its own on German soil alongside "narrated" or oral literature.

Another component of the Arab-German literary production is in the arena of "narrative" literature. I would like to feature several aspects from the broad spectrum of prose, starting with children's literature. Both Schami and Taufiq among the Arab authors have made significant contributions to this genre, Schami with several illustrated children's books and Taufiq with the bilingual picture-book *Oh wie schön ist Fliegen*[38] (Oh How Beautiful Is Flying).

Ghazi Abdel-Qadir is exclusively an author of books for children and adolescents.[39] His books are realistic and written in an exciting and vivid narrative style. They deal with actual themes, current happenings, culture, and politics in the Middle East from the point of view of children and young people. His book *Abdallah und ich* (Abdallah and I) depicts the daily life of Palestinian children in an Arab village. The novel *Mustafa mit dem Buchladen* (Mustafa and the Bookshop), honored in 1994 with the Austrian prize for children's and adolescents' books, revolves around the fate of a

Palestinian youth in Kuwait. The book *Die sprechenden Steine* (The Talking Stones) situates the Intifada—the Palestinian uprising in the occupied territories—in the center of the action. The setting in *Spatzenmilch und Teufelsdreck* (Sparrows' Milk and Devils' Filth) is moved to Germany. The day-to-day cultural misunderstandings and linguistic miscommunications of a German-Jordanian family are portrayed with much wit and humor from the viewpoint of an eleven-year-old German boy.

Satire is an additional focus in prose written by Arab authors. Wadi Soudah, a Palestinian from Jordan who has lived in Bielefeld since 1979, writes short prose and regards himself as a realistic-satiric author, not a storyteller. His book *Kafka und andere palästinensische Geschichten* (Kafka and Other Palestinian Stories) describes events in the life of the Palestinians on the West Bank and, at the same time, depicts in a humorous-satiric tone the experiences of a Palestinian living abroad. Daily life and politics are dealt with candidly and dispassionately; all that is oppressive in the stories is neutralized by ironic detachment. In this narrative style the autobiographical story "Blutwäsche" (Dialysis) describes the kidney disease of a Palestinian named "Wadi Soudah" and his experiences in German hospitals. At the end of the story the dialysis patient reports the failure of a kidney transplant as follows: "I kept the kidney five years. Unfortunately it got homesick and went back to its previous owner—and I went back to the washing machine [the dialysis unit]. There we celebrated our reunion. Now I must wait until Allah calls to him the next donor, and so on, from donation to donation, until Allah calls for me."[40] The author, himself a dialysis patient, delivers in this story a literary "satire on the German health-care system."[41]

In the area of realistic prose, the majority of the authors have written novels, novellas, or short stories. Suleman Taufiq's autobiographically based novella *Im Schatten der Gasse*[42] (In the Shadow of the Alley) appeared in an Arabic-German edition. In 1992 Huda Al-Hilali published her first work, *Von Bagdad nach Basra*[43] (From Baghdad to Basra), and the Moroccan Mohammed Mhaimah published his book *Wenn Dortmund an Casablanca grenzen würde*[44] (If Dortmund Bordered Casablanca). The Tunisian Hassouna Mosbahi made his debut in Germany as a writer of prose with a translation of his collection of novellas *So heiβ, so kalt, so hart*[45] (So Hot, So Cold, So Hard). So did the exiled Iraqi Najem Wali with his antiwar novel *Krieg im Vergnügungsviertel*[46] (War in the Amusement Quarter), which describes the senselessness of the Iran-Iraq war. Both novelists have since written in both German and Arabic. Wali, a resident of Hamburg, published in 1990

the book *Hier in dieser fernen Stadt*[47] (Here in This Distant City); some of its stories are written directly into German while others are translated from the Arabic to German. Mosbahi, who works in Munich, published a nonfiction book in 1993 in collaboration with the Orientalist Erdmute Heller entitled *Hinter den Schleiern des Islam: Erotik und Sexualität in der arabischen Kultur*[48] (Behind the Veil of Islam: Eroticism and Sexuality in Arabic Culture). Mosbahi and Wali are active in the areas of the essay and journalism and publish in both Arabic and German magazines. As a literary critic, Mosbahi writes essays about Arabic literature for, among others, *Die Zeit*,[49] the *Frankfurter Allgemeine Zeitung*,[50] and the *tageszeitung*.[51] This represents another focal point of the work of Arab authors in Germany. In my opinion, the literary translations done by Taufiq and Al-Maaly also belong in this category. They translate German poetry into Arabic and Arabic poetry into German, and together they edit the resulting anthologies.[52]

To my mind, the literary works of the Arab authors in Germany are also an important contribution to an extraliterary phenomenon. They question the stereotype of what is regarded in the West as "typically Oriental" and as the "typical Arab woman." However, it remains to be seen whether these factors can bring about a broadening of horizons for a wider audience in the sense used by Jauβ[53] and to what extent this can generate a revision of Western esthetic expectations adopted by the literary critics. Except in specialized academic circles, literary criteria tend, in general, to reduce Arab art and literature to its popular—that is to say, exotic-folkloric—elements. Hence, I believe that a meaningful achievement of the Arab authors is that they convey to the German readership, to whom they direct their work, not a one-dimensional literary production, but rather a variety of themes and styles, full of nuances. The diversity of the genres, the artistic devices and narrative strategies make the reader who may be less familiar with the culture of the authors aware of the fact that Arab literature encompasses more than simply popular literature and the stories of *A Thousand and One Nights*. At the same time this diversity supports—on an esthetic level and in the German language—Edward Said's assertion that the Orient does not represent a sterile, homogenous cultural entity[54] except as a figment of Western imagination and as an intellectual product of European Oriental studies in the nineteenth century.[55]

Iman O. Khalil, Summer 1995, translated by Jeannette Iocca

■ ABOUT THE AUTHORS

Abdel-Qadir, Ghazi. Born 1948 in Palestine; diploma in Jordan; German and English studies, evangelical theology and Islamic studies in Bonn and Siegen; has lived as a writer in Siegen since 1988. Several prizes for his children's books.

Alafenisch, Salim. Born 1948 as the son of a Bedouin sheik in the Negev Desert; resident in the Federal Republic since 1973. Studied ethnology, sociology, and psychology at the University of Heidelberg. Lives as a writer in Heidelberg.

Al-Hilali, Huda. Born 1947 in Baghdad; resident in Germany since 1976, currently in Hamburg. Studied film history and drama in Kassel, then Islamic and German studies in Hamburg; M.A. in 1993. Narrative performances (*Erzählabende*) since 1984.

Al-Maaly, Khalid. Born 1956 as the son of Bedouins in southern Iraq; since 1980 in exile in Germany. Several volumes of poetry in Arabic and in German translation. Lives as a poet, translator, editor, publisher, and graphic artist in Cologne.

Awad, Fouad. Born 1965 in Damascus, brother of Suleman Taufiq. Came to Aachen in 1986 to study architecture. Musician and poet.

Karasholi, Adel. Born 1936 in Damascus; resident in Leipzig since 1961. Dissertation on "Brecht und das arabische Theater." Lecturer at the University of Leipzig. Poet, essayist, recipient of the Adelbert von Chamisso Prize.

Mhaimah, Mohammed. Born 1957 in Morocco. Studied literature and was a teacher in Casablanca; has worked as a teacher in Hagen since 1978.

Mosbahi, Hassouna. Born 1950 in Kairouan, Tunisia. Novellas and poems; translator, literary critic, journalist. Has lived as a writer and correspondent in Munich since 1985.

Naoum, Jusuf. Born 1941 in Lebanon; came to the Federal Republic in 1964. Training in hotel and restaurant management; has worked as a waiter, masseur, and physical therapist. Has lived as a writer near Frankfurt since 1983.

Schami, Rafik. Born 1946 in Malula, Syria; resident in the Federal Republic since 1971. Holds a doctorate in chemistry from Heidelberg. Has worked as a writer since 1982; Adelbert von Chamisso Prize; Hermann Hesse Prize in 1994.

Soudah, Wadi. Born 1948 in Palestine (near Nablus on the West Bank, Jordan). Studied sociology and Islamic philosophy in Beirut; came to Germany in 1979; study of sociology discontinued due to kidney disease. Lives as a writer in Bielefeld.

Taufiq, Suleman. Born 1953 in Syria;, came to the Federal Republic for study in 1971. Has produced radio and television programs; lives as a writer, poet, editor, and translator in Aachen.

Wali, Najem. Born 1956 in southern Iraq. Studied German literature in Baghdad. Has lived in exile in Hamburg since 1980; M.A. in German studies from the University of Hamburg, 1988.

[1] would like to thank the German Academic Exchange Service (DAAD) in Bonn and in New York; the Center for Contemporary German Literature at Washington University in St. Louis, Missouri; the Charles Grawemeyer Committee of the University of Louisville, Kentucky; as well as the University of Missouri Research Board and the University of Missouri-Kansas City for the academic support and for the financing of several research trips and study visits to Germany, which made it possible for me to conduct interviews with most of the authors covered in this article. I would also like to thank Jeannette Iocca for the translation of this article from the German.

[2] The authors are Jusuf Naoum from Lebanon; Fouad Awad, Adel Karasholi, Rafik Schami, and Suleman Taufiq from Syria;

Huda Al-Hilali from Iraq and her three compatriots Khalid Al-Maaly, Abdul Jabir, and Najem Wali; Salim Alafenisch, a Palestinian Bedouin from the Negev Desert; and the two Palestinians from Jordan, Ghazi Abdel-Qadir and Wadi Soudah. From North Africa come Mohammed Mhaimah of Morocco and Hassouna Mosbahi of Tunisia.

[3] Alafenisch, Huda Al-Hilali, Schami, Soudah, Taufiq, and his brother Awad.

[4] For example, the exiled Iraqi authors Khalid Al-Maaly, Abdul Jabir, and Najem Wali, who escaped the Baath regime at the beginning of the eighties. The Syrian Adel Karasholi had to flee the Nasser government by the beginning of the sixties after the unification of his country with Egypt (1958–61).

[5] As an example I would also name Naoum, Schami, and Taufiq during their productive cooperation in the eighties as coeditors of the "Südwind-Gastarbeiterdeutsch" anthologies and the annuals of the Polynational Literature and Arts Association. Al-Maaly and Suleman Taufiq translate together; as a musician, Fouad Awad accompanies Jusuf Naoum in his readings.

[6] Alafenisch, Abdel-Qadir, Al-Hilali, Naoum, Schami, Soudah.

[7] Jusuf Naoum, *Der rote Hahn: Erzählungen des Fischers Sidaoui* (Darmstadt, Luchterhand, 1974); *Der Scharfschütze: Erzählungen aus dem libanesischen Bürgerkrieg* (Frankfurt a.M., Brandes & Apsel, 1988); *Kaktusfeigen: Erzählung* (Frankfurt a.M., Brandes & Apsel, 1989).

[8] Rafik Schami, *Eine Hand voller Sterne: Roman* (Weinheim, Beltz, 1987); *Erzähler der Nacht* (Weinheim, Beltz, 1989); *Der ehrliche Lügner: Roman von tausendundeiner Lüge* (Weinheim, Beltz, 1992).

[9] Rafik Schami, personal interview, Munich, 26 July 1993.

[10] Jusuf Naoum: "Television, this Western monster, has unfortunately destroyed our popular art." *Die Kaffeehausgeschichten des Abu al Abed,* unabridged edition (Munich, dtv, 1993), p. 3.

[11] Klaus Farin, "Märchen aus Malula: Sieben Nächte mit Rafik Schami," *die tageszeitung* (3 November 1987).

[12] Naoum, *Kaffeehausgeschichten,* pp. 5–7.

[13] Naoum, *Nacht der Phantasie: Der Kaffeehauserzähler Abu al Abed lädt ein* (Frankfurt a.M., Brandes & Apsel, 1994).

[14] Naoum, *Nacht der Phantasie* (cover; biographical information about the author).

[15] Huda Al-Hilali, personal interview, Hamburg, 12 August 1994.

[16] Al-Hilali, personal interview.

[17] Salim Alafenisch, personal interview, Heidelberg, 17 July 1994.

[18] Salim Alafenisch, *Das Kamel mit dem Nasenring* (Zurich, Unionsverlag, 1990), p. 7.

[19] Alafenisch, personal interview.

[20] Salim Alafenisch, *Das versteinerte Zelt* (Zurich, Unionsverlag, 1993).

[21] Jusuf Naoum, *Sand, Steine und Blumen: Gedichte aus drei Jahrzehnten* (Frankfurt a.M., Brandes & Apsel, 1991).

[22] Suleman Taufiq, *Layali: Gedichte* (Essen, Klartext, 1984); *Das Schweigen der Sprache: Gedichte* (Berlin, Orient, 1988); *Spiegel des Anblicks: Gedichte* (Meerbusch, Orient, 1993).

[23] Fouad Awad, *Gesicht der Nacht* (Aachen, Vlinder, 1991); *Am achten Tag: Lyrik* (Berlin, Das Arabische Buch, 1994).

[24] Among the tapes there are two with Jusuf Naoum—*Karakus und andere orientalische Märchen* and *Die Kaffeehausgeschichten des Abu al Abed* (Frankfurt a.M., Brandes & Apsel)—and one with singer Hiam Sayeg: *Die Neigung zur Liebe: Arabische Lieder* (Frankfurt a.M., Brandes & Apsel).

25 For example: Sami El-Sadiq, Jabir Abdul.

26 Abdul Jabir, *Zurück: Oh Zeit der grünen Zitronen* (Abdul Muneim Verlag, 1988). Abdul Jabir, exiled Iraqi poet, prefaces his volume of poetry with this dedication: "This is the second volume of poetry that I have written in the German language, in hopes that its poems written with an Oriental accent will shed enough light on the danger zones of our world and their dark corners. . . ."

27 Taufiq, *Spiegel des Anblicks*, p. 1.

28 Naoum, *Sand*, p. 9.

29 Taufiq, *Layali*, p. 58.

30 Heribert Becker, "Die Fremdheit des Dichters: Der irakische Schriftsteller Khalid Al-Maaly," *Studiozeit:* Radio broadcast, 17 October 1991 (unpublished manuscript, used by permission of the author), p. 2.

31 Khalid Al-Maaly, personal interview, Cologne, 8 August 1994.

32 Khalid Al-Maaly, *Gedanken über das Lauwarme: Prosa*, trs. Khalid Al-Maaly and Stefan Linster, 2d rev. ed. (Berlin, Das Arabische Buch, 1994).

33 Becker, p. 11.

34 Becker, p. 17.

35 Khalid Al-Maaly, *Klage eines Kehlkopfes: Gedichte*, trs. Khalid Al-Maaly, I. Knips, Stefan Linster, and Hiltrud Zierl (Cologne, fundamental, 1992), p. 20.

36 Adel Karasholi, *Umarmung der Meridiane: Gedichte* (Halle/Leipzig, Mitteldeutscher Verlag, 1978).

37 Adel Karasholi, *Daheim in der Fremde: Gedichte.* (Halle, Mitteldeutscher Verlag, 1984), p. 10.

38 Suleman Taufiq, *Oh wie schön ist Fliegen oder Wie die Ente den Mond sucht: Ein Märchen für deutsche und arabische Kinder* (Berlin, Orient, 1988).

39 Ghazi Abdel-Qadir, *Abdallah und ich* (Weinheim, Beltz & Gelberg, 1991); *Die sprechenden Steine* (Weinheim, Beltz & Gelberg, 1992); *Spatzenmilch und Teufelsdreck* (Munich, Erika Klopp, 1993); *Mustafa mit dem Buchladen* (Zürich, Nagel & Kimche, 1993); *Das Blechkamel* (Munich, Erika Klopp, 1994); *Der Wasserträger* (Jugend & Volk, 1994).

40 Wadi Soudah, *Kafka und andere palästinensische Geschichten.* (Frankfurt a.M., Brandes & Apsel, 1991), p. 73.

41 "Gedacht wird in Besatzungszeiten: Dichterlesung mit Wadi Soudah im Handewitt" (WO), *Flensburger Tageblatt* (22 May 1992).

42 Suleman Taufiq, *Im Schatten der Gasse: Erzählung* (Berlin, Orient, 1992).

43 Huda Al-Hilali, *Von Bagdad nach Basra: Geschichten aus dem Irak* (Heidelberg, Palmyra, 1992).

44 Mohammed Mhaimah, *Wenn Dortmund an Casablanca grenzen würde* (Herdecke, Scheffler, 1992).

45 Hassouna Mosbahi, *So heiβ, so kalt, so hart: Tunesische Erzählungen,* trs. Erdmute Heller and Mohamed Zrouki (Greno, 1989; Frankfurt a.M., Eichborn, 1991).

46 Najem Wali, *Krieg im Vergnügungsviertel: Roman,* tr. Jürgen Paul (Hamburg, perspol, 1989).

47 Najem Wali, *Hier in dieser fernen Stadt: Erzählungen* (Hamburg, Galgenberg, 1990).

48 Erdmute Heller and Hassouna Mosbahi, *Hinter den Schleiern des Islam: Erotik und Sexualität in der arabischen Kultur* (Munich, Beck, 1993).

49 Hassouna Mosbahi, "Die verratene Tradition" *Die Zeit,* 7 (18 February 1994), pp. 13–14.

50 Hassouna Mosbahi, "Die Kunst ist Phantasie und Vorstellung: Die Welt des Nagib Mahfuz," *Frankfurter Allgemeine Zeitung,* 270 (19 November 1988).

51 Hassouna Mosbahi, "Wir sind ein Teil des Okzidents: Der libanesische Dichter Adonis über das politische Exil," *die tageszeitung* (2 September 1992), p. 14.

52 Suleman Taufiq, personal interview, Aachen, 9 August 1994; Khalid Al-Maaly, personal Interview.

53 Hans Robert Jauβ, *Literaturgeschichte als Provokation* (Frankfurt a.M., Suhrkamp, 1970).

54 See especially Edward Said, *Orientalism* (New York, Random House, 1978).

55 See my article: "Narrative Strategies as Cultural Vehicles: On Rafik Schami's Novel *Erzähler der Nacht,*" *The German Mosaic: Cultural and Linguistic Diversity in Society,* ed. Carol A. Blackshire-Belay (Westport, Greenwood, 1994).

Confronting the Fascist Past and Coming to Terms with It

Anti-fascist themes have persisted in the literature of the German-speaking countries for over fifty years.[1] By this time we can distinguish three successive waves of this preoccupation. Even the earliest examples, Thomas Mann's *Mario and the Magician* (1929) or Brecht's *Roundheads and Peakheads* (1934), were didactic. The writer wished to teach his reader or audience to discern fascist techniques of manipulation, ways of thinking and behaving; he placed these in an imagined historical or realistic sociopolitical context and attempted to trace fascist psychology and interpersonal behavior to their politico-historical roots. A literature of consciousness-raising from the beginning, it briefly came to encompass all genres after World War II. The volume of poetry and drama remained slim, however. Poems *were* written after Auschwitz, but Celan's "Todesfuge" (Death Fugue; 1948) is still the unsurpassed elegy to the Holocaust's dead. Brecht's example in the drama of the thirties, for instance in *Fear and Misery of the Third Reich* (1938), found followers after the war (Dürrenmatt, Hochhuth, Weiss). But the stark facts needed weighty, undramatic documentation; they were so brutal that they eradicated character or distorted it into caricature. The most effective dramatic representation, Weiss's *Investigation* (1965), an oratorio based on the 1964 Munich trials, resolved the dilemma by using the testimony itself. In an epic recitation inspired by Dante, speakers measured out the circles of a concentration-camp hell. Prose narratives (novel, novella, short story) were most frequently used to confront and come to terms with the Nazi past. The traditional novel of development and its variants, the family novel and the social novel, easily lent themselves to the portrayal of characters crushed by the weight of economic-social-political determinants. The genre's psychological perspective accommodated itself to probe the individual's share in collective guilt, motives of actions or, more usually, accommodation to the regime. During three generations of writers the narratives, stock of characters, motifs and situations remained remarkably stable. Yet there are distinct and interesting differences which permit us to gain insight into different generational perspectives and allow us to gauge the individual author's achievement.

The works of several exile writers may stand as examples of the first wave.[2] As a trained Marxist, Bertolt Brecht concentrates his attention on the economic-historical forces underlying fascism which the enlightened socialist must combat (cf. *The Avoidable Rise of Arturo Ui,* 1941).[3] By means of his alienation techniques, Brecht propels the reader into an analytical stance which frees him to discern the economic-historical forces determining the characters' relationships to each other. Ui and his henchmen, themselves petits bourgeoises and victims of the previous epoch, in the course of the play become victimizers of their former exploiters, the profit-seeking middle class. The unaware masses are forced to submit to their terror. The reader who has gained awareness of the workings of this system and its relationships is free to resist or take sides.

To create choices in a situation which almost overwhelms the individual is also the intent of another socialist, Anna Seghers, in her novel *The Seventh Cross* (1942).[4] Describing the flight of seven men from a concentration camp, it established the point of view of a proletarian resistance within Germany. The camp commandant has seven crosses erected, on which the recaptured men, dead or alive, are crucified. Aided by a Jewish doctor, the communist resistance and other sympathizers, a single escapee eludes his persecutors, thus demonstrating that the system can be overcome. The single empty cross triumphs over the victors and reminds them that their downfall has begun. Seghers's novel found several Eastern and a very few Western imitators (e.g., F. J. Degenhardt's novel *Zündschnüre* [Fuses], 1973). What provides her socialist protagonist (and presumably Brecht's enlightened reader) with the strength to refuse victimization despite overwhelming odds is his consciousness of and hence control over his historical situation and mission.

Although he was a socialist sympathizer with a pedagogical intent fully as strong as Brecht and Seghers, Thomas Mann in his *Doktor Faustus* (1947)[5] does not concern himself with arousing resistance or increasing awareness of socioeconomic root causes. He attempts

rather to reveal the psychological motivations of nationalism and fascism and to trace their historical roots—still alive in the provincial backgrounds shaping his two protagonists—back to the Reformation. Mann finds the personal psychological motivation to be a conscious, Nietzschean will to power in the musician Adrian Leverkühn, and an unconscious will to power in the novel's narrator, the high-school teacher Serenus Zeitblom. The artist's will to power is directed toward an expansion of the boundaries of art into archaic and utopian directions. He controls the newly gained artistic territories by his own authoritarian esthetic order, his new musical system of "master and servant notes." This dictatorial manipulator of spiritual orders cannot and may not love and finds it easy to transgress, for the sake of his art, against fellow humans (e.g., his role in the death of Rudi Schwertfeger). The prototypical bourgeois Serenus Zeitblom is ruled by an unconscious political will to power which appears, for instance, when he describes the German invasions of World War I as a spiritual wish of the German people to break through to union with the world "out of an isolation of which we are painfully conscious" (306). Western interpreters of Mann's novel have overlooked the fact that its two protagonists are petits bourgeoises. As Eastern critics have been well aware, their provincialism, obsessive orderliness, inhibitions and secrecy make them so.[6] With the portrayal of these figures, both alter egos of himself, Mann confronts proto-fascist elements in his own background and psyche. He does this with some sympathy for Adrian's struggle and with irony toward Zeitblom's mendacity. Critics have faulted Mann for not portraying the industrial, technological, economic aspects of fascism in their particularly twentieth-century form, an omission due to Leverkühn's and Zeitblom's restricted view of the world, not Mann's. Mann wanted to undermine this point of view from within; hence there was no place in the novel for these perspectives. Mann's was the first attempt by a German writer to unmask fascist attitudes in himself, and by so doing he set an example which has been followed by the best writers since.

▪ ▪ ▪

The defeat of the fascist regime left Germans with a heritage they had to come to terms with. While the population as a whole, after a brief period of formal de-Nazification and of discussion of "collective guilt," reduced the Nazi past to historical explanations and forgot it in the scramble for economic recovery (a process memorably satirized in the beginning of Günter Grass's *The Tin Drum,* book three), the writers of the Group 47 made *Vergangenheitsbewältigung* (coming to terms with the Nazi past) part of their literary program and the basis of their political commitment to a democratic future. Theirs was the second wave of anti-fascist literature of (generally young) participants for participants in the events of 1933–45. It remained a literature by intellectuals for intellectuals, since the population and the popular press derogated these efforts as *Nestbeschmutzung* (dirtying one's own nest). The attitude of Group 47 reflected, however, the Federal Republic program, which included compensatory payments to victims of National Socialism and summary reparations to the state of Israel. The German Democratic Republic refused responsibility for Nazi crimes with the excuse that it was a new socialist state without roots in the Nazi past. Its authors, if they dealt with the Nazi period at all, portrayed the proletarian resistance in the footsteps of Anna Seghers (cf. Ludwig Turek's *Die Freunde* [Friends], 1947) or used the old form of the novel of development to show a young person's path to socialism through a passing Nazi phase (Günter de Bruyn's *Der Hohlweg* [Blind Alley], 1963).

The task of unmasking the fascist in oneself is of course immeasurably harder for an actual (even if young) participant and a legally responsible adult. Group 47 authors, born between 1920 and 1930, were in exactly this situation. Therefore they often used some device to put distance between themselves, their protagonists and those events or characters which might prove too shocking and painful to themselves or their readers. Moreover, they give no direct psychological portrayal of an outright Nazi. Many authors of this generation follow the well-worn scheme memorably established by *The Tin Drum* (1959).[7] What was perceptively analytical parody in Grass's novel became serious melodramatic pattern in such internationally famous examples as Heinrich Böll's *The Clown* (1963)[8] or Siegfried Lenz's *The German Lesson* (1968).[9] A narrator and outsider of post-World War II society searches back in his childhood to find the reasons for his present predicament: a patient in a mental hospital (Oskar in *The Tin Drum*), an inmate of a prison for juvenile offenders (Siggi of *The German Lesson*), an alcoholic in an empty hotel room (Hans Schnier of *The Clown*). As actual events of the Nazi period are seen from the child's perspective, the protagonist is a victim by definition.

The generational struggle for power which propels Mann's *Doktor Faustus* appears in these works as the child's resistance to petit-bourgeois, Nazified parents, their obsession with law and order, their narrow-mindedness, pretenses and ambitions. The child's restricted perspective has the advantage of portraying the petit-bourgeois family from within, probing it as a breeding ground of fascism even while observing the effects of events produced by fascism (the early prosperity and profiteering, the war, bombing, invasion, et cetera). Moreover, because the adults in these novels do not take the child seriously, they unguardedly reveal themselves as they are. The child observer, angry eyes keen in behalf of his own survival, dispassionately notes the parents' behavior and attitudes. Because of the naïve perspective, the parents' motivations are easily accessible to the reader—their insecurity, lack of feeling, rationalizations, denial of reality, their lovelessness and their sweltering anger against each other, their complete inability to express themselves. The child observer uncritically inserts into this milieu the slogans of the age as they blared from radios, adds songs learned in school and in the Hitler Youth and mimics newscasts of rallies, invasions and retreats. Noting the reactions of family members, he shows how fascist propaganda and symbols penetrated the family, drugged the adults and helped them disguise their personal un-happiness and responsibilities. By these authors' accounts, dissatisfaction, grievance and anger of the lower middle class furnished fuel for national causes.

In every case the anger of his parents turns easily against the child, and he perceives them as murderous. Nearly at war's end, when the parents are cornered, they turn their children over: Siggi's policeman father relinquishes his son Klaus to the military police; Oskar is handed over to health authorities for extermination; Hans Schnier's mother turns her daughter Henriette over to the doomed air defense to "defend" the country. It is curious that exile authors, a generation older than Grass, Böll and Lenz, created the Nazi child or Hitler Youth who reports his not altogether cooperative parents to the authorities. Mann's Zeitblom, for instance, fears his sons might inform against him if they discover his loyalty to the "degenerate" artist Leverkühn; Brecht's teacher Furcke, in *Fear and Misery of the Third Reich*, suspects that his son is an informer. Writers grown up under Nazism suspect the parents of their protagonists of such betrayals.

The accusations of the generations against each other reflect the climate of the German bourgeois family, which is the microcosm of a nation at war against itself. The feelings, wishes and fears repressed and denied by each member within the family in the actual political situation of 1933–43 are projected outward onto national external or internal "enemies." When this is no longer possible because the enemy can retaliate, the family members turn against each other, and against that member whose position is weakest—either morally or physically. Critics have faulted the literature of *Vergangenheitsbewältigung* for restricting itself to trivial daily struggles and idylls of the family and almost ignoring concentration camps, slave labor and the role of technology and industry in the Nazi events. Critics overlook the fact that these books, like Mann's *Faustus,* attempt to explore Nazism from within the person and from his limited personal relationships. They do this in order to render in a humanly understandable way, for which humans can take responsibility, the inhuman, hardly graspable events. Precisely because many Germans have not taken responsibility for their attitudes, feelings and actions during the Nazi years, Grass, Böll, Lenz and also the dramatists Hochhuth, Weiss, Dorst and others see the Nazi mentality surviving into the present Federal Republic.

A variant of the child hero is the adult outsider, victim and resister who often appears in Böll's stories (cf. *Billiards at Half Past Nine,* 1959, and *Group Portrait with Lady,* 1971). He/she is not a strong figure but rather a "lamb" who opposes the "buffaloes": both these emblems appear in *Billiards.*[10] Lambs of varying shades of a gray come in families. At most, one exceptional buffalo grows up in their midst. By assigning evil to abstract forces (the emblematic buffaloes) or to caricatured anonymous functionaries or thugs whose motivations remain outside the reader's ken, Böll rescues the family from the charge of being the breeding ground of fascist attitudes. Good and evil in Böll's narratives, much as in a modern miracle play, oppose each other right through to the present and are juxtaposed with an astonishing simple-mindedness.

In all these works the point-of-view character with whom the reader identifies is either not really a Nazi, or not really responsible, or actually victimized. To the critical reader, this makes even works with a clear antifascist, didactic intent somewhat suspect. No doubt authors so close to the attitudes and feelings of the period needed to protect themselves and their readers from insights too painful and overwhelming. It is probably only in Grass's later novels *Cat and Mouse* (1961) and *Dog Years* (1963) that the protagonists or writer assume all responsibility for participation in Nazi events. But even Grass in *The Tin Drum* uses Oskar's grotesqueness to protect his reader from too close an identification. Considering that the literature of preoccupation with the Nazi past is large, it is surprising that not a single serious inner picture of an environment or of individuals who were convinced and committed Nazis exists in the Federal Republic from the participant generation.

Christa Wolf's *Kindheitsmuster* (Childhood Patterns; 1976)[11]—misleadingly translated as *A Model Childhood*—from the GDR is therefore all the more remarkable. Wolf's heroine, born in 1929, although a child through most of the period, does declare herself a Nazi and feels that, but for the grace of no opportunity, she might have done almost anything she was or-

dered to do. She had the petit-bourgeois background and training, enthusiasm for her leaders and a willingness to commit herself to the Cause. Wolf's protagonist-narrator writes her account from her present ideological perspective of a committed socialist, but she is too alienated from her childhood self, called "Nelly," to write about her except in the third-person singular. Therefore, as an adult she cannot muster a personal identity solid enough to explore and confront her past self in the first person, as "I." Rather, she addresses herself as "you" in a kind of self-interrogation. Only at the end of the book, when she has relived the child's experiences and worked through those patterns of feeling, thinking and behavior which made her susceptible to Nazism, does she emerge as a person who calls herself "I." Hers is now a self which has been tested in the crucible of an acid self-examination.

The narrator does not consider herself and the child Nelly an isolated case. Rather she takes herself and the child as typical of their generation. In so doing she sheds some light on why it was and is so difficult for even the most responsible members of that generation to confront their participation, willing or unwilling, in Nazi events. "Here was a whole generation and not just one," she said in an interview, "which was severely damaged in its psychic existence. And that is not repaired easily. It is not done with when you say, two years after the events, 'Damn it, Marx was right.'"[12] Hers is no self-pitying attempt to excuse that damaged generation, but rather an attempt to teach it to respond to personal and political situations "with appropriate feelings and responsibly." The narrator's self-interrogation extends easily to the reader, who is also included in the "you" of the writer's self-address. Because Nelly's training, experience and responses are so very ordinary (how fear, obedience, denial, selective attention, opportunism, forgetting are learned), the reader of her generation can easily substitute his/her own particulars for Nelly's and recognize underlying conditioned patterns in them. The conditioning Nelly received from her mother encouraged her to be dishonest, unaware of what she feels, to avoid feelings except those tolerable to adults and therefore to remain emotionally undifferentiated, illiterate, unable to express herself. This kind of child training in being nothing but the responses conditioned by the petit-bourgeois environment leaves an emotional vacuum in Nelly which makes her susceptible to ideological enthusiasms, to irresponsibility, to a merging into groups and a denial of herself as a person with an identity and judgment of her own. Wolf's attempt is to get to the heart of Nazism in its earliest day-by-day, ordinary childhood patterns. Her attempt is especially successful when she deals with seemingly trivial childhood incidents which yet have momentous consequences. One example of Wolf's close attention to significant psychological detail may stand for many.

Obedience, the unquestioning and blind following of what she has been told to do, is the child Nelly's quality most disliked by the adult narrator. An incident of sibling rivalry resulting from the parents' ignorant over-taxing of her emotional resources indicates the source of her obedience. Because her mother does not take seriously Nelly's jealousy of her brother, who was born in her fourth year, Nelly herself must control it. As an adult, she remembers a waking dream in which a goblin with a knife threatened her sleeping infant brother. In a fright Nelly got her mother, who calmed her and rewarded her concern. The mother failed to understand why the child, "although everything was all right" (19), broke into tears at this praise. The child half understood that her own jealousy caused the fantasy. ("How could it be all right if she was not good?" she asked herself.) She needed her mother's help, not to save her brother, but to control her jealousy. As a consequence of the mother's failure to understand, Nelly's guilt about her feelings of jealousy and anger grew, and with the guilt, anger in turn increased. Because unconsciously she wished it so strongly, she became terrified of anything's happening to her brother. When finally, in an argument, she actually hurt him, the mother's reproof ("It'll be your fault if his arm remains stiff" [27]) was devastating because it confirmed her own worst fears about herself. As a consequence, Nelly does not learn to distinguish between wishes, fantasy and reality. On the contrary, she learns that murderous wishes can actually have disastrous effects. She does not learn that wishing, thinking or feeling something does not inevitably lead to action. Therefore, like her parents, she must control her feelings and thoughts by repressing or denying them. Hence she loses the knowledge of her feelings and the capacity to deal with them. Moreover, obedience that assigns responsibility for actions and feelings alike to someone in authority becomes easy for her. The intergenerational chain of obedience to authority rests on an intergenerational failure to acknowledge and deal with feeling.

The incident of sibling jealousy remains the paradigm for parental and societal attitudes to children's feelings. The adults in Nelly's environment have no empathy at all for children, who are supposed to be innocent and good. Nelly learns early that she has a "right face," a "soft, dear, obedient face" (20), which is the face the adults want to see. The face of sadness, unhappiness, anger is one "the child of a happy family does not learn, and in exchange the child takes on the difficult task of protecting her parents. Protect them from un-

happiness and shame" (33). As a consequence, the child's inner life is stunted. The child is not allowed to differentiate herself emotionally from her parents: "The everyday words predominate: eat, drink and take and please and thank you. Look, listen, smell, taste, touch, one's healthy five senses which better be in good shape. I believe that five pounds of beef make a good soup if you don't take too much water. Everything else is idle fantasy" (33). As the very tone of the quotation implies, this kind of petit-bourgeois realism hides anger and resentment. On the parents' side it implies that they have not been allowed the luxury of feeling, thought and imagination and do not allow their children to have them either. This realism forces Nelly either to deny as much feeling as her parents or to develop a secret life of her own at the price of dishonesty. As the choice presents itself to her, she realizes that she loses in any case: "Yes, to be rid of one's own soul, to look into mother's eyes undauntedly when she sits at your bedside at night and wants to know if you have told her everything: 'You know, don't you, that you are to tell me everything every night?' To lie shamelessly: Everything, yes! And to know in your mind: Never again everything. Because it is impossible" (22). Moreover, since the unacknowledged feelings, fantasies and thoughts must remain unconscious, Nelly becomes isolated and alone (which in turn she must not acknowledge). She cannot develop distinctions between feelings, fantasies and thoughts, hence acquires no language in which to speak of them. All the way through her account, the silence in her family is deafening.

Nelly is very much aware that her adult self stems from having been forced to deny too much too early, from having been taught too many techniques of rationalization, self-deception and dishonesty. The book is less successful in integrating facts and figures of the Nazi period into the narrative of childhood events and conditioning, and least convincing in its critique of fascist and imperialist tendencies of the present. In accordance with GDR dogma, Wolf attributes Vietnams and black ghettos only to the West. What is new and courageous in *Kindheitsmuster* is Wolf's attempt to confront the fascist in herself in all her banality (Hannah Arendt's "banality of evil" comes home here with a vengeance).[13]

▪ ▪ ▪

The postwar generation (authors born between 1940 and 1955) represents the third wave of antifascist writing and shows that literature is by no means finished with this theme. Having grown up during the period of recovery and the economic miracle after 1945, this generation observes its former Nazi parents in the late 1970s with feelings of embarrassed pity, distaste and total alienation. The narratives of these writers begin with the actual dying or death of the petit-bourgeois parent, in the present of the 1970s. The writer, who is himself becoming a parent or assuming a parental role toward a child, is forced to come to terms with his parent, and with that parent's heritage in himself. The writers restrict themselves to the lives of their parents; their own childhoods and present situations only appear in order to reveal something significant about the parent. A gulf created mostly by differences in class and education separates sons from parents. The parents came from the lower middle class and moved into the middle class during the Nazi years; the sons are middle-class. While the parents barely had a primary-school education, the sons are university-educated. The sons owe a debt of gratitude but find this hard to acknowledge, either by approval or imitation, since they like neither the way their parents moved up the social ladder nor the persons the parents became in so doing. Peter Handke's writer-protagonist in *Wunschloses Unglück* (*A Sorrow Beyond Dreams;* 1972)[14] sees his mother's life as a long-drawn-out death. The same applies to Paul Kersten in *Der alltägliche Tod meines Vaters* (My Father's Everyday Death; 1978)[15] and to Peter Henisch in *Die kleine Figur meines Vaters* (The Small Stature of My Father; 1975).[16] All through the stories these parents are dying—the mother in Handke's story by suicide following a depressive illness; the father in Kersten's by cancer; the father in Henisch's from cirrhosis of the liver. Handke's leitmotiv description of the mother's life—"she was, became, became nothing"—applies equally to the fathers of the other two. The price of bourgeois success was loss of personal identity. As a child and young woman, Handke's mother figure rebels against her lower-middle-class female destiny of becoming "nothing." She leaves home to become "something"—namely, manager of a small resort hotel. During the early Nazi years she comes into her own and feels herself "somebody," as the pleasant radio voice of Hitler buoys her spirit. The illusion of personal happiness, community and national greatness is quickly destroyed. Through war, a marriage of convenience and children she has become nothing at thirty. Later, as her growing son shares his reading with her, she attempts to become literate and expressive when she learns to identify with literary characters. But vicarious experience fails to free her. Neither does psychic illness or psychotherapy. According to her son, her self-chosen death frees her from nothingness.

Despite her lack of personhood, the mother figure is likable. Paul Kersten's father figure, a petty army officer during the Nazi period and an insurance controller afterward, is not. A bundle of prejudices, vengefulness, incompetence and submission, he leads an existence entirely without salvation, a self-poisoned, hellish life of utter banality. There is nothing left of him but his long dying, his son's embarrassed obligatory visits and a pity moderated by alienation.

While the Handke and Kersten parents, unwitting fellow travelers, hardly know what they are about, scarcely differentiated as they are from their social class, Peter Henisch's father, a photographer, artist and self-defined "tightrope walker," knows exactly who he is. Grown up in an orphanage, mistreated by a stepfather for being Czech or Jewish or both, small in stature like Goebbels, with only a primary-school education, he uses the Anschluss, the Nazis and the war to get ahead as a press photographer. The camera lens serves as a defense against others and a means to success. He judges everything—rallies, camps, ghettos, war, battles, invasions, retreats—in terms of photogenic potential. A complete opportunist, when the Nazis are no longer photogenic he turns communist. When the Austrian communists no longer provide photogenic spectacles, he becomes a social democrat.

Handke's and Kersten's parents are neither negative nor positive. Their children must come to terms with the fact that they were nothing except their social backgrounds—living clichés, so to speak. That is why Handke briefly experiences the death of his mother as her personal triumph, a liberation which makes her into someone more than the clichés she lived. His difficulty and Kersten's, as children of such parents, is precisely that very emptiness, that lack of personal identity and authenticity. By the act of writing, both attempt to fill this emptiness, to make the parent into someone who is at least a "case," someone who gives the artist son a pretext to overcome his own inexpressiveness (*Sprachlosigkeit*), emptiness and alienation. The theme of the twentieth-century writer's alienation and difficulty with language appears in these works as related to the parents' history. Making works of art is necessary to fill that emptiness and give expression to the *horror vacui*. Handke ends on a note ("I'll write more precisely about it later") indicating that the protagonist has not succeeded in overcoming his horror of empty lives. Both writers attempt to give an esthetic resolution to a psychological, political and moral problem.

Henisch's difficulty as a son is that his father has an unmistakable personality, that of the Nazi opportunist, and that the family recognizes the son as being like his father. He is faced with the task of becoming different. Though he becomes a writer rather than a photographer, the father insists on their likeness and calls them both "tightrope walkers." Hence the son must distance himself from the father. He does so by calling himself Jewish and by trying not to be an opportunist. Nevertheless he cannot convince himself that he is different. After all, he can afford to call himself Jewish now—he can afford not to be an opportunist because the times are better. At the end of the novel the son takes the fact that a daughter is born to him as a sign that he has begun to live his own life, an unsatisfactory ending at best. Although the novel ends on an optimistic note, the reader wonders what will happen if the times grow bad.

The reader of the books produced by these three waves of preoccupation with Nazism must ask himself, judging the books of the last wave, if the painful task taken on by writers of the German-speaking countries over the past fifty years has resulted in no more than a sociological explanation or rationalization of the phenomenon (Henisch) or in merely keeping a record of the way in which human beings can empty their lives of any personal content (Handke). If this is so, then the turning by many contemporary writers of the Federal Republic to the literature of the nineteenth century may be more than a simple escape into idylls or esthetic safety. This turn toward older literary models may also be a search for values to fill the moral void which is the heritage of writers of the present. We may hope that in their return to narrative forms of the nineteenth century, these authors will rediscover Thomas Mann's still most insightful works on Nazism. Through his work and the life he led, he has much to teach them. No literary theme shows as clearly as the confrontation with Nazism that a mere esthetic resolution will not do and that the life of letters and the satisfying, meaningful life alike demand a moral commitment.

Ursula Mahlendorf, Autumn 1981

1 Restrictions of space and time do not allow me to give a detailed and complete account of this important theme. The present essay is merely intended as a basis for further work and discussion. I have limited myself to works relatively well known to an English-speaking audience. Presently available critical studies mostly concern themselves with the period immediately following World War II: e.g., *Gegenwartsliteratur und Drittes Reich* [Contemporary Literature and the Third Reich], Hans Wagener, ed., Stuttgart, Reclam, 1977.

2 The historical (cf. Bergengruen's *Der Großtyrann und das Gericht* [A Matter of Conscience], 1935) and allegorical novels (e.g., Ernst Jünger's *Auf den Marmorklippen* [On the Marble Cliffs], 1939) of the "inner emigration," although antitotalitarian in intent, are themselves so permeated by nationalist and fascist attitudes that we cannot call them anti-fascist.

3 Bertolt Brecht, *Gesammelte Werke* [Collected Works], vol. 4, Frankfurt a.M., Suhrkamp, 1967, pp. 1719–1839.

4 Anna Seghers, *Das siebte Kreuz,* Mexico City, 1942.

5 Thomas Mann, *Doktor Faustus: The Life of the German Composer Adrian Leverkühn as Told by a Friend,* H. T. Lowe-Porter, tr., New York, Knopf, 1948. Quotation from this edition.

6 Eugen Barbu and Andrei Ian Deleanu, "Serenus Zeitblom," *Sinn und Form,* Special Thomas Mann Issue (1965), pp. 134–43. Ad-

orno's later equation of the petit-bourgeois mentality with fascism (cf. *The Authoritarian Personality,* 1950) makes its first literary appearance in Mann's *Faustus.*

7 Günter Grass, *The Tin Drum,* Ralph Manheim, tr., New York, Random House, 1961.

8 Heinrich Böll, *The Clown,* Leila Vennewitz, tr., New York, McGraw-Hill, 1971.

9 Siegfried Lenz, *The German Lesson,* Ernst Kaiser and Eithne Wilkins, trs., New York, Hill & Wang, 1971.

10 Heinrich Böll, *Billiards at Half-Past Nine,* Leila Vennewitz, tr., New York, McGraw-Hill, 1962.

11 Christa Wolf, *Kindheitsmuster,* Berlin/Darmstadt, Aufbau/-Luchterhand, 1976/1977. Translations from this work are my own. The English version, *A Model Childhood,* translated by Ursule Molinaro and Hedwig Rappolt, was published in New York by Farrar, Straus & Giroux in 1980.

12 *Sinn und Form,* 1976, no. 4, pp. 861–88.

13 Hannah Arendt, *Eichmann in Jerusalem: A Report on the Banality of Evil,* New York, Viking, 1963.

14 Peter Handke, *Wunschloses Unglück,* Salzburg, Residenz, 1972.

15 Paul Kersten, *Der alltägliche Tod meines Vaters,* Cologne, Kiepenheuer & Witsch, 1978.

16 Peter Henisch, *Die kleine Figur meines Vaters,* Frankfurt a.M., S. Fischer, 1975.

Disunitedly United: Literary Life in Germany

The business of literature today threatens to obstruct our view of the essentials of literary life, namely the author of a work of literature and his readers. Both the author and his readers share a desire to be left alone and undisturbed in order to concentrate—the former on writing, the latter on reading.

It is true that a new element of literary life begins with the process of writing every fictional text, since this writing is directed toward the publication and circulation of the completed work—that is, toward literary communication. However, the actual writing usually takes place in the antechamber of public literary life, just as reading generally calls for privacy.

I point all this out in advance, for in what follows there will be very little mention of private literary life; instead, attention will be focused almost exclusively on public literary life in a politically unified Germany. The promotion of literature and of authors by the state will be omitted from consideration, because it influences literary life only indirectly. The situation of authors in Germany, of publishing, of book-selling and of libraries, as well as of literary initiatives and institutions, will be accentuated.

In Germany, and in German-speaking areas generally, cultural life was decentrally organized until the second half of the nineteenth century as a result of the pre-vailing multistate system, and this remained so after the founding of the German Reich in 1871. The federalist structure of the Federal Republic (West Germany, the FRG) and its deliberate avoidance of a central ministry of culture prevent developments toward cultural cen-tralism. In German-speaking areas, literary life in partic-ular has never been oriented toward a single city, just as literature in the German language has never re-mained confined within specific national borders. Fic-tional literature has many locations in German-speaking areas, regional centers with supraregional influence: for example, Leipzig, Munich, Hamburg, Frankfurt am Main, and Berlin in Germany; Vienna in Austria; Zürich and Basel in Switzerland; and, at one time, the Czech capital, Prague.

Of course, such regional centers of literary life cor-respond with one another. And even during the four decades when there were two German states, each of which attempted to ostracize the other, a variety of rela-tions between the two literary societies could be ob-served. These played their part in ensuring that divisive thought did not become so firmly established that it could develop permanence. Although it was possible to observe an independent literary life in both states, it was the authors in particular who—far earlier than cultural policies—held on to the shared aspects of German-speaking literature and who continued or initiated dis-course with their colleagues in the other German state.

Those authors who could no longer remain in the Democratic Republic (East Germany, the GDR) after the expatriation of Wolf Biermann, and who had been obliged to find a new focal point for their lives in West Berlin or the FRG, played a leading role in this dis-course. But numerous authors from West Germany and West Berlin, prompted by a desire to manifest the com-mon aspects of language and literature, also visited col-leagues in their homes in the GDR regularly from the seventies onward, often reading there from literary works and discussing and debating literary matters with other GDR authors. For years this was a one-way street, since authors from the GDR were seldom permitted to travel to West Germany or West Berlin; but in the mideighties, cooperation also developed within the public sphere: the departments of literature at the Acad-emy of the Arts in West Berlin and at the GDR Academy of the Arts, for example, invited their respective mem-bers to public and semipublic meetings or even accept-ed certain individuals as members of the literary sec-tions in their respective institutions.

After the political unification of Germany, little of this will for cooperation remained—at least for the mo-ment. Suddenly, authors from both parts of Germany

Christa Wolf (*AP/Wide World Photos*)

overaccentuated all their past experiences, verifying a divergence which certainly had taken place—despite all the links forged—and recalling every possible divisive element. Some observers of this development trace it back to the authors' loss of social importance in a uni-fied Germany. Henning Ritter, for example, commented as follows on the fifth anniversary of reunification: "A divided Germany, and this has only emerged in retro-spect and through our experiences with reunification, was a paradise for politicized literati. In the West, they were always called upon to act as mediators at home, to forge links, to practice and to preach understanding for the other side, and they could provide that other side with a halo without having to assume liability for their praise." Moreover, continued Ritter, "Those GDR authors who were not strictly conformist, without being dissidents, enjoyed a double kind of attention. They were in the not always comfortable yet flattering posi-tion of never supporting their own side in an argument, a characteristic which the English attribute to the liber-al." The same commentator assumes that "the division, which was considered insurmountable, . . . was also welcome to the German character type with his tenden-cy toward ineffective commitment and the idealism of eternal problem-solving."[1] This reproach is directed at authors such as Günter Grass in the West and Christa

Wolf in the East. It seeks to expose the ridiculousness of a standpoint which enabled these authors to speak, in November 1989, of the possibility of a "socialist alternative to the Federal Republic," of a democratically legitimized GDR, a position which was taken up in the GDR by many authors, including Volker Braun, Stefan Heym, and Christa Wolf. A similar position was expressed in the appeal "Für unser Land" (For Our Country) seconded by Günter Grass, Günter Wallraff, and others in West Germany and by Max Frisch in Switzerland.[2]

The events of 3 October 1990 refuted such thinking once and for all. However, in their delight over their victory, apologists of a rapid unification of the two German states ought not to forget or attempt to obliterate the fact that precisely such authors as Stefan Heym, Stephan Hermlin, Christa Wolf, Christoph Hein, Helga Königsdorf, Heiner Müller, and Volker Braun had, both inside and from within the GDR during the second half of the eighties, contributed to the creation of preconditions for a liberalization of the East German government's cultural politics and had helped to give the wider population courage to alter their social conditions by means of their poems, novels, stories, plays, essays, and public speeches.

Authors in the GDR had this kind of influence, which should not be underestimated, for—as Rolf Schneider pointedly remarks—in the state "with the most idiotic journalistic system in the whole of the Eastern bloc . . . the fine arts were granted a function as a substitute and a safety valve. If all went well, people found out from films, the theater, and contemporary novels the information which the newspapers and the electronic media withheld from them."[3]

As early as the summer of 1990—that is, before the unification of Germany—leading influential figures from the cultural sections of national daily and weekly newspapers in the Federal Republic used a then recently published story by Christa Wolf as an occasion to insinuate that this author, highly esteemed in both German states, and a large number of other GDR authors, had dedicated themselves to the "esthetics of political convictions," had been "state poets" whose "rank as authors was much overestimated."[4] Christa Wolf's story reports on the surveillance that was conducted on her by the Ministry of State Security (Stasi) and was published under the title *Was bleibt* (Eng. *What Remains*) in May 1990 by the Luchterhand-Literaturverlag of Hamburg and Zürich.

Quite correctly, Reinhard Baumgart maintained of this "new German literary dispute" that it "was hardly a matter of those one hundred pages of prose, and not

even the settling of a score with Christa Wolf." Far more, "it was a question of the relationship between society and literature, between morality and esthetics, and so it also concerned the former literature of the FRG." Wolf, Baumgart went on to point out, "was and is the most representative figure of a position which is difficult to tie down to a single concept and to indivisible moral standards. She represents that both halfhearted yet determined form of dissent in which part of oneself was still sitting on the government benches as a result of unabandoned sympathy for the maltreated, wasted project of socialism, while the other part, possibly even for the same reasons, stood in the camp of those opposed to the system." Baumgart reduces these critics from the camp of "uniform and unambiguous thought" that was established in the winter of 1990/91 to a single common denominator when he adds ironically: "A totalitarian system, at least if the total morality of its rigorous observers has its way, should provoke total opposition."[5]

The "new German literary dispute" was replaced by the "Stasi debate," which had refused to die down even by the end of 1995. With justification, not only those authors who were compelled to leave the GDR critically questioned the attitude of colleagues who remained, and by the end of 1991, without justification, they had received scarcely any reply. The answers came only after Wolf Biermann, in a speech made upon receiving the prestigious Georg Büchner Prize in the autumn of 1991, had exposed the young poet Sascha Anderson—an author who had significantly shaped the art scene in the East Berlin district of Prenzlauer Berg during the first half of the eighties and who had lived as a dissident in West Berlin from the mideighties onward, founding a small literary publishing house in East Berlin immediately after the *Wende* (the political changes of 1989–91)—as an "unofficial collaborator" (*inoffizieller Mitarbeiter* or IM), and after the files from the Ministry of State Security were made accessible to the public. These answers caused many old friendships and long-lasting relationships to disintegrate. The author Hans Joachim Schädlich discovered that his own brother had been commissioned by the Stasi to spy on him, and the poet Reiner Kunze had been spied upon by his best friend, also at the urging of the Stasi. Jürgen Fuchs, who had spent nine months in appalling Stasi detention both because of his public protest after Biermann's expatriation and because of his own intention to publish in West Germany and who was afterward deported to West Berlin, maintained that Stasi activities had produced an "Auschwitz in the soul."[6]

The disappointment and bitter anger about "this kind of betrayal and poisoning" (Jürgen Fuchs) usually remain, even when the informers neither consciously nor unconsciously damaged their colleagues by what they reported to the Stasi, or even when they could claim that they had actually helped their colleagues through their cooperation with the Stasi. The psychologist Ursula Plog explains this, saying that the power of the state in the GDR "[had] taken control of its citizens' innermost being to an extent never seen before under any regime. When the GDR collapsed, there were no pictures of mass graves and concentration camps, but hundreds of thousands of destroyed souls."[7]

The fact that such leading literary figures of the GDR as Christa Wolf and Heiner Müller, of all people, were involved with the Stasi is a case of macabre dialectics: as IM's, they were initially on the side of the perpetrators, but subsequently became victims of the Stasi. The exposure, in the summer of 1995, of the author Monika Maron's brief activity as a Stasi informer at the end of the seventies and of her subsequent persecution by the Stasi was at last taken as a stimulus for some of the opinion makers who had instigated the "new German literary dispute" in 1990 to revise and correct themselves even more clearly than they had already done in 1993 in regard to the discussions over Heiner Müller. Frank Schirrmacher, for example, had warned in January 1993 against "an overhasty condemnation of authors" and called for a far more vital "political and esthetic discourse";[8] in August 1995 he took a position entirely different from that of 1990, writing: "No one has reproached the important authors of the GDR for the way they acted under the pressure of dictatorship—most of them as young people. In the field of literature, the essential point is who supported a dictatorship intellectually, and then in most cases—against their better judgment—to the very end. Monika Maron never did this."[9] One author who did was Hermann Kant, president of the GDR Writers Union from 1978 until the end of 1989, whose Stasi files were published in the autumn of 1995.[10]

It seems that the time is past when, as with Wolf Biermann's stance toward Sascha Anderson in 1991, an author exposed as a Stasi informer is denied the status of an artist because of his moral failure. What is still necessary is precise knowledge of the deeds for which authors in both German states and the associations or unions representing their interests must accept the responsibility. A prerequisite to this is publicity, and those who do not have the strength for this, because they have been debilitated by the injury done to them, should enable those with the strength to act tolerantly. The social aim must be reconciliation, and this applies to German literary life as well. Reconciliation does not mean forgetting; it is based upon a knowledge of what was and what is. The alternatives cannot therefore be "either lay the matter to rest or continue to dispute." Disputes cannot be avoided, but a climate of tolerance is necessary. Of course, this is an aim which can be achieved only up to a point. The psychologist Ursula Plog remarks: "Forgiveness heals. One aspect of forgiveness is that a person who has betrayed another does not gloss over it, does not pacify, but acknowledges that he is guilty of betrayal. And that someone else who has been betrayed says, 'I can forgive you.' Then they can begin to talk to each other again." Laconically, Plog adds, "Up until now, I don't know of any case where that has happened."[11]

As yet, there is no known case in German literary life which would offer hope for any improvement in the situation, although "history workshops" organized by the Verband deutscher Schriftsteller (the union organization of German authors) and the German PEN Center (East) or the Enquete Commission of the German Bundestag for the "Reappraisal of History and the Consequences of the SED [Social Unity Party] Dictatorship in Germany" have made efforts at clarification. Our aim should be to learn how to have normal dealings with each other, or at least to live and let live and not create new divisions which are simply a political or esthetic reversal of those which went before. In the literary field, this ought to be realistic if one recalls "that a process of emancipation from the conditions laid down by cultural policy is characteristic of GDR literature at its best, a process which could not be prevented by the measures of the Ministry of State Security." This is a quotation from The Mechtenberg's "Expertise," a report commissioned by and presented to the Enquete Commission. It closes with the following comments:

> The painful but artistically productive conflict between literature and doctrine which characterized the striving for autonomy not only produced works of literary merit, but also contributed to an intellectual development which was ultimately directed toward overcoming the repressive system. As a result, this striving for autonomy must be classed as an element of intellectual resistance, as opposed to a widespread tendency, following the discussion of Stasi influence on literature, to deny the authors who remained in the GDR their credibility and to classify their works as perpetuating the system.
>
> This evaluation means that GDR literature must now be integrated into the entire concept of German postwar literature, and that a corresponding educational policy must be adopted. It should take into account that the concept of "socialist national literature" and a centralized teaching curriculum determined by cultural politics ne-

glected to consider authors, works, conflicts, and developments significant to the process of emancipation. Without a concept of educational policy integrating certain aspects of GDR literature, a comprehensive reappraisal of the GDR dictatorship will prove very difficult, and an essential aid to the necessary intellectual convergence of the two parts of Germany will be lacking.[12]

This description of the task implies that a solution is still overdue. In fact, the beginning of Christa Wolf's *Kindheitsmuster* (Eng. *A Model Childhood*) might serve as a motto describing present literary life in Germany: "What is past is not dead; it is not even past. We cut ourselves off from it; we pretend to be strangers."[13] Many authors, like most Germans after the liberation from the National Socialist dictatorship in 1945, faced the dilemma "whether to remain silent or to live in the third person"[14] after the failure of the attempt at a socialist society. This applies not only to GDR authors, but also and in equal measure to many authors from West Germany, who may have rejected the GDR due to its Stalinist basis but who had hoped for an alternative to capitalist society.

Literary Germany seems to have been almost paralyzed in its attempt to unite the authors' organizations and institutions in the two former German states. It proved possible to fuse the two academies of the arts only by the skin of their teeth; members of the Western academy resigned in anger because they could not work, and did not want to work, under the same roof as certain colleagues from the Eastern academy. It was suggested to members of the academy in the East—if they did not, like Hermann Kant, for example, give up of their own accord any claim to membership in the unified academy—that they leave. In all these cases, the reasons were either involvement with the Stasi or a close relationship with leading organs of the SED (the Social Unity Party of [East] Germany) or of the GDR government.

The creation of a joint German PEN Club is proving a great deal more complicated than the unification of the two academies. In arguments about the correct approach, the Stasi IM activities of a relatively large number of members of the PEN Center of the GDR are again playing a significant part, but the fundamental objection, formulated by Hans Joachim Schädlich, as a representative of the PEN Center of the Federal Republic, is more important: "Essentially, the GDR-PEN, which gave itself the pleasant-sounding, prestigious name German PEN Center (East), was not a national center of the International PEN but rather a state organization of the GDR. This organization was financed by the GDR state budget, and was controlled by an internal SED group. The charter of the International PEN was withheld from the members of this organization; they were not intended or permitted to sign their names to the aims of the PEN charter, and in fact they were not members of PEN. The state organization called GDR-PEN became famous chiefly for its transgression of the principles of the International PEN; it grossly misused the name PEN and was in fact no more than an instrument of cultural policy under the GDR dictatorship."[15]

Countering the objection that the German PEN Center (East) with its headquarters in Berlin, which evolved from the PEN Center of the GDR, may be the latter's legal but not spiritual successor and therefore has "equal validity and equal rights" to the PEN Center of the Federal Republic, Schädlich points out: "The renaming of the GDR-PEN, the resignation of several particularly guilty functionaries (including the government official responsible for censorship), and the accepted membership of blameless authors cannot wipe out the history of this organization. Quite the contrary, that history is made all the more visible in the form of SED literary functionaries, Stasi informers, and leading figures of the past who still belong to the group. The unification of the GDR-PEN with the PEN Center of the Federal Republic would be a cynical mockery of all those PEN members who have committed and who continue to commit themselves to the aims of the PEN charter in both word and deed."[16]

Not all the members of the PEN Center of the Federal Republic share this viewpoint, which is held by a majority of the current presidium in Darmstadt. For example, eighty members of the Darmstadt PEN, who have belonged to both German PEN Clubs since the summer of 1995 in solidarity with the members of the Berlin PEN, adopted the following position, outlined by Klaus Staeck: "What can no longer be tolerated is the claim of an untiring moral committee to exclusive representation—by their own grace alone—and to final jurisdiction over all discourse. In the long term, it is impossible to accept that a group of fewer than twenty people should continue to determine in such an authoritarian fashion, by means of their connections in the media, what may or may not be the subject of discussion and debate in this country. What is especially shocking is the growing moral severity of those ex-GDR citizens among the accusers, some of whom might have reason to examine the black marks in their own biographies. In the currently prevailing climate of denunciation and suspicion, a serious discussion is hardly possible."[17] Staeck is referring to a number of authors in the Darmstadt PEN who were obliged to leave the GDR during the seventies and eighties. In particular, these include Günter Kunert, Sarah Kirsch, Jürgen Fuchs, Hans Joachim Schädlich, and Reiner Kunze.

By contrast, Jochen Laabs, the General Secretary of the German PEN Center (East), appears more conciliatory.

> There is no doubt that the GDR-PEN has some black marks against its name; but it was not the dark, horrid monster it is now made out to be. There is no question that the state and the party repeatedly interfered, and PEN officials certainly offered their assistance; but the state did not get a great deal out of it. The two attempts to found a party group came to nothing. The withholding of the charter was attempted with deceit and cunning, but in the long term it could not be imposed. PEN maintained the practice of secret elections for new members. All attempts to revoke this failed. Most of the acclaimed, genuinely socialist authors, of whom the party made considerable use, were not admitted to PEN. The state doctrine's pressure to take over the organization met with the literary, ethical, and moral claims of PEN, which had not been reduced to nothing. Not a single member, however much he or she displeased the party, was thrown out. PEN was an institution within a dictatorial system, but it did not become an instrument of dictatorship. It paid the price and led a peripheral existence. But the assertion that the East PEN is the same thing as the GDR-PEN is either a demonstration of ignorance or a deliberate attempt at defamation. Of the 144 current members of East PEN, 73 have joined since 1990. On the other hand, a number of members who would have had no reason to do so during the GDR era have now left PEN. Of the present presidium, I am the only one who was a member of the GDR-PEN at all.[18]

Clearly hurt, Laabs asks others to consider: "Some people are setting to work with dual standards, people who have left behind not only the GDR and its PEN, but also their seat at party meetings. They not only blame members of the new East PEN for things for which they themselves were responsible as former GDR-PEN members, but above all they lay claim to a considerable skill in transforming themselves, denying such skill to those who remained behind in the East. They pin the attitudes of that time not only on their opponents and tormentors of ten or fifteen years ago, but on almost all other Easterners as well."[19]

Jürgen Fuchs took the consequential next step when, at the beginning of 1995, he joined the PEN Center of German-Speaking Writers Abroad, headquartered in London—i.e., the "Exile PEN" founded sixty years ago by authors driven out of Nazi Germany. The two German PEN Clubs appear to have taken to heart Heiner Müller's "Plea for Dissent," which appeared in *Neues Deutschland* at the end of 1989: "What is needed now is not unity but the full expression of existing differences, not discipline but dissent, not the closing of ranks but an openness to the movement of contradictions, and not only in our country."[20] The decisive aspect for Müller—and this should be understood in the sense of *the principle of hope*—is that "finally, the mute will speak and the stones give voice."[21]

Things do not look any better within the authors' associations of the Federal Republic of Germany. There it is merely quieter, because the cultural-political importance of the authors' associations in the old FRG had already rapidly deteriorated during the eighties, just as that of the GDR associations collapsed along with the country. It is true that several competing organizations of authors exist in Germany, but for years they have all been so concerned with their own problems that they could not—either alongside one another or in true cooperation—forcibly represent the interests of their members in the face of the cultural policies of the federal government (the cultural departments of the Home Office and the Foreign Office), of the individual state governments, and of the respective local governments. And today, the rights of authors in the media industry are not as convincingly defended and developed as they were during the seventies in West Germany, when model contracts were fought for, social and health insurance for authors was established, and the right to a say in the decision-making processes of literary policy was obtained. Examples include the "Verband deutscher Schriftsteller" (Association of German Authors or VS) within the industrial media union (VS/IG Medien), the "Freier Deutscher Autorenverband" (Free German Authors Union or FDA)—the corporate organization with the most members—and the "Bundesverband deutscher Autoren" (Federal Union of German Authors or BA). In addition, there are other nationwide organizations such as the "Autorenkreis der Bundesrepublik" (Authors Circle of the Federal Republic), which does not exist as a legal entity but, like the "Gruppe 47" which was originally established around Hans Werner Richter, is a loose affiliation organized around the Berlin author Sigmar Schollack. Since the beginning of the nineties, this group has attempted to influence literary politics and esthetics nationwide.

On a regional level, there are numerous additional associations of authors in all the federal states, including the new ones, and these shape literary life with varying levels of effectiveness. The relative lack of significance of these authors' associations in cultural life may also be explained by the fact that writers have always been "loners," and even in 1970 Heinrich Böll's phrase "the union of loners"[22] was more an invocation than a description.

In a 1995 anthology titled "From Abraham to Zwerenz" and including contributions from over a hundred authors, mostly from the new federal states, the majority of contributors responded with considerable skepticism if not complete negativity to the question of how they rated solidarity among German authors. Fritz Rudolf Fries answered laconically, "There are friendships, mutual 'schools of admiration,' but no solidarity."[23] Peter Hacks seconded this: "Solidarity among authors of the same political tendency is, as it always has been, excellent."[24] Heiner Müller termed author unity "limited,"[25] Stephan Hermlin claimed that "there isn't any,"[26] and Hans Christoph Buch toned things down a bit by attributing the lack of solidarity among writers to "the lasting crisis of the VS, which has now taken over PEN."[27] Rolf Schneider, for whom writers are "individualists, a fact determined by their profession," comforted himself and his colleagues by remarking, "Where a large measure of solidarity emerges among authors, there must be great hardship, which I certainly do not wish to conjure up simply in order to arrive at greater solidarity."[28] By contrast, Günter Kunert's answer was more fundamental:

Solidarity exists only among those with the same attitudes. This means that an author who considers me a deviant from the mass of conformists classes me—and by "me" I mean anyone—as an opponent, an enemy, or the like. This means that in Germany, where democracy is only shallowly rooted in people's minds, intellectuals and writers, even when they consider themselves liberal, are strict dividers. The expression of a different notion of politics is already an offense against "solidarity." The German intellectual and writer, always on his high horse, cannot bear it if anyone does not pay due respect. But that implies a lack of democratic understanding, to which a contrary opinion appears suspect and worth fighting about (sometimes even worth destroying). In a word: even supposedly worldly-wise authors and intellectuals are not capable of valuing contradiction as an element of democratic conduct; they always view it as a personal attack against the opinion they themselves represent. That is the reason why there are no intellectual debates in Germany which could illuminate our path even a little.[29]

The lack of solidarity among writers is even more regrettable, since, in a unified Germany, far-reaching changes in the nature of publishing and bookselling, in radio and in television, and also in the library system are in need of correction by means of such a counterweight.

In the anthology quoted above, only a few authors make positive comments regarding their opportunities for publishing new manuscripts. It is true that Hans Christoph Buch from the West and Jan Faktor from the East see their professional position after the unification of Germany as at least no worse than before. The same goes for writers such as Fritz Rudolf Fries and Günter Kunert. Nevertheless, most contributors to the anthology complain of poor publishing opportunities. Walther Petri, who brought out several volumes of poetry and a number of children's books in the GDR and whose *DerdiedasBuch,* designed in collaboration with Egberth Herfurth, was awarded a prize as the most attractive book in the FRG during 1991, is representative of many of the contributors.

The hopes and expectations linked with political change meant that I personally hoped to realize all my publishing intentions—that is, no longer limiting myself to poetry and essays, but to take up and write about everyday political themes directly for radio and television to a greater extent than had been possible in the GDR era. But nothing came of this. There were and there are only "occupied chairs" and, at the core, the bitter experience that as an East German author I have not received the kind of training that would enable me to compete in the media market and the publishing business. By "competition" I mean only discourse of a professionally high standard with colleagues—that is, participation in a socially essential discourse, one that also involves East German themes. As a result of the pulping of my books and the dissolution of publishing contracts, I have almost become an author without a publisher; there is general agreement, as I have experienced from publishers, that my lyric work, even that aimed at children, is too sophisticated and thus constitutes too great a business risk. I experience an enormous divergence as far as the reception of my texts is concerned: on the one hand, the publishers declare it too big a business risk and reject it, even as it is met with a great deal of interest and involvement by audiences at a wide variety of readings. . . . In sum, the expectation that my work would at last get a chance to exert some influence in West Germany has remained an illusion. But it is equally true that since 1989 I have worked more than ever; the great changes have liberated themes and energies to such an extent that I am obliged to save my strength, for writing is an ambivalent process: the treatment of a given theme is equally liberating and self-destructive at the same time.[30]

Wolfgang Hilbig, one of the authors who were compelled to leave the GDR in the eighties, supplements Kunert's experience by concluding that there was an apparent "bonus to be had for authors from the GDR who were considered oppositional when there were still two German states. This bonus is gradually being lost."[31]

Apart from exceptions like Erwin Strittmatter, authors from the GDR, due to what is for them a completely new attitude on the part of potential purchasers of their books, have suffered considerably lower sales in the new federal states than was the case during the GDR era. And in the old states they have had to make themselves known, at least if they were not members of the circle of GDR authors already much read in the Federal Republic. Changes in the field of publishing throughout Germany and a restructuring of radio and television have caused all writers, including those from West Germany, considerable adjustment difficulties.

In the case of the reading public in the new federal states, two factors have contributed to the considerable reduction in the number of books bought in comparison to the GDR era. The most important factor, and fortunately a very positive one, is an evolution in the function of art: "The substratal function of art has ceased to apply. There is now a fully accessible and informative press available to all." Rolf Schneider, just cited, remarks coolly: "Art in the former GDR has lost its old function and is having difficulties finding a new one."[32] The second factor can be observed in the "new arrangement of all market structures": "As a rule, incomes remained well behind those in the old federal states, while almost all costs shot up to the level of those in the West."[33] The price of books also rose to astronomic levels, by GDR standards. With the gradual alignment of incomes in the old and new states and with the slow reduction in unemployment levels in the new states (bringing these into line with the still excessive level of unemployment in the old states), buying habits should improve somewhat in the foreseeable future.

With the unification of Germany, publishing was transformed in the new states almost overnight. In the GDR, publishers had belonged to the state (as "national properties"), to the parties (primarily the SED), or to social organizations like the "Kulturbund" (Cultural Alliance) of the GDR. After 3 October 1990, a large number of these publishers fell under the administration of the "Treuhand [Trustee] Commission," whose task it was to privatize these businesses—that is, to find solvent investors for them. Important publishing firms such as Aufbau, Rütten & Loening, and Volk & Welt almost fell victim to the initial brute force of the Treuhand. Memorials to the commission's infamy have already been constructed by Rolf Hochhuth (the play Wessis in Weimar [Westerners in Weimar], 1993) and Günter Grass (the novel Ein weites Feld [A Broad Field], 1995); so here it is possible to concentrate on the positive outcome of

several lengthy disputes over the future of GDR publishers. The three firms listed above, and several additional literary publishing houses from the GDR, are still in existence; none makes a profit, but their new owners are investing large sums of money in the belief that their firms will be "worth it" again in a few years' time. The constant, long-term fear for their very existence experienced by many GDR publishing houses has meant that in recent years only a very few young authors could be accepted into the publishing program, and also that these firms have now lost authors who had been linked with them for decades. Many GDR authors took refuge under the roofs of those West German publishers who had produced the licensed editions of their works prior to the end of 1989. Simultaneously. A large number of authors from the GDR had the experience of seeing their books printed by East German publishers, only to find them all but unavailable in bookstores. One example is the marvelous ten-volume edition of the works of Volker Braun, Texte in zeitlicher Reihenfolge (Texts in Chronological Order), issued by the Mitteldeutscher Verlag (Halle) between 1989 and 1993 but scarcely noticed at all. On the one hand, this was due to the fact that former GDR publishers were obliged to set up a completely new distribution network in order to establish a presence in the old Federal Republic and, as a rule, did not have a sufficient knowledge of marketing. On the other hand, booksellers in the new states, like their customers, had developed a completely new orientation: the books put on sale and bought were mostly by those authors who had only been rarely available—if at all—in the old GDR due to proscription by the censor. Quite apart from this, there was also an enormous desire to catch up, in quantitative terms, on popular literature. Then too, booksellers in the old states, like their customers, had first of all to learn to take notice of the expansion of the book market resulting from publishers' offerings from the new states. Certainly it is true that fiction from the GDR had "long been an integral part of the [West German] book market"[34] when the unification took place, but that did not apply to all the outstanding authors from the GDR. One striking example was the huge success of Erwin Strittmatter with booksellers and readers in the new states and his relative anonymity in the old states.

The publishing houses that survived the GDR are still today, in the midnineties, not yet fully competitive as a result of several strange regulations in the unification agreement. From 3 October 1990 onward, every allocation of a license to a GDR publisher by a West German publisher was rendered void, whereas the licenses allocated to Western houses by GDR firms remained valid. This has had a particularly strong effect on the large-circulation paperback market. The Fischer Taschenbuchverlag in Frankfurt am Main was thus able to use its licensing rights to German translations of works by the Japanese author Kenzaburō Ōe, granted during the GDR era by the GDR publishers Volk & Welt, to bring reasonably priced paperback editions of his work onto the market in the autumn of 1994, shortly after the announcement of Ōe's Nobel Prize in Literature; the granter of the license, Volk & Welt, could only offer new editions of the hardcover versions, which of course were considerably more expensive.

However, it is not only Eastern publishers who have been shaken by crises and have feared for their continued existence; publishing houses in the old Federal Republic of Germany have experienced similar agonies. The Luchterhand Literaturverlag, which has an excellent reputation, was having difficulties as early as 1987; it changed hands, lost a number of its important contemporary authors, relocated its headquarters numerous times (from Darmstadt to Frankfurt am Main to Hamburg and Zürich), only to change owners once again in Munich in 1994, winning back at least one "house author," Christa Wolf, in the process. One of the few family firms in the German publishing field, the Piper Verlag in Munich, was sold to a Swedish publishing group in the autumn of 1994. The (West) Berlin Rotbuch-Verlag was only able to save itself by taking refuge under the wing of a well-reputed publishing firm in Hamburg.

There has been a surprisingly large amount of activity within the publishing field in Germany. It is true that new publishers have been established which would scarcely have been conceivable without the political unification of the country. The many small houses which appear to have shot up overnight in the new federal states since 1990 should be mentioned, a development made possible by the cessation of state censorship. A great many of these newly established firms will probably not survive for long on their own, but the successful work of the Christoph Links Verlag in Berlin, for example, provides hope that not all of them will fail, a fate already suffered by the esthetically ambitious "Unabhängige Verlagsbuchhandlung Ackerstraße" (UVA), also in Berlin. In the long term, some publishers will certainly have to seek a solution similar to that found by Gerhard Wolf with his company "Janus Press": functioning as an independent series of imprints under the aegis of a financially secure publishing house.

Alongside such small presses, several new publishing houses are being founded which anticipate the relocation of Germany's capital to Berlin. "Rowohlt Berlin," founded in 1990, is independently directed, but like the Rowohlt Verlag in Reinbek (near Hamburg), it belongs to the Holzbrinck Group. The S. Fischer Verlag, originally founded in Berlin, will keep its headquarters in Frankfurt am Main, but it has considerably expanded and remodeled its Berlin offices. Finally, Arnulf Conradi, previously the editor-in-chief at S. Fischer, revived the "Berlin Verlag" in 1995.

Both large and small literary magazines are also important in the German publishing scene; as a rule, they prove to be financial burdens to their respective publishers but nevertheless play their role in establishing the firm's good name. The magazine *Sinn und Form* survived the collapse of the GDR and continues to be published by the Academy of the Arts (now with the addition "Berlin-Brandenburg") and the Aufbau Verlag. Aufbau also publishes the magazine *neue deutsche literatur,* which was the official organ of the GDR Writers Union, and the magazine *Sprache im technischen Zeitalter* (Language in a Technical Age). The fact that *Sprache im technischen Zeitalter* has been published by Aufbau since 1993 represents one of the few achievements in East-West integration within German literary life, for up until 1990 it would have been unthinkable that this magazine, founded at the beginning of the 1960s by Walter Höllerer and still edited at the Literarisches Colloquium Berlin, could ever appear under the auspices of the GDR's most prominent publishing house. And of course, literary debates in a united Germany are also influenced by literary magazines such as *Akzente* (produced by the Munich publisher Hanser); at the same time, magazines which are not exclusively dedicated to belles lettres also extend their influence into literary life: for example *Kursbuch* (Rowohlt, Berlin), *Freibeuter* (Wagenbach, Berlin), and *Merkur* (Klett-Cotta, Stuttgart).

In contrast to France, for one, book prices in Germany are "bound" or controlled—that is, no bookseller can sell a book for more or less than its publisher has determined. This practice has the advantage that books cannot be sold at an excessive price anywhere, not even in places where a particular bookstore enjoys a monopoly. At the same time, the fixed retail price lowers the calculated risk for both publishers and bookstores.

A few recent figures: in 1994 nearly 71,000 titles came onto the book market; of these, only a quarter were new editions of titles which had already appeared at some earlier date, meaning that almost 53,000 titles were issued for the first time. However—and this is a regular phenomenon over the years—the proportion of titles which were literary works, including literature for children and young people, was only around 21 percent. Nonfiction claimed the lion's share of production. Barely 4,500 literary titles were translations from other languages into German—and yet these represented a good 43 percent of all translations published in the year

1994. Among the literary works, translations from English dominated, with approximately 74 percent. Exactly 8.4 percent of the literary translations came from French; two years earlier, in 1992, the figure was 12.1 percent. However, the drop may not have any significance for the years ahead. As a comparison, only 2.5 percent of all literary translations were from Russian, 2.6 percent from Spanish, 2.4 percent from Italian. The number of translations from French may be much smaller than from English, but it is still well ahead of Spanish, the third most frequently translated language in the German-speaking countries. Conversely, around 13 percent of the translation rights granted to publishers abroad by German firms were for literary works. In this field too, appreciable changes in comparison to earlier years cannot be unequivocally determined. France was the primary licensee in 1993, but in 1994 it took sixth place. In the sphere of literary works, licenses for 55 titles were granted to French-speaking countries, for 62 titles to English, 45 to Spanish, and 43 to Italian in 1994. Only 19 licenses were granted for titles into Russian.[35]

One important factor for the widespread reception of literature is literary criticism, which is published chiefly in the national dailies and weeklies and also has its place—one not as poor as is often presumed—in radio and television. This criticism consists of a few literary "popes" (at least it is not just one pope) tossing balls back and forth to one another: *Die Zeit* and the *Frankfurter Allgemeine Zeitung,* the *Süddeutsche Zeitung* and the *Frankfurter Rundschau, Der Spiegel* and *Die Woche, Freitag* and *Die Wochenpost,* to name but a few of these press outlets. This certainly does not exclude the possibility of quality literary criticism in regional newspapers such as the *Stuttgarter Zeitung* or the Berlin *Tagesspiegel* and *Berliner Zeitung.* The *tageszeitung* has a small circulation, but for friends of literature, it plays a special role; in contrast to all the other daily and weekly papers, it regularly and courageously presents poets from all over the world, usually in very good German translations and usually in first-time publication within the German-speaking countries. The *tageszeitung* is also a paper which regularly takes a stand in support of writers who have been persecuted for political reasons or are imprisoned in their home countries.

On German television, the most popular and also most controversial forum of literary criticism is "Das literarische Quartett": six times a year, Marcel Reich-Ranicki, together with three other colleagues, revels in his "To be or not to be" criticism on this program. "Bücherjournal" (Book Journal), broadcast three times a year in the First German Televison Network (ARD), certainly cannot compete with Reich-Ranicki's Second Network (ZDF) series in terms of the number of viewers it attracts, but this televised literary review, in which—unlike "Das literarische Quartett"—both nonfiction and literary titles are presented, has yet to lose its influence on the literary life of Germany despite its late-evening time slot. The ARD also broadcasts longer programs to mark the Leipzig Book Fair each spring and the Frankfurt Book Fair each autumn. Third channels belonging to the regional companies of the ARD broadcast additional regular programs of literary criticism: for example, "Bücher, Bücher" (Books, Books), produced by "Hessen 3" and shown on forty-two Sundays a year from 6:00 to 6:35 P.M. Only "Das literarische Quartett" (with 2 percent or 710,000 viewers) and ARD's "Bücherjournal" and a program of the same name on the North 3 regional network (with 1 percent or 420,000 and 220,000 viewers respectively) can boast of notable ratings. All the other literary programs on German television attain ratings of 0 percent, which translates to an audience figure somewhere between 2,000 and 11,000.[36]

The situation does not appear any better with regard to radio, although there are some very stimulating and distinctive programs of literary criticism, particularly on regional radio networks. Of course there is not only literary *criticism* on German radio and television; there is also literature. Most of the films based on literary works seen on television, however, are not the networks' own productions, but rather films which have already been seen in cinemas and subsequently taken over by television. Oddly enough, the literary models, usually novels, are then extolled by publishers and booksellers as "the book of the film." Whether Fontane's *Effi Briest* or *The Tin Drum* by Günter Grass are bought and read as "the book of the film" or as the film's literary model and predecessor is probably a matter of no consequence to most readers. The decisive factor is that the filming of literature leads to a sudden rise in demand for the corresponding book in bookstores and public libraries.

The literary genre of the *Hörspiel* or "radio play" has a difficult time with radio companies. Just as the presentation of literary texts by young authors or of new texts by established authors and the public reading of world literature have been drastically reduced over the last three decades, so too has the radio play fallen victim to cuts in the "verbal shares" of radio networks. In contrast to "music," "words" do not ensure sufficiently high audience ratings. However, literature on the radio continues to be an important source of income for authors—and a no less important aid to orientation for listeners. It is possible that the increasingly popular "spoken book"—the recording on tape or CD of readings of unabridged literary texts (including longer novels) by the authors themselves or by trained speakers—will help literature regain a greater presence on radio. The "spoken book," distributed by booksellers and music shops alike, has a particularly large fan club among those people who wish to be pleasantly entertained on long car trips.

Literary life in Germany for the last hundred years would have been inconceivable without public libraries. As a rule, these are financed by district or county governments or by religious bodies. In addition to their traditional tasks, public libraries today are required to provide their constituencies with topical information. Indisputably, such libraries promote reading in a way matched only by schools and adult-education courses. They also prevent socially weak groups from being denied access to information, education, and entertainment.

This makes it all the more regrettable that after the political unification of Germany, the tighter network and greater number of libraries in the GDR (in comparison to the Federal Republic) could not be maintained. Even if, in comparison to West Germany, a wide variety of literature could not be found in the libraries of the GDR any more than in its bookstores, due to the censor, a unified Germany could have learned from the GDR that public lending libraries, for example, are useful institutions accepted by the populace. As a report on libraries in the FRG soberly states:

> For approximately every 17,000 inhabitants in the Federal Republic there is a public library with a collection of 1.7 media units per inhabitant. Per inhabitant, 3.7 media units are borrowed each year, which means that the collection of media has a turnover of 2.5 times per year. On average, parishes spend DM 17.80 per inhabitant on libraries, DM 2.40 on the purchase of new media. There are just under two library employees per 10,000 inhabitants. In order to clarify the true range of these figures, it must be recalled that, despite average statistics, there are numerous libraries which surpass these figures by more than twice as much, others which fail to reach them by half.

> The average public library in Germany is open 22 hours a week, and it is assumed that approximately 15 percent of the population use a public library. According to the understanding of "use," or to the way in which this percentage is ascertained, the figure may be estimated as higher in individual cases. In many cases, the use of a library is still free, but the number of libraries which charge a range of fees has risen continually over the last three years. The trend is clearly toward a user contribution to costs.[37]

A further set of figures may speak for literary life in the Federal Republic: in 1993, just under 244.4 million books were borrowed from public libraries; 56.2 million of these were literary works, 76.6 million were books for children and young people.[38]

"Erbepflege" (the cultivation of one's heritage) was the name given to the activities of literary archives and memorial institutes in the GDR, work which bore fruit not least in exemplary editions of texts by German and foreign authors. One good example of this was, and remains, the popular "Bibliothek deutscher Klassiker" (Library of German Classics) produced by the Aufbau-Verlag. In many communities there are smaller or larger archives specializing in the work, life, and reception of authors with links to those particular locales; schools, libraries, and similar institutions within the spheres of education and culture bear the names of important or at least regionally influential authors; regional and national literary societies devote themselves to "their authors." The federal structure of literary life in Germany is obvious here too. Nevertheless, there are also institutions of a more national scope working to maintain and develop the German literary heritage, preserving it and making it available for research. These institutions include the "Stiftung Weimarer Klassik" with its Goethe and Schiller archives, the German Literary Archive and the National Schiller Museum in Marbach am Neckar, the "Freie Deutsche Hochstift" with its Goethe-Haus and Goethe-Museum in Frankfurt am Main, and the foundation "Archiv der Akademie der Künste Berlin-Brandenburg" in Berlin. One characteristic shared by all these institutions is the fact that they do not simply seek to engage literary academics and researchers themselves, but are committed to an extensive array of public work, including events ranging from exhibitions to readings (some by contemporary authors)—i.e., they establish and maintain close contacts with the public.

This work is supported by literary societies throughout the Federal Republic. Almost 120 such societies have now joined the "Arbeitsgemeinschaft Literarischer Gesellschaften" (Labor Association of Literary Societies, ALG), which was founded in West Berlin in 1986. A further 80 literary societies do not yet employ the services offered by the ALG. One single literary society survived the division of Germany undivided: the Goethe Society, headquartered in Weimar and keenly observed by the state security services of both Germanies. Today it is almost unimaginable that a literary society was ever a political entity of the highest order.

After 1990, numerous literary societies were founded in the new states in order to replace memorial institutions and archives which had been lost with the collapse of the GDR. These included the Theodor Fontane Society in Potsdam, the Hans Fallada Society in Feldberg, and the Friedrich Wolf Society and the Anna Seghers Society in Berlin. The Fritz Reuter Society moved from Lübeck to Neubrandenburg, and the Shakespeare Societies West and East have been reunited. As a rule, it has not proved necessary for such societies—which usually lack the necessary financial means—to take over the fiscal direction of a memorial institute or archive. However, they support the state-financed institutions in mind and spirit and through the planning and staging of effective public events.

In addition to these author societies, open public literary societies and institutions in many locales throughout Germany are involved in making primarily contemporary literature from both home and abroad available to a wider public, endeavoring to awaken understanding for new esthetic forms by addressing readers directly but also offering further educational opportunities for critics of literature, for the editorial staffs of publishing firms, and for editors of literary magazines. They invite authors to read from their latest works. They organize symposia on specific literary themes. They invite publishers, radio editors, and critics to come together and share their experiences, something which, unexpectedly, would otherwise be a rare event. Literary societies of this kind are active in Leipzig and Marburg, in Berlin and Munich, in Neubrandenburg and Frankfurt am Main. And everywhere in Germany there are bookstores, art galleries, libraries, and sometimes even churches which invite people to readings by authors and to literary discussions. Authors regularly read—not least due to the efforts of the Friedrich Bödecker Circle—in schools and in youth centers. Local cultural centers everywhere also open their doors to literature.

The work of the few literary institutions found in Germany is outstanding. Traditionally, the first to come to mind are the Literary Academies in Darmstadt and Mainz and the Academies of (Fine) Arts in Munich and Berlin; their work continues to be irreplaceable. Without doubt, the most important is the Deutsche Akademie für Sprache und Dichtung (German Academy for Language and Literature) in Darmstadt, which, alongside its other work, awards the annual Georg Büchner Prize. But it is also important to remember those institutions which since the 1960s have been active in improving the reception of literature by the reading public, in qualifying literary criticism, and in promoting authors, usually by the awarding of suitable grants. The oldest institution of this kind is the Literarisches Colloquium Berlin, which was founded in Berlin by Walter Höllerer in 1963 and is housed in offices directly beside the Wannsee. In 1986 this was followed by the Litera-

turhaus Berlin, situated—in contrast to the Literarisches Colloquium—in the center of the city (west) on a side street off the Kurfürstendamm. The Literaturhaus is available free of charge to all literary organizations and groups in Berlin. A successful combination of its own programs and other events has been copied elsewhere: in Hamburg, in Frankfurt am Main, in Bonn, in Leipzig, and in Darmstadt, with Munich to follow. Since the reunification of Berlin, the Literaturforum im Brecht-Haus in the eastern part of the city near Friedrichstraße, and the "literaturWERKstatt berlin" in Berlin Pankow at the northern edge of the city have both been established. The "Berliner Zentrum für Kinder- und Jugendliteratur — 'LesArt'" was founded at the same time. "LesArt" grew out of the "Zentrum für Kinderliteratur der DDR," the "Literaturforum im Brecht-Haus" out of the "Brecht-Zentrum der DDR." The "literaturWERKstatt" occupies the same building that housed an authors' club during the eighties, a club which was not, however, open to the public.

In this context, it is important to mention the "Haus der Kulturen der Welt" (House of World Cultures), which is also based in Berlin and is unique in Germany. This interdisciplinary institution is dedicated to the propagation of the cultures of Africa, Asia, and Latin America, and its literature department has repeatedly succeeded in introducing literature previously unknown in Germany and in persuading publishers to take on books by one or another of the authors presented in their program.

The Federal Republic still basically lacks a training program for authors, although there have been numerous attempts since the early 1970s to set up an educational institute for that purpose. In the GDR there existed an institutionalized system of training for authors at the Johannes R. Becher Literary Institute in Leipzig. Although this institute had to be closed without replacement immediately after the political changes, the Free State of Saxony was able to establish a new institute for the training of authors following that closure. That new institute is called the "Deutsches Literaturinstitut Leipzig" and is affiliated with the University of Leipzig.

Of course, authors have a variety of possibilities for continued education and training within the private sector. The Bertelsmann Foundation, for example, regularly sponsors seminars for writers, and the Literarisches Colloquium Berlin organizes alternating annual seminars for dramatists and radio-play authors as well as for literary translators. At the end of the eighties, a diploma course in literary translation was established at the University of Düsseldorf. The "Europäischer Übersetzer Kollegium" (European Translators Collegium) in Straelen, North Rhine-Westphalia, also contributes to the continuing education and training of translators in the literary field; it was opened in 1985 in the presence of Heinrich Böll, who was also highly esteemed as a translator.

In today's unified Germany, it is apparent that translators in the two former German states had developed very different approaches toward their profession. In the GDR interlinear translations of poetry were quite common, for example, and served poets as the bases for new versions. In the Federal Republic such a procedure was considered quite old-fashioned. Rainer Kirsch, one of the most talented poets in Germany, was among the most prolific producers of such verse translations in the GDR. He has ironically caricatured his new experiences with colleagues in West Germany as follows:

> When I read a few [poems by Sergei Esenin] alongside the Russian original at a conference of translators at the Literarisches Colloquium Berlin in 1991, I noticed a strange expression of dissatisfaction on many faces. Was this due, I asked myself, to my untrained voice? Or to the person of Esenin, who had come from the provinces to conquer the St. Petersburg salons in 1913, had been received by the czarina in 1917, saw himself as "far left of the Bolsheviks" in 1922, and had stylized his home of Ryazan as a utopian landscape until his death? In addition, he drank, loved many women, dressed elegantly, and was very good-looking, even according to the judgment of his worst enemies. No, it had nothing to do with any of this. The problem was that I had read the poems in *verse*, whereas everyone knows that, since Ungaretti, poems are possible only in prose, and that the market demands this as well. All that was necessary, I see now, was to expunge the art from Esenin's texts; then they wouldn't have bothered anyone.[39]

Literary activity in Germany does not occur only in the German language. Authors from other countries, in particular from Turkey, the former Yugoslavia, Italy, Spain, and, since reunification, more and more from Poland, Lithuania, Russia, Hungary, the Czech Republic, and Romania, live and work as equals in the new united German state. They are members of writers' associations, they receive grants as citizens of those federal states where they have settled, and they are awarded literary prizes. Since 1990, more and more authors from France, the Netherlands, Great Britain, and the USA come to Germany—sometimes for a shorter period, sometimes for good. For these authors, it is often not Germany itself which they are seeking, but rather an encounter with artists from other countries and cultures. In Berlin, for example, writers from France can easily meet colleagues from Poland; for such writers, Germany is more a medium than an end.

At the same time, an increasing number of writers are seeking refuge in unified Germany, writers who are threatened in their home countries and who cannot continue their literary work there unimpeded. In the midnineties these include as well many authors from the former Yugoslavia, from Algeria, and from Pakistan. The International Parliament of Authors, based in Strasbourg, has begun to weave an international network known as "Cities of Refuge" for authors such as these whose lives have been threatened. Berlin, one of the first cities to join this network, has placed a furnished flat and a grant at the group's disposal. Berlin was able to react so quickly because, each year for the last three decades, the "Berliner Künstlerprogramm" (Berlin Artists Program) of the German Academic Exchange Service (DAAD) has invited five or six authors from all around the world to the city for a period of study; one of the flats reserved for these authors was immediately made available to Cities of Refuge. Experiences with foreign authors residing permanently in Germany were not as extensive in the GDR as in the FRG. However, we should not overlook the fact that writers from, for example, Chile and Vietnam found safe haven in the GDR.

Among authors, publishing employees, and booksellers there reigns an openness toward foreigners that is not found within the general population. However, a genuine hatred of strangers and of foreigners, which has led to murder and arson in both the old and the new federal states, fortunately remains the attitude of only a small minority. Literary Germany has attempted to respond to crimes perpetrated against foreigners, and while there is something touchingly helpless about the fact that authors and publishing employees alike have tried to confront the problem through books, it should be recalled that each of us can use only those instruments available to us.[40]

Literary life in Germany? Directly after the political changes occurred in the GDR, Françoise Bartheélemy and Lutz Winckler polled writers from both German states about their understanding of themselves. Question 5 was: "How can you explain to an outsider—for example, to a Frenchman—the particular nature of your situation as a German writer? (That is, if you feel that there is anything particular in your situation.)" The responses were as different as the writers questioned. Nevertheless, the reply given by Günter de Bruyn, from the GDR, appears exemplary: "It would not be enough to ask the Frenchman to imagine that both France and Paris were divided by fortified borders and by two different forms of government from this day forward; he would also have to be able to imagine that this had been the case for decades, that he had grown accustomed to it and had even come to see advantages in it; and then he would also have to be able to imagine a Hitler in the history of France, with all the consequences this entails—but that would surely be too much for him."[41] This reply was given without any knowledge of further political developments in Germany. We know about these now and can only ask, "Is it not still too much?"

Concerning literary life in Germany six years after the unification of the country—for writers as much as for readers—an observation by Helga Königsdorf is generally valid: "We have new biographies. Each of us sets the record of his own role straight just a little. No one can live with himself in a disintegrated condition. Life is unique and too valuable for a person to be able to say he has ruined it if nothing can be corrected. So ultimately everyone has his own truth. The truth of others causes him pain when it puts his life in question. In close-up, the mote in the eye of another becomes a beam."[42]

Dietger Pforte, Winter 1997

[1] Henning Ritter, "Endlich oder unendlich? Die deutsche Einheit nach fünf Jahren," *Frankfurter Allgemeine Zeitung,* 2 October 1995.

[2] The appeal "Für unser Land" was first published on 29 November 1989 in the *Frankfurter Allgemeine Zeitung.*

[3] Rolf Schneider, "Das Schweigen der Schafe: Über den ostdeutschen Kulturbetrieb," *Merkur,* 48:6 (1994), p. 538.

[4] Frank Schirrmacher: "'Dem Druck des härteren, strengeren Lebens standhalten.' Auch eine Studie über den autoritären Charakter: Christa Wolfs Aufsätze, Reden und ihre jüngste Erzählung 'Was bleibt'," *Frankfurter Allgemeine Zeitung,* 2 June 1990.

[5] Reinhard Baumgart: "Vom Widerstand des Besonderen: Der neudeutsche Literaturstreit," *Der Tagesspiegel* (Berlin), 9 October 1991.

[6] Quoted by Frank Schirrmacher, "Verdacht und Verrat," in *MachtSpiele: Literatur und Staatssicherheit im Fokus Prenzlauer Berg,* eds. Peter Böthig and Klaus Michael, Leipzig, Reklam, 1993, p. 306.

[7] Ursula Plog, "Immer auf der richtigen Seite stehen," *Der Spiegel,* 33 (1995), p. 62.

[8] Frank Schirrmacher, "Literatur und Staatssicherheit," *Frankfurter Allgemeine Zeitung,* 28 January 1993.

[9] Frank Schirrmacher, "Lebensläufe: Monika Maron und die Stasi," *Frankfurter Allgemeine Zeitung,* 7 August 1995.

[10] Karl Corino (ed.), *Die Akte Kant: IM 'Martin', die Stasi und die Literatur in Ost und West,* Reinbek bei Hamburg, Rowohlt, 1995.

[11] Plog, p. 64.

[12] Theo Mechtenberg, "Der Emanzipationsprozeß der DDR-Literatur von der Kulturpolitik unter Berücksichtigung repressiver Maßnahmen der Staatssicherheit: Expertise im Auftrag der Enquete Kommission des deutschen Bundestages 'Aufarbeitung von Geschichte und Folgen der SED-Diktatur in Deutschland'," MS, 1994, p. 30.

[13] Christa Wolf, *Kindheitsmuster,* Berlin/Weimar, Aufbau, 1976, p. 9. In English as *A Model Childhood,* tr. Ursula Molinaro, New York, Farrar Straus Giroux, 1980.

[14] Ibid.

[15] Hans Joachim Schädlich, 7 January 1995, as quoted in *europäische ideen,* 94 (1995), p. 41.

[16] Ibid.

[17] Klaus Staeck, 24 February 1995 in the *Süddeutsche Zeitung,* as quoted in *europäische ideen,* 94 (1995), p. 62.

[18] Jochen Laabs, 24 February 1995 in the *Süddeutsche Zeitung,* as quoted in *europäische ideen,* 94 (1995), p. 63.

[19] Ibid.

[20] Heiner Müller, *Zur Lage der Nation,* Berlin, Rotbuch, 1990, pp. 81–82.

[21] Ibid., p. 82.

[22] Heinrich Böll, "Einigkeit der Einzelgänger," in *Einigkeit der Einzelgänger: Dokumentation des ersten Schriftstellerkongresses des Verbands deutscher Schrifsteller (VS),* ed. Dieter Lattmann, Munich, Kindler, 1971, p. 21.

[23] In *Von Abraham bis Zwerenz: Eine Anthologie des Bundesministeriums für Bildung, Wissenschaft, Forschung und Technologie, Bonn, und des Ministeriums für Bildung, Wissenschaft und Weiterbildung des Landes Rheinland-Pfalz als Beitrag zur geistig-kulturellen Einheit in Deutschland,* 3 vols., Berlin, Cornelsen, 1995, vol. 1, p. 505.

[24] Ibid., vol. 1, p. 631.

[25] Ibid., vol. 2, p. 1382.

[26] Ibid., vol. 1, p. 688.

[27] Ibid., vol. 1, p. 248.

[28] Ibid., vol. 3, p. 1884.

[29] Ibid., vol. 2, p. 1060.

[30] Ibid., vol. 3, p. 1485.

[31] Ibid., vol. 2, p. 721.

[32] Schneider, p. 541.

[33] Ibid.

[34] *Geschichte der deutschen Literatur von 1945 bis zur Gegenwart,* ed. Wilfried Barner, Munich, Beck, 1994. *Geschichte der deutschen Literatur von den Anfängen bis zur Gegenwart,* vol. 12, p. 801.

[35] Cf. *Buch und Buchhandel in Zahlen 1995,* published by the Börsenverein des Deutschen Buchhandels, Frankfurt a.M., Buchhändler Vereinigung, 1995.

[36] Cf. Wolfgang Niess, "Im Getto der Nacht," *Börsenblatt für den Deutschen Buchhandel,* 64 (11 August 1995), pp. 12–14.

[37] Hans-Peter Thun, *Eine Einführung in das Bibliothekswesen der Bundesrepublik Deutschland,* Berlin, Deutsches Bibliotheksinstitut, 1995, p. 13.

[38] Cf. *DBS—Deutsche Bibliotheksstatistik 1993: Teil D—Gesamtstatistik,* Berlin, Deutsches Bibliotheksinstitut, 1994, p. 151.

[39] In *Neues Deutschland,* 30 September / 1 October 1991.

[40] The "Verlagsinitiative gegen Gewalt und Fremdenhaß" produced the anthology *Schweigen ist Schuld* in 1993 (available through the Piper Verlag, Munich); that same year Wolfgang

Balk and Sebastian Kleinschmidt produced the collection *Denk ich an Deutschland: Stimmen der Befremdung* for the Fischer Taschenbuchverlag, Frankfurt a.M., and Bahman Nirumand published the collection *Deutsche Zustände: Dialog über ein gefährdetes Land* with the Rowohlt Taschenbuchverlag, Reinbek bei Hamburg.

[41] Günter de Bruyn, "Die eine deutsche Kultur," in *Mein Deutschland findet sich in keinem Atlas,* eds. Françoise Barthélemy and Lutz Winckler, Frankfurt a.M., Luchterhand, 1990, p. 28.

[42] Helga Königsdorf, *Unterwegs nach Deutschland—Über die Schwierigkeiten, ein Volk zu sein: Protokolle eines Aufbruchs,"* Reinbek bei Hamburg, Rowohlt, 1995, p. 8.

Paul Celan and the Cult of Personality

A mere twenty years after the death of the Romanian-born but German-language poet Paul Celan (1920–70), his life and writings had already inspired almost as much comment as those of Federico García Lorca, Ernest Hemingway, James Joyce, or Ezra Pound. By the end of 1989 Jerry Glenn's excellent bibliography of the available biographical and critical publications devoted to Celan already listed more than three thousand items. Many of the increasingly numerous American, English, French, German, or Israeli publications devoted to Celan display, however, the unmistakable characteristics of a somewhat uncritical "cult of personality" rather than those of objective biographical or literary scholarship. On the one hand, far too many of these publications tend to neglect a few of the more significant biographical facts that had already been revealed as far back as 1979 by Israel Chalfen in *Paul Celan: Eine Biographie seiner Jugend,* which is now available also in Maximilian Bleyleben's remarkably faithful English translation, recently published in New York by Persea Books. On the other hand, practically none of Celan's American, English, French, German, or Israeli admirers appears to have yet taken the trouble to read Celan's few truly outstanding Romanian-language poems, yet these clearly mark a decisive break between the rather conventional, if not adolescent or even provincial postromantic mood of his earlier German-language lyrics, still written in his native Czernowitz, and the much more original and mature German-language poetry that he began to write in Bucharest and Vienna and ultimately published in 1952 in *Mohn und Gedächtnis.* Neither has the influence of the poetry of Celan's French friends and contemporaries on his own verse of the years that he later spent in Paris yet been at all seriously investigated.

Nearly all of Celan's earlier poetry displays indeed the influence of his readings of Rilke, Trakl, Eichendorff, Mörike, and of course Goethe too, but no influence of any readings of Heine. His curious reticence concerning the poetry of Heine and his exceptional talent as a multilingual translator of American, English, French, Hebrew, Italian, Portuguese, Romanian, and Russian poets into German are rare characteristics that he shared with only one other German poet, August Graf von Platen, whose *Venezianische Sonetten* I know that Celan admired, since we once read them aloud together in Paris after I had pointed out to him how much I felt that they had influenced some of Stefan George's early sonnets and perhaps Rilke's *Sonette an Orpheus* as well.

However, Celan's few Romanian-language poems and some of the German-language poems of *Mohn und Gedächtnis* suddenly display quite clearly the influence of the Romanian-language verse of such surrealist friends as Gherasim Luca, among others, with whom he was associating very closely in Bucharest between the spring of 1945 and the end of 1947. Celan can also be reasonably suspected of having then become acquainted with some of the Romanian-language poetry of two outstanding and slightly older Romanian-Jewish writers: the poet Benjamin Fundoianu (Benjamin Wechsler), who is more widely known as the French-language poet and philosopher Benjamin Fondane, deported from Paris by the Germans and murdered by them in the gas chambers of Auschwitz-Birkenau in October 1944; and the bilingual Romanian and French poet Ilarie Voronca (Eduard Marcus), whose grief and despair at the loss of so many relatives and friends as victims of the Holocaust led him to commit suicide in France in 1946. Long neglected in their native Romania under its anti-Semitic regime as an ally of Nazi Germany, these two poets were both being read and discussed again in 1945 in the Bucharest avant-garde literary circles that Celan frequented.

From readings of Fundoianu's less overtly dadaist or integralist Romanian-language poems of 1917 and 1918 about the rural life of his native province of Moldavia, grouped under the collective title "Hertza" in his first published collection, *Tagaduinta lui Petru* (Bucharest, 1918), Celan may well have learned to develop his own equally nostalgic kind of nature poetry inspired by memories of the countryside of his native Bukovina. Such poems as "Der Geheimnis der Farne" in *Mohn und Gedächtnis* are no longer at all like most of the more conventional lyrics he had still been writing a few years earlier in Czernowitz.

In the vault of swords the leaf-green heart of the
    shadows perceives its own reflection.
The blades are bright: in death, who wouldn't linger
    before mirrors?
Here too one toasts in mugs full of a living nostalgia

that froths high in dark blossoms before one drinks it
  as if it weren't water,
as though it were a daisy whose petals are questioned
  about an even darker love,
about a pillow more black for one's couch, about
  even heavier hair.

Translated here into English, these lines from Celan's
"Secret of the Ferns" might indeed remind one of the
mood of Fundoianu's "Hertza."

This autumn—one wonders why—the day shrank so
  much.
The barren field approached the village, so black and
  timid,
as if it wanted to slip through the undergrowth of
  fences
and set foot once more in the attics and barns.
And something here is missing from what once was:
behind the windows of houses one senses the
  presence of adobe hallways
and of roofs that jut over empty rooms and are full
of nettles and manure driven there by rains and
  wind.

A more systematic study of the writings of other Romanian-language poets with whom Celan is known to have
associated in Bucharest or whom one can reasonably
presume that he read would surely produce even more
convincing evidence of the importance of his own Romanian-language poems as a veritable turning-point in
his evolution as a German-language poet.

    Three further avenues of investigation which might
lead to an equally significant understanding of Celan's
overall evolution as a poet appear to remain likewise
unexplored by most of the more rhapsodic hierophants
of the cult of personality that has emerged about him.
The first of these would consist in a systematic study,
already undertaken to some extent by Jerry Glenn and
a few others, of the German-language poetry of two of
Celan's Czernowitz-born German-language contemporaries, the poets Immanuel Wasserglass and Alfred
Gong (Likornik), with both of whom he began to associate even in his adolescence, and of three older Czernowitz-born German-language poets of some distinction, Rose Ausländer, Alfred Kittner, and Alfred Margul-
Sperber, with all three of whom Celan is known to have
associated closely in Czernowitz on his return from a
Romanian forced-labor camp in Moldavia or later too
in Bucharest.

    The second generally neglected avenue of investi-
gation would consist in a systematic study of the writings of the few French poets, above all René Char,
André du Bouchet, and Jean Daive, with whom Celan
is known to have associated and sympathized in the

years that he later spent in Paris. One of the poems of
Von Schwelle zu Schwelle, the first volume of those composed in France, is indeed entitled "Argumentum e
Silentio" and is dedicated to Char, whom Celan translated and admired and who is recognized as having
been, in his own poetry of the decades that immediately
followed World War II, increasingly cryptic and a veritable apostle of the rhetorical trope known as aposiop-
sis, which consists in refraining from being more explicit and was then consistently practiced by Char's
younger disciples, above all by du Bouchet and Daive,
both of whom were close friends of Celan, who even
translated a number of their poems into German and
was translated in turn into French by Daive. Such a
study of the poetry of Char, du Bouchet, Daive, and
their friend Jean Dupin, who was also translated into
German by Celan, would surely yield some valid explanations for a few of the more cryptic statements or eva-
sions of overt statement—in fact, examples of aposiope-
sis—that can puzzle readers of much of Celan's later
German poetry.

    The third of the neglected avenues of investigation
might consist in a study of the very few poets who wrote
on specifically Jewish themes and with whose writings
Celan is known to have first become acquainted in Bucharest, Vienna, or Paris. These would include: Else
Lasker-Schüler, whom he had been urged to read by
Margul-Sperber in Bucharest and a few months later in
Innsbruck by Ludwig von Ficker and the latter's Swedish wife; Nelly Sachs, whom he is known to have met,
if only briefly, in Zürich; and finally the Egyptian-born
French-language poet Edmond Jabès, one of the very
last friends on whom Celan called in Paris shortly before
his suicide. Perhaps one should also include here Alexander Koval's German translation of my own *Three Hebrew Elegies,* published in Berlin by the Karlheinz Henssel Verlag and of which Koval gave Celan a copy in
Paris.

    Many of the increasingly cryptic references to any-
thing Jewish in Celan's later poetry display indeed very
little affinity with the more rationalistic and conventional Judaism of the German Haskalah in which he had
been schooled for his Bar Mitzvah or with the more
popular and folkloristic Yiddish writings of Itzik Manger and Elieser Steinbarg, for whose "jargon" Celan so
often expressed contempt in Czernowitz. On the contrary, most of the references to anything Jewish that appear in Celan's later poetry suggest a new interest in the
Cabala and perhaps in the writings of Gershom
Scholem, in fact in the kind of Jewish mysticism that
Celan could find in the poetry of Jabès and perhaps in
mine too. In addition, it might be of some interest to
investigate whether Celan was at all acquainted, before

his brief visit to Israel that so ominously preceded his suicide, with any of the truly great Hebrew poetry of Dan Pagis, a Bukovina-born Romanian-Jewish survivor of the Nazi extermination camps in Transnistria, who, like his compatriots the Hebrew novelist Aharon Appelfeld and the Israeli painters Avigdor Arikha and Arnold Dagani, preferred to turn his back on the German culture which had produced as its spellbound changelings so many vicious anti-Semites.

In all of Celan's earlier and more traditional German-language poetry written in Czernowitz before the summer of 1941, when the parents and sister of Celan's friend Alfred Gong were suddenly deported, together with some four thousand other Jews, by the Soviets from Czernowitz to Siberia, practically nothing displays his awareness of being a Jew, his fluency in the Yiddish that was still widely spoken in most Jewish homes of Bukovina, or his knowledge of Hebrew. Neither can one detect here much evidence of his fluency in Romanian, which allowed him a few years later to distinguish himself in Bucharest as a Romanian-language poet of some promise and as an exceptionally good literary translator of Russian classics.

Celan's early German-language lyrics display, of course, some evidence of his acquaintance with nineteenth-century French poetry. Even before the year that he spent in France as a student, preparing in Tours his admission to a medical school, he expressed in Czernowitz his admiration for Baudelaire and Verlaine, whom he would certainly have been inspired to read as a consequence of his great admiration for Rilke. It was only later, however, that he was exposed in Bucharest, through his Romanian friends Ghellu Naum, Gherasim Luca, Nina Cassian, Paul Paun (Zaharia Zaharia), and Petre Solomon, most of who were members of the Romanian surrealist group, not only to Romanian-language dadaist, integralist, or surrealist poetry such as that of Tristan Tzara (Samy Rosenstock), Ion Vinea, Ion Caraion, Benjamin Fundoianu, and Ilarie Voronca, but also to a certain amount of surrealist writing in French, including some of the works of André Breton. This certainly prepared him for his later confrontation in Paris, as a German translator, with the work of such French poets as Antonin Artaud, Breton, René Char, Robert Desnos, Paul Eluard, Henri Michaux, Benjamin Péret, and Aimé Césaire. The impact of his sudden confrontation in Bucharest with Romanian or French literary surrealism is most clearly illustrated, though, in the few lyrics or pieces of poetic prose that he now composed in Romanian, as well as in the German-language poetry that he wrote either while still living in Bucharest or in the course of his brief sojourn in Vienna, the cultural Mecca of both his poor mother's and his own dreams which

so bitterly disappointed him and Alfred Gong when they both managed at last to escape there from communist Bucharest.

Only in Romania have Celan's Romanian-language poems been so far granted the critical attention that they deserve. Elsewhere they have been almost scornfully neglected, probably as a consequence of Celan's oft-quoted but nevertheless absurd statement: "Only in one's mother's tongue can one express one's own truth. In a foreign language the poet lies." Were Dante and Milton lying when they wrote their magnificent poems in Latin? Is the "Dies irae" a lie, together with so much other great medieval poetry composed in Latin? Was Rilke likewise lying when he wrote his few exquisite but quite unpretentious poems in French? In expressing this opinion Celan was indeed voicing a critical prejudice that has its source in the attacks on classicism and humanism of those nineteenth-century romantics who were political and linguistic nationalists. Is a poet's language breast-fed to him by his mother? Why did Celan not choose to write his poetry in Yiddish, the language that his father often spoke, according to all available testimony, but that his purist mother abhorred? Celan's choice of the *Hochdeutsch* of traditional German literature rather than the local German dialect of Bukovina as his vehicle for poetic expression was certainly dictated to him by obscure psychoanalytic forces. For similar reasons other bilingual writers have chosen to express themselves in the language of their father, if offered such a choice.

Be that all as it may, Celan's two years spent among his Romanian surrealist friends in Bucharest appear to have exerted other and less strictly linguistic influences on his life. According to Chalfen's biography and the testimonies quoted there, Celan managed at last in Bucharest to free himself to some extent from the mother-fixation which, as long as he was still living in Czernowitz, led him to continue prudishly repressing most of his sexual urges. Suddenly Celan began to behave more freely in his relationships with women. From several of his Romanian-language writer friends who likewise happened to be Jews, among them Paul Paun and Ovid Crohmalnicianu, he also adopted the custom of adopting a pseudonym as a writer: first Paul Aurel, as a successful translator from Russian into Romanian; later A. Pavel; finally Paul Celan, an anagram of the Romanian spelling, Ancel, of his rather Germanic-Jewish family name, Antschel. This last pseudonym ultimately became his official name too. Tristan Tzara, Benjamin Fundoianu (or Fondane), Ilarie Voronca, Claude Sernet, and Celan's friend Paul Paun are all Romanian-Jewish poets who, in order not to attract too much attention as Jews in anti-Semitic Romania, published their writings under these pseudonyms, which sounded less Jewish than their Hebraic or Germanic family names.

Much of the impact of the Holocaust, of the murder of his parents in Transnistrian Nazi camps, and of his own experiences in a Romanian forced-labor camp on Celan's psyche was first expressed, above all, in "Todesfuge," the poem to which he soon began to owe his international reputation as "the true bard of the Holocaust" and, in some more skeptical than truly anti-Semitic West German literary circles as "unser Wiedergutmachungslyriker." However, Celan expressed here his awareness of the extermination camps mainly in terms and imagery borrowed from other poets: for example, Rose Ausländer, who saved her own life and that of her sick mother by living in hiding in the cellars of abandoned homes in the Czernowitz ghettos; or Immanuel Weissglass, who saved both himself and his mother from death in the Transnistrian camps where Celan's parents perished so miserably. Other details of "Todesfuge" are borrowed from the painter Arnold Dagani's oral accounts of his and his wife's survival and of the death, which he had witnessed in Transnistria, of Celan's young relative, the teenage German-language poet Selma Meerbaum-Eisinger. Dagani later wrote and published these accounts in an English translation as "The Grave in the Cherry Orchard" in numbers 291, 292, and 293 of volume year 29 of the English periodical *Adam.* As we know from Chalfen's biography, Celan had personally experienced only the rigors of a Romanian forced-labor camp in Moldavia, from which, according to testimony gathered by Chalfen, he was even occasionally able to return "on leave" to Czernowitz, perhaps thanks to the bribing of a Romanian guard.

A close friend of Celan while the latter was living in Bucharest immediately after World War II, the Romanian-language poet and scholar Petre Solomon, published a few years ago a remarkable book of personal memories of Celan, *Paul Celan: Dimensiunea românească* (Bucharest, Criterion, 1987), which includes as an appendix Celan's Romanian-language poems in verse and prose, his Romanian translations of four short prose texts by Franz Kafka, and his letters from Vienna and Paris to Solomon (written at first from 1948 to 1951 in Romanian but later in French), as well as his letters written from Vienna and Paris in German to the older Bukovina-born German-language poet Alfred Margul-Sperber, who had befriended Celan in Bucharest. All the letters originally written in French or German are published here in their original text, followed by a Romanian translation. Solomon's book was subsequently brought out in Paris in a French translation, which Celan's widow forced its publisher to withdraw from

circulation. Later she refused to permit the publication of an American translation of Solomon's book.

It is unfortunate that so few American scholars who display an interest in Celan can read Romanian. Solomon's book alone contains factual material which might usefully correct some of the characteristic absurdities of the cult of personality that detract from the value of much current Celan scholarship. One is even left wondering why so much pathos is now lavished in America, England, France, Germany, and Israel on Celan as a survivor of the Holocaust, rather than on any of the often equally gifted poets who can be numbered among its victims. It was of course easier to grant prestigious national prizes in West Germany to Celan, a survivor, then to grant them post-humously to Jakov van Hoddis, Alfred Grunewald, Alma Johanna König, Gertrud Kolmar, Alfred Mombert, or Juri Soyfer, who all died in Nazi concentration camps, or to Bruder Sonka (Josef Sonnenschein), who survived Auschwitz only to die as a Trotskyist in a Stalinist jail in his native Czechoslovakia. Both the gentile and the Jewish literary worlds needed a living poet on whom they could lavish their guilt feelings, the Germans above all for having failed to prevent the Holocaust and many Jews for not having morally deserved to survive it.

In the years that he lived in Paris and the course of his frequent trips from Paris to West Germany, Celan developed a sense of public relations that is well illustrated in most of the deliberately "soulful" photographs of him that are widely used for publicizing his works, contrasting so strikingly with the much happier and more relaxed photographs of him that were taken earlier in Bucharest and that illustrate Solomon's book. The original German edition of Chalfen's biography likewise offers us some refreshingly unassuming photographs of Celan as an apparently more normal and sometimes even quite happy young man. Chalfen also reveals, from the testimony of Celan's friends, that the poet already displayed as an adolescent in Czernowitz some talent and ambitions as an actor.

Both Chalfen and Solomon thus offer us valuable information on Celan's early life, literary tastes and activities, and friendships and associations in Czernowitz and Bucharest. It is in this respect all the more significant that the 1988 double issue of *Acts* (a periodical edited by Benjamin Hollander, published by David Levi Strauss in San Francisco), devoted entirely to Celan's activities as a translator, never mentions his activity as a translator of Romanian poetry into German or of German or Russian writers into Romanian. None of the contributors to this volume, entitled "Translating Tradition: Paul Celan in France," appears moreover to have dared discuss any of Celan's rare mistranslations, most of which might well be considered revealing as "Freud-ian slips." I must limit myself here to pointing out only two such mistranslations, both of them from French. In his German rendition of a none-too-significant little prose poem by his friend Henri Pastoureau, Celan mis-translated "un centaure pie" (meaning "a piebald cen-taur") as "ein frommer Kentaur" (meaning "a pious cen-taur") instead of "ein gescheckter Kentaur," thereby revealing his lack of any sense of irony or humor as well as his general tendency, displayed also in many of his other translations, to raise the tone of the original text in order to bring it closer to his own conception of "the sublime."

In his "Remarks on Celan's Last Translation," that of a very pretentious French poem, "Décimale blanche," by his French friend and translator Jean Daive, Bern-hard Böschenstein fails to point out that Celan likewise mistranslated "visage de grand large" (which clearly means "face of the high seas") as "Weit-drauβen-Gesicht" instead of "Hochseegesicht," thereby compli-cating Daive's image, whether consciously or uncon-sciously, by creating an unnecessary German neologism after the manner of the philosopher Martin Heidegger.

It has often been claimed that Celan's very cryptic poetic diction reveals his desire to purge his German of any of the linguistic heirlooms of Hitler's Third Reich; but Heidegger's German had already been condemned in Celan's lifetime, by the Heidelberg philosopher Dolf Sternberger, as typically National Socialist. This makes it all the more strange that René Char, a hero of the French Resistance during the German occupation of his fatherland, and Celan, a victim of the very worst mani-festations of Nazi anti-Semitism, should both have al-lowed themselves to be seduced by Heidegger's siren songs so soon after World War II. Such are, however, some of the more puzzling manifestations of the cult of personality in our age.

A few of the most egregious examples of the delib-erate disregard of available facts that such a cult can lead an otherwise reputable literary critic to display may be found in a review that George Steiner devoted, in the *New Yorker* of 28 August 1989, to the Persea Books edi-tion of Michael Hamburger's translations of a selection of Celan's poems. Steiner began there by referring to Celan's life "as a child during the Holocaust, as an exile in Paris, . . . as one inebriate with the light-bursts of Je-rusalem and of the beloved woman he encountered there." In point of fact, Celan was already over twenty years old when the Holocaust spread to his native Buko-vina; he lived in Paris, like Gertrude Stein, as a willing expatriate, having left Soviet-occupied Czernowitz, then communist Romania, and finally postwar Austria without ever being exiled; and his first and only visit to

Israel occurred a few months before he committed sui-cide in Paris as a married man and father of a French son, having met again in Israel only a couple of women whom he had once loved briefly in Czernowitz or Bu-charest but with whom he had long ceased to corre-spond at all.

In his dithyrambic article Steiner goes on to state that no one who met Celan "failed to sense the sombre radiance, the desolateness and apartness of his being," as if poor Celan had been the illstarred hero of a Gothic novel or a Byronic Manfred of sorts. Further on, Steiner lists the image "black milk," repeated several times in Celan's famous "Todesfuge," as one of the poet's "most famous finds"; but we now know, both from Chalfen's biography and from other sources such as the recent Insel Verlag reprint of the first volume of the collected poems of Rose Ausländer, that this image was borrowed by Celan from her poem "Ins Leben," first published in 1939 in Czernowitz in her collection *Der Regenbogen*: "Nur aus der Trauer Mutterinnigkeit / strömt mir das Vollmaβ des Erlebens ein. / Sie speist mir eine lange, trübe Zeit / mit *schwarzem Milch* und schwerem Wer-mutwein" (emphasis added).

Steiner also refers to "the inwoven multilingualism of Celan's idiom; Hebrew, Yiddish, Russian, French, and Italianate words, turns of phrase, acoustic transpar-encies abound in his German." He omits from this list, however, a language, Romanian, that Celan spoke and wrote fluently, as well as English, from which he trans-lated Shakespeare, Emily Dickinson, Andrew Marvell, John Donne, Alfred Housman, and Robert Frost, and which reappears occasionally in transparency in Celan's cryptic poem "Huhediblu" as well as elsewhere. Steiner then suggests that "the only legitimate reading" of Celan's best poems "is by Talmudic or Cabalist meth-ods," although none of Celan's German would lend it-self to the kind of legalistic commentary that character-izes the Talmud or to the gematria and notarikon that characterize Cabalist commentary founded on the numeric values of the Hebrew alphabet, which are not applicable to the Latin alphabet of German. Neither does Celan's poetry lend itself to another Cabalist sys-tem of interpretation, that of *pardes* or literal, allegori-cal, metaphorical, and anagogical meanings, which Dante too proposed for his *Divina Commedia* in his Latin letter to Can Grande de la Scala.

Much of what Steiner wrote here on Celan can thus be dismissed as but another example of the absurdities to which the cult of personality can lead. It is also signif-icant, however, as an example of the kind of argumenta-tion that can somehow be interpreted as an attempt to refute Theodor Adorno's widely quoted but neverthe-less nonsensical remark about the impossibility of writing poetry after Auschwitz, as if the Holocaust had struck all poets dumb but left all fiction writers, composers of music, painters, and sculptors still capable of expressing themselves adequately.

Because I devote here so much attention to George Steiner's article, some readers may begin to suspect me of harboring a personal grudge against him, but I have chosen to point out a few of the piece's more regrettable flaws for two reasons: it was certainly the most widely read of all articles of this length that had yet been devoted to Celan's life and poetry in English; and its author, both here and in his other writings, has so often displayed his exceptional knowledge of the German language and its literature that some aspects of his uncritical cult of personality in the case of poor Celan are unforgivable.

In his introduction to the American edition of Chalfen's biography John Felstiner of Stanford University likewise makes the following statement, as if he had not read the contents of the book: "Like millions of others in central and eastern Europe, Celan's family persistently saw their destiny there rather than in emigration." Chalfen states clearly and repeatedly, however, that Celan's father harbored Zionist ideals and was eager to emigrate with his wife and son to Palestine, which was still governed under a British mandate. This is also stated implicitly by Celan himself in the two poems where he refers to his father's tragic death. Both Celan and his mother opposed such a plan to emigrate, however, and there is even some evidence that Celan's mother remained overnight in their home until her actual deportation by the Germans to an extermination camp in Transnistria, still sincerely convinced that the *Volk der Dichter und Denker* could not possibly be the *Volk der Schinder und Henker* that it had actually turned out to be. For this very reason she may indeed have failed to follow Ruth Lackner's advice to hide (like Celan) overnight in a factory during those weekends when the Germans were proceeding with their deportations of Jews.

In the introduction to the revised and expanded edition of his *Poems of Paul Celan* Michael Hamburger refers in a footnote (page 21) to the German edition of Chalfen's biography but likewise still states, as if he had not read it, that Celan shared with Nelly Sachs "an obvious preoccupation with the mass killings he had physically survived but could never recover from," though Chalfen reports clearly that Celan had escaped these atrocities without ever witnessing them. The cult of personality can indeed induce writers to lapse into an often fancifully negligent handling of available facts.

In Celan's poem "Shibboleth," which clearly refers—with its references to Madrid, Extremadura, and the Loyalist slogan "No pasarán"—to the Spanish Civil War, Hamburger's mistranslation of Celan's "Einhorn" as "Unicorn" is frankly absurd: Chalfen's biography reveals without any possible doubt that the poet is here invoking his young communist friend Erich Einhorn, whose political sympathies with the Loyalists he then shared; but "Unicorn" is here more puzzling and, one presumes, more poetic.

I must admit that I too was originally inclined to become a victim of this same fatal cult of personality when I first met Celan in Paris in 1952, after reading his "Todesfuge" a couple of years earlier in Vienna. Eighteen years later, in 1970, Celan committed suicide by drowning in the Seine in Paris. At that time I happened to be at the other end of the world, on the shores of the Pacific Ocean, but I had continued to see Celan fairly often since our first meeting and even associated with him quite closely from time to time. I found him, however, increasingly self-centered as the years went by, often making such weird demands on me that it became more and more convenient to avoid involvement with him in any discussion whatsoever.

I had originally come across "Todesfuge" in an anthology of younger postwar Viennese writers given to me by its compiler and editor Hans Weigel, the *Hans-in-allen-Gassen* of Viennese literature who had already befriended the ill-starred Juri Soyfer, among other victims of Nazi persecution, in Vienna in the thirties. I was so impressed by this one poem of Celan's that I asked Weigel whether he could arrange for me to meet its author, only to be told that Celan had recently moved from Vienna to Paris. Weigel gave me his Paris address, however, so that I was soon able to write him, inviting him to contribute some poems to *Das Lot,* which the French poet Alain Bosquet, the German poet Alexander Koval, and I were still editing for the Karlheinz Henssel Verlag in West Berlin. We were thus the first to solicit contributions from Celan for a West German publication, but the Berlin Blockade delayed for a long while the publication of the issue of *Das Lot* that was to include his poems, so that *Die Wandlung,* published in Heidelberg by Dolf Sternberger, ultimately brought Celan into print ahead of us.

By 1952 both Bosquet and I had moved from Berlin to Paris, where I was editing the French, German, and Italian versions of the Ford Foundation's well-intentioned quarterly *Perspectives USA* under James Laughlin's general editorship of its original English-language edition. I contacted Celan and soon understood that he had no permanent job and was living rather precariously; so I began to commission him to undertake well-paid translations of American texts for the German edition of each issue of *Perspectives USA*. These translations included, in addition to some critical prose and a few captions for reproductions of works by Ben Shahn, two poems by Marianne Moore which are now included by the Suhrkamp Verlag in the posthumous edition of Celan's complete poems, prose, and verse translations, with the notable exception of his previously published translations of a series of French poems by Alain Bosquet (with whom, if I remember right, Celan had later quarreled). I must admit, however, that his translations of Marianne Moore displayed so little sense of her wit and irony that I had to correct them considerably with him before sending them to press. When I chanced to read many years later Celan's "Abzahlreime" and "Groβes Geburtstagsblaublau mit Reimzeug und Assonanz," I realized how ungifted he was for the kind of nonsense poetry in which Christian Morgenstern had already displayed so brilliantly in German the kind of wit and irony that one associates in English or American literature with such names as Edward Lear or Odgen Nash. Celan also proved to lack this sense of fun when I introduced him in Paris to the older German poet Peter Gan, once famous too for his wit and whom I also commissioned from time to time to translate American texts for the German edition of *Perspectives USA.* Celan and Gan appeared to be quite incapable of communicating at all, although Gan, who came from a family of Hamburg patricians, had never been a Nazi and, throughout the Nazi regime, remained in voluntary exile in Paris, then in Madrid when the Germans occupied the French capital.

These little jobs for the quarterly German issues of *Perspectives USA* were not enough to keep the wolf from poor Celan's door, however. Some time earlier *Das Lot* had already published in Berlin a German translation of selections from my friend E. M. Cioran's first French book, *Précis de décomposition.* These so impressed a major German publisher, the Ernst Rowohlt Verlag, that I was suddenly asked whether I could suggest another translator for the whole book, as the widow of the poet Joachim Ringelnatz, who had translated these selections for *Das Lot,* was now too ill to undertake the job of translating the whole book. I suggested Celan, who soon obtained the contract and subsequently continued to associate with Cioran as a friend until shortly before his suicide.

One of my friends as a part-time free-lance conference interpreter was Lydia Kerr, a passionate admirer of Rilke and herself a trilingual or quadrilingual poet of sorts, but above all chief of the translating and interpreting services of the International Labor Organization, a United Nations agency located in Geneva. She turned up for a few days in Paris and, in the course of a conversation, expressed to me her admiration for what little

of Celan's poetry she had managed to read. She was also seeking to recruit a new translator from English or French into German for her office, so that I promptly recommended Celan and invited them both to dine in my apartment. Lydia immediately engaged him, and he soon moved to a generously paid job in Geneva; but his work there proved before long to be beneath his dignity as a rhapsodic bard, and he returned to Paris, where he was fortunately offered, some time later, a steady but less demanding job as lecturer in German literature at the Ecole Normale Supérieure, a civil-service job similar to the one that Samuel Beckett had long held there in English literature. Celan retained this post until his death.

Rudolf Hirsch, the interim editor of the illustrious German literary journal *Die Neue Rundschau* for the S. Fischer Verlag in Frankfurt am Main, had meanwhile come across the English translations of a few Portuguese poems by Fernando Pessoa which I had published in the Chicago journal *Poetry: A Magazine of Verse.* He suddenly asked me whether I knew anyone who might now assist me in translating them into German too. I proposed Celan, of course, though he did not know any Portuguese. We undertook the task together, with me producing rough word-for-word translations into German, which he proceeded to rewrite in more poetic diction, though I sometimes found it difficult to convince him that Pessoa, especially under his "heteronyms" Álvaro de Campos and Alberto Caeiro, often very deliberately avoided expressing himself in traditionally poetic diction. Be that all as it may, Celan saw to it that our translations were published under his name "unter Mitarbeit von Edouard Roditi" rather than under our joint names. Under German copyright law, our translations are now reprinted in Celan's complete works without my being authorized to claim any royalties on them or to reprint them under our joint names in any similar edition of my own collected writings.

This collaboration with Celan proved at the time to be only one of the first among several incidents that gradually led me, and Bosquet too, to realize how pathologically egocentric poor Celan really was. Another and more embarrassing incident arose when *Poetry: A Magazine of Verse* asked me to contribute a selection of translations of new German poets. Without any hesitation, I selected and translated a couple of short poems by Celan, some by Koval (my close friend and coeditor of *Das Lot*), and some by Hans Magnus Enzensberger, whom I had but recently met in Paris. It never occurred to me that Celan would be mortally offended at finding himself published in such company, but the tone of his indignant protests warned me to avoid any further such attempts to promote him as the remarkably gifted poet

I still believe him to have been. Oddly enough, it was as a consequence of our collaboration on the Pessoa translations for a periodical published by the S. Fischer Verlag that Celan was soon able to transfer his allegiance from the Deutsche Verlagsanstalt Stuttgart, which had been his original publisher in West Germany, to the much more prestigious and powerful combine comprising the Insel Verlag, the S. Fischer Verlag, and the Suhrkamp Verlag that happens to publish me too, from time to time, in German.

I finally decided to avoid any further misunderstandings with Celan at the time of his truly absurd quarrel with Claire Goll, the widow of my very old friend the trilingual German, French, and American poet Yvan Goll. Some years earlier Celan had contacted Goll in Paris and, shortly before the sick older poet's death, promised to translate a few of his recent poems into German, a truly unnecessary task since Goll had originally made a considerable name for himself in Berlin as a leading younger German-language expressionist poet and was again writing some poetry in German, which Bosquet and I were proud to be able to publish in *Das Lot.*

After Goll's death, Claire began to find fault with Celan's translations and insisted, I understand, on revising them herself, having likewise originally been a German-language poet. Celan objected to her pretensions, and all this led to a major literary feud, in the course of which Claire accused Celan of having plagiarized some of Yvan's German poems in a few of his own. In the introduction to his volume of translations of selected poems by Celan, Michael Hamburger refers to "Claire Goll's maniacal accusations," but Celan's reactions to these were just as maniacal, as can be seen from the letters which he wrote at that time in German to Margul-Sperber about this whole episode and which Petre Solomon has now published in Bucharest. The fantasies Celan describes there, about an imaginary neo-Nazi conspiracy to discredit him as a poet, are quite as maniacal as some of the far more entertaining fantasies about her own love life that one can now find in Claire's published memoirs. There she boasts of having been the mistress of Rilke and Malraux, among others, but of having then experienced her first orgasms in her seventies with a new teenage lover.

Celan was ready to sue Claire Goll in court over this matter of her accusations of plagiarism and even began to ask some of his friends to appear in the proceedings as witnesses, or at least to file affidavits to the effect that no trace of Yvan Goll's poetry could be detected in any of his own. When Celan approached me as a potential witness, I was tactless enough to laugh the whole matter off while pointing out that all poets,

whether consciously or unconsciously, reflect some of their readings in their own poems. Virgil, I argued, thus remains a great poet in spite of his borrowings from Homer and Apollonius Rhodius and perhaps Ennius too in the *Aeneid,* or from Hesiod in the *Georgics* or Theocritus in his *Eclogues.* Should Milton have been ashamed of his borrowings from Dante or Tasso? Stravinsky, I tried to reassure Celan, would certainly refrain from suing anyone who might suggest that he had borrowed, in *Jeu de Cartes,* a musical theme from Rossini.

Celan's reactions to my remarks left me speechless. He accused me of now joining the pack of anti-Semites who, in the German press and elsewhere, were already beginning to accuse him—though I was not yet aware of this—of other and far more obvious borrowings. Only many years later, from my readings of Chalfen's biography, then of the first volume of the Insel Verlag edition of the poems of Celan's immensely gifted and even more unfortunate compatriot and former friend Immanuel Weissglass (born in Czernowitz the same year as both Celan and Alfred Gong), did I realize how much Celan borrowed in "Todesfuge" from other German-language Bukovina-born writers with whom he had associated in Czernowitz on his return from his Romanian forced-labor camp in Moldavia. In one of these poems in particular, Weissglass described, while still toiling there, his experience of the death camps in Transnistria where Celan's parents perished. Later too, I found much of this reported more factually and in greater detail in the previously mentioned journal of the painter Arnold Dagani, whom Chalfen also quotes as one of the sources for Celan's information about how his parents died in Transnistria.

In addition to his borrowing of "black blood" in "Todesfuge" from his friend Rose Ausländer's poem, Celan borrowed even more from the following poem, entitled "Er," which Weissglass had written in the Transnistrian death camp from which he managed to save both himself and his aging mother:

Wir heben Gräber in die Luft und siedeln
Mit Weib und Kind an den gebotnen Ort.
Wir schaufeln fleiβig, *und die andern fiedeln.*
Man schafft ein Grab und fährt im Tanzen fort.

Er will, daβ über diese Därme dreister
Der Bogen strenge wie sein Antlitz streiche:
Spielt sanft vom Tod, er ist ein deutscher Meister,
Der durch die Lande als ein Nebel schleicht.

Und wenn die Dämmrung blutig quilt am Abend,
Öffn' ich nachzehrend den verbissenen Mund,
Ein Haus für alle in die Lufte grabend:
Breit wie der Sarg, schmal wie die Todestund.

Er spielt im Haus mit Schlangen, draut und dichtet,
In Deutschland dämmert es wie Gretchens Haar.

Das Grab in Wolken wird nicht eng gerichtet:
Da weit der Tod ein deutscher Meister war.

For the poetry of Immanuel Weissglass, so different from his own in style in spite of occasional similarities in theme or imagery, Celan is reported to have expressed, whether in Czernowitz or later in Bucharest, at best a kind of somewhat patronizing condescension. The corrections in Celan's handwriting that Jerry Glenn has found on some of the surviving manuscripts of Alfred Gong suggest much the same kind of condescension of a master toward a disciple.

Oddly enough, Both Weissglass and Gong display, in the form of a few of their poems but above all in their bitter irony and occasional overt references to well-known lyrics by Heinrich Heine, their admiration for German literature's greatest Jewish poet, the cynosure of all anti-Semites for more than a hundred years. Some of their verse also appears to display the influence of a few of the expressionist poets of Berlin, such as Alfred Lichtenstein or Jacob van Hoddis, whose best-known poems were available in several popular anthologies of contemporary German poetry which had been published before 1933. Weissglass was obviously remembering Heine, for instance, when he began his own "Loreley" with the following overt parody: "Was soll es, daβ ich traurig bin, bedeuten? / Zur Tiefe lockt mich deine Fratze, Tyll! / Am Felsen ding ich, gleich verlassnen Brauten, / Und harr des Schelms, den ich verderben will." Gong likewise begins one of his early lyrics with a similar parody of another of Heine's most widely quoted poems: "In die Heimat kamen die Grenadier / Aus Krieg und Gefangenschaft. / Sie fanden sehr verdünnt das Bier, / Das Leben ohne Saft." Both Weissglass and Gong also repeatedly elide in their verse the mute vowels of literary *Hochdeutsch,* much as Heine did, again and again, in many of his most famous poems, such as "Atta Troll" or "Deutschland, ein Wintermärchen," where he allows himself to lapse into spoken German and even into rhymes, such as *bedeuten/Zeiten,* that betray his own accent as a native of Düsseldorf.

Nowhere, in all of Celan's poems, have I yet been able to detect a single hint of admiration for any of Heine's poems, a fact which may well explain his reported lack of sympathy for the poetry of Gong and Weissglass. Neither have I yet been able to discern in Celan's verse any evidence of an overt interest in the poetry of any of the major Berlin expressionists, except the very short poem from *Schneepart* where he deliberately parodies one of Brecht's most famous anti-Nazi songs:

Ein Blatt
für Bertolt Brecht:

Was sind das für Zeiten,
wo ein Gespräch

beinah ein Verbrechen ist,
weil es so viel Gesagtes
mit einschlieβt?

Celan is careful here, however, to strip Brecht's original statement of all its political significance and impact.

Celan is known, on the other hand, to have been acquainted with the poetry of Yvan Goll, of course, but also with that of Else Lasker-Schüler, and my admiration for her writings even occasioned my first unintentional moment of tension in my relations with Celan. I had known Lasker-Schüler briefly in Berlin before her first trip to Palestine, and we had then corresponded for a while about my proposed translations of some of her poems into French as well as into English. After first reading one of Celan's poems, "Ein Lied in der Wüste," in *Mohn und Gedächtnis,* I was tactless enough to remark delightedly to him that it reminded me of some of Lasker-Schüler's poetry. Celan's reaction to this truly innocent obiter dictum was almost as if I had accused him directly of plagiarism.

He appeared indeed to be at all times convinced of the absolute originality of everything that he wrote, to such an extent that his fears of displaying in his poems their biographical or literary sources may well have led him, as the years went by, to become increasingly cryptic. At best, he might admit to having emulated Hölderlin, Rilke, or Trakl, but never that he might have borrowed anything from them.

He was very secretive too about his own Jewish cultural background in Bukovina, especially after his Paris marriage to a French graphic artist who came from an aristocratic and reputedly anti-Semitic family. Chalfen thus reports in his biography that Celan displayed in his youth an admiration for the works of the older Jewish artist Artur Kolnik, at one time fairly widely known as "the Chagall of Galicia and Bukovina." A survivor of the Holocaust, Kolnik was living and exhibiting in Paris after World War II. Because I reviewed one of his shows favorably in *L'Arche,* the monthly periodical of the Jewish communities of France, Kolnik very kindly gave me one of his very fine lithographs in color, depicting a Purim scene in Galicia or Bukovina. When Celan saw it in my apartment, he displayed no interest in it; neither did he ever display any interest in meeting the immensely talented painter Avigdor Arikha, an Israeli resident of Paris but a Bukovina-born survivor of the death camps in Transnistria where Celan's parents perished.

More and more Celan appeared to behave as if he were the sole Jewish survivor of the Holocaust, or at least the only one authorized, as if by some divine election, to bear witness to it in writing. It is perhaps significant in this respect that, in the otherwise admirable speech he delivered in 1960 on the occasion of his acceptance of the prestigious Georg Büchner Prize, he refrained from mentioning the name of Karl Emil Franzos (1848–1904). This otherwise once widely read Austrian-Jewish writer was Galician-born but spent much of his childhood and adolescence in Czernowitz and is now remembered mainly for his single-handed literary resurrection of Georg Büchner, whose manuscripts Franzos retrieved, carefully transcribed, and finally published in 1879 in the first edition of Büchner's complete works. Franzos also happened to be the author of some very popular stories about the Jews of Galicia and Bukovina which were still read by Celan's elders in his boyhood and were despised by him, as were also the Yiddish writings of his compatriots Elieser Steinbarg and Itzik Manger.

What puzzled me most about Celan in this general context was his ever more overtly expressed admiration for the writings of Martin Heidegger, that arch-anti-Semite among contemporary philosophers. This admiration was all the more surprising when I began to realize, from my arguments with Celan on this subject, that he had only the very vaguest notions of the philosophies of Plato, Aristotle, Spinoza, Descartes, Kant, or Hegel. As for Ludwig Wittgenstein, some of whose works I happened to be reading when Celan and I were translating Pessoa together, he appeared to have never heard of him or not to be at all interested in reading him.

Long before meeting Celan, I wrote a series of aphorisms on poetry and poets. One of them was a parody of the once widely quoted Victorian remark, "Children should be seen but not heard." In spite of my truly formative friendships with T. S. Eliot, Paul Goodman, Kenneth Rexroth, Léon-Paul Fargue, and Alain Bosquet and my very pleasant though brief relationship with Dylan Thomas, I could not refrain from writing: "Great poets should be read, but not met." This has proven in my life to be particularly true of my few meetings with W. H. Auden and my far more numerous meetings with Celan, though I continue to read much of their poetry with delight.

A half-century ago I may well have been the very first American or English writer to develop suddenly a great and lasting interest in the poetry of Paul Celan, in fact an interest that managed to survive close to twenty years of an often very difficult personal relationship with him. Today Celan already shares the honor, with Rilke and Brecht, of being the most widely translated of all twentieth-century German-language poets, in spite of proving, in much of his poetry, to be one of the most untranslatable. He has even been translated, believe it or not, into Arabic and published privately in an edition in that language that bears no indication of copyright or of date of publication but reprints also the original German text of the twenty-one poems translated there by A. K. El Djanabi. Selected from *Mohn und Gedächtnis, Von Schwelle zu Schwelle, Sprachgitter, Die Niemandsrose, Atemwende, Fadensonnen, Lichtzwang, Schneepart,* and *Zeitgehoft,* these very ambitious translations include, of course, "Todesfuge," which may puzzle some readers in Baghdad, in the Gaza Strip, or elsewhere. My regrettable illiteracy in literary Arabic precludes, alas, my offering here an appreciation of El Djanabi's skill as a translator or of the critical acumen displayed in his brief introduction.

Edouard Roditi, Winter 1992

All My Foreigners

The topic of this conference and of this special issue appears to me like a beautiful, bright red apple promising the best of health, yet I have the feeling that I should be careful about biting into it. The author who is called to account will hardly be able to avoid leafing through his writings in his mind, searching for examples of intercultural encounters. If such are found, he will very easily run the risk of discovering in himself after the fact a pioneer of a multicultural society. If, in spite of a meticulous, even desperate search through his work, he does not come across a single foreigner, he will be tempted to give in either to self-justifications or to a deep depression.

I would like to take it upon myself to transform the topic of this conference back into the form of a question: is it true that we can find in contemporary German literature a presentation of intercultural encounters? I am not so sure. Perhaps I do not have the proper perspective. What I notice at first is an interesting inconsistency between literature and the mass media. At the latest, since the assaults in Hoyerswerda, Mölln, and Solingen, an enormous furor has developed on television and in the big newspapers around the issue of "foreigners." Even the physical presence of foreigners in the media has programmatically increased in the last few years. The television network ZDF initiated this trend in its morning broadcasts with the dark-skinned, accent-free newscaster Cerno Jobatai, whom even German nationalist audiences would presumably no longer want to do without. On the channel Pro 7, "Arabella" hosts a popular talk show dealing with intimate themes, and the successful Berlin radio station "Multi-Kulti" has existed for a year now, elevating the topic of this conference to an agenda.

However, we are still a long way from the situation in America, where for instance in police dramas on television a black detective regularly enters his squad car next to a white partner in order to launch their pursuit of a fugitive. When I first saw these programs, I asked myself what it might mean when the American screenplay writers planned a deadly end for the invariably sympathetic black detective while allowing his white partner to survive, grieving but unharmed. This is perhaps an initial indication that equal presence does not necessarily mean "equal opportunity."

All in all, no one will contest the fact that the mass media in Germany have taken up this topic swiftly and—at least in the case of the racist assaults—with a clear position in defense of the rights of our resident foreigners. The fact that the sensation value of the murder reports, a fear for the international reputation of the Germans, and a conformity to "political correctness" have all contributed to this reaction does not change the final result: the discussion concerning the "multicultural society"—though many are not happy with the concept—can no longer be silenced and will dominate the years to come.

But what is the situation in the theater, in literature, in film? Many artists and writers were among the first to react to the racist assaults of the neo-Nazis: they have taken and continue to take stands in newspaper articles, in public appeals, in campaigns, in solidarity concerts, in demonstrations, and in citizens' groups. But in our works one seldom encounters the people for whose civil rights we have committed ourselves. It is as if the millions of foreign inhabitants who have lived and worked with us for decades, whose children go to school with our own, in whose restaurants and bars we spend our evenings, whom we encounter on our soccer teams, at our conferences, and at our birthday parties had not yet found a place in our fantasy—they appear only infrequently as main characters.

I think that it would be fruitless to give a letter grade to this situation or to downplay it with hasty justifications. Writers are children of their times, and if it is true that art is anything but well-intentioned, then one should not scold artists for not fictionalizing "multicultural" experiences and contacts which they simply have not had. It does not occur to someone strolling across the Kurfürstendamm in Berlin that he is walking in the fourth or fifth largest Turkish city in the world. He might know or have learned that 170,000 Turks live in Berlin; but he does not see them in this area, and if he does, he can still exclude them from his perceptions. Presence, even a massive one, provides no guarantee of being noticed.

The complaint occurs to me which I constantly hear from foreign residents: even when they are born in Germany and speak German without an accent, the first question is always "What is your native country?" The answer—Germany—is always considered either an attempt to skirt the question or a joke. The implication behind this complaint is that in Germany one remains a foreigner all one's life, even when born there.

Finally, I am reminded of a sentence directed toward a friend of mine by one of his German guests after his fiftieth birthday: he was supposedly the sole intellectual who could invite almost as many foreigners as Germans to such a party without it appearing forced or programmatic. The sentence was obviously meant as a compliment, but it was depressing for my friend. If this compliment were true, which he contested, the only alternative would be to take to the hills.

Thus I arrive at a conjecture which I myself find difficult to accept: could it be that the weak presence of foreigners which I perceive in German literature and film says more about their social role up to now—namely, the level of their failure to be perceived and their limited presence in the collective imagination—than their momentary omnipresence in the mass media? The construction of a character in a film or a novel demands more personal familiarity and psychic effort than does a pamphlet or a declaration of solidarity. For the most part, art does not gain anything and loses a great deal when it attempts to compete with the news media; it loses itself. It is, incidentally, not uninteresting to pose the opposite question: which works by foreigners living with us, among whom there are of course many accomplished artists, have depicted the experience of immigration? There are, naturally, examples: the Turk Aras Ören, who writes in Turkish about Germany and became famous with his poem "Nyazi on Naunyn Street"; other, younger writers such as Zafer Cenosak and Zehra Cirak from Turkey; SAID, born in Iran; Gino Chiellino from Calabria; Fotini Ladaki, born in Greece; and many others who are second- or third-generation immigrants (Fritz Raddatz introduced many of them recently in *Die Zeit*). All these have been writing for a long time in the language of the country in which they reside, but are not recognized as natives. Most of them are published by small, alternative presses, often founded by compatriots living in Germany.

In our neighboring countries, France and Great Britain, the situation is different. There, writers such as Tahar Ben Jelloun or Salman Rushdie or V. S. Naipaul are naturally recognized and honored as French and British writers. One could even claim that the non-native writers have now become the most famous and most successful writers in these countries. One must add, however, that these writers are from the former colonies of these countries. A significant portion of

French and British cosmopolitanism is due to their colonial history and their laboriously achieved disengagement from it. The corresponding background is missing in Germany. One could partially explain the continuing German provincialism with the fact that the Germans never managed a comparable colonial history and, at a time when other peoples had begun to put such a history behind them, tried to catch up in the most horrifying way in the middle of Europe.

But let us come to the author who is being asked here to account for himself. In this case some biographical information is perhaps necessary. The author standing before you suffers from a sort of family illness against which he is helpless. All my siblings were born in April; all of them, except for one, write; and all, except for one, have chosen non-German life-companions. Please do not expect from me any explanation for this state of affairs. The only thing that is certain is that we did not arrange in advance to introduce one another to non-German partners.

With such a writer one is tempted to presume that foreigners might enter and leave his texts as if they were part of the family, so to speak. This is not the case. It is indeed true that in all of my longer essays and most fundamentally in the play *Totoloque* I have dealt with cultural borders: in *Die Botschaft des Pferdekopfs* (The Message of the Horse's Head), in three texts from *Extreme Mittellage* (Eng. *The German Comedy*), and in two essays from the collection *Vom Ende der Gewiβheit* (The End of Certainty).[1] But I repeat: the construction of a character demands more familiarity than does a political reflection. The clearest such attempt can be seen in the trio of friends from *Paarungen* (Couplings): Eduard, the German, confronts two Jewish Germans, André and Theo.[2] In *Lenz,* my first story, the hero, who has just presented himself for employment at an electronics firm, is on his way out when he meets a Turkish worker, who recounts to Lenz his path to Germany: "Lenz could hardly manage to listen. He paid most of his attention to the eyes of the Turk and to his powerful, boxer-like arm movements. He had the intense desire to see the world through his eyes. For a moment it seemed to him as if he must take him in his arms and make him into a friend."[3]

However, the desire to see the world through the eyes of the Turk is not so much the result of curiosity. It is solely a question of Lenz's attempt at salvation. He imagines that he will obtain relief, distance, and healing from the foreign gaze of the Turk. This foreigner, by virtue of the privilege of not belonging, would evaluate in a completely different way that which drives Lenz through the streets. At the same time there is, embedded in the desire to see the world through the eyes of

the Turk, something like an esthetic program: to view the familiar with a foreign gaze, with the gaze of the foreigner, in order to appropriate it via this roundabout path. "For a while he imagined that the houses and streets were rolling by on rails. He was surprised by the brightness which gave special prominence to every object: the windows of the upper floors, the crowns of the trees which from up here looked like bushes, the highways under the train—everything as if he were seeing them for the first time. A song from 'The Doors' went through his head briefly, first the melody, then the text: 'People are strange, when you're a stranger, faces look ugly, when you're alone.'"[4]

But this utilization of the foreigner, of the foreign gaze, has its price. Lenz is not interested in the foreigner, in that which is foreign in him, in his sensual, nonconceptual, and possibly incomprehensible aspects. He perceives the foreigner only with respect to himself, as a means of expanding his own gaze. I see this danger in the employment of the foreigner not only in *Lenz* and not only in my own texts. The foreigner, or the foreign, easily becomes an involuntarily expert witness. The foreigner is utilized in order to embody the opposite of everything which the author finds lacking at home. There is only one thing which the foreigner is not permitted to be: himself, unintentionally different and foreign. This energy dominates the last section of the book as well. The almost ideal picture of the Italian '68 movement which is painted there can only be justified by Lenz's hunger for an alternative to the unhappy Berlin world from which he flees: the depiction tends to slip into stereotypes. "He allowed himself to be caught up in their unaffected relations with him and with each other. He grew accustomed to the fact that everyone touched everyone else whenever one felt like it and without any type of further implications. It became for him a matter of course that others were as interested in his doubts and uncertainties as in his points of view."[5]

The limits of such a motivated interest in the "foreign" are self-evident: the foreign is perceived only to the extent that it can provide evidence in the form of counterexample against that which is one's own. A similar mechanism had already produced the figure of the "noble savage" which occupied the best minds of the European Enlightenment from Rousseau to Voltaire until it found its way to Potsdam, where it inspired Frederick the Great to compose an opera about Montezuma. It took centuries before solid anthropological research was able to liberate the Enlightenment transfiguration of the foreign from the grip of such goodwill. It became apparent that exploitation, slavery, rape—all those human vices allegedly imported from Europe—had already existed in the New World, though in alternative forms, long before the European conquerors had set foot there. And the anthropologists discovered something else after a long, hermeneutic controversy: a disinterested, completely objective gaze of the researcher upon the object of study—the savage, the foreign—never existed and never will exist. The only way to transcend one's own horizon of understanding is by naming and reflecting upon one's cultural conditioning instead of denying it.

The peculiar thing about the book *Lenz* is the foreigner who does not appear. I am referring to a friend of Lenz by the name of "B." The real model for B., the calm and fatherly, pleasantly German friend of Lenz, is a foreigner: a politically conscious and extremely active immigrant from Iran with whom I lived together for many years in a space measuring about 800 square feet. How is it to be explained that I Germanized this friend in my story many years before he himself obtained, with considerable aversion, a German passport? To be honest, I don't know. Perhaps I would have considered his depiction as a foreigner in a book which was already so populated by foreigners as obtrusive. Perhaps the real B., who came to Germany at sixteen and went to school here, seemed to me to be an especially typical German. The most important reason is probably a passion or caprice which one could describe as esthetic jealousy. The book *Lenz* lives off of that "foreign gaze," which the hero, by virtue of his distress, casts upon the world. Within such a project, foreigners—the natural owners of the foreign gaze—appear as potential competitors. This is perhaps the reason why so many authors have an instinctive fear of or aversion to depicting foreigners. They disturb, with their concrete difference, the foreign gaze through which the author seeks to make the world recognizable.

Der Mauerspringer (Eng. *The Wall Jumper*) is a book about a different kind of border; foreigners do not appear in it. That role is played here by the "other" Germans on the other side of the border, who live in the "shadow city" on that "other planet": "Life there didn't differ simply in outward organization; it obeyed another law. To attribute this to a different social order and pace of development was to label it too hastily. I could orient myself better in New York than in the half-city just a little over three miles from my apartment. . . . This other law within a similar life . . . made itself only slightly felt. It came through more in half-sentences, in a gesture which left something unsaid, a laugh where none was expected, a manner of looking around. Not just ways of talking, but even certain facial lines could be linked to compass points in Germany."[6] To make the claim that the wall in one's head would last longer than the

one made of concrete, it was not necessary even then to be a prophet, just a careful observer.

After this preparatory work it was natural to warn the West Germans after the fall of the wall to resist the temptation to regard the other Germans as images of themselves. The treatment of the other Germans will demonstrate whether Europe will be able to withstand the reunification: "A unity which flattens all differences would be something to be feared not just by our neighbors." Fritz Stern, the skeptical but ultimately benevolent observer of the German species, recently formulated his reservations in the following way: neighboring European countries are observing very carefully how the West Germans are treating their brothers and sisters from the East, for their behavior toward their weaker relatives shows how they would, in case of doubt, deal with their neighbors as well.

Measured according to this yardstick, the result is at best mixed. And it is not necessarily any comfort if I respond to Fritz Stern with the following: the West Germans do not deal with one another any better than they do with the East Germans. Every second German treats every third German like a foreigner, so that the silly statement of solidarity, "I am a foreigner too," unexpectedly makes sense: it says a great deal about the natives.

In the novel *Paarungen* I planned a kind of frontal attack against the indigenous view of things. I searched for another, external perspective on the preeminently German topic "Berlin—city of separations." To this end I invented an anthropologist from the Third World—a so-called love detective—whose research project had brought her to Berlin. In my notes about her I wrote:

> . . . That which causes the male passersby, who typically manifest their erotic interest here as in all parts of the city by aggressively looking away, to look up with consternation is the skin color of this in any case colorful creature. This color probably corresponds almost exactly to that average value which the population of the world would arrive at through a resolute intermixing: for every one part white in the world there are at present, as everyone knows, nine parts color, and the proportion of white continues to decline. Consequently, her conspicuousness was partly a result of the fact that the inhabitants of the city had kept themselves so amazingly white. . . .

No one would have believed her capable of the research project which had led her with an overseas business-class ticket to the Central European metropolis. Marina Cuautemoc of the Nahua tribe, after finishing her anthropology degree at the University of Belém with a thesis concerning the temple priestesses of Mexico-

Tenochtitlán, had won over the Humboldt Foundation with an unusual research proposal. Her project, for which the learned, entirely male commission had granted a full $75,000 from the Third World fund, would break new ground for science. After European scientists had researched for centuries the living habits of the so-called primitive peoples, the applicant claimed that it was time to reverse the point of view. Marina Cuautemoc, graduate of both the University of Belém and Harvard University, traveled to Berlin with the intention of researching the romantic life of Central European men. This project led her straight into the "Tent," in front of which the waiter had just set up six tables. Marina ordered a Campari and soda, then took and leafed through the notes which she had prepared the day before in another restaurant and sketched the neighboring table, true to scale, into a site plan. In this sketch the center of the city appeared as a single, gigantic restaurant zone in which only the names of individual bars and the table numbers offered any orientation. The quadrangle which Marina was now drawing remained, for the time being, empty, like the neighboring table which it represented. When the waiter set down a new glass of Campari and soda, he saw the adorned head bent over a book on the top end of which one could read *The Serapion Brothers*. One of the pearl-embellished braids threw, like a bookmark, a shadow on the words of the romantic writer.

The invention of the love detective was, like all my ideas, in no way a product of pure fantasy. In the mid-1980s a researcher from Ghana had undertaken an investigation of the festivals and family rituals of the working class in the Ruhr area. The only trace of Marina left in my novel is a single detail: the pearl-embellished head bent over a book by E. T. A. Hoffmann.

What happened? Why did I ban Marina Cuautemoc from the third version of the manuscript of my novel? Why did she have to go? The idea of depicting and evaluating the romantic troubles of my three protagonists from the perspective of this researcher only functioned in my mind. In the execution, I believed I could perceive myself becoming more and more the slave of my Indian anthropologist. One night I gathered up my courage and threw her out of the manuscript.

Not completely. Through a (I admit, rather conventional) back door my beautiful tyrant reentered. But, to be sure, in a radically transformed—or should I say, in an easier to control—version. On page 203 the exiled love detective reports back. The Indian anthropologist has become an opera singer of Italian descent, who constantly overtaxes her lover Eduard not only in conversa-

tion but also in love: "Laura was not fearless just in disputes, she was also fearless in love. Her desire, to the extent that Eduard was the addressee, excluded the bed as the site of the event. Telephone booths, toilets, seats in the cinema, his old Citroën—all were preferable to a bed for Laura." Her passion for spectacular locations leads Laura unerringly to the wall, which she resolutely uses for purposes other than originally intended.

With a single movement of her hand she freed Eduard's member from his pants and held the tip in the border light. Eduard leaned back against the wall and bore in this way the legs which Laura scissored around his hips. The wall held, but Eduard's knees began to yield. . . .

"Someone's out there!"

"You're not being very romantic!"

"What do you mean not romantic, this is dangerous!"

Eduard could not believe his eyes. Out of contrariness, with the carelessness of a stranger to the city, Laura took a shoe from her foot and threw it, just like that, over the wall.

"What are you doing?"

"I'm proving that no one's there!"

Laura had hardly reseated herself when something dark, about the size of a bird, flew over their heads and hit the ground several feet away.

"The shoe!"

"There really is someone there!"

"Well, so what!"

"Shameful!" you will say. What a decline! What a deterioration! The author began with a researcher from the Third World and leaves this former main character in the end with only an eccentric scene at the wall! But you are doing me an injustice. For I had put so much effort into this Laura! Devoted so much text to her! In thirty unpublished pages I granted her everything which a character might desire: an exciting biography, intelligence, wit, wickedness, and a never-ending quarrel with her German lover, Eduard. But these pages were never to receive the consecration of the bound book. This time it was not the author but an energetic reader who prevented Laura from taking on the proportions which were due to her. My reader found that the author's characterization of Laura was redundant, clichéd, and too dependent upon good intentions. After this judgment, she deleted everything that I had accomplished for Laura and left only the immoderate lover remaining. No one will ever know who was right, my reader or I, because the pages in question have been committed to a diskette not destined for printing. But wait! I have saved a small section. Judge for yourself.

(By the way, Laura, formerly Marina Cuautemoc, went by the name Malin in this intermediate version.)

A dark Mercedes with a customs number on the white strip stopped in front of the border café. A woman pushed her hair up over her ear, too early; the federally employed ear fetishists were sitting sixty feet away. Eduard looked at Malin's ear, from which a plastic turquoise triangle was dangling. Is it really true that the ears of six billion people are all distinguishable, and what kind of eye training would be necessary in order to be able to recognize the difference? Malin suddenly turned her head to the side, pushing her hair over her ear. In this moment Eduard believed himself capable of identifying Malin's ear among a thousand others.

"Is that me?" asked Malin and threw a brand-new green passport with the federal eagle in front of Eduard.

"No," said Eduard.

"I hate the thing, the gigantic size, this German forest green on the cover, and with the ugly bird as well, the whole document. But I had no other choice."

Until this moment Eduard had never given a thought to the question of which passport Malin had been using to live in Germany. She was an Oriental who spoke German better and had lived longer in this city than most Germans that Eduard knew. He could say just as easily that she was a German whose racial features set her clearly apart from the Germans. If anywhere, then she was at home in both countries. The fact that she had to decide between her German and her Turkish sides seemed as absurd to Eduard as being forced to choose between cheese and bologna for the rest of one's life. Good Eduard, you have no idea, you're dreaming. You live unsuspecting and unmolested with your green passport among the Germans and grant yourself now and then half a night with an Oriental princess. You know nothing about the rest. Let me inform you. The princess has passport problems. You don't know that she has to stand in line every three months—right around the corner from here, by the way, it's an old Nazi building—in order to extend her residence permit another three months. You don't know anything about the bureaucratic tone at the alien registration office either, about the everyday unfriendliness in the corridors. Not your problem.

Quietly and inconspicuously your country has changed. It is enough just to look; people hate for the sole reason that someone is obviously not German. Perhaps this hatred had never stopped, was merely suppressed by the grimace of tolerance which the victors demanded. But suddenly the Germans have taken courage again; they express it undisguisedly, their hate for the non-German. Some all too clever people say that it is good that such repressed errors can finally manifest themselves; one can only deal with them when they are out in the open. As far as I am concerned, the suppression of these errors is preferable to such honest demonstrations. Forced and, if necessary, obedient friendliness is better than a proclamatory mania for domination. They are beginning to speak again, openly but not freely: Turkish cunt! What do you want here! Go back home!

Eduard was startled. Malin spoke of an experience from which he himself had been sheltered, thanks to the biological accident that he belonged. However separate from the Germans he might be on the inside, it did not matter in the competition of daily life what he thought but how he looked. And in the visual estimation of other Germans he passed as someone who belonged to the club.

Perhaps this example shows how such a character can be smothered by prejudices and hugs of solidarity, how quickly justifications and explanations thrust themselves in front of the narration. Unbiased codes of perception probably need as much time in literature as in reality to establish themselves. Such bias is, incidentally, also evident in the other direction. The writer from Iran, Bahman Nirumand, recently suggested—as Marina had done earlier in my novel—finally turning the question around. The topic should no longer simply be the problems which Germans have in dealing with foreigners, but rather the difficulties foreigners have with the Germans. The project took on the predictable form of a book and has been published under the title *Deutsche Zustände* (German Conditions; 1993). Foreign writers from Iran, the U.S., Israel, Turkey, and France describe how they have experienced Germany and the Germans; German colleagues answer them. A fascinating and long-overdue project. But it becomes apparent—how could it have been otherwise?—that the respondents display incredibly limited views and prejudices. The Iranian Sonia Seddighi feels, for instance, that the following experiences of her son are appropriate for characterizing the Germans: "A friend of Zubin's is only allowed to chew gum for one or two hours on Saturday. Our son was astonished by this restriction. 'What if poor B. should happen to want to chew gum on Monday instead of Saturday?' he asks. The other day I overheard a dispute between Zubin and one of his friends. 'I get to eat more than you because I paid ten cents more than you did.' They were discussing a package of potato chips which the children had purchased with their pocket money. The parents of the child would presumably be proud that their son knew how to defend his rights so well. We in Iran have learned very different principles. For example, we were not permitted to bring particular kinds of fruit or candy to school because there were some children or their parents who could not afford to buy them."[7]

It would be difficult to claim that Sonia's perspective is free of resentment and fixations. This type of reduction leads unavoidably to the familiar opposition: we, the spontaneous, human, warmhearted, cooperative; you, the technically superior, cold, egotistical, unhappy, et cetera. The supply of such characterizations seems to be limited. For, indicatively, the quarrels between Germans from the East and the West are carried out using the same key words. It is interesting how self-consciously, if not to say disingenuously, some of the Germans so described react to their portrait. After Sonia Seddighi has completely denied to Germans any spontaneity, tranquillity, openness, and tolerance, after she has attested to their neurosis about security, their "calculated rationality," and their pathological egoism, her German dialogue partner answers in the following way: "The first thing which I noticed about your article was the discretion and caution with which you write. It is more than politeness, it is a way of thinking which is foreign to any type of polemic and aggressivity. . . . I am pleased at the friendliness with which you speak to us; you plead for understanding and almost excuse yourself for the shortcoming that what you have to say is critical. But it also causes me to reflect. Must the guest be friendlier than the host?"[8]

A German masochism manifests itself here which is indeed more pleasant than the German mania for domination but still not harmless. The willingness of many Germans to excuse themselves for their Germanness—"Foreigners, don't leave us alone with the Germans!"—does not in any way lead to a more relaxed or more precise perception of the non-Germans who live with us. A love of foreigners which is nourished by self-hatred employs foreigners for a narcissistic operation: it serves to improve the image that the enlightened Germans have of themselves.

After everything I have said here, it might surprise you to hear that, all in all, I am fairly optimistic. Yes, I maintain that German society will gradually notice—and slowly but inevitably profess—that which it has already become: a society in which many cultures live alongside one another and endure one another for better or for worse. I maintain this because the reality has gone farther and become crazier than that which one might be able to extract from the speeches of politicians, the German naturalization laws, and our novels. In Ber-

lin or in Frankfurt it has been normal for a long time that young Turkish women, who were born in Germany yet can only obtain a German passport after extensive efforts, teach German and even German cooking to immigrants of German ancestry from White Russia and the Volga.

Allow me to relate in conclusion a story from Dr. Jean Jerome Chico Kaleu-Muyemba of Zaire. He belongs to a group which several writers—I myself among them—founded in Berlin after the events in Hoyerswerda. The members, half of whom are foreigners, have been agitating in schools for a year and a half against violence and hatred of foreigners. Jean Jerome has lived in Germany for twenty years, possesses a German passport, and feels in many ways like a German. In 1990, after the German soccer team's victory at the World Cup, he wanted to go to his favorite Berlin bar and celebrate with the Germans. His German wife advised him against it: jet black as he was and is, he would certainly be in for a beating if he shouted hooray in a German bar. He stayed home that evening. But the rage over the justified warning drove him in the following months and years around the country. Since that time he has appeared in over 200 schools. In 1994 he ran in Potsdam for election to the German federal parliament as a member of the Green/Alliance 90 Party. At one of his campaign events he had to deal with a young neo-Nazi who publicly provoked him by saying that he did not want to be represented in the federal parliament by an ape. At the same time the man showed Jean Jerome his bicep, which was tattooed with a swastika and the words "Blood and Honor." Jean Jerome asked him to come closer and felt his muscle. After a compliment regarding its circumference, Chico informed the Nazi that he had overlooked a serious mistake in the tattoo. What kind of a German was he! Didn't he know that he had used Latin instead of German letters for his German motto! The alphabet of the former occupiers of Germania! Didn't he know the German alphabet! The foreign tattoo must be removed! He should also take off his combat boots, since the manufacturer was not German. The same holds for his pants. He should not appear before Jean Jerome's eyes again until properly equipped with purely German products. Jean Jerome said all this with such a calm and dry manner that not only the bystanders but also the unmasked Nazi had to laugh. I am not looking for your love, said Jean Jerome to him; I just want your vote. Jean Jerome was, with a handsome 4.4 percent of the vote, not elected.

Peter Schneider, Summer 1995, translated by David Pan

¹ Peter Schneider, *Totoloque: Das Geiseldrama von Mexiko-Tenochtitlan,* Darmstadt, Luchterhand, 1985; *Die Botschaft des*

Pferdekopfs und andere Essais aus einem friedlichen Jahrzehnt, Darmstadt, Luchterhand, 1981; *The German Comedy: Scenes of Life After the Wall,* New York, Farrar, Straus & Giroux, 1991; *Vom Ende der Gewißheit,* Berlin, Rowohlt, 1994.

2 Peter Schneider, *Paarungen,* Berlin, Rowohlt, 1992.

3 Peter Schneider, *Lenz,* Berlin, Rotbuch, 1973, p. 11.

4 Ibid., p. 6.

5 Ibid., p. 82.

6 Peter Schneider, *The Wall Jumper,* tr. Leigh Hafrey, New York, Pantheon, 1983, pp. 13–14.

7 *Deutsche Zustände: Dialog über ein gefährdetes Land,* ed. Bahman Nirumand, Reinbek bei Hamburg, Rowohlt, 1993, pp. 112–13.

8 Ibid., p. 118.

Entering the Eighties: The Mosaic of German Literatures

■ INTRODUCTION

The resurgence of German-language literature after 1945 has proceeded with a notable constancy for thirty-five years. Authors writing in exile and those who defied Nazi prohibition and wrote secretly for their desk drawers were reintegrated into the society of German-language authors to join new and younger writers. As the decade of the eighties begins, three distinct generations of authors live in four definable political and geographical areas, all writing in German. To an observer of the literature produced, several remarkable conclusions may be drawn concerning the form and content of contemporary German-language literature.

First, whereas in former decades scholars identified and labeled literary trends or schools with terms such as romanticism, Biedermeier, realism, neoromanticism, expressionism and so on, the stubborn efforts of contemporary critics to separate and classify groups of authors who follow particular tendencies have been a futile exercise in most instances—with the possible exceptions of the worker-authors of the Gruppe 61 (Group 61) and the brief trend toward documentary drama. In 1961 a group of factory workers and laborers began to meet and discuss their literary aspirations, which resulted in the Gruppe 61, a shortlived trend led by Max von der Grün and Dieter Wellershoff, both of whom later turned to other themes. In the sixties the so-called documentary drama startled and intrigued theatregoers and critics, initially with the immense work *Der Stellvertreter* (*The Deputy;* 1963) by Rolf Hochhuth and with Peter Weiss's *Die Ermittlung* (*The Investigation;* 1965); but other authors in the subgenre

had little success, and it faded steadily. The immensely influential Gruppe 47 was founded by Hans Werner Richter and the late Alfred Andersch in 1947, when their efforts to continue publication of *Der Ruf* (The Call) were frustrated and their intention to inaugurate a new journal, *Der Skorpion,* was prohibited by American military authorities in southern Germany. The avowedly untendentious assembly of authors collected in the Gruppe 47 cannot be subsumed under a common denominator. For twenty years the Gruppe 47 met, at first semiannually and then annually, to read from unpublished manuscripts and then subject themselves to often crushing and merciless criticism by their colleagues and by professional critics, while they sat passively—in accordance with the rules of Gruppe 47 meetings—on what came to be known as "the electric chair." But the Gruppe 47, which over two decades introduced authors who became literary bywords, never fostered trends in form or theme.

Perhaps the closest approach to a school was the short-lived Vienna Group, whose members were frankly experimental—writing in dialect and espousing concrete poetry—but these writers retained their original creative voices and avoided patterns that would identify them as a school. They were rebels and innovators. Other trends, such as the "long poem" advocated by Walter Höllerer, found a few strong supporters and practitioners (Rolf Bongs, the late Nicolas Born, Gerald Bisinger and the late, irrepressible Wolfgang Weyrauch); but there was never a formal association, and the long poem remained an isolated phenomenon.

A second characteristic to be noted concerning the German literary world is the vitality of publishing ventures, large—venerable houses like Rowohlt, Piper, Hoffmann & Campe and Hanser; an expanded publisher like Luchterhand; and enterprises re-formed or founded after 1945 like Suhrkamp, Kiepenheuer & Witsch (in West Germany), Diogenes (in Switzerland), Residenz (in Austria) and Aufbau and Hinstorff (in East Germany)—and small, especially the Eremiten-Presse (Hermit Press). Though all publishers delight in the discovery of an exciting new literary talent, the large publishers, while promoting the efforts of authors like Günter Grass, Peter Handke, Siegfried Lenz and Heinrich Böll, have occasionally lacked the daring to welcome new writers. The Eremiten-Presse, on the other hand, has consistently welcomed unknown authors since its founding by the late V. O. Stomps in 1949 in a shed called Schloß Sansouris (Mouseless Palace) in Stierstadt in the Taunus. Having established a unique publishing operation, in 1967 Stomps turned the enterprise over to two young assistants, Friedolin Reske and the late Dieter Hülsmanns, who moved the press to their hometown of Düsseldorf and continued the tradition of publishing beautiful, illustrated volumes, often the first works of unfamiliar writers. A list of writers first published by the Eremiten-Presse includes Hans Bender (until recently the distinguished editor and cofounder of West Germany's most prestigious literary magazine, *Akzente* [Accents]), the late Ernst Meister (with his second collection of lyrics and the first after 1945), the late Günter Bruno Fuchs, Horst Bingel, Christa Reinig, Christoph Meckel and Gabriele Wohmann. Whereas some publishers fail to develop close personal ties with authors—which sometimes results in authors' dissatisfaction and their move from one publisher to another—the Eremiten-Presse traditionally and convivially keeps in close contact with its authors, who return again and again, even though they may have a principal publisher elsewhere. Some authors have enduring ties with large publishers too—Max Frisch (Suhrkamp), Günter Grass (Luchterhand), Heinrich Böll (Kiepenheuer & Witsch), Friedrich Dürrenmatt (Diogenes) and Siegfried Lenz (Hoffmann & Campe)—but others move about. The Klaus Wagenbach Verlag of Berlin, which publishes *Tintenfisch* (Cuttlefish), an annual survey of German writing in anthology format, experimented with an arrangement of collective ownership and editorial direction by its employees; but the scheme failed to be workable, and the enterprise split in two, producing a new, leftist-oriented publishing organization called Rotbuch (Redbook).

A third aspect of German-language publishing is the ingathering of authors that has been accomplished by West Germany. West German publishers print works by Austrians (Peter Handke, Suhrkamp), Swiss (E. Y. Meyer, Suhrkamp) and even East Germans (Günter Kunert, Hanser; Heiner Müller, Rotbuch). Though intranational publishing arrangements exist in most cases, German-language authors are repeatedly drawn to West German publishers; many eventually even become residents of West Germany. Aside from distinctive emphasis on locale and occasional political or social precepts, many works press a reader hard to guess the origin of an author who writes in German, unless he has prior knowledge. The greatest gap in philosophy and practice exists between East and West Germany. Though a host of increasingly well-known and admired writers from East Germany found publication in West Germany, the mounting pressure on the part of East German authorities to prevent such border-crossing has resulted in notorious incidences of expatriation (Wolf Biermann), de facto expulsion (Sarah Kirsch), voluntary departure (Günter Kunert), contentious insistence on freedom of expression within East Germany (Stefan Heym) and investigative imprisonment (Lutz Rathenow and Thomas Erwin).

Lutz Rathenow, first appearing outside of East Germany with two prose pieces in the American literary magazine *Dimension* in 1978, published a collection of stories, *Mit dem Schlimmsten wurde schon gerechnet* (The Worst Was Already Expected), with Ullstein in 1980, which resulted in an investigation, two-week imprisonment and repressive measures in the fall of that year, measures such as the confiscation of personal papers and books. Thomas Erwin, barely twenty years old, an impressive poet with an original and distinctive style, was jailed in October 1980 and in the spring of 1981 was expelled from the East and given shelter by Walter Höllerer in the quarters of the Literarisches Colloquium Berlin. The first collection of poetry by this unknown writer was published defiantly by the West German Piper Verlag in the spring of 1981: *Der Tag will immer Morgen bleiben* (Day Always Wants to Stay Morning) contains short lyrics that are commentaries on the coming-of-age in an environment with which the author has ambivalent ties. The poem "Ernste Spielerei" (Serious Playfulness), published as an afterword on the back of the book's dust jacket, summarizes the dilemma of young Erwin.

Früher
    habe ich Ausrufezeichen geglaubt
dann
    habe ich einen Punkt gesetzt
jetzt
    liebe ich Fragezeichen
Ausrufezeichen

(Once
    I believed in exclamation points
then
    I put an end to that
now
    I love question marks
Exclamation point)

German-language literature since 1945 has in no way followed a progressive development resulting in a homogeneous body of literature. On the contrary, its broad variety extends from one end of the spectrum to the other, from traditional form to daring experimentation, from standard subject matter to extremist themes. It has, however, experienced convulsions similar to those found in American literature during the same decades: the generally reminiscent subject matter of the fifties (the war, postwar tensions), the upheavals in politics and the social reform of the sixties (East-West strains, Vietnam, a generation of dropouts) and the pressures in society of the seventies (ecology, militant feminism). On the eve of the eighties a chorus of new voices is being heard, now more often searching for their own distinct identities and exploring interpersonal relationships in an accelerated world. The middle generation of writers seem to be taking a long and critical but often loving look at their own parents and siblings in an effort to understand the past, themselves and their own roles as family members and citizens: Christoph Meckel, Peter Rühmkorf, Peter Handke, Erika Runge, Peter Härtling, H. J. Fröhlich and Peter Henisch, among others, have done so. But there are no uniform and widely hailed tendencies.

Probably no authors outside the United States are more fascinated with American writing than are German authors. Because of the long hiatus in contact with American literary works during the Nazi era, the immediate concern of postwar German writers (and readers as well) was to discover what had happened in American letters. Added to the discovery of Ernest Hemingway and Thornton Wilder was the recovery of some authors who wrote in German, authors either lately appreciated (Elias Canetti), scorned and banned by Nazi officialdom (Franz Kafka) or exiled (Bertolt Brecht). The late Rolf Dieter Brinkmann promulgated American poets of the sixties with his anthology *Acid;* Donald Barthelme was championed by Jürgen Becker.

A phenomenon of contemporary German literary life has been the heavy traffic (though in essence oneway) between Germany and America, in that German writers, generally sponsored by the Goethe Institute of Munich or the Austrian Institute, traveled through the United States reading from their works, most often on college campuses. That exchange was strengthened by programs of visiting writers, twice yearly since 1967 in the Department of Germanic Languages at the University of Texas at Austin and then annually in the spring at Oberlin College, with the recent addition of "the German month" in the spring at the University of Southern California, bringing dozens of writers for extended stays in the United States. Their experiences have produced, and continue to produce, an increasing amount of material reflecting various aspects of their American sojourns. Such tours increased the authors' acquaintance with American students, scholars and writers—though, unfortunately, seldom with readers of English because of the obstinate resistance of most American publishers to bring out translations of German-language authors.

German-language literary efforts in the traditional three genres of poetry, prose and drama have not been equally successful. Prose has blossomed, in part because of the vigorous writing of authors such as Günter Grass, Siegfried Lenz, Heinrich Böll, Martin Walser, Christa Wolf, Peter Handke, Uwe Johnson, Peter Härtling, Gabriele Wohmann and others of lesser fame. The international success of Grass, Lenz, Böll and Handke in particular reveals the strength of German prose. Short prose has also flourished in the hands of Günter Kunert, Reinhard Lettau, Christa Reinig, Ilse Aichinger and Christoph Meckel. For a time an illusory form practiced by Jürgen Becker and Helmut Heißenbüttel principally, a mixture of prose and poetry known as the *text,* engaged the attention of readers and critics, but its experimental nature and rather hermetic content prevented wide popularity.

Lyric poets abound, though lyric poetry tends more and more—with the exception of recent renewed interest in the sonnet form—to resemble typographically accommodated prose in form and rhythm. Paul Celan received international recognition as a powerful and unique poetic presence. Iconoclastic and immensely involved in social problems of the day, Rolf Dieter Brinkmann was approaching his zenith when he was struck down by a car on a London street in 1975. Heinz Piontek, Peter Rühmkorf, Horst Bienek, the late Ernst Meister, the late Günter Eich, Karl Krolow, Ernst Jandl, H. C. Artmann, Günter Kunert and Walter Helmut Fritz, among others, have produced lyric poetry of note. Wolf Wondratschek even became a bestselling poet with frankly tendentious poems addressed principally to readers in their twenties.

The genre that has suffered most and produced the fewest widely acclaimed works is drama. After the giant contributions to the dramatic opus of German by Bertolt Brecht, whose influence dominated the efforts of younger writers, only Max Frisch and Friedrich Dürrenmatt have produced matchless dramatic works. Though Peter Weiss achieved international attention with his *Marat/Sade* (1964), his subsequent dramatic works have been universally ignored, and he has returned to prose. Smaller groups of admirers enjoy dramas by Thomas Bernhard, Martin Walser and Peter Handke—but none has reached the height of popularity achieved by Brecht and the two Swiss authors Frisch and Dürrenmatt. East Germany seems to have produced the most lively contemporary dramatists otherwise: Peter Hacks, who remains difficult and struggles in a hostile environment; Thomas Brasch, increasingly visible in Western exile; and Heiner Müller, also in the West, probably the strongest and boldest voice, himself a Brecht protégé. German theatre, however, is dependent more on dramatic works by English and American authors, as well as on the German classics, than on contemporary dramatists writing in German.

One subgenre of drama found its true place after 1945 and has largely retained it despite the popularity of television: the radio play became the first vibrant literary form in Germany after 1945, and it remains popular, though few authors of radio plays after Günter Eich and Wolfgang Weyrauch have had wide performances, with the notable exception of the experimental work done by Ernst Jandl and Friederike Mayröcker, often in collaboration.

A distressing fact to the observer of the postwar German-language literary landscape is the neglect demonstrated by American and English publishers in regard to German works in translation. Less than a dozen German-language authors have become widely known and appreciated by English readers. Günter Grass, Heinrich Böll, Peter Handke, Max Frisch, Friedrich Dürrenmatt, Uwe Johnson, Siegfried Lenz and Peter Weiss generally receive immediate translation and wide circulation in America. Others such as Gisela Elsner, Jurek Becker, Christa Wolf, Ilse Aichinger, the late Ingeborg Bachmann, Dieter Wellershoff, Martin Walser, Horst Bienek and Reinhard Lettau have appeared sporadically or with a single volume. Still others, considered to be among the most talented of German-language authors, such as Günter Kunert, Christoph Meckel, Christa Reinig, Gabriele Wohmann and Angelika Mechtel, have yet to have a book appear in English translation. *Dimension*, a literary magazine that publishes works by contemporary German-language authors, founded and unabashedly edited by the present writer since 1968, has in more than a decade published over 300 authors in German and in English translation in an effort to interest readers of English in the vitality and excitement of contemporary German-language literature.

For three successive years German Book Week in New York, sponsored by the Deutsches Haus at New York, University and the German Book Trade Association, has been an occasion for mutual headshaking, handwringing and bewilderment about the lack of interest shown by American publishers and readers for contemporary German writing. The laments voiced by German publishers have encountered blank expressions and empty responses from their American counterparts and from academic theoreticians. To me, the question seems clear. Welcome or not, it can be explained by several conclusions arrived at after long observation and reflection. 1) The German language, once the second tongue in the United States, suffered an almost mortal blow with World War I, a shock and loss of popularity that was reinforced and extended by World War II, which cast a pall of abhorrence on a language that seemed to represent bestial inhumanity and ghastly aberration. German was reduced to a poor fourth in languages studied in the United States. 2) Despite the rehabilitation of German to the status of a leading literary vehicle in the world, the status of the language has not changed in America, at least in part because a great

many American Germanists today persist in using German itself as their preferred language for public lecture and publication, a practice that has exacerbated the essentially isolated condition of German and has denied the American public at large access to contemporary German literature and information about contemporary German-language authors. 3) When the awkward and negligible attempts by German publishers to place the works of their authors with American publishers are taken into consideration, and when the publication of German works that does occur is in tawdry and faulty American translation as in the past, it should be no surprise at all that German-language literature remains largely unknown and ignored in the United States. The situation will not change until American Germanists begin to take seriously a role of mediation between German authors and American readers, until American publishers make honest efforts to present palatable and accurate translations of works by German authors, until German teachers and scholars recognize the negative attitude still held by Americans toward the German language and endeavor to contravene that attitude, and until German publishers themselves promote their authors and more actively undertake an informed dissemination of German works *in English* to the American public. Handholding, shrugging, doleful grimacing contribute only to self-defeatism. Only excellent translations and a dynamic spirit of mutual cooperation among scholars, teachers, American and German publishers and heretofore self-serving literary agents will bring German-language writing the distribution and recognition it deserves in America.

When Hans Magnus Enzensberger in the late sixties proclaimed the death of belles lettres in Germany, the German literary heart skipped a beat. Enzensberger's provocative claim was a ruse—he did not believe his own words—but for a time the immediate effect was a tendency on the part of German publishers to be skeptical about the wisdom of publishing works by newer and younger writers and largely to ignore them. That trend began to be reversed in the late seventies when a number of publishers—Suhrkamp, S. Fischer, Hanser, Rowohlt and recently Schneekluth—began to publish series devoted principally to the introduction of works by unknown authors. On the eve of the eighties a new vitality seems to be visible in German letters. If the pattern of the past can be used as a measure to predict the future, the German-language literature of the eighties will continue to be diverse, challenging, disruptive of stale and inbred social and political thought— humanistic in the true sense of the word—and probing boldly in an experimental way. Given the opportunity, readers of English will perhaps finally discover contem-

Günter Grass (© Gerhard Steidl, 1997)

porary voices of German-language writing with which they can identify, which they can admire and which can be integrated at last into the larger body of world literature today.

A. Leslie Willson, Autumn 1981

Günter Grass's Century

In Günter Grass's novel *The Rat* (1986) Oskar Matzerath, whom readers last saw celebrating his thirtieth birthday at the end of *The Tin Drum* (1959), makes a surprise reappearance. Now sixty years old, bald, and suffering from prostate problems, Matzerath has prospered in postwar Germany — first as the maker of pornographic films and then as the producer of educational videos. Late in the novel, rendered irritable by the permanent catheter with which his author has chosen to encumber him, Matzerath accuses Grass of trying to kill him off: "You want to get rid of me. In the future you don't want people to be able to point at me when they mean you."

This remarkable scene, which parallels other encounters of authors with their fictional creations from Unamuno's *Mist* to Kurt Vonnegut's *Breakfast of Champions,* hints with delicious irony at a relationship going well beyond those represented by Unamuno and Vonnegut. Grass, like few other writers, has been identified in the minds of many readers almost wholly with his great first novel. When the Swedish Academy announced the awarding of the 1999 Nobel Prize in Literature to Grass, it singled out *The Tin Drum* for ushering in a new era for German literature: "It is not too audacious to assume that *The Tin Drum* will become one of the enduring literary works of the 20th century." Certainly that masterpiece, which has sold more than four million copies worldwide, deserves its fame. Grass cre-

ated a narrative standpoint absurd enough to come to grips with the often terrifying history of Germany in the first half of the twentieth century. Oskar Matzerath, reluctant to participate in the world into which he was born, at age three hurls himself down a cellar staircase and injures himself in such a manner that he remains an outsider with the body of a child, able to observe reality from his picaresque perspective (looking up from below and often unnoticed) and, at the same time, capable of influencing events through the magical power of his tin drum and his glass-shattering voice.

Even in the German literary *annus mirabilis* that witnessed the publication of Heinrich Böll's *Billiards at Half Past Nine* and Uwe Johnson's *Speculations About Jakob,* Grass's novel created a sensation with its fantastic account of the rise of Nazism, the horrors of the Second World War, and the beginnings of the postwar "economic miracle." Grass had already received the prestigious prize of the literary circle Gruppe 47 for an excerpt from *The Tin Drum* that he read at its meeting in 1958. That was followed in 1960 by the Berlin Critics Prize and in 1962 by the French Prix pour le Meilleur Livre Étranger. But the controversy that has swirled around Grass's career from the start began when, in 1959, the novel was awarded a prize by a panel of critics in the city of Bremen: the prize was rescinded by the municipal senate fathers in a move heralding some forty legal actions brought against Grass in the next few years on grounds of obscenity, pornography, and blasphemy. In his recent Nobel Prize lecture Grass reminisced that his early success taught him the sobering lesson that "books can give offense, can provoke rage and hatred."

All this publicity, symbolized by Grass's appearance on the cover of the German newsweekly *Der Spiegel* in September 1963, simply underscored the significance of his first novel and the identification of the author with that work, which has been acclaimed by admirers as the greatest novel by any living writer or even of the twentieth century. A recent issue of *Der Spiegel* (11 October 1999) dedicated to young writers in Germany reiterated the influence of Grass's novel by depicting on its cover six "grandchildren of Grass & Co." clutching tin drums. Further millions who did not read the novel have become acquainted with Oskar's story in Volker Schlöndorff's prizewinning film adaptation (1979). Critics and the reviewers of his subsequent works have often expressed their disappointment and frustration at the fact that Grass has not simply repeated that virtuoso debut by, in effect, writing another *Tin Drum.*

And yet! Oskar Matzerath burst into the international literary consciousness exactly forty years before Grass received the Nobel Prize, and in the intervening four decades Grass has steadily produced a truly astonishing record of accomplishments in an impressive variety of fields — as a sculptor, as a graphic artist in black-and-white media, as a poet and dramatist for radio and theater, as an essayist on literary and social topics, as a political speaker for the Social Democratic Party in several elections, and as an activist in defense of persecuted writers and in such causes as environmental degradation, the dangers of DNA research, the threat of nuclear disaster, and Third World poverty. In addition to the major German literary prizes (Büchner, Fontane, Heuss, Fallada, Thomas Mann, Frankfurt Poetics, Hamburg Academy of Arts, Bavarian Academy), Grass has received enthusiastic recognition abroad, prompting honorary degrees (Kenyon College, Harvard, Poznań, Gdańsk), prizes (Mondello, Viareggio, Feltrinelli, Cavour, Comites, Hidalgo, Čapek, Sonning), and election to the American Academy of Arts and Sciences. Since 1989 he has again provoked a national cause célèbre through his opposition to German reunification on the grounds that it is both anticonstitutional and that it represents an aggression of Western imperialism against the weaker Eastern states. (It is Grass's view that the two Germanies should have been permitted to retain their political and economic autonomy within a loose *Kulturnation* related through a common language and culture.)

Small wonder, then, that Oskar Matzerath suspects in 1986 that his creator is toying with the idea of doing away with him. For the deformed and morally evasive narrator of *The Tin Drum,* however timely he may have been as a spokesman for the Grass of the fifties, cannot possibly exhaust the exuberant genius of Grass's forty-year career.

Only weeks before the Nobel Prize was announced, Grass published his most recent fiction, titled *My Century* (Ger. *Mein Jahrhundert*), in which each year is typified in one of an even hundred brief (roughly three-page) "annual episodes" portraying German history "from below." The first recounts, for instance, from the standpoint of a German soldier the European expedition to put down the Boxer Rebellion in China; in 1910 the wife of an armament factory worker recalls how one of the products was named "Big Bertha" after her; another narrator works for the firm that provided the glass cage in which Eichmann stood trial in Jerusalem; the entry for 1970 depicts, with an accompanying illustration by Grass, the moving occasion when Willy Brandt spontaneously fell to his knees before the memorial to the victims of the Warsaw Ghetto; and in the 1999 episode Grass resurrects his own deceased mother to reflect on her (and his) life and to celebrate her 103rd birthday. While few readers would argue that the language of

these straightforward accounts can compete with the outrageous energy of *The Tin Drum,* the enterprise is revealing: far from limiting himself to the half-century encompassed by *The Tin Drum* (1899–1954), Grass announces his intention to reclaim the whole twentieth century in an imaginative coup, and not just the years immediately surrounding the Nazi era.

Yet even this bold project fails to exhaust the historical sweep of Grass's fiction. In *The Flounder* (1977) Grass widens his fictional focus to encompass in a dozen episodes the history of the Baltic basin from its earliest Neolithic inhabitants to the feminists of the 1970s. In *The Rat* he presents us not only with an apocryphal view of that same topography in the "posthuman" period following a nuclear holocaust, when the world is inhabited solely by rats; but in a weird time-warp that Grass calls "Vergegenkunft" (pastpresenture), he also seeks to show how the past and future are always implicit in the present, and the imaginative in the real, by depicting a contemporary Germany in which the chancellor and his children interact not only with the historical Grimm brothers but also with the figures from their best-loved fairy tales.

The locale in Grass's fictions is almost always his native Danzig (the present-day Gdańsk) and the Baltic rim: not only in the so-called Danzig Trilogy encompassing the three closely related early works *The Tin Drum, Cat and Mouse* (1961), and *Dog Years* (1963), but also in most of the later novels. In *Local Anaesthetic* (1969) the narrating high-school teacher is sitting in a dentist's chair in Berlin of the late 1960s and thinking about his students, but in his thoughts he returns time and again to his youth in Danzig, where as leader of a gang of teenagers he also knew Oskar Matzerath. *From the Diary of a Snail* (1972) combines an autobiographical account of Grass's 1969 campaign efforts on behalf of Willy Brandt and the Social Democratic Party with the (fictional) story of a Danzig high-school teacher who, for his efforts on behalf of the Jews, is persecuted by the Nazis and forced to go into hiding during the war years. *The Flounder* amounts to a fictionalized history of Danzig and *The Rat* to an apocryphal projection of its future, while *The Call of the Toad* (1992) takes place in present-day Danzig, where, in a wild travesty of the postcommunist diplomatic dilemma, an elderly German widower and a Polish widow found the enormously successful German-Polish Cemetery Association to repatriate the bodies of former Danzigers who died in exile.

Only a few shorter works are set elsewhere: *The Meeting at Telgte* (1979), takes place in Westphalia on the border between Protestant and Catholic Germany during the Thirty Years War; in *Headbirths* (1980) Grass reported on the trip to India that he and his wife had recently undertaken; and in *My Century* he imagines himself, like the hero/heroine of Virginia Woolf's *Orlando*, moving through time and space in a variety of metamorphoses.

As these examples suggest, the subject matter of Grass's fiction is to a conspicuous extent autobiographical. Grass writes with compelling authority about the German experiences of this century because his own participation during the crucial formative years was typical: "At fourteen I was a Hitler Youth, at sixteen a soldier, and at seventeen an American prisoner of war." He points out that he was too young to have been a Nazi but old enough to have been molded by a system that scandalized the world. He is convinced, as he again stressed in his Nobel Prize lecture, that German writing, after "the irreparable breach in the history of civilization" represented by Auschwitz, could justify itself only by internalizing the past so thoroughly that it could never be forgotten.

However, except in a few straightforward autobiographical accounts, such as his campaign activities in *From the Diary of a Snail,* the material is always imaginatively transformed. Thus Oskar, in [The Tin Drum, repeats many of Grass's own experiences in the immediate postwar world — attending school in Düsseldorf, apprenticing as a stonemason, working at the Art Academy (albeit as a model, not a student), playing drums in a jazz trio (Grass played the washboard) — but Oskar's dwarfish perspective utterly defamiliarizes the material. Elsewhere Grass makes use of conjectural biographies, as in *The Meeting at Telgte,* where he projects himself and his friends from Gruppe 47 some three hundred years into the past.

If, like Faulkner in his Yoknapatawpha County and Joyce in his Dublin, Grass manages in his Danzig to achieve universality of human experience, it is characteristic that our view of that experience is almost always refracted through a weird perspective anticipated by the drumming dwarf of his first novel, who writes his memoirs while interned in a hospital for the criminally insane (and who constantly undermines the reliability of his own account). In *Cat and Mouse* the story of Mahlke, the strange Jesus-like boy in wartime Danzig who through his feats of swimming (and masturbation!) gathers a group of admiring disciples, is narrated fifteen years later by Pilenz, the Judas who betrayed his friend and who, now plagued by his guilty conscience, haunts churches and meetings of former SS officers. The third novel of the Danzig Trilogy, *Dog Years,* is narrated from three different points of view, including those of two boys, persecutor and persecuted, whose relationship in Danzig and postwar Germany mirrors the Nazi persecu-

tion of the Jews and their subsequent efforts to achieve a reconciliation. In *Local Anaesthetic* the story of the teacher Starusch and his student, who wants to express his opposition to the American use of napalm in Vietnam by immolating his dog on the Kurfürstendamm in Berlin, is told through the visions that Starusch projects onto the television screen in his dentist's office and in phone calls to his dentist during the weeks between his two operations for a prognathous lower jaw. (The orthodontic procedures reflect sociodontically the events of the plot.)

From the Diary of a Snail conflates fiction, autobiography, politics, and historical reality in a mélange that culminates in a brilliant essay on Dürer's *Melencolia I.* In *The Flounder,* which matches for sheer gusto the conception and prose of *The Tin Drum,* the history of Danzig is recounted by a narrator who moves through the centuries, always associated with one of a dozen women who represent through their lives and their cooking the epochs of human development — from the semidivine matriarch of the Neolithic Age through medieval nuns down to the feminists of the 1970s — and with extensive recipes for the foods that reflect the history of human nourishment. His story is further complicated by the fact that he chats with and is advised through the ages by a fish — the talking flounder from the Grimms' fairy tale of the fisherman and his wife — which is finally caught in the 1970s by a group of feminists who put it on trial before a feminist tribunal in Berlin for having aided and abetted a patriarchal hegemony from the beginning of time. In *The Meeting at Telgte* Grass imagines a meeting of Gruppe 47 projected back into the year 1647: the historical situation of the Thirty Years' War provides the analogy to the postwar period in Grass's Germany, and the writers of the German Baroque provide ample possibilities for a roman à clef involving the most prominent writers of contemporary German literature. *Headbirths* estranges Grass's own trip to India with his wife by juxtaposing it to the imagined trip of another young German couple to the same country.

The Rat, which might more accurately be translated as "The Ratess" or "The Ratrix" or "The She-Rat" in order to convey the eccentric feminine form of Grass's German title *Die Rättin,* begins when the narrator receives a pet rat for Christmas. As he tells his tale — which involves a research trip by five contemporary feminists to study the surge of jellyfish in the Baltic as well as his project, along with video producer Oskar Matzerath, to produce an educational film on the death of the German forests — the rat begins to talk to him in his dreams: he dreams that he is in a space capsule circling the world in which the human race has been exterminated by a nuclear disaster and which is now populated only by rats. Grass's fondness for weird points of view is reflected in his obsession with eels (in *The Tin Drum*), snails, flatfish, rats, bats (in *Headbirths*), frogs, and other noncuddly animal species. (His graphic works contain numerous self-portraits with rats, flounders, snails, and others.)

As these topics suggest, Grass has been politically active and socially engaged for much of his career. In 1966, one year after he first campaigned for the Social Democratic Party, Grass gave an address at Princeton at a joint conference of American and German writers on the role of the writer in modern society. Poking gentle fun at those writers and intellectuals who incessantly call for proclamations and petitions for or against various causes, Grass points out that society poses problems that cannot be solved by position statements and petitions alone. Rejecting any aspiration to represent "the conscience of the nation," he urges participation in the nitty-gritty (Ger. *Kleinkram*) of the democratic process. But unlike literature, he warns, politics requires compromises.

Grass was arguing in that speech for a clear-cut distinction between the absoluteness of literature and the contingency of politics, between the separate roles of the individual as writer and as citizen. Accordingly, in the scores of political essays that he composed in the following decades — from 1970 to 1972 he contributed a biweekly political column to the *Süddeutsche Zeitung*— and in the hundreds of campaign speeches that he delivered for the SPD in the election campaigns from 1965 to 1980, Grass repeatedly stressed that he was speaking as a citizen and not from any imagined position of privileged insight as a writer. He realized, of course, that his celebrity attracted his large audiences; but he sought to persuade his fellow citizens from a standpoint of democratic equality. Above all, he wanted to dissociate himself from what, in another essay, he called the "intellectual sorcerer's apprentices" — that is, the intellectual elites motivated by ideologies of the Left or Right. His most powerful literary statement of this principle was the play *The Plebeians Rehearse the Uprising* (1966), which is based loosely on Bertolt Brecht's refusal to take an active part in the 1953 uprising of the workers in Berlin. But Grass takes that incident as an occasion to pillory all intellectuals who articulate ideological positions and yet refuse to take an active part in political action. His attack on ideologies, in turn, informs the satirizing portrayals of such thinkers as Hegel (in *The Flounder*) and Heidegger (in *Dog Years*).

The Nobel Prize committee accurately characterized Grass as "a late Enlightenment figure in an age grown weary of reason." He outlined his views most vividly perhaps in *From the Diary of a Snail,* whose fictional hero is nicknamed "Doubt" (Ger. *Zweifel*) and where Grass defines his position in politics and social action as skepticism. Grass began one of his 1969 campaign speeches by stating that it was his intention "to spread skepticism" and to invite his fellow citizens to question the values by which they had been living. Hence the symbolic significance of the snail, which moves slowly, by evolution and not by revolution. Grass's opposition to the hasty reunification of the two Germanies in 1990 was absolutely consistent with this skeptical position of slow but steady progress. (Post-Auschwitz Germany is a monster, he quipped, seeking to be a Great Power.) Hence his conviction, in an essay of that title, that "Our Fundamental Evil Is Idealism," that misguided idealism that has so often driven Germans and their intellectual ideologues to radical, destructive extremes. "I am a Social Democrat," he explained in *From the Diary of a Snail,* "because socialism without democracy is worthless in my opinion and because an unsocial democracy is no democracy."

At the same time, as a skeptical realist Grass realizes that his own reasoning doubts cannot always influence younger generations, who often regard him as a "dinosaur." His fictional reaction to the violent excesses among students in the later 1960s was reflected in *Local Anaesthetic,* in which the forty-year-old teacher fails to persuade his student through rational arguments to give up his violent protests against the war in Vietnam. When the student finally does desist, he does so, paradoxically, because he wants to avoid, when he himself is forty years old, the fate of his teacher, who is so utterly obsessed with the adventures of his own youth in Danzig that he cannot engage himself fully in the present.

When social and political concerns do occur in Grass's novels, then, they are distanced ironically by hypothetical biographies, by comic inversions, and other literary devices. They provide, in short, the material for his fictional imagination, but not the purpose or goal of the fiction. Yet, despite his sharp distinction between the work of the writer and the action of the citizen, Grass's literary career, notably in Germany, has been marked by political attacks. Indeed, his very moderation has infuriated critics on the Left as well as the Right. As Grass remarked in his Nobel Prize lecture, it is literature's most grievous offense in the eyes of those in power that it takes up the cause not of history's victors but of the losers standing at the edge of the historical process. Accordingly, his enemies have attacked his works from the outset on political grounds: from *The Tin Drum* and the other novels of the Danzig Trilogy, because they raised all the specters of Germany's Nazi past, down to *The Rat* with its forebodings of nuclear calamity, and *Headbirths* with its depiction of Third World misery. (Critics and readers outside Germany, in contrast, have tended to assess Grass on more purely literary terms.)

The anti-Grass crusade reached its nadir, however, with the campaign against his most recent novel, *Too Far Afield* (1995; Ger. *Ein weites Feld*), in which Grass gave fictional expression to his views on German reunification, distancing them through the collective narrative voice of "We from the archive" (as a satire on the depersonalization of life in societies regimented by the impersonal institutions of politics and economics). Spearheaded by Marcel Reich-Ranicki, Germany's so-called literature-pope, in a cover piece in *Der Spiegel*, the attacks were aimed at Grass's critical attitude toward the takeover of East Germany by the Federal Republic and, in particular, the Treuhandanstalt (Treuhand or True-Hand Commission), the institution charged with the privatization of former GDR properties and businesses. Focusing on the political implications, which again provide only the background of the novel and not its substance, West German critics tended to ignore its immense literary achievement and to dismiss it as political hackwork. Readers in the former GDR, in contrast, found Grass's depiction of conditions there much fairer, while reviewers outside Germany have often praised the novel on literary grounds as a match for *The Tin Drum*. It is Grass's achievement that he is able to represent and give equal weight to all opposing points of view, regardless of his own political views: *The Tin Drum* portrays with the same vividness the horrors of National Socialism and the appeal of the Nazis to lower-middle-class Germans; *The Flounder* respects and simultaneously ironizes the views and achievements of feminists.

Ultimately, Grass's reputation will rest not on his political views and activities but on his literary merits. And here, it seems safe to predict, his place in European literature of the late twentieth century is assured, as foreign admirers from Nadine Gordimer to Salman Rushdie attest. Grass has remarked that, influenced by his early training as a sculptor and graphic artist and by the estheticizing tendencies of the immediate postwar period, his early poems were exercises in formal virtuosity. Some of the poems in the volume *The Merits of Windfowl* (1956) suggest the absurdist strategies of the later fiction: e.g., the short poem "Family Affairs" (Ger. *familiär*), which reports on a new wing of the local museum that displays "our aborted children, pale serious embryos," which sit there in bottles and worry about the future of their parents. Initially, in fact, he contemplated writing the story of *The Tin Drum* as a long poem. It was only, he reports, when he finally found the proper fictional perspective and, with it, the first sentence —

"Granted: I am a patient in a mental institution" — that the work began to take shape as a novel. For that novel Grass created a prose of a vigor that had not been heard in Germany since the Bible translation of Martin Luther and the picaresque idiom of his revered model, the Baroque novelist Grimmelshausen, creator of Simplicissimus and Mother Courage. (Grimmelshausen subsequently turned up as one of the figures in *The Meeting at Telgte*.) Indeed, the earliest reviews focused with fascination on the power, the exuberance, the vitality of the language, which sprang like an exotic plant from the "forest clearing" (Ger. *Kahlschlag*) of the earliest postwar fiction as practiced by the writers of Gruppe 47. (Grass has suggested that his linguistic vigor may have benefited from the fact that, because of the war, his formal education was interrupted before he completed high school: the energy had not been trained out of his prose.)

At the same time, in its formal experimentation the novel reflects the bold complexities of the twentieth-century German writer whom Grass has repeatedly called his teacher: Alfred Döblin, the author of *Berlin Alexanderplatz*, in whose name Grass donated his house at Wewelsfleth in 1985 as a center for young writers. A sophisticated awareness of the formal potentialities of modern fiction is apparent in the opening pages of *The Tin Drum*, as Oskar debates the various ways of telling his story. "You can begin a story in the middle and create confusion by striking out boldly forwards and backwards," he reflects. "You can act modern, smooth away all times and distances and subsequently proclaim, or have proclaimed, that you have finally solved the time-space problem." (That is precisely what Grass self-ironizingly achieved in the "paspresenture" of *Headbirths* and *The Rat*.) It is in this connection that the odd form of *From the Diary of a Snail* has not always been fully appreciated in its mixture of autobiography, history, fiction, and art criticism. In a 1991 interview Grass remarked that he regarded it as, in many senses, his boldest formal experiment, without which he could never have written such later works as *The Flounder*.

Readers who approach Grass's most recent novel as a literary rather than a political statement cannot fail to appreciate its imaginative power. While *Too Far Afield* is on one level a critique of the consequences of the 1990 reunification of Germany, that critique is achieved by means of a startling literary technique: a sustained analogy between the history of Germany in the twentieth century and the nineteenth century. This effect is achieved by means of one of the two central figures, Theodore Wuttke, who, because of his obsession with the great nineteenth-century novelist Theodor Fontane, is known to his friends as Fonty. As Fonty's life is revealed — from his birth in 1919 precisely on the hundredth anniversary of Fontane's birth and in the same town of Neuruppin, through the Nazi years and his work as a cultural lecturer in the German Democratic Republic, down to his current position as a messenger in the Treuhandanstalt — we are constantly reminded of parallels in Fontane's life, times, and works, signaled by the title of Grass's work in German, *Ein weites Feld,* which is a familiar phrase from Fontane's novel *Effi Briest.* Fonty is of course ready on every occasion with an appropriate quotation from Fontane's works. This technique of fictional postfiguration — used, for instance, also in Thomas Mann's *Doktor Faustus*— enables Grass to suggest larger patterns in German history and, specifically, to enlist Fontane's reservations about Bismarck's unification of Germany in the service of his own critique of the 1990 reunification. But — and this must be stressed — it is first and foremost a critique by literary, not by political means. Grass is using the political materials in the service of fiction and not forcing fiction into the Procrustean bed of politics.

It seems reductive, therefore, to judge Grass's works from a political standpoint, for it is difficult to think of any other twentieth-century writer who has manifested such a universal interest in capturing life and history with all available means of expression. In addition to his typewriter, the tools of his graphic art, and the washboard of his early music-making, for instance, Grass has also chosen to express himself with the implements of the kitchen. From his early ballet *Five Cooks* (1959) and the play *The Wicked Cooks* (1961), Grass has been obsessed with cooking: "cuisine" would be too elegant a designation for the earthy ingredients that he prefers, including leg of mutton and lentils, calf's kidneys on celeriac, green eel, tripe, mussels, suckling pig, fish and mushroom soups, and minced lung. In those same years he also turned out many drawings of cooks: "A Grouping of Cooks," "Seven Cooks," "Small Cook," "Self-Portrait as Cook," and others. In *From the Diary of a Snail* he imagines that he might someday purchase one of the small churches standing empty all over Berlin and transform it into an inn "At the Sign of the Holy Ghost," where he would prepare all his favorite foods, which betray the same earthy quality as his prose. In that same work he expresses the wish, before he becomes old and wise, to write a "narrative cookbook" including over ninety-nine recipes and dealing also with the process of eating and the disposal of waste matter. This wish in fact developed into *The Flounder,* which includes dozens of recipes along with half-page hymns to such ingredients as millet, lentils, and potatoes. It is not utterly absurd to imagine that Grass, had he not received the Nobel Prize,

would have been equally happy with three stars from Michelin.

In forty years Günter Grass has advanced far beyond Oskar Matzerath and *The Tin Drum.* In a variety of media unmatched by any other contemporary artist and with a seemingly inexhaustible vigor and gusto, Grass has succeeded with incessant inventiveness and without self-repetition in stamping his artistic imprint on the century that he has documented so unforgettably. Does any other writer have equal claim to the last Nobel Prize of the twentieth century?

Theodore Ziolkowski, Winter 2000

IRELAND

Dwelling in Impossibility: Contemporary Irish Gaelic Literature and Séamas Mac Annaidh

For the last several years rumors of a revival of Irish Gaelic literature have wafted uneasily over the contemporary intellectual establishment. Heretofore it has been fashionable to dismiss the efforts to revive the language as second-rate cultural conservatism and to treat writings in Irish as schoolboy-level exercises. There has been much truth in these views, but it is time to revise them. Just as the most optimistic of native-language enthusiasts are admitting that the battle to save the language is a losing one, a new and vitalizing interest in it has arisen. This new interest is no longer fueled by any reasons of personal aggrandizement or social advancement. In addition and ironically, the intrinsic value of the language has been purified by tacit withdrawal of a large official commitment. The practical recognition of it as a lost cause has released an artistic commitment far more genuine and infinitely less insular than a political strategy. Denis Donoghue says in his discussion of "Romantic Ireland": "Lost causes are often known by others to be lost, but not by ourselves: we may think there is still time. But when we give ourselves to a lost cause which we know to be lost, we do so from a different structure of desires and needs; perhaps because we dwell in impossibility and would not live elsewhere even if we could."[1]

Donoghue's statement is apt when taking account of Irish artists who write for a mere handful of readers, and it is particularly so when applied to a young Irish writer who has broken the bounds of possibility and written a novel in Irish that reflects the influence of authors such as Joyce, Nabokov, and García Márquez.

Cuaifeach Mo Londubh Buí (My Yellow Blackbird Brain-storm) by Séamas Mac Annaidh, published in Dublin in 1983, is a fully realized self-conscious novel which brings together such a variety of influences and themes that it may be said to be the first work in Irish to transcend parochialism, provincialism, and even nationality, while retaining a firmly rooted basis in the native landscape.[2]

A self-conscious novel is one that constantly calls attention to itself as a literary artifice, thus undermining the traditional tacit agreement between author and reader that presupposes a suspension of disbelief on the part of the reader. In the usual sense, a reader accepts the fictional world laid out for him in a realistic novel as being indeed "real," and the author abets him in an exercise in mutual deception. In the self-conscious novel, however, this deception is constantly being undermined by the writer, who, by using a variety of literary sleights-of-hand, casts continual doubt on the "reality" of his fiction and at the same time unbalances belief in actual facts. In the words of the critic Robert Alter, "A fully self-conscious novel is one in which from beginning to end, through style, the handling of narrative view-point, the names and words imposed on the characters, the patterning of the narration, the nature of the characters and what befalls them, there is a consistent effort to convey to us a sense of the fictional world as an authorial construct set up against a background of literary tradition and convention."[3]

"My Yellow Blackbird Brainstorm" fulfills all these conditions to a greater or lesser degree, and my intention is to examine the work with them in mind and to show to what extent Mac Annaidh succeeds in combining them into a novel of great wit and wonder. An explication of the title will bring into prominence two of the principal elements of the story. "My yellow blackbird," a term of endearment in Irish, is that imaginative faculty in the author that enables him to deal with the world: "The blackbird was a symbol for the queer poetic something that was within him, the airy spirit that nothing could restrain" (69). A rallying cry throughout is "Blackbirds of the world, unite!"—a call to similarly unfettered souls. As for *brainstorm,* the Irish word signifies a whirlwind, vortex, or furious eddy and is physically present in the book as a blowhole on the island of Aranmore, the locale of a major thread of the story, as well as the deepest pothole in Ireland, Noone's Pot near the town of Enniskillen, the home ground of the book. Climaxes of the action take place at these hypnotic natural landmarks. Symbolically, the whirlwind force is the mental and emotional crisis the author is anticipating in his efforts to control his characters and conclude his book.

In essence, the novel is a juggling act with the author tangling nimbly with three story lines. A map of the plots of "Brainstorm" begins with the basic "real" account of a day in the life of the author. Mac Annaidh is at pains to ensure that the reader believe in this reality. "When Séamas says he had raisin bran for breakfast," he writes elsewhere, "you can be sure that he did indeed have raisin bran."[4] The date is 28 July 1982, the morning after Anwar Sadat's assassination. Séamas's day begins with the arrival of the post and his degree diploma from the university. He signs on at the labor exchange and gets a provisional driving license: "Re-rooting in his native town, this is what these formalities meant. He would be firmly tied down by them before long, with no road of escape" (6). It is an end to a carefree period in his life, particularly the summers he has spent on an island off the Donegal coast at an Irish summer school as a student teacher. All that remains are his suntan, the rhythms of conversation and music in his mind, and some dulse in his pocket to remind him of the taste of the island.

The events of the twenty-four-hour day are recounted in snatches throughout the book, but the sane beginning gradually builds in tension, while the author becomes increasingly eccentric in his behavior. He has promised himself to accomplish a mighty feat, to finish the book he is writing, but things do not go quite as he has planned. The effort of bringing the various threads of the stories together is too much for his mental equilibrium; hence his "brainstorm." His grasp on reality is shaken, his characters and plots get out of hand, and the ending of the book is not what he intended.

The shift from "real" to "fictional" narrative is prefaced throughout the novel by the repetition of curious little invocations. Before the act of creating begins, one of the author's selves addresses another, asking that they merge with each other but, at odds with what ought to be going on, repeating "Never mind about the story." This is the beginning of a mounting proliferation of perversities—signposted in the oxymoron of the book's title—that indicate the ambiguity lying at the core of the work.

Layered just a step away from the real world of Enniskillen is a second story with the appearance of reality, and thus resembling a traditional realistic fiction. It is the story of the student teacher Séamas and his days on the island of Aranmore off the coast of Donegal. This story is mainly concerned with his intense relationship with a student, Michael, and to a lesser extent with another student, Kevin. The author has been careful to tell us that his own name is Séamas Michael Kevin Mac Anna, and each of four main characters has one of these names. So, are Michael and Kevin "real" separate characters, or are they all aspects of one personality? Probably both.

The picture of a Gaeltacht summer school is rendered accurately, with no romantic blurring, but with a keen appreciation of the shedding of conventional shackles.[5] It is a community of schoolchildren and teachers bored with the obligatory classes, which attempt to drill into unwilling minds some smattering of the language. Strongly evoked is the atmosphere of anarchy that exists at these sessions. Rules are laxly enforced. Older students and teachers are hung over in the daytime and drunk at night. Adolescent sex preoccupies the teen-agers, while the younger children take advantage and make mischief to their hearts' content. The squalid elements in this laissez-faire environment are glazed over by the ennobling brightness of a midsummer sun. It transforms all it touches, making landscape and people alike beautiful. Summer life on the "Bright Island" may be a saturnalia, but it is a joyous one.

In this milieu Séamas is somewhat out of bounds, his judgment blurred by an alcoholic haze. He is in charge of one of the lodging houses that give bed and board to a group of the schoolchildren. The children observe his erratic conduct and goad and tease him to distraction. Foremost among them is Michael, a streetwise, unruly brat who jeers at everyone but who is still child enough to wail, when his teasing goes too far and he is threatened with retribution, "I always knew I'd end up with a pack of weirdos." Séamas is simultaneously compellingly attracted and driven mad by him. Michael knows no Irish, refuses to make the smallest attempt to learn any, and undercuts Séamas's authority at every hand. At the same time, he wheedles Séamas with provoking pleas to be taken into Séamas's confidence, to take the place of "best friend." The exchanges between Séamas and Michael are written in Irish and English, which gives them a resonance difficult to translate in a single language. In the following excerpt the italicized passages are in Irish in the original.

> Seamus (*it's Séamas, Michael*) is it true that you get drunk on coke? Coke-drunk? Honestly? You put aspirins in it? That's impossible. Is it that seaweed that makes you as high as a buckin' kite? *Ah, no, Michael, you don't understand the kind of person I am. I'm a blackbird. Séamas,* said Bucko, if you're a blackbird, then I'm a great tit. *Bucko understood the game perfectly.*

If I were a blackbird I'd whistle and sing,
And I'd follow the ship that my true love sails in.

> Delia Murphy. Seamus did anyone ever tell you that you were mad? *Michael, I have the 11-plus, ten O-levels, three A-levels, and an honors degree from the New University of Ulster.* But Kevin says you

get drunk on coke? *Michael,* I've more wit than you'll ever have—to-wit, to-woo. Seamus, you really are mad. I just knew that I'd end up livin' with a pack of weirdos. *Michael, it takes one to know one.* And what the hell does that mean? *You'll find out before long.* (57–58)

That Séamas's obsession with Michael (or the author's obsession with the Michael aspect of his own persona) is a strong one is reflected in the unexpected entry of Michael into the third layer of the book, the story of Gilly and his friends at a boarding school in Dublin. This is really the story that lifts the book from a fairly conventional rite-of-passage novel to an intricate imaginative fantasy, hilarious at one minute, deeply tragic the next. It is richly allusive, with a large cast of characters ranging from pop stars to grave-robbers. Most important of all, it is intricately embedded in a framework based on the ancient Sumerian epic *Gilgamesh.* So dependent is it on *Gilgamesh,* in fact, that it is impractical to discuss this story line without first referring to the early myth.

The invocation of the Gilgamesh story is apt, since one of the basic themes of "My Yellow Blackbird Brainstorm" is brotherly love. Gilgamesh, of the tribe of the goddess Anna and king of Uruk, has a beloved young friend, Enkidu, who dies. Having watched over the body of his friend until it turns to dust, Gilgamesh sets off on a heroic quest to find the secret of everlasting life. After various vicissitudes, he comes upon an ancient wise man, Utnapishtim, who tells him the secret: it lies in a small thorny plant that grows in water. Gilgamesh dives in and finds it, only to lose it almost immediately.

Mac Annaidh repeats sections of the *Gilgamesh* epic in short snatches, at first verbatim; but as the book progresses and the author begins to fall apart, the *Gilgamesh* retelling becomes increasingly confused (as do the other strands of the story).

> Once when Oisín Mac Fhinn was out hunting he saw the wild man, Enkidu, as the gods named him, and when he returned to the Mobile Fort his cheeks were drawn, his face was wasted, his brow shrunken, and his eyes were watering in their sockets, and his face that of a traveler who has gone on a long journey. Fionn spoke to him and said: "This story has nothing to do with us. . . ." [Oisín proceeds to Uruk and addresses Gilgamesh.] "Your story is gradually overpowering Irish Literature because there is a wild man in the northern mountains; he eats with the animals and protects them from the Fianna. There is an end to the hunt." And Gilgamesh says to him, "Young man, it is clear that you are not seeking the Wind if the hunt is at an end." (66)

There is a further deterioration in the epic still later, when Utnapishtim, the possessor of the secret of eternal life, thinks that Gilgamesh is an entrant in a Eurovision song contest.

In the story of the reincarnation of Gilgamesh in contemporary Dublin, he is the creation of a Middle Eastern doctor, Siamais, whose name is that of the Sumerian god of the sun, "judge and giver of life." Siamais is intent on performing a miraculous deed involving futuristic brain surgery and the secret formulae of ancient seers and wizards. He comes to Ireland, appropriately enough, from Philadelphia, city of brotherly love. Needing an Irish surname, the doctor visits the Irish center in that city and, finding a book inscribed "Máire a Scríobh" (Written by Mary), concludes that this constitutes the author's name. He decides that "Siamais a Scríobh" (literally "Written by Siamais") is a suitable name. Corrected by a helpful clerk, he emerges as Siamais Mac Grianna. There are many levels of punning going on in this passage alone, but it might be useful to point out that it contains an authorial acknowledgment of two of the best modern writers in Irish, Séamas Ó Grianna and his brother Seosamh Mac Grianna. Séamas Ó Grianna wrote under the rather curious pen name "Máire" (Mary). *Grian* is the Gaelic word for "sun."

Siamais, the Middle Eastern brain surgeon, is alone in the world, a "soul without a country, a soul without contacts"—a phrase echoing Patrick Pearse's ominous cry, "Tír gan teangan, tír gan anam" ("A country without a language, a country without a soul"; variations on the phrase reverberate throughout the book like a knell). Siamais arrives in Dublin to take up a post at a Dublin hospital as a surgeon (sawbones). He puts up on his door a sign representing a saw, the emblem of the god Siamais. He works quietly and secretively and obtains extraordinary results from his operations. He starts to gather the raw materials for his great experiment, the creation of a new life through surgery. He first obtains the unblemished face of a newsboy whose skull is shattered in Gardiner Street by a sports car. Most important is the brain, which he acquires from an old man, Pádraig, who has been killed by a Hell's Angel. Finally the doctor gets the body of a fourteen-year-old (by coincidence a grandnephew and namesake of Pádraig) who is killed in a freak accident precipitated by an elderly woman, Sally Holmes, once the elder Pádraig's great love. After much secret labor the doctor succeeds in bringing to life a being who has the body of a young boy but, in a hitch the doctor did not anticipate, the mind of an eighty-two-year-old man. Nevertheless he is triumphant.

All this may sound like campy sci-fi, but it is rendered with great humanity through the expedient of using the old man Pádraig as the narrator. His rage when he finds out that he is not dead, as he deserves to be, knows no bounds. His first waking moments convince him he is in hell. Siamais is recounting part of the story of Gilgamesh to him when he first regains consciousness.

> The patient listened to this storytelling and he became afraid. Maybe he was not alive any more, and if he were not alive it needs be he must be dead. Maybe the Evil Spirit was tormenting him with ridiculous folk stories. But only a died-in-the-wool Gaelgore[6] would think of such a penance. It couldn't be that there was an ex-monk, an ex-poet, or even worse again than those, an ex-Gaelic Leaguer acting as a devil in hell. He made a supreme effort to open his eyes. (35)

He remains convinced he is in hell and becomes bitterly iconoclastic. When he hears he is to be sent to a boarding school, he is indignant: "If I were really young, I'd have my head stuck in a bag of glue by this time. I admire the escapism of youth" (53). The doctor, Siamais, gives his "son" the name Gilgamesh, and gradually the born-again Pádraig develops into the stoical and warmly sympathetic character Gilly.

It is one of the triumphs of the novel, this creation of an old man's mind in a fourteen-year-old body. In a genre that typically inclines to two-dimensional characterization, Gilly is so fully realized as to be entirely believable. Part of his appeal is due to his belief in himself as far wiser and more knowledgeable than the cretinous adults in authority, a common belief of fourteen-year-olds but in this case justified by his having the experience of fourscore years of life. The progress of the Dublin school story is both vivid and devastating. While the principal, Father Humbaba, plays Gilbert and Sullivan records in his study, and as long as the students do not seriously bother the teachers, Gilly and his friends do much as they please. They grow marijuana on the windowsills of the dormitories, throw orgiastic transvestite parties, are devotees of punk music groups like Meatloaf and Hot Vomit, and hold seances in an effort to raise the spirit of Sid Vicious. Gilly's clique forms a music group calling itself "The Alter Boys" (*sic*). They consistently cut their Irish classes taught by Séamas a' Chaca (Séamas the Shit), the author in another role but offstage in this particular story.

The mythic Enkidu, the wild man who was Gilgamesh's beloved friend, is represented by John Power, nicknamed the Wanderer. The Wanderer is a beguiling and tragic character. His story is a common one. Growing steadily more alienated as the help he so badly needs is not forthcoming from careless grown-ups, he gives himself up to drugs and drink, and soon all he wants from life is to get his "kicks." Gilly watches, angry and helpless, as he sees his friend destroy himself. The Irish proverb "Beidh lá eile ag an bPaorach" (Power will have another day)[7] takes on a grim irony when the Wanderer kills himself in the grisly climax of a nightmarish joyride through Dublin.

As much a misfit in the boarding school as he is in the island summer school, Michael plays a peripheral role in this segment, but his cheeky mockery is undiminished. During the seance sequence he remains outside the circle of friends who are trying to raise the spirit of Sid Vicious. (Michael is continually an odd man out.) Whereas Gilly plays the role of leader, probably because of his curious origins—he is a creation of the "doctor" Siamais, i.e. the author Séamas—Michael mocks the proceedings and rudely interrupts conversations. Once again he has the ability to throw the equilibrium of the story out of kilter. The first figure to appear at the seance is Bishop Ever Matthews, executed in Enniskillen in 1650. Gilly knows his history and, incidentally, seems to have an unusual store of information about the history of Enniskillen. The bishop thinks the boys are English: "'Ye are not of the Gael for thou dost not spake the language of the Gael as she is spoke. Thou shalt not wrest the confession from me. My lips are sealed by Almighty God.' 'Piss off then!' said the voice from the bed" (13). The voice is of course Michael's and has the effect of dismissing the ghost.

The intrusion of Michael into the Gilly segment is a forewarning of the increasing confusion of the overlapping stories. The author's brainstorm is becoming worse. The "Alter Boys" are engaged by Séamas, now an entrepreneur, to play a gig in Enniskillen. As they journey north to the Fermanagh town, they are joined by all the characters from the various plots. Séamas, now in a state of great confusion, physically behaves in a manner representative of his state of mind. He spins himself around in whirling-dervish style, at length falling dizzy to the ground. The climax of the book is a Walpurgisnacht of classically grotesque catastrophe. Exactly twenty-four hours after he began, the author has somehow achieved his end and survived his brainstorm. He wakens in the morning, at peace with himself—and indeed with his selves.

A Self-Evident Sham. An integral attribute of the self-conscious novel is its foundation on literary bases which, far from being unconscious or even concealed, repeatedly call attention to themselves. These constant nudges to the reader force him to read beneath the surface and face the consequent meaning and double meaning of the most trivial references. Among the central symbols of the book are feathers, sand, seaweed, and, most prominently, stonecrop—*cliabhán na gcloch*. Another oxymoron, stonecrop, unwelcome in civilized gardens and flourishing on barren and sandy ground, is, in its simplest symbolic meaning, the plant holding the secret of eternal life which Gilgamesh finds and loses. In the garbled version of the Gilgamesh tale that begins to confuse both author and reader, the following incident occurs. Utnapishtim tells Gilgamesh that the secret of eternal life lies in the stonecrop growing on an island between Heaven and Erne. Gilgamesh travels to the island, where he meets the Guardian of the Island.

"I am the Guardian of this island, I am the giver of life. Name your business here."

And Gilgamesh said to him: "Oh, kind, quiet, brave Guardian, Utnapishtim sent me here to find an herb called stonecrop, a magic herb that is possessed of a strange power."

"That rascal Utnapishtim! You are the third person to come along in a couple of hundred years."

And Gilgamesh said to him: "Don't be anxious, as long as the people of Belfascist don't find out you needn't worry."

And the Guardian said to him: "I am the writer of this account, and the people of Belfascist will never gain entrance here, as long as I have the strength." (198–99)

Gilgamesh finds the stonecrop and, returning to the mainland, lays the plant out to dry in the sun on the boat deck, then falls asleep. While he is sleeping, it disappears; the author hazards a guess that it is stolen by a hen-blackbird.

It may be that at this point the guiding artistic impulse of the book passes into the Anna aspect of the author's character. Though it is not specified that the girl at the end of the book who steps in at a crucial moment is actually the character Anna who sings with the "Alter Boys," it may be someone who represents her, and it is she who restores balance to the author's world.

Stonecrop, true to its nature, repeatedly crops up throughout the novel. Most prominently, the author wears a sprig of it as he sets out on the last chapter of his odyssey, and predictably, he loses it. Similarly, feathers feature as a major symbolic link. They recall the journey of Gilgamesh in the wilderness, living on birds and beasts and clothing himself in their skins. Feathers are connected with the blackbird and in this respect are handed out to puzzled strangers by Séamas the author in his most manic phase. Finally, they make a quill, the writer's tool. All the symbols as well as the thematic center depend on the story of Gilgamesh. In addition to the actual retelling of the tale itself, versions of even relatively minor incidents within it recur in thinly disguised form—for instance, the ritual felling of Humbaba's cedar.

Deliberate and obvious is the use of an ancient epic to provide a theme and framework for a modern experimental novel. Joyce's *Ulysses* is the template, and it also provides the twenty-four-hour timetable. The saga of Leopold Bloom and Stephen Dedalus on 16 June 1904 is imitated in the precisely twenty-four-hour momentous day in the life of the author Séamas on 28 July 1982. What Dublin is to *Ulysses*, Enniskillen is to *Cuaifeach*. Enniskillen turns out to be surpirsingly rich in allusion and association, all precisely relevant to the author's aim and experience. A few examples will make the point. Royal Portora, a venerable boys' school in Enniskillen, has been attended by many literary luminaries, including Oscar Wilde and Samuel Beckett. Both writers are frequently invoked, and particular reference is made to their respective writings in French rather than English. (Wilde's *Salome* is re-created in one of Mac Annaidh's sprightly eccentrics, Sally Holmes.) It was in Enniskillen that Patrick Pearse, poet-leader of the 1916 rebellion, first delivered his famous indictment of the education system, "The Murder Machine." Mac Annaidh's portrait of the Dublin school is a similar indictment. In the boys' seance Patrick Pearse is one of the ghosts to appear, and he is wandering in Enniskillen— as is Oscar Wilde—on the night the author's brainstorm causes him to lose control of his characters. It is noteworthy that several of the historical characters presented in the book are associated with sexual ambiguity.

Linked to this is the rich allusive image of islands. Enniskillen is a town situated on an island on the River Erne. The summer school takes place on Aranmore Island. As we have seen, Gilgamesh finds the magic herb on an island, probably Enniskillen itself. The symbolic meaning of islands is a continual reminder of the author's isolation, both physical and psychic. This, in turn, is aggravated by the language problem, another island barrier that obsessively concerns the author. In particular the exchanges between Michael and himself, in which each speaks a different language, fairly represent the worlds that divide them.

The Irish writer who best made use of two languages to good effect, Brian O'Nolan, author of *At Swim-Two-Birds,* chose to write what many believe to be his best work, *An Béal Bocht* (Eng. *The Poor Mouth*) in Irish.[8] His influence on Mac Annaidh is, again, not something one has to dig for. *At Swim-Two-Birds* is acknowledged to be one of the most obvious examples of the self-conscious novel in Irish literature. The resemblances of *Cuaifeach* to it are mainly structural.

At Swim-Two-Birds is, seemingly, an autobiographical account of the author as student, engaged in writing a novel. Bored with conventional modes of fiction, he formulates his own rules.

> It was explained that a satisfactory novel should be a self-evident sham to which the reader could regulate at will the degree of his credulity. It was undemocratic to compel characters to be uniformly good or bad or poor or rich. Each should be allowed a private life, self-determination and a decent standard of living. This would make for self-respect, contentment and better service. It would be incorrect to say that it would lead to chaos. Characters should be interchangeable as between one book and another. The entire corpus of existing literature should be regarded as a limbo from which discerning authors could draw their characters as required, creating only when they failed to find a suitable existing character.[9]

Following his own guidelines, the real author invents a character, Dermot Trellis, who is engaged in writing a novel. He, in turn, compels his characters to lodge in the same house with him and locks them in their rooms at night so that he can sleep and still maintain control. However, they break out and submit the unfortunate Trellis to horrible punishments. Intertwined with this theme are several substories based on Irish legend and literature.

The similarity of this basic schema to *Cuaifeach* is clear. Séamas, the author, is writing a work of fiction in which the present reality is mingled with legend, fantasy, and myth. As in *At Swim-Two-Birds,* the characters get out of hand, and the novelist is at their mercy. Other marks of the self-conscious genre are to be found in both books: the fantastic names of characters, the pastiche of literary styles, the mockery of convention, elaborate wordplay. A marked cultural similarity is the tension of two languages at war with one another in both books. O'Nolan, who wrote with fluency and ease in both Irish and English, employs a stilted formal style in sections of *At Swim-Two-Birds* to give the effect of a bad translation, and although his book is ostensibly written in English, only a bilingual reader can be fully aware of its linguistic complexity, signposted by the apparently senseless title.

It would be unlikely for Mac Annaidh not to acknowledge the most prominent modern writer in Irish, Mártín Ó Cadhain, who wrote his difficult experimental narrative fiction *Cré na Cille* (Churchyard Clay) in the 1940s.[10] It was typical of Ó Cadhain's embittered personality to choose to make his long work as difficult and as impenetrable as possible. He was aware of this; "It is every inch as difficult for someone to read my work as it is to read poetry," he wrote.[11] Still, *Cré na Cille,* with all its difficulties, is a self-conscious fiction, although Ó Cadhain chose to ditch all fictional conventions and, ill-advisedly, some dramatic ones also. The result tends to alienate the reader, although it works well in oral presentation, where the myriad unnamed voices can be identified by ear alone. It is quite likely that Ó Cadhain had precisely this in mind.

Fortunately, Mac Annaidh has preserved enough conventionally acceptable modes to make his narrative methods quickly clear to the reader. Also, in place of Ó Cadhain's idiomatic linguistic peculiarities Mac Annaidh uses an easy, fluent style, rendering faithfully the modern vernacular English in Irish—no easy job. Inevitably, though, there are a few tips of the hat to Ó Cadhain. As concerned about the educational system as is Mac Annadih, Ó Cadhain also evokes Pearse's "Murder Machine" frequently. A more strict echo is in the personality of the old man, Patrick, before he is killed and reincarnated. As an old man, he is a typical Ó Cadhain character, rambling in his thoughts about the past, cranky and obstreperous, obsessively caught up in a few personal memories that have highlighted his life, such as the occasion when he heard Count John McCormack sing "Panis Angelicus" at the Eucharistic Congress in 1932 and, in a deliberate pastiche of Ó Cadhain, the number of times he dislocated his ankle.

The nods to Ó Cadhain are significant on another level. Although *Cré na Cille* was hailed as a master-work and remains the chief literary landmark in modern Irish, it has comparatively few readers and has not been published in English translation. Mac Annaidh is as stubborn as Ó Cadhain in his persistence in using Irish, though he makes it very clear what this costs him as a writer. The audience to which he most wants to appeal is represented by the egregious Michael, as the author addresses him on the page in English: "Anyway, to get back to the story . . . and just in case you're reading this, Mickey, though I very much doubt it, I'll put in a few more lines in English to give your dog-eared dictionary a rest . . . twill annoy the fascists too. Brucellosis an Bhéarlachais" (59).[12]

Why does he write in Irish at all? It is perhaps the most self-conscious gesture of all, to choose—some might think perversely—to write in a language which is not the writer's first language, and which is also not widely read by readers who appreciate his sophisticated verbal brio and literary groundbreaking. Whereas Ó Cadhain firmly resisted translation into English, however, Mac Annaidh is more tractable. Nevertheless, a certain nervousness remains. Brian Ó Nolan has been ill served by translators of *An Béal Bocht* and unfortunately

was no longer alive to put a stop to the pale imitations that have been published. Mac Annaidh will doubtless keep a close and critical eye on an English version of *Cuaifeach Mo Londubh Buí.*

It is no longer defensible for claimants to assert the existence of master literary works in Irish and deny their availability to the rest of the world. It is unnecessary here to go into detail about the validity of translation, but it has been the curious attitude of nationalists to resist efforts to translate works for which such large claims are made. In bringing to notice a novel which in many senses is "novel" in Irish, I should stress that both an English and a Russian translation are in preparation.

Joan Trodden Keefe, Winter 1989

[1] Denis Donoghue, *We Irish: Essays on Irish Literature and Society,* New York, Knopf, 1986, pp. 24–25. On the revival of Irish Gaelic in poetry and fiction, see also my essay "What Ish My Language?" *WLT* 59:1 (Winter 1985), pp. 5–8.

[2] Séamas Mac Annaidh, *Cuaifeach Mo Londubh Buí,* Dublin, Coiscéim, 1984. All parenthetic page references will be to this edition. The translations are my own.

[3] Robert Alter, *Partial Magic: The Novel as a Self-Conscious Genre,* Berkeley, University of California Press, 1975, p. xi.

[4] Séamas Mac Annaidh, letter to Joan Trodden Keefe, 31 January 1986.

[5] *Gaeltacht:* name for native Irish-speaking areas.

[6] A "Gaelgore" is an Irish-language enthusiast. The word is often used derogatorily.

[7] The saying has the meaning implicit in "Tomorrow is another day"—i.e., one always has another chance.

[8] Myles na gCopaleen (Brian O'Nolan), *An Béal Bocht,* Dublin, Dolmen, 1941.

[9] Flann O'Brien (Brian O'Nolan), *At Swim-Two-Birds,* London, MacGibbon & Kee, 1960 (first publication, 1939), p. 33.

[10] Máirtín Ó Cadhain, *Cré na Cille,* Dublin, Sairséal agus Dill, 1949. For a discussion of this novel, see *WLT* 59:3 (Summer 1985), pp. 363–73.

[11] Máirtín Ó Cadhain, in the pamphlet "Páipéir Bána agus Páipéir Breaca," Dublin, 1969, p. 38.

[12] *An Bhéarlachais* means "of the English language."

Re-Grafting a Severed Tongue: The Pains (and Politics) of Reviving Irish

The revival or development of modern literature in the Irish language cannot be separated from the fate of Irish as a vernacular. The situation of the language is quite peculiar. Nobody who has gone to school in Ireland since 1922 can have escaped some acquaintance with the language. For many, their school encounter with the language was unhappy, and they have gladly forgotten as much of the language as is possible while still living in Ireland. For most, perhaps, the language has slipped into a desuetude of which they pretend to be ashamed, as Americans do with their vague incomprehension of something they dimly think of as "good grammar." In a pinch these can muster enough to grasp the point of a simple witticism in Irish or, when abroad, exchange rudimentary confidences in the presence of foreigners. Others have a rusty but adequate command of the language, enough to follow the drift of a conversation or as a cultural exercise enjoy an occasional play at the Peacock or the Damer; they will often quote with pleasure favorite lines of verse remembered from school. There are also enthusiasts, who go out of their way to speak and read the language, who keep abreast of new literature and proselytize among the rusty. But only a small segment of the Irish people, in a number of geographically separate rural areas, experience Irish as a true vernacular, as a twenty-four-hours-a-day lived-in language. Such Irish-speaking districts are known, even in English, in the singular and also collectively, as *Gaeltacht.*

The Gaeltacht is too small an economic unit to support a separate literature financially, but fortunately it is not required to try. Some unreliable statistics will give a sense of the numbers involved. At the 1971 census, when about 25% of the population of the Irish Republic (in round numbers, about 750,000 people) by responses to questions about language use placed themselves in the class I have called "enthusiasts," the total Gaeltacht population was guessed to be in the neighborhood of 30,000, or only 1% of the total. The entire 1971 census is suspect, however, and a new census, just completed in 1979, shows an apparently huge growth in population in most categories—an incredible 13% for the entire Republic in just eight years. The Gaeltacht areas in Donegal and Galway have certainly increased greatly in population, though testimony is so far mixed as to the extent this has strengthened or diluted Irish as a vernacular.

The potential sales market for literature in Irish may then run as high as one million people, a sizable figure for a small language, several times the total population of Iceland. Yet if the true Gaeltacht fails to survive, Irish literature will diminish first to a parlor game for enthusiasts, then die forever. Modern spoken Irish divides readily into three main dialects. The Northern dialect, represented chiefly by the Donegal Gaeltacht —a fairly extensive range of coastal valleys in County Donegal—is the most linguistically distinct from the others, holding certain idiosyncrasies in common with

Scottish Gaidhlig. The Western dialect is spoken in parts of Co. Mayo and in a large region of Co. Galway extending westward from Galway City along the north shore of Galway Bay, and including the Aran Islands. The Southern dialect is spoken in several areas, notably the Decies in southern Co. Waterford, Muskerry in western Co. Cork, and Corca Dhuibhne, the Dingle Peninsula in Co. Kerry, southwesternmost county in Ireland. What the Gaeltacht regions have in common, aside from the survival of Irish as a vernacular, are the conditions for that survival—geographical isolation and extreme poverty of resources for earning a livelihood. They are rock-pools left from a vanished sea. Until the past decade they were isolated from one another as well as from the encroaching world of English, their young people emigrating, their old left behind as exhibits in a museum, tape-recording their memories for scholars before they dropped one by one into the grave. Second-hand awareness of the existence elsewhere of similar rock-pools did nothing to alleviate demoralization, accompanied as it was by the information those others spoke a different kind of Irish.

A recent dramatic reversal of these circumstances has two main aspects. One is that both Donegal and Galway have acquired a range of new modern industries, resulting in net immigration and population growth. Young people are returning to the Gaeltacht to good jobs, settling down and raising new families. A cloud in this sunny sky, however, is the fact that many have returned with English-speaking wives or husbands. It remains to be seen if the local vernacular is strong enough to assimilate the children of such households, or if the fruit of prosperity will be the final poison for Irish. The Southern Gaeltacht has seen no influx of outside industry, but the energetic people of Corca Dhuibhne have asserted themselves by organizing a Development Co-Operative that runs Irish-language courses and music festivals, fosters land reclamation and vegetable-growing efforts, and develops plant nurseries; it also owns and operates its own publishing house.

The second aspect, also a product of Gaeltacht initiative like the Kerry Co-Op, is the establishment of Radio na Gaeltachta. This is a daily broadcasting service, quite distinct from the national Radio-Telefís Éireann network, uniting all the Gaeltacht districts with news, current events and entertainment in Irish, drawing on all the dialects. In Kerry now people are exhilarated because Galway Irish has become familiar to them, and even Donegal Irish comprehensible. The Gaeltacht areas are now mentally united, the people feel part of a larger and stronger community than they did in the past; they no longer are isolated and hemmed in.

Listeners outside the Gaeltacht also tune in, and write or phone the stations. Nothing I had read had prepared me for the revolutionary impact of Radio na Gaeltachta on the morale of Irish speakers I encountered this year in visits to Galway, Kerry and Cork. The survival of Irish as a vernacular, then, continues to depend, as it has for a long time, on throws of the dice. At this time a little run of good luck might put it permanently out of danger; a run of bad luck could end the game.

■ ■ ■

I turn now to a consideration of literature in Irish with a historical survey to clarify our terms of reference. To speak of a revival of literature in Modern Irish should not be taken to imply that creation of literature in the language had ever completely ceased. What the Literary Revival in Irish meant was writing with the intention of being printed and reaching a fairly wide audience at one time, and also the reestablishment of what had almost disappeared, a canon of generally accepted critical standards. Old Irish and Middle Irish literature, which lie outside our present concern, had each its own distinct communal consensus on the canons of literary quality. Modern Irish, dating in its early phase from the mid-fourteenth century, is a product of the linguistic onslaught on Middle Irish by English and especially Norman French following the Anglo-Norman invasion in the twelfth century, and is characterized from the beginning by the destruction of the cultural institutions that had provided a consensus. Old rules became for some writers a pedantic fetish, while other writers never learned them.

The printing of Irish did not become commonplace until the later nineteenth century. Irish incunabula include one sixteenth-century Catechism from Dublin, and a seventeenth-century Bible and Prayer Book from London, all aiming to wean the Irish from the Church of Rome, and a number of seventeenth-century Counter-Reformation works from the Continent aiming at the opposite effect. None of these books had much effect on what Daniel Corkery called "The Hidden Ireland," where literature continued without access to print as in the Middle Ages, by manuscript transmission. That tradition survived to overlap the nineteenth-century opening to the press. The time span relative to one major work is instructive. Brian Merriman's comic epic poem *Cúirt an Mheán-Oíche* (The Midnight Court) was composed about 1780, and at least twenty-five manuscript copies have survived, although the work was printed, almost furtively, in Dublin in 1850, seventy years after its composition.

The writers of the Revival also differed from their immediate predecessors by turning to prose, of which

Modern Irish had no significant monument later than Geoffrey Keating's popular history of Ireland, *Forus Feasa ar Éirinn,* written about 1630 in an elevated vernacular. Keating's language was close enough to the living tongue to be appreciated by the hundreds of readers among whom copies circulated throughout the succeeding centuries. But his long periodic sentence, full of carefully balanced subordinate clauses, made a poor medium for modern fiction, and writers were baffled in the attempt to find an adequate prose style for Irish until the advent of Peadar ó Laoire, who wrote straightforwardly in his native Cork dialect, replacing Keating's long sentences with short sentences, and subordination with parataxis. O Laoire's short stories and his "folk-novel" *Séadna* are full of dialogue, the patterns of speech also molding the narrative. During the first three decades of this century the short story in colloquial language became the norm in Irish writing. The short stories in English of Liam ó Flaithertaigh (O'Flaherty) parallel the bulk of his work in Irish and illustrate that norm. Frank O'Connor also, although he has written only a few stories in Irish, conforms to the pattern. The Galway writer Pádraic ó Conaire, for the gallery of memorable characters in his stories, had become a sort of cult idol by the time of his death in 1928.

Within a year, however, a new genre appeared—the Blasket Book—initiated by Tomás ó Criomhtháin's *An tOileánach* (The Islander; 1929). This autobiographical retrospection on a life of seventy years upon the Great Blasket Island, three miles off the tip of the Dingle Peninsula, impressed by its spirited colloquial prose and the poetic response of its author to island, sea, weather and the communal spirit of the islanders. It also astonished as a depiction from the inside of a rich though primitive culture. Although the Blasket may never have held many more than 200 people, ó Criomhtháin's book was followed by a whole series of islanders' memoirs: Muiris ó Súileabháin's *Fiche Bliain ag Fás* (Twenty Years a-Growing) in 1933 and Peig Sayers's *Peig* in 1936. In 1953 the last islanders were evacuated to the mainland; but subsequently Seán Sheáin í Chearnaigh has produced several successive memoirs, and Seán ó Criomhtháin, son of the pioneer Tomás, in *Laetheanta dár Saol* (Days of Our Lives) has narrated his experience of the crises that forced abandonment of the island, as well as the life he and his fellows have since followed on the mainland. Pádraig ua Maoileoin, from neighboring mainland Corca Dhuibhne, has added to the Blasket literature *Na hAird ó Thuaidh* (The Hills to the North; 1960) and *Ár Leithéidí Arís* (Our Likes Again—an echo of ó Criomhtháin's favorite elegiac phrase—1978), objective and sympathetic appraisals of the islanders, their lives and their writings.

The real attractiveness of the Blasket books cast an evil spell on the development of modern Irish literature. They celebrate and lament a way of life their authors recognized was passing away even as they wrote; consequently they could point no way ahead for Irish writing. Worse, they effected in many minds an identity between the Irish language and the dying Blasket way of life. Those I have mentioned earlier who resented as time wasted and effort misdirected their compulsory learning of Irish at school had their "modernist" prejudices reinforced by an Irish literature devoted to the nostalgic maunderings of senile subhumans on a remote backward island. Those more concerned for the language, however, were delighted by Myles na gCopaleen's (Brian O'Nolan's) wicked backlash, *An Béal Bocht* (The Poor Mouth; 1940), the memoirs of one Bónapart ó Cúnasa, native of the most superlatively backward and benighted Gaeltacht a fiendish mind could imagine. This, one of the funniest books ever written in any language, parodies the whole genre of Blasket books, especially *An tOileánach*.

An Béal Bocht appeared early in World War II, an episode known in Ireland as "The Emergency," an ill wind that blew some benefits toward the Irish language and culture. The Irish were left to their own material and spiritual resources, isolated from the warring world, a state which brought new dimensions to Irish literature. At about the same time three excellent lyric poets began to write, reflecting in Irish verse modern everyday concerns: Máire mac an tSaoi from Corca Dhuibhne, Seán ó Ríordáin from west Cork and Máirtín ó Díreáin from Aran.

Prose in Irish also began to face the concerns of modern life but encountered a problem which verse escaped, one perhaps unique to Irish. The Irish short story in English or Irish, whatever it may owe to Continental example, is a natural outgrowth of traditional fireside storytelling. The form and content of William Carleton's *Traits & Stories of the Irish Peasantry* (1830) clearly reveal this ancestry. Canon Peadar ó Laoire's stories, like the more sophisticated work of Pádraic ó Conaire, still concern the lives of rural folk. But Ireland is becoming increasingly urban (today almost 40% of the Republic's people live in metropolitan Dublin alone). Irish prose writers began to engage urban topics in stories set in Dublin or Belfast, even Liverpool or London. The English settings lessened the problem, but a story set in Dublin carries always the distracting question: "What language are these people supposed to be actually speaking?" Plenty of people in Dublin carry on their home lives, and part of their social lives, in Irish, but the general life of the city is conducted in English. Since the greatest strength of Irish prose is the reproduction of living speech, how is a writer in Irish to convey the variety and the overtones of Dublin voices?

One or two writers have found ways to allow the Irish language to engage the whole gamut of human experience, to escape the trap of Irish as a medium for rural experience only. Máirtín ó Cadhain, the greatest twentieth-century writer of Irish, escapes not by muting the idiosyncrasy of voices that may be supposed to be speaking in English, but by enhancing it. His immense genius so refines and develops his perception of the human voice as the unique vehicle of each human personality that each of his characters speaks in his or her own individuated authentic voice. An ó Cadhain bus conductor or bartender does not speak like *a* bus conductor or bartender, but like *this* one particular unique bus conductor or bartender: the speech is reproduced in Irish; the language it may be supposed to have been uttered in scarcely matters. This solution to the problem of linguistic plausibility may be recommended to any writer who possesses ó Cadhain's genius to carry it out.

Ó Cadhain's radical individuation of human voices is the basis of his masterwork, a 350-page innovative novel called *Cré na Cille* (The Graveyard Clay; 1949). The book has no narrator and no stage directions; it is divided into ten "Interludes" of obsessional cross-talk among the corpses in a graveyard. The rules of their existence are that they can do nothing, see nothing and cannot communicate with the living. All they can do is talk and listen to one another; they depend upon the newly-buried for word of the living. They are in fact reduced to their own voices, talking endlessly and acrimoniously, locked in their own selves, unaltered and unimproved by death. Irony and humor and the sheer awfulness of the principal characters carry the reader to the ambiguous climax, the moral of which seems to be that even in death we can expect disappointment. *Cré na Cille* holds a position in Irish like that of *Finnegans Wake* or even *Ulysses* in English—not perhaps the model for other writers to imitate, but a reminder of what resourcefulness may achieve.

In addition to his fictions, Máirtín ó Cadhain has left an important body of literary theory and criticism, including the most valuable manifesto of his own commitment, *Páipéir Bhána agus Páipéir Bhreaca* (White Papers and Multicolored Papers). This concludes with words I must yield space to translate:

> Irish is a new medium even if it is a narrow one and it is a challenge to me. It is my own, something I cannot say about any other medium on earth. In the loneliness of my heart I heard—I always hear:
>
> > the warbling of the blackbird of the banks of Lee and the music of the Fenian chant.

I am as old as the Hag of Beare, as old as the Brugh on the Boyne, as old as the great doe. There are two thousand years of that filthy sow that Ireland has been, going round in my ears, in my mouth, in my eyes, in my head, in my dreams. A writer in a minor language, if it is a language at all, Hugh Mac Diarmid, said it better:

> The great rose of all the world is not for me
> For me the little white rose of Scotland
> That smells sweetly and breaks the heart.

Mention of the negative appeal to some of the Blasket books, and of the urban-rural gap Irish prose encounters, leads to the political aspect of Irish revival my title alludes to. The Young Ireland Movement of 1840 and the Gaelic League of 1893 both sought the revival of Irish as the normal medium for Irish life and culture. Both movements coincided with political movements aimed at national independence, but despite overlaps in membership, political and language movements were never identical. However, Patrick Pearse, figurehead of the 1916 Rebellion, though born an English-speaking Dubliner, was mystically devoted to the Irish language. Éamonn de Valéra, sole survivor of the 1916 leadership, professed throughout his long life the same devotion to the language, and during his regime firmly enforced its compulsory teaching in the schools. De Valéra unhappily was more adept with sticks than carrots, and political opposition to De Valéra sometimes crystallized into hostility to Irish, while resentment of compulsory Irish in school was exploited by De Valéra's political opposition.

For all his professions, it is dubitable that De Valéra really knew or loved Gaelic Ireland, since the drab clerical morality he imposed on the country is so much at odds with the earthiness of the language and the frame of mind it reflects. An equal duplicity haunts the rhetoric of those who abolished compulsory Irish in the name of freedom, with their pieties about uncoerced love rejuvenating the language. De Valéra's motives were obscure and contorted; those of his opponents rise from ill-concealed hate. The hope I can see for the language is in the increasing independence of those who speak it—those who organized the West Kerry Development Co-Operative and those who established Radio na Gaeltachta—not from the venal Tweedledum and Tweedledee of the alternate governing factions.

The politics of the language revival can be illustrated by the critical reception accorded a new novel, Lig Sinn i gCathú (1976), by Breandán ó hEithir, a journalist who was born in Aran. It is not a masterpiece, but has been a critical and commercial success, reaching a third printing by 1978. A boisterous, reasonably bawdy "good read" about student life at University College,

Galway, in 1949, it is something of a technical achievement in that it has naturalized for Irish the third-person narrative with focus on a single consciousness. This is no novelty in English, but its advantage in Irish becomes evident in that it allows the ubiquitous speakers even subgrammatical idiosyncrasy, while maintaining an unobtrusive narrative flow. Idiomatic unmannered narrative cannot be simply translated from one language into another. Ó hEithir could not simply imitate English. His success owes much to the slowly accruing body of scholarly prose in recent Irish—biography, history, literary criticism—for the development of effective narrative prose.

When in 1978 ó hEithir published his own translation of his book into English as Lead Us Into Temptation (the exact sense of the original title), the critical reception was just the reverse: "Is this all that the hoopla was about?" sums up the consensus. Never mentioned by either side is the fact that the book's plot is a satire on those forces in Irish political life I have above associated with hostility toward the Irish language. Applause for or condemnation of the book depended less on its literary values than on its ability to focus unspoken linguistic and political antipathies.

I should mention a final novel that has provoked less enthusiasm, though it attempts greater innovation. So far as I know, it has not been translated. That is Eoghan ó Tuairisc's An Lomnochtán (The Sheer Nude; 1977), a phantasmagoric story set in a country town about the end of the Irish Civil War of the early 1920s. The narrative style reminds me somewhat of Faulkner, and the effect may be the result of a continuing struggle to wrest new literary possibilities out of the language.

■ ■ ■

I shall conclude by raising the question: does Ireland need another literature, in Irish, on top of what has been produced in this century alone by Yeats, Synge, Joyce, O'Casey, Behan, Flann O'Brien—to name only the dead? Can Ireland afford to divert her stock of energy to a quixotic attempt to produce equally great literature in Irish? In one sense the question is pointless—the country does not produce the writers by her own will and purpose; they produce themselves. Nothing could have stopped Máirtín ó Cadhain from following his road, or Joyce from following his. But of the six writers in English I have named, only Yeats could not express himself in Irish—although his manifest engagement with native traditional themes might well deceive the world in the matter. Joyce as a young man, or at any rate his Stephen Dedalus, affected to despise the Irish Revival, but Joyce learned far more Irish than Stephen did, although it was Stephen's soul that fretted in the shadow of the English language, a foreign, "an acquired speech." Synge's best plays depend upon his knowledge of Irish; his idiom is inspired translation. O'Casey, a Dublin Protestant, learned Irish and continued to weave it through his plays to the end of his career, in allusive placenames and personal names he invented to convey sense only to those who shared the language. Behan wrote poetry in Irish, he wrote *The Hostage* originally in Irish (*An Giall*), and in *The Quare Fellow* entire conversations take place in Irish—I have no idea what non-Irish-speakers make of them in performance. Flann O'Brien was a multiple personality who as Myles na gCopaleen wrote the funniest novel in Irish, while *At Swim-Two-Birds* is unthinkable without a background in Irish.

For many Anglophone Irish, loss of the native tongue is no more than two or three generations old. Irish minds created the Irish language, as the Irish language has created the Irish consciousness. The language is the reservoir of Ireland's racial memories, its influence pervades the mental landscape: it is home, the starting place. I shall try, probably unsuccessfully, to show how the Irish language and its heritage works for a modern Irish mind by a clumsy analysis of a very short poem by Máire mac an tSaoi, "Athdheirdre." Even the title challenges—"Meta-Deirdre," perhaps, but that is too ugly; in Irish the sense is quite clear: another Deirdre, an other Deirdre; a second Deirdre, a replacement Deirdre. My translation of the poem:

"I will not cut my nails,"
That's what she said
And turned her back on life
On account of that one day—
With her clay
I would not claim,
Nor anyone like me, kinship—
    I comb my hair
    And I put paint on my lips.

The reticence of this poem does put its speaker on a par with Deirdre; we are never told what anguish of loss has made her think of the comparison. Because she is Irish, the example of Deirdre springs vividly to her mind in her moment of pain, as it would not naturally spring to the mind of a woman not Irish. Because she is a woman of the twentieth century, responding to heartbreak with the stoic gestures of vanity common to modern women of the Western world, she recognizes that she is not of the same clay as Deirdre. She is in the same predicament as Deirdre, but must react to it in *her* way: as a later Deirdre, *Athdheirdre*. That, I think, is the simple dialectic of the poem, and it shows Irish language and culture not as a retreat from the modern world, but as precisely

the best medium through which an Irishwoman can deal with the modern world.

I shall close this discussion with two quotations of poetry written in English, both by the eminent living Irish poet John Montague. Both reflect on the trauma inflicted on the Irish people by the loss of their own language. The first quotation is from the second sequence of "A Severed Head":

The whole landscape a manuscript
We had lost the skill to read,
A part of our past disinherited;
But fumbled, like a blind man,
Along the fingertips of instinct.

The last is from a poem, "A Grafted Tongue," from which I derived my title for this essay:

    To grow
a second tongue, as
harsh a humiliation
as twice to be born.

Brendan P. O Hehir, Spring 1980

The Great Irish Elk: Seamus Heaney's Personal Helicon

When Yeats received the Nobel Prize in Literature in 1923, he was fifty-eight and at the height of his poetic powers, which happily continued undiminished for another sixteen years. Yeats wrote some of his best poems in the last years of his life, the decade and a half that followed the Nobel Prize, and in his *Autobiographies* he even went so far as to say that "The Bounty of Sweden" made him feel that though he was old his Muse was young. Seamus Heaney has long been recognized as a worthy successor to Yeats; we can hope that, in receiving the Nobel Prize in Literature for 1995, he will share not only Yeats's honor but also his fate, and that, at the slightly younger age of fifty-six, Heaney will prove that he still has some of his best poems to write.

Yeats has been the undisputed Irish national poet for most of this century, a preeminence celebrated annually at the Yeats International Summer School in Sligo, but Heaney is the emergent Irish national poet, for whom another literary festival may well be founded some day. I remember it was at a Yeats International Summer School in Sligo that I first heard Seamus Heaney read his poems, and it was a moving experience because he reads so well, in a soft Ulster accent freighted with gravity but lightened by wry humor. I realized then that if Heaney could be compared with Yeats, the two poets must have more in common than their Irishness, for Yeats himself was never simply an Irish poet; he was one of the chief modern world poets as well. And if Heaney is really like Yeats, he may come to be seen as more significantly a Modern poet than an Irish poet. Indeed, it may already be happening: Heaney's poems appear regularly in such non-Irish places as the (London) *Times Literary Supplement* and the *New Yorker,* and his dual appointment to the prestigious Boylston Professorship of Rhetoric and Oratory at Harvard and the Chair of Poetry at Oxford are proof enough that he commands wide respect outside Ireland.

Americans especially appreciate Heaney, for he has lived long enough in Boston to become an honorary citizen, has had his picture in the *New York Times Sunday Magazine,* has delivered a commencement address—in verse, no less—at Fordham University, and has been featured on a special American television program for Saint Patrick's Day, introduced by his universally admired fellow-countryman, the flutist James Galway, as "everybody's favorite Irish poet," as he strolled beside a stone wall in the Boyne Valley, talking of Saint Patrick's conquest of Ireland as if it had happened the day before. His own conquest of America was pictured some time ago in the pages of *National Geographic* magazine, which ran a photographic essay on "The Mystery of the Bog," quoting Heaney's poetry almost as if it were scripture. He is already ahead of Yeats in recognition, for his honors at Oxford and Harvard elevated him to the highest position a poet can reach in the English-speaking world, before he won a still higher international honor from the Swedish Academy at Stockholm.

So there is justice as well as judgment in the award of a Nobel Prize in Literature to Seamus Heaney, and it is clearly a popular choice for the Swedish Academy to make. When Yeats received it, he was honest enough to admit that his lyric poetry alone would not have won him the honor, though it had given him greater distinction than anything else he wrote: he attributed the award as much to his identification with the cause of Irish Nationalism—which by 1923 had won independence from England and created a new Free State—and to his having helped found the Irish National Theatre, as to his lyric poems, because he knew patriotism and theatre appealed to a wider audience than poetry. Yeats was naturally suspect in his native country, belonging as he did to the Anglo-Irish Protestant Ascendancy, but he overcame the prejudices of his mainly Catholic countrymen by defining a new Irish consciousness rooted in Celtic myth as much as in Christian faith. He created a heroic character for Ireland out of mythical heroes like Oisin and Cuchulain and Queen Maeve, which allowed him to transform the very landscape into symbols of courage and patriotic pride: the Isle of Innisfree

was his youthful retreat; above his grave Under Ben Bulben is his own defiant epitaph.

Seamus Heaney has had less native prejudice to overcome, being born as he was into an Irish Catholic farming family; but he had greater literary prejudice to overcome, for he was destined to come after Yeats, and the new Irish poetic tradition of which Yeats was the master forced Heaney to wrestle through much of his career with the powerful ghost of Yeats. Indeed, he could only lay that ghost to rest by founding an Irish tradition of his own recognizably different from that of Yeats.

It is not surprising that there are echoes of older poets in Heaney's early poems: the Irish voice of Yeats, the English voices of Hopkins and W. H. Auden, the Welsh voice of Dylan Thomas, even the American voice of Robert Frost can be heard in them. But the strong voice of Heaney asserted itself above these echoes, from the time when he chose to open his first book, *Death of a Naturalist* (1966), with "Digging," an ancestral poem linking him with his father and his grandfather on the farm near Londonderry where he was raised. By the time he had written his next three books, *Door into the Dark* (1969), *Wintering Out* (1972), and *North* (1975), it was clear that Heaney had found his true subject and was no longer in debt to Yeats or any other poet, having at last made himself into an Irish Symbolist in his own right.

The bog is quite literally Heaney's turf, for he has come to join that distinguished line of modern poets who sought the prehistoric and primitive roots of civilization, following the lead of cultural anthropologists who went in search of the origins of all myths and the foundations of all religious beliefs. In the twentieth century, along with the Bible and epic poetry, *The Golden Bough* has been one of the primary sources for poetry, bringing back from deep in human memory vegetation rites that are even more ancient than the Trojan War. The poet's imagination, as another Nobel Prize-winning poet, T. S. Eliot, once said, must be at the same time primitive and sophisticated, extending human consciousness to the extreme limits of our encounter with the present and our knowledge of the past. Heaney, like other modern poets before him—like his fellow Irishman Yeats, but also like the American expatriates Eliot and Pound—has felt the need for recalling vividly and often painfully in his poems certain ancestral myths and rituals, apparently with the instinct to preserve the record of the remote past so that we will never forget it, knowing from somewhere deep inside, as Yeats once put it, that "we only begin to understand life when we conceive of it as tragedy."

Yeats achieved his first identity as an Irish poet, later as a Modern poet. So, in the first decade of Heaney's career, in the 1960s, he could be seen—indeed saw himself—as only one of several promising young Irish poets, maybe a little more ambitious than Thomas Kinsella or John Montague, but not necessarily more talented or more accomplished than they. His first book, *Death of a Naturalist* in 1966, evoked comparisons with Thomas Hardy and Robert Frost, high company for a beginner, but it was the voice of the Irish farm boy that was most distinctly heard. The really memorable poems in that volume were the opening poem, "Digging," and the closing poem, "Personal Helicon." The first was clearly autobiographical, since Heaney, having grown up on a farm in County Derry, portrayed himself in the poem as following his father, who dug for potatoes, and his grandfather, who dug for peat, by "digging" for words with his pen. It is a homely metaphor, but it suited his style well, signifying strength, skill, and earthiness. Heaney later said that

> 'Digging', in fact, was the name of the first poem I wrote where I thought my feelings had got into words, or to put it more accurately, where I thought my *feel* had got into words. Its rhythms and noises still please me. . . . I wrote it in the summer of 1964, almost two years after I had begun to 'dabble in verses'. This was the first place where I felt I had done more than make an arrangement of words: I felt that I had let down a shaft into real life.[1]

So his first poem came directly from life on the farm where he grew up, and his attitude in it seems almost the Irish equivalent of an American naturalist such as Thoreau or Frost; however, the last poem in that first collection, "Personal Helicon," speaks from a more sophisticated and literary background. Heaney had left the family farm to go to Belfast and earn a first-class honors degree in English literature from Queen's University, and the poem introduces more literary ancestors than his father and grandfather. Helicon, after all, is the sacred mountain in Greece where Apollo and the Muses were supposed to dwell, and where poetic inspiration was said to flow from the Fount of Hippocrene. In Heaney's poem, Helicon is transformed from a Greek fountain associated with the Muses into a sacred well associated with many Irish saints, but it is also unmistakably a real well on the farm where Heaney spent his boyhood: "As a child, they could not keep me from wells," he begins, and ends, as a man and a poet, still looking into them: "Now, to pry into roots, to finger slime, / To stare, big-eyed Narcissus, into some spring / Is beneath all adult dignity. I rhyme / To see myself, to set the darkness echoing."

To see the Irish holy well as also a Greek fount of inspiration, and to compare himself to Narcissus looking at his image in the water—of course, with the myth of destructive self-love staring straight back—sets up a parallel between ancients and moderns that Heaney found congenial to his poetic development. By placing the first poem, "Digging," beside the last poem, "Personal Helicon," we can see that in his first book Heaney was beginning to dig deep into the Irish landscape for his subjects, though he still had the Irish farmer's point of view chiefly in his mind, and County Derry, Northern Ireland, bore a strong resemblance to that other Derry in New Hampshire where Robert Frost had once kept farm and written poetry.

Then in his next book, *Door into the Dark,* in 1969, Heaney began digging deeper, and a new theme appeared in his poetry, which was barely discernible then but became more evident in *Wintering Out* in 1972 and was definitely confirmed by the publication in 1975 of his fourth collection of poems, called simply *North.* Heaney emerged in this fourth and most distinctive volume as a poet who had a special perspective on the stormy scene of Northern Ireland that came from the light of the remote past—not simply from the Irish past, though he knew it well, nor simply from the Western literary and historical past, which he also knew, but from the truly ancient, the ancestors, distant kinsmen connected to him in imagination only, as Homer was connected with Troy, Virgil with Greece, or Dante with Rome, a kinship of the spirit more than of the blood, a vital link with the whole heritage of his race. Heaney was not ostensibly writing an epic; yet his series of short poems seemed to have coherence, and a new kind of hero stepped forth in them, the unlikely figure of "The Tollund Man": "Some day I will go to Aarhus / To see his peat-brown head, / The mild pods of his eye-lids, / His pointed skin cap." After meditating on his kinship with this Danish corpse dredged up from a bog far from his own native Ireland, Heaney concludes the poem with a reference to the contemporary situation in Ireland: "Out there in Jutland / In the old man-killing parishes / I will feel lost, / Unhappy and at home."

What Seamus Heaney had stumbled upon, in the bogs of Denmark, was a man like himself, whose body had been miraculously preserved for two thousand years so that the features were still recognizable, and so was the cause of his death: ritual sacrifice. Around the Tollund Man's neck was a noose that had been twisted to resemble the torc necklace worn by the goddess for whom he had given his life. Heaney's sympathy for this ancient victim was strong, because it formed a connection in his mind with the deaths in his own North of Ireland, where the bogs also preserved organic material for centuries, as perfectly as if it had been mummified. Tollund Man as Heaney imagined him had willingly sacrificed himself to his goddess, the Bog Queen or Earth Mother, in a way that reminded Heaney of the deaths of contemporary Irish Catholics for the Virgin Mary; and so it seemed that the "Modern" was repeating the fatal action of the "Ancient." Heaney was not admiring their heroism so much as he was remarking on the similarity of their martyrdom, in "the old man-killing parishes" where he as a living Irishman felt both "Unhappy and at home."

Seamus Heaney did not claim that he had invented this figure, but freely admitted that he had discovered the Tollund Man in the illustrations and descriptions contained in a contemporary archeological treatise called *The Bog People: Iron-Age Man Preserved* by P. V. Glob, a Danish anthropologist, a work that had fascinated him when it first appeared in English translation in 1969. Heaney's poetic use of this book bears less resemblance to what Yeats did with early Irish mythology in his poetry and drama than to what Eliot did in adapting Sir James Frazer's *Golden Bough* and Jessie Weston's *From Ritual to Romance* to his purposes in *The Waste Land.* Indeed, Heaney's true Personal Helicon, his bog imagery, seems closer to Eliot's modern version of the Grail legend than to any of Yeats's poems, since it gives the reader the same uncanny sense of walking through a contemporary Irish landscape that is also an ancient Danish landscape, just as the reader of Eliot's poem looks at modern London as the Grail knight might have seen the Waste Land, a haunted and sterile landscape where the only voices are those of hollow men and women waiting for death to relieve the monotony of their futile lives. Heaney's Tollund Man has taken the place of Eliot's Fisher King, just as the bog has taken the place of the Waste Land. Furthermore, any possible hope for an end to the ancient sacrificial killing seems as remote in Heaney's bog as hope for the restoration of fertility seems in Eliot's Waste Land: the conjunction of the ancient and the modern has produced a purgative diagnosis of human suffering, but no relief or means of escape from it.

So, by the time he had written his fourth book, Seamus Heaney had made his difficult rite of passage and had come of age as a poet, and along the way he had raised Glob's *Bog People* to something like the status of Weston's *From Ritual to Romance.* But Eliot's Waste Land was as real as it was mythical, owing less to Jessie Weston than to his own acute observation of the lonely crowd which "Flowed up the hill and down King William Street / To where St. Mary Woolnoth kept the hours / With a dead sound on the final stroke of nine." And Heaney's bog was not purely literary, but came directly from his own observations of growing up on a farm in Ireland. As early as his second volume, *Door into the Dark,* even before he had read Glob's book, Heaney had already written a poem called "Bogland," which made the bog a symbol of the long Irish memory and contrasted it with the American frontier as a symbol of the wide-open spaces of the West, which Heaney says he had in mind because "at that time, I was teaching modern literature in Queen's University, Belfast, and had been reading about the frontier and the west as an important myth in the American consciousness, so I set up—or rather, laid down—the bog as an answering Irish myth."[2] It starts by looking at the American frontier from an Irishman's perspective.

We have no prairies
To slice a big sun at evening—
Everywhere the eye concedes to
Encroaching horizon,

Is wooed into the cyclops' eye
Of a tarn. Our unfenced country
Is bog that keeps crusting
Between the sights of the sun.

Then Heaney proceeds to raise up an Irish equivalent of the American Frontier from his bogland.

They've taken the skeleton
Of the Great Irish Elk
Out of the peat, set it up,
An astounding crate full of air.

The symbolic landscape of Seamus Heaney's poetry is a place where long-extinct animals like the Great Irish Elk may come to the surface when a farmer digs for peat in a bog, as if the earth itself had a faculty of memory like the minds of the men who live on it, and could draw them downward by the seductive appeal of its soft, dark body, by a feminine presence like the Bog Queen reincarnated. Heaney has said that "if you go round the National Museum in Dublin, you will realize that a great proportion of the most cherished material heritage of Ireland was 'found in a bog,'"[3] and he has described his own creative process as if it had lain for a while in the earth beside the Great Irish Elk: "I have always listened for poems, they come sometimes like bodies come out of a bog, almost complete, seeming to have been laid down a long time ago, surfacing with a touch of mystery."[4]

Certainly such a rebirth after long burial in the earth seems to fit the language of "Bog Queen," where Heaney replicates the voice of the Earth Goddess, to whom the Tollund Man long ago had been ritually married and then sacrificed.

I lay waiting
between turf-face and demesne wall,

between heathery levels
and glass-toothed stone.

. . . .

My diadem grew carious,
gemstones dropped
in the peat floe
like the bearings of history.

. . . .

My skull hibernated
in the wet nest of my hair.

Which they robbed.
I was barbered
and stripped
by a turfcutter's spade

. . . .

and I rose from the dark,
hacked bone, skull-ware,
frayed stitches, tufts,
small gleams on the bank.

The best footnote to this poem is a passage in *The Bog People* where Glob describes the figure of Nerthus, who was once depicted on bronze amulets as a naked woman, the primitive Danish personification of Mother Earth, a fertility goddess like the Middle Eastern Ishtar or Astarte or the Greek Aphrodite, to whom sacrifices were made in ancient vegetation rites in order to renew natural fertility. Glob concludes his book by linking the belief in the Bog Queen, or fertility goddess, with the sacrificial death of the Tollund Man, a real man who was ritually killed and buried in a bog to appease the Bog Queen and ensure the coming of spring.

Thus Heaney, in the poems about the bog which are his most memorable creations, completed something approaching an epic reconstruction of primitive man in his prehistoric, preliterate stage, and connected that remote and aboriginal tribal experience with his own experience as an Irishman living in the violence-torn North, the subject of so many terrible and shocking headline stories in the latter half of the twentieth century. In so doing, he drew a strong moral parallel between contemporary terrorism and ancient ritual sacrifice, or what in the poem "Punishment" he calls "the exact / and tribal, intimate revenge." It would be too easy to say that he has accounted for the causes of strife among the people of his native country, and too much to say that he has produced a cure for them, but he has humanized them by the power of poetic language and so made them more understandable, more capable of a sympathetic response, than they would otherwise be. Especially by transforming the Irish bogs into a symbolic landscape, Heaney has performed a feat of imagination which can justly be compared with Yeats's achievement

in making a symbolic landscape of the countryside around Sligo, the world of his childhood, so that readers far removed from Ireland could inhabit it and feel at home there. True, Yeats's Lake Isle of Innisfree and his mountains of Knocknarea and Ben Bulben are more beautiful than Heaney's bogs, and his rhythms are more lyrical; but there is something deeply elemental and instinctive in the appeal of Heaney's earthy language, nowhere more seductive than in the sequence in *North* called "Kinship," which may be his finest single poem to date, especially its second section, a relentless hammering of compound words that signify

. . .bog
meaning soft,
the fall of windless rain,
pupil of amber.

Ruminant ground,
digestion of mollusc
and seed-pod,
deep pollen bin.

Earth-pantry, bone-vault,
sun-bank, enbalmer
of votive goods
and sabred fugitives.

Insatiable bride.
Sword-swallower,
casket, midden,
floe of history.

Ground that will strip
its dark side,
nesting ground,
outback of my mind.

This is incantatory language, ritual verses for the Earth Goddess in which we hear what sounds like the song of the elements, the movement of wind and rain and rivers and tides above the earth and beneath it, a sort of ancient vegetation ceremony reenacted in the present, digging deep into the tribal memory for roots that connect the earliest generations with the latest generation, a distant and strange but still warm human kinship that is also a natural kinship renewed and reaffirmed.

Sound has always been an essential element in Heaney's poetry, and he seems to be aware of the incantatory power of his voice when he reads his poems. His meters are often regular enough to be called traditional but still free enough to be unpredictable, which makes his poems less easy to memorize than those of Yeats. Yet he is fond of Eliot's phrase "the auditory imagination" and listens for the music in poetry, attesting that "the grave inward melodies of Wallace Stevens become more available if we happen to have heard that Caedmon recording of him reading 'The Idea of Order at Key West.'"[5] The eloquence of Heaney in his bog poems arises as much from their sound as from their sense, and it is his ability to imitate the primitive ritualistic use of language that imbues his best poems with religious overtones which seem to evoke prehistoric ceremonies celebrating earth goddesses and sacrificial victims.

Few poets have written so eloquently as Heaney in recent years, and he himself has not surpassed the poems of *North* in his later books *Field Work* (1979), *Sweeney Astray* (1983), *Station Island* (1985), *The Haw Lantern* (1987), and *Seeing Things* (1991); nor has he achieved anything like the emotional coherence and depth of his bog poems. He says that he has been seeking a new direction out of the bog, understandably being reluctant to remain mired in his native sod forever: "I remembered writing a letter to Brian Friel just after 'North' was published, saying I no longer wanted a door into the dark—I want a door into the light. . . . I really wanted to come back to be able to use the first person singular to mean *me* and my lifetime."[6] The quest for a new tone and subject matter is understandable for a poet in middle age and again invites comparison with Yeats, who in his middle years deliberately strove for his Mask, in opposition to his earlier Irish Self, and who succeeded so heroically that he wrote much of his best poetry in his later years. All we can say so far is that Heaney has not found his Mask, whatever shape it might take, for neither the wildly comic persona of the medieval anti-Catholic Irish king Sweeney (the name rhymes with Heaney), whose mad wanderings about Ireland after being cursed by Saint Ronan are the subject of *Sweeney Astray,* nor the more personal and political poems of *Field Work* and *Station Island* and *The Haw Lantern* and *Seeing Things* have provided Heaney with a contrasting set of themes and imagery to put beside the bog poems. He is in everything he writes worth reading, but no more so than a score of contemporary poets, Irish, English, or American. His criticism is at its best when it is most personal, as in the self-exploratory essay "Feeling into Words," which traces his early development as a poet born into an Irish Catholic farming family in the Protestant North, an essay that appeared in his earlier collection, *Preoccupations* (1980); no essay in his more recent collection, *The Government of the Tongue* (1988), is as insightful as the earlier one, and when he writes about his contemporaries, Irish or English or American, he seems to have less important things to say than he has to say about himself.

Nevertheless, taking him at his best, Heaney has come as near to being the epic poet of the later twentieth century as any poet in the English language after Robert Lowell. So far his epic is more piecemeal than whole, and he has written no single poem of the scope of Lowell's *Quaker Graveyard in Nantucket,* though he may eventually find a new subject for epic outside the bog. *Sweeney Astray* was clearly meant to be a step in that direction, but it remains a translation from the Old Irish more than an authentic new poem in English; and *Station Island* also moves toward epic but is finally a long poem of personal pilgrimage to Saint Patrick's Purgatory—that is, to medieval, monastic, Catholic Ireland. Heaney can be as unreservedly candid and critical as Joyce about the Irish Catholic mind, but *Station Island,* in spite of some arresting passages, finally lacks the force of real belief that animates his poems about the Bog People. Perhaps Heaney is waiting for his imagination, which had seemed to sprout flippers in the bog, to grow wings and fly above it—that, at any rate, is an intriguing possibility, briefly tried in *Sweeney Astray* and in a few other poems, such as the one in *Station Island* called "Drifting Off," which is as good as any to be found in his more recent poems collected in *The Haw Lantern* and *Seeing Things*. In this later poem he names a number of birds he would like to be, starting with "The guttersnipe and the albatross" and going on to the gannet and the heron, "the allure of the cuckoo / and the gossip of starlings," and mentioning also the bullfinch and the wren, as well as waterhens and corncrakes, blackbirds and magpies, before concluding:

But when goldfinch or kingfisher rent
the veil of the usual,
pinions whispered and braced

as I stooped, unwieldy
and brimming,
my spurs at the ready.

In this poem Heaney does not try to become a golden nightingale, seated on a bough in Yeats's imaginary Byzantium; his mood is more playful than joyful, but having swum so long and successfully in his native bogs, he seems to be looking upward, perhaps to find the right bird for his reincarnation. If he finds it, it is more likely to resemble one of the wild Irish geese of the coastal slobs than one of Yeats's wild swans at Coole Park.

All that can be said with certainty at this pinnacle of his career is that Seamus Heaney has done one thing extremely well, enough to make him a worthy successor to Yeats: with his Irish bog poems he has created a symbol of human memory and imagination that goes far beyond Ireland in its significance, reestablishing the link between man and the natural world that we seem to have lost by single-mindedly pursuing a purely technological mastery of nature. For this achievement, he deserves the Nobel Prize in Literature as much as any living writer. We can hope that he will go on to emulate Yeats, meaning that he will write some of his best poems after winning the Nobel; but even lacking such a resurgence of inspiration—even if the rest of his writing, whether in poetry or in prose, is less consequential than a dozen of his earlier poems about the bog—he may be said, as Ezra Pound once memorably claimed, "To have gathered from the air a live tradition / Or from a fine old eye the unconquered flame," and as Pound added, "This is not vanity." No, Seamus Heaney's work is not an act of vanity, but an act of humanity, for which we can all feel grateful, whether we are Irish or not.

William Pratt, Spring 1996

[1] Seamus Heaney, *Preoccupations: Selected Prose 1968–1978*, London, Faber & Faber, 1980, p. 41.

[2] Ibid., p. 55.

[3] Ibid., p. 54.

[4] Ibid., p. 34.

[5] Ibid., p. 199.

[6] Quoted by Helen Vendler in "Echo Soundings, Searches, Probes," her review of Seamus Heaney's *Station Island*, in *The New Yorker*, 23 September 1985, p. 114.

Brian Friel's Imaginary Journeys to Nowhere

Brian Friel is arguably the best living playwright, a dramatist whose works attract immediate interest in Dublin, London, or New York whenever they are introduced in these major theatrical cities. He is thoroughly Irish, yet he writes often about faraway places, sometimes about places not even on a map, sometimes about places real on the map but imaginary in his plays. Such deliberate ambiguity about setting is notable in the title of his first successful play, *Philadelphia, Here I Come* (1964), as well as in the title of a more recent work, *Wonderful Tennessee* (1993), since in neither play do the characters ever get near Philadelphia or Tennessee. In his plays, the real setting is Ireland, but the other places are something more than fantasy.

One of his major accomplishments has been to make a believable place of the fictional Irish town of Ballybeg. *Baile Beag* means just "small town" in Irish, and there is in central Ireland a real town named "Littleton," which would be a literal translation of *Baile Beag;* but Littleton is not his fictional town. His Ballybeg is located on the coast of County Donegal, in northwestern Ireland, and has its provincial charm, but his characters are never happy there. His characters are always restless, and they move about in strange directions, dream-

ing of journeys that never take place and giving real American names to their destinations but seeming always to arrive at a dead end—that is, to go nowhere. Yet what is strange about Friel's dramas is that somehow "nowhere" exists: it is at the very least an intended destination, and at most it is a dreamworld beyond space and time, where the characters hope to find the kind of personal fulfillment impossible in the real world they know. The poignancy of Friel's plays has much to do with the native Irish wander-lust, which has made Ireland historically a nation of emigrants; but the plays have their universality as well, because his characters never really want to leave home, and they have a fierce loyalty to their homeland which appeals to the patriotic sentiment in people everywhere.

As an Irish playwright, Brian Friel is not a nihilist like Samuel Beckett; rather, he is a visionary, more like William Butler Yeats. His famous contemporary, the Irish poet Seamus Heaney, has written sympathetically of Friel that "we and our language still possess a religious unconscious, whether we are striving consciously to secularize ourselves or are being secularized, willynilly."[1] Friel's journeys to nowhere are part of his religious searching, and they appeal to audiences by propelling them into communion with their deeper, older selves. He can dramatize the journey as the historically familiar departure from Ireland to America, or as a more psychological excursion from present into past, or from life into death; but however he may dramatize it, every search leads from the plane of reality to the plane of mystery, from the familiar and known to the strange and unknown.

His first successful play was *Philadelphia, Here I Come* in 1964, written after a year of apprenticeship in 1963 at the Tyrone Guthrie Theater in Minneapolis, which Friel later said was "my first parole from inbred, claustrophobic Ireland." *Philadelphia, Here I Come,* an unlikely title for a very Irish play, presents the main character, Gar O'Donnell, on the eve of his departure from the familiar Old World of Ballybeg, County Donegal, to what he hopes will be the New World of America. He keeps singing "Philadelphia, Here I Come," consciously altering the original title of a popular American song, "California, Here I Come," because he plans to emigrate from Ballybeg to Philadelphia, a city he has never seen. There are, however, two sides to his consciousness, and by means of theatrical magic (there is some kind of inspired improvisation in every one of his plays), Friel personifies both the Public and the Private Gar O'Donnell, as if they were complementary characters who do not agree about what about what is going on inside the character's mind, and who exchange their contradictory opinions early in the First Episode (first act) of the play:

Private: You are fully conscious of all the
            consequences of your decision?

Public: Yessir.

Private: Of leaving the country of your birth, the
            land of the curlew and snipe, the Aran sweater
            and the Irish Sweepstakes?

Public: I have considered all these, Sir.

Private: Of going to a profane, irreligious, pagan
            country of gross materialism?

Public: I am fully sensitive to this, Sir.

Private: Where the devil himself holds sway, and
            lust—abhorrent lust—is everywhere indulged in
            shamelessly?

Public: Who are you tellin'? Shamelessly, Sir,
            shamelessly.

Private: And yet you persist in exposing yourself to
            these frightful dangers?

Public: I would submit, Sir, that these stories are
            slightly exaggerated.

At the end of the play, Gar O'Donnell has not decided to leave Ireland for America after all, though he swears, "I've stuck around this hole far too long. I'm telling you, it's a quagmire, a backwater, a dead end!" and "There's nothing about Ballybeg that I don't know already. I hate the place, every stone, every rock, every piece of heather around it." But with all these hostile feelings about his hometown, he stays where he is and never goes to Philadelphia, a name which he has wrongly sung of anyway as "Philadelphia, here I come" and which he pictures disdainfully in his mind: "Impermanence—anonymity —that's what I'm looking for; a vast restless place that doesn't give a damn about the past." The play ends with Private Gar imploring, "God, Boy, why do you have to leave? Why? Why?" and Public Gar replying rather reluctantly, "I don't know. I don't know." So it may be said that in his first successful play, Brian Friel dealt ambivalently with the familiar theme of Irish exile, which he took literally, while a less literal, more figurative kind of exile has dominated the best of his plays in the period of more than three decades since that time.

Lovers, in 1967, consisted of two short one-act plays, the first of which he called "Winners" (it is the better of the two, the other of which is called "Losers"). In it the two lovers, Joe and Mag, drown together in a boat, after they have been forced to become engaged because she is pregnant. They have chosen to make their journey to nowhere into death, because they see no hope for their future. As presented on stage, they quarrel and joke with each other, making light of their prob-

lems, but before the end of the play we know they have drowned, when the narrator reports that their boat has been discovered upturned in the lake and their bodies have been recovered; the inquest into their deaths proves they drowned together in what must have been a suicide pact, though this violent ending is not seen on stage, merely reported to have happened to them. Their journey thus ends in a final voyage to nowhere, leaving the audience to speculate that since they died together, death may have seemed a better place of union than any they could find in life.

The Mundy Scheme, produced in 1969, is Friel's most fantastic play, the plot of which turns on the proposal by an American millionaire developer to make Ireland as famous as other civilized nations by converting much of it into a huge graveyard. The preposterous schemer argues that "France is the recognized home of good food; America is the acknowledged center of art; Switzerland is the center of Europe's banking. Let's make the west of Ireland the acknowledged. . .eternal resting place." Hence, the outlandish "Mundy Scheme" is concocted as a way of transforming the desolate bogs in the west of Ireland into commercially valuable lands, by making them into one vast international cemetery. The plan is impractical, of course, but it is taken seriously by the reputed Prime Minister of Ireland as a cure for the poverty and emigration which have always plagued Ireland. He responds enthusiastically to the plan, saying, "In a nutshell, boys, the Mundy Scheme is a heart transplant at a critical time. It means a flood of capital investment, an immediate drop in emigration, full employment in depressed areas, new airstrips capable of carrying the biggest—" He can't finish his speech, but agrees to support a proposal for a new Irish motto: "Rest in Peace in Ireland." The play is too farfetched to hold the stage for long, and its scheme never materializes, of course; but it is significant that the proposed final journey to the west of Ireland turns out to be another of Friel's trips to nowhere, this time to an imaginary city of the dead, the sort of thing the ancient Irish constructed in their passage graves and the ancient Etruscans built in their elaborate *città della morte* or "cities of the dead" in Italy.

Of Brian Friel's later plays, the most dramatically successful have been *Translations* in 1980 and *Dancing at Lughnasa* in 1990. These are not literal journeys in the present, but figurative journeys into the past, and in each case the journey turns out to be futile. *Translations* is set in the Ireland of the early nineteenth century, 1833 to be exact, at a hedge school where Greek and Latin are taught along with Irish in order to maintain a native intellectual culture in the face of English dominance. The plot centers on a romance between an Irish girl and an English officer, which allows them briefly to bridge the gap between languages—her Irish and his English—and the theatrical marvel created in this play is that the audience believes the characters are speaking two languages when they are really speaking only one. But their interlingual communication, if successful on stage, does not result in a happy marriage, because at the end the English officer mysteriously disappears and is assumed to have been killed by Irish nationalists, who stubbornly and violently refuse to accept a permanent liaison between an Irish woman and an Englishman. The romance thus proves abortive, and the journey into the past has led to a dead end, though at its highest dramatic moment—a piece of Friel's magic, a love scene which consists almost entirely in the exchange of musical Irish place-names—the play is an appealing expression of interracial harmony, making credible an Anglo-Irish dreamworld that takes the stage for a brief moment, only to vanish in a realistic and tragic ending.

Dancing at Lughnasa has proved to be Friel's most successful play to date, as far as international audiences are concerned, and in fact was recently adapted for the screen, with a cast that included Oscar winner Meryl Streep. It is a memory play, in which the main character is also the narrator, who takes us back to his boyhood in the 1930s, when the old Celtic harvest festival of Lughnasa was still celebrated with dancing. The young boy's mother (his father, a charming ne'er-do-well, comes back to visit them, but has never bothered to marry his mother) joins her sisters in doing the harvest dance in their cottage beside the wheat fields, and their dance is the high moment of the play, a sudden spontaneous expression of feeling danced to the strains of radio music—coming out of "Marconi," as they have nicknamed their wireless set. The pathos of it is that they cannot go on dancing forever, and the narrator who was once a boy has now grown into a man and left home for good: the play is his recollection of a moment of his past that was happy but could not be sustained. So the tone of the play, like that which infuses many of Friel's dramas, is nostalgic and bittersweet, presenting a scene in which human beings experience bliss but cannot preserve it; their journey into the past is starkly contrasted with the death and dissolution of the entire Mundy family, which once consisted of five sisters and a brother but now exists only in the memory of the narrator, a man who lives in the past more than in the present, because the past was a happier time for him.

Of all Brian Friel's later plays, *Wonderful Tennessee* seems by its title to be the nearest equivalent to *Philadelphia, Here I Come*. It has unfortunately not proved as successful on stage as the earlier play, but symbolically, it takes its place as one of his most revealing dramas and

a serious expression of his most characteristic theme: the imaginary journey to nowhere. Produced by the Abbey Theatre in Dublin in 1993, it closed after some months despite favorable reviews, and it lasted only nine days on Broadway, though it was praised by New York critics as one of his finest works. The play is pure Friel: three couples sit at a dock and try all through the play to get to an island off the Irish coast, but they spend their time gazing out to sea and never leave the shore, waiting in vain all night for a boat to take them to the island—a familiar scene of anticipation and disappointment.

In his stage directions, Friel describes the setting so as to evoke the full Irish atmosphere:

> A stone pier at the end of a headland on the remote coast of north-west county Donegal. The stonework is grained with yellow and grey lichen. The pier was built in 1905 but has not been used since the hinterland became depopulated many decades ago. The pier extends across the full width of the stage. It begins stage left (the mainland) and juts out into the sea so that it is surrounded by water on three sides—the auditorium, the area stage right, and the back wall.

> There are some weather-bleached furnishings lying around the pier floor: fragments of fishing nets, pieces of lobster pots, broken fish-boxes. Some rusty bollards and rings. A drift of sand in the top right-hand corner. Stones once used as weights inside lobster pots. A listing and rotting wooden stand, cruciform in shape, on which hangs the remnant of a life-belt.

In this symbolic stretch of deserted Irish coast, the play opens with the characters looking around them in wonder and disbelief.

Trish (Terry's sister): Where are we, Terry?

Frank: Arcadia.

Terry: Ballybeg pier—where the boat picks us up.

Trish: County what?

Terry: County Donegal.

Trish: God. Bloody Indian territory.

Terry has invited them all to travel to the island with him, and he produces a picnic hamper full of champagne for them to drink while they are waiting at the dock for the boat to arrive that will take them out.

Trish: You never said it was a big island, Terry.

Terry: It's not big, is it?

Trish: That's a huge island.

Terry: Is it?

Frank: Hard to know what size it is—it keeps shimmering.

Angela: Has it a name, our destination?

Terry: Oilean Draoichta. What does that mean, all you educated people?

Trish: That rules me out. Where's our barrister?

Berna (Terry's wife): Island of Otherness; Island of Mystery.

When Trish asks Terry if it is only a mirage, Terry replies by giving a full description on of the island as he remembers it.

Terry: There is a legend that it was once a spectral, floating island that appeared out of the fog every seven years and that fishermen who sighted it saw a beautiful country of hills and valleys, with sheep browsing on the slopes, and cattle in green pastures, and clothes drying on the hedges.

> And they say they saw leaves of apple and oak, and heard a bell and the song of coloured birds. Then, as they watched it, the fog devoured it and nothing was seen but the foam swirling on the billow and the tumbling of the dolphins.

Terry, who alone of the six characters has visited the island, tells the others that he was taken there long ago, at the age of seven, by his father. He remembers the visit vividly still, recalling how he fasted the night before he went there, ate only bread and water while he was on the island, and prayed at the three mounds of stones he and his father found there. He also remembers a holy well on the island where his father filled a bottle with water and corked it with sea grass, and the ruins of a medieval church dedicated to an obscure Irish saint named Conall. The church was once the site of a pilgrimage, but now no one goes on pilgrimages because no one believes any longer in their efficacy. Terry says that his father had gone there to do penance, that is "to attest to the mystery," a mystery which may have been connected either with the Christian God or with Dionysus, the Greek god of wine; he is not sure which.

We learn in the course of the play that Terry has bought the island for sentimental reasons, and so he is taking his wife and sister and best friends with him out to see it, forty years after his first visit. For no particular reason, he sings a song his mother taught him, an antebellum American minstrel song of the 1850s called "Down in de Cane-brake" or "Nancy Till," which ends with the word he has never forgotten:

Come, my love, my boat lies low,
She lies high and dry on the O-hi-o.
Come, my love, come, and come along with me
And I'll take you back to Tennessee.

His dream of the island as "Wonderful Tennessee" has brought them to the Ballybeg dock, but they seem to

sense already that it is probably not going to come true; and so they have their party and sing their songs, sitting at the dock all night long, with Angela declaring, "So we're stuck here! We're going nowhere! We'll pass the night with stories." They do tell stories to pass the night, and the stories they invent are about the medieval monks who once inhabited the island they hope to visit; they even imagine the monks at their prayers day and night in the ruined church. One character, Frank, muses: "Maybe Saint Conall stood on the shores of the island there and gazed across here at Ballybeg and said to his monks, 'Oh, lads, lads, *there* is the end of desire. Whoever lives there lives at the still core of it all. Happy, happy, lucky people.' What do you think?" Terry replies, "That's us—happy people."

Happiness is clearly lacking in the six characters as they wait at the pier, but they try to make a brave front of it. In one dramatic scene Terry's wife suddenly dives off the pier into the sea for a swim, but soon comes back chilled and has to be warmed up after her sudden, unaccountable escapade Meanwhile the dawn has come, and Frank goes off to photograph the island in the morning mist, returning elated to tell them of his adventure.

Frank: Just as the last wisp of the veil was melting away, suddenly—as if it had been waiting for a sign—suddenly a dolphin rose up out of the sea. And for thirty seconds, maybe a minute, it danced for me. Like a faun, a satyr; with its manic, leering face. Danced with a deliberate, controlled, exquisite abandon. Leaping, twisting, tumbling gyrating in wild and intricate contortions. And for that thirty seconds, maybe a minute, I could swear it never once touched the water—was free of it—had nothing to do with water. A performance—that's what it was. A performance so considered, so aware, that you knew it knew it was being witnessed, wanted to be witnessed. Thrilling; and wonderful; and at the same time—I don't know why—at the same time. . .with that manic, leering face. . .somehow very disturbing.

Berna: Did you get pictures of it?

Frank: Nothing. You'd almost think it waited until my last shot was used up before it appeared.

So the "Ballybeg epiphany," as Frank calls it, has been witnessed only by him; the others are unaffected by it and give up their hope that a boat will ever come to take them to the island. They become so disillusioned that Angela finally cries out in disgust, "What a goddamn, useless, endless unhappy outing this has been!" Terry reacts by telling them a shocking story that he learned from the lawyer who arranged for him to buy the island. He was told that long years ago a young boy had been ritually sacrificed on the island, killed and dismembered by a group of friends who went out there on a religious pilgrimage; the bishop was so dismayed by the event that he sent the whole pack of young people away to Australia and organized annual pilgrimages to the island for penance, but the pilgrimages were discontinued. The play ends with a scene in which Terry's shirt is torn from him and hung up on the pier as a souvenir of their birthday party for him—and a reminder of the ritual slaughter that had once occurred on the island. Terry finally confesses that he has not bought the island outright, but has merely taken an option on it, which he now says he will never exercise. And so the island remains an unfulfilled destination for them all, and they laugh as they leave on the bus to go back to their homes, still singing "Down in the Cane-brake" with its haunting finish, "I'll take you back to Tennessee." The play is over and nothing has happened, but the characters' imaginations have been fired with the thought of an abortive pilgrimage to the Island of Mystery, and they carry this memory away with them, building a mound with stones to mark their night of waiting and promising to come back in a year for another birthday party by the sea.

The future of *Wonderful Tennessee* among Friel's plays remains somewhat uncertain, for the director of the Abbey Theatre, Patrick Mason, who produced the play in Dublin and New York, concluded from its hasty closing in New York that it is "not a commercial property." Still, it occupies a central place in Friel's dramatic corpus because of its symbolic use of setting—the real unhappy Ireland contrasted with the imaginary island paradise. *Dancing at Lughnasa* has been a phenomenally successful stage property ever since its premiere, and it has been revived in Dublin, New York, and London, winning the Tony Award in New York for the Best Play of 1992 and being produced at provincial theaters all over the world. *Wonderful Tennessee* should have capitalized on that success, but was perhaps too philosophical, for as the *New York Times* reported in October of 1993, "The play, about three middle-aged Irish couples who spend a night on a Donegal pier waiting for a boatman, drinking and philosophizing, received respectful but disappointing reviews." Frank Rich, the critic for the *New York Times,* concluded after the play closed in New York: "There will be better plays than *Wonderful Tennessee* this season, but how many of them will take us, however briefly, to that terrifying and hallowed place beyond words?"[2]

Another New York drama critic, Edwin Wilson, in the 29 June 1994 issue of the *Wall Street Journal,* argued for a reform of Broadway theater, on the ground that "two shows that opened and closed last fall, *The Kentucky Cycle* and *Wonderful Tennessee,* were worthy plays that in a healthy theater environment would unquestionably have run long enough to find their audiences— but a healthy environment is exactly what we do not have." In his view, the very success of the big musical show is a limiting factor in attracting audiences for serious drama, since "Theater owners and statisticians deduce from the dollar amounts that roll in that the theater is thriving, ignoring how limited Broadway's menu has become and forgetting that the musical cash cow cannot go on forever."

Brian Friel seems not to have been discouraged by the relative failure of *Wonderful Tennessee* after the success of *Dancing at Lughnasa,* because he produced another play, *Molly Sweeney,* in 1995, about a blind woman whose sight is restored by an operation but who surprisingly regrets it and wants to be blind again. For her, the journey to nowhere takes place inside the mind, not outside it, and so she discovers she is happier not seeing than seeing: the play offers the curiously appealing paradox that she loses her blindness only to wish that it could be restored. After the operation which has restored her sight, Molly says to herself (all three of the characters in the play talk to themselves rather than to one another) that "the only escape—the only way to live—was to sit absolutely still; and shut the eyes tight; and immerse yourself in darkness; and wait."

The doctor who operates on Molly sees that though she has sight at last after forty years of congenital blindness, "From a psychological point of view, she [is] still blind." Soon after the operation has finally made her see, Molly begins withdrawing into her formerly sightless world, leaving the light to stare in darkness into a black mirror; she eventually chooses to be blind again, repelled by the visual world that has been revealed by her miraculous eye operation. To her, the real world is terrifying, while the world of darkness familiar from childhood is comforting. "I seemed," she says to herself, "to be living on a borderline between fantasy and reality." At the end of the play, she has willingly become sightless again, and admits, "My borderline country is where I live now. I'm at home there." The difference between fantasy and reality no longer fascinates her, and she actually prefers the imaginative world of sightlessness to the dull hypocrisy of the real everyday world.

Original and touching though it is, unfortunately *Molly Sweeney* has not been received any more warmly by theater audiences than *Wonderful Tennessee,* despite considerable praise from drama critics in Dublin, London, and New York. But even if serious drama appears to go on losing the competition for audiences to big musicals, Brian Friel has demonstrated that he has the rare ability, beyond that of any living playwright, to use the magic of theater to plumb psychological and even religious depths in human experience. Joe Dowling, who directed an earlier Friel play about the Irish Catholic gentry, *Aristocrats,* and who is now director of the Tyrone Guthrie Theater in Minneapolis, takes the view that "Friel is not only one of the most significant voices in contemporary Irish theatre, he is also one of the most important writers on the world's stage."[3] And so Friel's journeys to nowhere could hardly be called futile, no matter how small or large the audiences may be for them. They take us outside ourselves to an unknown country, whether it is called Philadelphia or Tennessee or the Isle of Mystery, that has no corresponding spot on any map: his characters never reach the place they dream of, but their dreams form the heart of his dramas.

Friel's characters remain torn between the old world and the new, between a haunting religious belief and an overwhelming secular materialism. To his friend and fellow Irishman, Seamus Heaney, Friel's plays are proof that "we refuse to abandon ourselves totally to a relativistic flux even as we concede the inadequacy of older systems of order and authority, whether they were invested in a faith or a family or a motherland."[4] Friel has been hailed as "the foremost living Irish playwright" by the American poet Richard Tillinghast, because "Friel sees in Ireland an authenticity of culture and personality, an integral society, unchanged in essence since the Middle Ages."[5] Friel himself has expressed the wistful hope that his fictional Ballybeg might someday be compared with Faulkner's Yoknapatawpha County as an imaginary landscape, and the Irish critic Richard Pine has argued, "Like Winesburg, Ohio, the place Ballybeg—*baile beag,* small town—is a place of the imagination that the eye of the mind knows to be true and that the eye of the mind can recall at will."[6] To compare Friel's fictional west of Ireland with Faulkner's mythical kingdom in northern Mississippi or with Anderson's quintessential Midwestern Ohio town is to give credibility to his sense of place as a locale of the imagination, not simply Irish but universal in its symbolism.

What can also be said of his work is that in two of his most important plays, *Philadelphia, Here I Come* and *Wonderful Tennessee,* Friel has used American place-names both strategically and symbolically, as they could not be used by any American playwright, to evoke imaginary images of an exotic country toward which the audience is drawn irresistibly; but in the end the ties that bind his characters to their native country are too strong, and they find they cannot leave Ireland for any other place on earth. As Matt Wolf wrote in the April 1994 issue of *American Theatre,* "Friel has made a career

out of expressing the inexpressible—of giving voice via words, music and, most crucially, silence to those vast reaches which language cannot fill."[7] Indeed, in the one play which most competes with *Wonderful Tennessee* for philosophical import, and which despite its limited stage success some regard as his best, *Faith Healer* (1979), the characters are dead and speak from the grave, voicing an eerie communication from the dead to the living, which may be taken as an ultimate journey to nothingness, since these characters refuse to be silenced even posthumously, insisting instead on asserting beyond this life the mystery of another life.

Brian Friel himself has maintained that "drama is a fiction, with the authority of fiction,"[8] but it could be said that his dramas go beyond fiction into myth. He has connected a fictional Irish place called Ballybeg with authentic American places called Philadelphia and Tennessee, giving names to Nowhere that make it seem a reachable destination. This mysterious place of the imagination that Friel projects on stage is always beyond us but always beckons to us, as the Isle of Mystery beckons to the postulants at the end of *Wonderful Tennessee,* an unreal place in Ireland bearing the name of a real—but still mysterious—place in America.

William Pratt, Summer 1999

[1] Seamus Heaney, "For Liberation: Brian Friel and the Use of Memory," in *The Achievement of Brian Friel,* ed. Alan Peacock, Garrards Cross (Eng.), Colin Smythe, 1993, p. 239.

[2] Frank Rich, drama review in the *New York Times,* 25 October 1993.

[3] Joe Dowling, "Staging Friel," in Peacock, p. 187.

[4] Heaney, p. 240.

[5] Richard Tillinghast, "Brian Friel: Transcending the Irish National Pastime," *The New Criterion,* October 1991, p. 48.

[6] Richard Pine, "Brian Friel and Contemporary Irish Drama," *Colby Quarterly,* December 1991, pp. 190–201.

[7] Matt Wolf, "Epiphany's Threshold," *American Theatre,* April 1994, p. 14.

[8] Quoted by F. C. McGrath in "Language, Myth and History in the Later Plays of Brian Friel," *Contemporary Literature,* Winter 1989, pp. 534–45.

ITALY

Modern Poetry and Its Prospects in Italy

Literary history deals with a recent or remote past, whereas militant criticism tends to focus on the present and, by implication at least, on the future, for it stakes its value judgments against several odds. I have been asked by Ivar Ivask to take this kind of chance, and I am not sure that I am equal to the challenge. When we extrapolate our judgments into the future as professional readers, we may be in for surprises and disappointments by the time the next generations take over—if we are still around by then. In the 1890s, when Italo Svevo's first novels appeared in print and hardly anyone noticed them, who would have surmised that he was going to be a dominant figure in three or four decades? And who, on the other hand, would have imagined that Gabriele d'Annunzio's triumphant fiction (with part of his verse) was fated to undergo cold reappraisal? In early twentieth-century handbooks of literary history, Emily Dickinson was ignored, Hopkins had a diminutive niche if at all, and Melville was given short shrift. Until his death in 1952, Benedetto Croce, a giant of modern humanism, failed to recognize the significance of Eugenio Montale's poetry, which he could not help knowing (he had also met Montale a few times, and they shared basic political views). Back in early nineteenth-century times, Goethe's cold-shouldering of Hölderlin (despite Schiller's advocacy) made negative history, and Hölderlin had to settle for posthumous recognition. Let us piously forget as well Voltaire's treatment of Shakespeare and Dante (on the very eve of their big revival in Europe at large).

Rather, let me mention (to return to my own times) a private episode from the spring of 1984, when, after the successful defense of a doctoral dissertation on Vittorio Sereni's poetry for which I had served as major advisor, I was bluntly asked by a close relative of the new Ph.D. what guarantees I had that Sereni's poetry would still be deemed worth talking about a century hence. Of course I had no scientific proof to offer, of the kind my interlocutor seemed to expect, and I could honestly rely only on my inner certainty. Whatever the abstract possibility for a negative reassessment of Sereni's poetry, I had no hesitation in placing my bet in his favor. Flair or arrogance? I only know that I felt a genuine commitment.

For its success and survival, poetry (and art in general) depends on ever-renewed value judgments, whether analytically motivated or not, rather than on the confection of scientific testing formulas. A throw of the dice will never abolish chance, thank God, and that is what makes the game worthwhile. The production and sifting of literature have to do with the cumulative effect of such choices, and I could do worse than bet on the long survival of a poetry like that of my late friend Vittorio Sereni, who interpreted the predicament of our World War II generation with a low-keyed terseness that made his voice unique: "Non sa più nulla, è alto sulle ali / il primo caduto bocconi sulla spiaggia

normanna" (He knows nothing now, he is high on the wings, / the first soldier who fell on Normandy Beach). Is the memorability of this incipit from *Diario d'Algeria* (Algerian Diary) exclusively bound to the war experience of my generation, and therefore perishable in the long run, or does it also rest on felicity of articulation? I believe the latter is true, just as I believe that Sereni's epitaph for the poet Antonia Pozzi upon her suicide will survive its distressing occasion: "All'ultimo tumulto dei binari / hai la tua pace" (At the last tumult of the railway tracks / you have your peace). Even the Lombard quality of Sereni's writing, his albeit unparochial sense of place, contributes to its authenticity, however limiting it may turn out to be with regard to the audience.

A critical case in this respect is Pier Paolo Pasolini, best known outside Italy for his stark, compassionate neorealist movies and (to a lesser extent) for his even starker novels of lumpenproletarian life, yet almost unknown so far for what is the finest part of his versatile work, the poetry in his native Friulian dialect. Ruth Feldman and Brian Swann in their avant-garde anthology *Italian Poetry Today* and Lawrence Smith in his bilingual anthology *The New Italian Poetry* have offered translation samples which should begin to correct that imbalance as far as America's cultivated readership goes.[1] Even so, the sweet lilt of Friulian is too elusive for nonnative ears, and it happens to be the decisive factor in this part of Pasolini's lyrical writing, which can become accessible only to the reader (or listener) willing to undergo a prolonged linguistic initiation. That also applies, to some extent, to native Italian readers unacquainted with the local speech of the northeastern Italian enclave, Friuli, to which linguists grant independent language status within the Romance family. I am not Friulian; I am just a Lombard, and the unique Friulian cadence strikes me as something alien and close at the same time, something remote yet intimate. Perhaps this is why Pasolini's Friulian verse sounds to me like resurrected troubadour poetry. The closest analogue outside the Italian pale is to be recognized in the modern Provençal opus of Frédéric Mistral, whose poetic genius succeeded in raising from the dead what had once been, in medieval Europe, the first literary vernacular, the model and matrix of postclassical Western lyrical poetry; yet when one talks of nineteenth-century French poetry, his name never comes up along with those of Baudelaire, Nerval, or Mallarmé, either because French literature has become centralized on Paris since the time of King Louis XIV or because Provençal, the old langue d'oc, is felt to have independent status as a language vis-à-vis geographically hegemonic French, the erstwhile rival langue d'oïl. Be it as it may, the significance of what is loosely called "dialect" literature emerges only if we realize what a venerable cultural phenomenon dialect can be, and what an unsuspected dimension accrues thereby to the regionally confined but historically deep literary enterprise of a Pasolini, destined though it is to reach only a small minority of readers in the overinformed world of our time.

Not surprisingly, Pasolini himself has also given us a highly informative anthology of Italian dialect poetry in the twentieth century, in keeping with his populist, regionalist, pro-agrarian views; and regardless of his pessimistic anticipations for what he sees as a recessive phenomenon in the homogenizing context of today's mass-media culture, one can glean from this book abundant evidence of poetical vitality. Names like Virgilio Giotti, Albino Pierro, and Biagio Marin, among others, have found their way into handbooks of literary history and anthologies of important Italian poetry; the same kind of belated recognition had come to their nineteenth-century predecessors, Carlo Porta of Milan, Gioacchino Belli of Rome, Salvatore Di Giacomo of Naples.

All this may well sound like mere digression. On the contrary, it is essential to my purpose of evoking, even if by the sketchiest outline, a sense of the weltering richness of modern Italian poetry: pluralistic even in a linguistic sense, regionally rooted though inevitably gravitating toward the illustrious Tuscan tradition, experimental at times through sheer anachronism—for it was a daredevil anachronism, on the part of Pasolini, to recover a folksong kind of melody in this age of iconoclastic modernism, just as it was brilliantly anachronistic on Montale's part to revive the Beatrice myth in troubadour style. In the sphere of poetry, even today, Italy is more a subcontinent than a peninsula.

Italy contains its share of aboriginal as well as broadly European traditions, along with the ferments that can renew them or bring them to fruition. In such perspective, elements seemingly marginal turn out to be focal in the long run; thus the mysteriously archaic folk tunes of Pasolini (the Pasolini of the Friulian verse, of *La meglio gioventù,* so utterly different from the copious meditative and polemical vein in the official Italian language to which his translator Norman MacAfee has restricted the choice published by Vintage Books in 1982). Within the modern Italian context, Friulian Pasolini can be seen as the latest flourishing of an alternative poetical tradition that goes back to Piero Jahier in the World War I years and then Cesare Pavese, the Pavese of *Lavorare Stanca* (1936). I say "alternative tradition" by comparison to the "hermetic" or strongly intellectual and cosmopolitan, allusively textured poetry that came to the fore in the thirties, in the wake of Montale and Ungaretti, with sophisticated writers like Qua-

simodo, Gatto, Luzi, Parronchi, Sereni, or Bigongiari.[2] The political aftermath of World War II dethroned the hermetic movement, to the advantage of *engagé* writing (whether prose or verse) that came to be loosely labeled "neorealism" and to include such authors as Pavese, Vittorini, Pasolini, the early Calvino, Tobino, Roversi, Pratolini, and others.

The lines were not so sharply drawn, however, that mutual demarcation could become incontrovertible. Quasimodo, who had made a name for himself in the early thirties with quintessentially "hermetic" verse (*Acque e terre, Ed è subito sera*), took on a fighting "realist" stance while the equally committed Alfonso Gatto continued expressing himself in the metaphysical melody that is his signature; many of the new poets (as gathered in the 1954 anthology by Luciano Erba and Pietro Chiara, *Quarta Generazione*), meanwhile, showed little or no sign of revolt against the "poetics of the word" that had been hermeticism's basic bequest, even though they also heeded the "poetics of things" that was now in the air. This is particularly true of Andrea Zanzotto, who moved from a posthermetic style of polished verbal fastidiousness to an increasingly intellectual iconoclasm of the kind that the "Novissimi" avant-garde group was to proclaim in 1960 and 1963. Other exponents of the "fourth generation" group have kept up their discourse in stabler forms, achieving considerable results in a poetics of the explicit, whether virulent (as is the case with Nelo Risi), ironic (witness Giorgio Orelli's or Giovanni Giudici's unrelenting critique of the quotidian), or elegiac (Maria Luisa Spaziani).

Within and without the "Quarta Generazione" group, still another tendency has taken shape, one which crosses boundary lines between movements like hermeticism, neorealism, or the avant-garde and asserts the primacy of an existential theme that in turn fosters imagery of matchless intensity. This theme is the Mezzogiorno, the Italian South in its beauty and blight, the still-unsolved problem of Italian history, a love like an ancestral curse. From sunstruck Puglia, Lucania, or Sicily come the baroque voices of Vittorio Bodini, of Rocco Scotellaro, the prematurely deceased peasant poet discovered by Carlo Levi, of Lucio Piccolo, the dreamy Sicilian aristocrat, of Bartolo Cattafi, the restless Sicilian roamer who can assail our sensibility with searing emblems, as in "Agave."

Abbandona la sabbia siciliana, la musica e il miele
degli Arabi e dei Greci,
rompi i dolci legami, questo torpido
latte delle radiche,
discendi in mare regina sonnolenta
verde bestia con braccia di dolore

come chi è pronto al varco; nelle grandi
città, nelle nevi, nel bosco, nel deserto
carovane camminano in eterno.

(Abandon the Sicilian sand, the music and honey
of Arabs and Greeks,
break the sweet ties, this torpid
milk of roots,
go down to the sea sleep-ridden queen
green beast with arms of grief
like one ready for the crossing; in the big
cities, in the snows, in the wood, in the desert
caravans keep treading on forever.)

Yes, if accomplishment to date is an indication of more to come, if the unabating experimental restlessness that has futurist genes can be counted upon to do its gadfly work, the prospects for modern Italian poetry are far from bleak. It will be noticed that in my random coverage I have not banked on the grand old men (now deceased) of twentieth-century verse: Ungaretti, Montale, Saba, about whom my colleague Joseph Cary has eloquently written. I have preferred to take my cue from younger and lesser (if "lesser" they are) masters, because I am not concerned with comparative "greatness" but with authenticity; and so, when talking of Sereni or Pasolini or Cattafi, I intend to exemplify what I consider genuine voices, and if one wants to label them "minor," then let us remember that such "minor" voices are as essential to the vitality of a literature as are "major" ones. Where would seventeenth-century English poetry be without poets like Herrick or Herbert?

Another aspect I have deliberately ignored is the list of Nobel Prize recipients. The fact that three Italian poets were so honored in this century—Carducci in 1905, Quasimodo in 1959, Montale in 1975—matters much less than the fact that they (or rather, the two latter ones) have found increasing response outside Italy in translation and criticism. Speaking of which, the work of poet-translators such as Allen Mandelbaum, I. L. Solomon, Sonia Raiziss, Frank Judge, W. S. Di Piero, William Arrowsmith, and the tireless Ruth Feldman and Brian Swann above all, deserves a special place in American literature for its quality and range; in this context particularly, it amounts to a significant indication of the belated but hearty recognition that modern Italian poetry has managed to achieve in the U.S. Nor should we forget that poems by Ungaretti and Montale have found a translator (or "imitator") in Robert Lowell. Gone are the days when, as a newcomer to Columbia University in 1951, I realized that Montale was an unknown quantity to fine scholars of modern English poetry, or when, as a visiting lecturer at the University of Michigan in 1958, I found out that its rich library lacked the works of Montale, Ungaretti, Pavese, Quasimodo. . . .

Beyond the question of public recognition abroad, one must also accept the fact that some poets will seldom find a broad response, and that this in a way is the price of their greatness. Pasolini's Friulian verse remains great even if it can only have a few readers.

Finally, I leave open the question of the respective merits of poetry, drama, and fiction. It is not true in contemporary Italy, as Ivar Ivask says it is in contemporary Russia, Greece, and Spain, that poets "dominate entirely" the literary scene. The Italian contribution to modern drama rests chiefly on Pirandello, with Ugo Betti and Eduardo De Filippo for reinforcement; and here enduring quality has to compensate for small quantity, while prospects for the future remain uncertain. No one will seriously argue, however, that a pleiad of novelists like Svevo, Pirandello, Moravia, Deledda, Palazzeschi, Gadda, Morante, Alvaro, Pavese, and Calvino fail to hold their own vis-à-vis their fellow Italian poets. My point is only this: that all things considered, modern Italian poetry is alive and well.

Glauco Cambon, Spring 1985

1 *Italian Poetry Today,* Ruth Feldman and Brian Swann, eds. & trs., Berkeley, New Rivers, 1979; *The New Italian Poetry,* Lawrence Smith, ed., Berkeley, University of California Press, 1981.

2 On several of the Italian writers mentioned by name in this essay, see the following: on Calvino, *WLT* 57:2 (Spring 1983), pp. 195–201; on Luzi, *BA* 48:1 (Winter 1974), p. 78; on Montale, *BA* 45:4 (Autumn 1971), pp. 639–45, 50:1 (Winter 1976), pp. 7–15, and *WLT* 56:3 (Summer 1982), pp. 470–72; on Piccolo, *BA* 47:2 (Spring 1973), pp. 239–52; on Ungaretti, *BA* 44:4 (Autumn 1970), pp. 543–618.

Eugenio Montale's *Diario postumo*

Upon receiving the news that the Swedish Academy had assigned the 1975 Nobel Prize to him, Eugenio Montale was unable to say something memorable. He is reported to have remarked, "Usually in this world the imbeciles are the winners. Have I become one of them?"

He offered a more pensive reading of the event in a poem of that same year—"Telefoni per ricordarmi" (You Call to Remind Me)—published posthumously: recognition arrives always too late, when even a long-coveted title seems worthless; the succession of events is on a time line entirely separate from that of one's life. Though the beginning of the poem is colloquial and cordial, the gnomic conclusion, just paraphrased, is disheartening. The motif of the unremitting passage of time and the very same colloquial mode characterize Montale's last collection of poems.*

The timing of the publication of the poems is itself an amazing story. The eighty-four compositions, written between 1969 and 1979 alongside *Satura* and *Diario del '71 e del' 72* and *Quaderno a quattro mani,* remained unpublished for several years. In eleven sealed envelopes, they had been entrusted to Montale's friend, the poet Annalisa Cima. Each of the first ten envelopes contained six poems: the eleventh, besides the expected six poems, held an additional eighteen poems which presumably were to have been distributed in three other envelopes, but Montale never got to it. According to his instructions, the poems were to be published five years after his death, six poems every year. The first installment appeared in 1986, issued by the Fondazione Schlesinger, followed annually by the other ten booklets. The whole collection, together with the final installment and the eighteen additional poems, was published in 1996 by Mondadori under the title of *Diario postumo: 66 poesie e altre* (Posthumous Diary: 66 Poems and More).

Montale's singular project to be heard posthumously, in defiance of the march of time, was achieved. Perhaps his true intent was to furnish additional proof of poetry's power to vanquish time—to the point of activating an illusory dialogue, after death, with his readers and an elite of friends, all of whom are addressed or touched upon in these posthumous verses. Certainly the instructions for publication were a deliberate design to reinforce the underlying theme of the book: the old poet's daily struggle with time and his deeply felt need to prolong life, be it through remembrance or poetry or the poetic paternity that he bestowed on his disciple, Annalisa Cima.

Each poem is dedicated to A. Cima, and it has been assumed that the Montalean "Thou" is directed to her. Montale himself, in one of his last letters, suggests something more encompassing: "Of these poems you are the inspirer and the interlocutress: the epiphany that includes the preceding feminine presences." Obviously the feminine figure the poet addresses in these late poems is the "quintessential Muse" of his earlier works. She is the messenger who sparks his inspiration as he gropes his way through fleeting time.

Yet she no longer is the mysterious visionary figure, the "absent lady" or the "visiting angel" of his early works. Here the feminine presence revolves around familiar gestures. The lyric intensity and tension anticipating the possibility of revelation of the early Montale are replaced by an amiable and epigramatic tone. In a prosaic world, existential questions can be posed only in a conversational, ironic manner: "And if life were a vain mystery?"; the miracle ("il prodigio") is no longer possible.

Nevertheless, despite the humdrum nonsense of modern civilization and the provisionality of his own life, Montale's commitment to poetry remains unfaltering. In one of the final poems he even envisions a commune of friends dedicated to poetry. In a sort of modern Dantesque limbo, they are shielded from the vulgarity of modern times: "Will ever we live in our / commune of New York, / in a skyscraper, on the thirtieth floor, / together with our dearest friends?" The wish is expressed in a light jesting tone which belies the speaker's sincere yearning to "sail" (*veleggiare*), a recurring word-symbol for making poetry.

And the feminine presence, though placed in an everyday setting, still maintains her ineffable quality.

You come down the wide walkway,
the blue of the summer sky
overhangs you. The white
cloud of your linen refreshes
the canicular hour, on your arrival.

She is an "agile messenger," a mediator between the world and the poet. She can attenuate fear, open the Elysian doors, and even give, in the face of the world's refuse heap, an immaculate sense of life. Through dialogue with his interlocutress, the poet reasserts his faith in poetry and reiterates its redemptive values.

The poet's message to her is also a reminder for himself: stay anchored to the beauty, to the dream; do not fall into the trap of the present. Repeatedly the poet is on the alert for an intelligible sign that might give meaning to "all," and he finds moments in which the old fire is rekindled. On such occasions he reaches the heights of the early works, though very much within the parameters of the book. For example, the "fish imagery" of his well-known poem "The Eel" (from *The Storm and Other Things*) recurs in "Come madre" (As a Mother), but no longer to celebrate, as in the early poem, vitality and procreation: "afflicted by the daily routine /. . . / we live like trout embedded in mud. / Then, skimming the water, the delightful vision: / the opal wake of the trout's ova / in a flash leaves a furrow as remembrance. /. . . / I too will be a womb for him who has remembrance of me." Here the emphasis is on "remembrance," to reiterate the painful motif of book. Remembrance through the creative act of poetry is postulated as the only alternative to mundane reality and awaiting death.

Rosario Ferreri, Spring 1997

*Eugenio Montale. *Diario postumo: 66 poesie e altre*. Milan. Mondadori. 1996. xxvi + 117 pages. L.26,000. ISBN 88–04–41032–9.

Contemporary Italian Literature from a Comparatist's Perspective

In the culture of the Western world, the decade of the nineties—the last years of our century and of the second millennium of the Christian era—has been taken up by the postultimate postdebates on postmodernism and by the rising tide of conventions, books, polemics, journalistic inquiries, photographic exhibitions, and manifestations of the most diverse kinds dealing with the 1900s: the century that has come to an end before its time, the "brief century," in the words of the eminent English historian Eric J. Hobsbawn.

Toward the end of the first one thousand years, the apocalyptic sense of the millennium was of uppermost concern throughout Europe among both the leading classes and the common people. Today, what concerns us most is bringing the twentieth century to definition as well as to closure. Accordingly, the millennium is like a vague phantasm. At best, it is the subject of exercises in erudition for the sake of disquisitions of a historical or religious nature. In the final analysis, the millennium has an elusive quality to it. In a "secularized" society such as the one inhabiting the northern and western sectors of our planet, the advent of the third Christian millennium assumes a secondary role: indeed, it drifts unavoidably from the limelight toward the backstage area. A century, after all, is a unit of time, which we are best able to manage historically and subjectively.

We may recall, in this context, some facts that can show us, beyond any doubt, the "control" we exercise by measuring time in hundred-year stretches. Europe is still in the process of reconfiguring itself territorially in the wake of the balancing and unbalancing forces unleashed by the two world wars of the first half of the century and by the subsequent "cold war." The world is full of nonagenarians and centenarians who can tell us about the century firsthand. One example that readily comes to mind is the German philosopher Hans G. Gadamer, born precisely in 1900. Africa, even while trying to find liberation from the last vestiges of European imperialistic colonialism, falls back into the invisible, pernicious netting of global neocolonialism. Latin America still strives, in one way or another, for revolution in an effort to become, at long last, "nuestra America" (our America), as the Cuban writer Roberto Fernández Retamar puts it, borrowing the expression from the poet José Martí. China and Japan, the great civilizations of the Far East, have experienced modernization—not colonization—in their somewhat conflictive relation with the West and now are asserting upon the rest of the world the centrality of the Pacific region.[1]

The millennium, it bears repeating, seems to defy any attempt at a general synthesis as well as any possibility of direct experience. The only vestiges left of its course are ruins—traditions more or less fading away—and stories told in books.

Throughout the entire year 2000, Jerusalem and Rome will be again at the center of the world, the goal of pilgrimages from all around the globe. They will be the appropriate sites for an otherwise unthinkable phenomenon—the "festival" of the millennium—and will remind the whole world that time, which regulates our lives and affairs, the universal calendar, is wide open, kept in full operation by that Christian event. By the same token, Italy will be privileged to feel itself anew as the cradle and destination, the navel and boundary of world history, understood as Euro-Christian history.

However, Italy is, at the same time, a secularized land, and its culture has always been secular in a preponderant fashion. Despite the traditional stereotype espoused by the cultured elite and the belief held far and wide, Dante is not the father of Italian literature. Dante is the Catholic Church and the Holy Roman Empire, classical antiquity and the European and Florentine political life of the thirteenth century. These are the ingredients blended into the greatest poetic construction in finite form within the Western tradition—a perfect, unique edifice with its author smack in the middle. The *Divine Comedy* is text—macrotext, that is, and autotext all in one—in sharp contrast with Shakespeare's oeuvre, to which, passing over Dante's production, Harold Bloom accords a preeminently central position in the "Western Canon." With his dozens of plays, Shakespeare creates a macrotext of plurality—the macrotext of the *theatrum mundi*. I suggest that, not unlike Homer and Virgil with respect to the culture of ancient Greece and Rome, Dante and Shakespeare, with respect to European modernity, stand out as the two exemplary figures illustrating how a literary work and its author become *eminently* canonical: Virgil and Dante, historical figures, are authors of singular, perfect texts (no matter what else they wrote); Homer and Shakespeare, authors enveloped in legend, created pluralistic oeuvres.

But let us get back to the 1900s. For the past few years, Italian Italianists, a clever lot inured for centuries to arguing historiographically, have been very busy drawing up, with impressive skill, registries and balance sheets, synthetic accounts and full-fledged histories of our national literature. Since I am not an Italianist but instead a comparatist, what I will attempt to do in this brief essay is to project Italian literature of the last twenty-five years against the backdrop of the entire twentieth century. What I propose, for my part, is to appraise the literature in question by an analysis of wide dimensions.

An attempt such as mine will succeed only if we decide to adopt a truly ultranational perspective, *when and precisely when* we are dealing with the literature of our own country. This not-so-easy task remains completely neglected by specialists in national literatures in general and by Italian specialists in particular, who continue to think that comparative literature is an ancillary discipline, involved exclusively with the regulation and recording of the "foreign market" of national literatures.

If, whenever we deal with our own national literature of our time, we adopt a comparatist and ultra-nationalist point of view, we will find ourselves in a quasi-conflictive position vis-à-vis the specialists among our colleagues, with whom, because of several compelling circumstances, we come in close contact, whether at the university or in our day-to-day cultural life. I will try to make this kind of conflict as evident and exemplary as possible so that the issue may be better discussed or be more open to discussion and, last but not least, so that the two perspectives may be clearly brought to light and sharply contrasted one with the other, both methodologically and ideologically. The conflict, to be sure, has been exacerbated from the very start by the fact that all of us in both camps, nationalists and comparatists alike, have been operating on the territory of our choice and *of our property:* the field of our own national literature. Here *own,* for the specialist, points to the object to be studied, whereas, for the comparatist, it signifies exclusively the linguistic-literary tradition as a *mother* tradition. Yet *own* indicates also that the specialist in the literature of his or her own country regards himself or herself by definition as superior to all other literary scholars and will never accept being considered as just any other specialist.

The problem is serious enough and has hardly been explored at all; but to investigate it further here would lead us far afield. Let us return to the simple—apparently simple—topic of our discussion and ask how the judgment on contemporary Italian literature, as formulated by an Italian comparatist, differs from the one expressed by an Italian Italianist. A few words will suffice to address what, in my judgment, is the general position of the Italianists. All in all, they strive to produce a master list (an updated canon of sorts), which would include other lists: important authors, those not so important, those to be reconsidered, authors who are no longer important, those to be launched, those who have not yet made it to the list. These lists—more or less justifiable on the basis of some bland moralistic or esthetic criterion—are, by their very nature, fundamentally acritical. They are based on the unquestioned assumption that the mode of existence of contemporary literature is not any different from that of Florentine literature of the thirteenth century. To put it simply, what we have here is a distinctive phase (the last one, to be exact) of the same grand cultural parade: the parade of Perpetual Italian Literature.[2]

In order to develop a specific ultranational point of view concerning contemporary Italian literature, we must opt, in my opinion, for two wider (much wider) criteria than the ones adopted by the Italianists. The first criterion has to do with time: the Italianists envisage the century as the usual type of subject for investigation and regard as ingredients of the inner constitution of the century several time spans about which they can come to some agreement.[3] I will proceed in a contrary fashion for the purpose of understanding contemporary Italian literature and the twentieth century along the millenary course of the Western literary tradition. The second criterion deals with space: while the Italian Italianists have set up relationships, influences, reception theories, and links between Italian and foreign literatures of the twentieth century, I, for one, have been trying to understand how contemporary Italian literature has been dialoguing and is currently dialoguing with the worldwide network of literatures and whether it possesses the idiom or the idioms to conduct that dialogue.[4]

Let us begin, then, by situating contemporary Italian literature in the most convenient category within the century to which it belongs. Consequently, we can then judge that literature in the light of a long-term historical overview, encompassing the vicissitudes of the European literary tradition of Mediterranean and Christian origins.

We may safely state that the first Euro-Christian millennium (from A.D. 200 to approximately 1200) is characterized by the protection and preservation of the Greco-Roman legacy, which had to endure both strained relations with the new Christian culture and a melding with the cultures of the various Germanic peoples. The second millennium opens with the retrospective synthesis of Dante's divine poem and continues with the luminous season of Renaissance humanism. Eventually, the model of the revival/rebirth of the ancient world becomes entrenched by sheer repetition. That model, which from Petrarch onward may be appropriately called *classicism,* would come to a definitive close with the *neoclassicism* of the eighteenth century. Up until that delimiting period (*terminus ad quem*), Italian literary and artistic culture had been at the helm of European civilization, securing and redirecting its sway from the Mediterranean cradle, through central Europe, to the distant British Isles.

Beginning with the period of the Renaissance, which at its climactic point is marked, in the visual arts, by the masters of the "third manner" (Leonardo, Raphael, Michelangelo), Italian culture veers toward its irreversible decline. Gradually, it loses its role as active guardian of the Classical tradition. With the advent of Romanticism, no new "renaissances" of the ancient world are being proposed; instead, following Friedrich Schlegel's declarations of 1798, a new "universal, progressive" art is under foot, and the real essence of this art resides in the nature of becoming and futurity. By reaction, Italy is now seen by the rest of Europe as a park turned into a museum of every ruin of the past, a showcase of stuffed memories, a collection of statues, of "embalmed" classical masterpieces. Italy has become a marvelous cemetery to be visited. By now its civilization has been left with no voice, no living dignity—not even the voice or dignity of a custodian of its own memories. All this is duly noted, with precocious disdain, by two solitary men of genius: the Marquis de Sade and the Marquis Giacomo Leopardi.

From that point on, Italian literature has been on the skids along the slippery slope of Eurocentric (more often than not exclusively Francocentric) provincialism, which, despite some notable exceptions in the 1900s, ranging from Giuseppe Ungaretti to Luigi Pirandello, from Italo Svevo to Carlo Emilio Gadda and Ignazio Silone, from Eugenio Montale to Italo Calvino, has come to be mired, in more recent decades, in the doldrums of a posthumous, insignificant desolation. With a great deal of intellectual courage and historical clairvoyance concerning the *decayed*—not to mention *decaying*—Italian literature of our day and age, Cesare Segre, the eminent authority on Romance literatures, in his recent survey of twentieth-century Italian literature, has made the following statement:

> I have been asking myself if our literature has been fit to express to best effect the problems and anguish of our century, which is now in its hour of twilight. I must acknowledge that, by and large, our writers, with the exceptions I have highlighted, have not shown as wide a scope, as great a capacity for analysis and power of imagination as have the writers of other lands. Today the field of comparison has become very wide, indeed, because, besides the writers from Latin America, others from India and Pakistan, South Africa and Japan, Egypt and Israel, and so forth, have taken center stage. Thanks to this influx of writers, literature still eludes the flattening process of conforming to American models—a process which is virtually a fait accompli in the visual arts. I, for one, believe that any expression of confidence would be out of place at this point. The only thing that hope is good for is to lead us to dissolution in not quite so bitter a mood. (415–16)[5]

The millenary history of European literary civilization began in the eastern basin of the Mediterranean, transferred to the Italian peninsula at the center of the Mediterranean, and was spread by Italy to the four corners of another peninsula, situated in Eurasia's farthest reaches to the west. For quite some time that civilization has been expanding to other regions, has mixed with other civilizations, having been transfused into them. The Italian writers of our time go on tilling, over and over, the dry, barren soil of an exhausted tradition, which, in its finest moments, has come up with new ways of nourishing and reviving the legacy from the ancients but has never had any real success in opening up to modernity. For a change, some of these writers hang on, obstinately, to the same tiresome, obscure operations of the most hermetic and formalistic European modernism, including, now and then, an aftertaste—a reminiscence, perhaps—from the avant-garde.

Up until the waning of the Renaissance, the only language of Italian literary culture—the language of the management and the renewal of things ancient—was also the language of Europe, hence of the world, in view of the fact that Europe was the only world Europe knew about and had any consideration for. With the epoch-making unfolding of Romanticism and concomitant worldwide dissemination of literature hand in hand with bourgeois capitalism—not in vain do Marx and Engels, in their *Manifesto* of 1848, propound a strict, direct connection between the two—Italian literature cannot find and does not seek a new idiom by means of which to converse with the new global community.

I have now come to the second point of my discussion. We have seen that the only world language available to Italian literature is the one pertaining to the management and renewal of Greco-Roman antiquity. It is Dante who wedded the enterprise of Christianity to the age-old classical lineage, thus bequeathing to us a masterpiece which, for all its perfection, stands in isolation as a "noble failure" of sorts, since it does not broach any new universal idiom, whether in Italy or in Europe. Perhaps this is because the "good news" of Christianity does not tolerate the art of poetry or of narrative (witness those *figmenta poetarum,* which any good believer must avoid, as the saintly scholar Isidore of Seville duly warns us way back in the Middle Ages). Such "good news" is supposed to convey the truth directly. It is as if Dante had fulfilled and exhausted forevermore all the potential of a "Christian literature"—that is, for the period ranging from the birth of Christ to 1200 and from 1200 to the end of time. The era of the various, recurrent renaissances of the ancient cultures, the era of the regenerating power of the "Classics," had come to a close, and, with that, Italian literature sank into the abyss, its vitality depleted by its long, monotonous effort.

Let us ask: who are the Italian writers who in the last twenty-five years have attracted worldwide interest? We may answer, without fear of being contradicted: Umberto Eco and Italo Calvino. With his three novels of progressively decreasing interest and success—that is, *Il nome della rosa* (1980; Eng. *The Name of the Rose;* more than ten million copies sold), *Il pendolo di Foucault* (1988; Eng. *Foucault's Pendulum;* painful to read), and *L'isola del giorno dopo* (1994; Eng. *The Island of the Day Before;* very hard to wade through beyond the first eighteen pages)—Eco has joined the international grand tour of the best-seller industry. He has been imposed upon the entire world very much as have been Michael Crichton, Stephen King, Harold Robbins, and Ken Follett, rather than in the way that Salman Rushdie, Milan Kundera, Gabriel García Márquez, and Nadine Gordimer have been imposed. Having won big in Babel's sweepstakes, Eco has exploited in every way imaginable the advantages offered by the wheel of Fortune, that ultimate billionaire, and by his own impressive, versatile intelligence. His is an Italian style blended with "understatement" à la Oxbridge. He has become an eminent speaker on the grand lecture tour around the American universities, a scholar through and through of resounding success all over the planet. >From New York his lectures are being carried *urbi et orbi* on the Internet. In the light of all this publicity, the works he has authored as an astute student of semiotics, esthetics, and mass media have been reassessed and reprinted. All this has won him prominent mention in those books—so fashionable in the international trade—which list the forty-three or fifty-one major intellectuals of the last eighteen (or is it fifteen, twenty-one, seven?) years.

In Calvino's case, it is quite a different story. He is not an author of best sellers but, rather, an accomplished, refined storyteller, whom the international literary market has placed in a constellation invented by university professors and directors of publishing houses. I mean the pleiad of postmodern, somewhat fantastic metafiction, which includes Jorge Luis Borges (universally recognized as the leader of the group), Raymond Queneau, Julio Cortázar, and the Oulipo group's Georges Perec, among others. As for the remaining contemporary Italian writers, I don't think it makes too much sense to speak of them from a comparatist's point of view.

You may well ask: what, then, do the Italians read in Italian? A lot of rubbish and collections of funny stories—these are indisputably the greatest hits in our bookstores, according to sales records. And yet, to side-step this disgusting, horrible wasteland, the literate Italian reader has an invaluable recourse against the peddling of a national literature which is outmoded and insignificant, and against the despair of scholars such as Cesare Segre: thank heavens for those worthy translations of literary works from all over the world! In this fashion, at least, our reading public can participate in a colloquium of truly cosmopolitan range.

Armando Gnisci, Spring 1997, translated by Peter Cocozzella

▓ WORKS CITED

Bloom, Harold. *The Western Canon.* New York. Harcourt. 1994.

Caesar, A. Hallamore. "Post-War Italian Narrative: An Alternative Account." In *Italian Cultural Studies: An Introduction.* D. Forgacs and R. Lumley, eds. New York. Oxford University Press. 1996. Pp. 248–60.

Fernández Retamar, Roberto. *Para el perfil definitivo del hombre.* Havana. Letras Cubanas. 1981.

Gnisci, Armando. *Ascesi e decolonizzazione.* Rome. Lithos. 1996.

———. *Il rovescio del gioco.* Rome. Carucci. 1992.

Hobsbawn, Eric J. *Age of Extremes: The Short Twentieth Century, 1914–1991.* London. Michael Joseph. 1994.

Huntington, S. "The Clash of Civilizations?" *Foreign Affairs,* 72:3 (1993), pp. 22–49.

Segre, Cesare. "Letteratura." In *La cultura italiana del Novecento.* C. Stajano, ed. Rome/Bari. Laterza. 1996. Pp. 372–422.

Wang Ning. "Post-Colonial Theory and the Decolonizing of Chinese Culture." Fifth Meeting of the Chinese Comparative Literature Association. Changchun, August 1996.

[1] This is the thesis advanced, in the main, by the Chinese comparatists, particularly by Wang Ning from Peking University. Wang Ning takes up, in addition, some suggestions made in this respect by S. Huntington.

[2] Among foreign Italianists we may find several commendable attempts at a different reading of contemporary Italian literature. Of particular interest, for instance, is A. Hallamore Caesar's effort toward a fresh approach—fresh precisely because it arises from a circle of non-Italian Italianists in the realm of "Cultural Studies." The thesis of this English scholar is to "give greater emphasis to writing by women" within current Italian literature. This certainly constitutes a proposal for an alternative study.

[3] The current model seems to me to be as follows: first phase, the turn from the nineteenth to the twentieth century up to World War I; second phase, the period from World War I to World War II, including the epoch of Fascism; third phase, from the Resistance and postwar reconstruction up to 1968; fourth phase, from 1968 to the present—that is, the end of the century.

[4] The orientation of the Italianists in question is exclusively and obsessively Eurocentric (France being accorded the most privileged position), with extremely rare references to the Far East in line with German scholarship. Though largely ignored by Italian scholars, the latter field of study is the object of intense exploration by foreign (Hungarian, Croatian, Serbian, Czech, Slovak, Polish) Italianists.

Dario Fo *(Ola Torkelsson, EPA)*

[5] I must say that Segre's critique is certainly striking, even though I do not share his "desperate" conclusion. In dealing with the literature of immigration into Europe and, in particular, into Italy, I have identified and discussed this less-than-dignified condition of contemporary Italian literature in my book, *Il rovescio del gioco* (The Reverse Side of the Game; 1992). I take up this argument again in my latest book, *Ascesi e decolonizzazione* (Asceticism and Decolonization; 1996).

Dario Fo: Jester of the Working Class

Dio esiste e anche lui è un giullare. (God exists and he too is a jester.)[1]

■ **DARIO FO**

Although the proceedings for the selection of the Nobel Prizes are secret, intriguing information inevitably leaks. Apparently it was Italy's year to win the prize for literature. Dario Fo, however, was not considered a leading candidate, in part because of the paucity of support for Italy within the Academy. One of the few Italianists there in recent memory was the late Anders

Österling, the Swedish poet and editor of a well-known anthology of Italian verse covering the period between 1959 and 1975, years in which two Italian poets won the Nobel Prize in Literature (Salvatore Quasimodo in 1959, Eugenio Montale in 1975).[2] The only other major Italian literature supporter of late is Lars Forssell, the Swedish poet and songwriter and well-known Italophile. Thus, if an Italian were to be considered a serious contender, it would quite likely be a poet, and the name that everyone expected was Mario Luzi, who in fact did entertain hopes of winning the award. It is conceivable that the Academicians wanted to give the prize to Italy but that, since the last two Italian winners had been poets, they felt it needed to go a different route.

Ultimately, the Academy members may have wanted to stress content over form and bring attention to the struggle between the weak and the powerful, as they indicated in their press release. They praised Fo as an emulator of "the jesters of the Middle Ages in upholding the dignity of the downtrodden," a writer who "opens our eyes to the abuses and injustices in society." The Academy also stressed Fo's literary qualities, adding that "his works are open for creative additions, dislocations, continually encouraging the actors to improvise, which means the audience is activated in a remarkable way."

The reaction in Italy, from the world of "traditional" literature, was predictable. One critic called awarding the prize to Fo a slap in the face to all that Italian literature has accomplished in the second half of the century. Another said it was a choice having to do more with sociology than with literature. Another critic argued that Fo might have merited the prize if it had been awarded just for theater, but for literature another name was to be expected.[3]

Of course, the most renowned Italian winner of the Nobel Prize in Literature was a man of the theater. But in Luigi Pirandello's case (1934) no questions were raised as to his legitimate literary credentials, because, as the author of novels and short stories in addition to plays and his work as a director, he was obviously a man of letters. Fo's selection pushes the definition of literature into a broader context, for he is not strictly and only a man of letters. He is an actor, playwright, director, stage designer, popular songwriter, mime, TV personality, and political campaigner, a figure whose ideas have managed to antagonize such diverse groups as the Catholic Church and the Italian Communist Party. In fact, to understand all of Fo's "literary" qualities from written texts alone is not possible, for no written page contains what he is or what he does in his works. However, an examination of *Mistero buffo* (1973; the title would literally translate as "Comic Mystery," but Ed

Emery's English edition was published under the original Italian title)[4] and *Morte accidentale di un anarchico* (1974; Eng. *Accidental Death of an Anarchist*)[5] can give a good idea.

In his now classic study of Italian literature, Giuseppe Petronio argues that today's theater presents *directors'* interpretations of plays, rather than authors' or actors', and that even when the play is from the past, the emphasis is on today's problems (961). This is certainly true in Fo's case, although in *Mistero buffo* the roles of playwright, director, actor, stage designer, and mime blend, making it impossible to see where one role begins and the other ends. As the writer and sole performer of *Mistero buffo,* Fo manages to fulfill Pirandello's view that authors and actors should "immedesimarsi" (become the characters) with the work they are composing or performing (215). Fo becomes the characters every time he stages the play, each performance presenting a different and new work because of his improvisations, which show the audiences his creative powers in action.

Although the play is therefore never totally "finished," the working texts of *Mistero buffo* and *Morte accidentale di un anarchico* contain the fundamental elements of Fo's opus, and particularly his concern for the poor and their struggle against the political establishment, elements which to a certain extent reflect the author's working-class roots (his mother was a peasant, his father a railway worker). In addition, these two works attempt to "recover" the people's language and culture going back to the Middle Ages, his role as *giullare* (jester), and his ideas about theater as an art form.

Fo borrows both the title and the concept of *Mistero buffo* from *Misteriia-buff* (1918) by the Russian poet and playwright Vladimir Mayakovsky, who sought to rewrite sacred issues of history through parody and farce and to present the proletariat's struggle against the forces of tyranny. Fo's *Mistero buffo* returns his spectators to the Middle Ages, although he repeatedly makes pointed, often startling connections with the present. Echoing Gramsci's ideas, Fo believes in the importance of knowing oneself, which allows the self's authenticity and thus enables one to be the master of one's destiny. To accomplish this, one must know the past; thus in the 1950s Fo began a study of medieval culture, the beginnings of theater and of his Padan language, a blend of Northern Italian dialects, which he uses in *Mistero buffo.* Fo believes that the dominant Italian class has robbed poor people of their culture and their language (Hirst, 110).[6]

His return to the Middle Ages is also an attempt to recover the vital sources of theater in a precapitalistic society before the mass media turned culture into merchandise in the hands of the rich and powerful to control the working class (Ielo).[7] Applying the knowledge he gained as a result of his study, Fo creates a number of vignettes on topics with an ecclesiastical background to show not only the corruption and repressiveness of the Church but also the political implications of its power. Stressing popular, comic, and irreverent elements of medieval mystery plays and religious cycles,[8] Fo attacks the repressiveness of the Catholic Church and the land-owning classes, using the language of the Italian peasants, whom he sees as representatives of peasants all over the world.

At the root of Fo's world view is the idea that poor people's lives are controlled by the rich and powerful, who have stolen the downtrodden's culture. *Mistero buffo* will thus be the "giornale parlato e drammatizzato del popolo" (the people's spoken and dramatized newspaper; 9). People must retake possession of what their masters have stolen and made their own.

In the first of the vignettes of *Mistero buffo* Fo tries to do just that. He reinterprets the classical Italian poem "Rosa fresca aulentissima" ("Sweet-Smelling, Fresh Rose") with its famous contrast between a tax collector and a woman who initially rejects his advances, a poem familiar to every student of Italian literature. Critics believe the poem was written by an aristocratic author who used refined language to turn the trivial theme of physical love into elevated poetry. Traditionally, it is seen as the first example of Italian courtly love. Fo reveals the poem's popular origins. He asserts that the poem might have been sung as a ballad in public squares. By turning the piece into a theatrical text, Fo stresses the brutal sexual oppression the tax collector imposes upon the woman, a servant girl, when he says he may even be willing to pay the "difensa" of "dumili' agostari" or 2,000 gold coins ("Rosa fresca," 91)—an allusion to what noblemen used to pay the families of raped girls in order to avoid prosecution. Fo concludes that the verses were probably composed by a social critic who wanted to draw attention to abuses of the poor.

In "Nascita del villano" (Birth of the Peasant), another of *Mistero buffo*'s vignettes, Fo shows how the powerful control the poor with literature, defining the lower classes through the stories they tell about them. In Fo's version of Creation, Adam refuses to lend his rib for the creation of the peasant who is to do the master's unpleasant work; God therefore creates him from an ass's fart. Under the guise of religious instruction, the master teaches the peasant that his lot on earth is to be vulgar and repellent, though he has a soul, through which he can transcend his misery. However, an angel tells the peasant he has no soul, thus revealing the master's blackmail. The pungent satire and exaggerated low condition of the peasant's birth were designed to show the factory workers watching Fo how they lose control of their lives by accepting their bosses' stories, their oppressors' view of the world.

In Fo's opinion, the powerful classes also use religion to control the poor, and he makes the Catholic Church the subject of a vicious invective in the vignette titled "Bonifacio VIII," the most celebrated single episode of *Mistero buffo*. Beginning this section with a lecture on medieval history exalting the utopian movements of the period, Fo pits this idealized background against a portrayal of the infamous pope. As Bonifacio is preparing for a ceremony, Christ appears, turning the rite into an interrogation, as the Son of God questions the pontiff about an orgy of 1301 involving bishops, prostitutes, and cardinals which Bonifacio had organized. Fo does not act out Christ's role on stage; spectators "see" him only through Bonifacio's physical reactions and words. Eventually Christ kicks Bonifacio for his pretense of not having committed any sins.[9] Christ thus becomes a judge who punishes the pope and, by implication, the entire Church hierarchy.

This condemnation of the Church is extended to the present pontiff, as Fo embodies Pope John Paul II and mocks his right-wing ideas.[10] Spectators see John Paul II jetting around the world like some superman endeavoring to "help" the needy. Ultimately, through a pretended slip of the tongue, Fo confuses Bonifacio and John Paul II, then returns to the person of Bonifacio, who, despite the dressing down he has received from Jesus himself, continues his blasphemies. Even divine intervention, Fo suggests, cannot end the oppression. If there is going to be a solution, it must take place outside the theater, as the audience, having been made aware of the problem, takes action in real life.

Although Fo sympathizes with the lives of poor people, he does not present them idealistically. In "Moralità del cieco e dello zoppo"[11] (Morality of the Blind and the Lame), for example, neither the Blind nor the Lame wants to run into Christ, for fear that He might perform miracles on them and remove their income-producing afflictions. If that were to happen, they would have to get jobs with masters. As in the Bonifacio vignette, Christ does not actually appear but is instead "seen" as a presence which both the Blind and the Lame try to avoid. Through their actions and words he is also "seen" by the audience.

Poor people are also presented realistically in "Nozze di Canaan" (The Marriage at Cana), wherein a Drunkard and an Archangel vie for the right to tell the story, reminding us once again that there is more than one way to tell any tale, even one we have heard all our lives. Eventually the Archangel is driven off stage as the Drunkard plucks away at his plumes. When the Drunkard tells the familiar tale, his emphasis is on the delight of the feast, the food and drink, and other physical needs, and on the "tragedy" when the wine eventually turns into vinegar. For the Drunkard, wine solves everything and would have even prevented the fall of mankind. If Adam had had a glass of wine in his hand, he would not have fallen from grace.

In "Lazzaro" (Lazarus) a similar emphasis on the common people's world is shown. Here Fo plays the roles of mercenary, gatekeeper, sardine seller, and a man renting chairs, as well as many members of the crowd, including one who screams he has been robbed, as they all witness the miracle of Lazarus' revivification. Fo stresses again the secular qualities of the piece and of the crowd observing the miracle, as spectators see even at the end when someone comments on Lazarus' rotting and offensive-smelling body.

Although Fo presents the world of the poor in a realistic manner, stressing in part the positive aspects, he nevertheless does not allow the spectator to forget the injustices. To create a just world, the poor need help, specifically a Christ-like figure. For Fo, the *giullare* or jester must fill this role. In "Lanascita del giullare" (The Birth of the Jester) Fo paints an exaggerated view of the poor person's adversary. A peasant who has found a mountain and cultivated its land is robbed of all his efforts' rewards by a landowner, who also rapes his wife in front of him and his children. Seeking revenge, the peasant is stopped by his wife, who soon leaves him, and his children also die. Alone, with nothing to live for, he decides to hang himself, but a passerby, who turns out to be Christ, asks him for water. Eventually Christ kisses the peasant and saves him, giving him a gift: a language which will cut like a knife and which he will be able to use against the masters to crush them. Christ turns the peasant into a *giullare* and instructs him to spread the message of his oppression. Thus the mission is not religious but political, and Christ brings not a message of peace but a sword. However, the hero does not know how to act and does not have to, for Fo, as always, expects his *audience* to act, on the outside, in real life. His lack of convention is always a political technique, never a literary flaw.

Fo's *giullare* serves the people, entertains them, but especially uses satire to show them their condition and spur them to action. As Sogliuzzo asserts, Fo's *giullare* is not based on the commedia dell'arte (72). Fo sees the comics of the commedia as having become part of the establishment. From the point of view of content, the comics of the commedia dell'arte were reactionary, because they had cleaned up their acts to please the court and the bourgeoisie. Yet there was another tradition of comics within the commedia dell'arte which is not part of the official history; these comedians performed not at court but rather in public taverns, in town squares, and in even lowlier locales.[12] Binni asserts that it is this unofficial repertory of the *giullari* that Fo attempts to recover (52). It is in this tradition that Fo sees himself as a *giullare,* someone who "nasceva dal popolo e dal popolo prendeva la rabbia per ridarla ancora al popolo perché prendesse coscienza della propria condizione" (was born from the people and from the people he would seize their rage to give it back to the people so that they could become aware of their own condition; *Mistero buffo,* 15–16).

Ironically, early in his career Fo worked in the more well-known tradition of the commedia dell'arte— as jester of the powerful. He has described on many occasions his failed experience with being a *giullare* of the bourgeoisie. He and his wife Franca Rame, with their Fo-Rame Theater Company, enjoyed great popular success both on stage and on television, but their audience consisted of people who were part of the establishment, unable to comprehend or accept their radical ideas. Thus, in 1959, with Italy's left-center government opening national Italian television to artists from the Left, Fo was invited to be part of the extremely popular musical review *Canzonissima,* which boasted a viewership of up to fifteen million across Italy. Fo's sketches included satires on real-estate speculation and on the dehumanizing working conditions in factories, but the government found his subject matter unacceptable. After the eighth program, his sketches were censored, and soon he was fired for refusing to obey the censors and banished from Italian national television for fourteen years.

Fo, as *giullare,* needed an audience that allowed him creative independence and at the same time accepted his revolutionary messages. In 1968, after considerable success in commercial theater, he began looking for this audience. The year 1968 was, of course, a turbulent one, politically and culturally. The demonstrations in Berkeley spread to Paris and eventually to Italy. This political activism also affected theater. Supported in part by ARCI, the cultural wing of the Italian Communist Party,[13] Fo and Rame created a new company, Nuova Scena, and began staging their plays in such public venues as soccer stadiums, gyms, circus tents, and *case del popolo* (communist cultural centers) to audiences that may have never previously attended the theater. Fo now sees himself as Lungo, the protagonist in his first play, *Gli arcangeli non giocano al flipper* (1959; Eng. *Archangels Don't Play Pinball*), when he says to Antonia, his girlfriend, that since noblemen don't exist any

more, he himself makes his low-class buddies laugh; he is their jester. Although this worked for a while, even the limitations imposed on Fo by the communists were too restrictive, and he eventually set up his own theater company, La Comune, in an abandoned building in Milan. But now, to be able to create, Fo needed not only the right audience but the right text as well. *Mistero buffo* was that text.

Although a written version of the play exists, Fo recreates the work every time he stages it, based on what he perceives to be the audience's needs. For Fo, a theatrical text is like a musical score, with its rhythms, silences, and pauses. Little is gained from reading a score, because the work comes to life only in performance. *Mistero buffo* gives Fo the freedom to create on stage, without any political strings attached, whether from the Left or the Right. He is alone on a bare stage, wearing a black sweater, with no lighting effects, continually changing characters, going in and out of roles, the spareness of the stage setting reflecting the poverty of his audience. The effects are all created by allusions and gestures.[14] The audience must be active and involved. In the initial performances of *Mistero buffo,* Fo would start with a lecture on the Middle Ages and would show slides of paintings and drawings of the period to give an aura of authenticity to his material. Eventually, he dropped this artifice and introduced what have become "interventi"—discussions with the audience about the different vignettes and how they relate to current events.

Unlike television, where viewers see everything laid out in front of them, Fo's audiences must participate actively with their imagination and especially with their discussions once the performance is over. He expects them to continue thinking even the day after, when they go back to work in their factories. The performance never entirely ends. Television viewers, on the other hand, have everything set before their eyes, yet go back to work with nothing in their heads, ready to be exploited again, becoming merely means of production.

Ironically, *Mistero buffo* did end up on Italian television.[15] It was broadcast in 1977, the same year Franco Zeffirelli directed his celebrated *Jesus of Nazareth,* creating an inevitable comparison between the two artists' vision of Jesus. Zeffirelli criticized Fo's vision of Christ because of its overtly political qualities.[16] Fo's Christ is human and tells people to have fun, not to wait for paradise, but also to take an active role in the struggle on this earth. Fo replied that Zeffirelli's pious and meek Christ made as clear a political statement as his own: by bolstering the power of the church and the state, Zeffirelli had simply created a right-wing Jesus.

The *Osservatore Romano,* the Vatican newspaper, called *Mistero buffo* the most blasphemous show in history and accused Fo of ideological violence targeting the religious values of Italians but aiming really at the disintegration of the Italian state (quoted in *Avvenire*).[17] But if the Vatican believed that Fo had gone as far as he could in attacking Italian institutions and the political system, they were wrong. One year after *Mistero buffo,* in *Morte accidentale di un anarchico,* Fo struck directly at the system's heart.[18]

Morte accidentale di un anarchico is structurally a more "traditional" play than is *Mistero buffo* in that there are many characters, requiring a number of actors. The play is based on the death of Giuseppe Pinelli, a railway worker accused of having set off a bomb at Milan's Banca Nazionale dell'Agricoltura on 12 December 1969. The explosion killed sixteen people and wounded an additional eighty-four. After three days of interrogation, Pinelli "flew" out of a fifth-floor window at Milan's police headquarters. The government explained his death as a suicide provoked by his "guilt."

In the play Fo presents a grotesque farce which reveals the contradictions between the police officers' statements and their actions. Assuming the role of a *Matto* or Maniac, loose in police headquarters, Fo conducts an investigation into what might have really happened. By pretending to be, in turn, various figures of authority—psychiatrist, professor, magistrate, bishop, forensics expert—the Maniac forces officials to re-create the events with the purpose of showing the inconsistencies in the official reports of Pinelli's "leap" and to confess their responsibility in the anarchist's death.

At the very beginning of the play the Superintendent interrogates the *Matto,* who confesses his mental illness and explains it as "istrionamania. . .mania dei personaggi" (histrionic mania. . .mania of impersonating characters; 2). He acknowledges having received his training in a number of mental institutions. Kicked out of the office, the Maniac eventually sneaks back in and continues to impersonate different officials. After stealing a magistrate's coat and briefcase, he questions the police as if he were reopening an inquiry into the death of the anarchist. As the Magistrate, the Maniac corrects the police versions of the events. The "Magistrate" puts the police into the position in which the anarchist had found himself—having to explain what happened. In essence, he interrogates them. He even forces them to the window and tells them to jump, as they had probably done to the anarchist.

Eventually Fo pulls back when it becomes evident that the police were guilty of the anarchist's death and suggests that the police are really being used as scape-goats by the government. Here Fo attacks further by pointing a finger at the government as a whole. In essence, he uses one part of the establishment against another (*Morte accidentale,* epilogue, 117). Thus the Maniac-Magistrate will help the police extricate themselves by aiding them in the invention of acts of humanity toward the anarchist, such as offering him chewing-gum.

It is very easy to see through the Maniac's and the police officers' farce, but such lighter aspects of the play help balance the serious and tragic tones. For example, the Constable and the *Matto* try to concoct a story to explain how the police attempted to keep the anarchist from jumping: they held his foot, and the fact that they have the shoe that came off when he jumped bears witness to their efforts to save him. Unfortunately, the body was discovered on the ground with both shoes still on. But no matter, the "Magistrate" says; the anarchist must have been wearing three shoes. The system is quite reasonable, Fo suggests, if your standard is a madman's logic.

And the system is more than willing to accept insane logic when this suits its purpose. By the time a *Giornalista*[19] (Reporter) enters and begins asking questions, the police have already been made aware that the Maniac is not the forensics expert he claims to be. However, his explanations support their case—his madness is useful—and so they not only allow him to continue acting out his farce for the media's benefit, but they also urge the real forensics expert to play along with him, to back up his crazy stories. Still, Fo knows that the one who tells the story has the power, and handing control of the story over to a madman is not a wise choice—as the police discover when the Maniac begins to support the reporter's suggestion that there are obvious contradictions in the police report on the anarchist's death. In the end, the system's willingness to go along with any lie, any insane story, as long as it allows them to keep their power, defeats the system.

Although Fo certainly pokes fun at the police officials, he does not present them merely as comic figures but rather as devious abusers of power. Neither does he show great sympathy for the anarchist, whom he views as inept. On stage there are no clear heroes or villains, for Fo's primary interest is not in assigning blame but rather in opening a political dialogue. The Maniac, at the play's end, reveals that he has been recording the entire proceeding and threatens to send copies to the media, the political parties, and the government. He threatens, in essence, to do what Fo has just done: to put the insanity, injustice, and hypocrisy of the system before the people; to show the absurdity of the powerful to the powerless in his audience and let them decide what to do about it.

In the first two years after its première *Morte accidentale* was staged approximately two hundred times and more than 300,000 people saw the play. With each staging, Fo created a new and original work. However, his most original single performance was a staging of *Mistero buffo* in Vicenza. When the production was interrupted by rain one evening, Fo started talking with the thunder, addressing it as the voice of God and asking for lightning. Lightning in fact came, after a particularly provocative question to God. The spectators remained riveted to their seats, mesmerized, as Fo took a chance that nature or God would cooperate with him to create the desired effect. That night God himself was a jester, awarding the risk-taking Dario Fo a dramatic and most unexpected prize.

Domenico Maceri, Winter 1998

▪ WORKS CITED

Avvenire, 24 April 1977.

Binni, Lanfranco. *Attento a te. . .! Il teatro politico di Dario Fo.* Verona. Bertani. 1975.

D'Alcamo, Cielo. "Rosa fresca aulentissima." In *Antologia della letteratura italiana dalle origini al Quatttrocento.* Italo de Bernardi, Franco Lanza, eds. Turin. Società Editrice Internazionale. 1973.

Fo, Dario. *Gli arcangeli non giocano al flipper.* In his *Commedie,* vol. 1. Turin. Einaudi. 1984.

———. *Guerra di popolo in Cile.* Verona. Bertani. 1974.

———. *Mistero buffo: Giullarata popolare.* Verona. Bertani. 1973.

———. *Morte accidentale di un anarchico.* Turin. Einaudi. 1974.

Hirst, David. *Dario Fo and Franca Rame.* Basingstoke, Eng. Macmillan. 1989.

Ielo-Natsis, Mariangela. "Il teatro medievale come atttualità." Presentation at the 7th Conference on Theater and Semiology, University of Piraeus (Greece), 5–8 April 1996.

Petronio, Giuseppe. *L'attività letteraria in Italia.* Florence. Palumbo. 1973.

Pirandello, Luigi. "Illustratori, attori e traduttori." In his *Saggi, poesie e scritti varii.* Milan. Mondadori. 1965.

Puppa, Paolo. *Il teatro di Dario Fo: Dalla scena alla piazza.* Venice. Marsilio. 1978.

Sogliuzzo, A. Richard. "Dario Fo: Puppets for a Proletarian Revolution." *Drama Review,* 16:3, September 1972.

Swedish Academy press release, 9 October 1997.

Valentini, Chiara. *La storia di Dario Fo.* Milan. Feltrinelli. 1977.

[1] All translations from the Italian are my own.

[2] In 1975 the Italian PEN Club had submitted Fo's name as a candidate for the Nobel Prize, along with those of Simone de Beauvoir and Alberto Moravia. Asked how he would have felt if he had won the prize instead of Montale, Fo replied that it would have been like acting in one of his farces.

[3] Of course, a number of "theater" people including Giorgio Strehler and Maurizio Scaparro were very supportive of Fo. There was also unexpected support from the Paolini brothers, who praised Fo in spite of the official stand from the Vatican that he was unworthy of the prize.

[4] *Mistero buffo* was first staged in 1969.

[5] *Morte accidentale di un anarchico* was first staged in 1970.

[6] Although most Italians were and to a certain degree still are "bilingual," since they speak standard Italian and their native dialect, the vernaculars are in danger of disappearing.

[7] In *Grande pantomima con bandiere e pupazzi piccoli e medi* (Grand Pantomime with Flags and Small and Midsized Puppets; 1968) Fo presents a strong satire of the mass media.

[8] Although Fo claims to have used authentic materials in *Mistero buffo,* his own contributions are very significant (Valentini, 120).

[9] Dante in the *Divine Comedy* condemns Bonifacio to hell for his sins (*Inferno,* XIX).

[10] In 1980 Pope John Paul II disapproved of workers' strikes in Italy.

[11] Here Fo adapted a plot from Andrea della Vigna.

[12] As a child growing up in Northern Italy, Fo was an attentive listener to *fabulatori* and *cantastorie,* as these modern-day *giullari* would entertain peasants and fishermen in the area around Lake Maggiore.

[13] Fo never formally joined the Communist Party, although his wife did. She left it in 1970.

[14] The staging of *Mistero buffo* obviously requires talents that few performers possess, yet the play has been staged in several languages, including French, English, and Flemish.

[15] The TV presentation of *Mistero buffo* was a four-part program.

[16] The political qualities of Fo's works made him the target of the Italian government. In 1973 he was arrested for one day by Italian authorities for not allowing "real police" to enter his theater while staging *Guerra di popolo in Cile,* which included several policemen among the dramatis personae. The play deals with police brutality and conspiracies during Pinochet's coup in Chile. Fo also had trouble with the American authorities. In 1980, and again in 1983, he was refused a visa to enter the USA. He is in good company. Brecht, Chaplin, and García Márquez were also refused visas. However, in 1984 the Reagan government granted Fo a temporary visa.

[17] Ironically, the Vatican's outrage at Fo's *Mistero buffo* made the show even more popular because of all the free publicity. There was also an outcry against Fo from the Italian Communist Party.

[18] It is interesting to note that *Morte accidentale* also benefited from free publicity. When it was first staged, a lawsuit brought by Luigi Calabresi against the leftist newspaper *Lotta Continua* kept the subject alive, aiding the success of the production. The paper had accused Calabresi of direct responsibility in Giuseppe Pinelli's death.

[19] This character was based on Camilla Cederna, who recently passed away.

Italo Calvino: The Repeated Conquest of Contemporaneity

"With all the variety and innovation of your writing, how would you define your work as a whole? What would you see as the ultimate purpose of your writing?"

"I write each book as though it were the first I've ever written—as if it had no relation whatever to any of the others. I'd leave the task of defining my work to the critic."[1]

■ ITALO CALVINO

Like Pirandello, Italo Calvino has repeatedly insisted that his works originate in images and not in ideas. Both writers have wanted to shake off the straitjacket of philosophical and theoretical abstractions that critics—true to their vocation of intellectualizing art—have too often forced on them. Pirandello's expression of intolerance derives from an almost physical malaise, the fear of being imprisoned or limited; it is a cry for freedom, a passionate denunciation of the evil men do to one another. Calvino's statements are matter-of-fact, informative, not polemical. In speaking about his differences with a fellow writer, Carlo Cassola, he is amusingly self-revealing when he says that both of them in the course of a discussion tend to render their positions extreme: "I become more and more obstinate especially to get him angry and also a little because I believe in what I'm saying; he becomes even more obstinate because he believes in what he is saying and a little also to get me angry."[2] The contrast in attitudes between him and Cassola, the comparative dosage of belief and provocation, emphasizes Calvino's capacity for remaining cool, ironically detached, inclined to laugh where another person might burn with righteous indignation or become withdrawn in resigned melancholy. Calvino's joie de vivre—or joie d'écrire—in spite of disenchantment, his basic acceptance of things as they are without being blind to their insufficiencies, his ability to make the best of the ceaseless activity of modern life, to recharge his energy from the same sources that feed changes in industry, international relations, dominant ideologies, literary criticism, journalism and art—all these mark him as in tune with the contemporary world.

To a greater degree than most writers of fiction, perhaps, Calvino has been generous with a wide range of published comments on his works. They are often retrospective, accompanying a new edition of a work,[3] but they may also be contemporaneous with the work[4] or even precede it.[5] What distinguishes these writings is their direct confrontation with specific works and with the author's career as a writer. They are elaborate curricula vitae, presentations of work done or to be done, sophisticated blurbs, press releases—the unavoidable frame that modern mass communication and the rapid turnover in the production of the printed word demand and require. In comparison to the large quantity of material which could be subsumed under the rubric of "Calvino on Calvino"—and which makes the critic's work almost redundant—Pirandello's not infrequent comments on his writings shrink to near-insignificance. But in the one instance as in the other, whatever the impression at first sight, it would be improper to speak of self-promotion. Pirandello's rage to be heard, his vindication of man's right to assert his individuality, to speak his "reason," is paralleled by Calvino's impersonal chronicling of his literary and intellectual trajectory, by his factual, unemotional recounting of his professional activities. If the image of the romantic poet still hovers in the background of Pirandello's bourgeois persona, it has been completely replaced in Calvino's case by the gray suit of the businessman or the more informal turtleneck sweater of the professional intellectual (the *operatore culturale,* to use a recent expression). In this respect too Calvino is unmistakably contemporary.

In terms of literary career as measured by a writer's continued active presence on the literary scene, Calvino's has from the outset been a success story. The ebullient affirmation of storytelling which marked his debut as a writer immediately following the end of World War II reverberates in the apparent ease with which he has been able to renew himself for almost forty years now. Calvino's success is no literary "case." It is an extraordinarily fortunate beginning followed by continuing growth in an accretion and transformation of meanings won not by retreat from the surrounding world but by acceptance of its riches and contrasts, by exploiting it "to turn facts into words," constructing not "a duplicate copy of life" but an equivalent to it.[6] Calvino is neither a realist painter or photographer nor yet a poet turned storyteller; it is neither the world outside he wishes to capture and hold, nor the evanescence of his own states of consciousness, his inner self, that he is anxious to explore and express. He finds that the cinema and the press have successfully and definitively taken over the "task of the minute representation of their time which was the burden and the glory of literature in the nineteenth century."[7] And he has stated bluntly that he is not interested in "psychology, spiritual life, interiors, the family, customs, society."[8] When he is not telling stories, he functions as an intellectual, sometimes as a scholar: up-to-date on new works and ideas, in touch with what is being thought, written and read, engaged in the life of the mind not as introspection and meditation but as activity, productivity and performance.

More important in this respect than his formal education (he has a degree in English from the University of Turin, earned with a dissertation on Conrad) were his years of editorial work for the publisher Einaudi, which date from the publication of his first book, *Il sentiero dei nidi di ragno* (1947; translated as *The Path of the Nest of Spiders,* 1957), and his militant journalism, first in the pages of the Communist daily *L'Unità* and later, between 1959 and 1966, as co-director with Elio Vittorini of the journal *Il Menabò.* Indicative of the coherence of his literary career is the fact that virtually all his books have been published by Einaudi[9] in handsomely produced and for the most part inexpensive editions, distinguished by illustrated covers which propose visual equivalents to the text in vignettes taken from the minimal art of a Paul Klee or a Saul Steinberg.[10] It is customary to present the significance of the Einaudi imprint almost exclusively in terms of the writers and intellectuals who have gathered around the publishing house: Pavese and Vittorini, Natalia Ginzburg and Carlo Levi. But it is well to remember that Einaudi differs from other major Italian publishers not only in editorial policy, which determines the selection of titles (including translations) for publication, but also in the commitment to its writers, measured by its willingness to keep the backlist in print. To a greater degree than other commercial publishers Einaudi has interpreted its main function as that of serving Italian culture: first under Fascism by ensuring that the lines of communication with intellectual life outside Italy remained open, and later in the early post-World War II years by the massive introduction into Italy of works that had been excluded for political and ideological reasons during the preceding twenty years—Marx, Brecht, Lukács, Adorno, Aragon, Auerbach, Gramsci, Jung and Benjamin, among others. At Einaudi, then, Calvino found himself in a stimulating and formative environment, more an intellectual training ground than a moneymaking enterprise.[11]

As alluded to earlier, Calvino's literary production has almost from the beginning been accompanied by critical efforts to track its evolution. His precocious success (he was barely twenty-four when *Il sentiero dei nidi di ragno* was published) attracted more than the ordinary share of attention to each of his subsequent works. It came as a surprise when in 1952 he left his neorealist beginnings to veer full course into the realm of fantasy.[12] In the novel and in the short stories collected in *Ultimo viene il corvo* (1949; *Adam, One Afternoon and Other Stories,* 1957), the setting had been the Resistance, more precisely Partisan warfare in the mountainous terrain that presses upon the Ligurian shore of Genoa and San Remo (the latter the old European vacation paradise where Calvino grew up). The characters had been persons, recognizable individuals, involved in human situations and contemporary dilemmas. They may not have been presented with the full genealogy, personal history and psychological assessment of figures in nineteenth-century novels but instead with shorthand notations such as are used in drama or in the short narrative genres; still, they were not for that any the less "real." Their names were most frequently nicknames and epithets (Pin, il Dritto, Mancino, Maria la Matta), their features and gait sketched with a few strokes, their speech monosyllabic, full of expletives, colloquial. They had almost no revealed inner life. But these were familiar narrative procedures: the lack of depth in portrayal, of written density on the page, were part and parcel of the thinning out, the stripping down that the novel had begun to undergo even before neorealism.

As for the sentiments expressed in Calvino's early work, the positions taken, the ethical judgments made, the distinctions between right and wrong, good and bad, however superficial and unnuanced they actually were—the pronouncements of youth after all, no more than so many "givens"—they sounded right, and eventually he and others like him in the mainstream of postwar European literature ended up by imposing their view of recent history in creating the not yet exploded myth of the Resistance. In 1964, when Calvino wrote a preface to a new edition of *Il sentiero dei nidi di ragno,* he was still able to recapture effortlessly the euphoria of those years, the sense of a new beginning, of the "defiant gaiety" with which his generation faced the future, and the veritable explosion of storytelling that appeared to unite a whole people in the recounting of a common experience: "In the trains that were beginning to run again, crowded with people and sacks of flour and oil cans, every passenger was telling his neighbors what had happened to him, and the same was true of every customer in the workers' canteens, and of every woman queued at a store. The grayness of everyday life seemed a thing of the past. We moved in the multicolored universe of storytelling."[13] In the years that followed, one might say, it has been Calvino's self-imposed task to recreate the fullness of this initial period, and it has been his fortune to be successful each time in remounting the incline of diminishing creative energy, a hazard in the individual's life in general and an earmark—in the opinion of some at least—of our own troubled times.

The novel Calvino published in 1952, *Il visconte dimezzato* (*The Cloven Viscount,* 1962), turned its back not only on neorealism but even on verisimilitude. Set in the late seventeenth century during the Austro-Turkish Wars, it tells the unlikely story of a knight whose adventures continue even after he is cut in half by a cannonball. In 1957 it was joined by another piece of apparent escapism, *Il barone rampante* (*The Baron in the Trees,* 1959), whose protagonist as a boy of twelve, on 15 June 1767, leaves the family dinner table to climb up an oak tree in the garden and thereby begin a stubborn, uninterrupted arboreal life that will come to an end only with his death a half-century later. Finally, in *Il cavaliere inesistente* (1959; *The Non-Existent Knight,* 1962), Calvino dipped into the chivalric epic and invented a new paladin for Charlemagne, the warrior Agilulfo, who is an empty suit of shining armor, a being all spirit and will and entirely without body. Actually Calvino had thought of *Il visconte dimezzato* as no more than a "divertimento," and had he been able to impose that status on all three works (by publishing them in a periodical, for instance, as he had intended to do with *Il visconte,* or by turning them into children's books, as he did with *Il barone* in 1959 and *Il visconte* in 1975), he might have avoided the need to defend himself against the accusation of disengagement, of having rejected the literature of social consciousness for works of frivolous entertainment. His apologia is contained in the preface to *I nostri antenati* (Our Ancestors; 1960), the book that brought together the three novels as a trilogy and thus made them even more visible as turning points. It is a typical exposé of the latent ideological implications of a work of art: what Calvino says in essence is that because external circumstances had changed, he was no longer able to find the right tone for his old subject matter, but that, contrary to what it might seem, the new subject matter was by no means divorced from surrounding reality. Rearranging the three works to respect not the chronology of their composition but the chronology of the historical epochs in which they are set, Calvino was able to privilege the "message" of *Il barone rampante.* The argument runs like this: if in *Il cavaliere* the human experience depicted is that of the conquest of being and in *Il visconte* it is the aspiration to wholeness in spite of the mutilations imposed by society, then *Il barone* charts the way to an integrity that is not individualistic but is achieved through loyalty to personal self-determination.

■ ■ ■

So much for the ideological debate and the relation of Calvino's works of fantasy to it. But the preface to *I nostri antenati* and a number of essays that belong to the period of the trilogy reveal more than this.[14] They show Calvino to be conversant with the dominant trends in the study of literature and with the various "approaches" to the discussion of the work of art. If his concern with the relationship between literature and society betrays the leftist foundation of his intellectual orientation (he had resigned from the Communist Party in 1957), his dissection of the writer's craft, his ability to analyze his own and others' works as artifacts, as constructed forms, points to his having been in close contact with twentieth-century developments in the novel in Italy and the rest of Europe and with the various theories, historical and structural, that had been advanced to explicate them. He presents the trilogy on the one hand as a sequence of didactic models for self-realization, "three steps in the approach to freedom," part of the intellectual's program for influencing historical processes; but on the other hand he cannot let go of critical topoi such as narrative voice, identification of author and character, relationship between theme and plot, the fruition of the work of art in the act of reading and, finally, the self-conscious focusing on writing itself, on "the connection between the complexity of life and the sheet of paper on which this complexity comes to rest in the shape of alphabetical signs."[15]

A great leap forward in Calvino's appropriation of new subject matter, the next step in his constant *aggiornarsi* or repeated conquest of contemporaneity, comes with *Le cosmicomiche* (1965; *Cosmicomics,* 1968) and *Ti con zero* (1967; *t Zero,* 1969). In these works, according to some critics, Calvino has abandoned the anthropocentric view of the universe. And indeed, they mark a kind of final acceptance—in all its consequences—of the Copernican revolution, an inversion in values that Mattia Pascal (and with him Pirandello) had still considered a disaster for mankind but that Calvino is able to dominate with a buoyancy reminiscent of the apparent ease with which space exploration succeeded in finally putting man on the moon. The narrator of the stories, sketches, vignettes or (to use the term favored by the structuralists) "microtexts" that constitute *Le cosmicomiche,* and of two of the segments into which *Ti con zero* is divided, is a certain Qfwfq, a sentient, conscious being, sometimes a lowly organism floating in undifferentiated matter, sometimes a New York corporation executive caught in a traffic jam; through him the evolution of the universe, as it happened or might have happened, is recounted. Each "chapter" is introduced by a passage of scientific exposition such as might occur in one of the encyclopedia entries or works of popularization that Calvino refers to as having furnished the images out of which these stories grew, an imaginary space atlas, the modern counterpart to the geographical maps that gave impetus to stories of exploration in other centuries.

The successive conditions of the universe and the theories that account for them are the background for fictional episodes which dramatize and communicate the feeling of such temporally and spatially distant experiences for us as cataclysmic explosions, slow changes in the atmosphere and in the pull of gravitation, the passing of geological eras and periods, the extinction of species, the ever-recurrent alternation of assimilation and differentiation, the attractions and repulsions between like and unlike beings who often have only a residue of the human in them. "How could we get along with one another?" Qfwfq asks at a certain point apropos the clash in reactions between himself, now a New Jersey commuter, and Vug, his old girl friend, rediscovered in front of a Tiffany show window.

> For me only what has homogeneous growth, indistinctness, achieved repose has any value; for her what is disjoined or commingled, either one or the other, or preferably both together. . . . I imagined a slow, uniform expansion like that of crystals, until the "I"-crystal would become interpenetrated with the "she"-crystal and perhaps together we would become one with the world-crystal; she already seemed to know that the law of living matter would be to separate and to come together again endlessly.[16]

Thus the familiar everday causes of conflict between individuals, the recurrent strains in a marriage, the incompatibilities that exist because of different temperaments and different growth and maturation rates are here expressed with concepts derived not from psychology or sociology, as often in modern fiction, but from physics and chemistry, reminding one that Calvino's family background and his earliest education were in fact dominated by the natural rather than the human sciences.[17]

Like poets who try their hand at translating the poetry of others, Calvino has not only told his own stories, but he has also retold the stories of others. His most important retelling no doubt occurred in *Fiabe italiane* (1956; *Italian Folktales,* 1980), an Einaudi project that kept him occupied between 1954 and 1956. *Fiabe italiane* was first published in the series "I Millenni," a deluxe collection of world classics begun in 1947 that already included the Brothers Grimm's *Le fiabe del focolare* (1951) and a volume of *Fiabe africane* (1955), for which Calvino had written the preface. In 1957 a volume of *Fiabe francesi,* French folktales of the seventeenth and eighteenth centuries, joined these.[18] Calvino's task included collecting folktales in the various dialects of Italy and translating them into Italian, thus putting together a corpus that could take its place beside the most famous such European collection, the German one. *Fiabe*

italiane, which won recognition for its impeccable scholarship, brought Calvino into direct contact with the fund of (as he was himself to write) "the ever repeated and ever varied case histories of human vicissitudes. . .the catalogue of the possible destinies of a man or a woman. . .the drastic division of the living into kings and beggars; the persecution of the innocent . . . the common fate of succumbing to enchantments . . . and the effort to free oneself . . . loyalty to commitments . . . beauty as a sign of grace . . . and especially the unitary substance of all—men, beasts, plants, objects—the infinite possibility of metamorphosis in everything that exists."[19]

Orlando furioso di Ludovico Ariosto raccontato da Italo Calvino (1970) is a different kind of retelling. The work is patterned on those abridged versions of classics in which selected passages are connected by brief summaries of the intervening material. Ariosto's *ottave,* his eight-line stanzas, mingle with Calvino's prose in a reworking that both maintains and varies the structure of the original and emphasizes the reality of the poem as construct, as text. "At the beginning there is only a maiden who flees through the forest. . . . She is the protagonist of a poem that was left unfinished, and she is running to enter another poem barely begun"—thus Calvino begins his retelling, "translating" the recent critical discovery of literariness to indicate the *Furioso*'s link with the *Innamorato* and clearing the hurdle of historical, biographical and cultural contexts. The latter are dealt with in his "Presentation," which, as is usual in introductions to the *Furioso,* starts out with a review of the development of the Charlemagne cycle and continues with a brief sketch of Ariosto's life, culminating with the main themes of the poem and its form. (The indispensable notes, borrowed from Caretti's 1966 edition of *Orlando furioso,* are relegated to an appendix and round out the scholarly apparatus.) Calvino's perceptions of Ariosto's storytelling techniques interest us in particular for what they tell us about his own craft. Three points that he makes are especially worth noting: Ariosto added episodes to the *Innamorato* that spread out in all directions, "intersecting with one another and dividing up to create new symmetries and new contrasts"; the masterly heaping of *ottava* on *ottava* deflects attention from Ariosto himself, keeping him—"this crystal clear, cheerful poet, apparently without a care in the world"— hidden and mysterious; and finally, in the last canto, the poem ends in the presence of its own audience, welcomed by the ladies and gentlemen of the time of its telling, for whom it was composed, and by all those others, "readers present and future who will take part in its game, recognizing themselves in it."[20]

The next two major works are probably Calvino's most difficult ones yet published: *Le città invisibili* (1972; *Invisible Cities,* 1974) and *Il castello dei destini incrociati* (1973; *The Castle of Crossed Destinies,* 1977). Both are related to his retelling of the stories of others and to the structural analyses of storytelling which accompanied and grew out of the emergence of the *nouveau roman.* They have a programmatic, mediated origin; they are intentional more than spontaneous. In the postscript to *Il castello* Calvino himself has told about the double genesis of this work: a 1968 international seminar at which one of the contributors dealt with fortune-telling and the language of emblems; and the decision of the publisher Franco Maria Ricci to bring out an art book on the Visconti tarot cards preserved by museums in Bergamo and New York. When the assignment from the publisher came, Calvino had already been at work on another deck of tarots, the so-called Marseilles deck, which provided the visual stimuli for "La taverna dei destini incrociati" (The Tavern of Crossed Destinies), the second text of the completed work. Obviously the operative concept is that of "crossed destinies" rather than that of "castle" as opposed to "tavern" as cultural and sociological referents; this is corroborated by the fact that Calvino at one point planned a third text, "Il motel dei destini incrociati," built on vignettes from comic strips, which he describes as "the contemporary equivalent of the tarot cards as a representation of the collective unconscious."[21] Calvino's project was to let the cards tell the story, as in divination, bearing in mind that any single card has no inherent meaning, only one derived from its place in a sequence, and that at the end of the game all the cards must have been used. Reversing the usual order, instead of looking for pictorial illustrations for a text already written—as had been the case, for instance, in the "I Millenni" edition of the *Fiabe*—the starting point here is a picture, a sign with many meanings. The self-imposed rules, the many determinants, turned the assignment into a nightmare, a maddening puzzle, a placing and replacing of cards that was cut short only by publication.

The frame for both sets of stories in *Il castello* is embedded in a device of the fabulatory tradition of the West which goes back to the *Decameron* and the *Canterbury Tales* and which was still very much alive on the reduced scale of the single story in the flowering of short fiction in the nineteenth century. A group of travelers gathers about a table, and soon, as on the Italian trains after the war recalled earlier, they are deep in the exchange of tales. But the lightheartedness of that now distant experience is lacking in *Il castello,* whose special twist is that the travelers on their way through the forest—locus of the folktale but also of the *Divine Comedy*

and of many of the episodes of the *Furioso*—have lost their speech because of their horrible and fearful encounters. It is true that on the table—in one case richly set and lit by chandeliers, in the other strewn with rough bowls and mugs, the gloom barely dissipated by a smoky candle—each group finds a pack of cards through which to communicate. But the communication is difficult, and though the suspense generated by the successive emergence of cards is sufficient to keep the travelers alert, the reader must be endowed with an uncommon literary education to appreciate Calvino's sleights of hand—the evoking of Faust and Macbeth, Oedipus and Parsifal, Hamlet and Orlando. Thus this work has been received most enthusiastically by academic critics, whose intellectual pleasure in unraveling tight constructions may distort the total effect of this slim volume. The effect, for me at least, is not unlike that of "Il conte di Montecristo" (the last story in *Ti con zero*). In that retelling Calvino had emphasized the efforts of Edmond Dantès and of the Abbé Faria to escape from the Castle of If, relating them emblematically to the manner in which Dumas *père* and his assistants had put the novel together. Perhaps because the subject is the blocked liberation from an impregnable fortress, from an oppressive concentration-camplike environment, the proliferation of hypothetically possible but actually impossible escape routes and the repeated production and elimination of alternative developments in Dumas's compositional strategy are not accompanied by the usual ebullience, the youthful, life-affirming joyfulness we are accustomed to find in Calvino's coming to grips with diversity and open-endedness.

No such impediment to full enjoyment exists in *Le città invisibili* and in *Se una notte d'inverno un viaggiatore* (1979; *If on a Winter's Night a Traveler,* 1981). In the first work the brilliant writing and the optimistic "message" redeem the burden of an intellectual structure which plays with variations on the organizing themes modestly announced in the chapter headings. These imaginary Eastern cities, suggested by that mercantile version of *A Thousand and One Nights,* Marco Polo's *Il Milione,* have released an unsuspected richness of incantatory words, and the moral lesson—that one must learn to live in the midst of evil by recognizing the little that is not evil and making room for it to flourish—is sufficiently understated to appeal to a generation of readers suspicious of high-sounding promises and radical panaceas. In the second work, *Se una notte d'inverno un viaggiatore,* frame story and framed stories are finally, triumphantly integrated. The frame story is about nothing less than "ce vice impuni, la lecture," and in the early chapters we get an almost complete phenomenology of the book as artifact and text such as only someone who has been personally involved with all aspects of book production could so effortlessly provide. The framed stories are actually only beginnings of stories, interrupted novels, tantalizing way stations on the road that leads the Reader and that other reader, Ludmilla his beloved, to the large double bed where each is last seen reading his/her book. And thus, we may presume, they lived happily ever after.

■ ■ ■

It might be asked in conclusion: What are the chances of survival for an oeuvre so embedded in contemporaneity, so consequent in its denial of the weight and conditioning of the past, so successful in achieving freshness and novelty for its every new component? Calvino was admired from the start, and he now has a public that circles the globe. At the very time when the printed word is on so many sides beleaguered by other media, he has conquered the readers that count by taking them into his confidence, by showing them not the world, but the world of the writer. May the critic, that other kind of reader, that subversive spoilsport, deal lighthandedly with that world, guarding it against destruction.

Olga Ragusa, Spring 1983

1 Constance Markey, "Italo Calvino: The Contemporary Fabulist" [interview], *Italian Quarterly*, Spring 1982, p. 84.

2 Italo Calvino, "Dialogo di due scrittori in crisi," 1961; reprinted in *Una pietra sopra*, 1980, p. 64. All Italian originals of Calvino's books cited here were published by Einaudi in Turin unless otherwise noted. All translations are my own.

3 For example, the preface of *I nostri antenati* (1960) or the introductory note to *Gli amori difficili* (1970).

4 See the note published together with the first four "cosmicomics" in *Il caffè politico e letterario* (1964).

5 E.g., "Appunti sulla narrativa come processo combinatorio" (1968; translated as "Notes Towards a Definition of Narrative Form as a Combinative Process," *Twentieth Century Studies*, May 1970) in its relation to the major works after *Ti con zero* (1967).

6 The quoted words come from Cesare Pavese's 1947 review of *Il sentiero dei nidi ragno*, reprinted in his *La letteratura italiana e altri saggi*, Turin, Einaudi, 1951.

7 Calvino, "Dialogo di due scrittori in crisi," p. 67.

8 Calvino, *I nostri antenati*, p. ix.

9 Some exceptions are a school anthology, *La lettura*, edited by Calvino in collaboration with G. B. Salinari (Bologna, Zanichelli, 1969); the first edition of *Il castello dei destini incrociati* (1973), which functioned as an introduction and commentary for *Tarocchi: Il mazzo visconteo di Bergamo e New York* (Parma, Ricci, 1969); and introductions to books by Elio Vittorini (1967), Serafino Amabile Guastella (1969), G. Bonaviri (1971), F. Lanza (1971) and G. Basile (1974). The most recent instance is his edition of *Le più belle pagine di Tommaso Landolfi*, Milan, Rizzoli, 1983.

10 Klee has been used for *Il sentiero dei nidi di ragno* and *I racconti* (1958), for instance; Steinberg for *L'entrata in guerra* (1954) and *Una pietra sopra*; M. C. Escher for *Le cosmicomiche*. One exception was *Il cavaliere inesistente* (1959), which had a detail from Paolo Uccello on the cover.

11 In the biographical sketch which forms the introductory note to *Gli amori difficili*, Calvino recalls that *Il sentiero dei nidi di ragno* had been written in 1946 to compete for a prize offered by Mondadori for an unpublished novel by a "new" writer. The judges, Giansiro Ferrata and Vittorini, preferred the work of others (Milena Milani, Oreste Del Buono, Luigi Santucci), thus preparing the way for Calvino's joining the Einaudi roster of authors. A comparison of the four writers' careers suggested by this crossing of paths would make an interesting study in connection with the different identities of Italian publishers.

12 There are contrasting views of the reception of Calvino's change in direction. Whereas J. R. Woodhouse defended the trilogy against a "bizarre variety of reactions" (*Italo Calvino: A Reappraisal and an Appreciation of the Trilogy*, University of Hull, 1968), Calvino himself wrote in the introduction to *Gli amori difficili*: "Among the critics there was an unexpected consensus of favorable opinions."

13 Calvino, *Il sentiero dei nidi di ragno*, 1964 ed., p. 8.

14 See, for instance, Calvino's "Natura e storia nel romanzo" and "Tre correnti del romanzo italiano d'oggi," reprinted in *Una pietra sopra*.

15 Calvino, *I nostri antenati*, p. xviii.

16 Calvino, *Ti con zero*, p. 44.

17 Calvino's father was an agronomist, his mother a botanist; he himself started out studying agriculture at the university. Specifically on the reception of *Le cosmicomiche* and *Ti con zero* see *Una pietra sopra*, pp. 187–88.

18 Calvino was to have a hand in the later reissue of the German and French tales: he made a selection from the Grimm volume and presented it in J. and W. Grimm, *Fiabe* (1970), and he wrote an introduction to C. Perrault, *I racconti di Mamma Oca seguito de Le Fate alla moda di Madame d'Aulnoy* (1974). He also wrote an essay for Ovid's *Metamorfosi*, published in 1979 as part of the "I Millenni" series, and he contributed a chapter, "La tradizione popolare nelle fiabe," to *Documenti*, volume five of the Einaudi *Storia d'Italia*.

19 Calvino, *Fiabe italiane*, 1971, p. xviii.

20 From Calvino's introduction to his edition of *Orlando furioso*, Turin, Einaudi, 1970, pp. xvii, xvi, xxiv, xxvi.

21 Calvino, *Il castello dei destini incrociati*, p. 128.

The Poetry of "Limited" Exile and Its Revealing Trek among Italy's Small Presses

■ END-OF-MILLENNIUM ACCOUNTS

To speak of Italian matters from the American shore amounts to translating them, and translation is like kissing a woman through a veil. From my "little" or "limited" exile in America, which to date has enveloped me for more than thirty-five years, living now on the prairie, now in the vast city, contact with my nominal "origins"—standard Italian and my native dialect—takes place by telephone and electronic mail, in addition to the occasional trip back and forth. My most advanced and proficient correspondents are already "on line"—but, I must stress, only the most advanced practitioners, and these are not many. However, it is my good fortune that these people are well able to inform and enlighten me about tendencies and perspectives in Italian poetry at the end of our century. Indeed, writer/critics who frequently visit us in the United States, such as Giuliano Manacorda, who teaches at "La Sapienza" University in Rome, and Luigi Reina, from the University of Salerno, often enlighten me with their passion and great expertise.

With the anthology *I limoni: La poesia in Italia nel 1995* (Lemons: Poetry in Italy in 1995; Marina di Minturno, Caramanica, 1996), a sort of yearbook of poetry for the year 1995, Manacorda feels the poetic pulse of that year's poetic output; and in the little anthology *Disordinate convivenze* (Messy Cohabitations; Naples, Glaux, 1996), with unequivocal zeal, he presents a mere six poets, whom he defines, in his own end-of-the-millennium stock-taking, as *confrontanei* (confrontationalists), facing off against one another as well as against us: Mariella Bettarini, Milo De Angelis, Rodolfo Di Biasio, Luigi Fontanella, Vito Riviello, and Antonio Spagnuolo. This is what he writes: "The time for taking stock is approaching for poetry as well: in four years the century and the millennium will come to a close, and it is inevitable and appropriate that one look back and try to understand what has been accomplished and consequently how the future is likely to proceed. A stereotypical enterprise, perhaps, but one which is nevertheless difficult to avoid, not in order to mark impossible leaps, but in order not to miss a unique opportunity which is not only full of promise, but surely not to be repeated for all those whose name appears in this anthology."

As for Reina, in a recent wide-ranging essay in the journal *Periferia,* instead of identifying "troublesome new offerings" (what Manacorda calls "impossible leaps") in the poetry being published at the end of the millennium by both large and small presses, he discovers a sort of "minimal" disposition on the part of new poets: a postmodern minimalism with regard to objects (persons, ideas, feelings, and things), in the sense that these poets "turn practically any project aimed at linguistic sublimity on its head and do not always do so ironically as others have done before and continue to do: they deny mysteric Orphism, turn their backs on oratory, refuse all intellectualist poses as they refuse the

elegiac, and devote themselves to the word with an uncommon endeavor to retrieve its semantic force."

However, before jumping to drastic conclusions, Reina prefers to establish (and reconsider) the historico-linguistic "periods" of this poetry, or at least of that poetry which "exits from the allotropic tunnel and enters the world of human beings." Keeping in his sights the anthropological matrix of dialects and dialect poetry, reinvented to exploit its bi/univocal valences, he pauses to consider Calzavara, Franco Loi, Andrea Zanzotto, Dante Maffia, Achille Serrao, and Giose Rimanelli. By degrees, then, he dusts off and reveals the course which poetry took in Italy in the seventies and eighties, and eventually in the nineties. He thus arrives at an assessment, which he links with poetry's renewed relations with history and with the established "old masters," a dialogue between "a Montale, a Bertolucci, a Luzi, a Caproni, a Pagliarani, a Zanzotto, a Pierro, a Raboni, and a veritable army of young and not so young poets." Among current poets are to be found those devoted to pure experimentalism, those who advocate "the poetic gesture, according to whom poetry must be the expression of 'mental gest-a(c)tion' and therefore sign-gesture more than sign-writing," and those dedicated variously to "nonsense," to interlinguism, or to the "recovery of the word"—for example, Sebastiano Vassalli, Franco Cavallo, Luciano Caruso, Andrea Genovese, and Angelo Jacomuzzi.

As for the poets who base lyric expression on the "subjective line," Reina does not skimp on names, feeling that he cannot leave anyone out. Included here are Sandro Boccardi, Carlo Frixone, Grytzko Mascioni, Albino Pierro, Geri Morra, Giuseppe Rosato, Giuseppe Selvaggi, Ruggero Jacobbi, Sebastiano Grasso, Dante Maffia, Paolo Ruffilli, Maria Luisa Spaziani, Luciano Erba, Biagia Marniti, Alda Merini, Raffaele Nigro, Silvio Ramat, Giusi Verbaro, and Lucio Zaniboni. At this point, desiring more information, and mostly to thank him for having remembered my "little exile," I call him on the phone.

"And the others, Gigi?" I ask him, "Where are all the others, the young and the not so young who, whether within or outside the artificially contrived poetic schools, continue to cultivate their own little gardens?"

"Just like you in your little American exile, Giose, the young and the not so young cultivate their small plots in solitude despite the indifference with which the major publishers regard them. And for the very few who have ended up with the better-known mass publishers, there are many others who grace the catalogues of smaller presses. I'm just reiterating what I wrote."

"Your essay reached me in fragments. May I record you on tape?"

"Sure, if you wish. Let me drop a few names: Valerio Magrelli, who plays with existential absurdities and tends to delyricize poetry by restricting it to static objects which he barely infuses with metaphorical meanings—take a look at his *Nature e venature* (Natures and Striations; 1987); Carlo Villa, with his proposal for a hyperrealistic and distortional poetry; Maurizio Cucchi, sustained by a neutral narrative tension which aims to give a positive spin to an anxiety which warps our cognitive faculties; Cesare Viviani, eager to appropriate the *lapsus* or slip, the possibility of semantic amplification, the surplus, even in post-dadaist or psychoanalytic behaviors; Milo De Angelis, who effects a regression to the primal scene, to the cheerful consciousness of childhood, a little like the less successful Elio Tavilla, who works on language with a surgeon's scalpel; Giuseppe Conte, who weds love and desire in his search for an original vital energy, arriving at results full of excessive, neobaroque tropes; Fabio Doplicher, whose apparent rationality does not prevent leaps into the surreal or deter his structural and linguistic regressions back to the Middle Ages; Achille Serrao, intent on finding all possible harmonies between content and language, often with a cold rationality, but always with a steadfast yet open disposition; Umberto Piersanti, refusing any appropriation of poetry of a mystical nature, yet eager to use it as a medium to gain a road to salvation; Paolo Ruffilli, who sets up a dialogue between past and present, nostalgia and pleasure, love and death, making use of a crude, transitive language. And mind you, Giose, many others should be mentioned, each engaged on a different front, from Rodolfo Di Biasio to Biagia Marniti and Cristina Rosati, from Corrado Calabrò to Lucio Zinna, from Silvio Ramat to Leonardo Mancino, from Ciro Vitiello to Lucio Zaniboni, from Enzo Fabiani to Paolo Gentili. . . ."

"Too many, it sounds like, Gigi. And I will soon die here on my Black Sea. . . . But could you tell me something?"

"As for you, Giose, I see you in the company of Pierro, Zanzotto, Loi, Glazavara, Baldini, Scataglini, Giacomini, Grisoni, Maffia, Mare, Serrao, Naldini, Rosato. . . ."

"I meant to say women, Gigi. . . . Women poets, in your end-of-the-century analysis and stock-taking: where do they fit?"

"It's clear, and I've written as much: the indisputable fact is that poetry, even Italian poetry, recognizes no distinctions of sex. Elsewhere I have alluded to Rosselli, to Spaziani, Marniti, Merini, Maleti, to Verbaro. They are only the tip of the iceberg that is still being pushed along by the promotional fervor which developed in the seventies. But the role of certain individual poets is undeniable: for instance, Mariella Bettarini, Laura di Nola, Biancamaria Frabotta, Nicla Farini, and Mariella Gramaglia."

"She doesn't remember, I'm sure—because time is blind and she was very young at the time—when I used to play the organ in one of the two twin churches in the Piazza del Popolo, in Rome, and she would occasionally come to listen along with our mutual friend, the poet Rocco Scotellaro."

I've been talking to Luigi Reina by phone for years, and when, on rare occasions, we happen to see each other, night and day no longer exist, because we feel great friendship and the profound pulse of poetry.

■ LOVE AND POLITICS

From the provinces, my friends—not counting the more fortunate ones who come to America for conferences and research, such as Manacorda and Reina—write me letters every once in a while, when they put their mind to it, but generally they do not, for a variety of reasons: a) they don't have the time, since for them twenty-four hours aren't enough in a day, which they have to stretch to the brink of exhaustion in their work projects and meetings; b) stamps cost too much, and the mail isn't reliable; c) it's best, therefore, to kill what little time remains in arguments and serious business at the bar or in the *piazza,* which is a perennial stage, especially when the topic of discussion is politics, as is usual, or the attributes of that lovely young woman strolling past the shop window just now, rather than to remain shut up in a room, even if glued to the TV. With the exception of poets, of course, who live their "little" exile precisely in such lonely rooms, as Gigi Reina has recalled.

As a boy, while living in that small town where I was born, I would sometimes take a volume of Ovid down from the shelf and read out loud to keep myself company: "*Hic ego, finitimis quamvis circumsoner armis, / tristia. . .*"—"And here, although a din of arms surrounds me, / I try to uplift as best I can, / by writing verses, my sad tale. / And if there be no one ready to turn an ear / to hear them, nevertheless in this manner / I pass my day and deceive time."[1] And if a friend came and asked, "What are you doing, Giose?" I would show him the book. And he: "You're really nuts! There's a band in the *piazza.* Aren't you coming?" I would shake my head. Even as a boy, I never liked following the band. I am now a man in slippers, retired from work, if not from writing or from arguing by phone or by e-mail with compatriots and friends, perhaps with no other end in mind than to make peace. Often, from my residence in St. Paul, Minnesota, I phone or write to them, sometimes even sending gifts, as Petrarch used to do with his friends.

Recently I've taken to telephoning and writing more frequently to these friends, far and near, with the intention of learning a little more about the present state of small presses in Italy, since, before it's too late, I would like to publish a few tons of the unpublished manuscripts which have remained in my desk drawers as a result of what I might call my personal ingratitude toward my own work. At times, however, my Italian friends believe me to be so far away from Italy (and here Ovid comes to mind again: "The land where I dwell lies where the world ends, a land far from my own"), so very far that, in addition to informing me about the poetical situation, they deem it appropriate to apprise me of the political situation as well, politics being (along with love) the great wellspring of passion.

The patriarch Adolfo Polisena, poet and musician, who together with Giovanni Cerri has composed the most beautiful songs in the dialect of Casacalenda, our little town in the Molise region, writes to me in this guise, as if I were living in some distant galaxy: "You ask me about poetry and music, eh? Fine: it's all so simple that it's difficult to explain. Have you heard that a black woman was chosen as Miss Italy? An immigrant, in a country which is famous mostly for having scattered millions of our own people throughout the world! And have you heard about the danger of secession which exists in Italy? Poetry, huh? A fanatical parliamentarian from the North is a ferocious foe of the South and all those who live here, and he intends to found a region or nation called Padania and make it independent. This very day, on the banks of the Po River with his followers, he will make the proclamation, but with an ill wind. He risks being jailed! His name is Umberto Bossi and he is a senator from Milan, apparently lacking in love of country."

It's true that, traveling through northern Italy nowadays, it's not unusual to read signs on apartment windows which say things like: We Do Not Rent to Southerners [Terroni][2]—something akin to what used to confront people of color in America, at least until the sixties. The poet Fontanella from New York wonders, "But shouldn't Bossi be considered an outlaw in Italy?"

Love and politics, as I've said, are powerful forces, and the poet Giuseppe Jovine, who has a vast knowledge of both, keeps me informed about them through long telephone conversations. "Small presses, did you say? You have published with the *major* publishing houses, and now from America you want to inquire about the *minor* ones?"

"I've also published with minor ones, together with you, remember?"

"Well then, you are probably aware that Sellerio Publishers of Palermo has attained a certain national prominence. Going back to 1978, they could already boast of the collaboration they enjoyed with Leonardo Sciascia, and recently they published a book that has been quite a sensation: Michele Perreira's *Delirium cordis*. 'Delirium cordis' is what the ancients called fibrillation of the heart, and the author of this investigation into the chaos of a world in fibrillation sets his book in a southern city—Palermo, to be exact, symbol of the contradictions inherent in a society lacerated by questionable links between the Mafia and the government."

"But wasn't that very same topic, at least in its political dimensions, addressed by a leader of the Communist Party?"

"Emanuele Macaluso, of course, in *Giulio Andreotti tra Stato e Mafia* (Giulio Andreotti Between the State and the Mafia), published by Rubattino of Soveria Mannelli, in the province of Cosenza. The strange laissez-faire relationship existing between the Mafia and the Italian government was confirmed by Andreotti himself in a television interview with Giuliano Ferrara, which was ignored by the press. The problematic issue of the widespread practice of political patronage, which in its more extreme manifestations has much in common with Mafia-style behavior, is taken up by Maria C. Pitrone in *Il clientelismo tra teoria e ricerca* ([Political] Patronage Between Theory and Research), published by Bonanno Publishers of Acireale: the problem of patronage is viewed as an illegitimate form of political mediation, a type of behavior related to cultural codes derived from the behavior of families and clans and presented with impressive analytic rigor."

"Hasn't a book by Romano Prodi also just emerged out of this political quagmire?"

"Certainly! Let me tell you that among the twenty-five best-selling books from small publishers is Prodi's *Governare l'Italia: Manifesto per il cambiamento* (Governing Italy: A Manifesto for Change), published by Donzelli in Rome. As you surely know, in the field of economic research, Prodi was trained at the London School of Economics and at Stanford University in California, in the circle of those economists who pay particular attention to small and midsize businesses. As a result, Prodi, in his management of the government's power, tends to favor small and midsize businesses by supporting the free market and opposing monopolies, all within the framework of an antirestorational economic policy which ends up harming the less well-to-do classes. This topic is addressed at length by Massimo Nardi and Aldo De Jaco, president of the National Union of Writers, in their book *In viaggio con Prodi* (Traveling with Prodi), published by Monteleone (Vibo Valentia, 1996). They put into sharp focus the problem with Prodi's plan for renewal, on the basis of the mutual interests of the working class and the entrepreneurs, in addition to considering it in terms of a fiscally driven cooperativism, with organizational models, structures, and salaries identical to those found in noncooperative businesses."

"Those of us in America," I interject, "were deeply moved by the recent loss of Paolo Volponi. And, in his honor, let me ask you this question: what has happened these days to the relationship between industry and literature?"

"It's still the same old problem confronted by Volponi years ago, and now taken up by him again (posthumously) and dissected in *Scritti dal margine* (Writings from the Margin), issued by Manni Publishers from Lecce. The conditions of Italian industry are associated with the social crisis facing the Italian nation and with the crisis in the relationship between man and nature, brought about by commercial capitalism. I should also point out that in the field of literary production over the last few years the publishing houses which have distinguished themselves are Lacaita in Manduria, Empiria in Rome, Bastogi in Foggia, and Avagliano in Cava dei Tirreni, which has just published, in November 1996. . . ."

"Yes, I know, though I haven't seen it yet. . . ."

". . . your last novel to appear while you were still living in Italy, *Una posizione sociale* (Eng. *A Social Position;* 1959), reedited and introduced by Sebastiano Martelli and graced with a new title, *La stanza grande* (The Great Room). But I wanted to give you news of our mutual friend, Mario Lunetta, whose most recent book of poetry has come out with the publisher Lacaita, of Manduria, with the title *La presa di Palermo* (The Taking of Palermo); this is a work which reaffirms—I'm not sure with how much conviction—the new trend in Italian writing, the so-called 'Third Avant-garde Wave.' Lunetta, as you know, has proclaimed himself a 'heterodox avantgardist,' and Giuliano Gramigna, in his introduction to the volume, defines his position this way: 'In opposition to the comforting canon of poetry that pronounces the truth, this book lies; it obscures, under the apparent limitlessness of speech, the impossibility of speaking. But it does so by playing openly with a stacked deck.'"

As an expert linguist, Lunetta writes "political" poetry with sardonic cadences. His "anti-Western" polemics derive from the need to restore a human face to those societies which have been corrupted by consumerism, to revitalize an asphyxiated cultural landscape, and to put forth an influential literature of high quality, of the type hypothesized in the twenties by Walter Benjamin, based on "allegorical realism" and antithetical to the traditional symbolism of Orphic, hermetic, lyrical, consoling, and contemplative poetry. And so Rome, the center of all politics, inevitably becomes in Lunetta's poetry the symbol of modern decadence: "Rome is a livid Medusa / it's a wrinkled peach, a legging, a / dishpan, a casserole / deep fryer / with the climate and the people it deserves." It's the same Rome which is taken to task in *Saldi di fine stagione* (End-of-Season Sales), published by the Roman firm of Fermenti: "Once upon a time there was Rome / now it has no more lifeblood. / It used to be an Oriental sofa, a golden planet, a moon, / but now it's a great blotch of rags and murky plastic." It's the negative Rome of Maurizio Ferrara, "gorged with the vices and the infamies / of the well-to-do"; it's "the ugly old Rome with a sick body" of Antonello Trombadori; it's the Middle Eastern Rome of Giulio Carlo Argan, closer to Tehran than to Paris; and it's still the Rome of this man who is writing today from his "little" American exile, as described in the literary chronicles contained in his book *Il mestiere del furbo* (The Sneak's Craft; Milan, Sugar, 1959), an environment spoiled by an undergrowth of would-be writers anxiously scrambling for a measly scrap of fame at any cost, the Rome which is still torn today between the mirage of liberalization, à la Sir Karl Raimund Popper, and the vision of socialism's ghost still haunting the sacred texts of Marxism.

Directly opposed to Lunetta's "rationalistic materialism" is the work of Elio Pecora, author of *Interludio* (Interlude), published by Empiria in Rome. He too is opposed to a consumeristic society, but with an elegiac tone of recovered serenity and (perhaps) resignation: "Paradise is here / where we are made to live / and it's dear and dreadful." In this same "elegiac" and dramatic atmosphere characteristic of Pecora dwells the very melodious Elena Clementelli, whose *Vasi a Samo* (Vases to Samo) was issued by Bastogi in Foggia. She exclaims: "How can we accept Monte Mario? / We have been to Los Angeles / the total dimension of our American dream / lived by us without hope / on the domestic borders / of a seasonal Mediterranean."

But naturally, there is also a Rome in these authors which reflects the development of a new secular consciousness within a proletariat that wants to combine all available social and political forces in its struggle to thwart the direction imposed by a new, rich, "sordidly mercantile" bourgeoisie which is backed by political forces evoking that constant, intimidating alternative: "Either money and Christ, or the proletariat."

■ EPISTLES

Alongside the category "Love and Politics" I should now add the rubric "Love and Skirmishes." With this resolve in mind, but with a certain tact, I decide to call Nicola Iacobacci of Toro, in the Molise region, a man with a poetic vein which is thoughtful and radiant, gentle and experienced, full of faraway echoes of green, enchanted springtimes, full of life. He is the author of various books of poetry, among them *La parabola del volo* (The Parabola/Parable of Flight; 1992), as well as novels and radio dramas, including *Hàmichel* (1995), a story about a mouse and a boy, and *Monologo a quattro voci* (Monologue in Four Voices; 1996), published by one of my two Molisan houses, Cosmo Marinelli of Isernia. *Monologo* is a work which the critic Giorgio Barberi Squarotti describes as "the ordeal of the death and resurrection of writing, as it passes through that orality which was literature's primitive and original mode of being."

I called Iacobacci as my lips were pronouncing these verses of his: "Leave me at least the light of the Moon / and your shadow, faint, on the grass / fragrant of anemones and violets, / the voice of the wind / at the white springs of life." I asked him, "What are you doing, Nicola?" And he answered with the voice of exile, albeit very different from that of Ovid: "You know, I live, as poets live, silent and dreamy, content with my daily work at the service of poetry. My work compensates for all the bitterness, especially that of seeing 'parati a festa i buoni a nulla' (the good-for-nothing all adorned for celebration). I'm invoking Shakespeare. And there's nothing else I want to add from that sonnet."

"Which of the 154, Nicola?" A futile question. Besides, at this point, the line went dead. But I soon realized, as he himself doubtless did, that he must be referring to the opening lines of Sonet 66, one of the forty selected and so admirably translated by Giuseppe Ungaretti: "Tir'd with all these, for restful death I cry / As to behold desert a beggar born, / As needy nothing trimm'd in jollity, / And purest faith unhappily forsworn, / And gilded honour shamefully misplac'd."

Soon after, I called Giuseppe Jovine again, our "Peppe," my fraternal colleague who also writes poetry in our regional vernacular—he in the dialect of Castelmauro, and I in that of Casacalenda—an eloquent and learned man, especially when he is indulging in his predilections of a Catullan ilk, but always as sharp and penetrating as a scalpel; a mocker, an inveterate satirist, like all those who have been illuminated by a revelation of the nature of time, of the seasons, of the *brevitas* of all things in life and of their fateful recurrence. But he is also one of those who are blessed with the wisdom of metaphorical imagination, which is the key to understanding the thought of Vico, for whom the use of metaphors is the crux of the creative force in human imagination. Thus, Peppe murmurs on the page: "La vita sempe za rennova. / E' murte tata / e iè pens'a la giacchetta nova / che mmeia mette mò he vvè l'estate." In the translation of Luigi Bonaffini, another Molisan who has chosen America for his own "little" exile, these lines read: "Life always renews itself. / My father has died / and I'm thinking of the new jacket / I'll wear when summer comes." On the page, this magical page, Peppe carries on a dialogue with words which are tacitly explicit even in translation, words like those of a Sgruttendio, of a Basile or a Cortese, of the most noble dialect tradition. Let's listen to him:

> While hoeing, Zeppicoca inched shoulder to shoulder with Concettina.
>
> "It's cold, Concetti!"
>
> "Hoe and you'll get warm," answered Concettina.
>
> "I was just saying, Concetti . . . I know that you get warm hoeing . . . It's this work that's God's punishment."
>
> "For a lazy hoer lifting the hoe is always a real pain."
>
> "Concetti. . . Those who hoe drink water, those who don't drink wine."
>
> "Don't hoe, then. . . Sing and you'll get over it."
>
> "Should we sing? Let's sing then, Concetti."

I called Jovine for the twentieth time, with the usual question: "What are you doing?" And he, as if to cover up a voice even sadder than that of Ovid in his exile on the Black Sea, answered half sarcastically: "I'm going through a period of crisis because of excessive 'Augustinian wantonness.' I'm afflicted by a rash (urticaria) due to exegetic indigestion. I shall explain by epistle." And so it arrived, full of news—naturally—about poetry. "Bro', I always read you with great pleasure. That little book of yours with the cover by the painter Fratianni and with the little poem which you dedicated to me was shown to me by Achille Serrao, who, together with Franco Loi, the Lombard dialect poet, will go with me to Frosolone on August 4 for an evening of poetry. On July 27 I'll be in Guardialfiera, where Virginia Manuzio and Pietro Corsi will discuss your book, *I rascenije* [The Reasonings]."

Since dear Peppe lists collecting exotic "beauties" among his hobbies, I feel it my duty to send him postcards for "amateurs" from time to time. He mentions these in his postscript: "I've finally framed your naked California girls, who are now parading under the picture of the Madonna at the head of the bed which used to belong to my parents, and where I love to sleep. Franca, my wife, who was here for a few days, was shocked and took down those beautiful lasses, but I put them back in their place, under the Madonna, at the head of the bed, as soon as she went back to Rome."

And—speak of the devil!—at this point I receive a letter which fills me with a secret joy and makes my eyes glisten in this "little" exile of mine. It is dated "Milan, October 1996" and resounds with the deep voice of Franco Loi, high priest of neodialect poetry as Foscolo was of neoclassical poetry, whom the philological scholar and historian Pier Vincenzo Mengaldo defines as "the most powerful poetic personality of recent years." In Loi's poetry, according to the analysis of Franco Brevini, "communism and religion, libertarian impulses and evangelical propheticism, anarchic anxiety and utopian visionariness all overlap."[3]

"Dear Giose, even if that 'dear' is both too much and not enough. I still remember the Rimanelli of the 40s and 50s, the period of Unità (Unity) and Tiro al piccione (Eng. The Day of the Lion).[4] And it's a pleasure to notice that the threads of life are never cut completely loose and that there is a secret web which binds places and people, considering that, through a dear friend such as Achille [Serrao], we have now found each other again. It makes me very happy that Achille has been translated, and I hope that he will have good luck there. He is one of the few poets of real quality, and, as Stendhal used to say of 'dialect' Italians, 'he is also someone one is pleased to know in person.' It's also interesting to recall the distinction Stendhal makes between the arrogance of the poets who write in standard Italian and the modesty and quality of dialect poets such as Carlo Porta.[5]

"Apparently the poets who write in their regional languages are closer to prose and more respectful of the unknown which each person must face. There should not be, or, better yet, we should not cultivate bitterness. Love satisfies itself, if it is real love. Of course, it would be well if the gift of love were reciprocated. But we know that among men blindness and deafness are more widespread than concern, and that those who govern are generally more prone to violence than to poetry. Besides, ours is a decadent era: banks have taken the place of steeples and bell towers, and even of civic towers, and culture is out, with no social core. Maybe it's dead. Even Sartre, who was rather nearsighted, had foreseen that 'the culture of cemeteries serves to embellish violence.' The quotation marks aren't his, but they do convey one of his ideas.

"I'm anxiously expecting your three books. I was with Achille in Frosolone. We also met up with Jovine,

who was the organizer of a poetry reading in the piazza. It was a good evening. And so, for the first time, I set foot in his territory. I had read Le terre del sacramento [The Lands of the Sacrament], and yet Molise seemed even more rugged. And Frosolone, it turns out, is the home of knives. There was in fact a knife festival taking place. Therefore I can appreciate the harshness of his poetry even more now. A fond embrace. Franco."[6]

■ AN ITINERANT VOCATION

The Italian province has always put on airs to show the foreigner that it is not at all deprived of "news of the world," that it is "in the know" about the goings-on in the big city, and that it is proud of having preserved its "andirons," symbols of the hearth and the family, as well as good manners and civility and "culture." But this last element, "culture," was of the portable variety during my childhood in Molise, carried around with the comedies of Plautus and Goldoni, Shakespeare and Molière, on what was called the "Thespian Cart," with farmer-actors who often dressed up as satyrs and rural deities. Some were also puppeteers of the Podrecca school for handling marionettes, or storytellers who recited the feats of the knights, especially those of Ariosto's heroes Rinaldo and Orlando. They arrived in the town square and exhorted the crowd with a parlance that seemed a kind of folksy Latin: "Signuri, bbóna gènte / pónéte córe et mènte / alle sànte paróle" (Sirs, good people / lend your hearts and minds / to the sacred words). The intonation was the important thing. And they would come up with bewildering statements, usually incomprehensible, always at the outset of their poetic presentation: "And remember, ladies and gentlemen, that man is wolf to man: homo homini lupus"; or "Poetry is poetry when it is poetry, as in Dante, for example, who states: 'Amor con altro amor si paga. . .One pays for love with more love.' No, sorry! 'Amor ch'a nullo amato amar perdona. . . Love who forgives no loved one for loving.' Et cetera. Love is everything, ladies and gentlemen . . . because it is poetry and is made of poetry. As is music, for that matter. You all know how that French poet puts it: 'De la musique avant tout chose . . . Music above all.' Yet only the Latins knew precisely what love is. Amor vincit omnia . . . Love conquers all. Et cetera."

Back then the pipers, dressed as shepherds, would come along the old sheep trails, with their bagpipes, the snow of Christmas, and the music of "Tu scendi dalle stelle, o mio Signore" (You come down from the stars, o my Lord), which immediately brought to mind the generosity of the three Magi. This tradition still persists, but in today's absence of shepherds and with the old sheep trails covered over, a new generation of revelers has transformed it into a cosmopolitan, MTV-style celebration, with songs of the swing/rock variety and people dancing to them in the *piazze,* regardless of the cold. The master of this phenomenon of the "new bagpipers" is the clarinetist and composer Giovanni Borraro (leader of the quartet called Wafer), who majored in literature at the University of Salerno and graduated in 1993 with a thesis on "The Roots of Restlessness in the Narrative of the Early Rimanelli," a fact which led to our meeting and which allowed me (since jazz is my passion) to discern how much expertise and talent there is in his wide-ranging and eclectic playing, which presents/re-presents, both to those who are aware of it and to those who aren't, the clarinet of Sydney Bechet and Johnny Dodds, of Barney Bigard and Benny Goodman, of Artie Shaw and Tony Scott.

The festivities of Carnival and its masquerades which go back to antiquity, made famous in Renaissance Florence by the Carnival songs penned by Lorenzo the Magnificent, are still alive and flourishing today in the so-called "little" exile of the Italian provinces, where both greater and lesser poets abound (see the surprising anthology compiled by Vittoriano Esposito, *L'altro Novecento nella poesia italiana* [The Other Twentieth Century in Italian Poetry; Foggia, Bastogi, 1995]). It is there, along with and because of the presence of these many poets, that the so-called small presses are proliferating. In fact, it would be better to call them "special" presses, like those artisans who make precious pieces of furniture to order, in the sense that they have no set prices, no established book market, in many cases not even a catalogue. Nevertheless, today they constitute the "historical" mainstay of poetry, especially dialect poetry, where sensitivity and vitality are most likely to be found.

We of the Molise region proudly identify this vitality with people in general, the populace, figuratively linking it with a botanical metaphor rather than a literary one: the poplar, which in Latin is in fact called *populus.* "Alba populus," Horace hails the white poplar. Whenever the first son is born in one of the houses in our countryside, the head of the family plants a poplar. There are various types of poplars: the black poplar, which is the most common and has a very tall trunk, pale bark, straight branches which form a pyramid shape at the top, seeds wrapped in cottony flakes, and pale and light wood; the white poplar, commonly found in moist places, with a whitish trunk and leaves with dense white fibers; the quaking aspen, with its fluttering long-stemmed leaves. All of this suggests to us that poetry embodies strength, purity, and beauty, reaching for the sky like the trunk of that tall tree which stands out in the landscape, the poplar.

During one of my sabbaticals, in 1983, I returned to Molise to conduct research on a dialect—my own—on its way to extinction. Together with Benito Faraone, a famous singer and composer of the region, I covered hundreds of kilometers, on foot, on the backs of mules, by car, and on carts, to feel the pulse of the people, in taverns and on threshing floors, in towns and farmhouses, all the while composing ballads, madrigals, and tarantellas, a little like the troubadours of Provence before 1150—Marcabru, Jaufre Rudel, and Cercamon—or the minstrel-preachers and the converts such as Jacopone da Todi and Beato Colombini, and naturally the "Sicilians" Rinaldo d'Aquino, Guido delle Colonne, and Jacopo da Lentini. And so, reciting verses in the town squares, verses which I had composed feverishly, even when sleeping, verses of love, of sorrow, of travels, of binges, all with the aim of bringing poetry to the countryside, Faraone and I came up with the idea of reviving the techniques of the traveling salesmen and fortune-tellers of long ago. With the aid of a trained parrot, and for only a few lire, under the beneficent influence of the stars, they used to provide for the good gullible people a fortune printed out on a colored *cartellino* (small card), which was supposedly blind fortune but in fact always predicted good luck to come. With our *cartellino* we wanted to give them poetry for free. But we never did find the parrot.

I ended up writing over a hundred poems, short and long, in all possible meters, even monosyllabic songs, along with bi-and trisyllabic ones. They seemed like so much confetti sprinkled in the air, texts which were later gathered in a volume titled *Moliseide.* The first twelve poems, accompanied by a music cassette on which they are sung by Faraone, were published in October 1990 by Edizioni Enne of Campobasso, a firm run by Enzo Nocera, a pioneer of the small-press industry. The complete trilingual edition of Moliseide (dialect, standard Italian, and English) was published in 1992 as the first volume in the series "Studies in Southern Italian and Italian American Culture," issued by Peter Lang Publishing in New York. This series would soon distinguish itself with the publication of Dino Campana's *Canti orfici / Orphic Songs,* Giuseppe Jovine's *Lu Pavone / La sdrenga—The Peacock / The Scraper,* and Achille Serrao's *'A canniatura / The Crevice,* all masterfully translated into English by Luigi Bonaffini.

The people of Molise liked our poems, especially a ballad which I had written on 26 January 1985 from my "little" exile in Albany, New York. It was titled "Rè-pórtème nè càse" (Take Me Back Home), which I confess was inspired by Guido Cavalcanti's *ballatetta,* presumably written in 1300 while he was exiled from Florence, in Sarzana, whence he would return ill only to face a premature death, according to the testimony of Giovanni Villani (book 8, chapter 42). Here is a stanza of my ballad, in its English translation:

Take me home to Molise once again
down the narrow old country road.
I have drunk vinegar and champagne
with the good and the wicked of this world.
But time is not square, it isn't round:
it grabs you by the guts, it lays you out.
And now this life of mine looks for its home
to find a little rest. . . .

If I have lingered somewhat on this autobiographical anecdote, it is because the people there are still talking about it, so much so that those apparently extravagant minstrel shows of ours have spawned further research and studies, some recently published by Edizioni Enne, among them the *Vocabolario ragionato del dialetto di Casacalenda* (Dictionary of the Dialect of Casacalenda; 1991) by Antonio Vincelli, with an introduction by me; *Grammatica descrittiva del dialetto di Casacalenda* (Descriptive Grammar of the Dialect of Casacalenda; 1995) by the same author, introduced by Ugo Vignuzzi; and *Lessico del dialetto di Ripalimosani* (Lexicon of the Dialect of Ripalimosani; 1996) by Michele Minadeo. Because of the reborn euphoria for itinerant artists in Italy, and in order to make the pleasure of reading available to the public at low cost, the Commission for Educational Policies, along with the Italian Booksellers Association and the Italian Association of Publishers, has sponsored meetings between students and writers, as well as seminars for parents and teachers, under the tutelage of a board of directors headed by the dialectologist Tullio De Mauro.

The most striking fact which I have discovered from my persistent stalking of Italian people by phone and the occasional letters which they, in their goodness, send to me, is what the singer/composer Faraone has reported: namely, the return of the Thespian Cart of poetry, with Faraone himself riding in it, as it follows in our own footsteps of a decade ago and winds its way through the towns of Molise—Busso, Pietracatella, Castelmauro, Larino, Petrella Tifernina. With him rides the actor Pierluigi Giorgio, the head organizer, who in the town squares recites and performs Gibran, Pessoa, Hesse, Walcott, Castaneda, Justin Vitiello (a personal friend of ours at Temple University), whose *Vazetti's Fish Cart,* translated into Italian by himself, has achieved great success in Italy. Wasn't it the eternal Rousseau who wrote somewhere: "Place a pole adorned with flowers in the middle of a town square. Gather the people around it, and you'll have a feast. Better yet, present the spectators themselves as the spectacle, turn them into the actors"?

"Dearest friend, finally!" Faraone writes from Campobasso on 26 August 1996. "After being sick for a long time, I can now assure you that I'm getting better from day to day. The right carotid artery remains blocked, but the left one is clear. As long as it stays clear, I can get by. I've started to play the guitar again and to sing our songs, partly at the urging of Pierluigi Giorgio, a Molisan who resides in Rome as you do in America. He has invited me to perform with him on a gypsy cart drawn by a horse. As you and I used to do, we stop in the squares of the towns and the people flock around us. At Castelmauro we met up with Peppe Jovine, who recited one of his poems in dialect. In each town it's a huge success, with all the local people involved. Pierluigi would like to know you, and here's his address. Write to him."

▪ THE SMALL PRESSES

Molise is Italy's second smallest region, after the Val d'Aosta. This is one of the reasons why I chose to start my review of publishing ventures there. Actually, all my "journeys" begin from there. Molise, furthermore, because of its location in a central/southern pocket of the Apennines, provides me with a vantage point from which to explore the minor publishing sector, following the pattern of a swallow's erratic flight. The sector is flourishing today with more than 2,000 publishers, a phenomenon which first erupted in the late 1950s, in the beginning mostly as a reaction to and a demystification of the juggernaut of conformity and consumption which the major publishers had become in giving a semblance of legitimacy to products of scant cultural value. Eventually the small presses also developed as a response to the demand for diversity in communication and the need for writers and publishers to have a direct impact on their regional areas and these areas' problems, inevitably linked to those of the nation.

Considering that there were 2,705 publishers listed in the Italian census of September 1994, with a collective output estimated at 44,000 titles (with an average print run of 6,000 copies each), Molise might be considered the poor stepsister of the regions, akin to Perrault's Cinderella: only five publishers are active in the Molise region, producing less than 0.1 percent of the books published in Italy.[7] A number of factors might be responsible: 1) Molise's separation from Abruzzo and its subsequent autonomy, sanctioned only recently, on 27 December 1963, with Constitutional Law no. 3, left the new inexpert region to stand on its own feet, to decide its own political destiny and administer its sacred independence; 2) a serious shortage of adequate cultural institutions such as libraries (until now exclusively the patrimony of the "dons," the patricians of Bourbon/

liberal ancestry) and centers for cultural research and services, from which derives the need for the various Thespian Carts to undertake their cultural missions through the countryside; 3) and, as Sebastiano Martelli of the University of Salerno points out in his thorough presentation of the *Catalogo storico 1965–1995* (Historical Catalogue) of the Edizioni Enzo Nocera, "The university has been established in Molise for only a few years. It needs a long time to establish real and constructive roots in the territory. Because of the lack of bookstores and kiosks in many of the towns, and because Molise has one of the lowest rates of buying and reading books in southern Italy, it is certainly not easy to undertake a publishing project in the region, and it would be difficult to carry it forward for thirty years, if the person who had the idea and put it into practice did not possess a great passion and strong motivations." Giorgio Palmieri, director of the Central Library of the University of Molise, backs this assertion up with the following facts: "In his thirty years of activity, from June 1965 to June 1995, Enzo Nocera has produced 168 monographic publications—distributed among 38 series devoted to nonfiction, narrative fiction, poetry, theater—several important periodicals, and numerous pamphlets of graphic design, availing himself of hundreds of writers and collaborators."

In this portrait, expressions such as "great passion" and "strong motivations," applied to the publishing enterprise of Enzo Nocera in Molise, come to be emblematic of the sacrifices and the enthusiasm which characterize most or all of the small publishers in Italy, from the Alps to Sicily. They seem indeed no less than heroic in their commitment to elegance, refinement, and the constant search for new techniques, original graphic presentations, and new authors, especially young ones, who have a sacrosanct right to have their voices heard. I have a memory of Enzo Nocera, who does not drive, waiting for a bus along a dusty road in Molise, in order to reach some far-flung printer's shop or other in Rome or in Benevento or in Milan, where he could have his books printed, since he gets by with barely one or two apprentices to help him in his small two-or three-room office.

So, now it's clear to me how much small publishers, in one way or another, must make sacrifices and give of themselves. And yet they do their job honestly and enthusiastically, even in the face of very severe difficulties. Another testimonial reaches me from the estimable Guido Leotta, poet and publisher at Mobydick Editions in Faenza (province of Ravenna), whose select and rich catalogue, full of excellent names (including Serrao, Marcello Marciani, Tolmino Baldassari, and the Flemish writer Leonard Nolens), also includes my

name, with *I rascenije* (The Reasonings), perhaps the hundredth title! He writes me: "Dearest friend, first of all, please excuse my 'parliamentary' delay, but—believe me—it's not to make myself seem important. It's just that there are only three of us in this small publishing house, and we do the work for six for the collective salary of one. . .and at times we come close to being crushed by the overwhelming number of commitments, emergencies, disputes. . .a whole bunch of things, in other words, which furthermore often have very little to do with literature and the pleasant art of friendly correspondence."

Guido Leotta—who in a mysterious way reminds me of what Guido Compagni had to say of Guido Cavalcanti before his exile: "courteous and bold, and devoted to his studies"—owns among other things a prized goose quill, with which he writes his messages (they echo those of many other managers of small presses: "The tragic, fundamental problem consists of our financial situation, which is by no means rosy") on distinguished yellow-tinted paper, on which a demanding logo stands out: Il Mestiere Di Scrivere (The Labor of Writing).

Pleasure and labor, mostly the latter, radiate from the eyes and the sparsely cropped beard, in the guise of a ruff, of Giovanni Tesio of Turin, author of a fundamental study of the dialect of Piedmont and the influence of dialect in its literature, and of a book on the poetry of "little" exiles, titled *La provincia inventata* (The Invented Province; 1983), which has cemented our friendship. His letter of 3 September 1996 from Turin absorbs me in its verve and wistful brio: "Dear Giose, I'll be hanged if your little book isn't right bonny! All in all, delightful and well stacked, like one of those sandwiches you get on Fifth Avenue (I remember one under the Empire State Building that was fabulous—a metropolitan fable). I never know where you are. You assume that I know where you are only because you know where I am. But I am not a rover, like that proverbial Jack who's always hitting the road; I'm just a damned stay-at-home stick-in-the-mud! But really though, all hypotyposis aside, I really like your book. Yup, Serrao's preface is good, and even my own insignificant little words not half bad! To hell with understatement, at least this once, right? They may be few, but they say it all."[8]

Before concluding with "a great oceanic hug," Tesio informs me that he has just completed a commentary on Primo Levi's book *Se questo è un uomo* (Eng. *If This Is a Man*), which has absorbed him (made him "thin," as Dante would say) the entire summer, finally leaving him feeling somewhat disjointed. To be precise, Giovanni says: "And now that summer has vamoosed, I feel more dazed than usual. But life must be lived because—as imperfect as it is—it's the *only* miracle which has been meted out to us. Amen."

Amen. In addition to his work at the Centro Studi Piemontesi / Ca dë Studi Piemontèis (Center for Piedmontese Studies), Tesio is the editor of the prestigious series "Incontri" (Encounters) for the non-trade editions of Boetti & Co., inspired by "the great love for writing and poetizing" of a barber from the city of Mondovì, Domenico Boetti, and his associate Remigio Bertolino, both of them Piedmontese vernacular poets. These editions, which began in 1984 with the trademark "lj babi cheucc" ("cooked toads" in Piedmontese dialect) and which were intended for local poets, have now achieved national distribution and significance with Tesio's series. Several of its prominent titles come to mind: among them, *I loghi de l'omo* by S. Zanotto (from the Veneto region), *Passagi* by Bianca Dorato (Piedmont), *La prete de Bbacucche* by F. Granatiero (Puglia), *Memoria* by Franco Loi (Lombardy), *Lamentu Cubbu* by S. Calì (Sicily), *Cecatella* by Achille Serrao (Campania), and *Umbri* by Stefano Marino (Calabria).

In conclusion, it must be admitted that small presses constitute an Italian miracle. In addition to the publishers already mentioned, the list also includes "El Bagatt" Publications of Bergamo, Editore Caramanica of Marina di Minturno, The Gazebo of Florence (with series devoted both to prose and to poetry), Demetra of Bussolengo in the Varese province, Girasole (the sunflower) of Catania, Lampo of Campobasso, the Tracce Cooperative of Pescara (which has published a precious edition of the *Epitalamio* [Nuptial Ode] by Fernando Pessoa), Editrice "Il Libro Italiano" of Ragusa (which has printed *I miei set* [My Sets] by the film-maker Alberto Lattuada), Casa "Congedo" of Galatina (province of Lecce), Editrice "Osanna" of Verona, Cosmo Marinelli of Isernia, and Sestante di Ripatransone of Ascoli Piceno (which has published an enchanting first work by the vigorous young poet Roberto Deidier, *Il passo del giorno* [The Pace of the Day], the Mondello Prize winner in 1995). A few verses from Deidier's volume could appropriately serve to close this "narrated" survey of small publishers in Italy today. They suggest what a heroic tapestry such publishers constitute, with a vision projected toward the future: "This is the landscape, a field / which becomes sand which becomes sea / and at our back a road once narrow / which reaches where the North is barely sensed."

■ **POSTSCRIPT: SUMMARY OF THE STATUS OF SMALL PRESSES**

Recent investigations among publishers regarding their operations, budgets, and editorial projects have led to

the following conclusions. 1) The element of financial risk (one of the hazards which makes an enterprise truly an enterprise) is missing in small presses, since in most cases it's the author who pays the costs of publishing, in whole or in part. A sample survey of ten publishers revealed that only three of them (El Bagatt, Boetti, and Caramanica) did not require a contribution to defray publishing costs. 2) Small presses do not operate on a set annual budget, since their publishing projects are so varied. Their annual publishing program depends on the demand for publications on the part of the writers. 3) They enjoy limited, not to say negligible, distribution in bookstores, even though a few publishers (e.g., Mobydick), at great sacrifice and partly offset by printing subventions, do make an effort to have their published books included in important national exhibitions, such as Il Salone del Libro di Torino (The Book Salon of Turin), La Rassegna del Tascabile (The Paperback Display) in Belgioioso, and Galassia Gutemberg (The Gutenberg Galaxy) in Naples. 4) In most cases the small presses contract to consign all (or almost all) copies printed to the author, since they don't have warehouses or other adequate space to store residual copies. 5) Small presses exist somewhat precariously at the margins of fiscal legality, meaning that (in order to avoid the clutches of a tax code which would not otherwise allow them to survive) they are often forced to adopt the ploy of publishing books as "supplements" to an already existing and authorized literary periodical (e.g., Gazebo).

■ **COMMENTARY**

Nevertheless, it is precisely to this myriad of "obscure" cultural brokers that we owe the *perseverance,* the very survival, of what is (often) our best literature in prose and in verse. Frequently the small presses (for example, Mobydick but also Gazebo, the latter of which makes it clear that one of its main, if not exclusive, functions is to provide literary advice) exercise a meaningful, effective, preselective function by ushering into the book market texts which end up becoming "revelations," whether for content or for style. It is small presses, as a matter of fact, that have been the mainstay of the recent creative blossoming of dialects, which otherwise would have had serious difficulty in finding an outlet through the so-called major and medium-size presses.

Giose Rimanelli, Spring 1997

---

[1] See the translations by Enzio Cetrangolo in *La lirica latina,* Florence, Sansoni, 1993, pp. 882–85; the lines are from 4:10, vv. 111–14.

[2] The disparaging term *terrone* is used in the North to refer to southern Italians. It derives from the word *terra* (land) and im-

plies that Southerners are uneducated, ignorant farmers who know nothing beyond the tilling of the soil. While there is no exact English equivalent, analogous terms might be *hick, sodbuster, hillbilly,* et cetera.

[3] See Franco Brevini, *Le parole perdute: Dialetti e poesia del nostro secolo,* Turin, Piccola Biblioteca Einaudi, 1990, p. 318: "The poetry of Franco Loi is based on the reaffirmation of the full linguistic dignity, if not actually the primacy, of dialect, an affirmation which the poet would also defend through a heated publicity campaign, gathering around himself all the forces of neodialect poetry. With Loi. . .dialect becomes the language of an autobiography which communicates the experience of subalternity and marginalization of an entire social class."

[4] Those were the years of "my" Milan, of friendships with journalists, writers, and poets such as Davide Lajolo, Marcello Venturi, Guido Lopez, Mario Schettini, and the three Elios: Vittorini, Pagliarani, Bartolini. *Tiro al piccione,* my first novel, although written several years earlier and read and accepted for publication by Francesco Jovine and Cesare Pavese for the Einaudi publishing house in Turin, came out with Mondadori of Milan in 1953, and the following year in English with Random House in New York, bearing the title *The Day of the Lion.* But today Loi makes my ears prick up. His letter of 12 February 1997 to me ends with statistics from which he, fine poet that he is, derives the lesson that nowadays life in Milan is not exactly serendipitous. "There's not much to be happy about," he quips, for the "real Milanese" have either fled the city or remain stewing in their discontent. It is precisely this widespread disgruntlement that, one suspects, Senator Bossi has channeled into disturbing political actions. Loi, a poet I love and respect, writes to me with perplexing undertones: "And by the way, if you remember Milan in the old days, you wouldn't recognize it now. This very morning I went to the Mediaset headquarters and they showed me the shocking results of their recent survey on Milan. It's a city in decay. And this is not only my intuition but a general feeling among the Milanese. Just imagine. They represent merely 20 percent of the city's population; and the number of people over 64 is double that of the youth and children under 14 *and* double that of the average in all Italian cities. In addition, 60 percent of Milan's population would rather live somewhere else, and one third of its inhabitants live in poverty. Plus there's another alarming statistic: one in every four Milanese remembers his or her dreams every night—and most of these are nightmares! So you see there's not much to be happy about. How can we still count on Italians' enormous creative and productive capacities if they no longer have children? Take the Milanese: their birth rate is lower than the national median—which itself indicates a negative population growth. But don't think for a minute that I'll surrender to all these negative developments. I'll get by fighting these damned statistics!"

[5] It does the mind and the heart good to see the names of Carlo Porta (1776–1821) and Stendhal (Henri Marie Beyle, 1783–1842) together. Stendhal lived in Milan from 1814 to 1820 and knew Porta, the major dialect poet of the time. Soon afterward, in Rome, he met Belli (1791–1863), the most important poet of the time writing in the Roman dialect. The allusion by Franco Loi is revealing in how it identifies the relationship between regional languages and standard Italian and the comparison between "the arrogance of the poets who write in standard Italian and the modesty and quality of the poets" who write in regional languages—all this through his allusion to Porta/Stendhal and to the fact that the dialect poets are "closer to prose and more respectful of the unknown which each person must face." For

many years, during my adolescent youth, I traveled with Stendhal's story of Julien Sorel in my knapsack. And one day, late in my years, I went to Grenoble to read the headstone with the epitaph "Arrigo Bayle, milanese" (Italian for "Henri Beyle, citizen of Milan"), as dictated by Stendhal.

[6] There are two authors named Jovine: Francesco (1902–50), my mentor, author of the novel *Le terre del sacramento* (The Lands of the Sacrament), a classic of Italian literature, which I had the honor of typing for him as he dictated it to me; and Giuseppe, his nephew, a poet of vigor and taste, among the best.

[7] Giuliano Vigini, "Rapporto 1994 sullo stato dell'editoria in Italia" (1994 Report on the State of Publishing in Italy), printed as a preface to the *Catalogo degli editori italiani 1995* (1995 Catalogue of Italian Publishers), issued by the Italian Association of Publishers, Milan, Editrice Bibliografica, 1994, pp. ix-xlviii.

[8] Tesio is referring to my verse collection *I rascenije* (Faenza, Mobydick, 1996), which contains a preface by Achille Serrao and an afterword by Tesio himself.

NETHERLANDS

Jacques Hamelink: A Man Armed with the Imagination

In contemporary Dutch fiction there is a current, central in its popularity, which is roughly similar to the main current in modern American fiction. This is likely to take the form of a story about a somewhat hapless and inadequate central figure who endures a series of harrowing experiences and survives them, largely passively, perhaps with a modest flourish of triumph. In recent Dutch fiction the much-discussed work of Willem Brakman (b. 1922) has especially exemplifed this tendency. But there are other voices in Dutch literature today, more idiosyncratic and perhaps therefore less fashionable. Such a particular voice, a voice expressing a special vision at the same time both private and cosmic, is that of Jacques Hamelink.

He was born in 1939 in a region known as Zeeland Flanders. This is an area south of the Scheldt River, geographically isolated from the rest of the Netherlands and having strong cultural and dialectal affinities with nearby parts of Belgium. The consciousness of being a native of a border region has a great importance for Hamelink's work, and his most effective fiction is set in such border regions, although Hamelink is not in any real sense a regional writer. But the exploration of borders of all kinds and the irrational ambiguities associated with them is a persistent theme in his work. Hamelink's accomplishment has been significant both in prose fiction and in poetry, and his output is fairly extensive. There have been eight volumes of prose, plus two volumes of essays, ten volumes of poetry and a play and several translations as well. In the space I have here

I will choose from the works that indicate in important ways the directions his writing has taken, in the fiction and in the poetry as well.

■ ■ ■

Hamelink began his career in prose as a writer of short stories, some of the most impressive being of ample length, although he has thus far published nothing that he calls a novel. The stories that drew considerable attention to what was seen as a remarkable literary debut are carefully crafted and intensely absorbing narratives which show that the writer, at the beginning of his career, had already mastered the techniques of realistic fiction.

His first collection, which appeared in 1964, is called *Het plantaardige bewind* (Vegetable Rule), and the story in it which drew most notice is "Brandoffer op Zondag" (Burnt Offering on Sunday), a brief and powerful tale of how a group of boys on a camping trip decide to immolate one of their number as a kind of human sacrifice. The ambience is the aftermath of confused and unfocused emotions swirling in the wake of World War II (it is set in 1951), and it expertly probes the almost irresistible irrational feelings that motivate the most grotesque and horrible acts men commit. A parallel story from the author's second collection, *Horror Vacui* (1966), is "Spaldarg," about a remarkably precocious boy who startles a rural village on the border into which he has recently moved, and his unexpected and catastrophic confrontation with his own father, a convicted bank robber. From these stories a pattern emerges, that of a boy whose accomplishments set him apart from his contemporaries (the victim in the first story is envied by the others for his precocious sexual feats) but also draw him into inevitable if unpredictable disaster.

These stories, extremely effectively done, are relatively realistic in their subject matter. Certain other stories in these early volumes, however, attest to a more imaginative and more private vision which was to become the author's main concern. The combination of strange and fanciful subject and realistic narrative technique makes them remarkably gripping. Perhaps the most effective is "Een schijndode maan" (An Apparently Dead Moon) in *Horror Vacui,* a disturbing narrative of the experiences of a boy (again) who is sent for reasons of health to a wild and desolate border region, where in a setting reminiscent of gothic fiction, but exactly and tangibly rendered, he meets a mysterious and fascinating girl somewhat older than himself. In the course of the story, after a mysterious moonlight trip through the desolate countryside, she is literally devoured by a dimly perceived vegetative presence. At the end the boy

inexplicably finds himself in the presence of the people he was supposed to visit and their grotesquely deformed daughter. Abruptly the story ends. A hallucination? A dream? We are not told, but the combination of precision of detail and overall ambiguity, in a strange and unsettling context, here and elsewhere in Hamelink's fiction places him in the tradition of Kafka.

Both kinds of story are present in the third collection, *De rudimentaire mens* (The Rudimentary Man; 1968), although here even the more realistic stories are set in lands that clearly exist more in the realm of the imagination. "De boom Goliath" (The Tree Goliath) is set in a hot, dry Mediterranean plain and is an intensely sensual depiction of the frustrated passion of a mature woman for the wild shepherd who becomes her daughter's lover. The enormous isolated tree that broods over these events with superb indifference is the focus of the story's energies. In sharp contrast is "Het wenken der vogels" (The Beckoning of the Birds), set in the frozen winter of a northern country in the grip of a violent revolution, a tale of slow and careful revenge in which the frozen natural world, where only flocks of birds move and whirl, counterpoints in its indifference the savagery of human passions which intersect in complex ways.

Quite different is "Een voorbode van de civilisatie" (A Precursor of Civilization), a fantastical tale in which an exponent of modern technology is confronted with lunatic religious obsession in a dying forest. The curious result includes flashes of wild comedy which will perhaps remind an American reader of certain episodes in Flannery O'Connor. This story too, realistically begun, moves in the direction of startling fantasy, and its protagonist is finally absorbed, again literally, into a surrealistic explosion of vegetative rebirth.

What absolutely distinguishes the early Hamelink from his contemporaries, in Holland and elsewhere, is his obsession with the energy of vegetation. Parallel to this, but developing somewhat later, is a fascination with the energy of stone: the third collection also contains a story, "De huidaandoening" (Skin Trouble), in which a man turns into a stone, not entirely to his own dissatisfaction. Again and again in this body of writing, we are made aware of the presence of a world of vegetative power, of vigorous plants whose growth follows directions that are not those of man. This power is manifested in its most remarkable form when individuals are literally absorbed into the unchecked growth of plants, an experience increasingly seen as a kind of apotheosis, a way of man's entering into the very substance of myth.

Both of these tendencies are manifested in what is perhaps Hamelink's most ambitious work so far, *Ranonkel* (Ranunculus; 1969), a long piece of fiction which is not called a novel but is subtitled "The History of a Self-ing (A Kind of Epic)." The word *verzelving,* here translated as "selfing," is in fact an untranslatable pun, based as it is on the ordinary word in Dutch for "change," *verandering,* literally "other-ing."[1] A *verzelving* (the word is Hamelink's coinage) substitutes the world *zelf* and is thus a process of intensification of the self. This remarkable book focuses not on individual consciousness, but on a mosaic of consciousnesses intersecting in one place, the unnamed city which is its locale, and which itself undergoes a series of bizarre transformations until it ends as something very much like, but not precisely the same as, what it was to begin with.

The story, told in a sparer and leaner language, begins realistically enough as the tale of a retired mailman, Evarist Schouwvagher, who is married to an enormous woman who hates plants, which he therefore must grow secretly in the attic. When she dies, and the plants are brought into the sunlight, one—a simple Ranunculus or buttercup—begins an irresistible growth that engulfs not only the house but eventually, in spite of several episodes of official intervention, the entire city. The process is most strenuously resisted by a Catholic pastor, who sees the growth as diabolic. What follows is a series of strange and incredible but curiously fascinating episodes. The vegetation turns into a kind of stone, and the pastor gains control of the chastened inhabitants, who had moved into the trees and given themselves over to a life of sensual abandon. The work ends with a grotesque and blasphemous (and at times quite funny) parody of the Crucifixion, witnessed by a group of bewildered but energetic visiting American businessmen who at first think they are watching a Passion play.

The book is a complex and variegated work. In it Hamelink places himself in the line of those visionary writers such as Blake who attempt to shape a private mythology to express immense patterns that perhaps are better apprehended as mythic forms rather than admitting of rational explanation. It is worth noting that the work is dedicated to the memory of the Flemish painter Hieronymus Bosch, who lived and worked not far from Hamelink's native region, and in whose visionary and partly inexplicable work strange vegetative and other organic forms are present. At one level the work suggests an allegory of the rise—and inevitability—of revealed religion, culminating in a crucifixion as horrible and irrational as the event recounted in the Gospels. One may think of the Kafka of "The Penal Colony," but Kafka's work is not so drenched in Catholicism as is Hamelink's.

The grotesque is the mode of the book's exploration of the religious impulse, and the reader is impressed by the work's uncompromising refusal to arrive at any solution which denies the conflicting evidence of obsessive human passions the book catalogues. A number of characters weave in and out of the action, including a certain number of inhabitants of the city who adapt their private concerns to the amazing variety of events. The pastor, the carpenter, the butcher's apprentice, the gravediggers—all pursue the vocations that identify them until at the end they have become archetypes. Evarist Schouwvagher, the mild and humble mailman who is the early protector of the plant, is transformed into a mythic figure, perhaps to be identified with the one-eyed sleeping being whom we last see clearly when the energy of the upthrusting stones begins the process that will lead to a usurpation of the vegetative by the mineral. He lives on in the book as the dimly remembered Ranonkel, whose second coming a dwindling group of believers awaits, apparently in vain. It is their leader who is crucified.

In this book, as in some of his poetry, Hamelink plays with the idea of God as vegetation, a supreme force that operates in the universe in particular through the growth of plants. Yet this energy is inexplicably superseded by the triumph of the mineral. The enormous Ranunculus is coated with a hardening substance that falls out of the sky (like bird droppings), while other stones thrust themselves out of the ground to reconstitute the medieval Gothic cathedral at the city's center. The triumph of the mineral is complete when the pastor has gained almost complete control of the populace, who flock into the cathedral for a bizarre sequence of religious observances which include the presence of animals, the mystic transformation of plants into defective humans, a bloody gladiatorial exercise and the presence of an enormous chamberpot. The city is finally compared to an enormous empty flowerpot in which nothing grows.

Yet the vegetable faith is kept alive, incarnated, first underground, then in the sunlight, in a small plant in the shape of a man and in a pregnant woman who does not give birth. But the stone cathedral, and the return it represents to something like the absurdity and cruelty of life as we ordinarily experience it, also are associated with a kind of life, a life like that we know. So at the end the vegetable faith seems to be crushed, the man-plant is trampled into the ground, the last keeper of the old faith is crucified, and the pregnant woman's child, born at the foot of the cross, is cruelly destroyed. And all that is left at the end is a dim memory that children muse on as they fall asleep at night.

One mark of the triumph of the enormous plant is that the men living in it cease to die. And after the mineral has reasserted itself, men in the city begin dying once more. A central problem that our author wrestles with is the place of man in a world whose natural forces never give a sign of being concerned with him as an individual, and the mineral is perhaps ultimately no more under men's control than the vegetable. But it is easier for him to adapt himself to the forms of a mineral world. It looks like our world in a way that the world of the plants does not. One could also read the work as an allegory of the death of nature in a universe where human concerns, for better or worse—on the whole more clearly for worse—reassert their dominance. And one wonders whether we are left with a feeling, which in this context would be a hope, that where there is any kind of living there will be plants and all they represent. It is perhaps a sign of Hamelink's profoundly contemporary pessimism that in this work he puts his faith not in man but in the vegetable realm.

Such a brief discussion does not do justice to a work as complex as this, and in particular there is a richness of incident that cannot be dealt with in summary. The way in which the work juxtaposes layers of detail suggests an overall meaning which transcends the significance of each separate incident. In the articulation of detail, as well as in his fascination with the grotesque, we sense a kinship between Hamelink and Flemish painting. Another "Flemish" quality of Hamelink's work is the strong sense of corporality, of bodiliness, which is one of the basic obsessions of Flemish culture. The fascination with and simultaneous revulsion toward the body is an attitude expressed in many Flemish writers of this century (Hugo Claus, for instance) and even in writers of Flemish background writing in other languages, such as Michel de Ghelderode. Yet Hamelink is a writer who has lived his life in Holland, not in Belgium, and therefore in a more tolerant and more pluralistic culture. A writer who has chosen to live in Amsterdam is one who is especially exposed to all the manifestations of current life, from advanced technology to the Rolling Stones. The "modern" Hamelink is one who is constantly exploring the relationship between the individual and his context. The individual is a modern man and therefore isolated, contemporary and therefore stripped of any certainties, but he is armed with the imagination.

I will conclude my investigation of Hamelink's prose with a work as remarkable as *Ranonkel,* although very different from it, *Afdalingen in de ingewanden* (Descent into the Intestines; 1974). This is a work of fiction but is not primarily narrative. It suggests Borges, but a Borges stripped down, one in which the meditative impulse has all but smothered the storytelling tendency. It is a collection of imaginary anecdotes, each anecdote being an external projection of a whim, a feeling, a state of mind. The work was published with a quotation from

a letter of the author to the publisher on the back cover, in which Hamelink describes the work as "in various respects, an anatomy lesson." After *Ranonkel* he found it impossible for a time to write anything but poetry. This later book then is a kind of radical self-inspection, the knife cutting into "one's own incurable flesh." This is the writer's most anguished book and most introspective, although it is in no ordinary sense autobiographical.

Stylistically too, it is quite unlike the author's earlier prose. It is softly focused, without color, often gentle and always bleak. Here the specificity of detail blurs into a less well-defined background, which is more elusive and more suggestive. But this is a vision that is never vague. It is in fact one of the marks of Hamelink's toughness as a writer that however painful the object of his vision, he never takes refuge in vagueness.

The work is composed of a number of varied sections. It begins with "Visioenen van de stad Glamorrhee" (Visions of the City of Glamorrhee), a "superficial" city made up entirely of an immense series of numbered parallel streets, each with its own characteristic abnormality. In "Bericht uit een vreemd land" (Report from a Strange Country) we read of such places as Hernomorre, where men dream of whatever it is they are about to acquire but where counterfeit dreamers are punished by being made to eat their own excrement. The Borogguls are beings repulsively ugly in life who become inexplicably beautiful for an instant at the moment of death; but the sight is to be avoided, for to see it is to make one doubt one's own existence. Especially disturbing is the section called "In de hersenfabrieken" (In the Brain Factories), which tells of a realm dedicated to the "radical domestication of Utopia."[2] Here dreaming, viewed as basically antisocial, is rooted out, even if the dreamer dies. If the treatment is successful, he loses his *ikgevoel,* his sense of himself. (The word is another of Hamelink's coinages.) All this culminates in the enormous machines on the "Wearisome Plain" which are fed with human beings.

More appealing are the Rancofiers, described in a section of that name. They are birdlike beings who seem to have less tangible physical existence than men. Their cheerfulness, not accessible to men, is perhaps related to the fact that they have less corporality. They don't sleep. Especially whimsical is their attitude to their own progeny. Untroubled by sexual impulses, they don't beget their children, but simply breathe them out: "The Rancofiers consider their children not as the continuation of something but as an imperfection of their condition."[3] And since they don't grow accustomed to their children, ultimately they forget them.

The book ends with Hamelink's bleakest and most pessimistic utterances, in the section significantly titled "Het andere ik" (The Other I). Even the earlier pictures of the man who chews on his limbs with the idea of swallowing himself entirely, or the man who while shaving cuts off his head on impulse, then after a while misses it but can never find his own head again and, since he is without one, is very poorly equipped to hunt for it—even these are cheerful compared to the psychological surgery that this consciousness performs on itself at the end of the book. We are told that this is the beginning of true autobiography, "that is, pure crystallography,"[4] and what follows is indeed lapidary, the expression of a first-person voice full of rage at the essential meaninglessness of things and at the kindred meaninglessness which is at the center of himself. Almost at the end of the book is a curious image, projecting both inward and outward, the image of the speaker picking up a hammer and methodically smashing the fingers of his left hand, joint by joint, not, he says, out of any masochistic impulse but out of sympathy with anyone whose value depends on his work within a system he does not understand.

One can see in this book, full of fleshy, deformed beings, of isolated organs that have taken up a lively, independent existence of their own, the horror of the body which is the pendant of the fascination for it I have noted elsewhere in the author's work. ("De boom Goliath" with its vigorous, sturdy, well-shaped bodies in the dry summer heat is the most effective expression of this fascination.) But one can also see the impulse as expressing the central problem of the individual, defined by his own consciousness, trapped not now amid indifferent energies of nature, but desperately alone in the even more indifferent realm of technology. It is a realm in which only by an act of painful, self-inflicted suffering—such as, one might say, by the writing of this book—can one express sympathy for another caught in the same intolerable situation.

■ ■ ■

Afdalingen in de ingewanden, written out of a repulsion toward ordinary prose, comes close in the denseness and allusiveness of its language to the quality of prose poetry, and in it the twin careers of the author as writer of prose and of poetry converge, subsequently to diverge again. Hamelink's poetry, which began to appear in book form at the same time as his fiction, has from the beginning impressed readers as having at any given point close affinities in its themes and language with the prose he was writing at the same time. Yet there are noteworthy differences as well.

In the poetry Hamelink frequently luxuriates in language in a way he does not allow himself in his prose. He uses a large vocabulary with relatively little repetition and frequently takes advantage of the plastic qualities of the Dutch language to combine familiar words so as to create new and unfamiliar ones. He avoids recent loanwords, of which Dutch is normally very tolerant. He almost always avoids rhyme but at times makes subtle and effective use of assonance. The result is a body of poetry that is dense and rarely easy to penetrate on first reading. With rereading, however, it unfolds, and the sharpness and precision of the images make an impression that lingers with the reader after reading. Like the prose, the poetry can at times be quite funny.

There is not space here to trace the development of Hamelink's career as a poet, but I shall merely note some of its more characteristic features. Although there has been the evolution that one might expect over the course of almost twenty years of steady poetic production, there is a consistency of voice not paralleled in the prose. In surveying Hamelink's work as a whole, one may possibly get the impression that it is the very singular and ever-present voice in the poetry that serves to hold together the vision of a world where man's place is problematic. The prose veers out of the security of that constant voice, taking soundings in directions oblique to the main thrust. The prose moves abruptly from stage to stage, whereas the poetry evolves.

From the first volume, *De eeuwige dag* (The Eternal Day), which appeared in 1964 as did the first volume of stories, the verbal exuberance makes itself felt. Hamelink's evolution as a poet has been in the direction of tighter and more laconic form, and the early poems at times may remind the English-speaking reader of Dylan Thomas in their freewheeling use of language as well as in the theme of a boy disporting himself in a rural countryside and by the sea. Already, however, there is a careful discipline controlling these effects. As in the prose, Hamelink is not overtly autobiographical, yet most of his poems are in the first person. While they rarely tell us about his life, they give us glimpses of his world. The speaker is often isolated in the earlier poems, although the first book contains a remarkable group of poems, "De zomer jij" (The Summer You), addressed to a woman, which are sexual and direct and almost entirely physical in their expression of energy. In the poetry, in fact, the body is less of a problem, since it serves to link man to the natural world: its impulses are his impulses. In his poetry as in his prose, Hamelink will only gradually move into the city.

The poetry does, however, generally express a bleak view as it chips bits of meaning out of the intractable meaninglessness of the universe. In the second volume, *Een koude onrust* (A Cold Restlessness; 1967), Hamelink is more concerned with man as such: *de mens* is more often the subject of the poetry. The poet moves away from the erotic and the countryside and in *Geest van spraak en tegenspraak* (Spirit of Speech and Contradiction; 1971) comes into modern urban life, resentful and prophetic. Some of these poems are amusing. "The Poetical Genius" (its title is in English) compares the past, when poets wore heroic moustaches, traveled by train disguised as seals and dragged along hatboxes belonging to titled ladies, with the present, where the poet, in the lotus position, teaches himself a new game of patience. In "Anno Diaboli" the poet finally "provisionally" turns into "a glass of jenever distilled from a consciousness as clear as glass."[5]

The shift from the energies of the plant world to that of stone also occurs in the poetry, although the "stone" poetry is more geological in its concerns and is at times taken up with the paradoxes implicit in fossils. Curiously too, we get a view of the universe seen as a whole in the poetry in a way we do not in the prose. This is paradoxical because Hamelink prefers shorter poems, in recent years sometimes very short, and because the surface texture is at first glance so opaque. Yet, uncompromising as the poetry is in refusing to accept false comforts (no one has ever written poetry that is less sentimental), the very fact of the poetry's coming into being becomes a consolation. A theme in recent volumes is that of the hidden or invisible wing. An example from a prose poem will demonstrate its unexpectedness: "Just as the great homesick animal the whale preserves in his fat the remnants of hind feet, so we have at our disposal a hidden wing."[6]

It has become fashionable in recent years for poetry, like current criticism, to become tinged with self-reflexiveness. This can lead to a thin and bloodless poetry, however useful it may be as a critical concept. Hamelink touches on the idea, but in his poetry the use of the theme never leads to a loss of energy. He can speak, for instance, of "the profound / slow bled to iron growth / of poetry,"[7] an image not inappropriate to his own. What gives strength to the self-awareness his poetry has come to manifest is a quality peculiar to a writer so aware of the resources of the imagination in the face of the world we must live in: "Poetry / is only an imaginary doorway / but one you must go through concretely."[8] Most recently Hamelink has published *Responsoria* (1980), his most autobiographical poetry to date, where he expresses his deep and complicated feelings at the death of his mother. The parents whom we see in these poems are laconic and uncommunicative rural people,

but the poetry hints that in the purposeful inarticulateness of his mother lies the root of her son's poetry.

You had nothing to offer me
except that whatever was worthwhile
was unutterable, and that is true
even of these given poems
which I have you to thank for.[9]

This has not been an attempt to summarize Hamelink's career, but rather to illuminate certain salient works which show his most individual and significant qualities. I have neglected recent prose, his essays and translations, and the remarkable "mystery play for voices," *De betoverde bruidsnacht* (The Enchanted Wedding Night; 1970), his most charming work. What I have tried to emphasize are the qualities which set him apart from his contemporaries. Hamelink is still a relatively young man and has already produced a substantial body of work, work that is increasingly unlike anything in his immediate literary context. One thinks in reading him of Borges, of Calvino, perhaps of García Márquez, in the way the play of his imagination takes on such persuasively concrete forms. From time to time there is discussion in Dutch as well as in English of the fact that current Dutch writers are so little known in the English-speaking world. Writers, either those translated or potential candidates for translation, who have been mentioned as possibly appealing to British or American readers have generally been writers working along lines also being explored by American and British writers. Perhaps it is time to introduce to the outside world a Dutch writer who has chosen a solitary path.

Fred J. Nichols, Summer 1982

---

[1] I owe this observation to Anneke Prins, to whom I am generally indebted for help with the subtler nuances of Dutch.

[2] Jacques Hamelink, *Afdalingen in de ingewanden,* Amsterdam, De Bezige Bij, 1974, p. 97. All translations are my own.

[3] Ibid., p. 218.

[4] Ibid., p. 309.

[5] Jacques Hamelink, *Geest van spraak en tegenspraak,* Amsterdam, De Bezige Bij, 1971, p. 55.

[6] Jacques Hamelink, *Het rif,* Amsterdam, De Bezige Bij, 1979, p. 15.

[7] Jacques Hamelink, *Windwaarts, wortelher,* Amsterdam, De Bezige Bij, 1973, p. 43.

[8] *Het rif,* p. 19.

[9] Jacques Hamelink, *Responsoria,* Amsterdam, De Bezige Bij, 1980, p. 29.

On the Poetry of Albert Verwey

Popular perception of Albert Verwey (1865–1937) among the poetry-reading Dutch public has always been divisible into several categories. Some see him as "difficult," "a mystic," a poet who is often impenetrable and only worthwhile in such oft-anthologized "easy" poems as "O man van smarte" (Oh Man of Sorrow) and "De terrassen van Meudon." Others see him as a poet whose philosophy so dominated his poetry that his language became flat and better suited to prose. One particularly damaging image of Verwey as "cerebral" and "unpoetic" was perpetrated by his erstwhile friend and colleague in the Movement of Eighty, Willem Kloos, who had no doubt that Verwey's poetic flame waned in his youth.

To a large extent, the scholarship in the last half-century or so has had to combat these images. From the brilliant dissections of P. N. van Eyck to the loving biographical studies of Maurits Uyldert to the detailed comparative analyses of Jan Aler, these commentaries have helped uncover and illuminate an astonishing poetic creation. Verwey has been lucky in his commentators. Each has contributed toward the gradual rehabilitation of this great poet. Theodoor Weevers has perhaps done more than anyone else to set the record straight. In his earlier *Mythe en vorm in de gedichten van Albert Verwey* (Myth and Form in the Poems of Albert Verwey; 1965) he sketched Verwey's development and argued that it followed, after 1896, one clear, though not entirely unbroken line, which could be traced as an enduring and ever more intimate relationship with an apprehended but hidden power. The gathering strength of Verwey's poetry may have entailed an occasional difficulty, but it was an organic, necessary difficulty. Weevers's latest study *Droom en beeld* (Dream and Image)* is less concerned with the unity of Verwey's career than with providing some cornerstones of Verwey's poetic edifice and with Verwey as a creator of images whose thought is indivisible from his poetry.

Weevers's book is invaluable because it tackles so many of the problems that any reader of Verwey, whether influenced by false images or not, must have. The whole subject of Verwey as the poet of poetry, for instance, is here elucidated. Verwey, says Weevers, is in some sense a dramatic poet; the objectifying power of his poetry is such that the personal "I" has disappeared, and this new impersonal "I" is "the mythic figure of the poet who is the main character of Verwey's poetry" (24). Weevers, following Uyldert, emphasizes that Verwey's poetry is not confessional poetry but "een objectieve zelf-uitbeelding" (an objective self-portrayal; 25), a life lived in poetry. Weevers's first chapter, "Dichterschap," is especially helpful in showing the identity of Verwey's form and the myth of *dichterschap,* for the shape and imagery and expression of Verwey's poems directly relate to his sense of the poet's role, mission and destiny.

In part, this is a view of poetry, and indeed a theme for poetry, that belonged to Verwey's time. The late nineteenth and early twentieth century produced a whole host of poets who believed in the supremacy of Art and the miraculous divinity of poetry. Surely one of the things Verwey and his famous friend Stefan George had in common was the belief in the mission of the poet, and surely R. P. Meijer is right in associating the Movement of Eighty with the French symbolists in this regard, and in saying that "[the Kloos and Verwey of the eighties] made art into a religion, with Beauty and Self as its twin gods" (*Literature of the Low Countries,* Assen, 1971, p. 239).

Related to the myth of poetry, says Weevers, is the dialectic, serial character of Verwey's poetry. Verwey strongly emphasized this series aspect, and it has remained a major problem for his readers, since many of the connections he points to in, say, the titles of his various cycles seem obscure to all but the poet. And even where scholars remove the obscurity, the connections do not always seem worthwhile. Still, Weevers is particularly acute in revealing the links between poems, series, cycles; his chapter on the polar structure of Verwey's *Het blank heelal* (The Unmarked Universe) impressively shows how similar motifs are treated in different poems and how such opposites as Self and World are gradually reconciled. Recurring images—e.g., the island of the self, the garden in the world, the poet-king and his imaginative realm—as well as opposing figures, matching associations, related motifs, are all studied as part of the conception and structure of this volume.

Weevers's capacity to clarify real difficulties in the reading of Verwey is matched by his ability to discuss form and metrics in larger contexts. To be sure, this orientation leads him to an occasionally flaccid and impressionistic formulation, as when he struggles to define form as the "slechts halfbewust ontstane inwendige vorm, de gestalte" (the only half-consciously arisen inner form, the shape; 111); but his intentions here are admirable still, for they indicate that his emphasis is where it should be, making it easier for him to comment on such outer aspects of form as stanza structure and metrics. Not only do these observations surface again and again in his analyses, they also inform his comments about the kind of poetry Verwey wrote and the kind of poet he was. Verwey, like Wordsworth and unlike Milton or Stefan George, expresses himself so spontaneously that a form grows from the utterance (14), a style resulting organically from the conception. This discussion, fascinating in itself, also offers a telling rejection of some of the post-Kloosian images of Verwey as a tortured, cerebral poet.

Weevers's book does not provide a full commentary on Verwey's poetry, which would risk offering itself as a substitute for a reading of the poems. He intends to further that reading and, through his study of imagery and basic motifs, make Verwey's work more accessible. My one criticism of the book is that not all chapters do this equally: the two chapters on the origin and growth of the imagination are interesting in themselves but do not contribute enough to the overall presentation.

And there are other regrets. I would have liked a more elaborate discussion of "de schone vrouw" (the beautiful woman) who appears so mysteriously in some of Verwey's most appealing poems. Who is she? What is she? Weevers refers to this mythic woman in his discussion of "De gestalten van mijn levenstijd" (Figures from My Lifetime), while in his earlier book she had figured in his commentary on "Het ontwaken" (The Waking). Most welcome too would have been some discussion of this same personage in the "Epiloog" of *De kristaltwijg* (The Crystal Twig), especially in connection with the views of love in that poem.

But these are small complaints when put next to Weevers's achievement in solving problems for readers of Verwey. One final example: his treatment of "de idee" (especially pp. 241, 242) and his implicit rejection of some of Simon Vestdijk's *Albert Verwey en de Idee.* The Idea in Verwey is not a thought or a concept or an antinomy, but a current, an attitude, a well-spring. Weevers demonstrates in his last chapter as well as in the whole book that the unity of Verwey's poetry is predicated on the force blending "droom en beeld," dream and image, reconciling the dream that shapes images with the world that yields its life in imagery.

Manfred Wolf, Spring 1980

*Theodoor Weevers. *Droom en beeld: De poëzie van Albert Verwey.* Amsterdam. Arbeiderspers. 1979. 297 pages. 23.50 fl.

PORTUGAL

Some Considerations on Rodrigues Miguéis's "Léah"

The novelette "Léah" by the well-known Portuguese writer José Rodrigues Miguéis has attracted a considerable amount of published comment, but it has been reviewed almost exclusively in terms of the larger work of which it now forms a part.[1] Perhaps the only critic or reviewer to call attention to the fact that the story was first published separately in 1940, nearly two decades before its appearance in *Léah e Outras Histórias,* was Jorge de Sena, when he reviewed the main lines of Miguéis's literary career upon the occasion of the latter's winning the first Prémio Camilo Castelo Branco, Portugal's highest honor for writers of prose fiction at the time (1959). As far as its literary quality was concerned, this critic said that it was "sem dúvida uma obra-prima da literatura portuguesa."[2]

More specifically, Jaime Cortesão, writing in *O Primeiro de Janeiro* (29 April 1958, p. 3), saw it as a "representação da vida não só nos temas universais, mas em vários pontos do Universo." Several other reviewers pointed out that "Léah" was a work which revealed a sensitive comprehension of human problems and human psychology. Guedes de Amorim considered it a re-creation of Miguéis's own not-too-distant past.[3] In a similar vein, Armando Ferreira and Manuel Poppe found that the novelette was charged with a goodly admixture of *saudade.*[4]

However, it was Óscar Lopes, in *O Comércio do Porto* (13 May 1958, p. 6), who observed that Miguéis had made a small modification in the traditional Portuguese outlook on sex, love and marriage with his frank treatment of Léah's lack of sexual inhibitions. Massaud Moisés, in *O Estado de São Paulo, Suplemento Literário* (9 August 1958, p. 2), placed this facet of the story in a more universal context when he said that the girl Léah was "um simbolo perfeito da adolescencia impulsiva dos nossos dias." On another occasion he considered that Miguéis's treatment of the human condition was much more true to life than was that of Eça de Queiroz in "Singularidades de uma Rapariga Loura."[5] Miguéis therefore was being favorably compared with the nineteenth-century master.

In sum, then, the critical comment on this work has generally been both very favorable and quite far-ranging in scope. One wonders, though, given the autobiographical nature of many of Miguéis's works and the importance of social and psychological problems in their thematic content, just what the temporal indications, the locational referents and the social and psychological problem content of this work actually are. Therefore I offer below a brief examination of these aspects of "Léah," in that order and in some detail. First, however, a synopsis of the novelette.

■■■

As the story opens, we see Carlos, a young Portuguese scientist doing experimental research in Brussels, taking a chilly, drafty room on the top floor of a *pensão* run by a Madame Lambertin. In spite of its dubious cleanliness and the all-pervasive odor of stale fried potatoes, he allows a certain sense of inertia to take possession of him and stays on even after discovering its faults.

"Monsieur Carlôss," as he is called by the Belgians, soon develops an inertia of another sort. With the failure of his first laboratory experiments and a growing disillusionment with his foreign surroundings, he becomes gloomy and filled with a certain apathetic discontent. He shuns company, finds it impossible to keep up with his appointments or correspondence and cannot abide to read anything. Even a chance meeting with some fellow Portuguese at a Russian restaurant is of no help to him, because all they do is complain about the food.

One day Carlos returns to his room somewhat earlier than usual and finds it still untidy. His accumulated resentment boils up, and to this is added a certain jealousy at the assiduous manner in which the attractive chambermaid Léah has been attending to the other roomers, especially the homosexual Perlman and the mentally retarded Monsieur Albert. To Carlos, it suddenly seems that Léah spends far too much time with these two behind closed doors. All this comes to a head in a towering fit of anger, and he calls Léah, yelling her name down the stairwell at the top of his lungs.

Much to Carlos's surprise, Léah comes running upstairs at once. He starts to criticize her bitterly for the poor condition of the room, but his anger fades when he notices that the chambermaid is sincerely concerned. Besides, she is young and very pretty. They soon discuss the cleaning of the room somewhat more calmly, therefore, and quickly progress to other matters after Carlos is informed that it is Mme Lambertin, and not Léah, who usually cleans it. Furthermore, it turns out that the reason she has never before come to his room is that Carlos has never called for her until now. In fact, it transpires that she and Mme Lambertin have both thought that the young Portuguese *doutor* was terribly reserved, because he has never made much of an attempt to chat with anyone. And as Léah tells him about the other residents of the *pensão,* including the landlady and herself, Carlos feels himself falling in love. Léah, it is evident, is also beginning to feel the same way about Carlos. Time passes in an enjoyable exchange of confidences. Suddenly Mme Lambertin calls for the chambermaid. After another embrace and with a promise to return when she goes off duty at ten that night, she leaves.

The weeks pass, with Carlos and Léah enjoying the delights of being in love. Mme Lambertin drinks heavily. Ferdinand, Léah's boyfriend, lurks in the background as a stolid presence which occasionally causes Carlos a pang of remorse. One day, much to Carlos's surprise, Léah brings her younger sister to visit him. To Léah, everything that is beautiful or enjoyable is good. She loves both Carlos and her sister and, in her simple way, she wants them to feel the same way about each other. Thus she insists that Carlos not only admire her sister's legs but kiss her as well, much to their embarrassment and to her own discomfort at being outshone by her sister's greater physical attractiveness.

The idyllic relationship between Carlos and Léah does not last for long, however. As a result of her heavy drinking, Mme Lambertin cannot meet her debts. Léah eventually goes on strike, hoping that the guests will force Mme Lambertin to pay her. The *pensão* is filled with turmoil. The next day there is a terrible row. The landlady has called Ferdinand and, in a drunken rage, tells him that Léah has been unfaithful to him. Léah calls on Carlos to come to her rescue, and he does so immediately, after first reducing Mme Lambertin to a sobbing heap by reminding her of a sordid scene he once witnessed with an Indian and several female companions. Ferdinand, however, says that there is no need for explanations. In the end, Léah leaves the *pensão,* absolved of any wrongdoing but without her wages.

The relationship has almost ended. There remain only the dregs of Léah and Carlos's adventure together, a gradual, prolonged drifting apart. They meet furtively at ever-increasing intervals. Carlos finds his heart slowly hardening toward his lover, and there eventually comes the day when he fails to meet her as promised. Centripetal forces and his lack of initiative have won out, except for a fit of remorse from time to time. There have, however, been other consequences to their affair. More than a year later, Carlos sees Léah for the last time. She is accompanied by Ferdinand, who is now her husband, and his family. She seems outwardly happy and prosperous as she makes the necessary introductions, but Carlos notices that tears come to her eyes when she shows him her baby boy.

■ ■ ■

The novelette's temporal aspects can be summarized as follows: the setting in historical time is imprecise, but it obviously takes place over a period of about eighteen months at some time during the two decades between World Wars I and II. The action cannot take place earlier than the end of World War I, for Carlos's fellow boarder, Perlman, is suffering its political consequences.[6] There is no internal indication of the last date at which the action could take place, but this temporal limit is furnished by the date of the story's first publication: November 1940. Furthermore, one can logically push this limiting aspect of "Léah" backward to the last years of the decade of the 1920s or the first years of the 1930s, roughly speaking, by taking into consideration the fact that Miguéis spent the major portion of the years 1929–32 in Belgium and emigrated to the United States in 1935, not returning to Europe until 1946. In the absence of evidence to the contrary, therefore, it can be assumed that "Léah" is set during this general period of time and that the indistinctness of this aspect of the work is due to its thematic content, whose relevance transcends chronological time except in the most general way. Furthermore, even the outside temporal limits indicated in the work and by virtue of its first date of publication place the time of the story squarely in the middle of an extremely important portion of its author's life.[7]

The geographical location of "Léah" is quite clear: it is Brussels. On the second page of the novelette there is a reference to Mme Lambertin's being Flemish. Her husband is a Walloon, and in contrast to Léah, no mention is made of Mme Lambertin's being a foreigner. Concrete mention of place is first made with the reference to the Indian's drifting about Brussels. Léah herself is described as being "francesa, e não belga." Later, Carlos returns to Brussels after taking a trip. Finally, we last see Mme Lambertin after she has served six months' imprisonment in Saint-Gilles, a prison in the metropolitan area of Brussels. This story therefore is one of a great number of Miguéis's fictional works which are set in foreign places he knows from personal experience, in this case as a result of his years of study at the University of Brussels.

As might be expected from Miguéis's earlier works, "Léah" is replete with social problems. Many of them are familiar. There is, for example, the problem of the modest means of the protagonist. Carlos's genteel poverty has its effect in many ways, but with relation to the plot it is particularly important to note that it is his lack of money that first brings him to Mme Lambertin's *pensão,* where he takes a room which is far from being luxurious and is only passably clean. It is at the *pensão,* of course, that he meets and falls in love with Léah. Then, as Carlos and Léah's love affair progresses, it is primarily his impecuniousness that stops him from accompanying Léah to her native France, where she hopes they can marry and settle down. Thus poverty, or at least a certain lack of affluence, not only leads to Carlos's meeting his lover but also militates against the couple's regularizing their relationship.

Carlos's financial situation does not improve during the course of the novelette, but he has much company in this regard in the persons of the other boarders. Perlman, for example, has an even shabbier room, and mention is made of the general poverty of the others. Even his landlady Mme Lambertin is in the same, and very human, situation. In fact, this affects others as well, for she is unable to pay Léah her wages because of being in debt herself. By the end of the story she has gone bankrupt and her establishment has closed its doors. It is important to note, however, that even this one aspect of "Léah" has many ramifications and several levels of complexity. The protagonist's poverty can logically be ascribed to his years of study as well as to his travels abroad. His lack of affluence is thus a result of positive personal decisions, of an investment in his future, as it is often put, however much it may weigh upon him at the moment. Perlman, on the other hand, may be in an analogous financial position for different reasons, both of which are more difficult to remedy: his homosexuality and loss of nationality as a consequence of World War I. Thus he is not a free agent but is instead a pawn of destiny. Mme Lambertin is similarly fated to be and remain poor, but the cause of her penury is of another order entirely. It is her addiction to alcohol, which also leads her into a certain moral dissolution as well. Nor is the question of poverty approached only in terms of a positive causal relationship: Léah's boyfriend Ferdinand is not well off but is thought of by her as being an appropriate suitor because he has a steady job. Thus he is not poor in Léah's eyes, just as her sister does not show the effects of a life of hard work which are often observable among even young adults of the lower end of the socioeconomic scale. In this way Miguéis has highlighted certain aspects of a life of poverty through contrasting perceptions of reality. And finally, it is apparent that, even though the author has discussed the problem of poverty before and has dealt with it elsewhere from various points of view, it appears in "Léah" as yet another example of his complex treatment of a problem beneath the surface of a seemingly simple presentation.

While there is a wide range of other social problems which the author brings to the reader's attention in "Léah"—the dangers of coal-fired space heaters, vivisection, Mme Lambertin's imprisonment for debt and alcoholism and even the process of aging—the main social problem of which he treats is none of these. Rather, it consists of the whole complex episode centering about the fact that a man from a relatively higher socioeconomic class falls in love with, seduces and then abandons a girl from a lower socioeconomic class. As usual, Miguéis does not present the situation in simplistic terms, for in Carlos and Léah's case the process of falling in love and being seduced is a mutual affair. But in the end it is Carlos who abandons Léah. This is a very old theme in Miguéis's writings, for one can trace it back at least to "Poeira da Rua: Miss Dolorosa" and "Poeira da Rua: Meia Noite," both published in 1923 in the Lisbon daily *A Republica* (17 June 1923, p. 1 and 20 July 1923, p. 1 respectively).

Typically, too, Miguéis prepares the way for Carlos's final act of abandonment by pointing out early in the story the differences in social class that exist between him and Léah. These are due primarily to education, which Léah lacks almost entirely. This facet is given a neat, rationalizing twist, however, to obscure this basic incompatibility between the two lovers: Léah's lack of formal education is seen initially as a virtue because it results in her having a refreshing candor. In this manner Léah's innate attractiveness has been enhanced at the beginning of the episode, while the seed of future dissension and drawing apart has also been planted, all but unnoticed. Thus it can be seen that the author's subliminal infiltration, observable in such earlier works as *Páscoa Feliz,* continued to be an important part of his literary technique, at least up to the time of the first publication of "Léah."

The first blooming of the lovers' affair is what immediately catches and holds our attention, of course. The sailing is smooth as long as circumstances permit Carlos to continue it with no particular effort. As soon as difficulties appear, however, we notice that Carlos becomes hypocritical and progressively loses initiative with respect to his lover. Léah, on the other hand, tries to consolidate her position, making plans for the two of them to move to Paris. In spite of her efforts, however, the situation is steadily degraded, first to their spending the night together in a cheap hotel and then to Carlos's final failure to appear at a trysting-place.

The affair thus ends on a sordid note, with Carlos bearing most of the blame. And yet he is not intentionally an evildoer, for he at least thinks he has been in love with Léah and is left with a sense of permanent loss. He finds expiation in his work and encounters his retribution in seeing Ferdinand calmly playing the role of husband and father and supporting Léah in a thoroughly proper, if sedate, manner. Carlos is thus typical of the ordinary mortal, neither weak enough to be entirely evil nor strong enough to master all of life's temptations. He is, in sum, a very human character.

Regarding the psychological problems evident in the novelette's thematic content, we have noted Mme Lambertin's alcoholism and Perlman's homosexuality. By implication, we have also touched upon the whole range of transient emotional problems inherent in the course of a love affair, such as Carlos's jealousy, timidity and cowardice, as well as Léah's remorse at her treatment of Ferdinand.

There is, however, a group of psychological problems which is both central to the development of the plot of "Léah" and is observable in many other works by the same author: that is, the problems a foreigner has in adjusting to his new surroundings, which are manifested in Carlos by his disillusionment with his Belgian surroundings, a recurring sadness and loneliness and a longing for home. He is dissatisfied with life and even with his own compatriots. In this respect, then, Carlos is in a position analogous to that of the protagonist of "Cinzas de Incêndio": in many ways he could be the latter's twin except that he has scientific rather than artistic tendencies. Like his counterpart, Carlos is ripe for an amorous adventure—hence the importance of these problems to the story's development.

There are other psychological problems apparent in "Léah," such as the fact that Mme Lambertin's husband does not seem to care about anything that takes place around him, M. Albert's mental retardation and the emotional effects of a girl's loss of virginity prior to marriage. None of these, however, is as important to the progress of the story as those preparing the way for, and arising from, Carlos and Léah's love affair. And of course these have their social as well as their psychological importance: it is an added dimension which furnishes yet another bit of evidence that Miguéis is a writer of major talents.

Finally and perhaps most importantly, because one can note this point of view in earlier writings—as, for example, in *Páscoa Feliz* and "O Acidente"—the most striking of the various complementary aspects of "Léah" which come to the fore is the author's depiction of the worker as an essentially noble being. Thus the "operários do arrabalde [pass by with] passadas fortes no calçada sonora" (workers of the district [pass by with] firm steps ringing on the pavement) as they go to work. The theme of the nobility of work itself is incorporated into that of the nobility of love between man and woman as well. Thus, in speaking of Léah's dream of moving to Paris, Carlos says: "E tu, que querias tu? Libertarte da existência mesquinha?, de Ferdinand? Conhecer mundo, *as batalhas da vida, o sacrifício, a união firme de dois seres que labutam e gozam, criam e sofrem juntos?*" (And you, what did you want? To escape your wretched existence? To escape Ferdinand? To get to know the world, *life's battles, sacrifice and the strong union of two beings who work, enjoy things, create and suffer together?* [my emphasis]). As one can see, this aspect is hedged with rhetorical doubt and melded into a dream of a fuller life. But it is there, and it was perhaps one of the reasons why a critic of the stature of Adolfo Casais Monteiro could place on Miguéis's brow the perhaps unwanted laurel of being the true, if unacknowledged, mentor of the Portuguese neo-realist movement.[8]

John Austin Kerr, Jr., Spring 1977

[1] This paper was adapted from portions of my Ph.D. dissertation, "Aspects of Time, Place and Thematic Content in the Prose Fiction of José Rodrigues Miguéis as Indications of the Artist's Weltanschicht," University of Wisconsin, Madison, 1970. It was written under the direction of Professor Jorge de Sena, to whom I am greatly indebted for his kind advice and stimulation over a number of years. Any faults, of course, are my own.

[2] Jorge de Sena, "José Rodrigues Miguéis," *O Estado de São Paulo, Suplemento Literário,* 29 August 1959, p. 1. Miguéis's novelette was first published under the title "Léa" in Vitorino Nemésio's *Revista de Portugal,* no. 10 (November 1940), pp. 185–209.

[3] "'Léah' por José Rodrigues Miguéis," *O Século Ilustrado,* Lisbon, 14 June 1958, pp. 9 & 30.

[4] Armando Ferreira, "*Léah* por José Rodrigues Miguéis," *Jornal do Comércio,* Lisbon, April 5/6, 1958, p. 10; and Manuel Poppe, "*A Escola do Paraíso* de José Rodrigues Miguéis," *Rumo,* vol. 5, no. 57 (November 1961), p. 442.

[5] Massaud Moisés, "Considerações Sobre o Conto Moderno," *O Estado de São Paulo, Suplemento Literário,* 23 April 1960, p. 3; Eça de Queiroz, "Singularidades de uma Rapariga Loura," in *Contos,* Oporto, Lello & Irmão, n.d., pp. 9–43.

[6] José Rodrigues Miguéis, "Léah," in *Léah e Outras Histórias,* 4th ed., Lisbon, Estúdios Cor, 1968, pp. 9–35.

[7] For a brief biobibliographical résumé see my paper, "A Thumbnail Sketch of the Life and Works of José Rodrigues Miguéis," *Proceedings* of the Pacific Northwest Council on Foreign Languages, XXV:1, Literature and Linguistics 1974, pp. 35–39.

[8] Adolfo Casais Monteiro, "José Rodrigues Miguéis," *O Estado de São Paulo, Suplemento Literário,* 13 June 1959, p. 1.

José Saramago (*José Frade*)

José Saramago: Art for Reason's Sake

In his diary for 14 October 1997 José Saramago records a telephone call from Dario Fo. Even while savoring the pleasures associated with winning the Nobel Prize in Literature for 1997, the Italian dramatist promptly called the Portuguese writer to say: "I am a thief: I stole the prize from you. One day, though, it will be your turn."[1] And, in fact, twelve months later the two exchanged greetings once again on the occasion of the Nobel awards, this time to celebrate Saramago's victory of 8 October 1998. Obviously the two calls indicate a genuine camaraderie between the two Nobel laureates, who have shared similar political views and exchanged war stories over the years about their respective controversies. Dario Fo's initial call, however, also suggests

that Saramago had long been a serious contender prior to the decision of the Swedish Academy in the fall of 1998. Portugal's best seller for several years with most of his works available in translation in many languages, Saramago had become a point of reference in literary circles in both Europe and the Americas. According to all reports from Stockholm the decision was reached with remarkable unanimity among the judges and won strong support from public and press, quite unlike the situation of the previous year when Dario Fo made his call. Despite an occasional dissenting voice that I shall address presently, veteran observers of the prize hark back to 1978 and Isaac Bashevis Singer to find a similar example of such a positive atmosphere surrounding the literary prize.[2]

In light of the widespread support for Saramago and, at least for Dario Fo, the predictability of this year's award, it may seem paradoxical that the prize for 1998 occasioned the kind of jubilation that typically accompanies an unanticipated victory against overwhelming odds. It is also the case that Saramago's success has entailed a cultural dimension absent from the usual Nobel award in literature insofar as this is the first time the prize has gone to a writer of Portuguese. A language with a rich literary tradition beginning in the twelfth century, Portuguese is the official language of more than two hundred million speakers. When the British Hispanist Aubrey Fitzgerald Bell observed decades ago that Portuguese was the vehicle for one of the world's half-dozen major literatures, he could hardly have foreseen the extraordinary vitality that was beginning to emerge in Brazil, where a number of Nobel-quality contenders have appeared in this century, to say nothing of even more recent writers in Lusophone Africa. And yet the admirers of such talents as João Guimarães Rosa, Carlos Drummond de Andrade, Miguel Torga, Sophia de Mello Breyner, and many others have long come to dread October as the time when "Latin's last blossom" (as the Brazilian poet Olavo Bilac referred to his language) would once again be ignored by the Swedish Academy. Saramago's achievement, therefore, signifies a kind of recognition impossible to imagine had this year's laureate been from almost anywhere else besides a Portuguese-speaking country. Painfully aware of the many years of frustration and disappointment that had made October truly the cruelest month for Portuguese-speaking lovers of literature, José Saramago echoed Fernando Pessoa's "My country is my language" by dedicating his prize to Portuguese speakers everywhere (although he wryly added that he would keep the money for himself, thank you. . .). He was immediately showered with congratulations and gratitude from Manaus to Maputo, and the Portuguese government promptly declared that 8 October would henceforth be a holiday known as the Day of the Language. On his visit to the Portuguese capital the new laureate found the city awash in festive bunting in his honor. In short, one can hardly conceive of a more joyful or widespread celebration sparked by a Nobel Prize.[3]

Several commentators have tried to temper the festivities with reminders that a Nobel Prize in Literature is conferred to recognize an individual's merits and not to kindle linguistic pride or further patriotic agendas.[4] Such reminders are all the more timely given Saramago's own doubts with respect to any positive impact that a Nobel Prize in Literature might have on the prestige of Portuguese as a language, nor does he think that decisions reached in Stockholm will enhance the standing of a national literature in the international community.[5] Such lofty matters with all their rhetorical grandeur fail to impress this year's winner, who is little inclined toward bombast of any kind. Born in 1922 into a poor provincial family, José Saramago is hardly the product of the Portuguese establishment with its centuries of sharp class distinctions and social privilege. On the contrary, he is in every sense a self-made man whose future distinction was curiously foreshadowed when a civil functionary erroneously appended a family sobriquet to

the birth certificate of the infant José de Souza. Only when he was nine and living with his family in Lisbon did his father discover the mistake, and, rather than confront his country's bureaucracy, he decided to make the change official by assuming his son's name as his own. And so it is that the Nobel laureate in literature is not José de Souza but rather José Saramago, the first so named in his family and a constant reminder of some mysterious association linking his relatives to the lowly wild radish known in Portuguese as *saramago*. Such botanical bonds between clan and nature are by no means unusual in the peasant world of rural Portugal; moreover, our writer's modest origins have provided him with a civil identity while serving as a source of inspiration for much of his work.[6]

The young Saramago attended a "proper" school for barely two years before financial constraints forced his transfer at the age of twelve to a trade school, where he studied to become a locksmith. Testimony to the occasionally beneficial aspects of a reactionary social system was the heavily humanistic curriculum provided by a vocational-technological institution that offered classes in French and a decent library to working-class boys in overalls. The future writer drank deep from the classics, including a number of authors who have left their mark, such as Luis de Camões, António Vieira, Miguel de Cervantes, and Michel de Montaigne. The nearby library at the Galveias Palace further widened horizons that soon encompassed a certain Ricardo Reis, a fascinating poet whom only later the young industrial apprentice would recognize as a heteronym of Fernando Pessoa and an inspiration for one of his most acclaimed novels.

At the age of seventeen the future Nobel laureate was on his own, earning a livelihood as a locksmith, but his knowledge of French coupled with an unusual grasp of grammar and the principles of composition eventually led to a job with an insurance firm before earning him a position as a literary editor. During these early years he wrote his first novel, *Terra do Pecado* (Land of Sin; 1947), a realistic account of a widow's struggle with sexual and emotional needs in a rural setting. Recently reissued, the novel represents a respectable first step and was followed by a second novel, *Claraboia* (Skylight), which was sent to a prospective publisher only to disappear until resurfacing forty years later. To this day *Claraboia* remains in manuscript form: its author, doubting that this fruit of early labor would enhance his bibliography, has declined all offers of publication elicited by the renown of recent years.

José Saramago divides his life into two segments: "Until the age of fifty we have to learn, and after fifty we have to work until the end occurs."[7] As befits a self-confessed late bloomer, he wrote little in the fifties save for an occasional translation like his version of *Sisyphe et la mort,* a play by the French writer Robert Merle. In this account of heroic struggle for justice against the corruption of the powerful, Saramago would find a number of themes that he would later revisit. However, his next two endeavors were collections of poems, *Os Poemas Possíveis* (The Possible Poems; 1966) and *Provavelment Alegria* (Probably Joy; 1970). By this time Saramago was a contributor to the press, and he published four volumes of his columns from 1971 to 1976. The seventies also saw a third book of poetry, *O Ano de 1993* (The Year 1993; 1975), two collections of short stories, and, most significant, a novel, *Manual de Pintura e Caligrafia* (A Manual on Painting and Calligraphy; 1977). Into this account of a self-taught artist's growing awareness of his talents and his omnivorous curiosity the author put much of himself despite the plot's Italian setting. Not surprisingly, Saramago has referred to this realistic novel as perhaps his most autobiographical book.

The quickening tempo of Saramago's work during the seventies occurred against a background of important developments on the national scene, especially following the revolution of 25 April 1974 and the end of a repressive right-wing regime that had prevailed since the author's earliest years in elementary school. A member of the proscribed Communist Party since 1969, he emerged from the political shadows to become an editor of the newspaper *Diário de Notícias* during a brief period of communist control of editorial policy. During this time Saramago participated in the purge of a number of journalists associated with the previous regime's policies of censorship, colonial warfare, and reactionary social programs. When, however, his party lost power several months later, Saramago was himself dismissed and obliged to eke out a living as a freelance columnist and translator. But the decade ended on a decidedly positive note when his first play, *A Noite* (Night; 1979), won the Portuguese Critics Award. Recognizing a promising new talent, the publisher Caminho provided the fifty-seven-year-old rising star with an advance to write a travel book on Portugal directed to the Portuguese reader (eventually published in 1981 as *Viagem a Portugal* [A Trip to Portugal]). But even more auspicious was the publisher's support for a novel, *Levantado do Chão* (Up from the Earth; 1980), which won the City of Lisbon Prize and would ensure that the author become Caminho's most prominent writer to this day.

Inspired in part by the author's own forebears in a similar setting, *Levantado do Chão* is a saga of landless peasants who have toiled on the large estates of the Alentejo region since medieval times. Saramago follows the fortunes of a couple of families from 1900 to the revolution of 1974, and while doing so he hits his stride. For the first time we encounter his warm appreciation for simple men and women who attain a stature of heroic dignity as they doggedly persist, like Merle's Sisyphus of 1956, in a centuries-old struggle against misery and systemic humiliation. Perhaps even more remarkable is the author's development of a technique that has become his hallmark. Gone are the usual distinctions involving narrative, description, and dialogue: now all three are melded into an unbroken web spun by the intensely personal voice of a weaver of tales. The result with respect to the very format is unsettling as the reader opens to pages filled with lines of unbroken print. One may even lose one's way in the absence of capital letters, punctuation marks, and paragraph indentations. When a friend complained that he found the book impenetrable and difficult to read, the author suggested that he try reading aloud—sage advice most appropriate to a literary tone that is profoundly oral and quite often musical. On the following day the friend, now much relieved, called to say, "Now I realize what it is you expect [from the reader]."[8]

The breakthrough that was *Levantado do Chão* made José Saramago a familiar name at home. It fell to his next novel, *Memorial do Convento* (1982), to introduce him to an international public. The plot focuses on two lovers, Baltasar and Blimunda (their names constitute the title of the English translation). Baltasar is a maimed veteran of peninsular wars who decides to share his fate with Blimunda, a mysterious seer with the ability to divine the inner will of others. Against the background of early eighteenth-century Portugal the two join the thousands of mostly indentured workers who toil on the construction site of the enormous convent of Mafra, an absolute king's payment for answered prayers regarding an heir. Saramago balances the obscurantism of an ignorant and fanatical power structure comprising altar and throne against glimmers of intelligence and decency as represented by the lovers and their friend, an enlightened priest who enlists their aid in building a marvelous flying machine. The trio are joined by their confidant the musician Domenico Scarlatti as he plays the harpsichord in their secret workshop hidden away from the watchful eyes of the Inquisition. Once again employing his highly individualistic narrative technique, Saramago conflates past and present, marvelous events and rampant cruelty, mass hysteria and lightly worn erudition to create a modern masterpiece that has been translated around the world. The novel even inspired the Italian composer Azio Corghi to create an opera, *Blimunda,* which premiered in Milan in 1990. Notoriety of a different sort, however, followed when the conservative city fathers of Mafra, infuriated by the author's portrayal of the Church's historical role and by his denigration of their famous national monument, declared Saramago *persona non grata*. They also refused to grant a request by students and faculty who had asked that the local high school be renamed in the writer's honor. Only now, in the wake of his national acclaim following the awarding of the Nobel Prize, have they grudgingly relented in the face of official pressure.

With his next novel, *O Ano da Morte de Ricardo Reis* (1984; Eng. *The Year of the Death of Ricardo Reis;* 1990), Saramago shifts his gaze to 1936, the first year of the Spanish Civil War. We find Castilian aristocrats fleeing social upheaval to take refuge in a Lisbon hotel that is also home to a certain medical doctor newly repatriated after spending years in Rio de Janeiro. He is none other than Ricardo Reis, one of Fernando Pessoa's famous heteronyms who has decided to return to Portugal following the death of his creator in 1935. Probably the most acclaimed of Saramago's novels, the plot follows the doctor as he strolls along Lisbon's rain-swept streets, often in the company of his recently deceased (primary) creator, Fernando Pessoa, as they discuss life and literature against a background of Salazar at home and Franco, Hitler, and Mussolini abroad. Although he is known for his elegant neoclassical verses celebrating idealized aristocratic women in Attic settings, the doctor is an indifferent suitor of a handicapped and sad, if pretty, young woman while bedding the hotel maid who happens to bear the name of his muse. Pessoa himself would have marveled at the shifting moods, voices, and identities, and he would have thrilled to the author's wit and irony, which George Steiner has likened to the best of Robert Musil.[9] To be sure, the acclaim has not been universal: Mafra's conservative city council has found allies who take umbrage at Saramago's mordant views of Salazar's dreary New State and his portrayal of popular religious beliefs as depicted in Ricardo Reis's excursion to the national shrine at Fátima.

In one of his frequent interviews, which are usually delivered with such aplomb and linguistic precision that interviewers often dispense with editing before sending the transcript to a newspaper, Saramago has suggested that "perhaps I am not a novelist; perhaps I'm an essayist who has to write novels because he doesn't know how to write essays."[10] Even allowing for the conventional modesty of one who has contributed hundreds of essays and columns to journals and newspapers on as many topics, there is no doubt that his novels contain much erudite commentary and analysis of cultural patterns and contemporary issues. One such issue of central concern to the author is the role of his country in a world characterized by multinational entities and a global economy, a theme central to *A Jangada de Pedra* (1986; Eng. *The Stone Raft,* 1995), of all his novels the one most reminiscent of a thesis novel. Positing as his argument that Iberia represents something of an anomaly in Europe, the author initiates his demonstration on a fateful day when the peninsula is literally sundered along the Pyrenees from the rest of the continent. A little band of Spaniards and Portuguese, including both men and women, join forces on their panic-seized peninsula as it proceeds to float southwest before eventually coming to rest somewhere between Africa and South America. For the defenders of a united European Community, such a plot smacks of reactionary separatism even while they tend to look upon Iberia as an exotic appendage, remnants of the remote Roman provinces of Hispania and Lusitania more akin to North Africa than to the lands north of the Pyrenees. Even the inhabitants of Iberia itself may react with mixed feelings to Saramago's thesis: Portuguese take a dim view of alliances with their traditional and powerful enemy to the east, while Spaniards regard their smaller neighbor to the west with a mixture of condescension and indifference. At the same time, all would agree that Portugal and Spain share much in common.

Clearly *The Stone Raft* raises a number of issues fraught with complexity and contradiction, but the author makes a strong case for rendering highly problematic the European character of the Iberian peninsula as he sees it. For Saramago, "We [Spaniards and Portuguese] have always felt a pull to the south," whether in Africa or the Americas.[11] Even more fundamental, however, than a division between Iberia and the rest of the continent is Saramago's vision of two Europes, one powerful, prosperous, progressive, and cultivated, and the other confined to a peripheral reality of islanders, mountaineers, and semiliterate poor societies vulnerable to the designs of powerful neighbors. The author discerns an analogous dichotomy in European history as well, which is as brilliant in its cultural achievements as it is stained by war, genocide, economic exploitation, and other horrors that once crowded the nightmares from which James Joyce wanted to awaken. For the present, Saramago observes that, like the sea, the same continental space that provides a medium for communication can also be a barrier dividing peoples who remain stubbornly different with respect to one another. As for those who fault him for a lack of filial loyalty to Mother Europe, he counters that a true mother respects all her children equally. Until she does, he will continue to defend his sympathies for the lands to the south while remaining wary of the hegemony of one Europe over another. That his thesis strikes a responsive chord is evident in the popularity of *The Stone Raft,* and of the author's works in general, among Spaniards, Latin Americans, and Lusophone Africans. One might note that among the very first to congratulate the new laureate were the presidents of Argentina, Brazil, Cuba, and Nicaragua, all lands "to the south" that he regards as traditionally no less important to the cultures of Iberia than are England, France, and Germany.

In a curious way *The Stone Raft* has mirrored events in the author's personal life. In 1986 a Spanish journalist for *El País,* Pilar del Río, interviewed the author of *The Year of the Death of Ricardo Reis,* which she much admired. Each found the other charming, and within two years the distinguished author and the young journalist were married. In 1993 the couple decided to relocate to Lanzarote, one of the Canary Islands, thereby creating their own version of a Spanish-Portuguese space between Africa and the Americas. From all accounts the two remain devoted to each other, and Pilar del Río has become her husband's most loyal fan as well as the official translator of his works into Spanish.

In his next novel, *Historia do Cerco de Lisboa* (1989; Eng. *The History of the Siege of Lisbon,* 1997), our author delved into the parallels between past and present and between history and fiction. The protagonist, Raimundo da Silva, is a shy middle-aged bachelor employed as an editor in a large publishing house. Chafing at his colorless routine, he impulsively decides one day to insert a "not" into an account of the fall of Moslem Lisbon in 1147 to a Christian army. According to Raimundo's revision of the past, the latter did *not* contain a large contingent of English crusaders en route to the Holy Land: only local troops under the direction of the first Portuguese king were involved. In revising the past, Raimundo finds the will to revise his own life as well when he falls in love with the writer Sara, and their affair mirrors the loves of a twelfth-century soldier and a peasant girl. A besieged Lisbon beset by famine merges at times with its twentieth-century descendant in a plot that proceeds on several levels, bound together by a storyteller blending commentary, dialogue, narrative, and description.

If one were to evaluate the significance of a work by its appeal to a sensation-hungry media, one would have to confer the prize to *O Evangelho segundo Jesus Cristo* (1991; Eng. *The Gospel According to Jesus Christ,* 1994) as Saramago's most important novel. In retelling the life of Jesus, the atheist author draws heavily on biblical accounts while refining his own approach to magical realism to re-create the supernatural aspects of his subject's life. Saramago's Jesus is the eldest son of Joseph and protégé of a mysterious shepherd who turns out to be none other than Satan himself. In time Jesus becomes the lover of Mary Magdalene until God orders him to offer his life as an intermediary between Himself

as a vengeful judge and a sinful mankind. A very reluctant Messiah, Jesus is appalled to learn that he will be only the first to be sacrificed in a divine plan entailing centuries of suffering and death. Quite literally, the blood of martyrs (and of their adversaries as well) will nourish the Christian church. Saramago's God thus appears as a Moloch-like figure who wreaks havoc as He pleases to affirm His absolute power. Satan, on the other hand, represents the voice of common sense and reason in his defense of humanity.

Although Saramago's interpretation of the life of Jesus (which he describes as "really the Gospel according to José Saramago")[12] reflects a critical perspective reminiscent of certain authors of the eighteenth-century Enlightenment, its publication shocked and dismayed many believers and conservative commentators unaccustomed to critical appraisals of popular dogma. Many were especially incensed by the author's description of the Christian church as a divine instrument for war and repression in the form of crusades, inquisitions, and willful obscurantism. The Vatican especially registered a protest, echoed by members of the Portuguese hierarchy and clergy and their supporters. Arrayed against Saramago's critics were nonbelievers subscribing to an equally traditional strain of Portuguese anticlericalism that prevailed when the novel won the 1991 grand prize granted by the National Association of Portuguese Writers. However, in the following year the undersecretary for the Ministry of Culture denied the authorization necessary for the book's entry in a competition at the level of the European Community. His decision outraged many, including democratic believers, who saw in his opposition a return to the censorship that had stifled cultural expression for so many years under the Salazar regime. For Saramago the government's imposition of a heavy hand, following on the heels of the rebuke delivered by the right-wing officials of Mafra's city government, proved to be the last straw. It was at this point that he left his country to take up residence in the Canary Islands, thereby becoming one more Portuguese emigrant (and not, he observes, an exile).[13]

Not at all daunted by the controversy following publication of his life of Jesus, Saramago has continued to probe the marriage of religion and oppression, which he considers inseparable even while others may view the union as a scandalous paradox. He has written a number of plays on the topic, including *In Nomine Dei* (1993), a winner of Portugal's Grand Prize in Theater. Based on the bloody suppression of visionary Anabaptists in sixteenth-century Germany, the drama sparked a furious row when Portuguese national television refused to carry advertising promoting the published script. On the other hand, Will Humburg, the director of the Münster Opera, was so taken by the play that he commissioned an opera based on Saramago's account of the violent events which rocked the German city from 1532 to 1535. Once again, Azio Corghi collaborated with the author, who was joined by Claudio Abbado as director to compose and record a second major musical adaptation of a work by José Saramago. In the same year Corghi also composed a cantata, "La Morte di Lazzaro," inspired by an episode in *The Gospel According to Jesus Christ*. In Saramago's version of the famous miracle Jesus raises the dead Lazarus only to be chided by a reproachful Mary Magdalene, who reminds him that "no one is so sinful that he deserves to die a second time."

The current decade has seen no slackening in Saramago's creative drive, but some have discerned a move away from the author's elaborate (or, as some prefer, "baroque") brew of erudite commentary and narrative toward a more conventional novelistic structure. The change became apparent in *Ensaio sobre a Cegueira* (1995; Eng. *Blindness*, 1998), a novel some have described as harrowing in its vivid account of an unidentified society suddenly afflicted by a plague of blindness. The author describes a descent into terror and hysteria as all semblance of comity surrenders to unleashed savagery and wholesale cruelty. Only a small group guided by a woman who has somehow maintained her sight avoids succumbing to the reigning barbarism. When sight is abruptly restored, the survivors are faced with a devastated country that will have to be rebuilt.

The critical reaction to Saramago's parable of a society bereft of lucidity and any sense of shared interests met with favorable reviews, even while some commentators expressed misgivings over Saramago's expressionistic excesses in creating a vision of society's collapse. One might note, however, that the author entertained similar Dantean imagery twenty years earlier when he wrote the poems published in *O Ano de 1993* (The Year 1993; 1975). Here too one encounters plague-ridden cities where torture is officially sanctioned and social order collapses. The verses present horrific situations that even surpass *Blindness* in some ways, as we find in one poem where household pets turn on their masters with sadistic cruelty. And both the early poems and the recent novel suggest that wholesale mayhem may be a necessary prelude to restoring order and social tranquillity. Also, each work ends with a torrential downpour that washes away the debris of chaos. Only then can social harmony emerge from the ruins, an optimistic resolution expressed in the poems in the form of "a rainbow that appears each night / and that is a good sign."

In 1997 Saramago returned to allegory in the novel *Todos os Names* (All the Names), with its anonymous setting and characters. The protagonist, known only as José, is a spiritual twin of Raimundo de Silva from *The History of the Siege of Lisbon*, a colorless white-collar employee who one day arbitrarily makes a life-changing decision at his job as a clerk in the Ministry of Civil Records. But there will be no happy affair with a Sara; rather, José becomes obsessed with the history of a woman whose records he removes by mistake from the files. His search eventually reveals that she has recently died by her own hand. At novel's end parable and myth merge when, like Orpheus, José returns to the Ministry's labyrinth to remove her files from the records of the deceased, thus rescuing his unknown but beloved Eurydice from bureaucratic death.

Since moving to the Canary Islands the Nobel laureate has annually published a diary sequentially numbered with the title *Cadernos de Lanzarote* (Notebooks from Lanzarote). In this journal the reader finds the log of a man who is obviously very much at peace with himself and devoted to his wife in their new home "built entirely of books, from top to bottom" in a setting of volcanic hills, flowers, and the sea.[14] Never one to frequent the night life and cafés so dear to Southern European society, he is content to work on his writing each afternoon, with evenings devoted to nearby in-laws or to friends and admirers who visit from far and near. Saramago also expends considerable time and patience caring for several stray dogs that have availed themselves of his wife's open door to take up residence with the couple. The notebooks, however, are by no means limited to scenes of domestic bliss, for they include entries on current events, philosophical reveries, and many trips to international meetings. Our author is in constant demand for conferences, lectures, and honorary distinctions, and he provides the reader of his journal with summaries of many of the papers he delivers in the course of far-flung travels that he seems to find less satisfying with each passing year.

In its decision honoring Lanzarote's most distinguished resident the Swedish Academy cited Saramago's consistent excellence in fashioning parables that balance imagination, compassion, and irony to express an illusory reality. The judges have clearly recognized the laureate's penchant for allegorical structures founded on a striking original situation: a king's vow to build a massive convent, the separation of the Iberian peninsula from Europe, the conception of the Messiah, an arbitrary decision that alters history or one's life, the sudden outbreak of an epidemic of blindness, the repatriation of a dead poet's heteronym. . .Each unusual occurrence triggers a unique blend of the real and the fantastic leavened with lyrical sensitivity, wit, and an erudition that manages to be impressive without becoming obtrusive. At no time, however, does fantasy supplant the author's abiding respect for reason, and he is the first to follow his own advice: "Begin with the imagination, but from then on let reason prevail."[15] One might add that it is *his* reason which prevails: not for Saramago theories regarding intentional fallacy or disappearing authors, nor would he posit an unreliable narrator when an unreliable author will do just as well. Accordingly, none of his works is in danger of being orphaned by intertextuality, for, as he reminds us, in all his writings "there is at least one individual throughout—me!"[16] His voice forges an intimate bond as he leads his reader over a challenging course that is completely absorbing from start to finish.

In addition to a strong authorial presence, Saramago's works exhibit a sense of history that confers a kind of transcendent significance to his characters. Blimunda and Baltasar, for instance, are not only lovers but also paragons of humanity in an age that is found wanting, while even their fellow workers toiling on the Mafra site redeem a bleak time with their quiet heroism. Similarly, Saramago's Messiah is the first of many thousands of victims whose names and tribulations will fill the liturgical calendar, and the woman who leads a little band in the midst of a blind panic ensures that civility and social responsibility will endure. Each individual derives significance from a social context to which each contributes. One might even say that each derives *her* significance, since our author creates female characters who are never marginal or in any way inferior to men in their strength, dignity, and wisdom. They are clearly the creations of one who finds "women more fully human [than men]" and claims to have learned far more from the women he has known than from his fellow males in a distinctly Latin society.[17]

José Saramago imbues his characters, women as well as men, with his own respect for reason and clearheaded common sense, which stand in marked contrast to the foibles and failings of their times. Both intelligence and a sense of humor are essential as long as society continues to indulge what Bacon called the idols of the cave. This is not to imply, however, that mystery and wonder are absent from our author's works. Indeed, wonder and mystery abound in his portrayal of the relationships that make it possible for lovers to unite and individuals to form bonds of friendship and solidarity. There is a fertile tension between, on the one hand, the lucidity that dissolves illusion and, on the other, the kind of trust that asks no questions. Thus, while a verse from *O Ano de 1993* affirms that "people are by nature evasive," one reads in *Os Poemas Possíveis,* "Love is perhaps all we have / perhaps our crown, our mantle." Thus, even while the other is never really

known and opacity rather than transparency describes character, men and women fall in love and trusting friendships are formed. Somehow the two, opacity and trust, must be reconciled, and even the seer Blimunda, who divines the inner will of others, swears to respect Baltasar's intrinsic autonomy by never plumbing the depths of her lover's spirit. The reconciliation seems to come about thanks to an adaptation of the traditional believer's faith in things unseen. It may not be too much to say that Saramago's views regarding love and trust constitute a secular version of Pascal's appeal to heartfelt reasons that may elude reason itself. The wonder and mystery in his works, therefore, stem from the fact that lucid individuals free of illusion can live in the harmony of love and trust without succumbing to wishful thinking and superstition.

Given the complexity and versatility of the laureate's work, it is unfortunate that much of the international news concerning the 1998 Nobel Prize in Literature has focused on Saramago's membership in the Communist Party and on the Vatican's jaundiced view of his award. A case in point is the *Wall Street Journal*'s editorial "Another Nobel Laureate's Stalinist Past," where one looks in vain for a single positive statement. Even allowing for the media's preference for sound bites and, especially in the United States, despite a hoary hysteria regarding all things even remotely Marxist, one might have expected a modicum of nuance given the author's record of intellectual independence. When the communist-oriented journal *Seara Nova* sought compliance in matters of artistic liberty in 1964, the future laureate resigned in protest. More recently, he has publicly stated, "I do not regard my party as competent to decide on literary matters or artistic issues."[18] On the other hand, he obviously finds in Marxism insights useful for understanding social issues. When he learned of his award, he was attending the Frankfurt Book Fair to participate in a roundtable of Portuguese writers discussing "On Being a Communist Writer Today." Our author answered the question "Can one still be a communist?" in the affirmative with his usual irony, a sure defense against the dogmatism that the *Wall Street Journal* would impute to him. For Saramago, being a communist requires "a certain spirit (I grant that this is hardly a materialist condition)." At the Frankfurt meeting he proceeded to define such a spirit by invoking a Marxist dictum: "If man is shaped by circumstances, it behooves us to shape such circumstances humanely."[19] For his part, he sees little humanity in a world where market forces substitute for policies that are reasonable and rational and daily fluctuations of paper losses and gains on stock markets comprise the primary news of the day. He is therefore appalled that "the supreme superintendent of education in our time, including 'civic' and 'moral' education, is the shopping mall. We are being educated to be consumers. This is the basic education that we are transmitting to our children."[20] As for those who claim that the history of communism invalidates any moral authority claimed by its adherents, he counters with references to centuries of religious persecution, authoritarian oppression, and obscurantism, "but the Pope is still there" to speak on behalf of such ideals as the inviolable dignity of the individual.[21]

When one looks into the second major news item, the Vatican's reaction, it soon becomes apparent that the editorial in the *Osservatore Romano* turns out to be less severe in its criticism than has been reported. The Roman newspaper described the laureate as "anticlerical" and "an inveterate communist," a description that Saramago himself might consider neither unfair nor inaccurate, albeit terribly simplistic. In Portugal itself the Portuguese hierarchy exercised remarkable independence by publicly closing ranks in support of an honored favorite son despite Rome's disapproval, and the well-known Dominican intellectual, Brother Bento Domingues, went so far as to praise the laureate's courage in addressing "major world problems including issues dealing with human spirituality and life in society" and to fault the Vatican's newspaper for failing "to evaluate a literary body of work [in all its esthetic density] while criticizing someone for what he has every right to be—a communist. [The newspaper's reaction] is laughable."[22] A rare objection to Saramago's award based on religious reasons was expressed by Dom Duarte Po, the pretender to the Portuguese throne, who declared that "José Saramago openly insults [our] Christian sentiments." The prince was promptly excoriated in the press for assuming a religious homogeneity that many of his countrymen hotly dispute. It would appear that his attempt to deliver a royal scolding only served to validate a republican form of government, its drawbacks notwithstanding.[23]

For all his reputation in certain quarters as an anticlerical firebrand, Saramago has observed that "to be an atheist like me requires a high degree of religiosity."[24] One might add that it is *because* of his interest in questions of faith and reason that he insists on not confusing the two with ill-advised attempts to impose faith-based policies in the public domain where reason alone can appeal to all, believers and nonbelievers alike. To those who would argue that religion is essential to ensure social harmony and the general welfare, he looks to history and to his own experience as one who has lived much of his life under a conservative, religiously oriented regime to argue cogently that religious beliefs are neither necessary nor sufficient to achieve a society that is just,

peaceful, and moral. He is ruefully aware, however, that human nature remains perversely recalcitrant to reason, including the humanism inherent in his Marxist principles. Recently our author expressed more than a little pessimism in an interview: "The world is not going to improve. . . . We are returning to an intolerant time, one which is so not only politically or socially but also in a religious sense, the worst of all kinds of intolerance."[25] Like Sisyphus, though, José Saramago perseveres in his defense of reason as an alternative to the claims of religion and the nihilism of contemporary cynicism. His life and works demonstrate that even in the darkest of times the lives of ordinary people provide equal measures of delight, intellectual challenge, and a renewed conviction that "Each one of us is for the moment life itself, / Let that be enough for us."[26]

Richard A. Preto-Rodas, Winter 1999

[1] The incident will appear in the fifth volume of *Cadernos de Lanzarote*. It is cited in the newspaper *Destaque* for 10 October 1998, pp. 2–3. All translations are my own.

[2] See the article by the Stockholm-based correspondent Alexandre Pastor, "Um Prémio a Contento de Todos" (A Prize to Everyone's Liking), in the biweekly cultural review *JL (Jornal de Letras)* for 14 October 1998, p. 6.

[3] For a non-Portuguese view of the cultural dimensions of this year's Nobel Prize, see Luciana Stegagno Picchio, "A História e a Parábola" (History and Parable), in *JL* for 21 October 1998, p. 13. In the same issue see the comments of the president of the Brazilian Academy of Letters, Arnaldo Niskier, "Consagração da Língua" (Consecration of the Language), p. 14.

[4] See João Mário Grilo, "A Obra Explica o Autor" (The Work Explains the Author), in *JL* for 14 October 1998, pp. 16–17.

[5] In 1997 Saramago stated, "The Nobel Prize does not enhance the prestige of a nation's literature. . . . If tomorrow Portuguese literature were to win a Nobel Prize, it would not gain any more respect on the world stage." See *JL* for 14 October 1998, p. 27.

[6] For the genesis of "Saramago," see the author's interview with Carlos Reis, "O Momento Decisive" (The Decisive Moment), in *JL* for 14 October 1998, pp. 16–17.

[7] From an interview given in 1983, quoted in *JL* for 14 October 1998, p. 24.

[8] See Germano de Almeida, "Inventar a Escrita" (To Invent Writing), in *JL* for 21 October 1998, p. 14. See also the special edition of the news weekly *Visão,* 9 October 1998, p. 21.

[9] Steiner's comments, which appeared in the *Times Literary Supplement,* are quoted in *Visão*, p. 27.

[10] Quoted in Reis's essay, p. 17.

[11] See *Visão*, p. 19. See also the issue for 15 October 1998, p. 103: "I feel as though I were from a large country that extends from the Canary Islands to Brazil." And the feeling is mutual: Saramago has collaborated with the renowned Brazilian photographer Sebastião Salgado in the latter's *Terra,* and his *Levantado do Chão* provides the title and theme for a record by the Brazilian composer Chico Buarque de Holanda. See *JL* for 14 October

1998, p. 23. In the same issue there is an article written by Saramago in 1989 expressing his mixed feelings as a European. See "Europa sim, Europa não," pp. 29–30.

[12] See *Visão* for 9 October 1998, p. 22.

[13] See *Destaque* for 10 October 1998, p. 2.

[14] See *JL* for 14 October 1998, p. 27.

[15] See Maria Leonor Nunes, "Uma Vida com Palabras" (A Life with Words), in *JL* for 14 October 1998, pp. 8–9.

[16] See Alexandre Pinheiro Torres's column in *Destaque* for 9 October 1998, p. 6.

[17] From an interview in the literary journal *Ler,* quoted in *Visão* for 9 October 1998, p. 18.

[18] See the interview with Rodrigues da Silva in *JL* for 14 October 1998: "Um Escritor Confessa-se" (A Writer Makes a Confession), p. 25.

[19] For a summary of the panel's papers, see the newspaper *Público-Leituras* for 10 October 1998, pp. 2–3.

[20] See Saramago's essay "A Mão que Embala o Berço" (The Hand That Rocks the Cradle), reprinted in *Visão* for 9 October 1998, p. 34.

[21] From an interview in *Destaque* for 10 October, p. 3.

[22] See Frei Bento Domingues's essay, "Um Encontro com o Evangelho" (A Meeting with The Gospel), in *JL* for 21 October 1998, p. 15. Concerning the reaction of the *Osservatore Romano,* see also António Marujo's "Commentrio" (Commentary) in the news daily *Cultura* for 22 October 1998, p. 30.

[23] See Ferreira Fernandes's comments on Dom Po's objection in *Visão* for 15 October 1998, p. 12.

[24] From an article in *Ler* written in 1991, quoted in *Visão* for 9 October 1998, pp. 68–71.

[25] Quoted in *Visão* for 9 October 1998, p. 30.

[26] From Saramago's *Provavelmente Alegria* (1970).

Fernando Pessoa's Legacy: The *Presença* and After

To study the extent and character of Fernando Pessoa's legacy, it is necessary to consider the circumstances surrounding the publication of his work. Practically unknown at the time of his death, Pessoa (1888–1935) possessed a reputation based solely on *Mensagem* (Message; 1934), a book of nationalistic verse imbedded in the occult—a little-known facet of this multifaceted poet—as well as on several dozen poems scattered throughout short-lived, inaccessible journals such as *Orpheu* (1915), *Athena* (1924–25), *Contemporânea* (1922–26) and *Presença* (1927–40).

Nor did Pessoa's known work give the true measure of his legacy. *Mensagem* was not well received, not even by some of the poet's small band of admirers. They would have preferred that Pessoa introduce himself to the public with a work of a less patriotic nature. The steady collaboration he maintained in these other journals, on the other hand, could not overcome the scandalous behavior of years past, when those "lunatics" from *Orpheu* with whom he was associated stirred sleepy Lisbon into literary awareness. For years he was known as the poet of *Orpheu,* dismissed by some for the scandal he and others had caused, hailed by others as the poet most responsible for introducing Modernism into Portugal.

Until the late forties, when the bulk of his work began to be available to the public and to the critics not directly involved with Modernism, Fernando Pessoa was admired and imitated mostly because of the boldness of the technical innovations evident from the poems in *Orpheu.* We know now that formal experimentation was only one of his many facets, the one he had assigned to "Álvaro de Campos." Among the several other selves Pessoa invented to express his many moods—the heteronyms—Campos represented the Modernist outlook and style. It was left to later generations to discover that there were other important traits in Pessoa's poetry. To the free verse and structural audacity of the Modernist Campos were added the epigrams from the Latinist "Ricardo Reis," well-wrought poems carving contemporary themes in Horatian odes. Juxtaposed to these two poets was the matter-of-fact, almost careless free verse of "Alberto Caeiro," the anti-poet, for whom only the exterior world was real. And from this symphony of poets Pessoa himself emerged as conductor, striving toward what none of the others had dared to seek—to apprehend the ineffable world beyond words, the irrational made rational through language, the intensely musical verse akin to song. It is this legacy, the attempt to express the inexpressible through the power and mystery of language, that characterizes Fernando Pessoa's influence on Portuguese poetry today.

In such a broad topic as the study of sixty-three years of Fernando Pessoa's legacy, it would be impossible, within restricted space, to present more than a summarized account of the movements and poets involved. Rather than try to be superficially comprehensive, it seems advisable to concentrate on one particular movement, the *Presença,* and to study its pioneering role in making known the novelty and excellence of Pessoa's poetry. Moving beyond esthetic affinities, I shall examine those poets from *Presença* in whose work the Pessoa legacy is most evident.

■ ■ ■

The first literary movement in Portugal to recognize the importance of Fernando Pessoa was *Presença*. The name was derived from a journal which in the late twenties congregated a group of young students from the University of Coimbra who wanted to transform the quality of Portuguese literature, bringing it closer to echoing European trends. The journal lasted thirteen years (1927–40). Fifty-six numbers were issued in two different series: fifty-four in the first and two in the second. During those thirteen years *Presença* defended the literary artifact with unswerving devotion, rescuing Portuguese literature from the clutches of an autocratic government bent on using folksy, easily accessible art as a means of propaganda. A steady struggle was maintained in the pages of the journal to keep literature pure, that is, to make literature an earnest and sincere spiritual activity between the writer and his craft. Furthermore, *Presença* wanted to keep literature autonomous, free from any correlative purpose, such as being used as a vehicle for exposing sociopolitical ills. In time *Presença* would be accused of promoting art for art's sake by the proponents of committed literature beginning to be heard in Portugal after 1940.

As they looked for literary vocations as genuine as their own, the *Presença* group became interested in the poets from *Orpheu*. Theirs had been an authentic and sincere poetry, and as such it needed to be revived and their authors brought back from semi-oblivion into the Modernist fold. Therefore the group that called itself "the second Modernism" set out to promote the poets from the first Modernism. In one of the journal's first issues José Régio wrote in reference to Pessoa: "For all these advantages, Fernando Pessoa has the makings of a Master and is the richest in outlets of the so-called Modernists" (*Presença*, 3, 8 April 1927). Spurred by such acclaim, Fernando Pessoa went on to publish some of his best work in *Presença*.

Presença was founded, edited and directed at first by José Régio, a pseudonym for José Maria dos Reis Pereira (1901–69), the most gifted writer to have emerged from the group and its principal animator; João Gaspar Simões (b. 1903), novelist and foremost critic whose weekly columns appearing in leading newspapers have helped shape Portuguese letters for the past fifty years; and Branquinho da Fonseca (1905–74), poet and novelist, author of an excellent novel, *O barão* (The Baron; 1942). An important event occurred in the early stages of *Presença*'s history. Alleging that the journal's prevailing philosophy, as determined by Régio, smothered individual expression, Branquinho da Fonseca broke away from the group, taking with him Adolfo Rocha (better known as Miguel Torga, b. 1907) and Edmundo Bettancourt (1899–1973), leaving Régio and Simões to answer for the journal.

Fernando Pessoa became indirectly involved in the controversy. He was one of the "Masters" who were sup-posedly guiding *Presença* toward esthetic absolutism. Miguel Torga told him so in an angry letter written in reference to Pessoa's unfavorable opinion of his book *Rampa* (1930): "The era of the Masters has already passed," he wrote (*Cartas de Fernando Pessoa a João Gaspar Simões,* Lisbon, Europa-América, 1957, pp. 56–57). As a gesture of allegiance to Régio and Simões—they were later joined by Adolfo Casais Monteiro (1908–72)—Fernando Pessoa maintained from then on a steady presence in the journal. The *presencistas* in turn did all they could to make Pessoa's poetic genius known while he was alive and continued to do so even after his death. First they sought his active collaboration. Later, when *Presença* prospered enough to launch its own book series, the directors offered to publish his work. He declined, suggesting the publication of Mário de Sá-Carneiro's unpublished poems instead, which were in his keeping. Gaspar Simões wrote the first two critical essays on Pessoa to appear in book form—*Temas* (1929) and *O mistério da poesia* (1931).

After Fernando Pessoa died, Simões and Luis de Montalvor—the latter had been with him in *Orpheu*—went through his manuscripts and selected the poems which today make up the first four volumes of the "Complete Works," put out by Ática. Along with *Mensagem,* already published, these four volumes are the nucleus of Pessoa's poetry. Other volumes of unpublished works have since appeared. Their contents, however, have not revealed any better poems than the ones originally selected by Simões and Montalvor. Unfortunately, Simões's crowning effort on behalf of Pessoa, the monumental and controversial *Vida e obra de Fernando Pessoa* (Lisbon, Bertrand, 1951), fell short of expectations. Some of the conclusions reached are based on psychological probings into the human soul, difficult to assess. Nevertheless, in spite of the impressionistic methods used, Simões's biography is still the fundamental, most complete study of Fernando Pessoa's life and work available.

Simões looked at Pessoa from the point of view of a critic. Others in the *Presença* group saw him principally as a poet whose work offered rich possibilities for their own poetic growth. Such was José Régio, at least in the early stages of his poetic career, for after the praise he bestowed on Pessoa in the first three numbers of the journal, he never again wrote a line about him. After that, Régio would always consider Sá-Carneiro the better poet. According to Simões, the reason for the sudden reversal had to do with a meeting, the first between the two poets, or rather between Régio and Campos—elusive, impersonal Campos—who had on that occasion impersonated Pessoa. Hiding behind the mask of Álvaro de Campos, Pessoa answered the young poet's questions evasively, stating during the course of the conversation that he knew little about English literature, having read only two or three English novels. Régio took Pessoa-Campos's strange behavior to be a sign of insincerity and assumed he had been wrong in identifying Pessoa's poetry with his own. The two poets' views on art had collided. For Régio, art was a means of exploring the psyche, of revealing personality, the "I," conscious and subconscious. For Pessoa, art was a means of concealing personality. Art was for him the expression of many masks, of imagined personalities differing from his own, each paradoxically interpreting truth from many points of view.

Pessoa's influence on José Régio's poetry can be traced only to his early work and is evident in "Cântico negro" (Black Canticle), a poem inserted in his first book of poetry, *Poemas de deus e do diabo* (Poems from God and the Devil; Coimbra, 1925). This celebrated poem, written at a time when Régio was an ardent admirer of what little portion of Pessoa's poetry had appeared in print, reveals certain affinities with "Lisbon Revisited, 1923," published for the first time in *Contemporânea* in 1923. Joaquim Montezuma de Carvalho points this out in an article entitled "'Cântico negro,' um poema de José Régio," published in the literary supplement of *O Estado de São Paulo* (no. 769, 4 April 1972, p. 4). In spite of the similarities between the two poems, they differ in tone and style. Pessoa and Régio are, after all, quite different, as are the two movements they superiorly represented—*Orpheu* and *Presença*.

Régio's echoing of Pessoa-Campos—for it is the raving, defiant Campos who in the heteronymic family subscribes to "Lisbon Revisited, 1923"—may be detected in the use of free verse and irregular stanzaic form as well as, thematically speaking, in the tone of social defiance and individual affirmation, the assertion of self-reliance common to both poems. In the Campos poem, however, there is the underlying suggestion of a painful existential awareness which points to the futility of all protest. Protest is useless, according to Campos, in the face of the world's opacity. Where the poetic voice in Régio's poem is resolute, in Pessoa's it is, above all, metaphysically weary.

"Come this way!" some tell me with gentle eyes,
holding out their arms, so sure
that it would be good for me to hear them
when they say, "Come this way!"
I eye them with weary eyes
(fatigue and irony are in my eyes)
and fold my arms
and never go that way.[1]

And in Álvaro de Campos:

Don't take my arm!
I don't like you to take my arm. I want to be alone.
I said I am alone!
Oh what a bore, your wanting me to be with
  people![2]

Régio is confident of the course to be followed. He goes forth with "songs in his lips." The madness of which he speaks is the madness of the seer, the possessed, ready to pursue a vision with obstinate idealism: "I have my own madness." Although madness is never mentioned in the Campos poem, its imminence is implicit in the widely disparate irregularity of the stanzas—some of one or two lines—and the asymmetry of the verse line, abruptly long and short. Often an exclamation mark ends the incomplete thought, as if to sustain and even repress the catapult of feeling ready to burst forth. In the Campos poem the impending madness is the madness of the despondent, the defeated—a final refuge. Moreover, the poem's overall structure contrasts sharply with Régio's relative uniformity of line and stanza in spite of the free verse. In the Régio poem the subjective voice, the "I," never loses control; it imposes itself on the extrinsic reality, while in Campos the "I" is diminished and almost smothered by the overwhelming presence of the universe.

Pessoa and Régio are similar in their devotion to the prerogatives of art, though different in their way of expressing it. Pessoa explores many aspects of truth through the several personalities he has created, far removed from the empirical self. His aim is, as he has said, relating his method to Shakespeare's, to arrive at sincerity through multiple insincerity. By disappearing as an artistic entity, a self, he introduces conflicting realities created by many selves, each an infinitesimal segment of a universal truth. Rooted in emotions Pessoa himself has felt—he too once returned to Lisbon from South Africa after a long absence—"Lisbon Revisited, 1923," for example, interprets reality from the point of view of Campos. Circumscribed within the thematic and structural confines of the Campos poem, the resulting poetic reality has acquired a new dimension which is only faintly related to whatever sensations Pessoa might have felt. All the poetry written by Fernando Pessoa is characterized by this very same dramatic quality. It is the poetry of the other self; "I fly into another," Pessoa tells Simões in a letter regarding the dramatic quality of his verse (*Cartas a João Gaspar Simões,* p. 101).

Régio, on the other hand, is the poet of the empirical self. His poems are poetic "translations" of what he already carried inside himself when he was born, to evoke Régio's own statement in a famous essay included as a postscript to *Poemas de deus e do diabo,* beginning with the second edition. Although his declared intention is to refer his personal anguish and anxiety to that of all mankind, José Régio, like Walt Whitman, never quite succeeds in substituting the egotistical "I" for an egoism that would represent the overall human predicament. His most common theme, the myth of the "fallen angel," depicting the man who fell from grace to find the Devil, is pursued with considerable involvement of the self in spite of the intentions to relate to all mankind.

God and the Devil guide me, no one else!
Everyone has a father, everyone has a mother!
But I who have no beginning nor end
Was born of the love between God and the Devil.[3]

Orpheu and *Presença* are two closely associated literary movements. The latter sprang from the former and identified with it in the full commitment to literature and in the innovative poetic techniques meant to bring to the surface the formerly untapped human subconscious. At the same time they are two very different movements. On one hand is *Orpheu,* never quite falling into a group pattern, led by three highly individualistic poetic personalities: the enraging, vituperative Almada Negreiros, venting his fury against the Lisbon middle class; or the intellectual, multifaceted Pessoa, hiding behind the many masks; or Sá-Carneiro, himself a sheaf of metaphors, until he becomes one grandiose metaphor, killing himself. On the other hand is *Presença,* more cohesive, led by Régio and Torga, who reaffirm the hegemony of the indivisible self as they grope torturously with Christ's presence on earth: Régio, in anguish, seeking Christ and finding the Devil; Torga immersing himself in the midst of human suffering. His is a telluric mysticism rooted in the harsh, inhospitable region of his birth, the crags and arid valleys of northern Portugal.

It is regrettable that neither Régio nor Torga perceived the religious elements in Pessoa's poetry—regrettable but not surprising. Pessoan appreciation in those days was confined mostly to the question of the simulated selves, the heteronyms. It did not allow for the serious consideration of the poems written under Pessoa's own name, more specifically, the occult poems reflecting an earnest quest for an *Ente Supremo* (Superior Being) or for the intermediate superior beings Pessoa alludes to in a famous letter to Adolfo Casais Monteiro of 13 January 1935, transcribed in Simões's *Vida e obra* (1st ed., vol. 2, pp. 232–33). Although quite different from Régio's theocentricity, focused on Christ and on Catholicism, Pessoa's religiousness, as portrayed in his poems, is no less sincere than Régio's and its ultimate failure in offering an explanation just as poignant.

"I am basically a religious spirit," he confides to Armando Cortes-Rodrigues in a letter of 19 January 1915,

included in *Cartas a Armando Cortes-Rodrigues* (Lisbon, Inquérito, 1959, p. 72). The abiding quest for religious knowledge led him to the study of esoteric doctrines as expounded by such theosophical organizations as the Rosicrucians, the Knights Templars and the Theosophical Society, founded in 1888 by Madame Blavatsky, whose writings he translated into Portuguese. According to Pessoa, these writings were responsible for the reawakened spirituality he felt around 1915. Like Yeats, another convert to Madame Blavatsky's teachings, Pessoa sought solace for an avidly religious spirit in the principles and teachings of the non-Christian theosophical societies with their promise of semi-mystical thought.

The two *Presença* poets for whom the Pessoa legacy was most meaningful, playing an important role in their poetic accomplishments, were the younger poets Adolfo Casais Monteiro and Carlos Queiroz (1907–49). Both were attracted no less by his personality than by his poetic accomplishments, unlike Régio and Torga, whose initial interest in Pessoa waned for reasons other than artistic. As expected, the poetry written by Adolfo Casais Monteiro and Carlos Queiroz is influenced principally by Campos, the heteronym most likely to serve as the catalyst for the Pessoa legacy, given his alluring message of disaffected man, abandoned by God, by country and by family. However, it is possible to discern in their work the first traces of Pessoa himself—that is, the poet who chose to feign under Pessoa's own name but who was as much a heteronym as the others (to borrow an ingenious observation made by Jorge de Sena). Let us look at a poem by Casais and one by Queiroz where the Campos presence is evident. "Ode to the Tagus and to the Memory of Álvaro de Campos," the Casais poem, recalls "Lisbon Revisited," the poem discussed in connection with Régio's "Black Canticle." It is included in *Poesias completas* (Lisbon, Portugália, 1969, pp. 258–60), and once again we are indebted to Jean Longland's excellent translation.

Only after Álvaro de Campos' shadow sat down
   beside me
did I remember you were there, Tagus.
I passed and didn't see you.
I passed and came to shut myself up in four walls,
   Tagus!
No waiter came to tell me whether this was the table
   where Fernando Pessoa used to sit,
With you and the others invisible around him,
inventing lives he didn't want to have.[4]

In spite of the allusions to "Lisbon Revisited" and the long free-verse expansions, the Casais ode is quite different from Pessoa-Campos. There is a greater prosaic quality to the verse line, a conversational tone that imparts firmness and strength, whereas in "Lisbon Revisited," as in all of Campos, the abrupt, embittered exasperations such as "the only conclusion is to die" convey a sense of restrained despair. The voice is about to crack. The irony comes through in the contrasting lyrical passages allowing for the dilacerated self to emerge.

Oh blue sky—the same one of my childhood—,
Eternal, empty, perfect truth!
Oh sleek Tagus, ancestral and mute,
A small truth where the sky is reflected![5]

Curiously, Casais Monteiro's "Ode to Tagus," with its exaltation of the concrete—the Tagus—and the debasing of abstract thought, draws nearer Alberto Caeiro, the anti-metaphysical heteronym. The exaltation of the concrete and the resulting decrease of emphasis on the abstract is one of the characteristics of Casais's poetry. Another is his intimation of an intemporality and transcendence in the real which is not, however, pursued and apprehended, but remains luminously allusive throughout. The suggestion of an envisioned real irreality on the fringes of the tangible is an important aspect of Pessoa's legacy found in Casais.

With Carlos Queiroz, the Pessoa legacy is in full force. Not only has he inherited from Campos the free-verse technique and the short and long lines meant to convey uncontrolled emotion, but he has also made extensive use of understatement, which is a Campos trademark. His poems reflect the same sense of self-fragmentation to be found in Campos, caused by the impact of a seemingly overwhelming objective reality.

Although more sentimental than Pessoa and more preoccupied with love—a subject not too common in the poetry of his mentor—Queiroz is the first Portuguese poet to follow Pessoa's example of intellectually conceiving a poem, that is, of making each poetic element contribute toward the poem's organic whole. In Pessoa, language is carefully chosen, each word weighed against other words in the verse line, its connotations igniting realities which, based on language, go beyond language. As the poetry subscribed by Pessoa himself attracted the critics' attention, the subtle manipulation of language to describe the abstract and the mysterious lurking behind the senses became the most important aspect of Pessoa's legacy.

Presença ceased publication in 1940. World events such as the Spanish Civil War and World War II brought about a shift in literary taste which went from the esthetic and confessional to the militant. For almost forty years Pessoa's reputation as a poet became involved in the contention between the militant poets who saw literature, and poetry in particular, as a vehicle for social reform and the craftsmen who believed that the demands of form and structure were to be met in the creation of a poem.

Challenged by the so-called "new realists," who were further alienated by nationalistic *Mensagem* and its use by the government's propaganda machine, Fernando Pessoa lost favor with the general public and the young. On the other hand, his following increased among the estheticists, who had begun to discover artistic qualities in Pessoa which had been obscured by the Modernist breakthrough he had initiated. Neglected at home by the militant poets, Pessoa's poetry traveled to other lands. Brazil adopted him as its very own, his acclaim there reaching apotheosis. The foreign recognition has helped to solidify Pessoa's reputation at home, which today knows no bounds.

For this, *Presença* was greatly responsible. The critical excellence and the artistic integrity of such writers as José Régio, João Gaspar Simões, Adolfo Casais Monteiro, Carlos Queiroz and others helped to rescue Pessoa from oblivion while contributing in no small measure to the importance of his legacy in contemporary Portuguese poetry.

Alex Severino, Winter 1979

Ed. Note: Special thanks should be given to *WLT* Editorial Board member Klaus Müller-Bergh, who initially proposed the idea of a special Lusophone number and whose tireless efforts and expert advice have been instrumental in assembling this issue's essays, poetry selections and photographs. The editors of course bear the final responsibility for the appearance and selection of the material—and the blame for any omissions or inaccuracies.

[1] *Modern Poetry in Translation: Portugal,* vols. 13–14, London, 1972, pp. 16–17. The poems quoted have been admirably translated by Jean R. Longland, Curator of the Library of the Hispanic Society of New York and a renowned translator of Portuguese poetry.

[2] *Portuguese Essays,* Lisbon, pp. 55–56, 63–69.

[3] *Modern Poetry in Translation.*

[4] *The Journal of the American Portuguese Society,* 12:1, p. 21.

[5] *Portuguese Essays.*

Prodigious Exorcist: An Introduction to the Poetry of Jorge de Sena

"Nature interests me," he said, "but nature interests me if human beings or human marks are upon nature; otherwise, I'm not interested in nature at all." Earlier in the interview he'd said, "I always was against the idea that poets, to be considered important, must be stupid and illiterate."[1] These two statements, although mild by comparison, are typical of the iconoclastic candor evinced by Jorge de Sena throughout his life and go far in explaining the writer's prime matter: that substance from which he drew inspiration.

Jorge de Sena (1919–78) was, above all, a humanist, a critical observer of the human condition—and a poet (he was anything but stupid or illiterate). Throughout his life—and in this he saw no contradiction—it had been his experience that, along with living fully immersed in the present, he could cultivate the wisdom and learning of the past. This drive led him to become preeminent as a scholar, cultural historian and university professor. Without becoming confessional or yet psychological, he found he could also come closer to understanding mankind by penetrating into the deepest recesses of his own being, both mind and body, and so became Portugal's leading contemporary man of letters: poet, playwright and author of short fiction.

These two avenues to human understanding—from without and within—were made all the more efficacious in him by virtue of his diverse formal training: scientific, military and literary. He received an M.A. in civil engineering from the University of Oporto in 1944 and for fifteen years exercised his profession, building roads and bridges for the National Highway Commission. He spent five years in the military: first as a cadet in the naval academy, then four years as an army officer. He received a Ph.D. and Livre Docente (Brazil's highest degree) in literature from the University of São Paulo in 1964. This preparation in both the sciences and humanities made him an unconventional essayist, and he brought to Portuguese literary criticism a precision and exactness rarely seen before. In fact, his methods brought about a major reevaluation of the work of Camões.

Sena's personal experience with the world was likewise uncommonly broad. He lived on three continents and traveled extensively. He left Portugal and his engineering career in 1959 to accept a teaching position in literary theory at the University of São Paulo. He then accepted a professorship in Portuguese at the University of Wisconsin in 1965 and again at the University of California-Santa Barbara in 1970, where from 1975 until his untimely death at fifty-eight on 4 June 1978 he was concurrently chairman of the Department of Spanish & Portuguese and the Department of Comparative Literature. He was born in Lisbon on 2 November 1919 but in 1963 became a naturalized Brazilian citizen. Asked why he remained a Brazilian after thirteen years in the United States, he replied: "Being born a Portuguese, the Brazilians don't like it. And as I was born a Portuguese, the Portuguese don't like it either. So just to irritate both, I keep the citizenship" (Videotape interview, 4 May 1978). Sena wished to become personally acquainted with all present and former lands belonging to Portugal, and he nearly succeeded: he lacked Macao, on the Chinese mainland, and Timor, now part of Indonesia.

With such experience, training, insight and native intelligence, and with the further refinement of his sensibilities through a prolonged study of the thought and culture of Western civilization, it is little wonder that Jorge de Sena was regarded as Portugal's foremost intellectual and achieved an international reputation few Lusitanians have attained. Often compared to the sixteenth-century bard Camões and to the twentieth-century poet Fernando Pessoa, he also had something of the seventeenth-century cleric António Vieira. Neither of the first two had much impact during their lives. Vieira, on the other hand, was a power to be reckoned with throughout the Hispanic world, both as a writer and intellectual. So it was with Sena; but comparisons can be misleading. He worked at no man's bidding nor in the service of any party or philosophy. Neither did he appreciate the *préciosité* often implicit in a Gongoristic style. Sena prided himself on what he called his political and literary integrity. By political integrity he meant he had not compromised himself with either the right or left and was free to reprove them both (and anything in between that needed chastening), which he delighted in doing, to the irritation of nearly everyone. By literary integrity, he meant his style was his own—not borrowed—and that it had undergone few modifications from his first to his last books.

Jorge de Sena's scholarly and creative production is incredibly vast and varied and includes such genres as biography, criticism, essay, literary history, short fiction, theatre, the novel and poetry. He was one of the leading Camões and Pessoa scholars and had published several studies on each. His dedication to cultural history can be seen in the exhaustive study he made on Inês de Castro, which appears in two volumes. At home as well in Spanish literature and culture, he brought to his Iberian studies a breadth and balance rarely seen in either Spain or Portugal, as in his study of Francisco de la Torre, for example. He was one of perhaps two or at most three Portuguese who likewise knew the international bibliographies, the ancient as well as modern texts, which always situated his work in a comparative context.

Sena is the author of a standard text on English literature in use at Portuguese-speaking universities. His output in comparative literature includes book-length essays on authors ranging from Emily Dickinson and Shakespeare to Petrarch and Mauriac. In addition to translating more than twenty volumes by major French, British and American prose writers (including Malraux, Waugh, Greene, Poe, Caldwell, Hemingway, O'Neill and Faulkner), he wrote a one-volume work on the Greek poet Constantine Cavafy, which includes ninety-four translations. In three other volumes he has translated the major poets of the world in a work appropriately entitled "Twenty-Six Centuries of Poetry."

Sena's own creative prose comprised three volumes of short fiction, including the classic *O físico prodigioso* (The Prodigious Physician), and one novel (left unpublished, save for a few excerpts, and lacking its final chapters) entitled *Sinais de fogo* (Signs of Fire), which he had been working on for three decades. *O físico prodigioso* is a novelette that draws elements from two tales popular during the Latin Middle Ages. The first is about a young man who is able to cure a sick lady and bring 500 men of her court back to life with his blood, because he satisfies three conditions: he is handsome, a virgin and a physician. The second tells of a man who can never be hanged because he is protected by his master, the devil. In Sena's story the tales are combined: Satan is the force behind the young man's curative powers. In exchange for the miracle of life, the ability to become invisible, and all manner of magic (including the ability to control time and replay events, which allows him the opportunity to enjoy the pleasures of young women's company and then erase all memory of it, leaving him a virgin once more), the youth must periodically service Satan sexually. At key points the narration is divided into two columns on the page, each a separate account of the same reality, but from two perspectives. Besides entertaining the reader (which, as a consummate raconteur, Sena always does), he provides much food for thought on the nature of and relationship between good and evil, sin and responsibility.

Sena also wrote and published seven plays, one of which, *O indesejado* (The Unwanted King), is considered a masterpiece, the most significant play of the first half of this century. The four-act tragedy in verse explores the unsuccessful bid by the Prior do Crato for the Portuguese throne (it went instead to Phillip II of Spain in 1580, and thus began the sixty years of the so-called "Babylonian Captivity"). Sena had also been a theatre and movie critic, publishing his reviews in the leading newspapers of Portugal and Brazil. His major creative vein, however, was poetry, of which he published over a dozen volumes (of even quality) which I will presently consider. Taken together, his articles, essays, monographs and books number well over 200, and he left a dozen books ready for the press (both literary and scholarly); in the past decade it was common for him to publish six or more volumes a year.

He had been the recipient of numerous awards and prizes in various countries, including Italy's prestigious Etna Taormina International Poetry Prize in 1977. In 1976 he was selected as the keynote speaker for the International Convention of Writers at Grado, Italy. Canceled at the last minute, he would have shared the honors with three Nobel laureates: Solzhenitsyn, Böll and Montale. He delivered the keynote address at the 1977 Camões Day Celebration, which was presided over by the President of Portugal and televised nationwide. He was a member of the Lisbon Academy of Sciences, a member of the Hispanic Society of America, a Commander of the Order of Prince Henry the Navigator and a posthumous recipient of the Order of St. James. He was also a nominee for the Nobel Prize in Literature in 1978.

Jorge de Sena was regarded by many as not only the number one living poet of Portugal, but perhaps the third of all time, after Camões and Pessoa. Like theirs and Eliot's, Sena's poetry is in the mainstream of Western civilization, with each passage rich in allusions to our shared cultural heritage. Yet Sena is not merely a poet of thought and culture, but also of feeling and conscience, and of love, with an incredible variety of meter and verse, rhyme and form, from the classical sonnet sequence to concretism. He was first published on 13 March 1939 in *Movimento,* a student newspaper of the University of Lisbon, where his poem "Nevoeiro" (Dense Fog) appeared under the pseudonym Teles de Abreu. He became an editor of *Cadernos de Poesia,* a literary journal of great prestige in which some of the brightest members of Portugal's third Modernist generation published their work. They include José Blanc de Portugal (b. 1914), Tomás Kim (1915), Ruy Cinatti (1915), Sophia de Mello Breyner (1919) and Eugénio de Andrade (1923). With Sena, they sought to continue the most avant-garde tendencies of the poets in the first Modernist generation (Fernando Pessoa, Sá-Carneiro, Almada Negreiros), which in many ways meant reaching back over the work of most of the poets connected with *Presença* (members of the second Modernist generation), who had become too predisposed toward art for art's sake.

Perseguição (Persecution), his first volume, appeared in June of 1942 and contained a total of fifty-one poems arranged into three sections; nine sonnets appeared which contrasted sharply with the free-verse form of most of the other poems. But a variety of form (and content) would become his hallmark. The subjects ranged from man's relationship to man and the universe, to love, with much introspection and a marked tendency to explore surrealist and Modernist techniques such as free verse, juxtaposed thoughts and themes, truncated syntax and a slightly chaotic spatial arrangement. In those early years Sena also experimented with the more radical techniques of surrealism, such as suspending the conscious, logical and moral reason to allow free rein to the imaginings of the subconscious self. But he soon abandoned the experiments, explaining that he found them to be quite dangerous: "I got a big scare. I discovered they were no jokes. . .and one had to back away" (Video-tape interview, 4 May 1978). He did, however, retain the notion that a poem is autonomous and should be allowed to develop naturally, which sometimes meant unhurried over a long period of time. Once written, however, a poem was rarely changed.

Perseguição was followed by *Coroa da terra* (Crown of the Earth; 1946) and *Pedra filosofal* (Philosopher's Stone; 1950), with a special volume in 1955 containing a twenty-one-sonnet sequence entitled *As evidências* (The Evidences). When these four were collected and published as *Poesia I* in 1961, Sena included a section or volume entitled "Post-Scriptum," containing thirty-three unpublished or dispersed poems dating from the same periods as the other volumes. *Fidelidade* (Fidelity) was published in 1958, followed by *Metamorfoses* (Metamorphosis; 1963) and *Arte de música* (Art of Music; 1968), the last two, like *As evidências,* considered by Sena to be outside the mainstream of his poetic flow but running parallel to it. *Metamorfoses* contains evocations and impressions of or prompted by various art objects: paintings, buildings, statues, as well as poems and poets. It also includes a four-sonnet sequence to Aphrodite Anadyomene (rising from the water) that utilizes Greek and other ancient language forms which, while giving the impression of an ancient tongue, appear as near-words in Portuguese; they thus evoke the most erotic scenes which, if stated rather than suggested, would be blatantly obscene.

Arte de música, as its title suggests, contains evocations and impressions associated with or suggested by various musical compositions by the masters, including Bach, Händel, Mozart and Beethoven. In 1969 he published *Peregrinatio ad loca infecta* (Peregrination to the Polluted Regions), followed in 1972 by *Exorcismos* (Exorcisms) and in 1974 by *Conheço o sal* (I Know the Salt). Smaller collections include *Camões dirige-se aos seus contemporáneos* (Camões Addresses his Contemporaries), published in 1973, and *Sobre esta praia* (On this Shore), a series of eight meditative poems written on the shores of Santa Barbara, published in 1977. *Poesia II* and *Poesia III,* containing all his published volumes since *Poesia I,* appeared in 1978.

Unpublished at his death was *Quarenta anos de servidão* (Forty Years of Servitude), a selection made from his unpublished and uncollected poems written between 1938 and 1978 to celebrate his forty years of writing poetry. An anthology with a similar format—but using only poems that had appeared in the various published volumes—celebrated his thirty years as a poet, *Trinta anos de poesia* (Thirty Years of Poetry); it did not appear until 1972, however. Sena also left a volume entitled *Dedicácias* (Inscriptions), which are his scurrilous, satirical and obscene poems, very much in the tradition of the medieval *Cantigas de escárnio e maldizer* (Songs of Scorn and Slander), and a number of smaller collections, among them *América, América, I Love You* (ironic poems on life in the United States, especially during the Vietnam War) and *Invenções au goût du jour* (Inventions in Today's Style), concrete-like poems and experimentations on the poetry of various writers. Still remaining are folders with well over a hundred unpublished poems.[2]

■ **MAJOR THEMES**

Culture. As the above review of Sena's poetry has shown, references abound to the art, literature, music and history of ancient and modern civilizations. As might be expected, such allusions by one so thoroughly acquainted with Western culture have tended to intimidate his readers. But Sena could do no differently. He never apologized for his erudition and did not attempt to conceal it. To the contrary, he relished the arts. He had an immense personal library, with books and records overflowing the shelves that stood from floor to ceiling on every wall in nearly every room in his spacious house. In the poem "Mahler: Sinfonia da ressurreição" his contemplative spirit is set on fire by the beauty of the music, which in turn excites his mind with an appreciation of the grandeur and majesty of eternity. Still, he does not give himself over fully to faith in the resurrection, but is nonetheless compelled to declare belief in some paradise.

Mahler: Resurrection Symphony
Before this impetus of sounds and silence,
before such shouts of furious peace,
before this furor grand enough to coexist eternal
could there be Gates in boundless space that might
  withstand?
Could there be boundless space which might resist
  not having gates
that could be forced? And could there be a Paradise
that would not wish to be true? And what Paradise
could dream itself more real than this?[3]

Political Satire and Portugal. When asked what characterized his poetry most, whether love, music, politics or culture, Sena responded that all of them did, but then added that satire was clearly a dominant tone in many things he wrote. He was quite correct; nothing delighted him more than to goad or play the role of gadfly, particularly in regard to his country's politics. But though he attacked often and vehemently, it was only Portugal's meanness he decried. He was always proud of his Portuguese heritage. Classic is his poem "Os paraisos artificias" (The Artificial Paradises), where he bemoans the lack of liberty under Salazar's repressive government: "My country is not ineffable. / Life in my country is what is ineffable. / Ineffable is what cannot be said." In "Os ossos do imperador e de outros mais" (The Emperor's Bones and Some Others) he states that his countrymen have ceased to dream or think and only procreate.

Portugal is filled with soldiers, prostitutes and those who ride in new cars—a reference to the physical and moral toll the African wars had exacted—and all of them mediocre, says Sena in "L'été au Portugal" (Summer in Portugal). In another classic poem, "Uma pequenina luz" (A Very Little Light), he desperately and defiantly clings to the flickering flame of liberty, which he is determined will one day catch fire. Where is liberty? he asks in "Quem a tem?" (Who Has It?), and vows not to die before seeing what its colors are in his native land. His bittersweet relationship with Portugal is clearly expressed in "Aviso de porta de livraria" (Sign Over a Bookstore Door) where he confesses that his homeland, though she brings him pain, is the subject of much of his poetry. He cannot do otherwise; his soul is Portuguese: "Of love and of poetry and of having a homeland / are herein treated: /. . .where one dies in human dignity / the pain of having been born in Portugal / with no remedy but to carry her in one's soul."

Immediately after the 1974 revolution an exultant Sena celebrated the long-awaited advent of liberty in poem after poem: "Nunca pensei viver para isto" (I never thought I'd live to see this) was the first line of one poem. In another, "Cantiga de Abril" (Song of April), he is permitted to answer his own query on the color of liberty: it's green, green and red, he says, the colors of the Portuguese flag. But after nearly fifty years of dictatorship the people lacked confidence and were ill-prepared for self-government. In some poems Sena admonishes them to believe in themselves; in others he cautions that it will take courage to maintain liberty. With the passage of time he saw with great sorrow and disappointment the discrepancies and errors committed by would-be leaders, do-gooders, charlatans and divisive politicians of various philosophical persuasions; and the excitement of the early years turned to anxiety

in his later poems, as in this fragment from *Quarenta anos de servidão*:

Ah people, people, how they have misled you
dreaming the dreams that you had unlearned!
And how they've frightened you one and all,
with those dreams and with the fear of them!

. . . . .

Take into your own hands the Portugal you have
so divided amongst itself. Forward.
With tact and with firmness. And with hope.

Social Satire and the Dignity of Man. Sena did not confine his attacks to the foibles of his countrymen alone; he was forever satirizing mediocrity, falseness and hypocrisy, regardless of race, nationality, social position or age: "Women are viscerally dumb / Men are spiritually immoral / Old people are chronologically deaf / Children are intemporally foolish" ("Blind Alley"). He wrote an ode to lying ("Ode à mentira"), a poem in dispraise of old age ("Em des-louvor da velhice") and an "epigraph to the art of stealing" ("Epígrafe para a arte de furtar").

They rob me of God
and others the Devil
—whom shall I sing?

they rob me of Country;
Humanity also
others have robbed me
—whom shall I sing?

there's always a thief
for those whom I love;
and from myself
everyone robs me
—whom shall I sing?

they rob me of voice
if quiet and meek,
they rob me of silence
if I should then speak
—help, send for the king!

It was said of Sena that, once hurt, he would forgive but never forget. Sometimes just the opposite seemed true: he would not forgive but soon forget. However, if something reminded him of the old wound, all the feelings would return to him in a flood, prompting such masterful tirades as the following:

Camões Addresses His Contemporaries
You may well rob me of everything:
ideas, words, images,
as also metaphors, themes, motifs,
symbols, and of being first
in suffering the pangs of a new language,
in understanding others, in courage

to fight, to judge, to penetrate
into the recesses of love for which you are castrated.
And later you may well not credit me,
but suppress me, ignore me and even acclaim
other more fortunate thieves.
It matters not: for your punishment
shall be terrible. Not only will
your grandchildren no longer know who you are
they will have to know me far better
than what you pretend not to know,
since everything, just everything you so laboriously
     pilfer,
will revert to my name. And shall in fact be mine,
be taken as mine, accounted as mine,
even that miserable and precious little
which, on your very own, without stealing, you'll
     have fashioned.
You shall have nothing, but nothing; not even your
     bones,
for the very skeleton of one of you will be sought
     after,
so it may pass as my own. In order that other
     thieves,
just like you, on bended knees, may place flowers on
     the tomb.

In a more pensive mood, he would often reflect on the human condition generally—but nowhere better than in the series of poignant and often mordant "Natal" or Christmas poems, which for him constituted a kind of exorcism, an annual, year-end, state-of-the-world review. Although he nearly always concluded that there was little to rejoice in and rarely found answers to the meaning of life, still his meditations evinced a most lucid perplexity. And more importantly, he always resolved to continue the struggle to better mankind—no matter how depraved or hopeless—convinced that he was answerable for his own actions. Whether he was accountable to man as well, or even to God, did not necessarily concern him: he had to be true to his own inner light, his best self, and to the faithful who had preceded him.

Sena's appeal to human dignity stands out in such poems as "Carta aos meus filhos sobre *Os fusilamentos de Goya*" (Letter to My Children on *The Executions* by Goya), where he decries prejudice against race, religion, nationality or belief and lauds the martyrs' resolve to die for principle: "For being faithful to a god, to an idea / to a homeland, a hope, or just merely / to the unanswerable hunger which gnawed at their guts, / they were disemboweled, skinned, burned, gassed."

Love and Sex. Love was a subject which forever fascinated Sena, and he never tired of exploring its many aspects. He could be a poet of great tenderness and feeling, as in "Como quiras, amor" (As You Desire, Love), or as found in the sensitively drawn portrait series "Sete sonetos de visão perpetua" (Seven Sonnets of Perpetual Vision), where he reflects on the changing stages of love which time has wrought upon his conjugal partnership. He might proposition gently, as in "Na sombra, que dizes" (In the Shadows, How About It?), or be jocular and even scurrilous, as in "La dame à la licorne" or "Em Creta com o Minotaur" (In Crete with the Minotaur), where he "stirs the sugar in his coffee with a dirty finger sullied while investigating the origins of life."

He often reflected on the vicissitudes of an older man stirred sexually by a handsomely endowed young woman, as in "No comboio de Edimburgo a Londres" (On the Train from Edinburgh to London) and "Intriga-me o teu corpo" (Your Body Intrigues Me). He could be explicit, as in "Adivinha dupla" (The Double Guessing Game), even clinically descriptive, as in "Arquitectura do corpo" (Architecture of the Body) or "Filmes pornográficos." He was offended that love should be called dirty in "Arte de amar" (The Art of Love), and extolled the pleasures of undressing someone either with the eyes or by hand in "Despir alguém" (To Undress Someone). He therefore found it hard to understand the apparent lack of allurement a naked body holds for today's youth in "Sobre esta praia, II" (On this Shore, II). He viewed the human body as a thing of beauty and often used it as a symbol for truth and liberty against censorship, as in "Sobre a nudez" (On Nudity).

He could be shocking, as in "O hermafrodito do Museu do Prado" (The Little Hermaphrodite of the Prado Museum); rank, as when he describes the birth process in putrid, living colors in "Maternidade" (Maternity); and pornographic (almost), as in the poems belonging to the Aphrodite Anadyomene series. But most often he was erotic, leaving it up to the imagination of the reader to fill in the details only hinted at by his words. Here is one of the most beautiful:

I Know the Salt
I know the salty taste of your warm skin
when summer ends and slowly turns to winter
your resting body bathed in its nocturnal sweat.

I know the salty taste in milk we drink
when from our eager mouths the lips would tighten
and beating hearts would throb within the groin.

I know the salty taste of your dark hair
or light or gray which softly tumbles down
in this the bluish brilliance of repose.

I know the salt that's left upon my hands
as on the shores a sweet perfume remains
whenever tides recede and then withdraw.

I know the salt within your mouth, the salt
found on your tongue, the salt around your nipples,
and round your waistline curving to the thighs.

I know each salty taste that's yours alone,
or which is mine in you, or yours in me,
a particle of crystal formed by lovers.

For Sena, sex could either be alluring or mechanical, intense or calm, even vulgar and hurtful, but always titillating and a little wicked. And while its urgings could be temporarily satisfied, it was insatiable. Love, on the other hand, was enduring, always tender and thoughtful and strong, forming a bond which even death could not break: "I will come, my love, even after death," he writes in "Tenção do amor nocturno" (Tension of Nocturnal Love).

Death, God and Religion Death intrigued Sena. He refers to it repeatedly, sometimes mockingly, as when he witnesses the decomposition of the body in "Restos mortais" (Mortal Remains), or irreverently, as in "Envoi," where he declares that he wants to be buried naked just below the surface of the sand (so his limbs can poke out to be washed clean by the sea, and his smiling skull warmed by the sun), or even scandalously, as in "O desejado tumulo" (The Desired Tomb), in which he asks to be buried in a hidden shady lane on the outskirts of town, where desperate, lonely youths can secretly masturbate, kidnapped virgins can be despoiled and laughing children can urinate.

He also would take death quite seriously, questioning the process ("I don't know if I think/or will think when I slip from myself"—Sonnet XXI, *As evidências*), asking departed friends how one dies ("A memória de Adolfo Casais Monteiro") and dedicating several long poems to it in which he meditates on its meaning and relationship to the hereafter, as in "A morte, o espaço e a eternidade" (Death, Space and Eternity). In "Fidelidade" he asks to be told the words "that would be told to death, if it could hear, or to the dead, if they could return." In his self-portrait, "Quem muito viu" (He Who Saw Much), he states, a little sadly, that when death comes for him, it will find him already dead. And in his long final poem on death (after a lifetime of musings and jestings about it) all he can be sure of is that "the dead die dead" ("Post-mortem") and that no one escapes. He also suspects, in "Quando o poeta" (When the Poet), that his contemporaries already wish him dead.

Although Sena had been reared in a religious home, he had not been trained to observe the practices of traditional Christianity in his youth. His grandmother was a Positivist matriarch who during most of her life assumed an agnostic attitude; his (for many years) absentee and now disabled old salt of a father was, at best,

indifferent; and his mother, though religious, was the type who continually practiced a self-serving form of self-mortification which was personally abhorrent to Sena. But religion, and especially the rituals, interested him. Man's belief in God (or gods)—no less than his belief in devils, numerology and the occult—was a matter not to be taken lightly, and he studied them all, both ancient and modern. As to his own belief, Sena lived by a high-principled code of morality which, among other things, dictated that he should not seek God through any form of organized religion (though their various services could be very moving to him), while at the same time he should not discount any religious beliefs: he was a true catholic who half-believed in even his own childhood superstitions about the workings of the underworld and the supernatural. He also believed that we pay for our sins while yet in this life.

He admitted once, in "Declaração" (Declaration), a lengthy exposition of his religious convictions, that if he did not at that moment believe in God, he was nevertheless resigned to the fact that he someday would: "I feel I will turn to Thee, / . . . Indeed what I feel / is that, sooner or later, I'll fall prostrate. / . . . I know that I shall believe." In his early poems he questioned the existence of God, suspecting that He was nothing more than man's invention ("Cinco natais de guerra . . . 1944" [Five Wartime Christmases]), and therefore the poet neither needed nor wanted to believe in Him ("Unidade" [Unity]). In "Transepto" (Transept) he systematically searches for God in a church. Seemingly alive with the presence of God when he entered the nave, the church becomes progressively filled with the stench of death, until in the end "God is extinguished." In "Glosa à chegada de Godot" (Gloss on the Arrival of Godot) he frankly states his belief that no God can save mankind from its evil, concluding his thoughts by saying that it is as easy to despair as it is to have hope.

Although Sena sometimes vacillates about God's existence, he nevertheless repeatedly affirms his belief in some form of immortality, and he lived a faithful and God-fearing life. This was not through fear of some future punishment, but from a conviction stemming in part from his personal testimony of the existence of an independent evil power (and if *it* exists, then its opposite exists as well) and partly out of his own integrity to live life the best it can be lived, which meant in justice and truth: honestly, unashamedly, fully. He expressed his belief in immortality in several poems, but nowhere more beautifully than in the following selection, "Madrugada" (Dawn):

One must leave on earth the weeds and sorrow,
and on the water's surface leave the gall of life.
We should, when dead, take with us the desire

and sense of our existence which, while reaching
out beyond the mire below the deepest waters,
shall be as green as age-old hope eternal
upon the bitter meadows now in bloom.

One must leave the trees on earth erect,
and, of trembling flesh, the foolish caverns,
destined now for others and for mountains
which snows will cover with their chilly absence.
To carry in our high resistant bones
an unknown quantity of tranquil peace.

And on the water's surface leave the gall of life.

Frederick G. Williams, Winter 1979

[1] "Jorge de Sena Reads His Own Poetry," a video-tape interview
in color by Frederick G. Williams, conducted 4 May 1978 at
the University of California, Santa Barbara.

[2] In addition to the collections listed in this essay (all published
in Portugal), I am at present preparing a bilingual (Portuguese-
English) anthology of Sena's poetry, which will be published
by Mudborn Press of Santa Barbara. This had been arranged for
prior to his death. The same press is publishing *Sobre esta praia*
with translations by Jonathan Griffin.

[3] All translations from the Portuguese are my own.

SPAIN

Spain's Vernacular Literatures in the Post-Franco Era

Literarily—in terms of development of their own literatures—Gallego, Catalan and Castilian are of comparable
age, although Gallego was first to become a refined instrument of artistic expression. Accidents of history determined that Castilian became dominant within the
peninsula and subsequently in Spain's overseas domains, with Gallego and Catalan restricted almost entirely to their regions of origin (the Northwest and
Northeast of the peninsula, respectively). The rich medieval literatures of Catalan and Gallego declined after
the fifteenth century (a decadence coincident with
Spain's political unification and the hegemony of Castilian). Both enjoyed a modern renaissance beginning in
the nineteenth century, extending into the twentieth.
Truncated by the Civil War and suppressed for over
three decades under Franco, the literatures in Catalan
and Gallego, together with Euskera (Basque) and some
dialectal literatures as well—especially those in *valenciano* and *mallorquín* (dialects of Catalan) and *andalán*
(Aragonese)—are currently experiencing a new flowering, intense activity and enhanced visibility. It would be
inaccurate to imply, however, that this phenomenon is

the result simply of the death of Franco; beginning in
the late sixties and early seventies, this resurgence is
part of a complex politico-cultural whole which merits
scrutiny.

Historically and culturally, the several languages of
the Iberian Peninsula have long been identified with
local autonomy movements in their respective regions.
Political unity in the peninsula was short-lived, ending
when Portugal threw off Spanish domination. Whether
or not the example of Portuguese independence was an
important factor, Galicia, Cataluña, the Basque provinces and occasionally other linguistically distinct sub-
groupings have aspired to break away from the central
government to establish political entities bounded by
the "natural" limits of language and culture. So much
a feature of Spanish history are these divisive tendencies
that Ganivet in *Idearium español* (1896) identified "local
rights" as one of a cluster of peculiarly Spanish characteristics, while Ortega y Gasset in his meditations upon
history (notably in *España invertebrada,* 1921, and *La re-
belión de las masas,* 1929) pointed out that separatism
and extreme individualism constituted perennial national ills.

During the Second Republic and the chaos before
and during the Civil War, regional autonomy groups
were especially active, with vocal proponents seeking
independence from Castile; Cataluña's experiment in
autonomy would likely have succeeded had it not been
for the war, and Galician voters overwhelmingly approved a Statute of Autonomy in July of 1936, shortly
after the Nationalist uprising (Article 4 established the
legality of Gallego, in an officially bilingual context).
Once in power, Franco outlawed not only the regional
separatist parties—together with all other political organizations save the Falange—but also the languages of
local autonomy, the vernacular tongues. Although himself Galician, Franco imposed Castilian as the one legal
national language. Some trace of the resentment produced thereby is still evident four decades later in an
article by the renowned Catalan linguïst Joan Coromines: "Castilian and Galician-Portuguese are sister languages which I have studied profoundly; for Galician-
Portuguese my *profound* sympathy, for Castilian the distrust deserved by a language which attempts to devour
the others."[1]

In the postwar era the vernacular languages could
not be taught in the schools, be used for public functions, publish their own newspapers, et cetera. Logically, the outlawed tongues became the idiom of opposition to the extent that ultimately, for example, songs in
Catalan and Gallego, regardless of theme or content, acquired the status of protest songs by virtue of the language alone. The vernacular literatures suffered by asso-

ciation, and even when not prohibited, faced stricter and more capricious censorship than comparable compositions in Castilian.

Given the impossibility of policing the use of the minority languages within the home, the vernacular tongues survived the years of prohibition, albeit not unscathed. Educational reform legislation approved in the early seventies included authorization of classroom use of the vernacular languages, but after more than thirty years of illegality, no qualified teachers remained. The need to institute courses to prepare them suggests a major problem of Spain's vernacular cultures: because of their minority status during much of the nation's history (and for Galician, centuries of illegality), the vernacular languages have lacked basic grammatical texts,[2] becoming at times the idiom primarily of the untutored, with corresponding internal disparities, manifest not only in the numerous local dialects but in disagreement among "experts" as to spelling, phonetic variants, lexical forms and syntactic principles.

Reintroduction of the vernaculars in the schools necessarily has been hampered by the scarcity or nonexistence of basic teaching tools. As recently as the end of 1977, Xesús Alonso Montero[3] mentioned the absence of a single Galician-language primary school as a key factor in the difficulties experienced by *Vagalume,* the only periodical in Gallego for children. Similarly, the lack of a literate public for vernacular writing afflicts other periodicals and the literature in general.[4] In Galicia especially, where the language has survived primarily among the rural population and illiterates ("a language systematically spoken by those social classes which cannot read"),[5] problems both of the literature and unification of the language are acute.

Minority status down through the years has resulted in untold losses for the vernacular literatures, even in those relatively peaceful periods when they were not rigorously suppressed. Of writers currently in Spain, only the oldest generation—those born around the turn of the century—has experienced anything approaching the context of vernacular culture, a situation wherein the minority literatures labored under no restrictions other than those inherent in the vehicle of a minor tongue: limited public diffusion, greater difficulties in translation, restricted critical recognition. Such limitations led ambitious and talented writers of many generations to write in Castilian. The Galician Countess Pardo-Bazán, Spain's most important woman writer in the nineteenth century, not only wrote in Castilian but avoided intellectual identification with Gallego. Another Galician, Valle-Inclán—one of this century's towering literary geniuses—published entirely in Castilian, and an overwhelming majority of Galicia's prose writ-

ers, even those most involved in regional causes, have tended to write in Castilian.[6] Basque literature was denied the contributions of figures of the stature and fecundity of Unamuno, Baroja and Maeztu, to mention only a few. It can be said without exaggeration that if "Spanish" literature in the twentieth century has achieved world prominence, it has done so at the expense of the peninsula's vernacular literatures. Catalan, with its relatively larger public and more secure economic base, has suffered comparably less attrition than have Basque and Gallego.

Severely restricted, literature in the vernacular languages languished during much of the Franco regime (books being economically beyond the reach of all but a few, occasional literary works were authorized as an escape valve). Official tolerance included a large dose of contempt, as seen in these words by Juan Aparicio, Spain's Director General de Prensa in the fifties: "The writer who publishes in the Grial collection of the Galaxia publishing house in Vigo, or drafts verses in the old-fashioned *d'oc* language [an allusion to Catalán] or in the still more archaic Basque because Castilian seems to him harsh, inaccurate or inexpressive, is a writer who suffers spelling faults in his pen and in his soul and is ashamed of exhibiting his shame openly."[7] The Vigo publishing house Galaxia, for many years the only source of Galician-language works in Spain, was established in 1951 with official tolerance so long as its output was limited to poetry, folklore and the like, but the use of Gallego for more "intellectual," philosophical topics was not allowed (e.g., the Galician translation of a lecture by Heidegger was prohibited).

Those works published in the vernacular languages were allowed little if any publicity in the nation at large; study and criticism were discouraged via censorial prohibitions, and an entire generation of Spaniards grew to maturity unaware of the existence of "other literatures" within the country. The fact that Catalan, with nearly nine million speakers, had become the seventh language of Europe with a literature of international significance was unknown to the average educated Spaniard; dramatists such as Manuel Pedrolo— highly esteemed in England and France—were ignored in Spain, together with poets of the importance of J. V. Foix, Salvador Espriu (see *WLT* 51:2, pp. 224–27) and "Pere Quart" (Joan Oliver). Poet-dramatist Joan Brossa, considered by Pere Gimferrer to have produced the peninsula's most valuable and innovative theatre in any language,[8] suffered more than the others cited, as systematic suppression of vanguardism resulted in the greater part of his drama and poetry remaining unpublished.[9]

Just as political factors produced a relative eclipse of literatures in the vernacular tongues, subsequent political events have contributed to produce their present prominence, vigor and interest. More crucial perhaps than the death of Franco, though comparatively unnoticed, was the concession of legal (if not equal) status to the minority languages some three years prior to the end of the dictator's regime. The impressive quantity and quality of writers currently employing the vernacular tongues did not appear miraculously upon the demise of *el gran Prohibidor*. Essential is the fact that vernacular literary activity, frequently clandestine or semiclandestine under Franco, continued; works produced earlier and either prohibited by the censors or voluntarily withheld by the authors constitute a sizeable percentage of post-Franco publications.

The more moderate political climate in Spain since November 1975 has unquestionably stimulated interest —not purely intellectual—in the vernacular languages and literatures. Regional autonomy movements have recovered great momentum, accompanied by a fever of related cultural activity, the proliferation of vernacular journals, the growth of existing vernacular publishing houses and the founding of new ones, the establishment of a chair of Galician Language and Literature at the University of Santiago, and so on. After years of efforts, perennially frustrated by the old regime, a daily newspaper in Catalan, *Avui*, began publication in April 1976. As yet no Galician daily exists, although a number of articles in Gallego are carried by *La voz de Galicia* and other regional newspapers.[10] *Grial*, a Galician cultural periodical, came into being several years ago, and *Verba*, a philological quarterly in Galician, published its first number in 1974. Catalan periodicals are far more numerous and varied.

The vernacular literatures have benefited not only from relaxed restraints during Franco's twilight years and the liberalizations introduced by the monarchy— most notably the abolishment of censorship in December of 1977— but are riding the crest of an insatiable public appetite for things previously prohibited (the case also of literature in Castilian). This, however, is a mixed blessing: works are not good simply because once censored, or because their authors were exiles or their language identified with opposition to a given regime. Works of protest are guaranteed some measure of success with a certain public—other protesters—but only so long as the situation protested continues to exist; the interest generated by whipping a dead horse is short-lived, and ultimately writings in the vernaculars like those in Castilian must stand on merits extrinsic to a specific political context.

It is not only within regional confines that interest in the vernacular literatures thrives: periodicals and scholarly publications in Castilian are devoting increas-

ing attention to writing in the peninsula's other languages. When Editorial Castalia revived the literary almanac or yearbook some four years ago, *El año literario español 1974* included essays on Galician and Catalan literature (officially permitted more visibility following the educational reform legislation authorizing their pedagogical use, but still bureaucratically hampered and discouraged). In the more propitious atmosphere after the death of the dictator, the volumes of *El año literario* corresponding to 1976 and 1977 expanded their sections devoted to "Literatura Gallega" and "Literatura Catalana," adding a separate essay on Catalan theatre in the latter. Another symptomatic and important innovation is the expansion in 1975 of the Premios de la Crítica (awarded annually by a panel of over thirty professional critics and formerly limited to works in Castilian) to include recognition for the outstanding works of poetry and narrative in Catalan and Gallego. Euskera was added in 1976 (see *WLT* 53:1, p. 191 for a listing of the most recent winners).

Publishing output has soared in the vernacular literatures; even Basque publications have mushroomed. Many of the Franco years saw the printing of only two or three titles in Euskera; last year the total passed 100, a tremendous increase in comparative order of magnitude. Publications in Catalan are especially voluminous, the result not only of current writing by the mature generation and a large and vigorous component of new writers but (as elsewhere) of the reintegration of exiles as well. Many works published previously in Buenos Aires, Montevideo, Havana and Mexico City have been printed for the first time in Spain; returned exiles are likewise bringing out unpublished titles or new works and seeing their earlier writings anthologized or reprinted as complete works, selected works and the like. Similarly, the literature of "internal exile"—unpublishable under Franco—is appearing in print, in some cases for the first time, while private editions tolerated for limited circulation are being reissued commercially, becoming available after as a quarter-century to the general public.

Politics, sex, religion—themes previously taboo (in addition to the obviously taboo question of regional autonomy)—are not only tolerated but are undergoing an exploitation which relegates all else to the background. As with publications in Castilian, ideologically tendentious writing predominates, rivaled only by the erotic (a more distant second in the vernacular languages). The most cursory and haphazard perusal of best-seller lists for the past three years reveals the overwhelming preponderance of the porno-political, often of inferior or subliterary quality. More serene critical observers of the several peninsular literatures applaud the advent of freedom but look forward with undisguised eagerness to the eventual separation of things political and artistic, to what is somewhat wistfully termed "normalization."

Just as there seem to be an insufficient number of Spaniards writing of things political to sate the public demand after years of enforced abstention, so the number of contemporary writers established as cultivators of Gallego and Catalan appears suddenly too few for a newly aware, fervent and enlarged public. One consequence is the translation into the vernaculars of a wide range of "classics" of all eras, ranging from the *Iliad* (version in Gallego by Evaristo de Sela, 1977) to Shakespeare, Yeats and T. S. Eliot.

Similarly, there is a trend to translate into the vernacular many works composed in Castilian by writers who had abandoned their mother tongue, sometimes accompanied by the physical return of such authors to their regions of origin. Such is the case, for example, of Gonzalo Torrente Ballester and Camilo José Cela, native Galicians who have achieved the nation's ultimate literary recognition via election to the Royal Spanish Academy for their accomplishments in the novel (both have published only in Castilian, although a majority of Torrente's works present Galician ambient and themes). Cela's best-known novel, *La familia de Pascual Duarte* (1942), was published in Galician translation by the late novelist of the "Xeneración Nós," Vicente Risco, in 1976 with a prologue by another returned Galician exile, Rafael Dieste.

Risco and Dieste, Galician literati of some distinction who were previously known for their works in Castilian, are now being recognized for their vernacular writings, as is the case with many other writers. What has changed is not the literature in question but its visibility and acceptability, presently inseparable from political considerations. Writers whose work is largely apolitical continue to be underesteemed, as is the case of Alvaro Cunqueiro, talented and erudite Galician and Castilian writer of novels of fantasy; he is probably the greatest "undiscovered" novelist currently in Spain.

Intriguing indeed is the speculation as to just where the novel in Castilian would be today without the more or less forcible incorporation of Galician and Catalan writers during the Franco era. Had Cela, Torrente, Elena Quiroga, Cunqueiro and other Galicians produced their works in Gallego, Ana María Matute and the Goytisolos in Catalan, Delibes would be left almost alone for many years in the forefront of the Spanish narrative. Most recent trends seem to foreshadow a reversal for the foreseeable future, as the new generation contains a large percentage of emerging writers who are either resolutely bilingual or who have deliberately chosen to write in the minority language.

The point at which the situations of Gallego and Catalan cease to be comparable is precisely that point at which political and more specifically literary factors diverge. The very existence of Gallego is precarious, while Catalan demands recognition not of its linguistic identity but of its sometimes stellar role in European literature. During the present century Catalan figures in the forefront of the artistic vanguard (including drama and poetry) while Galicia usually lags behind. What passes for vanguardist or *novísimo* in Galicia in this decade is essentially—literarily, sociologically, esthetically—undifferentiated from Castilian social literature of the fifties (an affirmation especially applicable to poetry and theatre; a degree of formal experimentation exists in the narrative, but its thematics echo those of the *novela social* in Castilian nearly a quarter-century ago). Social preoccupation is something of a constant in Galician literature, however, not merely from Rosalía de Castro henceforth, but from remote origins; there is a degree of continuity in Galician thematics unaffected by fashion, especially the preoccupation with linguistic and cultural identity and the note of protest.

Catalan, linguistically more distinct from Castilian than is Gallego and thus less threatened by absorption, with the advantages of its larger area and number of speakers, has benefited because Barcelona is one of the two literary centers of the country. Spain's publishing industry is divided between Madrid and Barcelona, perhaps more concentrated in the latter; an overwhelming majority of the country's intellectuals, artists and writers reside in these two cities, where theatrical activity is also centered (under Franco, theatre in the provinces disappeared, with the exception of one in Valencia which functioned approximately a month each year). While only one or two theatres in Barcelona were authorized for productions in Catalan, theatre in this language—semi-clandestine, semi-tolerated—attained exceptional achievements on the level of the text; Cataluña's flourishing dramatic production was frequently confined to the artificial ambient of print (and even in the post-Franco era, many significant works have not yet found producers).

The works of Manuel Pedrolo, Salvador Espriu and Joan Brossa not infrequently surpass the literary attainments of dramatic authors in Castilian. The Catalan works are generally more innovative, daring and experimental, with greater affinity to new developments in Europe and elsewhere. Numerically also, the complement of dramatists in Catalan is imposing, with scores of young playwrights emerging during the last decade of the old regime. In a panorama including close to a hundred writers,[11] Jaume Melendres, Jordi Teixidor and Terenci Moix seem especially promising. The single most important event for Catalan drama to date in the post-Franco era is the publication in 1976 of the second volume of Brossa's *Teatre complet*,[12] although of great interest as a phenomenon is the proliferation of activity in areas away from the metropolis, in Valencia, the Balearic Islands and many smaller towns, particularly in the north of Cataluña.

Galician theatre, deprived of production and reduced to the printed page when it existed at all, began to display new vigor in 1973 when the Asociación Cultural Abrente de Ribadavia (dramatic center of Galicia) announced the first postwar theatrical contest. The seven largely amateur groups then involved in Galician theatre grew to forty by 1977,[13] a figure indicative of the upsurge in interest. The increased activity is a positive sign, although the quality of writing occasionally leaves something to be desired. Younger playwrights especially (together with many of their counterparts in Catalan) cultivate political or sociopolitical themes with a tendentiousness, belligerence and truculence which redound to the detriment of esthetics and transcendent values. The influence and example of Valle-Inclán is often in evidence, particularly in the *esperpento* quality of works by one of Galicia's best young dramatists, Euloxio Ruibal. Other significant dramatists now writing in Gallego include Blanco Amor, Carballo Calero, Mariñas del Valle and Varela Buxán.

The narrative in Gallego and Catalan is perhaps of comparably less interest than either the theatre or poetry. Characterized by frequent irony or sarcasm, socioeconomic and political concerns and a good deal of *costumbrismo,* most vernacular novels lack the experimental and vanguardist preoccupations of the novel in Castilian, relegating formal innovation to secondary position. However, the mass of material being turned out is impressive, especially in Catalan: the overall bulk rivals that of the novel in Castilian,[14] and the numerous novelists in Catalan include many writing in the dialects of *valenciano* and *mallorquín* (at least one novelist of international significance, Llorenç Villalonga, does his writing in *mallorquín*).

Many of the younger poets are also fiction writers, some of them involved in formal experimentation, as is the dramatist Pedrolo with his "simultaneous" novels. Younger experimenters include Montserrat Roig, Carme Riera, Quim Monzó, Brel Mesquida, Pi de Cabanyes, Josep Albanell, Ilsa Trolèc (pseud.) and Carles Reig, all in the "anti-novel" camp, while more recognizable forms are ably represented by Joan Perucho, Guillen Frontera, Janer Manila, Pau Faner, Jordi Sarsanedas, Mercè Rodoreda, Terenci Moix and Baltasar Porcel, many of whom obsessively analyze the *educación sentimental* under Franco. In Galicia, where experimentation

usually takes the form of multiple time planes and non-linear narration or fades into the background of pressing socioeconomic issues, there have emerged a number of novelists worthy of further observation: Méndez Ferrín, Anxel Fole, Xan Guisan Seixas, Xosé Neira Vilas, Silvio Santiago, Xosé M. Martínez Oca, Eliseo Alonso, Carlos Casares, Anxel A. Rei Ballesteros, Blanco Amor and Xohana Torres, in addition to those cited earlier. The most durable indigenous influence is that of Castelao.

Poetry is the predominant genre in both Catalan and Galician literature, in terms of the number of cultivators, intrinsic level of achievement, and innovativeness (especially in the case of Catalan lyricists). Logically enough, poetry is also the genre which has been most frequently studied and the subject of anthologies.[15] Poetic activity in Catalan is intense, embracing the publication of collections, numerous reviews, recitals and books; the scene boasts several first-rate poets, beginning with Foix, Espriu and Brossa, all of European stature. Among a legion of other versifiers, some who particularly bear watching are Miquel Martí y Pol, the painter Albert Rafols Casamada, Feliu Formosa, Joan Ferraté, Bernat Meix (pseud.), A. Tàpies-Barba, Narcís Comadira, Joan Vinyoli, Agusti Bartra (see BA 50:1, p. 94 and 50:2, pp. 266–67), Jaume Pont, Francesc Parcerisas, Pere Gimferrer and the Valencian Vicent Estellés.

Celso Emilio Ferreiro, patriarch of Galician poetry, is, like most of the younger lyricists in Gallego, rather traditional in handling of form; they are uniformly less interested in theory and experimentation than in engagement, protest and ideological exposition. Common to the several generations of poets presently on the scene in Galicia is an attitude of belligerence, the desire to denounce conditions in the region, the marginal level at which Galicians subsist, with a corresponding indifference toward literary modes and fashions. Irony, violence and sarcasm are frequent—imitations of Celso Emilio by many younger poets, but lacking his subtlety, balance and shadings. Anti-rhetorical almost without exception, their focus is less artistic than ideological. Formally and on the lexical level, conscious effort is made by some younger poets to incorporate rural and popular elements in their writing. Exile, not political but economic (i.e., forced migration), loneliness and *saudade* are also frequent themes.

Less versatile than the Catalan poets (who are both more numerous and more concerned with esthetics), the Galicians experiment less with form, with vanguardist tendencies and the anti-poem—isolated instances of which do occur in Gallego, usually without being identified as such. Especially worthy of note in a rather populous panorama are Arcadio López Casanova of the older generation and Manuel María among younger poets; others include Luis Pimentel, Méndez Ferrín, Aquilino Iglesia Alvariño, Emilio Pita, Luis Seoane, Cunqueiro, Díaz Castro, Alvarez Blázquez, Lorenzo Varela, Pura Vázquez, María Mariño, Antonio Tovar, Tomás Barros, Luz Pozo Garza, Uxío Novoneira, Xohana Torres, Xosé Luis Franco Grande, Salvador García Bodaño, María del Carmen Kruckenberg Sanxurxo and Xosé María García Rodríguez.

Spain in the post-Franco era is filled with excitement, literary and cultural as well as political. The vernacular or minority literatures are undergoing an "explosion" without precedent in history, particularly in regard to the numbers of exponents of the various genres currently publishing in these languages. Public receptivity is similarly at an all-time high, due not only to the increase in the number of readers in modern times but also to the political factors previously mentioned. Excellent writers can be found in both Catalan and Gallego, the most outstanding being poets and dramatists; the future of the narrative seems promising, given the extent and variety of practitioners, although this genre is esthetically the weaker at present. Excitement is generated both by the vigorous revival of the vernacular languages and cultures and by the return or recuperation of literary works previously exiled or censored; but the present is marred somewhat by the almost exclusive predominance of political thematics, tendentious works and ideological conceptions which, no matter how understandable in their context, limit the artistic potential and progress. We can hope that a decrease in political tension in the not-too-distant future will permit the vernacular literatures to realize the potentials of their cultures and idioms, free of partisan servitude.

Janet W. Díaz, Spring 1979

1 Joan Coromines, "Sobre a unificación ortográfica galego-portuguesa," *Grial,* 53 (1976), p. 278 (my translation).

2 *Picariños,* billed as the first "método galego de lectura i escritura prás nosas escolas," was announced for publication in 1975, a pioneering effort in developing a text for teaching Gallego in the primary schools.

3 Xesús Alonso Montero, "Literatura gallega," in *El año literario español 1977,* Madrid, Castalia, 1977, p. 126.

4 *Teima,* a Gallego weekly introduced late in 1976, disappeared in less than ten months; many other serials are of intermittent publication.

5 Xesús Alonso Montero, "La literatura gallega," in *El año literario español 1974,* Madrid, Castalia, 1974, p. 123 (my translation). Symptomatic of the same situation is Celso Emilio Ferreiro's qualification of Gallego as a "proletarian language" in a now-famous poem. The language's survival among the underprivi-

leged has strengthened its association with protest and, more recently, with leftist politics.

6 Alonso Montero terms Gallego "una lengua, salvo circunstancias excepcionales, inescrita durante más de cuatro siglos," alluding to the all but total disappearance of Galician literature during the four centuries prior to its literary rebirth or *Rexurdimiento* in the second half of the nineteenth century (ibid.). The literary survival of Gallego until well into this century depended largely upon the poets.

7 In *Pueblo* (Madrid), 21 June 1951; reprinted in *Encuesta mundial sobre la lengua y la cultura gallegas,* Madrid, Arealonga, 1974, pp. 212–13 (my translation).

8 Pere Gimferrer, "Literatura catalana," in *El año literario español 1976,* Madrid, Castalia, 1976, p. 126.

9 Experimental drama in all languages of the peninsula, including Castilian, labored under especially heavy restraints and found little support from the public, even in Barcelona, Spain's center of vanguardism in this century. Many dramatists saw most, even all, of their work denied production, although some were allowed publication.

10 It was largely through control of the mass media—radio, television, movies, newspapers—that the Franco regime came close to accomplishing what vernacular opponents of *castellanización* termed *lingüicidio;* minority publications were tolerated in inverse ratio to their expected circulation.

11 As included by Xavier Fábregas, *Aproximació a la història del teatre català modern,* Barcelona, Curial, 1972.

12 In the opinion of Pere Gimferrer, loc. cit.

13 Alonso Montero, "Literatura gallega," *El año literario español 1977,* p. 144.

14 According to Gimferrer, op. cit., p. 121.

15 ADDITIONAL READINGS. For Galician, see: Miguel González Garcés, *Poesía gallega contemporánea,* Barcelona, Plaza & Janés, 1972 (anthology), and *Poesía gallega de posguerra (1939–1975),* 2 vols., La Coruña, Castro, 1976 (bilingual anthology of twenty-six poets); Ramón González Alegre, *Antología de la poesía gallega contemporánea,* Madrid, Rialp, 1957; Basilio Losada, *Poetas gallegos de la postguerra,* Barcelona, Ocnos, 1971; Carmen Martín Gaite, Andrés Ruiz Tarazona, *Ocho siglos de poesía gallega,* Madrid, Alianza, 1973; María Victoria Moreno Márquez, *Os novísimos da poesía gallega,* Madrid, Akal, 1973 (anthology); and J. P. González Martín, *Ensayo sobre la poesía gallega contemporánea,* La Coruña, Castro, 1972, the second part of which deals with this century.

For Valencian poetry, see particularly: Amadeu Fabregat, *Carn fresca,* Valencia, L'Estel, 1974, an anthology of informative rather than selective principles. Catalan poetry is represented by *Tres escritores catalanes: Carner, Riba, Pla,* Madrid, Gredos, 1973; *Cinc poetes,* Barcelona, Destino, 1969; books devoted to J. V. Foix include *Antologia poética,* Barcelona, Àymà, 1973 and *J. V. Foix en els seus millors escrits,* Barcelona, Arimany, 1973, as well as Pere Gimferrer, *La poesía de J. V. Foix,* Barcelona, Edicions 62, 1974; on Espriu, *Obres completes* (with an introduction by J. M. Castellet), Barcelona, Edicions 62, 1968 and Castellet, *Iniciació a la poesía de Salvador Espriu,* Barcelona, Edicions 62, 1971; also *De Joan Oliver a Pere Quart,* Barcelona, Edicions 62, 1969 and M. Arimany, *L'avantaguardisme en la poesía catalana actual,* Barcelona, Pòrtic, 1972; see also J. Folguera, *Les noves valors de la poesía catalana,* Barcelona, La Revista, 1919 and more generally, Joan Triadú, *Nova antologia de la poesía catalana (1900–1964),* Barcelona, Selecta, 1965.

Also recommended, Joan Fuster, *Literatura catalana contemporanea*, Barcelona, Curial, 1972; J. Castellanos, ed., *Guia de literatura catalana contemporània*, Barcelona, Edicions 62, 1973; F. Curet, *Historia del teatre català*, Barcelona, Aedos, 1969; J. Molas, *Literatura catalana de postguerra*, Barcelona, Dalmau, 1966. And for an impression of the narrative, see Prudenci Bertrana, *Obres completes*, Barcelona, Selecta, 1965; S. Juan Arbó, *Obra catalana completa*, Barcelona, Edicions 62, 1966; Mercè Rodoresda, *La Plaça del Diamant*, Barcelona, B. Club, 1969; M. A. Capmany, *Obra completa*, vol. 1, Barcelona, Nova Terra, 1974.

Vicente Aleixandre, Last of the Romantics: The 1977 Nobel Prize for Literature

Why Aleixandre? More explicitly, why should the Nobel Prize for literature be awarded to Vicente Aleixandre in 1977? Barbara Walters, speaking through a nationwide television program, declared that the poet was virtually unknown outside his native Spain (which only proves the lack of intellectual preparedness of our television announcers). And yet, if Lorca had been alive today, there is no question that the prize would have been his. The prize belongs not to a man, in this case, but to a whole generation, the generation of Lorca, Jorge Guillén, Rafael Alberti—perhaps the brightest and most original poetic generation in twentieth-century Western Europe. Not a restricted, disciplined group, as the French surrealists became, but rather a band of friends open to all influences.

I remember Aleixandre in the courtyard of his Madrid house, a great conversationalist who also knew when to listen. We talked about the romantics, dada, surrealism, the new trends: his blue eyes sparkled as he claimed that he had inherited from all movements, and by investing wisely he had increased the capital of poetry as a whole. Aleixandre is a tall man, with a noble face that seems to come out of a Michelangelo fresco, a modern prophet with a gravel voice and slow gestures. Wit and charm are part of his personality, and also personal warmth, yet the first impression is hard, almost overwhelming. The visitor is facing a giant, a giant who has attained the heights of poetic genius and is aware of it. Only slowly, step by step, the giant unwinds and becomes the most generous and cordial of hosts.

During our conversation I asked Aleixandre whether he could feel at home within any specific literary movement: he claimed the romantic movement came closest to his ideals. I both agreed and disagreed with his statement. Compared to an urbane and witty poet such as Pope, both Blake and Aleixandre, Keats and Baudelaire are brothers: a vast vision, a romantic sensi-

tivity unites them. Yet compared to the other romantics, the style of Aleixandre's poems is clearly different. More difficult, more illogical, more mysterious, it is a style that has been profoundly influenced by surrealism.

There is an image which I feel can help us to understand the role of surrealism in contemporary poetry. If we think of a huge rocket as standing for the poetic vanguard movements in our century, then surrealism stands for the third stage of the rocket, the fastest and brightest stage. Every stage is marked by an increase in the anti-rational, illogical, subjective elements. Futurism, launched in 1909 by the Italian poet Marinetti in a manifesto written in French, wants to revolutionize subject matter, rhythm, rhyme, typography. Machines should be put on a pedestal; old legends and monuments should be put to the torch. Dadaism is invented by a Romanian, Tristan Tzara, in Zurich in 1916. Its aims are still more radical. As Stephen Spender puts it:

> Dada began in 1916, and consisted of the cultivated madness of gestures directed against the madness of the war. Although Dada called itself revolutionary, its politics were not realistic or intended to be. Dada had no political program. The attitude of Dadaists was that mad and subversive and childish protests against the bourgeoisie were in themselves an already accomplished revolution in the lives of those who participated in them.[1]

We are dealing, of course, with international movements. Writers such as Apollinaire, Alfred Jarry and Pierre Reverdy contributed to their launching, just at the time when the poems of the Chilean author Vicente Huidobro were helping to create a propitious climate for change both in Latin America and in Spain. And just as Picasso found inspiration in primitive American sculpture, Aleixandre brings to his observation of modern society the freedom, the power and the audacious sexual overtones that characterize his poems about the primitive world and the animals in the prehistoric jungle. In his poem "The Waltz," for instance, the poet's X-ray eyes discover under the elegance and refinement of a modern ballroom, with ladies and gentlemen dancing faster and faster, carried away by the tidal wave of music, the passion of sexual desires, their pubic hair carefully hidden under the formal dress, the same heady mixture of sex and death:

This is the instant the moment to say the word that
  explodes
the moment when long skirts become birds
windows scream out
light yells "help"
and the kiss waiting in the corner between two
  mouths turns into a thorn

that will give out death by saying
I love you.[2]

In this poem, as in most other poems, Aleixandre destroys the distinction between subjectivity and objectivity, fuses the ideal and the real, the imaginary and everyday experience: these two realms are shown to be one and the same. This is why he can be at the same time a great poet of nature—nature as the outside world of spaces, rivers, forests, seas, dawns, animal life—and a great surrealist poet, delving into the unconscious, swimming in the stream of his own mind. He realizes, as most surrealist poets did, that the conventions of the rational world, as opposed to the desires and visions of the subconscious world of dreams and fantasies, tend to split into two mutilated halves what for primitive man was a whole and sound universe; hence the cult of voluntary hallucination and the sudden changes of subject and perspective, which can be baffling indeed to the average reader. There can be no doubt that Aleixandre is one of the most difficult poets ever to use the Spanish language. More than Lorca, Guillén and even Cernuda, in his generation, he employs every device that can free the mind of its rational categories. He wills a new reality whose truth is poetic rather than scientific, universal rather than particular. His main tool is his uncommon imagination, which faces the ordinary world and "derealizes" it. In other words, the conventional boundaries between ordinary perception and delirious hallucination are broken down, and every conceivable approach to experience becomes permissible.

Aleixandre knows instinctively that the modern poet must grow wings, must soar beyond everyday life, must see reality both from above and from below. He goes back in time and plunges into an abyss that opens both in the past and in his inner self. As a great critic of contemporary Spanish literature, Ricardo Gullón, puts it:

> Logically such an intense dreamer had to search for an answer where so many other poets before him looked for it, in the descent into Hell, in the underground where strange passions shed their dark light. Hell is now called the Subconscious, and the poet's guide is no longer Vergil or Orpheus but Rimbaud—yet a new name does not mean a new identity. And the traveler is called Surrealist, since under the outer layer of reality, beyond rational attitudes, in the abysses of dream, he is trying to discover the secret of Life and Death. From this dive into darkness Aleixandre came back a richer poet, both mysterious and lucid. His poems, like rivers, surround the reader slowly and inexorably, making him feel how much strength and vitality sparkle under the smooth surface of every word.[3]

It is difficult to know whether to characterize much of the nineteenth-century romantic verse as "religious." On the one hand, there is little overt reference to God or to religious subjects; on the other, many of the poems deal with experiences of a spiritual nature. Wordsworth, for instance, in "Lines Composed a Few Miles above Tintern Abbey," describes

. . . that serene and blessed mood
In which the affections gently lead us on,—
Until, the breath of this corporeal frame
And even the motion of our human blood
Almost suspended, we are laid asleep
In body, and become a living soul:
While with an eye made quiet by the power
Of harmony, and the deep power of joy,
We see into the life of things.

These lines are inspired not by a supernatural power but by nature itself. What has caused in the poet an almost mystical trance are the trees, the fields, the sky.

The parallel between Aleixandre's poetry and William Blake's writings is even closer. They are both mystical and cosmic poets, visionary adventurers into the unknown. Blake's prophetic poems, like "The Four Zoas" and "The Book of Los" are extraordinarily complex, full of strange symbolism and self-created cosmologies. Aleixandre, in his "The Jungle and the Sea" (from *Destruction or Love*), likewise builds a vision of a primitive world through strange and powerful similes:

Far away in a remote
splendor of still virgin steel
there are tigers as large as hatred,
lions looking like a hirsute heart,
blood like placated sadness,
fighting against a yellow hyena shaped like the
   greedy
sunset.

Aleixandre's cosmos, like Blake's, is animated by love. Yet the human elements in Blake are ever-present. His angels and titans are man himself writ large. Aleixandre goes back in his poetry to a primeval age in which man is a newcomer, almost an intruder. It is nature that rules man, not the other way around. And nature is restless—often, to the untrained human eye, pitiless. But there is love behind the destructive forces of nature. As I have noted elsewhere,

> [Aleixandre's] poems, if read from beginning to end, evaluate man's place in the cosmos, define all creation, and sing of the communion of men, as temporal beings, with the universe and with other men; only in such communion can man endure and become eternal. Through his difficult symbolic and visionary imagery, derived mainly

from dreams and surrealism, Aleixandre has managed to unify realities that seemed irreconcilable. Not unlike William Blake, in Aleixandre the "marriage of Heaven and Hell" appears as a possibility; chaos is but one aspect of order; love and communion accept— and transcend—death.[4]

Everything in nature is alive, as Keats knew, as Baudelaire and Rubén Darío had proclaimed (let us add here that Darío was for Aleixandre the poet who taught him the true meaning of poetry). Aleixandre writes:

In the forest the trees sing just like birds do.
An immense embrace caresses the jungle's waist.
A bird that the unending light has turned to gold
is still seeking the lips that will free him from his jail.
("Come, Come Now," from *Destruction or Love*)

Perhaps the greatest book written by Aleixandre in the surrealist vein is *Sombre del paraíso* (Shadow of Paradise), begun in 1939, a year in which the whole of Spanish society lay in shambles. Jails and concentration camps were crowded. Most of the poet's close friends were dead or in exile. Life had to begin again from ground zero. Aleixandre took refuge in his memories of a happy childhood by the shores of the Mediterranean. As the critic Kessel Schwartz points out:

Aleixandre deviates somewhat from the tumultuous and disparate ambivalence of *Destruction or Love,* but in the old familiar distinctions between man and nature, he continues to denigrate the former. The old fire remains in sublimated form, although from time to time the frenzy and naked passion of *Destruction or Love* shine through, and the poet employs new dimensions of supplementary imagery. He returns to his innocent world of infancy, to a Paradise beyond original sin and knowledge, to be one with the heavens and the creatures of the dawn.[5]

Cosmic unity is the underlying theme of the book:

Yes, poet: cast off this book which pretends to enclose
in its pages a sparkle of sunlight,
and look at the light face to face, while your head is supported on this rock,
while your feet so far away feel the final kiss of the setting sun
and your uplifted hands sweetly touch the moon,
and your hanging hair leaves a wake among the stars.
("The Poet")

The poet is surrounded by innocent, virginal creatures. Hatred and sin have not yet been invented by Man:

There each morning the birds were born,
surprising, all new, full of life, celestial.
Their tongues of innocence

said no words . . .
Birds of initial happiness, opening their selves,
trying out their wings, without losing the virginal drop
of dew!
("Creatures in the Dawn")

Yet the poet's journey is not at an end. In *Historia del corazón* (History of the Heart), written between 1945 and 1953, Aleixandre comes back from Paradise in order to face all the ambiguity and anguish of our own times. As Kessel Schwartz describes it:

The central theme concerns human solidarity and compassion for the victims of injustice. . . . Although he reserves his deepest and subtlest meanings for the description of historical and existential man, the poet also portrays his own life and personal past. No longer the creature of telluric forces . . . the poet, as a man, becomes all men, destined like him to live and die, without the assurance of Paradise or eternal life, in a world where death is always with us.[6]

Nevertheless, it is not necessary to live desperate solitary lives, the poet exclaims with tenderness and optimism, as he sings for all mankind of fleeting time and human solidarity. Infants and oldsters mark the boundaries between being and not being, life and death. The poet recognizes that he is aging, but is without despair, empathizing with his neighbor who must also stoically face the end.

Rebellion, love and death are fused in one single existential vision:

the lover knows that he passes and disappears,
that love itself passes
and that this generous fire that still endures in him
witnesses pure the sweet passage of that which eternally passes.
("Like the Thistledown")

The message is clear: man must learn to say "yes" both to life and love, on the one hand, and on the other, when it comes, to death and oblivion: "Oh dark night. I no longer expect anything. / Solitude does not lie to my senses. / The pure, calm shadow reigns" ("Final Shadow").

A Poetry with Open Arms. Perhaps the main feature of Aleixandre's poetry is the feeling of unity and organic growth that it creates in its readers. We are aware that each book has its own style, its peculiar characteristics, and at the same time that each book has a role to play in the corpus of Aleixandre's writings. The motto of this corpus could be "order and wisdom out of chaos"—yet an order and a wisdom that do not mask or conceal at any time the persistence of chaos, violence, anguish and ultimately death. Aleixandre's youthful poetry can be compared to a tornado, a nova exploding in the sky, a torrent of lava pouring into a primeval jungle. His later books are less violent and more nostalgic, as the poet opens his heart toward his own past and toward the suffering of his fellowmen.

The first period would stretch from 1928, the date of publication of his first book, *Ambito* (Space), to 1953, with *Nacimiento último* (The Last Epiphany). Its dominant trait is power: immense telluric and cosmic forces are deployed before us. They look for unity, love, ultimate fusion. The spectacle is at the same time fascinating and terrifying. The masterpieces of this period, *La destrucción o el amor* (*Destruction or Love;* 1935) and *Sombra del paraíso* (Shadow of Paradise; 1944), are organized around a main character which is basically not a human being but rather the whole cosmos, nature, the primeval creation of natural forces: man is only one of the many forces that nature deploys in its search for unity.

The second period, from *Historia del corazón* (1953) to *Poemas de la consumación* (Poems of Consummation; 1968), is less subjective, less irrational. The wild visions are replaced by an awareness of human time and human suffering. The first book belonging to this period, *Historia del corazón,* is basically the story of a love affair, in its daily moments of joy and anguish, and also the story of a growing awareness, a solidarity: the poet realizes that he is only one member of a vast society, the Spanish people, and that ultimately he is a part of mankind. Solidarity means a realization of finitude—the small, finite self is bound to disappear soon—and at the same time a source of strength: other human beings, very much like the poet, will go on living and loving. To this period belongs the book *Retratos con nombre* (Portraits with Names), thirty-seven poems each of which captures the physical and psychic essence of a friend of the poet: the poet's pen becomes a camera, one with great sensitivity and clear focus. One of the poems, "Birthday," is a self-portrait: in it Aleixandre retraces step by step his own life as objectively and dispassionately as possible, and not without humor.

Self-knowledge is a door to wisdom: the last books by Aleixandre, *Poemas de la consumación* and *Diálogos del conocimiento* (Dialogues of Knowledge; 1974), are often desolate and tragic, yet serene. Human life has an end, old age is but the prelude to death, nothing —and nothingness—awaits us. The poet speaks with a soft voice, as in a confession or in evoking a memory too painful to explain in full detail. Often his sentences become brief, mysterious, contradictory. They remind us of the fragments of Heraclitus. Perhaps paradox and contradiction are the only weapons left to our mind: knowledge has to be paid for; logic can lead us only so far. For this last stretch of the journey the poet's mind must turn once again to irrational utterings. Yet the meaning of these books is not obscure: one must learn to say both "yes" and "no" to death and nothingness, the poet tells us. We must bow to what is and will be, and at the same time, as Dylan Thomas advised, we must not go too gently, too meekly, into the dark night of death: life is too precious for us not to regret its passing.

Organic growth is, as we have seen, the key feature in Aleixandre's poetry: *plus ça change, plus c'est la même chose,* since even in his philosophical poems dealing with death and old age we feel the fires of youth and desire burning under the smooth surface of each poem. Aleixandre's books encompass the "seven ages of man," and the remarkable feeling of unity, of growth within the frame of one individuality and one style, can be generated only because the poet is a master of Spanish poetic language and can thus clearly etch his own personality, his own vision of life, into each book, whether the book deals with the world as seen by an enthusiastic adolescent or whether we are listening to an old man waiting for death.

This is in itself a great merit—and yet it does not fully explain the range of Aleixandre's style. His poems are above all noble, "large," uplifting: we are always facing giants, a larger-than-life vision of the landscape and the figures in it. This feeling of *grandeur* can be attributed in part to some of the subjects; the sea, for instance, is a recurring theme. Yet there is more: Aleixandre has created, out of the influence of surrealism, a multilayered style, one in which symbols are hidden behind words, and each line calls to mind a new group of symbols flying through the air toward the reader. For example, many of his nature poems can be read three ways, the first interpretation being that of a dream, a vision. And then the symbols begin to appear, both the Freudian and Jungian variety. The poem unfolds, new dimensions are added to it: it is a poem about a visionary poet, who at the same time is a child looking for his mother— and afraid of his parents—and a whole people remembering its past and the origins of the world. Thus in one of his earliest poems, in which he describes a stormy sea, menacing yet somehow attractive:

The bituminous sea crushes shadows
against itself. Hollows of deep blue
remain frozen in every arch of the waves . . .
Under lofty black skies the deep mouth bellows
and demands night. The mouth, the sea, everything
calls for darkness, deep, huge darkness,
the horrible jaws want to eat, they show us
all their white teeth of foam.

A tongue huge as a pyramid, ominous, cold,
rises up, demands . . . .
("Sea and Night")

We see here how a positive symbol can acquire dramatically negative characteristics. The sea, symbol of fertility, of the feminine principle of fertility, is presented as something dark and menacing. In Cirlot's *Dictionary of Symbols* we read that the symbolic meaning of the sea "corresponds to the 'lower ocean,' to waters in motion. It is a transitive and mediating agent between the shapeless elements (air, gas) and the elements solidly shaped (earth, solidity) and by analogy between life and death. The sea, the oceans, are thus considered to be the fountain of life and also its end. 'To return to the sea' is like 'to return to the mother,' that is, to die." In Aleixandre the traditional symbols of the collective unconscious, the Jungian symbols, are reinforced very often, in a parallel system, by Freudian symbols: are not the "white teeth of foam" and the "tongue huge as a pyramid" the clearest poetic definitions of the "vagina dentata" which is a frequent motif of Freud's clinical writings?

Nostalgia is for the poet a normal and healthy reaching from our present consciousness toward the past, toward our roots. Human life is like a tree: its vast trunk, its leaves and flowers are easily seen, yet the roots are invisible, underground. We must always remember them, for without them, without the lost paradise of our unconscious world, our world of dreams, our childhood memories, we are no longer fully human. And yet another movement, a movement forward and upward, must also be emphasized: the open hand, the open arms, the solidarity with other human beings. After being long confined in his room, the poet goes out to the street, to the square, in order to mingle with other human beings and be a part of humanity:

It is a beautiful feeling, beautifully humble and
  buoyant,
life-giving and deep,
to feel yourself beneath the sun among other people,
propelled, carried forward, conducted,
blended, softly carried along.

    It is not good
to remain on the shore
like the jetty or like the mollusk stonily aping the
  rock.
Rather it is pure and serene to drown in happiness,
in the happiness of flowing and oblivion,
finding oneself in the movement with which the great
  heart of all men beats everywhere . . .
Don't look for yourself in the mirror,
in a dead dialogue where you cannot hear yourself.
Go down, go down slowly and search for yourself
  among the others.

There they all are, and you among them.
Get undressed, and fuse, and recognize yourself.
("In the Square")

The poet can become a full-fledged member of mankind, can feel at home with the crowd, without losing his individuality. Paradise lost was not completely lost: a glimmer of the ancient light can be seen when we join arms with other human beings. The inescapable—and welcome—message is, we are not alone, if only we look around. This message is made even more explicit in his next book, *En un vasto dominio* (In a Vast Dominion; 1962). Again we can find in Aleixandre's poetry an echo of the great romantic poets. Wordsworth had written,

Our birth is but a sleep and a forgetting;
The soul that rises with us, our life's Star,
    Hath had elsewhere its setting,
        And cometh from afar.
("Intimations of Immortality")

Man is not alone, because—as Plato believed, as the theory of reincarnation holds—much wisdom, the untold knowledge of many previous lives, of previous beings, the experience even of animals, stones, water, infinite space, travels in our veins into our mind and heart. Man appears as an atom in a vast cosmos, but if the universe is curved about itself, man daring the vastness of time and space would then return on himself, perhaps from the route of the infinitesimally small.

> Finally, if the world is created by the effort of arms and hands, and the earth itself, in a sense, is a product, a town also becomes a living unit, as do its citizens, a part of the landscape as they perform their daily tasks. Since things, life, man, love, history, spirit, and flesh are all material . . . Aleixandre stresses the need for collective participation in the process of salvation. Human life is still an arduous effort, but with the aid of men, both present and past, we may achieve continuity.[7]

■ ■ ■

In his recent work Aleixandre, once more, renews himself without changing his poetic personality. His two last books, *Poemas de la consumación* and *Diálogos del conocimiento,* with their short sentences, their paradoxes, their moments (flashes) of illumination, remind me of Heraclitus, of the Oriental mystics, of Schopenhauer. Wisdom, resignation, a sad acceptance, a stubborn resistance. From surrealism to wisdom: this is the trajectory—a long and fruitful journey—of our poet. As Robert Bly has written: "For the Nobel Prize to come to Aleixandre now is fitting, not only because of the energy and intensity of his own poetry, but because it comes at this moment in Spanish history. Spain is waking up after years of sleep, and Aleixandre's poetry and stubborn presence have a strong part in that awakening."[8]

Manuel Durán, Spring 1978

[1] Stephen Spender, "Life Wasn't a Cabaret," *The New York Times Magazine,* 30 October 1977, pp. 20–65.

[2] All the translations in this article are mine, not because I disagree with the translations by Stephen Kessler, Lewis Hyde and Robert Bly, but rather because I have always found both pleasure and challenge in translating Aleixandre.

[3] Ricardo Gullón, *Literatura española contemporánea,* New York, Scribner's, 1965, p. 533.

[4] Manuel Durán-Gili, "Spanish and Catalan Literature," *World Literature Since 1945,* Ivar Ivask, Gero von Wilpert, eds., New York, Ungar, 1973, p. 611.

[5] Kessel Schwartz, *Vicente Aleixandre,* Boston, Twayne, 1970, p. 99. This is still the only book of criticism in English on Aleixandre. The critical bibliography in Spanish is of course extensive: see especially Carlos Bousoño, *La poesía de Vicente Aleixandre,* Madrid, Gredos, 1956; and José Olivio Jiménez devotes a long chapter to Aleixandre in his *Cinco poetas del tiempo,* Madrid, Insula, 1964. In Italian there is Vittorio Bodini, *La parola poetica di Vicente Aleixandre,* Rome, Bulzoni, 1971. A chapter on Aleixandre can also be found, in English, in C. B. Morris, *A Generation of Spanish Poets: 1920–1936,* Cambridge, Cambridge University Press, 1969. As for translations of Aleixandre's poetry into English, we have Stephen Kessler's translation of twenty-two poems from the poet's fourth book, *Destruction or Love,* Santa Cruz, Ca., Green Horse; *The Cave of Night,* Joeffrey Bartman, tr., Solo, 1976; and Lewis Hyde and Robert Bly have recently issued *Twenty Poems of Vicente Aleixandre,* a selection from several periods and books (available at 8 Donnell St. / Cambridge, Ma.).

[6] Schwartz, p. 119.

[7] Ibid., pp. 130–31.

[8] *The New York Times Book Review,* 30 October 1977, p. 52.

Fiction and Metafiction in Contemporary Spanish Letters

Slowly but steadily the Spanish novel has been changing course during the last decade. The trend is toward a more complex, less realistic narrative, one in which the author is often obviously present, pulling the strings and organizing the scene. We may call this new Spanish novel a "self-referential novel," as does Robert Spires,[1] or, as other critics do, "metafiction." It is useful to compare this trend with the origins of modern Spanish fiction, the picaresque novel and Cervantes's *Don Quixote.* Indeed, many contemporary Spanish novels are indebted to these classic works, and even when they conquer new literary spaces, the extent of the conquest can only be judged by looking at the point of departure. Many of the best Spanish novelists of our time, writers such as Juan Goytisolo, Carmen Martín Gaite, Juan Benet, Gonzalo Torrente Ballester, and even the older novelist Camilo José Cela, have been practicing the challenging art of metafiction, and in every case it may be possible to trace a link between their recent works and Cervantes's masterpiece.

Cervantes was not only a great writer of fiction but also a theoretician of literature: his ideas about fiction and about the theatre helped him in the writing of *Don Quixote.* The two outstanding literary events that took place in Spain during Cervantes's lifetime were the creation of a Spanish national theatre by Lope de Vega and, of course, the creation of the modern novel by Cervantes himself. These two events are basically antithetical but not unrelated. It can be said that all the critical statements made by Cervantes about the romances of chivalry can be applied as well to Lope de Vega's *comedias,* which are also an idealization of Spanish society and distort many aspects of daily life.

Cervantes had tried his hand at playwriting and failed to win the approval of the Spanish public: hence a psychological need to succeed as a novelist by writing a novel that is implicitly a criticism of the games of illusion which are at the heart of Lope's theatre. Ironically, this rejection of Lope as a model brings Cervantes to a close examination of daily life and the creation of the first realistic novel, yet he is forced to reproduce in it many instances of theatricality, because Spanish society had been thoroughly pervaded by the theatre and play-acting had become the rule even in daily life. In *Don Quixote* it is not only the hidalgo who acts out his fantasies. Many secondary characters, such as Marcela and Grisóstomo, play at being what they are not, assume roles and don disguises. The spirit of carnival, as described by Bakhtin, pervades several chapters of the novel. Finally, in part 2 all the events in the Duke's palace are theatrical and can be compared to the "play within a play" in *Hamlet.*

As a keen observer and critic of Spanish society, Cervantes was aware that its obsession with the theatre and with playacting was sacrificing truth to illusion and blurring the borders between the real self and the self created by convention or by fantasy. Moreover, an important feature of baroque art is the blurring of the frontiers between the beholder and the work of art. Thus in Velázquez's painting *Las Meninas* the artist includes himself, and the act of painting the picture, in the picture, and the public, moreover, is also invited to enter the space which the artist is depicting, since the painter is facing and "observing" the spectator. Don Quixote, commenting upon the first part of *Don Quixote,* is simultaneously *within* and *outside* the novel, and Cervantes converts his hero into a reader, just like us, just as real—or, conversely, just as fictitious—as we ourselves are. This means that the games of illusion can be used to make statements about society and ultimately about epistemology and metaphysics.

As the gifted Mexican novelist Carlos Fuentes puts it, "for me, the modern world begins when Don Quixote de la Mancha, in 1605, leaves his village, goes out into the world and discovers that the world does not resemble what he has read about it."[2] Lionel Trilling once wrote, "All prose fiction is a variation on the theme of *Don Quixote:* . . . the problem of appearance and reality." And in *The Order of Things* Michel Foucault writes, "Don Quixote is the sign of a modern divorce between words and things." Both the glory and the misery of our era are involved in this divorce, this bitter and perhaps hopeless separation. It opens the doors to modern philosophy, modern criticism, modern fiction. The Spanish hidalgo is both noble and pathetic in his naïve attempt to make words mean what they are supposed to mean and thus restore virtue and courage to a society that can only talk about such virtues. We know better, yet literature will be forever in his debt. In his obsession with books and the value of words, Don Quixote helps us understand our new obsession with literature as texts and intertextuality. Julia Kristeva's ideas about intertextuality, ideas which by the way are essential to our interpretation of the latest novels by Goytisolo such as *Count Julian* and *Juan the Landless,* also help us understand why Don Quixote thought knights-errant and their fabulous exploits had really existed, since they were mentioned by these same texts that talked about Charlemagne, whose existence chronicles had established as certain. All the traits of metafiction—the intruding author, discussion of the work's creation within the work itself, criticism of fiction and even criticism of the novel we are reading by the characters in the novel, the stepping out of the novel by the characters in the novel—are already present in *Don Quixote.* Such a fascinating subject allows for infinite variations, and contemporary Spanish fiction offers not a few.

Now, fifty years after Lorca's death, Spain is becoming in literature as well as in economics and politics an important part of Western Europe. It was Franco and his totalitarian regime that had drawn around Spain a wall of barren isolation; not even that wall could keep Spain apart for too many years, and by the sixties and the seventies international currents and fashions could be clearly detected on the local scene. Nowadays the doors and windows are wide open, and the predictable result is a joyous chaos.

Only textbooks explain literary history in terms of clearly defined waves of thought and feeling, of style and ideology, arriving neatly one after another and spreading their white and blue foam onto the sandy beaches of history. More often what we really see is a period of transition, hard to define and offering a blurred outline; several rival trends clash and mix before our eyes. This is what is happening now in Spain in the field of narrative literature. The novel and the short story dominate the literary scene; no main trend can be discerned, and no one can suggest a headline that summarizes the current situation.

For many years there was indeed a dominant trend: the gifted writers of the post-civil war period knew that they had to keep score; they were the only witnesses able to write down what was happening: newspapers and magazines were too heavily censored to be truthful. The avant-garde literature that had flourished in Spain in the twenties and the thirties, the golden era of Lorca, Alberti, and Aleixandre, was thus superseded by an era of realism. The labels were of course new: existentialism, *tremendismo,* et cetera. At bottom, however, it was old-fashioned nineteenth-century realism. There was no need to apologize, since Spain in many ways had invented realism way back in the sixteenth and seventeenth centuries with the picaresque novel and *Don Quixote.* Realism was needed once more, and it was readily available. Many excellent novels were written under this mantle. We need only mention the names of Camilo José Cela, Miguel Delibes, Ana María Matute, Ignacio Aldecoa, even the young Juan Goytisolo.

We all remember the first Italian films after Mussolini: *The Bicycle Thief, Rome, Open City,* the great fresh wave of films created by De Sica, Rossellini, Fellini. The best Spanish novels of the forties and fifties were very much in that vein, and they accomplished much the same task—with less ease, since Franco's censorship was always there to hinder the writers. As censorship weakened and Franco's ideology receded, the realistic novel lost its main raison d'être. Today both the press and the media in general can pinpoint the highlights and the shortcomings of the political and social situation, and therefore literature has been freed from the burden of having to say what no one else dares to state. (We remember how harsh censorship could be with respect to the theatre, movies, television, the daily press; it was much more lenient with the novel and even more so with poetry, the assumption being that poetry was read only by the "happy few.")

Elsewhere the novel had abandoned on the whole the realistic paths so often and so successfully followed by the nineteenth-century novelists. Joyce, Proust, and Kafka had pointed out new roads. Both the French *nou-*

veau roman and the Latin American *nueva novela* offered a challenge. With Borges, Cortázar, Rulfo, Fuentes, García Márquez, and Donoso active in Latin America, the Spanish novel was being pressured into a change of course.

Camilo José Cela, one of the most popular and prolific writers during the last several decades, joined the challenge with his *Mazurka para dos muertos* (Mazurka for Two Dead Bodies), which appeared in 1983.[3] It became an instant success, was awarded a prestigious prize, and was reprinted ten times in two years: a best seller by Spanish standards, this novel is more than a rural recycling of Cela's early city novel, *La colmena* (1951; Eng. *The Hive*), a work which is still judged by many critics to be one of his best. *Mazurca* moves at a Proustian, deliberate, noble, slow pace. It is a novel composed of brief vignettes that fade out only to present the same character again a few pages later. A mosaic of people and situations, it demands strict attention from the reader and can at times become irritating because of the large number of non-Castilian words included; these are, of course, Galician words, but the reader is not aware that a glossary at the end of the novel explains and translates them. The result is a tense, mysterious style and a climate of magic and mystery, upon which the developments of Franco's uprising and the Spanish Civil War are superimposed and projected. The final impression is more heartening and pleasurable than the mood created by *The Hive*. *Mazurca* is a novel in which the presence of its author is felt on each page. We see him at each turn of the action, asking questions and soon afterward answering them, manipulating his readers in a good-humored way. We realize at last that we are reading literature, not a chronicle of real-life events, and that in literature human beings are always assured of having the last word.

One more step toward fantasy and away from realism is taken by Carlos Rojas in his novel *El sueño de Sarajevo* (The Dream of Sarajevo; 1982). Almost from the beginning, Rojas's novel reminds us of the celebrated masterpiece by Thomas Mann, *The Magic Mountain*. We are in a private clinic, high in the mountains (although this time in the Pyrenees), and the essential ingredient is to be found in the conversations between the patients, the interplay of personalities, memories, value systems. Rojas's clinic is much more fantastic and Kafkaesque than Mann's, however. Within its impeccably white walls we hear dialogues in which the dead debate the living; we hear the voices of Descartes, Proust, and an enigmatic monk, Fray Antonio Azorín; we see and hear the ghost of Spain's most execrable king, Ferdinand VII, among many other voices belonging to the living and the dead. Fantasy and history mingle on each page until we are no longer sure of our own sanity.

Lest one think this novel is a new departure for Rojas—the winner of Spain's National Literature Prize in 1968 for the novel *Auto de fé*, the Planeta Prize in 1973 for *Azaña*, and the Nadal Prize in 1979 for *El ingenioso hidalgo y poeta Federico García Lorca asciende a los infiernos* (The Ingenious Gentleman and Poet Federico García Lorca Ascends to Hell)—I should state that this last novel is perhaps as complex and mysterious as "The Dream of Sarajevo." Its main characters are Don Quixote, Lorca, and Sandro Vasari, who has written Lorca's biography. Hell, Rojas states, is nothing but an eternal memory. The novel offers us three different and irreconcilable versions of Lorca's life. We witness his last hours in Granada, surrounded by cruel and stupid killers. Other pages describe his escape and his life in the United States, where he has become a professor. The third version is perhaps closer to historical truth and describes his days of hiding in the house of his fellow poet Luis Rosales. We find in this novel echoes of Dante, Sartre, and Carlos Fuentes at his most complex and mysterious. It is an ambitious work, full of unexpected turns and dramatic climaxes, and reading only a few pages of it will give us the conviction that the time for realism is now irrevocably past in Spanish letters.

Another writer whose reputation has grown fast in recent years is Gonzalo Torrente Ballester, whose book *La saga/fuga de J.B.* (J.B.'s Saga/Flight; 1972) has become, according to a poll published in the magazine *Hispania,* one of the ten most popular novels in the Hispanic world during the last decade. Among his latest titles are *Fragmentos de apocalipsis* (Fragments of an Apocalypse; 1977) and *La isla de los jacintos cortados* (The Island Where Hyacinths Are Cut; 1980).[5] Fantastic and whimsical details are so abundant that it is impossible to find a parallel to these novels in the whole panorama of Spanish contemporary fiction, unless we compare them to those of Alvaro Cunqueiro, to which they have a certain resemblance.

"Fragments of an Apocalypse" begins with the diary of a novelist who is describing his efforts and his creative process in trying to write a novel, all of which may remind us of Gide's book *Les faux-monnayeurs* and of a famous sonnet by Lope de Vega which tells us how to write a sonnet. Matters become complicated when we realize that the diary's writer, Justo Samaniego, is a professor who studies medieval manuscripts and that the texts of his diary are intermingled with fragments of manuscripts containing apocalyptic texts. These texts were written to explain and predict the future, a future which would already be our present, and in this approaching present we understand that the Vikings are planning to return to Villasanta de la Estrella in order to avenge their ancient defeat when they invaded the region in order to capture Esclaramunda, the beautiful mistress of Bishop Sisnando.

The scattered and contradictory fragments of this strange novel are finally fused, and the puzzle begins to take shape and make sense. In the meantime other strange events take place. Lenucka, the writer's mistress, disappears before his very eyes when he decides that he no longer will believe in her existence. Villasanta is destroyed because of the ringing of a gigantic bell, which descends in a huge parachute after the funeral of the Viking king Olaf, who is killed by Samaniego, who is eager to rid himself of his Oedipus complex. The characters travel through time toward the past and toward the future.

There is more: a card game in a cathedral, where an archbishop plays with several anarchists and finally exits, flying with the narrator and his lover on a sunbeam to bring to Mallorca an old and horrible dragon. After all these "happenings," a Spanish Buddhist priest in a trance experiences a vision and speaks to us about the infinity of stars and the cosmos, a cosmos in which we search in vain for a nonexistent God. There is also a factory of female robots, of erotic dolls, made necessary because the conquering Vikings have captured all the real women. All this should make us declare once and for all that the famous old "realism" of Spanish narrative prose which Menéndez Pidal and other critics thought so basic and essential is definitely dead.

In "The Island Where Hyacinths Are Cut" we are again dealing with the diary of a writer, intended this time for his beloved Ariadna, who in her turn is interested in a professor of history. The professor's latest book tries to prove that Napoleon never existed but was the end product of a huge joke carried out by Nelson, Metternich, Chateaubriand, the English ambassador to La Gorgona, and all their respective mistresses during a long orgy. Even if Napoleon does not exist, however, we find in him the key to the plot and the guiding thread along a corridor of events that seems made out of soft, distorting mirrors. We realize at the end that this is a roman à clef which portrays real-life characters whom the author has known as a visiting professor at an American university. The plot and the complex intertwining tales, however, remind us most of a modern version of the *Arabian Nights*. In sum, any resemblance between Rojas's work and a realistic novel is pure coincidence.

An author whose name could not be absent from my panoramic survey is Juan Goytisolo, as well known abroad as he is in Spain. His "Trilogy of Treason"— *Señas de identidad* (Identification Papers; 1966), *Re-*

ivindicación del Conde Don Julián (1969; Eng. *Count Julian*), and *Juan sin tierra* (1975; Eng. *Juan the Landless*)[6]—has become a modern classic, a must on the reading lists of all graduate Spanish programs. The last two novels of the trilogy especially offer poignant, subjective visions that express social criticism through fantasy in a masterful way that has no parallel in Spanish literature, and very few rivals in world literature. The last novel seems to close a cycle; the author has spoken, for the moment at least, his final word about Spanish life and culture. His new books, published in the eighties—*Makbara* (1980),[7] *Paisaje después de la batalla* (Landscape after a Battle), and *Coto vedado* (Hunting Preserve; 1985)—are clearly less powerful than the novels of the trilogy. The author is groping for a new beginning, identifying with the Third World, criticizing Western values, but his new works lack the intensity that his complex love-hate relationship with his native land gave to most of his earlier novels. Only a few "true confessions" in his last book, essentially an autobiography, are of genuine interest to his many aficionados. His trilogy remains his best work and also the clearest example of the self-referential novel in recent Spanish literature, with the constant presence of the author as one more character or as the main character in the novel. In *Juan the Landless* he introduces us to his private world of dreams, fantasies, and nightmares, and toward the end of the novel we even attend a curious roundtable, a television talk show in which the author and his novels, including the one we are reading, are strongly criticized, even denigrated, by a panel of critics and average readers.

Another prolific novelist, one whose works are always highly original, mysterious, and baffling, is Juan Benet. He has successfully combined the gothic novel, allegory, fantasy, and social criticism in a series of novels each related to the others yet individual and unique. Benet is often obscure and has not yet had the chance to reach a vast audience, though most critics are aware that he is an important writer who deserves attention and needs critical elaboration. Benet's latest novel, *Herrumbrosas lanzas* (Rusty Lances; 1983)[8] is perhaps one of the best of the series that starts with *Volverás a Región* (1967; Eng. *Return to Región*). The American critic and *WLT* collaborator Catherine G. Bellver, who teaches at the University of Nevada in Las Vegas, has this to say about Benet's long (310 pages) 1983 novel:

> Faulkner has his Yoknapatawpha County, García Márquez his Macondo, and Benet his Región— fictional places of personal invention nonetheless identifiable with geographical areas known to the authors. In his latest novel, Benet attempts to negate this duplicity by creating a momentarily credible and even palpable illusion of real places,

people, and events. Benet, the civil engineer, goes beyond his previous precise lexical descriptions of the geography and geology of Región to provide us with a supplementary 1:150,000 scaled map of Región that seemingly establishes the authenticity of his setting but at the same time reminds the alert reader of the author's efforts at intellectual entrapment.

The Spanish Civil War, present already in Benet's first novel, *Volverás a Región* (1967), becomes the central issue in *Herrumbrosas lanzas,* the 1984 recipient of the Premio de la Crítica. This most recent novel by Benet traces the strategy planning, the conflicts and battles, and the personalities involved in the civil war as it unfolded in the mythical Región area. Early in the war, the city of Macerta succumbs to the fascists, but the capital city, Región, stays loyal to the Republican cause. For some, this work is an allegorical analysis in microcosmic form of the whole of the Spanish Civil War, whereas for others it may be a study of war on a more universal plane.

The world brought to life in these pages always remains Benet's very own, however. Despite the veracity given it by exact dates and allusions to the war elsewhere, Región is the same strange geographical place, isolated from the rest of Spain and forgotten by history. As the author affirms early in the novel, Región, the drifting remains of the Republican shipwreck, floated along peacefully during the war and, to the consternation of its nucleus of resisters, was ignored by the enemy because of its lack of strategic importance. This peripheral historical role helps to complete the vision of ruin and decadence Benet began painting in his first novel. The structural complications of his earliest work give way here to clarity and simplicity, but the underlying syntax of his prose reveals the hand of a literate and polished stylist.

I have included this review in its entirety because it gives us the flavor of a difficult writer, one who seems to want to create distance and suspicion between himself and his readers.

Finally, a first-rate novelist, Carmen Martín Gaite, has continued to produce excellent books during the eighties, including *El cuarto de atrás* (1980; Eng. *The Back Room*), which reminds us of one of her first works, *El balneario* (At the Spa), inasmuch as it is also a mystery novel. *El cuarto,* however, is much more complex and impressive. Its sources are found in Lewis Carroll and in Tzvetan Todorov's essays on fantastic literature, the dialogue is convincing and occasionally brilliant, and the mixture of realism and hallucination belongs to the great romantic tradition, the gothic novel, and Edgar Allan Poe.

To sum up, the cornucopia keeps pouring out hundreds of novels, many of which are very good by international standards. Among these novels the objective observer will find many divergent trends. Realism has not disappeared altogether, yet the present, and probably the future, belongs to an experimental and adventurous type of novel, one which combines realism and fantasy, everyday life and wild dreams. Cervantes found a viable formula a long time ago. Today each novelist strives for a personal, original approach. If only a few of them succeed, as they seem to be doing in recent years, the Spanish novel will enter the new Golden Age which many of us have anticipated for some time. The best is yet to come.

Manuel Durán, Summer 1986

[1] See Robert C. Spires, "From Neorealism and the New Novel to the Self-Referential Novel: Juan Goytisolo's *Juan sin tierra,*" *Anales de la narrativa española contemporánea,* 5 (1980), pp. 73–82. Also, *From Fiction to Metafiction: Essays in Honor of Carmen Martin Gaite,* Mirella Servodidio and Marcia L. Welles, eds., Lincoln, Ne., Society of Spanish and Spanish-American Studies, 1983, especially the essays by Manuel Durán (pp. 129–38), Robert Spires (pp. 139–48), and Ruth El Saffar (pp. 185–96), and also the excellent essay by Marcia Welles (pp. 197–208).

[2] Carlos Fuentes, "When Don Quixote Left His Village, the Modern World Began," *New York Times Book Review,* 23 March 1986, p. 15.

[3] Camilo José Cela, *Mazurca para dos muertos,* Barcelona, Seix Barral, 1983. For a review, see *WLT* 58:4 (Autumn 1984), p. 571.

[4] Carlos Rojas, *El ingenioso hidalgo y poeta Federico García Lorca asciende a los infiernos,* Barcelona, Destino, 1980. For a review, see *WLT* 55:2 (Spring 1981), p. 282.

[5] Gonzalo Torrente Ballester, *Fragmentos de apocalipsis* (1977) and *La isla de los jacintos cortados* (1980), both published by Destino in Barcelona. For reviews, see *WLT* 52:3 (Summer 1978), p. 439, and 55:4 (Autumn 1981), p. 645 respectively.

[6] Juan Goytisolo, *Juan sin tierra,* Barcelona, Seix Barral, 1975. For a review, see *WLT* 51:1 (Winter 1977), p. 67.

[7] Juan Goytisolo, *Makbara,* Barcelona, Seix Barral, 1980. For a review, see *WLT* 55:2 (Spring 1981), p. 281.

[8] Juan Benet, *Herrumbrosas lanzas,* books 1–6, Madrid, Alfaguara, 1983. The review cited in the text is from *WLT* 59:1 (Winter 1985), p. 57.

Camilo José Cela: 1989 Nobel Prize in Literature

From the perspective of 1989 it is difficult to imagine what Spain was like in 1942, when Camilo José Cela published *La familia de Pascual Duarte.* Barely three years after the cessation of one of the bloodiest conflicts of the twentieth century (the Spanish Civil War has often been called the dress rehearsal for World War II), Cela's novel appeared in the midst of some of the bleakest years in Spanish history. On the one hand, daily life was dreadfully difficult, as Spain, with its back to the war being fought in the rest of Europe, experienced both the scarcity occasioned by the interruption of a complex economy by its own civil war and the unavailability of many essential products from its former trading partners, now themselves at war. On the other hand, the triumph of the fascists unleased one of the worst examples of sociopolitical repression in modern Europe, a mechanism both of revenge and ideological confirmation clearly modeled after what Hitler had exemplified in Germany and in concert with numerous international models of how to bring—or at least how to attempt to bring—order out of the chaos of a multifaceted twentieth-century society. Franco's Spain in the forties was unswervingly committed to dictating a new social order based on the fantasies of reactionary Catholicism, and there was little room for even the slightest manifestations of dissent from this program, which El Caudillo himself touted as divinely inspired and the only way to save Spain from the evils of the modern world.

Tyrannies, whether from the right or from the left, never seem to learn the lessons of history: cultural expression cannot be effectively silenced, nor is it possible to impose, no matter how Draconian the methods employed, a totalitarian cultural ideology. Culture, by its very nature, embodies an opening toward the contestatorial, the demythificational, the deconstructive, and the disruptional. Even the sincerest attempts to toe the line of ideological uniformity fail in speaking clearly with one voice, and one of the few hopes for humankind in the nightmare of its contemporary history is the fact that culture cannot be other than now a reluctant, now a shameless reflection on the failures of the social contract.

Cela and his publisher, although hardly standing alone among an underground of voices from the pre-Franco cultural legacy (a period of intense brilliance in Spain) and from those both excluded by the system of revenge or simply unable to assimilate to a prescribed cultural voice, were able to prevail against the many formal and informal mechanisms of censorship to bring out *Pascual Duarte* at a time when Spanish readers where hardly disposed to contemplate a rewriting of their social body that went so dramatically against the grain of the official versions of Catholic Spain, the sanctity of the family, the benevolent nature of the social hierarchy, and the acquiesence of individuals in the face of their assigned lot in life. Or at least, the Franco cultural establishment assumed there could not be—ought

not to be, was not probably—any space in the new Spanish consciousness for *Pascual Duarte:* the official versions were viewed as so patently self-evident and so persuasively prevalent that such a narrative could only be viewed as fanciful, as so much a distortion of reigning social reality as to be fantastic at best and scurrilously prevaricating at worst.

Such was not to be the case: Cela's novel so effectively challenged the fantasies of the mythic never-never land of Franco's image of Spain for export—the bargain-basement Spain that he tried successfully to sell for business investments, military bases, neo-Hollywoodian filmmaking, and gum-chewing tourism —that it inaugurated the entire tradition of anti-Franco cultural honesty which has affirmed itself with such emphasis in present-day constitutional, socialized Spain. A cultural producer like Pedro Almodóvar may be the international darling of the hour because of his audacious film interpretations of the social myths that still cling like lint to the Spanish social fabric, but it must be understood that it was authors like Cela who made the first strategic moves to defy and to counter a cynical cultural policy that rewrote in overpowering large letters whatever reality Spain was in fact experiencing in those intolerable days fifty years ago.

Pascual Duarte is the story of a young man who is a witness to all the unrelenting brutality of social life and who, in turn, becomes yet one more unreflecting instrument of that brutality. The fact that Pascual narrates his own story is a dramatically ironic index of his essential separation from any awareness of the dynamics of his social existence, while at the same time allowing for some glimmer of an inherent redemptive grace beyond the swagger of his words. An assassin of both his mother and the local patriarch, potent symbols in the mythology of the nuclear and social family, Pascual, as his name suggests, is a sacrificial victim to a system of justice that condemns and punishes the crime but is incapable of reflecting on the sources of the antisocial behavior to which it attests. That the local patriarch, no matter how benevolent, is a token of an oppressive economic order and that his mother is, in her maliciousness, the antithesis of the Marian image cannot be computed in the calculus of Pascual's behavior—or so at least it would seem on the surface of the relentless chronicle of the harsh facts of life he has witnessed and his own deeds that defy the institutionalized code of Christian charity.

Cela's novel, of course, is a challenge to his readers to perceive the fissures in the social discourse that surrounds them in the carefully orchestrated rhetoric of Franco's eternally Catholic Spain. Against the first hypothesis that Pascual Duarte is the sort of sinner who must be extirpated in order to consolidate the triumph of traditional morality and the reciprocal social order it implies, the novel postulates a counter-discourse, especially in its unremittingly stark descriptive and narrative registers, whose effective resonance must be both the recollection of the social injustices that culminated in the civil war in the first place and the terrible social contract its aftermath sought to enforce. It is not so much that Cela's was a lone voice. Indeed, the forties and fifties in Spain present a rich inventory of cultural producers in all genres who cast light on the darkest corners of the Franco social edifice. The stark naturalism of *Pascual Duarte,* however, its unrelenting reality effect, so to speak, was an especially forceful articulation of the horrors of life in Spain at the time, particularly in its most impoverished regions like Extremadura, where the novel takes place, as it signaled the recovery in Spanish fiction of a registry of colloquial authenticity that official discourse both diligently belied and strove to drown out.

Authenticity in the literary representation of social discourse is, in fact, a key to much of Cela's subsequent writings. It has often been stated that the themes and characters in Cela's works are grotesque, verging on the repugnant, and exemplary all too often of gross vulgarity. Such a complaint derives from the abiding conflict between an ethics of culture that proposes to contemplate unflinchingly the life humankind is obliged to live and an ethics of culture that postulates a Utopia of society reconstructed or redeemed. The latter is always a valid program for culture, as long as the Utopia it proposes makes some sort of sense within the concrete physical and social parameters of existence. Clearly, for Cela and the many other writers who spoke against the official discourse of the tyranny, the romantic myth of an eternally Catholic Spain, sanitized whenever necessary as the gaily painted scrim of the tourist industry (medieval castles, stomping Gypsy dancers, black-clad reverent peasants, and taut-liveried bullfighters), simply had nothing to do with the daily lives of the battered Pascual Duartes.

Pascual Duarte provided the rural dimension of life in Franco's Spain. The neorealist novel *La colmena* (1951; Eng. *The Hive,* 1953) turned attention to the more contemporary reality of the difficulties of urban existence. Combining images of the migration of people into the cities (the consequence of both the devastation of the countryside by war and the concentration of the postwar economy on city-based capitalist expansion), of the meanness of quotidian human commerce as the reflex of the scarcity of jobs and goods, of the omnipresence of moral righteousness as a mechanism to enforce irreflective conformity, and of all manner of degrading

Camilo José Cela (*Lütfi Özkök*)

exploitation in the context of a social reality that did not have much to do with the Christian virtues routinely invoked by the righteous defenders of the faith, *La colmena,* not surprisingly, was banned in Spain, to be published in Buenos Aires.

The title of Cela's novel invokes the socialist icon of the beehive as the buzzingly harmonious abode of a smoothly integrated and productive society, with every member-individual given over selflessly to the pursuit of the common weal. Perhaps such was one of the fantasies of Franco's new order, and the icon of the beehive has an indisputable eloquence within the fascist mythology of the frictionless social hierarchy. Nevertheless, the tenement that is the real-life manifestation of the apian icon is instead a cockroach- and fly-infested dungheap where the sweet harmony of the productive bees is replaced by the hideous noises of the pariahs in a world in which the distinction between those who are bestialized because of their spiritual corruption and those who are bestialized because they have been victimized is a sentimental nicety to which this mosaic of urban chaos gives short shrift.

The portrayal of social intercourse as cacophony is one of the most powerful dimensions of Cela's writing, as well as it is one aspect of both his expressive range and the sense of the grotesque that emanates from his texts. No writer in twentieth-century Spain since Ramón del Valle-Inclán (1866–1936) has had the command over the vast lexicon of Spanish evinced by Cela's writings. The *Diccionario* of the Spanish Royal Academy affords only a minimalist's appreciation of the semic wealth of the Spanish language along its multiple regional, class, and stylistic dimensions. Indeed, one of the goals of the Academy has been traditionally to codify—that is, to circumscribe—this wealth in favor of the fixed (if yet still flexible) standard required by contemporary socioeconomic needs: language too is a capital that must be rationally controlled. Cela's confrontation with this goal has been threefold.

In the first place, in consonance with his depiction of the vast panorama of social reality that overflows the narrow confines of the Franco and sundry other neofascist containments, he has assumed the task of demonstrating the cynical manipulation of language in the interests of that containment and the mythologies it propagates; this is the case, certainly, of his handling of the icon of the beehive and its derivations, or of his deconstruction of pastoral tropes in *Pascual Duarte*. Second, in repudiating the tinny sounds of a Spanish language denatured by bureaucratization and the exigencies of a repressive official discourse, Cela has worked indefatigably to recover the echoes of Spanish as it is actually used by people all of whose languages, verbal as well as not linguistically symbolic, have been excluded from the new order. This means not only calling things by their rightful names, as in his outrageous picturebook on whores and the lexicon of their trade (*Izas, rabizas y colipoterras,* 1964) or when his characters speak a language that denotes, in painfully graphic detail, the humiliations of their life, as well as evoking at the same time, with joyful ebullience, the ways in which popular language creatively metaphorizes the processes of daily existence. Concomitantly, Cela's *Diccionario secreto* (1968), easily his most ambitious and original undertaking, is an impressive interpretive compilation of the history and derivation of taboo words in Spanish, sort of the lexical outhouse of the Royal Spanish Academy and an eloquent demonstration of all the real-life manifestations of language that such institutions, by their very nature, cannot address. One interesting example of Cela's commitment to non-Academic Spanish has been (and in this he also follows Valle-Inclán) an exploration of the complex projections of the language outside Spain, as in his Venezuelan novel *La catira* (The Blonde; 1955) and his American novel *Cristo versus Arizona* (Christ versus Arizona; 1988).

Finally, Cela himself has been an assiduous contributor to the evolution of the Spanish language. His writings abound with neologisms, complex figures of diction that both reproduce the metaphorical processes of the language of everyday people and add their own poetic dimension to the ongoing project of finding adequate linguistic expression for the intricacies of daily experiences, and the ingenious deployment of fruits of his philological fieldwork among all the strata of spoken and written Spanish. Cela's writing oscillates (not always felicitously) between the poles of a naturalistic depiction of the richness of Spanish as it is used by his characters to speak their lives and what often verges on a Byzantine *préciosité,* a vertigo of linguistic foregrounding that brings the reader back to the inevitable—and, of course, salutary—realization that what is being read is a highly acculturated text and not, after all, social reality itself. If there is any significant ideological slippage in Cela's writing, it may well be found in the perhaps unresolvable tension between a commitment to rewriting for the reader the Book of Life for post-civil-war Spain and in indulging in all the feverish enterprises (here concentrated in linguistic pyrotechnics) late capitalism promotes. This is evident not only in the enormous verbal energy unleashed by his writing, but also in the dizzying frequency with which he startles the reader with shifts in the structure of his works and his experimentation with the considerable range of narrative models offered by modern fiction. (The foregoing observation probably means that one should talk about Cela as the paradigmatic Spanish postmodernist, as far as literature is concerned, but it is not crucial to pursue such a critical option at this point.)

I have stated that one might consider the *Diccionario secreto* to be Cela's masterpiece, not only because of the philological research it implies but, more important, for its central role in his view that the Spanish language must be rescued from the Academy and from the repressive bureaucratization of culture—linguistic in the first instance, comprehensive in the final analysis—that the Academy serves. (The Academy is, after all, an official government entity, as are the universities and other scientific institutions with which it enjoys interdependence; Cela, in the usual evolution of cultural history, is now a member of the Spanish Royal Academy and has held employment as a servant of the government, serving also as one of the king's appointed senators.) Still, the *Diccionario secreto* has rarely been given more than passing commentary in studies of Cela's writing, as though it were somehow parenthetical to his major titles. The same can be said of Cela's extensive bibliography of travel sketches, which were inaugurated in 1948 with *Viaje a la Alcarria* (1964; Eng. *Journey to the Alcarria*) and extend through the early 1970s.

These books were, at least in the beginning, based on Cela's journey by foot through areas he describes, and their importance lies in the implied effort to recover in another dimension an authentic image of Spanish society beyond the confines of a new order that either flattened out the rough texture of lives conducted in the only way they could be conducted under the difficult circumstances of the time or repressed whatever those lives contained that did not conform to the official sociocultural ideology that had been securely locked into place. Cela sought to listen to the real language of the people, with all its rough edges, and he sought to provide a nonromanticized depiction of what they lived by, what they thought, and what the contradictions of their not always, not usually lovely existence were. Although these sketches have not enjoyed the fame his novels have, the latter being written in conformance with the contemporary priorities of "elaborated" art, they too constitute very significant elements in Cela's enterprise of countering the totalizing official discourse.

One can be pardoned for entertaining many objections to Cela's works published during the last twenty years, although some come near to reproducing the brilliance of his early production. Perhaps this is only because there is so much outstanding writing coming out of Spain in recent decades, as well as from the many other Spanish-language countries. The over-whelming coherence that can be attributed to Cela's writing from its earliest manifestations, however, and the role his work has played in defining what literary culture in Spain might be since the worst days of the postwar period lend his texts the singular distinction the Nobel Prize serves to confirm.

David William Foster, Winter 1990

■ CAMILO JOSÉ CELA IN BA/WLT

La colmena, reviewed by H. C. Ladewig in *BA* 26:1 (Winter 1952), p. 35.

Jacob Ornstein and James Y. Causey, "Camilo José Cela: Spain's New Novelist," *BA* 27:2 (Spring 1953), pp. 136–37.

Esas nubes que pasan, reviewed by Jacob Ornstein in *BA* 28:1 (Winter 1954), p. 31.

Mrs. Caldwell habla con su hijo, reviewed by Gerald E. Wade in *BA* 28:3 (Summer 1954), p. 304.

Baraja de invenciones, reviewed by Terrell Louise Tatum in *BA* 29:1 (Winter 1955), p. 45.

El gallego y su cuadrilla, reviewed by Jacob Ornstein in *BA* 30:3 (Summer 1956), p. 290.

La catira: Historias de Venezuela, reviewed by Jacob Ornstein in *BA* 30:4 (Autumn 1956), p. 401.

La rueda de los ocios, reviewed by Terrell Tatum in *BA* 33:3 (Summer 1959), p. 288.

Historias de España, reviewed by Robert G. Mead Jr. in *BA* 33:4 (Autumn 1959), p. 408.

Recuerdo de don Pío Baroja, reviewed by David Griffen in *BA* 34:4 (Autumn 1960), p. 387.

Primer viaje andaluz: Notas de un vagabundaje, reviewed by Rodolfo Cardona in *BA* 35:2 (Spring 1961), p. 137.

La familia del héroe reviewed by David William Foster in *BA* 40:3 (Summer 1966), p. 318.

Diccionario secreto 1, reviewed by Charles L. King in *BA* 43:3 (Summer 1969), p. 389.

Al servicio de algo, reviewed by David William Foster in *BA* 44:2 (Spring 1970), p. 281.

Vísperas, festividad y octava de San Camilo del año 1936 en Madrid, reviewed by David William Foster in *BA* 45:1 (Winter 1971), p. 79.

Oficio de tinieblas 5, reviewed by Joan T. Cain in *BA* 49:1 (Winter 1975), p. 92.

Rol de cornudos, reviewed by William R. Risley in *WLT* 51:4 (Autumn 1977), p. 598.

Vuelta de hoja, reviewed by Luis Larios in *WLT* 56:3 (Summer 1982), p. 489.

El juego de los tres madroños, reviewed by Ricardo Landeira in *WLT* 58:1 (Winter 1984), p. 76.

Once cuentos de fútbol, reviewed by Joan T. Cain in *WLT* 62:1 (Winter 1988), p. 96.

Twentieth-Century Spanish Poetry

The twentieth century in Spain has been dominated by poetry, especially during its first half, gloriously marked by the work of Miguel de Unamuno, Ramón del Valle-Inclán, Antonio and Manuel Machado, Juan Ramón Jiménez, Jorge Guillén, Federico García Lorca, Vicente Aleixandre, and others whom I shall discuss throughout the course of this paper. Two causes decisively influenced the rise of lyric poetry: first, the quality and variety of the works produced by the aforementioned poets; and second, the establishment of a critical context in which the poets found comprehension and elucidation, appraisal and support. The result was that the years 1900–50 were as stimulating and productive as the best years of the Hispanic past. The works appearing during those decades were so outstanding that they were considered by some to represent a new Golden Age in Spanish literature. To convey such literary splendor, it would be worthwhile to detail specific examples, precisely because each is unique and very different from the others, although alike in renovative intent. It is obvious that that kind of detailed treatment, however, is not possible in an essay which, by necessity, must be limited.

I would place Unamuno in the position attributed to him by critical consensus: that of the great primary figure of the age. He did not enter into literature through the door of poetry but instead through that of the journalistic article, the essay, the short story, and the novel. His first book of poems appeared late, in 1907, when the author was forty and had achieved the renown and popularity that would remain with him until his death. He was viewed by the majority and by many in the minority as the great patron of Spanish letters. Ortega, however, called him "Morabito Máximo" (The Ultimate Mohammedan Hermit), denigratingly. A renovator rooted in tradition, Unamuno was recognized as a master by Antonio Machado, in whose work he left his own visible traces. Juan Ramón Jiménez declared more than once that contemporary poetry in Spanish originated with the dual mastery of Unamuno and Rubén Darío. If poetry acquired from one the rhythm of idea, it found in the other the idea of rhythm. The verbalization and the impulse which governed it were indistinguishable. Thus, internalized rhythm came to govern poetry.

The early years of the century were characterized by the propagation of modernism, a romanticism reactivated by adaptation to a new age, Parnassian modes of writing, and the rise of symbolism, which characterized the best lyric poetry of the times. The swan, multivalent symbol of beauty, grace, youth, and the poet himself, was an emblem which Darío felt to be at the same time a representative of the Maker and a maker itself. The poet, "torre de Dios" (tower of God) opposite the dominant vulgarity, was a creator and not merely a transcriber of experiences that were realized in the poem, even if woven with the fragile substance of dreams.

Unamuno was Basque; the Machado brothers and Jiménez, Andalusians; Valle-Inclán, Galician. Men on the periphery, they moved to the central region of Castile in order to be better heard. They contributed to poetry the accents of their regions, languages, or dialects and cooperated, via different routes, in the renovative undertaking. Gustavo Adolfo Bécquer was their distant inspiration and on occasion also their model. Unamuno and Valle-Inclán wrote plays and novels, the Machado brothers drama and criticism, and Jiménez brought poetry to the short story and lyrical autobiography, in addition to writing very astute criticism. In a country like ours, the writer must attend to everything: he must ignite a fire, keep watch over those already burning, and rekindle the one that has gone out. New styles were arriving while traditional ones were still popular with most of the public.

Following the example of the plastic artists (Picasso, Gris, and later Miró), the poets let themselves get caught up in the atmosphere of change, which sometimes proceeded from outside Spain. Juan Ramón Jimé-

nez, who at that time was becoming ever more successful, served as an example if not as a model to young writers. The Iberian landscape became populated with magazines that waved like flags, with Juan Ramón himself launching some of the most interesting ones. A spirit of optimism prevailed throughout the country. The avant-garde "had arrived" and, with them, the hope that Spain was about to come of age or, as Machado described it, rise to the level of the circumstances. Through the patronage of Ortega at *Revista de Occidente,* of Manuel Azaña at *La Pluma,* and of Jiménez at *Indice,* young voices were allowed to be heard (not just poets but, above all, poets of quality).

In *Diario de un poeta recién casado* (Diary of a New-lywed Poet; 1916) Jiménez revived the prose poem and wrote poetry founded on a generative and constituently textual rhythm that, according to the poet, was inspired by the sea on his trip to the United States to get married and on the return trip to Spain. In this book the sea is the protagonist as much as are the poet and his wife. No book delineates so clearly the break with the past, and in it one is informed how, through a change in the flow of the text, the substance is altered, in this case charged by a lyricism which is sufficient in itself, reducing referent and incident to the condition of pre-text. The will to create persisted, and creative conscience had become keener and more precise. To create was to name: "Inteligencia dame el nombre exacto de la cosas / que mi palabra sea la cosa misma creada por mi alma nuevamente" (Intelligence, give me the exact name for things / so that my word may be that thing itself newly created by my soul). Here, the soul is the superspiritual-ized synecdoche of being, the word, expression of being, expression of feeling, feeling itself; and woman, love, illusion.

One poet who achieved serenity of mind and precision in writing recaptured the legacy. "Creemos los nombres" (Let us create names), advised Jorge Guillén.[1] (He advised and did not "state"—everything about this enthusiastic man was joyfully determined to elevate poetry to pure song.) *Cántico* (Canticle; 1928) was the name of his first book, an expression of exaltation and enthusiasm moderated by the rigor of the poetic word and crystallized in poems par excellence in the art of condensation. Everything—being, time, life—was concentrated in verses that reflected on themselves in order better to challenge the perceptions of the reader by an accumulation of verbal expressivity, which in no way is magical. Two words— exclamatory indeed—were sufficient to situate spring in the poem, if not with "su caballo blanco," as with Jiménez, then with the transparency and beauty with which he fills his universe. The poetic space vibrates with the resonance of the poetry which occupies it.

I have cited two books, the most singularly important of Spanish poetry during the first half of the century, and I like to recall the fact that both were written against the current: *Diario* against the general line of traditional verse, *Cántico* in open opposition to those who viewed existence in terms of anguish and who thought that one had to live on the edge of despair. The vitality of Guillén's poems incites optimism and for many has been a decisive stimulus. The pain of a "poorly conceived" world, of the social world, Guillén would write of elsewhere—namely, in *Clamor*. His *aire*, which is *nuestro*, does not exclude anything.

The avant-garde had indeed arrived, and if the Spanish were setting the pace in painting, they were not far behind in poetry. With the exception of the *ultraístas*, Spaniards did not align themselves with isms as did the French on the other side of the border. After Jiménez, and then with Guillén, poets could not deviate from the path of renovation. I shall resist the temptation to mention the many individuals who made their own contribution to the change and enrichment of poetic language and to the exploration of what Antonio Machado called the chambers and corridors of the soul, or what others have defined as the unconscious.

A lyricism of Bécquerian resonances linked the new poetry with the old. There was variation but no break between them. The new arrivals recognized their masters for what they were and sometimes viewed them as models. Bonds of friendship and coincidences of a different order united the poets, though not all. Antonio Espina, ironic, sarcastic, heretical (in poetry and in everything else), was cast out and subjected to the law of silence, as was Juan José Domenchina and others. Azorín invented the so-called generation of '98—later the "generations" arose at the convenience of those who formed them. Within or outside these groups, poetry grew, and in the case of Federico García Lorca, it invaded neighboring territories, such as the theatre, which through his words was filled with a lyricism that, allied with fantasy, at times inclined toward farce and at others toward tragedy. The transformation of the theatre was effected through poetry, and it imposed on both characters and incident a truly unique perspective: that of the poet himself.

The year 1936 is for Spaniards that terrible date of confrontation: a long and cruel civil war, compounded by revolution and counterrevolution which converted civilian life into a hellish nightmare. A great many of the writers were dead or exiled, and, as León Felipe declared from Mexico, for a moment it seemed that poetry had abandoned Spain. A mirage of the exile, poetry was the first thing to reflourish in the devastated homeland after the conflict. Poets whom geography, and at times ideology, placed on the side of the victors and poets who remained on the Republican side slowly took up current poetics again in the more widely circulated magazines and books, on occasion in clandestine alliance with the losing side. Miguel Hernández wrote his last poems in prison, and there he died. The older writers joined with the young writers, and in the early postwar years there appeared books such as *Hijos de la ira* (1944; Eng., *Children of Wrath*) by Dámaso Alonso[2] and *Sombra del paraíso* (Shadow of Paradise; 1944) by Vicente Aleixandre, who later would receive the Nobel Prize and whose influence went further than what today would have been imagined.[3]

Literary currents became more diversified, and the poetry magazines reflected this diversification, as seen in the renewed interest in Garcilaso de la Vega in Madrid, in poetry that was ignited by underground protest in León, in fragile intimism in Córdoba, in passion and sensibility in Santander. The provinces competed in promoting their own poets, who, although different, participated in a community of interests and especially in the desire to forge, where possible, a climate of freedom.

When linked with the names of yesterday, the new names did not compare unfavorably: names like Rosales, Panero, Nora, Otero, Hierro, and García Nieto, who were as different as one could hope for, yet were all committed, nonetheless, to the common enterprise of reimplanting poetry in Spain. During the war, poetry had lost its unity and, in more than a few cases, was corrupted and converted into an instrument of propaganda or a weapon to serve some cause. Later, the courage of the best had a tendency to reconstruct the fragmented unity, and even though the fragmentation subsisted, the courage to overcome it was worth the pain and did not cease to produce the desired results.

In establishing somewhat sketchily the manner in which that fundamental unity tended to be divided, one is obliged to admit that, for some, poetry should identify with social issues, while for others it should identify with esthetic matters, the will of artistic creation taking precedence over any other requirement. All poetry is, by its production and direction, social poetry; it is born of society, and through the individual it returns to society. The texts protected by this rubric during the forties and fifties were in reality political poetry that did not dare give its name. Even a trend as heterodox, refreshing, and perturbing as that which dubbed itself *postismo* disguised its character, in labeling itself in this way, as a later form of surrealism, a school which in those times was unmentionable in Spain.

Perhaps the rise in poetry was aided by its minority status; what was expressed in verse aroused the least suspicion among the censors and was permitted to see the light of day with much less difficulty than was prose. The opportunity of living a secret life was afforded the poets—but not so the prose writers. The cause of the disparity is clear: the elusive, periphrastic, and metaphorical language of the lyric poets allowed them to go unnoticed by the watchdogs of orthodoxy, or at least kept them from directly confronting those authorities as frequently as did the novelists and essayists. Poetry, therefore, caught on earlier than did the novel (there were one or two exceptions, but they were nothing more than that) and soon recovered without great difficulty the creative tension of the years preceding the war. Young poets, followed in turn by not-so-young poets, discovered Antonio Machado through his poetry and his character. He was an example of singular integrity to many and, for some, a model of conduct. Who, therefore, should be surprised that this happened, given the unequivocal position of the author of *La guerra,* who remained so close to his countrymen during the most difficult years in contemporary history? Through Machado, César Vallejo, and Pablo Neruda, the great patriotic theme asserted itself with irresistible force: Spain was a nation filled with passion and rage. The Spain of Leopoldo Panero, Eugenio de Nora, and Blas de Otero had nothing to do with the cultural purism and Hispanism that had become part of the official rhetoric and had little in common with the picturesque *colorismo* that in former times had attracted Théophile Gautier and Prosper Mérimée. The abovementioned poets and many others wrote lyrically of the Spain of courage and suffering, the Spain that offered its chalice to the Peruvian Vallejo, and the Spain of men with first and last names whom Neruda brought to his verses and whom Unamuno called *intrahistóricos.*

The country became a compelling lesson, profiting by the fact that no one could obstruct her praise, the exaltation of her people, both humble and great alike. No one could reproach the poet who shared and expressed the pain of his fellow man and, less still, identified with his hope. In a very different way, "cantos de vida y esperanza" (songs of life and hope) reappeared, and readers identified themselves with the songs and what was sung.

The symbolic representation, which transformed the swan into an emblem of an epoch, revealed untapped wealth in regard to Spain. The word alluded, of course, to the *patria*—not to the abstraction manipulated by the politicians, but to very specific realities. When one spoke of Spain, one had also to speak of country, independence, liberty, love for tangible life and things not alien to the poet, who experimented very deep inside with what existed outside himself. *Spain,* sacred and untouchable word, served to give meaning to the poets (and, perhaps, can still be very important inasmuch as politicians and hack journalists substitute this beautiful, meaningful word for that worn-out expression, the Spanish State).

For two, perhaps three decades the memory of the civil war was present, elusively or directly, in poetry and the novel (and it even arises with excessive frequency in what is written today). As a result of such prolonged recollection of suffering, poetry continued to be devoid of any foundation or calm. I have already pointed out that in Córdoba a group of poets tried to be read in a different way—poets of sensibility and silence had to be listened to carefully in order to be heard. These voices were not discordant, although internalized they did represent a break with lyrical tradition in that the canto became all-important. It is logical that the magazine of the group was called *Cántico.*

The paths of compromise and esthetics presented themselves to Spanish poetry and, with them, diversity and ornateness, two most enriching variations. These two paths were not the Scylla and Charybdis about which Dámaso Alonso wrote in a very famous essay, but instead were signs of the double tradition by which the lyric poetry of this country (and I would even say the entire Spanish language, with exceptions imposed by geography and history) is generally categorized. Unamuno and Darío, Antonio Machado and Juan Ramón Jiménez, leading figures whom time could replace, were immutable as archetypes of creative behavior, if not unchanging as examples.

It seems possible to establish as a third course for contemporary lyric poetry the so-called *culturalista* route. In it grand reminiscences, fascinations, and homages to diverse heroes of the arts are expressed. Turn to any page of such poetry and on it you can find reference to Luis de Baviera, to de Quincey on the next page, and to Novalis, Mozart, and Vermeer van Delft on the pages that follow. These poems are filled with evocative resonances and personalities in which the imagined is as important as who or what the poems really were about. Represented was a reality of clear, sparkling, diverse beauty, in which the romantic existed alongside the sardonic and ambiguity served as background.

I see Spanish poetry—not only of this century—as being very conspicuously contemporary, like a dialogue between diverse parties who complement rather than oppose each other. We witness in the text a conversation between the text's author and the distant poet (i.e., Luis Cernuda and Lope de Vega, Blas de Otero and Quevedo), yesterday's poet (José Hierro with Jiménez and Gerardo Diego), or today's poet, alongside whom he exists but who proceeds down a different path. In a very subtle way verbal bridges are laid between distant poems, successfully allowing open questions in one poem to find answers in another written from some other perspective. In this way, the text operates as a point of encounter, coincidence, dissidence, and contact, so that it can just as easily represent appreciation as contention. Are these contradictions? Hierro writes against an esthete, while alongside him Julio Maruri personifies with nimble grace the man who persists in "living" art with absolute purity.

The fact that poets of a different language share these conversations and secret dialogues is natural. The boundaries of language do not constitute a barrier, and in the world of culture it is incongruous to establish divisions. Many years ago in Puerto Rico the well-known North American writer Alfred Kazin asked my opinion concerning the two cultures that thrive on the isle, the Hispanic and the Anglo-Saxon. I did not hesitate in telling him that those who express themselves in such a way are actually referring to two noncultures lacking in refinement and to the partial ignorance or knowledge of one or the other, two parts of a greater whole.

During the Renaissance, the rhythms of the new style of writing poetry made its way from Italy. Centuries later the meditative seriousness of Leopardi and the eloquence of Victor Hugo enriched our culture. Toward the end of the century Verlainesque harmonies were heard. Why is it surprising then to see the influence of Paul Claudel in Luis Felipe Vivanco, of Pessoa in Angel Crespo, of Cavafy in Luis Antonio de Villena? I cite these as just a few examples of the many that could be mentioned which deal with the communication across borders that exists among poets. It doesn't make sense to talk about influences, although they exist and can be very profound, in pointing out the community of lyric poets to which they all belong.

Through a logical fluctuation in the pendular movement which governs poetry, the young poets currently profess purity of diction, a clarity and rigor that cannot be acquired but is, instead, inherent. The transparency of Antonio Colinas and, quite different in tone, that of Claudio Rodríguez[4] inherit and surpass the "audacity" of the new young writers, *los novísimos*. This is neither easy nor difficult. These terms no longer had meaning as seen, for example, in the last works of Juan Ramón and Guillén. What José Angel Valente called "infinite indetermination" opened up the poem to maximum freedom, which amounted to a maximum under-

standing of knowledge. To comprehend this phenomenon, it is appropriate to refer to a noun that has fallen into disuse—and been subjected to abuse—the noun *mystery*. The search for knowledge implies an investigation into shadowy areas in which what is termed *mystery* seems to be preserved. To understand this most secret reality is the legitimate desire of the poet, who, thanks to his own instrument, the poem, manages through the act of expression, simultaneously to achieve understanding. It is no coincidence that this word appears in titles and texts by Aleixandre, Valente, and Brines (in Brines it is associated with methods, "methods of understanding").

Lyrical confidence holds out a mirror to whoever places it on the page out of the need and desire to recognize himself; this is certainly nothing new. Such a phenomenon underlines a constant in literary creation. *Search, penetration, investigation,* and, in other respects, *revelation* are terms which promote critical discourse in imposing reason on an activity whose meaning is constantly in question.

The invention of poetic personas, emblematic incarnations of the speaker and his counterparts (or of his inclinations, of the diverse attitudes of being), is an experiment in which, for reasons already suggested, other poets, other voices, collaborate with the inventor. Certain deviations, like certain affirmations, are less a product of what Harold Bloom called "the anxiety of influence" than the natural and mental verbal fluctuation imposed on whoever is included (anyone living) in the vast realm of literature's overflowing possibilities. Within this realm is Antonio Carvajal, one of the most appealing poets to appear within the the last ten years, whom the reader welcomes as he would a friend. Once again poetic vigor and control of form were recognized, just as they had been not long ago with Rafael Morales and Miguel Hernández and centuries before, in almost mythical times, with Quevedo and Góngora. Carvajal maintains a distance from the writers of his time in order better to approach writers of the past and energetically underscore his affinity with them. *Extravagante jerarquía* (Extravagant Hierarchy; 1983), like *Abril* (April; 1936) by Luis Rosales, incorporates a discrepancy that I shall call "heterodox purely orthodox" in the panorama of experimentation.

Perhaps (and I dare not judge too conclusively) poets of the renovative tradition and the endless experiment such as Carvajal, the Andalusian, and Alejandro Amusco, the Northerner, are today the most interesting to those of us who continue to believe in work well done and who feel its attraction. A sad loss came with the death of Ignacio Prat, whose critical dialogue with Carvajal is included in the epilogue of *Extravagante* and who was preparing to launch poetry down risky and uncharted paths when death came and took him away. A small book, scarcely half a hundred poems and prose pieces, is as much as his creation could bestow upon us. Imaginative audacity, irony, difficulty, and even obscurity are all brought together in these pieces of enigmatic intensity and occasional sarcastic disdain for the possible "serious" reader.

No, as long as tradition persists, experimentation will not die. Guillermo de Torre, commenting on Apollinaire, imparted a lesson on the theme of adventure and order that is worth remembering, even if it comes to us via André Gide's observation that, "since no one is listening, it is necessary to begin again continually." On this level, experimentation possesses a tradition, and tradition becomes experimental. Could it be any other way when tradition can be named after Góngora and experimentation (from a hundred sources) has established García Lorca and Aleixandre as patron saints? When now I meet poets like Julio Llamazares, who was born in 1955 and in whom the mythic is expressed (as in the novels of his countryman from León, José María Merino) with delicate simplicity, I think that perhaps in a book like *Memoria de la nieve* (Memory of Snow; 1982) and in other similar books, a poetry is beginning to be forged that will link the end of our century with the beginning of the next, which is almost within sight.

Ricardo Gullón, Spring 1985, Authorized translation
by David Draper Clark

[1] On Jorge Guillén, see *BA* 42:1 (Winter 1968), pp. 7–60, and *WLT* 58:2 (Spring 1984), pp. 228–39.

[2] On Dámaso Alonso, see *BA* 48:2 (Spring 1974), pp. 231–320.

[3] On Vicente Aleixandre, see *WLT* 52:2 (Spring 1978), pp. 203–208.

[4] On Claudio Rodríguez and Francisco Brines, see *BA* 42:2 (Spring 1968), pp. 211–14.

The Poetry of J. V. Foix

L'antic museu, les madones borroses,
I el pintar extrem d'avui! Càndid rampell:
M'exalta el nou i m'enamora el vell.

(The ancient museums, the faded madonnas,
And today's extreme painting! A naïve sudden impulse;
The new inflames me and I'm in love with the old.)[1]

■ J. V. FOIX

At the venerable age of eighty-eight, J. V. Foix remains the acknowledged master of avant-garde Catalan poetry. Since 1917 he has been closely associated with Cata-

lonia's artistic vanguard, including internationally known painters like Joan Miró and Salvador Dalí, both of whom he presented in their first one-man shows. In addition to his poetic and journalistic activities (he has edited magazines like *Trossos* [Pieces], *La Revista Catalana* and *Monitor*), Foix is also the prosperous owner of two fine pastry shops. His customers sometimes ask him if by any chance he has a son who writes those strange poems with the long titles.

Foix and Joan Salvat-Papasseit, both of whom emerged in the 1910s, were the first truly modern Catalan poets. While Salvat died in 1924, Foix went on to forge a style and vision that have made him a leading figure in modern European literature. In a fictitious "Lletra d'Itàlia" (Letter from Italy) at the beginning of his book *Poems en ondes herzianes* (Poems in Electric Waves; 1919), Salvat commented, "Here in Rome people murmur that to understand Mr. Foix of Sarrià one should first read Sophocles."[2] The choice of Sophocles is somewhat arbitrary, but Salvat's meaning is clear enough: part of Foix's subject matter is culture itself.

Foix was indeed far more cultured than his friend Salvat. Like more traditional Catalan poets such as Josep Carner and Carles Riba, Foix sought to established direct links with the Catalan past, drawing into his work what he conceived to be an entire Mediterranean tradition. This synthetic effort is perhaps clearest in early sonnets like "If I Could Reconcile Reason and Madness . . ." At the time of its composition (between 1913 and 1927, according to an introductory note), Foix was also writing experimental prose poems. Yet the form of "If I Could Reconcile" is classically Petrachan and uses Ausiàs March's characteristic decasyllables.

Si pogués acordar Raó i Follia,
I en clar matí, no lluny de la mar clara,
La meva ment, que de goig és avara,
Em fes present l'Etern. I amb fantasia

—Que el cor encén i el meu neguit desvia—
De mots, sons i tons, adesiara
Fes permanent l'avui, i l'ombra rara
Que m'estrafà pels murs, fos seny i guia

Del meu errar per tamarius i lloses;
—Oh dolços pensaments!, dolçors en boca!—
Tornessin ver l'Abscon, i en cales closes,

Les imatges del son que l'ull evoca,
Vivents; i el Temps no fos; i l'esperança
En Immortals Absents, fos llum i dansa!

(If I could reconcile Reason and Madness
And in clear morning, not far from clear sea
My mind, avaricious for joy,
Could make the Eternal present. And with Fantasy

—That the heart inflames and my uneasiness turns

aside—
Of words, sounds and tones, could
Occasionally make today permanent, and that strange
  shadow
That mimicked me on walls, be good sense and
  guide
For my wanderings through tamarisks and
  tombstones;
—Oh sweet thoughts! Sweetness in mouth!—
They might make the Secret true, and in sheltered
  inlets
Bring alive sleep's eye-evoked images;
And time might not be; and the hope
Of Absent Immortals, light and dancing!)

Broken into two sentences, the sonnet really makes one long, closely-knit period. The tone is meditative, philosophical and suggestive of Ramon Llull's efforts to join intellect and feeling: "Acompanyaren-se memòria e voluntat, e pujaren en lo munt de l'amat, per ço que l'enteniment s'exalças, e l'amor se doblas en amar l'amat"[3] (Memory and desire came together and climbed the Beloved's [i.e. God's] mountain, so that understanding might increase and love be redoubled in loving the Beloved). In this context the word *follia* (madness) also suggests Llull, who often apprears in his own books under the *senhal* of Ramon lo Foll (Ramon the Mad).[4]

Also evoked, however, are a series of "classical" equilibria between Apollonian and Dionysian, transience and eternity, imagination and reality. Thus, in the poem, Reason and Madness are followed by a subtler dichotomy: on one hand, the clear morning air and the Mediterranean Sea, symbolic of Greek rationality; on the other hand, Foix's own individual sensibility, "avaricious for joy." These dichotomies are joined together by the creative act itself. The Eternal can be made concrete thorough the poet's "fantasy . . . of words, sounds and tones."

The argument, explained in this way, sounds rather dry. In the poem itself, however, Foix manages to impart a sense of breathless intellectual adventure that keeps the reader deeply involved. This is accomplished, in part, by the constant linking of abstractions with emotionally charged language. Two examples are "my mind, avaricious for joy" and "with Fantasy / That the heart inflames." Another instance is the fascinating shift from the abstract "Oh sweet thoughts!" to the vividly sensory "Sweetness in mouth!" The poem's syntactical structure—the way it slowly builds toward its final "light and dancing!" —also contributes to the emotional impact.

A glance at the quotations Foix uses to introduce his early sonnet sequences—Guido Cavalcanti and Dante, Ausiàs March and Llull, Bernart de Ventadorn and Jordi de Sant Jordi—will suggest some of his poetic models and give a more precise idea of what "Mediterranean tradition" means here. The link to the *stilnovisti* and to March and Llull is particularly evident. Like their work, Foix's poetry is at once densely speculative and passionate. Foix seeks what T. S. Eliot, speaking of the English metaphysical poets, called "a direct sensuous apprehension of thought, or a recreation of thought into feeling."[5] In addition to Foix's medieval and early Renaissance sources, there is also a strong effort to reach back toward classical antiquity. This aspect is most obvious in the juggling of opposites ("make the Eternal present," "make today permanent," "and that strange shadow be good sense and guide"). In "If I Could Reconcile" Reason/Madness also suggests Nietzsche's Dionysus/Apollo dichotomy. In the sonnet's final tercet these opposites are linked and brought into a kind of Platonic tension by the imagination: "Bring alive sleep's eye-evoked images; / And time might not be; and the hope / Of Absent Immortals, light and dancing!" In these lines Foix condenses a tremendous amount of thought and feeling. The imagination, conceived of here as closely akin to dreams, can make the transient permanent and turn the idea of the gods into a concrete ritual of artistic celebration.

Foix's sonnet-writing period ended in the late 1920s. Since then most of his work has been unrhymed, structurally more open and often distinguished by long, explanatory or scene-setting titles. When the poetry has a specific historical context, these titles—together with the dates at the end—can be very useful. One poem, dated September 1936, opens with a scene from the outbreak of the Spanish Civil War.

AT THE ENTRANCE TO AN UNDERGROUND STATION, BOUND HAND AND FOOT BY BEARDED CUSTOMS OFFICIALS, I SAW HOW MARTA SET OFF IN A TRAIN FOR THE FRONTIER. I WANTED TO SMILE AT HER, BUT A POLICELIKE MILITIAMAN CARRIED ME OFF WITH HIS OWN FAMILY, AND SET FIRE TO THE WOODS

In other cases the titles may be more complicated, but they usually attempt to orient the reader. "At the Foot of a Cyclopean Wall" (1935) opens with a clearly etched scene involving two figures: a pulley-adjusting mechanic and an uneasy observer, perhaps the poet himself, "watching the sea with an old book in my hand."

AT THE FOOT OF A CYCLOPEAN WALL, THE MAN IN THE BLUE WORKSUIT, TALLEST OF ALL, WAS POLISHING LEATHER STRAPS AND ADJUSTING PULLEYS. FROM TIME TO TIME HE LOOKED AT ME FROM BENEATH HIS

STRANGE VISOR, TACITURN. I PRETENDED
NOT TO NOTICE, WHILE WATCHING THE
SEA WITH AN OLD BOOK IN MY HAND

In fable and sleep I know that man who,
Among ancient rocks near the open sea,
scatters fake faded stars covered with printed sheets.
Torch in hand, I've followed him among twin-engine
       planes
When in secret he anoints their gears
In elliptical hangars and sacred watch-posts.
I've seen him, regal, in a cave of the sea
As if dressed in moss
beneath a stifling sun
            —when the hand-shaped shadows
Retire into streams and see births—
Or within a closed wall
            —when the hours anchor
In mental harbors—
            humming and surrounded by tools,
Measuring stellar chasms and their foliage.

It's the menhir of forested dawn
Rustling with waterflowers and scented light,
Muscle, adolescent and bloody, of midday,
Bird of the afternoon, exiled
Among wandering propellers, mortal
And evanescent motors, on the captive runway.
Night's androgyne, generous with seed,
Darkening solitude of primitive meadows,
Present wherever we covet the body,
Perennial flame on the battlements of calm,
A singing breeze in the leafy blueness,
Ancestral form in the nocturnes of inlets,
Brightness of ash trees in the passages of dreams.

It's the Eternal Ungraspable wandering through
   dunes:
"Light on your face when you see me and grow silent."
Or it pierces the boulders with impalpable drills:
*"It opens infinite vistas above the red seas
When the night-fishing boats set sail from port
and deep humid voices modulate their chants."*
It evokes new gods on the abstract beaches:
*"Your name exalted by gay northwinds
when joy runs to seed you faint and you pray."*
Immortal burning speck in the ocean's ravines:
Your body bursts forth in unseen leaves and flowers."
It bears secret creatures in immanent groves:
"When the shadow of both is the Single Shadow."

It is helpful to know here that Foix was an aficiona-
do of amateur aviation and a member of the Catalan
Aviation Circle or Penya de l'Aire.[6] "At the Foot" opens
in a mood of mystical adulation for the mechanic. Foix
knows hims "in fable and sleep," describes him in terms

suggesting Poseidon ("regal, in a cave of the sea") and
Hephaestus ("Humming and surrounded by tools, /
Measuring stellar chasms and their foliage") and even
follows him "torch in hand." In the poem's first section
the literal mechanic in his worksuit gradually evolves
into a god of airplanes who "anoints their gears / In elliptical hangars and sacred watch-posts." At the same
time, Foix develops a strain of natural imagery centered
on the sea. This imagery is woven into the portrait of
the mechanic and is played off against the artificial
world of tools and planes just as the clear sea, tamarisks
and sheltered inlets interact with Platonic ideas in "If I
Could Reconcile." The mechanic is slowly enveloped in
a nimbus of magic and ancient Mediterranean myth.

The second stanza continues and deepens this pattern, with natural and sexual imagery gradually gaining
dominance over the mechanical. The mechanic, as a
character, disappears entirely, and we are left with the
plane, which by now is as much a sexual presence as
a machine. The plane itself has become alive, a "bird of
the afternoon" as well as a divine presence, beautiful
and frightening, an "ancestral form" or "menhir."

This series of mystical parallels and correspondences is reinforced by the poem's incantatory quality.
Though there is no rhyme scheme, the meter (decasyllables and Alexandrines) is regular within each stanza and
underlines the mysterious, prayerlike intonation. Another element in this atmosphere is the series of syntac-
tically parallel lines beginning with nouns, as in the
conclusion of the second stanza.

flamma perenne . . .
brisca cantaire . . .
forma ancestral . . .
claror de freixe . . .

These nouns are then linked to another series of nouns
that locate them in imaginative space.

. . . als merlets de les calmes,
. . . a les blavors boscoses,
. . . als nocturns de les cales,
. . . en el congest del somni.

A final element—the most obvious but the most important of all—is Foix's intensely lyrical imagery in lines
like "Darkening solitude of primitive meadows" or "A
singing breeze in the leafy blueness." Such lines are at
once literal descriptions of a plane and magical inter-
penetrations among mechanical, natural and emotional
worlds.

The poem's last stanza introduces still another element, "the Eternal Ungraspable." With this transcendent abstraction, another speaking voice also enters the
poem, first addressing the poet and then gradually

merging with him in a final chant. Here images of the sea mingle with images of fertility and birth (*"when joy runs to seed,"* "It bears secret creatures") and with the repetitive songs of night fishermen. The result is a sense both of the oneness of everything and of the miraculous possibilities of each individual object.

Though "At the Foot" is formally quite distinct from "If I Could Reconcile," the two poems do have a number of interesting similarities: in particular, their effort to bind together such opposites as imagination and reality, the concrete and the abstract, the old and the new. The effort, in both poems, ends in Platonic unity and in the synthesizing nature of art, an art that makes the intangible specific and brings together all of man's experience. In the often-quoted "Lletra a Clara Sobirós" (Letter to Clara Sobirós; 7–9) Foix describes the poet as "mag, especulador del mot, pelegrí de l'invisible, insatisfet, aventurer o investigador a la ratlla del son" (magician, word-speculator, pilgrim of the invisible, unsatisfied, adventurer or investigator on the border of sleep). Though the word *magician* seems to emphasize the poet's role as inventor, the succeeding terms suggest that he is the revealer of a world that already exists, independent of his verse. This conviction of a prior poetic reality is even more explicitly stated in the preceding paragraph.

> If you read me—and I'm afraid you're thinking of it like someone determined to cross against a traffic light—always remember that I'm a witness to what I tell of, and the real, from which I depart and live, with my insides burning as you know; and the unreal you think you'll find there, are the same.

To achieve this synthesis, Foix relies heavily on the Catalan cultural, historical and physical landscape. One aspect of this landscape is the Hellenic and Renaissance tradition, which I have already discussed in some detail. Another is the world of Pyrenean shepherds from which Foix's own ancestors came. This world forms the focal point of "El meu país és un roc" (My Country Is a Rock), a poem dedicated to his family line and to Catalonia's rough mountain folk in general.

Lliberts, i durs, amb alous,
Llur fona en rosa de cercles
Colpia el menhir dels segles
En una tardor de bous.
O mels pures del paratge!
Recobrar, dels meus, l'imatge,
Aigua enllá de l'hort furtiu,
Molls de rou de la caverna,
Hereus de la nit eterna
Amb els astres per caliu! (159)

(Freedmen, tough, with freeheld land

In a circle of rhumbs their slingshot
Smote the centuries' menhir
In an autumn of oxen.
Oh, the pure honeys of that spot!
Rediscovering my people's image
Water beyond the furtive garden,
Wet with dew from the cavern,
Eternal night's heirs
With the stars for hot ashes!)

As is often the case with Foix, the date at the end—August 1939, immediately following the end of the Spanish Civil War—is significant. The poem's last four lines, coming after the celebration of a heritage that seemed mortally threatened, form one of the most poignant expressions of Catalan postwar sensibility.

Vaig i vinc de roc a roc
—O pasturo palets tosos
En un bosc de crits confosos—
I, en ser fosc, hi vento foc. (159–60)

(I come and go from rock to rock
—Or I pasture shaved pebbles
In a woods of confused cries—
And when it's dark, I fan the fire.)

The end of the war evoked some of Foix's very best verses. Prior to 1939 he had been an ardent Catalanist and one of the leaders of Acció Catalana (Catalan Action), a conservative nationalist group that included a number of prominent intellectuals. An admirer of the French reactionary Charles Maurras, Foix had denounced the Catalan anarchists. He accused them, both in poetry and in prose, of destroying the nation's classically balanced heritage and replacing it with Iberian fanaticism. Despite his often conservative positions, Foix was a highly respected figure during the 1930s. He led the separate Catalan delegation at the 1934 PEN Club Conference in Dubrovnik. He was also the literary director of and a frequent columnist for *La Publicitat* (Publicity), a daily Barcelona newspaper.

With Franco's victory, of course, all this came to an end. For a time the future of Catalan literature itself seemed in doubt. Foix, whose verse had been so allusive and philosophical, would have seemed to be among those least equipped to express the mood of the postwar period. In fact, he did it better than virtually anyone else. Perhaps his outstanding poem of this period is "I Arrived in That Town . . ." Once again the date (1942) situates the piece historically, and the title establishes the tone of disorientation and nightmare.

> I ARRIVED IN THATTOWN, EVERYONE
> GREETED ME AND I KNEW NO ONE; WHEN
> I WAS GOING TO READ MY VERSES, THE

DEVIL, HIDDEN BEHIND A TREE, CALLED
OUT TO ME SARCASTICALLY AND FILLED MY
HANDS WITH NEWSPAPER CLIPPINGS

The clear, simple images that follow, and the innocent speaking voice, help create a mood of childlike bewilderment. Beneath this mood, there is also Foix's condition as a poet suddenly deprived of his audience: "Such crowds there are in the square! / They must be waiting for me; / I, who read them verses; / they're laughing as they leave." It is not just poetry, however, but an entire culture that has been dislocated. Foix's portrait flutters on a scrap of newspaper, perhaps symbolizing the end of the Catalan press and of his position as a public figure. An entire national identity—and with it memory itself—has been obliterated. And Foix, who had striven to reconcile Reason and Madness, has now become a madman, a memoryless imbecile wandering through a town he does not recognize.

This atmosphere of disorientation is made grimmer by lines hinting at the poverty and bloodshed that followed the war: "I look at my bare foot: / in the shadow of a barrel / a puddle of blood is shining." In general Foix plays down this element, allowing the panic to build as the half-naked speaker is mocked by the townspeople and cannot find his way home. Only in the penultimate stanza do public events burst suddenly into the open: "What do they say on the radio? / I'm cold, I'm scared, I'm hungry." And in the final lines the devil, whom we had met in the title, reappears: He awaits the amnesiac speaker "around the corner," consummating the feeling of infantile terror.

"I Arrived" is one of Foix's most famous poems. Surrealistic imagery is played off against a colloquially direct tone in the same way that it was earlier against accumulated literary tradition. Whether Foix really is a surrealist has been debated among Catalan critics, but the poet himself has always denied it. Though in isolation some of his images may seem rationally inexplicable, they usually do fit into a coherent system of ideas, conceits and personal myths. In an excellent study of Foix's work, the poet Pere Gimferrer describes his poems as transposing "into metaphorical or visionary terms data from the poet's individual or social experience."[7]

The best explanations, however, come from the poet's own writings. Foix describes himself as an "investigador en poesia," one who "finds, by means of new symbols, the permanent."[8] For him, the experimental verse of the 1920s was not so much a new form of consciousness as a new set of genres in which he could work. These genres demand the same poetic discipline and craft as any other kind of verse. Thus Foix admonishes his fellow avant-gardists, "In your verses be hard and precise."[9]

The language here is similar to much of Ezra Pound's criticism.[10] Though it seems improbable that either poet influenced the other, there are a number of parallels between them. Both writers drew on the Mediterranean Middle Ages and Renaissance for inspiration, while using experimental techniques in highly individual ways. Both attempted to reunite a Western culture they saw as fragmented and decaying, and knitted together art and social reality partly by applying artistic standards to the latter. In Foix this is expressed by his "poetic real" in the "Letter to Clara Sobirós." But above all, the two authors both possessed a literary kind of perfect pitch: an ability to write verse at once lyrical and precise, intellectually demanding yet dense with feeling.

Beyond certain superficialities (such as his famous long titles), Foix has had no imitators in Catalonia. His poetry is perhaps both too rigorous and too idiosyncratic to form the center of a school. Nonetheless, he is recognized by younger poets and by the reading public as a monumental figure. Appearing early in this century, he—along with Salvat—marked off a broad area of sensibility that Catalan poets have been exploring ever since. This area, which ranges from the most immediate daily impressions to intricate philosophical speculation, is partly responsible for Catalan poetry's rich diversity in the last fifty years.

David H. Rosenthal, Winter 1983

[1] J. V. Foix, "Em plau, d'atzar . . ." [I like, at random . . .], in his *Obres poètiques,* Barcelona, Nauta, 1964. Unless otherwise noted, all citations are taken from this text. Translations are my own.

[2] Joan Salvat-Papasseit, *Poesies,* Barcelona, Ariel, 1962, p. 89.

[3] Ramon Llull, "Llibre d'amic e amat," in his *Obres essencials,* Barcelona, Selecta, 1957, vol. 1, p. 265.

[4] Foix frequently cites Llull at the beginnings of his books. The most significant of these citations comes at the beginning of *Les irreals omegues (Obres poètiques,* 104): "Where the semblance is most obscure the understanding that comprehends that semblance is most elevated."

[5] T. S. Eliot, *Selected Essays,* New York, Harcourt Brace, 1950, p. 246.

[6] This and other biographical details about Foix are taken from Joan Colomines's introduction to *Catalans de 1918,* Barcelona, Edicions 62, 1965.

[7] Pere Gimferrer, *La poesia de J. V. Foix,* Barcelona, Edicions 62, 1974, p. 192.

[8] J. V. Foix, *Tocant a mà,* Barcelona, Edicions 62, 1972, p. 8.

[9] Ibid., p. 9.

[10] E.g., Pound's "Second Set of Composition Exercises," in *ABC of Reading,* Norfolk, New Directions, 1951, p. 66, where he be-

gins: "1) Let the pupil write the description of a tree. 2) Of a tree without mentioning the name of the tree (larch, pine, etc.) so that the reader will not mistake it for the description of some other kind of tree. 3) Try some object in the classroom. 4) Describe the light and shadow on the school-room clock of some other object."

SWITZERLAND

Gauging Existential Space: The Emergence of Women Writers in Switzerland

For quite some time, modern Swiss-German literature was considered as practically tantamount to the writings of Max Frisch and Friedrich Dürrenmatt. Emerging at the end of World War II on a literary scene that had been impoverished by exile and forced silence, the two Swiss rapidly gained fame through their ingenious mixture of small-town Swiss atmosphere and global significance. During the 1950s and into the 1960s their imposing prominence was, however, also felt as a certain impediment for the development of younger writers. Yet with works like Hugo Loetscher's *Abwässer* (Waste Water; 1963), Peter Bichsel's *Eigentlich möchte Frau Blum den Milchmann kennen lernen* (*And Really Frau Blum Would Very Much Like to Meet the Milkman;* 1964), Adolf Muschg's *Im Sommer des Hasen* (In the Summer of the Hare; 1965) and Kurt Marti's dialect poems *rosa loui* (1967), a new generation asserted itself. Thenceforward, Swiss writers showed continued lively activities at a level that had been rare in Swiss literary life. Signs of this varied creativity are the many anthologies that appeared in the wake of the first such venture, *Bestand und Versuch* (Tradition and Experiment), which was prepared for the Swiss National Exhibit in 1964.[1]

When surveying all this literary production, one is struck by the scarcity of women's contributions. And it is only when checking through new publications or the standard reference work *Die zeitgenössischen Literaturen der Schweiz*[2] that more names of women authors come to the fore. Obviously, the work of Swiss women writers in the past and the present still constitutes a terra incognita for literary scholars. In this respect, the Solothurner Literaturtage, literary festivals held in 1979 and 1980, brought some innovation, since they included a relatively high number of women writers.[3] Among the eleven and thirteen authors invited to the two festivals were four and five women respectively, setting their participation at 36–38%, an appreciable increase from the rather constant 8–11% in the preceding collections.[4] Sparse as they are, these figures signal an expansion of women's literary contributions which is more than just

coincidence; rather, it marks a point that, upon closer examination, seems to be both an end and a new opening—an end of the first real expansion of women's writing in the 1970s, and an opening to a broader contribution of women to Swiss literature in the 1980s.

A remark about the definition of "Swiss" is called for: in doubtful cases the decisive factor is not simply that of Swiss nationality, but rather that of whether an author has spent a considerable part of her creative life in Switzerland. Thus, for example, Ingeborg Kaiser, born in southern Germany, is seen as Swiss, while Swiss-born Verena Stefan, who has lived in Berlin since 1968, is not.[5]

A glance at Swiss literary history reveals not only the extent to which the increased female presence around 1980 is indicative, but also points up some historical particularities in the emerging of women writers: While women have published literary works since around 1900,[6] their small number does not show any noticeable growth until the 1970s, when suddenly an entire group appears on the scene:[7] Erica Pedretti (b. 1930) in 1970, Margrit Baur (b. 1937) in 1971, Elisabeth Meylan (b. 1937) in 1972, Ingeborg Kaiser (b. 1935) and Gertrud Leutenegger (b. 1948) in 1975, Maja Beutler (b. 1936) and Margrit Schriber (b. 1939) in 1976, Adelheid Duvanel (b. 1936) and Claudia Storz (b. 1948) in 1979. Though publishing some years earlier, Gertrud Wilker (b. 1924) should also be included, since it is in the 1970s that she unfolded her talent to its full breadth.

It is interesting to note that all but three authors were born in the 1930s: when publishing their respective first independent books, they were between thirty-four and forty-three years of age, thus starting their careers clearly later than their male counterparts.[8] The most obvious reason for this delay, the obligations as wife and mother, applies, however, only to two cases, namely those of Ingeborg Kaiser and Erica Pedretti. Therefore it becomes clear that the difficulty to be overcome by all is ultimately one of tradition and psychology. In Switzerland, with its predominantly rural culture and its lack of aristocratic patronage of the arts, creative careers are less prestigious and even harder to achieve than in Germany and Austria. There are no Swiss female models who could even faintly compare with Bettina von Arnim, Annette von Droste-Hülshoff, Marie von Ebner-Eschenbach or Else Lasker-Schüler, to name only those German and Austrian women who did acquire a relatively widespread literary reputation. Thus it is understandable that even unmarried women in the 1960s and 1970s hesitated to embark on a writing career with all its uncertainties.

The fact that the generation of the 1930s did not become active until roughly forty years later[9] also emphasizes a specific historical element. Since Switzerland was spared the ravages of World War II with its brutal interruption of daily routine, the traditional life patterns in this generally conservative country could continue undisturbed far longer than in Germany and Austria, where the first generation of modern women authors emerged much sooner: Ilse Aichinger in 1948, Ingeborg Bachmann in 1953, Gabriele Wohmann and Barbara König in 1958, Christa Reinig and Christa Wolf in 1961.[10] The two Swiss women entering the literary scene in this period cannot really be compared to them: Silja Walter (b. 1919), the sister of the writer Otto F. Walter, published her first book in 1944; yet since 1948 she has been living as a nun in a convent, placing her work within the confines of religious experience.[11] Starting in 1953, Erika Burkart (b. 1922) produced a distinguished, mostly lyric oeuvre.[12] Though she is imbued with the modern skepsis toward language and meaning, she mainly draws her inspiration and material from the rural landscape where she spent most of her life. While these authors are well known in Switzerland, they are creative in a limited area whose characteristics—religion, nature, lyric form—least contradict conventional views of women's strength and competence. Therefore their work does not assume exemplary status for women trying to portray the experience of modern life with all its complexities caused by a technological age and societal change.

Neither guided nor bound by strong precursors, Swiss women writing in the 1970s had to strike out on their own. They achieved this in ways that are related and make them appear, despite their differences in style and individuality, as a rather cohesive group, although there seems to be little personal contact between them. Their works show a significant thematic link since, in one way or another, these authors are taking measure of space, the space in which they live and write. The group that at first was delineated only by such external criteria as birth and publication dates thus reveals an inner connection in that the writers share, be it consciously or unconsciously—a common preoccupation with the house as the space of human existence.

References to rooms, houses and places appear in many titles. Elisabeth Meylan's first stories bear the title *Räume, unmöbliert* (Rooms, Unfurnished), and her subsequent novel is called *Die Dauer der Fassaden* (The Permanence of Façades). Margrit Schriber chose the titles *Aussicht gerahmt* (Framed View) and *Kartenhaus* (House of Cards), and Adelheid Duvanel collected stories under the title *Wände, dünn wie Haut* (Walls Thin as Skin). Places figure in titles by Margrit Baur (*Von Straßen, Plät-*

zen und ferneren Umständen [Of Streets, Squares and Further Circumstances]), by Maja Beutler (*Flissingen fehlt auf der Karte* [Flissingen Is Not on the Map]) and by Gertrud Wilker (*Altläger bei kleinem Feuer* [Altläger with a Small Fire] and *Winterdorf* [Winter Village]). Yet even in works without specific spatial references, the exploration of living-space plays a role: in her first novel, *Elegie auf die Zukunft* (Elegy to the Future), Gertrud Wilker narrates how a family takes possession of and exploits a small place in a Jura valley, while in her story "Warum denn darum" (Why Then Because; in *Winterdorf*) she portrays the town of her childhood; and Gertrud Leutenegger, in her novel *Ninive*, meditates about modes of existing in several closely delineated, insular places. Yet what lies behind the images of these titles? What significance do the authors ascribe to the portrayed living-spaces? And what might this thematic preoccupation reveal about the authors' situation as women writing in the Switzerland of today?

■ ■ ■

It is appropriate to begin a *tour d'horizon* of specific works with Elisabeth Meylan, who has the most obvious propensity to rooms and houses, exploring them as the immediate encasings of people's daily existence. At first the title of her story collection *Räume, unmöbliert* (Zürich, Artemis, 1972) might seem contradictory since all the rooms described are furnished in such a fashion as to emit the well-tendered solidity so typical for the snug comfort of contemporary Swiss life-style. Yet the tasteful arrangements cannot hide, but rather lend emphasis to, an ever-present vacuum that envelops human relationships and chills life into clockwork order. For Nelly Griesser in "Das Haus," her home—inherited from her parents—becomes a shell filled with stagnant trappings. Not surprisingly, Rau in "Die Fahrkarte" (The Ticket) yearns for his boyhood room, where a wide sky stood in a curtainless window and where many a night he was absorbed in developing his own photographs—which, contrary to his present life, held "einen unheimlichen Wirklichkeits-anspruch," an uncanny claim to reality.

In her novel *Die Dauer der Fassaden* (Zürich, Arche, 1975) Meylan creates a wider scene of life and work in the city. The protagonists, a man (W.) and a woman (Helen), are part of the impersonal work world with its hectic pace. As recent divorcees, they are both newcomers to this city and try to carve out a suitable new space. Alone and together they probe all sorts of spaces, from their apartments to the various parts of the sprawling agglomeration. Yet the façades they encounter provide only specious support. Helen's old apartment house with its appealing stucco falls prey to unchecked construction activity. W.'s fascination with his new job of creating unorthodox large-scale rooms for industry fades away with the realization that they too do not furnish an atmosphere conducive to lively activity, but rather constitute another type of façade surrounding emptiness. Thus it is fitting that the novel begins and ends with W.'s visits to a decaying suburban spot where obvious emptiness is strangely supplemented by the signs of invincible life bursting forth from *Schrebergärten,* the small private garden plots now cultivated there.

Meylan's latest novel, *Bis zum Anbruch des Morgens* (Until the Break of Day; Zürich, Arche, 1980), scrutinizes modern city life in yet another way, namely by correlating the city's crowded but impersonal outer space with the still furrowless, noncommittal inner space that the nameless female "I" is exploring upon her divorce. The city's anonymity with its fleeting encounters and the very insignificance of her job enwrap the protagonist in a muffling but translucent distance which allows her to start shaping her own personal space, wherein inside and outside eventually can intermingle. Thus Elisabeth Meylan gives form to the experiences of both men and women in the contemporary urban setting. Tinging her cool precision with a hidden, vibrant sensitivity, she captures the peculiar, vapid feeling of empty spaces and of people lost in them. In Meylan's latest novel the central spatial metaphor of unfurnished and stagnant rooms seems to lose importance and to make way for more temporally-oriented images, as evidenced by the title. This might indicate the possibility of change for the characters described as well as the possibility that Meylan herself is in transition, reaching out for wider realms.

Among the titles referring to houses and places are those of two story collections: Maja Beutler's *Flissingen fehlt auf der Karte* (Bern, Zytglogge, 1976) and Adelheid Duvanel's *Wände, dünn wie Haut* (Basel, GS-Verlag, 1979). Though using different imagery in their titles, two further collections must be mentioned along with them: Duvanel's *Windgeschichten* (Darmstadt, Luchterhand, 1980) and Margrit Schriber's *Außer Saison* (Out of Season; Frauenfeld, Huber, 1977). All these stories share a basic thematic concern for outsiders whose existential space is drastically curtailed, for unloved children, stranded women and neglected older people. Adelheid Duvanel adumbrates the experiences of children in pictures which an almost uncanny empathy and dreamlike evanescence make translucent for the deeply but not yet consciously felt pains of emotional deprivation. Narrow external circumstances and human callousness surround these children with walls as thin as skin—that is to say, porous for manifold pains.

In her short texts Maja Beutler intertwines realistic description with an often surrealist story line, embodying thoughts directly in action and representing the lack of communication and true feeling in spatial arrangements. A fascinating example of her spatialization of abstract concepts is "Das Wortmuseum" (The Word Museum). In a building, words, the individual particles of human speech, are exhibited, ordered in ascending groups—from the invented, personal words and names in the basement to the everyday vocabulary, lying on coarse burlap, to the solemn phrases of emotion draped in red velvet. Thus language is spatialized as "Sprach-Bau," which, for those sensitive to its changing nuances, becomes a frightening prison. Beutler also shows people caught in the spaces of their role. Irma Kramer, a second-rate ballet dancer now settled as wife and mother of two, reenacts every morning, in the three meters behind her locked bedroom door, the moment of her stage triumph. Or there is the teen-age boy Jakob in "Die Jakobsleiter" (Jacob's Ladder): his mother's refusal to let him live on his own is translated into Jakob's being walled into his room. Though he can leave it on a board through the window and enter the apartment from outside, he is separated from yet filled with the desire to be with the family he formerly wanted to leave. In a terrifying way, distance and closeness within the confines of an urban apartment are painfully bound together. Recently Beutler published the novel *Fußfassen* (Taking Hold; Bern, Zytglogge, 1980). Casting her net wider, she describes—possibly autobiographically—the experiences of a woman's battle with the horrors of cancer. In a series of haunting scenes she unfolds the dramatic confrontations of the protagonist with recklessly changing external circumstances and with the demands of her creative self. Here the mixture of the real and the surreal appears in widening images and a hectically driven language. If Beutler's stories present battles against immovable spatial order, her novel enacts a war against time.

Margrit Schriber's collection *Außer Saison* shows the most realistic style; her stories focus most often on older people. She represents the limitations and emptiness of their space in bare images and a language whose reflected sobriety is permeated with veiled, pent-up sadness. Schriber has also published two novels in which she makes interesting statements about women per se as well as the woman writer. In her first book *Aussicht gerahmt* (Frauenfeld, Huber, 1976) she portrays the existence of a young woman writer in a modern subdivision on the outskirts of a small town. As a resident, she experiences the monotony of life between glass walls and neatly spaced garden hedges. As a writer, describing the life around her as seen through the window and overheard through the walls, she finds herself in the position of an observer. This position could be called classic were it not for a significant variation: though uninvolved, the woman is nevertheless situated inside rather than outside or opposite her object, and thus she is also part of what she describes. She knows that for the sociologist studying the subdivision from the outside she is but a fixed feature in a window. Whereas his gaze at least encompasses the whole surface of the subdivision, her view is always framed by the window, by her position inside, and thus allows only a limited vision, albeit one enriched with inner perceptions. In this position Schriber conjoins a modern, distanced writing stance with the basic situation of the woman, who is the constant feature of the house, reduced to observing life outside without really being able to reach beyond her limited realm. This is also reflected in the form of Schriber's text, which consists of short individual passages strung together by observation, not by any action, and presenting framed views that have a certain depth but cannot acquire an unencumbered perspective.

Kartenhaus (Frauenfeld, Huber, 1978) narrates Schriber's childhood spent in the large red house of her father, who was a renowned quack and avid hunter. The experiences of the ebullient child are related in a style of richly colored, vivid evocation. Yet Schriber's sober precision, so characteristic of her earlier works, is present too, since the story of the child is framed by a visit of the grown woman to her mother, who is still living in the father's house, which is now white and whose attic, formerly a place of abundant treasures, is now swept bare and clean. In an extraordinary manner Schriber re-creates the house as the central symbol of her own and her mother's life. A bright sign of the father's wealth and vitality, it silently collapses when he leaves, having built a new house in a different town. For the mother, bearing the withering stigma of divorce in a staunchly Catholic region, the house represents the last bit of security, to which she clings in paralyzing fear. For the daughter, the house becomes evermore an illusion of security; its earlier splendor is extinguished, and its rich treasure of life flounders like a house of cards.

As the writer Schriber creatively confronts the house of her childhood, establishing it as an existential space that is dramatically structured by gender role models—the father is the freely roaming hunter, gregarious storyteller and authoritarian master while the mother shrinks more and more into the role of his silent, obedient helpmate within the house. In writing this book, Schriber transcends the exact gauging of a living-space—"dieses exakte Vermessen des Lebensraumes" (165)—which could be likened to her mother's desire to secure a threatened abode. Instead she pushes ahead to an incisive analysis of existential dimensions, to an act of scrutiny which, in itself, constitutes a way

of measuring her own, new possibilities. Having revisited and fully explored the house of cards, she might now be ready to leave her window and face a larger world.

The house as the particular space for the role of wife and mother also plays a crucial part in Ingeborg Kaiser's *Die Ermittlung über Bork* (The Bork Inquiry; Aarau, Sauerländer, 1978). The use of the last name "Bork" for the protagonist is the linguistic sign for her role as the average, full-time housewife, a specimen of the statistical norm whose life and reactions are to be examined. Kaiser gives Bork an identity, a family and childhood memories, yet despite all this, Bork never steps out of her traditional female behavior to assume an independent individuality. Therefore Bork's comfortable house becomes "a cell, a coffin, a museum" (43) smothering life. Kaiser's book is striking since it combines vivid personification of a stereotype with a dismantling of this type in a fast-moving narrative that translates theory into a more than plausible piece of chilling reality.

As mentioned earlier, Gertrud Wilker is not naturally part of the writers' group born in the 1930s: born in 1924, she published a small book in 1959, a novel in 1966 and a travel diary in 1968. However, the bulk of her oeuvre and her most characteristic contributions belong to the seventies, for which reason her work merits attention here. Although somewhat older, Wilker is by no means more old-fashioned. On the contrary, she has repeatedly addressed the most current issues—the problem of the younger generation's dissatisfaction and the rapid change from peasant culture to industrial society in *Altläger bei kleinem Feuer* (Zürich, Flamberg, 1971), the aftermath of a nuclear explosion in "Flaschenpost" (Message in a Bottle; in *Winterdorf*) and the questions related to the education and socialization of women in *Blick auf meinesgleichen* (A Look at My Peers; Frauenfeld, Huber, 1979). This collection of short stories offers poignantly condensed glimpses of the lives of women from different walks of life. Despite their topical and formal diversity, these stories have a common denominator; they show women held in silence and passivity dictated by role expectations. Houses play a minor part, yet the female role model itself emerges metaphorically as a confined house, a domesticated structure from which escape is difficult and terrifying.

Here as in earlier works Wilker uses the form of dialogue in a special way. Focusing on groups of various people, she interweaves the different voices, creating a complex web of pronouncements and thoughts that delineate the confines of the existential space. In *Altläger* townspeople speculate about the sudden disappearance of a young woman writer, and in so doing they are led to probe the possibilities for a meaningful life in their community, to question the traditional order as well as the seemingly boundless openness introduced by industrialization. In "Warum denn darum" (*Winterdorf*) two voices explore, in past and present images, the formative forces of the speakers' hometown. Thus Wilker actually transforms the structural and geographical space of house and town into a figurative space of resonance where possibilities and limitations are signaled by resounding voices.

Wilker's latest book, the novel *Nachleben* (Afterlife; Frauenfeld, Huber, 1980), narrates the life of her aunt Emmy K., an unmarried home-economics teacher who died in 1977 at the age of eighty-six. The author combines several narrative strands: Emmy's past life as mirrored in her diaries, the author's present life while writing the novel, and her changing relationship with a male friend, Jutzi, who constantly reads, comments upon and questions the emerging text. Thus Emmy appears in a triple image. The richly quoted diaries capture, artlessly enough, her existence, which was limited by external circumstances. Within these limitations Wilker unfolds the hidden drama of Emmy's lifelong yearning for better education and of her tenacious, even radical belief in the values of spirit and individuality. The author elucidates all of Emmy's "text," that is to say, not only her diaries, but all expressions of her life-her apartment, her relations with family and friends, the pictures taken of her. This interpreting is fraught with Wilker's own reactions of saddened empathy, admiration and rejection, affinity and distance. Through this emotional and analytic process, the author exposes the intricate forces—historical, social, personal—that enclosed Emmy's existential space. On the third level, in the dialogue between the writer and Jutzi, Emmy is reflected in a still larger context that includes not only a male reading of her, but also the world of male interest: Wilker skillfully uses Jutzi's political and economic concerns to highlight the full but usually overlooked dimension of Emmy's problems. Thus the description of this one woman's life extends into a far larger picture.

The book's title *Nachleben* carries an echo of Christa Wolf's novel *Nachdenken über Christa T.* (*The Quest for Christa T.;* 1968), which today appears as a new beginning of the serious but all too long overdue quest for fully reincorporating women's lives in literature. Encompassing social and historical elements as well as the formal problem of how to reenact a person's life in mere words, Wilker's book might, on a modest scale, be a similar sign of the coming of age of Swiss women's writing. *Nachleben,* Schriber's *Kartenhaus* and Meylan's *Bis zum Anbruch des Morgens* seem to indicate that these women are now transcending the first stage of their writing, the richly explored but externally narrow topic of the house as existential space.

▪ ▪ ▪

Looking at these Swiss writers as a group leads to some interesting observations. Women assert themselves relatively late as writers due to the specific, historical continuity of traditional life patterns in Switzerland. And once a larger number of women emerges, they show a surprising unity in topical and symbolic orientation toward all forms of houses and places as closely structured living-spaces that define and confine existential possibilities. The reason for such a preoccupation is obviously the basic experience of, and the generally decreed task for, women in the European bourgeoisie: to be assigned to the circumscribed space of the house and to realize their lives in the prescribed female role by tendering and preserving the small inner realm that men have come to regard as refuge from the outside world.[13] Women are not allowed, much less enjoined—as are men—to enlarge this given space or to go beyond it. In the case of women, this is seen as an undue transgression, while for men it is interpreted as an admirable conquest. It is no wonder, then, that the women of a conservative culture such as that of Switzerland feel compelled to gauge the confines of this existential space before venturing into wider realms. It is also interesting to note that there is not, to my knowledge, a comparable focus on the house in the writings of Austrian, East and West German women writers.

It goes without saying that the experience of confining spaces is not exclusive to women. Schriber, Wilker and Meylan often choose male protagonists. Yet the problem of the living-space is, on balance, only one aspect of man's existential complex. Therefore Swiss men writers express the spatial experience with its difficulties far less on this private, interpersonal level than on the larger plane structured by historical and political forces as well as by the opposition between the small town—symbolic of Switzerland—and the wide world. When discussing this concept of *Enge* or "narrowness," so important for Swiss literature,[14] it should therefore be noted that this narrowness is experienced, and thus symbolized, differently by men and women writers.

At present Swiss women writers do not seem interested in the political dimension. To what extent this aspect is foreign to the female experience becomes clear in women's works that stand outside the topical realm of the house. Erica Pedretti, who was born in Moravia but has lived in Switzerland since 1950, encompasses in her works the world from Sternberg in the East to New York in the West. Yet even in this wide arena the idea of an inner space narrowly marked off by one's abilities—or lack thereof—is a central element. In Pedretti's surrealist novel *Heiliger Sebastian* (Saint Sebastian; Frankfurt, Suhrkamp, 1973) the main female character cannot believe in her own greater possibilities, not even in New York while working in public as a silversmith, and she decorates all the different places she lives in with the same pictures, terming them "her snail's shell" ("Die Bilder: ihr Schneckenhaus"; p. 171). Thus it is not surprising that she finds herself again and again at roads and in tunnels without exit. And her later novel *Veränderung* (Change; Frankfurt, Suhrkamp, 1977) is concerned mostly with almost inperceptible changes leading to the destruction of people. Gertrud Leutenegger's first novel *Vorabend* (Eve; Frankfurt, Suhrkamp, 1975) is set in a potentially highly political situation, namely on the eve of a big demonstration. The narrator describes her way through the streets chosen for next day's demonstration; however, she adduces personal memories and scenes from her individual development without realizing the political dimension in the book's plan.

Of course, the absence of the political, or other wider dimensions, is not a lack per se. It lies within every writer's discretion to choose a large or small realm. Yet, as the presentation of this group of modern Swiss women illustrates with almost uncanny clarity, women do not yet have the liberty of choosing any subject, any realm for their works; they still are confined, even in their imagination. But just as these Swiss women have started, though slowly, moving into the domain of literature, they now seem to be transcending this stage and moving forward into new topics. And it is to be hoped that Swiss women writers will also gain more exposure beyond their own country and be appreciated for their particular contribution to the literature of German expression.

Marianne Burkhard, Autumn 1981

[1] *Bestand und Versuch,* Bruno Mariacher and Friedrich Witz, eds., Zürich, Artemis, 1964, includes all four literatures of Switzerland. On Swiss-German literature see: *Gut zum Druck,* Dieter Fringeli, ed., Zürich, Artemis, 1972; *Lyrik aus der Schweiz,* Frank Geerk, ed., Zürich, Benziger, 1974; *Fortschreiben,* Dieter Bachmann, ed., Zürich, Artemis, 1977; *Belege,* Werner Weber, ed., Zürich, Artemis, 1978; and *Literatur aus der Schweiz,* Egon Ammann and Eugen Faes, eds., Frankfurt a.M., Suhrkamp, 1978.

[2] *Die zeitgenössischen Literaturen der Schweiz,* Manfred Gsteiger, ed., Zürich, Kindler, 1974. Two new anthologies are especially helpful in identifying women writers in the earlier twentieth century: *Unruhige Landsleute,* Beatrice von Matt, ed., Zürich, Artemis, 1980; and *Helvetische Steckbriefe,* Zürich, Artemis, 1981. The latter is the catalogue of an exhibit covering forty-seven Swiss authors in the nineteenth and twentieth centuries.

[3] Cf. the published programs in *drehpunkt,* 11 (1979), no. 44/45, and in *Neue Schweizer Literatur: Die Solothurner Literaturtage in*

Wort und Bild, Vrony Jaeggy, Arnold Lüthy and Hanspeter Rederlechner, eds, Basel, Jenny, 1980.

[4] In the anthologies published between 1964 and 1978 the proportion of female to male authors remains quite constant: shorter anthologies of about twenty writers feature two to three women, larger ones of eighty to 100 feature between eight and eleven.

[5] An interesting case not included here for lack of time is Hanna Johansen, born in 1939 in Bremen and now married to the Swiss writer Adolf Muschg.

[6] My stay in Switzerland in the summer of 1980 did not permit me to gather complete bibliographical information for the older authors; thus I must depend on von Matt's bibliography, which lists only the "most important works." Yet on this basis the year 1900 seems to emerge as something of a *terminus ante quem.* Johanna Spyri (1827–1901), the author of *Heidi,* who started publishing in 1871, could be seen as an exception; however, her works, written for children, constitute a separate category of literature.

[7] The appearance date refers to the author's first book-length publication.

[8] Of the eleven male authors born in the 1930s, all but one made their literary debut before reaching thirty-four: Jörg Steiner at twenty-six, Werner Schmidli and Beat Brechbühl at twenty-seven, Peter Bichsel at twenty-nine, Urs Widmer and Jörg Federspiel at thirty, Ernst Eggimann, Adolf Muschg and Gerold Späth at thirty-one, Urs Jaeggi at thirty-two and Ernst Halter at thirty-four.

[9] Two exceptions are not considered here since they have so far published only intermittently: Brigitte Meng (b. 1932) won a drama competition in 1957, yet her first book did not appear until 1966; I have found no publications by her since 1970. Magdalena Vogel (b. 1932) published four small volumes between 1961 and 1971.

[10] Whereas all but one of these authors were born in the 1920s—Aichinger in 1921, König in 1925, Bachmann and Reinig in 1926, Wolf in 1929, Wohmann in 1932—they started publishing comparatively earlier: i.e., between twenty-six and thirty-five.

[11] Cf. Silja Walter's statement in *Gegenwartsliteratur: Mittel und Bedingungen ihrer Produktion,* Peter André Bloch, ed., Bern, Francke, 1975, pp. 195–96.

[12] Only in her second novel *Der Weg zu den Schafen* (Zürich, Artemis, 1979) does Burkart find a truly narrative stance; in her first novel *Moräne* (Olten, Walter, 1970) the lyric element prevails.

[13] Cf. Barbara Duden, "Das schöne Eigentum: Zur Herausbildung des bürgerlichen Frauenbildes an der Wende vom 18. zum 19. Jahrhundert," *Kursbuch,* 47 (1977), pp. 125–40.

[14] Cf. Karl Schmid, *Unbehagen im Kleinstaat,* Zürich, Artemis, 1963; Paul Nizon, *Diskurs in der Enge,* Bern, Kandelaber, 1970.

Max Frisch: A Writer in a Technological Age

Freud believed that the discovery of the role of the unconscious was destined to count among the fundamental insults to man's self-love in the history of science, an elemental affront to his perception of mastery over his own psychic life. It would rank, he wrote in *A General Introduction to Psychoanalysis* in 1917, alongside the blows to human narcissism delivered by Copernicus and Darwin, which removed man from the center of universal attention and robbed him of his special creation. Despite the loss to the gradiosity of his self-image, man has shown a remarkable capacity to rebound from these assaults. Developments in modern physics that began during Freud's lifetime, however, and reached a critical stage one year before his death with the discovery of nuclear fission (1938) may, in their applied forms, ultimately defeat this capacity. Hiroshima and Nagasaki have given man good cause to doubt his very ability to survive as a species.

By the end of World War II the threat of nuclear extinction overshadowed all other catastrophic visions that have traditionally found expression in myth and literature.[1] Of the German-speaking writers who touched on the theme during and after the war, Max

Frisch was, along with Brecht and his *Galileo Galilei* (1943), one of the first. Still, his early play *Die Chinesische Mauer* (1946; Eng. *The Great Wall of China*)[2] has not enjoyed the popular success of Dürrenmatt's comedy *Die Physiker* (1962; Eng. *The Physicists*) or Kipphardt's documentary drama *In der Sache J. Robert Oppenheimer* (1964; Eng. *In the Matter of J. Robert Oppenheimer*). Since that time Frisch has continued to ponder openly, through works of the imagination as well as in his journals, the ramifications of scientific and technological advance in the twentieth century. In *The Great Wall of China* he warns of the dangerous collusion now possible between technological knowledge and political power. Works from later in his writing career, *Homo faber* (1957; Eng. *Homo Faber* and *Der Mensch erscheint im Holozän* (1979; Eng. *Man in the Holocene*), shift the focus from the public to the private sphere, from the effect of technology on politics and thus on the masses to its effect on the individual. Frisch has no illusions about the cultural role of literature relative to that of the hard and soft sciences and has clearly sober expectations of his craft. Although it can and does reflect the large shifts of intellectual paradigms called world views Frisch wrote in his *Tagebuch 1966–1971* (1972; Eng. *Sketchbook 1966–1971*), it is incapable of setting these in motion: "Literature that is deserving of its name does in fact mirror the metamorphoses of our consciousness, but it only mirrors them; the impetuses toward the metamorphosis of one's world view come from elsewhere" (11:88).[3]

For Frisch, the airplane has assumed the special significance that the train held for writers in the late nineteenth and early twentieth centuries and represents the prototypical encounter of contemporary man with technology. Without the daily flights of commercial airlines, which have reduced the world to a global nation if not a village, the career and travels of the engineer Walter Faber would be unthinkable. The thin white vapor trail of the jet is visible high above the Alps, even in the remote Swiss valley to which Herr Geiser, the main character in *Man in the Holocene,* has retired. In an extended entry in his early journal, *Tagebuch 1946–1949* (1950; Eng. *Sketchbook 1946–1949*), Frisch records his ambivalent reactions to an air excursion over these same Alps with a group of painters and writers in 1946 (4:386–93). Like the fictional Faber of his later novel, he has implicit trust in the machine that suspends him above a granitic reality. Unlike Faber, he senses a shamelessness, an impropriety underlying this trust in a conveyance that has carried him outside the limits of experience that are meaningful in human terms. He contrasts the safe but unreal experience in the plane with the palpable danger he would face if he were climbing at the same hour on the mountain ridges below. He interprets the need of the group to pronounce the names of the features on the Alpine landscape as a vain attempt to overcome the experiential estrangement of their perspective. In the suspension of perceptual conditions natural to human experience lies the diabolical aspect of technology. Removed by innumerable contrivances from immediate contact with the other, man's capacity for inhumanity rises all too easily to the behavioral surface. In a moment of startling frankness, Frisch confesses the involuntary realization that he feels himself potentially capable of dropping bombs on a populated area at the "inhuman distance" that flight allows (4:388). The imagination seems incapable of narrowing the distance that technical means create.

Although staged in its original form in 1946, *The Great Wall of China* underwent revisions into the seventies, a textual history that accounts for its allusions to computers and the moon landing. The basic artifice of what Frisch labels a "farce" is the suspension of historical time in order to introduce an array of personages onstage ranging from the Chinese emperor responsible for completing the Great Wall to Napoleon Bonaparte, from Pontius Pilate to King Philip of Spain and Ivan the Terrible. Armed with knowledge that none of the others can have, "the Modern Man" (*der Heutige*), the central dramatic persona, moves from conversation to conversation, warning the tyrants and politically powerful of the past not to return to the present. He sketches with catchwords and in handbook fashion the complicated and involved state of knowledge in modern physics for Mee Lan, daughter of the Chinese emperor. When she presses him for his knowledge of man, his answer is the single remark that he lives in "a state of alienation" (3:164). By juxtaposing the profundity in one area with the superficiality in the other, Frisch underlines the one-sidedness of contemporary intellectual achievement, the discrepancy between an advanced knowledge of nature and a primitive knowledge of man. Even in her day the Modern Man points out to the two-thousand-year-old princess, wise men of her father's court had had substantial insight into the cause and cure of alienation.

The Great Wall of China is an admonitory play. To a world that possesses the expertise to produce the hydrogen and cobalt bombs, a world that for the first time in the history of mankind can stage its own version of the Flood, the playwright Frisch underscores the danger of an alliance of this expertise with modern incarnations of past tyrannies. Still, he has only exceptionally been a writer of public warnings through his imaginative works. The province of literature, he wrote in his journal, is the private sphere of the individual encounter with the world that the natural and social sciences cannot grasp: "Domains of literature: everything that people experience, sex, technology, politics, but in contrast to science, related to the experiencing human being" (11:89). Whereas the sciences can only capture this individual as a silent statistic, the literary work can give audible expression to his experience. Neither the first-person voice of the engineer Walter Faber in *Homo Faber* nor that of the sculptor and title figure in *Stiller* (1954; Eng. *I'm Not Stiller*) is that of Max Frisch himself, yet each encompasses an essential aspect of the man who graduated from the Technological Institute in Zürich and successfully practiced architecture before devoting his talents exclusively to literature.

In the opening scene of *Homo Faber,* the itinerant technologist, an employee of UNESCO, sits aboard a Super Constellation at La Guardia in New York anticipating clearance of his flight to Mexico City. From there he expects to fly on to Venezuela and the turbines that await his technical expertise. A chance meeting on the plane with the brother of a long-lost friend and a forced landing in the desert, however, radically alter the nature of Faber's travels. What began as a professional trip becomes the first stage of an odyssey back into his past. Instead of flying directly to Caracas from Mexico City, he accompanies his new acquaintance to the jungles of Guatemala, where his friend Joachim manages an experimental tobacco plantation. By the time they arrive, however, Joachim has committed suicide and the first stage of Faber's odyssey comes to an abrupt end. Psychologically, it has been significant in preparing him for the fateful coincidence that will make his further jour-

ney a tragic one. The prospect of seeing Joachim again had flooded his mind with memories of their youth, particularly of Hanna, the one woman in his life he had truly loved. After the episode in Guatemala and on board a ship returning to Europe, Faber is strongly attracted to a young woman whose uncanny resemblance to Hanna he tries to suppress but which continues to exert an unconscious power over him. In the further course of the novel he plays out a modern version of the Oedipal myth in which he falls in love with Sabeth, a daughter he never knew existed, and becomes responsible for her death.

Written as a "report" by an engineer who makes no secret of his disdain for literature and who tries to reconstruct the events of his life into a rational pattern, *Homo Faber* includes a meticulous delineation of time as well as references to scholarly works on mathematics and cybernetics. In making his argument, for example, against the influence of metaphysical forces on this pattern, he cites four standard works on mathematical probability as the fundamental basis of his technological credo (7:22). At least on the surface, Faber protests with conviction against the mystical or miraculous and places his faith firmly in statistics, which, he points out, account for even the most extreme improbability. This faith falters, however, at the end of the novel when he faces an operation that, despite the favorable statistics, he knows he will not survive. It has been critically shaken earlier by the failure of numbers to predict the outcome of his daughter's injuries. The odds had overwhelmingly favored her recovery from a snakebite, the apparent threat to her life, but she had died from an undiagnosed skull fracture accidentally caused by Faber himself. In her case, as he seems to fear in his own, the numbers may be valid but not applicable.

After the death of Sabeth, the grieving Faber contemplates physically blinding himself and carries out, in thought at least, the self-punishment of his mythological model, who put out his own eyes for the unwitting crimes against his father and mother. Faber has suffered, however, throughout his life from a figurative blindness, a flaw rooted deep in his character and nurtured by a professional training that has limited him to a restricted area of human experience. Art or any other experience with a strongly emotional component lies outside this area. He imagines himself to be a "blind man" (7:111), for example, when someone tells him how he should inwardly react to a work of art. He sees, but only on a superficial level. Concerning his lack of insight into human relationships and his uncomprehending attitude toward Hanna's life, he is "stone-blind" (7:144), she maintains; and toward his mother, in whom Hanna had confided for years without his knowledge, he feels "like a blind man" (7:184) when he learns of their intimacy. Frisch further contrasts the limitations of Faber's sight with the real blindness and imaginative powers of Armin, an old man and childhood friend of Hanna: *"Armin was totally blind, but he could picture everything that was described to him."*[4] For Faber, by contrast, it is futile to try to imagine a concrete situation for which he lacks the data of the senses.

Early in the novel, after the plane has made an emergency landing on the desert floor, Faber reacts with irritation to the gushing of the other passengers about the surrounding landscape (7:24–25). He finds preposterous their transformation of empirical observation into an experience of the fantastic or supernatural. Although he again pointedly denies it, he is blind precisely to this kind of symbolic projection onto the environment that in a higher form allows the artistic and artistically receptive eye to see the universe in a grain of sand. His is a materialistic vision which presumes a human faculty that can clearly distinguish between perceiver and perceived, between the subjectively insubstantial and insignificant and the objectively concrete and meaningful. To Faber, the moon over the desert is no longer a romantic symbol that fascinates the beholder because of the inexhaustibility of its allusions, but a "calculable mass" (7:24) that can be translated into the unambiguous figures and formulae of mathematics. In the moral order that Frisch constructs in *Homo Faber,* the presumption of the technologist to know the universe from its surface, to build an epistemology based on appearances, is not only blindness to the symbolic perception of its multifarious levels, but hubris as well. Faber embodies both the disability and culpability characteristic of contemporary technological man.

Faber's guilt stems from interactions with other human beings as well as from an attitude that values machines as inherently superior to mortal man, since they function without emotion according to the laws of probability (7:75). Relationships with machines offer Faber certainty, calculability; relationships with people do not. "People are tiring," he comments on more than one occasion, and he avoids close or extended human contact, declaring that after three weeks with a woman, he yearns for his turbines (7:91). They are the perfect companions for Faber, who remembers with irritation the "incalculable temperament" (7:46) of Hanna that he associates with her interest and training in art history. In his comedy *Don Juan oder die Liebe zur Geometrie* (1953; Eng. *Don Juan, or The Love of Geometry*) Frisch portrays the legendary figure driven to his unfaithfulness not by an unbridled sexual drive, but by a love for something pure (*lauter*), something temperate (*nüchtern*), something exact (*genau*)—a love, that is, for ge-

ometry. "I have a horror of the morass of our emotions,"[5] he tells an incredulous Don Roderigo. His flight from his bride is a flight to cold but determinate relationships with circles and triangles. As Sabeth's amused reaction in *Homo Faber* illustrates, Faber's discourse on machines strikes a comic vein very close to that in Frisch's play, yet in the novel the comic vein inevitably merges with the tragic.

C. P. Snow first published his controversial essay on the two distinct cultures of Western society in 1959.[6] At one pole he placed what he termed the "traditional" culture of literary intellectuals, and at the other the community of scientists, although at points he simply juxtaposed scientist to nonscientist. Topics and perspectives of the one culture naturally predominate in *Homo Faber,* since the narrator himself is an engineer. Representatives of the nonscientific culture, however, primarily Hanna and the musician Marcel, function as a refractive medium that relativizes Faber's views and points to the inadequacies of his life. Underlying the considerable reaction that Snow's essay provoked in the intellectual community was his observation that neither culture knew much about the other, a determination that has subsequently evolved into a platitude. A central scene on board the ship in Frisch's novel reflects in miniature the simultaneous but separate dialogues of these two cultures. While Faber and his roommate Mr. Lewin, an Israeli farmer, discuss diesel engines, Sabeth carries on the other half of the *Doppelgespräch* (7:78) with a Baptist minister about the Louvre and Van Gogh.

Only a few days before his operation, Faber finds himself on his "last flight" (7:194), again in a Super Constellation, but this time on his way from Zürich to Athens and back to Hanna. As he flies for the first time over the Alps that he had known in his youth, he reacts much as did the group of artists and painters in Frisch's journals, naming the features of the landscape still familiar to him. In both autobiographical and fictional works, Frisch comments on the incredibly narrow band of atmosphere around the earth upon which life depends (4:389, 7:195). Even at an altitude of a few hundred meters, Faber ponders, this "zone of life" becomes too "thin" to sustain living organisms. He is suddenly beset by a powerful desire to be on the ground, feeling, smelling, hearing, tasting its realities and never to fly again. Instead, he registers with poignant regret, "we rise higher and higher" (*HF,* 206). On a level of meaning at which flight is a metaphor for man's technological adventure in Frisch's grand design, Faber's regrets extend beyond the concrete moment and express the general tragedy of a life lived at rarefied heights where experience is diluted from the human norm. Only when death has become a certainty is Faber vaguely conscious of a sense of remorse for having lived at a distance, for having narrowed the spectrum of human experience by a blind faith in technology. As technologist, he is a modern Icarus in danger not of falling back to earth, but of climbing past the point of no return to its "zone of life."

Along with the rest of the world in December 1968, Max Frisch followed via television the flight of three American engineers as they soared higher above this zone than any man had ever done before. During the few days around Christmas of that year, the Apollo 8 with its crew of Borman, Anders, and Lovell completed its orbital flight around the moon. The entries in Frisch's journal (11:183–84) are detached, objective remarks, and he shares with his neighbors not only a sense of relief at the flight's success, but also a curiously flat response to a monumental undertaking and historical milestone. Indirectly, he explains this detachment as a natural reaction to an "anonymous adventure," an accomplishment that belonged to science, technology, and the computer rather than to the astronauts. Although confronting incredible peril, they were removed from its immediacy by the intercession of technology, and their enterprise lacked the human drama of explorers directly braving the elements. Buffered from natural forces by their spacecraft and its myriad support systems, the astronauts experienced their journey in a manner similar to the technological estrangement from lunar reality which the viewer Frisch sensed as he watched the moon craters glide by on the television screen: "Excitement comes only from imagining one were there."[7] Seven months later, on 21 July, the diarist Frisch devoted only a single line to the first landing on the moon.

Herr Geiser, the seventy-four-year-old retiree in Frisch's narrative *Man in the Holocene,* has withdrawn in his old age to a remote Swiss village without industry and precariously tied to the larger world. He has consciously put the mountainous natural barriers of his homeland between himself and his native Basel. By setting his story at the edge of civilization, where the only evidence of flight is the vapor trail of the jet high overhead, Frisch confronts Geiser with an environment of minimal technological intrusion and protection. As in his play thirty-three years earlier, the threat of a second Flood hangs over the landscape, but no longer as a metaphor for man's nuclear self-destruction. For the several days of torrential rains during the narrative, nature herself appears intent upon literally restaging the biblical scene. The single road to the village is washed out, the electric power is sporadic, and small landslides seem portents of a larger cataclysm.

Although Geiser, the narrator assures the reader, does not believe that the downpour signals the world's end in imitation of the biblical model, he is uncomfortably reminded by the storm of his own vulnerability to nature's inevitable claim. Prone to confusion and loss of memory, he employs two basic strategies to counter this claim. However characteristically human, both are futile, even foolish attempts in Frisch's eyes to exploit man's accumulated knowledge, particularly in its technical and applied forms, in a struggle with the vastly superior forces of nature. For most of the first part of the narrative, Geiser spends his time copying data from an encyclopedia, which he then tacks to the walls, a ritual he later makes more efficient by cutting the scraps of information directly out of his source books. With the names, facts, figures, and historical information from diverse branches of learning surrounding him, he seeks to ward off the forgetfulness that signifies his aging and thus his mortality. At the midpoint in the narrative, Geiser makes an abortive attempt to flee through the mountains back to Basel, a symbolic return to a world cushioned against the ravages of nature by man's inventions.

Neither Geiser's scraps of knowledge, scattered onto the carpet by the wind, nor this knowledge in its applied form as the superstructure of civilization can finally shield him from his own mortality. The sights and sounds of this civilization have returned even to his valley by the end of the narrative, but a stroke has paralyzed Geiser's eyelid and the corner of his mouth during his strenuous mountain hike, an ominous sign of what Faber had called the "curse" of human flesh (7:171). The reader learns relatively little about Geiser compared to the information he acquires about the fictional engineer's life and past. Frisch declines even to supply Geiser with a first name or former occupation, an omission designed to underscore the symbolic extension that the title of the narrative suggests. Geiser's growing doubts about the final value of his knowledge are inherent in the species he represents, the species whose appearance marks the major event on that short stretch of time on the geological clock called the Holocene epoch: "Now and again Geiser finds himself wondering what he really wants to know, what he hopes to gain from all this knowledge."[8]

Frisch's concerns about technology over the course of his literary career have been large ones. From his anxiety about man's newfound potential to commit generic suicide grew an existential question about technological man and his way of being in the world. According to Frisch's novelistic analysis, Faber is fundamentally incapacitated and unable to grasp the full measure of humanly accessible experience. More than twenty years after *Homo Faber,* Frisch's attention shifted from this subtype of Homo sapiens to an exemplar of the species itself. Geiser learns the distinctly unique lesson of old age in the world of contemporary technology that despite man's capacity to subjugate nature, this capacity cannot grant him the ancient dream of immortality. If his destiny is to "appear" in the Holocene, as the German title indicates, it is also to disappear.

Francis Michael Sharp, Autumn 1986

[1] Reinhold Grimm, "Eiszeit und Untergang: Zu einem Motivkomplex in der deutschen Gegenwartsliteratur," *Monatshefte,* 73 (1981), p. 176.

[2] Only the dates of the original publications are given in parentheses. For all original individual texts by Frisch except *Der Mensch erscheint im Holozän,* reference is made to volume and page numbers of the twelve-volume pocketbook edition, *Gesammelte Werke in zeitlicher Folge,* Frankfurt a. M., Suhrkamp, 1976. Unless noted, the occasional translations of words and phrases are my own.

[3] This and the subsequent quotation from the *Tagebuch 1966–1971* were omitted from Geoffrey Skelton's English translation, published in 1974 by Harcourt Brace Jovanovich as *Sketchbook 1966–1971.*

[4] Max Frisch, *Homo Faber,* Michael Bullock, tr., New York, Harcourt Brace Jovanovich, 1959, p. 193 (italics in original). Subsequent citations use the abbreviation *HF.*

[5] Max Frisch, *Don Juan, or The Love of Geometry,* in his *Four Plays,* Michael Bullock, tr., London, Methuen, 1969, p. 119.

[6] C. P. Snow, *The Two Cultures,* New York, Cambridge University Press, 1959.

[7] Frisch, *Sketchbook 1966–1971,* p. 151.

[8] Max Frisch, *Man in the Holocene,* Geoffrey Skelton, tr., New York, Harcourt Brace Jovanovich, 1980, p. 90.

Silvio Blatter: Realism and Society in Modern Switzerland

Silvio Blatter grew up in Bremgarten and trained as a teacher; he was also a factory worker for some time and a student at Zürich University, then worked as a radio producer. His collection of sketches *Brände kommen unerwartet* (1968) indicated that here was a writer with a distinctive voice who could quickly give life to the people he wrote about and their environment. The writing was simple but precise. The scenes often imply sympathy for those who are at a disadvantage in society: for the stranger who is mistaken by local people for somebody else more important than he is; for the woman crossing a frontier into Switzerland to take up work there; for those over whose faces a shadow falls shortly before their death; for the maid who loses her job because she has forgotten to close a door and a dog has gone astray. At other times the sketches are briefly evoc-ative: an aunt comes to tea to meet the mother of the boy narrator; a fire which unexpectedly starts in an afternoon causes widespread damage; a mother worries when her son stays out late. The author, as the dust jacket claims, has an eye for the details which surround and define a human being. Another early work by Blatter is the narrative in free verse *Flucht und Tod des Daniel Zoff,* which asks the reader to share the author's indignation at the unnecessary death of a youth who was taking flight from a detention center. It is a theme which Blatter also develops in his later writings, notably in the two major works *Zunehmendes Heimweh* and *Kein schöner Land.*

Blatter first showed himself to be in command of wide-ranging material and to possess an approach of his own in *Schaltfehler* (1972), a volume of fifteen short stories, each of which focuses attention on a different person. The protagonists are all employees in the same factory and are likely to have comparable relations with its management; the preoccupations and crises of their working hours are skillfully varied by the author. The first story and the last supplement each other and draw attention to very different attitudes toward factory life. Margrit B. has been esteemed for her reliability and loyalty. She drew the management's attention to a time-saving procedure of her own discovery and was given a gratuity of 120 francs. The procedure is then introduced as general practice but is administered in such a way that the workers must put in more effort for less reward. After giving up work in the factory (she no longer needs the money), Margrit continues to be attached to the factory environment and pays frequent social calls there. In the final story Fritz H. has tendered his resignation because he finds the work boring and repellent. He does not complain about the factory's management, but although he has had varied experience with different operations and even, as a maintenance worker, has been able to travel to Lisbon and other foreign places, at the age of twenty-six he is determined to leave factory work for good; perhaps he will become a furniture salesman. He is going to go his own way, without explanations to his employers and colleagues. Some men are keen to identity themselves with their roles at work: Peter T. is proud to be a foreman and has an annual holiday in the Ticino which is a form of further service to and dependence on management. Another foreman, Markus H., has to take time off for illness but knows that without supervision "his" workers will get into mischief. Oskar V. has been working in the factory for thirty-two years, and in his retirement he will be able to give more attention to his eighty rabbits, which are a supplement to his income. Bruno G. has been married for five years; his wife grumbles about the inadequacy of his pay, for all their careful management and Bruno's refraining from going out in the evening. Steady and experienced workers feel humiliated at petty reproofs: Marco P. for washing his hands in the wrong cloakroom, or Walter U. for lateness when the train was at fault. Heinz L. prefers to be at his machine rather than to have the responsibilities and worries that promotion would bring: "Die gute Laune abends ist ihm wichtiger als ein paar Franken Lohnerhöhung." Jürg A. is not keen on change either and is scornful of office workers. Rolf K. is distracted from paying full attention to his machine by an Italian foreign worker who plays a trick on him. Martin B., age seventeen, finds himself almost the only Swiss in a room full of Italian and other immigrant workers.

Women are more vulnerable than men in the factory community. Pia F. dislikes her job of removing oil and metal shavings from one of the machines; she feels ill with the smell of oil and the difficulty of getting clean; however, she succeeds in obtaining a transfer to another type of work. Rosa D., a secretary, is irritated by the detailed paperwork she has to do and by the dirty, oily, confined condition of the changing room. Elisabeth is badly shocked but not physically injured when she comes too close to a machine which seizes and damages part of her clothing; she is allowed to transfer to another working group where she can be with her man friend. The stories show workers who are in the grip of their machines and of the expectations which the management has of them. Narrated mainly in the present tense, these pieces usually employ noncolloquial language with very little use of dialect, and so their protagonists make a formal, at times statuesque impression. The sentences convey an immediate impression of clarity and precision. A series of individuals are hemmed in by the program of their machines and the regulations of the management; they suffer constraints at work and are too tired to be able to express their personalities with a spirit of independent thought and interest in their free time.

The novel *Mary Long* (1973) provides something of a contrast to the short stories of factory life in *Schaltfehler,* which had preceded it. The narrator's voice is soon heard as he apologizes to those of his readers who had expected him to choose factory workers as protagonists again and declares his reluctance to be confined to any particular subject matter: "Ich bin keine Maschine, ICH MUβ ETWAS ANDERES MACHEN." The restrictiveness of the machine-operator's way of life is put aside, and in its place there is an opting-out of society's pressure to conform, an emphasis on exotic milieus and on often playful irony and fantasy. The narrative form tends not to be linear, but rather to leap from one episode to another, ignoring chronology. The narrator writes that he is in the process of inventing "a novel character of paper and printer's ink" (31).

> Springer ist aufgestanden bleich hat das Zimmer verlassen wort- und gruβlos Springer war nie da war Einbildung war Methode Springer ist verschwunden entkommen verschollen hat sich dünn gemacht sich verdrückt ist weggelaufen Springer war wirklich nie da wohnt nicht mit mir im Zimmer wohnt in meinem Kopf haust körperlos und braucht darum keine Satzzeichen ist Hirngespinst aus Wörtern gemacht ist Zeichen statt Blut Buchstabe statt Knochen Springer ist ein Papiermensch nein Springer ist nur aus dem Zimmer nur kurz aus dem Zimmer war im. . . . (31)

Another time the narrator declares that he met Springer on a skiing holiday and shared accommodations with him. Springer works in the office of the Building Department of Schorheim, a fictitious Swiss town which contains both Protestant and Catholic confessions, has problems with building plans and car parking, and has a local newspaper, a football team (with Springer as one of its members), and a male choir.

Markus Springer visits America on impulse, and his three years there are summed up in the second chapter (where, we have been told at the end of the first chapter, we can count on "the orderly sequence of a story"). Soon after his arrival in America he is robbed of his papers and can consequently only get work there illegally. In New York he lives with Mary Long, who guides and protects him; in Maine he works as a woodcutter, and elsewhere he works in a slaughterhouse and as a target for a knife-thrower in a variety theater; his return journey to Europe is made as a stowaway on a ship bound for France. Having finally swum in the Rhine from French to Swiss territory at Basel, he comes back to Switzerland without clothes as well as without identification papers. The events leading to the death of Rita Bucher, whose stabbed body is found on the town football field, dominate the subsequent action. Rita is discovered to have been pregnant and involved with drugs. Markus Springer has had a passing relationship with her and is for a time wrongly suspected of being her murderer. Rita Bucher becomes a more familiar and more three-dimensional character in the novel than does Mary Long, who remains a shadowy figure. She finally agrees to marry Markus and live with him permanently. Mary Long is necessary to Markus, but her particular personality is left to the reader's imagination.

Genormte Tage, verschüttete Zeit (1976), a short novel, can be seen as a return to the main issues of *Schaltfehler.* The earlier volume presents the separate points of view of a number of factory workers in self-contained short stories. In the later book we sense the passing of time as experienced by Stöhr, a machine operator, and we note the sobriety of the realism. Stöhr, age twenty-eight, is introduced to us as he gets up in the morning and prepares for a day's work at the job he has held for the last six years. The narrative ends with Stöhr's return to Lis, about whom we learn little; but she remains his principal support, both outside and enclosing factory life. Of the characters in *Schaltfehler,* Fritz H. is closest to Stöhr in his determination to get out of factory work; both are seen on the last day of their employment at a factory. As he changes his clothes and puts on his overalls at the factory, he has a feeling of bewilderment and resentment: "Alles erscheint ihm sinnlos und fremd. Wie schon oft überfält ihn Ratlosigkeit, und er fragt sich, warum er sich nicht schon früher dagegen aufgelehnt hat" (35). In his interview with the works manager he expresses his dislike of the nature of the work and of management's indifference to the workers. After the long morning he takes his lunch break in the company of three colleagues. In the course of the afternoon session he takes a break, but as he walks to a vending machine in search of a cup of tea, he is negligent and causes the driver of a forklift to have an accident which involves various large tins' being thrown on to the floor. After this incident Stöhr receives immediate dismissal. The later part of the afternoon he spends in a café, where he wins money at an automatic gaming machine, and subsequently in the company of an acquaintance, a revolutionary socialist whose political mission he rejects. After the factory shift is over, he meets a number of his fellow workers at another café, by arrangement, for a final drink together. His colleagues think him foolish to have given up a safe job in a difficult time, and fairly soon he is left on his own. He returns home to Lis, fearful of what new work in the future may involve and at the same time afraid that he may not find work; he has no constructive vision of his future, at least not as yet. He reveals his state of bewilderment in emotional, subjective terms which enable the reader to identify himself effortlessly with this figure.

Love Me Tender (1980) is designated on the title page as an *Erzählung,* but it is somewhat longer than *Genormte Tage, verschüttete Zeit* and might well be thought of as a novel rather than as a "tale." Whereas the action of *Genormte Tage* takes place within the space of fourteen hours, *Love Me Tender* has a duration of several months, from the time when the first-person narrator becomes secretary and assistant to Surina to the time of the conclusion of the latter's venture. Surina is devoting his resources and energy to promoting an athletes' gathering of international status in the vicinity of his hometown, the fictitious Meldorf. The narrator had a marriage, a house, and a secure job when he was twenty-six, but eight years later he has started afresh, divorced. It now suits him to accept the essentially temporary work of helping to organize a sporting event under Surina, a successful building contractor who came from Italy in the 1950s and who now, over forty, sets about organizing the event with flair and determination; he had been impressed by the protagonist's earlier newspaper articles on sports. In the early stages of his involvement with him, the narrator imagines that Surina's lonely strength is doomed to failure: "Er ist ein starker Mann, dachte ich, und darum wohl zum Scheitern verurteilt" (113). Surina inspires the narrator to further achievement by his own greater-than-normal capacity for work: "Die Veranstaltung sog mich auf. Ich war Surina—ganz Arbeit!" Surina can also be cordial and friendly, however: "Ich war jedesmal neu verblüfft, wie herzlich er sein konnte, wie offen-sichtlich er sich freute, wenn man ihm eine gute Nachricht brachte" (133).

The other characters around Surina also depend upon him and are aware of his power to dominate. Frau Surina confides to the protagonist that her husband is ruthless and ambitious; she and the narrator share a liking for a record of Elvis Presley's, "Love Me Tender." Markus, Surina's schoolboy son, is addicted to pills, which help him forget his fears and his lack of direction. Surina has a mistress, Esther, a woman of thirty who runs a restaurant and travels with him on journeys made in preparation for the games and also on a holiday; shortly before the games take place, it becomes clear that the relationship is coming to an end. He offers the narrator a permanent job after the games are finished, but the latter refuses. Much of the text describes how Surina organizes the run-up to the games: obtaining the cooperation of the local gymnastics association; securing the participation of three leading champions from America, West Germany, and East Germany; his plans for a shopping center at the stadium; his negotiations with a Swedish furniture manufacturer and a Japanese car firm for sponsorship and with Omega for the timing of the events. Surina denies rumors that he is running the games for business purposes, as he also denies that the German Democratic Republic's representatives have an unusual hold on him. He is, however, hoping to be accepted as a local councilor on behalf of the Christian Party. He fears deliberately provoked disturbances will upset the undertaking, but these do not become significant. Finally, there is the problem of the weather; but when the time comes in September, it is hot and sunny and all tickets are sold. The narrative concludes just after the finish of the 1,500-meter race, with Surina in triumph. The games have successfully taken place, even if no personal emotional problems have been resolved.

In *Die Schneefalle* Blatter turns to the crime story. It is the author's first and so far his only venture onto the terrain of Friedrich Glauser's *Wachtmeister Studer* and Friedrich Dürrenmatt's Kommissär Barlach. In introducing the Swiss detective Walker, the author provides him with a human-story background. He must give up his plans to have lunch at home with his wife and daughter and enjoy a restful Christmas when he is summoned to an emergency; German terrorists have raided a bank in the Federal Republic, and Anna Schnell, an individual much wanted by the police, is believed to have fled to Switzerland. Jansen, Walker's counterpart in Germany, lives alone since his divorce; he is seconded to the Swiss police. A young couple, Rolf and Priska, plan to spend Christmas in the now-deserted climbers' hut some distance from the village of Rinell. This is not known to the police, who are persuaded by Jansen to believe that the terrorists have set out for the Alpine hut with the expectation of finding shelter there and then of escaping to Italy across the mountains. A local guide accompanies Walker and Jansen as far as the hut, while a group of ninety-seven policemen are kept in reserve in the village. The tension mounts as the three men struggle upward to the hut and see a light there. The narrative concludes rather abruptly with the revelation that there are no criminals at the hut, simply a pair of lovers. Jansen's hunch that Anna Schnell would be rounded up here has proved erroneous, and the complex police operation has been a waste of time and resources; the wanted criminal is still at large. Walker is at home in these mountains, however, and Jansen learns to respect him as they are climbing, while Walker appreciates Jansen's fitness and concentration: "Walker liebte diese Berglandschaft. In einem Dorf auf der anderen Talseite war er aufgewachsen. Aus den Fenstern der Stube hatte er als Junge zu den Hägen und zum Gipfel des Piz Rosei hinübergeschaut" (112). Jansen also responds to the mountain landscape with keenness and insight: "Des Gebirge imponierte ihm, das schon. Das Karge, die bizarren Formen, die kraftvolle Landschaft. Jansen liebte die Extreme: Nordsee und Gebirge. Die spürbare Härte verband. In diesen Verhältnissen überlebte nur, was auch den Willen dazu hatte, was überleben wollte" (114).

Zunehmendes Heimweh is, with the 476 pages of the first edition of 1978, considerably longer than Blatter's previous novels and stories. For the first time he commits himself to a broad panorama of contemporary life and establishes it firmly in his home area of Canton Aargau. This canton is probably less familiar to readers of

Swiss literature than are Basel and Zürich, which flank it on either side, but in Blatter's writing the terrain comes to life and acquires an identity of its own with considerable vigor. The novel is thus located in the contemporary scene and presents with precise attention to detail the backgrounds of its main protagonists, whose point of view we share. Most of these figures come across as well-intentioned, sincere people whose lives are likely to be played out against a backdrop of respectability and sameness, or else to be profoundly disturbed if they lose this support. The principal action, in a contemporary setting, is spread over seven days, during which time fundamental changes in the lives of the characters take place. There are also episodes from earlier periods of local history which accompany the main narrative and provide additional dimensions to it.

Margrit Fischer, whose husband is a bank employee, is expecting her first child after being married four years; as she recalls it now, the formal and conventional nature of her wedding remains in her mind. She works in a chocolate factory and only gives this up shortly before the birth of her baby. Margrit is friendly with Anna Villiger, a widow in her early sixties who also works in the chocolate factory. Anna has an urge to fill up her free time in order to avoid being on her own too much; she also finds herself looking back to the past: "Seit ein paar Jahren verspürte sie ein zunehmendes Heimweh nach den Tagen ihrer Kindheit" (167). Her husband died eight years previously. Like most people in this part of Canton Aargau, Anna was brought up as a Catholic; she has retained her faith. On Friday afternoon she learns that she is to lose her job, although she is an efficient worker. She is very hurt at this and is conscious of time's being in allotted spans: "Der Kerze ist eine Zeit bemessen, dachte sie. Wie mir auch. Und wie die Zeit ihre Zeit verbraucht, wenn sie abbrennt, habe ich einen großen Teil meiner Zeit verbraucht. . . . Du wirst pensioniert. Jetzt beginnt das Leben erst recht. Anna Villiger wußte, daß das nicht stimmte." She feels a need to go out and to spend her time in some sort of action, but after hurrying to a railway station in the late evening, she has a heart attack and dies on the train. She is desirous of being helpful to others, is very attached to her friends, and is open and well-meaning; hers is altogether a sympathetic portrait.

Anna is attached to the teen-ager Anita, who works in the same factory and confides to her her anxieties about her relationship with Pep and Lur, two youths who have reacted with hostility to the form of life that society expects of them. Pep and Anita are in love; Lur has been rejected by her. Lur is much more dangerous than Pep and has established a gang of motorcycling "Blackbirds" who menace the public. Lur's childhood, as the illegitimate son of a mother who has had many sexual partners and who dies at age forty, is unstable. He has become violently aggressive and, having escaped from prison with Pep's help, is on the run from the police for several days before being recaptured. Soon after his escape, Lur feels an impulse to visit his mother with "increasing nostalgia"; he decides against entering the hospital to see her and learns subsequently that she has taken her own life. Lur's early years have made of him an antisocial and criminal figure. Pep is someone who, we soon come to believe, will regain normal equanimity; his father, confident that his work and office-furniture factory constitute a model way of life, is angered that his son has done badly at school and is working as a filling-station attendant contrary to his father's wishes; his mother regrets that he does not share her Catholic piety. Pep is part of a family home, however, and can regain social stability much more easily than can Lur. The latter will be required to pay his debt to society at much greater cost than Pep; he is to find support in Lisa, a young woman whom he meets shortly before he is rearrested.

Hans Villiger, nephew of Anna, is a substitute teacher, living as a bachelor in a furnished room at a farmer's house. He taught Lur at school a few years previously, and gives the boy food and opportunity to rest when he comes to his window, though he does not condone his behavior. Hans dislikes the conservative Catholicism that has been very influential in this region, the "Freiamt," and the time he has spent in Amsterdam represents an intellectually liberating episode, especially as it was then that he was first attracted to Maria Cohen, whom he wishes to invite to live with him in Switzerland. Writing to Maria, he comments that anyone who has been born in this particular region and has many ancestors there will feel lonely at night and will recognize this loneliness as a nostalgia that becomes "increasingly stronger."

Anna and Hans Villiger are particularly important to the novel because they convey to the reader not only the quality of contemporary life, but also a critical awareness of life in Canton Aargau in earlier times and a strong sense of historical continuity. Anna's thoughts turn toward the time of her birth, 1914, and she recalls—or the novel recalls on her behalf—her father's experiences as a border guard. He has to leave his home and farm when he is summoned to military service, just before his child is born. Although he is physically strong and can keep up with the exercises he must perform as a soldier, he soon becomes mistrustful and hostile toward the army and its ethos. On one occasion he refuses to take part in bayonet practice and is punished with five days of solitary confinement; he then becomes

more silent than ever. While now taking care to avoid any further punitive responses from authority, he is quietly resentful of all military activity: "Geselligkeit war ihm nie leicht gefallen, die Kameradschaft einer Armee widersprach seinem Wesen" (300). He spends his various times on leave with his family and farm. He too can experience "increasing nostalgia" (344). Toward the end of the war there is talk of the Social Democrats' opposition to the existing structure of Swiss society, and troops advance toward Zürich, where revolution has seemed possible. Anna's father is not actively involved in these events, however, or in the general strike of November 1918.

Hans Villiger occupies some of his free time writing an account of political disturbances in Aargau in January 1841, for publication in the press. This report is presented in installments at various points in the main narrative, as is the description of Anna Villiger's father's way of life during World War I. The confusions of 1841 arise from the hostility between rebellious Catholics and the controlling Protestant government of the canton. When the Aargau authorities order the arrest of specific leaders of the opposition in Bremgarten, a crowd maltreats the district administrator and the jailer's wife and kills the jailer. The government commissioner is sent from Aargau with twelve constables; he holds out for a time against the crowd but ultimately gives way and authorizes the release of the captives. Then troops are sent off to restore order in the region. The village of Villmergen is the battlefield where the appearance of military strength puts the rebels to flight; had they known that the soldiers had an inadequate provision of arms, munition, and horses, they could most probably have won the day. The defeated rebels subsequently look toward the Catholic cantons for solidarity and support, thus anticipating the Sonderbund War of 1847. Blatter succeeds particularly in conveying a sense of dramatic tension in the narrative of the events of 1841; but throughout the novel situations of conflict are carefully calculated for their effectiveness in promoting the movement of the action. Blatter evidently finds that the larger-scale novel can realize successfully the ways in which a community can respond to critical situations.

Kein schöner Land (1983) is to some extent a sequel to *Zunehmendes Heimweh*. It is again a lengthy work (there are 545 pages in the paperback edition), with a broad sweep in its delineation of a group of characters, a number of whom are members of the Villiger family and whose location and movements are mostly in Canton Aargau. Hans Villiger appears again; he is now married to Maria Cohen, and they have a two-year-old daughter. Local people think of Maria as frivolous and obstinate, and she considers them to be lacking in sociability. Her husband continues to be preoccupied with his historical studies; he has been working on the period of the strike of 1918, he would also like to know more about Hitler's visit to Zürich in 1924, and he has traced some of the movements of right-wing groups in Switzerland in the 1930s. Hans recalls a song he learned at school, which is quoted in other contexts in the novel as well: "Kein schöner Land in dieser Zeit / als hier das unsre weit und breit." It is Hans Villiger who is invited to give the traditional festive and patriotic speech in his locality on 1 August.

The novel closes in the late evening of the national holiday, when he can to some extent take stock and tell his sister that, in order to avoid despair and fear and to have confidence in life in spite of the terrifying state of the world, he needs to have reliable people around him, people who give him support (*Rückhalt*). Katrin, age thirty-four, has been divorced for four years and has recently begun a relationship with Pablo, an artist, but she and her brother Hans are close and respond to each other at an intuitive level. They can quietly support each other at the time when they together break the news to their parents that their brother René has been killed in a car crash. The death of René Villiger is a shock to the neighborhood. His particular success has been the invention of a type of barbed wire that has been widely used by the police and the army and to cordon off roadworks. He has built himself a bungalow (which his wife Barbara silently considers to be pretentious), drives an expensive car, and has annoyed Hans by his hostility to the liberal causes with which the latter sympathizes. Barbara (age thirty-eight) is first encountered as she receives the news of her husband's death; she accepts what she considers to be the social obligations of her bereavement, including the long drawn-out formal meal with fellow mourners in a restaurant. She is surprised by the amount of money René has had to leave, but is soon glad to be able to move to the more anonymous environment of a flat in Zürich. Her loyalty to her late husband's memory is much shaken when she learns that he was frequently unfaithful to her. Three months after René's death, she burns all her mourning clothes, and at the end of the novel her friendship with Fred indicates to her daughter Jo that her mother has transformed her way of life radically.

There are a number of parallel actions that are linked together somewhat, though they can be viewed as separate strands of narrative. As in *Zunehmendes Heimweh*, two youths are at a vulnerable stage in their development and are in part victims of their early family conditions. Flip and Daniel are brothers whose parents have proved negligent and irresponsible as guardians of the young. Flip (age nineteen), who works as an auto

mechanic, is directly responsible, by his careless driving, for the death of René Villiger. He confides his guilt to Daniel and later to Jo, but neither of them considers the issue important. He is not suspected, and when he takes up a new job as a salesman of safety locks, he quickly shows a flair for business and soon establishes his economic independence. He accepts the status quo in Switzerland as a way of life and finds himself in strong disagreement with Jo, who believes ardently in radical change. In Sonja, the girl from the Philippines, Flip finds a partner who can gratefully accept the stability he can offer. Daniel, his younger brother, absconds in order to avoid school commitments, has to be "talked down" when he threatens to jump from a high crane, and is placed in supervisory care by the authorities; he makes off a second time, and there is little expectation of his developing into a cooperative member of society in the short term. At thirteen Daniel feels let down, not only by his parents and his brother, but also by "his" social worker, Lea Berger, for whom he has formed a positive regard. She and the priest Francis Fischer (who officiated at René's funeral) become attracted to each other so strongly that he leaves the priesthood and they emigrate to Canada.

René, Hans, and Katrin have had to overcome the lack of balance and harmony in their parents' relationship. Emma Villiger (at sixty-one) has been conciously self-sacrificing as a mother and at the same time possessive. Her husband has had a stroke and is confined to a wheelchair; he had earlier been silent and uncommunicative and is now mute at all times, though insistent on drink, tobacco, and other distractions to which he has become habituated. One member of the older generation is taken as a positive example by Jo: he is David Goldfarb (born in 1899), who has been placed by his sons in a retirement home and whose colorful eccentricities endear him to Jo and to a community of squatters, who accept him as one of their own.

The individual's dependence on and acceptance of the idea of home and home country is seen as inevitable by Hans Villiger: "Du lebst hier, dachte er manchmal, du hast dich eingerichtet, einrichten müssen . . . hier ist deine Heimat, und er verstand das weder ironisch noch zynisch, er war nicht dem Irrtum unterworfen, hier sei alles gut, im Freiamt sei es gut und besser als an anderen Orten" (435). The author's ability to sustain life and shape in a largescale, realistic portrait of the society that forms home and home country for him is convincingly demonstrated in *Zunehmendes Heimweh* and *Kein schöner Land*.

The three sections into which *Wassermann* (1986) is divided describe events that take place in Zürich, then in Canton Aargau, and finally in Egypt. Christian, the narrator, lives with Nora and their five-year-old child Mimi in a ground-floor apartment of a block of flats where the cellar is used as a toilet and where wine and bicycles are liable to be stolen. Christian relies on valium and sherry to keep him going. Nora is lively and full of laughter, and also generous; but she is often impatient at being dependent upon and bound up with Christian and Mimi. The constant stream of traffic nearby gets on Nora's nerves. Both adults are tempted to buy goods on credit cards which they cannot afford; they mistrust bureaucracy. Christian entertains Mimi with stories or takes her out into the night to see the first snow of winter.

The second section focuses on Christian's solitary day's walk to revisit the land of his and Nora's childhood. He is the illegitimate child of a Swiss mother and a German father who had been refused asylum in Switzerland in wartime and sent back over the border. His mother marries another much less sympathetic man and bears him children. Christian has had little fondness for his stepfather and preferred to turn to his grandfather, an assertive and willful man, for guidance. The final section takes place in Egypt, where the Nile, the desert, and Cairo are described with as much detail as is the inner-city Swiss life in the opening part. Christian is now training an Egyptian football team, and his daughter, now called Tina, is at seventeen having her first love affair, with a young Egyptian; she is precociously intelligent and is fully at home with a computer. *Wassermann* is more static than, for instance, *Zunehmendes Heimweh,* and one misses the busy outward action of the plot, the gallery of different characters, and the smooth fluency of *Heimweh's* style. Instead there is much dwelling on detail and a harsher portrayal of human shortcomings. However, hope remains: "Was, um Himmels willen, wollte ich erzählen? Daß wir niemals aufgeben. Daß wir einen Schritt weiter sind und wieder hoffen? Weil wir eingesehen haben, daß die Fähigkeit zu hoffen zur Konstitution des Menschen gehört" (332).

Silvio Blatter has built up a very considerable oeuvre in the last twenty years. After the disciplined nature of the narrator's approach in *Schaltfehler* follows the willful fantasy in the first novel, *Mary Long,* where the author is trying out a more experimental attitude to his narrative material. *Genormte Tage, verschüttete Zeit* and *Love Me Tender* are fairly straightforward stories, on a smaller scale and of more limited scope than the two volumes of the Villiger family chronicle, *Zunehmendes Heimweh* and *Kein schöner Land;* here the reader's continuing interest is ensured by the skill and smoothness with which the author binds together many strands of narrative. *Wassermann* moves from the two previous novels' extended portrayal of a family and their friends and associates to the lives of an essentially isolated couple and their one child; again Blatter is essaying another style of novel. With their direct, unsensational, and balanced approach, *Zunehmendes Heimweh* and *Kein schöner Land* seem to be the most satisfying and mature of his works thus far. Blatter has already made a varied and impressive contribution to modern Swiss prose writing.

H. M. Waidson, Winter 1990

▪ SELECTED WORKS

Brände kommen unerwartet. Zürich. 1968.

Flucht und Tod des Daniel Zoff: Vorläufiges Protokoll eines ländlichen Tages.

Schaltfehler: Erzählung. Zürich. 1972.

Mary Long: Roman. Zürich. 1973.

Genormte Tage, verschüttete Zeit: Eine Erzählung. Frankfurt a.M. 1976.

Zunehmendes Heimweh: Roman. Frankfurt a.M. Suhrkamp. 1978. For a review, see WLT 54:1 (Winter 1980), p. 104.

Love Me Tender: Erzählung. Frankfurt. 1980.

Die Schneefalle: Roman. Zürich. 1981.

Kein schöner Land: Roman. Frankfurt a.M. Suhrkamp. 1983. For a review, see WLT 58:4 (Autumn 1984), p. 588.

Wassermann: Roman. Frankfurt a.M. Suhrkamp. 1986. For a review, see WLT 61:4 (Autumn 1987), p. 618.

UNITED KINGDOM

Barbara Pym's Women

Since the Barbara Pym revival, begun in 1977 when Philip Larkin and Lord David Cecil independently cited her in the *Times Literary Supplement* as one of the most underrated novelists of the twentieth century, surprisingly little of consequence has been written about one of this century's great writers. Most of the criticisms of Pym's novels have consisted of brief articles and book reviews in publications such as the *TLS* and the *New York Times Book Review*. Most of these have demonstrated only a shallow understanding of Pym, and some have actually been wrong. They have concentrated on the superficial similarities between Jane Austen and Pym, on Pym's vain clergy and her churchgoing spinsters, and on the high Anglican comedy of her novels. Some critics even make the mistake of saying that Pym writes about marriage and marriageability or of suggesting that she writes feminist novels.

The essence of Pym has either been glossed over or misunderstood. She is not a twentieth-century Jane

Austen. Pym's heroines, who are past their prime, do not have the same concerns as Austen's heroines, who are between the ages of seventeen and twenty-one. Pym does write about churchgoing spinsters; but the lives of many of her women do not revolve around the church, and not all her novels are centered on a clergyman and his parish. It is not about marriage and marriageability that Pym writes, but about spinsterhood and unmarriageability, and there is a great deal of disappointment, despair, failure, and loneliness in her works. The essence of Pym's answer to the feminist characterization can be found in a letter to Philip Larkin, where she wrote: "I did at least save myself once when a question about my treatment of men characters suggested that I had a low opinion of the sex. My instinctive reply sprang to my lips, 'Oh, but I *love* men,' but luckily I realized how ridiculous it would sound" (*A Very Private Eye,* 303).

In most of her eleven published novels[1] Pym's main character is in the position of the unmarried, unattached, aging woman, and it is this character's condition, thoughts, desires, and emotions that interest the author. In the following study I hope to illuminate the condition of the Pym woman, her identity and experience; the quest of the Pym woman, her search and failure; the predicament of the Pym woman, her disappointments and illusions; and finally, Pym's attitude toward her characters and their condition, the sympathy and irony.

■ THE CONDITION OF THE PYM WOMAN: HER IDENTITY AND EXPERIENCE

The vast majority of Pym's women are spinsters. For the most part they are past their prime or at least have missed out on life. Pym has only three main female characters under thirty years of age; the others are in their thirties, forties, and fifties. They live in middle-class areas of London or small English villages such as West Oxfordshire, and they lead mundane, unexciting, and lonely lives.

Of Pym's main female characters, three are "excellent women" (Belinda and Harriet in *Some Tame Gazelle* and Mildred Lathbury in *Excellent Women*), defined by the characters in the Pym world as a certain group of unmarried women who are sensible and good and who spend their time involved with "clergymen and jumble sales and church services and good works" (*EW*, 138). Five of Pym's main female characters are spinsters who work either in offices (Prudence in *Jane and Prudence,* Penelope in *An Unsuitable Attachment,* and Marcia and Letty in *Quartet in Autumn*) or at home doing odd jobs and making indexes (Dulcie in *No Fond Return of Love*). One is a spinster who is financially well off and does not

work (Lenora in *The Sweet Dove Died*); one is a spinster who is not financially well off and is a companion to an older woman (Jessie Morrow in *Crampton Hodnet*); and two are spinsters with careers (Catherine, the writer, in *Less Than Angels,* and Emma, the anthropologist, in *A Few Green Leaves*). Only three of her main female characters are married, two of them to vicars (Jane in *Jane and Prudence* and Sophia in *An Unsuitable Attachment*) and one to a civil servant (Wilmet in *A Glass of Blessings*).

In Pym's seventh published novel, *Quartet in Autumn,* Letty, a spinster in her fifties, asks, "Might not the experience of 'not having' be regarded as something with its own validity?" (25). To this question Pym answers "Yes," for the experience of not having is precisely what her novels are about. Whether the Pym women spend their day doing domestic chores and church tasks, or editing and proofreading manuscripts, or working in offices or libraries, or even pursuing careers as writers or anthropologists, they are lonely, restless, unhappy, and unfulfilled. Spinsters such as Rhoda Wellcome in *Less Than Angels* attribute their feelings of inadequacy and unfulfillment to having not had "'the experience of marriage,' a vague phrase which seemed to cover all those aspects which one didn't talk about" (*LTA,* 36). In the Pym world "all those aspects which one didn't talk about" are passion and romance, the experiences and emotions a Pym woman, as a respectable spinster, is not supposed to know or speak about. Even Pym's married main characters—Jane Cleveland, Wilmet Forsyth, and Sophia Ainger—feel that they have missed something. They are restless and lonely since their husbands do not pay them much attention.

In the Pym world marriage forms the basis of the social scale, with married women at the top and spinsters at the bottom. Pym's spinsters confess to feeling "like an inferior person," "not socially equal," or "inadequate." They equate marriage with a full life and spinsterhood with an empty life. The fear of being passed over is prominent in the thoughts of Pym's two youngest main characters, Prudence Bates of *Jane and Prudence* and Penelope Grandison of *Unsuitable Attachment.* At twenty-five Penelope had "reached the age when one starts looking for a husband rather more systematically than one does at 19 or even at 21" (37–38). And at twenty-nine Prudence had reached "an age that is often rather desperate for a woman who has not yet married" (7). As Pym's characters get older, the fear of being passed over becomes reality. *Excellent Women's* Mildred Lathbury, having just attended a school reunion with her old friend Dora, also a spinster, reflects, "We had not made particularly brilliant careers for ourselves, and, most important of all, we had neither of us married. That was really it" (112). Marriage is an achievement, and it is the experience the Pym spinster wants; she never questions whether marriage will dispel her loneliness and make her happy.

The irony of the spinsters' perception of marriage is shown by the experience of Pym's married women. Marriage does not make them happy, and it is not filled with passion and romance. In *Excellent Women* Helena Napier is dissatisfied with her husband Rocky and leaves him. In *A Glass of Blessings* Wilmet Forsyth is bored with her husband and seeks attention from other men. Marriage also does not guarantee passion and romance, the experiences and feelings the Pym spinsters are aware of having missed. In *Jane and Prudence* Jane, realizing that the passion in her marriage has faded, looks at her husband and thinks, "Mild, kindly looks and spectacles. . .this was what it all came to in the end" (48). Pym's spinsters do not recognize that they are searching for the same things as Pym's married women: love and happiness. Pym's single women believe marriage will bring them all they do not have, but Pym's married women know marriage does not bring all these things.

Despite being denied certain of life's experiences, the Pym spinsters do not give up their interest in them. Spinsters such as Prudence, Emma, and Penelope are not so confined as the others by models of respectability, and they actively seek passion and romance. The excellent women are curious about passion and romance.[2] The Pym women are openly interested in whether a clergyman is celibate. Comments and questions such as that by Ianthe Pott, a spinster in *A Few Green Leaves,* "Your vicar's good-looking isn't he?. . .Is he a celibate?" (123), are scattered throughout the novels. Mildred Lathbury, at her annual luncheon with William Caldicote, the brother of her good friend Dora, finishes a quotation begun by William, saying, *"Drink deep, or taste not the Pierian spring"* (*EW,* 67). Mildred personalizes this statement by commenting, "But I'm afraid I shall never have the chance to drink deep so I must remain ignorant."

Just as Pym's spinsters do not give up thoughts of passion and romance, they also do not give up hopes of marriage. They keep these longings private, however, for in the Pym world, once a woman is resigned to being a spinster, she is expected to give up such hopes of marriage. At the annual luncheon between Mildred and William Caldicote, William tells Mildred that he and she are "the observers of life" (*EW,* 70) and that marriage is for other people. Nonetheless, Mildred does not give up hope, although she cloaks it. She admits to herself, "But I have never been very much given to falling in love and have often felt sorry that I have so far

missed. . .the experience of marriage" (44). The use of the phrase "so far" indicates that she has not abandoned hope. When William questions her, "I do hope you're *not* thinking of getting married?," Mildred, reverting to the attitude her role requires, responds, "Oh, no, of course not!" (69). She knows that a respectable spinster should not openly confess her desire for marriage.

▪ THE QUEST OF THE PYM WOMAN: HER SEARCH AND FAILURE

The Pym spinster, not content with her station in life, looks for marriage, or at least attention from men, but she has to be either cautious or clever in the way that she does it. As a respectable spinster, she offers her services, whether typing, editing, making casseroles, knitting socks, or doing churchwork. As Belinda notes, she has to consider what is "fitting to her own years and position" (*STG,* 131).

The main focus of Pym's excellent woman is usually her clergyman. Her efforts to get his attention are often cloaked in the guise of church work. As Wilmet notes in *A Glass of Blessings,* most of the excellent women are devoted rather than devout. The excellent women are fierce competitors for the attention of the clergy, and most of them harbor hopes of being chosen by a single clergyman for marriage. In fact, in one of the novels a character explicitly mentions the irate women a clergyman would have to contend with if he came to a parish already engaged.

The Pym women who work in offices are just as eager as the excellent women to find love and happiness. Their methods of finding men range from those of Dulcie, who stalks Aylwin Forbes like a detective, to Prudence Bates, who overdresses and applies a green, "greasy preparation which had little flecks of silver in it" (*J&P,* 84) to her eyelids. Instead of offering to knit socks or to do church work, they offer to type, edit, or make indexes. They also do other chores for men in exchange for attention and affection. For example, Emma Howick, the anthropologist in *A Few Green Leaves,* picks up groceries for Graham Pettifer and takes casseroles to his cottage. In *Less Than Angels,* Pym's novel about a community of anthropologists, Dierdre, a young student of anthropology, accurately describes how the Pym women seek love and happiness: "They had learned early in life what it is to bear love's burdens, listening patiently to their men's troubles and ever ready at their typewriters, should a manuscript or even a short article get to the stage of being written down" (49). One can see that the relationships are sought after in a barterlike system, with Pym women applying the rules of trade to their struggles to escape their loneliness and unhappiness.

Still, the ways in which Pym's women seek love are not consonant with what they seek. Indeed, their choice of language reveals that their relationships are to be engineered by manipulation. In *Some Tame Gazelle* Edith, in speaking about Harriet and the bishop, comments, "I don't think Harriet will get him." She continues, "I think he has successfully avoided so many women in his life that not even Harriet will be able to catch him" (192). In *Excellent Women* Sister Blatt decides, "Oh they [widows] have the knack of catching a man. Having done it once I suppose they can do it again" (120). With language such as this, the ulterior motives behind these single women's typing and cooking become more apparent.

Despite the casseroles, knitted socks, indexes, typed manuscripts, and editing, the Pym woman never gets what she wants—love and happiness. The excellent women who hope to win the heart of their clergyman or some other suitable man perform tasks which more often than not confirm their position as excellent women. The spinsters who are not excellent women, like Prudence and Penelope, are usually rejected by men as being either so overdone in their makeup and dress as to be "formidable rather than feminine and desirable" (*J&P,* 159) or as the type of women who "would have wanted so much" (189).

Although the Pym women never get what they seek—love and happiness—some of Pym's spinsters find mild flirtations, lukewarm affairs, or suitable attachments. The experience that all the Pym women seem to crave is one that they have not had, since their "hearts mend too easily." *Jane and Prudence*'s twenty-nine-year-old spinster, Prudence Bates, one of Pym's favorite characters, is also one of her most promiscuous.[3] Prudence enjoys affairs, and she is even described by her close friend Jane as having gotten "into the way of preferring unsatisfactory love affairs to any others, so that it was becoming almost a bad habit" (9). The lack of emotion and feeling in Prudence's affairs is revealed by her ability to recover so quickly when they are over. Shortly after being jilted by Fabian Driver, she looks forward to having an affair with Gerry Manifold, although, as she tells Jane, "we shall probably hurt each other very much before it's finished" (217).

More often than not, the Pym woman has, like Leonora, "never been badly treated or rejected by a man—perhaps she had never loved another person with enough intensity for such a thing [love wasted] to be possible" (*SDD,* 58). When Emma struggles to find the correct phrase to define her relationship with Graham, the description deflates from "brief love affair" to "mild affection" to "knew him quite well." Mildred admits that she "had once imagined [herself] to be in love"

(*EW,* 122) with Bernard Hatherley. When Dulcie meets Maurice Clive, the man who formerly had rejected her, she feels indifferent toward him. And when Tom Mallow, a young anthropologist, is killed in Africa, his girlfriend Dierdre is upset over not being upset. She tells Catherine, "I know you won't be too shocked when I say I can't really *feel* anything about Tom" (*NFR,* 240). More often than not, if a Pym woman has loved and lost, the love proves to have been so lukewarm and one-sided that she really had nothing to lose in the first place. In *Less Than Angels* Mark Penfold, a fledgling anthropologist, describes this kind of tepid affair: "It is commoner in our society than many people would suppose. . .the woman giving the food and shelter and doing some typing for him and the man giving the priceless gift of himself" (76). Mark is speaking of the relationship between Catherine Oliphant and Tom Mallow, two of his friends who live together. His description, which recognizes primarily the convenience of the relationship instead of the romance, is an accurate one. When Tom leaves Catherine, there are no outbursts of emotion, but rather perfunctory acceptance of a lack of interest.

When marriages occur in Pym's novels, they are generally the type of relationship known in the Pym world as a "suitable attachment." In *No Fond Return of Love* Dulcie describes this type of relationship. Quickly informing middle-aged Aylwin Forbes that any thoughts of marrying her nineteen-year-old niece are clearly out of place, Dulcie boldly instructs him in what is suitable: he should make a "sensible marriage," a marriage with "somebody who can appreciate [his] work and help [him] with it" (223). In *A Few Green Leaves* Emma, who at times views her condition as objectively as any of the Pym characters, expresses the essence of the suitable attachment in her assessment of her situation with Tom: "After all, they were two lonely people now, and as such should get together" (193). In thinking of a possible union between herself and Tom, Emma appeals to logic, not to romantic notions.

For the most part, these suitable attachments occur between minor characters and are mentioned only in passing. Such attachments for Pym's main characters never occur in full focus in the individual novels in which the characters appear. If there is hope of a possible marriage for the Pym spinster, it is suggested only at the end of the novel. For example, at the respective conclusions of *Excellent Women, No Fond Return of Love,* and *A Few Green Leaves,* the possible marriages of Mildred Lathbury and Everard Bone, Dulcie Mainwaring and Aylwin Forbes, and Emma Howick and Tom Dagnall are suggested but left in question. By only suggesting marriages at the end of her novels, Pym downgrades the importance of these less-than-ideal relationships. In fact, this is one of the ways she shows that these relationships are less than ideal.

The grimness of the suitable attachment is recognized by Ianthe Broome, one of the main characters in *An Unsuitable Attachment*. On learning of the engagement of Miss Grimes, a retired elderly spinster, to a Polish widower, she thinks:

> At that moment life seemed very dark; Ianthe was perhaps too rigid in her views to reflect that a woman might have worse things to look forward to than the prospect of marriage to a Polish widower and a life in Ealing, or even a quick drink in one's own room at the end of a hard day. (244)

Having "worse things to look forward to" is a condition in which many of the Pym women find themselves. However, Ianthe knows and on one occasion admits that life can be very lonely for a woman, and that is "why it's better to marry when one has the chance—or perhaps I should say *if* one has the chance" (243). The spinsters do not all have the chance to escape loneliness by marriage, for, more often than not, the relationship peters out. In *Jane and Prudence* Fabian Driver loses interest in Prudence; in *Less Than Angels* Tom loses interest in Catherine; in *An Unsuitable Attachment* Rupert never really has any interest in Penelope; in *The Sweet Dove Died* James leaves Leonora for a homosexual; and in *A Few Green Leaves* Graham Pettifer loses interest in Emma.

Having found neither lukewarm love affairs nor suitable attachments, most Pym women are so desperate for affection that they will content themselves with illusions. Viola Dace, a character in *No Fond Return of Love,* had "offered to do Aylwin's index, unfairly waylaying him on the steps of the British Museum so that he could hardly have refused" (75). Viola creates an illusion out of this incident and smugly tells Dulcie, "Aylwin has asked me to do the index for his new book" (74). She even drops the line, "I shall be rather busy. . .so you may not see very much of me," as a way of "casually" (74) telling Dulcie this news. Dulcie's accurate judgment about Viola, which is applicable to many of Pym's women, is: "Just to be allowed to love them [men such as Aylwin Forbes] is enough" (75). The Pym women have no other choice, since they, like Viola, can expect nothing more. Furthermore, "to be allowed to love them" is essential.

Dulcie discovers why "to love them is enough" for the Pym women: she understands that "perhaps women enjoy that [doing what they could] most of all—to feel that they are needed and doing good" (*NFR,* 22). This observation of Dulcie's is confirmed by another Pym

character. Wilmet, in *A Glass of Blessings,* admits, "Everybody wants to be needed, women especially" (165). From Wilmet's statement we begin to realize that one of the reasons women want to be needed is that it makes them feel important or at least useful. Feeling needed is a way of hedging against the fear, as Mildred puts it, of "being unwanted," the terror of knowing that one, like a photo in a picture frame at a jumble sale, "could so very easily be replaced" (*EW,* 39).

▪ THE PREDICAMENT OF THE PYM WOMAN: HER DISAPPOINTMENTS AND ILLUSIONS

In *Less Than Angels* Catherine describes the life that she herself knows and observes around her: "It's comic and sad and indefinite—dull, sometimes, but seldom really tragic or deliriously happy, except when one's very young" (89). This description could apply to the lives of all Pym's main female characters. In every Pym novel a character makes a similar confession: "We can't expect to get everything we want. . .we know that life isn't like that" (*FGL,* 159); "Life hasn't turned out quite as she meant it to" (*J&P,* 102). If a character does not admit this in words, we nonetheless sense that she feels it.

Pym's characters assuage their disappointment by fostering vague hopes. On several occasions throughout *A Few Green Leaves* Emma wonders, "Who knew what might come of it?" (4), and "There was no knowing what it might lead to" (145). When Letty, after retirement, is "settled in Mrs. Pope's back room," she thinks, "There was no knowing how her life would change" (*QA,* 75), and she retains these illusions. *Quartet in Autumn* ends with Letty thinking, "At least it made one realise that life still held infinite possibilities for change" (218). The "it" refers to Letty's choice of either remaining with her London landlady or joining Marjorie, a friend who has recently been jilted by her fiancé. Letty's possibilities are hardly "infinite," for the available change is not significant. The reader therefore understands Letty's perception of "infinite possibilities of change" as illusory. There is no hope for real change in her life. The only change that will occur is the change all the characters in this novel fear: aging and death.

The Pym woman adopts certain attitudes as camouflage for the despair and loneliness she feels. The fierceness of her determination to keep up appearances is virtually a barometer of the extent of her unhappiness. For example, after her retirement, Letty feels that "she must never give the slightest hint of loneliness or boredom, the sense of time hanging heavy" (*QA,* 134). Letty is not the only character who "made up her mind to face Christmas with courage and a kind of deliberate boldness, a determination to hold the prospect of loneliness at bay" (87). Christmas is the one holiday that most of

Pym's spinsters dread, for, as Pym tells us in *Quartet in Autumn,* it is "a difficult time for those who are no longer young and are without close relatives or dependents" (83). Letty herself admits that she is "dutifully assuming the suggested attitude towards retirement that life was full of possibilities" (106). Letty's situation seems even grimmer, because she admits for a moment that even she does not believe in the attitude she is expected to adopt. We see a paradox: she is expected to expect the unexpected.

Presenting optimistic attitudes for the future is not enough for the Pym women. They must also dampen the disappointments of the past with convenient fictions. This conversation between Mildred and Dora could easily occur among other Pym spinsters.

> 'There's not much you can do when you're over thirty,' she went on complacently. 'You get too set in your ways, really. Besides, marriage isn't everything.'
>
> 'No, it certainly isn't,' I agreed, 'and there's nobody I want to marry that I can think of. Not even William.'
>
> 'I don't know anyone either, at the moment,' said Dora.
>
> We lapsed into a comfortable silence. It was a kind of fiction that we had always kept up, this not knowing anyone at the moment that we wanted to marry, as if there had been in the past and would be in the future. (*EW*, 101)

Mildred recognizes these shared illusions, these fictions, for what they are. She does not dispel them, however, for she feels the essential comfort and compensation they provide.

Pym's characters frequently escape rejection and unhappiness by reshaping disappointing circumstances. With the aid of rationalizations they create consolations. In *Less Than Angels* Catherine views an example of this type of consolation in Rhoda's response to Mabel as they discuss Dierdre's reaction to the death of her boyfriend Tom Mallow.

> 'You must allow Dierdre her grief,' said Mabel almost sharply. 'You don't know what it is to lose somebody you love.'
>
> 'You've no right to say that, of course I do'. . . Rhoda's voice trembled and she began to refill the teacups in an agitated way.
>
> Catherine noticed her confusion and wondered if she were trying to justify herself, to think of some kind of compensation for the shame of not having lost lover or husband, but only parents and others who had died at their natural and proper time. *If women could not expect to savour*

all experiences that life could offer, perhaps they did want the sad ones—not necessarily to have loved or been loved, but at least to have lost, she thought simply and without cynicism. (238; emphasis mine.)

The only sustainable fiction the Pym woman can create is the belief that she has loved and lost, thereby justifying her existence as a spinster. What becomes clear is that the Pym spinster's delusion about romance, loving, and losing is a way to see herself as someone she is not, to distinguish herself from others, to embellish or even invent reality and thereby, if only as an illusion, create some of the experience she has not had. These illusions are more pathetic and difficult to sustain as the Pym women grow older. Aging means a loss of one's self-esteem as well as one's ability to attract men, or at least the hope of being able to attract men. Thus, as Pym's women grow older and less attractive, they begin to see loneliness as a permanent condition.

Still, sometimes these illusions catch up with their creators, as in Belinda's effort to console Count Bianco for his unrequited love for Harriet.

> Her eyes lighted on the works of Alfred, Lord Tennyson 'that it is better to have loved and lost than never to have loved at all. I always think those lines are such a great comfort; so many of us loved and lost.' She frowned: nobody wanted to be one of the many, and she did not like this picture of herself, only one of a great crowd of dreary women. Perhaps Tennyson was rather hackneyed after all. (*STG*, 213–14)

Belinda shifts the blame to Tennyson and refuses to see herself as one of a great crowd. She dodges the implication and avoids having her comfortable illusion melt.

The grim reality, however, is probably as Letty sees it: "Even Marcia had once hinted at something in her own life, long ago. No doubt everybody had once had something in their lives? Certainly it was the kind of thing people liked to imply, making one suspect that a good deal was being made out of almost nothing" (*QA*, 36–37). Catherine, in *Less Than Angels,* notices that the experience that the Pym woman wants is at least "to have lost." In *Some Tame Gazelle* Belinda expresses a related belief shared by many of Pym's women. She is "sure that our greater English poets had written much about unhappy lovers *not* dying of grief, although it was of course more romantic when they did" (130). There is no logic in her idea that to die for grief is romantic. Having loved and lost is to the Pym character both tragic and romantic; indeed, *tragic* and *romantic* seem almost to be synonyms. The irony is that the condition she desires would bring her only that from which she wants to escape: loneliness, unhappiness, and despair.

▪ THE ATTITUDE OF THE AUTHOR PYM: THE SYMPATHY AND IRONY

Pym states the cases of types of women who have not, at least in the twentieth century, often found their way into literature. She writes the novels that Letty in *Quartet in Autumn* looked for but could not find: "[Letty] had always been an unashamed reader of novels, but if she hoped to find one which reflected her own sort of life she had come to realise that the position of an unmarried, unattached, ageing woman is of no interest whatever to the writer of modern fiction" (3). In stating the case of the lonely women who are not regarded with much concern even in their world, Pym is sympathetic to her characters' plight. For all her sympathy, she writes realistic, indeed ironic novels, not sentimental ones. For all her characters' loneliness, they are women who are, for the most part, selfish and self-concerned. The Pym woman is observant of those who surround her, but her awareness does not stem from concern about others, only curiosity. In fact, when Pym women become aware of situations in which they might be expected to help, they recoil. After her brother's engagement is announced, Winifred tells Mildred, "I hoped I would come and live with you." Mildred confesses that the thought of Winifred staying with her "filled [her] with sinking apprehension," and she is careful in her answer because she realizes that "easy excuses. . . would not do here" (*EW,* 207). And when Letty and Marcia, two of the quartet in *Quartet in Autumn,* retire, Marcia fears that Letty will ask her if she can come and live with her.

Thus the Pym women, although they recognize the loneliness of others, do not exhibit real compassion or sympathy. Their thoughts remain centered on themselves, and they remain detached and aloof. Indeed, the Pym women even see each other as rivals, natural antagonists in a world where pettiness has replaced compassion. When a woman is successful in getting "the desired object," the other women reveal their jealousy. For example, in discussing Mildred Lathbury's marriage to Everard Bone, Miss Morrow learns from Miss Bonner that "Mildred helped him a good deal in his work" and that "she even learned to type so that she could type his manuscripts for him." Miss Morrow immediately decides, "Oh, then he had to marry her. . . . That kind of devotion is worse than blackmail—a man has no escape from that" (*J&P,* 126).

Pym's works are infused with irony. The criticism that "nothing ever happens" is often applied to her novels. Nothing much happens in them, and thus the reality of the characters' lives is just what makes their statements that "anything might happen" ironic. Despite their unhappy circumstances, Pym's women cling to their illusions. Belinda observes, "But there was always hope springing eternal in the human breast, which kept one alive, often unhappily . . . it would be an interesting subject on which to read a paper to the Literary Society" (*STG,* 130). The works of Barbara Pym are "papers on this interesting subject." While we laugh with Pym as she exposes, in her witty way, her characters' minor foibles and petty machinations, we should not gloss over the darker side of her writing or ignore the grim reality of her characters' conditions. She shows us women who search for love and happiness. In their quest they offer their services and compete fiercely among themselves to gain attention and affection. Not finding what they seek, her women remain unhappy and lonely. Self-centered and self-concerned, and at times petty, they are painfully aware of having missed out on life. To fend off their disappointments, they occupy themselves with trivial chores and minor tasks, and they fortify themselves with vague hopes and small consolations. Pym's women have failed at romance and love, and they grow old suffering the fears of aging and the terrors of loneliness. They cling to pathetic illusions and look to the future with vain expectations that "anything could happen." To protect their optimistic attitudes and to ward off potential disappointments, they have learned to keep their hopes vague and unspecific.

Margaret C. Bradham, Winter 1987

1   Pym's eleven novels, in order of publication, are: *Some Tame Gazelle,* 1950 (parenthetic references in the text are abbreviated as *STG*); *Excellent Women,* 1952 (*EW*); *Jane and Prudence,* 1953 (*J&P*); *Less Than Angels,* 1955 (*LTA*); *A Glass of Blessings,* 1958 (*GB*); *No Fond Return of Love,* 1961 (*NFR*); *Quartet in Autumn,* 1977 (*QA*); *The Sweet Dove Died,* 1978 (*SDD*); *A Few Green Leaves,* 1980 (*FGL*); *An Unsuitable Attachment,* 1982 (*UA*); and *Crampton Hodnet,* 1985 (*CH*). In 1986, a twelfth novel, *An Academic Question,* was published posthumously. Hazel Holt, Pym's friend and literary executor, prepared the work for publication by amalgamating and editing two of Pym's unfinished manuscripts, I have chosen not to include *An Academic Question* in this paper for purposes of discussion for two reasons: first, during her lifetime (1913–80) Pym chose not to prepare the two manuscripts for publication; second and more important, the novel is not solely the work of Barbara Pym.

2   The topic of sex and sexuality in Pym's women deserves to be given full attention in another article. Critics have tended to ignore this aspect of Pym. In *A Few Green Leaves* Avice Scrubsole diagnoses Emma Howick's depression as either "unrequited love" or "frustrated sex." The two alternative conditions are related. Although many of Pym's women are chaste, they at times feel embarrassed about their lack of experience. They giggle nervously when sex or passion is mentioned or when a word or phrase is used that has a secondary sexual connotation. Other Pym women seek affairs and enjoy the physical aspect of them. The reader learns about the physical intimacy of Pym's characters' various relationships not from Pym's description of them, but through unintentional discoveries by other characters: for example, in *Excellent Women* Mildred Lathbury finds

Julian Malory and Allegra Gray holding hands; in *Quartet in Autumn* Letty Crowe awakes to see Marjorie and Father David Lydell kissing; and in *A Few Green Leaves* Adam Prince discovers Emma Howick and Graham Pettifer "canoodling on the grass."

3 Until the publication in 1984 of *A Very Private Eye: An Autobiography in Diaries and Letters* by Pym's sister Hilary Pym Walton and her literary executor Hazel Holt, the image persisted of Barbara Pym as a typical English spinster, a retiring, gentle woman who lived a life of the utmost respectability. In the introduction of *A Very Private Eye,* Hilary Pym Walton tells us that Barbara was a tall, good-looking girl who was very extroverted and entertaining and who had many admirers as an undergraduate at Oxford. Although she never married, she had a number of love affairs. Pym chose to allow rather than deny herself experiences. In a diary entry of March 1940 she wrote, "Oh how absurd and delicious it is to be in love with somebody younger than yourself! Everybody should try it—no life can be complete without it" (101). Thus the Pym reader is not surprised to find in another entry Pym's revelation that Prudence Bates, one of her most promiscuous characters, was one of her favorites.

Legend and Legacy: Some Bloomsbury Diaries

"I have had to write a memoir of Old Bloomsbury—from 1904 to 1916," Virginia Woolf stated. "We were extremely social—forever lunching and dining out and loitering about the book shops. . . . Thursday evening parties were. . .the germ from which sprang all that has since come to be called—in newspapers, in novels, in Germany and in France—even, I daresay, in Turkey and Timbuktu—by the name of Bloomsbury."[1] Frances Partridge recalls that Bloomsbury consisted of "a number of individuals who shared certain attitudes to life and happened to be friends or lovers. . . . Conventions did not interest them—ideas were their passion. They were mostly left-wing and atheists, and during the first World War, pacifists. They loved art and travel, avidly enjoyed their work as well as talk, laughter, French cuisine; and owned fine libraries. They set great store in friendship. Marriage was a convenience, never celebrated in church. Love, hetero and homo, took precedence over it. There was nothing sacrosanct, or immune from mockery."[2]

Bloomsbury, according to Leonard Woolf, began with "a small number of persons living in or around Bloomsbury during the years 1912–1914." The term was used by them "before it was used by the outside world." In the 1920s and 1930s they talked of " 'Old Bloomsbury,' meaning the original members of our group of friends"—i.e., the three Stephens (Vanessa, married to Clive Bell; Virginia, married to Leonard Woolf; and Adrian Stephen, who married Karin Costelloe), Lytton Strachey, Roger Fry, Desmond MacCarthy, and Molly.[3] "Its basis was [founded on] friendship,

which in some cases developed into love and marriage" (LW, 25). Their minds were colored by Cambridge and the philosophy of G. E. Moore. Afterward the group expanded and became New Bloomsbury.

It can be said that love and/or marriage proliferated, with relationships crisscrossing and interconnecting, widening and stretching the orbit and reaching the outermost bounds, forming a Bloomsbury galaxy with many keepers of diaries. "Diaries now pullulate," Virginia Woolf wrote in her own diary in 1939.[4] This sui-generis genre, the diary, is first cousin to letter writing, biography, autobiography, history, and even the novel and the play. It partakes a little of them all yet remains distinct, a kind of letter to oneself or "a soliloquy," as Virginia Woolf calls it, "written in gulps and jerks," or it is "gossip and comment." Diaries can be records: of Jane Clark's social engagements, of her husband Kenneth Clark's career in art, of Harold Nicolson's diplomatic and political activities, of Peter Hall's directorship of London's National Theatre, of Siegfried Sassoon's war years (1915–18). A diary helped Alice James overcome loneliness, Carrington to pour out her love, May Sarton to describe solitude and advancing years, Katherine Mansfield to observe and endure her illness, Frances Partridge to take up her Bloomsbury legacy. As for Virginia Woolf, her diary made "each day longer," was a "dialogue," a clearinghouse for her "many selves," a place for "expressing feelings," to work things out, to "decramp," an outlet for "an inveterate writer," a practice sheet for her novels and memoirs. One quality which all these diaries—and all diaries in general—have in common is that none of them, unless interrupted by death or abandoned, has an ending.

From this bounty of diaries, let us consider several, beginning with the one penned by Virginia Woolf, which Quentin Bell pronounced "a major work" and "a masterpiece" in his foreword to volume 1. Amazingly enough, the entries in this monumental journal were written largely in bits and snatches of five or ten minutes because of the pressures placed upon the author and her writing schedule: interruptions caused by illness, visitors, house parties, and other social exigencies. Recognizing the drawbacks of this strict limitation, Virginia Woolf admitted that "many deep thoughts have visited me and fled," that her diary is "stifled with too much life," that she can only write when "in the mood" and when there is no one else in the room. "Ottoline Morrell kept a journal devoted. . .to her 'inner life,'" Woolf notes, "which made me reflect that I haven't an inner life." What could be better evidence of an inner life, however, than Woolf's decision to break the rule and write about "the soul"? Once, when overcome by gloom, she writes: "I pitched into my great lake of melancholy. Lord how deep it is! What a born melancholiac I am! . . . What a terrific capacity I possess for feeling with intensity. . .the inane pointlessness of all this existence." Still, courageously, she vows, "This tragedy of despair shall not engulf me. I will go down with my colours flying. . . . What I want is a season of contemplation. I get this about 3 A.M. when I. . .open my window and look at the sky over the apple trees."

Then there is Virginia Woolf's inner life concerning the creation of her novels and other books, the ideas, traumas, and dilemmas connected with her work. Her brain threatens "to split . . . with the combination of the external and the internal. . . . I still struggle and still feel the rush and the glory and the agony. . . . Few people can be as tormented about writing as I am." Writing, for Woolf, was a kind of mediumship ("I become the person"), likened to a long childbirth. The reader assists at many a parturition, that of *To the Lighthouse, The Waves, The Years,* and so many other books. Still, Woolf enjoyed her writing and depended upon it for her sanity: "The only way to keep afloat is by working. . . . Life suddenly becomes thin" otherwise. More drastically and ominously, she agrees with Duncan Grant's assertion that if one cannot write, "one may as well kill oneself."

Doubts concerning the diary did trouble Woolf. She wondered, for example, what it all amounted to and what its fate would be: "What is the point of all these notes?. . .Who's going to read it? . . . I have half a mind one of these days to explain what my intention is in writing these continual diaries. . . , no publication. . . . A memoir of my life? Perhaps." Nonetheless, there are light moments, with her "disporting" herself while writing her diary, which "Thank God in heaven needs no re-writing." Rereading her diaries "amuses" her and leaves her "much refreshed." The reader senses the same enjoyment in perusing Woolf's diary, from her wry comments to her brilliant metaphors, her portraits of people, her naturally elegant style. "I am in danger, indeed," she avers after being praised by a provincial critic, "of becoming our leading novelist and not with the highbrows alone." There is hardly a line that is not quotable, hardly a sentence that is not memorable: "I will now snatch a moment from what Morgan calls 'life' to enter a hurried note. My notes have been few; life a cascade, a glissade, a torrent"; the queen "is like a lit up street in diamonds"; E. M. Forster "blew in like thistle-down." If Woolf were never to write again, we read elsewhere, she would "whizz into extinction like an electric globe fused"; and alluding to one of her feminist books, she claimed to have "enough ammunition to blow up St. Paul's."

Some people remind Woolf of fish, fowl, insects, and other animals: Edith Sitwell is "an ivory elephant,"

Clive Bell a "poor parakeet"; T. S. Eliot is "supple as an eel. . .tight as a wood louse," Maynard Keynes "a gorged seal," Duncan Grant a "shabby moth," Saxon Sydney-Turner "a hen who has laid an egg," Lytton Strachey "my old serpent," Arnold Bennett a "lovable sea lion," Aldous Huxley a "giant grasshopper," Ray Strachey "a very fine tabby. . .castrated." Woolf spares not even herself, describing, for example, the back of her newly shingled head as "the rump of a partridge"; and when the Huxleys travel around the world, she complains, "And here I live like a weevil in a biscuit." Well aware of her tartness and "cruelty with my friends," she makes up for it with affection. Her highest praise is reserved for her sister Vanessa Bell and her dear friend Vita Sackville-West: "Nessa's charms rising resplendent like the harvest moon"; and "Vita. . .free and easy. . .recalling some image of a ship breasting a sea, nobly, magnificently, with all sails spread and the gold sunlight on them."

References to the sun and moon and to the sea reveal Woolf's susceptibility to nature: "The harvest is positively orange on the hill, and the country divinely coloured ripe ash. . .and gold, as I came through Tristram's grove up the river." On long walks over moor and marsh she observes a kingfisher, a stoat, the first flowers of spring. In Greece she is enchanted: "I looked up and saw the mountains across the bay, knife-shaped, coloured, and the sea, brimming smooth. . . . I could find nothing lacking in that . . . beauty, every inch has its wild flowers. . . . I could love Greece, as an old woman . . . as I once loved Cornwall as a child." Travel held great attraction for Woolf, but she also loved London: "I went on the roof . . . and saw all London—a magnificent metropolis, so ornate, so continental and cosmopolitan. . . . Why do I love it so much? London thou art a jewel of jewels and a Jasper of Jocunditie."[5] The two world wars devastated large areas of London. Woolf records the nightly bombing raids, bringing the experience very close to the reader: great holes in the streets, crammed underground shelters, thousands of evacuees, gutted buildings, a hospital train bringing the wounded—"the slowness, cadaverousness, grief of the long train taking its burden through the fields." Elsewhere we read: "Damage considerable to Bloomsbury. . . . Rubble where I wrote so many books. Open air where we sat so many nights, gave so many parties . . . books all over the floor. I began to hunt out diaries. . . 24 volumes salved; a great mass for my memoirs. . . . L. says he has petrol in the car for suicide shd Hitler win."

"After 25 years," Woolf wrote in 1937, she and Leonard "can't bear to be separate. . . . How moving to find this warmth. . .in being alone with L. If I had dared,

I would investigate my own sensations with respect to him, but out of . . . I don't know what reticence—refrain." Later: "L. and I too happy. . . . How sweet life is with Leonard. . . . I am the happiest wife. . . . It has not been dull, my marriage. . . . L. may be severe; but he stimulates. . . . Oh and L. . . . divinely good . . . and I have him every day."

The Woolfs' social life, what Virginia called "the flutter and clutter of engagements," comprised not only theatre, concerts, lunches, dinners, teas, and weekend and house parties, but also the Bloomsbury Memoir Club meetings: "The usual people there, the usual sensation of being in a familiar but stimulating atmosphere. . . . Old Bloomsbury relationships flourish," despite its haters and baiters, and despite the death of several of its members. In 1934 Woolf wrote of Roger Fry: "The poverty of life now . . . comes to me. . . . Desmond came up, I laid my hand on his shoulder said dont die yet nor you either he said we have had wonderful friends he said." In 1938 Woolf paid tribute to Ottoline Morrell, who had entertained so many at Garsington Manor: "She created her own world." From a 1932 entry on Lytton Strachey we read: "Lytton died yesterday . . . a sense of something spent, gone . . . to me so intolerable. . .the impoverishment. . .20 years of Lytton lost to us." The cruelest bereavement, however, was the loss of the bright young idealist Julian Bell, elder son of Vanessa Bell and beloved nephew of Virginia Woolf, killed in the Spanish Civil War in 1937: "I can hardly bring myself to say anything about Julian's death . . . like a blow on the head . . . incredible suffering . . . brings close the immense vacancy and our short little run into inanity." Woolf's diary stops short on 24 March 1941. Death came to her of her own will four days later.

This depiction of the diary of Virginia Woolf is a pale rainbow compared to the aurora borealis. In such a short study it is not possible to gather all the colorfulness and variety and flavor of the immense cast of characters and the vast number of events which distinguish this vivid work. Vita Sackville-West, in an entry for 14 October 1953 in her own diary, writes: "Oh God, how I wish I could get Virginia back! Reading her diary makes me regret her so poignantly; and also feeling that towards the end I might have done something to stop her from taking her life."[6] Harold Nicolson noted in his diary: "I work at my lecture . . . then read Virginia Woolf. She rightly says that to a diary one entrusts a mood rather than the expression of continuous personality. There is nothing of her distinction, charm and occasional affection and kindness in her diary. She seems neurotic, vain and envious. But it is fascinating." The diary that they read was A Writer's Diary, edited by Leonard Woolf, a Hogarth Press prepublication edition

which showed only one aspect of Virginia's "many selves." Nicolson—writer, diplomat, politician, husband of Vita Sackville-West—kept a diary for over forty years. In an entry dated 26 February 1941 he commented: "I am rather fussed about this diary. It is not intimate enough to give a personal picture. . . . I feel this diary will be for me a record from which I can fill in remembered details . . . and some relief in putting down on paper the momentary spurts and gushes of this cataract of history." In his journal the reader becomes acquainted with a scholar and a gentleman as well as a statesman, a loving father, and, with his wife, the creator of the famous gardens of Sissinghurst, their country home. The spurts and gushes he puts down on paper—from an inside view of politics and politicians, to history as it unfolded during the World War II years, to his achievements as a writer—contain much valuable information and interest.

Quite another kind of diary is that of Evelyn Waugh, chronicler of London's Bright Young People and Smart Set of the 1920s and 1930s.[7] Waugh's link with Bloomsbury is very slender, and he serves mostly to demonstrate the diversity of the friends of Virginia Woolf who were also friends of Waugh. The aunt of his second wife Laura Herbert was Lady Margaret Duckworth, wife of George Duckworth, half brother of Virginia. Waugh's dealings with the Woolfs were not of the best. He had sent the manuscript of The Balance to Leonard, only to have it returned; and elsewhere we read, "Claud lent me a novel by Virginia Woolf which I refuse to believe is good." Arthur Waley makes him think of Bloomsbury, and he finds Clive Bell "ingratiating." In 1930 he went to "a cocktail party at Francis Meynell's. He has taken Duncan Grant's house which was covered in frescoes by him and Vanessa Bell and has painted them all out except one"; gratuitously and maliciously, he adds, "So sensible." Despite cocktail parties and other social functions and his "heavy drinking" and "hangovers," he managed to write novels and serve in the Royal Marines during World War II. His diary gives a good account of the segment of society in which he moved.

No contemporary writer of fiction was more of a rival to Virginia Woolf than the New Zealander Katherine Mansfield. On 28 January 1923 Woolf noted in her diary: "Katherine Mansfield has been dead a week, and how far am I obeying her 'do not quite forget Katherine.'. . . Katherine's my rival no longer. . . . I was jealous of her writing—the only writer I have ever been jealous of. . . . I shall think of her at intervals all through life. . . . We had something in common I shall never find in anyone else." There is no mention of Woolf in Mansfield's diary,[8] although she was the recipient of many letters from the latter. Mansfield's diary is almost wholly subjective, taken up with her illness, her invalidism, thoughts of death, her fears for her mental health, her struggles with her writing, her many loves, her many changes of country and domicile, her constant hotel-hopping, her status as a woman and a writer, her attitude toward art, her reading, her relations with her husband John Middleton Murry, her observations of people, animals, places, and things, her imagination and mysticism. She felt ambivalent about Bloomsbury: "If one wasn't afraid—why should I be? this isn't going to be read by Bloomsbury & Cie." There is frankness in her journal: "I reproach myself for my 'private life' which, were I to die, *would* astonish even those nearest to me." Grave illness and excruciating pain could not stifle her innate sense of humor, her gratitude for even intermittent moments of happiness, her deep appreciation of nature, her loving memories of her homeland and childhood there, her enthusiasm for Chekhov, her enjoyment of friendship, her delight in animals. Neither did she lose her gallant courage, but that courage did not halt death from tuberculosis at the age of thirty-five.

What of Bloomsbury after the death of Virginia Woolf? There is a good narrative of the succeeding years in the diary of Frances Partridge (née Marshall), the wife of Ralph Partridge, who worked briefly for the Woolfs' Hogarth Press. He and Lytton Strachey purchased Ham Spray, a country house in Wiltshire, where they lived with the painter from the Slade Art School, Dora Carrington, to whom Ralph was once married. The Bloomsbury Memoir Club was very hospitable to Frances. She went to London regularly for its meetings and eventually became its secretary. Two papers or memoirs were read at each meeting—for example, by Vanessa Bell on Virginia as a child and Virginia's own account of her early days. Frances lists the members of New Bloomsbury: "By the time I was elected it had been augmented by Bunny Garnett, Adrian Stephen, Olivier Strachey, Janie Bussy, Quentin Bell. . . . Later on, in the teeth of fierce black balling. . .Dermod MacCarthy, Julia Strachey, Olivier Bell, Angelica Garnett, Sebastian Sprott, Denis Proctor. Dinner at a Soho restaurant, then to rooms of a member." As to the sexual mores of Bloomsbury, Frances asserts: "I think they are less promiscuous than their image in the eyes of the more conventional. . . . The Bloomsbury philosophy of sex by which Ralph and I have lived for 20 years, disregards convention, but not human feelings. . . . There were no divorces in Bloomsbury, but there were re-shuffles in which we ourselves had taken part." This alluded to their affair while Ralph was still married to Carrington. He married Frances after Carrington died.

The Partridges saw a lot of the Bloomsbury set, lunching regularly with Clive Bell, having Saxon Sydney-Turner resume his erstwhile weekends at Ham Spray, inviting Vanessa Bell and Duncan Grant as houseguests: "The best company we have had for ages. . . . Spiritually, Vanessa is ageless. . .nothing to remind us that he is seventy." Alix and James Strachey, friends of old, were "ever true to themselves. Though admitting that Bloomsbury was now in a trough they were convinced they would rise again." In 1955 Frances noted: "The weeklies are very full these days of cynical abuse of our Gods, the Bloomsbury ones, both of what they stand for and the characters themselves—Virginia, Maynard and Roger. I feel as certain as anything that the journalists are wrong, and that one day it will be seen that they played an important part in the history of civilization."

Bloomsbury *has* risen again, it seems, now that Charleston, the home of Vanessa Bell and Duncan Grant, has been restored and opened to the public. Its rooms have been repainted with Grant's murals, and its chairs have been reupholstered with fabric printed with Vanessa's designs. Let us hope that the bookcases hold—or will hold—all the many diaries from the golden age of Bloomsbury, those that have been mentioned here as well as those of others connected to the group: Mary Pearsall-Smith Berenson, wife of Bernard Berenson, an art critic living in Italy, where Virginia Woolf visited them in 1904; Dora Carrington, who lived and loved at Ham Spray and took care of Lytton Strachey and who, when he died, shot herself; Beatrice Webb, one of the Fabians with whom Leonard Woolf allied himself; Stephen Spender and W. H. Auden, the young poets who intrigued Virginia Woolf; . . . and so many more.

Are diaries literature? Do they have a form? Are they timeless? If one uses Virginia Woolf's standards, the others will be found wanting. Each diary should be judged by its own standards. What one looks for in a good diary are improvisation, spontaneity, reasonable truthfulness, a trustworthy picture of the period in which it is written, and a good idea of the character of the writer. It should also be enjoyable or at least informative, read well, and have not less than a modicum of elegant language, form, or style. The criterion, then, is *quality,* irrespective of the nature of the diary. Form is usually decided upon by the compiler, timelessness by the interest it evokes years hence. Like any other literary work, a *good* diary, no matter what its category, will qualify.

Kathleen Chase, Spring 1987

[1] Virginia Woolf, *Moments of Being: Unpublished Autobiographical Writings,* Jeanne Schulkind, ed., New York, Harcourt Brace Jovanovich, 1976, pp. 159, 163, 164.

[2] Frances Partridge, *Love in Bloomsbury,* New York, Little, Brown, 1981.

[3] Leonard Woolf, *Beginning Again: An Autobiography of the Years 1911–1918,* London, Hogarth, 1964, p. 22. Subsequent references use the abbreviation LW.

[4] This and other citations are taken from *The Diary of Virginia Woolf, 1915–1941,* 5 vols., Anne Olivier Bell, Andrew McNeillie, eds., San Diego, Harcourt Brace Jovanovich, 1977, 1978, 1980, 1982, 1984. For reviews, see *WLT* 52:4 (Autumn 1978), p. 636; 55:2 (Spring 1981), p. 328; 57:2 (Spring 1983), p. 295; and 59:2 (Spring 1985), p. 292.

[5] William Dunbar, *In Honour of the City of London.*

[6] From *The Diary of Vita Sackville-West 1930–1962,* included with Harold Nicolson, *Diaries and Letters,* 3 vols., Nigel Nicolson, ed., 1966–67.

[7] *The Diaries of Evelyn Waugh,* Michael Davie, ed., London, Weidenfeld & Nicolson, 1976. For a review, see *WLT* 52:4 (Autumn 1978), p.635.

[8] *The Journal of Katherine Mansfield, 1904–1922,* John Middleton Murray, ed., New York, Knopf, 1959.

Recovering a Tradition: *Anglo-Welsh Poetry 1480– 1980*

Almost fifty years ago now, on 10 December 1938, the great Welsh poet and dramatist Saunders Lewis delivered to the Cardiff branch of the Guild of Graduates of the University of Wales its annual lecture, which he called "Is There an Anglo-Welsh Literature?" Contrasting the Welsh with the Irish, the answer, he said, was no, first because the literature people called Anglo-Welsh was written in a language and for a community that were largely indistinguishable from those of industrial England, and then because it sought its audience not among the Welsh but the English. "I conclude . . . that there is not a separate literature that is Anglo-Welsh," he said, "and that it is improbable that there ever can be that."[1]

Even as Lewis spoke, however, Welsh writing in English was moving in new directions. In 1937 Keidrych Rhys brought out the first issue of *Wales,* whose goal was "to be a sort of forum where the 'Anglo-Welsh' have their say"[2] and which published the work of such early English-language poets as Dylan Thomas, Vernon Watkins, and Idris Davies. More important for the future of Anglo-Welsh literature, in the same year as *Wales* was founded, David Jones published *In Parenthesis,* a "writing" which, in its allusive and sympathetic reflection of the history and heritage of Wales, looked forward to a new perspective in Anglo-Welsh literature. If earlier (although not necessarily older) writers like Davies and Dylan Thomas, whether consciously or unconsciously, made Wales seem backward and exotic, those who came later—Jones, R. S. Thomas, Roland Mathias, Emyr Humphreys in his novels, Gwyn Williams in his translations of ancient Welsh poetry—all sought individually to conserve the culture and traditions of Wales and to interpret them sympathetically for the English-speaking Welsh.

Although the early 1950s were, as Roland Mathias has pointed out, transitional years[3] (Dylan Thomas was at the end of his career, David Jones and R. S. Thomas were scarcely known, the great contemporary flowering of Anglo-Welsh poetry would not begin until the mid-1960s), even then Lewis's conclusions were being implicitly challenged by the work of Welsh writers in English. An editorial in the Spring 1952 issue of *Dock Leaves* (now the *Anglo-Welsh Review*), which had been founded in 1949, expressed the hope that "'someone will persuade a publishing house to put forth a badly needed anthology of Anglo-Welsh poetry from the seventeenth century to the twentieth' such as might be used in school and college courses."[4] The motive, of course, was not simply to make known to students a body of often distinguished poetry, but to acquaint them as well with a major part of their history and cultural heritage. Now, more than thirty years later, the anthology has at last appeared. Edited by Raymond Garlick and Roland Mathias, two of the founders of *Dock Leaves,* and published by Poetry Wales Press with the financial assistance of the Welsh Arts Council, *Anglo-Welsh Poetry 1480–1980* includes the work of 124 poets, from Ieuan ap Hywel Swrdwal (fl. 1430–80) to Robert Minhinnick (b. 1952) and Mike Jenkins (b. 1953). The collection is doubly valuable, for it both represents clearly the long tradition of Anglo-Welsh poetry and brings together at last generous and judicious selections from the work of the important Anglo-Welsh poets of our time.

Although, as the editors explain, the seventeenth century seemed, in 1952, the obvious point at which to begin the anthology, in the following year D. M. and E. H. Lloyd edited *A Book of Wales,* whose introduction suggested that Anglo-Welsh poetry had its origins not with the Herberts and Vaughans of the seventeenth century, but in 1470, more than a hundred years before: "The earliest effort at literary composition in English by a Welshman, of which we have any record, is very much a *tour-de-force.* It is an eulogistic poem to the Virgin by an Oxford student, composed in the fifteenth century."[5] The poem, written by Ieuan ap Hywel Swrdwal, was published in the *Transactions of the Honourable Society of Cymmrodorian* in 1955 with a linguistic study by E. J. Dobson of Jesus College, Oxford. "The Hymm to the Virgin," which uses a traditional verse pattern, alliteration, and a rhyme scheme of Welsh poetry, encouraged further search for genuine Anglo-Welsh writing prior to the twentieth century. Though some critics still locate its beginnings only within the last seventy years, both Raymond Garlick and Roland Mathias have argued convincingly for a five-hundred-year tradition of Anglo-Welsh literature (the former in his groundbreaking volume in the Writers of Wales series, *An Introduction to Anglo-Welsh Literature,* first published in 1970; the latter in his recently published *Anglo-Welsh Literature: An Illustrated History*), and their anthology provides the empirical evidence for it.

Anglo-Welsh poetry, at least as the editors define it in their introduction, is poetry written in English by those who "either had indissoluble connections with the Wales of the past or see themselves as part of the Welsh literary scene in the present" (43). If the definition, as they recognize, is a generous one, it can include, as it should, such poets as Jon Dressel, who was born in St. Louis of Welsh-immigrant parents; Joseph Clancy, an Irish-American poet from the Bronx who has distinguished himself as a translator of Welsh poetry; Jeremy Hooker, an Englishman who has taught at University College Wales in Aberystwyth; and Raymond Garlick himself, who was born in London of English parents but raised and educated in Wales. (The two puzzling absences are Gerard Manley Hopkins and Edward Thomas, each of whom, in different ways, had strong connections to Wales.) Still, for all the generosity of their definition, the poems here seem more closely related than one might at first expect. Anglo-Welsh poetry is different from English or American poetry first of all because it is the work of a minority, written more often than not out of the experience of being Welsh and of living, actually or imaginatively, in Wales, and also because it is shaped, in part at least, by the indigenous language and the heritage of the place out of which it is written.

The troubled relation of the two languages in Wales has generally been the argument advanced against an Anglo-Welsh poetic tradition. It presents itself roughly in the form of three questions. First, does not a Welsh poet, by writing poetry in English, actually contribute to the displacement of Welsh—help, in R. S. Thomas's words, to dig a grave for the language? Second, can one actually write about Wales and the experience of being Welsh in a language that expresses an alien tradition and thus necessarily lacks the rich resonance, for Wales and its people, of the Welsh language? (Some would ask the second question a little differently: can a poet write

about his heritage and his own experience of it in the language of its oppressor?) Third, can one really know what it is to be Welsh without knowing the language of Wales? As R. S. Thomas has written, "Let nobody imagine that because there is so much English elsewhere in Wales it is not a foreign language. . . . I have neither the instinct nor the confidence (in Welsh) which are essential for anyone who wishes to use language in the most skillful ways possible, namely in writing poetry. . . . I have had to steep myself in the history and traditions of Wales, but I am quite conscious of the way in which the contemporary cosmopolitan world has shattered these traditions. . . . In the Wales in which we live there is no literary answer to the literary problem."[6]

Although there is indeed no answer, such arguments have not prevented Welsh men and women from writing, out of their experience of Wales, a distinct body of often distinguished poetry in English. In an essay that admittedly looked (if one can make such a distinction) at the allusive rather than the political or ideological dimensions of language, David Jones suggested perhaps the only answer possible.

> I see it as a civilizational situation—of traditions wholly or partly lost—of linguistic changes that can't be overcome. And, after all, all "artists" or "poets" of whatever sort can best work within the civilizational or cultural setting in which they find themselves. They are not responsible for the particular circumstances into which they were born. So I suppose the most that any of us can do is to "show forth" the things that seem real to us and which we have inherited by this accident or that. It does not matter much whether it's appreciated at all. What does matter is that one feels oneself that it is *valid*.[7]

Although they have had no choice but to write in English, the poets one would call Anglo-Welsh have created, in English, a recognizable body of poetry whose formal, functional, and thematic characteristics have been shaped and conditioned by Welsh-language poetry and by the place in and about which it is written.

The Anglo-Welsh poet, like his or her Welsh-language counterpart, tends to think of himself as a bard, a poet who plays a public role in his community and is responsible to celebrate or criticize it. As Welsh poetry has from its beginnings, Anglo-Welsh poetry reflects the particular world in which it is written, the particular community to which the poet belongs. At the same time, Anglo-Welsh poetry is also characterized by what Roland Mathias once called "the affection it continues to demonstrate for comparatively severe structural forms."[8] Although it is rarely as formally demanding as traditional Welsh poetry, it is generally more aware of time and place, of history and geography, than is American or English poetry. The history may be only personal, the place simply some small village somewhere in Wales, but the Anglo-Welsh poem characteristically reflects "a local habitation and a name." While the poetry is usually not explicitly political, it often has political implications and, for a variety of reasons, an elegiac tone. Though he would probably have never claimed it, the intricate aural and stanzaic patterns, the strong sense of place, and the elegiac remembrance of things past make Dylan Thomas's magnificent "Fern Hill" an unmistakably Anglo-Welsh poem.

The great value of Garlick and Mathias's much-needed and long-awaited anthology is that it can provide entry into a poetic tradition about which very little is known, either in or out of Wales. (Soon after its publication, a generous patron of Anglo-Welsh literature offered to pay the cost of placing a copy of the book in every school library in Wales so that young Welsh men and women will have an opportunity to discover the English-language poetry of their nation.) On the one hand, the collection makes it possible to read such relatively better known poets as George Herbert, Henry Vaughan, Dylan Thomas, Vernon Watkins, and R. S. Thomas not as English poets, but in the context of the tradition to which they belong and which they themselves have shaped. (George Herbert's picture poems "The Altar" and "Easter Wings" seem much more at home in Wales than in England.) On the other hand, the collection at last makes easily available in the appropriate context a wise and representative selection of the work of such distinguished contemporary Anglo-Welsh poets as Roland Mathias, Dannie Abse, Leslie Norris, John Ormond, and Gillian Clarke, whose work deserves a wider reading than it has so far received. For the contemporary poets as well the collection makes at least partially possible what Roland Mathias once insisted readers of Anglo-Welsh poetry need: "a recognition of the special qualities of the Welsh-English background and its historical and literary ancestry. The basic fault is to imagine that one can deal with a text *in vacuo,* even if one does manage to identify what the poet means to say. The validity of that meaning can only be judged satisfactorily against an understanding of the society that produced it. . . . Anglo-Welsh writing suffers continually from the assumption that its origins differ so little from those of, let us say, an ex-Mercian society that no examination of them is necessary."[9]

To call these poets Anglo-Welsh is, as Roland Mathias implies, in no sense to narrow or depreciate their achievement, for the distinct characteristics of Anglo-Welsh poetry work themselves out in a wide and resonant variety of ways. Although their poems are often set in Wales and grow out of the experience of being Welsh, they consistently transcend their particular settings quietly and skillfully to speak, with great power and eloquence, of significant human experience. "The Key" by John Ormond, for example, is set in the small Welsh village in which the poet was born and recalls the way life was once lived there, but the poem is finally a deft and resonant evocation of the joy and fragility of ordinary life.

The key was as long as my hand,
The ring of it the size
Of a girl's bangle. The bit
Was inches square. A grandiose key
Fit for a castle, yet our terraced
House was two rooms up, two down;
Flung there by sullen pit-owners
In a spasm of petulance, discovering
That colliers could not live
On the bare Welsh mountain:
Like any other house in the domino
Row, except that our door
Was nearly always on the latch.
Most people just walked in, with
'Anybody home?' in greeting
To the kitchen. This room
Saw paths of generations cross;
This was the place to which we all came
Back to talk by the oven, on the white
Bench. This was the home patch.
. . . .
The others have gone for the long
Night away. The evidence of grass
Re-growing insists on it. This time
I come back to dispose of what there is.
The knack's still with me. I plunge home
The key's great stem, insinuate
Something that was myself between
The two old litigants. The key
Engages and the bolt gives to me
Some walls enclosing furniture.

Roland Mathias's "Brechfa Chapel" takes its title and setting from a place not far from the poet's home, yet the poem, which continues what Raymond Garlick calls the "preoccupation"[10] of Anglo-Welsh poetry "with the metaphysical," confronts the loss of belief and of a sense of community in the fragmented world in which all of us, like the Welsh, now, in one way or another, live.

The farmers, separate in their lands, hedge,
Ditch, no doubt, and keep tight pasture. Uphill
They trudge on seventh days, singly, putting
Their heads to the pews as habit bids them to,
And keep counsel. The books, in pyramid, sit tidy

On the pulpit. The back gallery looks
Swept. But the old iron gate to the common,
Rusted a little, affords not a glimpse
Of the swan in her dream on the reed-knot
Nor of the anxious coot enquiring of the grasses.
The hellish noise it is appals, the intolerable shilly-
Shally of birds quitting the nearer mud
For the farther, harrying the conversation
Of faith. Each on his own must stand and conjure
The strong remembered words, the unanswerable
Texts against chaos.

Leslie Norris's "Elegy for David Beynon," which takes the familiar Anglo-Welsh form of a portrait poem, grows out of the death of a teacher and his pupils in a schoolhouse destroyed by a landslide in Merthyr Tydfil but ends with the poet's inevitably human inability to find words to pay tribute to his dead friend.

I think those children, those who died
under your arms in the crushed school,

would understand that I make this
your elegy. I know the face you had,
have walked with you enough mornings
under the fallen leaves. Theirs is
the great anonymous tragedy one word
will summarise. Aberfan, I write it
for them here, knowing we've paid to it
our shabby pence, and now it can be stored

with whatever names there are where
children end their briefest pilgrimage.
I cannot find the words for you, David. These
are too long, too many; and not enough.

Glyn Jones's extraordinarily moving poem "The Common Path," which describes some chance meetings of a schoolboy on the common with a school-mistress, mourns all our terrible failures of sympathy and concern for other human beings.

On one side the hedge, on the other the brook:
Each afternoon I passed, unnoticed,
The middle-aged schoolmistress, grey-haired,
Gay, loving, who went home along the path.

That spring she walked briskly, carrying her bag
With the long ledger, the ruler, the catkin twigs,
Two excited little girls from her class
Chattering around their smiling teacher.

Summer returned, each day then she approached
     slowly,
     Alone, wholly absorbed, as though in defeat
Between water and hazels, her eyes heedless,
     Her grey face deeply cast down. Could it be
Grief at the great universal agony had begun
     To feed upon her heart—war, imbecility,

Old age, starving, children's deaths, deformities?
     I, free, white, gentile, born neither
Dwarf nor idiot, passed her by, drawing in
     The skirts of my satisfaction, on the other side.
One day, at the last instant of our passing,
     She became, suddenly, aware of me
And, as her withdrawn glance met my eyes,
     Her whole face kindled into life, I heard
From large brown eyes a blare of terror, anguished
     Supplication, her cry of doom, death, despair.
And in the warmth of that path's sunshine
     And of my small and manageable success
I felt at once repelled, affronted by her suffering,
     The naked shamelessness of that wild despair.
Troubled, I avoided the common until I heard
     Soon, very soon, the schoolmistress, not from
Any agony of remote and universal suffering
     Or unendurable grief for others, but
Private, middle-aged, rectal cancer, was dead.
What I remember, and in twenty years have
     Never expiated, is that my impatience,
That one glance of my intolerance,
     Rejected her, and so rejected all
The sufferings of wars, imprisonments,
     Deformities, starvation, idiocy, old age—
Because fortune, sunlight, meaningless success,
     Comforted an instant what must not be comforted.

Though these poems are all (to borrow the words of John Ormond) set on "the home patch" and draw their power from it, they have been written by poets whose craft and vision make clear, through the concrete particulars of their poems, that the central, abiding truths of our lives are seen and felt in the ordinary events that engage them and the familiar places in which we live them.

As the collection of poems in the anthology makes clear, the greatest achievements of Anglo-Welsh poetry have been reached in the last fifty years. In addition to the work of the distinguished poets already mentioned, the volume includes fine pieces by such other Anglo-Welsh poets as Idris Davies, Harri Webb, T. Harri Jones, Raymond Garlick, John Tripp, Anthony Conran, Meic Stephens, Jeremy Hooker, Tony Curtis, Sheenagh Pugh, and Robert Minhinnick, to name only a few. Many of the earlier poems are only historically interesting; the excellent work in the latter part of the volume is characteristic of the achievement of Anglo-Welsh poetry in our own time, however, and one can only hope it will help make this rich and distinguished body of modern poetry more widely known throughout the English-speaking world.

The appearance of an anthology of Anglo-Welsh poetry in 1984 inevitably raises a question which cannot, at this point, be answered with any certainty: can we reasonably expect that something we might fairly call Anglo-Welsh poetry will continue much longer to be written in Wales? The answer, of course, depends in part on whether the Welsh language itself will survive and in part on whether Wales will succeed in conserving whatever remains of its distinct culture and heritage despite the countless pressures against it. Still, if the future of Wales is by no means assured, it is not yet lost either. The work of the younger writers in the anthology suggests that Anglo-Welsh (rather than English) poetry is still being written in Wales, and the efforts of many to foster its language and culture may yet keep Wales out of the Anglo-American melting pot. One hopes they will, for Wales continues to give the world two distinguished bodies of literature, one in Welsh and the other in English. The dragon, as Glyn Jones put it in the title of his book, has two tongues, and when it speaks in English, as the Garlick/Mathias collection makes clear, it speaks with great beauty and resonance, not just of itself, but (to use the words of Dylan Thomas) of the "heart's truth" in the world at large. Here is the next-to-last poem in the anthology, "Chartist Meeting," an Anglo-Welsh poem by Mike Jenkins, who was born in Aberystwyth in 1953 and now teaches in Merthyr Tydfil. It suggests, I think, that thus far Anglo-Welsh poetry survives.

The people came to listen
looking down valley as they tramped;
the iron track was a ladder
from a loft to the open sea—
salt filling the air like pollen.

Each wheel was held fast
as you would grip a coin;
yet everything went away from them.
The black kernel of the mountains
seemed endless, but still in their stomachs
a furnace-fire roared,
and their children's eyes hammered
and turned and hollowed out a cannon.

Steam was like a spiral of wool
threaded straight down the valley,
lost past a colliery.
The tramways held the slope
as though they were wood of a pen.
Wives and children were miniatures
of the hill, the coal engrained
in enclosures on their skin.

They shook hands with the sky
an old friend; there, at the field,
oak trees turned to crosses
their trunks bent with the weight
of cloud and wind, and harsh grass

from marshes that Morgan Williams,
the weaver, could raise into a pulpit.

A thousand listened, as way below them
Cyfarthfa Castle was set like a diamond
in a ring of green,
and the stalks of chimneys
bloomed continuous smoke and flame.

The Welsh that was spoken
chuckled with streams, plucked bare rock,
and men like Morgan Williams
saw in the burnt hands a harvest of votes.

Michael J. Collins, Winter 1989

1 Saunders Lewis, "Is There an Anglo-Welsh Literature?," Cardiff, University of Wales Press, 1939, p. 13.

2 Quoted in Raymond Garlick, *An Introduction to Anglo-Welsh Literature*, 2d ed., Cardiff, University of Wales Press, 1972, p. 11.

3 Roland Mathias, "Literature in English," in *The Arts in Wales: 1950–1975*, Meic Stephens, ed., Cardiff, Welsh Arts Council, 1979.

4 Quoted in the "Introduction" to *Anglo-Welsh Poetry 1480–1980*, Raymond Garlick and Roland Mathias, eds., Bridgend, Mid Glamorgan, Poetry Wales, 1984, p. 27. For a review, see *WLT* 59:2 (Spring 1985), p. 305.

5 Quoted in the "Introduction" to *Anglo-Welsh Poetry 1480–1980*, p. 28.

6 R. S. Thomas, in *Planet*, 41 (January 1978). Quoted in David Smith, "Confronting the Minotaur: Politics and Poetry in 20th Century Wales," *Poetry Wales*, 15:3 (Winter 1979/80), p. 11.

7 David Jones, "On the Difficulties of One Writer of Welsh Affinity Whose Language is English," in his book *The Dying Gaul and Other Writings*, London, Faber & Faber, 1978, p. 34.

8 Roland Mathias, "Introduction" to *Green Horse: An Anthology by Young Poets of Wales*, Meic Stephens and Peter Finch, eds., Swansea, Christopher Davies, 1978, p. 17.

9 Roland Mathias, in "Anglo-Welsh Symposium on Critical Issues: Pieces from Seventeen Anglo-Welsh Poets, Critics, and Academics," *Poetry Wales* 15:2 (Autumn 1979), p. 27.

10 Garlick, *An Introduction to Anglo-Welsh Literature*, p. 60.

Place and Displacement in Salman Rushdie's Work

Salman Rushdie is not only an "almost textbook example" of a self-reflexive postmodern novelist;[1] he is also—not coincidentally—one of the most persuasive spokesmen we have for the benefits, in increased tolerance and moral understanding, of cultural displacement. Because he has been forced "to find new ways of describing himself, new ways of being human,"[2] Rushdie argues, the immigrant or expatriate is in a better position than the rest of us to appreciate the pluralistic, contradictory nature of contemporary experience: to accept the fact that "reality is an artefact," for example, or that "meaning is a shaky edifice we build out of scraps, dogmas, childhood injuries, newspaper articles, chance remarks, old films, small victories, people hated, people loved" (*IH*, 12). Particularly in this "century of wandering," in this age when traditional cultures are being drawn more and more into conflict and confrontation, it is the immigrant writer who is best equipped, by the kind of "double vision" attributed to Gibreel Farishta and Saladin Chamcha in *The Satanic Verses*,[3] to come up with the corresponding new literary forms: "the mingling of fantasy and naturalism" (*IH*, 19), say, or the patching together of a narrative out of the "shards of memory" (*IH*, 11–12). Indeed, in Rushdie's view, the immigrant has become "the central or defining figure of the twentieth century" (*IH*, 177), dramatizing "in an intensified form" the sense of alienation, of cultural discontinuity, to which, as "immigrants from the past," we are all increasingly prone (*IH*, 12).

Of all Rushdie's books, it is probably in *Shame* that the effects of cultural displacement are most fully discussed, that the benefits of an alienated "off-centering" perspective are most persuasively argued. Not only is the book narrated primarily from the point of view of its "peripheral" or repressed or rejected characters, "its 'male' plot refracted, so to speak, through the prisms of its reverse and 'female' side."[4] Not only does it return, over and over again, to the theme of cultural dislocation, to the sense of "a world turned upside-down": "the fear that one is living at the edge of the world, so close that he might fall off at any moment: (*S*, 15). But it also attempts, through what Aruna Srivastava describes as "acts of reader estrangement,"[5] to infect its audience with this same sense of cultural "vertigo": jolting us (for example) with its unexpected shifts from the Western to the "Hegiran" calendar (*S*, 6), with its casual introduction into a realistic modern narrative of fairy-tale motifs long ago "consigned to peripheries by conventions of disbelief" (*S*, 219), with its teasing "metafictive" asides on the novel that it might have become instead of this one (*S*, 70–72)—with, above all perhaps, its superbly incongruous metaphors: its description of Isky Harappa's death cell as an "inverse womb" (*S*, 254) or of battered women and children as "janitors of the unseen," vessels for all the "unfelt shame" in the world, "their souls the buckets into which squeegees drip what-was-spilled" (*S*, 131–32).

Although he is obviously aware of the pain and disorientation involved, Rushdie seems to regard cultural displacement as essentially a positive and liberating experience, one of the best ways in the world "of seeking freedom" (*S*, 90). To people "living in the aftermath of

the death of God and of tragedy," for example, it must seem inconceivable "that men will sacrifice their dearest love on the implacable altars of their pride": that they will physically abuse and humiliate their daughter for having been born female or murder her "because by making love to a white boy she has brought such dishonour upon her family that only her blood can wash away the stain." Such behavior is conceivable only to people brought up in traditional patriarchal or authoritarian societies, to people raised "on a diet of honour and shame" (*S*, 123–24). In helping to free us from such a society, therefore, in offering us an "anti-belonging" pill that will allow us to "float upwards from history, from memory, from Time" (*S*, 91), Rushdie feels that he is performing a positive moral and intellectual service. As Mark Edmundson has observed concerning *The Satanic Verses*, homelessness in Rushdie's view seems to be a condition "to be affirmed, because it allows for more metamorphosis, change, the ability (and the need) to be other than one was."[6] In *The Satanic Verses* in particular, one of the central questions is how "newness" comes into the world: "Of what fusions, translations, conjoinings is it made?" (*SV*, 8).

Helpful as such an alienated "off-centering" perspective can be in understanding Rushdie, however, it is equally illuminating to take the opposite approach: to consider his work from the point of view of someone like Wendell Berry, who is a critic of our "'pluralistic,' displaced global economy," a defender instead of "all rooted, locally adapted cultures that know what works and what doesn't work in a given place."[7] Far from simply advocating the benefits of cultural dislocation, it can be seen from this perspective that Rushdie is just as concerned with its social or psychological dangers. In the same passage in *Shame* in which he equates migration with freedom, in which he speculates on the possibility of an antigravity pill that "would make migrants of us all," he goes on to reflect, more soberly, on the price of such mobility: on the loss of moral meaning, the lapse of cultural continuity. If the best thing about "migrant peoples and seceded nations" is their "hopefulness," he concedes, then the worst is "the emptiness of [their] luggage. I'm speaking of invisible suitcases, not the physical, perhaps cardboard variety containing a few meaning-drained mementoes" (*S*, 91). In *Midnight's Children* Saleem Sinai's displacement from his "Bombay roots" results in a "haze of unreality," in his being completely "emptied of history" and plunged, like India itself, into a state of moral amnesia.[8] "Nothing was real; nothing certain," Saleem observes of the "diseased reality" of his Pakistani years (*MC*, 406).

Far from embracing the "simplistic idea of 'freedom'" attributed by Berry to alienated modernists and romantics like Shelley—the belief that "the human place is any place," that "we can fulfill a high human destiny anywhere, any way"[9]—Rushdie seems in passages such as these to be as concerned as Berry himself about whether, having been uprooted from its native soil, having been "driven into the mind" by the conditions of modern "careerism and specialization," it is possible for a cultural heritage to survive: "The mere memory of a place cannot preserve it, nor apart from the place can it long survive in the mind."[10] Even when migrants pack their past "into bundles and boxes" and try to take it with them, Rushdie points out, "on the journey something seeps out of the treasured mementoes and old photographs, until even their owners fail to recognize them." What from one point of view seems to be an opportunity for change and moral transformation is from another a process of cultural dispossession and degradation, for "it is the fate of migrants to be stripped of history, to stand naked amidst the scorn of strangers upon whom they see the rich clothing, the brocades of continuity and the eyebrows of belonging" (S, 64). Saleem Sinai's grandmother is not unusual at all among Rushdie's characters in feeling that, "for all her presence and bulk, she was adrift in the universe" (MC, 42).

One indication of Rushdie's ambivalence about the ultimate value of cultural alienation is his preoccupation throughout Shame with the relationship between the imaginary country of his novel, his "fairyland" or "looking-glass Pakistan," and its real-life counterpart. Writers and politicians are alike, he maintains—they are "natural rivals" of one another—because they are both always trying to impose their vision on reality, "to make the world over in their own image" (IH, 14). Pakistan, in particular, is an example of a country which, instead of evolving naturally out of a local native culture, was dreamed up by expatriate Muslim politicians in London and then "was borne-across or trans-lated, and imposed itself on history; a returning migrant, settling down on partitioned land, forming a palimpsest on the past." Instead of accommodating itself to existing cultural realities, instead of incorporating "parts and relics of its own history,"[11] it was invented precisely in order to suppress and conceal that past, in order "to cover up Indian history, to deny that Indian centuries lay just beneath the surface of Pakistani Standard Time." That is why today Pakistan can be described as a "peeling, fragmenting palimpsest, increasingly at war with itself," as a country in which the repressed element is always struggling to force "its way back through what-had-been-imposed" (S, 91–92).

What is the difference, though, between an alien political idea like Pakistan that has been imposed by outsiders on an indigenous local culture and the "imaginary countries" which, according to Rushdie's own account, expatriate writers like himself are always trying "to impose on the ones that exist"? If one can be criticized as a "palimpsest on the past," as a political fiction designed to conceal and suppress the truth, why can the same objection not be made to the other, to what Rushdie himself candidly describes as "my story's palimpsest-country"? (S, 92). This is the question that seems to nag Rushdie from beginning to end in Shame, that has him brooding in one passage over the adequacy of his language ("this Angrezi in which I am forced to write and so for ever alter what is written") to his central theme—"Sharam, that's the word. For which this paltry 'shame' is a wholly inadequate translation" (S, 34)—and has him squirming in another over imagined challenges by indignant native critics to his authority as a writer, to his right (as an "Outsider! Trespasser!") to his subject matter: "you, with your foreign language wrapped around you like a flag: speaking about us in your forked tongue, what can you tell but lies?" (S, 23). What if it is really the case, Rushdie seems to be wondering in passages such as these, that as an emigrant writer he is nothing but a fantasist, cut off by his "physical alienation" from telling the truth about his subject and condemned to the fabrication of fictions, "not actual cities or villages, but invisible ones, imaginary homelands, Indias of the mind" (IH, 10)? How is he any better than the repressive political leaders attacked in Shame or Midnight's Children for their efforts to abolish history, to impose political and moral amnesia on an entire nation?

Broadly considered, the question to which Rushdie keeps returning in Shame as well as in his other novels is that of the mimetic or referential function of art: whether the literary work can be regarded more plausibly as being about external reality or about its own internal literary or linguistic or semiotic processes. Considering the position he takes on cultural displacement, it is probably not surprising that, on the surface at least, Rushdie seems to endorse the familiar postmodern belief that the literary work is "an autonomous, self-sufficient 'world' or law unto itself, independent of the external world."[12] "The migrant intellect roots itself in itself," he observes approvingly, "in its own capacity for imagining and reimagining the world" (IH, 280), and from the way he talks about "imaginary homelands" and "Indias of the mind"—from the way he conjures up fanciful "Peccavistans" (S, 93) or "Peristans" (MC, 486)—it seems likely that he might say the same thing about the artistic imagination in general.

Not only does Rushdie like to emphasize the extent to which real people and places have been imaginatively "off-centered" in his work in order to satisfy the requirements of art—the fact that his fictional country is "not quite" Pakistan, for example, or that Omar's hometown is "not really" Quetta (S, 23–24)—he also likes to emphasize the fallibility of the human intellect or memory, describing it as a "broken mirror" or "cracked lens," capable only of "fractured perceptions" (IH, 10–12). Instead of being concerned primarily with his subject matter or themes, he is often more preoccupied in his novels with what he refers to as "the process of filtration itself": with the way in which memory "selects, eliminates, alters, exaggerates, minimizes, glorifies, and vilifies," in which "in the end it creates its own reality, its heterogeneous but usually coherent version of events" (MC, 253). At times, in fact, Rushdie seems to have taken what Gerald Graff regards as the inevitable next step for an antimimetic postmodernist:[13] that of deciding that reality itself is a construct or fiction, "that it does not exist until it is made, and that, like any other artefact, it can be made well or badly" (IH, 280). He seems to have succumbed to what Saleem Sinai describes as "the temptation of every autobiographer, to the illusion that since the past exists only in one's memories and the words which strive vainly to encapsulate them, it is possible to create past events simply by saying they occurred" (MC, 529).

Though the self-reflexive, antimimetic strain in Rushdie should not be ignored, however, neither should the emphasis in his work on "the communal nature of the artistic process"—on the obligation of the writer "to preserve memory against disintegration, 'to save a nation from amnesia,' by creating a repository of the past."[14] Everywhere in Rushdie's books we find indications of his continuing attachment to "the East": Saleem Sinai's joy on returning to Bombay from Pakistan and rediscovering "the rainbow riot of the city" (MC, 356), Saladin Chamcha's frustration on coming back for a visit and finding that the city "isn't home" any more (SV, 58), Rushdie's own reported feeling of outrage on hearing that his father had sold his boyhood home (S, 90). "What to do?" he asks about such feelings of estrangement and alienation: "Shrug. And pickle the past in books" (IH, 277).

One of the most compelling motives for any expatriate writer, Rushdie maintains, is the "urge to reclaim, to look back, even at the risk of being mutated into pillars of salt." Like James Joyce or Günter Grass or Milan Kundera—"like many people who have lost a city"—the reason he turned to writing to begin with was his love of place, his need to "restore the past to [himself], not in the faded greys of old family album snapshots, but whole, in CinemaScope and glorious Technicolor" (IH, 10). This is why he refers to his books as "novels of memory"—because they are designed to fulfill basically

the same function that Wendell Berry assigns to the writer: that of reminding us of "what is remembered and ought to be remembered."[15] Far from treating the world simply as a construct, in fact, Rushdie's books should be read as indictments of those forces in modern politics and economics that threaten to subvert our sense of reality. It is necessary for writers to resort to their "pickling of Time" in the first place, after all, only because "in a country where the truth is what it is instructed to be, reality quite literally ceases to exist" (MC, 389).

If it really is Rushdie's view that the function of the writer is to preserve or reclaim the past, however, then what are we to make of the belief, evident throughout his work, that one "version" of the past is just as valid or defensible as another—that the writer and the politician are perfectly equivalent in their desire "to make the world in their own image"? Can Rushdie really believe, when he focuses in Shame on the experience of the "peripheral" or repressed characters, for example, that the resulting "version" is no more balanced or complete than the "official, politicians' version" that it was designed to correct—that it is "no more than one version of all the hundreds of millions of possible versions" (IH, 10)? If he does believe this, then how can he turn around, in the same passage, and attack the state for "distorting reality, altering the past to fit its present needs"? How can he characterize the writer's resistance to state power as being, in Milan Kundera's phrase, "the struggle of memory against forgetting"? (IH, 14). Surely either of these descriptions implies a distinction of some sort in the truth or adequacy or coherence of different "versions." Surely it implies some standard of reference, independent of any particular "version," by which its adequacy or truth could be determined.[16]

One indication that Rushdie does in fact believe in a reality independent of our minds, to which the literary work might be thought of as in some sense referring, can be seen in the form of Shame: in the way in which, instead of concealing its internal consistencies beneath a "palimpsest" of stylistic coherence or unity, the book deliberately presents itself as a product of conflicting inspirations, as the result of revision and reconsideration. By its nature, Rushdie points out, the decision by a writer to tell one particular story, to employ one point of view or one specific set of stylistic conventions, tends to function as a "kind of censorship," precluding the telling of any other story, the exploration of all other formal or stylistic possibilities (S, 72–73). Like the physicist or sociologist, the writer tends to become a victim of what Kenneth Burke refers to as the "impulse to perfection":[17] the temptation, inherent in all language, to reduce a complex, multifarious reality to the dimensions of a single metaphor or model, to pretend (as Wayne Booth puts it) that "all life, the entire world, is *like* this piece of it."[18] It is because he is so sensitive to this danger, of course, that Saleem Sinai agonizes throughout *Midnight's Children* over the demands imposed on him as a story-teller by "the world of linear narrative, the universe of what-happened-next" (*MC,* 38).

One method employed by Rushdie to combat this "terministic compulsion"—to introduce into *Shame* a "sense of the complexity, the cross-graining, of real experience"[19]—is that of preserving in the final form of the book many of the earlier or alternative "versions" normally discarded in the process of revision, many of the "ghosts of the stories" that it might have become. Instead of letting the work become a palimpsest in the sense applied to Pakistan, in other words, he has turned it into a palimpsest as Wendell Berry defines the term: something which (like a handwritten page or a "well-crafted table or cabinet") "contains parts and relics of its own history—erasures, passages crossed out, interlineations, suggesting that there is something to go back to as well as something to go forward to."[20] To use Saleem Sinai's favorite analogy for the self-conscious narrator, he performs in the novel "like an incompetent puppeteer," always revealing "the hands holding the strings" (*MC,* 72).

In one characteristic passage, for example, Rushdie speculates at length on some of the "real-life material" that he might have felt compelled to include if, instead of the present book, he had decided to write a realistic novel about Pakistan: the subterranean water pumps installed in his parents' Karachi suburb to steal water from their neighbors; the sign in front of the Sind Club in Karachi that reads "Women and Dogs Not Allowed Beyond This Point"; "the film censor who took his red pencil to each frame of the scene in the film *Night of the Generals* in which Peter O'Toole visits an art gallery, and scratched out all the paintings of naked ladies hanging on the walls" (*S,* 71–72). The only problem with such material, Rushdie points out after a couple of pages, is that the book would almost certainly have been banned in Pakistan—"banned, dumped in the bin, burned. All that effort for nothing!" It is for this reason, he coyly concludes, that he decided on writing a "sort of modern fairy-tale" instead: "nobody need get upset, or take anything I say too seriously. No drastic action need be taken, either. What a relief!" (*S,* 72).

Meanwhile, though, Rushdie has succeeded in smuggling into his "fairy-story" whole pages of a book which, since it is almost the exact generic antithesis of this one, ought logically to have been completely suppressed. Rather than following the option attributed by

Wendell Berry to Hemingway in "Big Two-Hearted River" of sacrificing depth and scope of understanding for the sake of "literary purity,"[21] he seems to have adopted precisely the opposite approach: that of incorporating into the fabric of his work a suggestion of "the doubleness, the essential mysteriousness" of human experience itself.[22] In doing so, of course, he has imaginatively reaffirmed that skepticism—that suspicion of "all total explanations, all systems of thought which purport to be complete" (*IH,* 280)—which he maintains is the principal legacy of the immigrant's "double vision."

Even more important perhaps than the passages in which he speculates on the books he might have written instead of this one are those in which Rushdie discusses the real-life sources or inspiration for his novel. The passage, for example, in which he tells us about his friend, the Pakistani poet, who was "hung upside-down by the ankles and beaten" in Zia's prison "as if he were a new-born baby whose lungs had to be coerced into action so he could squeal" (*S,* 22). It is this friend, Rushdie feels, who probably should be telling the present story ("or another one, his own"), and in one of his first important passages emphasizing the "off-centering" effects of the poetic imagination, he goes on to point out some of the parallels between his friend's experience and that of his fictional hero Omar Khayyam Shakil: the fact that the latter has also been "ankle-hung" as a baby, for example, or—though "no quatrains ever issued or will issue from his pen"—that he bears the same name as a famous poet (*S,* 23). Though Rushdie likes to emphasize the extent to which it has been fictionally "off-centered" or "displaced"—to which it now exists, "like [himself], at a slight angle to reality" (*S,* 24)—in passages such as this one he seems to be reminding us that in fact his "looking-glass Pakistan" is firmly rooted in real experience,[23] that in contrast to the autonomous "word-worlds" of Berry's "specialist-poets" it actually does represent "a point of clarification between [himself] and the world . . . an adventure into [the] reality or mystery outside [himself]."[24] The same sort of reminder is provided in *Midnight's Children* by the references to parallel political events going on simultaneously with Saleem Sinai's life.

The most obvious exploration in *Shame* of the relationship between fiction and reality is probably the passage in which Rushdie describes the real-life origins of his heroine Sufiya Zinobia, beginning with the case—"not so long ago, in the East of London"—in which a young Pakistani girl was murdered by her father "because by making love to a white boy she had brought such dishonour upon her family that only her blood could wash away the stain" (*S,* 123). Interested in writing a story about shame, Rushdie recalls, he found himself "haunted by the imagined spectre of that dead [girl's] body, its throat slit like a halal chicken, lying in a London night across a zebra crossing." At first, apparently, he thought he could write about her realistically: her East London accent, her jeans ("blue brown pink"), her contempt for her parents' native language. "Anna Muhammad: lively, no doubt attractive, a little too dangerously so at sixteen. Mecca meant ballrooms to her, rotating silver balls, strobe lighting, youth." Eventually, however, the girl eluded him— "she became a ghost"— and Rushdie decided that "to write about her, about shame, [he] would have to go back East, to let the idea breathe its favorite air." That is how his character came to be "deported, repatriated to a country she had never seen," how she "caught brain-fever and turned into a sort of idiot"—in response not so much to the exigencies of art, apparently, as to those of place (S, 124–25).

Not that the process of fictional "off-centering" ended there, of course, for Rushdie goes on to tell the stories of at least two other "phantoms"—from "Proper London" instead of "spectral 'Pecca-vistan'"—who also "haunt" his book, who, as he describes them, are also "inside my heroine" waiting to "pop out": that of a boy found burning in a parking lot one day who, as the experts were forced to conclude, must "simply [have] ignited of his own accord, without dousing himself in petrol or applying external flame"; and that of an "Asian" girl "set upon" in a late-night subway by a gang of white boys, whom Rushdie gleefully imagines lashing back at her assailants, "breaking arms legs noses balls, without knowing whence the violence came, without seeing how she, so slight in figure, could command such awesome strength" (S, 125–26). The purpose of such stories, of course, is to illustrate the way in which, as they are refracted through the "cracked lens" of art, the facts of experience wind up being imaginatively "displaced": in Rushdie's own novel, for example, the way in which the fury of the rioters rampaging across his television screen has been displaced, first to the "Asian" girl humiliated in the subway and then, through her, to Sufiya Zinobia as "shame's avatar"; or the way in which Anna Muhammad's ignominious death by stabbing has been deflected, first to victims like Sindbad Mengal or Little Mir Harappa and then, in one of the supreme ironies of the novel, back to the tyrannical father who originally perpetrated it and who, in the fictional guise of Raza ("Razor Guts") Hyder, is finally sliced to ribbons by the spring-release stiletto blades concealed in the Shakil sisters' dumbwaiter (S, 312).

Even if Rushdie's main purpose in telling such stories is to emphasize the difference between art and reality, however—even if he is interested primarily in the "off-centering" or "defamiliarizing" effects of the artistic

imagination—it is still the case that, every time he interrupts his narrative with one of these illusion-shattering, self-reflexive asides, he is directing our attention back to the real-life sources of his work, reminding us that, for all his talk of "fairylands" or "looking-glass Pakistans," his book is still basically mimetic or referential in nature. Perhaps there are writers, like Jean Genet in The Balcony or John Barth in Chimera, who make use of such passages mainly in order to dramatize the autonomous, convention-governed nature of the literary work—or, even more radically, the fictive nature of reality itself, what Gerald Graff refers to as "the fictionality of everything."[25] If so, however, Rushdie is clearly not one of them. In his work there always seems to come a recognition, at some point, of the larger, extraliterary context of the work, a recognition of its dependence, for meaning and value, on some sort of nonverbal reality. In other words, there always seems to be a release at some point from "the prison-house of language," a return to what Rushdie himself describes as the "existential question: How are we to live in the world?" (IH, 18). Far from antimimetic, in fact, one of Rushdie's obvious purposes as a writer is to warn against the breakdown of reality in contemporary society, to expose the promoters like Hal Valence (SV, 267–70), the tyrants like General Zulfikar or Indira Gandhi, who manipulate and subvert history for their own ends.

Having cautioned us, for example, that the country in Shame is "not quite" Pakistan, that Omar's hometown of Q. is "not really" Quetta, Rushdie goes on to acknowledge the limits of this sort of fictional "displacement." "But I don't want to be too precious about this," he concedes. "When I arrive at the big city, I shall call it Karachi. And it will have a Defence" (S, 24). Ultimately, the issues we are confronted with in Rushdie's work are not epistemological or semiotic at all; they are political or social or moral issues: problems like child abuse or sexual exploitation, like censorship or political assassination—all the real-life consequences of shame or shamelessness (S, 71–72).

This is hardly surprising, of course, when we recall that Rushdie makes use of his self-reflexive, "off-centering" narrative technique in the first place mainly in order to make his work more responsive to the complexities of real experience, in order to satisfy what Saleem Sinai describes as "an Indian disease, this urge to encapsulate the whole of reality" (MC, 84). As Rushdie sees it, all of life can be described in the same terms that he applies to Pakistan (or, in Midnight's Children, to India): as a "peeling, fragmenting palimpsest" or as "a picture full of conflicting elements" (S, 92). Instead of being like Robespierre or Danton from Büchner's play, either a puritan or an epicurean, a real person is always an internally divided, self-conflicted amalgam of such tendencies, a sort of "Robeston" or "Danpierre" (*S*, 267). In *The Satanic Verses,* for example, Saladin Chamcha is aware of dozens of "old, rejected selves," "alternative Saladins . . . which had split off from himself as he made his various life choices but which had apparently continued to exist, perhaps in the parallel universes of quantum theory" (*SV*, 523). Similarly, in *Midnight's Children,* Saleem Sinai is aware that, "inside himself," he is "anything but a whole, anything but homogeneous; all kinds of everywhichthing are jumbled up inside him, and he is one person one minute and another the next" (*MC*, 283).

It is in order to mirror this fact—in order "not to falsify reality with patterns too neat, too inclusive"[26] —that Rushdie has infused *Shame* with an element of the same complexity, that he has turned it, in fact, into the same kind of "peeling, fragmenting palimpsest" as the country that it describes. Formally, in fact, all of Rushdie's novels can be read as an acknowledgment that reality takes precedence over art, that "the unchanging twoness of things" can never be reconciled to "the universe of what-happened-next" (*MC*, 38), to "the narrow one-dimensionality of a straight line" (*MC*, 178).

Rufus Cook, Winter 1994

[1] James Harrison, "Reconstructing *Midnight's Children* and *Shame*," *University of Toronto Quarterly*, 39:3 (Spring 1990), p. 399.

[2] Salman Rushdie, *Imaginary Homelands: Essays and Criticism 1981–1991*, New York, Viking Penguin, 1992, p. 287. Subsequent references use the abbreviation *IH*.

[3] Salman Rushdie, *The Satanic Verses*, New York, Viking Penguin, 1989, pp. 351, 416. Subsequent references use the abbreviation *SV*.

[4] Salman Rushdie, *Shame*, New York, Random House, 1983, p. 189. Subsequent references use the abbreviation *S*.

[5] Aruna Srivastava, "'The Empire Writes Back': Language and History in *Shame* and *Midnight's Children*," *Ariel*, 20:4 (October 1989), p. 76.

[6] Mark Edmundson, "Prophet of a New Postmodernism," *Harper's Magazine*, December 1989, p. 70.

[7] Wendell Berry, "The Art of Place," *New Perspectives Quarterly*, 9:2 (Spring 1992), p. 29.

[8] Salman Rushdie, *Midnight's Children*, New York, Viking Penguin, 1981, pp. 419–20. Subsequent references use the abbreviation *MC*.

[9] Wendell Berry, *Standing by Words*, Berkeley, Ca., North Point, 1983, p. 57.

[10] Ibid., p. 58.

[11] Wendell Berry, *What Are People For?*, Berkeley, Ca., North Point, 1990, p. 193. Berry's view is that "[all] good human work remembers its history. The best writing is full of intima-

tions that it is the present version of earlier versions of itself, and that its maker inherited the work and ways of earlier makers."

[12] Gerald Graff, *Literature Against Itself: Literary Ideas in Modern Society*, Chicago, University of Chicago Press, 1979, p. 13.

[13] Ibid., pp. 60–62.

[14] Kelly Hewson, "Opening Up the Universe a Little More: Salman Rushdie and the Migrant as Story-Teller," *Span: Journal of the South Pacific Association for Commonwealth Literature and Language*, 29 (October 1989), p. 88.

[15] Berry, *What Are People For?*, p. 89.

[16] See Graff, pp. 70, 90.

[17] Kenneth Burke, *Language as Symbolic Action: Essays in Life, Literature, and Method*, Berkeley, University of California Press, 1966, p. 17.

[18] Wayne C. Booth, *The Company We Keep: An Ethics of Fiction*, Berkeley University of California Press, 1988, pp. 340–41.

[19] Berry, *Standing by Words*, p. 35.

[20] Berry, *What Are People For?*, p. 193.

[21] Ibid., p. 69.

[22] Ibid., p. 67.

[23] Helen Watson-Williams, "An Antique Land: Salman Rushdie's *Shame*," *Westerly: A Quarterly Review*, 29:4 (December 1984) p. 38.

[24] Berry, *Standing by Words*, p. 7.

[25] Graff, p. 15.

[26] Frank Kermode, *The Sense of an Ending: Studies in the Theory of Fiction*, New York, Oxford University Press, 1966, p. 130.

The Renaissance of Welsh Letters

Although Welsh literature has an ancient and honorable history, the performance of its writers in the twentieth century has not been spectacular. The impact of Welsh-language works on other world literatures has not been great in any period of history, and its readership has been confined basically to the one small area of Britain where Welsh is spoken and read. This lack of impact has been due not only to the limited knowledge of the language outside Wales, but also to the restricted, provincial nature of the culture which produced the literature. It is the geographical isolation and the special theocratic ambience which account for the survival of Welsh in an era which has seen the almost total disappearance of the other Celtic languages, so that the mere existence of a Cymric literature is due to its traditional insulation from the outside world. The outside world, if it was conscious at all of this literature's existence, considered it to be merely a production of primitive stories and poems interesting chiefly because they were composed in a quaint, archaic language which it was not worth the while of anyone to learn. Contrary to this belief, there have been decades and even generations in which works of genius and inspiration flowered profusely in Wales; the nineteenth century was one such period.

Although the twentieth century saw a marked downturn in the quantity and quality of Welsh-language literary output, the years between the turn of the century and 1960 were not totally devoid of production, and even a few geniuses emerged, such as Saunders Lewis, Kate Roberts, Gwenallt, T. Roland Hughes, Cynan and D. J. Williams. Nevertheless an impartial observer would have to conclude that the vast majority of the output of bound books, periodical contributions and Eisteddfod Prize pieces was banal and provincial and that it was hogtied by the powerful religious establishment which controlled thought and letters. In theory, Wales does official homage to literature in the form of the National Eisteddfod, an annual musical and literary competition. With its prizes the Eisteddfod has kept literary creation alive during periods of dearth in commercial endeavors. However, the quality of a novel written for a prize competition rather than to please a public is almost by definition inferior, and the novels crowned by the Eisteddfodau have been uniformly mediocre.

Any modern literature must stand or fall on its prose fiction, particularly the novel. Poetry is an archaic art form which has little impact on today's readers. The fact that the high point in the yearly Eisteddfod is the Chairing of the Bard, and that the prize poem receives the bulk of the publicity about awards, shows how far out of step with the times this venerable institution is. Like the forty "Immortals" of the French Academy (who can remember the name of an academician of fifty years ago?), the poets crowned by the Eisteddfod are soon forgotten and their "masterpieces" disappear into oblivion.

However, in spite of the fact that less than 25% of Welshmen today are speakers of the language, since about 1960 a tremendous upsurge in literary production in Welsh has taken place—an upsurge in both quantity and quality, giving Welsh letters an éclat which rivals that of its most brilliant century, the nineteenth. This renaissance—for such it seems without doubt to be—can be attributed to a number of factors. Firstly, it is connected with the worldwide phenomenon of nationalism in provinces having a traditional historic identity, such as French Canada and Brittany. Secondly, the British government has pursued a policy of financially supporting the arts, the theatre and letters in all parts of the island, through the several Arts Councils. Thirdly, several native Welsh organizations have come into

being to promote Welsh-language books and culture (among them the Welsh Books Council and the Welsh Academy). Fourthly, there is little doubt that the exposure of Welsh servicemen to foreign cultures in World War II resulted in a more cosmopolitan approach to literature by native authors (Hydwedd Boyer is the prime example). Fifthly, the relative affluence of the reading public has created a wider market for Welsh books than at any time in the past. Lastly, while religion is perhaps more lively today in Wales than in other parts of Britain, it has lost the near-absolute hold it once had on the thought and writing of the Principality, and a free literature is more apt to be a creative and articulate one than is a strait-jacketed, censored one.

There is little doubt that the agency most responsible for this literary revival of the 1960s and 1970s is the Cyngor Llyfrau Cymraeg or Welsh Books Council, with headquarters in Aberystwyth. Organized in 1963, it has branch book societies in each county and is governed by a council of representatives of the local authorities, the Welsh Arts Council, the University of Wales, the Academi Gymreig, the National Library of Wales, the Union of Welsh Authors and the Union of Welsh Publishers and Booksellers. All of these bodies offer financial support of the Council's endeavors, which include a central marketing and ordering depot for all Welsh publishers; yearly publication of the *Catalog Llyfrau Cymraeg*; receiving, editing and marketing of manuscripts from aspiring Welsh writers; school competitions; publishing of some works on its own (including incidentally a handbook on creative writing); and direct grants to authors. Grants to authors by the Welsh Books Council amounted to £6,000 in the 1976–77 fiscal year.

According to a recent report compiled by Gwerfyl Pierce Jones, head of the Editorial and Publicity Section of the Council, the total number of Welsh-language books published in 1976 amounted to 312, compared to 177 in 1971, 239 in 1973 and 308 in 1975. It is thus clear that the quantity of literary output is steadily increasing. This report breaks the production down further into twenty categories such as memoirs, poetry, religion, novels and short stories, plays and essays. All except two categories register an increase in number in 1976 over 1971. For example, poetry collections numbered 11 in 1971, 27 in 1976; plays numbered 2 in 1971, 12 in 1976; novels and collections of short stories numbered 24 in 1971, 30 in 1976; collections of essays numbered 8 in 1971, 9 in 1976.

Compared with the 20,000 new titles published each year in the United States, 300-plus new Welsh-language titles annually may not seem impressive. It must be remembered, however, that American authors are writing for a nation that numbers 220 million, not to mention their overseas markets like Britain, and that English is a world language. Welsh writers are addressing a public of only 700,000 Welsh speakers, some of whom also buy books in English. (There is a flourishing contemporary Anglo-Welsh literature which competes for readers with the Welsh-language literature, although it seems that the latter has a certain edge because it is now "in" and therefore has a snob appeal that its rival lacks. This is an ironic turnabout in a land where children were once punished for using Welsh in school. Dylan Thomas, now deceased, is the most famous product of Anglo-Welsh letters.)* Welsh, far from being a world language, is little known outside the Principality. Some 300-plus new titles per year represent a substantial figure in proportion to potential readership, and this figure is phenomenal compared to the annual production of any previous literary period, even the most brilliant ones.

Quantity, however, is no guarantee of quality, and today's Welsh authors are turning out their fair share of banal, badly-written, absurd and even juvenile prose. But the renaissance of the last two decades has produced four novelists of genuine talent, all of whom have even shown flashes of genuine at times. These four are Islwyn Ffowc Elis, W. Leslie Richards, Hydwedd Boyer and Selyf Roberts. Significantly, only one is a minister, and even he (Elis) has left the pulpit and is now a college lecturer. Historically, most Welsh authors have been Protestant ministers, so this departure from tradition brings a secularization to the novel which could do nothing but improve it.

The most prolific and most popular of today's novelists is Islwyn Ffowc Elis. His work runs the gamut of the subgenres, from farce (*Tabyrddau'r Babongo*) to science fiction (*Y Blaned Dirion*) to Plaid Cymru propaganda (*Wythnos yng Nghymru Fydd*). His books are very uneven in quality, but his audience of readers is very faithful and continues to buy even his mediocre ones. His chief fault lies in his excessive use of irrelevant dialogue; we find a good example of this in *Y Blaned Dirion* (The Tender Planet). *Tabyrddau'r Babongo* (Drums of the Babongo), set in Africa, is the best-crafted novel. *Wythnos yng Nghymru Fydd* (A Week in the Wales of the Future) is good science fiction as well as religious and political propaganda. Other novels are *Cysgod y Cryman* (Shadow of the Sickle), *Ffenestri tua'r Gwyll* (Windows toward the Darkness), *Yn Ôl i Leifior* (Back to Lleifior), *Blas y Cynfyd* (Taste of the Primitive Life), *Y Gromlech yn yr Haidd* (The Cromlech in the Barley) and *Eira Mawr* (Great Snow). He has also produced a volume of fine essays, *Cyn Oeri'r Gwaed* (Before the Blood Cools).

The most promising novelist of today's renaissance was W. Leslie Richards, who produced three minor

masterpieces: *Yr Etifeddion* (The Heirs), *Llanw a Thrai* (High Tide and Low Tide), and *Cynffon o Wellt* (Tail of Straw). It is necessary to use the past tense "was," as Richards, who is a schoolmaster in Llandeilo, near Carmarthen, Dyfed, has stopped writing novels. He has published several volumes of verse, but he is wasting his talents on this archaic literary medium. Richards's novels are well crafted, intelligently plotted and free from the theocratic trammels that still afflict and inhibit much Welsh-language prose.

Hydwedd Boyer, now deceased (he died in 1970), has produced the most original form of novel in the literature. He served abroad in the British army in World War II, and his stories have the war as a background and soldiers as protagonists. *Ym Mhoethder y Tywod* (In the Heat of the Sand) is laid in North Africa, and *Ffarwel Ha'* (Farewell Summer) is set in wartime Wales. Boyer's realism breaks with local conventions, and his military-oriented novels are unique in the literature. It is amazing how little impact the greatest conflict of our century had on Welsh letters. Boyer is the exception, and his work would be important for this reason alone, quite apart from his other qualities. He is the link between a provincial, introspective culture and the wide, wide outside world.

The novels of Selyf Roberts are likewise a venture into a new arena, that of the business world. Such an innovation in itself is worthy of note and would claim for Roberts a place in the forefront of the contemporary renaissance, even if his skill as a novelist did not give him a solid place as one of the premier writers of today. He has produced four novels: *Helynt ar Hoelion* (Trouble on Nails), *Cysgod yw Arian* (Money is a Shadow), *A Eilw ar Ddyfnder* (Which Calls on the Deep) and *Wythnos o Hydref* (A Week in October). Unfortunately Roberts, like Richards, has given up novel writing; a book of essays, *Mesur Byr* (Short Measure), is his sole recent contribution to the literary scene. He is a banker by profession and lives in Oswestry, on the English border.

One of the most popular novels of the last decade is Caradog Pritchard's *Un Nos Ola Leuad* (One Moonlit Night), laid in the quarry region of Arfon, North Wales. It was dramatized in serial form by the BBC in August 1977. Marian Eames has produced two historical novels, *Y Stafell Ddirgel* (The Secret Room) and *Yr Rhandir Mwyn* (The Gentle Region), both set in Pennsylvania in the eighteenth century. They are well researched and well written. A historical novel laid in the Middle Ages, Beti Hughes's *Aderyn o Ddyfed,* is unfortunately a rather amateurish production; as it was a prize winner of the Flint National Eisteddfod, perhaps this is to be expected.

Science fiction, the detective novel and the novel of protest are all represented in the revival. In the first group we might mention W. J. Jones's *Rhwng y Sêr* (Among the Stars), in the second John Edwards's *Y Bobl Beryglus* (The Dangerous People) and in the third Meg Elis's *I'r Gad* (Into Battle; see *WLT* 51:3, pp. 486–87). Besides these giants or near-giants, there is a host of authors of lesser stature turning out prose year after year, some of it good, some of it eminently forgettable. The most difficult task of one who wishes to keep abreast of literary developments in the Principality is to separate the wheat from the chaff. There are a number of periodicals publishing reviews which can assist the reader, including *Barn, Taliesin, Y Cymro, Y Faner* and *Yr Herald Gymraeg.*

From the standpoint of quality, the Welsh Renaissance may have peaked in the late 1960s and early 70s, as it seems now to be on a plateau. From the standpoint of quantity, it is still going full blast and getting more voluminous each year. Those who have been predicting the disappearance of Welsh language and literature will probably have to wait a few more years yet before they see their prophecy fulfilled.

John M. Jones, Spring 1978

*Ed. Note: See *WLT* 51:4 (Autumn 1977), pp. 534–37 for an essay by Michael J. Collins on the Anglo-Welsh poet John Ormond.

Welsh Writing in English

Wales is a nation enriched, and conflicted, by two literatures: one in Welsh, one in English. Welsh-language literature is among the oldest of Europe, its writers having produced masterworks in all genres, from *The Gododdin,* a sixth-century long poem in the heroic tradition, to the medieval prose masterpieces of *The Mabinogion,* to the modern dramas of Saunders Lewis, the greatest of Welsh playwrights.[1] English-language literature, on the other hand, came into prominence in Wales during the twentieth century. It is thus a young body of work, with major achievements primarily reflected in the works of poets, notably Dylan Thomas, R. S. Thomas, and David Jones. Despite its brief existence, this new literature has become the subject of sometimes fierce debate in Wales, with critics disagreeing on not only what the future holds for Anglo-Welsh literature, but also on how this literature is to be defined in the present.

Whereas Welsh-language literature was preeminent in Wales through the nineteenth century, by the early decades of the twentieth century enough Welsh men and women were writing in English, especially in the south of Wales, to give birth to a new literature. Complex and controversial issues have helped shape Anglo-Welsh writing from the 1920s to the present, and will surely help determine its future. The main issues include the claim of some Welsh-language writers to represent the only authentic literature of Wales, the question of whether or not an extended literary tradition in English has existed in Wales, the absence (until recently) of a publishing apparatus for English-language writers, the rise of a Welsh nationalism committed to preserving the Welsh language, and the question of whether English-language literature in Wales can be distinguished from English literature proper.

To understand the development and current status of Welsh writing in English, one must first know something of Welsh culture and Welsh-language literature—for whatever makes English-language writing from Wales distinct from English literature proper must relate to the degree of its "Welshness," however that might be defined. Also, Welsh and Anglo-Welsh writers of the twentieth century have been very conscious of the actual and the potential tensions and conflicts resulting from the presence of two language communities, and two literatures, within a single nation. That consciousness has exerted a powerful influence on the development of Welsh writing in English.

Outside Britain, it is not widely known that a distinctive and vibrant Welsh-language culture and literature has survived through the twentieth century, despite English control of educational, religious, and governing institutions during the centuries subsequent to Edward I's defeat of Prince Llewelyn ap Gruffydd in 1282. Although the number of Welsh speakers has declined through the nineteenth and twentieth centuries, Welsh literature in all genres continues to be written, with novels, critical and scholarly works, and collections of poetry published in the Welsh language, reviewed in Welsh-language newspapers and literary journals (such as *Y Cymro* and *Barn*), and discussed in Welsh on Radio Cymru. A Welsh-language TV station, Sianel Pedwar Cymru (S4C), has broadcast news, cultural programs, and even soap operas and game shows from the capital city of Cardiff since 1982, when proponents of Welsh-language TV won a decade-long battle with Margaret Thatcher's government over the issue.[2] One indication of the unexpected success of Sianel Pedwar Cymru is its ability to sell its productions to overseas markets for translation and rebroadcast.[3]

Despite these signs of literary and cultural vitality in the Welsh-language community, today only about 500,000 of the 2,500,000 people living in Wales speak Welsh. Reasons for the decrease in the number of Welsh speakers over the last two hundred years have been analyzed and documented and include economic, political, and educational factors.[4] The comparative resilience of the Welsh language through centuries when related minority languages—Cornish, Manx, Scots Gaelic, and Irish Gaelic—were in decline toward virtual or complete extinction has also been described in a number of studies. The struggle to preserve the Welsh language, and so preserve Welsh literature and culture, continues, though with somewhat less of the militancy that characterized the Welsh-language movement during the 1960s and 1970s, when language protestors were regularly put on trial for acts of civil disobedience as well as occasional acts of violence.

It was also the 1960s and 1970s that saw Anglo-Welsh literature firmly established in Wales, with its own publishing vehicles and Welsh Arts Council financial support—and with a distinctly nationalist bias. Though the amount of English-language poetry and fiction written in Wales prior to the twentieth century is small, Raymond Garlick and Roland Mathias, among others, have shown that works in English have been written in Wales since the fifteenth century. The anthology *Anglo-Welsh Poetry 1480–1980* (edited by Garlick and Mathias) provides a selection of such writing, while critical works such as *Anglo-Welsh Literature: An Illustrated History,* by Mathias, and *An Introduction to Anglo-Welsh Literature,* by Garlick, describe its development.

Those who see Anglo-Welsh literature as distinct from provincial English writings argue that the sensibilities of Welsh writers in English have been fundamentally shaped by the Welsh culture, landscape, and language. Anthony Conran, for example, argues that interaction "between the two language-groups of Wales" occurs "on all cultural levels" (35). It is difficult to ascertain the extent, or even the existence, of complex and subtle cultural interactions, but one powerful force—the Welsh language itself—has certainly shaped, and will continue to shape, Anglo-Welsh literature and attitudes toward that literature. A few Welsh writers in English have spoken Welsh since birth (e.g., Caradoc Evans and Glyn Jones); some have acquired the language as adults (R. S. Thomas, Emyr Humfreys, Gillian Clarke, Christopher Meredith); others speak little or no Welsh (Tony Curtis and Robert Minhinnick). No matter what their relation to the Welsh language and its literature, all Welsh writers are affected by the tensions between the two literatures and cultures, for language has long been a political battleground in Wales. Speaking or writing Welsh communicates cultural—even political—allegiance, which partly accounts for the increasing numbers of contemporary English-language writers who have learned, or are learning, the language. One

such writer is Oliver Reynolds, whose poem "Dysgu" (which means "learning" in Welsh) describes his motivation for attending a class for Welsh-learners: "Each has his reason to be here / Speaking through declenched teeth: / I'd thought it time to stop / Welshing on the language / And learn about roots, / If only etymological ones" (stanza 4).

Despite the creation in Wales over the last three decades of a viable publishing apparatus for English-language poetry, fiction, and criticism, acceptance of the idea that these writings constitute a separate literature with an extended tradition has been slow. The existence of Anglo-Welsh writings from at least the fifteenth century is not disputed; it is their nature and significance that have become matters of debate. Whereas some critics, such as Garlick and Mathias, argue for critical and academic acceptance of Anglo-Welsh literature as a second literature of Wales with its own extended literary tradition, others such as the Welsh poet and critic Bobi Jones contend that Anglo-Welsh writings constitute a provincial English literature that cannot be described as a literature on a par with Welsh literature in the Welsh language (47).[5] Some writers who initially supported the development of an English-language literature later came to disavow and then attack it. Harri Webb, for example, and English-language Welsh poet and political nationalist, declared in 1985 (*Western Mail,* 2 April) that he would no longer contribute to the "load of rubbish" that constitutes Anglo-Welsh literature.

The term *Anglo-Welsh* itself reflects the complexities of literary and cultural identity in Wales. Coined by H. Idris Bell in 1922 to refer to Welsh writing in English, it was in common use by the 1930s[6] and actively promoted (especially in the pages of the *Anglo-Welsh Review*) during the 1950s and 1960s to distinguish that literature from, and out of deference to, Welsh-language literature, a point made by Garlick and Mathias: "By long usage the term Welsh poetry is properly understood to denote poetry in the Welsh language. To apply it to the poetry of Wales composed in English is confusing and, to some Welsh-language writers and readers, offensive" (27). Though still in use, the term is rejected by writers and critics who dislike its implications of divided national allegiance or who see the term as an acceptance of colonial linkage to England.[7] This political dimension has led many writers in Wales to prefer the descriptive phrase "Welsh writer in English" to "Anglo-Welsh writer."

Modern Welsh literature in English was, in fact, born out of a political environment, for the coalproducing valleys of south Wales, centers of labor unrest and political organizing during the 1920s and 1930s, provided the intellectual and artistic ferment out of which the "first flowering" of Anglo-Welsh writers developed.[8] The short stories of Caradoc Evans, the poetry of Idris Davies and Glyn Jones, and the novels of Jack Jones and Gwyn Thomas are the most acclaimed early representatives of this writing.[9] Whereas English outlets published by far the greatest number of Anglo-Welsh writers prior to the development of sufficient outlets in Wales, Irish—and, to a lesser extent, Scottish—literary magazines also published Welsh writers and served as models for those trying to launch a Welsh equivalent of the Irish or Scottish literary renaissance.[10]

Many English-language Welsh writers may have preferred access to the readership and financial opportunities of a London publisher and, possibly, to the American market. Whether or not Anglo-Welsh writers of the 1930s and 1940s believed a London-based literary career to be preferable to one based in Wales, they had little choice but to send work to English magazines and presses for publication—and so essentially write for an English readership. Although R. S. Thomas, for example, published his earliest poems in the *Dublin Magazine* and his first book, *The Stones of the Field* (1946), with a small press in west Wales (Druid's Press), he received critical attention only when his later books were handled by English publishers, first Hart-Davis and then Macmillan. Although two important English-language literary magazines appeared in Wales during the late 1930s and early 1940s—*Wales,* edited by Keidrych Rhys, and the *Welsh Review,* under Gwyn Jones—it was not until the mid-1960s that a sufficient number existed, along with viable book publishers, to sustain a developing literature and readership in Wales.

The "second flowering" of Welsh writing in English, occurring during the 1960s, was spearheaded by a group of committed nationalists, including Anthony Conran, Meic Stephens, and Harri Webb. Stephens founded the Triskel Press in 1963 and *Poetry Wales* magazine in 1965 to promote writing in English that was distinctively Welsh in character. His efforts were encouraged by eminent Welsh-speakers such as Aneirin Talfan Davies and Jac L. Williams, "who gave favorable attention to *Poetry Wales* in the Welsh-language press."[11] Under Meic Stephens, the first director of the Literature Committee of the Welsh Arts Council, the Arts Council allocation to literature grew from £18,000 in 1967 to £850,000 in 1990, with most of the monies supporting bursaries for writers, publication grants for magazines and books, and vehicles for public access to literature, such as readings and the Arts Council Bookshop in Cardiff. Today three literary magazines (the *New Welsh Review, Planet,* and *Poetry Wales*) and two presses (Gomer Press and Seren Books) constitute the primary Arts Council-supported Anglo-Welsh outlets, publishing the great majority of English-language poetry and fiction appearing in Wales.[12] Alternative magazines and presses, with little or no grant support, also exist sporadically.

With the establishment of viable literary magazines and presses and access to development capital through Arts Council funding, most publishing of literary and critical texts in English by Welsh writers now takes place in Wales.[13] The successful development of an English-language publishing industry has itself come under attack, however, in part because editorial decision-making is concentrated in the hands of a very few editors and publishers. This criticism is made by many of those commenting on the achievements of Seren Books, which has established itself as the premier publisher of English-language poetry and fiction in Wales, issuing its one-hundredth title in 1990. The problem of editorial monopoly is lessened, however, by the activities of small-scale magazines and presses that often promote highly specific, "corrective" editorial agendas. The recent establishing of Honno, the Welsh women's press, along with the publication of a number of young women writers by Seren Books,[14] signals that the historical exclusion of women from publishing outlets is being challenged.[15] Activities of small-press publishers and magazines not supported—or supported only sporadically—by the Arts Council attempt to broaden the range of editorial tastes shaping contemporary writing.[16]

Despite this impressive superstructure, Anglo-Welsh literature has not gained recognition, much less acceptance, easily, either within Wales or abroad —for complex reasons. While using the medium of English, it is written out of a Welsh milieu, physically and culturally distant from the centers of English-language literary activity in London and New York. Consequently, Welsh writing in English has been largely ignored by the English and American critical establishments, except for attention to a few authors such as Dylan Thomas, R. S. Thomas, and David Jones.[17] At the same time, this literature is often seen as peripheral, even antithetical, to the culture and literature of Welsh-speaking Wales, despite the nationalist political sympathies of many English-language authors. This view of Welsh writing in English is held by a number of Welsh-language writers, among them Bobi Jones,[18] but also by some English-language writers of Wales.[19]

The fact that R. S. Thomas, the most acclaimed Welsh poet writing in English, remains antagonistic to the idea of Anglo-Welsh literature has certainly contributed to the slow acceptance of Anglo-Welsh writing abroad and in Wales itself. Early in his career Thomas supported the idea that Welsh writers could produce a literature in English "compatible with the literary tradition in Welsh" ("Llenyddiaeth," 53). However, Thomas's developing political convictions, centering on the need to preserve a distinct Welsh-language culture, eventually led him to reject that idea.[20] When asked about the issue in a recent interview, Thomas responded, "What is written in Welsh is Welsh literature of varying quality. What is written in English has to strain very hard indeed to merit the description of Welsh writing in English, which is nonsense anyway" (Ned Thomas and John Barnie, 35). In his essay "The Creative Writer's Suicide" (from *Selected Prose*) Thomas describes his own painful struggle with the contradiction between writing in English and remaining politically committed to the Welsh language and culture.

In 1991 the minister of arts for the United Kingdom asked major arts-funding bodies of Britain to prepare strategic plans establishing priorities and objectives for the coming decade. The issues facing those involved in contemporary literature are especially complex, volatile, and urgent in Wales, as evidenced by the energetic responses to the minister's request. Tony Bianchi, literature director of the Welsh Arts Council, has commissioned papers (two in English and two in Welsh) on literature in Wales in the 1990s, and editors of the literary magazines have been publishing numerous articles and interviews addressing the same topic.[21] Against a backdrop of cultural division, political struggle, and nationalist resurgence, the writers, publishers, editors, and critics of both language communities are debating fundamental issues of literary and national identity—issues particular to Wales but relevant to any nation struggling to maintain its distinctive cultural and literary traditions.

David Lloyd, Summer 1992

■ WORKS CITED

Barnie, John. "The Anglo-Welsh Tradition." In his book *The King of Ashes*. Llandysul. Gomer. 1990.

Collins, Michael. "Keeping the Flag Flying: Anglo-Welsh Poetry in the Twentieth Century." *WLT* 56:1 (Winter 1982), pp. 36–40.

———. "Recovering a Tradition: Anglo-Welsh Poetry 1480–1980." *WLT* 63:1 (Winter 1989), pp. 55–59.

Conran, Anthony. *The Cost of Strangeness*. Llandysul. Gomer. 1982.

Garlick, Raymond, and Roland Mathias. *Anglo-Welsh Poetry 1480–1980*. Bridgend, Wales. Poetry Wales Press. 1984.

Jones, Bobi. "Anglo-Welsh: More Definition." *Planet,* 16, pp. 11–21.

Mathias, Roland. *Anglo-Welsh Literature: An Illustrated History.* Bridgend, Wales. Poetry Wales Press. 1987.

Reynolds, Oliver. *Skevington's Daughter*. London: Faber & Faber. 1985.

Stephens, Elan Closs. "View from the Quadrant." *Planet,* 84, pp. 30–33.

Thomas, Ned. "S4C and Europe." *Planet,* 66, pp. 3–8.

———, and John Barnie. "Probings: An Interview with R. S. Thomas." *Planet,* 80, pp. 28–52.

Thomas, R.S. "R. S. Thomas." *Contemporary Authors Autobiography Series*. Vol. 4. Adele Sarkissian, ed. Detroit. Gale Research. 1986.

———. "The Creative Writer's Suicide." In his *Selected Prose.* Bridgend, Wales. Poetry Wales Press. 1983.

———. "Llenyddiaeth Eingle-Gymreig" (Anglo-Welsh Literature). In his *Selected Prose*. Bridgend, Wales. Poetry Wales Press. 1983.

[1] *A History of Welsh Literature* by Thomas Parry (first published in 1944 as *Hanes Llenyddiaeth Gymraeg hyd 1900* and translated into English by H. Idris Bell in 1955) is still the most comprehensive history of Welsh literature. Bell provides a critical survey of Welsh literature of the twentieth century as an appendix to Parry's work.

[2] The "best-loved programmes" on S4C "reach audiences of 100,000 on a Welsh-speaking base of half a million" (Elan Stephens, 31).

[3] Animated productions for children top the list of "most widely sold programmes," but "the majority of programmes sold by S4C have appealed in other countries not particularly because they are about Wales or because they are Celtic Exotica, but on their merits as drama or documentary which convey life experience across boundaries of language and country through being themselves and then being translated" (Ned Thomas, "S4C and Europe," 7).

[4] The census of 1901 first documented the decline in the number of Welsh speakers to under 50 percent. The number has declined further in every subsequent census. For an outline of the causes of decline, see Bud Khleif, *Language, Ethnicity and Education in Wales,* New York, Mouton, 1980, pp. 55–56. Other relevant sources include *Welsh in Education and Life* (1927), *The Welsh Language Today* (1973), and *The Welsh Language 1961–1981: An Interpretive Atlas* (1985).

[5] Jones argues his case in "Anglo-Welsh: More Definition," in *Planet,* no. 16, pp. 11–23.

[6] According to the *Oxford Companion to the Literature of Wales.*

[7] In his introduction to *Ten Anglo-Welsh Poets* Sam Adams notes "Emyr Humphreys's decision to dissociate himself from any collection bearing the words 'Anglo-Welsh'" (3).

[8] The phrase "the first flowering" was coined to distinguish between writers who published their major works between 1915 and 1945 and those who emerged during the 1960s. The best introduction to Anglo-Welsh writers of the "first flowering" remains Glyn Jones's book *The Dragon Has Two Tongues: Essays on Anglo-Welsh Writers and Writing,* London, Dent, 1968.

[9] Caradoc Evans's first collection of stories, *My People,* published in 1915, is generally seen to mark the beginning of a distinctive Anglo-Welsh literature. The bitter tone and eccentric style of Evans's work, as well as its early date, separate this writer from other early Welsh writers in English. A Welsh-speaker, Evans grew up in west Wales and was not associated with the later group of English-language writers from the mining valleys of south Wales.

[10] Glyn Jones and R. S. Thomas have applauded the support given to Welsh writers by *Dublin Magazine* editor Seamus O'Sullivan (Jones, 31; Thomas, *CA,* 305). Thomas also mentions the interest in his early work demonstrated by those involved with the Scottish literary renaissance (Thomas and Barnie, *Planet,* 33).

[11] This quotation and related material in the paragraph derive from an unpublished interview I conducted with Stephens.

[12] When the *Anglo-Welsh Review* ceased publication in 1988, the *New Welsh Review* was launched with the support of the Arts Council. The *NWR* publishes fiction, poetry, and criticism. *Planet* covers literature and culture. *Poetry Wales* covers poetry and criticism.

[13] This is not, however, to deny the influence of literary movements from abroad or that talented writers from Wales often choose English or American rather than Welsh publishers. Publishing in the Welsh language has, of course, always been centered in Wales.

[14] Christine Evans and Hilary Llewelyn-Williams are two notable examples.

[15] Until recent years women have been consistently underrepresented in Anglo-Welsh anthologies published in Wales and England. For examples, see *Ten Anglo-Welsh Poets* (Carcanet, 1974) and *Twelve Modern Anglo-Welsh Poets* (University of London Press, 1975).

[16] For a discussion of writing workshops, performance poetry, and small-magazine activity in south Wales, see "Sounding the Work" by Phil Maillard in *Planet,* 51 (1985), pp. 49–56.

[17] In terms of American coverage of Anglo-Welsh literature, recent exceptions to the general ignorance include articles by Michael Collins in *World Literature Today* (see 63:1 [Winter 1989], pp. 55–64], a "Writers of Wales" special issue of the *New England Review / Bread Loaf Quarterly* (10:4, [1988]), and a section of a *North Dakota Quarterly* issue providing a selection of Anglo-Welsh poetry (57:2, [1989]).

[18] See "Anglo-Welsh: More Definition," in *Planet,* no. 16 (1973).

[19] For an example, see John Barnie's review article "The Anglo-Welsh Tradition," published in *Poetry Wales* and reprinted in his collection of essays *The King of Ashes* (Llandysul, Gomer Press, 1989).

[20] See R. S. Thomas's article "Reflections on a Speech at Machynlleth" (*Planet,* 84 [1990]) for an example of the poet defending nationalist opinions criticized as inflammatory in the Welsh press. See Toni Bianchi's essay "R. S. Thomas and His Readers," in *Wales: The Imagined Nation* (Tony Curtis, ed., Seren, 1986), for a discussion of Thomas's relationship to Welsh- and English-language critics and readers.

[21] Recent examples of English-language responses include Dai Smith, "Silent Readers: Invisible Writing," *Planet,* 90 (1991), pp. 7–12; Anthony Conran, "A Welsh Strategy for Literature," *New Welsh Review,* 4:3 (1991–92), pp. 52–58; and John Barnie, "Where Next? The Direction of Welsh Writing in English," *Planet,* 91 (1992), pp. 3–10.

The Thorn on Scotland's Rose: Hugh MacDiarmid

The rose of all the world is not for me.
I want for my part

Only the little white rose of Scotland
That smells sharp and sweet—and breaks the heart.

■ HUGH MACDIARMID

After being pretty well ignored during much of his life, and all of his most creative period, Hugh MacDiarmid (pen name of Christopher Murray Grieve; 1892–1978) achieved a good measure of fame in his later years: a festschrift in his honor for his seventieth birthday, so-called "collected" editions of his poetry in 1962 and again in 1967, a genuine *Complete Poems* in two volumes in 1978, and a course on him offered over the BBC by the Open University. The *Complete Poems* was essential to serious study of the poet, because it made widely available the entire output of MacDiarmid, rendering accessible some works which had been published originally in very small editions. The earlier *Collected Poems* were not at all what the edition purported to be; therein we read MacDiarmid's statement that the volume contains all the poems "I think worth including in a definitive edition." The fact is quite otherwise; MacDiarmid told me that the collection as he originally prepared it was much larger but that the publisher (Macmillan) decided that it must be cut down. The poet, of course, assumed that his prefatory statement would be suppressed and was quite annoyed when it appeared in print. Armed with the poetic output, scholars are now going to work to try to disentangle some of the puzzles of this complex man. Having a complete text, it should be recalled, does not give us the true story of the text, because by the expressed dictate of the author the editors of the *Complete Poems* (Michael Grieve and W. R. Aitken) were allowed to present the text only, bare of any annotation. Any reader familiar with MacDiarmid's work will recognize the need for a critical edition of the poetry.

In addition to the festschrift, there have been a book and a collection of essays by divers hands edited by Duncan Glen (1964, 1972), a short monograph by John Weston on *A Drunk Man Looks at the Thistle* (1970), a book by Kenneth Buthlay (1964), as well as a good assortment of articles and taped interviews. Not much, one may say, for a major world poet who was proposed for the Nobel Prize and who was the major force behind the Scottish Renaissance. At hand we have two books which will go some way to redress this situation. *Thistle and Rose* by Ann Edwards Boutelle[1] is a general study of MacDiarmid's poetry, as the book's subtitle tells us—a pretty large undertaking, it must be admitted. In fact Boutelle's book does not live up to its subtitle. She devotes seven of the eight chapters to poetry published by 1935. Admittedly, most critics agree, this was his period of greatest creativity, but it still includes only about half his published work. Furthermore, Mac-

Diarmid frequently said that his most important poetry was the later material. One would probably find readers agreeing or disagreeing with MacDiarmid according to their political and social outlook and not strictly according to what qualities the verse itself possesses. The author himself was probably undecided on the point; he included a very ample selection of the early poetry in the *Collected Poems* of 1962, proportionately more than was taken from his later work, emphasizing for us the contradictions of which he was made.

These contradictions are briefly examined in Boutelle's first two chapters: "Thistle and Rose: The Paradoxical Vision" and "Trembling Sunbeams: The Vision and the Poetry." The England/Scotland theme was to preoccupy MacDiarmid for most of his adult life, as was the Scottish Nationalist/world brotherhood or communist theme. I wonder how one can, as Boutelle says she has, have the "passions respond to the poetry" while avoiding "embroilment in issues other than the poetry" when her subject was so firmly convinced that poetry and life are one. How does one judge as poetry only a work like *First Hymn to Lenin* with its opening stanza,

Few even o' the criminals, cravens, and fools
Wha's voices vilify a man they ken
They've cause to fear and are unfit to judge
As they're to stem his influence again
But in the hollows where their herts should be
  Foresee your victory

and which in the following stanza roundly condemns Churchill, Locker-Lampson and Beaverbrook? To attempt to do so risks a serious misreading of the poetry. In chapter seven, which is devoted to the *First* and *Second Hymn to Lenin,* Boutelle suggests that these volumes (1931, 1935) and the Marxism which they extol gave him "an emotional strength and courage that would otherwise be missing." I read a statement such as this as admitting the close bond between art and life which became increasingly apparent in MacDiarmid's work. One might even speculate that a recognition of the fusion of poetry and politics in its broadest sense in the poet's later work was what decided Boutelle to concentrate on the earlier publications.

It is well known that MacDiarmid's poetic output underwent a major change after the mid-thirties; from this date onward most of his poetry was written in English. There are theories aplenty why this change took place, but no certainties. The author was very reticent about discussing this in depth. Typical of his response to questions was an interview which was published in *Studies in Scottish Literature:* "Scots is an impossible medium for any poems on scientific and modern subjects that I have been writing; you couldn't write *On a Raised Beach* in Scots at all, but you couldn't write it in English either, of course." Must we conclude that MacDiarmid was finally defeated in his use of the Scots language, which he had so passionately advocated? Is it really true that *On a Raised Beach* could not have been written in Scots, or is it that the poet was himself unable to do it? To argue that the multitude of geological terms to be found in the poem required that the remainder of the language be English is to ignore that there are a very large number of words used by Scots which are common to both languages; this has never prevented poets from using Scots when they wished to do so, and I do not accept that as a reason why MacDiarmid had to write the poem in English. Surely the answer lies much more deeply hidden in the mind of the author. We may never know the full reason for MacDiarmid's switch to English, but this should not be used as a reason for ignoring the English poems. Why is there, for example, no commentary on, and barely even mention of, *In Memoriam James Joyce?* This poem, published in 1955, merits attention in any study of MacDiarmid, no matter what the feeling of the author may be about the relative merits of the English poems.

It would be wrong to condemn *Thistle and Rose* for a misleading subtitle or for what the author does *not* do; what she does write about, the early work through the Scots period, she does well. Boutelle devotes about a third of the book to each of the three periods of the poet's work: early books, *A Drunk Man Looks at the Thistle* and later work to 1935. This appears to me to be a judicious division of attention; we move rapidly from the apprenticeship of *Annals of the Five Senses* (1923) to the astonishing control of Lallans in *Sangshaw* (1925) with such gems as "The Bonnie Broukit Bairn," "The Watergaw" and "I Heard Christ Sing" (how did an avowed atheist write such a superb religious poem?). The middle of the book (chapter four) is devoted to MacDiarmid's crowning achievement, *A Drunk Man* (1926). Boutelle calls the work "one of Scotland's chefs d'oeuvre, one of the most interesting pieces of modern poetry," and goes on to point out that it has influenced almost every Scottish poet since. In my opinion she understates the case—I think that it is one of the most important long poems of the century. And yet it was not at first recognized as such; *The Glasgow Herald* reviewed it "very unfavorably," according to MacDiarmid, and *The Scotsman* did not review it at all. The book cannot have sold well; the publishers (Blackwood) bound up the unsold sheets at a later date in order to dispose of remaining stock, and it was 1953 before a second edition was published.

It seems likely that the language question played some role in the slow appreciation of *A Drunk Man.*

Once he turned to the use of Scots for his poetry, Mac-Diarmid went at it with a vengeance; he tells of scouring J. Jamieson's *Etymological Dictionary of the Scottish Tongue* (there was no *Dictionary of the Older Scottish Tongue* or *Scottish National Dictionary* in those days) to find new words. From this study he evolved "synthetic" Scots, which differed from dialects in that it was completely eclectic. Now the well-entrenched "Kailyarders" of the time were dedicated to producing poetry, and prose, in the dialect of a particular district, so that we find such titles as James Davidson's *Poems: Chiefly in the Buchan Dialect* (the title, of course, from Burns's *Poems, Chiefly in the Scottish Dialect*) or William Farquhar's *The Fyvie Lintie: A Collection of Original Poems, and Songs, Partly in the Aberdeenshire Dialect,* to name but two among dozens. It may be that these authors saw what MacDiarmid was doing as a threat to their sort of poetry, or it may have been the poetry itself—in any case, *A Drunk Man* met with scant approval. Boutelle says that the "kailyard tradition quailed before MacDiarmid's singlehanded establishment of a new tradition in Scottish literature."

▪ ▪ ▪

"The Language Problem" by David Murison is one of the most important essays in another book about MacDiarmid, *The Age of MacDiarmid: Essays on Hugh MacDiarmid and His Influence on Contemporary Scotland,* edited by P. H. Scott and A. C. Davis.[2] Murison edited the last eight volumes of the *Scottish National Dictionary,* and so he speaks with real authority on the subject. Unfortunately the essay tries to do in sixteen pages what it would take a large volume to explore comprehensively; we are left with tantalizing observations which cry out for elaboration. In one paragraph Murison mentions that MacDiarmid was playing with the idea of "scientific didacticism" before his Scots period, that his switch to English coincided with his joining the Communist Party and that the bitterness in the introduction to *Lucky Poet* showed signs of a "psychological trauma." Murison also points to an irony in the poet when he reminds us that Scottish poetry had fallen into a tradition of "the short simple lyrical and balladic mode . . . which MacDiarmid fought tooth and nail to change," but he does not remind us that much of the poet's finest work is short lyrics; like Wordsworth, he sprinkled them throughout his longer works—the incomparable "O wha's been here afore me, lass" from *A Drunk Man* springs to mind.

The doyen of Scottish literary critics, David Daiches, situates MacDiarmid in the Scottish literary tradition, pointing out that "self-contradiction for Grieve [MacDiarmid] is a mode of poetic awareness." In reaching for an adequate image to describe the earth (in "The

Bonnie Broukit Bairn"), MacDiarmid uses a "sudden shift in scale that shows eternity and the single individual thing as somehow illuminating each other . . . linking the moment with eternity." This traditionally Scottish trait Daiches finds in the long poem as well as the short ones. He follows the poet's call "Back to Dunbar" by claiming that MacDiarmid's "verbal exuberance" is to be found also in the Makar; in addition he sees Mac-Diarmid indulging in "exhibitionist use of technical terms, in verbal playfulness . . . even in a sort of 'mouth music' where language becomes essentially varied rhythmic sound." And so back to the language question once more.

Like Boutelle's book. *The Age of MacDiarmid* work is tripartite. The first group of essays consists of personal assessments; there are contributions by Sorley MacLean (see *WLT* 52:2, pp. 229–32), who has frequently admitted the formative influence MacDiarmid's work had on his own development as a poet; by J. K. Annand; by Duncan Glen, who has done so much to further Mac-Diarmid's international reputation; by Alan Bold, a poet of the second generation of followers of MacDiarmid and whose essay "Dr Grieve and Mr MacDiarmid" takes up again the divided self of Scotland and Scottish literature; and finally by Tom Scott, who writes on "The Influence of Hugh MacDiarmid," himself not the least of the group.

The second group of essays consists of critical assessments of MacDiarmid's work. In addition to the pieces by Murison and Daiches, there are essays by George Bruce, Kenneth Buthlay, Iain Crichton Smith, Ronald Stevenson and John Wain. Three of these contributors are poets of acknowledged standing, and it is interesting to see how they assess a member of their own craft. Bruce examines, partly from personal reminiscence, partly from published sources, one of the best-known causes which MacDiarmid took up with Edwin Muir as his target—one wishes one could call it a "flyting," but this supposes a response, and Muir wisely chose not to answer his friend. It started in 1936, when Muir's *Scott and Scotland* appeared; the gist of Muir's argument was that the Scottish writer must write in English, for if he writes in Scots there is "neither an organic community . . . nor a major literary tradition to support him." MacDiarmid felt that Muir had betrayed Scotland, even though, as we have seen, he was himself no longer writing much in Scots. The real problem lay in the suggestion Muir made that not only must Scottish poets write in English, but that Scots should not seek any sort of separate national identity.

Kenneth Buthlay, whose 1964 study of the poet broke new ground, contributes the longest essay, a study of the sources of *To Circumjack Cencrastus* (1930).

Buthlay is able only to touch upon them in just one work, but the essay forms an eloquent plea for a full-scale study of the multitude of influences which were to shape the poetry of Hugh MacDiarmid and ultimately to shape the whole course of the Scottish Renaissance. A close study by Iain Crichton Smith of *On a Raised Beach,* a short note on symbols in MacDiarmid by Ronald Stevenson, and an imaginary dialogue between Roy Campbell and Hugh MacDiarmid by John Wain make up the remainder of this section.

The third section of this book is concerned with quite another Hugh MacDiarmid—the man and his politics. Grieve/MacDiarmid is probably the only Scotsman ever to have been expelled by both the Communist Party and the Scottish Nationalist Party, and at a later date to have been proudly claimed as a member. How are we to account for a person who at the same time espouses the ideal of worldwide internationalism and the fragmentation of one of Europe's smaller countries? (The breakup would not have ended with Scotland—there were Ireland, Wales, Cornwall, northern England—the list seems limitless.) I have puzzled over this contradiction for a long time and have no ready answer—not the least puzzling part of the question is the fact that Grieve/MacDiarmid steadfastly maintained that no contradiction existed and thus sidestepped repeated questions about it. One cannot dismiss his attachment to the cause of Scottish Nationalism, even though he added to it more than a touch of showmanship. Anyone, for example, who can describe his recreation as "Anglophobia," as he did in *Scottish Biographies 1938,* cannot expect to be taken entirely seriously, even though a deadly seriousness underlay his every political statement. In his perceptive essay "Prose and Polemic" Owen Dudley Edwards puts it this way: "But he did say things he believed with only part of his mind, usually the uppermost and most superficial part." Edwards also makes the point, debatable I believe, that MacDiarmid's prose was for those "too stupid to understand his poetry." To accept this statement would be to relegate Grieve to the rank of a second-order MacDiarmid, and I do not believe this to be the case. Neal Ascherson has some useful points to make (and perceptive questions to ask) about MacDiarmid and real politics, those issues about which he wrote and talked: Leninism, Stalinism, Social Credit, the Nazi-Soviet Pact. "MacDiarmid took from Communism what he needed and fancied," he writes correctly. Stephen Maxwell claims that MacDiarmid saw that "the motive force of radical change had henceforth to be sought in Scotland's political needs rather than in her distinctive linguistic or cultural heritage." Something of a synthesis of poetry and politics in MacDiarmid is attempted by Edwin Morgan.

Almost every one of the essays in this book stresses the difficulty of pinning down MacDiarmid; as soon as the reader thinks he has done so, up pops the poet with a statement which appears completely to belie his own writing. Cantankerous, contradictory, obstinate visionary with a pen of gold, MacDiarmid can probably best be summed up in his own words:

So I have gathered unto myself
All the loose ends of Scotland,
And by naming them and accepting them,
Loving them and identifying myself with them,
Attempt to express the whole.

If anyone could express the whole, Hugh MacDiarmid could.

G. Ross Roy, Winter 1982

---

[1] Ann Edwards Boutelle. *Thistle and Rose: A Study of Hugh Mac-Diarmid's Poetry.* Loanhead, Midlothian, Scotland. Macdonald. 1981. 259 pages. £12.50.

[2] *The Age of MacDiarmid: Essays on Hugh MacDiarmid and His Influence on Contemporary Scotland.* P. H. Scott, A. C. Davis, eds. Edinburgh. Mainstream (Barnes & Noble, distr.). 1981. 268 pages. £7.95/$22.50.

The Last Romantic: Henry Boot, Alias Tom Stoppard

The Real Thing represents a midcareer conjunction of two elements that have been a force both in many of Stoppard's plays and *on* his writing in general. The result of this merger is a play whose sobered-down ideas and language contrast sharply with the parodic brilliance of *Rosencrantz and Guildenstern Are Dead, Jumpers,* and *Travesties.* The first, an internal element, is the main character of Henry Boot, a dramatist in the image of his author. As dramatist, he embodies Stoppard's view of the artist and his function in society, a view already argued in earlier plays such as *Artist Descending a Staircase* and *Travesties.* More importantly, he is the culmination of a long series of Stoppardian heroes, from George Riley in the television play *A Walk on the Water* (later changed on the stage to *Enter a Free Man*) to Malquist in *Lord Malquist and Mr. Moon,* Stoppard's only novel. As protagonist, the Boot character is challenged either within himself or by another character, a Moon. He may be a Boot in one situation and a Moon in another; occasionally he is both at once.

In *Travesties* Lenin divides all men into two groups: those who do and those to whom things are done, the former constituting the Boots of Stoppard's plays and the latter the Moons. Contrasting with Lenin's hero as social activist, however, are Stoppard's stylists: the Lord Malquists, James Joyces, and Tristan Tzaras. Their heroism consists not of action but of style over substance and the consequent detachment from personal and political involvement. As a result, critics have called attention to the missing dimensions of conscience and emotional credibility in Stoppard's characters.

The origin of the Boot character is the reporter in Evelyn Waugh's *Scoop,* a novel that has directly influenced *Night and Day,* Stoppard's drama about journalists caught up in an African revolution. In his days as a journalist, Stoppard wrote under the pseudonym of William Boot. The name recurs in early television and radio plays of the 1960s: *The Way Out with Samuel Boot* and *The Dissolution of Dominic Boot.* Moon references similarly occur in the early plays *'M' Is for Moon among Other Things* and *Another Moon Called Earth.* Stoppard attributes his naming a critic Moon in *The Real Inspector Hound* to a Paul Newman movie, *Left-Handed Gun,* in which drunk cowboys shoot at the moon's reflection in a watering trough.[1] (These cowboys appear also in Stoppard's novel.) Similar de-mystifications of romantic moon mythology occur prominently in *Another Moon Called Earth* and *Jumpers* in the persons of women characters who are disillusioned as a result of watching quarreling lunanauts on television.

The purest expression of the Boot character is Lord Malquist, who rides through congested modern London streets around Buckingham Palace in a horse-drawn carriage and conducts himself in the style of an eighteenth-century gentleman, scornfully detached from the chaos of his time. He hires a secretary, Mr. Moon, to ride with him and function as Boswell to his Johnson, in order to record for posterity his pronouncements on a dying age. Beset with Prufrockian uncertainties, Moon himself intends to write a history of the world, only to be destroyed by the accidental explosion of a bomb which he carries around with him through the novel. The carriage journey of the two men takes place on the day of the funeral of the last great traditional hero, a man of action, presumably Winston Churchill. As Malquist dictates to his secretary, the new hero, hereafter, is the spectator-stylist which the new age demands. Moon, on the other hand, in his increasingly frustrating attempts to write, disappears into his uncertainties and is eventually destroyed. Malquist survives. Thus the construction and subsequent dismantling of artistic, ethical, and philosophical systems through his Boots and Moons by means of linguistic and intellectual exuberance, bizarre events, and successfully daring parodies of Shakespeare, Beckett, Wilde, Eliot, and others have established Stoppard as the spectator-stylist dramatist whose characters lack emotional or moral conviction.

This second, subtle but consistent force has haunted the productions of Stoppard's plays, and some critics remain unconvinced where character credibility is concerned. In his three major plays to date, mentioned above, characters are dominated by the spectacular fireworks of ideas and language that have become Stoppard's dramatic hallmark. Endowed with brilliant intellectual arguments, dazzling language, and the fantasy-defying events of their lives, they attempt to construct personal or philosophical order from the chaos around them, only to see their attempts dismantled by other characters or events. Rosencrantz and Guildenstern, George Moore, and Henry Carr—of *Rosencrantz and Guildenstern Are Dead, Jumpers,* and *Travesties* respectively—search for certainties with varying degrees of failure, yet do so in ingeniously entertaining ways. They make a stab at understanding the world and at gaining some control in their destiny, but fail except in the brilliance of their attempts. In the late 1970s, however, Stoppard wrote dramas about human-rights violations in Eastern Europe. On television he dramatized the plight of dissidents in his native Czechoslovakia in *Professional Foul.* On the stage, *Every Good Boy Deserves Favour* and *Dogg's Hamlet, Cahoot's Macbeth* continued his response to the criticism that he lacked conscience and commitment. *Night and Day,* however, while helping to silence one criticism, evoked another, this time of his conservative position on closed shops. The liberal union journalist, Wagner, receives harsh treatment as opposed to that of the young nonunion, idealistic journalist, Milne. No secret to those who knew him, one journalist wrote, Stoppard's "argument may have gained ferocity during his talks with his friend . . . 'Mrs. Thatcher's swooning disciple.' The play is dedicated to him."[2]

Nevertheless, having dealt with the social-commitment criticism, that regarding the emotional dimensions of Stoppard's characters remained until 1982, when *The Real Thing* opened at the Strand Theatre in London. *The Real Thing* dramatizes a painful emotional education of a dramatist named Henry, as that education is implemented by his current wife Annie, an actress, his ex-wife Charlotte, also an actress, and his precocious seventeen-year-old and very modern daughter Debbie.

Although the play reviews were mixed, Stoppard's attempt at the realization of an emotionally plausible character was noted in every instance. Some critics, like Irving Wardle, who described it as "cleverness with its back to the wall," remained unconvinced. In New York, however, there was near unanimity in the acclaim of the critics. Attributed to the tightening of the pace of the dialogue and action by director Mike Nichols and to some rewriting by Stoppard, the contrast between the London and New York productions was more subdued when Jeremy Irons and Glenn Close left the cast. The interesting history of the play on stage is traceable in the reviews of Frank Rich, who saw the London version as one in which "Mr. Stoppard's old and new obsessions fight to a fitfully engaging draw."[3] In its transitional and tentative nature, "its sincere feelings and potentially dazzling theatrical devices buckle out of shape as the author veers between fresh territory and familiar ground." However, in New York Rich noted that the play "is not only Stoppard's most moving play, but also the most bracing play that anyone has written about love and marriage in years."[4] Rich's enthusiasm moderated with the play's second New York cast, as he noticed "the flaws in Mr. Stoppard's play on another visit," even while gaining "renewed respect for its many strengths."[5]

The fresh territory referred to involves Stoppard's first creation of a convincingly emotional character. The familiar ground consists of the expected Stoppardian debates (here about love, of course), wit, and parody. The blend of the two results in the toning down of the spectacular displays of language and ideas of earlier dramas and also in the broader appeal of the play, on a realistic level, to a commercial and more romantically inclined audience.

The new realism of the American production was realized in several ways. One of these was the elimination of screen images after many of the scenes. In London the projected images distracted some, seemed too arty to others, and clearly slowed down the action of the play. Also eliminated in New York were the individual panels raised or lowered to indicate scene changes. In New York changes were achieved by the use of a revolving stage, effectively tightening the pace of the action. Technical matters such as these are only a part of the revisions occasioned by the play's crossing of the Atlantic.

Although the revised text is not available and thus cannot be quoted or referred to, one of the few substantive sea changes, at least to my mind, occurs in the penultimate scene, in which Annie clearly and unequivocally informs Henry that she cannot casually stop her current affair with Billy. The New York revision of this confrontation blurs and blunts Annie's honesty, making her like the more traditional fictional Charlotte of Henry's *House of Cards.* As such, she confirms the real Charlotte's description of Henry as the last romantic and weakens the final impact of Henry's emotional education.

Additional weakening occurs in the structural change involving the merging of two scenes: that between Henry and Charlotte (scene 7) and that between Henry and Debbie (scene 9). Originally each scene builds to Annie's revelation to Henry of her attraction toward Billy. The New York version, in the interest of speeding up the pace of the action, sacrifices or at least de-emphasizes subtle ironies, reducing again the painful impact of the reality of Henry's situation on his traditional romanticism. Even Annie's throwing the bowl of dip in Brodie's face (an ironic variation of the dip scene early in the play) loses its force and imposes a farcical tone on the play at the end.

These losses are balanced, however, by a gain in Stoppard's rewriting of Henry's rewriting of the Brodie play (scene 11 in the original). In a stroke of genius, the wordy version is cut to a few lines, and the scene ends ambiguously as the lights dim out. Preceding Annie's climactic confrontations with Henry and Brodie, the tightened version results in a fluidity lacking in the original.

The new emotional realism of *The Real Thing,* however, still relies on familiar Stoppardian devices. Among these are what the author has called ambushes for the audience. The latest variation of this ambush consists of the onstage performance of a fictional play, *The House of Cards,* by Henry. Not until the second scene is the audience let in on this bit of deception, enhanced by the fact that the characters in the scene carry their real-life names. Thus begins a familiar Pirandellian game of role playing.

The presentation of a West End scene within another West End play is a clever parodic device whose fictional truths remain to be played out in the real lives of Henry, his first and second wives, Charlotte and Annie, as well as his daughter Debbie. Like the toppling of the house of cards which the architect of the fictional play constructs as a model for his new building, Henry's ideas of marriage must fall as he is painfully educated into what the real thing is. The dramatization of that education is realized in the style of the nested Russian dolls or Chinese boxes contained one within another. Scenes or parts of scenes from the actual performance of *The House of Cards* and from readings or rehearsals of Strindberg's *Miss Julie,* Ford's *'Tis a Pity She's a Whore,* and still another fictional inner play by Brodie (Henry's antagonist in love and in writing) nest within one another.

An example of thematic nesting is Charlotte's complaint to Henry of her dissatisfaction with the phantom lover provided for her in *The House of Cards.* Her complaint carries over into real life, not only for her but for

Annie, her successor as wife to Henry. Shortly after she and Henry are comfortably ensconced, Annie refers to their honeymoon as being over, since Henry's late working habits restrict their lovemaking. He is becoming for her that same phantom lover found in his play and in his marriage to Charlotte.

He also becomes the jealous husband of that play. The fictional Charlotte returns from Switzerland to a suspicious husband who has gone through her recipe file and discovered her passport, thinking to catch her in her infidelity. Charlotte later reveals to Henry that her current lover, an architect, had rifled her bathroom cabinet, accusing her of taking her diaphragm with her on one of her acting jobs. In the ultimate imitation of art by life, Annie, also an actress, returns from one of her many trips to Glasgow, where she has been performing, to find that Henry has disturbed her belongings.

Henry, who describes himself "as an ironist in public though a prig in private,"[6] both writes about and becomes that suspicious husband. Slowly, however, the detachment of the ironist-author from the prig-husband grinds to a halt as the women in his life conspire in his emotional education. To begin, Annie does not share Henry's contempt for the left-wing dramatist Brodie or for the committed playwright in general. Having made the acquaintance of Brodie on a train en route to an antinuclear rally, she champions his cause and seduces Henry into rewriting his bad television play about social change. In the meantime, she has taken on another lover, a younger actor, Billy, to whose Giovanni she plays Annabella in 'Tis a Pity She's a Whore. She and Billy also play the leads in Henry's revision of Brodie's play.

Henry's education in love begins innocently enough when he "reads" with Annie a scene from Miss Julie, a play about seduction. She is irritated with his inability to read subtext and, consequently, accuses him of not being able to write it. More importantly, she suggests he cannot read between the lines in real life, for whenever she makes sexual overtures, he becomes moody as a result of being seduced from his work, making her feel that she is "just a relief after Charlotte, and a novelty" (44). Just the opposite occurs between Annie and Billy on train rides to Glasgow and in rehearsals, as they subtextually communicate a mutual attraction by using lines from the plays in which they appear together. In a rehearsal scene in Glasgow, Annie returns Billy's kiss in earnest.

Henry's painful suspicions gain momentum in short scenes with his ex-wife Charlotte and his daughter Debbie. He discovers that one of Charlotte's lovers was

an actor who had played Giovanni to her Annabella, much as in the current situation between Annie and Billy. Debbie rejects Henry's traditional arguments about love, informing him that "exclusive rights isn't love, it's colonization" (69). She chides her father for writing about nothing in The House of Cards except "did she have it off or didn't she? . . . Infidelity among the architect class" (67). She repeats Annie's earlier charge of Henry's insensitivity, finally cutting through his intellectual arguments about love with her penetrating question, "Annie got someone else, then?" (69).

The scenes with Charlotte and Debbie precede the one in which Henry is similarly confronted by Annie and in which the action of The House of Cards repeats itself closely in real life. Annie has returned from Glasgow to find her room in disarray. Irritated further by Henry's close interrogation about her movements from Glasgow to London, she admits to lying but makes it clear that she won't have him playing on her guilt or remorse, insisting equally that she does love him.

Like Charlotte in The House of Cards, Annie brings her husband a gift. Unlike her fictional prototype, however, she has a real lover. Also unlike the fictional heroine, she is pushed into taking a lover out of need, not by her husband's jealousy and suspicions. With total honesty, she informs Henry that her affair with Billy is not a threat, but neither is it over.

> I didn't want to start it casually, and I can't stop it casually. I can't, and I don't want to go. I go around all the time saying 'Thank you' like a child because I can't behave well towards you both, and you allow me to behave well towards him without having to be furtive, so I'm grateful and I say thank you. I need you. Please don't let it wear away what you feel for me. It won't, will it? (79)

In the final scene, Henry, Brodie, and Annie watch a video cassette of Brodie's play. When Brodie coarsely recounts his liaison with Annie and questions her relationship with Billy, she smashes the bowl of dip in his face, and he leaves. Henry's jealousy of Brodie vanishes, and he (Henry) now declares that he can "write love." He understands Annie and Billy, and, as well, Charlotte and her many lovers, about whom she has only recently informed him. Perhaps his hardest lesson is Annie's plea that he must find a part of himself where she is unimportant, if their love is to survive. Henry the ironist remains, but no longer is he a spectator. Henry the prig, however, has changed. For the first time a Boot character changes into a Moon without being destroyed by or disappearing into his uncertainties.

As stylist, Henry remains intact. His earlier claim that writing about love was embarrassing, childish, or rude and that loving and being loved are unliterary seems to have dissolved. His creator, Tom Stoppard, has similarly illustrated that love can be both literate and literary. Henry's views on the author as stylist are those of Stoppard. In response to Annie's defense of Brodie's right to write about something real, even if he isn't the wordsmith that Henry is, the latter picks up his cricket bat to explain the difference between a wooden club and a bat, and also the difference between his writing style and Brodie's.

> This thing here, which looks like a wooden club is actually several pieces of particular wood cunningly put together in a certain way so that the whole thing is sprung, like a dance floor. . . . What we're trying to do is to write cricket bats, so that when we throw up an idea and give it a little knock, it might . . . travel. . . . Now, what we've got here is a lump of wood of roughly the same shape trying to be a cricket bat, and if you hit a ball with it, the ball will travel ten feet and you will drop the bat and dance about shouting 'Ouch!' with your hands stuck into your armpits. (53)

Henry's debate with Annie over the matter of Brodie's art occurs early in act 2 and is the same view of art that Stoppard has aired through characters in other plays, such as Joyce in *Travesties*. Here, however, the debate is part of his increasing personal jealousy of Brodie. Since the argument about style is so obvious, in fact, that it is no argument at all, it does seem overdrawn and awkward in and of itself. It seems so at least until out of sheer exasperation at Annie's stubbornness in insisting that he rewrite the play, Henry's detachment suddenly breaks and he exclaims: "Why Brodie? Do you fancy him or what?" Too late he takes back his question, and Annie leaves, replying as she does, "Too late" (56).

The metaphor of the cricket bat as art is followed by several long diatribes by Henry on Brodie's prejudices that "patriotism is propaganda, religion is a con trick, royalty is an anachronism" (54). Evoking lines from an early short story, "Reunion," Stoppard concludes Henry's harangue with his very strong feeling about the overriding importance of language: "If you get the right ones [words] in the right order, you can nudge the world a little or make a poem which children will speak for you when you're dead" (55). In *Travesties* Joyce defines the artist as "the magician put among men to gratify—capriciously—their urge for immortality."

> The temples are built and brought down around him, continuously and contiguously, from Troy to the fields of Flanders. If there is any meaning in any of it, it is in what survives as art, yes even in the celebration of tyrants, yes in the celebration of nonentities. What now of the Trojan War if it had been passed over by the artist's touch? Dust. . . . And yet I with my Dublin Odyssey will double that immortality, yes by God there's a *corpse* that will dance for some time yet and *leave the world precisely as it finds it.*[7]

What stands out prominently as a difference between *Travesties* and *The Real Thing* in the debate about the function of art in life is that in the former the characters, as debaters and antagonists, are equally matched. In *The Real Thing* Henry and Brodie are mismatched both as lovers of Annie and as writers of plays. Herein lies a major flaw in the play. Henry is characterized fully, whereas his antagonist Brodie remains a caricature. What still remains unliterary for Stoppard is the modern liberal philosopher or activist, much as characters with conscience and emotion once seemed. Despite the flaw, however, Henry's emotional adjustment, brought on by a painfully acquired understanding, can claim a credibility not present in previous Stoppardian characters.

Susan Rusinko, Winter 1985

[1] Tom Stoppard, "Ambushes for the Audience," *Theatre Quarterly,* May–June 1974, p. 17.

[2] Marc, "A Play for Paul," *Sunday Times,* 29 October 1978, p. 32; Irving Wardle, "Cleverness with Its Back to the Wall," *Times,* 18 November 1982.

[3] Frank Rich, "Stoppard's *Real Thing* in London," *New York Times,* 23 June 1983, p. C15.

[4] Frank Rich, "Love Lost and Found," *New York Times,* 6 January 1984, p. C3.

[5] Frank Rich, "Plays-Within-Plays are Doubling the Theatregoer's Pleasure," *New York Times,* 12 January 1984, p. C17.

[6] Tom Stoppard, *The Real Thing,* London, Faber & Faber, 1982, p. 66. All subsequent references are indicated parenthetically.

[7] Tom Stoppard, *Travesties,* London, Faber & Faber, 1975, pp. 62–63.

The Best of *Books Abroad*

World Literature Today, 63:2 (Spring 1989)

INTRODUCING OUR 250TH ISSUE

This issue represents a moment of reflection, a halt along our way from season to season, accumulating ever new perspectives, an opportunity to look back at the road behind us. As *Books Abroad,* our journal published two hundred issues during the half-century 1927–76. In its new format as *World Literature Today* it has reached herewith its fiftieth number. It seemed a good idea to mark the occasion by reprinting several of the memorable essays and surveys from previous issues—not from *WLT,* which is still readily available (with only a very few exceptions), but from *BA,* complete sets of which have become collectors' items. Consequently, what follows is one hundred pages of criticism culled from the years 1934–76, grouped as "Writers" and "Topics." Why no articles from the quarterly's first seven years? Because there were very few articles included with the reviews during those years, and those few tended to be short, more of the purely informative than essayistic kind. After 1934 the choice became increasingly difficult and inevitably more subjective. Still, I hope there are enough highlights and variety to make the reading—or rereading—of our small anthology a cumulative pleasure.

There is quite a range of modern literary history, and of our journal's history too, gathered in these essays. Stylistic preferences and critical approaches have naturally changed over the decades, all reflected in the texts. (We have made only minimal changes in spelling, punctuation, and style and have added but a handful of notes for updates and clarification; only the Taha Hussein essay has been shortened.) Nevertheless, one feature has remained constant through the years: a sense of genuine excitement, of personal involvement with literature. In the opening piece we visit the first Russian Nobel laureate, Ivan Bunin, at his exile home in Grasse, Provence: "Before the evening meal you take a stroll with the host, and whether he talks or gazes about in alert silence, your senses are sharpened. Somehow he imparts to you his own extraordinary receptivity, and with Bunin at your side you respond more keenly to land and sea and sky at twilight," writes Alexander Kaun back in 1934. Together with Domenico Vittorini we meet the Italian Nobelist Luigi Pirandello "at the reception tendered him aboard the *S. S. Conte di Savoia* on 20 July 1935, when he arrived in New York on his way to Hollywood, where he was to take part in the filming of his play *Six Characters in Search of an Author.*" From these impressionistic vignettes we are soon led into an encounter not only with the writer but with the essential aspects of his work and thought. The appreciation of Kafka's classical achievement is as perceptive today as it was when Werner Neuse formulated it in 1935 and when it was still new and not yet the staple grist of the Kafka industry, which would be so hilariously parodied twenty-two years later in this same journal by Charles Willeford ("To a Nephew in College"). The tragic loss of Lorca is evoked by another early contributor, while a Hungarian critic laments the linguistic inaccessibility of such a major Hungarian literary figure as Mihály Babits—a red thread running through many a subsequent essay presenting poets from this Finno-Ugric language. There cannot be too many who could claim Sigmund Freud as an uncle, as is done by Ernst Waldinger. It was quite a satisfaction for me to come across Robert Ray's laudatory 1966 interpretation of Raja Rao's novels, long before Rao received our Neustadt Prize. Other editors can take credit for commissioning the articles on Yiddish, Anglo-Irish (by Seán O'Faoláin no less), English Canadian (by Northrop Frye), and Arabic literature (by Taha Hussein, thanks to Bernice Duncan), and on West African writing in English. It was my immediate predecessor as editor, Dr. Robert Vlach, who sponsored the 1967 Nobel Prize symposium introduced by Herbert Howarth's seminal

Ivar Ivask *(Gil Jain)*

"Petition to the Swedish Academy," the formulations of which not only subsequently influenced the choices of the Swedish Academy but also led to the establishment in 1969 of our own Neustadt International Prize for Literature.

The Swedish author and critic Olof Lagercrantz recounts his impressions from the third Neustadt jury meeting and its selection of Francis Ponge in "A Literary Prize in Oklahoma" (1974), and elsewhere Harry Levin takes us to meet Ponge in his own Parisian home at 34 rue Lhomond. Other Neustadt laureates such as Giuseppe Ungaretti and the later Nobelist Czesław Miłosz are represented respectively with a text on Allen Ginsberg and a thoughtful evaluation of another Nobel winner, Boris Pasternak. Since we have long made a point of highlighting each year's Nobel recipient, other articles selected here deal with the two Greek laureates (Seferis and Elytis) and the only Japanese honoree (Kawabata). Neither René Char nor Heimito von Doderer garnered either prize, yet they are lovingly presented to our readers by Paulène Aspel, a specialist on the former, and Helen Wolff, the latter's American publisher, respectively.

There still remains another category of authors associated with this journal, individuals to whom we have dedicated one of the biennial Puterbaugh Conferences on Writers of the French-Speaking and Hispanic World. The first poet honored in this series cosponsored by *BA/WLT* was Jorge Guillén in 1968. Since he was well known as a translator and disciple of Valéry (though always disputing the latter fact), I asked him to write down his reminiscences of the French poet for an issue I had planned to dedicate to Valéry. Guillén surprisingly agreed (we had been friends and correspondents since 1952), and the Spanish original was beautifully translated by the Lithuanian-American Hispanist Birutė Ciplijauskaitė. Mario Vargas Llosa was the special guest for the 1977 conference, but seven years earlier he had written for our special issue on "The Latin American Novel Today" an introductory essay which has been widely acclaimed as the most brilliant exposition of the Boom phenomenon in Latin American fiction.

The Estonian critic Alexander Aspel, a specialist on modern French poets such as Char, Bonnefoy, and Jaccottet, participated in our issue "A Look at Baltic Letters Today" with an essay that analyzed the present editor's poetry alongside that of two other Estonian émigré authors. I have published several more collections of verse since 1976, but Aspel's focus on my essential preoccupations as a poet still is to the point. Bernice Duncan, an associate editor of the quarterly who served under all five editors and kept the journal going during the interregnum between Vlach's death and my own appointment, concludes the article section, which justly spans all five decades of *BA*, including my own arrival, in the history of the journal. Indeed, "And So It Grew" is a most apt formula for the 250 issues of *Books Abroad,* now *World Literature Today.*

Our faithful readers will notice the absence on the back inside cover of our customary "Notes on Contributors" column. The passing of several of the contributors has been noted in our pages, either in separate articles or within our annual necrologies. Finding out about several of the others would have entailed research which our small, overburdened staff could not have accomplished easily. So let their presence in this selection, with their one-time academic affiliations, serve as our tribute to their collaboration and, in several cases, to their memory. The journal has reached this point thanks to their and their many other colleagues' faithful service over more than six decades, work done with faith in and enthusiasm for living letters. All this was fostered by the five editors of the journal thus far: Roy Temple House (1927–49), Ernst Erich Noth (1949–59), Wolfgang Bernard Fleischmann (1959–61), Robert Vlach (1961–66), and myself (1967-), with Bernice Duncan serving as acting editor in 1966–67. None of my predecessors is today among the living. The present critical anthology is one way of paying tribute to their faith in literature as a living force, which is shared by the contributors chosen to stand for so many others in this our 250th issue.

Ivar Ivask

WRITERS

Ivan Bunin [1934]

On an October morning he met my train at Cannes. Even if he did not hold in his hands a copy of *Posledniia Novosti,* as previously agreed upon, I should have recognized his face, certainly his eyes. From my early boyhood I have been familiar with the strong features of Bunin's face, youthful and bearded at the time of his companionship with such "rising" authors as Gorky and Andreyev, clean-shaven and haggard since the Revolution and his emigration. His gray eyes have always struck me with their composite expression of severity, haughtiness, and melancholy. As time went on, and as his life became enriched with chagrin and vicissitudes, his photographs betrayed a growing intensity of that expression.

For some ten years Bunin has been living in Grasse, about an hour's ride from Cannes. When he did not come to see me, in the annoyingly anglicized Cannes, I took the bus to Grasse, where after a long and winding climb I would reach his Villa Belvedere. Quiet, isolated, high in the hills overlooking the verdant town and the distant Mediterranean, Bunin's home has the air of a cloister. A rough simplicity reigns in the place, and a Provençal geniality, even to the stocky landlord who on occasion turns cook and butler. Before the evening meal you take a stroll with the host, and whether he talks or gazes about in alert silence, your senses are sharpened. Somehow he imparts to you his own extraordinary receptivity, and with Bunin at your side you respond more keenly to land and sea and sky at twilight.

You try to make him reminisce, describe. With him the two are synonymous; his art is extremely close to that of the painter, at times disconcertingly so. He perceives and records the finest details of color and line, taxing both your vision and memory, forgetting that literary composition differs from one on canvas, which permits your eyes to rove up and down, back and forth, simultaneously observing both the details and the ensemble. If possible, Bunin is even more sensitive to odors. In his verse and in his prose he uses odor to evoke a multiple variety of sensations. Who can forget the blossoming orchard in *Mitya's Love,* the sensuous

aromas of pears and acacias in their effect on adolescent passion gone wild? And Bunin's is a most catholic bouquet: his hypersensitive nostrils have inhaled the scents of vast stretches of land and sea, from Russia's fields and steppes, through Western Europe, to exotic Asia and Africa.

Still, his life, like his stories, has been rich but not eventful, in the sense of "plot," of recountable episodes. The autobiographical work in which he is engaged at present (the first volume has appeared in English as *The Well of Days,* Knopf), and which promises to be his masterpiece, makes you feel and smell his boyhood and youth, but not as a specifically human life. Man is seldom an isolated entity in Bunin's scheme; he appears as a component part of the setting, of the landscape or seascape, and is not endowed with any relatively greater significance. He has already shown us in *The Gentleman from San Francisco* how puny and fragile looks the strutting biped against a background of elements—the ocean, and death.

His reminiscences are thus poor in plot. His life can be told in a few sentences. He was born (1870) in central Russia, Turgenev's Russia, whose nonspectacular landscape both these writers have loved and have made live as much as its exquisitely melancholy folk song. In 1891 his first book of verse was published, and within a decade he took his place along with the leading Russian authors. This in spite of the fact that he kept aloof from political parties and literary schools, an extremely difficult position in Russia. In a cool, crystallike verse, and in as fastidious a rhythmic prose, Bunin went his own way, voicing lyrically what he thought and felt, regardless of contemporary tendencies. His great curiosity for life in its variegated forms may explain his prodigious travels in faraway lands, as well as his ventures into foreign literatures. During that same decade he translated Longfellow's *Hiawatha* into a racy Russian of such excellencies as one may not easily find in the original. He also translated Byron's *Manfred* and *Cain.* In 1903 he was given the highest literary award, the Pushkin Prize, and six years later he became one of the twelve members of the literature section of the Imperial Academy of Sciences. Bunin's indifference to political problems was shown by his acceptance of this honor, despite the resignation from the Academy, a few years previously, of Korolenko and Chekhov as a protest against the treatment of Gorky (Nicholas II had the Academy cancel the election of Gorky, after it had been officially announced).

In 1910 appeared Bunin's first novel, *The Village.* Unlike most of the gentry writers, who idealized the Russian peasants, Bunin drew a gloomy picture of the economic and moral disintegration of rural Russia. As if in answer to his critics who accused him of bias, he followed this novel with another, *Sukhodol,* in which he portrayed as mercilessly the decay of his own class. While remaining delicately lyrical and sensitive, Bunin displayed in these and other works a keen eye for human folly and banality that reminded one of Gogol and Sologub. Bunin, however, is not a satirist. A deep melancholy suffuses his canvases, a brooding nostalgia. In his poetry and in his prose one senses the pathos of the irretrievable past. Himself a member of an impoverished noble family, he lived from his childhood in a moribund atmosphere. Turgenev's Russia, the land of large estates, of ancestral parks, of charming futility, of quixotic Hamlets, was passing. Patriarchal rusticity was disintegrating, and being replaced by a swiftly advancing industrialism, which provoked ruthless class conflicts and which bore the seeds of the inevitable collapse of the old order. One hears in Bunin the note of the Last Mohican of gentry Russia.

The Bolshevik victory jolted Bunin out of his political detachment. He took definite sides. To this day he is one of the most irreconcilable enemies of the new order. Russia ceased to live for him in 1917. The pathos of the dying gentry was now augmented by the pathos of a dead country. Bolshevik Russia is to Bunin "the snout of a pig." The past acquires a multiplied charm, a splendor seen through tears of chagrin and regret. The present he brands, in his verses, as "a shameless and contemptible age." He entertains no hopes for the restoration of the old: "There is no return to that by which we once lived. Our losses cannot be counted, nor forgotten. The blows on the face by the soldiers of Pilate cannot be washed off, nor forgiven. As one can forgive neither the pain nor the blood nor the convulsions on the cross of those murdered in Christ. As one cannot accept the coming new order in its repellent nakedness".

In his bitter hatred of the new Russia Bunin is unreasoningly blind. This is one subject on which you cannot fruitfully converse with him: his fine baritone breaks into a falsetto, his gray eyes lose their haughty melancholy and shoot ire, his noble nose twists and wrinkles, and his delectable sense of humor forsakes him utterly. I have met other intransigent haters among Russian emigrants; most of these have so completely severed themselves from Russia that their minds have become hollow and sterile. Bunin alone has kept his talent alive and creatively welling. Perhaps this is due to the profound religiosity which permeates all his work and his whole being. The sense of divinity imbuing all nature, all life, must keep him afloat, must give him hope, must urge him to go on, to fulfill his mission as a creative artist. One can only regret that, unlike the ex-

uberant Soviet writers, Bunin can look only backward. How much more vital his work might be if his vision were not so circumscribed!

Alexander Kaun

Franz Kafka [1935]

When Franz Kafka died in 1924, at the age of forty-one years old, he left only six slim volumes of stories behind him. Three novels and a collection of prose writings were published posthumously, and we are still waiting for the publication of other material from his manuscripts, among which his correspondence will be especially interesting because of the light it may throw upon his thought. An unprinted chapter from the novel *Der Prozeß* appeared recently in the periodical *Die Sammlung.*

The world that Franz Kafka pictures in his stories and novels is a strange world, and a great many commentators have tried to explain it. Written in a prose style the lucidity and rhythm of which remind us of Stifter's novels, his works reveal the relentless searching of a troubled soul. Nowhere does he give us a clue to his stories, and although we may understand the importance of the details so clearly set forth, only he himself could have given the final key to their meaning. Undoubtedly we are dealing with the product of a restless conscience which did not seem to find an answer to its penetrating self-search. This explains why he never felt that any of his books was ready for publication; in his lifetime one story was printed as a fragment, some others were meant as parts of later novels. Most of the stories are written in monologue form, either using the first-person singular or the form of discourse called "erlebte Rede." It is also noteworthy that the first chapters of the novel *Das Schloß* were originally written in the "I" form for which later the letter "K" was substituted. Not action but discussion and meditation abound. *Betrachtung* [Contemplation] was the name of Kafka's first book (1913), and the name fits as a subtitle to many others.

Kafka's realism is the realism of the parable which undertakes to show, according to his own words, "that the inconceivable is inconceivable." His world seems to move continually from reality into an atmosphere which with its impressive and depressing realism makes the reader feel as if he were moving in a dreamworld. His world of reality is strangely invaded by another world which destroys it more and more. The traditional values do not seem to count any longer. In this transformed world the most unexpected may happen: a man finds himself changed into an animal, an ape chooses to take over the role of a man. We meet a cross-breed between a lamb and a cat. Also the laws of reason and morality are neutralized; space and time become relative to the absoluteness of new conceptions and undergo peculiar changes. The width of the places of action is narrowed incredibly. The sky is the vault of the circus tent, and oftener still the perspective is that of animals like mice or moles. Horses emerge from a pigsty in the story "Ein Landarzt." The village in the novel *Der Prozeβ* might just as well lie in a desert as in Bohemia, since there is no connection between it and the outside world. Time as a unit has only relative importance. History is upside down: to the Chinese people living emperors are long dead, and those long dead have ascended the throne again. The moment widens into an eternity, and time, intead of a measurement of the past or the present, becomes a projection into the future.

Thus Kafka succeeds, by upsetting the natural laws that govern our daily life, in smashing the world of reality as it presents itself to our senses. It becomes the playground for a spiritual inner drama whose end lies far beyond the duration of our lives, whose direction [lies] far beyond our comprehension. Another "Law" or other "Laws" control our lives. Nobody knows these laws; they have been there ever since people can remember. Indeed the existence of these laws is above our understanding; it can only be guessed from those who act as their guardians or interpreters (cf. "Zur Frage der Gesetze" in *Beim Bau der chinesischen Mauer*). Kafka calls the representatives of the Law by various names: guard, father, lawyer, officer, messenger. But it would be futile to try to imagine the next highest authority on the Law. Beyond them everything becomes hearsay, and Kafka develops with great ingenuity an elaborate system of competencies which eventually may lead to the highest competent authority, the judge, the count, the emperor, the Law. In various instances he has pointed out how the human mind is unable to comprehend the other, the "real" world. Only through conception of minute parts for the whole is man capable of grasping the universe and eternity. He is like the animal in the story "Der Bau" (in *Beim Bau der chinesischen Mauer*) who has lost control over his own complicated construction of tunnels and holes. The Great Wall of China can be erected only in small sections.

Similarly the individual is unable to think in the form of *we*, but only in the form of *I*. The individual is strangely isolated in this world. His realization that he is part of another kind of existence is a sudden one and throws his whole life into a turmoil. His life has turned into a "case" which cannot be concealed from the rest. Sooner or later everybody hears of the transformation of Gregor Samsa in "Die Verwandlung," the fictitious claim of the surveyor Josef K. in *Das Schloβ* is reiterated by all who recognize him, and the bank clerk K. in *Der Prozeβ* discovers that almost everybody is informed about his lawsuit. In face of the new personal situation the individual feels an urge not only to conceal his plight but also to deny his identity, yet inwardly there is no escape; for at the very moment when the individual is brought into contact with the other absoluteness—and here Kafka comes close to Kierkegaard's explanation of fear—a terrible uncertainty begins to take hold of him, an apprehension of guilt. However, what we are guilty of we do not know and may not know until we die. Fear will become almost unbearable, for we do not know whether our efforts lead us upward or downward, toward Heaven or toward Hell. Death alone ends the inner struggle. Our duty is to recognize our guilt and to accept the punishment. Life therefore shall lift itself to the fatal moment when we face God. "How long did you hesitate until you matured!" says the father in "Das Urteil" before pronouncing the verdict which the son himself immediately executes. Gregor Samsa, the traveling salesman in "Die Verwandlung," who has found himself transformed into a big bug, accepts his sister's word: he must disappear! A happy expression comes over the faces of the prisoners in "In der Strafkolonie," whose guilt is written upon their backs with the help of an intricate machine shortly before they die.

Still, Kafka is not entirely pessimistic about man's future life. As human beings we might be inclined to argue along logical, moral, or other lines with God, and our viewpoint is like that of an animal measured with His incomprehensibility. Hence Kafka's frequent use of the animal symbol. Nevertheless, the very danger of drifting helplessly and aimlessly before some absolute power is in itself evidence of the religious character of the relationship. Again, as Kierkegaard sees it: the absolute difficulty indicates the connection with the absolute Good. "Sein," says Kafka in one of the aphorisms in *Beim Bau der chinesischen Mauer*, in the German language means two things: "to be" and "to belong to Him." Life in this world, according to another aphorism, as proof of the perpetual repetition of the loss of paradise, indicates that we are eternally there no matter whether we know it here or not; and Life, as the everlasting process of existence, forms the end to many of Kafka's stories. At the end of an ordeal of fear the individual seems to find contact with humanity, and Kafka has given most eloquent expression to a bright outlook in the final chapter of his last novel, *Amerika*, called "Das Naturtheater von Oklahoma," a place of no local or temporal definition, where no questions are asked, and where the individual meets everybody, especially the beloved ones whom he had to leave behind. This is the end to Kafka's own inner struggles as we can see it: a world like a prison in which the individual is confined and kept in ever narrower cells widens into infinity and eternity.

Whatever the forces were that broke through Kafka's writings, whether Neo-Platonism, Romanticism, Mysticism, Judaism, Cabala, or others, the fact remains that his art has completely succeeded in tearing down the everyday aspect of the world and in setting in its place a reality in the face of which no other reality can exist. One may call this way of looking at the world religious or philosophical; it certainly represents an attitude that few poets have presented with such consistency, such uniformity, and such sincerity. Perhaps no other man has felt so keenly the modern profound fear called "Weltangst."

Werner Neuse

Mihály Babits [1935]

1. From a literary point of view Hungary's tragedy consists in the uniqueness of the Hungarian language. This handicap is less felt as far as Hungarian prose is concerned; although the *par excellence* artists of Hungarian prose are not often enough translated into foreign languages, yet they enjoy a certain advantage compared with the Hungarian poets. It is a truism to say that poetry, especially lyric poetry, cannot be translated, because the translation requires such an operation on the original spirit and expression of the poem that its genuine freshness is apt to suffer on account of it. The justice of this statement is quite obvious when, for example, the lyric poems of Sándor Petöfi, Hungary's greatest lyric poet of the nineteenth century, are read in translation. They affect one as if fresh flowers were sprinkled with perfume; and frequently the personality of the translator is so much emphasized that the real atmosphere of Petöfi's poems seems to disappear.

Probably this is one reason why the most outstanding poet of contemporary Hungary, Mihály Babits, has not been, as yet, introduced to the world outside his country. Some of his novels and stories, of which I shall speak later, were translated into French, German, and Italian; their esthetic success cannot be denied; and while these prose works of Mihály Babits do not detract anything from the depth of his creative genius, they do not completely reflect the manifold facets of his art, in which poetry plays an important part. Mihály Babits is a *poeta doctus,* which, however, should not lead one to conclude that his poetic genius moves exclusively in the

realm of intellectual awareness; his thoughts are richly colored with feelings. Naturally, the intellectual element of his work is comparatively easy to express in a foreign tongue; it is the subtleness of his magnificently suggested emotions, the profoundness of his artistically portrayed complicated self, the indestructible restlessness of his sensitive soul, wearing the garment of delicately yet energetically selected words which is difficult to convey in a foreign language. Babits himself is a master of translations. His Hungarian renderings of certain plays of ancient Greece, of Dante's *Divine Comedy,* of medieval Latin hymns, of Shakespeare, Baudelaire, Wilde, and Meredith indicate his capacity for translation. Perhaps a congenial foreigner endowed with the genius of this Hungarian poet could be capable of bringing him nearer through translations to foreigners who do not read Hungarian.

Babits is fifty-two years old. As the editor of Hungary's leading literary periodical, *Nyugat* (West), he exerts a profound influence over the literary life of the country. As a critic and essayist, he compels the admiration of many for his reliable esthetic evaluations and for his ability to decipher from facts the living spirit of mankind, as proved by his extraordinary book that deals with the history of European literature. His erudition is amazing, yet free from stiltedness, evidently because of the vitality of his imagination. If he were writing in a world-known language, nothing could prevent his international recognition.

2. As a poet Babits is a contemporary of Endre Ady, the most feverish poet of modern Hungary, who died in 1919. No two poets could have been more dissimilar than these two. Ady's poetry is the dynamic visualization of an extremely erratic personality's fermentation. Ady was the cursing visionary prophet of his people, the crystallization of an apocalyptic uneasiness. He lacked classical calm, psychological evenness; his subjectivity knew no bounds. On the other hand Babits is universal, his taste is catholic, his restlessness is so much tempered by intellectual discipline, his philosophical knowledge is so all-embracing that, while the first may be called the jeremiad voice of his people, the latter must surely be called the jeremiad voice of mankind in general. Ady's humanity is racial; Babits's is universal. Ady stirs the emotions; Babits humiliates the incompetence of the intellect. Ady's range of poetic forms was rather meager; Babits's range of poetic forms includes every traditional and modern form. Ady's language is often close to the Hungarian translation of the Protestant Bible; he was a Calvinist. Babits, who received a Catholic education, is much nearer to that Europe in which Latinity predominated. Ady is the singer of the word; Babits, the artist of the word. The two poets com-

plete each other, however: both are characteristic voices of modern Hungary; both of them deserve the attention of the world.

When Babits's first volume of poetry, entitled *Levelek Irisz koszorujából* (Leaves from the Wreath of Iris), appeared, the conservative critics of Hungary either ignored the work or criticized it with the superiority of ignorance. Why? Because his poetry was new; because he gave a new rhythm, new intonation to the Hungarian language; and because he broadened the subject matter of Hungarian poetry. Like every poet, he was seeking order in the midst of disorder; he was searching for an illuminating justification of being. While he was accused of violating the traditions of Hungarian poetry, which, no doubt, in the *fin de siécle* period and before the appearance of Ady and Babits, was merely a repetition of stereotyped notions and emotions, he had no intention of destroying values deserving consideration. Even as a young man, and much more so with his ripening, he differentiated between the dignity of conservatism, which recognizes the permanency of values despite the changing trend of merits which are merely expressions of moods in vogue, and that dilettante complacency of conservatism which is uncritical to the status quo when it serves the interests of its own exponents. It is quite characteristic that, while Babits was considered an iconoclast, he emphasized his debt to János Arany, the poet laureate of nineteenth-century Hungary who is included in every Hungarian literary textbook; but his adherence to Arany did not prevent him from following the voice of his own genius and giving expression to it with the undeniable magnetism of his own creative personality. In his later works of poetry, like *Herceg, hátha megjön a tél is* (Prince, Perhaps Winter Will Come), *Recitativ, Sziget és tenger* (Island and Ocean), *Nyugtalanság völgye* (The Valley of Restlessness), *Az istenek halnak, as emberek élnek* (Gods Die, Man Lives), and in his last collection of poems, we are confronted with the same frankness of the spirit that determined his early poetry. Babits reflects the introspective uneasiness of the modern man, his attempts to find meaning in the meaninglessness of life, his heroic struggle with the dark phantoms of destiny. His modernity is not "up to date," however; his taste is too sure, his mastery of expression too deeply rooted in the past, his vision too much in the realm of eternity to succumb to the *tour de force* cleverness of a great many of his contemporaries.

3. The same high-mindedness that characterizes Babits's poetry and his translations characterizes his original prose work. He may be called a realist, but his realism is impregnated with such vivid and sometimes grotesque imagination that even his pronounced realis-

tic works give one the impression of a romantic experience. With a magic touch he probes the soul of matter. No doubt some contemporary psychological theories influenced him; but this influence is hardly worth mentioning, as it is the intuition of Babits that verifies some modern psychological theories, chiefly those related to the "split soul." In his prose the language is more decorative than in his poetry; but even his prose is essentially the work of a poet and not of a man who writes to sell. Ibsen stated that he considered himself a poet, although his writing was cast in the form of plays. This "poetic self" runs through everything that Babits has written. His verbal virtuosity is unusual; but what is even more surprising is his ability to defy the tempting superficiality of mere verbal virtuosity.

As in his poetry, so in his prose he searches for the interdependence of things. His goal is unity in art, coherence in life. Regardless of whether he selects a purely fantastic subject, such as *Karácsonyi Madonna* (The Christmas Madonna), or whether he enters into the subconscious self of his heroes, as in *Gólyakalifa* (The Stork-Caliph), or whether he chooses a tender yet tragic subject, as in *Timár Virgil fia* (The Son of Virgil Timár), in each one of his stories we are aware of a deeply stirred creative mind that wishes to eliminate confusion and convulsion. Even in his novels dealing with social problems, like *Kártyavár* (Castle of Cards), *Halálfiai* (The Sons of Death), *Elza pilóta vagy a tökéletes társadalom* (Pilot Elsa or the Perfect Society), within the structure of an ironically or pathetically crumbling social order he recognizes the loneliness of the human soul, the incredible struggle of the *homo sapiens*. Babits the artist demands form from formlessness, and Babits the man admits the tragic privilege of thinking and feeling.

4. It is obvious that Babits cannot be a poet and a writer recognized by vulgar popularity. Goethe says somewhere that nothing is more horrible than imagination without good taste. Babits's imagination is fertile, but supported always by good taste. Under such circumstances it is comprehensible that his recognition is reduced to the understanding of a relatively small but still very substantial number of connoisseurs. I said before that if he were writing in a world-known tongue, he would be known all over the world. But I would also add that, even then, his international reputation would not reach a great mass of readers; he is too complicated to be exploited for average reading consumption. His microscopical mind makes the insignificant significant; his seismographlike sensitiveness observes the invisible, thus making it visible; he has no "message," with the exception of repeatedly recognizing the fact that to be is

a tragic obligation and to express being is the singer's duty.

Joseph Remenyi

Spain Loses a Great Poet [1937]

Spain has suffered many tragedies since the beginning of the "rightist" rebellion, but to lovers of her literature one of the saddest is the loss of Federico García Lorca, shot down in September by a rebel firing squad. In poetry and in drama he was the most promising writer of his generation in Spain. I am not using "promising" in the usual critical sense of the word—to describe an artist who gives fairly reliable indications that he may become a great poet; his position as the leading and most universally popular poet of present-day Spain was already firmly established at the time of his death. He was a young man and vitally active; and the steadily increasing scope of his more recent work gave every promise of his becoming an even greater one.

His short life was devoted to the emergent modern Spain for which he died, and it was filled with the most intense and manifold activity. Federico García Lorca was born in Fuente Vaqueros (near Granada) on the fifth of June, 1899. He was a precocious child and early in his life became passionately devoted to poetry, music, and the theater—the three arts that were to become integrated in a life devoted to their service. As a youth, he studied philosophy and law in Madrid and returned to his native Andalusia, where he took his degree in law at the University of Granada. The quality of his work there attracted the attention of Fernando de los Ríos, now the Spanish ambassador to the United States.

At the age of twenty he moved his residence to Madrid, where he became intensely occupied in dramatic activities at the Residencia de Estudiantes. From this time on, his genius was widely recognized, even though he had not yet produced his first significant book. His case presents the remarkable phenomenon of a poet whose youthful energy, rare poetic spirit, and unfailing *simpatía* had caused him to be known and loved by Spain's leading men of letters before the publication of his first verse; for his *Impresiones y paisajes* (1918)—the recording in an insecure and oversentimental prose of his first impressions of Castile—gave slight indication of the burning and original genius which was to mark his later, more creative work. However, in his first collection of verse, *Libro de poemas* (1921), it is evident that, although he knew and had assimilated the ultramodern tendencies flourishing in France and Spain at

that time, the book marked the advent of an essentially Spanish poet. The identifying trait of García Lorca's later work, the depurate *andalucismo* in which are combined a truly popular inspiration with a sure sense of form and a great creative gift, is scarcely discernable in his *Libro de poemas;* but its embryo is already there.

His next work, *Poema del cante jondo,* was not published until ten years later, but he had won fame in the intervening years through the publication of *Canciones* (1927; written 1921–23) and *Romancero gitano* (1928; written 1924–27). It is not surprising that García Lorca, profound student of folklore and recognized authority on folk music, should have chosen the "deep song" of the Andalusian gypsy for the theme of his first essentially Spanish work. With his compatriot Manuel de Falla, he had loved and studied this "deep song" so characteristic of the south; and in 1922 he, Falla, and Zuloaga organized the first great fiesta of these folk songs, in Granada. The themes which make up the *Poema del cante jondo* are the familiar ones of the "deep song" of the people: passion, suffering, death. Without sacrificing the genuinely popular note, García Lorca the poet added to these brief scenes all the music and variety of an unfailing rhythmic sense, all the warm glow of a rich imagination. The playful intimacy, the new and subtle imagery, the graceful irony, the fresh and lyrical evocation of the Andalusian scene of this book and of *Canciones* are also present in his masterpiece, *Romancero gitano,* in which García Lorca gave new life to that most classical of Spanish literary genres, the *romance* (ballad). Not since Góngora had such esprit and such creative genius been summoned to the service of the *romance,* and critics and public alike hailed the new favorite who knew the spirit of the people yet possessed all the finesse of the new poetry. The influence of this collection of ballads is difficult to estimate, but it is safe to affirm that in Spain and in Latin America the *Romancero gitano* had been read and imitated by more poets than any other single collection of poems published in the last decade. The poetry of García Lorca contains more that is truly popular than that of any of his Spanish contemporaries, but the high regard in which his work is held by a generation of poets whose poetry is preeminently intellectual is a testimony to his mastery of the pure form for which they strive. In García Lorca's case, the new poet of the people had long been the poet's poet.

That he knew and appropriated the best of such widely different movements as surrealism and the neoclassicism of a Paul Valéry will at once suggest itself to the reader of his four odes: to Salvador Dalí (1926), to the Blessed Sacrament (1928), to Walt Whitman (1933), to the King of Harlem (1933). The bizarre metaphors of the one are often fused with the disciplined structure of the other; but one feels throughout the commanding presence of the poet's own individuality. Even here he showed himself the true son of the Spanish tradition. He would not break with it. Rather he sought to revive and enrich it.

The poet who in childhood had gathered together brothers and classmates to give popular plays in his home, and who had later been a leading spirit in dramatics at the Residencia de Estudiantes, could hardly do otherwise than turn playwright. Already at twenty-one he had produced a symbolic piece, *El maleficio de la mariposa,* and in 1927 the great Spanish tragedienne Margarita Xirgu chose his dramatic ballad *Mariana Pineda* for production in Madrid. Two short guignolesque farces followed, and in 1933 his *Bodas de sangre* won an extraordinary success. The Neighborhood Playhouse selected this play for the celebration of its twentieth anniversary and in February 1935 presented it in the translation of José Weissberger under the title *Bitter Oleander.* This production did not finish its fourth week in New York, although Clayton Hamilton found the play "a beautiful expression of the poetry of primitive passion" and Richard Loveridge pronounced it an "intense and moving drama." Jo Davidson and Will Irwin confirmed such favorable comment, but the poignancy of García Lorca's conception and the dark beauty of his poetry could hardly be judged by critics forced to sit through a play cumbersomely translated and produced in a manner entirely out of keeping with the earthy simplicity of its story. As Brooks Atkinson remarked, it had been "removed from the soil and clapped into the straitjacket of style." *Bodas de sangre* was followed in 1935 by the equally successful dramatic poem *Yerma,* in which the fusing of real folk poetry and intense drama recalls the best plays of Lope de Vega, of whose *La dama boba* García Lorca made a notable adaptation. Had he lived, García Lorca would doubtless have continued writing dramas, for he said that he felt himself drawn more and more to that form; his keen dramatic sense had been apparent from the days of his early Andalusian poems.

García Lorca's versatility was remarkable. He was a gifted pianist and musicologist: his transcriptions of the finest old Spanish songs won him the grateful applause of his people and the admiration of so serious a musician as Falla, and he proved himself an able accompanist to La Argentinita in her recordings of his settings of early songs. In 1927 the exhibition of his paintings and sketches at Barcelona showed him to be a painter of merit with something fresh and vital to say regarding his own country. His fame as informal lecturer in Madrid spread abroad, and he made thousands of friends through his new interpretations of folklore and Spanish classics, in New York, in Cuba, in Mexico, in Argentina, in Uruguay. Ever alert to the possibilities of new material, he received some new stimulus, some new enriching influence for his own work from each country he visited. The published parts of his *Nueva York* revealed how deep an impression his visit to that city in 1929–30 had made on him. Since 1932 his activities as head of his government's student theater La Barraca have brought him the gratitude of numberless isolated districts, to which he introduced the best plays from Spain's past, and additional admiration from literary compeers. For years he was one of the most important and hardworking advocates of the new poetry, and almost none of the magazines of verse which have arisen in Spain in the last decade has been organized without his collaboration. He has always used folklore, not as the subtle tool of the return to feudalism, but as the living expression of the people whose individuality he respected and whose ultimate freedom he sought to bring about. Not the least of García Lorca's contributions to the literature of his land was fresh and chastened interpretation of the Andalusian theme. As Falla had done in music, he proved in poetry that the real Andalusia could be a source of profound and noble beauties and was something more than the land of garish warmth of color, of facile humor, of conventional picturesqueness.

To the student of Spanish literature, the death of García Lorca will mean the loss of the leading poet of his generation at the very moment when his work had attained its surest form and deepest inspiration and his vision was steadily broadening. To the millions sympathetic with the Spanish government in its present struggle for life, it will mean the loss of a leading spirit in that government's admirable program of culture. But to the Spanish people and their brothers in the New World, the death of García Lorca will mean far more than that. It will mean that their most eloquent spokesman, the poet who knew them best and re-created their life with the greatest beauty, has been shot down by a squad of fascist usurpers because he was a part of the new Spain they had fought long to create. García Lorca's unequaled popularity as a man both in Spain and in Latin America was the result of his having lived for poetry, for music, and for the people he represented. To the end he lavished prodigally his almost superhuman vitality on the cause of creating a new popular art for Spain and reviving the best art of her past. Now less than ever could she afford to lose him.

The increasingly discouraging news from Spain leads one to wonder what fate awaits other leading Spanish writers, the majority of them sympathetic with the constitutional government, in the event the mercenaries of General Franco win. The fate of artists in other dictator-ridden countries is painfully fresh in our memories. By force of protest, the writers of Chile recently saved Magda Portal from the despotism of the Civilista government of Peru. Should we not be preparing now to make every effort to save the lives of other loyal Spanish artists, in case the rebels finally become the rulers of Spain? However distasteful it may be to entertain such a possibility, we must not allow the repetition of a crime like the loss of a García Lorca.

William Berrien

Luigi Pirandello at Close Range [1937]

I first met Luigi Pirandello at the reception tendered him aboard the *S.S. Conte di Savoia* on 20 July 1935, when he arrived in New York on his way to Hollywood, where he was to take part in the filming of his play *Six Characters in Search of an Author*. As I stood on the pier bewitched by the beauty of the New York skyline, the majestic ship slowly advanced like a fantastic and huge bird, dazzlingly white, and moored at the Eighteenth Street dock. Once on the ship, the thought that I was so shortly to see the man whose works I had always admired keyed me to a high nervous tension. When I confided my nervousness to a young colleague of mine, he, with characteristic modern indifference toward greatness, almost shouted, "For heaven's sake, man, do you think Pirandello is a god?" Tartly replying that I did not know that God had ever written plays, I hastened toward the other end of the hall, where the smiling countenance of the Maestro had appeared. He was accompanied by ship officers and the New York dignitaries who had gone to meet him at quarantine.

Pirandello was of medium height, rather heavy-set, with an oval face and a short, pointed gray beard. Although sixty-seven years of age, he moved very swiftly and his person bore the marks of a robust manhood. His lips were still fresh; his eyes were most mobile and full of life, and their intensity was so great as to attract one's attention to the exclusion of the rest of his physical being. They converged on you as if to penetrate your innermost thoughts, and then they suddenly became hidden by an impenetrable veil as he relaxed his attention to withdraw within himself. Introspection was not a pose with Pirandello. It was an instinct and it was the habit of long years. He lived within himself just as do the characters in whom he had mirrored himself. There was something shy and timid in the way he moved in a crowd. While grateful for the recognition accorded him, he seemed to have to force himself to listen to the oratory poured forth in his praise.

As I stood a little to one side, studying Pirandello's reaction in meeting the people who swarmed around him, I saw him turn and beckon to me with his crooked finger, evidently having been told that I was eager to have an interview with him. Pirandello was very cordial. He thanked me for my interest in his writings and expressed gratification at the manner in which I had presented him in a long article that I had recently published in Italy. He gave me an appointment for the following day at the Waldorf-Astoria at ten o'clock.

The next morning, as I waited in the magnificent lobby, it was hard for me to picture Pirandello, who has always indicted the splendor and bustle of modern civilization, on the forty-first floor of a hotel that has no rival anywhere in the world for size, beauty, luxury, and comfort. Pirandello greeted me cordially, and we sat near a window in the large living room of his apartment. The Maestro was seated in a rather high chair against the open window, and I was happy to look up to him. As we discussed his art and plays he seemed gradually to recede miles and miles from the luxury that the richest country in the world has provided for those who are desirous of grasping and enjoying the gifts of our materialistic civilization.

At the very outset of our interview, in reply to my question, Pirandello very emphatically disclaimed connection with any literary movement. "Even with naturalism?" I queried. "Yes, indeed. Giovanni Verga, the great representative of that movement, wrote me that there was a new force, a new light in my art. I have a letter written to me by him after the publication of my novel *L'esclusa*. Indeed, I feel that I am at the opposite pole from naturalism. I have battered down blind faith in clumsy, tangible reality. Man can, indeed must, through his imagination, conquer and break the fetters of everyday reality. Why cling so steadfastly to it? Its experience is so short-lived. When my characters cling to their illusion, they do so because to accept historical reality is to sink more deeply into their torment." As he spoke, the Pirandello living at the Waldorf-Astoria had altogether disappeared, and I could now follow the artist into a world of his own, cheered by the light of his art and illuminated by the new values, tragic and lofty, that he has given to his sense of humanity.

In proclaiming the independence of his art Pirandello shows his intense individualism. As an artist he is only himself, and it is hard, indeed impossible, to consider him a part of that static whole that is a man-made system, be it in religion, art, or politics. His statement upon his arrival in New York that art and politics do not mix was dictated by his unbounded individualism. The same deep sense of individualism caused him to be vexed when recently a newspaper man asked him whether it could be said that he is the Bernard Shaw of Italy. Pirandello shrugged his shoulders and shook his head in an emphatic negative. The reporter, to make up for his lack of tact, queried again whether he thought that Bernard Shaw was the Pirandello of England. There was the same movement of repressed annoyance on the part of Pirandello: "Dear, dear, no. Shaw is Shaw and I am I. We are two distinct individuals."

In discussing his art during our interview, Pirandello insisted on the predominating and unchanging character of his art. He stated, "My art never has changed because I have never changed. I have always felt that man is a restless wanderer on this earth, a dreaming vagabond, almost always outside of himself, which means that he is not fully conscious of himself and of his acts." I must have looked a bit perplexed, for he proceeded to expound his philosophy of life, saying that to him there are four great forces whose urge man constantly feels: love, hatred, mystery, and the right of possession. "We fiercely say this book is mine, this ashtray is mine." He turned toward the little table near which we were seated and grasped a small exquisite ash receiver that was there.

> We say as fiercely as in the days of the cave man: "This woman is mine." As to mystery, this is to me the greatest force of all. Man speaks and he does not know whence his words come. He does not know whether they are an echo of words spoken a hundred years before or words that will be uttered a hundred years hence. We are the prey of forces emanating from a world that we feel moving beyond the arched blue line of the sky, beyond time and space, a world whence all life springs, whence all the forces of instinct issue. We feel and think and act seemingly as if we were the masters of our own emotions and deeds, but actually we are under the complete sway of these forces. We pass the greatest part of our lives outside of ourselves, lost in the flow of primeval life, out of which a strange and ironical god has fashioned this universe of ours. Most of the contradictions of man are caused by the clash between the individualistic and the eternal elements in him. The sex instinct is a primeval force in man, yet it leads him into terrifying complications. It makes a traitor out of him; it urges him irresistibly to break laws and conventions and finally leaves him desolate on the bleak shore of despair. This is what I have tried to express in my art. A man, I have attempted to say something to other men, with no other intention except perhaps that of avenging myself for having been born.

"Would you say that in your works you spurn life?" "Oh no," replied Pirandello.

In spite of all that it has made me suffer, life is beautiful. While this may seem absurd from the point of view of the philosopher, an artist can, with the privilege that art grants him, move in an atmosphere of dualism and create. What critics have not seen in me is the undercurrent of seriousness and of deep thought that flows through my art. Even when I laugh there is a tragic grief behind the grotesque mask that I lend to my characters. Critics want positive statements from a writer. Only the abstract thinker will make these positive statements about life and will enclose them in immutable formulas. A man who has suffered a great deal is reluctant to make categorical statements. Life is so fluid, so shifting, so illusory, when seen at close range, that an artist can well claim the right to express a tragedy in which artistic truth defies and surpasses actual truth.

In his conversation he referred again to what he calls the world of mystery. Speaking with vehemence, his eyes flashing with enthusiasm, he added: "The sense of human personality that one finds in my works is the result of my harkening to strange voices and impulses that come from a mysterious distance. I am filled with a sense of awe before the portals of the Unknown." His countenance actually expressed awe; his arms were open and raised, his body slightly bent forward, as if laboring under the crushing weight of mystery. He continued: "The world that we know is a small part of the universe. We live in a world within a world. Untold distances and depths are yet to be explored. The present state of progress is but the dawn of a distant and never-to-be-realized tomorrow."

I suggested that this was a sort of mysticism. Pirandello's ecstatic mood changed to one of cold objectivity. He said that critics of today, especially Professor Pietro Mignosi of the University of Palermo, were trying to make a Catholic mystic out of him but that he could not recognize himself in the image that they placed before him. This reaction allowed me to peer into the great dramatist's soul and art better than the reading of any of his books. One finds in him a tendency toward an evanescent mysticism. He is constantly aware of an infinite and boundless life from which man and earthly existence have been excluded. At the same time one notices in him the cold power of his intellect, which dissects the aspiration of his soul and chills its enthusiasm. The result of this clash is humor. Had Pirandello listened to his soul only, he would have been merely a dreamer. Had he followed only the dissecting force of his intellect, he would have been a heartless cynic. However, he strikes a happy balance between the warmth of his soul and the aloofness of his intellect, with the result that one of the greatest humorists of all times has appeared. Pirandello's fertility of imagination has no match in the history of Italian humor.

I confessed to him that I had been very eager to account for the strange adventures of his characters. How was it that such tragic figures were born in his mind, and what had determined the tortuous course of their existence and their pitiful plights? "It must have been your own life," I ventured, fearful of being too personal. "That's art," Pirandello replied. "The artist receives an inspiration from life, a suggestion, out of which he weaves a pattern where the original impulses are hardly recognizable. But experience plays a great part in the quality and temper of one's art. Life has made me suffer a great deal." I did not wish to indiscreetly reopen the wound of his wife's long madness, nor did I like to bring his thoughts back to his distant childhood, passed in the sluggish atmosphere of a Sicilian town. Why remind him of his father-in-law, who, with Pirandello's father, a partner in the sulphur business, had sealed a contract binding their children's lives without ever consulting them? There was no need of delving into the great writer's personal life. It was necessary only to look at his wistful and sensitive face to see that life had tried him in a bitter and even cruel manner.

"Isn't the oustanding feature of your art that process of self-deception that you, in your picturesque way, have called 'building up oneself'?" He agreed. As he had moved among men, he had noticed the mask of respectability that we place on our faces in order to hide the moral ugliness that offends us. At the same time he could not help noticing a sharp differentiation between the mask and the face, and he had used this contrast in many of his plays.

I admiringly pointed out some of the best characters that were born out of this tragic intuition: Ciampa in *Cap and Bells,* Ersilia Drei in *Naked,* Baldovino in *The Pleasure of Honesty.* Pirandello agreed that unquestionably that motif of "building up oneself" recurs more often than any other in his plays. "But don't you see what happens even to God when he 'builds up Himself'?" he queried. He spoke with deep conviction, and there was not the slightest hint of irreverence in his voice. He meant that when the universal idea of God becomes enclosed in a religious formula, we have the Christian God, the Hindu God, and as many Gods as there are tribes in Africa and peoples on the earth. Although natural enough, this diffusing process dwarfs the idea of a universal God in breaking it into the various concepts of the Deity that form the basis of religions.

"But," I added, "critics have accused you of not having distinguished between the mask and the face,

and of having played ball with two irridescent celluloid globes: reality and unreality. According to them you do not distinguish between the two entities, nor is there for you a boundary line that marks the point at which reality ends and unreality begins."

Pirandello moved quickly toward me and, gesticulating with great vehemence, said, "Unfortunately I have been accused of walking in the clouds and of vainly reaching out toward evanescent unrealities. That's what has hurt me very deeply. Critics do not see that they destroy the very soul of my drama, or rather that they obscure for themselves the most salient feature of my art. My drama *is,* after all, independently of their interpretations." "Think of Henry IV," I suggested.

Yes. There was a man whom the stupid accident of striking his head on a stone had separated from life. He was a madman for twelve years and lived, in an old castle, not his own life, but the superinduced life of the German Emperor. One day he opened his eyes and he was terrified by the appalling realization that he was not Henry IV. He was himself, a man of today, whom life had left behind just as a stream leaves in a deep bay a piece of wood that lies in the stagnant waters till it disintegrates. What could he do? How could he reenter life? He clung to his madness by continuing to play the role of Henry IV. His lucid madness was more bearable than the torment of his life. But I have never denied the original ego in my characters. How could I? How can anyone deny the historical actuality of human personality? What I notice is that at times actuality is so bitter and tragic that we must attempt to obliterate it, and for a moment of glorious exaltation we succeed in doing it. Soon, however, the illusory reality is overcome by the actual one, and this sudden replunging from the stars into the mud is the source of a greater tragedy.

"I am playing the role of *advocatus diaboli,*" I prefaced what I was about to say. "If you point out the harm of social hypocrisy and self-deception, don't you assume a moralistic attitude in your art?" "No," he replied. "When I see a man donning his mask I do not inveigh against him as a moralist would. Far from it. I grieve with him because I know that that is the common lot of humanity, and I pity in him also the frailties that I share."

I was conscious of having the rare opportunity of standing before the very source whence the majestic stream of Pirandellian art has originated. I wanted to assure myself of the absurdity of many of the charges against Pirandello the artist. I asked, "If you lend to your characters a goal that you know is unattainable, if you direct their eyes toward an illusion that both you and they know has no reality, don't you deprive your art of the element of truth and of realism?" The creator of Henry IV turned rather sharply toward me: "Why don't you critics look at the question from the point of view of my characters? The world of illusion is a real world to my characters. The solace that they derive from illusion makes illusion real. It is at any rate the only ointment that my human sympathy can pour over the wounds that life inflicts on us."

"Isn't the process of 'seeing oneself in a mirror' the next act of your tragic humanity?" Again the Maestro nodded assent. "Do you mean," I continued, "that when the warmth of sentiment recedes from our actions, then cold reason and the infernal contrivance of a little machine called logic are set in motion, and they transform our sentiment of life into a concept of life?" "Yes," he replied. "We live enclosed in concepts formed about us by our friends, our family, and even by ourselves. When the stage of exaltation is over, we see ourselves wearing the tinsel and trappings of our intellectual constructions as if in a mirror. Then we hate our images just as we hate to see ourselves reflected in a looking glass that deforms our features. We are both grotesque and pitiful. We are tragic."

"If 'reason' is the cold wind that chills sentiment and freezes our feelings into an inert mass," I continued, "then 'reason' is most certainly a negative attribute." Pirandello nodded approval. "To live is to navigate unconsciously in the swift current of life. Only children and animals and a few privileged beings really live because they can abandon themselves to the flux of primeval life. 'Reason' is the handmaid of fraud, and fraud creates the web of intricate evil where my plays begin. When we enclose a human being in a concept that is not natural to him, we follow the dictates of fraud, and evil is born. I find evil in situations that are made to appear moral, when inwardly they are putrid. I have always hated fraud, be it in our social relations and institutions, or in art."

There was in him a flame of genuine moral indignation as he spoke. He agreed that the motivation of *Six Characters in Search of an Author* was the contrast between the reality of life and of the ingenious tricks of art as compared with the reality that true art lends to human vicissitudes when the divine afflatus of fancy raises them to a higher plane.

I was eager to reach the basis of Pirandello's art: his philosophy of life. I asked him, "If the process of 'building oneself' is natural but dwarfing, why have you not afforded to man a firmer basis on which to stand? Surely there is something better for man than to be tragic with reality or ludicrous with fiction." Pirandello liked the latter phrase. I told him that I had coined it after a long study of his works and that it in a sense belonged to him too. He smiled affectionately. "But to go back to the original question," I repeated, "have you not pointed out that the reason why so many characters assume the postures and looks of exasperated marionettes is because they lack humility?" "I am no philosopher," he said; "I am only an artist, but that is my philosophy of life. If life is a tragic experience, humility is the only shield that can protect us against the onslaught of daily experience."

"It is very important to point this out," I insisted. "It transforms your thought from negative into positive. You differentiate yourself from those characters that have negative traits, that 'build up themselves.' Your characters are your antagonists." He shook his head in a negative. His characters were his children. He loved them all. I was surprised to notice the intensity with which he referred to them. I suggested that someday in his quixotic mind a story depicting a clash between his real children and the children of his imagination might appear. He smiled and suddenly his thoughts seemed to wander far away to the distant land where his children Stefano, Fausto, and Lietta were awaiting his return.

There was another question that I wanted to ask him, but it was of such an intimate nature that I hesitated. It concerned Marta Abba, who is now playing in New York in *Tovarich;* the young and beautiful actress who has brought to life so many of Pirandello's ideas and about whose relationship with Pirandello international gossip has found ample food for its degrading hunger. I broached the subject by mentioning an occasion on which I had lunch with exambassador to Italy Richard Washburn Child. The ambassador and I were discussing a lecture which I had given at Buck Hill Falls, in which I had presented Pirandello as the embodiment of the new consciousness that had dawned in Italy out of the tragic destruction and ruin of the world war. Mr. Child jokingly warned me not to be so sure about the new consciousness as embodied in Pirandello, and added, "He is having a good time just now with a young and beautiful actress." Pirandello interrupted me, "Why didn't you tell him that Pirandello has never had a good time in his life?" I felt the unbreakable moral strength of the man in those words that summed up the whole of his tragic existence.

Pirandello expressed indignation at the aspersions cast over his relationship with Marta Abba. He confided, "She is like a daughter to me. She is younger than my own children. She is twenty-seven years old and I am an old man of nearly seventy. She comes of a very distinguished family, and the senseless gossip has been a cruel blow to her."

I asked, "Did you have in mind Marta Abba when you wrote your play *The Wives' Friend* in which the heroine, Marta, is a lofty woman condemned to loneliness by her spiritual superiority over the people who surround her?" Pirandello nodded and smiled assent. "Did you think of Marta Abba in *She Wanted to Find Herself,* where a great actress is denied the joy of love of normal human relationships by the fact that her life is entirely absorbed by her art?" Pirandello again nodded agreement. I took courage. "Did you not wish to silence those malignant voices when in your latest play, *When One Is Somebody,* you depict the love of young Veroccia and of the old poet and you have the latter say to her, 'It would have seemed to me to have contaminated your youth, had I failed to keep my love on a lofty level'?" Pirandello smiled, and there was a light of gratitude in his brown eyes, which were now soft and affectionate.

I had never realized more clearly than now how close is the relation between Pirandello the artist and Pirandello the man. As long as I live I shall remember that I have lived in the vivid light that emanates from the man's soul and that the artist in him has made eternal in his works. I had never known that greatness could be so human and approachable.

The recent passing of Luigi Pirandello has deprived Italy, and the world, of one of the most significant expressions of modern art. There is no one in contemporary Italy who measures up to our beloved Maestro. In the unassuming simplicity of his personality as well as in the unadorned naturalness of his art he struck a deep vein in the mysterious depths of the soul of man and revealed terrifying truths to our generation, truths that are bitter at first but which are made acceptable to thoughtful beings if they learn how to be humble of heart before the gigantic sphinx of life.

Domenico Vittorini

My Uncle Sigmund Freud [1941]

When I am asked for recollections of Sigmund Freud, I find it hard to single out separate traits. I can describe his everyday life only in the frame of his whole personality and his extraordinary activities, so that I am always led into a discussion of his achievements; but I shall try to give an idea of the appearance and the way of living of this heroic personality who, like an intrepid Homeric hero, dared descend into the Tartarus of our ego.

It may be worth mentioning that the section of Vienna in which he lived was not the most aristocratic part of the city. The cool, quiet house which bears the number 19 lies at the foot of the steeply rising Berggasse and is close to the Trödelmarkt and the police station. The Danube Canal separates this part of the Ninth Bezirk from the Ghetto proper, but a large number of its residents are Jews, Jews of the better class, so that the section is often jocularly called the "Nobelghetto." To translate all this into terms of New York geography, it was somewhat as if a physician of Freud's standing were to office not on Park Avenue but somewhere over in the Bronx, which this hypothetical American physician's clientele might put up with as an angle of the great man's stubborn eccentricity. The old Vienna doctors have always had the habit of officing in their homes; and Freud was a doctor of the good old Vienna school, however much his method has revolutionized not only our thinking but our whole way of living. The old socialistic Vienna government, which had voted Freud a sort of honorary citizenship, had planned to change the name of the Berggasse to Sigmund Freud-gasse. The retiring psychiatrist, although he was grateful for the honor, which was all the more welcome in view of the long hard struggle he had had before he had secured recognition for his discoveries, was embarrassed by the plan and succeeded in having it abandoned. He disliked nothing so much as noisy notoriety, although he was the unwilling center of notoriety for years. We learn from *The Life of Madame Curie* by her daughter Eve how annoying publicity becomes when a scholar has once stepped out of the quiet of his laboratory and stirred the curiosity of the multitude by a striking discovery, how ruthlessly it disturbs his fruitful peace and interferes with his labor.

In Freud's case this curiosity was pretty effectively discouraged. Very rarely did a visitor who had no definite business cross his threshold. It was on one of the rare occasions when this happened that I saw him violently angry for the only time in all my contacts with him, although he could be impatient and excited now and then. He had occasion enough for exasperation in the malicious and unreasonable attacks to which he was frequently exposed.

It was at the end of May in the year 1938, after the terrible incidents which followed the entry of the Hitler cohorts into Vienna. The Gestapo, which had first planned to throw the eighty-two-year-old scientist into prison, had finally relented to the extent of merely forbidding him to continue his labors and confiscating his property. Eventually he was allowed permission to leave the country which for years had basked in the reflected glory of his name. When he received permission, the old man, who loved his familiar surroundings so dearly that he had lived for fifty years in the same house, cried gaily, with a whiff of recollection of the folklore of his childhood: "Now I'm Hans im Glück!" The Gestapo had graciously left him in possession of a sufficient sum of money to tide him over the first days of his exile. Shall we call it naïveté or shamelessness when a Nazi official visited him in London a long time afterward and demanded this amount back? On the gloomy May day of which I speak, everything in his Vienna home was packed ready for his departure. The old gentleman, who was bearing up remarkably well under the excitement and the torment of his disease, insisted on showing me his archeological collection before it was shipped to London. As we left the great comfortable dining room with its old-fashioned rosewood furniture, on our way to his work rooms, we passed through an anteroom into which the usually discreet servant had admitted a stranger as the result of a misunderstanding in a telephone conversation. Freud asked the intruder what he wanted. The man, who had come from Berlin expressly for the purpose of reassuring himself as to the safety of his revered Master, about whom all sorts of alarming rumors were afloat, stammered in confusion: "I only wanted to see you!"—"There isn't anything to see about me!" Freud snapped violenty, and went on, calling back to me to follow him. One can understand why it was almost or quite impossible to elicit an autograph from him. A letter of recommendation from him was a rarity. He rarely wrote a recommendation—never unless the case was one in which he was profoundly interested.

Freud did not like journalists. He is said to have told Dorothy Thompson very frankly what he thought about her profession, at the beginning of a conversation which, it is true, turned out very harmonious and profitable. He has often been reproached with coolness toward America, but he never forgot that at a relatively early stage in his career the Americans gave him the opportunity to present in four public addresses the results of his investigations in new psychological territory, and that they awarded him an honorary doctorate. No one could blame him for a degree of sensitiveness to the danger to which his doctrines were exposed in this country from irresponsible disciples and popular distortion; but he constantly had American students, and there were several of them whom he valued very highly and who remained faithful to his Vienna group to the last.

Freud was not only one of the last of the European sages. He was one of the greatest lovers of his kind whom the nineteenth centry bequeathed to a century which has thus far produced so many enemies of the race. His knowledge of the turbid depths of human nature and his far from optimistic life philosophy never made him a hater of men. The great Vienna comedian and playwright Johann Nestroy declared, long before Freud's time, that he always believed the worst of every human being, himself included, and that he had seldom found himself wrong in that belief. Although Freud's works, especially the later ones, share this characteristically Viennese melancholy and ironical wariness, the fundamental ideal of psychoanalysis would seem to justify a less hopeless view of mankind. The fact that the relief or even the healing of a disease can be accomplished by the clearing up of certain obscurities (Stefan Zweig calls this process "Healing through the Spirit") speaks for the great Vienna physician's belief in progress, although he was fated to end his life in an age of mass madness.

It was another Viennese, Nothnagel, who uttered the famous dictum: "Only a good man can be a good physician." Freud, who knew as much about the diseases of the social organism as he did about those of the soul—they are often of the same origin—was an exceptionally good man. He was generous, and he exercised his charity with unusual tact. It was through his initiative that psychotherapy was made available to the poor, at least in Vienna. Every member of the Vienna Psychoanalytic Union was under obligation to treat gratuitously a certain number of patients who were turned over to him from the Ambulatorium. Freud was always very appreciative of the remarkable social services of the Vienna city government, although he was not of the same political party as its officials.

It was natural that the great scientist was a lover of nature. He always came back from the long walks in the Wienerwald and the forests of the Salzkammergut which he kept up in the company of his children as long as his health allowed (he spent several summers in Hitler's Berchtesgaden) laden with flowers, fungi, and berries. In the last year of his life he took pleasure in the flowers of his little London garden, and his writing table was almost always brightened with a bouquet of his favorite orchids.

In his vigorous early years he took a long trip every year, often to Italy, once to Greece. I have mentioned the archeological collection which meant so much to him—small articles of Chinese, Etruscan, Egyptian, Hellenic, and Roman art, statuettes, rings, amulets, and the like. The remark has often been made that his enthusiasm for the treasures of past ages, which can be recovered only with great ingenuity and endless labor from thousand-year-old tombs, fits appropriately into the life of this student of the soul, who listened with patient attention for the elemental secrets that had been buried just as deeply and just as long as the others till he had brought them to the light of day. The smallest and most incidental hobbies fit perfectly into the marvelous melody of this life, which in spite of its tragic end, in spite of the struggles which were his lot, must nevertheless be deemed a happy one, since it bears witness to the greatness of an original and independent personality who knew how to defend the truth which he had discovered against a world of mockery and hate. His love of riddles and his skill in solving them, an occupation which he followed long before it became a modish diversion, was an appropriate pastime for a man whose serious labor was the solving of riddles. He loved too to play solitaire with cards, sitting in front of his table with his legs high on the back of a neighboring chair, smoking his eternal cigar. He was amused by the clever combinations of Mah-Jongg, and all the year round his weekly tarok game with old friends was an invariable institution. He found no recreation in the theater or the movies. Music had no place in his life. Still, he occasionally attended the performances of Yvette Guilbert, who was a good friend of his and whose art afforded him much pleasure.

Except in the summer, Freud's day was crammed with work. His day's program was very carefully mapped out. He lived by the clock. His forenoons were devoted to patients and his lecture-analyses. After his midday meal, he kept up as long as he was able his habit of an afternoon walk, and many of his fellow townsmen will remember how he covered his one invariable route every day, a little bent forward but walking rapidly, somehow always giving the impression of uprightness. He usually walked alone. The remark of Adler (or was it some other individual-psychologist?) that when Freud walked he always crept along close to the houses, from which one could infer his natural cowardice, is completely ridiculous. I do not believe there ever was a braver soul than his. A feeble old man, suffering the torments of a terrible disease, he did not hesitate to shock his beloved Jewish people with the declaration of his belief that their hero Moses was an Egyptian, adding thus—as many believed, gratuitously, but impelled by his passion for truth—to the phalanxes of the enemies which his antireligious position had made for him among the orthodox Jews a formidable reinforcement from the Jewish Nationalists. There is no sort of justification for Adler's slur. Freud loved to walk while he meditated, as most of us need a physical escape valve when we endeavor to collect our thoughts. When his physical condition made it necessary for him to forgo his daily walk, he was reduced for exercise to a circuit of his roomy apartment, taken at the end of each hour of work.

The period after his evening meal belonged to his organizing labors. His activity as leader of the psychoanalytic movement speaks eloquently of his organizing ability. There were conferences with his fellow workers, and last of all there was his writing, to which he devoted more time in the summer. This is doubtless the place to say something of Freud as a writer. His contribution to the development of German as a scientific language is traceable first of all to the clarity of his thinking. The darker his field, the more cavernous and rugged the inferno through which his path led, the more brightly did the calm light of his phraseology illumine the way. No language is more difficult, more perverse, more obscure and obscuring than this German speech of ours. The regret has often been expressed that the German savants use this language as if they were trying to conceal their thoughts rather than to make them clear, and many foreign students who find it necessary to read scientific German books in the original could tell a sad tale of the riddles which scientific German has set for them. Freud's style is so natural and simple that his ideas were completely accessible to laymen and seemed to them reasonable. This, it is true, led to the danger that the half-educated and the bluestockings of both sexes would seize on psychoanalysis as a sort of glorified parlor game and make trouble. Allied to this clarity of expression was the ease with which Freud wrote. His manuscripts show very few corrections; he wrote his works down in one draft and never found it necessary to rewrite them. He had his whole plan clearly in mind when he sat down to write.

Very late, usually about two o'clock in the morning, Freud retired after such a day as I have described. He went to sleep instantly and slept soundly for five hours. This scientist who had lifted the dream out of the sphere of the Egyptian dreambooks and professional fortune-tellers and made it scientifically productive was not himself much of a dreamer—not necessarily because he accepted Kierkegaard's theory that the epicure does his delightful dreaming in the daytime, but it would seem that his attention to the trains of thought of his patients and of their reports of their dreaming sufficed for him without dreams of his own. Moreover, his rigidly rationalistic conception of life did not leave much room for fantasy. One of the important factors in his greatness was that through all the bewildering multiplicity of the dream symbols which occupied him, he remained the clear-headed rationalist; that in the inferno of instincts, which he understood as no one else had ever done, and whose peril is becoming more than ever evident today in certain uncanny mass movements, he steadily kept faith with reason; that he remained a sober and cautious man of science, never deserting the ranks of the men of the other century, in which he stood firmly planted with both feet, although he helped this century to the birth more effectively than any other had done.

Neither is Freud the zealot and the spiteful nature which he has been accused of being. How could a man in whose vocabulary the word *love* plays so dominant a role be a blind, raging fanatic? Educators in all lands have come to realize that he understood child-nature particularly well. No one who has ever seen him with children will ever forget the old man's charming naturalness and amiability in their company. It is true that he would stand for no trifling where the purity of his doctrines was in question. This thinker who in his old age was inclined to mildness and silence, who weighed an idea long and conscientiously before he gave it his approval, yet who was anything but a dogmatist, since he never hesitated to admit that he was in the wrong and to correct an error, was very careful to hold his overreckless disciples in leash. Caution was not the least of his virtues. The reader will recall in the much-assailed Moses book he is constantly warning him to follow his arguments carefully. Freud was as cautious and prudent as a surgeon who has a delicate operation to perform. A psychoanalytic treatment can be as perilous as a major operation, and it is unfair to blame the surgeon if in some unpromising cases his operation is not successful. It was Freud's special achievement to unite the exactness of the inductive method with which he began his life work, and a creative boldness which completely changed our conception of the world.

I could mention a long list of instances of how Freud, theoretician of wit, enlivened his conversations with witty illustrations and similes, but the best of his witticisms are so local in their flavor that they would be difficult in translation. Freud's wit was probably *wienerisch* at bottom—it certainly was Jewish. It is obvious that he was always very consciously a Jew. It is well known too that he steadily refused baptism, although in prewar Vienna that ceremonial was a tacitly agreed-on prerequisite for the attainment of the highest academic positions. After the Great War, even before Hitler, racial anti-Semitism, which had previously been limited to academic circles and certain narrow official strata, grew steadily, so that it no longer helped a Jew to become a Christian. This is why Freud was never made an *ordentlicher Professor*. In liberal Vienna it was common to lay ironic emphasis on his status as *außerordentlich*. He was never what is called "religious." In his book *Die Zukunft einer Illusion* he took a position at variance with that of many of his disciples and supporters and urged the abandonment of religion as a dangerous error. However, his pupil Pastor Pfister of Zürich sent him on his sixtieth birthday a telegram which I found

among his papers and which ran: "May God leave you with us for many years, even though you don't believe in Him!"

He was driven out of the city in which he had spent a long and fruitful life, the city which he had done almost as much as the great Viennese musicians to make famous in every corner of the world. They are still treating patients in Germany by his method, just as they are still using the Wassermann blood tests and Ehrlich's salvarsan, although their discoverers were Jews. His name is immortal. Of course that does not necessarily mean a great deal. There is a negative immortality, such as Attila and Genghis Khan have attained, and such as will one day be accorded to Adolf Hitler. Freud's immortal achievement was not destructive, although he uncovered the sources of destruction; reaching out beyond the narrow field of psychology and medicine, it is a Copernican discovery whose full significance is still far from having been exhausted.

Ernst Waldinger

The Novels of Raja Rao [1966]

One of the most satisfying of vicarious literary experiences is the close scrutiny of an author's development from rudimentary beginnings to artistic fulfillment. Such development is manifested in form and structure, in characters, in them and plot, in symbolism, and especially in style. With a novelist like Raja Rao,[1] whose native language is not English, style becomes particularly important, because he is attempting to embody within written English the rhythms of Indian life and the traditional qualities of Sanskrit. As he says in his introduction to *Kanthapura*, his first novel (1938):

> The tempo of Indian life must be infused into our English expression, even as the tempo of American or Irish life has gone into has making of theirs. We, in India, think quickly, we talk quickly, and when we move we move quickly. . . . We have neither punctuation nor the treacherous "ats" and "ons" to bother us—we tell one interminable tale. Episode follows episode, and when our thoughts stop our breath stops, and we move on to another thought. This was and is the ordinary style of our storytelling.[2]

In *Kanthapura* what Raja Rao produced from such a theory is a stylistic texture dominated by *and, then, but, when,* and *now.* One sequence follows another without emphasis or control, and the result is a book that reads much like the following passage, which describes a typical scene in the South Indian village of Kanthapura:

. . . and they clapped hands again, and they wiped the tears out of their eyes, and more and more women flowed out of the Pariah street and the Potters' street and the Weavers' street, and they beat their mouths the louder, and the children ran behind the fences and slipped into the gutters and threw stones at the police, and a soldier got a stone in his face and the police rushed this side and that and caught this girl and that. And the women . . . . (148)

The description loses force at *this side and that;* it becomes completely diffuse at *this girl and that.* The effect, of course, is breadth: violence touched all sides (places, areas, et cetera) at all times, and all violence was equal, and the police and the soldiers were all equally violent, and the people were all equally victimized, but especially some of the girls. For a novel of almost two hundred pages, the effect is not speed, as Raja Rao hoped in his introduction, but monotony, and even the most socially concerned reader has trouble digging into the story.

Like most Indo-Anglian novels, *Kanthapura* is a didactic work of social criticism, and its message to the world of India in the troubled thirties is reinforced and clarified by some fifty-odd pages of notes. These notes provide necessary historical and cultural background on the Gandhi movement, which motivated the villagers of Kanthapura to action against the British-controlled government. Unfortunately, the clarity of meaning is contained not in the novel itself, but in these notes, where the didactic voice of the novelist is stronger and more convincing than the sonorous tones of the female narrator. These notes, when added to the monotonous style and the plural point of view ("and we rushed down the aloe lane"), make *Kanthapura* an artistic failure.

More than twenty years separate *Kanthapura* and *The Serpent and the Rope* (1960), Raja Rao's second novel. During this time the novelist went through a psychological and spiritual transformation, and the subsequent change in his artistic craft is the most profound in the history of Indo-Anglian literature, perhaps even in the history of contemporary literature. He has replaced the obvious theme of social criticism with a probing examination of the human psyche. The limited setting of the tiny village of Kanthapura he has expanded into a gigantic geographical triangle that covers England, France, and India. He has embodied new power in conventional symbols (like city, bridge, mirror, mountain), and the fifty-odd pages of notes have shrunk to a glossary of two pages. But the most significant difference in the two novels, and the key to the change in the novelist himself, is style; through his new first-person narrator (a South Indian Brahmin historian

named Ramaswamy), Raja Rao moves far beyond monotonous coordination to paradoxical language patterns that are stunning, subtle, profound, and beautiful. The explanation for this change is simple enough and occurs as part of the texture of the novel, not in an introduction.

All books are autobiographies. . . . They all represent a bit of oneself, and for those who can read rightly, the whole of oneself. The style of a man—whether he writes on the Aztecs or on pelargonium—the way he weaves word against word, intricates the existence of sentences with the values of *sound,* makes a comma here, puts a dash there: all are signs of his inner movement, the speed of his life, his breath (*prana*), the nature of his thought, the ardour and age of his soul. Short sentences and long sentences, parentheses and points of interrogation, are not only curves in the architecture of thought, but have an intimate, a private relation with your navel, your genitals, the vibrance of your eyesight.[3]

Instead of simply reflecting Indian life (the stylistic credo of 1938), style is completely a part of the author; and this is the change that made *The Serpent and the Rope* Raja Rao's best novel and one of the deepest and most serious literary efforts of the twentieth century.

As we discover the stylistic elements of *The Serpent and the Rope,* we must remember that they belong deep in the texture of the novel, and when we isolate and describe them we are not describing *the* novel, but only a part that reveals significant tone, atmosphere, or essence. For the novel's style is a complex network of subtle repetitions, crossing pronoun references, rhythmic parallels, and delicate (and impossibly paradoxical) equations. All of the style is a part of Raja Rao himself, and as the novel is one long human perception, so the style mirrors the nature of that perception:

Nothing more had happened, in fact, than if you see deep and long at silence you perceive an orb of centripetal sound which explains why Parvathi is daughter of Himalay, and Sita born to the furrow of the field. I heard myself say I heard myself. Or I saw my eyes see that I saw.

Backing off from the synesthetic word *orb,* we arrive at Ramaswamy's perception of perception. This particular kind of statement is developed by repetition ("I heard myself, I heard myself," "I saw, I saw") and by syntactic balance: "I heard myself *say* I heard myself." The rhythm of the prose brushes us across the impossibility of the paradox, and the careful syntax coils our thoughts into a double circle that begins and ends with the reflexive pronoun. Tautologies like these pervade the book and often wind themselves down into ironic commentary on the very nature of tautology.

Love demands nothing, it *says* nothing, it knows nothing; it lives for itself, like the Seine does, for whom the buildings rise on either side and the parks and the Renault factory farther downstream make no difference. Who can take away love, who give it, who receive? I could not even say that I loved Savithri. It is just like saying 'I love myself' or 'Love loves Love.' 'Tautology! Absurdity!' I cried.

The epistrophe that develops at *nothing* contrasts in form with the parallel segments of the rhetorical question that gets shorter; yet both support the abstract autonomous (*itself*) qualities of Love. The tautological repetition of "Love loves Love" clarifies Ramaswamy's relationship with Savithri (his female student friend from Allahabad) and at the same time turns our focus on the circle of the more obvious pronoun tautology: "I love myself."

If the stylistic essence of any book is revealed more by one pattern or part of speech than another, then the essence of *The Serpent and the Rope* is revealed by reflexive pronouns. As in the passages above, the reflexives control the metaphoric center of Ramaswamy's philosophy and turn even his most carefully contrived objective symbols into extensions of the self. This symbolic extension is evident in the development of Ramaswamy's concept of Love ("Love, my love, is the self") and of Woman ("Woman shows that the world is oneself seen as the other"); but it is especially apparent in his Brahmanic view of Benares, Paris, and London. Benares, where Ramaswamy flies from Europe to cremate his father, is "indeed nowhere but inside oneself." When he returns to Europe, he finds the same to be true of Paris—"Paris somehow is not a city; it is an area in oneself"—and when he looks again, he sees Paris as "a sort of Benares turned outward," the whole image mirroring the spatiality of the reflection of perception. As Paris is for Ramaswamy, so London is for Savithri.

> For Savithri London was not a city, a place in geography—it was somewhere, a spot, maybe a red spot in herself. Like the London traffic lights, it might suddenly grow red, and then like a kunkum, a large one on the face of a Bengali woman, would the green go up, the cool, round, auspicious green of London.

Just following a long politico-philosophical discussion that terminates in Savithri's pronouncement of Love, Ramaswamy excitedly perceives London as himself: "London was no longer a city for me, it was myself." The essence of the symbolic city emanates from the true perception of self, this perception is the constant major question of the narrator, and the moment of perception is both illusory and eternal: "Seeing oneself is what we always seek; the world, as the great Sage Sankara said, is like a city seen in a mirror." The circle that binds the narrator to style is constantly turning inward, and it is this same motion that characterizes our perception of *The Serpent and the Rope*. Discovering the "reality" of the novel is like Raja Rao's mythical man "trying to walk into a road that he sees in a hall of mirrors." We can see the details, and we can isolate them on the page and in the mind; but the total pattern of the whole is obscured in the paradox of their presentation.

Raja Rao's third novel, *The Cat and Shakespeare* (1965), is an extension of *The Serpent and the Rope;* the narrator is an unnamed South Indian; the controlling symbols (wall, house, cat) are simple and strong; the main subjects are women, philosophy, and the paradox of the perception of perception; and the key to the novel is again the reflexive pronoun. *The Cat and Shakespeare* takes its name from a symbolic cat and a parody of Hamlet's soliloquy. The cat is symbolic of motherhood in all its protective qualities, even when it is eliminated from the Shakespeare parody. The parody itself is delivered by Govindan Nair, neighbor of the narrator and the central character in the novel: "A kitten sans cat, kitten being the diminutive for cat. *Vide* Prescott of the great grammatical fame. A kitten sans cat, that is the question."[4] This speech by Govindan Nair occurs in the Ration Office where he works, and it occurs just before Boothalinga Iyer, the head of the Ration Office, dies. From Raja Rao's oblique prose, we can only assume that the cat *and* Shakespeare were the cause of death.

> "I'll tell you a story," said Govindan Nair, and lifted the cat and placed her upon his shoulder.
>
> "Once upon a time," he began, and before he could go on, the cat jumped onto Boothalinga Iyer's head. Boothalinga Iyer opened his eyes wide and said, "Shiva, Shiva," and he was dead.

This scene in the Ration Office is typical of the key scenes in the novel: linked together only by the voice of the narrator, Govindan Nair, and the tricks of illusory perception, they form points of intensity at different levels in the network of action that is almost a nonplot. A short time later, for example, Govindan Nair is arrested, "not on a charge of attempted homicide [for the death of Boothalinga Iyer?] . . . but on a charge of bribery," and the trial that follows forms another point of intensity in the narrator's reverie. The most striking point of intensity, however, is Govindan Nair's visit to a doctor's office, which turns out to be a brothel, Govindan Nair the symbolic doctor, and the dancing prostitute a patient in disguise: "The patient may undress while the doctor is getting ready."

With the illusory nonplot of *The Cat and Shakespeare* held together only by these mystifying points of extreme intensity, the texture of the novel becomes even more important: symbols and elements of style turn in on themselves, mirroring each other as they disclose paradoxical data about Govindan Nair, the narrator, and our illusory perceptions of perception. Govindan Nair, for example, transports himself from place to place across a wall that becomes gradually a symbol. The wall exists at the edge of the narrator's garden, and Govindan Nair jumps across it so that he can philosophize with the narrator. He jumps back across it to go into the world and into the several intense scenes of the nonplot; but when the narrator himself crosses the wall near the end of the novel, we see the return of the mirrored self, a symbol from *The Serpent and the Rope*.

> That was the first time I went across the wall. I found a garden all rosy and gentle. . . . The air was so like a mirror you just walked toward yourself. How is it I never knew my neighboring wall went up and down the road, and up again toward the hospital.

The wall extends to the narrator's experience of Woman, as he learns from his beloved not-wife Shantha, who says: "I can see you have never been across the wall. For there you could touch me and see yourself touch me." The wall is also the symbolic resting place and transit point for the kittens: "What is death to a kitten that walks on the wall? Have you ever seen a kitten fall? You could fall. I could fall. But the kittens walk on the wall." The singular kitten on the wall is probably representative of the dimensions of the self, which Raja Rao carries with the familiar reflexive from *The Serpent and the Rope*: "There's only one depth and one extensivity and that's (in) oneself. It's like a kitten on a garden wall. It's like kittens walking on the garden wall."

In a sense the reflexive pronoun is the key symbol of *The Cat and Shakespeare*, linking the objects of the universe to mankind, the obvious center. A watch, for instance, is "a thing that turns on itself and shows the moon"; the moon is "the thing that turns on itself and (elliptically) goes around the sun." The reflexive pronoun is the beginning and end of all things, forming a convenient circle for all didactic problems raised by the narrator's conversations with Govindan Nair and with himself.

> A child for a woman is always her own child. All children belong to her by right. Who made the world thus? I say you made it. Whoever said it was made, made it. Otherwise how can you say it was made? Making itself is an idea born of the world. When making seeks making in making, pray, who sees a world?

Intuitive recognition of such a device reveals the depth of Raja Rao's understanding of English, which is, I re-peat for emphasis, not his native tongue. Our problems with such a device, if we have them, reveal our lack of understanding of our native tongue and produce other problems with philosophy and world view. We are perhaps more at home with abstractions such as "perfection of perfection," but Raja Rao's deepest talent is in the concrete.

> Looking at the rope from the serpent is to see paradise, saints, avatars, gods, heroes, universes. For wheresoever you go, you see only with the serpent's eyes. . . . You see the serpent and in fear you feel you are it, the serpent, the saint. One—the Guru—brings you the lantern; the road is seen, the long, white road, going with the statutory stars. "It's only the rope." He shows it to you. And you touch your eyes and *know* there never was a serpent.

> *Robert J. Ray*

1 Raja Rao is the author of three novels: *Kanthapura* (1938), *The Serpent and the Rope* (1960), and *The Cat and Shakespeare* (1965).

2 *Kanthapura,* New York, New Directions, 1963.

3 *The Serpent and the Rope,* London, John Murray, 1960.

4 *The Cat and Shakespeare,* New York, Macmillan, 1965.

George Seferis: Myth and History [1968]

No Greek poet is more intensely aware of the abyss between a great past and a dismal present than George Seferis, winner of the Nobel Prize in Literature in 1963.[1] "Wherever I travel, Greece wounds me still," the poet laments as he peers into Greek realities and recoils in agony at what he finds there. In his speech of acceptance on receiving the Nobel Prize in Stockholm, Seferis expressed above all the dilemma of being Greek.

> I belong to a small country. It is a rocky projection in the Mediterranean that has in its favor only the effort of its people, the sea and the light of its bright sun. It is a small country, but its tradition is immense.

The attraction of George Seferis for American readers may lie therefore in his poetic concern with Greece, just as the attraction of William Faulkner for foreign readers lies partly in his commitment to the Deep South. The circumstances of the Deep South and Greece, the matrices of Faulkner's prose and Seferis's verse, define tragic moments in history when a frustrated region lives in the shadow of its legendary past and, inevitably, traditional values lose their power to comfort or sustain.

The Swedish Academy cited Seferis's treatment of the Greek landscape and especially his concentration on the deep mystery of stones, marble fragments, and silent smiling statues. These grounds littered with ruins, ancient marine kingdoms, empty harbors, the trail of arid mountains, slow-moving ships, abandoned homesites, together with the Aegean Sea, the bright sun, and the maddening wind, are woven into a symbolic net, the tangled web of the Hellenic experience. Moreover, the Hellenic experience embraces the moral conflicts and existential doubts that characterize much of the problematic literature of our times. The poet usually gazes at stone images and searches for some identity with past values; but statues do not always reveal their hidden truths, and man must face the mystery alone, maimed, as it were.

I woke with this marble head in my hands
which exhausts my elbows and I don't know where
  to prop it.
It was falling into the dream as I was coming out of
  the dream
so our lives joined and it'll be hard to part again.
I look into the eyes; neither shut nor open,
I speak to the mouth which always strives to speak,
I hold the cheeks which have grown beyond the
  skin.
I can do no more;
my hands vanish and then approach me mutilated.

The irresoluble contrast between man and statue accents the yearning for some answers to our existence and symbolizes the predicament of man trapped by his past. "He sinks who lifts the great stones" is the refrain of *Santorin* and *Mycenae;* yet man somehow accepts the burden, for he needs the kinship with his historical and legendary past: "These stones I have lifted as long as I was able, / these stones I have loved as long as I was able, / these stones, my fate." Thus through broken stones, marble fragments, or confined spaces, indigenous sights of the Greek ambience, the dispersement, alienation, or the flow of time, typical motifs of contemporary literature, stand out. The search amidst ruins and the tormenting self-questioning together form a permanent backdrop of Seferis's verse and are a steady reminder of the tragic predicament of finding a way to be and a way to die.

Because we have known so well this fate of ours,
wandering through broken stones, three or six
  thousand years,

. . . .

shall we be able?
Because we have been bound, because we have been
  scattered,

and have struggled with unreal difficulties, as they
 put it

. . . .

shall we be able to die according to the rules?

Whether the answer is yes or no, whether the gap between heroic memories and present breakdowns can ever be bridged, what stands out in the poetry of Seferis is the painful trial of a man who, by seeking, asking, wandering, and enduring, tries to find his center, to come to terms with some viable truth among the heaps of uncertainty.

George Seferis was a career diplomat, and he has said, half serious, half tongue-in-cheek, that he never regrets having chosen a profession that is totally divorced from poetry. We must see him under this double aspect: a sensitive poet attracted by myths but also a commonsensical man of affairs grounded in history. The biographical facts are significant. He was born George Seferiadhis in 1900 in Smyrna and spent his childhood on the Asiatic seacoast where the Greeks, despite a long Turkish rule, had kept their language, their religion, and their traditions. In 1914 he left because of the war, and in 1922 the Greeks were ousted from Asia Minor, Smyrna was destroyed, and Seferis was never to see his birthplace again. The shock of the disaster, the pain of exile, and the general disillusion became strong shaping influences upon his poetry; and his professional duties enabled him to assess with objectivity the problem of a country more and more isolated in the world.

The situation of Seferis as poet only bears out his experience as diplomat. He opened his acceptance speech at Stockholm, delivered ironically in French, with an acute and poignant statement of a Greek writer's frustration.

> At this moment I feel that I am a contradiction. The Swedish Academy has, in fact, decided that my efforts within a language famous for many centuries but of little if any extension in its present form, were worthy of this high distinction. The Academy wished to honor my native language, yet here I am thanking you for the honor in a foreign tongue. Please accept the excuses that I must also make for myself.

Seferis is both a spokesman and a symptom of the Greek condition. Unlike other Nobel winners, who elaborated universal problems, he discussed the development and importance of modern Greek poetry. It was an act of solidarity: "I need this solidarity," he concluded in Stockholm, "because if I do not understand my own people, with all their virtues and their vices, I feel that I shall not be able to understand the other people of this big world." Thus the first Greek ever to win the Nobel Prize happens to embody most purely and persuasively the Greek sense of acceptance and fellowship—crystallized in the tragic myth of Oedipus and the tragic history of Socrates.

▓ I

Seferis is an unusual Greek in that he is not a prolific writer. In three decades he has written one volume of poetry, one of critical essays, and one of translations.[2] His style is economical and simple: "I want nothing more but to speak simply; may I be given this grace. / Because we load the song with so much music that little by little it is sinking." His poetic expression is deliberately condensed and gnomic, and consequently his simple phrases carry a weight beyond their ostensible meaning; each poem is pure, the result of a careful, conscious word-for-word technique that makes heavy demands upon the reader.

His first book of poems, *Strophé,* was published in 1931; the title means "Stanza" but also "Turning Point," a prophetic term since the collection opened new directions for Greek poetry. Seferis initiates here themes like the passing of time, the anxiety of death, sensuality and sterility. In "Rima," for example, he juxtaposes life's vital activities with the consideration that man dies a little every day until he dies for good: "'Tis the time when dusk is drowned / and I tire searching in darkness . . . / (Our life diminishes a little every day)." Recollection of past activities (loving, hunting, sunbathing) leads to a meditation on the preciousness of experience now reluctantly surrendered. The only long poem in the first collection, "Erotikós Logos" (Song of Love), is an account of passion in time: the poet evokes something beloved and is briefly in an intoxicated state of expectancy but eventually realizes that the changes of time are final: "Red rose of wind and fate / you only remained in memory, a heavy cadence, / rose of the night you passed by, a purpureal tempest, / a tempest of the sea . . . And the world, it is simple." Recalled experience is maddeningly incomplete because something lost cannot be summoned up again in its dazzling actuality. As with Proust, spots of time (here "corals of memory" or "dense flutterings") overcome temporarily the ravages of oblivion and bring about the miracle of identity with one's past. The psychological development of exaltation and letdown ends in the matter-of-fact acceptance that the world is simple after all. The implication is that man outgrows his dreams. Seferis brings to the retrospective meaning of time a gentle and somber resignation which will become central in his later poetry.

The anxieties of *Strophé* and "Song of Love" assume by 1932 a tragic vision in "Sterna" (Cistern): "Here on the ground taking roots, a cistern, / a cave of hidden water collecting treasures." The underground, sealed reservoir is like man's sleepless consciousness; above, one hears footsteps of crowds marching silently, blindly through a mysteriously unreal, hell-like atmosphere of "ebony darkness." If we could only forget and "Let roses blossom in the blood of our wound." The poet recalls anxiously pleasure, fertility, blooming lemon trees, and suddenly envisions a spring procession: "Mournful shadows upon dead wreaths / footsteps . . . footsteps . . . the slow bell / unwinds a dark chain." The spectacle is Christ's funeral as re-created in Athens every year two days before Easter. Crowds move slowly, holding candles and singing laments which nevertheless betray the hope of redemption, and all the while the cortege has been passing, ironically, under the Acropolis.

"We are dying! Our gods are dying! . . ."
And the marbles know it as they gaze
like a white dawn upon the victim,
strange to us, full of eyelids, broken pieces,
as the crowds of death wind by.

Visually, a telling scene: the Parthenon columns gaze silently upon this mournful march toward Resurrection; as the wise silence of pagan stones makes clear, there is no Resurrection. Footsteps are both those of the cortege and the ones that echo over the cistern which patiently bides it time: "'Tis a cistern that teaches silence / inside the lighted city." The crisis before the cistern—that is, the moment before man crosses the ultimate frontier of life on to death—is here magnified into a majestic awareness of the pattern of history, balancing the hope of Christianity with the finality of paganism.

Seferis undercuts rhetoric or patriotic bombast while his simplicity deflates exaggerated notions of Greece's "destiny" and heroic grandeur. He offers an antiheroic vision of life, a skeptical appraisal of rampant heroism, and a concern more about the predicament of the Greeks than their heroism. This explains why Seferis did not plunge into partisan commentary upon the political, social, and literary conflicts of contemporary Greece, an extraordinary feat considering the temptations and pressures for involvement. He distrusts easy commitment and concentrates on the anonymous participants that few care to remember: "Again and again the same things, you will tell me, friend. / Yet the thought of the exile, the thought of the prisoner, the thought / of man become mere commodity / try and change that, you cannot." I suspect, moreover, that his concern for the young of Greece (he considers his Nobel award one of their few victories) is part of his commitment to those who are ground to oblivion by history, to the anonymous and the insignificant.

▪ II

Following his first poems, Seferis abandons rhyme, eliminates whatever smacks of tour de force, and concentrates on simple, dense, subtle musical expressions. The combination of austere form and the Greek circumstance leads in 1935 to the famous *Mithistórema*. The work consists of twenty-four poems complete in themselves but also part of a unified whole. The title is ambiguous, meaning, variously, myth and history, myth of history, mythical story, novel, or romance. Perhaps "legend" is more appropriate—that is, a true or fictional account that comes down from the past. "The immemorial drama" that is to "begin once more" is a trying journey, while the actors are voyagers who suffer physical deprivations and hopeless yearning. Each poem is about a visited spot, a relic found, a misadventure, a recollection, an observation, a lament. The characters are ancient or modern Argonauts "sweating at the oars," exiles "tasting the bitter bread," pilgrims "in aimless pilgrimages," harassed Orestes circling "onto the track," expectant Odysseus, refugees, and several others. The narrator speaks as "I" or "we," and this compound voice of multiple identities moves back and forth in time until the border line between past and present is completely blurred. Thus the voyage is also an act of self-examination and a meditation upon the human condition by straddling, as it were, the diverse times of civilization, by wandering among the various mirrors of myth and reality.

Mithistórema stands to an epic as an oratorio to an opera. There are no glorious actions and no glamorous figures, but rather silent sufferers ("They did not complain / because of weariness or because of thirst or because of frost") not recorded in history and referred to only in passing in the legends about Jason and Odysseus: "They had the bearing of trees and waves / that accept the wind and the rain, / accept the night and the sun, / without changing in the midst of change." The "mythistorical" voyager is the common man found anywhere in all times of Greek history, who endures through time and survives the changes in political, social, and religious philosophies because he lives, necessarily, by a basic philosophy which is a law of life: one lives as one can. The Argonauts toil submissively, endure all humbly, die a death that is, justly, forgotten: "The companions expired, one after the other / with downcast eyes. Their oars / indicate the places where they sleep on the shore. // And no one remembers them. Justice." We remember Jason or Odysseus but not the lads who followed them. The last word, *justice,* is the awareness that these are after all the rules of the game, but it is also a questioning of the fairness of these rules.

Justice and injustice are here inextricably mingled, as in all Greek tragedies.

The title indicates the poetic structure, because myth and history are juxtaposed so that they make their own comment on each other. There is an oscillation between modern Greece, where seamen live in a concrete world, and ancient Greece, where Argonauts live in a legendary world. The condition of modern seamen and ancient Argonauts is alike in that it is a tragic condition, but their reality differs in that one is real and the other fabricated in the mind of some poet. Seferis presses this boundary situation of history and myth for its total yield. In the invented world of myth the Argonaut is anonymous, and his is the fiction of a nonexistent character; in the real world of history the anonymous Argonaut is only a shadow of reality, he is only a myth; but also in the world of history the anonymous Argonaut, as a tragic spirit, exists—he endures beyond myth and belongs to the world in which the common Greek seaman exists. Each one suffers and endures anonymously like the other; that is, the tragic pattern of anonymous toil, effort, and death gives unity to myth and history. The Argonaut or the modern Greek, "we," are all such stuff as myths are made on, even if our life is surrounded by history. Our legendary past casts light on our tragedy just as our history substantiates the tragic stuff of past myths. Tragic fellowship is the bridge that Seferis constructs so that one can cross the abyss between myth and history.

After being led slowly but remorselessly toward the meaning of the ancient dead who "smile in a strange silence," and after being confronted with the tantalizing question whether one can die according to the rules, *Mithistórema* ends with two poems that balance each other.

Only a little more
And we shall see the almond trees in bloom
the marbles shining in the sun
the sea rippling

only a little more,
let us rise a little higher.

Finally, lucidity is comforting and painful awareness is a movement toward recovery, a turning toward acceptance where consolation is not completely shut out. We are made to take a glimpse at the abyss but also at the possibilities of hope. The vision of *Mithistórema* is thus neither of total despair nor of total redemption but, as with Greek tragedies, of something tantalizingly, precariously in between. The end is deliberately one of ambiguous calm.

Here comes to an end the works of the sea, the
  works of

love.
Those who some day shall live here where we end,
if by chance the blood should darken in their
   memory
and overflows
let them not forget us, the feeble souls among the
asphodels.
Let them turn the victim head toward the weird
   darkness:

we who had nothing shall teach them peace.

The calm melancholy of leave-taking seals *Mithistórema* with a new sense of contact between life and death. The peace offered is that of "strange silence," a reminder of the mystery of our lot. The Greeks saw the human predicament "shining in the sun" as part of the order of things. The choice involves finality and hope in an unclear mixture and leads to the awareness that there is some principle of order within the haphazard scheme of things.

   Mithistórema is, despite "purity" and "modern" techniques, circumstantial poetry, for Seferis is committed to Greece as Antonio Machado was committed to Spain and W. B. Yeats to Ireland. In all three there is a strong sense of the regional particularity. Spain, Ireland, and Greece are, to paraphrase Hawthorne, quite as large a lump of earth as the heart can really take in. When a Greek poet journeys on a little steamship from port to port and sees the "curtains of mountains, archipelagoes, naked granite," observes "the bitterness of the harbor once all the ships are gone," overhears social trivialities, and feels the banality, waste, sterility, frustration, and misery of provincial Greece, naturally Greece wounds him and "They call the ship that travels, Agony 937"—that is, the poet always mingles in "agony" the private world, the Greek world, and the big world. The combination of regionalism and universality makes his poems engrossing, utterly faithful to their own terms. Seferis invents a mythical Aegean world complete and living in all its details, and his journeys into the Aegean Sea stand as a parable or legend of Greek history and man's history.

▪ III

Seferis strove constantly to make his poems move upon several planes, and in *The King of Asine,* his acknowledged masterpiece written on the eve of World War II, he perfects the technique of transition from one plane to another. The poet searches around a ruined fortress in the small sea kingdom of Asine near Nauplion for its old king, "unknown, forgotten by all, even by Homer / just one word in the *Iliad* and that uncertain." The allusion is to "Asinen té" in Homer's list of those heroes who

came to fight against Troy. It means "and Asine"—that is, let me tell you of one more king who took part in the battle. The search underlines the changes: ruins in place of a fortress, a name for a king, and a bat, symbol of uninhabitedness, in place of the kingdom's activity. Seferis constructs his modern Greek poem around the ancient Greek phrase "Asinen té": "The king of Asine a void under the mask, / everywhere with us, everywhere with us, under a name: / 'Asinen té . . . Asinen té . . .'" He converts Homer's line into a refrain and skillfully grafts it into a modernized elegy. The effect is striking, and the Homeric affirmation "and of another hero" reads as an ambiguous lamentory query: "What of Asine, the hero hardly mentioned by Homer?" The lament for the king leads to a question about the tangible and intangible realities that vanish, recalling François Villon's "But where are the snows of yesteryear?": "Do they exist, the movement of the face the form of affection / of those who dwindled so strangely in our life, / of those who remained wave-shadows and thoughts like the endless sea?"

   The recollection of past splendor is a reminder that, in the face of death and annihilation, all pretensions of glory are puny and futile. And the refrain "Asinen té" is so placed that it draws all the attention and infuses an ironic reality both into Villon's elegiac motif and into the Homeric epic formula: "Asinen té . . . Asinen té . . . / Could this have been the king of Asine / for whom we search so carefully about the acropolis / feeling sometimes with our fingers his very touch upon the stones?" Echoes from *Macbeth*: Asine was but a walking shadow after all, one more player on a big stage and then was heard no more. And heroism is one more illusion. Asine was listed and sought out as a great king, but Asine is in fact a shadow of a king, a shadow of a hero—"a void under the mask"—with only one phrase in an epic, no more, for his heroic identity.

   "The *Thrush*" is Seferis's best-known work after the war. It is a very dense poem wherein everything can be read as an account of postwar experience or as an extensive structure of existence and is held together by a whole network of real and symbolic references. Its literary and contemporary allusions, something like Joyce's *Ulysses,* will be resolved only with the passing of years. The setting is the picturesque island of Poros (Seferis spends most of his summers there), where one could still see after the war the hull of a small ship, the *Thrush,* sunk by the Germans in 1941. The half-submerged boat punctuates the waste and the bitter memories of the war as well as man's precarious position. The narrator is here a mature Ulysses back from the war, the witness to many absurdities and to many bitter experiences, now skeptical, stoical, tolerant. The surroundings provide a canvas for his inner conflicts and his meditations on the human condition: a house near the sea focuses on the idea of stability and emptiness; a conversation between a young war companion who recalls Elpenor in Homer's *Odyssey* and a capricious woman who recalls Circe dramatizes the irony of physical proximity and spiritual distance; a radio by the beach is a reminder of inanities and mechanized conventionalities; the wreck of the *Thrush* points to the imminence of death; finally, a little girl on the beach, called Antigone, symbolizes the hope for regeneration. The older Ulysses is mature but unable to indulge in life as before; in short, the restless seeker is now restlessly remembering, and everything in his mind turns into a network of symbols as in the works of Aeschylus. Life and death, past and present, war and peace, myth and reality, time and eternity, memory and oblivion, passion and inadequacy, and many more universal themes are perfectly integrated somehow and viewed in terms of Greek symbols, Greek landscape, and Greek traditions.

As the poet observes the sunken *Thrush,* he hears voices coming from the bottom of the boat as if from Hades. He is especially drawn by one "calm, changeless, still" voice: "And if you sentence me to drink poison, I thank you; / your law shall be my law; for where should I go / wandering about in foreign lands, a rolling stone. / I choose death rather." He recognizes Socrates, the wronged one. The implications of injustice, exile, and death lead to introspection, and in a moving review of his past we see all the echoes of existential anguish: "As the years go by / so increase in number the judges who condemn you; / as the years go by and you converse with fewer voices, / you gaze with other eyes upon the sun." The poet sees clearly all malevolence, frauds, privations, the sting of criticism, the mockery of friends; but the personal drama is superseded by the awesome drama of the war.

What conclusion can result from this abyss of private and general catastrophes? The poem is resolved in a series of dualities.

Angelic and bright light,
daughter of waves on playgrounds of the sea,
tearful laughter,
the old man looks on you, suppliant
ready to make his way over invisible slabs,
light mirrored in his blood
that gave birth to Eteocles and Polynikes.
Angelic and black day. . . .

Light and darkness are symbolic of the circle of man's life. The old man is Oedipus, who in darkness saw light, who has just begun on the hard road to understanding the true meaning of his answer—*man*—to the riddle of the Sphinx. The poet next addresses Antigone, a little girl on the beach as well as a figure of tragic ambivalence.

O sing, little Antigone, sing O sing . . .
I do not speak of things past, I speak of love;
crown your hair with thorns of the sun,
dark girl. . . .
he who has never loved shall love,
in the light. . . .

Antigone carries within her the two worlds of man, the two brothers Eteocles and Polynikes, the angelic and the black light. "The Tyrant inside man has left," and there is time for one to love in these difficult days; but this is not an easily accessible love, for one must experience the light—that is, the total awareness of our lot with its vulnerabilities and all its direness. Seferis provides that satisfying and perfected embodiment of a long-sought truth which gives at once the impression of recognition and discovery. The sustained quest of the poet-Ulysses and the appearance of Antigone set everything in the light of Greek tragedy: man's sorry lot and his capacity to learn, to "see in his blood," as Oedipus, the angelic and the black light. The resolution emerges in a kind of dark luminousness, the characteristic half-light of Greek tragedy.

After many years of self-search and a terrible war, "The *Thrush*" seems to be both a comment and an answer to the question raised by *Mithistórema.* Man can die according to the rules, of course, but the road is difficult, full of fragmentary, tentative, and precarious truths. Suffering will not be avoided, but suffering can lead to light, to the knowledge of what one is and what it means to be.

No single work sums up Seferis better than "Makriyanis: One Greek," an essay about a hero in the struggle for independence of the 1820s. John Makriyanis was an illiterate who somehow left behind a remarkable book of memoirs: "And whatever I mark down here," he explains, "I mark down because I cannot stand to see injustice choke what is just. For this reason I learned letters in my old days and I jot these notes here gross and raw because as a child there was no way for me to learn." Seferis is awed by the sheer will of this illiterate fighter to express himself and by the literary quality of the memoirs written under personal limitations, historical conditions, and private dangers that would have reduced any lesser man to silence. Makriyanis's passionate need for expression is for Seferis like "these stubborn plants that, once their roots take hold, go on overcoming walls, stones, and graveyards."

Makriyanis was in later years persecuted by his liberated countrymen, and Seferis sees in this ironic twist of fate the makings of a significant, tragic action, as in ancient drama—not because of the lamentable blows that fell upon a heroic figure, but because of his counterthrust that makes for authentic drama. This counterthrust can be seen in Makriyanis's lifelong, innocent conversations with God, which he records in the memoirs whenever he encounters difficulties. In one such confrontation with God he comes face to face with his destiny and strikes back, as in a play, with words. The harassed national hero addresses God pitifully but also firmly: "And you don't hear us and you don't see us. . . . And me groaning night and day with my wounds. And I have to see my miserable family and my children choking in tears and without shoes. And six months jailed in a cramped dungeon. And unable to see a doctor, and they don't let anyone come near us or see us. All wish that we should perish. They question all of us, they search our houses, our basements, our roofs, our boxes . . . even your own icons."

Makriyanis was no longer able to come to an understanding with God. The times had changed. The national hero was now imprisoned, beaten, tried, and convicted, but he stood his ground, in the words of Seferis, "a man reaching the heights of man." He is for Seferis the image of Greece, for Makriyanis finds out, like the "companions" of myth and history, that the world is not always reasonable and not always just. Still, unjustified suffering must be endured and accepted as part of the mystery, and Makriyanis—a sort of Oedipus and Job put into one modern dress—can do no more than persevere in the pride of his convictions and to understand. In his appeal to God against God, in seeing the "angelic and black light" of his lot, he has learned, like Greece, to live and die according to the rules.

Anthony N. Zahareas

¹ See "Seferis," by John E. Rexine, *BA* 41:1 (Winter 1967), pp. 37–38.

² Seferis's poems are available in English: *Poems,* Rex Warner, tr., Boston, Atlantic-Little, Brown, 1964; and *Collected Poems 1924–1955,* Edmond Keeley, Phillipe Sherrard, trs., Princeton, N.J., Princeton University Press, 1967.

The Poetry of René Char, or Man Reconciled [1968]

At the age of sixty, with twenty volumes of poetry published, René Char is considered by more and more critics in France as the greatest living French poet. Albert Camus had made such a claim for him as early as 1951, in *L'homme révolté,* when he greeted him as "poète de

notre renaissance," and in the preface he wrote for Char's *Dichtungen,* an anthology compiled in Germany in 1959, he declared that no such voice had been heard since the pre-Socratics. In 1962 Char was placed among the constellations whose "feux sont sûrs et durables," and in 1966 he was awarded the Prix des Critiques for his latest volume of poems, *Retour amont.* A film was made by the Télévision Suisse de Genève the same year. Last August his prominent position was highlighted by a "Soirée René Char," an event that took place at the Fondation Maeght's new fine-arts center and museum. Char is now achieving international recognition as well, with translations and critical anthologies published in a dozen European countries, in the United States, Canada, Argentina, and Japan.

The poet's life is spent chiefly between Provence and Paris. Near L'Isle-sur-Sorgue, his birthplace and the cradle of his family, is Les Busclats, a white Provençal house surrounded by a large garden of cosmos, hollyhocks, and lavender. A short distance away, one has a view of the Mont Ventoux, whose summits have a prestigious presence in Char's poetry. Three miles west, at Fontaine-de-Vaucluse, where Petrarch lived and wrote, the soaring Sorgue, with its heavy cubelike waters, springs from a vertical rock. The swift river has been for the poet, since his childhood, an infinite source of inspiration.

Although several American universities have invited him to read or discuss his poetry, he has declined. It seems that he wants above all to preserve his freedom and independence. Meanwhile, Les Busclats is becoming a high place, with Char sought out by a growing number of visitors from the world of art and literature. When Heidegger came to France in 1955, the two individuals he wanted to meet first were René Char and Georges Braque.

Today, when we look back over forty years of production, the striking constant we can observe is Char's fidelity. From his early books *Arsenal* (1929) and *Le marteau sans maître* (1934), an enigmatic, unoriented, but radiant current which hammered down the author's young beliefs with even more rage than *Fureur et mystère* of fifteen years later (1948), to his latest volumes *Retour amont* (see *BA* 41:1, p. 56) and the 1967 reedition of his plays, *Trois coups sous les arbres* (see *BA* 42:2, p. 236), Char has remained remarkably faithful to his themes. If a continuous line of major trends can generally be seen in every great writer, the fact is indeed especially true of Char, who has not zigzagged between political affiliations and would not let himself be enslaved by the most tempting ideologies. He parted from his surrealist *bons compagnons de révolte* only after five years of comradeship when he found André Breton becoming too dogmatic and, later, his best friend Paul El-uard turning into a hopelessly committed communist. Moreover, two important breaks in Char's life, which could have developed into a complete change of out-look, in the end were not ruptures. Rather, they helped him elaborate and reinforce the themes he had already anticipated in his early works. The first break was in 1936–37, a septicemia followed by a long recovery. The other was *la grande épreuve de Céreste* (1941–44) when, hemmed in by Vichy police, he organized and directed the Maquis in Basses-Alpes. In each case Char was en-gaged in a struggle against monsters, disease or oppres-sor; he went through "l'halucinante expérience de l'homme noué au Mal, de l'homme massacré et pourtant victorieux." Char's merit was, in the course of a perilous moral itinerary comparable to Camus's of the same time, to have reconciled two opposite, demanding truths: revolt and happiness. It was to wager in favor of man when man everywhere sank, to speak up for beau-ty when beauty was obscured by darkness. Char was to emerge from the Résistance as a genuine moralist and a greater poet.

His first major works then, *Seuls demeurent* (1945) and the famous journal of a Résistance fighter, *Feuillets d'Hypnos* (1946), reveal his important themes. These appear with mixed ethical and poetic concepts, in long poems as well as in simple little ones close to nature and daily life. They are tightly interwoven, sharing their bril-liant, challenging images. Poetry, the making of the poem, the poet's function, is regarded by all Char's exe-getes as his predominant, richest theme. Char says in "Mirage des aiguilles," a poem in *Retour amont:* "Fidèle à son amour comme le ciel l'est au rocher." Tender lov-ing expressions, such as *mon amour, l'Amie, ma martelée, la Rencontrée,* apply most often to poetry in this poet's world, and not to woman, as more than one unaware reader has been misled to think. The decisive, magic en-counter between poetry and poet had already taken place in childhood: "Tout enfant, j'ai senti, réellement, quelqu'un, qui se tenait à mon côté, invisible—qui n'était pas Dieu." The theme runs through many differ-ent kinds of texts in prose and verse, in poems and even in pamphlets, letters, or homages to other poets, like those in a book which can be said to represent Char's credo: *Recherche de la base et du sommet*. This theme is also the very topic of special long poems made up of short numbered sequences, which can be read as a se-ries of aphorisms or a continuous poem, such as *Partage formel* (1945), *A une sérénité crispée* (1951), *A la santé du serpent* (1954), *L'âge cassant* (1965). One characteris-tic Charian definition in the fifty-five dazzling sentences of *Partage formel* presents the poem as a free unifying force of ethics and esthetics: "Cette forteresse épanchant

la liberté par toutes ses poternes, cette fourche de vapeur qui tient dans l'air un corps d'une envergure prométhéenne que la foudre illumine et évite, c'est le poème, aux caprices exorbitants, qui, dans l'instant, nous obtient puis s'efface."

In *Arrière-histoire du poème pulvérisé,* which consists of comments added to a 1947 plaquette called *Le poème pulvérisé,* Char explains how a poem is born: "J'ai pris ma tête comme on saisit une motte de sel et je l'ai littér-alement pulvérisée: de cette illusion atroce est né 'J'habite une douleur,' plus quelque calme. C'est là, je crois, l'un de mes poèmes les plus achevés." Hence the nature of Charian poems, which indeed bear traces of this pulverization, somehow become *fragments* scat-tered over the world, but paradoxically remain solid, re-sistant entities. These fragments are island-poems, made of small blocks, prose paragraphs, boldly emerg-ing from silence. In fact, the entire work of the poet is in the form of an archipelago. *La parole en archipel* (see BA 36:4, p. 393) is the title of a book published in 1962, but it had been Char's program long before that date. Moreover, the compact quality of the fragment is all the more striking because so many polyvalent images are condensed in it. The word is taut with poetic charge, or, in Char's terms, "La constellation du solitaire est ten-due." Immense perspectives and opposite metaphors in a short, elliptic sentence constitute the Charian explo-sive aphorism. In brief, it can be said that the chief theme of Char is a complete monography of the Poem, its genesis, form, function, and aims. A passage written by Maurice Blanchot in *La part du feu* and often quoted since it was first published in 1946 sums up the poet's originality and work: "L'une des grandeurs de René Char, celle par laquelle il n'a pas d'égal en ce temps, c'est que sa poésie est révélation de la poésie, poésie de la poésie, et comme le dit à peu près Heidegger de Hölderlin, poème de l'essence du poème."

The second essential theme in Char's poetry is that of rebirth, a theme which has been somewhat neglected by criticism but will demand more and more attention since it has gained more importance in the poet's latest works. Frequently it appears together with hymns to nature and spring life, as in "Le bois de l'Epte," or it bor-rows the paths of his ars poetica, as in "La bibliothèque est en feu." The theme is confirmed and amplified in *Re-tour amont,* a book which is, as defined by the author, "a tentative crossing beyond springs," "vers ce qui per-met aux sources de se refaire." In a central piece, "Le nu perdu," the instant is revealed when the living, the creators, "those who will bear boughs," are touched by the down of black night that precedes the lightning flash of illumination.

The theme of rebirth is generally apprehended in its full scope, as the dialectical operation of destruction and renaissance. It is supported, in the tradition of mythology and alchemy, by multiple images of fire. Fire is the one of the four elements which lends itself best to symbolizing opposite, ambiguous human behaviors, a large variety of which can be found in Char's poetry. The word *feu* achieves indeed a high frequency, which is surpassed only by the word *soleil*. The terms have many related ones, such as wheels, stars, peacocks, light, dawn, warmth, the famous lightning, et cetera. Numerous references are also made to their opposites, shadow and light. The "feu-chaleur" is associated with the expression of friendship and brotherhood, whereas *l'éclair,* the quick happening of which lasts a little longer for the privileged poet, brings knowledge, uncovers a brilliant and beloved country, and finally becomes *le cœur de l'éternel.*

Fire is so precious, however, that we want to preserve, condense it in a form and space as small as possible. What could such a compact dynamic entity be? Bird, of course. A variety of birds, as well as the word *oiseau,* appear in numerous texts. Above all of them flies the eagle. In a typical taut Charian metaphor, "l'aigle solaire," encompassing the two main types of fire, represents the thinker Heraclitus, whose "exaltante alliance des contraires" has forever inspired the poet.

Both closely related major themes of regeneration and the essence of the poem are essential in forming the meaning of one of the greatest poems by Char: "La bibliothèque est en feu" in *Poèmes et prose choisis* (1957). The flawless *poème en archipel* also combines three other chief Charian themes: the problems of knowledge and time, and especially the beautiful and frail fraternity among men of this earth. The poet dances with his fellow man: "Torche, je ne valse qu'avec lui." Man, "le bel homme déconcertant et fragile," has been for Char an object of long-range attention and care. The poet often seems to imply that his preferred friends are "les amis au sol," his Vauclusian compatriots, who partake of qualities of earth itself, serenity, solidarity, warmth, and who can also understand the language of the Provençal sun. The native soil is rarely used as topic itself for a poem, but it pervades all works, with its mountains, rivers, and fauna contributing their own personalities to that of the poem, the geographic elements being thus transcended and humanized. The *pays* leads one to other regions, especially the *Pays* with a capital *P,* which is poetry land.

Knowledge, with its traditional meaning of a vast, baffling, and misleading endeavor, is also for Char "la connaisance aux cents passages," a dispenser of vertigo to the one who has climbed it up to its crest and is fasci-

nated by the abyss. Another type of knowledge, however, one which is more specifically Char's, aims at being productive, ultimately resulting in the poem itself. It can be at the same time defined by a strange aspect of unpredictability. Events are always surrounded with mystery, and a few unexpected encounters are truly privileged moments in Char's world. It is, for instance, at the turn of a road, a girl walking on a country trail after picking mimosas during the day: profiled against sunset, her figure appears as a lamp of perfume, ("Congé au vent"); but the apparition could have been poetry herself. Knowledge and poetry are sisters, even if, according to Heidegger, they like to live on separate summits. In "La bibliothèque est en feu," one day in winter, poetry manifested itself, with another one of its touching ways, as bird down on the windowpane; it announced spring and a life of writing: "Comment me vint l'écriture? Comme un duvet d'oiseau sur ma vitre en hiver."

Most Charian happenings take place in an absolute present. By the emphasis given to the use of that tense and time in his work, Char reveals himself as a true existential poet. Georges Poulet, who has made a thorough study of Char's time, has stressed the compact, tense, full quality of a "présent essentiel," that culminates into instant. Things are given very little time "pour faire leur entrée dans le champ de la conscience." Many metamorphoses, many contradictory events are accomplished in no time at all, in what Char himself calls "raccourci fascinateur." Hence the continuous trembling of a crowded instant under the pressure of such forces; hence the constantly explosive quality of this poetry.

Among the many polyvalent images, *l'éclair, le serpent, la rose, l'oiseau* offer probably the richest symbols. Among all birds, unique is the eagle, which can be said to combine and condense the main Charian themes. It is a small, live fragment, endowed with a furious power, that of creation, of the poet himself. He is freedom as well as free encounter of knowledge with all its frailty; but he never means escape. On the contrary, watching is his concern and duty; his view and views are sharp. Proudly flying high, or staying on summits, he is closer to the sun than anyone else; but dwelling in rocks, he draws links between sun and earth, thus symbolizing the dynamic unified man. Finally the eagle is to come, and, like the Nietzschean superman, only in the future will he be ideally realized.

In the past twenty years Char's poetry has challenged the foremost critics to write an ever-increasing number of penetrating analyses; but for all the excellent decoding they have done, Charian studies are only beginning. For instance, no stylistic study has yet been made on the famous aphorism, allegedly inherited from

Heraclitus, but which also bears resemblances to those of several French moralists. In numerous homage poems, recently thoroughly classified by the author in *Commune présence* (1964) and the second edition of *Recherche de la base et du sommet* (1965), the poet has acknowledged his debt to Heraclitus, Rimbaud, Mallarmé, and Nietzsche, among others, and also to his great friends of the postwar period, Albert Camus and Georges Braque. Criticism so far has merely repeated these opinions. It has insisted on Heraclitean as well as surrealist influences but has hardly touched the Nietzschean. That influence, however, will undoubtedly be found far greater and more durable than the others. A study should compare Char and the author of *Also sprach Zarathustra*. Let us remember, for example, the latter's interrogation to the sky after hearing the cry of an animal: "And behold! An eagle was sweeping through the air in wide circles, and from it was hanging a serpent, not like a prey, but like a friend, for it was coiled around the eagle's neck." "The proudest animal under the sun and the wisest animal under the sun" appear in Char's poetry with similar and even richer implications. Among all known serpents in mythologies and poetries, Char's snake is indeed the most akin to Zarathustra's. The eagle occupies the privileged place we know. Concerning the "unvollständiger Nihilismus," which is one of the evils confronting our human condition, as also denounced especially by the existentialists, the poet repeatedly challenges us to perform the necessary task of destroying harmful, worn-out values. *La parole en archipel* echoes Nietzsche's "fragmentary language" which urged us first to reduce the universe to crumbs. Thus numerous tentative questions posed by the philosopher are tentatively answered by the poet. To the madman's burning one, why earth and sun are being tragically divorced, several poems, among them "La bibliothèque est en feu," do indicate the way to reconciliation. The reconciliation is also symbolized by the eagle of the summits and the terrestrial snake as friends. The poet himself participates as a "liana" of the sun.

This reconciliation, however, goes further than Nietzschean or existential philosophy, by its encompassing and understanding of the unknown. Char does not feel any nostalgia or anxiety about it. Char, "poète du devenir," praises it as being "l'inconnu équilibrant." He recommends it, in fact. The "Argument" of *Poème pulvérisé* begins with these words: "Comment vivre sans inconnu devant soi?" The unknown might well be the region where brilliant rebirth will take place after the darkness of our lives, where miraculous fragments of poems can be collected, love for the fellow man reach its zenith, and man his unity. The firm young voice of the great poet achieves indeed an "Umwertung aller

Werte," the striking change in life which our times demand. His poetry teaches the way to reconciliation: "En poésie, devenir c'est réconcilier."

Paulène Aspel

Heimito von Doderer [1968]

Asked, as his last American editor-publisher, to contribute to a memorial issue on Heimito von Doderer, I am, naturally, concerned with his reception by the American public, critics, and readers. Doderer is one of the major European writers most difficult to "put across" the cultural wall that divides the two continents. That this should be so is easy to understand: he is overwhelmingly an Austrian writer. I suspect that even in his native language he can be read in the right way only by "South Germans," and not for nothing is his German publisher located in Munich. He belongs to that cultural group "which built cathedrals when in the north they were still eating their grandmothers," as the somewhat arrogant saying goes.

What do I mean by "read in the right way"? To me, an Austrian on my mother's side, it means that I do not read Doderer as I read any other writer; in fact, a new verb entered our private language with the first Doderer novel, *Die Strudlhofstiege*. As one or the other took the volume to his room, he announced: "I am going to doderer." That term expressed a delectable process: meandering, loitering, inquisitively turning corners for unexpected views, somewhat like taking a walk in Venice. No one in his right mind would read Doderer for plot, would hasten ahead to find the why and wherefore—any more than one would Proust, with whom Doderer has a great deal in common, except that his world is as much outdoors as indoors, if not more so, his society more ramified and stratified. The way in which he goes fishing in the waters of the past is Proustian, using memory rather than imagination for creative production. If, he tells us, there are gaps at some point of the past under scrutiny, he concentrates the light of consciousness on the dark spot and sends "a messenger" into the unconscious who dives down, probing around until he rises to the surface with the lost piece retrieved.

Like Proust, Doderer has been served extremely well by the locus of his remembrance. As an Austrian, he had—and I use his own words—"a ground to stand upon, a noted, honorable ground, known throughout the world, as legitimate as that of an Englishman, a Dane, a Spaniard." He is complex with the complexity of the Austro-Hungarian Empire, its people and lands, and makes sovereign use of its oddities, linguistic as well as ethnological, sometimes, as I reluctantly admit, with a somewhat irritating touch of whimsy which is not Proustian and does not get across in English at all.

One American critic said of Doderer's last published novel, *The Waterfalls of Slunj,* that it is an example of how *not* to write a novel. He might as well have said that an intricately constructed labyrinth is an artless mess produced by a mindless creature running around in circles, for in this, as in his great earlier book *Die Dämonen* and the as yet untranslated *Strudlhofstiege,* Doderer did far more than retrace the vagaries of a set of characters. He reproduced the quality of time at a certain suspended moment in history: a time, he says somewhere, which in contrast to the coming cataracts was still like a pond, "had time," reflected movement in slow, concentric circles; a time that allowed for the apperception of nuances, for the aimless yet subtly revealing gossip of coffeehouses and open-air taverns; a time when empires seemed solid, trade was eternally expanding, life and property reasonably safe, when war was not often thought of and extinction not conceived of at all. Yet this amiable and ambling world was in fact pregnant with war, sliding toward doom, as every reader knows, supplying, as Doderer ingeniously anticipated, his own clouds to the cloudless sky.

One of the chief attractions of "doderering" is this constant awareness that here is a writer who engages his reader in conversation, who plays in order to produce echoes, who calls for interlinear reading. In his deliberate ramblings, gaps are left on purpose for his audience to fill. One of the charms on entering his atmosphere is the encounter with aperçus sprouting, provocative and delightful, out of the even texture of the narrative. It is this, incidentally, that makes "doderering" such an irritating hazard to all non-doderers in the vicinity. The reader is tempted, and cannot always resist the temptation, to interrupt whatever another is thinking, reading, or doing, with the unpardonable "Listen to this!"

The "this" may be a singularly acute light thrown on such various issues as the victory of the Greeks over the Persians or the origins of Austrian coffee-drinking habits, casually thrown into light conversation. Doderer is too much of a Viennese to be truly didactic. He is merely civilized, thoroughly educated, not just "informed." As no one should read him for plot, so no one should read him for information, though his facts could not be more exact, down to the weather at a certain hour of a certain day. He should be read for what he calls the "indirect lighting" that falls obliquely on the scenery and scenes that have always been there but which now become visible. What fascinates him is not so much one character or the other, but the net of relations by which they meet and cross—their junction.

Throughout his works, the moments and places of meetings, the fateful yet casual oddity of coincidences, are strikingly prominent. The then and there is more important than the why and wherefore.

Whoever surrenders to Doderer enters a considerable world that had reality once and is given by him a reflective reality, an eternal present. For the American reader it is an alien reality, his surrender to it therefore more difficult, more in the nature of a journey than of a homecoming; but it might have all the fascination of a journey not just in space but also in time, an experience of styles of living and being that throw light on what is as much as on what was. The final word belongs to the author (listen to this!): "The only book I wish to write is one I would like to read myself. A book that would captivate me, that would show me the radiant points in the world, not merely the problematical darkness in the heart of the author."

Helen Wolff

Kawabata: Achievements of the Nobel Laureate [1969]

Although Yasunari Kawabata has for years been considered the most distinguished member of the Japanese world of letters, the news of the selection of the sixty-nine-year-old author as the recipient of the 1968 Nobel Prize in Literature—a surprise to readers throughout much of the world—was initially received with a sense of disbelief by his countrymen. The insight revealed in the citation by the Nobel Committee, which praised the author for "his narrative mastership, which with great sensibility expressed the essence of the Japanese mind," seemed to mystify all but the most sensitive readers and critics, to whom the judgment seemed incredibly astute.

The typical Japanese reader tends, like readers elsewhere, to favor a well-paced narrative designed to quicken his interest in the story. He has been content to accept the high evaluation of Kawabata by professional critics and, rather than read his stories, has been inclined to enjoy them through the modified medium of the cinema. Indeed, Japanese movie-makers since the early fifties have produced some twenty film versions of his novels. The general reader in Japan has probably regarded Kawabata as a modernist rather than a traditionalist, for his stories are often difficult to apprehend fully, owing to the rich, allusive imagery, a suggestive quality that requires a matured sensibility of the reader, an elliptical sentence style, and a mode of story progression that often relies on linking through imagery rather than through contextual or sentence logic—a technique of the traditional *renga* or "linked verse." Many native readers are now avidly reading Kawabata novels to discover for themselves the traditional Japanese qualities that foreign readers were able to perceive through the reading of translations.

Snow Country (*Yukiguni*, published in 1948), *Thousand Cranes* (*Semazuru*, 1952) and *The Old Capital* (*Koto*, 1962) are the novels by which the Nobel Committee judged Kawabata's worth as a writer of fiction. These are novels in which the author's bent for the traditional is particularly evident, in depiction of outward forms of traditional culture (the tea ceremony, folk art, Shinto festivals, Buddhist temples) and the use of nature imagery for their cumulative, traditional lyrical implications, yet they do not fully represent the vast range of the author's creative capacity. . . . Translations of several of Kawabata's short stories have appeared in anthologies or magazines—among them, "The Izu Dancer" ("Izu no odoriko," 1926), "The Mole" ("Hokuro no tegami," 1940) "Reencounter" ("Saikai," 1946), and "Moon on the Water" ("Suigetsu," 1953).

In Japan, in the twentieth century, new literary trends were frequently set by coteries of writers who cooperated in the publication of literary journals. A particularly memorable year was 1924, when, in June, "Literary Battle Line" (*Bungei Sensen*) was founded as a monthly for Marxist writers and, in October, the publication of "Literary Era" (*Bungei Jidai*) was inaugurated by a group of young authors who were concerned primarily with the esthetics of literature. Yokomitsu Toshikazu (1898–1947) and Kawabata were the prime movers of the latter group, who were promptly labeled the "neoperceptionists" by the critic Kameo Chiba. In an essay, "The Birth of the Neoperceptionists" (in *Seiki*, November 1924), Chiba stated, "There is no doubt whatever that these writers, whom we might call the 'Literary Era' coterie, are sensually alert to diction, lyricism, and rhythm that are far fresher than anything ever before expressed by any of our sensitive artists." The expressive style of the neoperceptionists, literary historians tell us, was influenced considerably by the many startling examples of figurative language those young writers discovered in Paul Morand's *Ouvert la nuit*, which had appeared in Japanese translation that year.

Kawabata, by his own admission, has probably participated in the setting of more new trends than any other living writer. More important, however, has been his ability to experiment with new approaches and techniques and to adopt them into a larger embodiment which can be identified as a style uniquely his own; and his many years of experience, starting in his twenties, as a practicing critic have without doubt contributed much to the development of his own literary sensibility.

Although imprints of literary expressionism and psychological realism are rather clearly evident in Kawabata's stories, traditional Japanese themes have been more subtly infused into his writings. We may note coursing through all his major novels a sense of sorrow and loneliness, a recognition of an emotional and spiritual vacuity in man, and the recurring theme of the evanescence and meaninglessness of passion, even of temporal existence. The general tenor of the author's outlook has much in common with that of the *Tale of Genji* and diaries of the Late Classical Era (10th-12th century), with much of the prose of the Medieval Era (12th-16th century), and with traditional poetry. Because Kawabata avoids the explicit, his stories often seem veiled by vagueness, a quality that the native reader finds attractive. Because his writings contain so many diverse elements, they are at once subtle and complex, and they can be enjoyed for their sheer tonal and textural beauty.

Reading Kawabata's major works in chronological sequence, one may note a steady progression in the refinement of his technical mastery and a development of the ability to enter deeply into his characters. "The Izu Dancer" (1926), best known among his earliest writings, is a lyric description of a journey made by a high-school student, from the vicinity of Mount Fuji to the lower tip of Izu Peninsula, in the company of a troupe of traveling entertainers. Narrated in the first person and in a confessional vein, the short tale depicts a love that stirs the heart of the youth, whose eyes filter out the unsightly and create an idealized image of a lovely dancer who is about to blossom into womanhood. The inevitable parting and the lonely aftertaste remind him of the sorrow of having grown up an orphan, yet the memory of the fleeting encounter becomes a pleasurable one even while he continues to shed tears of regret. In composing this attractive tale, the author employed none of the techniques that were to characterize his later writings.

Kawabata's first full-length novel, "The Crimson Gang of Asakusa" (*Asakusa kurenaidan*), published in 1930, is considered the only noteworthy product of a short-lived movement for modernity and artistry that was launched by a loosely organized group of writers intent on stemming the tide of proletarian literature. This novel is in many respects antithetical to "The Izu Dancer." The Crimson Gang is a band of delinquents whose members are caught in a web of sex and violence. The setting is Asakusa, the colorful, raucous and sinful center of urban entertainment for the middle and lower classes of Tokyo. The author presents a panorama which unfolds in a series of rapidly changing scenes sketching various aspects of life in Asakusa. The ugly and evil are depicted along with the innocent and beautiful. Descriptions of the activities of the gang are woven into the panorama so that some semblance of unity is achieved. The author is a keenly sensitive observer, uninvolved in the story.

Snow Country (1948), which was written sporadically between 1934 and 1937 and expanded into its present form after the war, is the first novel in which we find all the artistic elements, both modern and traditional, that have since characterized the distinctive style of Kawabata. Rich in imagery and symbolism, suggestive by association, the novel can be reexplored through repeated readings to new discoveries of meaning. The opening passage is arresting: "When the train came out of the long tunnel separating the provinces, it was in the snow country. The bottomless depth of the night was imbued with whiteness." Typical of the author's style is the delicacy of expression that verbalizes the profundity of a common winter scene, the subtle contrast between black sky and night-darkened snow.

The hero, Shimamura, studies the face of a girl reflected in the train window. The mirror filters out the ugly and the unpleasant; what remains for Shimamura to observe is only the beautiful, detached from those associations of sadness and pain that are evident in the totality of the image. As Shimamura concentrates on the reflected face, his time track shifts from the external to the "concrete" or internal psychological time; we are presented with a flashback, and then a flashback within a flashback, as the image evokes one recollection and then another in his mind.

Even though the point of view of *Snow Country* is essentially that of Shimamura, the author does not enter deeply into him. The novel can hardly be considered autobiographical. Shimamura is the observer of two women—the innocent Yōko, whose reflected image has fascinated him, and the sensual geisha Komako. Through his characterization of these two, the author describes the eternal sorrow of the Japanese woman as well as his admiration for her quality of forlornness and passivity. The vacuity in Shimamura's heart, however, may well be the vacuity in the heart of the author, or of an archetype of the modern Japanese male. The concluding paragraph presents the reader with an example of the author's elliptical sentence style: "The voice that shouted the half-crazed Komako Shimamura tried to get nearer to . . ." This English approximates the syntactic and idiomatic level of the original. A Japanese would reread and ponder it before he could grasp the intended meaning: "The voice that shouted was Komako's; Shimamura recognized it and tried to get nearer to the half-crazed Komako. . . ." The concluding sentence, "The River of Heaven (the Milky Way) seemed to flow down

with a roar into Shimamura," seems to be an expressionistic attempt to objectify an inexpressibly complex state of mind.

Thousand Cranes (1952) is a novel that exhibits many of the qualities of *Snow Country*, but we note a bolder approach to the topic of eroticism. The mode of fiction is that of imaginative storytelling, the author being nowhere evident. The relationship depicted is at best an unhealthy one—that between a young man and the women who had been mistresses to his late father. The motif is similar to that in Maupassant's "Hautot and His Son," but the eroticism in *Thousand Cranes* is more explicit, and is pervaded by a sense of sin and guilt which is absent from the French story. Kawabata adds to the complexity of incestuous relationship by involving the young hero in carnal association with the daughter of his father's former mistress. Here, as in *Snow Country,* we are afforded glimpses of traditional esthetic forms—graphic patterns, the tea ceremony, ceramics—often invested with symbolic suggestion. The instant transitions and fantastic leaps in time are techniques that anticipated those used many years later in films—recently in *The Graduate,* for instance.

Kawabata's finest novel in his unique modernist-traditionalist mode of fiction is *Sound of the Mountain* (*Yama no oto*), published in 1954. Because the novel sheds much light on the immemorial Japanese household—an extended family—and on the often fast-and-loose world of Japanese business, we may say that it resembles the "novel of manners," which Japanese literary critics tend to regard with disdain. *Sound of the Mountain,* however, is essentially a psychological novel in which the process and effects of aging are drawn with remarkable sensitivity.

The narrative point of view is that of the sixty-year-old Ogata, who might be a fictional extension of the youthful "I" of "The Izu Dancer" and Shimamura of *Snow Country.* Like the shadowy hero of *Snow Country,* the gentle, aging Ogata is constantly observing and listening, absorbing all that happens about him, but, unlike Shimamura, he is keenly aware of his own reactions and gropes to identify the motives for his own thoughts and actions. His married son is involved in a sordid extramarital liaison with a war widow. Kikuko, the son's neglected wife, has a beauty that symbolizes purity and innocence—womanly qualities attractive to Ogata—and a mutual bond of sympathy and understanding draws the two close together. Kikuko shares Ogata's sensibilities, which his wife does not. The Western reader might be amused to note the corresponding levels of perceptivity assigned to Ogata, his daughter-in-law, and Mrs. Ogata, and to Mr. Bennet, Elizabeth, and Mrs. Bennet in *Pride and Prejudice.* The fading but persistent yearning for youthful femininity in Ogata's unconscious is revealed to him occasionally in erotic dreams. In a moment of stupefying realization, Ogata identifies the faceless woman he has often embraced in dreams with his own daughter-in-law. The eroticism, however, is presented subtly, and the texture of *Sound of the Mountain* is softened considerably by frequent references to traditional esthetics.

Although, having completed *Sound of the Mountain,* Kawabata could have rested on his laurels, he was busily at work in 1954 writing *The Lake* (*Mizu'umi*), a novel of stark psychological realism, infused with a dark lyricism which places it a fictional world apart from *Sound of the Mountain* and marks the beginning of yet another phase in the author's creative career. It is remarkable for its absence of references to traditional beauty. Instead, its emphasis is on symbolism, the bold use of interior monologue, the constantly shifting time track, and particularly the characterization of the hero: Gimpei's overpowering desire for beautiful women will never be fulfilled because of the ugliness of his feet—feet which he himself can regard only with morbid fascination, if not with abhorrence.

Another novel in a similar vein, *House of the Sleeping Beauties* (*Nemureru bijo*), depicting the behavioral and psychological manifestations of eroticism in the aging male, was published in 1961 and was immediately acclaimed as Kawabata's major work by a number of critics and authors. The novelist Yukio Mishima, among others, expressed regret that the Nobel Committee could not have read *Sleeping Beauties* to learn how the passing years had served to hone, rather than to dull, Kawabata's perceptivity and to enrich his creative and expressive capacities.

In *The Old Capital* (*Koto*), published in 1962, Kawabata reverted abruptly to the beauty and sadness he sees in youth and innocence. As in "The Crimson Gang of Asakusa," the story itself is less important than the traditional beauty of Kyoto, which is woven into a soft brocade, attractive for its sheer textural elegance.

Thanks to the Nobel Committee, readers of English should soon be given access by our commercial publishers to translations of Kawabata novels which have won praise for their literary quality but have seldom been published in large editions in Japan. The reader might be forewarned, however, of one peculiarity of Kawabata's stories that is distinctly Japanese. Almost all of his stories represent a non-dramatic mode of fiction and remain unresolved. There is no explicit statement of what the tomorrow will bring to Shimamura, Ogata, Gimpei, "old" Eguchi of *Sleeping Beauties,* or the many women in his stories. Most Japanese readers enjoy the

pathos born of such vagueness. We too might learn to enjoy pondering the eventual fates of characters in novels. Their lives are no less real than our own. No one, after all, lives quite happily or unhappily ever after.

James T. Araki

Presentation of Allen Ginsberg's Poems (Naples 1966)* [1970]

Three happy occasions are offered to me here tonight. First, to find myself once again in Naples, in one of the cities of the world I love most (he who has been tossed about continuously from one continent to another can use this expression "of the world"). Second, to be called upon to speak of an extraordinary poet, a dear friend, and an extremely generous man. Third, in praising Allen Ginsberg, to stand beside Fernanda Pivano, to whom I am not only deeply devoted but whom I also increasingly admire for her long activity as a scholar and translator. I am very moved to find myself in conversation with a Neapolitan public. I was in Naples the other evening, but it was not the same thing: it was in a courtly theater, a small theater, if you prefer, and I acted only as a reciter of verses; and even though the verses were mine, it was more like a museum statue that has a guide.

Naples is for me a great memory which begins with the birth of my fame as a poet. In 1916, exactly fifty years ago, I came here; I came here from the trenches, dressed as a shabby soldier, with the eighty copies printed in Udine of my first book, *Il porto sepolto*. I had contributed to *Voce* and to *Lacerba,* but it had been the *Diana* of Gherardo Marone which was to publish one by one those poems as soon as I succeeded in putting them on paper; it had been Gherardo who had made the novelty of them felt before I could collect them in a volume. Gherardo gave me hospitality in his home, and from that Neapolitan home gave to Italy and to the world *Il porto sepolto*. Unexpected glory smiled at me; but glory and easy life do not go hand in hand, and I chose a life of privations.

Later I read and commented on, in public here at the Circolo degli Illusi, which was a center of noble and bold culture, my poems of *Sentimento del tempo* as soon as I composed them. To Naples I have returned almost every year, for other lectures, always by invitation of the circle of the Illusi.

I still see myself, here in Naples, at Fuorigrotta, on the steps of the church, where perhaps they preserved his remains, called upon to commemorate Giacomo Leopardi one hundred years after his death. I had just recovered from a bad case of pneumonia, I was all wrapped up as for crossing Siberia, and from every side hands rose to offer me every type of cough drops. The windows facing the square were full of people, the square was crowded, but, although hoarse and faint, I seemed to possess in my voice that day the thundering of a crowd, marvelous in clarity, to celebrate fittingly Giacomo Leopardi, the Leopardi who had loved Naples so much, to celebrate him as a fellow citizen of yours for always, just as Vergil is a fellow citizen of yours for always.

Forgive me for having lost myself in melancholy. I will speak immediately of Ginsberg. I know very well that a poet is never the measure of another poet; if it was not so, there wouldn't be any more poetry, and it would not be right to pause to listen to Ginsberg, having spoken of Leopardi.

Nevertheless it seems right to me at the same time to walk in the company of Jacopone and of Francesco Petrarca, of Villon and of Leopardi, of Ginsberg and Mallarmé. Each of them has his truth to tell me, and from each the truth he manifests requires that he sacrifice his entire life to it without any ulterior motives. Fernanda Pivano has already told, as only she knows how, the literary facts, without neglecting anything worthwhile, the story of the Beat Generation, and perhaps she will not neglect to return to that story tonight.

I do not care much about schools; one can only give importance to people, and to works. By the way, talking of schools, in America another one is already in fashion; it is composed of the Vietniks. Like the Beats, but by imitation, and badly, they propose by interpreting themselves to interpret him who finds himself in a state of apprehension and refusal of society; yet, for example, the poetry of their Bob Dylan, who sends the young people into raptures in the United States, is the poetry of a singer certainly infinitely more gifted than those who scream at San Remo, but it is an ingenuous poetry, emphatic, banal, coarse. Think of it in comparison to the experience of Ginsberg; the comparison is an insult for which I hope Ginsberg will not hold a grudge against me. Ginsberg has traveled through Africa and Asia. He is always traveling. Upon arriving in a country, the first thing that he looks for is the place where the starving are; it is the place of those suffering from calamities; these are the places where he can bend down to touch, to caress, to comfort the inconsolable, the resigned. In this manner he has acquired his experience; in this manner he has learned to know the true way of poetry. It is impossible that on earth, for always, the great majority cannot do anything but stifle their shouts

for fear of increasing their suffering; he has aroused that shout; it can be seen in all his poems, and we will see before ending our speech how it will reach us in *Kaddish*.

In order to proceed better, it is necessary that I read you a poem of the not yet twenty-four-year-old and already very celebrated Bob Dylan. He sings it; I have to limit myself to reading it, never having been able to sing or accompany myself on the guitar. The words of the song, which is dedicated to the manufacturers of bombs, say: "And I hope that you die / And your death will come soon / I'll follow your casket / On a pale afternoon / I'll watch while you're lowered / Down to your deathbed / And I'll stand over your grave till I'm sure that you're dead."

It is a Beat poem, rather common; but at this point news of the day will allow you to imagine the importance assumed by Beat poetry, even if unfortunately it has assumed it especially by means of remakings passed with a different name. The American magazine *Esquire* circulated among the students of the universities of the United States the following question: "Who is the most remarkable personality of our times?" The greatest part of the answers gave: 1) Kennedy, 2) Bob Dylan, 3) Fidel Castro. A few weeks later, of the same students, the same magazine asked: "Who is the greatest of the writers living today in the United States?" Answer almost unanimous: "Bob Dylan." The *New York Times,* amazed, dedicated an article to the matter.

The United States is the most complex nation that can exist, because of the variety of the peoples that have formed it in the past and are still forming it. Innumerable varieties of opinion, of passions which are continually changing, mingle there and ferment. Excessive importance therefore should be not given to that conviction of young people who, however, will furnish in part the elements of formation of the ruling class of tomorrow. Infatuation of young people like the one our young people have for the Inter and the Fiorentina or Bobby Solo? Witty remark? Maybe. Or maybe because a truth is not accepted until one finds him who repeats it in comic-strip form? Let us return to the point. Poetry expresses, through personal facts, the aspiration and desperation that at a given moment are common to every one. It is the thermometer, poetry, from which one can read the degree of temperature. The root of poetry sinks down into the private events of a person to sink itself in the history of a period, to illuminate itself behind and above history. Is such the poetic recipe of the Beat Generation? A very effective recipe. Only the true poets resort to it.

The Beat Generation includes, by means of their accepted reciprocal solidarity from the beginning, if I am not mistaken—but in the introduction of Fernanda Pivano, you will have, I repeat, every information—the following writers: Gregory Corso, Lawrence Ferlinghetti, William Burroughs, Allen Ginsberg. Before going on, I have the duty, concerning Ferlinghetti, to express a disappointment which is not only mine but also that of my young friends of *Tel Quel,* and of whoever is well informed. Ferlinghetti in his anthology of the works of Antonin Artaud (City Lights Books) misrepresents their nature, character, and importance, even using documents of doubtful authenticity. I have been on terms of close cordiality with Artaud, and you should forgive me therefore if I intervene. One does not question the good faith of Ferlinghetti; on the contrary, I want to seize this opportunity to confirm my sincere esteem for him, yet one doubts, and has reason to doubt, the validity of his information. Considered on the level of the aims of poetry of a Rimbaud, Artaud is the greatest poet who has appeared in the world since Rimbaud, and he is, as by now everyone admits, the greatest modern innovator, for theory and for experiments, of the present art of the theater. I would ask Ferlinghetti and everyone else, if I have any qualification to do so: let no one dare to use, even if they were true and declared—and he who has frequented much Artaud knows that various were his obsessions and his attempts to save himself from anguish—let no one dare to make himself the preacher of special inclinations which could be the price imposed upon this or that poet, to deceive him that they might redeem him by helping him escape from an intolerable and implacable unhappiness. Weaknesses will remain weaknesses even in those boasting of irregularity, to deface a hateful system of placing people in line; even if from these poetic challenges to injustice, from those impudent imprecations slipped out against one's will against the implacable affronts of hate is born poetry. To make oneself the propagandist of them would be to offend that expressive freedom of which each one has the right to dispose in his own way, as constant impetuosity and so much sublimity of poetry shows in Allen Ginsberg.

In connection with Ginsberg, the name of Walt Whitman is mentioned. Even Fernanda Pivano mentions it, and gives, as always, convincing reasons for her opinion. Certainly that of Whitman is the only voice of American poetry preceding his own which could persuade Ginsberg. It is a voice which does not believe that it humiliates itself by taking as its own the voice of the poor, by tearing out from his soul the shout of his own spirit and his own tormented flesh.

However, would throwing himself in the furnace of the maturing summer have cauterized the wounds of Whitman and offered him the balm to soothe them, if he had not been a romantic or a downright follower of Victor Hugo? Ginsberg is thirsty only for sadness, even if always it tortures him more and makes him shout in repugnance and nausea. His is an unlimited desolation, and no escape is allowed him, except the anxiety to provide new punishment for himself. To Ginsberg the reading of Blake is customary, I believe. Blake is the poet that he quotes the most, and certain poems—"Wild Orphan," "An Asphodel," "In Back of the Real"—are very similar with respect to the cadence and fragmentation into brief segments of the historic phraseology, the sought-for simplicity, of the *Songs of Innocence and Experience.* The Blake of the prophetic poems will not be very far from him. It is natural that the verse of the Bible should be familiar to both of them. Even Whitman had it always present in his ear.

The Bible of Blake is that to which the hermetism of the eighteenth century turns and goes through its pages. Job and Isaiah become instead apocalyptics in Ginsberg, and, it may seem strange, in the rare passages of surrealistic transfiguration of his most terribly realistic poetry, the only hint of an example to which they can be referred is that of some paragraphs of the Apocalypse of Saint John. In the raw realism of Ginsberg the cruelty of a human fate can only disintegrate in a vision of the apocalypse.

It should not seem strange that the Cabala should be and will be and is a book meditated over for centuries and centuries in the ambient of Ginsberg and around Ginsberg and by Ginsberg himself: but it is Blake who has availed himself of it through that culture of the darkness that in his time stood up to the philosophy of enlightenment. After all, Cabala and apocalypse belong to the same tradition, which the apocalypse restores and the Cabala brings to supreme consequences of doctrine and images.

The poet closest to Blake is Guillaume Apollinaire. Would Ginsberg ever have written that unfathomable vision of the Pietà which is *Kaddish* without Apollinaire? Certainly not, but not without Blake either. The words of Apollinaire were light; he had such a grace for words that even in describing war, everything ended composed in a melodious sign, enchanting, in a rapture. The technique of simultaneousness, introduced in poetry by Apollinaire, consists in joining the events, not by giving them an order of place and time, by registering them successively as they come to mind, in the presence of a given face, or a given idea, or a given recollection of a person. It has been used, in a more elaborate way, by Joyce; it has by now been used by many, and it is used also by Ginsberg. It is the greatest presence of Apollinaire in poems of Ginsberg such as *Kaddish.*

The word of Ginsberg is atrocious like no other, and it becomes always more angry and ardent as he proceeds in laying bare the road, the long road of human suffering, reflected in the body, in the mind, in the feelings of the mother that dies, in the events of a victim of the mother that dies. Listen: [Here Ungaretti recited a fragment of *Kaddish*.]

In a vast hall of the Village, crowded with the curious, Ginsberg and I met in New York to read together, each some of his own poems. I believe I have returned this evening, and I would be proud of it, that tribute of brotherly enthusiasm that he wanted then, through his kindness, to offer to me.

Giuseppe Ungaretti, translated by Italo Romano

*This article by Ungaretti was taken from the stenographic transcript of an improvised discourse on the occasion of presenting a selection of Ginsberg's poems translated into Italian by Fernanda Pivano in Naples, 1966. The poet had intended to rewrite the text for publication in the present issue of *Books Abroad*, but illness and death prevented him.—A. Marianni

On Pasternak Soberly [1970]

For those who were familiar with the poetry of Boris Pasternak long before he acquired international fame, the Nobel Prize given to him in 1958 had something ironic in it. A poet whose equal in Russia was only Akhmatova, and a congenial translator of Shakespeare, had to write a big novel, and that novel had to become a sensation and a best seller before poets of the Slavic countries were honored for the first time in his person by the jury of Stockholm. Had the prize been awarded to Pasternak a few years earlier, no misgivings would have been possible. As it was, the honor had a bitter taste and could hardly be considered as proof of genuine interest in Eastern European literatures on the part of the Western reading public—this quite apart from the good intentions of the Swedish Academy.

After *Doctor Zhivago* Pasternak found himself entangled in the kind of ambiguity that ought to be a nightmare of every author. While he always stressed the unity of his work, that unity was broken by circumstances. Abuse was heaped on him in Russia for a novel nobody had ever read. Praise was lavished on him in the West for a novel isolated from his lifelong labors: his poetry is nearly untranslatable. No man wishes to be changed into a symbol, whether the symbolic features lent him are those of a valiant knight or of a bugaboo: in such cases he is not judged by what he cherishes as

his achievement but becomes a focal point of forces largely external to his will. In the last years of his life Pasternak lost, so to speak, the right to his personality, and his name served to designate a cause. I am far from intending to reduce that cause to political games of the moment. Pasternak stood for the individual against whom the large state apparatus turns in hatred with all its police, armies, and rockets. The emotional response to such a predicament was rooted in deep-seated fears so justified in our time. The ignominious behavior of Pasternak's Russian colleagues, writers who took the side of power against a man armed only with his pen, created a Shakespearean situation; no wonder if in the West sympathies went to Hamlet and not to the courtiers of Elsinore.

The attention the critics centered on *Doctor Zhivago* has delayed, however, an assessment of Pasternak's work as a whole. It is possible that we are now witnessing only the first gropings in that direction. My attempt here is not so much to make a neatly balanced appraisal as to stress a few aspects of his writings.

I became acquainted with his poetry in the thirties when he was highly regarded in Polish literary circles. This was the Pasternak of *The Second Birth* (1934); the rhythm of certain "ballads" printed in that volume has been haunting me ever since. Yet Pasternak did not appear to his Polish readers as an exotic animal; it was precisely what was familiar in his poems that created some obstacles to unqualified approval. In spite of the considerable differences between Polish and Russian poetry, the poets who had been shaped by "modernistic" trends victorious at the beginning of the century showed striking similarities due to their quite cosmopolitan formation. Pasternak, through his very treatment of verse, could be placed within a spiritual family, somewhere between Bolesław Leśmian, who achieved maturity when Pasternak was an adolescent, and Jarosław Iwaszkiewicz or Julian Tuwim, Pasternak's juniors by a few years. Now the fact is that in the thirties the poetics represented by those eminent figures was breaking down. The young poets who claimed the name of "avant-garde" paid lip-service to the recognized brilliance of their elders, but looked at them with suspicion and often attacked them openly. In spite of all the loose talk proper to so-called literary movements, some serious matters were at stake, though veiled by disputes over metaphor and syntax. Those quarrels proved to be fruitful and later gave a new perspective on the writers then in combat. Pasternak, however, to the extent that he was used as an argument by the traditionalists, partisans of the "sonorous" verse inherited from symbolism, had to share the fate of his allies, venerated and mistrusted at the same time by the young.

I say all this in order to show that my approach to Pasternak is colored by developments within Polish poetry of the last decades. Also, my approach is different for other reasons, both from that of an American knowing Russian and from that of a Russian. My Slavic ear is sensitive to pulsations of Russian verse, yet I remain on my guard and submit myself with reluctance to the rhythmical spell inherent in the language, which reluctance can be explained by the basically atonal character of Western Slavic tongues like Polish or Czech. Perhaps I lose a good deal that way, but it makes me more resistant to the gestures of a mesmerizer. Of Pasternak's eminence, I have never had any doubts. In an article written in 1954 (before *Doctor Zhivago*) I predicted that a statue of Pasternak would stand one day in Moscow.

▪ THE IMAGE OF THE POET

Half a century separates us from the Russian Revolution. When we consider that the Revolution was expected to bring about the end of the alienation of the writer and of the artist, and consequently to inaugurate new poetry of a kind never known before, the place Pasternak occupies today in Russian poetry is astounding. After all, his formative years preceded World War I, and his craft retained some habits of that era. Like many of his contemporaries in various countries, he drew upon the heritage of French *poètes maudits*. In every avant-garde movement native traditions expressed through the exploration of linguistic possibilities are perhaps more important than any foreign influences. I am not concerned, however, with literary genealogy but with an image which determines the poet's tactics—an image of himself and of his role. A peculiar image was created by French poets of the nineteenth century, not without help from the minor German romantics and Edgar Allan Poe; this image soon became common property of the international avant-garde. The poet saw himself as a man estranged from a society serving false values, an inhabitant of *la cité infernale,* or, if you prefer, of the wasteland and passionately opposed to it. He was the only man in quest of true values, aware of surrounding falsity, and had to suffer because of his awareness. Whether he chose rebellion or contemplative art for art's sake, his revolutionary technique of writing served a double purpose: to destroy automatism of opinions and beliefs transmitted through a frozen, inherited style; to mark his distance from the idiom of those who lived false lives. Speculative thought, monopolized by optimistic Philistines, was proclaimed taboo: the poet moved in another realm, nearer to the heart of things. Thoeries of two languages were elaborated: *le language lyrique* was presented as autonomous, not translatable into any logical terms which are proper to *le langage scientifique*. Yet the poet had to pay the price. There are limits beyond which the poet cannot go and maintain communication with his readers. Few are connoisseurs. Sophistication, or as Tolstoy called it, *utonchenie,* is self-perpetuating, like drug addiction.

This dilemma of the poet is still with us; that is why we tend to project it into the past. Yet great poets of other epochs did not know it at all. We saw how in our century poets of the communist obedience, disgusted by the increasingly narrow scope of modern poetry, turned to the camp of speculative thought, endowed, as it were, with a new prestige since it dealt in historical optimism (but no longer of the bourgeois variety); and speculative thought, whether incarnated in the police or simply installed in poets' minds, destroyed their art, often also their persons. As for the West, sophistication or *utonchenie* has been destroying poets so successfully that a poem on the page of a magazine is avoided by every self-respecting reader.

The image of the poet that we find in the early poems of Pasternak corresponds to the pattern dear to literary schools at the turn of the century: the poet is a mysterious, elusive creature living in accordance with his own laws which are not the laws of ordinary mortals. To quote Pasternak: "When a poet is in love, a displaced god falls in love and chaos crawls out into the world again as in the time of fossils." A man born with an ultraperceptive sensory apparatus gradually discovers that personal destiny which estranges him from the world and transforms a familiar reality into phantasmagoria: "Thus the seas, sudden as a sigh, open up flowing over the fences, to where houses should have stood; thus the iambs start." The weird, incongruous core of things unveils itself to the poet. He is overpowered by elemental forces speaking through him, his words are magical incantation, he is a shaman, a witch doctor.

Here I can refer to my experience. What my generation reproached Polish contemporaries of Pasternak for was less a certain literary technique than a certain philosophy underlying the rocking singsong of their verse. For instance, Julian Tuwim, who shows hallucinating similarities to Pasternak, was shaped by a programmatic scorn for all the programs, by a cult of "life," of an élan vital, by the cultural atmosphere permeated with the direct or indirect influence of Henri Bergson. He evolved from the enthusiastic vitality of his youth toward the horrified screams of a Cassandra tortured by Apollo, but had always been a shaman in trance. Intellectual helplessness, a "sacred naïveté" jealously defended, were typical of him no less than of nearly all his Polish colleagues who started to write about 1912 or 1913. They seemed to elude the dilemma which for my generation was insoluble but oppressive: for us a lyrical stream, a poetic idiom liberated from the chores of the discourse was not enough: the poet should be also a *thinking* creature; yet in our efforts to build up a poem as an "act of the mind" we encountered an obstacle: speculative thought is vile, cunning, it eats up the internal resources of a poet from inside. In any case, if modern poetry has been moving away from traditional meter and rhyme, it was not because of fads and fashions, but in the hope of elaborating a new style which would restore an equilibrium between emotional and intellectual elements.

Pasternak achieved perfection within the framework of traditional meter; one can also say that the wisdom of his maturity grew slowly and organically out of the image of the poet he shared in his youth with many poets. His poetry is written in rhymed stanzas, mostly quatrains. His experimentation consisted in inventing incredible assonances and in weighting every line to the breaking point with metaphors. Such a superabundance should have inclined him, it seems, to search for a principle of construction other than that of pure musicality. Perhaps Pasternak was afraid that his world of flickering bits of colors, of lights and of shadows would disintegrate if deprived of a unifying singsong. He is often a prestidigitator in a corset, which he wears as if to enhance his skill in the reader's eyes. It so happened that in this attachment to meter he fulfilled, at least outwardly, the official requirements. Strangely enough, in Russia meter and rhyme acceded to political dignity through the rulers' decision to freeze art and literature in their "healthy" stages of the past. Here an analogy between poetry and painting imposes itself: certain popular notions of the distinctive marks proper to the poet and to the painter have been carefully preserved; the poet is a man who writes columns of rhymed lines; the painter is a man who puts people and landscapes on his canvas "as if they were alive." Those who depart from that rule lack the necessary artistic qualities.

Pasternak's poetry is antispeculative, antiintellectual. It is poetry of sensory perception. His worship of life meant a fascination with what can be called nature's moods: air, rain, clouds, snow in the streets, a detail changing, thanks to the time of the day or night, to the season. Yet this is a very *linguistic* nature. In the Slavic languages words denoting planets, plants, and animals preserve their ancient power; they are loaded with a prestige of their femininity or masculinity. Hence the obsessive desire to identify the word with the object. Julian Tuwim, for instance, wrote a long poem consisting of variations on the word *green*. "Greenery," in its double meaning of a quality and of the vegetation, together with its retinue of names, adjectives, and verbs stemming from the same root, was for him a sort of vegetable goddess of the dictionary.

Pasternak gradually modified for his peculiar use his image of the poet as an exceptional being in direct contact with the forces of universal life. He stressed more and more passive receptivity as the poet's greatest virtue. The following pronouncement (from 1922) is characteristic: "Contemporary trends conceived art as a fountain though it is a sponge. They decided it should spring forth, though it should absorb and become saturated. In their estimation it can be decomposed into inventive procedures, though it is made of the organs of reception. Art should always be among the spectators and should look in a purer, more receptive, truer way than any spectator does; yet in our days art got acquainted with powder and the dressing room; it showed itself upon the stage as if there were in the world two arts, and one of them, since the other was always in reserve, could afford the luxury of self-distortion, equal to a suicide. It shows itself off, though it should hide itself up in the gallery, in anonymity."

Did Pasternak when writing these words think of himself in contrast with Vladimir Mayakovsky? Perhaps. Mayakovsky wanted to smash to pieces the image of the poet as a man who withdraws. He wanted to be a Walt Whitman—as the Europeans imagined Walt Whitman. We are not concerned here with his illusions and his tragedy. Let us note only that the instinctive sympathy many of us feel when reading those words of Pasternak can be misleading. We have been trained to identify a poet's purity with his withdrawal up into the gallery seat of a theater, where in addition he wears a mask. Already some hundred years ago poetry had been assigned a kind of reservation for a perishing tribe; having conditioned reflexes, we, of course, admire "pure lyricism."

Not all Pasternak's poems are personal notes from his private diary or, to put it differently, "Les jardins sous la pluie" of Claude Debussy. As befitted a poet in the Soviet Union, in the twenties he took to vast historical panoramas, foretelling *Doctor Zhivago*. He enlivened a textbook cliché (I do not pretend to judge that cliché; it can be quite close to reality and be sublime) with all the treasures of detail registered by the eye of an adolescent witness; Pasternak was fifteen when the revolutionary events occurred that are described in the long poems: "The Year 1905" and "Lieutenant Schmidt." Compared with his short poems, they seem to me failures. The technique of patches and glimpses does not fit the subject. There is no overall commitment; the intellect is recognized as inferior to the five senses and is refused access to the material. As a result, we have the theme and the embroidery; the theme, by contrast, returns to its quality of a cliché.

Thus I tend to accuse Pasternak, as I accused his contemporaries in Poland, of a programmatic helplessness in the face of the world, of a carefully cultivated irrational attitude. Yet it was exactly this attitude that saved Pasternak's art and perhaps his life in the sad Stalinist era. Pasternak's more intellectually inclined colleagues answered argument by argument, and in consequence they were either liquidated or they accepted the supreme wisdom of the official doctrine. Pasternak eluded all categories; the "meaning" of his poems was that of lizards or butterflies—and who could pin down such phenomena using Hegelian terms? He did not pluck fruits from the Tree of Reason. The Tree of Life was enough for him. Confronted by argument, he replied with his sacred dance.

We can agree that in the given conditions that was the only victory possible. Yet if we assume that those epochs when poetry is amputated, forbidden thought, reduced to imagery and musicality, are not the most healthy, then Pasternak's was a Pyrrhic victory. When a poet can preserve his freedom only if he is deemed a harmless fool, a *iurodivyi,* holy because bereft of reason, his society is sick. Pasternak noticed that he had been maneuvered into Hamlet's position. As a weird being, he was protected from the ruler's answer, and he had to play the card of his weirdness; but what could he do with his moral indignation at the sight of the crime perpetrated upon millions of people? What could he do with his love for suffering Russia? That was the question.

His mature poetry underwent a serious evolution. He was right, I feel, when at the end of his life he confessed that he did not like his style prior to 1940: "My hearing was spoiled then by the general freakishness and the breakage of everything customary—procedures ruling then around me. Anything said in a normal way shocked me. I used to forget that words can contain something and mean something in themselves, apart from the trinkets with which they are adorned." "I searched everywhere not for essence but for extraneous pungency." We can read into that judgment more than a farewell to a technique. He never lost his belief in the redeeming power of art understood as a moral discipline, but his late poems can be called Tolstoyan in their nakedness. He strives to give in them explicitly a certain vision of the human condition.

I did not find in Pasternak's work any hint of his philosophical opposition to the official Soviet doctrine, unless his reluctance to deal with abstractions, so that the terms *abstract* and *false* were for him synonymous, is a proof of his resistance. The life of Soviet citizens was, however, his life, and in his patriotic poems he was not paying mere lip service. He was no more rebellious than any average Russian. *Doctor Zhivago* is a Christian book, yet there is no trace in it of that polemic with the anti-Christian concept of man, which makes the strength of Dostoevsky. Pasternak's Christianity is atheological. It is very difficult to analyze a Weltanschauung which pretends not to be a Weltanschauung at all, but simply "closeness to life," while in fact it blends contradictory ideas borrowed from extensive readings. Perhaps we should not analyze. Pasternak was a man spellbound by reality, which was for him miraculous. He accepted suffering because the very essence of life is suffering, death, and rebirth; and he treated art as a gift of the Holy Spirit.

We would not know, however, of his hidden faith without *Doctor Zhivago.* His poetry—even if we put aside the question of censorship—was too fragile an instrument to express, after all, ideas. To do his Hamlet deed, Pasternak had to write a big novel. By that deed he created a new myth of the writer, and we may conjecture that it will endure in Russian literature like other already mythical events: Pushkin's duels, Gogol's struggles with the devil, Tolstoy's escape from Yasnaya Poliana.

■ **A NOVEL OF ADVENTURES, RECOGNITIONS, HORRORS, AND SECRETS**

The success of *Doctor Zhivago* in the West cannot be explained by the scandal accompanying its publication or by political thrills. Western novel-readers have been reduced in our times to quite lean fare, for the novel, beset by its enemy, psychology, has been moving toward the programmatic leanness of the antinovel. *Doctor Zhivago* satisfied a legitimate yearning for a narrative full of extraordinary happenings, narrow escapes, crisscrossing plots, and, contrary to the microscopic analyses of Western novelists, open to huge vistas of space and historical time. The novel-reader is a glutton, and he knows immediately whether a writer is one also. In his desire to embrace the unexpectedness and wonderful fluidity of life, Pasternak showed a gluttony equal to that of his nineteenth-century predecessors.

Critics have not been able to agree how *Doctor Zhivago* should be classified. The most obvious thing was to speak of a revival of great Russian prose and to invoke the name of Tolstoy; but then the improbable encounters and nearly miraculous interventions Pasternak is so fond of had to be dismissed as mistakes and offenses against realism. Other critics, like Edmund Wilson, treated the novel as a web of symbols, going so far sometimes in this direction that Pasternak in his letters had to deny he ever meant all that. Still other critics, like Gleb Struve, tried to mitigate this tendency, yet conceded that *Doctor Zhivago* was related to Russian symbolist prose of the beginning of the century. The suggestion I am going to make has been advanced by no one, as far as I know.

It is appropriate, I feel, to start with a simple fact: Pasternak was a Soviet writer. One may add, to displease his enemies and some of his friends, that he was not an "internal émigré," but shared the joys and sorrows of the writers' community in Moscow. If his community turned against him in a decisive moment, it proves only that every literary confraternity is a nest of vipers and that servile vipers can be particularly nasty. Unavoidably he followed interminable discussions in the literary press and at meetings—discussions lasting over the years and arising from the zigzags of the political line. He must also have read many theoretical books—and theory of literature in the Soviet Union is not an innocent lotus-eaters' pastime but more like acrobatics on a tightrope with a precipice below. Since of all the literary genres fiction has the widest appeal and can best be used as an ideological weapon, many of these studies were dedicated to prose.

According to the official doctrine, in a class society vigorous literature could be produced only by a vigorous, ascending class. The novel, as a new literary genre, swept eighteenth-century England. Thanks to its buoyant realism it was a weapon of the ascending bourgeoisie and served to debunk the receding aristocratic order. Since the proletariat is a victorious class, it should have an appropriate literature: namely, a literature as vigorous as the bourgeoisie had in its upsurge. This is the era of socialist realism, and Soviet writers should learn from "healthy" novelists of the past centuries while avoiding neurotic writings produced in the West by the bourgeoisie in its decline. This reasoning, which I oversimplify for the sake of clarity, but not too much, explains the enormous prestige of the English eighteenth-century novel in the Soviet Union.

Pasternak did not have to share the official opinions as to the economic causes and literary effects in order to feel pleasure in reading English "classics," as they are called in Russia. A professional translator for many years, mostly from English, he probably had them all in his own library in the original. While the idea of his major work was slowly maturing in his mind, he must often have thought of the disquieting trends in modern Western fiction. In the West fiction lived by denying more and more its nature, or even by behaving like the magician whose last trick is to unveil how his tricks were done. Yet in Russia socialist realism was an artistic flop, and nobody heeded, of course, the repeated advice to learn from the "classics": an invitation to joyous movement addressed to people in straitjackets

is nothing more than a crude joke; and what if somebody, in the spirit of spite, tried to learn?

Doctor Zhivago, a book of hide-and-seek with fate, reminds me irresistibly of one English novel: Fielding's *Tom Jones.* True, we may have to make some effort to connect the horses and inns of a countryside England with the railroads and woods of Russia, yet we are forced to do so by the travel through enigmas in both novels. Were the devices applied mechanically by Pasternak, the parallel with Fielding would be of no consequence; but in *Doctor Zhivago* they become signs which convey his affirmation of the universe, of life, to use his preferred word. They hint at his sly denial of the trim, rationalized, ordered reality of the Marxist philosophers and reclaim another richer subterranean reality. Moreover, the devices correspond perfectly to the experience of Pasternak himself and of all the Russians. Anyone who has lived through wars and revolutions knows that in a human anthill on fire the number of extraordinary meetings, unbelievable coincidences, multiplies tremendously in comparison with periods of peace and everyday routine. One survives because one was five minutes late at a given address, where everybody got arrested, or because one did not catch a train which was soon to be blown to pieces. Was that an accident, Fate, or Providence?

If we assume that Pasternak consciously borrowed his devices from the eighteenth-century novel, his supposed sins against realism will not seem so disquieting. He had his own views on realism. Also we shall be less tempted to hunt for symbols in *Doctor Zhivago,* as if for raisins in a cake. Pasternak perceived the very texture of life as symbolic, so its description did not call for those protruding and all too obvious allegories. Situations and characters sufficed; to those who do not feel the eighteenth-century flavor in the novel, I can point to the interventions of the enigmatic Yevgraf, half-Asiatic, the natural brother of Yuri Zhivago, who emerges from the crowd every time the hero is in extreme danger and, after having accomplished what he had to, returns to anonymity. He is a benevolent lord protector of Yuri; instead of an aristocratic title, he has connections at the top of the Communist Party. Here again the situation is realistic: to secure an ally at the top of the hierarchy is the first rule of behavior in such countries as the Soviet Union.

▪ THE POET AS A HERO

Yuri Zhivago is a poet, a successor to the West European bohemian, torn asunder by two contradictory urges: withdrawal into himself, the only receptacle or creator of value; movement toward society, which has to be saved. He is also a successor to the Russian "superfluous man." As for virtues, he cannot be said to possess much initiative and manliness. Nevertheless, the reader is in deep sympathy with Yuri, since he, the author affirms, is a bearer of charisma, a defender of vegetal "inner freedom." A passive witness of bloodshed, of lies and debasement, Yuri must do something to deny the utter insignificance of the individual. Two ways are offered to him: either the way of Eastern Christianity or the way of Hamlet.

Pity and respect for the *iurodivyi,* a halfwit in tatters, a being at the very bottom of the social scale, has ancient roots in Russia. The *iurodivyi,* protected by his madness, spoke truth in the teeth of the powerful and wealthy. He was outside society and denounced it in the name of God's ideal order. Possibly in many cases his madness was only a mask. In some respects he recalls Shakespeare's fools; in fact, Pushkin merges the two figures in his *Boris Godunov,* where the halfwit Nikolka is the only man bold enough to shout the ruler's crimes in the streets.

Yuri Zhivago in the years following the civil war makes a plunge to the bottom of the social pyramid. He forgets his medical diploma and leads a shady existence as the husband of the daughter of his former janitor, doing menial jobs, provided with what in the political slang of Eastern Europe are called "madman's papers." His refusal to become a member of the "new intelligentsia" implies that withdrawal from the world is the only way to preserve integrity in a city that is ruled by falsehood. Nevertheless, in Yuri Zhivago there is another trait. He writes poems on Hamlet and sees himself as Hamlet. Yes, but Hamlet is basically a man with a goal, and action is inseparable from understanding the game. Yuri has an intuitive grasp of good and evil but is no more able to understand what is going on in Russia than a bee can analyze chemically the glass of a windowpane against which it is beating. Thus the only act left to Yuri is a poetic act, equated with the defense of the language menaced by the totalitarian doubletalk or, in other words, with the defense of authenticity. The circle closes; a poet who rushed out of his tower is back in his tower.

Yuri's difficulty is that of Pasternak and of his Soviet contemporaries. Pasternak solved it a little better than his hero—by writing not poems but a novel, his Hamletic act. The difficulty persists, though, throughout the book. It is engendered by the acceptance of a view of history so widespread in the Soviet Union that it is a part of the air one breathes. According to this view, history proceeds along preordained tracks, it moves forward by "jumps," and the Russian Revolution (together with what followed) was such a jump of cosmic dimension. To be for or against an explosion of historical

forces is as ridiculous as to be for or against a tempest or the rotation of the seasons. The human will does not count in such a cataclysm, since even the leaders are but tools of mighty "processes." As many pages of his work testify, Pasternak did not question that view. Did he not say in one of his poems that everything by which this century will live is in Moscow? He seemed to be interpreting Marxism in a religious way; and is not Marxism a secularized biblical faith in the final accomplishment, implying a providential plan? No wonder that Pasternak, as he says in his letter to Jacqueline de Proyart, liked the writings of Teilhard de Chardin so much. The French Jesuit also believed in the Christological chracter of lay history and curiously combined Christianity with the Bergsonian "creative evolution" as well as with the Hegelian ascending movement.

Let us note that Pasternak was probably the first to read Teilhard de Chardin in Russia. One may be justly puzzled by the influence of that poet-anthropologist, growing in the last decade both in the West and in the countries of the Soviet bloc. Perhaps man in our century is longing for solace at any price—even at the price of sheer romanticism in theology. Teilhard de Chardin has predecessors in Russia—to mention only Alexander Blok's "music of history" or some pages of Berdiaev. The latent "Teilhardism" of *Doctor Zhivago* makes it a Soviet novel—in the sense that one might read into it an esoteric interpretation offered by official pronouncements. The historical tragedy is endowed with all the trappings of necessity working toward the ultimate good. Perhaps the novel is a tale about the individual versus Caesar, but with a difference: the new Caesar's might has its source not only in his legions.

What could poor Yuri Zhivago do in the face of a system blessed by history and yet repugnant to his notions of good and evil? Intellectually, he was paralyzed. He could only rely on his subliminal self, descend deeper than thought monopolized by the state. Being a poet, he clutches at his belief in communion with ever-reborn life. Life will take care of itself. Persephone always comes back from the underground, winter's ice is dissolved, dark eras are necessary as stages of preparation, life and history have a hidden Christian meaning—and suffering purifies.

Pasternak overcame his isolation by listening to the silent complaint of the Russian people; we respond strongly to the atmosphere of hope pervading *Doctor Zhivago.* Not without some doubts, however. Life rarely takes care of itself, unless human beings decide to take care of themselves. Sufferings can either purify or corrupt, and too great suffering too often corrupts. Of course, hope itself, if it is shared by all the nation, may be a powerful factor for change. Yet, when at the end of the novel friends of the long-dead Yuri Zhivago console themselves with timid expectations, they are counting upon an indefinite something (death of the tyrant?), and their political thinking is not far from the grim Soviet joke about the best constitution in the world being one that grants to every citizen the right to a postmortem rehabilitation.

However, Pasternak's weaknesses are dialectically bound up with his great discovery. He conceded so much to his adversary, speculative thought, that what remained was to make a jump into a completely different dimension. *Doctor Zhivago* is not a novel of social criticism; it does not advocate a return to Lenin or to the young Marx. It is profoundly arevisionist. Its message summarizes the experience of Pasternak the poet: whoever engages in a polemic with the thought embodied in the state will destroy himself, for he will become a hollow man. It is impossible to talk to the new Caesar, for then you choose the encounter on his ground. What is needed is a new beginning, new in the present conditions but not new in Russia, marked as it is by centuries of Christianity. Literature of socialist realism should be shelved and forgotten. The new dimension is that of every man's mysterious destiny, of compassion and faith. In this, Pasternak revived the best traditions of Russian literature, and he will have successors. He already has one in Solzhenitsyn.

The paradox of Pasternak lies in his narcissistic art leading him behind the confines of his ego. Also in his reedlike pliability, so that he often absorbed *les idées reçues* without examining them throughly as ideas but without being crushed by them either. Probably no reader of Russian poets resists a temptation to juxtapose the two fates: Pasternak's and Mandelstam's. The survival of the first and the death in a concentration camp of the second may be ascribed to various factors, to good luck and bad luck. Still, there is something in Mandelstam's poetry, intellectually structured, that doomed him in advance. From what I have said about my generation's quarrel with worshipers of Life, it should be obvious that Mandelstam, not Pasternak, is for me the ideal of a modern classical poet; but he had too few weaknesses, was crystalline, resistant, and therefore fragile. Pasternak, more exuberant, less exacting, uneven, was called to write a novel which, in spite and because of its contradictions, is a great book.

Czesław Miłosz

Remembering Valéry [1971]

The author of these lines met Valéry around 1920. The first encounter escapes recollection. It was undoubtedly most superficial and became absorbed by subsequent conversations. The setting never changed. The visitor used to call at the poet's home, 40 rue de Villejust. (Today named Paul Valéry, a side street off Avenue Victor Hugo, it is a bus stop. The conductor calls out in his customary voice: "Paul Valéry!" All this would have amused the essentially ironic spirit of that man.) One called at his door between ten and eleven in the morning, without previous appointment. Valéry had already finished his work, which had begun—a well-known fact—at dawn by lamplight, and it was not his custom to make one wait. Sometimes he would be in a small adjoining room, and one could see him slowly putting on his jacket as if he were going to some formal meeting. Although he believed in practically nothing, only in intellect and form, the official world—consisting (in his words) of "idols"—did exist, and he accommodated himself to it without aversion. After so many years of silence on the part of the public, in sharp contrast to his daily morning-writing, "vacarme" (so he called it) was beginning[1]: the bustle of celebrity. The visitor waiting in the living room was, in spite of his modesty and reticence, part of the noisy periphery. Then Valéry would enter: simple, affable, smiling, with a composure that had a calming effect on the caller. He bore no sign, in dress or hairstyle, of the proverbial Poet. Nor did his gestures ever suggest a possible major poet: strictly Low Church. Valéry's skepticism and good taste forbade all theatricality. A voice would surge, a brisk average voice that did not enunciate with precision—so different in this respect from Gide, his best friend, an artist of the well-articulated word. (Pronunciation of a good actor: "Familles, je vous hais!" with an aspirated *h*.)

The conversation would evolve most amiably. Valéry would listen, ask questions. Since he had, however, to act the part of a writer already threatened by great fame, he would answer inquisitive questions. About a poem, a verse, Mallarmé . . . . Seldom would he fail to mention the master. To him there was none greater. Valéry used to talk about what he had already written, about what he would write: a literary zone carefully inserted between his intimate life and his admirer. There was hardly any mention of the present in these conversations. The past under Mallarmé's authority was predominant. It may well be that the following anecdote, because of its humble nature, has not yet been recorded anywhere. Taking a walk in the countryside of Valvins with his teacher, the young disciple inquired: "What is this?" "Mais c'est du blé!" "Mallarmé," jokingly concluded Valéry, "taught me to recognize wheat."[2] This joking tone recurred frequently: "Il est resté chocolat!" It would be impossible to find a more colloquial equivalent of "thunderstruck, dumbfounded, bowled over." He who masters the most delicate subtleties of language shows equal interest in jargon, dialects, in the lowliest expressions.

But the caller would turn to literature again. Valéry used to refer to his own work soberly, often with a certain humor that was the exact opposite of pomposity. "*La Jeune Parque?* C'est une jeune fille," and he would lower his voice, "qui a ses règles." "Narcisse" would remain unfinished; there was no possible ending. *Le cimetière marin* was, according to the author, a poem with very personal roots. As a matter of fact, nothing could be more remote from that entelechy called "pure poetry."[3] There, in that "Cemetery," are found the native city—Cette, now Sète—and the man, with his impiety, his Greek philosophy, his biographical allusions, and the Mediterranean of his childhood. "Il faut tenter de vivre!" exclaims the poet. This will to live, renewed by the fresh breeze from the sea, is better understood if one recalls his roots, and if his juvenile suicide attempt in London one day in 1894 is not forgotten. On one intimate occasion he confessed that it was physical fright that prevented him from taking his own life.[4] Naturally, a man and his work represent different stages. "Il faut tenter de vivre!" in its value per se does not need biographical elucidation. By the way: what does a poem mean? Valéry *did not believe* in subject matter: it was of no importance and subject to equally legitimate individual interpretations. Gustave Cohen gave a solemn lecture on *Le cimetière marin* on 24 February 1928. The poet was present at the commentary. His critic tried to find out what he had thought of that exegesis. Valéry answered, but with a line of the poem that has been prey to endless disputes among the readers: "Je hume ici ma future fumée" (stanza 5). "An alliteration in *u*," commented Cohen, "intended to imitate the act of breathing."[5] Theory and application did not turn out to be compatible.

Valéry's poetry abounds in ideas and arguments, be they but indirectly suggested. He never abdicated his first convictions. *L'après-midi d'un faune* remained in the eyes of the disciple a most exquisite landmark in literary history—a history that interested him only as far as poetry was concerned. Dramatic dialogue or narrative techniques of the novel almost never touched him. Thus, in his homage to Proust he confessed that the art of the novelist was almost inconceivable to him.[6] An example of his lack of comprehension is a sentence that André Breton recorded from his lips: "Paul Valéry . . . would never condescend to write: "The marquise left

the house at five.' "He was forgetting that the word is dependent on its context. This sentence—as it is, without anything to lean on—does not necessarily imply a refutation of the novel: Cervantes, Balzac. (Nor of the ultimate limits of the poetic: Hölderlin, Baudelaire.)[7] He never ceased to admire Baudelaire. Even in Madrid—in the Residencia de Estudiantes, in May of 1924—Valéry gave a lecture on the author of *Les fleurs du mal,* and he recited with great sobriety of expression the famous sonnet "Sois sage, ô ma douleur." One great poet's reading of a page by another great poet is always an event. The final line, "Entends, ma chère, entends la douce nuit qui marche,"[8] was very effective. (Our traveler made an excursion to the gardens of Aranjuez and asked his young friends: what do you prefer, trees or flowers? The reply was obvious: trees!)[9]

Valéry's conversation flowed in perfect harmony with his thoughts as expressed in writing, a way of thinking that had been shaped in his youth, between 1892 and 1893.[10] There were no fluctuations in his general skepticism, in his love for intelligence as potential and form as result. A great formalist he was! Quite close to the very recent formulators of the doctrines of "structure."[11] When he spoke, he was always alluding to his unwavering principles[12] without revealing anything new to the anxious listener attracted—definitely so—by the anecdote, by the little everyday happening. In that living room tinged with yellow a large book rested—or resided—on the grand piano: the first volume of *Racine* edited by Bodoni, a really fine specimen. The owner would leaf through it, praising this masterpiece of typography. (Bodoni in his Parma had been the supreme printer between the very first, Gutenberg, and today's Mardersteig.)[13] Valéry had the good fortune of seeing his works published in admirable, deluxe editions. Bibliophilism is a passion. An author for select minorities in the beginning, he was, logically, helping himself in this way. An encounter with Valéry one early summer afternoon near *La Nouvelle Revue Française,* rue de Grenelle, where the poet was going out for a walk, comes to mind: the young Castilian lamented not being able to acquire such costly books. Valéry blushed and almost stammered apologies. More accessible volumes were to be published very soon.

One of those mornings at rue de Villejust he complained of the speculations about his writings, even those of a private nature. For instance, "a symbolist colleague" wrote to him demanding a reply. Valéry replied and the friend instantly sold the letter to a bookseller who in his turn gave it back to Valéry. The market was burgeoning; the celebrity had already become glory. Then came the moment for the Academy. Anatole France had died. He took over France's chair, although he was not happy to succeed one who had been so unjust to Mallarmé. He could not forgive the famous prose writer for having voted—as did Coppée—against accepting "Improvisation d'un Faune," the second stage of *L'après-midi,* for the third *Parnasse contemporain* (1875). Anatole France had insisted: "Non, on se moquerait de nous!"[14] The poet showed disdainful irony for all this. The partner of these conversations did not get involved in disputes with the eminent writer. If at times he insinuated some objection, most often it was dismissed with a gesture—never with a word—of displeasure. In his public appearances he was even more abrupt. Spring 1923, Vieux-Colombier theater: Valéry starts his lecture and, after repeating some of his antiromantic concepts, suddenly becomes silent. A spectator, a young man with a bohemian look, has raised an indignant voice: "No, no! 'Les plus désespérés sont les chants les plus beaux, / Et j'en sais d'immortels qui sont de purs sanglots!'" Faced with this vulgar objection sustained by Musset's lines (who does not, or did not, know them by heart?), the poet, nervous, lighted a cigarette, left the stage, and refused to continue the lecture. Was a debate impossible?[15] Like many front-rank figures, he was used to soliloquy, the soliloquy of a solitary pen throughout many laborious years. In this ascetic retreat juvenile pride affirmed itself. The I—perhaps called Narcissus—subsisted as the only secure foundation of an always uncertain reality, but Narcissus, the mythological Narcissus, was not an adequate designation. Valéry was striving for "le moi pur."[16] Did the "pure I" not belong as well to the realm of fable? To feel one's own value as potential rather than act must lead to a relentless pride! "Après tant d'orgueil, après tant d'étrange / oisiveté, mais pleine de pouvoir." Pure power that was not ignored among immediate friends. None more faithful or passionate than the friendship of André Gide. (One should not forget the importance of Pierre Louÿs.) Before the definite public emergence of the poet, at a "soirée" at a friend's house, recalls the unforgettable Pierre de Lanux, Gide pointed at an unknown figure, adding: "Don't you know who that is? One who has more talent than all of us." Valéry never failed to refer to his friend in his conversations. "We are very different, but we understand each other perfectly." When Gide received the Nobel Prize (1947), he paused and wrote: "It is Valéry who deserved it." A touching proof of friendship.

On these visits I met no one else. Only the admirable critic Albert Thibaudet appeared one day as an exception: joyful, debonair, a perfect figure of a "gendarme" with his poised stature and his moustache. (Even shorter was the coincidental encounter with Jean Royère, a minor figure among the symbolists.) None of

Valéry's family ever joined in the conversations. (It was outside that house that I had opportunity to meet his wife, who died in 1970, and his daughter Agathe Rouart-Valéry, closely associated with the literary activities of her father.) But let us return to rue de Villejust. The visitor used to take up the oft-repeated subjects. The poet would sometimes remember a line of his own. Thus, as an example of form achieved through toil, that alexandrine of *La Jeune Parque* (224) composed with all the modulations on the French *e:* "Le gel cède à regret ses derniers diamants." (It is one of the "secret movements" of imminent spring.) He was not satisfied with the closing lines of this poem. (More than once he said this.) Finally, he did change it almost entirely.[17] *Eupalinos,* he would say complacently, was a commissioned work: with a definite number of letters. He was also attracted by a "Dialogue sur les choses divines." Although written, possibly unfinished, it has never been published.[18]

What was totally lacking in Valéry was literary small talk and slander. He did not pursue details of contemporary literary trends. Novelties did not attract his attention. "Le moderne se contente de peu," he had noted already in his *Cahier B, 1910.*[19] One morning he spoke of Claudel: "Claudel s'est installé dans le génie." In spite of everything, the sentence sounded respectful. The so-called "vacarme" was growing. It is probable that he was more sensitive to the reputation that was affirming itself abroad: "the first manifestation of posterity." He was not indifferent to translations. He knew, of course, that a poetic version is a chimerical ideal. His young visitor did succumb to such temptation: he translated into Spanish "Les grenades," "Le cimetière marin," and, years later, "Le sylphe" and "Dormeuse." Les grenades" was rendered in an approximate version in prose and another in verse. The incisive "Sylphe"—"Aux meilleurs esprits / Que d'erreurs promises!"—was followed by four variations on "La dormeuse," which prompted the delightful Herbert Steiner to comment: "Vous n'avez pas fait plus de variations de peur qu'elle ne se réveille!" "El cementerio marino" resulted in a letter in which Valéry showed his gentility as well as the delight produced in him by the Spanish language perceived *through* Italian, his mother's tongue.

Paris 22 juillet 29

Muy querido amigo,

quel plaisir vous me faites!

Ebria de carne azul, . . . Je m'adore en espagnol! El viento vuelve, intentemos vivir!

C'est magnifique! Il me semble que musique et transposition sont l'une et l'autre parfaites!

Allez vous faire de ce chef d'œuvre une édition séparée? Ou bien—puis-je espérer d'autres hauts faits de cette espèce, *La Jeune Parque,*—ou *Charmes?*

Sachez que vous m'avez enchanté. Ce poème tant commenté, ressassé et que son père oubliait, il a pu et dû le relire en même temps que le vôtre pour mieux saisir l'espagnol.

Je vous prie de croire à toute ma reconnaissance et à mes sentiments très affectueux et très dévoués.

Ne m'oubliez pas auprès de Madame Jorge Guillén.

Tout Vôtre,

Paul Valéry

To the Castilian translator, Valéry's work represented a stimulating, exacting experience, aspiring toward elevation in subject matter and rigorous form. The essential diversity was, of course, almost always evident. "Subject matter" did not matter, or existed only as a subordinate: theory that was in contradiction with unavoidable practice.[20] Few poems are more loaded with content than that meditation on life, death, and immortality between the Mediterranean and the cemetery of the native city. Fortunately, we contradict ourselves. A totally consistent person would be the cause of his own serious impoverishment. The character created in his youth, Monsieur Teste, an enchanting monster, represented a superhuman and inhuman goal. His inventor was different. He would ask himself: "Why is Monsieur Teste impossible?" "Because he is only the demon of possibility." Our ghostlike characters reveal us in all seriousness. This paragon—far removed—of man reduced to a cruel mind, intent on sacrificing all the spiritual and corporal remainder, had to bear some details analogous to those of his father, or "step-father": "La parole était extraordinairement rapide, et sa voix sourde." Just the same in Valéry, although probably not as impetuous or as subdued. There is no reader, of course, who would imagine that Don Quixote is Cervantes, Werther Goethe, or Valéry Monsieur Teste.[21] Valéry's cordiality was authentic, evident, spontaneous, capable of faithful affection rather than only polite relationships. Passing through Genoa in 1924, a city that had been the delight of his childhood and adolescence, he confessed being "content et ému de retrouver ma vieille Gênes. Tout me parle ici. Je préfère ceci à toutes les Romes."[22] A sentimental—and very legitimate—preference. Valéry, like Monsieur Teste, was reserved. Serenity and curiosity shone in his blue eyes. A natural, innate distinction associated itself with simplicity. How well he rolled his cigarettes! A great sense of humor maintained the equilibrium between the assumed role of poet and his most intimate inclinations.1

The world did not leave him in peace. As a consequence, the visitor decided to space out his visits. "Les fâcheux, n'est-ce pas? Oui." The wars came, then death—1945—with full national honors (who could have predicted this!), as in the case of Victor Hugo. The glory irradiated from Paris had a local focus: the cemetery of Sète. Many tourists desired to see the tomb of the poet. The caretaker would call a dog, the daily guide, with a robust voice, "Dick! Valéry!" and the fervent admirer would follow the animal. What delight the poet would have taken in this custom! Let us stop here, with this smile—or laughter—from Valéry.

Jorge Guillén

[1] "Vacarme": *Œuvres complètes de Valery Larbaud,* vol. 7, *Ce vice impuni, la lecture, Domaine français,* Paris, Gallimard, 1953, "Paul Valéry," p. 332: "Notes autobiographiques, qu'il a bien voulu rédiger pour moi, et qui s'arrêtent à la date de la publication de *La Jeune Parque,* avec cette conclusion: 'Et le reste est vacarme!'" That study was published in *Fauteuil XXXVIII: Paul Valéry,* Paris, Alcan, 1931, p. 12.

[2] "Du blé": one should probably place this anecdote on a day like the one evoked by Valéry in his conversation with Paul Claudel. It was 14 July 1898 in Valvins: "Puis nous avons été cueillir des bleuets, des coquelicots, dans un jour de soleil éblouissant." Henri Mondor, *Propos familiers de Paul Valéry,* Paris, Grasset, 1957, p. 212 (24 November 1943).

[3] "Poésie pure": see E. Noulet, *Paul Valéry (Etudes),* Edition définitive, Brussels, La Renaissance du Livre, 1951, p. 46: "L'extravagante erreur de ranger sa poésie dans la poésie pure."

[4] On the attempt at suicide, see Pierre-Olivier Walzer, *La poésie de Valéry,* Geneva, Slatkine Reprints, 1966, pp. 385–86.

[5] Exegesis: Gustave Cohen, *Essai d'explication du Cimetière marin,* Gallimard, 1933. Valéry wrote as a preface to this study "Au sujet du Cimetière marin," *Œuvres,* Pléiade, I, pp. 1496–1507. The poet concludes: "C'est pourquoi le travail de M. Cohen . . . m'est singulièrement précieux." On the next page, he affirms again: "Il n'y a pas de vrai sens d'un texte" (underlined by the author). Affirmation—inadmissible—repeatedly stressed on various occasions: "Mes vers ont le sens qu'on leur prête. Celui que je leur donne ne s'ajuste qu'à moi, et n'est opposable à personne. C'est une erreur contraire à la nature de la poésie, et qui lui serait même mortelle, que de prétendre qu'à tout poème correspond un sens véritable, unique, et conforme ou identique à quelque pensée de l'auteur." *Charmes . . . commentés par* Alain, Gallimard, 1929, *préface de* Valéry, p. xix. To this T.S. Eliot wisely responds in *On Poetry and Poets,* New York, 1957, p. 113: "The meaning is what the poem means to different sensitive readers." Competent readers.

[6] Novel: "Hommage à Marcel Proust", *Œuvres,* 1, p. 769: "Quoique je connaisse à peine un seul tome de la grande œuvre de Marcel Proust, et que l'art même du romancier me soit un art presque inconcevable."

[7] The marquise: André Breton, *Manifeste du Surréalisme,* Nouvelle édition, Paris, Kra, 1929, p. 16: "Paul Valéry qui, naguère, à propos des romans, m'assurait qu'en ce qui le concerne, il se refuserait toujours à écrire: 'La marquise sortit à cinq heures.' Mais a-t-il tenu la parole?" Breton, in his first period, lived in

an atmosphere of symbolism and maintained a relationship with Valéry, whose *Monsieur Teste* he knew almost by heart. He dedicated to Valéry a completely symbolist sonnet in 1913, "Rieuse et si peut-être imprudemment laurée." In 1952 Breton declared: "il n'en reste pas moins que Valéry m'a beaucoup appris. Avec une patience inlassable, des années durant, il a répondu à toutes mes questions." It is in this context that the already famous sentence against the marquise who could not leave her house belongs: at a certain literary level she does not, she should not, exist; yet, in spite of everything, she exists and goes out. (André Breton, *Entretiens* avec André Parinaud, Gallimard, 1952, p. 17.)

8 The trip to Spain: in the "Introductions biographique," written by his daughter Agathe Rouart-Valéry for the edition of La Pléiade, 1, p. 48, one reads: "17 avril. Conférence à Madrid, à Barcelone. . . . Il est reçu par le poète [*sic*] Ortega y Gasset." Valéry went to Madrid in May, and as a reply to roses sent him by Juan Ramón Jiménez he composed verses dated as follows: "Madrid, Wednesday 21 May 1924" (originally in French). The poem forms part of *Mélanges*, "Petites choses," *Œuvres*, 1, p. 302. The lecture on Baudelaire was first "performed" in Monaco on 14 February that year and appears in *Variété II*. "Receuillement" is mentioned there without quoting the sonnet.

9 Aranjuez: these young friends were José Bergamín, Antonio Marichalar, and J.G.

10 Thought formation: Jean Hytier, *Questions de littérature: Etudes Valéryennes et autres*, New York, Columbia University Press, 1967, p. 59: "Mes idées se sont faites entre 1892 et 1893. J'entends ma manière ou méthode de juger."

11

Form: for example, among the numerous possible quotations: "La substance du poème doit s'opposer à la transformation immédiate de la parole en signification. Il y faut des similitudes de sonorité, de rythme, de forme etc . . . qui devront se correspondre et ramener l'attention à la forme." From "Réflexions sur l'art," in *Bulletin de la Société Française de Philosophie*, March-April 1935. (In Walzer, p. 230.)

Structure: For example, "*La Littérature est, et ne peut être autre chose qu'une sorte d'extension et d'application de certaines propriétés de Langage*" (underlined by the author). From *L'enseignement de la poétique au Collège de France*, 1937, in *Œuvres*, 1, p. 1440. Another example: "Ce qui est la 'forme' pour qui-conque, est le 'fond' pour moi." "Calepin d'un poète," 1928, in *Œuvres*, 1, p. 1416. Form as content, even more: as substance or the only reality of importance in the poem— another definition of the impossible pure poetry.

12 Convictions: J. P. Monod, a great friend (as well as "secretary" and "Maecenas") of Valéry, reports, referring to his last days: "Je veux seulement citer une des dernières paroles qu'il m'a adressées, en y insistant avec force, comme s'il s'agissait d'un message qu'il m'aurait chargé de répéter: 'Les principaux thèmes autour desquels j'ai ordonné ma pensée depuis cinquante ans demeurent pour moi i-né-bran-la-bles,' me dit-il." Valéry was a skeptic in general but had his own dogmas. (*Regard sur P.V.*, Lausanne, Editions des Terraux, 1947, pp. 47–48.)

13 Bodoni: "1813. *Théâtre complet de Jean Racine*, in-folio, vol. 1, 432 pages: vol. 2, 448 pages; vol. 3, 516 pages. Bodoni morì prima che fosse terminata la tiratura dell'ultimo volume. Stupenda edizione correttissima nel testo e degna di gareggiare con le più autorevoli d'oltre Alpe." In *Catalogo delle autentiche edizioni bodoniane*, Giampiero Giani, ed., Milan, Conchiglia, 1948, pp. 78–79. This *Racine* was, as a consequence, the last work

printed in the "Particolare Officina Tipografica" of Giovanni Battista Bodoni.

14 *Parnasse Contemporain*: Henri Mondor, *Histoire d'un Faune*, Gallimard, 1948, pp. 186–95.

15 Interrupted lecture: *Œuvres*, 1, "Introduction biographique," p. 46; "1923. 23, et 25 Mai: Conférence de Paul Valéry au Vieux Colombier."

16 "Le moi pur": *Œuvres de Paul Valéry*, *Les Divers Essais sur Léonard de Vinci*, Paris, N.R.F., 1938, *Note et Digression*, 1919, pp. 48–49: "Mais chaque vie si particulière possède toutefois, à la profondeur d'un trésor, la permanence fondamentale d'une conscience que rien ne supporte . . . le *moi* pur, élément unique et monotone de l'être même dans le monde, retrouvé, reperdu par lui-même, habite éternellement notre sens; cette profonde *note* de l'existence domine, dès qu'on l'écoute, toute la complication des conditions et des variétés de l'existence."

17 *La Jeune Parque*: see the great edition of the poem— manuscripts, texts, and study—by Octave Nadal, Le Club du Meilleur Livre, Gallimard, 1957.

18 *Dialogues*: J. P. Monod, p. 42: "Telle page du 'Manuscrit trouvé dans une Cervelle' ou du 'Dialogue des Choses divines' . . . qui n'ont pas vu le jour et ne le verront peut-être jamais."

19 *Cahier B-1910*: Gallimard, 1930, p. 64.

20 Subject matter: in one of the best commentaries of *Le cimetière marin* Oreste Macrí says: "Ricordo la poesia teologica de l'Ebauche d'un Serpent." (*Il cimitero marino*, Florence, Sansoni, 1947, p. 81.)

21 Teste: "Préface" à *La soirée avec Monsieur Teste*, *Œuvres*, 2, p. 14: "Pourquoi M. Teste est-il impossible? C'est son âme que cette question. *Elle vous change en M. Teste*. Car il n'est point autre que le démon même de la possibilité." In *La soirée*, p. 17: "Sa parole était extraordinairement rapide et sa voix sourde."

22 Genoa: *Œuvres*, 1, A-R-V, "Introduction biographique," p. 41.

Ice, Stars, Stones, Birds, Trees: Three Major Postwar Estonian Poets Abroad [1973]

The remarkable postwar efflorescence of Estonian literature in exile was initiated by writers who had achieved recognition before the war or at least had begun publishing in their native country (independent from 1918 to 1940). Eventually a new generation of writers emerged whose entire output was produced in exile. Among these writers, three poets who were born in the twenties command special attention for the scope as well as the significance of their oeuvre. Kalju Lepik, born in 1920 in Koeru, a rural community, studied for a year at Tartu University before being mobilized in 1943 by the Germans, who occupied Estonia at that time. In 1944 he fled to Sweden, finding employment first as a factory worker and later as a bookkeeper. At present he lives in Stockholm. Ivar Grünthal, son of a justice of the Estonian supreme court, was born in 1924 in Tartu. In 1943 he escaped to Finland and fought in the Estonian Volunteer regiment of the Finnish army. In 1944 he too fled to Sweden, where he studied medicine. He is now a practicing physician in Gothenburg. In 1957 he founded and for several years was the editor of the literary journal *Mana*. The youngest representative of this generation, Ivar Ivask, was born in 1927 in Riga as the only son of an Estonian businessman living in the Latvian capital. Next to Estonian and Latvian, German was one of the languages of his childhood. In 1944 his family fled to Germany, where he graduated from the Estonian Gymnasium in Wiesbaden and studied at the University of Marburg. In 1949 he immigrated to the United States, where he obtained his Ph.D. in German literature and art history at the University of Minnesota. For a number of years he was professor of German at St. Olaf College in Northfield, Minnesota, and in 1967 he joined the Department of Modern Languages at the University of Oklahoma, assuming the editorship of the international literary quarterly *Books Abroad*.

All three of these poets share the crucial experiences of the war, the destruction of their country, and exile at the very beginning of their adult lives. All of them have had bitter but unusually rich international experiences and have been remarkably productive—Lepik has published eight collections of verse, Grünthal seven (one of which is a novel in verse) Ivask five (one of which is in German). Their books have won an ever wider audience among the 75,000 Estonians who found refuge after World War II, chiefly in Sweden, the USA, Canada, and Australia; Lepik has found recognition and readers even in Soviet Estonia, where, by official decree, exile literature is virtually inaccessible. However, the chief interest of their work lies in the vigorous poetic personalities which by now seem to have fully developed. These three poets reflect the tragic fact of exile and integration into a new world, yet they always express it in the particular context of very individual diction and thematics.

▪ ▪ ▪

Kalju Lepik's first book of verse, "A Face in a Window of the Home" (1946), offers a collection of vivid, sharply focused, often playful recollections of his rural boyhood. Conscious of his modest origins and of the prevailing sophistication of recent Estonian poetry (e.g., the group of poets represented in the anthology "Magicians of the Word," 1938, and the publication of a surrealist volume of verse by Ilmar Laaban, "The End of the Anchor Chain Is the Beginning of Song," in 1946),

Lepik seeks to assert himself through simplicity of diction, laconic statements, and casual descriptions of remembered everyday events. Touches of robust humor and of restrained tenderness enliven the deliberately sober manner of his verse: "I have hairy legs / and a hairy chest. / the whole village thinks I'm / an ape . . . But my heart is free, / free as a bird. / Still nobody thinks I'm / a bird."[1] The absence of a confessional note, of any complaint or accusation, causes the few indirect hints at a tragic past, from which images of a poor but acceptable and warm life emerge, to have a deeply moving resonance. Thus the title poem, "A Face in a Window of the Home," which begins with the expression of a wish to listen through the broken windowpane to the cuckoo clock in order to feel the permanence of a home, describes the son's hesitant approach to the lonely home, and ends with these lines: "In the window of the home grimaces / the bloodstained face of a stranger." In a similar way, a whole poem entitled "My Country, You Are Screaming" seems to rise like a scream from the background of deepening silence: "My screaming shreds the sky, / my screaming blackens the sun. / I scream and you are ashamed / of the suffering and sorrow / of a small and courageous / country and people." This makes us aware that Lepik's silence is to a large extent a stark and choked silence. It is not the attitude of a detached conscience, but that of a militant one, very much aware of our limitations and of the vanity of all words. At the same time he remains faithful to his country, its right to freedom and its language as its way of life. In short, he affirms his faith in truth and justice as the inalienable rights of our conscience.

Such a conjunction of skepticism and militancy, of critical awareness and lyric endeavor is not new to Estonian literature. At the turn of the century the initiator of modernism and leading Estonian poet Gustav Suits drew much of the emotional tension of his work from the same fundamental dichotomy. In many ways Lepik's poetry resembles that of Gustav Suits, while at the same time it seeks to link up with the earlier, discreetly earthbound lyricism of Juhan Liiv. Later, Lepik's development also leads him to assimilate the particularly modernistic perception of a disrupted, fragmentary, and unstable reality. In "The Fiddler" (1948), his second collection of verse, Lepik finds adequate expression for his fractured vision in short unrhymed stanzas, sustained by discreet sound repetitions. However, fragmentation is only part of a more general intuition of the void which from then on colors Lepik's view of the world: "Suddenly the light is splintering / on the broken windowpane. / It flares, like embers, one more time / then turns to ashes." This shattering of light on a windowpane is a prelude to a widening perception of the void, of absence and death as final truths of experience.

The loss of his childhood faith is the leading theme of Lepik's third collection, "Beggars on the Stairs" (1949), although for Lepik's ceaseless search nothing is final. Out of death itself emerges a new depth, a promise or hope. "Sea Bottom" (1951), his fourth book of poems, becomes the very symbol of this hidden promise, "My death is spring / which yearns for / the song of running brooks. // My death is the innocent joy of melting / white snowdrifts. Why does ice still / conceal the blue depths of the sea? / The depth of the sea is death." Thus Lepik's poetry opens out to a transcendental vision, inherited from a Christian childhood and rekindled by the spiritual inspiration inherent in his poetic experience. At the same time Lepik assimilates thoroughly the Estonian folk-song tradition with its allusive, alliterative style and its naïvely animistic vision. He blends this smoothly with modernistic concentration and surprising turns of expression. Death is a life under ground; the dead are birds singing, and song is the voice of death: "Death has a child's eyes, / when I peer into death. / Am I peering into perdition? // . . . You went under the earth. / Where the houses of death are, / where the old white houses are. // There you warble like a bird" ("Death Has a Child's Eyes"). Death is part of an imaginary flow of metamorphoses which may grant us the ultimate freedom of joyful play within sorrow and mourning itself. Thus the void becomes the very condition of innocence, of a gentle light that emanates from it or, then, from its symbol, the tree of light which grows from the folded wings associated with churchbells heard in childhood. All this finds beautiful expression in the sequence of poems entitled "Velkar-Songs" in his book "Stone Quarry" (1958): "I looked into the rustle of your wings. / Two lambs looked back at me. / One was black as the earth under your feet / and the other was white as the light on your hands / . . . The light is an emptiness within the light. / Darkness is an emptiness within the darkness / . . . Your wings folded into a tree / and a rustling alighted like a bird on its branches." In the next poem the same tree is envisioned. "In a high and narrow window: / the red color of rowanberries, / the blue color of heaven's gates / the old tree of light. / . . . I myself sit on the long bench, / watching the window of light. / I have the kind mouth of a child, singing myself away in songs. / I could give myself to you, / old tree of light." Sorrow thus breeds a land of wonder where trees lit by song point the way to a childhood heaven. Similarly, in the poem "With Closed Eyes" God's absence leads to the credo, "I believe, you are not. / I believe, you still are. / You are good." In a much more somber mood we read in his volume "The Marble Emigré" (1968), "Dead birds overhead: / they cannot live. / Yet one lives nonetheless. /

I can tell from its beating wings: / it lives nonetheless. / . . . Above me dead birds. / Those birds fly."

Often the easy and playful modifications of images in Lepik's wonderland poems convey a humoristic touch. The humor may on occasion reach metaphysical dimensions. In "A Fairytale about Tigerland" (1955) the whole fabric of reality is reversed and dissolved through a breathless sequence of metamorphoses: an alligator swallows a flute player, and a dancing cobra becomes a tiger's tale, told by the poet who paints night, his topic, in the shape of tigerlike stripes, then includes himself in the tale as flute player, goat, and tiger, whereupon the latter, appeased by the ageless lullaby of the poet, plays with his tail on the huge harp of his own stripes. The poem ends with a restatement: "My feet are bare / when I touch water. / All else is a fairytale for childish minds, / even the shadow of footsteps / on the flute-player's face." Such a return to common "barefoot" reality is typical of Lepik's ironic stance toward the world and himself. In all his books we find, next to purely lyric verses, pieces of grotesque irony or sarcastic denunciation. Rough, bloody, and lowly reality serves as background to flashes of dreams and transcendental intuition; but above all, Lepik's sturdy sense of reality and an inborn feeling of decency keep his poetry within the limits of a restrained mood of expression. Humor and irony are his best allies against overstatement and pretension. In this his art touches that of his master, Gustav Suits, as well as that of another exile poet, Arno Vihalemm (b. 1911). Both of them have known how to build, with the help of humor, an effective shield against the bitterness of exile and retrospective illusions about the homeland. In fact, they have overcome the trauma and separation and can stand by themselves on the new ground offered them by their land of refuge. The song of these three poets is that of the common man, instrument and victim of the history of a tragically and ruthlessly divided mankind. Therefore, quite naturally, Lepik's emblem is not the nightingale or even the skylark, but the raven: "The raven is a bird. / Even the raven is a songbird."

■ ■ ■

Ivar Grünthal, young rebel since high-school days, underwent the experience of war and exile at the early age of nineteen. He published his first book of verse, "Sleeping with Open Eyes," in 1951, when he had completed his medical studies in Sweden. From this first collection down to his sixth and latest published volume to date, "The Measure is Full" (1964), his poetic output is marked by the impact of his early harrowing experience. Well read, well informed about contemporary literary trends in the main European languages, Grünthal begins his work fully aware of the avant-garde of modern classicism, as exemplified in such modern classics as Paul Valéry, Ezra Pound, T. S. Eliot, and, in Estonian literature after G. Suits, by the group called "Magicians of the Word" (1938) led by Heiti Talvik. Indeed, Grünthal's well-constructed stanzas with impeccable rhymes and clear-cut narrative outlines are in perfect agreement with Talvik's dictum "that it is the poet's duty to force the blind raving of the elements into slender stanzas."[2] However, Grünthal's stylization of inner turmoil and rage is less a purification and sublimation than a self-defense, a way of keeping distance vis-à-vis haunting memories of unfulfilled love and of death surrounding and smothering any hope in us. A series of statements in his first book, "Sleeping with Open Eyes," gives expression to this: "And still, love and medicine / are obviously an impractical combination: / out of the clash of poetry and the laws of nature / has come my hangover." Or in the poem "The Road of Freedom" we read, "Not to be bound / by any impulse or serenity . . . / Let thought be cold, sight clear, / blood cool. / This, perhaps this / is the road to freedom." In "We and I" we again find, "I, Ivar Grünthal, like ancient China, / keep from desires and self-torture: / I am neither industrious nor careless, / neither unfeeling nor indifferent: / I read in the setting stars, / daβ ich hab mein Sach auf nichts gestellt."

To be sure, such desperate detachment is more easily said than done. On a purely formal level it functions as commitment to a literary tradition and mental discipline, but in Grünthal's poetry it actually produces an increasing inner tension which leads to an explosive diction that makes his verse akin to surrealist and post-surrealist outbursts of aggressive and subversive imagery. The very conjunction of the two main themes, love and war, maintains throughout his entire production a taut polarity of opposites; yet far from laying a foundation for romantic plenitude, Grünthal's polarity suggests from the very beginning an irreversible doom. In an early poem he speaks about his almost religious adoration of the beloved: "Alone in the room, I feel that this is not faithfulness at all / . . . What is bliss in imagination, in reality is horror." The same poems ends with a harrowing stanza: "Of course there is hope, inexhaustible hope, / there are mystically simple escapes. / Even from the tundra and wastelands where people perished full of expectation, / souls are saved, but we are not." It is within the strict form of fifteen sonnets, dedicated to the same love, that the poet's diction achieves in his second collection, "Myths about a Land That Vanished into the Swamp" (1953), its particular surrealistic poignancy: "Love beyond reason is a force of nature; / you set boiling lava against the Arctic seas. / The destruction of our twin star, ripped / into your brain, imprisons volcanoes. // When every fading echo from your mouth, / that beautiful and sometimes filthy lover, / turns into myths about the land that vanished in the swamp, / you undulate within my soul, oh holy scum." Through his beloved's absence and the memory of their young and frustrated love, the poet searches for a foothold in the general shipwreck of his own life and of our world. At the same time he plumbs the depth of our physical and moral callousness by confronting it with the harsh truth of a front-line soldier's life as revealed in the casual deaths of fellow human beings, their cheap momentary compensations with prostitutes while on leave, or through their sudden flare-ups of despair. Grünthal knows well how to break moral, social, and esthetic taboos, in this way making us feel the lacerating truth of repugnant circumstances. A visit to "A Soldier's Bride" ends with the following lines, "Here's five hundred, beat it, broad! / You choke on mascaraed tears; / shut up, kettle, don't accuse the pot of being black!" Indeed, those who are victimized are not impressed with tears; nor is Grünthal's profoundly hurt conscience. One can only guess at the extent of disillusionment and loss of faith that lies behind the following lines of "Vocation": "Equality and fraternity are out of fashion, / everybody's fate lies in his cerebral cortex, / but we are free to see things our way. // This is the last thing still sacred to me, / taking one's stand in the tracks of Sisyphus: / to find through the Dead Sea's growing roar / the approximate, perhaps uncertain truth."

This radical search for truth culminates in Grünthal's third collection of verse, "Black Sunday" (1954), which contains a visionary kind of poetry where the previously parallel but separate themes of love and the universe are linked by strikingly powerful clusters of images: "When you laughed with eyes of melting snow, / you thrust yourself against me like a reef / and deep within you boulders were crucified / and from the rock spurted the miracle of springs." However, this miracle of love which gushes forth from crucified boulders within the lovers is doomed to destruction by a release of cosmic hostility. The bridges of night that connect him with his past collapse one after another under the relentless shower of stars, so that "He who asked for mercy from Hades, / turns to stone through the brutal fireworks of the sky." It seems that the higher powers revealed here are not only the religious but also the spiritual and historical forces which direct universal cataclysms: "We only wanted to stay in the shadows, / to find ourselves in the shadow of evening's black wing, / but amidst raging hordes of angels / we perish in quicksand from the Milky Way." Nevertheless, because salvation through love is doomed, erotic desire takes on the intense ring of a desperate, sardonic, and satanic re-volt: "My cruel curiosity / seeks to see your nocturnal hope of salvation / gushing forth like oil in a desert . . . / rubbing our mouths together like Friday's dry twigs, / you flow over my loins like oil into fire: / let dark Sun-days flare, / our godless inheritance." Then the poet chokes again on endless icebergs from an immensely black Antarctica; on piles of dead with bullet holes be-tween their eyes; on the hands of a girl with only eight fingernails—the other two having been pulled off dur-ing an interrogation—who scratches a hole for her mother's body, hung by her feet. With a taste of blood in his mouth, the poet discovers the meaning of his dead bride: she is the very vessel in which he under-takes his last journey around Cape Horn to Tierra del Fuego. Characteristically, Grünthal makes the parts of her body correspond to those of the vessel: "Delivered by night, your tanned skin / will be hoisted as a sail, / your spine become the mast, / your heavy breasts an-chors being weighed . . ." In this way parts of the female body become archetypal images for a new erotic my-thology and the vessel and sea become central images in Grünthal's subsequent poetry.

The poet's search for truth becomes Ulysses' jour-ney through seven seas with no Ithaca in sight. This is a direction taken by the complex and highly concise po-etry of "The Sea" (1958). A sense of balance between the powers of life and death, or uncertainty about our fate, allows the poet some statements of a contemplative na-ture: "I have got rid of truths with a capital T. / I long for the kingdom of heaven. / Andrey and Austerlitz. / Andrey and Austerlitz." The contemplation of the infi-nite sky by the wounded Prince Andrey Bolkonsky on the battlefield of Austerlitz in Tolsoy's *War and Peace* serves Grünthal here as an archetype for spiritual aspi-ration in the midst of gloom. In the poem "Meaning," where Captain Ahab's battle with the white whale is en-visioned, Grünthal feels close to the whale's path, sym-bolizing the light of eternal snows in which the captain's bloodbaths dissolve like fleeting instants: "Freedom's desert road is harsh: / Don't lose sight of the Arctic Sea in a stream of blood." The Arctic Sea seems to refer to eternity as a void which is the ultimate meaning of death. Simultaneously it is also a purification, an intu-ition which allows us to rise above the suffocating effect of immediate dissolution: "When blind hope is your only suspension cable / expectation of death is no lon-ger suffocating" (from the poem "Hope").

The very title of Grünthal's next volume of verse, "Snow and Lime" (1960), emphasizes the radically puri-fying function of poetry. Moving away from valleys to bare tundras, the poet approaches the white realm of lime, "which burns off the faces of the murdered." He

advocates the use of acids and alkaline solutions against the return of deadly nightmares. New sea voyages through the past and the dark areas of impossibility lead to new dawns "without the truth of yesterday" and to the freedom of flying: "But I dare not fly; / do my eyes hurt too much?" In spite of this restriction, the conclud-ing lines of "Snow and Lime" reverse the feeling of cos-mic doom which was so prevalent in earlier collections such as "Black Sunday." A sense of rebirth replaces the anguish of destruction: "The falling stars of July / glide like flakes from the choke-cherry, / the rigidity of snow, the severity of lime / melts, catching fire from the new moon."

In Grünthal's world of irreconcilable contradictions rebirth, however, is not deliverance. Therefore his last collection to date, "The Measure Is Full" (1964), takes us back again to the bitter struggle for truth. The hostile substances of snow and ice, acid and man find in "Counterpoint" their unifying image in the stone which stands still yet also rolls in order to "Rise like a moon / at the end of Terra Firma." The stone is also the symbol of "the life-giving force of endless revolt," on which note the poet ends his book.

The center of Grünthal's poetic thought is not an allegory of refusal and seclusion, but rather a symbol of concentrated energy ready to explode at any significant provocation. This is exactly what his poetry has done for fifteen years of tense development while at the same time being galvanized and held in check by an orphic awareness that "Too deeply buried is the blue height of life."

⬛ ⬛ ⬛

Ivar Ivask's first volume of verse in Estonian, "The Meaning of Stars," appeared in 1964 (see *BA* 39:3, p. 374), the same year as Grünthal published his last col-lection. However, Ivask had been writing poetry in Ger-man for some twenty years prior to this date. A collec-tion of his German poems, "The Mirrored Earth," was published in 1967, but the poems were actually written during the decade 1953–63 (see *BA* 42:1, p. 116). It seems therefore legitimate to consider here first of all Ivask's "Mirrored Earth," particularly since it contains in compressed form many of the main themes and indi-vidual perspectives of his later poetry. This seems justi-fied even if the form of his German verse does not al-ways correspond to that of his later Estonian poems. Employing traditional German verse forms, at times even sonnets, the poet proclaims himself a child born by the sea, in the port city of Riga, open to the wide world and the strange salty element of the sea: "Born by a sweeping, open bay, / nothing accidental disturbs your perspective. / The bustling port is an unfermented dish of distant countries / for your young tongue to taste . . . // You are struck by a hundred impressions / moved by ebb and tide, deeply moved." Not surprisingly, this poem, "Harbor Childhood," is followed by one entitled "Southern Estonian Landscape," the home of his father: "All day long larks keep courting spring. / Fields like cloth shot through with green. / Women watching birch sap ooze / harvest the sweetness of a world being born. / . . . No one is absent, not even the dead. / The Earth in a sky full of growing light." This open and harmoniously expanding world of shared happiness which moves toward light in a cosmic brotherhood—Earth in heaven—will remain at the heart of Ivask's poetry as his *Urerlebnis,* a gift from a seemingly happy early childhood which at the same time does reflect ancestral beliefs. Significantly, the trauma of separation from his homeland is touched upon only very discreetly in "The Refuge," a short poem which describes his arrival on a remote island with only sparse grass to meet him, yet a refuge from persecution where "your freedom lies sighing at your feet." From now on the island will remain a symbol of refuge, inner truth, or life's essence throughout the poetry of Ivar Ivask.

There are other recurring motifs which later acquire the significance of dominant themes. These are geographic locations interpreted as centers of fundamental experience and relationships, not merely captions of fleeting impressions. As the poet was later to state in the Estonian collection "Day Comes with a Rooster's Step," "To write poetry is to draw maps / always another map on another page." This charting of the poet's world is a way of formulating a universe created by him in response to the constantly changing flow of life in which he is caught. Indeed, "The Mirrored Earth" seems to chart a poetic topography of Europe which extends from the Northeast (Finland and the Baltic countries) to the Southwest (Spain, Italy, and Greece) and is centered in Marburg and Vienna. As a result, the impression of a manifold yet unifying poetic space with mythical implications is created. This helps to understand the meaning of the poem "Vision of Vienna," from which the title of the book derives: "Mirrored earth! underscored by the river, / clouds pursue the fleeing valley. / Time has faded along the slopes, / with blood-stained grape leaves as its coat of arms." The earth is mirrored by the sky, which responds, through clouds and reflections, to the fleeing valley, while another movement of time, symbolized by the endless plains rolling in from the East, stops at the foothills of the mountains, thus joining the eternity of the skies. A parallel, even more explicit vision of universal plenitude with mythical connotations can be found in the following lines of "Greek Perspective: Day": "Yet islands spring from the tide of noon / glowing green with rotund fertility. / Seagulls stretch out their wings / and stay still—white fans—in mid-air, / touching sea and cloud, sand and foam." Thus an image of cosmic fulfillment, a union of sea, sky, and islands, experienced in later years, echoes exactly the childhood vision of cosmic brotherhood of earth and heaven at the beginning of the book. When the collection ends with the lines "Every question becomes irrelevant. / No more answers are needed. / Clear bright days / are anchored like islands in the sea," we keep the feeling of serenity within an open, responding world where the "clear days" stand out like beacons of confident maturity. The entire collection is a web of corresponding landscapes and seasons, frequently animated by air-inspired imagery in which clouds, birds, and winds, as well as blue, white, or dark distances, form a counterpoint to fiery, watery, and vegetal substances.

Throughout the four subsequent collections, all written in Estonian, Ivask's poetry fully unfolds in the gravitational field charted by "The Mirrored Earth," yet at the same time searches relentlessly for new approaches, new confirmations, and new forms in order to express an increasingly intense contact with the world and his own inner truth. The very title of his first Estonian collection, "The Meaning of Stars" (1964), refers to a sentence written long ago by the grandmother of the poet and to the Milky Way, to the correspondence between macrocosm and microcosm, and thus it introduces us to the very heart of the poet's struggle for identity and his relation to the world. The descriptions of his confrontation with the woods, lakes, and rivers of Finland and Minnesota are strikingly dramatic. Stripped of his outer self, the poet discovers his foundations in the bare granite rock that rises from the bottom of Finnish lakes and becomes fused with the swarm of mosquitoes circling over fresh blood or with cold fish blood dripping slowly into the lukewarm lake that hangs from the tip of the promontory like a kettle of chowder. Rapid motions on horizontal and vertical planes crisscross the poems. In "Vision of August" the heat of the sun and an upcoming storm merge with the purifying effect of the sauna, reducing everything to ashes, with only the full moon in the end picking up its silver coins "mumbling to itself in the water." A splendid destruction leads to magic fulfillment. One recognizes here the pattern of rebirth myths.

It is "the axe of the sun," another symbol of fertile hostility, which measures in "Autumn's Weave" the length of the fir trees that immediately float down the rivers and lakes as logs while an island pushes its iron wedge between the sky and the waves. Finally, the moon rides over the mythical Finnish bridge, referred to in Estonian folk song, "Straight into the yard of winter." Here the rebirth is delayed, but the moon's easy voyage is itself a mythical feast. In Ivask's poetic universe, even the Ice Age is "a nice age": "The earth lies in shadow death. / The caveveins underground pulsate with blood warmth." Just as the cold anger of the Deluge was overcome by Noah's ark, which traversed it like a "hot coffin full of screaming life," so life seeps through between the "swords of icicles" ("Variations on Winter, Cold and Ice"). In such images the consecutive stages of the rebirth sequence (first destruction, then rebirth) are condensed into simultaneous events, which intensely vibrate in our mind due to their implicit opposition. Furthermore, the image of polar ice, packed with teeming life underground, produces a powerful cultural echo in any native Estonian, because it will remind him of Kalev's Son, the folk-epic hero who is held captive for many years in the underworld before he can escape to liberate his people. Linked with the theme of cosmic fulfillment discussed earlier, the theme of rebirth expands most fully in "Waterfall at Dusk": "Birches cascade down the slopes. / Churning rivers heave up birches of foam . . . // Drawn by the tenderness of waveleaves, / you float along, a clumsy skiff. // The foaming birch-bark of light went down. / . . . You don't need the Earth. You have a place in the sky: / you are a gleaming point in the Milky Way." This cascading fury of a waterfall in northern Minnesota, which erupts in birches made of foam, kindles a still more dynamic dream of ascension, liberation, and cosmic union. Just as in other poems, here too at the crucial moment, at sunset, the waterbound forces are transformed into an aerial upsurge, reminding us of another poem in this same collection which defines the poet's own situation: "Whatever comes with the wind, disappears in the wind / . . . I am not a fallow field / . . . But whirl, a seed in the wind's hand, / and await a new sowing" ("Three Truths: About the Lake, the Wind, and the Rock"). Active freedom, the dynamics of wind animate Ivask's poetic world. His Milky Way is not a static symbol of eternity but a flow like the original waterfall. The whirling seed and the gleaming point are in turn equally active agents within a general unifying context.

In Ivask's second collection of Estonian verse, "Day Comes with a Rooster's Step" (1966; see *BA* 41:3, p. 373), Finnish, Esto-Latvian, Spanish, Mediterranean, and Minnesotan visions are again woven into a resonant space of fundamental relationships. The rebirth theme receives a particularly explosive expression when the spectral reflection of the moon in a dormant lake full of fish is suddenly shattered into a thousand swarming fish-fragments by the fir tree's harpoon: "Then the lake darkens in the moon's craters, / high above circle fins,

/ scales of light shimmer in the distance, / the tide of the sky lapping in the night" ("Finland and Island, VII"). Thus a plain fishing event achieves profound cosmic resonance. The intimate participation with the natural world around us allows the poet to recover the ritualistic meaning of everyday events. A simple meal becomes a communication with the lake itself: "When in the soft evening dusk / we ate of the lake's heart in the whitefish." Or: "The wedding feast of earth and lake / was held at our table today: / into the earthen loaf / melted fiery fish!" ("Vaahersalo Variations"). The coming of twilight is a ritual of transition toward another world; but above all the frequent use of aerial images maintains a sense of alert expectation and promise all through this volume. "Fragment" gives beautiful expression to this element: "The thousand possibilities of this day / —before you have risen— / surround you like a thousand birds / whose song in the lap of night / still awaits the flight-signal of the sun."

In "The Gardens of History" (1970; see *BA* 45:3, p. 543), Ivask's third collection of verse, the song of a thousand birds takes off in an apparently opposite direction. Instead of rising, these poems dive into the depth of water pursuing a beloved born in the sign of Pisces. This time the poet himself sees the event as a rebirth: "Lightning-illuminated fishes / disappear into the depths of thought / I don't think but feel / a new being / which by destroying me / saves me." Among the forty-one short, one-to-eight-line unrhymed yet melodious stanzas of this sequence, which seem to grope for words under the impact of an unexpected emotional strain, some flashing fragments release an unusual amount of imaginative energy: "A shaman rarely falls in love / twice an eternity / when he does mountains explode / chunks of the landscape rise into the air / trees take root in the sky / flower right into your face." An exploded and reversed universe flowers magnificently downward. Packed with still tauter energy is the vision of the poet's own symbol, the bird, when confronted with fire, the substance of love, and the watery depths of the beloved: "In the underwater light it may seem / that one flash of lightning after another / is one long unbroken flash / but the bird sees the lightning-split fir / down to its roots." Marriage of fire and water thus becomes the leitmotiv of the cycle of love poems in this book, yet it also directs the following poems toward a Heraclitan hymn to everlasting, elemental motion, as exemplified by a poem in which Ivask addresses whole forests of spruces, firs, alders, and birches. It is an evocation of trees which symbolize "powerfully alternating" existence between the opposing poles of day and night, height and depth, with the four elements ordering our movement and fire as the cause of transformations. In this book the secret alliance of fire and water transforms the former dynamics of renewal through destruction and rebirth into a decidedly metaphysical pursuit: "All meaning can be found beyond boundaries / . . . We will ride straight through Hades / our eyes smarting from the rose of stardust / rising and sinking into timeless time / where the dolphins' flight hits the mark." The dolphins' flight that merges with the stardust suggests a fusion of water and fire, which was for Rimbaud too the most adequate approximation of eternity, defined by him as "Sun gone with the sea." At the same time this poem exemplifies a new function for poetry which becomes increasingly apparent: the poem actually participates in the magic forces active in the universe. As a descendant of the ancient shamans, the poet reigns over invisible inner powers that galvanize the words he employs. Their sound and meaning are directly related to the poet's experience in the world and derive much of their power from the beliefs and intuitions embedded in the language shaped by his ancestors. Therefore, writing poetry is tantamount to salvation of self and the world.

At a time when confidence in man and the world has been almost destroyed, when the poet's own life has taught him that death, loss, separation, and destruction are the primary evidence of human truth, Ivask's ability to restore a coherent universe may seem almost miraculous. Nevertheless, his own poetry bears witness to how the relatively late encounter with the landscape and language of Finland—"An invisible armor / Finland surrounds me"—led him to discover in Estonian the very resources of his renewal as poet. This in turn released new energies for a magic re-creation of a livable space inspired by the concept of meaningful universal existence as embodied in folklore. The best proof that it is a livable space can be found in Ivask's most recent book of poetry, "October in Oklahoma" (1973; see *BA* 47:3, p. 590), where a pervading mood of serenity—"The heart turns into a translucent autumn leaf"—enables him to celebrate everyday events in a series of haikus from Finland, such as, "When fetching from the well / our daily water / I kneel," or "Eight summers / three books much rain / maybe I was born here." In this collection the center of the poet's imaginary world is back on earth, and he finds a convincing symbol for this in four prose poems which evoke four trees of his childhood home in southern Estonia. The apple tree, mountain ash, birch, and plum tree are each envisioned as separate individual nests, thus assuming the symbolic function of islands in his earlier poetry (yet they are not self-sufficient because they are linked to their environment). A new dimension of intimate warmth and security is added, as well as an expansion toward the sky, the depth of the earth, and the surrounding world. Together-

er they constitute a sort of mandala of selfhood, and since a well-imagined nest contains in itself the entire universe, the four native trees are also symbols of the continually renewed creative gift. The creative surge from the four trees carries the poet ever deeper into himself and into the realization of silence and solitude as the most direct road toward communication with his fellow men.

After Lepik's reluctant struggle against the void and adversity and Grünthal's grim rage in the search for lost love and truth under the banner of irreconcilable revolt, Ivask's poetry of rebirth, salvation, and reunion with the world has a different, more positive ring. Still, it remains linked by numerous ties to the poetry of his two contemporaries. Just as theirs, his is also a poetry of struggle against a crushing fate, but his struggle is expressed through a denial of historical destiny and the rediscovery of the elemental sources of life which transcend present circumstances. It is above all a reaffirmation of earthly existence as the true ground of our being and his faith in the power of words to actually save us. Characteristic of these three Estonian poet is their intuitive awareness of archetypes and the mythical scope of their imagery. They activate in their poetry the four elements as carriers of primary truth and foundation of man's hope.

Alexander Aspel

1 This and all the following quotes from poems are prose translations by Ivar and Astrid Ivask, with the assistance of Tom J. Lewis.

2 See Ivar Ivask, "A Note on the Contemporary Estonian Poet Ivar Grünthal," in Ivar Grünthal, *Poèmes/Gedichte/Dikter*, Stockholm, 1964, pp. 7–10.

Francis Ponge, 34 rue Lhomond [1974]

Can it really have been all of twenty-one years since we became acquainted? Yes, in sober fact, plus a few months. As it happened, I was a professor on exchange from Harvard to the Sorbonne, looking for quarters in Paris at a time when they were scarce. The apartment that turned up was rather crowded for the three of us: my wife, our eleven-year-old daughter, and myself. It constituted most of the cement-floored *rez-de-chaussée* of a small and shored-up building which dated from the fifteenth century, and indeed had been condemned to be torn down almost forty years before. It faced toward a pleasant courtyard and away from the street, which was aptly named—as I was to realize—for an eighteenth-century grammarian, the Abbé Lhomond. One direction led there from official Paris: the *grandes écoles,* the Pantheon, the University. The other dipped down into the winding market of the rue Mouffetard and into the very oldest part of the city, with its Roman arenas and other ruins. Across our corner ran the rue de Pot-de-Fer, where the language heard was Arabic. Near the head of the street was the Ecole Normale, and at that conjunction two *clochards* slept regularly over a Métro grating. Our distinguished neighbor, when we got to know him, proved to be a proud and knowledgeable guide to his *quartier*. Here if anywhere was the ancient Lutetia, he liked to point out, as well as the medieval Latin Quarter that harbored François Villon. Jean Valjean had once escaped from Inspector Javert by climbing over the convent wall across the street, and a stone's throw away was the *pension* where Eugène de Rastignac had met Père Goriot.

We were determined to put up with the constriction because we were attracted by the location, and because we did not have much choice. We had no conception in advance of the luminously silver lining that lay behind our little cloud, until at the booth of the concierge we glimpsed the name of our fellow tenant and at certain times the exquisite politeness of his person. The name was not, of course, unknown to me. Francis Ponge's reputation had crystallized during World War II, with *Le parti pris des choses*. As between French and Anglo-American poetry there has been a fruitful cycle of interaction (e.g., Poe-Baudelaire-Laforgue-Eliot), Ponge, although completely original, struck a note which was evoked in English a generation earlier by Pound, by T. E. Hulme, by the imagists, and by the red wheelbarrow of William Carlos Williams—generally speaking, by a rededication to visual perceptiveness and verbal exactitude. My own long correspondence with Marianne Moore over her translation of Lafontaine had greatly sharpened my appreciation of this modern poet, who has been called "le Lafontaine des choses." Neglected in his youth, he was being hailed in his middle years as a fellow existentialist by Sartre and Camus. Still later years have shown him to be a precursor of the *nouveau roman* on the one hand and of structuralist criticism on the other. As a student of realism, which finds a semantic parallel in *chosisme,* I had been acutely impressed by his example. The exact delineation of particularities—the quest for what Joyce, in his scholastic jargon, termed *quiddity*—had found no more rigorous proponent.

This was the man who, as we so happily discovered, was now living just above us, on the *piano nobile* of our decaying edifice—in a flat inherited not too long before, with artistic appurtenances left over from the previous occupant, Jean Dubuffet. We had mutual friends in two brilliant young men who had recently studied with me at Harvard and were just then setting out on their careers as French writers, the poet André Du Bouchet and the art critic Pierre Schneider. We must have been introduced by one or the other, or possibly both. In any case, the Ponges were the kindest and friendliest of neighbors. They comprised, like ourselves, a closely knit circle of three. Odette was the gracious and intelligent wife, who coped with everything for her two charges. Armande was the charming *lycéenne,* who worked hard at her English and amiably consented to become the perfect babysitter and the adored companion of our little girl. (Does she still have the battered *Concise Oxford Dictionary* we left with her as a memento of that year?) Francis was not publishing very much except for an occasional and felicitous venture into art criticism, and he was supporting his family by teaching at the Alliance Française. (How he ever could have sold insurance, in his prior job, is beyond surmise.) German was his modern language, not English; "My Creative Method" was a title which he had accepted—unfortunately, I think—from a commentary by Betty Miller. We conversed in French; but I shall not try to render his conversation verbatim because, after the interval of years, I could not recapture the precision, the elegance, or the suecinctness of his phrasing.

The everlasting relation of words to things, than which life could scarcely hold a more critical relationship, was for him both a perpetual challenge and a persistent criterion, and if he saw the word as an object, he envisioned "l'objet comme idée." His talk—like so much of his writing, wherein he talks about writing—took the French language as its habitual point of departure and of return. Littré was his breviary; he was adept at glossing the archaic twists of Villon; his gift for explication was to unfold itself monumentally in *Pour un Malherbe*. It was characteristic of him to note that *oiseau* contains each one of the five vowels, as well as to speculate on alternatives for its single consonant. All such speculations, however, ended by bringing home the linguistic elusiveness and the inherent reality of the bird itself—or whatever theme he was contemplating, animate or inanimate, grand or minuscule. *Le savon* and "La pomme de terre" had virtually changed into crystal balls in his firm hands and under his penetrating eyes. It was good to be dwelling in quotidian proximity with one who could confer such depth and dignity on the humble and solid things of every day. Given the intensity of his gaze, it could become a short leap from the familiar to the cosmic, not to say the apocalyptic: *Le soleil placé en abîme*. Observing the behavior of a fly, he discerned an analogue in the figure of Coriolanus, during a year when the Comédie Française was interpreting Shakespeare's plays as a portent of authoritarianism. (Could that fly also be interpreted as a portent of Robbe-Grillet's centipede?) With what interest Monsieur Ponge would savor the Parisian locutions of our common *femme de ménage,* Madame Tissot!

Usually we encountered one another in the hallway, where he would often stop for a cordial interchange. Occasionally, after our respective family dinners, we would get together upstairs or downstairs for a demitasse and a liqueur. One of those occasions has lingered in my memory with a special glow. That afternoon I had attended the funeral of Paul Eluard, where the flamboyant Louis Aragon and other communist orators had tried to turn the crowd at Père-Lachaise into something like a political manifestation. Ponge, who had been a close friend of Eluard's for many years and was godfather to his daughter, had seen little or nothing of his fellow poet since he himself had resigned from the Communist Party. Having missed the ceremony on principle, he was nonetheless sympathetic and eager to hear about it in some detail and was ruefully meditative in his comments. Then, upon our questioning, he launched into a candid, eloquent, and excruciating account of his own experiences as a party member. After he had spoken at some length, my wife, whose Russian revolutionary background made her a particularly attentive listener, voiced two questions which he had aroused in her mind. If the discipline was as shackling as he attested, why had he joined the party in the first place? And how, if he had been so intricately involved, had he ever managed to get out? His reply was a clear-eyed self-appraisal and likewise a reverberating confession: "There is one thing you must understand about me. I was born and bred a Protestant. Hence what is difficult for me is what I must undertake." His difficulties were not those of Gide or Rousseau, but it is easy to understand what he means when he says that poetry, for him, is "un besoin, un engagement, une colère, une affaire d'amour-propre et voilà tout."

At the end of the term we took our leave from the address that we had shared with the Ponges, rather precipitously because of the housing pressures; and, although we exchanged publications and New Year's greetings, we did not see them during the next twelve years. Then, in 1965, our old neighbors made their first visit to the United States. Ponge was on a heavy schedule of public readings at colleges and other institutions. However, they were able to save a weekend for reunion and relaxation in what he would describe as "ce bel automne de la Nouvelle Angleterre." Though the fringe around his head was no longer so dark, his eyes were as sharp as ever and his voice was as clarifying. It was

an enormous pleasure to witness his spontaneous reactions, at the age of sixty-six, to our American vistas. Fall is the best season in New England; the leaves were outdoing themselves in their annual spectacle. We took them on our standard tour for European friends—Concord, Lexington, and Walden Pond. We tested them on clam chowder, which they enjoyed. What seemed to please him best was the North End of Boston; its Italian markets and eighteenth-century houses appealed to sensibilities deeply rooted in the Midi. Though he has returned to this country since, we have not seen him again, and I was at Oxford when he came back this past summer to receive the international prize he has so richly deserved. Still, I continue to cherish vivid and frequent recollections of those privileged months we spent on the rue Lhomond. It was the closest approximation that I can imagine, as a stranger who came along two generations afterward, to having been a guest of Mallarmé's at his Tuesdays on the rue de Rome.

Harry Levin

The Imagery and Collages of Odysseus Elytis [1975]

Just as Cavafis felt that, given other circumstances, he might have developed into a fine historian, so Elytis has felt that, had he been taught the rudiments of drawing at an early age, he might have developed into a fine painter. He does not regret, of course, that having had no other means, he turned to poetry. Indeed, he came to see that poetry, in its imagery, tones, and compositional structure, contained elements of painting and architecture; in its phonetic orchestration and arrangements, the instrumentation and the forms of music; in dialogue, narrative, or montage, techniques from the other arts.

Elytis's imagination always was—and continues to be—primarily an imagistic one. From the very first verses he wrote ("time is a swift shadow of birds / my eyes wide open within its images") to an as yet unpublished verse recently written ("one must transform every moment into an image") he finds that he has been impelled to apprehend mental, emotional, and physical phenomena in no other way but through visualization and imagery. This is what gives his poetry its pictorial quality, its concreteness, its lack of generalization.

Nonetheless, a strong abstract element, even in his earlier verses, finds an outlet in the extraordinarily complicated, almost mathematically composed structures he has invented for many of his later poems, in "The

Kimon Friar (© *Raphaelidis, Athens*)

Monogram," "The Light Tree and the Fourteenth Beauty," "The Stepchildren," and particularly in *The Axion Esti,* one of the most complicatedly constructed poems in modern times. "Image!" he exclaims, "O unvarying / outpouring of light / you enclose each hovering meaning / that allures our hope / toward composure"—and, it might be added, toward composition. Yet abstract design, proportion, synthesis are only the skeletal outlines of his poetic anatomy, fleshed out, given color, identification, and analogy by a select and strange imagery of dreamlike invocation, supported, extended, and given an esthetic base in early adolescence by his discovery of and dedication to surrealism.

At the age of eighteen, in 1929, he chanced upon a book of poems by Paul Eluard. In 1935 he heard a lecture on surrealism by Andréas Embirikos, who in that same year was to publish the first book of "automatic writing" poems in Greece, "Blast Furnace." In Embirikos's house the young man also saw for the first time original paintings by Max Ernst, Yves Tanguy, and Oscar Dominguez. He discovered the fascination of collage and threw himself passionately into the creation of such puzzles, pasting together cutouts from various periodicals, letters of different colored inks, with strings,

pebbles, wood. His first creations were the purely orthodox ones of paradoxical juxtapositions in imitation of the collages of Max Ernst, who, from engravings out of old books, put together strange and fantastic enigmas, much as in Lautréamont's revolutionary image, "as beautiful as the chance encounter on a dissecting table of a sewing machine and an umbrella." A few of these he exhibited at the First International Surrealist Exhibition in Athens (1935): amputated hands hanging from branches of trees, women with the heads of birds or horses.

Even at this period, however, the young inventor realized that, though fascinated by these chance and curious propinquities, he must later give them more formal organization and yoke their uninhibited flight to some central theme, some purification of meaning. After the publication in 1939 of "Orientations," in which he gathered together his surrealist experiments in poetry, he devoted himself exclusively to the evolution of his imagination in the imagery of poetry and not of painting. It was not until many years later, in 1966, that he felt the need once again to return to pictorial expression. This time he painted some thirty-odd gouaches, which in their freshness and translucency, their clear colors and purity, reflected the poems he had been writing about the apotheosis of youth amid a dazzlement of Aegean seascape. Among these are 1) "Athos": red roofs in the foreground, a sea for background on which Byzantine saints are arranged in ceremonial order as on an iconostasis. Boats disproportionately large sail between them, for, as he wrote in "Anniversary," "keels pass by, splitting some new obstacle / with passion and conquest." 2) "The Baptism": a facsimile of a Byzantine icon, but the one baptized is a lovely and naked adolescent girl. 3) "Mnisareti": divided into two unequal and vertical sections. In the left section is Mnisareti as we know her in the famous stele of the early fourth century B.C., and in the right section are boats that sail above roofs and terraces. 4) "The Sorceress of the Trees": a whitewashed wall implanted in the sea; to the left schematized shrubs and trees of various sizes; to the right a seated woman who holds a flame in her open palm, much as Elytis's mother, as he relates in his collection of prose writings, "Open Book," "kept vigil all night long, holding a fragment of moon in her hands." The image reflects that contained in an early poem, "Dionysos"—"scintillating in the palms of women who have embellished translucency"—and looks forward to another in *The Axion Esti:* "the stone hand of noon holding the sun in its open palm." These gouaches purified the absurdly contradictory images of his early collages into the fanciful reconstructions characteristic also of his imagistic development as a poet.

A year later, in April, the colonels were to stomp over Greece with their tanks, their tortures, and their censorship in an attempt to choke off all vital and therefore dangerous creative expression. The chance compilation in his flat of piles of periodicals with colored illustrations, a reluctance to publish, and an inability to think or create the more difficult imagery of poetry during a time of tyranny made Elytis turn once again to collage as a way out of his impasse. During the seven years from 1967 to the fall of the dictatorship in 1974, he created a series of about forty works, most of them in color and a few in black and white. Among those which I have had at my disposal are the nine published in his book of songs *Ta ro tou érota* (The Ro of Eros; 1972), the nineteen in Ilías Petrópoulos's book *Elýtis, Móralis, Tsaroúhis* (1966), and many unpublished works shown me by the poet.

During his direct experimentations with painting in his gouaches, Elytis came to realize that it had become too late for him to attain to anything which might satisfy him technically as a painter. At the same time, he found that by setting aside the extravagances and curious juxtapositions of his earlier work, by concerning himself with purely plastic and compositional problems of color, synthesis, design, line, space, mass, and proportion, and by utilizing the basic imagery of his poetry—seas, skies, shells, pebbles, waterdrops, stones, plants, flowers, fishes, birds, whitewashed island walls and homes, naked girls, ancient ruins and artifacts, Byzantine icons—he could, without treading on the claims of the painter, continue in another manner and in his own way the expressions of the same world which preoccupied him in his poetry and which corresponded to the same ideas. He found that he could now use the fully perfected images of painters and photographers and rearrange them to parallel the imagery of his poetry. He struggled within certain confines, for he had to work with whatever material was at hand, sometimes putting together these ready-made objects in ways to conform to a preconceived idea, but more often than not being directed by them, much as a sculptor may be directed by the quality, grain, or size of a block of marble or of wood. Except for some occasional frustrations (he could not realize all he imagined or create works of large size), he found, as in his poetry, that such restrictions more often freed than hampered his imagination. Also, the element of chance, the necessity of creating out of the arbitrary and the ephemeral, had always fascinated him as one of the basic tenets of surrealism.

Although no clear division is possible, or even desirable, Elytis's collages may roughly be divided into two groups: 1) those that are somewhat abstract and modern, and 2) those that are poetically and Hellenically centered. Characteristic of both groups are an opposition to the contorted and the entangled and a tendency toward the Greek and the composed. In the more "abstract" collages he approaches his materials much as a painter sets out to solve problems of composition and synthesis. Colors and form must be placed just so and in no other way. A curve must find its analogy in some other curve, space must be balanced by space, mass by mass; line must be related to line, whether horizontally, vertically or obliquely; a bit of red must be adjusted with another red or a color of equal weight or intensity. As in cubism, as in architecture, as in poetry itself, one image, one mass must structurally be related to another. "Theme," if there is a theme at all, plays a minor role as such and is subordinated to the pure pleasures of esthetic canons.

In "Embroidery and Bird," for instance (1974; *Elýtis, Móralis, Tsaroúhis,* p. 99), he cut out from a book of fabrics a rectangular sheet of light gray paper along whose bottom border was printed a horizontal wide band of woven crimson cloth with a geometric design in black, the handicraft of some Greek island, and from whose left edge hangs a wide tassel that not only breaks the symmetry of the design but also overlaps a narrower band of the same cloth without design a bit below and almost sheer with the end of the paper. Over this Elytis pasted, from a French book, the hollowed-out cross section of an oval semiprecious stone whose inner outline suggests the shape of a bird embryo within an egg. The effect is that of an abstract composition with a hint of the representational.

In "Red Composition with Bicycle" (1974; ibid., p. 111) Elytis started out with a stylized outline drawing of the front section of a bicycle tied firmly with lock and chain to a pole, both against a yellow background. This he placed in the upper right of a dull, mottled red cutout, and this again on a vivid red sheet of paper broken along its length by a white vertical line placed almost at the far left. Below the bicycle he placed a black-green rectangle, interrupted in its lower left-hand corner by an elongated section of a brick wall, against which is silhouetted in black the head of a child. Black is continued obliquely and below to the left by what seems to be a section of a window or skylight opening into a dark night. At the bottom of the composition, an elongated black strip that slants up at the far right and then breaks into fragments completes and balances the dark tones. Stretched across the top of the bicycle and continued vertically down and below its left side in a wider swath is a part of a gray-green wall with open windows revealing an azure sky with a hint of clouds. The effect is purely that of colors and proportions esthetically arranged, with the suggestion of a theme that relates the child's head with the bicycle and the fettered wheel with the open windows of freedom and escape, for nothing is *completely* abstract in any of Elytis's compositions. He is content, as in his poetry, to indulge his play with esthetics in the overall structure of his collages or poems that always contain some human or natural element.

In several instances Elytis has taken the well-known abstract paintings of Rothko as expressions of the modern spirit and imposed on them ancient archetypes, so as to place both in a timeless relationship, rendering them simultaneous and giving them another dimension through this conjoining. In "Delos" (1967; ibid., p. 106) he has placed the head and neck of one of the immediately recognizable lions of Delos in the upper of two blue-green rectangles followed by a third of mottled white, all set against an intense blue background. The two hues slightly suggest the colors of Greece, the mottled white the breaking foam of the sea. In "Idol" (1974; black-and-white; ibid., p. 109) he has adjusted an equally well-known Cycladic figure (c. 2000 B.C.) against a Rothko abstraction and further emphasized the amalgamation of times by bordering this along both sides with columnar cutouts taken from a scientific journal of modern abstract machines. In setting himself the problems of harmoniously wedding the archaic with the modern, time present with time past, he has unwittingly illustrated Eliot's proposition in "Burnt Norton" that "If all time is eternally present / All time is irredeemable. / What might have been is an abstraction" that remains "a perpetual possibility." This "perpetual possibility" is what has always fascinated Elytis's imagination. This same sense of condensed time has also impelled Elytis to use symbol or simile sparingly in his poems, for to him one object does not *represent* another nor is it *like* another. Rather, in an instantaneous identification, one object *is* the other, as in dream. So, in his collages, his girls are not symbols but simply *are*. When he places various cutouts side by side, they do not assume a metaphoric relationship but become fused into one another and exist monolithically in a newly created identity.

A similar sense of abstract design governs the collages that most imagistically correspond to Elytis's poetry of the Aegean. In "Aegean" (1974; ibid., p. 115) cutouts of whitewashed church domes from Santorini set against the sea, portions of whitewashed islandic walls, fragments of dappled green and gold sections taken from unrepresentational segments of Mycenaean death masks are all carefully balanced on an intense blue background. On the lower right of the rectangular depiction, hip and arm protruding slightly and thus breaking the vertical line, Elytis has tried, successfully, to combine a summery girl in rose (taken from Matisse)

with photographic cutouts. To carry her color into the sky, he cut out the outline of a flying bird from a similar rose-colored paper and placed it in the air above the sea. Such birds abound in Elytis's poems as "infants of the wind" that "go to the morning inaugurations of the sea," that "nullify on high the weights of our hearts / and so much blue we have loved," whose song "hovers in mid-air / sowing the golden barley of fire / to the five winds / setting free a terrestrial beauty." In this collage, as in his poem "Event in August," "the girl's bird took a crumb of the sea and ascended."

In another collage, "Votive Offering" (1973; reproduced in BA 49:4, p. 626), the whitewashed cubical houses of Skyros are viewed from the mountain on whose slope the village lies, so that their flat gray roofs form a jigsaw pattern of rectangles. In Elytis's creation, however, the mountain has vanished, and in its stead above the roof extends a deep blue sea with a bare rugged island and a flat blue sky. To the left, emerging above the roofs from the waist up against sea, rock and sky, a Byzantine angel extends a hand as in a votive offering, which may be the triangular cluster of seashells turned inside out, resembling a group of white angel trumpets announcing one of the Aegean's mysteries. Together with a few open-mouthed, reddish flowers, these cascade down from the roofs into another added sea, so that the town floats like a white island in an aqueous element. In one of his poems Elytis writes of "two seas again on either side," and of a "channel high above / changing the sky's ozone," for Greece is almost completely encircled by the sea. It is as if Elytis had depicted for us a variant of that lovely demotic distich: "Amid the blue Aegean waters come angels fluttering / And from the pulsing of their wings fall roses scattering." Two colorful strips from folk embroidery frame the collage at top and bottom, and above it rises the intricately carved woodwork of a Byzantine crown, from whose medallion Christ blesses a seascape which the poet and not His Father had created.

Perhaps the most enchanting and representative of all these collages, though, is "Hovering Landscape with Angel" (1975; unpublished), which depicts Lasithi, that inland green valley of innumerable windmills in Crete, beloved by Elytis as the island of his birth and which he has always wished had been implanted by the sea. Rectifying an error made by nature, he has wedged onto this inland landscape a harbor filled with multicolored boats anchored on its created shores, and below the sea he has placed an inverted mountain and sky again, so that both landscape and seascape float suspended in air. Indeed, in his poems, mulberry trees set sail on the grass's foam, the sun plants gardens on the surf, gardens enter the sea like promontories or bridal beds, and a cereal sea sustains huge cowsheds. Sea, sky, and land in Greece are One. In the sky above the windmills is a young, angelic, full-breasted girl encased in a rosy seashell (heavenly Aphrodite born not out of the sea but out of the sky) whose wings are made of other seashells turned inside out to reveal their gloss of mother-of-pearl. She comes flying, bringing a message, her hand raised in benediction.

Somewhat similar is the "Angel of Astypalea" (1967; "The Ro of Eros," p. 12), where the hilltopped town of that Aegean island has been turned upside-down and wedged with its sky against whitewashed island houses, while a Byzantine angel floats against the landscape between the two skies. An island church floats across the top sky, balanced by a strip of bluish land that cuts across the bottom sky.

This brings us to the main motif of Elytis's collages: the apotheosis of naked young girls, of Eros, and of girl-angels bringing mysterious and mystic messages, annunciations, and benedictions, for they are the "Vessels of the Mysteries." "Angel," the poet exclaims in the poem *Villa Natacha,* "hover in flight around me somewhere . . . take me by the hand." This Angel with her "lean boyish body" is Arete in "Sleep of the Valiant," both Greece and the Virgin Mary, all goodness, moral virtue, valor, glory, excellence of every kind, who descends to the Vast Dark Places of the world and labors to turn darkness into light.

In "The Fruit" (1974; *Elýtis, Móralis, Tsaroúhis,* p. 97) the face of a handsome dreaming girl has been substituted for that of the Virgin Mary in a holy icon. Before her have been placed, not church offerings of candles or incense, but nature's offerings of fruits, although flowers, shells, or pebbles would have been equally appropriate for Elytis, as are the "leaves, fruits, flowers, many-branched dreams" he lists in "Pellucid Skies." As in his poems, this is "the girl who has not yet entered into love / but holds in her apron an acrid orchard of fruit" or gives "to the ritual of difficult dream a sure restoration." Her face, the "innocence we had found so enigmatic," is "washed by a dawn we loved because we did not know that within us, even deeper still, we were preparing other larger dreams that must hug in their arms more earth, more blood, more water, more fire, more Love." "In the arms of the Virgin," Elytis writes in "Open Book," "I placed flowers, and in the arms of Saints, girls and birds."

In "Girl on a Calyx" (1974; ibid., p. 98), reclining on a huge red calyx growing out of luxurious green leaves on a black background, a girl is sleeping naked in the sun. She is "the blond and sunburnt girl" we meet in Elytis's poems sleeping in "the azure light on the stone steps of August," the one who is "intoxicated with the sun's juices," the "sunburnt and scintillating girl—lullaby of eyelids on the mythical spaciousness of the world." Elytis's collages are not literal depictions of his poems but simply utilize similar images, adapted as his materials direct. At times, indeed, he may take over into his poetry an image he has first created in a collage, as in a recent unpublished poem using this image of a sleeping girl sunning herself on the calyx of a red flower. There has always been an interchange flowing from his poems to his collages; now an opposite flow is beginning, thus establishing a genuine interrelationship.

"The Railing" (1975; ibid., p. 105) depicts a bare-breasted woman enclosed in railings cut out of mottled paper in various lights and shades. Her flimsy flowery shawl reveals a hint of "that bit of black in the nook" of the thighs, a "glimpse of the sea-urchin / for a moment / in sea-depths unexplored." On her right, from top to bottom, falls a cascade of large leaves, from highly polished, glossy green to dappled shades of rose and yellow. She is indeed that "patrician lady of grasses," that green girl of whom the poet says "I shall enter from the door that a plain leaf protects." Although the leaves are not those of a "celestial eucalyptus," they too are bitten by the poet, so that "the holy day of sensual pleasure may emit its fragrance." But most inspiringly, this is the woman whom the bearded man in "On the Republic" frees from her cage, who then turns into a bird that hovers motionless above the peristyle of the poet's Temple and becomes a naked woman again "with a green mist on her hair and a jacket of golden wire," sitting on the tiles "with her thighs half open." And this, says the poet, "in my consciousness took on the meaning of a flower when danger opens with it its first tenderness." He receives this celestial vision as in a wet dream, and then continues to write frenziedly "among large transparent leaves" to sanction and bless all forms of lovemaking in his Republic of poetry and collage, as diversified as "the various ways birds have of flying little by little / as far as the infinite." "When you glitter in the sun that on you glides water-drops, and deathless hyacinths, and silences," the poet exclaims in "The Concert of Hyacinths," "I proclaim you the only reality."

One is almost convinced, both in Elytis's poems and in his collages, that the beautiful, naked body of a young girl, a distillation of sunlight and dewdrops, is indeed the only reality; that in its purity and innocence it arouses sexual desire to the highest pitch of holiness. A girl-angel in flight bringing benediction is surely, and not only in Freudian terms, an intense if unconscious symbol of erotic sanctity. "A naked body," he writes in a yet unpublished poem, "is the only extension of that immaterial line that unites us with the Mystery." These are his "grapehard girls," "seablue to the bone," who "run naked in men's eyes" while "innocence / strips itself of its last lie." These "naked bodies carved on the pediments of time" are Ersi, Mirto, Roxani, Fotini, Anna, Alexandra, Cynthia, whom he invokes and glorifies in the last section of *The Axion Esti,* "Marina as she was before she existed." For Elytis, whatever is natural is holy, and the five or more senses are sacred portals to an earthly as well as to a celestial paradise. "I have never as yet found sorrow in the flesh," he writes in "Open Book," contradicting Mallarmé. For a love to be truly love, it must be "true and free, above and beyond the rumpled bedsheets of religion and country."

In "The Small Rose" (1967; ibid., p. 100) a naked girl wearing a necklace of leaves and what may be a semiprecious stone or seashell resembling a large drop of water and crowned with a huge rose rises out of rock and sea and extends into a classic Doric temple. In "Nude" (1974; ibid., p. 104) a naked girl with head bowed and hands hanging limply before her in the posture of reverence in church is placed against the backdrop of a huge angel's hand from some Byzantine icon in the ceremonious gesture of benediction. In the collage which is deceptively yet appropriately entitled "Portrait" (1968; ibid., p. 114) we are pleasingly startled to find in a golden Byzantine icon the clear-eyed face of a lovely girl with flowing blond hair gazing at us from where the face of Christ should have been, thus identifying male and female in that pristine stage of their early origins as related by Diotima in Plato's *Symposium.* In "The Two Friends" (1974; ibid., p. 112) two naked girls are placed side by side, their loving and joyous glances intertwined, while around their hands float orbs of mosaic stone and erect, slender, dark leaves rise like phalli. Encircling their heads, as in a single halo, is the gold-framed painting of a Renaissance angel kneeling before the lilies of annunciation. These girls, like the one in "The Small Rose," wear between their breasts what may be a semiprecious stone but which, in effect, for Elytis, is a large luminous drop of water, the "clover of light" which Marina of the Rocks wears in his poem by that name. In "Open Book" he writes of "naked girls flying and unwinding blond manes made of thousands of glittering water-drops." The various orbs which at times surround his girls or angels and which they often carry also resemble floating drops of water that have captured the essence of light.

In "Open Book" Elytis recalls how his island nurses exorcised the Evil Eye by babbling incoherent words while holding in their hands the small leaf of some humble plant. "This small leaf with the unknown powers of innocence," he writes, "and the strange words that accompany it, is Poetry herself." In his travels through-

out Greece he ascertained that its landscapes and seascapes were laden with secret messages expressed in what seemed to be incoherent sounds, yet heavy with "the meaning and weight of a secret and mystic mission." Voices "arrived from the unknown, half questions and half tyrannical oracles, meteors of the middle distance, fragments of consciousness that glide on the lips of Sirens and which the wind reaped." In his dreams he heard leaves speaking, one by one. When he gazed mesmerized on a lizard palpitating in a shaft of sun on a rock, or on dolphins in starlight stitching a ceaseless embroidery in and out of the sea, or on a butterfly alighting on the heaving breast of a young girl sleeping in the sun, it was as if an archangel, in the form of a beautiful young girl, had come to bring, not an annunciation for the Virgin only, but messages from nature as well, in sounds which, if rightly deciphered, would reveal the mystery of this life, of "this small, this great world."

It is, of course, the nature of these revelations to be forgotten the moment they are instinctively decoded. The only thing the poet can do is try to catch their revelations in the half-notation that is poetry, to catch "a metaphysic wherein the phenomenon of language is a musical notation of many meanings . . . an ethical power which the human mind invokes, in exactly the same manner in which a landscape is not at all the rustling of a few trees." Many of the poems in "The Light Tree and the Fourteenth Beauty" deal with this theme. In "Three Times the Truth" we read: "The wild bird *pit-pit* shifted truth from one rock to another / . . . Something must *assuredly* exist / . . . And everywhere out of springs and rosemary an *Our Father* rose like a confession / . . . Something dæmonic but which can be caught in the shape of an Archangel as in a net / . . . I didn't hear / what did you say? /—*Adýss, adýss, adize* / Until . . . I felt . . . that out of nothing is born our Paradise." And in "The Odyssey" we find: "A girl suddenly / struck by an Archangel's glance / whom I took as my slave / and even today as I write only she has stood by me." But it is particularly in "The Girl the North Wind Brought" that the girl-angel appears in annunciation to the poet: "up there . . . gaining in height / and as beautiful as can be / with all the whimsies of birds in her movements . . . / leaning her small breasts for the wind to withstand." In startled revelation, the poet testifies: "a terrified joy within me mounted to my eyelids and fluttered there / . . . / Kindred orbs of light burst behind her and left in the sky / something like the elusive signs of Paradise."

In "Sophia Erect" (1974; ibid., p. 101) an archangel with the face of a girl is holding in her left hand an "orb of light" much like a radiating star, while below and around her float other orbs—stars, planets, or dew-drops. The girls in "The Two Friends" have such orbs at their sides. In "Inverted Landscape" (1968; "The Ro of Eros," p. 68) an angel comes bearing such an orb, while others fall like huge drops of water from one sky to another. "Nude," "Portrait," "The Angel of Asty-palea," and "Hovering Landscape with Angel" all realize in collage Elytis's apotheosis of girls receiving or be-stowing benediction and bringing revelations of na-ture's divinity.

It remains only to note that the most prominent image by far in Elytis's poetry—the Sovereign Sun, in-carnation of all metaphysical and ethical light, of all Jus-tice—is nowhere to be found in any of his collages. It may be that this poet, this "sun-drinker" who has rarely seen a sunrise, who writes best far into the night, for whom the sun's "divine vertical," in Alexander Mátsas's phrase, is not shaken "in the purification of absolute noon," finds the sun too banal as a photographed or painted image, where it is deprived of its metaphysical extensions. And though he has equally hymned the ad-olescent Aegean lad, the "patriot of the sun," the "gamin of the white cloud," the "child with skinned knee," the "sailor boy of the garden," and the young second lieu-tenant of the Albanian campaign who "ascends alone and blazing with light," only one very lovely collage, "Small Eros" (1967; ibid., p. 57), depicts a small boy with trefoil wings rimmed with large drops of water as he treads the air over a mountain slope that descends in terraces from powdered blue to powdered green. Per-haps all the boys, all the young men in his poems, are the poet himself, narcissistically one, while his girls are all women everywhere, all revelation, all angels an-nouncing the holy wedding of the flesh and the spirit.

Kimon Friar

TOPICS

Yiddish Writing in America [1934]

While every nook and corner of American literature is being searched and explored, every bit of gossip exam-ined and dwelt on, there is one section of it, at least, which has been wholly neglected in American literary circles, in spite of the vitality and lustiness which it has been exhibiting on its own territory. I am referring to Yiddish literature, the literature of the two million American Jews who have not yet strayed from the cul-tural fold of their people. The Jews are paradoxical in more than one way, both actively and passively. They are ubiquitous, mix with all other peoples. You meet

them in every walk of life, even in church, yet their cul-tural life remains as much hidden from the view of the average American as the Buddhist gospel.

If the Yiddish literature of which I speak here were a foreign importation, its unfamiliarity at least could be understood. It so happens that American Yiddish litera-ture is, in a sense, flesh of America's flesh and bone of America's bone. Having been produced on American soil, even if it does not always portray American life, it must necessarily represent, in some degree, the Ameri-can viewpoint. Moreover, a large part of the younger Yiddish literature *does* depict American life and is even identified with American ideals. Epic poems like I. J. Schwartz's *Kentucky* and *George Washington* are surely part and parcel of American literature, even though they are composed in Yiddish. The line of cleavage between the American literature and the English seems to be a geographic demarcation and not a linguistic differentia-tion. When Raboy tells about life on the prairies, and Halperin apostrophizes the sidewalks of New York, they are essentially contributing to the literature of America in a language which is spoken in America.

The foreign elements of American literature (from the linguistic angle) have not yet been done justice to. Not only is it a desideratum to investigate the racial in-fluences of Dreiser and Mencken, Hergesheimer, Unter-meyer, Lewisohn and Benét, Kreymborg and Sandburg, but the very foreign adjuncts which have crept up in this country among the various racial units (German, Polish, Lithuanian, Italian) should receive at least a modicum of attention. Yiddish literature is superior in one respect to the other adjuncts in that it is no mere hangover or moribund survival of an established litera-ture in Europe, but is a full-fledged literature able to stand on its own feet and possibly leading in the world federation of Yiddish literatures, which extends from Soviet Russia to South Africa and from Canada to the Argentine.

Until very recently, Yiddish America still looked to Russia and Poland for its beacons. The three giants of Yiddish letters, Mendele, Sholem Aleikhem and Peretz, all died within two years of each other and all three dur-ing the World War. The epigones, Asch and Reisen, had already emigrated to America, where they served to magnify the galaxy of writers and poets that had already formed during the latter part of the nineteenth century.

Yiddish literature in America is scarcely fifty years old. Fifty years is certainly not a long period historically considered, only a generation and a half. In these five decades a powerful press has been established which numbers even today, with the tendency toward assimi-lation and the restriction in immigration, an array of half a million readers. Yiddish journalism, from the very beginning, found a fruitful soil in the United States, where the fugitives from Russian tyranny and persecution could both satisfy their craving for knowledge and at the same time learn from the articles in their newspapers how to ameliorate their economic condition.

The outsider little realizes how vast an edifice American Yiddish literature is. Not only does it comprise some hundred newspapers and periodicals, several hundred plays, collections of poetry by the scores, novels by the hundreds, but even a library of essays, scientific works, books of criticism, treatises on music (harmony), excellent memoirs, art—in short, all that goes to make up the literature of a cultured people.

It was in America that the first history of Yiddish literature was written, that the first history of the Yiddish theater was published, and, what is more, that the first adequate Yiddish translation of the Bible appeared, an undertaking of twenty years by the poet Yehoash, who, together with Morris Rosenfeld, dominated Yiddish poetry for a generation. In this connection, it is noteworthy that Yiddish poetry flourished in the United States more than anywhere else. The earlier tendentious notes of Edelstadt and Winchevski, which called the workingmen to combat for better social conditions and a more equitable economic system, gave way to the more lyric strains of the reflective Yehoash and the impassioned Rosenfeld, in whom the national tendency blended with the personal. Rosenfeld, too, complained of the sweatshop which prevented him from seeing his child awake, but he was no agitator. Among living Yiddish poets in America today, Leivick perhaps stands out because of the lofty conception of his *Golem,* a mystic play in verse, which has been rendered into English as well as into several other languages. This pillar of contemporary Yiddish literature, until his recent retreat to a sanitarium for tuberculosis, was compelled to work as a paperhanger for his daily bread.

The novel and the short story have not fared so well as poetry, strange as it may seem. With Asch residing in Paris, the number of good Yiddish fiction writers reduces itself to Opatoshu, Jonah Rosenfeld, Shapiro, and Raboy among the older men, and Chanukoff and Glassman among the younger set. David Pinski, whose reputation as a dramatist resounded far and wide in non-Jewish circles, has recently entered the domain of the novel, bringing out his *Noah Eden's Generations,* first as a serial in Yiddish and subsequently in book form in English. The book is a sort of *Forsyte Saga* on a restricted scale, but bristling with conflicts not only between the old and the new, but between two divergent civilizations in different parts of the world.

The Yiddish theater, founded about fifty-five years ago in Romania, flourished on the East Side more than anywhere else in Jewry because it served as an agency both for amusement and self-development, and furthermore its program was not impeded by oppressive government measures as in Russia or by the poverty of the masses. It was here that great actors like Jacob Adler, David Kessler, and Morrison began to thrive, and it was here that Jacob Gordin undertook to reform the Yiddish drama; but his productions were not American either in spirit or in content. Kobrin and Libin were the first to write on American Jewish subjects: life in the tenement houses of the lower East Side, problems between immigrant parents and the children weaned away from them by the environment. They were, and are still, the "presentialists," i.e., those who react to the present environment, as compared with Pinski, Hershbein, and others of a higher caliber who hark back to the past, in some cases the remote past.

When we ask ourselves whether the American Yiddish writer is more akin to the older Yiddish writer or to the non-Jewish American writer of today, we find the question difficult to answer. For the younger American Yiddish writer, the surroundings are distinctly American, the environment is a Jewish figuration against a multicolored American background, but the spirit, nonetheless, the conception, the Weltanschauung is rather Jewish—not that one can speak of an American or Jewish point of view of poetics, as if dealing with political parties, but rather in the sense that the composite picture of Yiddish writing and the synthetic makeup of American writings do not coincide. Yiddish fiction written in this country, let alone that of the Old Country, will not appear in *Liberty* or the *Saturday Evening Post.* Similarly, Yiddish readers, even of the less-educated classes, will not take a fancy to the stories printed in the average American magazine. At the same time, the American reader will read a translation of Chanukoff's *Submarine Z-1* without being aware that this is not a novel originally written by an American writer, a circumstance which is not possible with the works of the classical Yiddish writers.

The word *extinct* suggests the most vital question of all: what prospect is there of Yiddish literature surviving in the New World? This question has been posed and debated back and forth for more than a quarter of a century. Indeed, it was the author of the first history of Yiddish literature, Professor Wiener of Harvard, who prophesied its disappearance. It was long before there was any notion of restricting immigration and certainly when there was no anticipation of an economic debacle such as we are experiencing, that Wiener, with reference to the Yiddish theater in America, wrote: "It is very doubtful whether the Jewish theater can subsist in America another ten years" (*History of the Yiddish Literature in the Nineteenth Century*, p. 242).

A whole generation has passed since these words appeared in print in 1899. For two decades the gates of America had been practically closed to Yiddish-speaking newcomers, and to boot, within the last two years, the Yiddish theater, together with Broadway's White Way, has been undergoing a most critical period which bids fair to stifle the creative impulses of dramatic talent as well as the ambitions of producers, directors, and actors. With all these handicaps and drawbacks, both general and specific, it is estimated on the basis of actual box-office receipts that in the first half of the 1931–32 season alone, consisting of twenty weeks, the Yiddish-speaking public in greater New York paid over three-quarters of a million dollars in admission fees, which means that the receipts for the entire season would aggregate well over a million dollars in greater New York—only one, although of course the largest, Jewish center.

Prophets of doom are just as often wrong as prophets of boom and probably for the same reasons. Both see before them a regular slope, either uphill or downhill, and mistake the probable trend for an absolute certainty. Prophets of conditions involving human relations all too frequently are prompted by too much self-confidence and wishfulness, on the one hand, and too little knowledge of psychological laws and historical events on the other. When Professor Wiener predicted that 1909 would usher in the finale of the Yiddish theater, it was probably because he himself was preparing to bid adieu to Yiddish literature.

A. A. Roback

Ireland after Yeats [1952]

The story of Irish writing during the last fifty years falls into two parts: growth and decline. Though nobody could have observed it at the time, the causes for this decline began to operate immediately the Irish Free State was founded, in 1921. Their effects were, however, held at bay for a time by the continuing momentum of nationalist excitement persisting after the revolution was over. Seán O'Casey's plays illustrate this. His *Juno and the Paycock* was staged in 1924, and *The Plough and the Stars* in 1926, both of them dealing with the revolutionary period which was finished and done with. It is true that there was a theatre riot over the latter play, but nobody attached any special significance to it. If anything, one took it for a good omen. It was like the old

days of the *Playboy* riots. It promised a continuity of tradition. *Plus ça change,* we said, but we were wrong. It was not *la même chose.* There was a fundamental difference between the circumstances surrounding O'Casey and those surrounding Synge. One might build on the two riots a parable of the reasons for the latter-day decline in Irish writing.

In the old days—to keep, for the moment, to the example of the Theatre—an elite had been in the saddle. The whole of Yeats's outlook had been aristocratic though nationalistic, just as he had always been both European and Irish, or as excited by the *Axel* of Villiers de l'Isle Adam as by the peasant folktales of Biddy Early. He had said several times that his sort of theatre should be as hard to get into as a secret society. He liked small audiences. The poetic drama he admired could never have become popular, and insofar as the Abbey Theatre did become a popular or people's theatre, he felt that he had failed to create what he set out to create. So, he had always struggled against the popular taste for realistic drama; in spite of every inevitable concession to that taste, he dominated his ambiguous creation as a poet with a poet's ideals. This all began to change immediately a native government was established. The type of people who had, long ago, protested against Synge's *Playboy* had had no political power. The poeple who objected to O'Casey had political power. (It is to be remembered that the new Irish government decided to subsidise the Abbey Theatre; which at the time seemed to us all a splendid gesture—disillusion was to come slowly with the gradual realisation that when governments give money they receive influence in exchange.)

Moreover, in those "old days" the Catholic Church had had only a limited amount of political power, because the government had been an alien and non-Catholic government, and the foreign Gallio, like all proconsuls, had kept the ring with the tolerance of total indifference. Now the Church could wield almost unlimited power, becaused the native government was composed of men who respected, loved, and feared it. It is evident that the new intellectual atmosphere depended on the sophistication, cultivation, and tolerance of both the native government and the Church, the new elite. Unfortunately, centuries of oppression had bred in both not only a passionate desire for liberty but the antithesis of that natural desire. It had induced a nervy, sensitive, touchy, defensive-aggressive, on-guard mentality, as a result of which patriotism became infected by chauvinism and true religious feeling by puritanism. I imagine that I am describing something which happens commonly in all countries which have emerged from a revolutionary phase, and that it does not involve any special criticism of the Irish nature. (An intellectual

Jew in contemporary Palestine would probably nod his head in a clear understanding and sympathy if he were to read my summary.)

The simplest illustration of what happened was the establishment of a severe Literary Censorship, in 1929. Its aim was, and its aim no doubt still is, a blending of the moral and the patriotic: the desire to protect from corruption this infant nation born out of so much hardship. In a little over twenty years thousands of books have been banned as indecent or obscene. It will be noted that the reason for banning is not political; and it is social only insofar as books and periodicals are banned if they advocate, or advertise, contraception, abortion, or the artificial insemination of humans. Most of the books on the banned list are ephemeral, and their absence from the public libraries and bookshops is no loss; but there have been two particularly bad results for Irish literature: within a few years there was scarcely an Irish writer of distinction who had not, at least once, been declared the author of obscenity—and he was denied recourse to the courts of the land in self-defence. The worst feature of the Censorship, however, has been that with it there has arisen a private censorship all over the country in the form of a witch hunt which no librarian or bookseller could dare to resist by storing books objected to by these unofficial censors. Demos was in the saddle.[1]

To form a picture of this new intellectual atmosphere it is essential to grasp one other point. The revolution of 1916–21 had been a social revolution. This fact lifts the history of Irish writing over the past twenty-five years out of its apparently local setting and puts it in its proper place as part of a general world tendency. The idealists who inspired the people to rise against British rule were unaware of the social forces they were working with and releasing. In the nineteenth century these forces had been personified by the impoverished farming community in the Land League's fight for decent conditions of land tenure. In our day the social forces behind the last stage of the Irish Revolution were personified by the sons and daughters of those farmers—surplus children squeezed into the towns and cities and finding there that all the power and most of the wealth was in the hands of people of a different religion, racial origin, or political loyalty.

Seán O'Casey's plays are thus an exactly true statement of the Irish Revolution, whose flag should be, not the tricolour, but the plough and the stars of the labouring classes. We must, finally, understand that the class that thus came to power and influence was not a labouring class; the more able among them changed their nature by changing their place in life—they graduated rapidly into petit bourgeois, middlemen, importers,

small manufacturers, thus forming a new middle class to fill the vacuum formed by the departure or depression of the alien middle class. These men, naturally, had had very little education and could have only a slight interest in the intellectuals' fight for liberty of expression. They were ordinary, decent, kindly, self-seeking men who had no intention of jeopardising their mushroom-prosperity by gratuitous displays of moral courage. In any case, since they were rising to sudden wealth behind protective tariff walls, they had a vested interest in nationalism and even in isolationism. The upshot of it was a holy alliance between the Church, the new businessmen, and the politicians, all three nationalist-isolationist for, respectively, moral reasons, commercial reasons, and politico-patriotic reasons. The intellectuals became a depressed group. Possibly they were also infected by the atmosphere around them.

For completeness let us try to look sympathetically on the other side of the picture. Ireland is not a publishing country. All but a number of books, so few that it would be an exaggeration to call them a handful, are published abroad, apart from all primary-school texts and most secondary-school texts. Practically all our mental food is therefore imported: good food but not native. If there is such a thing as a racial Irish quality of life, it is very difficult for it to resist almost overwhelming external influences, since this local way of life is not equipped intellectually, and neither the Church nor the State is equipped intellectually, to support it. The intellectuals cry out for a bold, adventurous, and thorough system of popular education, but both the Church and the state fear the results. It is to be said that the Irish way of life, though poor, indeed impoverished as to institutions fit to represent it—e.g., publishing houses, periodicals, rich universities—is atavistically powerful, spiritually obstinate, strongly resistant, in a great many ways appealing; it represents precious and lovable qualities and is eminently worth preservation, provided it expresses itself in achievement and not merely in emotional declaration. The intellectuals' position is that it cannot and will not preserve itself by negative methods and that it is, in practice, being undermined and corrupted by a lack of moral and intellectual courage.

We can now look at Irish writing against this social, political, and religious background. First, the Theatre:

As we look back over the plays produced in the Abbey Theatre since World War I, we find that the Theatre was still lively almost up to 1932. (This suggests that the momentum of the revolutionary stimulus went on for some ten years.) The lists include first productions of plays by Lady Gregory, Brinsley MacNamara, Padraic Colum, Daniel Corkery, Shaw, Lord Dunsany,

Lennox Robinson, George Shiels, Seán O'Casey, T. C. Murray, Yeats, Wilde, Rutherford Mayne, Teresa Deevy, Denis Johnston, and Paul Vincent Carroll. Lady Gregory died in 1932. From then onward two or three plays of distinction were produced but no outstanding name is added to the list. In 1935 Yeats, who was aging and ailing, felt that the theatre needed younger men. His friend, the poet Frederick Robert Higgins, was appointed director; so was Frank O'Connor; and a significant name also appeared among the directors, an ex-cabinet minister, Mr. Ernest Blythe, a man with no experience of the drama. Mr. Hugh Hunt, now producer at the Old Vic Theatre, London, was brought in as producer, and from 1935 to 1938 the combination of Higgins, O'Connor, and Hunt gave the theatre a new and exciting spurt. It is of interest that in those three years the Abbey produced several non-Irish plays—including plays by Shakespeare, Flecker, Toller, Shaw, André Obey. Yeats died in 1939. O'Connor, feeling unable to cope with the influences of which he disapproved, resigned in 1939. Higgins died in 1941. Mr. Blythe became managing director. Thus, there remained on the board, to represent old tradition, only Mr. Lennox Robinson. Otherwise the bridge with the past was down.

Unless we imagine that literature exists in a vacuum, we must see what sort of official influences played on the Theatre at this period. I will give two examples. In 1932 when the Abbey Theatre visited the United States, the usual hyperpatriotic societies protested against some of the plays, including O'Casey's, and at home deputies were prompted to ask awkward questions in the Dail. In reply to one questioner, the prime minister, De Valera, said (26 April 1933) that the government had made indirect representations to the Abbey Theatre and that it was hoped that if the company visited America again, plays of the kind objected to by the American Irish would not be produced. In that year the official subsidy was reduced. In 1934 a similar angry question received a similar reply, De Valera then saying that such plays damage the good name of Ireland. Yeats stood his ground and was attacked bitterly by the popular press.

The second significant incident occurred in 1938, when the board of the Theatre decided that plays in the Irish language should henceforth become a regular feature of the work of the Theatre. This was a retrograde step artistically, however laudable from the patriotic point of view, since there happened to be no Gaelic-writing playwrights worth mentioning and most of the trained actors could not speak Gaelic. The result showed itself in 1942, when the government again interfered to ask the Theatre to take over the work of an existing company of Gaelic players called "An Comhar Dramuiochta" (The Drama Cooperative). With Yeats and Higgins dead and O'Connor gone, the board, now dominated by the ex-politician Mr. Blythe, decided that in the future no junior players would be employed unless they could speak Gaelic, an accomplishment which had about as much to do with acting as if they could dance the can-can. I record this incident solely to give the foreign reader an impression of the lowering of intellectual standards after Yeats.

Let us now try to define the precise effect on the arts. Fundamentally what had happened was that the social concept of the function of literature was beginning to replace the individualist concept. Compare Yeats, taking him as representative of the first twenty-five years of the Anglo-Irish revival. Yeats had loved all art that was remote and uncommon, "distinguished and lonely." He had seen the element of nobility in the simplest people, but he had never permitted his affection for familiar life to be confused with a preoccupation with the common or the popular. Thus, writing of the Theatre, he had said:

> The modern author, if he be a man of genius, is a solitary, he does not know the everchanging public well enough to be its servant. He cannot learn their convention; they must learn his. All that is greatest in modern literature is soliloquy, or, at most, words addressed to a few friends.

This dislike of realism had always been with him. He sought always to sublimate reality, and it was in that search for a dissolvent of the flesh that he had formed the distinction between Character, that is, the social, public, moral thing, formed by and for the purposes of organised society, and Personality, which is what appears in all the great moments of drama when this social, functional thing drops away and a man's spirit burns with a pure, gemlike flame. So, he had found inspiration in the ancient mind of his people, but it was not a political mind, or a social mind, but a mystical memory, linking man to those ages when life was still a unity, before he became fissured by rationalism and splintered by what we nowadays call psychological analysis.

The new, raw, ambitious, hardfaced democracy understood none of this. It is an aristocratic concept. It understood only realistic plays, political plays, representationalism, characterisation, explanations, social comedies and tragedies, preferably embodying what might be called the new synthetic orthodoxy, at least not diverging radically from it, not denying it, certainly not criticising or satirising it.[2] It is to the credit of some Irish playwrights resident in Ireland that they took the risks of criticism and satire, and it is to the credit of the Abbey Theatre, even in its decline, that it staged these plays. The risks were great and the penalties were severe: hardship, by disemployment or ostracism, or forced exile.

Still, there are even greater and deeper dangers in the writers' battle for honesty. The danger of becoming embittered or twisted threatens creativity itself, and here we come onto the real battleground of contemporary Irish writing. For the first time Irish writers have had to think—not just write—themselves into a personal release. Disillusion is also a form of revelation. There is no longer any question of dishing up local colour. The Noble Peasant is as dead as the Noble Savage. Poems about fairies and leprechauns, about misted lakes, old symbols of national longing, are over and done with. We have explored Irish life with an objectivity never hitherto applied to it, and in this Joyce rather than Yeats is our inspiration. To see clearly is not to write passionately, however. An artist must, in some fashion, love his material, and his material must, in some fashion, cooperate with him. It is not enough for an artist to be clinically interested in life: he must take fire from it. This has been the great rub in Ireland for some twenty years. It is not confined to Ireland. Everywhere today, as I see it, literature is facing the same problem: how to transmute into permanent forms a life that one sees critically rather than lovingly.

If this is really a universal problem, why is it so? I think it is because writers everywhere feel that life no longer has any sense of Pattern and Destination. The argosies set out. They forget why. I am not sure that I understand exactly what Flaubert meant when he said that the idea is born of the form, but I think it may have been something like this: that the pattern of any work is inherent in the subject as the artist sees it; that this fated movement of any subject in the creator's mind traces its parallel pattern on the page or the canvas. But if man is bewildered, insecure, faithless, how can his life suggest any pattern? Yeats's lines have almost become as near cliché as Gray's *Elegy,* they are so pat to our dilemma: "Things fall apart, the centre cannot hold. / Mere anarchy is loosed upon the world; / The blood-dimmed tide is loosed and everywhere / The ceremony of innocence is drowned." To give the most naïve example possible of Pattern and Destination, time was when novelists moved their men and women, with a sense of completion, toward a home and a family in love and marriage. Countless is the number of novels and plays shaped about the thwarting of this journey, writers still dare to play this old tune; but who cares? Yeats foretold this contemporary failure of Pattern and Destination when he said that life broke into a series of fragments between Chaucer and Shakespeare: a fissuration that has since broken us down to a series of complexes or

isolated receptivities. We play with mastery on a single string. I express my being, says a painter, with this picture of a saucepan; he expresses minute, if intense, portions of his being. The result is that men of genius have been writing as the matador kills bulls, by virtuosity or by savagery (Joyce, Hemingway, Anouilh, Aymé, Bazin, Julien Green), or they impose Pattern and Destination by sheer force: Lagerkvist by his symbolism, Malraux by his mysticism, Sartre by his existentialism, Bernanos, Greene, or Mauriac by their Catholicism, the later O'Casey by his communism. One must be lost in admiration of this forcible handling of intractable material, though one does sometimes wonder whether humanity has not emerged from their work literally manhandled, moulded to shape, intellectualised, not men but puppets. The regionalists are in the happier position. Faulkner may still find Pattern and Destination about him.

An Irish writer might expect to find old patterns persisting in his region also, but the dilemma has here taken a particularly sardonic form, very much the same form that it has taken in Soviet Russia. My countrymen are so satisfied with their Pattern that they have no interest in Destination. Everything having been solved, they have no further to go—except to Heaven. Like all peoples who have accepted a rigid ideology, they are frustrated by the completeness of their own conventions. The novel elsewhere may be frustrated by the certainties of men lost; here it is frustrated by the certainties of men saved. We read with an excited absorption the work of Catholic novelists elsewhere—that is, novelists who work within the frame of the struggle between God and the Devil, rather than the struggle of man with material evil or impersonal misfortune—and we observe that they deal with characters who are wilful, rebellious, passionate, arrogant, conscious, persistent, reckless. We turn, hopefully, to the potential material of Irish novels on the lines of Bernanos or Mauriac. We discover to our dismay that no error has been so great the popular conception of the Irishman as rebellious, passionate, reckless, wilful, and so on.

I may be permitted to give a personal illustration. About sixteen years ago (1935–36) I wrote a novel (*Bird Alone*) about a man who seduced a girl, who died in childbirth, and whom the seducer should, in his faith, believe damned. The probable effect on his life interested me. It was only necessary that the girl should sin once; it was necessary that she should sin only once—to underline the horror of the idea of eternal damnation for a single sin. It was with the greatest difficulty that I made it seem plausible that she should allow herself to be seduced at all, so powerful are the religious beliefs and social conventions of modern Ireland (I may add that the novel was banned as indecent.) It is obviously admirable from the religious point of view that this should be so; it is even splendid from the literary point of view, insofar as it means that this is a region in which sex does mean something. However, one cannot, it is equally obvious, get very far or achieve much variety of action with so strict a morality. We are, in effect, very much in the same position as Hawthorne, who managed to squeeze one great novel out of equally unmalleable material, in a society where, also, sin was furtive, revolt slight and brief, and convention rigid. As I have said, communist writers are in an identical straitjacket. The personalities of their dramatis personae are not free.

The Irish novelist who has been most successful, over the last twenty-five years, in mining for revolt and passion has been Liam O'Flaherty. He has found his passionate creatures in the west of Ireland and in the Revolution. His best-known novel, *The Informer* (1925), is just before our period; *The Assassin* (1928) is just within it, or *The Martyr* (1932); each deals with the same revolutionary upheaval, which was a god-send to all Irish writers until, as in the Theatre, the vein became exhausted around 1932, ten years after the Revolution ended. In that year O'Flaherty wrote *The Puritan,* a study of the new Irish rigorism, and thereafter he chose, with one exception, which was a failure, historical subjects. It is most revealing that all of O'Flaherty's work is shot through by a wild romanticism—to put it crudely, the romanticism of the Noble Savage. He had to write in this way to gear his people up to action.

I think my reader will have begun to realise the difficulties of writing in a country where the policeman and the priest are in a perpetual glow of satisfaction. He must, however, also see that, to a real extent, Irish novelists have failed to solve a problem. I will illustrate this problem by quoting the comment of an intelligent American critic on his first visit to Ireland. He said: "This seems to be a very prosperous, comfortable, well-to-do country. We do not get that picture from your writers. Why not?" His comment was, in every point, quite fair. I have failed to present an intelligible picture of contemporary Irish society—acquisitive, bourgeois, unsophisticated, intellectually conservative and unadventurous, rigidly controlled by a Church which is at once loved and feared—if the answer to that "Why not?" is not now apparent. I will underline it only by pointing out that the changeover from a stratified society—ranging from aristocrat to outcast—to a one-class society, where there are no native aristocrats and no outcasts, and where the hard, traditional core is in a farming population, rarely induces a fertile awareness either among its people or its writers. Even before the Revolution Irish writers—Joyce, Shaw, Wilde, dozens besides—felt this, insofar as our awareness was then all going down the drain of politics and nationalism, and left Ireland for the more interesting life of the island next door. It will be clear why the one prose-form which has flourished best during this quarter of a century is the short story. There are always small, revealing themes, rarely large ones.[3]

One other obstacle, and of all perhaps the most difficult to surmount, has come between the Irish writer, whether poet, dramatist, or novelist, and his normal material in Irish life. It may be expressed in the words of a younger Irish poet, Robert Graecen, in a poem significantly entitled "Written on the Sense of Isolation in Contemporary Ireland." Having called up the "unfettered great in heart and mind who gave no inch to fate"—Swift, Burke, Sheridan, Congreve, Goldsmith, Moore, and Yeats—he says: "Yet all of these the world for subject took / And wed the fearless thesis to their book." We have partly forgotten how to be, as Yeats was, European though nationalist. In some strange way all that revolutionary, nationalist period, self-absorbed as it was, gave to literary Ireland a world-sense, now lost. Whatever the cause, Irish writers, still tuning-in, as writers always do, to the intellectual stations of the world, do so now almost like men in an occupied country listening to forbidden voices. The writer who has the feel of the world rises from his grapevine excited by the sense of the world and turns to his page to write as he feels. But with what? With whom? What characters will act and speak fo rhim, in his poem, play, or novel? The dramatis personae are otherwise engaged. It is a story of an author in search of six characters. I feel this profoundly in contemporary Irish poetry. There is no loss of technical skill—if anything, a far greater verbal sophistication has arrived in Irish poetry over the last twenty-five years than existed previously. There is no decline in receptiveness. The later work of Austin Clarke, the poems of Patrick Kavanagh and Padraic Fallon, to name only three, show poetry just as much on tiptoe, ready for flight, as it ever was. All that is lacking is significant subject, and one rarely hears a modern idiom, a modern speech. (I find it in the tense poetry of W. R. Rodgers and in the hesitating rhythm of Valentin Iremonger.) The voltage of life is low. It suffices to illuminate the local. Beyond are shadows.

Only time, and its vicissitudes, will change all this, but men of genius accelerate the processes of time for their country, if (which is a challenging and often the most dismaying conjecture) they can cope with their country. The problem is up to the writers themselves. Nobody outside can help them; nobody inside will help them. They will not evade it be exile—Ibsen did not, and did not wish to. Nobody need pity them either, since by the grace of God and Oliver Cromwell their language is the English language, and if they have anything worth saying that they can say well, the periodicals and publishers of Britain and America are waiting for them with open arms and purses. If they feel that exile is necessary, they may, alone among the writers of the small countries of the world, emigrate freely. What they have to cope with is complex enough, but was there ever a writer whose life and work was plain sailing? Their main worry must be that their worse enemies are impalpable and insinuating: self-pity, bitterness, sentimentality, cynisicm, their own unsophistication, barren rage, even their love of country, their love of friends. (It was Ibsen who said that he had to leave Norway because friendship was too expensive: meaning that, for friendship's sake, one refrained from saying things that should be said.) It is improper for any critic to probe into these struggles. They are delicate, intimate, and fearful.

Seán O'Faoláin

[1] A typical list of Banned Books was published in February 1952. Eighty-nine books were banned. The greater number included cheap American importations of a popular nature, thrillers with sexy titles on the lines of *Make Mine a Virgin*. One Irish novelist was listed, Francis Stuart, for *Good Friday's Daughter*. The list also included: John Steinbeck's *Tortilla Flat*, Anita Loos's *A Mouse is Born*, André Gide's *Les nourritures terrestres*, Carson McCuller's *Reflections in a Golden Eye*. There has been, for some years, an Appeal Board which has unbanned a small proportion of books. They are usually out-of-print by the time they are unbanned. The Censorship Board is immune from legal action. In any case, writers have no money for prolonged action against the State.

[2] So, O'Casey's early plays are now enormously popular in Ireland—but, I fear, for reasons that do little justice to his passion and his poetry. His later plays make little appeal.

[3] The main novelists of the last twenty-five years have been: Liam O'Flaherty, Francis Stuart, Austin Clarke, Kate O'Brien, Peader O'Donnell, Norah Hoult, Elizabeth Connor, Frank O'Connor, Lord Dunsany, Walter Macken, Benedict Kiely, Francis McManus, Mervyn Wall, Joseph Tomelty, Sam Hanna Bell. The writer of this article has published three novels.

English Canadian Literature, 1929–1954 [1955]

Canada is such a huge and sprawling country that only a tremendous effort of will has made and kept it a single environmental unit. It has a prodigious interior but almost no coastline, and hence has had nothing to correspond to the Atlantic seaboard culture of the United States. It has the handicap of two languages; it has an almost uninhabited wilderness in northern Ontario sep-

arating the East from the West; and it exists in practically one dimension, like a bigger Chile. With all this, its primary problems of communication have long overshadowed the secondary ones connected with culture and literary expression. Up to World War I, English Canada was a scattered series of British colonies, of which only those close to Toronto and Montréal could get far enough above the cultural subsistence level to keep a literary output going. After 1918 the colonial phase of Canadian culture began to give way to a more distinctive growth, in which the pioneering art was landscape painting. American influences slowly began to appear beside British ones, and both in the prosperity of the twenties and the depression of the thirties English Canadian culture began to assume the appearance of northern spurs of the United States—the Maritimes of New England, Ontario of the Great Lakes region, the Canadian West and Pacific coast of their American counterparts.

With World War II a tremendous growth of industry, the rise of air transport, and the exploiting of natural resources deep in the North brought about a further change in the Canadian spirit. Since 1812 the most dangerous enemy of Canada was been not a foreign invader but its own geography, and with the overcoming of this the feeling of expectancy about Canadian culture has been given a new concreteness and immediacy. Canadian intellectuals have always been, for the most part, cultural nationalists, fostering a Messianic hope that something of major importance is just about to happen in Canada, but they have never been more so than at present.

The foregoing may help to explain a fact that might otherwise puzzle an outsider. During the past twenty-five years the most impressive literary achievements in English Canada have not been in the imaginative fields, but in scholarship. The bulk of this scholarship has been Canadian in reference. Canadian history and the new techniques of study provided by the social sciences constitute a scholarly basic industry in Canada, paralleling the rise of "American civilization" studies across the border. Similarly, Canadian critics no longer contribute essays to small periodicals under the title "Is There a Canadian Literature?" The question itself may be as relevant as ever, but whatever the answer, Canadian poems and short stories are anthologized and literary histories and bibliographies are appearing, along with some critical monographs. The best of the latter are E. K. Brown's *On Canadian Poetry* (1944) and W. E. Collin's *White Savannahs* (1936); the most recent history of Canadian literature is Desmond Pacey's *Creative Writing in Canada* (1952); an exhaustive annual survey, including French and other languages, has been provided by "Letters in

Canada," in the April issue of the *University of Toronto Quarterly,* since 1935. Tentative beginnings toward Canadian literature courses have been made in universities. As yet, all this activity is largely sociological: Canadian culture is studied because it is the actual cultural environment, not because it presents cultural phenomena of worldwide importance; but if such phenomena do appear—and the argument that a country with such pulpwood resources must produce great literature sooner or later is probably quite a sound one—a critical and scholarly apparatus has been set up which is ready to receive it.

English Canadian poetry up to 1929 was dominated by what had then become the clichés of English romantic and Victorian poetry. Apart from Whitman, there was little American influence, and the American poetic renaissance that began around 1912 was unfelt in Canada for a long time. The most strikingly original of Canadian poets, E. J. Pratt, began his productive career in the twenties, somewhat late in life. A Newfoundlander by birth, he chose the unfashionable heroic narrative for his medium and tales of shipwreck, whale hunts, and extravagant maritime fantasy for his themes. The narrative has always been a favorite form of expression in Canada, but Pratt gave it zest and bounce, a humor and a hyperbole that were all his own. In a series of poems climaxed by *The Titanic* (1935) and *Bréboeuf and His Brethren* (1940), he established himself as the dominating personality in Canadian poetry and as almost the only important connecting link between the old school and the newer writers. His *Collected Poems* appeared in the United States and Canada in 1944, and little that is essentially new in his work has succeeded it. His later position as a sort of unofficial Canadian poet laureate, devoting himself mainly to themes of national heroism, has not been an unmixed blessing for his purely poetic reputation; but in few parts of the world today can we find a poet so genuinely popular, in the classical and uncondescending sense of the word, as Pratt is in Canada.

In the year 1936 a small and somewhat belated publication entitled *New Provinces* indicated the rise of a new group of poets representing more international influences and showing less of the poetry of facile romantic and patriotic formulas that had come to be called the "maple leaf school." The contributors to this volume included Pratt himself (in a new, quieter, and more subtle lyrical vein), Leo Kennedy, A. J. M. Smith, A. M. Klein, F. R. Scott, and Robert Finch. Leo Kennedy, whose *Shrouding* (1932) was one of the most remarkable volumes of poetry in the period, gave an original turn to the wasteland and death-and-resurrection themes popularized by Eliot but has unfortunately written little poetry in recent years. A. J. M. Smith, who has also published very little since his *News of the Phoenix* (1943), showed the influence of metaphysical poets, the later Yeats, and an attraction to what he called, in a phrase his critics were quick to seize on, "difficult, lonely music." Abraham Klein has been declared to be the finest Jewish poet of the century, and his *Hath Not a Jew* (1940) and *Hitleriad* (1944) are full of the rabbinical spirit of erudition, humor, kindliness, and charity under pathological and meaningless hatred. He refused, however, to settle into this ethnical mould, and *The Rocking Chair* (1948) is full of brilliant and sympathetic studies of French Canada, some of them written in a curious bilingual vocabulary which is one of the liveliest poetic experiments yet made in the country. F. R. Scott, whose *Overture* appeared in 1945, is more politically minded; his poems combine a sharp social awareness with a kind of intellectual austerity that is difficult to characterize. Robert Finch, a professor of French, has brought some of the discipline of *symbolisme* to his *Poems* (1946) and *The Strength of the Hills* (1948). All of the above except Kennedy, and including Pratt, are university professors, mainly at Toronto and McGill, and are actively engaged in criticism as well. *A Book of Canadian Poetry* (1943) compiled by A. J. M. Smith is the best and most scholarly anthology of Canadian poetry. Klein has published a strange symbolic novel called *The Second Scroll* (1951), a tale of modern Zionism, and is now engaged in what seems a definitive critique of Joyce's *Ulysses.*

Of those who belong to the New Provinces generation, though not to their group, the most notable are two British Columbia poets, Dorothy Livesay and Earle Birney. The former was, during the thirties, the Canadian poet most deeply touched by the moral and political challenges presented by the rise of fascism and the Spanish Civil War. The latter has in some respects followed the Pratt tradition, both in his frequent use of the narrative genre, as in his remarkable poem *David* (1942), and in his attraction to national themes, though he makes much more use of satire than Pratt. *Now Is Time* (1945), *The Straits of Anian* (1948), and *Trial of a City* (1952) are his later volumes of poetry; he has also published a novel, a war satire in the picaresque tradition called *Turvey* (1949). Louis Mackay, who has also lived in British Columbia, has, in *Viper's Bugloss* (1938) and *The Ill-Tempered Lover* (1948), produced some of the best verse satire and some of the most beautiful "anthology pieces" in Canadian poetry.

In a still later group, Patrick Anderson has shown, in *The White Centre* (1946) and *The Color as Naked* (1953), a gift for pastoral lyric somewhat akin to that of Dylan Thomas, who has, of course, influenced him.

In Douglas LePan's collections *The Wounded Prince* (1948) and *The Net and the Sword* (1953) the tone is more romantic and elegiac and the chief influence Eliot; the earlier book deals with the Canadian landscape and the later one with the Italian campaign, in which the poet served. Louis Dudek is the center of an active Montréal group of poets whose main interests are social and realistic, though his *East of the City* (1946) still represents his best work. The most gifted, subtle, and technically expert of all the younger Canadian poets, Margaret Avison, has appeared in *Poetry* and elsewhere, but her work has not yet been published in a single volume.

In drama there is less to report; there has been an extraordinary amount of dramatic activity, but the number of good, indigenous stage dramatists is very small. In the earlier period the most serious dramatist was Gwen Pharis, who lives in Alberta and whose plays, the best of which are perhaps *Still Stands the House* (1938), *Dark Harvest* (1939), and *Stampede* (1946), usually have a Western setting. More recently Robertson Davies, an Ontario essayist and newspaper editor, has given us in *Fortune My Foe* (1948), *Eros at Breakfast* (1949), and *At My Heart's Core* (1950), the last on the 1837 Rebellion, a series of lively topical plays with unusually literate and urbane dialogue. John Coulter is perhaps more an Irish than a Canadian dramatist, except for a play on the Riel Rebellion (1950), which may well be his best work.

Every aspect of Canadian culture has been affected by the enormously beneficent influence of the Canadian Broadcasting Corporation. However one may criticize the CBC in detail, there is no reasonable doubt that without the steady employment it has given to writers, actors, musicians, and composers, and without its consistent efforts to guide as well as reflect popular taste, Canadian culture would be in a desperate state. American influences are frequently decried in Canada: this is not the result of any chauvinistic or anti-American feeling but arises from the simple perception that Canada's position is such that it gets, culturally, all the disadvantages of being so close to the United States without sharing in the important compensations. The CBC is one of the major defenses behind which a Canadian culture can survive; and nowhere has the radio been so important as in the field of drama. Len Peterson, Lister Sinclair, Tommy Tweed, Bernie Braden, Joseph Schull, and Graham Ferguson are a few whose names are household words in Canada and who have provided a consistently superior brand of radio drama in every genre. Dorothy Livesay's *Call My People Home* (1950) and Earle Birney's brilliant fantasy *Trial of a City* (1952) are poetic dramas written for radio. The radio has exploited and publicized the narrative talents of Pratt also, and through its poetry readings it has not only increased the audience of younger poets but encouraged them to think in less involuted terms than they might do if their communication were confined to the printed page.

In the field of fiction the short stories represent, on the whole, a higher level of competence than the novel. Here again we have to recognize the influence of the radio as a medium for reading stories aloud. Two good collections are Desmond Pacey's anthology *A Book of Canadian Short Stories* (1949) and *Canadian Short Stories,* edited by Robert Weaver and Helen James (1952). The former is historical and comprehensive, but most of the stories belong to the last twenty-five years; the editors of the latter are CBC producers, and the stories in their book were written for radio.

The Canadian novelist who is perhaps best known outside Canada is Mazo de la Roche, whose long "Jalna" series of stories began in 1927. The formidable family with which these books deal is well representative of the colonial phase of Canadian development and of the ability of well-to-do families during that phase to live apart from, and almost in defiance of, the real life of the nation around them. There are not many other good popular novelists. There is in Canada, as elsewhere, a voluminous romance factory turning out historical tales of all sorts and periods: tales of the French and Indian wars, of the early days in Québec, of pioneer life in Ontario, of adventure in the far North, of the intricate relationships between Canadian fauna and the nature-faker. Occasionally a historical novel of genuine literary merit turns up—an example is Thomas Raddall's *His Majesty's Yankees* (1942)—but the bulk of such work consists of antiquarian information on filing cards interspersed with erotic stimuli. The serious novel in Canada is therefore frequently marked by a militant realism, an emphatic underlining of the contemporary relevance of the theme.

The most impressive figure in Canadian fiction before 1929 was Frederick Philip Grove, who produced some extraordinary descriptive writing and some rather more maladroit fiction, mostly with a Western setting. His fame was obscured by an innocence of the world which bordered on perversity—it is said that he would have been the pioneer of naturalistic fiction, antedating even Dreiser, if he had understood the prejudice of publishers against huge manuscripts handwritten on both sides of the page. After 1929 he lived in Ontario, and his novel *Two Generations* (1939) has an Ontario setting. His last work was the awkward, unsuccessful, yet haunting powerful allegorical fantasy *The Master of the Mill* (1944).

Fiction of the prairies has manifested a number of lively and readable variations on what used to be profanely called the "no fun on the farm" formula. Frederick Niven, a writer of brilliant promise, used both Canadian and Scottish settings; his *Story of Their Days* (1939) is one of his best works. Edward McCourt's *Music at the Close* (1947) and *Home Is the Stranger* (1950) and W. O. Mitchell's remarkable *Who Has Seen the Wind* (1947) also belong to the West, as does Henry Kreisel's *Rich Man* (1948), which has a Viennese setting and is generally an expertly turned German *Novelle* written in English. In British Columbia, Ethel Wilson, by virtue of *Hetty Dorval* (1947), *The Innocent Traveller* (1949), and *The Equations of Love* (1952), is the leading fiction writer. She is less a "Canadian novelist" than a very good writer who happens to live in Canada and is better known outside the country than in it. Roderick Haig-Brown's *On the Highest Hill* (1949) records an unusually sensitive and intimate communion with nature, and the famous British Columbia painter Emily Carr produced in *Klee Wyck* (1941) the best collection of essays and descriptive pieces that appeared in Canada during the period under review.

In the east, Morley Callaghan had by 1929 established himself as perhaps the best short-story writer in Canadian fiction; a collection of his stories, under the title *Now That April's Here* (1936), is still representative of his best work. He has been less consistently successful in the novel, although *Such Is My Beloved* (1934), *They Shall Inherit the Earth* (1935), and *More Joy in Heaven* (1937) are head and shoulders above anything contemporary with them in Canadian writing. After a long silence, Callaghan returned to the novel in a half-symbolic, half-realistic tale of mean streats in Montréal, *The Loved and the Lost* (1951), a work of impressive if not wholly realized strength. Hugh Maclennan, a Maritimer, began his career with a lively story of the Halifax explosion, *Barometer Rising* (1941), and followed it with a more ambitious study of religious and cultural conflicts between English and French in Québec, *Two Solitudes* (1945), one of the most deeply interesting of Canadian novels for Canadian readers. A similar conflict between Jew and gentile in Montréal forms the theme of Gwethalyn Graham's *Earth and High Heaven* (1944), and the conflict of white and half-breed the theme of Christine van der Mark's *In Due Season* (1947). Other excellent one-shot novels are Selwyn Dewdney's *Wind without Rain* (1946), a story of the totalitarian trends in education that masquerade as progressive, and Ernest Buckler's violent and somber tale of Nova Scotia, *The Mountain and the Valley* (1953). Of war novels, among the best are Ralph Allen's *Home Made Banners* (1946) and Hugh Garner's *Storm Below* (1949). The latter's *Yellow Sweater* is perhaps the most distinguished one-man collection of short stories since the Callaghan book referred to above.

As the above catalogue implies, there is much eloquent and intelligent writing going on in Canada, without anything as yet having achieved the kind of greatness that would raise a different set of standards altogether. English Canada offers the writer a restricted market but a maximum of recognition within it, along with the opportunity to expand into the whole English-reading world. Canada's possessive attitude to its literature is frankly provincial, but the assumption that such provincialism is always and everywhere wrong is merely an assumption based on a different kind of provincialism. It would be wrong if it tried to limit the variety of Canadian writing to a few acceptable formulas; there is something of this in Canada, but the philistine resistance to imaginative literature seems to be gradually weakening. The result is a body of work which is partly a miscellany with no definite characteristics, except that it happens to be Canadian by one definition or another of that word, and partly the expression of a recognizable type of English literature which is steadily growing in articulateness and power.

Northrop Frye

The Modern Renaissance of Arabic Literature [1955]

To appreciate the true worth—and it is not at all negligible—of the renaissance of Arabic literature during the last quarter of a century, we must first make certain observations which bring themselves to our attention. They all go back to the many difficulties which for a long time prevented this literature from freely reaching its full scope. If we consider that it begins about 1925, we must state at once those obstacles which, for centuries, hindered the flowering of Arabic letters. They are of two kinds. The first are internal; they are concerned with an inherent difficulty of Arabic literature which, weighted down with a tradition more than a thousand years old, could not throw off the heavy burden of its complex heritage.

First, there was the pre-Islamic tradition: it imposed its imperious tyranny on every man of letters, be he prose writer or poet. Indeed, to be really literary an Arabic text had to have more or less the flavor of the desert, as much from the point of view of content as of form. Something of Bedouin nostalgia had to permeate every poem; a vague "something" had to be felt through everything written in prose; and the poetic forms which the Arabs learned toward the sixth century of the Christian era had to be respected. The slightest deviation was severely condemned. Not that several poets did not try sometimes to move away timidly from these desert forms; but they found that they always had to come back to them, take up the beaten path, and follow what the ancient critics called "the traditional column of poetry." Prose itself has developed only within a very rigid framework. It is known only through books of history, literary criticism, science, and philosophy; it lives too, thanks to certain translations from Hindu or Persian wisdom, thanks to epistolary literature, and thanks to what one might call official literature: decrees, proclamations, and discourses of the caliphs. Yet short stories, novelettes, even the saga novel were considered as belonging to the domain of popular literature, which had nothing in common with genuine classical literature, the only kind worthy of interesting the intellectuals— that is to say, people of good taste.

The second difficulty, no less despotic, is, however, of an external character. I would like to call it the "Hellenistic difficulty." It was induced by the translation into Arabic, during the course of the eighth and ninth centuries, of the philosophy of Aristotle, but particularly by the translation of his *Rhetoric*. This work quickly familiarized the Arabs with the famous *fleurs,* artificial figures, and verbal ornamentation. That is, as time went on, poets and prose writers rivaled in the creation of a literature where the classicism of the desert and Greek rhetoric were more or less harmoniously wedded.

There remains a third and last difficulty, likewise of an external nature: the stagnation imposed upon the whole Arabic world by the Turkish-Ottoman domination. Indeed, for several centuries all relations between the Arab world and the outside world were cut off. Iraqis, Syrians, Lebanese, and Egyptians were obliged to fall back upon themselves and be content with the heritage that they had received, without any hope of renewal. Their literature became formal and lost practically all its vigor. It was not until the nineteenth century that contact was reinstated between this closed world and the Occident, and this communication was finally to bring a breath of fresh air into the too-long closed world of Arabic literature.

There is still one other obstacle to be pointed out which is really neither internal nor external. It is difficult to define. I mean the restraints caused by a religion badly understood by people long condemned to ignorance and withdrawn into gross conservatism. People believed, a little naïvely, that the Arabic language, since it was the language of the Koran, was a sacred language. Now, a sacred language controls those who speak it and leaves little liberty to those who make use of it. It becomes forbidden to invent. Therefore the Arabs, instead of using their language, became its docile slaves. All innovation in expression was looked upon with a prejudiced eye and labeled near-heresy.

That, then, is the heritage left to the generation of the end of the last century and the beginning of this one. Indeed, an Arabic language existed, but it was paralyzed; there was still an Arabic literature, but it was enslaved. This generation had the gigantic task of liberating language and literature from their heavy chains. It was engaged in doing so during the first quarter of this century. Its work was not easy, and the political circumstances made it still more arduous. It was not until the victory of the Allies in 1918 that first Egypt, then the other Arab nations, recovered a little of their personality. Ottoman Turkey had just been conquered: its domination over the Arabic world came definitely to a close. On their side, the Allies had made fine promises to the Arabic peoples—too many, really, for them ever to be able to keep them all; but at the time of the victory the Arabs took these Western commitments very seriously, for they certainly did not intend to be freed from Ottoman slavery to fall under English rule in Iraq and Egypt or French rule in Syria and Lebanon.

Also, we were going to witness a double struggle, begun in Egypt. From 1919 until today the Arabic nations have fought in the political arena to obtain their complete independence, and they are likewise engaged in an intellectual battle to shake off the stifling traditions and the old prejudices. The story of this spiritual freedom is, then, closely linked with that of physical liberation.

It was on the morrow of the Armistice of 1918 that Egypt began the struggle, and the other Arab countries followed. The Egyptian impetus was of importance: the breath of revolution animated the Egyptians, men and women, young and old. Everyone was proud to fight against the formidable British Empire, which had just conquered Germany and Austria-Hungary in Europe, Turkey in Asia. The Egyptian people, in order to win their independence, agreed to enormous sacrifices and smilingly accepted British repression. However, in the wake of that revolt against foreign domination, another kind of reaction was born and developed rather rapidly to attain its first objective: I mean that revolution of the mind which soon secured liberty of thought and expression. In reality, parallel to the armed uprising against political oppression, a rebellion spread out against a long past laden with medieval traditions as irritating as military violence.

The first phase of this battle took place in 1920–21. A bitter argument began between young partisans of innovations in the domain of literature in particular and more generally in the things of the spirit, and the old conservatives, partisans of literary as well as religious tradition. The former maintained that the Arabic language should be considered like the other living languages—that is to say, as the servant of those who used it and not like a despotic mistress. Also, they assumed the prerogative of creating new words, ones that were not found in the dictionaries, and of adopting from the current dialect terms which were more suitable to their new manner of expression, even of borrowing from Occidental languages a certain number of terms which had no equivalent in the traditional Arabic language. They declared, then, that living in the twentieth century, it was right that they should express themselves and that they should think according to their period and no longer according to bygone times.

The struggle in which they engaged was difficult; it was above all impassioned, and for several years the Arab world was absorbed in this great quarrel between the Ancients and the Moderns, which was reminiscent of that which stirred French intellectuals at the end of the seventeenth century and the beginning of the eighteenth. Naturally, this quarrel soon crossed the borders of Egypt, where it had begun, and inflamed the whole Near East. Mustapha Al-Raf'l, Ahmad Al-Sakandari, and their disciples labored in vain to defend the Ancients. Victory belonged, according to the nature of things, to the spirited partisans of the Moderns; 'Abbas Al-'Akkad, Ibrahim Al-Mazni, Hessein Heikal, Salama Mussa, and Taha Hussein won over to their cause not only all the youth of that day, but also some old poets who undertook, after the revolution, a complete renovation of their technique.

So it is that our great Chawki, official court poet in his youth, completely renounced his first manner from then on. He became modern and, in company with Hafez Ibrahim and Khalil Mutran, became the precentor of the national movement in Egypt as well as in the other Arab nations. Chawki went even further; not content with celebrating in his verse the Egyptian Revolution and the Arab liberation, he wanted also to praise the Turkish Kemalist movement, and I do not think that the Turks themselves have praised their victory in Asia Minor more highly than the Egyptian poet did. Moreover, Chawki introduced into Arabic literature a genre that it did not know until then: the drama in verse. It was in the ancient history of his country that he first found his dramatic subjects. He chose Cambyses, for example, because the invasion of the Persians permitted him to make the glorious resistance of Egypt to foreign armies live again. He also composed an "Antony and Cleopatra," which sets forth Egyptian nationalism against a conquering Rome; but he knew also how to draw from the ancient history of the Arabs: *Madjnun*

Laïla (The Madman of Laïla) evokes the Arab empire at the height of its glory, when it imposed its peace upon the ancient world, thus permitting citizens to devote themselves to a life of leisure and praise of the passionate mysticism of platonic love.

There was not only Chawki and poetry. An extraordinary renovation manifested itself in all branches of classical Arabic literature. To analyze that real "rebirth" of Arabic letters, which occurred almost suddenly in the years 1920–30, it would be necessary first to point out the principal causes. They are three in number. In the first place must be mentioned that reaction against what was foreign, a reaction which resulted in liberating minds and consciences. Then came the publication, thanks to the progress and amazing extension of printing, of classical works of the true Arab period. Finally, one must not underestimate the influence of the translation into Arabic of the great masterpieces of foreign literatures, notably French and English. Doubtless, it is only justice to remark that the printing of ancient books and the translation of Western works had begun and had been increasing since the middle of the nineteenth century. Nevertheless, it must be emphasized that they yielded their finest fruits only after the Arabs secured that requisite to the existence of all literature: physical and moral liberty.

In 1923 the first Egyptian constitution was promulgated. It guaranteed, among other things, liberty of thought, expression, and assembly. Thus it is that the history of Arabic literature from this moment, particularly in Egypt, exactly coincides with the history of Arab liberty. . . . Two incidents, one involving 'Ali 'Abdel-Razek's book "Islam and the Principles of Power" and the other my own study, "Pre-Islamic Poetry," resulted in encouraging the Egyptian intellectuals, especially writers, to claim a greater liberty of thought as well as of expression. No censorship ought to be imposed upon them. They should not be exposed to annoying reactions from anyone. These Egyptian intellectuals knew indeed that liberty is not granted but won. That is why they undertook then to attack on all fronts, regardless of whether they were political, social, literary, moral. They finally won. Moreover, they now gained the support of the readers, who were at first most obstinate, and their public grew from day to day. So it happened that after a few years, the ideas of 'Abdel-Razek and myself, which were fought against so strongly, became classic, so to speak; they are generally accepted now. No Egyptian of today—and I would go so far as to say no Arab—thinks seriously of the reestablishment of the caliphate; and wherever classical Arabic literature is taught, the authenticity of "pre-Islamic" poetry is considered questionable.

The twelve years that followed World War I were prolific years. Everybody seemed drunk with liberty, and each tried to prove to himself and to show others that he was free. So-called "vulgar" speech also experienced a new vigor and especially in Egypt was given such an impetus that a whole literature written in colloquial language became abundant. People who scarcely knew how to read and write began to compose verse in current speech; they told of the renter's hate, their enthusiasm for an independence finally within their grasp, their admiration for the leaders exiled by the British or even put in prison in Egypt; or else they criticized the ministers who deserved it, and some of them had no fear of loosing satiric thrusts at the king and his court. Thus a new genre found its place in popular literature: satire, the pamphlet, and the lampoon enjoyed more favor with the public at large than these same literary forms in the classical domain; and thanks to the satiric comedy, many spectators laughed every evening at the expense of the occupying English and the men in power. Later, when spirits were more calm, this theater evolved and was transformed into social satire, which rendered important services in stimulating a national conscience, sometimes a little numbed, and in pointing out certain vices and wretchedness; but its principal value was to dazzle the eyes of the Egyptians with a vast program of reforms and a whole ideal of social justice not yet dreamed of but never again forgotten. On the one hand, consequently, the intellectuals who expressed themselves in a classical fashion moved the enlightened class of Arab society by their books, their poems, their novels, their articles; on the other hand, those of popular talent who made use of their dialects stirred the simplest hearts by their poems, their songs, and periodicals anyone could buy. There were not only the quasi-illiterates to be thus reached: the intellectuals themselves were interested to the point that about 1928–30 it was feared in the Arab world that there might be two literatures: the first, classical but renewed; the second, popular, more expressive, and more suitable for moving people.

Even a few classical writers almost went over to popular literature, and it is in this light that we see our great novelist and short-story writer Mahmud Teymour begin to write stories in the common tongue. That was not all; after the Congress of Orientalists held at Oxford in 1928, we witnessed a scientific defense of popular speech. Fortunately, as soon as Egypt had made a start toward independence and was consequently engaged in problems of public instruction, she exerted praiseworthy efforts to extend education as much as possible. About this time she created thousands of primary schools and hundreds of secondary schools, and thanks

to this double undertaking classical Arabic could predominate.

We have just seen that these twelve years were largely given over to two important quarrels: first, the one that can be called "The Quarrel of the Ancients and the Moderns"; later, the one which arose between the partisans of the popular language and the defenders of the classical language. Things could not remain in that state. Some time later a third quarrel arose; it brought into conflict only the classical writers, one against the other. This dispute was of long duration, and fortunately it was finally recognized that it was vain and sterile. In it the champions of French literature opposed the supporters of Anglo-Saxon letters. Indeed, until then the Arabs in general and the Egyptians in particular cultivated only these two literatures for the good reason that only the English and French languages were then taught in the schools; and naturally those who knew one of these two literatures, often to the detriment of the other, gave that one the preference and did all they could to aid in its expansion. Neither side stopped with writing polemics; they tried to make the great masterpieces of these two important literatures known by means of translations or studies. However, there were Egyptians who went to Germany and Italy, and they introduced Goethe and Dante to the Orient. They even translated Tolstoy and Dostoevsky into Arabic, and it is then that we understood that a country which wanted to be really free must not give her spirit solely to one rather than to another of the numerous foreign literatures. Quite to the contrary, this country ought to welcome all forms of civilization and culture, lend itself to absorbing all literatures and all ideas, wherever they may come from.

Just at this point these Egyptians began to demand the teaching of the principal foreign languages in the schools. In addition, the creation in 1926 of the first large university in Cairo (there are two today) implied that the teaching of the two classical languages, Greek and Latin, was indispensable for all real culture. The student body was in that way put in contact with two essential literatures. It was not long before some translations of Greek works into Arabic were published, thus tying up again with the medieval Arabic tradition. I translated Sophocles, and *Antigone* and *Oedipus* were played in Cairo. Then the rising generation understood that not only living languages and literatures were worthy of interest, but that there were likewise among the Ancients, Greek or Roman, things which, just like the Arabic culture of antiquity, were worthy of attention and of careful cultivation.

The founding of the University of Cairo also brought the young people into contact with professors who came from almost all the nations of Europe. Egypt, in reality, in order to enrich the staffs of its new faculties, called upon French, English, Belgian, Swiss, German, and Italian scholars as well as Austrian, Russian, Spanish, Dutch, and Swedish. The result of this intelligent planning policy was that many Egyptian minds were broadened by contact with these exchanges from the West and that, finally emerging from its too-long solitude, our country could meet on its own territory intellectuals and scholars of the entire world. This imperative need for universalism did not stop there. Egypt sent her children to further or complete their higher studies first in Europe, then more and more students crossed the Atlantic to finish their work in America. By so doing, Egypt (and other countries of the Middle East followed her example) established solid cultural relations with Europe and the New World. They continue to grow stronger and to bear encouraging fruits. Egypt did more; at the same time she opened her schools and her universities to the pupils and students of the Oriental world, from Morocco to China, and she sent her own teachers to teach in all the Arabic countries of the East. In this way, Egypt reestablished her historic mission: to serve as a bridge between the East and the West, a spiritual vocation which the Ottoman Conquest first, then the British Occupation, had tried to stifle. Thanks to Egypt, the whole Arab world, until then open to the politics and economy of the West, assimilated also its culture. The role assumed by Egypt deserves to be emphasized, for it has not ceased to have a considerable influence on the Arab literature of these last twenty-five years.

To complete, in so far as it possible, this brief picture of foreign contributions to Arabic literature, one must mention a phenomenon which concerns Syria and Lebanon exclusively. It is the Syro-Lebanese immigration to America, notably South America. This goes back to a former period, it is true, before the time which concerns us; however, these Eastern immigrants who settled more or less permanently in that part of the New World certainly did not forget their mother tongue. On the contrary, they preserved it jealously, and some of them devoted themselves to literature. Doubtless they were strongly affected by the American physical and social influences; they made, in any case, an important contribution, in verse as well as in prose, very different from that which was written in the countries of their origin, both in form and content. In fact, these writers of the immigration attacked in their works metaphysical problems to which the writers and poets of the Arabic Orient no longer hardly paid any attention. When one reads Gibran Khalil Gibran, Amin Al-Rihani, or Fawzi Al-Ma'louf, one feels a little expatriated, their thought

seems so much fashioned in the mold of the American concepts which surround them. The form, also, which they use seems to have undergone a foreign imprint; so one frequently sees the writers and poets doing violence to the Arabic language and breaking more or less with the classic traditions; often also they set aside the rules of grammar. Nevertheless, thanks to the renaissance of literature in the East and to the shortening of distances, these émigré writers find themselves more and more in close communication with the country of their origin, with the literary works which are published there. So they cannot fail to return to the essentials of the general character of modern Oriental Arabic literature.

These permanent and close contacts of Egypt and the Arab world with the contemporary universe have had marvelous results. Arabic literature had to renew itself and harmonize itself, so to speak, with literature as such, and that is the real miracle which the generation of the last twenty-five years succeeded in accomplishing. It is enough, in fact, to compare the acquisitions of Arabic literature of today with the products of traditional Arabic literature (and I speak naturally of only the best, that which covers the first four centuries of Islam) in order to realize the truly extraordinary advance of our literature in just a quarter of a century. This notable progress can be seen in four well-defined quarters: prose, drama, novel, and criticism, whether it be literary, political, or social.

Arab prose had never attained the abundance it enjoys today. The Ancients did not know either the journalistic article, or the literary essay, or the critique (in the modern sense of the word), or the novel, or even the short story or novelette, not even the drama. Now all the various genres are employed with success by contemporaries. I have already remarked that this same ancient Arab world never wanted to give literary freedom to narrative, whether it be short story, novelette, or novel, although these existed without name among the common classes. It will be the great privilege and honor of the contemporary Arabic writers to have literally reinstated this genre by making it the most important in the realm of modern prose.

The Ancients did not know the theater any better. When they began to translate the works of the Greeks, they hit only upon philosophical or scientific works. They became familiar with the metaphysics, ethics, politics, mathematics, and medicine of ancient Greece; but its real literature and particularly its theater having been condemned by Byzantine Christianity, the Arab translators were guilty of gross misinterpretations. Not all those who adhered to Aristotle understood his books, nor could they find terms, for example, to translate exactly the words *tragedy* and *comedy*. Thus they called the former "eulogy" and the latter "satire." The moderns knew the Western theater, however; they became acquainted with it in school. Some of them read it in the original and tried to translate plays, especially French and English. Adaptations were made and produced. A little later, in the period which interests us more particularly, Egyptian writers began to imitate the European theater. I have mentioned above the theater in verse of our great poet Ahmad Chawki; it must be said, however, that his plays, a little difficult for the most part, confused the average public, who admired them without understanding them. I have likewise said a word about this satiric theater in popular language, which came in time to be the true expression of the soul of a people but which cannot be truly integrated into what is strictly literature. Thus it seemed necessary to create a theater which, without really moving away from the classical form, was within the grasp of the public at large; and it is another credit due the Egyptian writers of this last quarter-century to recognize that they were able to give that sort of theater to contemporary Arabic literature. The real creator of this contemporary Arabic prose theater is Tawfik El-Hakim whose first play, "The Cavern People," dates from 1933. This Egyptian dramatist has not since ceased to produce dramatic works, and many have followed in his trail. However, they have continued to translate Western plays, doing it with more exactness and fewer adaptations. Moreover, the theater in popular speech has lived on and still amuses spectators today. Above all, there has been in the course of these last twenty-five years one man of genius: Naguib Al-Rihani. He was a kind of popular Molière: author, producer, adapter, comedian; he did it all himself. For nearly thirty years he enlivened the Egyptian scene with his extraordinary talent. He possessed the art of seizing upon any subject, a Parisian vaudeville for instance, and of transforming it into a typically Egyptian comedy of manners. In short, let us add that the theater in verse itself did not die after the passing of Chawki, since 'Aziz Abaza continues to work this vein and produces from time to time poetic dramas much appreciated by the literati of Cairo.

The writers of the last quarter of a century have thus to their credit the introduction of an entirely new genre in classical Arabic literature, the narrative genre: that is, the short story, the novelette, and the novel. It appeared, moreover, as the theater had appeared. First, translations of Western stories were made; they were soon liked, and attempts were made to do the same in Arabic. It was Hessein Heikal who first published before World War I a novel, *Zeinab,* an attempt to evoke the life of the Egyptian countryside. This example was not followed, and we had to wait for the postwar renais-

sance to see the Arabic novel develop in an interesting way. Today there are many Egyptian novelists in particular, Arabic in general. A special place belongs to Mahmud Teymour; he began by writing novelettes and short stories in which it was easy to trace the influence of certain French masters, notably Guy de Maupassant; little by little his personality evolved and took shape about 1935–40; then the novels of Teymour became the most authentic expression of Egyptian life in its commonplace aspects.

There were other novelists, and they won more and more favor with readers, to the extent that since the end of World War II, the novel has become the most important literary product of Egypt as well as of all the other Arabic countries. Indeed, a young author, if he wishes to try his talent today, begins by composing a short story; then he specializes in the short satiric and social piece; then he launches into a big novel, which, if it is well received, establishes him as a novelist.

However, it should be noted that if the generation which we call that of 1900 wrote many novels from 1925 to 1940, it did not limit itself to that genre. Heikal issued only *Zeinab;* 'Abbas Al-'Akkad published only one novel, *Sarah,* in which he analyzed with finesse the psychology of love. Ibrahim Al-Mazni did more, and I myself wrote a number of novels and narratives, such as the "Book of Days," "The Call of Karawan," "The Tree of Misery," *Adib,* et cetera; but we all thought of our novelistic production as only accidental in our literary life, and we preferred to devote ourselves to works which, rightly or wrongly, we considered more important. Let us say, rather, that the political and social circumstances of these last twenty-five years obliged writers of this generation to occupy themselves more with criticism than with personal creation. Between 1920 and 1940 it was much more a question of clearing the ground and preparing minds to receive than of building a new literature; it was especially a matter of "revising values," as they said, and of adjusting modern Western values to the traditional Eastern way of thinking. Politics was then the essential problem; so the intellectuals had to introduce the minds of their fellow citizens to the new aspects of European politics. It was likewise indispensable to apply almost all one's attention and efforts to literary things and consequently to devote oneself especially to criticism. That is the reason why these writers examined ancient Arabic literature minutely; they wanted to know what was worth keeping. They proposed, moreover, to give to their fellow citizens an intelligent taste for Occidental cultures, and that is why they translated and analyzed so many European works. Finally, it was fitting to examine carefully the new products of Arabic literature in order to channel it in a direction that would avoid the excesses of the Orient. In short, this generation took on the task of freeing the modern Arab mind from the chains of tradition as well as from the encroaching siege of Western materialism, by giving back to it—or more exactly, permitting it to find again—its true personality. If we add that certain of these writers were both men of thought and men of action, since the best known among them were members of Parliament and ministers, we will recognize, I think, without difficulty that their task was rather heavy and that, on the whole, they performed it with distinction.

I see one proof, among others, of my theory in a rather significant little fact: contemporary Arabic literature is beginning to interest the Western world, from Europe to America. Formerly the Orientalists, usually Europeans, concerned themselves only with *ancient* Arabic literature, either of the Orient proper or of Moslem Spain. One could really say that Arabic letters of the end of the nineteenth century and the beginning of the twentieth century did not exist in their eyes. Now, shortly after World War I, these Orientalists suddenly began to take an interest in what was being written in Egypt. Professor Gibb devoted a series of studies, which are not without interest, to contemporary Arabic writers. The German Kamphmayer brought out in collaboration with a Tunisian writer, Khamiri, a volume on the contemporary writers and their works. The Italian Francesco Gabrieli soon did the same, and in his recent book on Arabic literature in general he furnishes a great number of details on the present aspects of Arabic letters. In addition, some works of Egyptian authors, and likewise Lebanese, have been translated into French, English, Russian, Italian, German, Spanish. There are not many, to be sure, but we hope that it is only a beginning and that this regrettable lacuna of the West will soon be overcome, to repay us a little for the warm interest we have always borne it.

Thus, this generation, whose history I am trying to sketch broadly, will not only have given back to Arabic literature the splendor that belonged to it when it was at its epopee, but will have begun to make it a world literature. We have it translated or in the process of being translated into several Western languages and naturally, several Eastern ones, and this new phenomenon must be emphasized: everywhere that Arabic is taught in European and American universities it is the texts of contemporary Arabic writers, especially Egyptian, which are being explained, commented on, and taken as models of style.

Obviously, it would be unjust to think and to claim that this Arabic literary renaissance came *ex nihilo*, as the philosophers say. In human affairs, nothing comes from

nothing. If we want to know the real promoters of this sudden spiritual blooming, it is at least their due to name those who have struggled, according to their modest means, to liberate the Arabic mind, and who did so long before the conflict of 1914. Their merit is all the greater because they did not have, to aid them in their task, those political circumstances that I have mentioned at the beginning of this article: the revolutionary movements which followed the Armistice of 1918 were favorable to our generation, which drew upon them as much as possible. Let us mention in first place Sheik Muhammed 'Abdo, who freed intelligence from religious traditions, thus opening the way to the spiritual progress of the Arab world. Let us name also Kassem Amin, who proposed social reforms and courageously recommended the emancipation of women in the Orient; if there are today in Egypt many young women in the universities, women lawyers, Ph.D.'s, and administrators, our country owes to him that moral development. Let us not forget either Mustafa Kemal, who prepared minds for the political struggle against the British Occupation. Let us make a place, a large place, for Lutfi Al-Sayed, philosopher, man of letters, scholar, statesman, president of the Egyptian Academy, who familiarized the youth of the beginning of this century with the philosophical systems of the West and made it acquainted especially with those famous French philosophers of the eighteenth century who laid the foundations for the Revolution of 1789. These men are the masters who permitted this youth (the generation of 1900) to become aware of itself, its duties, its rights, and its responsibilities. Without them, it would not have triumphed over the difficulties I have mentioned. . . .

Does this mean that contemporary Arabic literature has really attained its full maturity and surmounted all the obstacles which prevented its free unfolding? I do not think so. There are many paths yet to be trod, many problems to be solved before that literature may fulfill the dreams we hold for it. Let us take a quick glance at the shackles. First, Arabic poetry is very far from coming up to our expectations. It cannot be compared with ancient Arabic poetry, which played a preponderant role. In honesty it must be confessed that our poetry has shown an undeniable decadence in the last twenty-five years. That is easily explained: to flourish, poetry doubtless needs a real equilibrium between men and life, an equilibrium of an inner nature, obviously. Now, the Arabic world of today has completely broken with its classical traditions of feeling and thinking and has not yet sufficiently assimilated new ways of living; for the moment it is lost between a heavy past of prejudices and traditions and a present which forces it to an adaptation not yet completed. That is why it is to be feared that so long as a modern way of life is not acclimated in the Arabic Orient, its poetry will remain without vigor. Let us notice, besides, that prose accommodates itself much more easily than poetry to this unbalance between what one has been and what one hopes to be. It even becomes a valid solution for achieving that difficult balance and for making the transition from secular tradition to present reality less painful. Naturally, there was a fine flourishing of Arabic poetry so long as the Arabs sought their literary ideal in the classics of an earlier day; thus it flowered only in the restricted milieu of scholars. Therefore, in Iraq, Djamil Al-Zahawi (who died about thirty years ago) sought his inspiration in the Arab philosopher-poets of the tenth and eleventh centuries of the Christian era. Am'rul Al-Rassafi (who died about twenty years ago) turned toward the pure sources of archaic classicism of the seventh and eighth centuries of the Christian era. Let us not omit some poets, Egyptian and Lebanese, who, without forgetting ancient classicism, cast a glance now and then toward the European and American West and more or less succeeded in effecting a certain harmony between these two modes of feeling and of expressing oneself; but they were not at ease in this genre and, moreover, did not awaken profound or lasting response in the society which surrounded them. It is only after World War I and the revolutionary movements to which I have referred that these poets succeeded in drawing closer to the masses and in moving them more. This generation of poets which attempted to compose verse by following two contradictory models—classical Arabic in form, classical European in content—disappeared with the death of the two great Egyptian poets Hafez and Chawki and with the recent passing of the very remarkable Lebanese-Egyptian poet Khalil Mutran. The young poets are today buffeted between an ancient classicism to which they do not sincerely belong and a Western modernism without roots. In conclusion, present-day Arabic poetry is groping its way, and I am confident that it will find itself someday, sooner or later.

These, then, are some of the many difficulties which contemporary Arabic literature has not yet surmounted. There are others, such as the question of illiteracy. That plague is still much too extensive in the Arab world, thanks to English colonial policy, on the one hand, and to the despotic and feudal regime still in force in the majority of Arabic nations, on the other hand. It is a sad fact that 60 percent of the Arab world does not know how to read or write: that is to say, they remain complete strangers to literature. The primary result is that literature enormously loses its effectiveness, since at present it can reach only a minority—those who

can read. In the second place, Arab writers are deprived of essential liberties, for, not being able to expect to be read by the majority, they find themselves constrained to seek other means of livelihood and consequently to earn their living outside literature. Moreover, if it is true that in Europe, and elsewhere, literature does not "feed the man," it is still more true that an Arab writer who would expect his books to support him would be in grave danger of dying of hunger. Such a situation sometimes requires compromises, even surrender harmful to real intellectual liberty. It is only fair to mention that the governments of the Arab countries of the Orient are today expending greater and greater efforts to fight illiteracy and that it is reasonable to hope that in ten or fifteen years to come they will succeed.

However, although illiteracy should be checked and the number of Arab readers considerably increased, a serious handicap would remain to be solved: our literature will remain ineffective for a long time, even if more people know how to read and write, so long as the knotty problem of the writing is not solved. A literature is first made by being easy of access; it is not so if it is not readable. That is a material condition of vital importance to the written book. Now, Arabic writing is difficult to decipher. It has remained, as it was in ancient times, a kind of shorthand which rebuffs the noninitiated. It is by nature destined for an elite—that is to say, a minority. It absolutely does not correspond to a democratic life, which stipulates that instruction is a right of everyone and that the governments have the duty to dispense it to everyone. Arabic writing is not vocalized and demands, to be read correctly, a sum of knowledge and culture sufficient to permit one to understand first and to read accordingly what one has previously understood. That ability cannot be required of every man. It is then imperative, if one desires that Arabic literature be read and appreciated by the greatest number, that our writing be reformed, democratized, and placed within the grasp of the masses who are in the process of overcoming illiteracy. They are now looking for a way to transform this writing without being forced to break with the past or to renounce the lofty Arab-Moslem heritage. The liberty and effectiveness of Arabic literature will not be assured until the day when the masses can read correctly and enjoy what they read.

There will remain, after all, a last difficulty. It is of a material sort, and I do not think that it is peculiar to the Arab world. I am speaking of the standard of living of the average reader. It is difficult for men now to find the necessary leisure to cultivate their minds. In the state of the Oriental world today, the worker, the laborer, the artisan, or the farmer is obliged to live an existence which leaves him just enough time to earn sufficient for the bare necessities—when he can get them. He certainly does not have time to read. A tired man, whose daily concern is to assure his family a little bread, cares little for literature.

Finally, when all these obstacles have been conquered, Arabic literature will find itself, like all the other literatures, moreover, at grips with a last obstacle arising from the mechanical progress of the modern world: the difficulty which exists already and which is becoming intensified of coming to terms with radio, press, movies, television, and the future inventions of the human species. Naturally, Arabic literature suffers the consequences of these discoveries, which become more widespread every day; but I see in it a stimulating proof of its success. Hence-forth it is in a position to tackle the questions posed by the other great world literatures. The lag is largely caught up, and our literature is testing now its young strength, its renascent virtues, and its new vigor.

Taha Hussein

To a Nephew in College [1957]

Dear Wesley: I am taking advantage of the new postal rate to enclose this letter with the book I've sent you. The book will come as a surprise, I know. Not merely because it is *Metamorphosis,* or because it is by Franz Kafka, but because it is from me, an old uncle you haven't heard from in five years.

But threads of conscience have been bothering me since your mother wrote to me three weeks ago and informed me that you were barely hanging on to a "D" average. Not that it bothers me too much; a "D" average means that you have a great many friends, but what does make me feel remorseful is that I have neglected you so completely for so many years. Of course, I thought of you a year ago when your mother told me of your decision to attend an Ivy League school instead of one of our fine Florida universities, but to tell you the truth, I haven't thought of you since. I am trying to make up for it now.

Examine the book. Observe how *slim* it is, how easy to read. It is set in ten-point type, the way all books should be set. Although this edition was published in 1946 and is not a first edition, it is worth fifty cents more now than it was then. If you keep it for twenty more years it will quadruple in value. The only flaw is a small spot on page 67. Because this is a very sad part in the story—where an apple has pierced Gregor's

back—you may think this blemish was caused by a tear falling onto the page. This is not the case; it is a drop of gin from an overflowing martini.

There is a purpose in my sending you *Metamorphosis,* although this rambling letter may seem a bit pointless at this stage, but as Kafka once remarked, "We must break the frozen sea within us."

You are now in your sophomore year, and it is time you became an expert. Inasmuch as you are not an athlete, and obviously not a scholar, I am recommending to you, out of the wealth of knowledge gained by twenty-four years in the public relations business, that you become an expert on Franz Kafka.

I am giving you this advice with the sincerity that I give $5,000 retainers, and I want you to pay attention to my instructions. To get by in this world, and to have the slightly sharpened edge on his fellow men that means the difference between mediocrity and success, a man, since he cannot be an expert on everything, must be expert in at least *one* thing. Kafka will not sustain you throughout your entire life, but an extensive knowledge of his works will bring your average in college up to a "C" or possibly a "B" before you graduate. No teacher in his right mind would dare to give the grade of "D" to a Kafka scholar.

Not only is it very easy to become an expert on Kafka, it is inexpensive. To my knowledge, there are only thirteen of Kafka's books printed in English, and all of them are available with very little searching. In addition to the small book I've included here, you only have to purchase Modern Library's *Selected Stories,* Knopf's *The Trial* and *The Castle,* and Schocken Books' *The Great Wall of China, The Penal Colony, Parables, Letters to Milena, The Diaries 1910–1913* and *1914–1923,* and *Dearest Father.* An arduous search will unearth *A Franz Kafka Miscellany,* published by Twice a Year Press, and to round out your library, complete it with a copy of *Franz Kafka: A Biography* by Max Brod.

Today you can obtain this entire list, secondhand, for less than fifty dollars. Now let me impress you: with this rack of books purchased and in plain sight in your room at college, *you do even not have to open one of them to obtain a "C" average by the end of the year!*

Such is the power of Franz Kafka in an academic setting. The mere fact that you have these books in your room will spread by word of mouth to every ivy-covered corner of the campus. But the setting is still incomplete. There is a scene in *The Trial* where K., the protagonist, buys three heathscapes from Tito-relli, the court painter. It isn't possible for you to go right out and buy heathscapes for your room, but for three dollars apiece you can get one of the fine-arts students at school to paint you three of them. If you know a female art student you can probably get them done for nothing. Unfortunately, none of the do-it-yourself painting kits feature heathscapes, or you could paint your own. Heathscapes are quite depressing; two gnarled trees in the foreground, a patch of gray-green grass, and a sunset. Three of these paintings, exactly alike, hanging side by side in your room, will speed your reputation as a Kafka expert considerably. They will also serve to remind you how bleak your prospects will be if you get bounced out of college.

Next, you must read all of Kafka's books. This will take time, but you have almost three more years to go in college and there are only thirteen books. After reading *The Metamorphosis,* read *The Trial* and then *The Castle.* Most readers stop halfway through *The Castle,* so if you continue on you will be way out in front. Many Kafka experts specialize by reading only one book over and over again. But this is the coward's way, and not for you.

Always carry a Kafka book with you from class to class. By reading a page at a time you will eventually get through them all. By doing so you will gain the awe of your fellow students and the admiration of your instructors.

As soon as you have finished reading at least three books you must write an article on some fragment of Kafka's works and have it published in the college magazine. I must caution you here: write it yourself. A ghost-written article could destroy you overnight. I have known many ghost writers and not one of them could keep his mouth shut. An as-told-to article is valueless, for obvious reasons. At this early stage I know it sounds difficult even to think about writing an article on a man you haven't even read yet, but Kafka experts *have to* write about him. In fact, after reading his books, you won't be able to prevent yourself from writing about Kafka.

To get started, choose any phrase or paragraph that interests you and explain it as well as you can, giving it your own interpretation. Your interpretation will be valid, and will not brook contradiction. Kafka's *Hunger Artist* interested me very much at one time, and I wrote seven different interpretations for my own elucidation. Every one of them was valid.

You won't have to bribe the editor of your college magazine to publish your article. He will be delighted to get it. An article on Kafka gives automatic distinction to any college publication. Everything written about Kafka is eventually published somewhere. Even if I were to send this letter to a magazine, it would be published immediately.

After the publication of your article in the magazine you will be invited to join all of the college literary societies. Join them, by all means, but do not take an active part in their activities. This calls for some preparation, however. It will be necessary for you to memorize several quotations from Kafka's works. To avoid being elected to any office, a good quotation is, "One must not cheat anyone, not even the world of its victory." I doubt if a Phi Beta Kappa could give you a comeback on that one. Or you could refuse just as gracefully by saying, "Beyond a certain point there is no return. This point has to be reached."

It will be better for your studies if you do not join any of the fraternities. To turn down the many requests you will receive after your article appears, quote, "What is gayer than believing in a household god?" You will, of course, lose a great many friends this way, but you will soon have ample time for studies.

As I remember college, the Sunday morning chapel was a bore. Kafka can release you from attendance when you tell the minister, "Heaven is dumb, echoing only to the dumb." There are many more, but you will find it fun to look them up for yourself. Kafka has quotations to fit every situation; however, they must be delivered deadpan to obtain maximum effectiveness. When you reach your senior year it will be best if you quote Kafka in German . . . but I am getting too far ahead for you, I'm afraid.

Your work is cut out for you, Wesley, but you will never regret the effort. As Kafka stated in *In the Penal Colony,* "Up till now a few things still had to be set by hand, but from this moment it works all by itself."

Fraternally,

Uncle Charles

Charles Willeford

Contemporary West African Writing in English [1966]

The last decade has seen the beginning of a literature in West Africa. The four ex-colonies of Britain (Gambia, Sierra Leone, Ghana, and Nigeria) have all added to the creation of a new development of world literature—an African literature in English. Some, very few, writers such as the Yoruba novelist Fagunwa, have chosen to write in the vernacular, but to all intents, it is clear, the African writers of those countries have made a fundamental decision: to use English, the old colonial language, as the vehicle for their writing. In a similar way, other artists in Senegal and Ivory Coast have decided upon French for their creativity. Some writers make this choice with regret that there is no adequately extensive African vernacular. Others welcome the linguistic flexibility and the international acceptability of the European tongue.

In a brief survey the significance of this choice for their writing cannot be debated fully, but it must be mentioned in passing that this decision carries with it a series of special difficulties. A writer by this choice is accepting a limitation in his local audience in exchange for an extension of his international reading public. More important than the numerical significance of this fact must be his realization that this other, external audience shares no cultural affinity with him. The awareness of the existence of these readers cannot but influence the construction of his novels. Sometimes this is shown in the unabashed addition of a terminal vocabulary of African words—a device employed by Nwankwo and Ike. At other times, pages of anthropological information which could be taken for granted with a local audience are awkwardly inserted in the plot, as in the novels of Nzekwu. Occasionally, too, it must be tempting to introduce the falsely exotic to delight the non-African. This other audience may have some effect also on language, but the English of these writers is rarely official British. It is not static but derives a new resilience and color from the local usage. While the English language is becoming more African, while the reading audience in the country grows with education, the problems of the African writer will diminish and a truly African style for an African audience will be achieved.

The first novel in English to receive London publication was Amos Tutuola's *Palm-Wine Drinkard* of 1952 (see *BA* 39:4, p. 413). This exotic and ghostly tale was written in a broken idiom that Europeans (including Dylan Thomas) found primitive poetry and the Nigerians found exasperatingly illiterate. Subsequent debate on this issue has become quite heated. Since this publication Tutuola has written three other books (see *BA* 39:4, p. 413): *Simbi and the Satyr of the Dark Jungle, Feather Woman of the Jungle* (see *BA* 37:4, p. 480), and *My Life in the Bush of Ghosts*. His exotic flower proved to be only a sport, and though he has not deserved the assaults of his Nigerian denigrators, none have appeared influenced by his extraordinary and personal idiom.

Another novel from West Africa was something of a dead end. *The African* by William Conton remains so far the only novel from Sierra Leone, and its writer has never attempted a second. It does exhibit characteristics which were to typify much West African writing. It begins with warm and effective scenes of early childhood memory, lovingly recorded, then develops into a plot

of grossest melodrama. As the book had no progeny, it is back in Nigeria that we can begin to trace a continuing line of development in the African novel form. The predominance of Nigeria in African writing is as obvious as it is inexplicable in literary terms. Sociologists may attempt to explain it with reference to the encouraging maturity of political development in that country, but it remains remarkable.

The Nigerian novel begins, almost simultaneously, with the work of three men: Chinua Achebe, Cyprian Ekwensi, and Onuora Nzekwu. Achebe has been most highly praised—partly, I suspect, because his work can be praised for its European caliber of technique in structure and characterization while it remains true to the strength and integrity of the African situation. Achebe's writing is based on a clear knowledge of the English novel: *The Great Tradition* of F. R. Leavis. Hardy is an obvious influence that comes to mind. Because of its appropriateness his first novel is a widely used book in Africa. Achebe is working on a tetralogy of which three volumes are in print so far: *Things Fall Apart, No Longer at Ease, Arrow of God* (see *BA* 39:4, pp. 411–13). These novels are all tragedies, though the second is a lighter situation derived from modern times. The first and third novels reconstruct the impact of change on the Africa of fifty years ago. Achebe describes the effect of British missionaries and administrators on a typical village tribal society: the dislocation that change, religious and educational, brings to historic certainties. Against the inevitable disintegration Achebe sets heroes of tragic dimension, Okonkwo and Ezeulu, but their integrity and courage are no match for the powers ranged against them by history. When the two opposing forces grind together, both are crushed. In a way, both sides in this struggle are destroyed; for the amalgam that is achieved between Europe and Africa joins the weaknesses of both traditions, and only those without nobility survive successfully. Instead of the confidence and security of village life, there is soon only a rootless alien existence. They are freed from conservative restriction to search aimlessly for new values in the moral chaos of developing cities. Achebe's conclusions are honest but pessimistic. It is this new generation, the fast-living transients of Lagos, who are the subject of the novels of Cyprian Ekwensi (see *BA* 39:4, p. 413).

Besides an unexpectedly tender story of the Fulani cattle men, *Burning Grass*, Ekwensi's novels have contemporary and urban themes: *People of the City, Jagua Nana,* and *Beautiful Feathers*. Ekwensi does not touch upon Achebe's world of tribal priests; his characters exist by different standards. He draws upon the Lagos nightclubs; their high-life dancing, their cheap whores. He writes of the slums, of commercial and political exploitation against a background of the false dazzle of chaotic but exciting urban change. With such subject matter it is easy to see how his style will differ from Achebe's respected prose. Not for Ekwensi the analysis of profound and inexorable event; his novels are sometimes glib, even superficial. The influences upon his writing are the movies and the cheap paperbacks from America. His plots are violent, complex, highly melodramatic stories of rape, lust, and murder. *Jagua Nana*, the life-loving prostitute with a heart of gold, is a conventional-enough figure, but Ekwensi cannot be dismissed by such remarks. He is a popular writer but a highly professional one. The growing confidence he exhibits as he describes the world of political corruption of modern Lagos holds promise of a really significant novel. The characters of Uncle Taiwo, Brother Jacob, and the Minister of Consolation are evidence of a gift for political satire unequaled by another West African writer.

Onuora Nzekwu's two novels, *Wand of Noble Wood* (see *BA* 39:4, p. 413) and *Blade among the Boys* (see *BA* 37:4, p. 480, and 39:4, p. 413), both exhibit a single, similar difficulty. In an endeavor to explain to his foreign audience the religious background of his incidents, his plots become little more than pegs on which to hang long explanations of aspects of Nigerian anthropology. The protagonists seem only to act in ways which allow Nzekwu to inform us about bride price, secret societies, sacrifices. When he avoids this teaching, he can create the African scene as well as any writer. No one has more sardonically exposed the conditions of missionary education.

At the moment these seem to be the major figures if only measured by the professionalism of their productivity. Each has another book in press. However, a large number of novelists from Nigeria have written only a single novel so far. Their work exhibits such range that it at least demonstrates a flourishing variety. T. M. Aluko's novel *One Man, One Matchet* (see *BA* 39:4, p. 413) is part comic satire, part a serious questioning of Yoruba tradition. It is made memorable for the satiric caricature of Benjamin Benjamin, verbose demagogue, wily opportunist, and rogue extraordinary of the Autolycus school. Nkem Nwankwo's novel *Danda* (see *BA* 39:4, p. 412) has another character who remains in the memory; it has been adapted very successfully for the stage. Danda is a picaresque figure, a flute-playing adventurer traveling Ibo land, outraging the stuffy and delighting the genuine. Both *Danda* and *One Man, One Matchet* concern themselves with tradition and change; it is an inescapable theme. It is more central to the debate (almost literally that) which makes up Obi Egbuna's first novel *Wind versus Polygamy* (see *BA* 39:4, p.

412). This describes with serious intent but with wild comedy (occasionally accidental) the effect of "the wind of change" blowing on the old tribal custom of polygamy and bride price.

A more recent novel has the unexpected title *Toads for Supper* (see *BA* 39:4, p. 413)—the phrase derives from an Ibo proverb. Its author, Chukwuemeka Ike, is at present registrar of the new University of Nsukka. I might observe in passing how many African novelists hold substantial administrative positions. Achebe is head of external broadcasting of Nigeria radio. Ekwensi is head of the government information services, and Okara holds a similar position with the provincial government. Conton is permanent secretary to the Sierra Leone Ministry of Education. In Ike's novel the debate again revolves around an aspect of change. Students at college, liberated from conventional assumptions by their widening education, find themselves still tied to the traditional customs of their homes. They cannot, as in this book, express their Western independence by marrying someone from a different tribe.

One first novel stands out from all the rest. It may suggest a new direction or perhaps a dead end. In this respect only it might be likened to the place of the later writing of James Joyce in English literature. Gabriel Okara, already a substantial poet, called his first novel *The Voice* (see *BA* 39:3, p. 367, and 39:4, p. 413). It has a common international theme, the quest for enlightenment—as he puts it, the search for "it." The style is claimed to be a literal translation from Ijaw idiom, but one is sure that a highly poetic sensibility has modified it considerably. The style is poetic and exotic, with repetitions, inversions, and parallelisms of form, and employs curiously concrete terms for inner reactions. Of the hero the townsfolk observe, "Okolo had no chest." It is too early to say what development may be expected along the lines of this experiment. Other recent novelists have not ventured into experiments along these lines.

Since *The African*—incredibly, in view of the spate of books from Nigeria—there have been only two novels from the rest of West Africa, and both were published this year. *Second Round* (see *BA* 40:2, p. 233) by Lenrie Peters, a Gambian poet, gives a highly autobiographical account of the problems faced by a doctor who tries to reestablish himself in Sierra Leone after study abroad. *The Catechist* (see *BA* 40:2, p. 229) by J. M. Abruquah of Ghana is only part novel, for it is a loving record in fiction of his father's life as a humble member of the mission church.

From such a collection it is not possible to see clearly the directions that the West African novel will ultimately take. Too much exploration and too many first attempts have made it difficult for a clear picture to emerge. Speculation at this stage may be rapidly contradicted by events in a field where one novel can suggest decisive change. It seems that few will follow Achebe's interest in recording the past; the Nigerian present attracts too strongly and dynamically. The novelists' subjects will probably remain the local, contemporary events drawn from immediate and personal description. Literary maturity will come as these writers achieve a greater detachment from their heroes, as novels begin to exist more in their own artistic right and less as an extension of the writer's own living. The first novel of that Nigerian man of letters Wole Soyinka, *The Interpreters* (see BA 39:4, p. 413), suggests what is possible. Here an urbane and sophisticated skill has been brought to bear on the usual Lagos theme, raising it to a dimension of comprehensiveness and universal subtlety. This book may stand as a goal for other novelists. Since there is so much vitality and variety in both language and subject, the future of the African novel seems certain to be both prolific and significant.

The short story has been curiously neglected in West Africa. A number of stories have appeared in the pages of *Black Orpheus,* the vital literary journal from the Mbari Society of Ibadan. Achebe has tried his hand in this genre, and so has Ekwensi. Abioseh Nicol from Sierra Leone is the only writer who has utlized this genre widely. In 1964 a collection titled *Modern African Stories* was edited in England by Ellis Komey and Ezekiel Mphahlele (see BA 39:3, p. 370). It includes some West African stories. The Nigerian concentration on the novel form is doubly surprising in contrast to Negro writing in South Africa, which has almost invariably found expression in the short story. Perhaps the different publication possibilities may be in part an explanation.

The drama has been slightly less exclusively a Nigerian fief than the novel, though that country remains dominant through the plays of Wole Soyinka and J. P. Clark. Ghana has also developed a significant school of drama under the ambitious direction of Joe De Graft and Efua Sutherland. The drama has two advantages in Africa compared to the novel form. First, there is some local tradition upon which it may draw. It may not exactly compare to the Western concept of drama, but there is a whole traditional ritual which approximates a kind of dramatic production, with dancing, drumming, and mime. Second, although some plays have been very successfully produced abroad, they do have a first audience in their writers' country. Thus there is a closer identification between the dramatist and his audience than between the novelist and his readers. These facts create two special limitations for an American

when he reads these plays from the printed script. He may feel much more at a loss for background information than when reading a novel, because a play, by the nature of its dramatic structure, does not permit the author to stop and offer elucidation and explanation. He will also miss all the theatrical elements that make African drama such an exciting revelation to Western eyes. The 1964 Berlin Festival of African Arts displayed Aimé Césaire's *Roi Christophe* (see BA 39:4, p. 481) and Duro Ladipo's *Obo Kosa* in productions that made the theater throb with sound, color, and movement. However, these plays must rest ultimately on their texts. We must be aware—as Soyinka has often chided us—that African drama is more than dancers with bare breasts. We must not mistake the merely exotic for the truly original.

The only vernacular dramatist available in English translation is Duro Ladipo. His *Three Plays* (see BA 39:3, p. 367), published in Nigeria by the Mbari Press, may more properly be defined as folk operas. As with the novel, most writers are prepared to use English or French as their language vehicle—and for similar reasons.

The published drama from West Africa can most conveniently be divided for consideration into two groups. There are the playwrights who accept the conventional tradition of the British West End play for their theme and technique. Others extend the range of drama by following the experiments of the poetic dramatists with evocative language and symbolic situations. The former writers lean heavily on the J. M. Barrie tradition, on Noel Coward, or Terence Rattigan. The latter draw upon the suggestive experiment of the Irish playwrights—and of Beckett and T. S. Eliot. African sensitivity to the exoticism of words makes such poetic drama far less self-conscious and awkward than some recent American attempts.

The traditions from which these two styles of drama derive suggest, in advance, their likely strengths and weaknesses. The traditional plays avoid the fuzzy symbol and intangible language of poetic drama and offer the old advantages of plot development and a coherent and comprehensible denouement; but they are also following a tradition that even in England is tired, overworked, stale. Their concerns are those of the middle classes, unconsciously snobby and prejudiced; their issues are trivial, a contrived domestic situation; their language is stagey in that unrealistic English of the "Who's for a jolly game of tennis?" variety. All these things seem doubly incongruous in the African setting.

The most competent of such plays is the one from Sierra Leone by R. Sharif Easmon, *Dear Parent and Ogre* (see BA 40:1, p. 115). Will the kindhearted but fierceexteriored father be able to manage his lively family as effectively as he can handle his political affairs? Is he really an ogre or a cuddly dear parent? Joe De Graft's play *Sons and Daughters* (see *BA* 39:3, p. 364) rides upon a similarly stock situation. A nouveau-riche businessman wants his children to take up professional careers in some occupation suitable to his new status in the community. His children, to his horror, want to be artistic, to study painting and dance. James Henshaw's best play *Medicine for Love* evokes a similar tradition, though with a satiric force that lends his play an extra heartiness and activity to set against the encroaching sentimentality.

Although these plays have been popular, more impressive perhaps have been the plays in the poetic tradition, and the major works in this style have been written by two important poets of Nigeria, John Pepper Clark and Wole Soyinka. Clark has written three plays. *Song of a Goat* (see *BA* 38:2, p. 211) was first published separately by Mbari and then was gathered with two others, *The Raft* and *The Masquerade*, into a collection for the Oxford University Press, *Three Plays* (see *BA* 39:2, p. 238). The most remarkable of this trio is *Song of a Goat*, produced as the official Nigerian entry in the Commonwealth drama festival in London last October. It has a splendid ironic theme couched in profound poetry. The title hints, of course, at the origin of Greek tragic drama (*tragoidia:* goat song). It describes implacably the conflict between two traditions. Zifa's wife is barren because of his impotence. In despair, she seduces his younger brother, and the end is the double suicide of the two brothers, each acknowledging that they have sinned against circumstance. *The Masquerade* ends in violent and bloody murder. In *The Raft* the men are condemned by the too-powerful forces of nature. Clark's plots have a ferocious, inexorable theme, but it is the language that gives these plays their impact. Echoing, a little, the dramatic verse of Eliot are lines like these that liken the barrenness of the woman to the seasons: "She has waited too long already, / Too long in the harmattan. The rains / Are here once more and the forest getting / Moist." If Clark can write powerful plays, however, it is Wole Soyinka who most obviously represents the range of the Nigerian drama. He is the complete man of the theater: actor, producer, director, writer. He was responsible for the forming of the 1960 Masks, the first attempt at a continuous theater company in West Africa. This group was recently reformed into the Orisun Players, the beginning of professional theater in West Africa.

Soyinka's theme is always that which haunts all African writing and was so omnipresent in the novel: the conflict between tribal cohesion and Western disinte-

gration, between custom and progress. The old certainties are destroyed, robbed of credibility; but no substitute to replace them can be found in changing Africa. Soyinka can employ both the comic and the tragic modes to elaborate on this division. Oxford's collection *Five Plays* (see *BA* 38:1, p. 92) includes two plays in the comic vein: *Brother Jero,* about a beach gospeller, mountebank, and rogue; and *The Lion and the Jewel,* Soyinka's most popular play. In the latter he contrasts progressive and traditionalist through the persons of the local schoolmaster and the leonine old chief. They compete for the jewel of the village, Sidi. Delightfully, the situation is developed so that the wily, tough passion of the old lion is victorious over the feeble follies of the teacher. Two other plays are in a darker vein: *The Strong Breed* and *The Swamp Dwellers* (see *BA* 38:1, p. 92 on both). They describe the pervasive world of superstition in the villages, the dark misery brought about by violence and ritual death; the corroding grip of false priests. The fifth play, *A Dance of the Forests* (see *BA* 38:1, p. 92) was commissioned for the independence ceremonies of Nigeria. It contains both tones; for if it warns of the dangers inherent in the African past, it does this partly through ridicule, and the last frenzied symbolic dance affirms the possibility of man remaking the future free from restrictive tradition. This was an especially bold thing to say to an audience expecting the easy heroics. Soyinka's recent play *The Road* (see *BA* 40:2, p. 360) has been produced in London to critical acclaim.

Both these writers are quite young, and since the theater is receiving support from audiences that allow it to be founded on a more continuous financial basis, the potential of Nigerian theater is likely to be as valuable and extensive as the future promised in the novel.

Poetry can be approached with an observation somewhat similar to the one made about the drama. The genre merges with the dual aspects of Europe and Africa. There is a very obvious African element. There has always been an elaborate and continuous tradition of oral poetry in the heroic vein throughout the continent. Much of this vernacular poetry is now being made available through the new African literature series from Oxford edited by Wilfred Whitely; but only on rare occasions can it be asserted that contemporary African poetry derives from this source. The new poets are African, but they are also very sophisticated men, often read in English studies at the university. Their subects are African and their experience is African, but their language and technique demonstrate another source of influence. Like many young poets in England and America, they respond to the pervasive influences of Ezra Pound, T. S. Eliot, Dylan Thomas, et alia. This discovery in itself suggests the way in which such writers are attempting to harmonize within themselves the apparently contradictory worlds of Africa and the West.

Another significant fact about poetry in English from West Africa is that it plays none of the intellectual games of the French. It is not written at the behest of some arcane thesis of the intelligentsia. Césaire and Senghor initiated the concept of Negritude, and its principle dominates the rhetoric of many French poets. Negritude, as an assertion of the positive qualities of the African, his Negroness, is justified. In repudiating the assimilating process, the implication that the African is a kind of inferior European, it effected a salutary rebalance of worn-out racial concepts. When this idea became, however, the basis for a virtual dictation of appropriate themes and attitudes for African writers, it was dangerously and pointlessly restrictive; it led to a declamatory verse style, hectoring rhetoric rather than poetry. The English poets from West Africa repudiated this whole stance, both by implication in a very different kind of precise, pragmatic, and personal poetry, and by the cheerfully deflating ridicule with which they attacked the subject in debate. Soyinka's famous analogy mocked the need to postulate a Negritude by observing that a tiger does not have to proclaim his tigritude.

The writing of poetry is widespread in West Africa, and we may here limit our attention to the professionals, arbitrarily defined as those who have written sufficiently to have their poetry published in a separate collection, no matter how slender its format. In passing, however, mention should be made of two good and readily available paperback anthologies: John Reed's *Book of African Verse* in the Heinemann's series and Gerald Moore's Penguin collection *Modern Poetry from Africa* (with Ulli Beier; see *BA* 38:2, p. 214). Interestingly enough, there is not a great deal of duplication in these two collections. Two significant poets fall outside the definition in these selections: Wole Soyinka and Gabriel Okara. Soyinka's style is urbane and sardonic in such masterly poems as "Telephone Conversation" which deride racial prejudices. Okara's work is cryptic and evocative. He encompasses the whole conflict in the educated African's dual allegiance in the last lines of his poem called "Piano and Drums." The poet responds to both traditions as he finds himself "wandering in the mystic rhythm of jungle drums and the concerto."

From Gambia there is the slim Mbari collection of Lenrie Peters, *Poems* (see *BA* 39:3, p. 367). His themes are in part conventional—time and the changing seasons, love and rejection—but it is still an African world, and there are "Cannibals' ghosts." He reverses the influence of Africa on European art by observing his world "wearing the Modigliani face." His vision of the mind

likens it to "the purdahed moon" and "a superconcentration Pile." Here two worlds abut within the imagery of a single poem.

Ghana's major contemporary poet is George Awoonor Williams. His Mbari collection is entitled *Rediscovery* (see *BA* 39:3, p. 367), and this word may say a good deal about the way Williams has reapproached the Africa of his childhood, with the sophistication of his European education. Whatever change he experiences, "there shall still linger the communion we forged / the feats of oneness whose ritual we partook of." Probably it is this sense of oneness that releases him from much allegiance to European styles. Some of his imagery is drawn from his mother tongue, Togo, and some lines sound like laments in traditional oral poetry, as in the repetition of "My people, I have been somewhere / If I turn here, the rain beats me / If I turn there the sun burns me." Such a style also owes something to the Bible, but there is always the Africa of such observation as "that girl with the neck like a desert tree." There is also a typical African mockery. In "The Weaver Bird" he likens this pushy intruder to the European colonial "Preaching salvation to us that owned the house."

In Nigeria, which is again the major country in contemporary African poetry, Christopher Okigbo has published two collections, *Heavensgate* and *Limits*. In these poems he makes a reconciliation between Africa and the West in a way that appears similar to Williams's writing; but Okigbo works in a reverse way, not by borrowing elements of African traditional techniques but by assimilating African philosophic ideas. If Williams merges African technique with European ideas, Okigbo joins African ideas with European technique. Unlike Williams's, Okigbo's verse shows a considerable impact of Western form; he is obviously influenced by Ezra Pound. His spiritual adjustment incorporates the religion of both continents: "Heavensgate" begins with the African symbol, "Before you, mother Idoto, naked I stand," and continues with the Christian: "watchman for the watchword at heavensgate; / out of the depths my cry." Equally dual, "Limits" owes its construction to Pound's "Cantos," but in it Okigbo's most famous image is purely African: "Bright with the armpit dazzle of a lioness she answers."

John Pepper Clark has perhaps the most substantial poetic achievement. At the moment there is only the Mbari collection *Poems* (see *BA* 38:1, p. 92), but a *Collected Poetry* published in England is due shortly. It is occasionally easy to pick up echoes in Clark's verse. There is Dylan Thomas behind the lines "Doped out of the deep / I have bobbed up bellywise"; Hopkins is often present, either deliberately, in "Variations on Hopkins" ("Ama are you gall bitter pent? / Have paltry pittance spent"), or less deliberately but clearly in such a sonnet as "Of Faith": "Faith can move mountains, will move whole mountain." Clark's themes are Africa, however, and an Africa recalled with loving and exact precision. "For Granny (From Hospital)" is warm without being maudlin; "Night Rain" moves us with its acute child memory of waking in a storm and finding mother setting her bowls out of range of the leaks: "out of the run of water / that like ants filing out of wood / will scatter and gain possession of the floor." "Girl Bathing" and "Fulani Cattle" both exemplify his involvement in the African scene. A famous poem describes the city of Ibadan with an almost haiku-like perfection of brevity.

Ibadan,
running splash of rust
and gold—flung and scattered
among seven hills like broken
china in the sun.

It is not yet certain how Clark's poetry will develop with maturity, but he is simultaneously exact and evocative; he explores both the African experience and the European poetic technique to form a poetic sensibility that makes him unique and among the most interesting of contemporary poets in English.

Regularly now one is confronted with new books from Africa, and as the novelty grows less, one's judgment grows more just. Already American learned societies and universities are beginning to see this as a significant and valid field of literature. Janheinz Jahn's recent *Bibliography of Neo-African Writing* (New York, 1965), though it makes a somewhat individualistic selection, has over 130 pages of listings from African sources. Clearly we are already at that exciting point where we are witnessing the *naissance* of a literature: that moment that the Americans knew, scarce realizing, some 150 years ago, and that the Australians recognized a bare fifty years ago. No one can say yet what direction this writing will ultimately take. There is a good deal of vivid experiment, some of which may, in the final elucidation, prove to have been abortive. Many young writers as yet unknown abroad are no doubt at the moment publishing their first efforts in some ephemeral student magazine. Some mute African Milton may become suddenly both articulate and available to us. For the moment it must be enough to point out the dramatic potential that we may expect from the literature in English produced in this part of the world. If there will be individual failures and inadequacies, new names and changing reputations, there will also be a developing body of literature worthy to be assessed against any other contemporary writing. For an infant only a decade old this is a remarkable achievement.

John F. Povey

A Petition to the Swedish Academy [1967]

This issue of *Books Abroad* [41:1] is devoted to the Nobel Prize in Literature. It examines the roll of prize-men and attempts to estimate the success with which the Swedish Academy has recognized the great modern writers since 1901. The prize-men have been grouped by languages, and in each of the longer papers a scholar reports on the literature of the language or family of languages in which he is most expert. In the shorter papers experts in large language groups not yet represented in the awards consider whether in their territories any major candidates for the prize have been overlooked by the judges and what signs there may be of the emergence of a future prize-man.

The symposium first took form at the MLA Annual Meeting in 1964, when, as chairman of the comparatists dealing with prose fiction, I invited six of the present contributors to revaluate the novelists on the Nobel Prize list. However, it is insufficient to appraise the awards in one genre alone; the speakers at the conference naturally gravitated toward a full inquiry into the whole list; and we agreed to extend the study. Dr. Robert Vlach, a passionate lover of books and a friend of Sweden, offered the pages of this journal for the undertaking and drew up the detailed design for the issue. We have thought of him in writing the papers, and we hope—but how can we know since his tragic death?—that we have neither said anything that his keen discrimination would have rejected nor failed to say anything that his courage would have required.

My part is to chronicle the reflections which underlay the inquiry at its outset and to translate into constructive terms the intenser reflections that come with the completed project. I speak out of regard for the Nobel Prize as an institution, out of a willingness to believe in its international value. I am one of the uncounted number of people, scattered everywhere, who find strength in literature, are glad to see it rewarded, and rejoice when latent literary greatness is transplanted to the light and grows there more vigorously. I would like to see the Swedish Academy less often fix the crown, and sometimes the death-mask, on fulfilled grandeur, more often go ranging for the discovery and reinforcement of genius which is still on the advance.

When the Academy gives the prize to a familiar figure whose excellence is a matter of general consent, there is a public sigh of acceptance, half-gratified, half-regretful. When it chooses a strange writer of whom little is known outside his own country, there is a stir of curiosity, and whatever the verdict eventually reached as to his quality, there is gratitude for the enlargement of the periphery of international vision. If it chooses a man whose literary level is mediocre, there is a recoil of distress. Twice in my London years, between 1946 and 1955, I opened an evening paper and learned, coming to an angry halt in the street, of the award of the Nobel Prize in Literature to a figure famous and admirable for achievements in other fields; it seemed evident that these divagations from pure literature must weaken the significance of the Prize. Later came another election which, though made on literary grounds, was scarcely the best available to the judges. In the last three or four years a general need has been felt for a survey of the whole record, to determine how often the judges have chosen badly, how often they have chosen well. Therefore this symposium

The contributors (whose revaluations of the prize-men will be useful alike to their fellow specialists and to the common reader) are now and again severe with the judges but on the whole find much to approve. Possibly they should have been more severe. Possibly their verdicts have been mitigated by two factors inherent in the method of the inquiry. First: as soon as one man asks about a prize-man not "Was he the best man?" but "Why did the judges select him?" one is likely to perceive that he was chosen for reasonable reasons, and one reports these and, in so doing, willy-nilly defends the good instead of demanding the best. Second: each contributor is limited to a single family of languages and is deprived of the opportunity to speculate whether, when a good candidate from his group was elected, the election was made at the expense of a better candidate from a different group. Compensating for the intervention of these factors, I summarize the findings of the symposium in fifty-two words with which the individual contributors might not concur: *The Swedish Academy has done well, but could have done far better; the list of prize-men is blemished by errors of commission and omission: includes nonliterary figures who should have been nonstarters; includes mediocrities; omits some writers of the highest rank; and where it names the best men, names them too late.*

How might the awards be distributed to more vital effect? I submit five suggestions:

1) It is time to disregard Nobel's preference for idealism. Alfred Nobel told the judges to look for works of "idealistic intent," and I am not generally in favor of overriding the wishes of a testator; but two strong reasons apply in this case. We no longer feel sure what Nobel meant by idealism: the evidence of common sense collides with the impressions of Mittag-Leffler. . . . We can maintain that all literature induces the development of the human consciousness, and does

so the more effectively in proportion as it is the better literature—that is, in proportion as it plays with language and experience more energetically—and that Nobel's penitent longing for a better world will be answered whenever the Academy gives the Prize not to the best-*wishing* maker but to the best *maker*—even if the best maker appears to wish ill.

2) The Academy should ponder the advantages of a different system of priorities than that which it has, presumably unawares, adopted hitherto. Analyze the record, and it looks as if the judges have either thought prose more beneficial to the world than poetry or have found it easier to reach conclusions about prose and particularly about the novel. The novelists outnumber the prize-men from other genres. The Academy has chosen few dramatists, few poets.

During the last ten years there has been a hint of change: a new care for poetry. It is a change in the right direction and should continue. How much better the whole Nobel list would look if poets had been better represented: if Stefan George or Claudel had been chosen instead of Eucken; if Rilke or Hofmannsthal had been chosen instead of Anatole France or Reymont; if Palestine's Bialik or Egypt's Shawky had been chosen instead of Sinclair Lewis; if Frost or Pound or Cavafy had been chosen instead of Galsworthy. By and large, the poet is the purest and most sensitive and subtle commentator on life, and the least rewarded. The publishers help the novelists, the theaters help the dramatists, the poet lacks all but an odd quixotic publisher for escort to his audience. Let the Academy seek the best poet of the year and prefer him to his rivals in other genres. If a good poet cannot be found, then let it seek a dramatist. Novelists should wait their turn somewhere to the rear.

The Academy has occasionally diverted the Prize in Literature to other disciplines, but with imperfect felicity. Eucken seems to me to have been wrong for a literary or any other place in the pantheon; Mommsen and Churchill and Bertrand Russell wrong for a literary place. I am happier about Bergson, but not completely happy. The Academy should be cautious to the point of abstinence with writers who are not first and entirely writers of literature.

3) The Academy might do more often what it has sometimes done so well: exert itself to discover writers outside the domains of the Big Powers and the current languages of diplomacy. It has been an advantage to the common reader that the judges have been immediately able to recognize a dozen Scandinavian prize-men, whom other regions might not have come to know without their championship. It has been an advantage

that they have extended themselves to recognize the writers of Chile, Greece, Poland, Israel, and Yugoslavia. When regional work is carried beyond its confines and put at the disposal of all, the world is a little more closely integrated. To read a people's literature is to be drawn into its rhythms and to sense its history and potentialities.

A working-rule for the Academy: that if ever there is an even choice between competitors from the supreme nations and competitors from others, the latter be preferred.

4) Only with hesitation and restraint should the Academy endorse a writer already widely recognized and rewarded. Nobel did not instruct his judges to catch every great master in the net, nor to heed that rather timid inner rebuke which says, "We mustn't be guilty of appearing not to know what everybody else knows." Perhaps the Academy should only crown an Old Master when he has performed a lifetime of work but received no adequate recognition or reward, or has lost his reward and security by some violence of fortune. Of course, if an Old Master writes in one of the little-disseminated languages discussed under the preceding head, it will be appropriate for the Academy to conduct him to the international forum; but a man as old and famous as Shaw was in 1925, Gide in 1947, Eliot in 1948, Hemingway in 1954, should for all his merits be bypassed. The Academy should have recognized Bergson in 1914, not in 1927; Gide in 1927, not in 1947; Quasimodo in 1947, not 1959. (This sequence illustrates how every overdeferred election defers the election of some younger writer at a time when it would be helpful and give him impetus; and it will be noticed that my dates are conservative, and that yet earlier election would be possible and more helpful still). If the judges miss a man in his best years, let them stay away afterward, as they stayed away from Hardy; but when has the Academy managed to identify a writer in his first brilliance? Never a man younger than 40! Kipling at 42 was, singularly enough, the nearest shot; he had begun early and spun prolifically, so that by 1907 his shelf had the deceptive length of a veteran's. It appears that the judges do not feel sure of quality unless they see it confirmed by quantity. They should allow the old standard: "Few but good."

5) But there is a different situation in which quantity interfused with a degree of quality may be the token of cultural health. E. M. Forster once said that a nation might be richest not by virtue of "the great poet who shall voice her" but by "the thousand little poets whose voices shall pass into our common talk." We need not look far for proof. The United States at this moment has no preeminent poet but is alive with thousands of gifted poets. England at the moment has no great novelist and no Shakespeare but has a sound culture of good novelists and a vigorous drama. I do not propose that the Swedish Academy should invent a way of awarding the Nobel Prize to American poetry at large or to the English novel at large—but I forbear only because these two countries possess well-established and smooth-functioning media through which their literature may radiate: publishing trades of immense enterprise and governmental information services. Let us imagine, however, that the Swedish Academy learns of a cultural renaissance in a country too small to maintain tentacular publishers and information agencies. It might vote a collective award. It could, for example, sponsor the translation of five hundred poems, and their publication in an edition to be distributed among the university libraries of the world. Or there may be more significant ways of executing the collective award. I am concerned here only to urge the principle, that the judges may be prepared if the occasion arises.

These recommendations are offered to the Swedish Acadmy with respect, with affection, and with the petition that they be read, considered, and—not adopted as a program, but—assimilated to the thoughts of the judges or sometimes remembered when nominations for the Nobel Prize in Literature are sought and sifted.

They can no more armor the Academy against mistakes than the old procedures could. Indeed, because they involve the renunciation of some of the Celebrated Masters, they may result in a record which, after another fifty years, will sound less magniloquent than the present record. They may even lead to more mistakes: to acts of faith in young men who later fail to live up to promise; but there is such a thing as a fertile mistake. To canonize the already-canonized fertilizes no one, whereas the mistaken election of a writer from an obscure culture, or of an innovatory young writer who eventually fades, may lead to controversy, to creative imitation, to analysis, to fresh departures and penetrations. . . . The new mistakes may be more fertile than the old.

Herbert Howarth

The Latin American Novel Today [1970]

The novel is the Cinderella of the literary genres of Latin America. Considered subversive by the Spanish authorities (and indeed it was), the novel was banned during the colonial centuries and did not come to life until the nineteenth century, after independence had been achieved. Once born, the novel in Latin America suffered a precarious infancy, except in Brazil, where the work of Machado de Assis endowed prose fiction with a dimension which would not be attained in Spanish America until the twentieth century. In Spanish South America, the most representative works up to the end of the nineteenth century were mere echoes of French, English, or, at worst, Spanish writings. Our "romantic" and our "realist" novels dramatically reflect the colonial temper of the Latin American novelist of the last century whose gaze remained firmly fixed on Europe. Naturally predisposed to assimilate the themes, techniques, and styles of the European masters, the early novelist refused to recognize the literary worth of his own American reality. The most notable nineteenth-century Latin American novel, *María* (1867) by the Colombian Jorge Isaacs, is little more than an opportune adaptation of Bernardin de Saint Pierre's *Paul et Virginie*. The prose fiction which Latin America inspired prior to 1900 gave the singular impression that Latin America was a continent of "whites": Indians, Negroes, and mestizos were incorporated into the novel only during the last decades of the nineteenth century, and even then they were little more than picturesque and distant elements, indistinguishable from the flora and fauna which served as the frame-work for the action of the novel. Even while essayists such as Sarmiento, González Prada, or Martí and poets such as José Hernández rediscovered Latin America and enriched our language, giving it an autonomous personality distinct from peninsular models, the novel remained an imitative and submissive genre, stripped of originality and creative inspiration.

After imitating Europe, the Latin American novelist attempted to photograph the reality that surrounded him: folklore replaced mimicry. From invertebrate cosmopolitanism, the Latin American novel evolved to aggressive provincialism. This tendency, initiated by the Peruvian Clorinda Matto de Turner, was given new impetus by the novel of the Mexican Revolution, and it achieved its highest expression with such writers as Mariano Azuela, Alcides Arguedas, Eustasio Rivera, Ricardo Güiraldes, Rómulo Gallegos, and Ciro Alegría. Historically this represented a step forward, a tapping of the conscience of autochthonous reality, a willingness to reclaim the indigenous and mestizo cultures and, through them, to find national identity; and in some cases it represented a political awareness of the social problems of the continent, problems such as agrarian feudalism, the selfishness of the oligarchic castes, and imperialistic penetration. However, from a literary point of view, the primitive novel confused creation with information, art with artifice. As is well known, good novels cannot be written with good intentions

alone. Freed from the domination of the anecdote based on European models, the primitive novelists nevertheless remained bound by the methods of composition and the narrative language of the writers of Europe, principally the naturalists. Painstaking in the description of landscapes and picturesque customs and manners, purists in the portrayal of nature, extremists in the use of the vernacular in dialogue, Manichean in the presentation of social conflicts, the primitive novelists present a view of reality that is at best vividly colorful but which is nevertheless decorative and superficial. The primitive novels are valid geographic testimonials, important documentaries, but their esthetic significance is nevertheless slight. Although they are enlightening with regard to historical and social reality, the primitive novels do not succeed in creating an autonomous and sovereign world of their own. The quality of a novel is not measured by the greater or lesser degree of correlation between the story and its real-life model; rather it is measured by the story's intrinsic power of persuasion, by its ability to impose itself upon the reader as a living and coherent reality *in and of itself*. In other words, the authenticity of a story is not dependent upon its plot but rather upon the means by which the plot is embodied in a particular written form and in a particular structure. The failure of the primitive novel is to a great extent the result of the disdain which its authors demonstrated toward the strictly technical problems of artistic creation. The parochial horizon of their vision, their epidermic notion of man, did not emanate from the themes which they adopted but rather from their incapacity to express these themes in a language and a structure sufficiently functional to elevate them to a universal plane.

The creative novel is thus a relatively recent phenomenon in Latin America. Only within the last twenty years has narration come to occupy the same plane of dignity and originality that the poem and the essay had already achieved previously (in general, the theater continues to flounder in a primitive state). Writers such as Borges, Onetti, Fuentes, Carpentier, Guimarães Rosa, Cortázar, and García Márquez have not only put our novel, bluntly speaking, on an equal footing with even the best of other countries; they have in addition made the narration of the twenties and thirties appear in comparison to be as anachronistic as that of the nineteenth century. Curiously enough, the qualitative change experienced by Latin American fiction during the postwar period parallels a certain stagnation of the European and North American novel which, after a period of notable splendor—culminating in the works of Joyce, Proust, Kafka, Faulkner—lost its impetus and was either debilitated by formalistic experiments (the French *nouveau roman*) or else languished in passive conformity with tradition (the current English novel). This fact has undoubtedly contributed to the popularity abroad of the new Latin American novelists ("new" in a literary sense, not generational, since the ages of these novelists range from thirty to sixty years). However, the principal reason behind the acceptance that our narrative has achieved is not of external origin, but rather is essentially a result of its own maturity.

What constitutes maturity? Thanks to the new writers, it consists primarily of a thematic shift in the axis of Latin American fiction from nature to man. Man's problems, his nightmares, and his ambitions are the essential themes of this fiction, rather than the pampas, the plateaus, or the cane fields, as was the case in the primitive novel. "Indigenous" themes have not been excluded but have been intensified and framed within a perspective that is no longer regional but rather universal. The literary worth of Guimarães Rosa's *Grande Sertão: Veredas* and of Juan Rulfo's *Pedro Páramo* does not reside in the fact that both novels accurately describe the rural worlds of Minas Gerais and of Jalisco, but rather in the fact that, drawing on firsthand knowledge of life in these regions, the authors have created *additionally* worlds which are soverign and autonomous, worlds endowed with their own significance and mythology, and with the verbal persuasion that allows readers of any country or language to recognize themselves and identify with the characters that populate this fictional world. Just as the Bolivian or Paraguayan reader has little difficulty identifying with a Mr. Bloom and empathizing with his Dublinesque odyssey, so also can the reader from Norway or Finland live vicariously the life of the "yagunzo" Riobaldo and share in his adventures as a highwayman of the *sertão*. This is possible because, regardless of differences in time and place, the two characters express two equally complex paths that human destiny can take.

In addition to becoming "more human," the new Latin American novel has expanded its concept of reality. In the primitive novel reality consisted solely of geography and history; nature and social concerns delimited its field of action. The new novelists have incorporated into fiction other dimensions of human existence, such as imagination and dreams; and themes of fantasy have invaded the short story as well as the novel. In the case of Miguel Asturias these new thematic devices do not exclude the more traditional themes exploited in the Latin American novel. Asturias blends the two in a curious baroque symbiosis in which social protest and political satire alternate with the evocation of indigenous myths, witchcraft, and magic. Hypercivilized surrealist prose, composed of unexpected associa-

tions and nourished by the free flow of subconscious images, is the instrument that Asturias utilizes to reconstruct allegorically—with varying degrees of success—the most primitive of worlds. Jorge Luis Borges, another major representative of the literature of fantasy, adopts techniques diametrically opposed to those of Asturias. His fiction contains nothing that is spontaneous or irrational; everything is the result of intimate knowledge and of maximum intellectual effort. His working materials do not consist of indigenous traditions or social protest, but rather of literary myths, philosophical systems, metaphysics, and the concept of time. Borges is the writer who best symbolizes the end of Latin America's inferiority complex vis-à-vis Europe. Previously, there was a tacit agreement among our writers that certain themes were taboo, beyond their capabilities: how could they possibly traverse the same paths as a Valéry, an Eliot, or a Gide? The great themes of Western culture were considered untouchable; they were the exclusive domain of the European writers. Borges was the first to expose this fallacy and to demonstrate that a Latin American intellectual could also make original statements concerning Shakespeare or Goethe and conceive credible stories set in the Middle Ages or Turkey.

In the case of some Latin American prose writers—Julio Cortázar, Gabriel García Márquez, and José Lezama Lima, for example—themes of fantasy have not replaced the purely realistic ones, but rather coexist with them, often in the same work. This fusion of objectivity and fantasy, of myth and history, of dreamed experience and lived experience, crystallizes in literary worlds in which the mysterious and unusual do not destroy objective reality; they are not open doors to mental escape. Quite the contrary, they embody the most urgent problems confronting contemporary man, illuminating those problems with heretofore unknown perspective (the best examples of this are *Rayuela* and *Cien años de soledad*). Lezama Lima's only novel, *Paradiso*, is, in addition, interesting for its "backward" exoticism: it does with Europe and Asia what the surrealists did with Japan; what writers such as Paul Morand or Joseph Kessel did with Africa, Latin America, and Asia; what Pierre Louÿs and Marcel Schwob did with ancient Greece. Just as the exotic worlds in the works of these authors served to mold a "European" interpretation or a superficial "European" view of exotic reality, in the same way, in *Paradiso,* the history, the literature, and the thought of Europe and Asia are exploited by the author as nothing more than decorative motifs or pretexts to construct a monumental fable of truly American origin (perhaps it would be more correct to say of "Antillean" origin).

Just as the countryside was the immutable setting of the primitive novel, the city is the permanent setting of the creative novel. Among the new novelists there are impassioned interpreters and inventors of cities. The first novel by Carlos Fuentes, *La región más transparente,* is a biography of the author's own Mexico City; it is a meticulous study of its human types, of its dramas and frustrations, of its myths, and of the concerns and the ideological battles which are waged within its confines. On the other hand, the novels of José Donoso bring about a confrontation between ruffians and aristocrats in a poetically conceived Santiago which has been stripped of its middle class, a Santiago in which everything collapses in a prolonged and elegant neurosis; and in the demented Caracas of the novels and short stories of Salvador Garmendia, all but the most cruel and sordid of human experience has disappeared. In *Sobre héroes y tumbas,* by Ernesto Sábato, Buenos Aires appears as a kaleidoscope of images that emanate at times from historical reconstruction, at times from direct observation, and at times from hallucination. On the other hand, other writers have invented cities: Juan Carlos Onetti sets his stories in a gray and nebulous Puerto de Santa María on the Río de la Plata, and García Márquez sets his in a mythical tropical hamlet, Macondo.

The primitive novel conformed to the prototype: the predominance of landscape over the individual, of content over form, of objective life over the subjective. Its language was impressionistic and rhetorical, its technique naturalistic. All the primitive novels were more or less successful variations of this same prototype. On the other hand, it is impossible to establish a common denominator for the creative novel in which the most heterogeneous themes, purposes, styles, and structures compete with one another; but beneath this diversity, which is the novel's greatest asset, there is one central and unifying element: an awareness of form, an artistic impulse. The new Latin American novelist recognizes that his success or failure as a creator will be decided not by the themes he selects, nor by the emotions or obsessions he expresses, but rather by the formal elements—words and structure—that are adopted to develop those themes, emotions, or obsessions. In the final analysis, the maturity of the Latin American novel signifies the achievement of esthetic independence. The Latin American novelist now explores not only untapped areas of reality with a view toward transforming them into literary myth; he also explores language. Not only does he invent characters or situations; he likewise invents new narrative techniques. In the case of writers such as Guillermo Cabrera Infante, Severo Sarduy, and Carlos Fuentes in his last novel, *Cambio de piel,* this increasing concern for narrative form has been translated into works which are above all linguistic experiments, novels whose heroes are not men but rather words. This

inclination toward esthetic originality which characterizes the new Latin American writer obviously should not be construed as a return to provincialism or as a total denial of Europe. On the contrary, the curiosity and the interest that exist in Latin America with regard to the new tendencies in narration in the rest of the world are perhaps even more intense than in the past. The one difference is that now the Latin American novelist no longer imitates; he assimilates, he adapts, he modifies, he discriminates and puts to use those imported models that are most consistent with his own literary objectives. Communication has replaced subordination; mutual exchange has replaced dependence. For the first time, literary influences do not operate in only one direction: it is no longer surprising to detect in the works of young European writers a resemblance to the work of Cortázar or to discover in the pages of *Tel Quel* of Paris that a French essayist repeats as his own the literary opinions that Borges formulated ten years ago.

Nevertheless, the preceding is not sufficient to explain the principal difference between Latin American narrative and what is written today in the rest of the Western world. There is nothing unique about the fact that our novel has substituted man for nature as the central concern; that it has expanded its perception of reality to include the social and the cultural, the imagined and the dreamlike; that the city has become the setting of the story; or that the Latin American novelist has recognized the irrevocable importance of form in the creative process. These developments signify nothing more than that our novel has arrived at a stage of development which had been achieved years ago in Europe and the United States. The circumstances that have stimulated the development of the Latin American novel are of a varied nature, most of them having already been pointed out by the critics. From a literary point of view, the Latin American writer considers himself a "professional" in the most flattering sense of the word, whereas his predecessors were rather like dilettantes or amateurs. The latter exercised their talent as creative writers while at the same time pursuing careers as politicians, diplomats, merchants, or adventurers. On the other hand, the contemporary authors are, first and foremost, writers. A vocation embraced in an exclusive and all-encompassing way should logically produce more vigorous and lasting fruits than one which is exercised only on Sundays and holidays. From a social point of view the growth of the Latin American cities in the last twenty years, a growth which has proceeded at a staggering pace, has contributed to the creation of a heretofore nonexistent reading public. This same phenomenon is also partly responsible for the establishment of new publishing firms. Half a century ago, writers in most of the Latin American countries did not write novels for the simple reason that there was no way to publish them: a short story or a poem at least had the advantage of fitting into the Sunday edition of the newspaper. Emir Rodríguez Monegal feels that World War II, which interrupted for several years the importation of European novels into Latin America, should also be included among the factors that stimulated the advance of our prose fiction. The void caused by the war forced the reading public to turn its eyes toward "indigenous" writers, thereby discovering that an Argentine or a Mexican novel could be just as attractive as an Italian or French one. There is a good deal of truth in this observation. I remember, for example, that fifteen years ago, in Lima, the attitude with which my university friends and I confronted a new novel was summarized by the following prejudiced formula: "All Latin American novels are bad until they prove themselves otherwise; all French and North American novels are good until they prove themselves otherwise." The attitude of Peruvian youth today is still prejudiced, but in the opposite sense: they await the appearance of the most recent work of García Márquez or of Carpentier with the same impatience that we awaited new works by Sartre or Camus.

In addition, there is a different type of factor which seems to me to be just as important—if not more so—as previous ones, in explaining the qualitative change in Latin American narration in the last few years. It is advisable to examine this in detail because, without a doubt, it is on the basis of this factor that the primary difference between today's Latin American novel and the novels of Europe and North America can be traced. It is neither a literary nor a sociological factor; rather it is a historical one. Unlike poetry or drama, whose origin coincides with the origin of all civilizations, the novel is the most "historic" of all literary genres to the extent that it has a definite place and date of birth. This disinterested verbal representation of human reality that portrays the world at the same time that it denies the world, that re-creates by destroying; this subtle murderer of gods that we call the novel, perpetrated by a man who serves as a substitute for God, was born in the West, in the high Middle Ages, when faith was dying and human reason was replacing God as the instrument for understanding life and as the guiding principle for the government of human society. Malraux has commented that Western civilization is the only one which has slain its gods without replacing them with others. The appearance of the novel, that deicide, and the appearance of the novelist, that substitute for God, are to a certain extent the result of that crime. Since the time when the novel of chivalry transposed in fiction the medieval cas-

tle which the winds of the Renaissance had already begun to erode, the novel has continued to represent a curious attempt at historical recuperation and exorcism, and it has achieved its most glorious heights when the reality that inspired it was on the verge of apocalypse, when the society that served as its source and paradigm was dying. Rescuer and verbal gravedigger of an epoch, the great novelist is a kind of vulture: the putrid flesh of history is his favorite nourishment and has served to inspire him to his most audacious undertakings. The literary worlds of a Tolstoy, of a Proust, or of a Kafka are monumental verbal images that have been inspired by societies in periods of decadence immediately preceding historical collapse. Like the moribund Spanish Middle Ages which produced the turbulent stories of Amadises, Palmarines, and Tirant lo Blanch; and like the condemned Russia in which Tolstoy and Dostoevsky were reared; and like the anachronistic Deep South which supplied Faulkner with the raw material for the invention of the saga of Yoknapatawpha County, Latin America is today a continent that is changing its skin, that is becoming the subject rather than the object of history. The impetuous explosion of novels that have welled up within its breast is the parting gesture of a dying continent.

Of course, this relationship between the historical evolution of a society and the refinement of its novelistic expertise cannot be measured with scientific precision; it is not as rapid a process as it might appear when described with such brevity. What I have described above is a predominant tendency and not a dogmatic formula. This tendency may be defined by asserting that the most propitious moment for the development of prose fiction is when reality ceases to have precise meaning for a historic community because the society's religious, moral, or political values, which once provided the foundation for social life and the master key for perceiving reality, have entered upon a period of crisis and no longer enjoy the faithful support of the collectivity. As a result, great novels normally do not appear in times of revolutionary fervor when the entire society is united behind one great cause. Not a single outstanding novel was written during the French Revolution, or during the Russian Revolution, or during the wars for independence in either North or South America, or during the Chinese revolution. Great novels never appear in these moments of optimistic exultation, of hope and faith in a country's destiny; rather, they appear in the preceding period, when the erosion of the old order permits the community to perceive only confusion and chaos in the reality that surrounds them.

This crisis of faith that accompanies the decay of historical reality, this skepticism toward the guiding values of the world, which is the most overt symptom of the decomposition of a society, curiously enough awakens an increasing receptivity, an appetite, an intense need for fiction, for narrative images that are capable of creating a new reality inherently different from the one in which it is no longer possible to believe. God is assassinated and the cult of the imposter begins; reality is distrusted and faith is sparked in reality's verbal manifestations. It is as if these reserves of faith which had been withdrawn from the real world were, in compensation, redirected toward the novels which the ruins of this world engendered. This is the phenomenon that is currently taking place in Latin America. The Latin American countries today are experiencing the most disturbing crisis in their history. All agree that one period is closing and that another, for better or worse, will soon open up; but no one has the courage to face up to the reality of today. Nevertheless, the narrative images inspired by this offensive reality which all despise have been received with greedy enthusiasm, with unprecedented credulity. Not only are novels circulating in greater numbers (previously an Argentine, Chilean, or Colombian novelist could expect to sell only 1,000 copies if his work were a success; now an edition of 20,000 copies is not exceptional); but also the novelist has become a popular figure whose picture appears in newspapers and who is met in the streets by autograph seekers.

Of course, this social phenomenon has a literary counterpart: at a moment when circumstances are favorable to the novel, the same gratuitous transference of faith on the part of the readers toward the novel serves at the same time as a stimulus for the author in his creative activity; it is what compels him to assume his role as a substitute for God through undertakings increasingly more daring and ambitious. The abundance of these better novels which are stimulated by the confidence of a whole community is itself a result of the unlimited confidence with which they were created. The quality of a novel stems, above all, from its power of persuasion. This power is only as great as the confidence (not the intelligence, or the ingenuity, or the skill) with which the novelist executes the creative act; and the societies in crisis are precisely those in which the literary vocation has adopted an almost religious and messianic character. These societies are the ones that have inspired the most daring and total novels ever conceived. The novels of stable societies which are inspired by a historic reality that is not threatened by an imminent radical change—that is to say, by the type of reality which is still sustained by the confidence of the society—tend to be characterized by a stamp of irony, by formalistic games, by either excessive intellectualism

or cynical nihilism. These characteristics reveal an attitude of rejection by the artist when confronted by reality. The author does not dare pretend to be God, he does not compete with reality on equal terms, he makes no attempt to create worlds as vast and complex as the real world. He has no faith in his own powers, and such an enterprise seems to him both absurd and naive. To a certain extent he is right: all novelistic projects that crystallize in a work of art involve a large dosage of both madness and innocence. The novelist in a stable society takes refuge in brilliance, in formalistic sophistication, and he proclaims that the function of the novelist is not "to compete with the Civil Code," but rather to create new techniques and to reinvent language.

This, I think, is the basic distinction that exists in our day between the best representatives of the European and North American novel. The differences of form, content, and purpose that separate them are a consequence of a more profound difference that is related to the evolution of the respective societies. The historical reality, the framework of experiences within which the Latin American novelist writes, is a reality threatened with extinction. This perspective is traditionally the one which has nurtured the illusion—naïve, demented, but nevertheless formidable—of wishing to recapture with fantasy and words the total image of a world, of seeking to write novels that express this total reality not only qualitatively, but also quantitatively. To this devilish and unrealistic impulse we owe the existence of such novels as *The Human Comedy*, *The Man without Qualities*, and *Ulysses*, novels which represent the highest achievement of European literature. The same holds true today in Latin America with works such as *Los pasos perdidos*, *Rayuela*, and *Cien años de soledad*. The European or North American novelist in our day rarely attempts to write a "total" novel. The crises that agitate their societies are different from those that are currently disrupting Latin American society. The former affect only the surface or marginal strata of historical reality; the foundations of that reality remain essentially untouched. This reality, which is still thought to be viable, does not awaken the same "total" rejection which compels today's Latin American novelist to attempt "totally" to replace reality with "total" novels. Quite the contrary, the historical reality currently found in Europe and North America evokes only mocking withdrawal and condescending criticism from the writers of those areas, postures which are translated into novels at times brilliant but nevertheless modest and skeptical, and at times luxuriously gratuitous. What is involved here is a profound difference, but at the same time it is provisional and precarious. Latin America will not continue to languish indefinitely, nor will the European countries and the United States always be able to assimilate their inherent historical contradictions; and these changes will undoubtedly be reflected in the novelistic production of the respective countries. Likewise, a period of historical stability and its corresponding narrative modesty will one day arrive in Latin America. Edmund Wilson boasted several years ago of never having been interested in the Latin American novel. I wonder if he would repeat today with the same conviction this somewhat abrupt remark.

Mario Vargas Llosa, translated by Nick Mills

A Literary Prize in Oklahoma [1974]

Books Abroad is an American journal published by the University of Oklahoma and edited by the poet and critic Ivar Ivask. Founded in 1927, the journal specializes in reviewing literature of the entire world. In a very recent issue, it reviews books from some twenty language areas. Ten new Swedish works of belles lettres are considered. In addition to this, Professor Richard B. Vowles from the University of Wisconsin offers a perceptive article on the mystical element in Sven Delblanc's novel *Homunculus*. *Books Abroad* is an almost sensational, unusual occurrence in the United States and the entire English-speaking world. The English language is a Chinese wall which is difficult to penetrate from either direction. In England and the United States, one finds little curiosity about other nations. The United States sits pondering its own mighty contradictory face with no time to brood about others. *Books Abroad* represents an attempt to breach this self-absorption.

Some years ago the journal was fortunate to interest the wealthy Neustadt family in donating a large sum of money to be used for an international literary prize. Every other year $10,000 is awarded by a jury made up of writers from the entire world.[1] They meet in the university town of Norman, a few miles outside of Oklahoma City.

This year I represented Sweden. My fellow jurors were the novelist Chinua Achebe from Nigeria—Per Wästberg has written many times about him in *Dagens Nyheter*[2]—Michel Butor from France, the poet Ernst Jandl from Austria, the playwright Ferenc Karinthy from Hungary, George Loghin from Romania, the poet Mario Luzi from Italy, John Gardner from the United States—Bengt Holmqvist presented him in this paper last year—Andri Peer from Switzerland, and the critic John Willett from England.

Oklahoma does not sound like world culture or literature. Mark Twain's *Huckleberry Finn* ends with Huck

saying that he wants to light out for the Territory, which was Oklahoma before it became a state. In the Territory adventure and freedom were alive among Indians and buffaloes. When civilization arrived, it was time for another kind of adventure. There were oil and gas in the ground.

Today the skyline of Oklahoma City is dominated by a mighty skyscraper. In the top storey there is a Renaissance hall with a ceiling twelve meters high and Gobelin tapestries covering the walls. On the floors stand wardrobes from the baroque period, monumental sculptures, carved chests, and marble-topped tables. There the members of the Petroleum Club gather and are served drinks by beautiful black girls.

Here Nixon is not considered a menace, while California's Reagan is expected to speak at a luncheon for 6,000 persons. This evening I have as my table partner the amiable lady who will be Reagan's hostess. I asked her whether Watergate has weakened the Republican party. This she denies. But then, after Agnew, what? I continue. At that moment a charming introspective smile appears on the lady's face. "Poor Spiro," she exclaims in a charming manner and in the tone of a mother who has caught her ten-year-old son in the act of stealing an apple. "Naturally that was not right," she admitted. "But then everybody does it."

In spite of such adventures in Oklahoma, Norman was nevertheless for several days in February a world literary center. Every juror had informed the others beforehand about his candidate and had given a written explanation of the reasons for his choice. I had come out for Eyvind Johnson.

Chaired by Ivar Ivask, the jury proceedings were pleasant but with somewhat unusual happenings. We came from very different backgrounds and had not met one another before. The majority of us were not specialists of literature but simply writers with the customary one-sided reading habits. Only a few jurors seemed to have read carefully several works by all the candidates. We sat there with the various names before us and talked into the air about him or her.

When it came to the actual "selling" of our candidates, those who had chosen poets had a head start. Every reviewer knows that if you wish to convince a reader of the value of a book, you must be able to describe concretely its form and language. Praise alone is ineffective. The reader must come into direct contact with the author discussed in the review.

Those who had chosen novelists or playwrights, such as Doris Lessing, Wole Soyinka, Anna Seghers, or Zaharia Stancu, had difficulty in offering comprehensible descriptions. As I talked about Eyvind Johnson, I felt

I was not succeeding before this international gathering in distinguishing him from Thomas Mann and other writers who blend fiction and essay. Ernst Jandl, on the other hand, a gentleman full of vigor and talent, came close to swaying us all toward a poet whom few of us knew, the Scotsman Ian Hamilton Finlay. Words form only one part of Finlay's "poems." His poetry is "concrete" in the sense that he builds artistic objects by using stones, cardboard, glass, wood, even ponds. His "poems" become riddles reminiscent of the emblematic art beloved by the Renaissance, where meaning was found in a combination of word and image. Jandl was able to place Finlay's poems on the table in front of us. He produced a cardboard sail with a few words printed on it and demonstrated to us how it worked.

Jandl might well have convinced us, had it not been for Michel Butor from France. This famous author is an indisputable proof of Rilke's contention that angels are human beings. His eyes, his smile, his entire being was exceptionally charming. It was impossible to take one's eyes off him. This is not to say that he convinced us merely by his appearance. His French was as luminous and effective as the Archangel Michael's sword. He had chosen as his candidate the French poet Francis Ponge, who will be seventy-five this year. When Butor took the floor, Jandl had already prepared the way for this year's prize to go to a lyric poet. Like Jandl, Butor was able to place Ponge in our midst by quoting some of his poems. Ponge is a prose poet in the tradition of Baudelaire and Mallarmé. His themes are simple. He selects things or animals which he describes in detail. From these descriptions he draws a moral. Butor called him a master of still life in the tradition of Gauguin or Monet. He also compared Ponge to La Fontaine, I believe with good reason.

One poem by Ponge is called "The Snail." On four pages he describes the snail's nature and way of life. It kisses the ground with its entire body and with its secretion, its cold blood, leaves a silvery trail behind. Its incredible nakedness forces it into constant movement while outside its shell, but it can always withdraw into its home, lock itself up in its shell, and shut out intruders. It moves with majestic slowness, which is all the more admirable since it is so vulnerable and its eyeballs so sensitive. It shies away both from excessive dryness and from too much water. Should it be angered, it has no means to express it wrath, except by letting its slime flow more abundantly. The shell which it carries with itself is a part of itself and at the same time a work of art, a monument which will outlast the animal. The snail transforms its life into a work of art, and this work of art has the right proportions, is not something apart from itself but is created for its real needs, and fits its

body exactly. Snails are saints because they obey their own innate laws. They know and accept themselves the way they are. They affirm even their own frailty.

We decided to award Ponge the prize and the silver eagle feather, which has exactly the same form as the feather Strindberg took from Harriet Bosse's hat and which he used to write poems to her. Ivar Ivask added, in announcing the decision, that in this age of environmental destruction we need poets who defend things and animals. Through Ponge we perceive nature from a new perspective.

This was the first time I had participated in a jury of this kind. I am skeptical toward literary prizes, and I have an especially low opinion of the Nobel Prize. The latter creates in many people the idea that it is a competition which the best writer wins. Ponge is of course not a greater writer than Eyvind Johnson or Michaux, who were also candidates. Writers are incomparable magnitudes. Due to the enormous and growing publicity value of the Nobel Prize, certain writers are singled out in the opinion of the general public and elevated to a status above all others. It is really absurd to see how throughout the world a Nobel Prize-winning writer is constantly coupled with the prize, so much so that Solzhenitsyn, for example, has been renamed Nobel Prize-winner Solzhenitsyn.

The *Books Abroad* Prize, however, lacks this prestige. It is not a medal which is to hang forever around the laureate's neck. It can serve as a corrective to the Nobel Prize. To conclude in the spirit of Ponge, the Nobel Prize is a "shell" that is out of proportion to the creature chosen to bear it. The Oklahoma prize has more reasonable proportions.

Olof Lagercrantz, translated by Ivar and Astrid Ivask

---

[1] The cash value of the Neustadt Prize has since been raised to $25,000.

[2] *Dagens Nyheter* is Sweden's largest daily newspaper. Olof Lagercrantz was one of its editors-in-chief in the 1970s, and this article first appeared there on 3 March 1974.

Recollections of *Books Abroad*: And So It Grew [1976]

If anyone had been asked in 1927 to predict a place likely to produce an internationally oriented literary publication, the choice would certainly not have been a small university town in the middle of the United States; but Dr. Roy Temple House, then Professor of

German and Chairman of the Modern Languages Department at the University of Oklahoma (1918–42),
had the idea of founding a literary journal that would
review new books in the principal European languages
and present articles on prominent foreign writers. In
this undertaking he was assisted by his colleagues Professors W. A. Willibrand, K. Kaufman, S. Scatori, A. M.
de la Torre, J. Malthaner, and others. The first issue was
indeed a modest one, only thirty-two pages, and it was
distributed gratis.

Dr. House was a quiet, unassuming man, born on
a Nebraska farm (see *BA* 38:2, p. 113) and, according
to his own account, a frail child, shy, rather introverted
and bookish. After securing his doctorate from the University of Chicago, he taught at Southwestern State College at Weatherford, Oklahoma, which was at that time
a Normal School whose main function was teacher
training. He married a colleague, a number of years
older than he, who taught French. During or following
World War I he was associated with the Hoover Commission in Belgium for the assistance of orphans and
war refugees and was awarded two medals from the Belgian government and the French award, Chevalier of
the Legion of Honor. A later honor was his induction
in 1948 into the Oklahoma Hall of Fame. The period
with the Hoover Commission was the last time he traveled abroad, in spite of his continuing international interest. Indeed, he never took a vacation and could not
understand why anyone else would insist on having
one.

Dr. House was kind to students and persons in
need of financial help. He lent or gave money to a number of people, although he lived very frugally himself.
Among those he assisted was a music student, who in
a recent newspaper article said of her own experience
on the occasion of her awarding a scholarship to a top
student in the OU School of Music, "When things were
looking the bleakest . . . Dr. House, a professor of modern languages, gave me a scholarship to complete my
work in Arts and Sciences." She had determined she
would help a student as she had been aided.

In person, Dr. House was fairly tall, slender, and
had sparse gray hair and a neatly trimmed moustache.
His pale, gray-blue, bespectacled eyes were sensitive to
light, and he usually wore an eyeshade while working.
He was a gentle, mild-mannered man, although at times
he could be authoritarian and a rigid disciplinarian, as
some of his students and colleagues learned. On the
other hand, he was often personally sympathetic and
generous.

Dr. House worked seven days a week with *Books
Abroad*. It was so much his primary interest that the

work became his pleasure, and since he had no children, he gave it his full devotion. Always a thrifty soul,
he used to write his reviews (of which there were many)
on the backs of old letters, saved string and paper for
the mailing of books to other reviewers, and used index
cards discarded by other departments of the university
for *Books Abroad*'s file records and annual index. At that
time there was practically no money for its operating
costs, and its survival then is to be credited largely to
a former president, Joseph Brandt, who also established
the University of Oklahoma Press.

A light, witty touch characterized Dr. House's style.
It was his philosophy that literary criticism could be serious without being dull or pedantic. By 1942, when he
gave up the chairmanship of the Modern Languages Department, the quarterly had grown to 116 pages and
had enlarged its scope. Many well-known authors and
critics of the day had become his friends through correspondence: Alfonso Reyes, Constant Burniaux, Aubrey
F. G. Bell, Albert Guérard Sr., Rafael Heliodoro Valle,
Gastón Figueira, Victoria Ocampo, and a great many
others. Although businesslike, his letters had a personal
warmth that elicited responses in the same vein.

When *Books Abroad* was twenty years old, my association with it began. I had been teaching Spanish after
coming to the University when my husband had accepted a position on the Political Science faculty in 1946.
Dr. House asked me to join the staff of the periodical
after hearing me read a paper on Federico García Lorca,
all of whose works I had read and in whom I was intensely interested. *Books Abroad* was a thriving journal
by this time with a fairly wide reputation and covered
books in many languages, including some non-
European. It comprised four or five principal articles,
a following section of brief articles or notes under the
rubric "Not in the Reviews," then "Headliners" (reviews
of books which the editor considered most important).
Then came the bulk of the reviews divided into French,
Spanish, German, and Books in Various Languages.
These were followed by a page or two entitled "The Editor Parenthesizes," giving the editor a chance to essay
briefly on whatever topic he wished.

In the summer of 1949 Dr. House, then seventy-
three, suffered a nervous breakdown. His wife had recently died and he faced retirement from his beloved
brainchild. Separation from *Books Abroad* was so painful
that his mental distress reacted to bring about physical
illness; but he had faced the reality of imminent retirement and had chosen his successor. Dr. House lived
until December of 1963 and from time to time contributed to *Books Abroad,* where he was always made welcome.

Ernst Erich Noth arrived in September 1949 from New York City, where he had been associated with the Voice of America, broadcasting in German. The arrangement was that he should teach a class in German for the Modern Languages Department, as I did in Spanish, and assume the editorship of *Books Abroad.* He had attended the Free University in Berlin, where he was born, and had fled before the onslaught of the Nazis. As a student, he had been outspoken, was a leader of opposition to the Nazis, and was on their "wanted" list. For a time he lived in the Provence, married, and was helped to escape to America by Father Baldensperger and the Dominicans.

Under Dr. Noth's editorship the scope of *Books Abroad* was considerably broadened. Reviews of books on art, politics, religion, philosophy, and various other subjects were included. As might be expected, greater emphasis was now given to German literature. A new feature was now (see *BA* 24:2) introduced, called "Periodicals at Large," which mentioned for each succeeding issue of a wide spectrum of foreign and American periodicals the articles of particular significance or the outstanding features. This proved to be mutually beneficial for *Books Abroad* and the periodicals noted. For them it provided a free international showcase for their periodicals, and for our quarterly it supplied important literary information on new currents in world literature and new books to request for review which might have been overlooked. Another innovation that came in volume 24 (1950) was an index of reviewers, enabling readers to find their respective contributions.

On the occasion of the twenty-fifth anniversary of the quarterly a commemorative booklet was issued containing twenty-five tributes from prominent literary persons, brief essays by the editor, the founder, persons associated with the early issues, and myself, plus "A *Books Abroad* calendar" by Dr. House noting the outstanding feature of each previous issue. Thus the Silver Jubilee booklet was a brief survey of the first twenty-five years.

It was at this time that Dr. Noth conceived the brilliant idea of presenting a survey of world literature during these twenty-five years, which would be authored by outstanding writers in their respective language areas. He had a wide international acquaintance with many writers, like the other editors, and drew them into the family of contributors. To implement this survey, Dr. Noth obtained a grant from the Rockefeller foundation, and more than forty survey articles were published between 1952 (see *BA* 26:4) and 1957 (see *BA* 31:1). However, few changes in format or organization of material were made during his editorship.

Besides his native German, Dr. Noth wrote and spoke fluently in French and English. Grasset Publishers had already issued his book *La tragédie de la jeunesse allemande* and *L'homme contre le partisan;* Plon his *Enfant écartelé, Un homme à part,* and *La voie barrée;* Gallimard *Le désert;* and Editions Méditerranéennes the trilogy *Ponts sur le Rhin.* He was a perfectionist in the copy-editing of articles and reviews. We would usually spend an hour or two settling the questions that each of us raised in our reading of the material for a particular issue. Not a comma escaped his attention apparently. So involved was he with every detail that for a number of years he made up the dummy himself, except in the summer, when he was usually in Europe for several weeks and this task was turned over to me. Finally, he turned it over completely—to the joy, I imagine, of the janitor who previously had found at the end of the day enormous cuttings of paper all over the floor around his desk instead of in a wastebasket.

Dr. Noth was rather blond, of no more than average height, somewhat heavy-set, fair-skinned, with very blue eyes. He dressed quite casually and would have been in style with the young genereation of today. He did not like the life-style of a rather small American town like Norman after having lived and Europe and would sometimes become depressed and nostalgic; but he took his work quite seriously and gave it great effort. Always considerate of his fellow workers, he kindly gave me a year's leave of absence with the permission of the administration to accompany my husband to Egypt when the latter was awarded a Fulbright Lectureship, and this gave me the opportunity to obtain the survey article on Egyptian literature from Dr. Taha Hussein (see *BA* 29:1; (1955; [see this issue, pp. 249–56]).

In 1959 Dr. Noth accepted an offer from Marquette University and assumed the Chair of Comparative Literature there, after having first served as chairman of the German Department. He and his family (wife, three sons, and a daughter) purchased a large house in Milwaukee near the lake; but the pull toward Europe later became too strong for him to resist, and after several years at Marquette he returned to Europe.

The next editor was a young Austrian, Wolfgang Bernard Fleischmann, who was born in Vienna and whose parents brought him to the United States in 1940 when he was twelve, at the time when many Jewish people were emigrating. He attended St. John's College and did graduate work at the University of North Carolina. His thesis and Ph.D. dissertation dealt with Lucretius. When he returned from U.S. military service in 1957, he became an instructor in the English Department at the University of North Carolina and succeeded Werner Friederich as editor of the *Yearbook of Comparative and*

General Literature. >From here Dr. Fleischmann came to *Books Abroad.* He and his mother established their home in Norman; his father, a physician, was on the staff of a Veterans Administration Hospital elsewhere in the United States.

Now it was the turn of Austrian writers to come to the forefront in *Books Abroad.* Articles on Austrian writers were given prominence, and reviews of books by Austrian authors received more attention. By volume 34 the rubric of the periodicals section was changed to "Periodicals Survey" as being more appropriate, but volume 35 dropped this section, which was not thereafter revived. Dr. Fleischmann's real interest was teaching comparative literature, and after two years he accepted an offer from Emory University in that field, bringing his editorship to a close.

Dr. Fleischmann was followed by Dr. Robert Vlach, a native of Czechoslovakia who had fled to Sweden by hiding on a Polish coal barge. He taught in Sweden and produced several books of poetry, plus a number of books which he edited. He came to the University of Oklahoma as a professor of Russian, but when Dr. Fleischmann resigned he sought and received the editorship of *Books Abroad.* He continued to teach classes in Russian and greatly built up the program of courses offered in that area. Dr. Fleischmann had planned to have a special issue commemorating the 700th anniversary of the birth of Dante but had left before it could be accomplished. This became the project of Dr. Vlach, who devoted much hard work to carrying out his predecessor's commitment. The special issue was printed in Sweden, and in the summer of 1964 Dr. Vlach spent a number of weeks in Sweden, from where he mailed sets of galley proof to the office for me and the others on the staff to make editorial corrections. The proof was then mailed back to him, and so the job was completed and the special Dante issue was published in May 1965. Thus its publication date did not conflict with the regular issue, which was in preparation at the same time, and nobody minded too much the extra workload.

Dr. Vlach added to *Books Abroad* in 1963 an independent section of reviews of books in Slavic languages—formerly included under "Various Languages"—and also a separate section devoted to books from and on Asia and Africa. It was about this time that a "Recommended" feature was added to each language section to provide brief notices on books not reviewed in the regular review section. It was not found necessary to restrict the book coverage to areas more closely allied to literature and omit those having to do with science, technology, religion, politics, and other such subjects.

Dr. Vlach was a small, slender, wiry man of enormous nervous energy. Having weak eyes, he wore dark glasses almost constantly, even indoors. He seemed to be a person whose ambition and intellectual fire drove him beyond his physical strength. Soon after he took over the editorship, it was my pleasure to take him, his wife, and their two daughters to Oklahoma City for their examination for citizenship and later also for the ceremony of induction into United States citizenship, a proud event for them.

Dr. Vlach seemed to be stronger physically than he actually was, for he walked back and forth from the office every day except when the weather was unusually cold or hot, at which times he rode with me. One cold, snowy Saturday afternoon in January of 1966 he was working late in the office (although it was not our custom to work on Saturday afternoon, we occasionally did so.) My husband and I were invited to some friends' house for dinner, and when we returned shortly before midnight I was informed by a phone call that Dr. Vlach had walked home around six o'clock and had immediately collapsed and died.

For the next eighteen months I was Acting Editor. The aim was then to keep the periodical alive; and since the feeling was that the next editor would see the need for wide-ranging changes to give the quarterly a more contemporary character, few changes were made, in order not to disrupt the format twice within a short period (although it was longer than anticipated). Months passed without the administration's making any effort to secure a new editor. Finally I asked Dr. Ivar Ivask, a multilingual Estonian poet (who also writes poetry in German—see *Gespiegelte Erde*) and already a contributor to the publication, to apply for the editorship. He was then teaching at St. Olaf College. He began his tenure in the fall of 1967. He and his wife Astrid, a Latvian poet, have become valuable participants in our community.

Now *Books Abroad* came into full bloom. Dr. Ivask's creativity and imagination produced step by step a totally new look. The cover was dressed in bright color, its design was modernized, large excellent photographs added personal interest, the article section became much larger and more important, more reviews were included, and each issue enlarged the journal to its present size of more than two hundred pages. Dr. Ivask brought to *Books Abroad* qualities that Dr. Vlach would have called "pluses" in relationships furthering the interests of the quarterly. His urbanity, sophistication, and personal charm opened doors to smooth the path of the publication. Under Dr. Ivask's guidance new sources of national literatures have been tapped, particularly those of the Third World, whose literary riches had been long overlooked; and in accordance with his ethnic heritage a section on books in Finno-Ugric and

Baltic languages was added. Likewise, a number of changes in type style have brought smartness and elegance to the quarterly. Dr. Ivask is continuing to do great things, and this article should not close without mentioning two other innovations to be credited to him: the Oklahoma Conferences on Writers of the Hispanic World, cosponsored by *Books Abroad* and the Modern Languages Department [now the Puter-baugh Conferences on Writers of the French-Speaking and Hispanic World], which bring various Hispanic writers to the OU campus every two years; and the establish-

ment by *Books Abroad,* together with the Neustadt family of Ardmore, Oklahoma, of a biennial literary prize of $10,000 [now $25,000] awarded for exceptional literary merit without geographic or political considerations.

In these fifty years *Books Abroad* has established a fine tradition, one in which each editor has made a significant contribution. We trust it will continue on the path so brilliantly followed during a splendid half-century.

Bernice G. Duncan

World Literature in Review

A Selection of Book Reviews

1977–2001

1977

■ **MICHEL BUTOR**. *Matière de rêves*. Paris. Gallimard. 1975. 139 pages.

With *Matière de rêves* Michel Butor, well-known novelist, essayist and critic associated with the new novel but transcending its scope by far, has added a new dimension to his multifaceted work.

In his latest book the author for the first time uses highly personal materials—dreams, memories—to create the five stories of the work. Each has a title and a recognizable story line, but the action is interrupted and diffused by a host of substructures. Many of these often minute subsections begin with the name of a city—for instance, Leningrad, Tirnovo, Chicago—visited by the narrator. Another device used by the narrator is to enclose a slide in a letter, a slide that may evoke associations or a name in literature, such as Chateaubriand, Balzac, Stendhal, Constant, Kafka or Zola. The text is studded with the words or names of members of the author's family that constantly arise in his mind and let him express his love for them or make him call out for their help when he is in anguish. Also used are such techniques of the new novel as repetition, regression and intertextuality. The whole kaleidoscopic view is imbued with mystery and rapidly changing images that defy rational explanation and startle the narrator as well as the reader because they are truly "such stuff as dreams are made on."

The narrator, who calls himself Michel Butor most of the time, seems to be asking the same unanswerable questions that appeared in his earlier *A Change of Heart:* "Who are you? Where are you going?" With anguish he "watches the screen" where his life story is shown. Simultaneously viewer and person viewed, he experiences rational and irrational forces from the most secret recesses of his mind. As the film progresses, he tries to describe and comment on what he sees. Speaking of "feverish, contaminated or agitated texts," he still strives to interpret what he sees. But unconscious, irrational behavior usually represses critical thinking.

There are also scenes of lovemaking, of being abandoned in a hut during a tropical rainstorm and of intense feelings of guilt or fear. Horror dominates other scenes when, swept away by masses of water, the narrator floats in a stream near dismembered bodies and crocodiles. Elsewhere he stands in front of an audience, incapable of saying a word, drooling. One night as he hides, unclothed, from the police on a lonely beach, he sinks into sticky mud. Although in *A Change of Heart* Butor has already used a dream in which the narrator wanders through a forest that keeps closing up behind him, nothing he has ever written equals the horror of these nightmares. Nowhere has he bared his nonrational side and libidinal drives so fully. In fact, he has always endeavored to avoid confrontation with the irrational, unconscious side of life.

Understandably, Butor dedicates *Matière de rêves* to "the psychoanalysts, among others," where "others" should be taken to refer to the large audience of all those interested in "seeing" what happens on levels of insight revealed only in dreams as described by a lucid man who possesses the words both to convey the experience and the courage to render it in powerful images.

Anna Otten

■ **NADINE GORDIMER**. *Selected Stories*. New York. Viking. 1976. 381 pages.

Commentators on Nadine Gordimer's fiction embroil themselves inevitably in the social and political milieu which is her ostensible subject. It would be well to remember her own conception of the artistic role of a writer who, as it happens, has involved herself to some degree in the liberal politics of South Africa: "An imaginative writer must not allow a political bias to intrude in the creation of characters—because the whole value of writing should be its dispassionate view. The injustices will come through."

Thus while it is true that Viking's selection provides a social history of the development of apartheid during the last thirty-five years, our first concern should be the growth in the powers of a writer who has achieved extraordinary artistic success in a difficult form which, considering the achievements of her predecessors, we might otherwise consider to be exhausted. From her early story of the black servant who bemoans her lot while struggling heroically to achieve the education of her children ("Ah, Woe Is Me") to the final story of a sculptor driven by his art and by injustice to exile and suicide while his more action-minded friend is suspected of being a police spy and must "prove" himself by going to jail under the Detention Act ("Africa Emergent"), throughout this career we see a true artist whose disgust for injustice is transformed by irony and by a real affection for human beings into a vision of her time and place which we must call wise.

Gordimer's vision is not one of villains and saints, but of fully realized individuals who are cowardly when they can afford to be and courageous when they have no other choice—in other words, of people who, whatever their race, class or political persuasion, are basically like the great majority of us. Nadine Gordimer is one of the most distinguished practitioners of the short story—perhaps the most distinguished—writing in English today. This retrospective of her work, which she has selected in approximately equal parts from her five collections, is an appropriate monument to her achievement.

Robert L. Berner

■ **ADIL JUSSAWALLA**. *Missing Person*. Bombay. Clearing House. 1976. 58 pages.

Jussawalla is among the important Indian poets writing in English, and the publication of this second collection of his is something of an event, for it comes fourteen years after his first. Among Indian poets in English he stands out as a poet with the strongest awareness of contemporary social and political realities.

Jussawalla's is a world of floods, famines, wars, riots, student posters, Five Year Plans, colonial apes, police dogs, running dogs, cell-mates, stone-throwers, refugees, immigrants, high-bottomed foreign-returneds

and a steel-genitaled Jaguar with Miss India at the wheel. Jussawalla brings this newspaper vocabulary to life, chiefly through his almost visceral rage, bitterness and irony. His particular achievement in *Missing Person* is a blend of public and private worlds. This is most evident in the ambitious long poem "Missing Person." Significantly, however, the poem is not just a rendering of sociopolitical and personal detail; it is an essay in mythmaking. References to the "saviour," "the broken tribe," "bright angels," Satan, Caliban, et cetera, ironic though they may be, indicate the poet's attempt to transform the "missing person" into an archetype.

As a "committed" poet Jussawalla demands change: "Restore us to fire." He complains that the sight of new refugees from Tibet does not ruffle our tempers, does not set us "adrift of the mainland's histories." In spite of his intense awareness of the "human pall," Jussawalla conveys a sense of hope: "Back / Where I was born / I may yet observe my own birth." This is personal, but Jussawalla's "I" is also the mythic "missing person." Jussawalla lived for over ten years in England before returning to India in 1970, and not surprisingly, a dominant theme in this volume is exile. The tension between alienation and belonging gives power to a number of poems.

The volume displays a mature talent, though Jussawalla does not quite seem to have outgrown influences. "The Raising of Lazarus" is too Eliotic in its rhetoric, and Auden, whom Jussawalla resembles in some ways, is echoed: "Exile's a broken axle" (see Auden's "The Exiles"), "The free / Couples in their chains" (see Auden's elegy on Yeats).

Vilas Sarang

■ **PRIMO LEVI**. *Il sistema periodico*. Turin. Einaudi. 1975. 241 pages.

Reviewers who had thought that the research chemist Primo Levi had exhausted his talent as a writer after *Se questo è un uomo* (recalling the eleven months he spent in Auschwitz) and *La tregua* (describing the nine months he spent getting back from Auschwitz to Turin via most of the Soviet Union) and who reacted fairly coldly to his subsequent collections of science fiction short stories had to change their minds after reading *Il sistema periodico*. The title of this collection of twenty-one stories, which refers to Mendeleev's táble of elements, suggests a thematic unity: every story is titled after the element closest to its theme. The first one, "Argon," compares this so-called inert gas to Levi's own Jewish ancestors, likable eccentrics who had in common "un atteggiamento di dignitosa astensione, di volontaria (o accettata) relegazione al margine del gran fiume della vita." The other stories are moments of Levi's experiences as a student, as a prisoner in Auschwitz, as a writer and most of all as a chemist: "Vincere la materia è comprenderla, e comprendere la materia è necessario per comprendere l'universo e noi stessi." "Chromium," possibly the best piece, describes Levi's return to chemical research after the concentration camp and his need to communicate what he had experienced, so as to rediscover humanity in himself. His passion for solving chemical problems and his frantic writing worked simultaneously to help him reenter life with enthusiasm: "Lo stesso mio scrivere diventò . . .un'opera di chimico che pesa e divide, misura e giudica su prove certe, e s'industria di rispondere ai perché."

But the book is something more than just an autobiography; it mirrors continuously the historical events of the author's generation—Fascism, the Resistance, the postwar years, people who died, people who kept on working. And another thread runs through the stories, as can best be seen in the last of them, "Carbon." The chemical history of an atom of carbon is followed through the centuries, till it eventually enters Levi's own brain, gives Levi's hand a certain impulse and leads it to impress the final full stop of the book on paper. There is no divorce between matter ("la Materia-Mater, la madre nemica") and spirit; only through mutual interaction does man develop.

The language is clear, lucid, always extremely concrete; it adds to the fascination of the book because of its very concreteness and nonliterariness.

Mirna Risk

■ **FLANN O'BRIEN**. *Stories and Plays*. New York. Viking. 1976. 208 pages.

■ **ANNE CLISSMANN**. *Flann O'Brien: A Critical Introduction to His Writings*. Dublin/New York. Gill & MacMillan/Barnes & Noble. 1975. xiv + 370 pages.

Brian O'Nolan (1912–66) wrote his novels under the pen name "Flann O'Brien" and signed his Gaelic novel and his famous newspaper column with the stage-Irish sobriquet "Myles na gCopaleen." He wrote with equal grace in Irish (Gaelic) and English and put his bilingualism to comic use in an elaborate pattern of wordplay based on the two languages. His first novel, *At Swim-Two-Birds* (the title is an example of tortured English resulting from literal translation from the Irish), was originally published by Longmans in 1939 to immediate critical acclaim. Graham Greene was enthusiastic, and the young Dylan Thomas said, "He could, I believe, be-

come a great comic writer, but this alone establishes him in the forefront of contemporary Irish literature." The book reached only a small public because, as V. S. Pritchett explained in a 1960 review, "1939 was a bad year for originality and laughter." His second novel, written in Gaelic, *An Béal Bocht (The Poor Mouth)* was also a hit with the small audience qualified to understand it. Beginning in 1940, his column of witty vituperation in the *Irish Times* made the name of Myles na gCopaleen a household word.

In O'Brien's early writing the surface brilliance of his invention is underscored with an affectionate concern for "the plain people of Ireland," but a harshly bitter quality seeps into his later work, probably because of professional and personal disappointments. He can be compared to Joyce, Beckett and James Stephens. All of them display an obsession with physical details of ludicrous discomfort vividly presented, often to comic effect. O'Brien always angrily rejected the comparison to Joyce, but certainly he shares what he himself described as "Joyce's almost supernatural skill in conveying Dublin dialogue." His method of creating a grotesque reality heightened by details of surpassing ordinariness can be compared to Beckett's, while his use of fantastic Irish mythological motifs has some of the poetical wit of Stephens. Add to these the intricately constructed bilingual dimension of his work, and a unique comic genius emerges.

In recent years O'Brien's books have been reissued, and *The Poor Mouth* is now available in English translation. *Stories and Plays* are minor pieces consisting of a fragment of an unfinished novel, two slight short stories, two plays and a deceptively perverse critique of Joyce. They all, however, bear the mark of his individual style, and the play, *Faustus Kelly,* is a leisurely but deadly dissection of bourgeois pretention, political corruption and nonsensical national shibboleths.

Comic writers are notoriously subject to mishandling by biographers and critics. Anne Clissmann, in her *Critical Introduction* to O'Brien's writings, skirts the biographical problems with a brief sketch and approaches her critical task cautiously. In the overall view she fails to come to grips with her subject, and a conclusion like

> It is very difficult to attempt a summation of O'Brien's unique qualities. The unevenness of his output and the extensiveness of his interests precluded that discipline and obsessiveness which often make the truly great writer. O'Brien is not in the first rank of creative artists, yet he could at times meet their measure.

is so diffuse and so hedged with qualifiers that in the end it tells us very little about anything. Granted, she admits in her introduction that her book is organized into separate essays because "it is my experience that students tend to read relevant chapters rather than complete books." Given this stance, it is perhaps understandable that the book is somewhat repetitive and lacks a unifying philosophy or idea. Her inability to recognize or appreciate the double-language dimension of O'Brien's writing is explained by her admission that she is ignorant of the Irish language. Certainly O'Brien is accessible to readers of English, in which language he is a superb stylist with an uncannily true ear for usage. That he had the same gifted way with Irish must be taken on trust by many.

Joan Keefe

■ **CHRISTA WOLF**. *Kindheitsmuster*. Berlin. Aufbau. 1976. 534 pages.

The reconstruction of developmental years lived in the arena dominated by National Socialism once again proves itself a valid literary undertaking. The success of Wolf's new book—neither repetitive nor imitative despite numerous related efforts by other authors—affirms the durability of this thematic material.

The narrative-time structure of this work, the length of which equals the total of Wolf's previous creative output, is as complex as it is successful. The focal point is a two-day visit by narrator and family to the small town of her birth—now in Poland—in July 1971. This brief span of hours retrospectively becomes the threshold from which the narrator reenters her early life at that point in 1932 when, at the age of three, she consciously used the word "I" for the first time. Recollection is pursued through her departure from the town before Russian troops in January 1945 and terminates in 1947 with the return of a somewhat normal life to the region of her relocation in the present-day DDR. The manuscript published here was begun in November 1972 and completed in May 1975; the growth of the narrative is painstakingly dated through contrapuntal references to events in Vietnam and Chile and to such dissimilar persons as General Pinochet and Daniel Ellsberg. The account gains further tension through a fourth time dimension, centered upon the narrator's teen-age daughter, in whose eyes are reflected events of which she has no direct experience.

This careful study of the past results in a panorama of historical universality; the review of these events from an adult perspective places central emphasis upon the nature and function of the individual within this context. The major question, "How did we become what we are?" is confronted by the disturbing inquiry: "Can every human being be turned into a beast?"

The overall success of the work lies in Wolf's fresh view upon the crisis of expression. She assumes that, in an ideal case, total correspondence between the structures of experience and those of narration would be possible; this would permit the "precision of imagination" which she seeks. Such a technique, she concludes, cannot exist, for life is a dynamic process which continues beyond and thus invalidates even the most sophisticated narrative structure. Faced by this dilemma, only two choices seem indicated: "To remain speechless or to live in the third person." In her quest for expression, however, Wolf finds a third possibility in a variation upon the Wittgensteinian theme: "About that of which one cannot speak, one must gradually cease being silent." Resignation before this task is not permissible: "We shall never succeed in explaining why things have gone the way they have and not differently; nonetheless, we must not hesitate to undertake at least the preliminaries for future explanations." The writer, through the exercise of "moral memory," mediates between past and present.

Only a hint of the grandiose dimensions of this work and the achievement involved can be given here. It is regrettable that Wolf has chosen to alloy such narrative gold with the propagandistic dross of repeated references to American political machinations. Unjust as the deeds mentioned may have been, the manner in which Wolf has employed them cheapens her work. On the other side of the coin, her mention of events in Czechoslovakia in 1968 is almost unrecognizable behind the melodramatic slag with which it is veiled.

W. V. Blomster

1978

■ **GÜNTER GRASS**. *Der Butt*. Darmstadt. Luchterhand. 1977. 699 pages.

Der Butt (The Flounder) may well be Grass's most innovative work since *The Tin Drum*. He has selected "The Fisherman and His Wife," one of the finest tales in the Grimms' *Märchen,* as the model or first cell of an elaborate novel of over 100 brief sections and almost 700 pages. The brief sections are distributed among nine major parts, which are explicitly linked to the nine months of pregnancy. In the Grimms' didactic fairy tale the spinelessness of the fisherman is almost as much to blame for the final catastrophe as is the insatiable greed of his wife. Although the magically endowed flounder, an enchanted prince who speaks like a human, has made her empress and pope, she desires to be God Himself; that is the wife's undoing, and her husband's too.

Grass has drawn on highly sophisticated representatives of recent literature and psychology—Joyce and Jung—as well as on the Grimms. Thus time is merely a convention to be played with at will; the narration may range backward 2,000 years to a matriarchal society located on the eastern Prussian plains, or ignore time entirely, as in the story of the fisherman and Ilsebill, his calamitous wife. (The narrator's own wife is called by that improbable name.) All of the nine—or rather eleven—cooks are in a sense within him, forming perhaps a collective anima. Aua, the first of the sequence of women to whom the seemingly indestructible "I" of the story is attached, is distinguished by having three breasts: she is the arch-arche-type of mother and matriarch. Yet in a sense all of Grass's women are one: "In those (neolithic) days Ilsebill was called Aua. I too had another name."

Doubtless, the narrator's attitude toward women and the feminist movement, from Aua to the present, will provoke heated discussion in many countries, as it has already done in Germany. Clearly Grass is highly critical of women, but no more so than he is of males. The two sexes are about equal in their (generally modest) intelligence. Women apparently love to make love, give suck and cook; men have corresponding drives and suffer moreover from "titmania" and "tit-trauma" (sic Grass). Whereas the matriarchs were reactionary, forbidding men artistic production and any traffic with metal objects, restless "Faustian" males tend to get involved in wars; here the Manzis (emancipated women) appear in a good light. Nuns are authentically emancipated. On balance, the women really rule; the mighty flounder himself proclaims the end of masculine domination. Women in power are most unscrupulous; thus the female tribunal or "feminal" is utterly one-sided; there is, moreover, a lesbian trend within the movement. By far the worst offense in the novel, however, is committed by men—on Fathers' Day. Basically Grass is much more conciliatory than Strindberg; it is his irony rather than any polemics which may cause Amazonian wrath. May he avoid the fate of Kleist's Achilles!

Some sixty prose episodes are balanced by about forty passages of poetry, all in Grass's free verse, low-keyed and often witty manner. Not a few of the latter are extremely successful. The strategy was a happy one; monotony is greatly reduced. Without the poetry, the adventures of the nameless "fisherman with a thousand faces" and the long series of friendly or hostile women might have palled. Despite the verse, there is a certain sense of choppy repetition.

The fisherman, who is also the narrator, makes generous use of the third person as well as the first: he quotes at length from a galaxy of characters, ranging from the flounder to the twentieth-century version of Ilsebill. Grass's wit adds spice to almost every section; expectably enough, it is often Rabelaisian, even extreme. A very few mild bits: the beautifully informed flounder is compared to a swimming newspaper; a nasty sort of headache is personified as Helene Migräne; an embrace is lapidarily evoked by the two-word phrase "umarmt, umbeint" (put both arms and legs around someone; the latter term is almost certainly Grass's coinage). An entity called "Marxengels" appears briefly. German "newspeak" is parodied: Aua's third breast is "dialectically" explained, and the speeches at the feminal are sheer jargon, reminiscent of the rhetoric of the late 1960s.

"The Flounder" is an extraordinarily rich book; certain aspects, like the critique of Communist rule in Gdańsk (Grass's native Danzig), have not been touched on here. The novelist is often at his best when returning to his grass roots, the southern shore of the Baltic. In tracing the careers of his many cooks, he gives us a tour of 2,000 years of German history. His account of the seventeenth century is the most interesting, perhaps because this artist has important affinities with the baroque.

After two readings, I cannot claim to have "mastered" this novel; but a few tentative conclusions may be drawn. While the discussions of women, singly and collectively, are interesting and at times enlightening, the main value of "The Flounder" seems to lie in its wit and comic vigor. One might guess that much of the thrust of Grass's account—woman through the millennia—is aimed at épater les femmes. Every one of the some sixty sections is highly readable; several are brilliant. If there were fewer short units, there would be less sense of repetitiousness. Yet as Hermann Weigand wrote of another comic novel: "It is still the hand of the master which guides the pen."

Henry Hatfield

▪ **VÁCLAV HAVEL.** *Hry 1970–1976.* Toronto. Sixty-Eight. 1977. 312 pages.

Both Jiří Voskovec's eloquent foreword and Havel's forthright afterword stress the difficulty of writing plays "for the drawer": more than any genre drama must see the light of day. Four of the five plays in this handsome volume have been produced—in Germany, Austria, Italy, Great Britain—but none may appear on the Czech stage: they date from the post-1968 period. Each in its own way reveals the political and ethical decay the playwright has witnessed in the past few years.

In the rather too abstract "Conspirators" Havel explores the absolute lack of moral fiber among a group of would-be putsch leaders. His adaptation of John Gay's *Beggar's Opera* has as much to say to his Czechoslovakia as the Brecht-Weill adaptation had to say to Weimar Germany. "Mountain Hotel" recalls Havel's earlier absurdist works, but by shifting the brunt of his irony from the bureaucracy to a group of convalescents at a health resort he generalizes his despair over man's willingness to surrender his identity. The characters not only talk nonsense and non sequiturs; they repeat one another's nonsense and non sequiturs. An apocalyptic round-robin waltz makes a highly theatrical finale.

"The Audience" and "The Opening," two one-act plays, are much more personal: into each one Havel has written a version of himself—a Czech intellectual forced by circumstance to earn his keep by working in a brewery. (On Havel and Czech theatre in general, see *BA* 41:2, pp. 157–63 and 46:3, pp. 387–92.) The first play consists entirely of the "audience" the intellectual has with his superior at the brewery. As the dialogue develops, it becomes clear that the proletarian master feels every bit as unhappy, out of place and alienated as his charge. In the second play the intellectual attends a private "opening" of the newly decorated apartment of some good friends. Their desperate plea for the consumer values they have substituted for their former humanitarian values is the epitome of intellectual capitulation.

Michael Heim

■**KENZABURO ŌE**. *Teach Us to Outgrow Our Madness*. John Nathan, tr. New York. Grove. 1977. xxv + 261 pages.

Teach Us to Outgrow Our Madness is the third publication in English of the extraordinary works of Kenzaburo Ōe, the most talented writer to emerge in Japan after World War II. Like his previous publications (*A Personal Matter*, 1968, also translated by John Nathan, and *The Silent Cry*, 1975), this book is certain to surprise some Western readers who have come to expect delicate prose and exquisite imagery from a Japanese novelist. Having learned his craft from postwar American authors such as Norman Mailer and French existentialists such as Jean-Paul Sartre, rather than from *The Tale of Genji*, Ōe writes fiction that is more brutal and savage than exquisite or quaint. He was a twenty-two-year-old French major at Tokyo University when he won his first literary prize. Since then he has won virtually every literary award offered in Japan, including the coveted Akutagawa Prize in 1958 for "Prize Stock," the earliest composition among the four short novels contained in the present book.

"Prize Stock" is a tightly knit tale of a black American flier's captivity in a mountain village during the War. Ōe referred to it as a "pastoral." But what a pastoral! Ōe superimposes a mythic, primeval society on the village and reveals the nature of man and conditions of human existence through a densely woven pattern of animal images. "Chilly, sweating stones" jut "like the swollen belly of a pupa," and "skin flush[es] hot as the innards of a freshly killed chicken." Symbolism is apparent as little boys in the opening scene "collect" well-shaped bones at a makeshift crematorium to use as medals and the black captive with a boar trap around his ankles is "reared" in the cellar. It is a powerful story that exploits all the elements of fiction.

The imagery of "The Day He Himself Shall Wipe My Tears Away" is just as striking. The narrator lies in a hospital wearing a pair of underwater goggles covered in dark cellophane and singing the song "Happy Days Are Here Again" in anticipation of death from liver cancer and return to an event in 1945 that ended his happy days. It is a technical as well as imagistic triumph. "Aghwee the Sky Monster" tells of a young composer haunted by the phantom of a kangaroo-sized baby in a white nightgown. "Teach Us to Outgrow Our Madness" is a tragicomic story of a fat man's obsession with his mentally defective son and the imagined madness of his own dead father. Both are original, well-plotted tales with vivid, if not likable characters and memorable scenes.

The four novellas vary in technique and style as well as subject matter but are alike in the theme of alienation (apparent in the images of the chained captive and the cancer patient waiting for liberation), in their absurdist, ironic, black-comic view of life and the use of anti-heroes. Artistic excellence characterizes all four. The translation is accurate and conveys the essence of the original, although some readers may prefer a more Anglicized, smooth-flowing rendition to Nathan's faithful-to-the-last-comma approach. *Teach Us to Outgrow Our Madness* is a book that should be read by everyone interested in contemporary fiction, for Ōe is as important a writer as Mailer or Updike.

Emiko Sakurai

■**SAINT-JOHN PERSE**. *Chant pour un Equinoxe—Song for an Equinox*. Richard Howard, tr. Princeton, N.J. Princeton University Press. 1977. 31 pages.

The four poems which make up *Song for an Equinox* are relatively short compared to Saint-John Perse's other works such as *Winds, Seamarks* or *Chronique*. "Drouth," which is the longest of the new book, is only six pages long, and "Nocturne," the shortest, is a one-page poem. The title poem has a little more than one page, and the fourth poem, "Chanté par celle qui fut là," covers two-

and-one-half pages. It is interesting to note that all of these poems remind us of some previous ones which they more or less complete. "Drouth" is an addition to the list of meteorological works such as *Snows, Rains, Winds.*

While the last three poems use the American background, "Drouth" draws a great deal of its material from the Mediterranean environment with which the poet became familiar during the last years of his life. Fascinated with water as he was, he must have been struck by the dryness and aridity of that region, elements of which can be found in the poem—for example, maquis, junipers of Phoenicia, yews, scrub, thorns and briars, rockrose and buckthorn. The poet also mentions some species of the Mediterranean fauna such as blowflies, Talitrae, Cantharides, blue Lycaenidae, grass-snakes. "The pink crystals in the salt-beds," which refers to one of the main resources of Hyère, is part of the setting at the very beginning of the poem. But as usual, Perse goes beyond these physical and local references, which are only props to convey his poetic message. For this is a song to spiritual life where the poet praises the effort of man to use his spirit to overcome his time-bound condition.

The passionate love expressed by a woman to her lover seems to be the main concern of "Sung by one who was there"; but if we read between the lines, we see that it is not devoid of some allusions to poetry itself. "Song for an Equinox" may well be the answer of the lover to whom the woman expressed her passion: "My love, the downpour from that sky was with us, / God's night was our foul weather, / and love, in all places, rose again toward its sources."

On the other hand this poem, which refers to the painful changes from autumn to winter and next to spring, with the resulting fecundity of "The Earth, our Mother," is akin to *Chronique,* which is devoted to the earth and its relationship with mankind. No doubt the poet also refers to the transition from life to death. Life has an origin and an end; it is "an equinox of an hour between Earth and man." But man's action, like the song of the poet, is continuous and eternal, having no "source," no "estuary." And mankind is seen as a homogeneous, innocent and intelligent entity: "a child is born into the world whose race nor rank is known, and genius knocks infallibly at the lobes of a pure forehead."

The volume closes with "Nocturne," another poem which is in the spirit of *Chronique* and also reminds us of Keat's "To Autumn," because it deals with harvest and fruits. But these are related to Perse's "imperious fate" and are produced by his dreams in the "abyss of his nights." They belong to another shore; they are "scattered," "without honour" and cannot be "harvested." This poem is obviously a meditation of the aged poet on his fate. Experiencing the autumn of his own life which "goes without hatred or ransom," he shows great serenity and dignity.

The volume of the four last poems has the same pleasant format and colors (blue and purple) as the former bilingual one of Saint-John Perse's *Collected Poems* published by Princeton University Press, which they complete. Let us hope that in the near future they will merge into one volume to which the poet's correspondence and other prose works of the La Pléiade edition will be added. These are presently being translated for this purpose.

Daniel L. Racine

■**TOM STOPPARD.** *Dirty Linen and New-Found-Land.* New York. Grove. 1976. 75 pages.

Tom Stoppard's rollicking double bill ostensibly takes place in London in the House of Commons. One need not be reminded that it was commissioned by London's "Almost Free Theatre" as a token gesture to the American Bicentennial in order to recognize that sex scandals, congressional investigations and incompetence in government do not respect national boundaries. The two short plays are not the demonstrations in complex plotting that we have come to expect from the author of the Tony Award-winning *Rosencrantz and Guildenstern Are Dead* and *Travesties,* but Stoppard once again proves himself unrivaled as the verbal acrobat and master of briskly timed incident of the modern theatre.

Dirty Linen springs through the antics of seven proper M. P.'s as they try to hide their association with the secretary Maddie Gotobed from each other and from the rest of Parliament. The lunatic obsessions, the puns, the bravura passages, the repetitions, the odd mixture of literary allusions, legal jargon and listings of magnificent trivia are reminiscent of the best of Ionesco (particularly the Ionesco of *The Bald Soprano*), liberally flanked with rapid-fire vaudeville routines. *New-Found-Land,* a slighter work, propels two members of Parliament into discussing an application for British naturalization. Since one of the actors is very old and very deaf, each is in dialogue with himself, and the speeches eventually become shaggy-dog stories, with the final "My America, my new-found-land" speech lasting six pages, a tour de force of place-names and keenly timed breath notes. One marvels at a comedy that is so unremittingly good-natured and unflinchingly observant.

Francine Leffler Ringold

■MARIO VARGAS LLOSA. *La tía Julia y el escribidor*. Barcelona. Seix Barral. 1977. 447 pages.

If writing about himself, exposing himself as in "una ceremonia parecida al *strip tease*" (*Historia secreta de una novela*), is what Vargas Llosa has done up to now under various disguises, then this recent novel constitutes an exercise in boldness and brazenness. Half of *La tía Julia* is the account of an episode from the writer's youth (his first marriage remembered in minute detail, with proper names and indiscreet data), and the writer does not even hide behind a character: the protagonist is unmistakably named Varguitas o Marito, which introduces a perturbing element in the work of a novelist who has made Flaubertian objectivity a trademark in his writing. The other half of the novel (that which corresponds to the *escribidor* of the title) presents the story of Pedro Camacho, a picturesque type who earns his living as a writer of soap operas and whose "texts" are of a morbid and exaggerated unreality.

This bipolar structure (similar to that of *La ciudad y los perros*) has an appearance of simplicity at the beginning: a clear contrast between the episodes that we can call "autobiographical" (the odd chapters) and the "imaginary" episodes (the even chapters, with the exception of chapter twenty, and the conclusion), between the private life of one protagonist and the outrageous fantasies of another, encouraged and shared by a mass audience. But both sides of the novel could be arranged in another way, permitting another possibility in the reading. To begin with, Marito, who talks about his plans to marry a woman much older than he and also divorced and related by marriage to his own family (Julia "era hermana de la mujer de mi tío Lucho"), also tells of his other adventure: a literary one, in that formative stage of adolescence in which he painstakingly struggles through failures and rejections for affirmation in his endeavors. This explains the continuous reference to the short stories that Marito writes (or tries to write), without achieving even a moderate satisfaction from them. This facet of the autobiographical part of the novel is important, because it progressively connects—thanks to a favorite technique of the author (the *vasos comunicantes*)—with the world of Camacho, where everything is efficient and submitted toward an end: to feed the voracious public that listens to his soap operas. There is a comic paradox in the novel: on the one hand we see a writer who scarcely writes, who speaks of writing but engages in other activities; on the other hand we see someone who evidently does not have anything to do with literature but who is highly productive and enjoys all the status of that métier.

There are two basic elements in Camacho that make him a parody of the real writer: the *distortion* that his life suffers as a consequence of his writing, making everything appear as a stimulus for him to produce his stories; and the *methodological excess*, the endless fanatical devotion which he uses to write his lamentable scripts. The narrator focuses on this intellectual rigor of the character: "Su concentración era absoluta, no advertía mi presencia pese a estar a su lado. Tenía los desorbitados ojos fijos en el papel, tecleaba con dos dedos, se mordía la lengua." Through Camacho, Vargas Llosa not only has made a tragicomic and melodramatic portrait of the writer of novels; he has gone even further and has produced a criticism of realism in the novel, of *his* realism.

Throughout the book we are shown how the willingness of the narrator to remain strictly faithful to the episodes of his adolescence is inevitably impeded: the filtering of the novelistic structure changes the meaning of the real experience and transforms it into "literature," as if this linking with life were nothing more than an accident. And, at the same time, Camacho's world of fantasy, which appears disconnected not only from his life but from any contact with reality, shows fissures through which are revealed secret obsessions, aversions and perversions that allow us to view his soap operas as the story of his disturbed mind. A victim of the vicious activity of writing, ascetic in his morals but perverse in his dealing with reality, Camacho is the living incarnation of Vargas Llosa's well-known theory of the novelist and his *demonios*.

It is especially this level of autoanalysis by the writer in the act of writing, this operation by which fiction consumes itself, which makes *La tía Julia y el escribidor* interesting and which compensates in part for the absence of something which until now has been typical of the author: intense technical innovation. Curiously, more than his previous novels, *La tía Julia* should be read in light of Vargas Llosa's two books of criticism, *Historia de un deicidio* and *La orgía perpetua*, because it answers the same two questions: how and why someone writes a novel.

José Miguel Oviedo

1979

■SAMUEL BECKETT. *Collected Poems in English and French*. New York. Grove. 1977. ix + 147 pages.

■———. *Poèmes suivi de Mirlitonnades*. Paris. Minuit. 1978. 44 pages.

Samuel Beckett (*Lütfi Özkök*)

"Abstracted to death!" was Beckett's judgment of the English language during the 1930s. Surfeited by the over-rich diet of Irish rhetoric, he sought and found a pauciloquy in the French language that filled his hunger for economy and conciseness of expression.

This collection arranged chronologically from 1930 to 1976 consists of previously published poetry originally composed in English from 1930 to 1976, poems originally in French with translations from 1937 to 1976, and translations and originals of French poems by Éluard, Rimbaud, Apollinaire and Chamfort in 1975 and 1976. The text begins with the florid *Whoroscope,* Beckett's first publication, over-embellished, studded with scholarly footnotes of historic allusion. The early "Gnome," "Home Olga" and thirteen poems under the heading "Echo's Bones" which follow are written over a five-year period in Ireland, England, France and Germany and show Beckett's first serious craftsmanship as a poet. The next six poems from 1936 to 1976 include the elegant four-line miniature "St. Lô," written from Beckett's wartime experience in Normandy, which burns into the mind the image of the ruined city and

its yet unborn lights reflected in the river Vire. "Dread Nay" (first published in "New Directions" in 1974 and which includes Dantean allusions), the graceful "Roundelay" and "Thither" from 1976 follow deceptively simple forms sharpened by inner echoes, subtle assonances, alliteration and phrasing that bends in on itself.

Part two, the poems in French with translations, written from 1937 to 1976, clearly demonstrates a musical ability to transpose as well as to translate from one language to another. Beckett's earlier pronouncement, "My work is a matter of fundamental sounds," is unmistakably evident here. The subject matter is love, isolation, time, emptiness, death. The structure is often circular and frequently spiralistic. The author is the hidden, sometimes imprisoned observer seeking freedom in poetic metaphor. Part three consists of scrupulously faithful readings in translation of the original poems. Words are measured carefully; there is no extravagance or excess anywhere in this workmanlike section. The final grouping, "Adaptations from Chamfort," is a refreshing fillip, and Beckett's sense of humor and fun is put into full play. Beckett has said of one of his plays that it was intended for the "nerves not the intellect." In this series of poetry, as is so often the case with this great writer, the objective seems double-edged. He strikes the mind, but once engaged it comprehends how the rapier has cut close to the nerve.

Six of the poems appearing in the Grove edition of *Collected Poems in English and French* are included in *Poèmes suivi de Mirlitonnades* as well: "Elles viennent" (translated in 1946 from the original English) "Ascension," "La mouche," "Dieppe," "Arènes de Lutèce," "Mort de A.D." "Je suis ce cours de sable qui glisse," composed between 1937 and 1939, appeared in *Les Temps Modernes* in 1946. The second section, entitled *Mirlitonnades,* is of particular interest. It contains thirty-five selections, some only four lines long, one a rhymed couplet. Beckett seems involved in self-mockery here—*mirliton* being the toy paper trumpet sold in fairs and carnivals decorated with curling lines of doggerel. Once again ironic surprise undercuts emotion, as in "en face / le pire / jusqu'à ce / qu'il fasse rire." The images are familiar ones: the face stuck to the window, the head first reassuring then admonishing the eye, the whisper of words wearing away silence, swearing never to stop, light borders of a moving shuttle, an extremity allowing its opposite, the imagining of the end, the presence of nothing, no one.

These short poems taken as a whole seem designed to put last things first. There is a discarding of all but the essential content, a final running out and summing up, a pasting in order, a tidying of life preparing for death. Beckett has said these poems are "only in French"; perhaps they are untranslatable. The English approximation does not equal the balance, the asymmetry of the original. The sounds when transposed are not analogous—the rhythm is altered, alliteration sacrificed, the echoes blurred or entirely lost. In *Mirlitonnades* the author is not composing in one language with an eye (and an ear) on a future translation. His focus appears to be the French language. And it is these sounds, rhythms, echoes, alliterations, circularities he has used to shape his ironic endgame reckoning.

Martha Fehsenfeld

■ **MAX FRISCH**. *Triptychon*. Frankfurt a.M. Suhrkamp. 1978. 115 pages.

"To die, to sleep— / To sleep—perchance to dream: ay, there's the rub, / For in that sleep of death what dreams may come / When we have shuffled off this mortal coil, / Must give us pause." In his *Triptychon* Frisch provides his answer regarding those dreams. In the first of these "three tableaux for the stage" one of the key characters defines eternity by saying that "the individual events of our life, each one in its place within time, do not change."

The dramatic action, such as it is, consists of a funeral during the first tableau, a series of conversations in Hades during the second one, and a conversation on a park bench in Paris between a couple of lovers (one alive, one dead) during the last one. The innovative device which Frisch uses to propel his "action" and to advance his thesis is to have dead and living characters intermingle and even speak to each other. The dead retain the age which they had at the moment of death; the living continue to grow old. This device results in some comic relief in the second tableau, as when a seventy-year-old son encounters his forty-one-year-old father who scolds him for still not being able to fish properly.

Essentially, though, this is a very serious work. As the eighteen disparate yet related characters confront each other in Hades, as they recount important events in their lives, as they try to justify their acts and omissions to each other, Frisch's familiar themes reappear: his condemnation of social injustice and of prejudice, but most prominently his exhortation that we should love a person without trying to change him or her, without forcing him or her into a preconceived mold. The eighteen characters in the second tableau had been unable to live up to Frisch's standards while they were alive, and they persist in their imperfections even in Hades. This is why Hamlet's question (uttered by a clochard) is answered at the end of the second tableau with the lapidary phrase: "Eternity is banal."

The banality of the characters in the second tableau is contrasted to the seemingly extraordinary couple in the third one. They are intellectuals who had thought for a while that they shared a perfect love. Then they had separated and she had died at the age of thirty-three. At the moment of their nocturnal discussion on the park bench he is fifty years old. During this discussion he comes to realize that she is right when she says, "You have never loved anyone, you are not able to love." Having failed in this fundamental aspect of his being, he shoots himself. His last words are: "And this is what remains."

And the rest is not silence. Frisch's stage directions specify that the banality of life is to assert itself: the very last sounds of the third tableau are the roaring noises of contemporary city traffic.

Franz P. Haberl

■ **PATRICK MODIANO**. *Rue des Boutiques Obscures*. Paris. Gallimard. 1978. 214 pages.

In the self-centered seventies the most sacred quest seems to be that of one's real identity, one's inner self.

Though he begins his tale with the phrase "I am nothing," the narrator of *Rue des Boutiques Obscures* shows nothing of the self-indulgence and self-dramatization common to works on this theme. His search is—in all senses of the word—essential; for "Guy Roland," who works with a detective (seeker of lost souls, finder of missing persons), is an amnesiac, in search of his name, his past, his true self. Free of a remembered personal history, he is caught up in the need to know who, where and what he was. Expatriated from his past, he discovers that the person he might have been had been one of a group of expatriates in Paris, whose names (or aliases) had been strange mixtures of nationalities and whose passports had been issued by the Dominican Republic.

Wandering souls in the early 1940s, they had necessarily left shadowed traces. Seeking, following, across a good part of the world and a quarter of a century, those who might remember, he finds that the person who might most readily have confirmed the story he has with difficulty pieced together has just disappeared. Hell—nothingness—might just be the absence of other people, in whose memories reside the sole vestiges of one's passage on earth.

Modiano's latest novel, again treating the search for remembrance, for a past, for the significance of a life and, by extension, of life itself, has many aspects of a mystery, a detective story. Mystery/detective stories become "serious" literature when legitimized by critics. *Rue des Boutiques Obscures* is the 1978 Goncourt laureate.

Judith L. Greenberg

■ **VLADIMIR NABOKOV.** *Sogliadatai*. Ann Arbor, Mi. Ardis. 1978. 253 pages.

Ardis Press is providing a much-needed service by issuing reprints of Vladimir Nabokov's Russian works. This volume is a reprint of the original edition of *Sogliadatai* which was published in limited edition in Paris in 1938. It was Nabokov's second collection of short fiction and includes a novella and twelve short stories. All the pieces first appeared individually in various émigré publications between 1930 and 1935, and all are now available in English translation.

"Sogliadatai," the title piece (rendered in English as "The Eye"), is a strange and fascinating novella with echoes of Gogol and Dostoevsky in its presentation of Smurov, the hyperconscious narrator who has lost his identity and who concludes that "the only happiness in this world is to observe, to spy, to watch, to scrutinize oneself and others, to be nothing but a big, slightly vitreous, somewhat bloodshot, unblinking eye." The dozen stories which follow display the full range of Nabokov's themes—exile, memory, travel, butterflies, Russia, loss, death, love, art and the supremacy of individual consciousness.

At the time when these stories were appearing, Nabokov had already written twenty-two stories and was completing his fifth novel. His prose apprenticeship, as it were, was well over, and these pieces demonstrate the mature fullness and richness of his Russian prose style. Indeed, the volume contains some of his best short fiction.

Stephen Jan Parker

■ **V. S. NAIPAUL.** *A Bend in the River*. New York. Knopf. 1979. 278 pages.

A Bend in the River, Naipaul's first novel since *Guerrillas* (1975; see *WLT* 51:1, p. 149), offers an even bleaker picture of postcolonial societies than we have come to expect from him. Africa, which Naipaul first used as a setting in *In a Free State* (1971), takes its place beside the West Indies and India as one of Naipaul's "new worlds" (see *WLT* 51:4, p. 581). As a character says of the town at the river's bend, "This isn't property. This is just bush. This has always been bush." And it will remain bush as well; as Naipaul asserted in a recent interview, "Africa has no future."

Like the other focal figures in Naipaul's novels since *The Mimic Men* (1967), Salim in this one is a sojourner. The narrative opens with his arrival at the town on the river's bend and concludes with his departure for points unknown. His is the story of a man who fails to find a sense of place. Salim establishes only uneasy alliances with several of the town's factions: the young Africans striving to fit into the newly independent nation, the colonial remnant (proprietors of restaurants named Bigburger and Tivoli) and the new elite. While Salim has an affair and is briefly engaged, he is a man almost without a private life. He functions primarily as a recorder of the town's social texture.

Naipaul's vision is particularly dark because the novel details both the destruction of the few who had flourished even in the bush culture of the town, such as the missionary Father Huismans, and the growing enervation of the young Africans seeking to establish themselves in the newly independent country. The vitality of all such figures is sapped by the Big Man, who creates a state at once highly regimented and unstable. His vision of a new society is represented by the New Domain, a flashy suburb for the country's new elite which is already returning to bush at the novel's close.

While *A Bend in the River* treats the disintegration of a foundationless "free state," the novel differs from Naipaul's preceding works by showing the decay spreading to metropolitan London, which has been the center of Naipaul's world. Where the earlier protagonists had sought refuge in London, a place with a culture founded on a developing history, such escape is no longer possible here. Nazruddin, Salim's mentor, tells of all the colonials "coming to the centre because it is all they know and because they think it's smart," only to find that they came "at the wrong time." There are Arabs with slaves in the streets and, Naipaul implies, the bush is beginning to grow around London. With this new novel, Naipaul's dark vision becomes all-encompassing.

John Cooke

■ **MICHEL TOURNIER.** *Le coq de bruyère.* Paris. Gallimard. 1978. 305 pages.

Le coq de bruyère, by one of France's most gifted novelists, is a collection of tales, some of which have been published separately. Tournier's first novel *Robinson ou Les limbes du Pacifique* marks a turning point in French literature by showing a way out of the labyrinthine *nouveau roman* and by stating once more that the novel is communication. His second novel *Le roi des aulnes* unanimously won the Goncourt Prize in 1970 and conferred on the writer a worldwide fame. Tournier's stylistic virtuosity, his erudition and precise documentation earned him the title of "le Flaubert de notre temps" (*Nouvelles Littéraires,* 1972, p. 2316), though his vision encompasses a metaphysical and imaginary world broader and richer than that of the Hermit of Croisset.

Narrated with subtle variations of tone, the fourteen short stories are modern parables and fairy tales, a genre natural to Tournier's art, rich in symbols and images. Lucid and realistic in the midst of fantasy, the stories are told from the point of view of the hero, generally a child, an adolescent or an underdog, who encounters a series of dramatic adventures. As in the traditional fairy tale, external events and roles achieve a greater relevancy than their immediate signification in the unfolding of the particular story. Many of the tales which show the protagonist leaving behind a secure and familiar way of life and stepping into a different age—adolescence, adulthood or senescence—may be interpreted as initiations. The development and outcome of the hero's confrontations, however shocking they may be, provide for the reader an aid to find himself, integrate the discordant aspects of his personality and proceed toward the laborious, and impoverished, path of maturity.

Though their quest is not a chivalrous one, the protagonists long for the renewal of a pre-Christian culture. Along with the regret for a golden age, nostalgia for childhood is keenly felt. Exiled into maturity and urbanism, the characters dream of rediscovering the purity, intensity and acuity of a child's experiences. An Orphic vision of the world prevails in Tournier's work, which adds a mystical and lyrical dimension to the tales.

> Voici donc la malédiction des Hommes: ils sont sortis du règne végétal. Ils sont tombés dans le règne animal. Or, qu'est-ce que le règne animal? C'est la chasse, la violence, le meurtre, la peur. Le règne végétal, au contraire, c'est la calme croissance dans une union de la terre et du soleil. C'est pourquoi toute sagesse ne peut se fonder que sur une méditation de l'arbre, poursuivie dans une forêt par des hommes végétariens.

Though not meat-eaters, the protagonists are often solitary predators whose love and affection can only be devouring and deadly, even when it is self-inflicted. The satanic dwarf who murders the woman he loves and enslaves her lover, the lady photographer who transforms her model and eventually kills him in her search for the ultimate photograph, the neglected wife of the fickle colonel and the grouse of the title who causes him to become crippled in order to "love" him better are some of the ogres, a theme Tournier fully developed in *Le roi des aulnes.* On the other hand, Monsieur Logre, in the modern transposition of *Tom Thumb,* is a priapic hippie who bequeaths to the child his magnificent embroidered boots that will carry him beyond seven leagues into the enchanted *Pays des Arbres.*

Tournier's tales in their symbolic significance are more convincing than realistic fiction. They represent a poetic rendering of his relationship to the world. Concretizing arcane reality through delusion or enchantment, Tournier is a magician who gives us the reassurance that there is a secret garden next to our backyard, that there is another world behind the mirror and that there is a small island in the Pacific Ocean where we lived happily once upon a time.

Danièle McDowell

1980

■ **ANDRÉ BRINK.** *A Dry White Season.* New York. Morrow. 1980. 316 pages.

Even though Brink allows his readers to discover within the first chapter of the book that Ben du Toit, the protagonist, will be killed by the South African secret police, the novel maintains its tension and suspense. Perhaps because Ben's innocence is also established very early in the book, the reader continues with shocked fascination, interested to discover *how,* in fact, a decent citizen of a so-called democratic country can be victimized and murdered by its law-enforcers.

If this predictability is regarded as a weakness, then the second weakness in *A Dry White Season* is that Brink does not vary his narrative style to give Ben a tone of voice, a diction or a syntax distinctive from that of the hack writer who sometimes tells his story and sometimes allows Ben to speak for himself. The reader has on more than one occasion to stop and reread in order to establish which of the two narrators is speaking.

This is the fourth novel which André Brink has himself written in both English and Afrikaans (see *WLT* 53:4, pp. 628–29). The degree of his bilingualism is extraordinary. Yet, although Brink's English is smooth and idiomatic, he is not able to manipulate the language in fresh and artistic ways. His style, unconsciously clichéd, flows on pedestrianly, rendering his books boring for a native English reader looking for more than a shocking plot. This was the case with *Looking on Darkness, An Instant in the Wind* and *Rumours of Rain* (see respectively *BA* 50:3, p. 705, *WLT* 51:4, p. 668 and 53:3, p. 549)—the latter heavily influenced by the plot line of Nadine Gordimer's *The Conservationist* (see *BA* 49:3, p. 597) but, unfortunately, not by her artistry.

I am always irritated by Brink's sometimes slighting, sometimes contemptuous depiction of women. The only worthwhile woman in this book is Melanie Bruwer, another of Brink's girl-women with small, prepubescent bodies and frank eyes. The black woman, Emily, an obviously approvable person, remains shadowy.

"Liberal" has become a comforting catchword among South Africans, radicals and Afrikaners alike with which to denigrate someone, though the definition of the word varies from speaker to speaker. The idea of the liberal again comes in for castigation in *A Dry White Season;* yet Ben du Toit, the hero we are to sympathize with, is himself an example of one definition of the word. He wants humane treatment, justice and fair play for all, and dies because of his insistence that justice can be done. But he never subjects his political stance to close scrutiny: he deplores the way he has grown up ignorant of the lives of black people, yet he never adequately questions the political structure that enforces this ignorance and to which he gives his tacit adherence throughout the book.

André Brink is considered by many to be an Afrikaner intent on rousing the conscience of his fellows. His novels certainly confront the horrors of the South African situation, and this one, showing a *white* Afrikaner preyed upon by the secret police, should be disturbing indeed to many South Africans. But it is difficult, if not impossible, to assess the impact of the arts on political thinking. In spite of their wide popularity in their own times of *Cry, the Beloved Country, Sizwe Bansi Is Dead* (see *BA* 50:1, pp. 81–84) and *Die swerfjare van Poppie Nongema* (see *WLT* 53:4, p. 735), it does not appear that political attitudes in South Africa have changed significantly since 1948. André Brink's outspoken and accusatory writing is perhaps most effective in the annoyance it must present to the South African Publications Control Board. Brink is irrepressible: he has not only arranged for private circulation of his books—e.g., *An Instant in the Wind*—but he has also challenged bannings (*Looking on Darkness*); and his great productivity means that the authorities have barely finished handling one offensive book before another is at the booksellers' in Johannesburg, London and New York.

Sheila Roberts

▪ **MARNIX GIJSEN**. *Rustoord.* The Hague. Nijgh & van Ditmar. 1979. 127 pages.

"Marnix Gijsen" is the pen name of Jan-Albert Goris (b. 1899). a Belgian whose literary output is especially impressive in view of his fifty-year pursuit of a career in politics and diplomacy. He once held a ministerial portfolio and for some thirty-five years served as cultural attaché to his country's embassies in Ottawa and Washington. More than a decade ago, however, he withdrew from public affairs. From his pen have come approximately thirty volumes of fiction, several collections of verse, memoirs, one play, and a virtual library of expository works touching nearly every aspect of Belgian culture. His readership is extensive, and he has long enjoyed high critical acclaim.

Like most of Gijsen's fiction, *Rustoord* (Nursing Home) contains conspicuous autobiographical elements. The narrator-protagonist is a man of approximately the author's age; presumably he is a Belgian; he has returned to Europe after a long residence in the United States. Perhaps the similarities between writer and fictional character end there, perhaps not. At any rate, the novelette is the fictional octogenarian's day-by-day account of his sojourn in a Swiss nursing home, where he lands by mistake while "still" in good health and whimsically decides to stay two months. Having been a mortician by profession, he at first displays a callous attitude toward death, but observation of the ways in which it comes to other occupants of the home soon affects him deeply. He departs seemingly obsessed by a dread not of death itself, but of the loss of dignity which so often accompanies the decline of health in advanced age.

Particularly since Gijsen has claimed elsewhere to lack imagination and to cultivate literature principally as a means to self-understanding, I conjecture that he has had personal experiences somewhat like those described in this book and that he wrote it in an effort to come to terms with impressions they left. It is a most depressing story but one undeniably told with feeling.

Philip Smyth

■ **LAO SHE**. *Rickshaw: The Novel* Lo-t'o Hsiang Tzu. Jean M. James, tr. Honolulu. University Press of Hawaii. 1979. xiii + 249 pages.

The appearance of a second translation of a work more often than not implies some degree of dissatisfaction with the original translation. Such is the case here with Jean M. James's translation of Lao She's (pen name of Shu Ch'ing-ch'un, 1898–1966) well-known novel, which was previously translated by Evan King (pen name of Robert Spencer Ward, b. 1906) and published under the title *Rickshaw Boy* (New York, Reynal & Hitchcock, 1945). In her "Note on the Text and Translation" James asks whether "those who have read Evan King's translation in 1945 as *Rickshaw Boy* will wonder if *Rickshaw* is the same novel." This is because King cut, rewrote, invented new characters and, as incredible as it may seem, changed the ending in the original story! Fortunately for modern readers, a most capable translator has successfully undertaken the arduous task of giving us a new rendition which not only reads well against the original, but also one that "omits nothing and alters nothing."

Rickshaw is an important novel in modern Chinese literature. This is because it offers the first in-depth portrayal of a Chinese workingman. Essentially, it is the story of an illiterate rickshaw puller in the 1930s Beijing and his hopeless struggle to survive in a cruel and corrupt society, one in which (as the Chinese describe it) "people eat people." Although Hsiang Tzu's (Lo-t'o, which means "camel," is his nickname) struggle ultimately leads to failure and corruption, the author's main point is that there are many lessons to be learned from his experiences. Comparatists will be interested to know that Lao She's biting description of Beijing is strongly reminiscent of Dickens's chronicles describing London.

Perhaps the most difficult task facing the translator of *Rickshaw* is the language of the original, which is Beijing colloquial. Chock-full of lively idioms and "street

talk," the work contains passages which seem to defy translation into English. Generally, James has handled her task well, and she is to be commended especially for her apt renderings of the many colloquial expressions. Finally, anyone who wishes to gain insight into and understanding of China's turbulent capital of the thirties and the people who lived there will want to read *Rickshaw*.

James M. Hargett

■ **STANISLAW LEM**. *The Chain of Chance.* Louis Iribarne, tr. New York. Harcourt Brace Jovanovich. 1978. v + 179 pages.

Known to his English-reading public primarily as a writer of science fiction, Stanislaw Lem has in fact reached far beyond the bounds of that genre to embrace the detective novel, philosophy, medicine, science and even the art of reviewing books, although the books he reviews are imaginary works by imaginary authors. In many respects Lem appears to be a Polish variant of Argentina's Jorge Luis Borges.

In *The Chain of Chance* we have a detective novel unlike most others. The detective, an aging astronaut, has embarked upon an investigation into the deaths of a number of people at an Italian resort. His method of investigation is to pose as a prospective victim and then to analyze the results of his experience. The outcome, as we might suspect, is unexpected. It hinges upon the application of information theory and probability theory to a multitude of related and unrelated characteristics and events. What makes all this immensely challenging is the extent to which chance and pure accident have become intertwined with the actual cause of death. In today's world it is more difficult to sort out chains of events brought about by chance occurrence from those produced by cause and effect than it was in the past because the density of random events has become so great. Death by accident becomes indistinguishable from death at the hands of a murderer.

The information overload of our modern world impinges upon the reader from the very outset, and it is disconcerting. As the astronaut-detective retraces the itinerary of one of the victims, every occurrence, however minor, however random, must nevertheless be regarded as concealing a potential threat. Lem loads the narrative with sharply defined details and events, yet he refrains from investing any one of them with more importance than the others. Thus a dirty windshield may seem to us to harbor as much of a threat to the detective as a sudden glint of sunlight from among the branches of a tree.

Making one's way through such a world, whether as reader or as detective, is a laborious and exhausting process, but it is not uneventful, as we come to appreciate. In fact, just the opposite proves to be the case, for, as is explained on the last page, "we now live in such a dense world of random chance, in a molecular and chaotic gas whose 'improbabilities' are amazing only to the individual human atoms. It's a world where yesterday's rarity becomes today's cliché, and where today's exception becomes tomorrow's rule." This may be owing, we suspect, to the fact that modern man perceives his world in much finer detail than did his predecessors, a tendency that may impede his apprehension of the larger patterns and their significance.

Tom J. Lewis

■ **DORIS LESSING**. *Shikasta*. New York. Knopf. 1979. xi + 365 pages.

Shikasta is the planet Earth. It was colonized a very long time ago by the highly advanced civilization of Canopus. The original colonizers were giants. Canopus fed Shikasta with a rich and vigorous air that kept everyone safe, healthy and made them love one another. But due to two factors—first the activity of the evil Sirian civilization, and second, a malalignment of the stars that cut off the good air from Canopus—Shikasta began a terrible and total decline.

Shikasta is the "documented" account of that decline. It begins with a report from Johor, an agent of Canopus, who has been sent to bring the bad news to the giants (who are huge, black, powerful, intelligent, noble, innocent) that they are finished as a race. The planet is soon to be short of fuel. Disintegration has set in enough so that some of the giants refuse to obey orders to leave. Those who stay merge with the "natives" and participate in the coming decline.

After skipping some millennia, the documents take up again, and the planet is roller-coasting to disaster. It has had World Wars I and II. The totally destructive World War III is to come, along with devastating famine, environmental poisoning and strange diseases. We are given case histories: the rich girl turned revolutionary; the devoted servant abandoned after fifty years of faithful service. We are told that the North-West (white) has been exploiting the rest of Shikasta (dark) for centuries. Johor returns in the form of George Sherban, and we watch the last years through the eyes of George's family, particularly through his sister Rachel. After the final calamity, Johor/George leads the remaining few Shikastans to begin a new, calm, hate-free world.

What are we to make of all this? Like Yeats and Lawrence, Lessing has obviously felt the need to imag-

ine an otherworldly dimension, something outside of and larger than the self (gyres, dark gods, Canopus), to give her fiction power. Here the extra dimension appears to be something like an interplanetary collective unconscious, a remembrance in the deep unconscious, of a powerful past civilization, millions of years old. *Shikasta* is the story of a Fall from this past grace: the loss of the life-enhancing air from Canopus via the agency of evil.

The frame Lessing has erected both does and does not work. It results in large sections of tedium. Lessing has never been an economical novelist, and the combination of a blue pencil and a sense of humor would do this novel wonders. But the frame also gives an urgency and power to the various images of greed, anger and self-love that contribute to the Shikastan decline. My chief difficulty with *Shikasta* has to do not with boredom, but with the unrealized quality of the alternative—Canopus, where the most important emotion seems to be calm. The novel's utopian vision seems to center around and escape from emotion, an escape from struggle, tension and, therefore, passion. This does not bode well for the works in this series to come.

Shernaz Mollinger

■ **EDWIN THUMBOO**. *Ulysses by the Merlion*. Singapore. Heinemann. 1979. 34 pages.

Edwin Thumboo's poetry, comprising three small volumes, is elegantly humanistic. Critic of African literature and editor of Malaysian poetry, he brings detachment and objectivity also to his own creative work. Lee Tzu Pheng notes "Thumboo's ease in moving among diverse images and themes, the ability to compare different cultural standpoints." A Singaporean of Chinese and Indian extraction, Thumboo stresses diversity and cultural richness, past and present. Earlier, in *Gods Can Die,* he claimed, "We are broken shadows / of giants and old gods," and that "we have to work at a destiny." Concerned for ordinary people, Thumboo found that leaders can become blind, corrupt, and gods, unseeing, can die. There he ridiculed "Ulysses, / such a fool to think the stars would sweat knowledge. He never knew that all our dreams / are edged with yesterdays."

In his new collection Thumboo sees himself in the title figure of *Ulysses by the Merlion,* who "Met strange people singing / New myths; made myths myself." Returning to Singapore and its harbor statue, a mythical lion of the sea, Thumboo thinks of the people: "despite unequal ways / Together they mutate, / Explore the edges of harmony, / Search for a center . . . Good ancestral dreams / Within new visions." Thumboo's eighteen poems here, though pictorial, are philosophical rather than lyric or dramatic. He envisages a global setting for world art: "Among / Sensitive vases / Silken birds /. . . This jade pomegranate / Is succulent; that ivory boat / Will always sail to Mogadishu." He enjoys cross-communication. "As Thai, Bahasa, Filipino, / Mandarin and English meet / . . . Come alive, flex themselves, ruminate / Converse." Personal friendships give him the means to surmount geographical, ideological and linguistic barriers. He imagines nine friends named John together, discovering a "special harvest / As they. . . / Remark upon Kissinger's / Shuttle in the crypt; / Christ on the Mount of Olive, / Harambee the burning spear, / They find common cause in / The tragic shower of / Post-Vietnam refugees."

Hope for the future rests with ordinary people. To the Bengal tigers and Serengeti lions at the zoo, Thumboo prefers "the meek of the earth—/ Gazelles, antelopes, that man / nursing a bent umbrella." >From the mighty, fighting tedium in complexity, he turns to those underprivileged who "Harvest with a sickle, pluck coffee, / Mine rubies, diamonds, gold, / Sew patchwork, embroider soft linen . . . thankful that six children survive / The long hard darkness of each day." His work is compassionate but restrained, thoughtful and coherent, a harmony of image and purpose.

Charlotte H. Bruner

1981

■ **SIMONE DE BEAUVOIR.** *Quand prime le spirituel.* Paris. Gallimard. 1979. vi + 251 pages.

In *La force de l'âge,* her second volume of memoirs, Simone de Beauvoir noted that she had written a work in 1937 to express her revolt against the spiritualism which had oppressed her for a long time. She entitled this book *La primauté du spirituel,* an ironic reference to Jacques Maritain's essay in defense of Christian democracy. Both Grasset and Gallimard rejected the manuscript, which, fortunately, has been published after forty-two years under the revised title *Quand prime le spirituel.* The book is composed of the stories of five victims of spiritualism which serve to express the author's disgust with the bad faith, lies and delusions inherent in it. While the same characters appear in the five stories, they do not form an ensemble that can be classified as a novel. Each young woman remains the center of her story, and the other characters appear and reappear in the background, as in Balzac's *Comédie humaine.*

The first story shows Marcelle's spiritual desire to be the tender inspiration of a weak man of genius as it

degenerates into meanness; the second describes the bad faith of the teacher Chantal, whose obstinacy in playing the role she has assumed helps bring disaster upon two of her admiring students; the third demonstrates the atrophy of Lise's mind at the Sainte-Marie Institute. In the fourth story Beauvoir relates the tragic account of the death of her childhood friend Zaza. The fictional re-creation of this death is less successful than the one in the autobiographical *Mémoires d'une jeune fille rangée.* Marguerite's story, a satire of the author's childhood and a description of her adolescent crisis provoked by the discovery of the death of God, is the last and, according to the author, the best of the five. Her realization that "no one ordered the trees, the sky, the grass to exist and [that she]. . .was floating gratuitously among those vague appearances of nothingness" made her determine to look things straight in the face, to refuse to accept either the pronouncements of oracles or ready-made values and to reinvent her own values.

Lucille Becker

■ **J. M. COETZEE.** *Waiting for the Barbarians.* London. Secker & Warburg. 1980. 156 pages.

Coetzee's is a remarkably rich and mature talent. In this his third novel he continues to explore the psychosis accompanying the forced contact between primitive and advanced societies. His first book, *Dusklands* (1974), contained a remarkable novella dealing with an early journey of exploration beyond the frontier of the Cape Colony. The second, *From the Heart of the Country* (1977; see *WLT* 52:3, p. 510), showed the dominant white society teetering toward collapse.

In his new book the frontiers are succumbing to on-slaughts of the "barbarians," and the "empire" is caving in. Although time and place are kept vague and the location is somewhere in an inhospitable corner of the northern hemisphere, the application to South Africa, Coetzee's country of birth and residence, is hard to ignore. For this—like his previous books—is an allegory of sorts. Books on the demise of white South Africa by other South Africans come to mind: Karel Schoeman's *Promised Land* (see *WLT* 53:4, p. 736) and Nadine Gordimer's recent *July's People,* to name a few.

The title is probably taken from Cavafy's poem which concluded that the barbarians were "a kind of solution": that their threat had served to justify stern measures by the central government. The book makes for compelling reading, largely due to the successful use of the present tense throughout and the vivid presentation of unfolding events. The story is told in the first person by a minor official, a magistrate on the distant frontier whose tolerant administration had become suspect by the government, bent on suppressing any indication of restiveness. The magistrate, weak, ineffective, but a decent human being, shoulders the guilt of the atrocities committed by his government and is destroyed in the process. The tightly controlled writing as well as the theme brings to mind Graham Greene's *The Power and the Glory* with its "whiskey priest." The book won the James Tait Black Memorial Prize, the Geoffry Faber Award, as well as the South African CNA Literary Award for 1980.

Barend J. Toerien

■ **ASSIA DJÉBAR.** *Femmes d'Alger dans leur appartement.* Paris. Des Femmes. 1980. 193 pages.

The cover of this book has a reproduction of Delacroix's famous painting *Femmes d'Alger dans leur appartement.* A century-and-a-half later Assia Djébar gives us an interesting literary variation on the same theme—and keeps the same title, as Picasso had some twenty-five years earlier with his reinvention of Delacroix's painting.

At the age of forty-four, Assia Djébar has reached the peak of her intellectual maturity and has tried her hand at every conceivable genre. Her first book *La soif* (1957) brought her instant celebrity. She was hailed by many critics—mainly because of her youth—as the new Françoise Sagan of Algerian letters. From the beginning and in all her work (four novels, a volume of poetry, a play, essays and several articles) Djébar's obsession is women. Yet *Femmes d'Alger,* a collection of short stories which are, as she defines them, "repères sur un trajet d'écoute, de 1958 à 1978," represents a landmark in her career as a writer and in Maghrebine esthetics in general.

Femmes d'Alger appears after an eleven-year voluntary silence on Djébar's part. Like many of her Francophone colleagues, Djébar faced the excruciating drama of writing in the Other's language and thus the impossibility of communicating with her public. As a woman writer she was all the more frustrated because she could not reach her female compatriots. The stories of *Femmes d'Alger* recount the daily life of Algerian women and their desperate attempt at reaching out to one another. The two main divisions in the book are significantly entitled "Aujourd'hui" and "Hier." By reversing the chronological order, Djébar seems to suggest that women's lot has not changed very much. Two decades after the bloody Independence war, the women who had played an important role, the "porteuses de feu" as made famous by the documentary film "Battle of Algiers," have mysteriously disappeared or have been silenced. What

has become of them? In today's Algeria, even though the harem curtains and doors have been flung open, there still surrounds the Algerian woman (and, for that matter, the Arab and Muslim woman) a conspiracy of silence. After eleven years of relative silence, Assia Djébar takes up her pen once more to give women the voice that society has denied them. Yet the author is relentless. Although the general tone is tragic, there is no pleading and no sensibility. She simply recounts the humdrum of women's daily life. In the second part, entitled "Hier," Djébar vividly resuscitates the language of the past. In "Les morts parlent," the most significant story in this collection, she conjures up a gallery of portraits and investigates a series of conditions and plights of Algerian women, in both near and distant history, as Djébar remembers them and as they are portrayed by oral and popular literatures.

Esthetically, *Femmes d'Alger* inaugurates a new dimension in Maghrebine literature: the painter's perspective. Djébar is offering a new portrayal, a reinterpretation and inevitably an updating of the original *Femmes d'Alger.* The author's postface is the most interesting part of the book. It is a fine piece of literature and a brilliant esthetic commentary on the theme of Algerian women as conceived by Delacroix, Picasso and the author herself. Delacroix's painting is fascinating not so much because it is exotic or offers a first look at an Algerian harem, but—and this is the source of its beauty and interest—"parce que nous mettant devant ces femmes en position de regard, Delacroix nous rappelle qu'ordinairement nous n'avons pas le droit. Ce tableau lui-même est un regard volé." The eye motif is central to Djébar. For the voiceless woman, "le regard" is the only means of communication. In 1955, on the eve of the Algerian War, Picasso reinvents Delacroix's masterpiece in fifteen canvases and two lithographs. Of the harem Picasso makes an open space and replaces sequestration by total nudity, "Comme si Picasso retrouvait la vérité du langage usuel qui, en arabe désigne les 'dévoilées' comme des 'dénudées.'"

Djébar's *Femmes d'Alger* resembles more Picasso's than Delacroix's. It offers an optimistic outlook and a brighter vision of the future: that of "une libération concrète et quotidienne des femmes." Underlying Djébar's "feminism" is not simply the affirmation of a new hope for women, but as illustrated in the stories of *Femmes d'Alger,* a hope of a new world for both men and women.

Hedi Abdeljaouad

■ **UMBERTO ECO.** *Il nome della rosa.* Milan. Bompiani. 1980. 503 pages.

On the cover of Eco's novel *Il nome della rosa* there is the outline of the labyrinth which once appeared on the floor of the Reims cathedral, and which was destroyed during the eighteenth century because children made a playful use of the maze and disturbed the sacred functions "for evidently perverse ends." Hence, from its very appearance, Eco's novel is posited under two signs: the labyrinth as an artistic structure, and play as transgression. Both are at the core of the book and explain its powerful appeal.

Thematically, the labyrinth is the form of the library of an abbey in northern Italy in the year of the Lord 1327, where seven consecutive murders take place in a mysterious connection with the quest for a lost (and forbidden) volume, Aristotle's second book of poetics, dealing with laughter and comedy. Almost until the end, a blind and fearsome Benedictine friar, Jorges da Burgos, defies the reasoned efforts of a Sherlock-Holmesian Dominican friar, Guglielmo da Baskerville, to trace the murders to the lost volume in the labyrinthine library. The events are faithfully recorded by another friar, the old Adso da Melck, who witnessed them as a young novice (notice that his name, Adso, probably derives from *adsum,* Latin "I am present," i.e. I am the witness). But in the process the narrator conveys an incredible mass of *medievalia,* from treatises on herbs and gems and their symbolic meanings to the organization of a medieval library built to mirror the world literally, from a terrifying sermon with apocalyptic tones to the subtlest theological and esthetic discussions, from the historical contrast between Pope and Emperor to the "political" role of Catholic inquisitors, from the stories of many a heresy to the conditions of poor villagers, tillers of the soil and ignorant workers who appear as defenseless pawns in the hands of both ecclesiastic and temporal power.

Play is at the core of the plot because it is forbidden and hidden in the abbey's library, the site of serious knowledge (Bakhtin had theorized laughter as the submerged culture of the Middle Ages). But play should also be considered at a metanarrative level. In fact Eco, who started his scholarly career with a study of Thomas Aquinas, won many bets with his latest book: *Il nome della rosa* can be read as a gothic novel, a thriller, a novel of ideas, even an allegory. Although the author disclaims any intention of having written something that connects his fictional world with our own present, it is sufficient to go back and read an essay of his, "Il Medioevo è già cominciato" (*L'Espresso/Colore,* 7, 13 February 1972, pp. 4–23), to see that for Eco "the model of the Middle Ages can be useful for understanding what is happening today"; just to give two examples, the reciprocal accusations between Benedictines and Do-

minicans are compared to those between Stalinists and Trotskyites, and medieval logic is said to be "close" to structuralism. Eco also won a linguistic bet: his novel is filled with Latin quotations, yet it is pleasant and easy to read, highly communicative; the logic of the plot with its denouements does not detract anything from pensive and poetic moments (and vice versa). For instance, here is the conclusion, which throws light on the whole book and its title: "It is cold in the scriptorium, my thumb aches. I leave my writing, I don't know for whom, I no longer know about what: stat rosa pristina nomine, nomina nuda tenemus." The words of the Latin quotation (not italicized in the text because they have to appear natural for the friar-narrator) seem to echo the concerns of the modern semiotician: the primeval rose stands, exists as a name, we only have bare names. That is the serious conclusion of an extended, literate, learned, labyrinthine play.

Gian-Paolo Biasin

■ **PABLO NERUDA**. *El río invisible: Poesía y prosa de juventud.* Matilde Urrutia, Jorge Edwards, eds. Barcelona. Seix Barral. 1980. 212 pages.

Only readers familiar with the work of Pablo Neruda will fully appreciate the publication of the book under review, which contains both poetry and prose produced by Neruda between 1918 and 1923. All the materials here appeared first in provincial newspapers or small literary reviews; few pieces, however, made their way into the author's poetic collections (and those bore notable emendations).

One might at first glance question the value of this book; the quality of the work is unquestionably inferior to *Crepusculario* (1923), Neruda's first collection. If its author declared that such a book "lacked literary value and was no more than a poetic diary," what then might he have said of this edition of rather uneven and hesitant early work? Modesty would have prevented him from removing them from oblivion; still, we readers of Neruda owe a debt of gratitude to our devoted editors, Matilde Urrutia and Jorge Edwards. The unassailable fame of a Nobel laureate will not suffer, and we are privileged to view the precious awakening of a supreme talent.

The coherent world view informing Neruda's later books is here as yet undeveloped. Instead we find the vacillations and contradictions typical of a developing and juvenile personality. Even this early, however, we find traces of the poet's lifelong creative evolution, marked in mature works by well-defined poetic stages or cycles. Form progressively frees itself from the tyranny of rhyme and the structured rigidity of the sonnet in favor of personal expression. Certain thematic leit-motivs here are surprising. The poet clearly longs for love but finds himself frustrated by his own character and views—his timidity and his idealization of women, for example, and also his dissatisfaction both with the provincial society of Temuco and with the life of the capital, Santiago.

All of this, including a subtle consciousness of his literary calling and complex personality, joined by a vague feeling of guilt (perhaps tied to his mother's death), confers upon these juvenilia a veil of melancholy and grief. The poet is conscious of embarking on a wandering search, a search without a clear and certain goal and without real hope of success. The poet's soul receives universal sorrow. Only simple people and objects deserve his praise: peasants, blind men, the sick, a crushed grasshopper, an old wall. These are far from the despised world of bureaucrats and the bourgeoisie, uniformed scouts and soldiers. After his elusive and fantasmal beloved, nature alone (sun, sea, night, tree) stirs the poet's admiration. In the first bloom of his poetic youth, then, Neruda knew both friend and polemical enemy.

I am far from suggesting that everything here is insignificant or of only documentary value. In certain selections, when the poet writes with assurance on matters on the far side or on the near side of literature, there are moments of profound truth. It is revealing that these moments focus on the intensity of opposing feelings: the poet's love for nature and woman ("Aquel bote salvavidas"), his guilt ("Luna" and "Un hombre anda bajo la luna"), his gratitude and admiration for his stepmother ("Humildes versos para que descanse mi madre") and his disenchantment with the mediocrity of provincial life ("Día miércoles" and "Poema en la provincia"). Here the reader very nearly forgets he is not reading the mature Neruda.

Carlos Cortínez

▪ **SIMONE SCHWARZ-BART.** *Ti Jean L'Horizon.* Paris. Seuil. 1979. 286 pages.

The problems of alienation and troubled consciousness; the awareness of past victimization, present disarray and future uncertainty; and the urgency of the quest for self and group identity are themes that have been consistently explored by Simone Schwarz-Bart in her first two novels, *Un plat de porc aux bananes vertes* (1967) and *Pluie et vent sur Télumée Miracle* (1972). Her latest novel *Ti Jean L'Horizon* mirrors her continuing concern with the cultural and psychic legacy accumulated in the history of her native Guadeloupe in particular, in the French Antilles in general and, by extension, in all the former European colonies of the Caribbean. But whereas *Un plat de porc aux bananes vertes* and even more so *Pluie et vent sur Télumée Miracle* limit their perspective in space and time, *Ti Jean L'Horizon,* beginning from a specific locus, explores the outer limits of the primordial. Taking its inspiration from the magical world of the Antillean stories, the novel, divided into nine books, follows the fabulous adventures of the mythical hero in his quest for lost identity and lost love.

The novel opens in Fond-Zombi, Guadeloupe. The inhabitants are polarized into two distinct groups, those living in the forested plateau (the "gens d'En-haut") and those on the neighboring lowlands (the "gens d'En-bas"). The forest dwellers, retaining almost intact their ancestral African culture and their tradition of revolt against plantation life, lead a rude, uncultured existence under the domination of the last of the maroons, Wademba. The more "civilized" plains dwellers are despised by the mountain folk, who believe that they have lost their original identity as they continue a precarious existence as serfs of the plantation owners. However, the easy existence of the villagers proves attractive to some of the forest dwellers. Thus the companion of Wademba and later his daughter Awa leave the mountain hideout to settle on the lowlands. Ti Jean L'Horizon, born of the union of Awa and a lowland dweller, represents a synthesis of the two polarized cultures.

In the course of his initiation, Ti Jean receives from Wademba the magical objects and powers that he will need in his mission to find the Beast which has swallowed the sun and plunged Fond-Zombi into total darkness. His journey, accomplished partially with the wings of a bird, takes him to Africa, where he confronts his ancestors, questions the living as well as the dead, animals as well as things. He witnesses the destructive impact of slavery as practiced by Africans as well as whites. He has numerous amorous encounters but maintains his desire for his beloved Égée. After visiting the Kingdom of the Dead, he finally returns to Guadeloupe, where he slays the Beast, finds again his beloved Égée and realizes that his mission is not over, since conditions have not changed.

Moving as it does from realistic detail of everyday life, geography, flora and fauna, historical events and personages to explicit symbols and identifiable allegory, Schwarz-Bart's novel maintains a textual density which does not render it readily comprehensible to the uninitiated reader.

Wilbert J. Roget

1982

■ **CAMILO JOSÉ CELA**. *Vuelta de hoja*.
Barcelona. Destino. 1981. 218 pages.

Camilo José Cela is probably one of the best-known
contemporary novelists from Spain. One area, however,
which has not received the attention it deserves is his
journalistic writing. *Vuelta de hoja* is a selection of his
articles published in the Madrid newspaper *Cambio 16*
during the year 1976 shortly after the monarchy was reestablished in his country. After so many years of oppressive dictatorship, Spain finally began then to experience the various consequences of freedom and
democracy. For that reason alone the present volume
has tremendously important value, as it reflects current
events from the point of view of a Spaniard from within
his own country. In the past, readers were frequently
treated to the opinions and views on Spain of exiles who
by and large lacked understanding of the currents operating within.

Cela is obviously well informed and knowledgeable
of what worries his fellow countrymen. Due to his popularity with the average man in the street, his position
at the Royal Academy of the Spanish Language and his
own political appointment by the King, Cela is probably
better qualified than any other writer or journalist to
write on the political panorama facing his homeland.

Cela's literary style—simple and rich at the same
time—makes this book ideal for use in intermediate and
advanced language classes. If an American edition is
published, it should contain, in addition to the traditional introduction and vocabulary, some historical information to facilitate the reader's understanding of the
content and frame of reference from which Cela was
writing. In *Vuelta de hoja* Cela compares most favorably
to his fellow citizen Mariano José de Larra, who also
wrote concerning the political situation of his country
at a crucial point in history.

Luis Larios, translated by San Xavier Translating
Services

■ **MARIA JULIETA DRUMMOND DE
ANDRADE**. *Um buquê de alcachofras*. 2nd ed.
Rio de Janeiro. Olympio. 1981. 165 pages.

Um buquê de alcachofras is a collection of *crônicas* written between 1978 and 1980 by Maria Drummond de
Andrade for her Saturday column in *O Globo*. As befits
a well-crafted *crônica,* the pieces gathered here are hybrid products in which one can easily detect certain aspects of other literary genres, such as the short story,

the essay and the epistle. The writing, a consistently
lively and fresh Brazilian Portuguese, is a pleasing mixture of everyday usages and more erudite forms. Andrade's subject matter varies greatly, as do her modes
of expression, which range from the whimsical and satiric to the contemplative and serious. Some of the most
interesting selections deal with the personal reactions of
the author upon meeting such literary celebrities as Borges, Sábato and Clarice Lispector.

Another singular feature of *Um buquê de alcachofras*
is the way that Andrade imparts to the reader a strong
sense of contrast between contemporary life in Buenos
Aires, where the author resides, and in Rio de Janeiro,
where she spends her holidays. In "Coisas de antes e
agora," for example, Andrade muses about how much
Buenos Aires has changed in the last few years, while
in "Almoço no Leblon" she gives us a telling glimpse of
the urban scene—the delightful and the pathetic—in
present-day Rio.

Maria Julieta Drummond de Andrade is a talented
writer, one whose sensitivity to both life and language
allows her to discern what is unique and valuable in
seemingly banal events and then to frame this for us,
often by means of a gentle humor, in a humane and
sympathetic fashion.

Earl E. Fitz

■ **NURUDDIN FARAH**. *Sweet and Sour Milk*.
New York. Schocken. 1981. 237 pages.

Soyaan dies mysteriously. Who or what killed him? His
twin brother Loyaan is determined to find out. The
clues come in from Soyaan's half-Italian, half-Somali
lover and from his friends and colleagues. Loyaan begins to close in on the truth, and the truth begins to
close in on him. For this is Somalia of today, ruled by
the General with the assistance of the Soviet Union. The
setting is local, the horror general.

> Keynaan and Loyaan fell silent as they heard the
> Green Guard rehearse the National Anthem of
> Uganda. Tomorrow or the day after, Idi Amin
> would come as the honoured guest of the Somali
> Democratic Republic. A week or so before: Ga-
> daffi. A month before that: Bokassa. *Garland these
> generals, these colonels with a necklace of haemhor-
> raged intestines. Quench Numeiry's power-thirst
> with a Nile of communist blood,* thought Loyaan.
> *Issue to N——a Union Jack of power-coupons. To
> K——: a queen of elephant-pouches and hard
> tusks of currency.*

It makes no difference whether the generals were
helped into power by the West (Amin, Bokassa) or the
East. Farah is as hard on Soviet involvement in his part

of Africa as Cyprian Ekwensi is in *Divided We Stand* (1980): modern Somalia is a Gulag. However, Farah is not putting the blame entirely on outside forces. On the contrary, he presents the internal forces of Somalia to show how such a dictatorship was possible: for example, tribal allegiances, as well as a tendency to obey the powers-that-be because everything comes from the government. Equally important is the age-old exploitation of women in this Islamic society. No society can be a just one if it exploits women, says Farah; his first novel, *From a Crooked Rib,* exposed the low status of Somali women. Keynaan, Loyaan's father, treats his wives like dirt. It is knowledge of Somali society that the illiterate General is able to exploit cunningly.

Loyaan finds a trail of people tortured for being involved with his brother. His brother, he discovers, had joined a group of young people building up a documented case against the General: knowing that the people were oral, the General had created a system of oral commands which could then be forgotten or wiped out without trace. Was that why Soyaan was killed and officially declared a hero of the republic? Because in Somalia even one's soul belonged to the General? The newspaper report said that Soyaan's last words were, "Labour is honour and there is no General but our General." With its sacrilegious echo of the Koran, this lie had come from Keynaan, anxious to get back his old job in the office of torturers, which he had lost (as a scapegoat) when a man had been tortured to death. Keynaan had been forced to marry the widow Beydan.

But Loyaan is not innocent either: he has too orderly a mind—which means, Soyaan's lover says, that it is unlikely he would let something forgotten enter his set world view and shake it up. As his investigation brings results, the secret police close in. We think he is taken to be tortured. Instead he is told that his brother had been about to become Ambassador to Yugoslavia, and Loyaan must take his place at short notice. What will Loyaan do? Will he choose to resist or will he accept? The latter, it seems. His resistance to the system, however moral a gesture when it finally came, was naïve, ineffective and dangerous. The whole society contributes to its own destruction by the General.

Farah's fourth novel, *Sardines,* has just been published in England. *Sweet and Sour Milk* is enough to stake his claim as one of the important novelists of modern, suffering Africa.

Peter Nazareth

■ **GEORGES PEREC**. *Théâtre I: La poche parmentier précédé de L'augmentation.* Paris. Hachette. 1981. 132 pages.

Théâtre I contains two plays, one with no stage directions, the other with many. They both belong to the familiar absurdist tradition, and they are particularly reminiscent of plays by Ionesco and Arrabal, of Beckett's three-character *Acte sans paroles* and of Sartre's *Huis-clos.*

L'augmentation is a repetitive litany in which a timid functionary tries to see his boss in order to ask for a raise. The whole play is a variation on this theme: "The boss will either be in or he won't. Let's assume he is; he will then either see me now or tell me to come back tomorrow. Let's assume he does the latter," and so on. The ratiocination has the effect of dehumanizing the language, a phenomenon encountered in the early absurdist plays by Ionesco (*La cantatrice chauve*) and Beckett (*En attendant Godot*). It cannot be said that *L'augmentation* is a good or a bad play, for it is so skeletal that its success must depend on interpretation, on the mise-en-scène and on histrionic execution. It fits comfortably into the paradigm of hopelessness so familiar in other absurdist plays.

The main text, *La poche parmentier,* is a curious play in which a group of people find themselves trapped in a house from which they cannot escape and which some of them vaguely recall having known in other times. As in *Huis-clos,* the characters seem to be in some sort of hell contrived out of their own lives and memories. However, given the opportunity to leave, they see no purpose in leaving, for outside the door are stairs, more stairs and a guard. As one character comments, it is difficult to tell if it is those inside or those outside who are confined. The final moments of the play find the characters acting out a variation on the Hamlet-Laertes death scene. A closing comment by an old servant suggests that the house is an insane asylum, but also that its inmates are wiser than the wise.

The absurdist quality of the play is enhanced by the recurrent theme of the potato. Periodically, characters peel potatoes, eat potatoes, discuss the relative merits of potatoes and give lengthy scholarly dissertations on the potato. The potato forms an armature for and gives some sort of rational meaning to the otherwise arbitrary and often confused recollections of the characters.

Eric Sellin

■ **MARTA TRABA**. *Conversación al sur.* Mexico City. Siglo XXI. 1981. 170 pages.

In a paradox no less troubling for being familiar, the experiences that would most demand a literary response prove difficult to elaborate in literary fashion. Such is the case with the upheaval produced by the mid-1970s rise of the new regimes in Argentina, Chile and Uruguay and the contemporary implementation of unwontedly massive anti-radical drives. The astonishing zeal with which official forces sought the extermination of leftist activity, the doomed persistence of radicalism, the involvement of numerous previously apolitical individuals in politically charged and violent events—all this demands a suitable narrative reflection. Marta Traba's *Conversación al sur* stands at a midpoint between the raw, denunciatory mode of testimonial writing (Alegría, Valdés, Skármeta) and the personal, somewhat apolitical reflections of such authors as Elvira Orphée and Marta Lynch. Traba's new novel gains a measure of detachment by commenting upon the chaotic years of the anti-radical crackdowns from a certain removal in time; the conversation that constitutes the essence of the book takes place in a Montevideo that, while definitely the worse for the disruption, is no longer a city in crisis. A second distancing factor is the generalization of the critical experience of repression to include events taking place in all three countries (the collectively fated *sur* [South] of the title) and having an impact on various persons belonging to two distinct social generations and unlike social strata.

The two who converse stand on opposite sides of this significant generational divide. An older woman, representative of three characters in the book, comes from a background that stresses the importance of making life stylish and amusing. At the same time, it is her concern with matters of style and art that lead her to an involvement with youthful radicalism; as a performing artist on tour, she comes in contact with student activists and unexpectedly discovers a bond of sympathy. Her interlocutor is of a younger, grimmer outlook, accustomed to the notion that the very struggle for survival will consume a good deal of life's energies, haggard after years in the lower middle class and the underground and the direct experience of torture and harassment. While this opposition between the woman of allure and the woman of steely purpose could be tediously schematic, Traba in a fascinating way explores affinities and likenesses that exist within this dichotomy. As the two meet to exchange memories and reflections, it becomes gradually evident that the radical harbors a considerable, if seldom-expressed capacity for the playful and joyful, while the glamorous actress understands more about the nature of the liberation struggle than her outward persona would suggest.

While these interpersonal considerations give the novel its form, it would be a mistake to call *Conversación* a personalized view of political events. The contents of denunciatory reports are in plain view throughout the novel: specific descriptions of torture and of other procedures designed to disrupt the lives of radicals and their suspected associates; accounts of the frustration of relatives seeking information about "disappeared" persons; characterizations of the havoc wreaked upon individual lives, whether those of the intentionally or accidentally involved. Traba has succeeded in creating a fitting narrative context in which this testimony may be embedded without the work itself losing its character as a satisfyingly literary work. And although she has been careful not to overwork this theme, she deserves credit for focusing specifically upon the experience of women involved in radical activity.

Naomi Lindstrom

■ **WANG WEI**. *The Poetry of Wang Wei: New Translations and Commentary*. Pauline Yu, ed. & tr. Bloomington, In. Indiana University Press. 1980. xiii + 274 pages.

During the last decade the poetry of Wang Wei (701–761) has attracted a host of different translators of Chinese poetry in the West. While the reasons which account for this important Tang poet's popularity with Western translators and audiences are varied and many (Yu discusses these in her preface), two immediately stand out. First, the language of Wang Wei's verse, especially his nature poetry, is (deceptively) simple and translates rather easily into English; and second, the poet's concrete and precise visual imagery is immediately appealing to almost all audiences. As an example, consider the following quatrain (in Yu's translation) entitled "Deer Enclosure," surely one of the most popular anthology pieces found in Western translations of Chinese poetry.

Empty mountain, no man is seen.
Only heard are echoes of men's talk.
Reflected light enters the deep wood
And shines again on blue-green moss.

The underlying assumption of Yu's study is that, largely as a result of the popularity of works such as that cited above, Wang Wei has heretofore been considered only a nature poet. Further, Yu contends that such an outlook does not take into account the other types of verse Wang Wei composed in addition to his nature poems, most notably his "Juvenilia and Other Literary Exercises" (which comprise chapter two of Yu's book), "Court Poems" (chapter three), and "Buddhist Poems" (chapter four). A selection of Wang Wei's nature poems is presented in the fifth and final chapter. Without a doubt, the 150 annotated translations appearing in this volume are the most representative selection of Wang Wei's complete oeuvre to appear in English translation to date.

Despite the great popularity of Wang Wei in China and the West, he has been the subject of very few critical studies in any language. Perhaps the primary reason which accounts for this neglect is that the apparent surface simplicity of much of his poetry on second glance "reveals disturbingly elusive philosophical underpinnings, grounded in Buddhist metaphysics, and the difficulty of grappling with these concepts and relating them to his poetry may have discouraged critical analysis." Students of Chinese poetry and comparatists will thus particularly appreciate the first chapter of *The Poetry of Wang Wei,* in which Yu offers a detailed and scholarly discussion of the Taoist and "metaphysical" traditions in Chinese literature as well as Western symbolist, post-symbolist and phenomenological theories as they pertain to the works of Wang Wei. While I have reservations about the usefulness and applicability of such theories in approaching works such as the "Court Poems" discussed in chapter three, Yu's brilliant essay does successfully create a meaningful critical framework in which to approach much of Wang Wei's verse. Unlike other critics in recent years who have tried to apply Western theories of literature to Chinese poetry, Yu does not allow her critical approach to overwhelm the material at hand. In all cases the poems are allowed to "speak" for themselves.

All the translations appearing in this volume are rendered faithfully into readable English. Those readers who know Chinese will particularly appreciate the punctuated original texts and character glossary of key names and terms included in the appendices. Pauline Yu's volume is a unique and important work among studies and translations of Wang Wei's poetry, one which deserves the attention of all serious students of Chinese verse.

James M. Hargett

1983

■**JOSÉ MANUEL CABALLERO BONALD.** *Toda la noche oyeron pasar pájaros.* Barcelona. Planeta. 1981. 318 pages.

José Manuel Caballero Bonald was born in Jerez de la Frontera in 1928. After completing his studies at the universities of Seville and Madrid, he taught Spanish literature for three years at the National University of Colombia. He returned to Spain in 1962 and joined the Department of Lexicography at the Spanish Royal Language Academy. He has previously published eight volumes of poetry and two important novels: *Dos días de setiembre* (1962) and *Agata ojo de gato* (1974).

Toda la noche oyeron pasar pájaros relates the story of a southern Spanish port town and slowly details the total disintegration of the local society. The novel centers on an English family who have set up residence in the town due to their maritime business interests. The plot does not follow the traditional order; instead a series of short vignettes are provided which, as in a collage, form the total picture. The characters in this small town live practically cut off from the rest of the world; this isolation, however, does not seem to bother them much. Theirs is at least a familiar world, and they have learned the rules of the game, with the exception of Mr. Leiston. As is to be expected, of course, there are references to a conflict, a war being fought somewhere else, but it does not seem to play such a dramatic role as one is led to believe by contemporary Spanish novelists.

The author, by means of skillful and powerful narrative technique, is able to portray a world in the various phases of collapse with all its degrading consequences. The reader comprehends the absurdity which envelops both the characters and their world by realizing the human treachery which at times appears to be the real protagonist. The insistence on various forms of contradictions emphasizes the internal chaos in which all the characters are forced to live. None is aware of the nature of the surrounding world, and none tries to escape from it. For that reason, the reader senses the alienation which denies them all any choice or alternative.

The language is strikingly rich with abundant regional and nautical terms. *Toda la noche oyeron pasar pájaros* was awarded the 1981 Ateneo de Sevilla Prize and is indeed a very good choice.

Luis Larios Vendrell

■**NIKOS KAZANTZAKIS.** *Two Plays: "Sodom and Gomorrah" and "Comedy: A Tragedy in One Act."* Kimon Friar, ed. & tr. Minneapolis. North Central. 1982. 120 pages.

The Saviors of God: Spiritual Exercises (translated by Kimon Friar in 1960) no doubt provides the key to understanding Kazantzakis's visionary philosophy. The play *Sodom and Gomorrah,* originally written in 1948, and *Comedy: A Tragedy in One Act,* originally written in 1909, appeared in Friar's translation in the Summer 1975 and Winter 1976 issues of *The Literary Review* and very much represent the dramatic embodiment of Kazantzakis's philosophy.

Even though Kazantzakis is well known for his novels and his epic *Odyssey* (translated by Friar in 1958), he also wrote nineteen plays but never considered himself a playwright. In Kimon Friar's words: "He saw himself, I believe, as a visionary, a prophet, as a soldier who seized whatever was most readily at hand—paper, ink, action—in order to do battle. But his was essentially a dramatic view of life, and whatever he touched crackled with emotion, tension, antithesis, upheaval, conflict. His plays are dramatic not because he was a man of the theater, but because he saw all of life in terms of protagonist and antagonist. The protagonist was Man, the antagonist was God." So it is with *Sodom and Gomorrah*: man is engaged in a fierce battle with God to the death. In Kazantzakis, God has an elusive, elastic and constantly changing meaning, but it is clear that for him it is man who has conceived of goodness, justice, truth, beauty and the standards of morality. God is an infinite power, surging throughout nature, forever creating but unconcerned with human ideals, a pitiless tyrant of whom Lot says, "He is not just. He is not good. He is only Almighty. Almighty, but He's nothing else!" As elsewhere in Kazantzakis, it is man who must save God.

The shorter play (a mere twenty-two pages in Friar's translation) anticipated the theatrical possibilities of Sartre's *No Exit* (1944) and Beckett's *Waiting for Godot* (1952) decades before these works were written and produced. The play takes place inside a man's mind at the moment of his death, according to the author himself, "when the soul rises to the summation and supreme summit of life." Kazantzakis exploits the idea that "the individual," in the words of Karl Kerenyi in his introduction to this play (translated by Peter Bien), "through his death-throes, reaches an existential state valid for all men and all times; also, that this state, since it is a perception shared by all men, can be transferred to the stage in intelligible form." In Kazantzakis's play the characters wait in vain for a God who does not come. The hour of death is every individual's great existential moment of waiting.

Friar has once again given us clear, crisp English translations of hitherto not readily available works of Kazantzakis. They are sure to enhance our understanding and appreciation of one of Greece's greatest literary figures.

John E. Rexine

■ **GEORGE KONRÁD.** *The Loser.* Ivan Sanders, tr. San Diego. Harcourt Brace Jovanovich. 1982. 315 pages.

The Loser is George Konrád's third novel and in some ways his most traditional one to date. Like his previous novel *A városalapító* (*The City Builder*; 1977; see *WLT* 52:1, p. 151), it was originally written in Hungarian but

published in German and French; moreover, while *A városalapító,* with some minor cuts, did eventually see publication in Budapest, *The Loser* (which is, by the way, not the literal translation of the Hungarian title *A cinkos*) has absolutely no hope of getting published in Konrád's native land. This statement, however, begs qualification: according to the London-based review *Index on Censorship* (April 1983), Konrád's new novel has been available in Hungary for some time thanks to the unofficial "publishing house" AB.

While the actual time of Konrád's previous novels was the continuous present, *The Loser* is more segmented and diachronic; it consists more of past reminiscences than sophisticated commentaries on an elusively rich present. Such handling of one's literary material diminishes and, to some extent, compromises the unity of Konrád's vision. The narrator K., an aging, half-Jewish ex-communist (now a "different-thinking" intellectual), remains the same throughout the book, but the narrative modes adopted by him change perceptibly. Of the five parts of the novel, the first brings us into a psychiatric hospital somewhere in Hungary in the 1970s, where K. is recovering from a nervous breakdown; the second deals with his family background; the third and fourth present chunks of experience from the prewar period, the war years and the aftermath of Hungary's liberation from the Germans and simultaneous occupation by the Red Army; and finally, the fifth part presents a chaotic finale in which various strands are brought together, including K.'s politics, his relationship with his now estranged wife and the problems caused by his younger brother Dani. This brother can be seen as K.'s alter ego; he is a reckless, unreliable, cheeky, hotheaded lunatic who apparently also possesses great charm; yet even this cannot quite save him from the consequences of murdering his whorish wife in a frenzy of excessive jealousy. In the last chapter of the book Dani is seen making preparations to kill himself, with K.'s quiet assistance. There may be good reasons for inventing the figure of Dani, yet in the end he strikes us as largely irrelevant in a novel which is, after all, meant to center on the hero's love affair with history—a love affair that starts out boisterously but ends in something approaching tragedy.

Konrád is predictably most impressive when writing out of his own experience. This is why the best parts of *The Loser* are the vivid description of the narrator's provincial childhood and his account of the 1956 uprising. In the latter instance Konrád manages to give a reasonably faithful and complete picture of the days that "shook the world." All the important protagonists and events are there, yet the reader is not overburdened with detail. This in itself is an achievement, and it is a pity that these excellent pages are followed by a kind of anticlimax in the form of the rambling, psychologizing final section of an otherwise very readable, well-translated and stimulating modern novel. (On Konrád see WLT 57:2, pp. 210–14.)

George Gömöri

■ **BERNARD MALAMUD**. *God's Grace*. New York. Farrar, Straus & Giroux. 1982. 223 pages.

The voice of God: "I made man to be free, but his freedom, badly used, destroyed him. In some, the evil overwhelmed the good." The voice of Cohn: "God made us who we are." Thus Malamud introduces the dilemma of Calvin Cohn, a paleologist and the only survivor of a thermonuclear war between the Djanks and the Druzhkies. Cohn finds himself adrift in the ocean with only a chimpanzee named Buz for companionship. Their ship eventually runs aground, and Buz and Cohn set up housekeeping on an apparently deserted island. Luckily for Cohn, Dr. Walter Bünder, who had been experimenting with giving primates the gift of language, equipped Buz with wires attached to his larynx that enable him to speak.

If this tale is beginning to sound fabulous, that is because it is. The form Malamud is experimenting with here is the fable, with all its attendant morals and lessons. The novel is clearly an experiment and as such deserves the kind of notice which befits the risk-taking of an established and intelligent contemporary novelist. Unfortunately, the rewards do not justify the risk.

The novel explores the reshaping of a world with Cohn as leader and teacher and with chimps, a gorilla and several baboons as his class—and, at times, as his congregation. Cohn tries to construct a civilized society and encounters the same problems that the Prime Mover, no doubt, did. The chimps and baboons are Hobbesian natural enemies vying over food, shelter and sexual property.

Cohn attempts to groom and guide Buz, his most loyal follower, in the ways of the world and of courtship; Buz focuses on Mary Madelyn, the female chimp. Cohn's speech reveals the ludicrous juxtaposition of civilized culture and natural instinct: "My sense of it is she would like to be courted, not gunned down by an ambitious phallus. Talk to her about *Romeo and Juliet*. She admires the play." But of course Mary Madelyn mostly admires Cohn, the bearer of romantic culture. They eventually mate, to the dismay of all the chimp males. All this activity ends in disaster. It is no surprise that culture, romantic or otherwise, is no antidote for the brutality often necessary for survival.

Although this fable soon wears thin, there are moments of insight and humor in the novel. The sustained insight and character study found in Malamud's previous work, *Dubin's Lives* (see *WLT* 53:4, p. 682), are not to be found here, though. The best one can expect is a curious foray into a modern morality fable which offers few revelations.

Rita D. Jacobs

■ **EUGENIO MONTALE**. *Altri versi*. Milan. Mondadori. 1981. 196 pages.

Just a few months before he died, Montale had the satisfaction of seeing his last book, *Altri versi*, in print (see *WLT* 56:3, pp. 470–72). About eighty poems in it were written during the last two years of his life; another forty-five date from the years 1969–77, and a group of two dozen poems stem from the first decade of his career (1918–28). One justification for putting them all together could well be that they illustrate the distinctively personal timbre fround in all Montale's poetry—there being something about its style, imagery and inflection (as about Pound's, for example) which is unmistakable and which no other poet in Italy has achieved since Leopardi. His infallible eye for detail, his concrete hold on what is most subtle and delicate and his indefatigable probing for meaning in what is apparently meaningless characterized Montale's poetry until the very end. And informing all the poems was what F. R. Leavis, in his memorable critique of *Xenia*, called Montale's use of intelligence in rendering with delicacy and precision not only his intensely personal experience (as in *Xenia*), but also "a profound and moving impersonality."

Through his earlier verse Montale had modernized Italian poetry; through his later (from *Satura* in 1971 to *Altri versi*) he added a new dimension to the Italian poetic tradition by injecting into it such elements as wit, irony, satire and paradox that had not been exploited—or exploited to the same effect—before. And yet Montale never founded a school. More imitated than matched, his "isolated superiority"—one can aptly apply to Montale the phrase used by Eliot vis-à-vis Pound—was never challenged. However, Montale's search for his own moral and poetic identity, which had started in *Ossi di seppia* (1925), continued unabated, and so did his search for words that could adhere to what he had to say. In other words, his wrestling with words and meanings was no less intolerable than Eliot's, and each book he brought out signaled a new stage in his poetic development and experimentation.

In *Altri versi* there are poems dealing with contemporary events as they impinged upon Montale's life and art. In "Quando il mio nome apparve," for instance, he comments wryly on the impact which winning the 1975 Nobel Prize had on him (see *BA* 50:1, pp. 7–15): "Quando il mio nome apparve in quasi tutti i giornali / una gazzetta francese avanzò l'ipotesi / che non fossi mai esistito. / Non mancarono rapide smentite. / Ma la falsa notizia era più vera." And in "Piccolo diario" he stands away from what fame meant to him and judges it in an almost sardonic vein: "Si accumula la posta / 'invasa' sul tavolo. Parebbe / che io sia molto importante / ma non l'ho fatto apposta. / Dio mio, se fosse vero / che mai saranno gli altri." The theme of love too is looked at from a new angle, translated into new accents and new concepts. He tells his beloved, "l'ago della bilancia sei sempre tu. / M'hanno chiesto chi sei. Se lo sapessi / lo direi a gran voce. E sarei chiuso / tra quelle sbarre donde non s'esce più" ("Per me"). As to the possibility of meeting her in the eternal life, he hasn't much hope. Moreover, there is a snag—how to communicate with her during such a meeting: "Era già problematico parlarti / nella terrena. / La colpa è nel sistema / delle communicazioni. / Se ne scoprono molte ma non quella / che farebbe ridicole nonchè inutili / le altre."

As to the truth he has been searching for all his life, the poet is no wiser now toward the end of his life then he was when he began. For "la verità è nelle nostre mani / ma è inafferrabile e sguscia come um'anguilla. / Neppure i morti l'hanno mai compresa / per non ricadere tra i viventi, là / dove tutto è difficile, tutto è inutile" ("Amici non credete"). And talking to "Mosca," his wife, whose death moved him to write *Xenia,* he tells her he finds it impossible to believe that "di te resti meno / del fuoco rosso verdognolo / di una lucciola fuori stagione. / La verità è che nemmeno / l'incorporeo / può eguagliare il tuo cielo / e solo i refusi del cosmo / spropositando dicono qualcosa / che ti riguardi." The subtle interplay of imagery and concept, hope and incredulity, gives these verses, as it gives the whole volume they come from, their unmistakably Montalean quality based on the poet's unpedantic use of wit, irony and paradox which characterized the latest stage of development in an art that was, even at the very outset (in *Ossi di seppia*), already, so mature and so accomplished: "Non a torto / mi avevano raccomandato, / se andavo a cena dal diavolo, / di usare il cucchiaio lungo. / Purtroppo / in quelle rare occasioni / il solo a disposizione / era corto."

G. Singh

■ **PHILIPPE SOLLERS**. *Femmes*. Paris. Gallimard. 1983. 570 pages.

Perhaps as a respite from or necessary break with the intense, concentrated scription of *Paradis,* Sollers has delivered himself of a different (for him) sort of book, one in which he gives us a personal prospect of the intellectual, literary and political scene during the past few years as well as an account of his own concerns and obsessions. In some ways it reminds me of Simone de Beauvoir's *Les Mandarins,* published nearly thirty years ago; I am of course aware of the gulf that separates the personalities and texts of the two writers. Interestingly enough, both have been greeted by the same prurient desire to decipher the work as a roman à clef and to sniff out scandalous bits of gossip; both should nevertheless be read as works of fiction, even though, as Marx said of Balzac's novels, they might teach us more about contemporary reality than the ponderous writings of historians could do.

The narrator of *Femmes* is an American newspaperman, a Southerner (possibly in homage to Faulkner and Flannery O'Connor) who works in Paris and travels much. We follow him to New York, of course, but also to Israel, Italy and Spain; the resulting political overview covers a great deal. He is a friend of S., a fictionalized version of Sollers himself, who has agreed to sign the narrator's novel. A schizophrenic text in which the writing subject is split between S. and the narrator? Would that things were so simple! The novel's title points to another split, for its characters significantly agree that it is not adequate. Among others that are bandied about there is *La fin du monde,* and also *La clé de l'abime* as well as *Bacchanale.* The unifying topic of the novel is not really women or even Woman but Sex in relation to Death: sex both as a form of *préciosité*—that is, a guardrail on the edge of the abyss—and its antithesis, a pessimistic rush into the abyss. The narrative is androcratic and conveys more than overtones of macho rhythm; it also harbors a female tide that gives it a complex, perplexing quality. Regardless of one's opinion concerning Sollers's previous literary and political stances, *Femmes* is a book that should be read by all those interested in the contemporary scene as well as those who might be troubled by Bataille's notion of eroticism as "the sanctioning of life unto death."

Leon S. Roudiez

1984

▪ **SILVIO BLATTER**. *Kein schöner Land.*
Frankfurt a.M. Suhrkamp. 1983. 545 pages.

"Kein schöner Land in dieser Zeit," the opening line of
a folk song, is meant to refer, both literally and skepti-
cally, to Silvio Blatter's homeland, the *Freiamt* (a county) in the canton of Aargau in Switzerland, the main setting of this novel (the same one he chose for his
previous novel, *Zunehmendes Heimweh;* see WLT 54:1,
p. 104), with Bremgarten (his hometown, where he still
lives), on the looping river Reuβ, as its center. The novel
is a saga of the present-day *Freiamt* and its people. But
it is not a *Heimatroman;* the author immediately raises
the question—implicitly at first, explicitly later on—in
what respects the *Freiamt,* which is at least in part representative of the Swiss Confederation, may or may not
be called one of the most beautiful places "in these
times."

One of the more calmly reflective characters in the
novel, Hans Villiger, a schoolteacher and a private historian of his canton, says to himself, "You live here,
. . . you have settled down, you have simply had to. . .
here is your home [*Heimat*], and he meant it neither
ironically nor cynically, he was under no illusion
that. . . in the *Freiamt* things were good and better than
elsewhere." In fact, to him, the *Freiamt* "is often a hell
(a ghetto)." What appears to disturb him most is that
"the history of modern technology" is "a history of unparalleled destruction." He feels that for this reason he
needs genuine support from people living with and near
him. In order to understand and accept the present as
much as possible, he is convinced that he must study
the past, perhaps the time between the world wars; he
suspects and then discovers the existence of crucial
analogies between that past and this present.

Another native of the *Freiamt,* Pablo, a painter,
shudders at the thought of looking at reality only
through the eyes of an artist and putting it only at the
service of art, while being eager to find that everything
is related to everything else. He experiences, among
other things, a fundamental kind of kinship with Pieter
Bruegel and believes it is legitimate for him to create
modernized adaptations of some of Bruegel's group pictures.

Blatter's work is a verbal realization of Hans Villiger's and Pablo's views and goals. It is, of course, a
novel, not a history or a journalistic report. For Blatter,
his *Freiamt* provides a valid illustration of the rather
"frightening condition" of the world at large, or certainly, at least, that of the Western industrialized nations.

In the role of an omniscient narrator, he tells us the intricately intertwined life stories of the members of a few
families, who maintain quite different attitudes and
habits. He records their experiences and activities over
the span of about a year in the early 1980s, with an intimate knowledge and a warm understanding of older
and younger generations, boys and girls, women and
men from various walks of life. Though the characters
are different from one another, the majority of them are
torn between the same opposite states of mind: stunted
emotion and sensuous love; imprisonment and freedom; alienation and rootedness, trendiness and independence; trust in technology and concern about nature's ecology. But each one of the characters has his or
her own personality.

Blatter's favorite literary techniques are juxtaposing
and weaving together aspects of the whole story and
thus achieving the effect of simultaneity and coherence.
His language is both lucid and unabashedly romantic
("New Romanticism"?). He uses strong symbols to the
point of over-indulgence; some of these symbols, especially the leitmotivic ones, come perilously close to
kitsch. The novel is composed of five eight-part chapters, whose titles are taken from those of certain paintings by Bruegel and whose thematic "points of gravity"
are early summer harvest, ceremonies around a funeral,
the annual *Freiamt* county fair, Carnival and the Swiss
national holiday. Once again, Blatter has demonstrated
his solid literary craftsmanship.

Peter Spycher

▪ **LAWRENCE DURRELL**. *Constance, or
Solitary Practices.* New York. Penguin. 1982. xiv
+ 394 pages.

▪ ———. *Sebastian, or Ruling Passions.* New York.
Viking. 1984. xiv + 202 pages.

Constance, or Solitary Practices and *Sebastian, or Ruling
Passions* are the third and fourth novels, respectively, of
Lawrence Durrell's Avignon Quintet, following *Livia*
(1979; see WLT 54:1, p. 107) and *Monsieur* (1975).
With *Constance,* the scene moves from Avignon to Paris,
Geneva and Egypt; *Sebastian,* set mostly in Geneva,
moves to the familiar Alexandria.

Although the geographical scope of the novels widens, the emotional range remains constricted. Future
graduate students will puzzle why the Avignon Quintet
(so far we lack a final volume and thus a complete judgment) seems so markedly inferior to the masterly Alexandria Quartet. Like that earlier work, these novels are
complex, erudite, sometimes illuminating, sometimes
touched by magic. The moments of artistic splendor,

however, are rarer. In spite of isolated scenes of brilliance (in *Constance*, e.g., Sutcliff's view of the girls selling apple fritters and the memories that the image conjures up; in *Sebastian*, the comic-tragic suicide of Dr. Schwarz), much of the writing seems forced, pedantic, burdened by a fable that—stretched over the volumes—diminishes rather than sustains credulity. One obvious flaw is that the characters are wooden. In Livia, Durrell has a poor substitute for Justine; in Constance, a far less interesting version of Clea. And Sebastian falls short of Darley as a center of the author's fictitious alter ego. Perhaps the quality of subdued melancholy, of poetical intensity pervading the earlier work has been replaced by a more detached, more brittle narrative quality.

Parody sketches and literary echoes abound: of D. H. Lawrence, Conrad ("She heard the incongruous voice of the negro stretcher-bearer Emmanuel saying hoarsely, '*Mister Schwarz he dead*'"), T. S. Eliot, Henry Miller, even of Durrell ("He studied the spatulate hands of the one who had spoken his name and felt the vague stirrings of familiarity. Could it be Faraj? Neguid? Perhaps Capodistria?"). Other verbal echoes are unconscious and annoying self-parody, as in the case of a once exquisitely tuned writer who has lost the music of his ear: "'But that is Culture,' said Sutcliffe in his most reproachful manner. 'Or if you prefer Erutluc. You see, we have never been interested in the real world—we see it through a cloud of disbelief. Ni eht gninnigeb saw eht drow!' He intoned the phrase majestically and explained that it was simply the backspelling of "In the beginning was the Word!"" It is sad. But one hopes—against the evidence so far—that Durrell can restore some harmony in his final volume.

Leslie B. Mittleman

■**YUKIO MISHIMA**. *Cinq Nô modernes*. Marguerite Yourcenar, Jun Shiragi (Silla), eds. & trs. Paris. Gallimard. 1984. 172 pages.

Yukio Mishima's (see *WLT* 57:3, pp. 409–11) five extraordinary Nô plays have finally been translated into French. It is high time. They are fascinating, hypnotic, unique. Referred to as Nô, they do not, however, retain the ritual quality of this composite art form, which dates back to fourteenth-century Japan. There are no painted pine trees or bamboo accessories; nor are there five musicians seated on stage, sung recitatives, dance sequences, gestural language or hieratic stances. Moreover, both women and men perform in these plays; and out of forty characters featured in his stage pieces, only five wear traditional Japanese clothes.

Although the locales featured in Mishima's plays are concrete and certainly banal in appearance (a park,

a psychiatric hospital, an office building, et cetera), his beings inhabit a spaceless area in a cyclical time scheme. His themes deal with present-day situations, yet their essence is Nô Buddhist priests no longer people the stage attempting, as they once did, to tranquilize aching souls, and ghosts do not emanate from some vague past. Mishima does introduce us to a poet and an old woman whose beauty remains eternally captivating, a geisha, a handyman who personifies a plant, and many more creatures who live in a fluid, vaporous and dreamlike atmosphere.

Mishima does not seek to renew what was but rather to impress new amalgams upon audiences, fresh brews—controlled, tremulously, exciting—always an aspect of his own cruel vision of life. Dreamlike realities are transformed into tension-provoking moments as past incidents are integrated into present realities, bringing into existence a whole metaphysical—sacred—climate. One must, however, be familiar with Nô themes to realize how deeply these are imbedded in Mishima's texts: pace, tone and temper, a detail borrowed from an ancient play but worked into a modern atmosphere. In *Sotoba komachi* five couples are seated irreverently on five benches in a public park, as once others had sat on a stele in a cemetery. A poet and a hag speak about a past, and in so doing, she is transformed in his eyes into that archetypal beauty which reigns supreme in the psyche of so many males. In *Le tambourin de soie*, which takes place in an empty space separating two office buildings, one intrudes upon the world of an old man who cares ever so gently for a laurel plant he identifies with his beloved. A soundless drum in all its symbolism occupies the stage area. *Hanjo*, about a young woman painter who falls in love with a geisha and buys her from the owner of a teahouse, takes place in a kind of no-man's land.

Mishima's Nô plays are dense, concentrated. Not one extraneous word is daubed onto his canvas, not a single sequence that does not reach into the very heart of the mysterious world he conjures forth. His dramas should be performed in the West, where such theatrical aridity reigns. Instead of countless and pointless vicissitudes accompanied by scatological dialogue repeated ad nauseam, Mishima invites us to witness *real* theatre, which mesmerizes and haunts—visually, poetically, viscerally!

Bettina L. Knapp

■**HAROLD PINTER**. *Other Places: A Kind of Alaska; Victoria Station; Family Voices*. New York. Grove. 1983. viii + 83 pages.

A triptych of short plays, one of which (*Family Voices* was originally broadcast on radio, *Other Places* is quintessentially Pinterese, without the theatricality that characterizes his major plays. Especially effective is *A Kind of Alaska,* which struck one critic, Michael Billington, "on instant acquaintance as a masterpiece."

In the style of short pieces such as *Landscape* and *Silence,* in which Pinter paints the interior landscape of his characters, *A Kind of Alaska* concerns the awakening of a patient from thirty years of sleeping sickness. The familiar themes of menace, usurper, the past as a strange country, the habitation of a no-man's land and the interchangeability of lies and truth are there. They converge in the psychological conflict between patient and those (doctor and sister) who are present at her re-emergence into life. The doctor's reference to her thirty-year sleep as a suspension, "a temporary habitation. . . in a kind of Alaska," is Pinter's latest metaphor for the kind of private security which his characters guard so zealously. Like *Old Times, A Kind of Alaska* concerns a reunion among two women and a man, whose relationships are threaded with sexual innuendoes and whose memories of the past vary widely and, indeed, conflict.

Similarly, *Family Voices* is about a trio, this time a son, mother and dead father who converse as though through letters. Most of the conversing is done by the son, who has gone to the city and become involved with a bizarre family with whom he lives. As he discovers their identities one by one, he becomes an intruder. They turn out to have the same last name, Withers. The catalyst for the son's desire to come home at the end is his experience with a black-haired man named Riley, who appeared one day while the son was taking a bath and threatened him, as did a bald relative named Withers. One recognizes at once the same confrontation as that between Bert Hudd and the black, Riley, in Pinter's first play, *The Room,* as well as that between the brothers and Davies in *The Caretaker* and between the McCann-Goldberg duo and Stanley in *The Birthday Party.* Both of these family plays tread familiar Pinterian territory: the first in a poetically realistic style, the second in the surrealistic mode.

The third play, *Victoria Station,* is a comedy about a controller who has lost touch with his cab driver and attempts frantically to identify the driver's location for him. Unable to do so, he becomes frustrated until in their radio contact the term "Crystal Palace" is mentioned and the driver recognizes his location. Having earlier threatened the driver, the controller is now caught up in the fantasy of the latter, who has admitted to having a female passenger in his cab, planning to stay with her the rest of his life in the car and wanting to marry her in the car and die with her in the car. The controller, completely ignoring other calls, tells the

driver to stay where he is so that they might celebrate the latter's good fortune.

Pinter's triptych is a refreshing and highly satisfying group of plays, particularly in the wake of *Betrayal* (1978), whose stage production received mixed (some negative) notices for its gimmicky structure and realistic style.

Susan Rusinko

▪ **SALMAN RUSHDIE.** *Shame.* London. Cape. 1983. 287 pages.

The bizarre saga *Shame* is set in the fourteenth and in the twentieth century. The "hero" of the piece, Omar Khayyam Shakil, is nursed at the six breasts of his three mothers: Chhunni, Munnee and Bunny. But is Omar really the central character? He tells us near the end of this grotesque tale, "I am a peripheral man. . . . Other persons have been the principal actors in my life-story." Indeed, Omar does disappear from the story for disturbingly long stretches. Other characters—Raza Hyder, military man and president, and Iskander Harappa, a civilian leader deposed and executed by Hyder—are equally elusive figures appearing also at intervals throughout the story. Salman Rushdie has attempted in *Shame* to illuminate Pakistan's hideous political realities in an extravagant satire in which Raza acts out the role of the Pakistani general Zia ul-Haq, while Iskander represents the deposed (and later executed) head of state, Zulfikar Ali Bhutto. But one might fairly ask how many readers will know enough of the inside details of these men's lives and of the grim events of the new nation of Pakistan to appreciate a satire on them?

Another problem in Rushdie's book is identified by the narrator: "I build imaginary countries and try to impose them on the ones that exist. I, too, face the problem of history: what to retain, and what to dump." The story ends neatly, where it began, at the home of Omar's three mothers, in the "remote border town of Q," but aside from that circle, all is tangled. The reader might have had a better line through the novel if Rushdie had in fact "dumped" some people and events. The author indeed must have been uneasy about the profusion of characters in his book, for he saw fit to provide a genealogy chart to help us keep the characters straight.

In some respects Rushdie is as brilliant as ever. He has a hundred throwaway lines in the book: "There is no country poorer than Escape." And there is a lot of clever narrative play suggesting that Rushdie's writing is in great part *about* writing: "But suppose this were a realistic novel! Just think what else I might have to put in." Despite many stunning passages, *Shame* finally does not work. In *Midnight's Children* (1981; see *WLT* 56:1, p. 181) Rushdie showed himself a master of building meaning and humor incrementally throughout a sustained work of fiction. Although he brings the same dazzling verbal sheen and Shandyan mythmaking skills to *Shame,* the novel's parts do not combine brilliantly into the satisfying whole that they created in the former novel. *Shame* is a disjointed nightmare about human animals who do not seem very real to us, and who therefore do not seem to matter much.

Robert E. McDowell

■**AMINATA SOW FALL.** *L'appel des arènes.* Dakar. Les Nouvelles Éditions Africaines. 1982. 144 pages.

With this her third novel, Aminata Sow Fall provides yet another view of what is developing into a multifaceted portrait of contemporary Senegalese society. It constitutes, at the same time, a continuation of her acerbic criticism of that society and especially of its urbanized and privileged upper and middle bourgeoisie. While her first two books, *Le revenant* (1976) and *La grève des Bàttu* (1979; see *WLT* 54:2, p. 327), depicted respectively the ruinous penchant of the Senegalese for ostentatious public generosity and the world of urban beggars harassed by self-important and hypocritical government officials, *L'appel des arènes* is set against the backdrop of the milieu of traditional wrestling, an ancient national sport. The plot revolves around the conflict between the adolescent Nalla and his parents over Nalla's neglect of his studies in favor of an almost obsessive fascination with the world of wrestling and his adoring devotion to his newfound friend Malaw, champion of the arena.

It eventually becomes apparent, however, that wrestling, with all its attendant color, ritual and mystery, becomes for the author, and indeed for the protagonists themselves, emblematic of tradition as a whole. For ultimately, it is tradition and its present tragic degradation that this book is about. Nalla's parents are guilty of a perverted assimilation of Western ideas with a concomitant rejection of traditional ways; hence the boy's instinctive craving for a more authentic and satisfying existence.

As if to underline the value of tradition, the author often assumes a distinctly oral tone: use of the present tense in descriptions, repetitions, conversations spiced with words in the original Wolof and traditional praise songs interspersed throughout. Used with more consistency and smoother integration into the whole, these and other such techniques could put Sow Fall into the forefront of those writers who are forging European

words and genres into an authentically modern African art form.

Fredric Michelman

1985

■**ITALO CALVINO.** *Palomar.* Turin. Einaudi. 1983. iv + 136 pages.

In Calvino's steadily growing list of intertwined stories, texts in ever-changing combinations with one another, *Palomar* is most reminiscent of *Marcovaldo* (1963). In both works, shadowy protagonists serve as catalysts for everyday experiences that mirror and stimulate reflection upon the surrounding world. True, these protagonists belong to different social and economic milieus, to different moments in the evolution of modern Italy. Marcovaldo is a country fellow uprooted by urbanization, Palomar an intellectual adrift in the world of technology. For the former, every city landscape evokes some lost aspect of nature; for the latter, every object, natural or man-made, cries out to be located in its proper place on the all-encompassing map of the known and knowable. Through both, however, Calvino projects his own melancholy portrait: "il suo malinconico autoritratto," as Pietro Citati has it in an emblematic formulation of an aspect of Calvino's work which it is probably time to put beside Pavese's much-quoted eipthet, "scoiattolo della penna."

As in other works, Calvino (see *WLT* 57:2, pp. 195–201) here provides a blueprint of the structure, while the reproduction of a Dürer drawing on the jacket brings into relief analogically the author's will to dispassionate, scientific precision in the observation of the phenomena of a "restless, twisted, unsteady universe." The book consists of three parts, each subdivided three times, with each subdivision composed of three variations on the same subject. "Palomar Shopping," for instance, finds him by turn in a Paris *charcuterie,* a cheese store, and a butcher shop. In a postscript Calvino himself points to the regular recurrence of three types of experience, each of which results in a different genre (or kind of knowing): the visual experience of the surface of things that leads to description; the cultural experience of relationships that leads to narrative; and the speculative experience, which tries to come to grips with imponderables such as time, mind, and the infinite, which leads to contemplation in the literary forms of meditations, reflections, et cetera.

Although the twenty-seven texts of *Palomar* are embedded in this master plan, they also lend themselves to being read singly, like so many *terza pagina* articles. As a matter of fact, they reveal, perhaps unexpectedly, Calvino's flair for what once went under the name of *prosa d'arte*. The pieces on Palomar's view from his rooftop terrace in Rome, his visit to the giraffes at the Vincennes zoo, the shopping expeditions already referred to, the gecko lizard whose feeding habits are revealed by the window pane to which it clings, the incongruent mass tourism expedition to a Zen temple in Kyoto are little gems. It is amazing that so much creative energy should spring from what is more and more showing itself to be not only a materialistic but also a nihilistic view of the universe: Palomar's last meditation, under the heading of "Palomar's Silences," is on the ultimate refusal, "How to Learn Being Dead."

Olga Ragusa

■ **MARGUERITE DURAS**. *L'amant*. Paris. Minuit. 1984. 144 pages.

"What I have most in common with Proust," wrote François Mauriac, is that "I do not observe, I do not describe, I rediscover, and what I rediscover is the . . . world of my childhood." Similarly, Marguerite Duras rediscovers in *L'amant* the world of her childhood in French Indochina and reveals to the reader a part of her life that she has kept hidden for almost fifty years. Although she did write about her mother and brothers before, she did so when they were still alive, and she merely hinted at the truth. Now she hides nothing; in this extraordinary, erotic confession, she provides the key to the themes and images that run throughout her work.

In a series of paragraphs of unequal length in which the chronology follows the order of memory, the author presents an album of pictures of her childhood. The pauses between the paragraphs function as fadeouts between the scenes of a film. The verbal images here, more vivid than any photographs, also evoke the sounds and smells of colonial outposts in the bush, "lost in the quadrilateral expanses of rice, of fear, of madness, of fever, and of forgetfulness."

In *L'amant* Duras reveals that the stifling, almost unbearable family situation that exists in her early novels, as well as the desperate desire of her protagonists to escape from unbearable poverty, an unstable mother, and a despicable older brother, was based on her own experience. She reveals too that she effected her escape from her family at the age of fifteen and a half, when she became the mistress of a Chinese multimillionaire whom she met on the ferryboat crossing the Mekong River. It was this crossing of the river between adolescence and adulthood and between the races which the

author considers to be the decisive event in her life and which constitutes the leitmotiv of *L'amant*.

Lucille F. Becker

■ **YŪSUF IDRĪS**. *The Sinners*. Kristin Peterson-Ishaq, tr. Max Winkler, ill. Washington, D.C. Three Continents. 1984. xiv + 116 pages.

The Sinners is a translation of Yūsuf Idrīs's novel *Al-Harām*, an interesting work in which the author, a child of the Egyptian Delta himself, manages to portray the inner workings of a provincial microcosm with all his skill and artistry. A newborn baby is found dead on a country estate where numerous peasant families live and work. The search for the culprit who has committed this taboo act is complicated by the presence of seasonal workers from elsewhere. Idrīs captures brilliantly the suspicions which initially flow in the direction of the migrant workers, then back to the girls of the estate itself, and finally to the "culprit," who turns out to have been the victim of a rape.

This is a novel by a prominent short-story writer (see *WLT* 55:1, pp. 43–47); the problems associated with that fact are evident in the construction of the work as a whole and in the emphasis given (or not given) to the various aspects of the novelist's craft. As noted above, the *atmosphere* of the provincial estate, the ingrained attitudes and biases, are presented with all the mastery that we have come to expect from readings of Idrīs's shorter works and, in particular, his early short stories, where he often broke new ground by presenting a whole series of vignettes of country life and the characters and attitudes to be found there. What is lacking in *Al-Harām* is a sense of cohesion in the plot. The chapters are all extremely short, and characters are depicted with that economy which is so necessary in the short story but which in the novel often leaves the reader perplexed about motivations and indeed sequence. The story also suffers from a certain amount of digression (such as the episode involving Mahboob), authorial intrusion (the disquisition on faith on page 79), and carelessness in construction: how, for example, can it be of any value to the reader to be told in anticipation that the "criminal" will be discovered on page 57?

All this, of course, is by no means a criticism of the translation under review here, which is, in general, of a very high standard of accuracy and readability. There is a useful list of readings at the end of the volume, plus a careful analysis of the plot with some useful insights as an introduction. After a somewhat heavy start, the translation itself settles down and provides a fluent version of the original. My only quibble is with the title itself. The word *Harām* in Arabic implies more than merely "sin," and indeed is an abstract concept. The implication intended in the title and indeed used by the translator thoughout the English text is "forbidden," and my own translation of this title has always been "The Taboo." I concentrate on this thought not simply out of academic pedantry but because Idrīs has written another (admittedly inferior) novel entitled *Al-'Ayb* which *does* translate as "The Sin." Retaining the title "The Taboo" would also avoid the need to use the human plural "Sinners," which is nowhere implied in the original and which, in my opinion, radically alters the impact of the title. Peterson-Ishaq's translation is nonetheless a most welcome addition to the list of modern Arabic fiction in English. Its attractive presentation and reasonable price should ensure its acquisition by all those with an interest in literatures of the non-Western world.

Roger Allen

■ **YASHAR KEMAL**. *The Sea-Crossed Fisherman*. Thilda Kemal, tr. London. Collins-Harvill. 1985. 287 pages.

Although *The Sea-Crossed Fisherman* is the tenth of Yashar Kemal's novels to appear in English in London, only *Memed, My Hawk,* his first novel, has so far been published in America too—first by Pantheon Books in a very successful hardcover edition, then in an equally successful paperback reprint as a Pantheon Modern Classic. Several of Kemal's other novels, however, have already proved to be bestsellers, not only in his native Turkey but also in France, Sweden, and West Germany. One thus has good reason to wonder why American publishers still show so little interest in his work.

Kemal has hitherto been known to English readers only for his tales of peasant life in Anatolia (see e.g. *WLT* 58:2, p. 323). In recent years, however, he has begun to shift his attention to the lowlife of Istanbul and its suburbs, and especially to life in the villages of fisherfolk on the shores of the Bosporus or the Sea of Marmara, on which the expanding metropolis is rapidly encroaching. The finest example of this new trend in his work is *Kuşlar da Gitti* (see *WLT* 52:4, p. 689), a short and very lyrical novel which has been translated, as far as I know, only into French (*Alors, les oiseaux sont partis,* Gallimard, 1983).

In spite of its many fine lyrical passages, *The Sea-Crossed Fisherman* may well perplex most of its English or American readers. In his pursuit of a gigantic swordfish, the fisherman Selim has much in common with the hero of Melville's *Moby Dick* or Hemingway's *Old Man and the Sea*. The motivations of most of its other characters, especially those of Zeynel, a petty murderer and bank robber, remain at all times obscure, unless one interprets his actions as diseased manifestations of *furor epilepticus,* in which case he may be guided mainly by hallucinations. Kemal refrains from making this at all clear, while at the same time appearing to approve of Zeynel's criminal actions and to sympathize with his excesses of often totally unjustified panic.

Many of the novel's other characters seem, moreover, to act mainly on similarly irrational impulses. Few of them ever think rationally, and they all believe quite uncritically every word of idle gossip that reaches their ears, so that one soon wearies of many of their conversations. Even the novel's plot is often chaotic. In this respect, it has more in common, at its best, with some of the dream sequences of Nerval's *Aurélia* or Lautréamont's *Maldoror* than with any more traditionally romantic work of fiction such as the wilder novels of Balzac or Maturin's *Melmoth the Wanderer*.

Kemal's emotional attitude as a writer appears indeed to be undergoing a kind of crisis. As a populist, he displays in some of his more recent works an increasingly reactionary nostalgia for the imagined virtues of the traditional Turkish past as represented, above all, by the peasantry of Anatolia or the fishermen of the villages now threatened by the expansion of Istanbul. At the same time, he expresses an almost revolutionary hostility toward all manifestations of Turkey's present economic and political evolution. He thus describes all Turkish policemen as fascists intentionally indoctrinated in racist theories, all Turks of any wealth as black marketeers, speculators, or misers, and only marginal paupers as being at all worthy of sympathy and respect. It never occurs to him that over a million Turkish peasants and other workers have chosen to better their skills and their fate by emigrating as laborers to West Germany, Belgium, or France. Although thousands of them have already returned to Turkey to invest their savings in modestly modern homes and become self-employed, often as cab drivers, Kemal has so far avoided choosing any of these more progressive-minded peasants or workers as characters in his novels.

The almost rabble-rousing quality of much of *The Sea-Crossed Fisherman* will of course appeal to many of the author's more simple-minded leftist readers, especially in Turkey. To most of his potential Western readers, however, the psychology of Zeynel in particular will remain as contradictorily unfathomable as that of the Turkish fascist who, apparently as a willing tool of the communists, attempted to murder the pope and now claims somewhat absurdly to be a messiah.

Edouard Roditi

■ **ALAIN ROBBE-GRILLET**. *Le miroir qui revient*. Paris. Minuit. 1984. 232 pages.

Unlike the rigorously structured, precise, restrictive, detailed, and frequently pedantic novels of Robbe-Grillet—*Les gommes, Le voyeur, La jalousie*—*Le miroir qui revient* introduces readers to a new literary genre of his own manufacture. This freely felt, imagistic, and poetic autobiography differs from the conventional type à la Stendhal, with its causal, chronological, and systematized recording of events. Such an approach Robbe-Grillet considers false. *Le miroir qui revient* is a composite of mirror images, as the title suggests: interlocking visions, sequences of refrains which emerge and vanish prismatically. Consciously organized, it is not weighted down with a burdensome vocabulary; rather, words seem to float, to touch, to feel, despite the fact that Robbe-Grillet remains entrenched behind his objective and relatively feelingless façade. His story deals with the problematics of writing, displacements, alterations, referentials inherent in stylistic innovations and conformities.

Robbe-Grillet began writing *Le miroir qui revient* in 1976, but in a desultory manner, since his other novels were also published during this period. He does not believe in Truth, he states categorically, or in dogma. No sooner is a theory concretized than it is ossified. New ideas, fresh ways of envisaging literary art, cannot emerge in such restrictive terrain—only a reinforcement of established order. He still questions, probes, tries to understand the meaning of projection, both conscious and unconscious.

As a child, he tells us, he used to love gardens, not seas or oceans. Their tumultuous and uncertain natures represented perils for him; his nightmares were fraught with such pounding sensations. As a child, he lived part of the year in Brest, in the Jura, and in Paris. His parents were anarchists belonging to the extreme right. They sided with Pétain during the German Occupation, but most overtly during the Liberation and afterward, when they placed Pétain's picture in the most conspicuous area of their apartment. They were Anglophobes, believing that France and Germany should be united as they once had been under Charlemagne. They were anti-Semitic, and Robbe-Grillet's mother never believed in the reality of the concentration camps; as for the extermination of the Jews, that was all merely Zionist propaganda.

Critics and writers such as Sartre, Camus, Barthes, Ricardou, and more are discussed. Barthes's dislike of "the three policemen" (Marx, Freud, and Saussure) also comes under scrutiny; their rigidity and imperialism are considered unbearable. For Robbe-Grillet, constant re-

newal and variety, as in *Last Year at Marienbad,* can transform the banal into the exciting, the well-worn into the fresh and provocative, blending new and old into new alchemical mixtures—as Robbe-Grillet has accomplished with such felicity in *Le miroir qui revient.*

Bettina L. Knapp

■ **RAMÓN RUBÍN**. *El canto de la grilla*. Mexico City. Fondo de Cultura Económica. 1984. 163 pages.

Ramón Rubín (b. 1912) is well known to connoisseurs of Mexican *indigenista* fiction, his most popular novel being *El callado dolor de los tzotziles* (1949). *El canto de la grilla* (1952), another of his major novels, has been reissued in a handsome illustrated paperback with a glossary of Indian words. Narrated in lineal form by an omniscient narrator, the plot of *El canto* takes place in the state of Nayarit among the primitive Cora Indians. The protagonists are Mateo, the son of a Cora *curandero* named Esmeraldo Mayordomo, and Iyali Quehuizarauta, a Huichol Indian girl baptized as a Christian. Because he opposes his son's marriage to one of another tribe and religion, Esmeraldo poisons his daughter-in-law during the couple's wedding celebration—described in elaborate detail—which leads to a heated dispute with his son. Accused unjustly of the heinous crime of striking his father, Mateo is sentenced by a body of Cora elders to hang by his hands until death. The author describes his protagonist's agony and then, in the epilogue, offers the reader three possible conclusions to his tale.

Elements of *El canto* that typify *indigenista* literature include its exotic Indian vocabulary, its detailed depictions of tribal customs, and its dramatization of the clash between white and native cultures. Indeed, the conflict here is not so much between the Coras and the Huicholes as it is between the Coras on the one hand and the Catholic priest and the government troops garrisoned in the vicinity on the other.

To the reader attuned to the literary sophistication of Borges, Cortázar, and Fuentes, Rubín's style will probably seem outdated. Still, it may come as a welcome respite to enjoy passively a simple, well-told yarn about an unknown culture without having to assume the role of accomplice to a sly creator in search of originality.

George R. McMurray

1986

■ **HEINRICH BÖLL.** *Frauen vor Fluβlandschaft.* Cologne. Kiepenheuer & Witsch. 1985. 254 pages.

Böll's last novel, posthumously published after the Nobel Prize winner's death on 16 July 1985, amounts to a vast prose drama written entirely in monologues and dialogues. The twelve chapters cover essentially one late-summer day on the outskirts of Bonn, in the course of which a variety of episodes linking several political leaders and their families reach an almost operatic conclusion. All the familiar figures of Böll's "Northmainia" are there: the ex-Nazis who have attained high office; the knowing wives whose despair drives them to drown themselves in the Rhine or to hang themselves in the rest homes to which they are consigned; the sons and daughters who dream of escape from the constraints of Germany to the socialist societies of Cuba or into flamboyant gestures of opposition.

Perhaps no contemporary writer has analyzed more incisively than Böll the corruption and compromises of a Germany that has moved so far from the principles of true Christianity and has so thoroughly repressed its Nazi past that it regards critics as mad. The solutions he offers, however, rarely go beyond a melancholy resignation or ultimately ineffectual gestures. That holds true in *Frauen vor Fluβlandschaft* for two of the central figures. Graf Heinrich von Kreyl, who is offered the highest office of his party, decides not to accept rather than compromise his principles. His son Karl, who has lived with his common-law wife in a trailer and eked out an existence by selling stolen hood ornaments from Mercedes automobiles, decides to work as a legal aide for an honest politician.

So typical is the novel that one can already imagine the seminar topics it will elicit. Compare the structure of the work—forty years of history narrated through interior monologues taking place on one climactic day—with that of *Billard um halbzehn.* Examine the gestures of protest (one character dismantles the grand pianos of rich bankers) with the "happening" (burning a military jeep) that dominates *Ende einer Dienstfahrt.* Compare the destiny of the foreign workers in *Gruppenbild mit Dame* with that of the lower-class Germans who find their own "Nicaragua in Germany." Compare the bitter ironies of Karl von Kreyl with those of Hans Schnier in *Ansichten eines Clowns.* Discuss the appropriateness of the Nibelungen images as an analogy to the events on the Rhine today. And so forth.

Frauen vor Fluβlandschaft will probably not be ranked along with Böll's most powerful works. For one

thing, the technique of exposition by means of pure dialogue and monologue becomes awkward from time to time; for another, the conclusion is too predictably constructed and melodramatic. Nevertheless, to the extent that it recapitulates the essence of Böll's style and themes, the novel constitutes the remarkable summa of a notable literary career that extended over almost forty years. Böll's voice will be missed.

Theodore Ziolkowski

■ **JORGE LUIS BORGES.** *Los conjurados.* Madrid. Alianza. 1985. 98 pages.

There are a few surprises in the most recent collection of Borges's poems. One is the title piece, which all but foretells the eventual domination of the planet by Switzerland; another is "Juan López y John Ward," in which an Argentine and a Briton, two young men who in a saner world might have been friends, instead meet tragically on a battlefield. The latter poem's evenhandedness ("cada uno de los dos fue Caín, y cada uno, Abel"), though certain to anger partisans on both sides of the Falklands/Malvinas question, seems refreshingly sane.

Most of the poems, in spite of their particular novelties, will sound deeply familiar to those who know the canon ("Doomsday," "César," "Son los ríos"). In "Góngora" the most difficult of poets is made to complain that he feels constrained by mythology or, more precisely, by the metonymic replacements it constantly suggests: "Marte, la guerra. Febo, el sol. Neptuno, / el mar que ya no pueden ver mis ojos / porque lo borra el dios." It is only a step to the intuition that all language is a kind of barrier between man and the physical world ("quiero volver a las cosas comunes"); here Borges's musings, ostensibly directed toward the *cultista* extravagance, shade quickly through autobiography into the universal.

In other poems a sense of historical dread is somehow fused with its antidote, an ecstatic idealism that seeks to prove all history false. "La tarde elemental ronda la casa," the poet writes in a fine sonnet, "la de ayer, la de hoy, la que no pasa." This powerful theme was sounded over sixty years ago in Borges's first book, *Fervor de Buenos Aires.* It is unmistakably preserved in the far stricter craft of his later years: a denial of time's passing, one might say, that grows more affecting as time goes by. (On Borges, see *WLT* 60:1, pp. 39–40.)

William Ferguson

■ **CARLOS FUENTES.** *Gringo viejo.* Mexico City. Fondo de Cultura Económica. 1985. 192 pages.

"Memory weaves and traps us at the same time according to a scheme in which we do not participate: we should never speak of *our* memory, for it is anything but ours; it works on its own terms, it assists us while deceiving us or perhaps deceives us to assist us." With his new novel, Carlos Fuentes (see *WLT* 57:4, pp. 529–98) gives us yet another intricate memory book. The triad of protagonists all search for a personal destiny, and in the fleeting encounters during the Mexican Revolution each finds and somehow loses again a fate as equivocal as those of García Márquez's characters plagued by erroneous readings of the tarot cards. Harriet Winslow, the Gibson girl from Washington, has entered Mexico as a tutor for the children of the wealthy Miranda family. She is surprised by the revolution, and because of its apocalypse, she encounters the rising military commander Tomás Arroyo. Arroyo had been a *peón* in the household of the Mirandas, and his circular fate has returned him to his point of departure. The North American journalist Ambrose Bierce makes of these two an unlikely new family and thereby seals his fate.

The most Joycean of Latin American narrators, Fuentes reveals the dilemmas of the trio through interwoven monologues, parts of conversations, and multiple layers of memory—all retained in the feverish consciousness of Harriet Winslow, now returned to North America, condemned to decipher the pattern beneath the several time levels of character. To help her and the reader, Fuentes incorporates symbolic actions and highly allusive space (crossing the river, entering the desert, facing the firing squad's wall), as is his custom. Mexico is the perfect setting, "tierra de memoria," and Fuentes configures its atmosphere laden with "polvo memorioso."

As is often the case with Fuentes's characters, irony is the hazardous realm in which destiny must be met. Artemio Cruz became a slave of his own success, and Ambrose Bierce enters Mexico as a creature he himself has created through his texts. One of the books in his valise is *Don Quijote,* and his character finds the perfect analogue in Fuentes's interpretation of the *Quijote.*

> Like Philip II, the necrophiliac monarch secluded in El Escorial, Don Quijote both pawns and pledges his life to the restoration of the world of unified certainty. He pawns and pledges himself, both physically and symbolically, to the univocal reading of the texts and attempts to translate this reading into a reality that has become multiple, equivocal, ambiguous. But because he possesses his readings, Don Quijote possesses his identity: that of the knight errant, that of the ancient epic hero. (*New York Times Book Review,* 23 March 1986)

With Arroyo as his unwilling Sancho and Harriet as a bewildered Dulcinea, the Old Gringo finds meaning for the adventures of his life, and he, of course, becomes a literary hero, as did his model.

The histories of both Mexico and the United States limit the possibilities and simultaneously provoke the characters to extreme actions. To give density to his three principal personae, Fuentes includes characters from *Los de abajo* (the archetypal novel of the Mexican Revolution), figures who may have strayed from Hemingway's narratives of other revolutions, characters from Bierce's story "An Occurrence at Owl Creek Bridge," personages from *Alice in Wonderland,* analogues of Faulkner's Gail Hightower, a child made of glass reminiscent of Cervantes's "licenciado Vidriera," and he allows Harriet to summarize Lowry's theme in *Under the Volcano,* "No se puede vivir sin amar."

In the mirrored ballroom of the old Miranda mansion, Fuentes allows memory to entrap Arroyo as it weaves for him a heroic destiny. That magical stage provides a new role for Arroyo and for Harriet. For Bierce, the possibilities of that stage are too small. Harriet went to Mexico looking for a new self; she finds a father and a potential husband. Arroyo entered the revolution looking for an escape from slavery; he finds death, a new family, death in two guises, and mysterious fame. As Harriet solves the enigma of triple memories, the reader must decipher the texts that are Bierce's final mystery.

Mary E. Davis

▪ **MAVIS GALLANT.** *Home Truths.* New York. Random House. 1985. vi + 330 pages.

The key to Mavis Gallant's incredibly powerful style may well be British short-story writer Katherine Mansfield, whose grave two young girls sojourning in France visit in "Virus X," a pivotal story in *Home Truths.* Future critics will have to decide whether Gallant uses the short story because it is a woman's writing style or because it allows her to focus on her fellow Canadians' elusive vulnerability. Gallant (see *WLT* 60:1, pp. 44–45), who in 1981 was made an Officer of the Order of Canada, is at her best in the longer short story, as in the cycle "Canadians Abroad."

Gallant's characters echo the conflict of cultural assimilation and the difficulty of being Canadian during and shortly after World War II. In a conformist, hopelessly materialistic, provincial environment, in which even a smile is suspect, indifference only covers up wounds endured by hopeless, futureless emigrants or by mediocre bureaucrats who save to buy their sons a

Mavis Gallant (*AP/Wide World Photos*)

"good, Protestant education," Ukrainians shipping abroad the unwed daughter after having forced her to put her child up for adoption, Winnipeg citizens caught in the "gold rush" of Canadian bureaucrats in postwar Europe. There were few contacts then between English and French Canadians, says Gallant, only pioneers such as Linnet Muir's parents, who mixed English Canadian puritanism with the soft luxuries of the soon-to-be-extinct Québécois bourgeoisie.

It is the odd side of the coin that Gallant chose to depict, the by-products of narrow-mindedness: young girls in love with older, married professors and confronted with half-baked intellectual truths and the dim prospect of becoming a woman in a society which has room only for monstrous wives and mothers; British "remittance men," unsettled artists, leftist marginals, provincial misfits, all in search of grandeur and uniqueness, lookers and dreamers caught in the sea of shapeless internal time. Heavy is the price for Canada to come of age in the midst of missed love and missed friendship, in sterile offices and hotel rooms, dirty restaurant tables, stifling flats.

Gallant's numerous references to abused childhood have been dubbed autobiographical. Rather, they are a parable about Canada. The autobiographical touches can be found in the composite portrait of a feminine

character, Linnet and Lottie, Sarah and Agnes. Hers is the apprenticeship of life through "haughtiness and cunning silence," through naïveté and perseverance. Gallant's is a feminist voice, but one caught by love, with no other alternative than to look at males with compassion.

Emotional displays are scarce. Gallant's stories are like minefields, ready to explode, yet with no closeness, sentimentality, or warmth in sight. True feeling surges out of emptiness, loneliness, and mediocrity, self-contained awareness or confession shedding a disquieting light on a story that seemed to have told it all. With her sociological scalpel, Gallant cuts through layers of appearance and offers a vision of mankind that is neither reassuring nor futile.

Alice-Catherine Carls

■**MILAN KUNDERA**. *Nesnesitelná lehkost bytí*. Toronto. Sixty-Eight. 1985. 296 pages.

■———. *The Unbearable Lightness of Being*. Michael Henry Heim, tr. New York. Harper & Row. 1984. vi + 314 pages.

Here at last is the Czech text of Kundera's latest novel, which appeared in English a year earlier. Czech readers had a preview of it the same year, when a portion of the fourth chapter was published in *Listy* (May 1984), a Munich émigré journal that circulates clandestinely in Czechoslovakia. Kundera has been well served by Michael Heim's translation, which gives us a novel whose easy, elegant articulation, especially in the discursive passages, creates the illusion of being the only possible original. Indeed, it was something of a shock to rediscover the same passages in Czech, with its startlingly raw, more concrete quality.

Ever since he settled permanently in France in the mid-seventies, Kundera's reputation has continued to grow, until he has become one of the most-discussed authors in France today. In this country, after Heim's translation of *The Joke* (1982), he has generated a tremendous interest not only as a novelist, but also as an eloquent spokesman for the submerged culture of Central Europe (see *WLT* 57:2, pp. 206–209). He has, however, kept scrupulously aloof from the Cold War alignment of intellectuals. Kundera is a man of letters in the grand European manner, a critic of the society he lives in as well as a storyteller. His main passion today, in the age of collapsed ideologies, seems to be the defense of the values of high culture against the encroaching barbarism of mass entertainment, which has become the degenerate kitsch of Western modernism. He is also a formidable literary and music critic, who has recently contributed major articles on Kafka, Broch, and Janáček.

While adamantly refusing to talk about himself and his life, Kundera is supremely at ease discussing the art of the novel and, in particular, his own conception of the genre's possibilities. In the address he gave in Jerusalem last year after receiving the Jerusalem Prize for Literature on the Freedom of Man in Society ("Man Thinks, God Laughs," *New York Review of Books,* 13 June 1985), he placed himself in the tradition of Rabelais, who conducted a dialogue between philosophy and fiction from the edge of the nonserious spirit of laughter. The novel, as Kundera sees it, is a form uniquely suited for our age, because it permits an intellectual synthesis proceeding from the assumption of unlimited freedom and unhampered by any obligation to reach a conclusion about the object of its inquiry.

The Unbearable Lightness of Being is, like *The Joke,* a love story, but one that takes its course on both sides of the borders of Czechoslovakia. The interlocking fates of two pairs of lovers, Tomáš and Tereza and Sabina with her Swiss lover Franz, raise the question of the possibility and the implications of love in a society of a waning twentieth century. The Toronto edition is accompanied by a fine interpretive essay written by Květoslav Chvatík, a structuralist critic from Prague now living in Switzerland. Chvatík seems to share Kundera's assumptions about the form of the novel, but he fleshes out the theoretical scheme with perceptive comments on the characters and the themes. He calls Tomáš, the central character, a combination of Don Juan and Tristan, whose fate illustrates the paradoxical nature of both libertinism and tragic romance, two extreme expressions of sexual love. When Tomáš finally opts for fidelity to Tereza, his life becomes irrevocably deathward bound. His death, like that of the other faithful lover Franz, is characterized by its casual, provocatively accidental quality. It is that combination of triviality and meaningfulness which is at the heart of Kundera's dark comedy of love.

Chvatík considers this fifth novel to be an integral part of a cycle that began with the first book of *Laughable Loves* in 1963. He ranks Kundera among the greatest writers of the second half of the century.

Maria Němcová Banerjee

▪ **HENRI MICHAUX**. *Déplacements dégagements*. Paris. Gallimard. 1985. 143 pages.

That Henri Michaux (see *WLT* 58:2, pp. 209–15) was a great poet has, of course, long been beyond all doubt. His mind was forever open, always aware, to be sure,

of the endless traps that beset the articulation of being yet constantly alert to the teeming wealth of those countless enigmas, banalities though they may be, that found and refound our streaming *passage.* Not unlike his contemporary, Beckett, Michaux often thrives on paradox, contradiction, tension. Deeply distrustful, sharply ironic, his gesture can suddenly assume a compassion, a smiling sense of what the other could be. The many "surprises" to which his remarkable *disponibilité* exposes him allow him, however, rapidly to outstrip Beckett in profound experiences of quick though tranquil passion and exaltation, of dynamic ontic consciousness beyond all esotericism, all clinging narcissism or materialism.

Michaux's perhaps most central thrust thus tended to throw him out of all readily definable cultural orbits. His perceptions and his vision retain a curiously uncongealed, unbound quality. *Déplacements dégagements,* for example, contains explorations of the shifting phenomena that draw his attention: sensations at a film showing, a visit to a friend in Belgium, meditations upon a chance "encounter" with an old African *sanza,* poetic sequences drifting between the real and the unreal, the drawings of young children, an accidental narcotic "trip" painstakingly annotated, a more deliberate plunge into the unknown, with "poetic" evocations. Such perceptions and vision follow no set, predictable line, obey no special intention even, inserting themselves rather into the seething flux of being that knows no special order, no particular reason, other than those that a bare, precarious naming can allow.

Michaux will be missed. Perhaps he knows more now about "la disparition des disparités" than he did in his final "Postures."

Michael Bishop

1987

▪ **MARYSE CONDÉ**. *Moi, Tituba, sorcière noire de Salem*. Paris. Mercure de France. 1986. 276 pages.

All of Maryse Condé's major fiction is rooted in a study of power (see *WLT* 59:1, pp. 9–13). Her protagonists—fictional, legendary, or historical—appear to emerge almost haphazardly as heroes, martyrs, saints, or sacrificial victims. In tracing their lives, Condé shows the formative influence of their fervors upon a mass of characters. Somehow some very human individuals seem singled out for eminence or persecution. In her two-volume epic *Ségou* (see *WLT* 60:3, p. 509, and 59:2, p.

309), for example, she portrays three generations of a Bambara royal dynasty at the time the march of Islam pushed aside the traditional animist empire of Ségou. The many family members in the novels undergo psychological, cultural, and geographic uprooting as they experience cultural change. Power is traced mainly through the male protagonists, a natural consequence of historical accuracy.

In Condé's latest novel, *Moi, Tituba, sorcière noire de Salem,* she introduces an interesting variant of her power theme. The actual historical Tituba was a West Indian slave who confessed to witchcraft during the Salem witch trials of 1692. Records of her part in this Salem power struggle are full and well documented. However, her history before and after the trials is conjectural only. Several legends conflict as to her death or her disappearance from Salem following the trials. In a brilliant re-creation Condé shows Tituba's early life in Barbados. Conceived on a slave ship in a public rape of a black slave by a white sailor, Tituba is forever an outcast from both black and white worlds. As a little girl she escapes servitude by running away when her mother is hanged for resisting and knifing her white owner. The girl is sheltered by an old herbalist in a remote area of the island, where she learns the healing arts, communication with the dead, and the exhilaration of freedom. Her passion for a métis slave, John Indian, drives her back to plantation life in slave quarters. However, her rebellious spirit outrages the owner, who sells the couple to the Reverend Samuel Parris, a Puritan minister on his way to Boston and, later, to Salem village. Condé convincingly draws together the traits of Tituba's personality to explain her use of the healing arts for the Parris children, her "false" confession after they betray her as a witch, her visitations with the spirits of the executed witches, et cetera.

Condé goes beyond the historical record in her new novel. Her Tituba becomes a martyr to Barbadian independence. Condé's own Guadeloupe has had its female martyrs in independence struggles; Simone Schwarz-Bart, also from Guadeloupe, has commemorated an ancestral female martyr in *La mulâtresse solitude.* As a critic, Condé has often commented on the social, literary, and political power of West Indian women. In *Ségou* she presented many linkages between Africans, West Indians, and Brazilians of the black diaspora. In *Tituba* she again links the Americas to Africa in the history of power struggles. Tituba, witch or saint, rebel or martyr, did exert actual power over Salem village in one of the few ways women activists of her time were able to influence their culture.

Charlotte H. Bruner

■**ODYSSEAS ELYTIS**. *What I Love: Selected Poems of Odysseas Elytis.* Olga Broumas, tr. Port Townsend, Wa. Copper Canyon. 1986. 96 pages.

Odysseas (or Odysseus) Elytis's great poetry is so rooted in the Greek language that transplantation into the alien soil of English is unlikely to take. How can one make readers unrooted in his Aegean world feel his seeming abstractions as emotions or respond deeply to "olive-tree," "whitewash," "Kore"? Each new graft by a serious translator brings fresh hope that the shoots will live, that more of Elytis will leaf in our foreign air.

Elytis's Greek varies, often in a single strophe, from literary to slang, from rhetorical to simple, from learned to folksong-like. Profoundly personal without being at all confessional, he requires us to make the harsh and timeless Hellenic world of the poems into our own truth, and so professes a Shelleyan belief in Poetry's transforming magic. His poetry depends on musical values for its urgency and to conjoin word and inner feeling, so to change us through our relationship with language—something like a mixture of Stevens and the Pound of "Drafts and Fragments."

Thus Elytis demands more than the translator's usual patience and discipline, a discipline to which Olga Broumas has evidently not submitted herself. Since all but two early pieces in *What I Love* have been accurately translated by others, one wonders why her translations are shockingly innacurate. There is not one poem in the book that is carefully or skillfully rendered. Examples of lapses in simple accuracy, giving one per page (there are many more on each page cited here, as on every page) from the first four pages: "greens" for "garden-patch" (p. 5), "arbor" for "grapevine" or "vineyard" (7), "drawing" for "dreaming" (9), "sharing" for "portioning out" (11). Printing the Greek en face amounts to hubris.

Such inaccuracy would be somewhat less culpable if the translations captured Elytis's rich, allusive poetic sensibility or were themselves at least good English. They fail in both respects. Let us examine one of Elytis's most graceful lyrics, the twenty-two-line "Small Green Sea" (translated by others twice before). The image of Kore, the maiden, is crucial to all of Elytis's books. She embodies the beginnings of fertility, fresh and virginal: she is Poetry herself. He calls her by many names. Here she is Sea (*Thalassa*), whom he wishes to educate in Ionia, where so much of the Greek miracle began. He would have her inspire him through all of Greek history with divinity, to be communicated in a sexual embrace. In the second line Broumas tones down Elytis's urgent phrasing: her "I want to adopt you" ought to be "How I would like to adopt you." Four lines later Broumas renders the simple word for "little tower" as "tight tower," whatever that may mean. Two lines later Elytis wants Sea to learn "to turn [rotate] the sun," not, as Broumas has it, "turn to the sun." In line 14 Broumas writes, "Go through Smyrna's window" for Elytis's "Enter Smyrna by the window." Her line 17 reads, "With a little north a little levantine." What she wants with the north and a diminutive Eastern gentleman I cannot tell: Elytis wants Sea to return "With a little bit of Northwind a little Eastwind." When the poet sleeps with Sea to get the essence of Ionia, Broumas either misunderstands or (as I suspect) suppresses this act. Broumas's "come back/ Illegally to me to sleep / To find deep in your keep / Pieces of stone the talk of the Gods" (the clanging rhymes are gratuitous) should be something like "come back / Little Green Sea thirteen years old [this line is omitted by Broumas] / So I may sleep with you illicitly / And find deep in your arms / Pieces of stones the words of the Gods." Broumas has lost the poem. This is not an isolated instance of bowdlerization. In the last stanza of "Ode to Picasso" and in the biting fourth stanza of "Maria Nefele's Song" (whose astringent meter and rhyme are not even suggested), Broumas again alters the sexual imagery Elytis clearly intends, and on page 71 she translates "buttocks" as "thighs." If Elytis's sexuality discomfits or offends her, she should leave his work, drenched in the erotic, alone.

Half of *What I Love* is made up of out-of-sequence selections from Elytis's book-length poem *Maria Nefele* (see *WLT* 54:2, pp. 196–201). Broumas strives for a punchy sytle; this could have been appropriate here. To see why it is not, let us look at "Nefelegeretes" (Cloud-Gatherer). The ancient Greek word is a frequent Homeric epithet for Zeus. The first line literally is, "Ah how beautiful to be cloudgatherer." Broumas translates this as "Ah how beautiful to hang out with the clouds." The slang does not fit. In the next line her word-for-word translation "on old shoes" misses the idiomatic meaning Elytis intends, "for the heck of it." In the first line of this poem's second stanza, Broumas's "to reap unpopularity" should be "enjoy unpopularity." Nine lines later, "the fat people" should be subject, not object, as here. Broumas's penultimate line, "and with large leagues open yourself freely to cry," is incomprehensible; an idiom, the Greek means, "and with great strokes you swim out to weep freely." As translated here, the poem is unintelligible. Broumas has not worked out the poem's meaning before translating.

Perhaps Broumas's own grammar is insecure: "don't be afraid / of what is written you to feel" (89); "I they threw me from the doors outside" (87). Her "It's me to who shouts" (43) must be making Elytis sad. If

sometimes her style is usefully crisp and direct, as in certain lines of the difficult piece titled "The Monogram," in no poem is her version superior to her predecessors', although improvement is the point of retranslation.

What I Love has a handsome cover, but the words "Nobel Laureate" on it may mystify the reader who finds the book's contents unworthy of that award. May I recommend Kimon Friar's Elytis translations *The Sovereign Sun* (1974; see *BA* 49:4, p. 830), which is what the Nobel Committee read? (On Elytis see also *BA* 49:4, pp. 627–716, and *WLT* 59:2, pp. 226–29.)

Jeffrey Carson

■ **EUGÈNE IONESCO.** *Non.* Marie-France Ionesco, tr. Paris. Gallimard. 1986. 310 pages.

Surfacing in Marie-France Ionesco's excellent translation half a century after the scandal it caused upon its original publication in Bucharest in 1934, the mélange of literary criticism, texts on Romanian literature and culture, and philosophic and existential notes titled *Non* is, more than anything else, a contribution to an inquiry into creativity, as we observe the metamorphoses that a writer's themes and motifs undergo with time and in relation to the circumstances of his life. Among writers in exile, displaced and alienated, with their struggle to adjust or resist adjustment and their performance in a foreign language from within a foreign culture, Eugène Ionesco (see *WLT* 60:1, pp. 34–36) is yet another extraordinary case: perfectly bilingual, taking his French from his mother and his Romanian from his father, Ionesco spent his childhood in France and his adolescence and youth in Romania, in the midst of Romanian literary life. He returned to France as a mature man and an obscure Romanian writer to become the plaaywright who has altered contemporary theatre. *Non* is a book from Ionesco's first literary career in Romania, an episode practically unknown to his Western readers.

Without much concern for structure, the kaleidoscopic material of the book is divided into two parts: a series of critical essays intended to demolish the glory of three literary lions of the time, the poets Tudor Arghezi and Ion Barbu and the novelist Camil Petrescu; and a collection of texts on Romanian culture and literature attempting a methodology of literary criticism. The work's unity resides in the aggressive and contemptuous tone of the young author, who does not hesitate to provoke and insult his readers while making his point, and in the young Ionesco's theory of "the identity of opposites," which he develops and applies throughout. The theory demonstrates gleefully—and brilliantly at times—the vanity of attempting to take a position in literary criticism, as Ionesco writes parallel reviews on the same subject and demolishes in one what he has just praised in the other.

The theatre seems absent from the preoccupations in *Non,* yet one can sense the future dramatist in the language always at high tide and in the way Ionesco stages his argumentations. It is this verbal energy, undiscovered at the time, which often thrusts the book out of its intended literary genre and into the realm of drama.

Written in the early thirties, the essays on Romanian culture should be read in the context of that time. In the disenchanted aftermath of World War I the generation of Romanian intellectuals concerned with the cultural crisis of their country are faced with two choices: cultural isolation brought on by an emphasis on Romanian traditional values as a source of creativity or an adaptation of Western values to Romanian cultural life, resulting in "cultural colonization." Ionesco offers the second alternative as a remedial program to what he believes to be a second-rate culture. His attitude is dictated not only by his bilingual and bicultural makeup, but also by a reaction to the tragic and complex circumstances of the thirties, when the ideologues of the rising Romanian fascism began to adapt some of the ideas of this generation, particularly the ones which exalt Romanian traditional values.

If the demolition of Romanian literary idols and the literary gossip of the thirties are less interesting to Ionesco's readers today, the personal notes scattered throughout *Non* complete the author's Romanian diaries, published partially in his *Présent passé, passé présent* and in *Journal en miettes* and invite a rereading of the interviews in *Entre la vie et le rêve* (see *WLT* 52:2, p. 258). Disengaged from the catcalls and the grimaces of the enfant terrible, they disclose the terrors and epiphanies of the writer and offer the fragile and vibrant poetry of Ionesco's future prose, a poetry which does not surface in his theatre. His feud with the terror of dying and the betrayal of language, two of the themes of his future plays, are also sketched here.

Non is a book against literature, a paradox sustained by the verbal energy of its author. "It was written by an angry adolescent," Ionesco warns in his 1986 preface, but "aside from some clumsiness and incoherences, what was said then, I continue to say and write, in the deepest and most spiritual sense, throughout my life." Indeed, one of the more recent interviews with Ionesco (in *Writers at Work,* 1986) contains almost word for word a leitmotiv from *Non:* "The basic problem is that if God exists, what is the point of literature? And if He doesn't exist, what is the point of literature? Either way," adds the present-day Ionesco, "my writing, the only thing I have succeeded in doing, is invalidated."

Two helpful essays, "Portrait of an Epoch" by E. Simionescu and "The Irony in *Non*" by I. Gregori, provide the necessary background information and a knowledgeable commentary.

Marguerite Dorian

■ **CLARICE LISPECTOR.** *An Apprenticeship, or The Book of Delights.* Richard A. Mazzara, Lorri A. Parris, trs. Austin. University of Texas Press. 1986. xiv + 126 pages.

Well known for her novels on the subject of love in the context of existential and metaphysical inquiry, Clarice Lispector here continues this quest, which she began with *A maçāno escuro* (1961) and *A paixāo segundo G.H.* (1964). First published in Portuguese in 1969, *Uma aprendizagem ou o Livro dos prazeres* narrates, via stream of consciousness, interior monologue, and primarily dialogue, the story of Lori (Lorelei), an elementary-school teacher who searches for a way to give of herself through love without losing her independence. However, in order to find love and take charge of her own life, Lori must, in true existential fashion, first learn to be free by not depending upon others to help her assuage the pain of life. As she learns to face life's burdens and ultimately the responsibility of living, characteristic of existential heroes, Lori, beset by a traditional family's ways and her condition as a woman, yearns to become a free and more authentic individual.

This lesson or "apprenticeship" is achieved via Lori's relationship with Ulysses, a young philosophy professor, who will consent to consummate their love only when she in turn becomes as psychologically free as he. Their relationship develops over long discussions during which Lori expands her consciousness and gradually—through a series of mystical and transcendental episodes symbolized by several images, including the sea and the biblical apple—achieves a "new realism" and eventually makes a choice. Her revelation or epiphany leads her straight to Ulysses' bed, where their lovemaking represents the type of spiritual and physical union that translates into hope.

Focusing upon the inner worlds of two people, the novel harbors many of the intimist qualities and philosophic ideas readers have customarily associated with Lispector's narratives. However, in this instance there also exists a strong undercurrent of social statement as to women's roles within a male-dominated society. Lori's past inability to free herself from society's male and repressive norms suggests that she is decidedly taking a risk with Ulysses, despite his apparent honesty. Curiously, the sentimental, romantic ending, uncommon with Lispector's heroines, closes with Ulysses' words and Lori's submissive behavior. To interpret this ending as upbeat may be premature, given the protagonists' natures and the implicit irony echoed in their names—Lorelei and Ulysses. As opposites of the luring siren and cunning leader of legend, Lori and Ulysses may in fact constitute a parody of individual existential freedom in a society where feminine independence may not always be possible.

Except for a few irritating footnotes in the text instead of elsewhere in a translator's note or preface, the translation is a fine tribute to Lispector's mastery of language and imagery. In short, the edition contributes handsomely to the ever-expanding publications in English of Clarice Lispector's important work.

Nelson H. Vieira

■ **BIENVENIDO N. SANTOS.** *The Volcano.* 2d rev. ed. Quezon City, Phil. New Day (Cellar Book Shop, distr.). 1986. viii + 242 pages.

■ ———. *Villa Magdalena.* 2d rev. ed. Leonor Aureus-Briscoe, foreword. Quezon City, Phil. New Day (Cellar Book Shop, distr.). 1986. viii + 286 pages.

Along with N. V. M. Gonzalez, Edilberto Tiempo, Sionil Jose, and Nick Joaquin, one must rank Bienvenido N. Santos among the "grand old men" of Philippine writing in English. Santos's literary career covers more than fifty-five years and includes two collections of poetry, five volumes of short stories, and four novels. (A fifth novel is being revised for publication.) He has received Rockefeller and Guggenheim fellowships for writing and was granted the Philippine Cultural Heritage Award in Literature. He has been accorded honorary degrees from the University of the Philippines and from Bicol University. For most of his career, he has divided his time between the Philippines and the United States. He taught at Wichita State for many years and now resides in Greeley, Colorado.

It is this cultural dualism which underlies a good deal of Santos's fiction. That duality is expressed most poignantly in three of his early collections of short stories: *Scent of Apples, You Lovely People,* and *The Day the Dancers Came.* It reappears more bitterly and cynically perhaps and is crafted with a sharper scalpel in *The Man Who (Thought He) Looked like Robert Taylor* and the forthcoming *What for You Left Your Heart in San Francisco,* which reflect the changed social conditions of the Philippines and the Filipino in America. The reissue of *The Volcano* and *Villa Magdalena* makes Santos's two early novels available to critics and readers of Philippine literature in English and reintroduces the two works to

a generation familiar only with the aforementioned later novels. The two earlier books are less skillfully written but have a gentler approach to the social problems Santos chooses to portray.

There has been no definitive study of *The Volcano* since its first appearance in 1965, perhaps because it is the weaker of the two rereleases. The best piece of criticism available is the short introduction to the New Day edition, written by Santos's son Tomas, a member of the English Department at the University of Northern Colorado. Tomas Santos reads the novel as basically a historical symbol for the themes of cultural identification and colonialism, with the intrusion, acceptance, and final rejection of the colonizer symbolized in the story of Dr. Hunter and his family. Underlying the symbol of colonizer and colonized is the main symbol of the volcano. The brief critique is all the more valuable for its presumable reflection of the author's own thoughts.

The best criticism on *Villa Magdalena* is the article by Soledad S. Reyes of the Ateneo de Manila in *Essays on the Philippine Novel in English* (1979; see WLT 55:3, p. 533), which outlines the journey theme and the "almost obsessive search for self" of the hero Alfredo Medallada, which is played out against the images of Magdalene, the sinner, and the physical corruption of both the Conde family and Philippine society. "*Villa Magdalena* is far from being a perfect work of art," Reyes states. The characters do not always ring true, and the symbolism is often too carefully and too obviously managed. Nevertheless, she adds, the work "still stands out as one of the most significant novels to come out of the 60s." In the foreword to the new edition Leonor Aureus-Briscoe notes that, "although *Villa Magdalena* has the deficiencies of a first novel, it is the closest to Santos's best."

When the two earlier novels are examined in light of Santos's later fiction, it can be seen that his themes remain essentially the same: the Philippine hero as pilgrim in search of personal and national identity and, in many cases, a stranger in his own land. Santos's basic technique, the sometimes exaggerated and obvious use of symbol, also remains. The later novels, however, have taken on a more sharply critical tone, which reflects what has been happening in his homeland over the past thirty years. Indications are that *What for You Left Your Heart in San Francisco* will continue the development begun in *The Volcano* and *Villa Magdalena* and modified in *The Praying Man* and *The Man Who (Thought He) Looked like Robert Taylor.* Perhaps in this fifth novel the "gentle people" of the earlier works will have grown old and bitter in exile from their native land. It is of that tension, the duality of cultural ambiguity, that Bienvenido Santos writes so well.

Joseph A. Galdon, S.J.

■ **DEREK WALCOTT**. *Three Plays*. New York. Farrar, Straus & Giroux. 1986. 312 pages.

One of Karl Marx's well-known sayings is that history repeats itself, the first time as tragedy, the second as farce. Derek Walcott's dramatic vision of the recent history of Trinidad, as represented in his new collection of plays, seems to be that it is both tragedy and farce simultaneously. The first selection in *Three plays, The Last Carnival,* is distinctly tragic in genre; the second, *Beef, No Chicken,* is distinctly a farce. Tragedy in *The Last Carnival* stems from the existence of groups or classes with no viable role to play in the historical situation in which they find themselves. The two most striking characters in the play are Victor de la Fontaine, a French Creole sugar planter and painter whose class, way of life, and aspirations toward European culture seem irrelevant in an independent, black-ruled Trinidad, and Brown, the nephew of Victor's loyal servant, who becomes a Black Power activist seeking to overthrow that same black rule for its timidity and subservience to white interests. Both characters die—Victor a suicide, Brown killed by the security forces but in essence a suicide—and though at first they might seem to be opposites, they share a great deal, as both are idealists seeking to make Trinidad a place far nobler and more principled than it is or can be.

The comedy of *Beef, No Chicken* is precisely that its characters fit with so little tension into the roles that their historical situation allows them. Set in a rural Trinidad being overwhelmed by modernization in the form of new roads and television, the play diagnoses the corruption of the new without any particular nostalgia for the old. Everyone here is quite willing, even eager, to be corrupted, with the possible exception of the protagonist, the mechanic and restaurant owner Otto Hogan, who sometimes seems to resist the new road from a sincere critique of the form "progress" is taking and sometimes just seems to be holding out for a better bribe. He alone, however, has any critical perspective on—or lack of fit with—the "commodification" of Trinidad which Walcott portrays with such zest and amused disdain.

Of the two modes, farce seems better suited to Walcott's dramatic talents, as *Beef, No Chicken* is much the stronger work. This is partly because Walcott's attempt to chronicle twenty-five years of Trinidad history in *The Last Carnival* means that it lacks the dramatic compression of *Beef, No Chicken.* More important is the fact that the farcical mode allows Walcott much greater freedom with language, as *Beef, No Chicken* fully exploits the poetic and comic resources of West Indian English. In this, though Walcott's nondramatic poetry is deeply influenced by Yeats, his forerunner is Synge, whose poetic drama—like Walcott's—relied not upon an admixture of high poetry in Yeats's vein, but upon the richly poetic and comic idiom of his own people. Walcott's mastery here seems as sure as Synge's.

The final play of the collection, *A Branch of the Blue Nile,* about conflict in a small theatrical troupe in Trinidad, is less compelling, at least for those of us who are not part of the theatre world. Nonetheless, it is revealing about the difficult conditions under which Walcott works in trying to sustain serious theatre in the West Indies. A recurrent question in the play is whether one should go abroad, to the U.S., Britain, or even other West Indian islands in search of better working conditions, more money, and fame. Here Walcott (see *WLT* 51:4, pp. 580–81, and 56:1, pp. 51–53) seems to be wrestling with the consequences for his art of his own long residence in the U.S. On the evidence found here and in his recent *Collected Poems 1948–1984* (see *WLT* 60:3, p. 512), Walcott has no cause to worry.

Reed Way Dasenbrock

1988

■ **CHINGIZ AITMATOV**. *Plakha*. Moscow. Molodaia Gvardiia. 1987. 302 pages.

Originally appearing in 1986 in the leading Soviet literary journal *Novyi Mir,* Chingiz Aitmatov's latest novel seems to have been written *po zakazu* (to order) in support of Gorbachev's *glasnost'* campaign. *Plakha* (The Block) represents the first depiction in Soviet letters of a hitherto taboo theme: narcotics trafficking and abuse in the Soviet Union. The novel is not limited solely to that theme, however. More important, it expands Edigei's philosophical reflections about Soviet man's need of God, which conclude the burial scene in Aitmatov's novel *The Day Lasts More Than a Hundred Years* (1980; see *WLT* 56:3, pp. 435–39). The hero of "The Block," Avdi Kallistratov, probes deeper into the woes of contemporary Soviet society, directly challenging the materialistic ideology upon which it is founded.

The son of an Orthodox deacon, Aitmatov's Avdi (English: Obadiah) rejects the conservative theology of his father while at the same time decrying the vacuum in Soviet society engendered by the state's atheistic ideology. Expelled from the seminary for his heresy of "immanent Messianism" (the belief that God is not transcendent but exists and reveals himself in the words and deeds of men), Avdi dedicates his life to saving the souls of a gang of young drug addicts en route to Central Asia to harvest the wild hashish crop. Casting his hero in a Christ-like mold, Aitmatov leads him down the thorny path to a Soviet Golgotha. Avdi's appeals for the most part fall on deaf ears, and in the end he is beaten and killed by the very people he would save. As he lies half dead after being thrown off a train by the addicts he hoped to convert, he imagines witnessing the conversation between Christ and Pontius Pilate on the day of the Crucifixion. The dynamics of the novel stem from this fictionalized rendition of the Gospel. In Aitmatov's dramatization of the meeting, tailored to condemn Soviet materialism parabolically, Christ rejects Pilate's cult of world power and proposes instead the preeminence of the spirit: "The meaning of human existence lies in the self-perfection of the spirit; there can be no loftier goal in this world." This dialogue of opposites is repeated in different form several times throughout the novel. For example, Avdi argues along similar lines with the leader of the hashish runners, Grishan, who represents the Antichrist of Soviet mass ideology in the novel. Like Dostoevsky's Grand Inquisitor, Grishan proposes making men happy on earth through deceit—in this case, giving them the *kaif* (high) easily available in narcotics. Grishan's deception is equated in the novel with the corruptive deception of materialistic ideology.

The various narrative planes in "The Block" are linked by a subplot that runs through the entire novel and depicts a family of wolves fighting to survive in a world continually violated by insensitive, depraved men. The fact that the wolf was once a totemic animal of the Turkic peoples of Central Asia heightens its symbolic significance for the novel. The mistreatment and eventual extermination of the wolf family in "The Block" thus cannot fail to touch a sensitive national nerve in Aitmatov's Central Asian readers. Still, the symbolism of the wolves also has broader ecological significance. In the novel's opening apocalyptic scene depicting the mass slaughter of the antelope—a crime ordered by party officials to make up for their inability to fulfill the plan for meat production in the republic—the wolves become inadvertent victims. The threat of nature's vengeance on man is implied in the concluding pages of the novel, when the last remaining member of the wolf family, the she-wolf Akbara, drags away the two-year-old son of a Kirghiz shepherd.

Stylistically, "The Block" is an uneven work. Too often the language becomes unduly pathetic. The novel also suffers from a high degree of disjointedness, an unfinished quality caused, no doubt, by the author's desire to take timely advantage of the changing political climate in the Soviet Union. The strength of the novel lies in its muckraking depiction of the sociopolitical evil pervading Soviet society. In this context Avdi's call for repentance can be seen as an appeal to the Soviet leadership to confront and overcome the intolerance and in-

humanity of the Stalinist legacy as a prerequisite to social progress in the Soviet Union. The open discussion of religious thought and the condemnation of scientific atheism in *Plakha* will certainly have an impact on Soviet letters in the future. The novel is a "must" for anyone interested in contemporary Soviet literature and society.

Joseph Mozur

■ E D W A R D   K A M A U   B R A T H W A I T E . *Roots.* Havana. Casa de las Américas. 1986. 308 pages.

Academically trained as a historian, Edward Kamau Brathwaite has become perhaps the world's most articulate and provocative social historian of the Caribbean and one of the region's important poets (see e.g. *WLT* 57:3, p. 500). In the tradition of C. L. R. James and Eric Williams, he has challenged long-established, Eurocentric theories of West Indian history, religion, art, politics, and music, and though iconoclastic, has been granted the position of public voice and advocate of the Caribbean folk.

Earlier in his career a critic of emigrant West Indian intellectuals, Brathwaite now sees that the "shortage of material on which the spirit is sustained becomes a famine in the soul of the West Indian artist. . . . He comes to seek a solution in moving away." He can never move away, however, from the African roots (particularly the religious underpinnings) of his culture and the "nation language" in which this is best expressed, so that physical migration is not necessarily destructive to writer or culture.

Brathwaite acknowledges V. S. Naipaul's novel *A House for Mr. Biswas* as "the first significant artistic expression of a minority culture in the West Indies" and looks for similar works; he believes, though, that Naipaul (see *WLT* 57:3, pp. 223–27) displays a reprehensible undervaluation of black culture. Of the other West Indian writers, he particularly values John Hearne, Derek Walcott (see *WLT* 56:1, pp. 51–53), George Lamming, (see this issue, p. 70), and Roger Mais. Unfortunately, the essays that constitute the volume (all written originally between 1957 and 1981) have not been brought up to date; hence many of the vital new West Indian artists, writers, and critics—including a large number of women—are not considered, and this is a weakness. Still, the bringing together of the eight essays (some really monographs) that make up *Roots* allows readers to consider Brathwaite's views as a philosophy of black Caribbean culture based on extensive research.

The book is heavily documented: it alludes to almost every study of consequence on the topics considered, whether Caribbean literary critics, creative writing during the era of slavery, jazz and the West Indian novel, or the development of "nation language," which has its own rhythms, its "collective forms, ridiculing individualism, singing the praises of eccentricity." *Roots* is, in effect, a study in the search for a genuine West Indian esthetic.

A. L. McLeod

■**BRUCE CHATWIN.** *Songlines.* New York. Viking. 1987. 293 pages.

Alice Springs in the center of Australia is the starting point for Bruce Chatwin's "walkabout," drive about, muse about the Aboriginals and their past and present way of life. As he joins his Australian friend Arcady on his official trips from one Aboriginal settlement to another on business for the railroad, Chatwin weaves together immediate observations and anecdotes of Aboriginal life with Aboriginal history and a discussion of the way in which the Aboriginals relate to the earth, to their ancestors, and to one another. Central to Aboriginal life and to Chatwin's book is the Aboriginal concept of "songlines" or "dreaming tracks," invisible pathways made by the ancestors across Australia, pathways recorded in songs linking modern man to ancient man, territory to territory, idea to idea, spirit to eternity.

Although Chatwin's book is filled with the people he meets in central Australia—teachers, art dealers, truck drivers, missionaries, and a wide variety of Aboriginals—his primary concern takes the reader beyond contemporary Australia and backward through the millennia to pose questions about man's basic nature. Is man at heart aggressive or passive? Is not the sedentary life conducive to greed, possessiveness, territoriality, and warfare? Does the nomadic life produce a different kind of man, one who sees the world as being perfect as it is, with no desire to change it—i.e., ruin it?

In one long section Chatwin breaks his immediate narrative and records a collage of ideas about man and his evolutionary characteristics, quoting from contradictory anthropological research, from philosophy, from history, and from his own travel diary. After the presentation of all his gathered insights in praise of the nomadic way, he returns the reader to the present and to the Aboriginals, indicating their admirable approach to the One, their passivity, reverence, awe, and acceptance. *Songlines* will no doubt anger critics by its structure and its assumptions, but it will delight the reader with the clarity of its prose and with the shared wisdom and humanity of the author as observer.

Ray Willbanks

■**MOHAMMED DIB.** *O Vive.* Paris. Sindbad. 1987. 136 pages.

The poems of *O Vive* are Mohammed Dib's most tantalizing to date (on his earlier prose and poetry, see *WLT* 58:1, p. 55, 59:1, p. 143, and 61:1, p. 141). They are elliptical and full of fascinating and sometimes maddeningly elusive syntactical and semantic lacunae.

The word *Vive* appears in many of the poems, and it is not always clear how we are to take it. It is obviously given two functions in the title with its pun (typical of Dib's later poems, especially in *Omneros*): 1) the value of a name as a result of the vocative *O* and the use of a capital *V* in a book otherwise devoid of capitals; and 2) the value of an adjective, as in its homonym "eau vive." The haunting recurrence of the word soon sent me to the library to consult the Littré dictionary. There were four pages on *vif, vive,* including *eau vive* and *eaux vives.* I also discovered that a *vive* (fem.) is a long, thin fish. To which we might add, of course, the subjunctive-imperative *Vive!*

The rarefied nature of the volume's brief poems and Dib's hermeticism load each word with connotation. As the immediate meaning eludes the reader, he turns to surface signs for guidance. Thus we find more "echoes" in Dib's poetry than we might notice in another poet's work. For example, when Dib uses the feminine adjective *oisive,* we sense traces of *oiseau* and *vive* as well as other words which he has used repeatedly in the poems: *givre, grive, oiselle,* et cetera. The final poem is entitled "à nuit vat," and Grevisse's *Bon usage* tells us that *vat* is found in "A Dieu vat!," which he says is the usual written form of "adieu-va!" or "A Dieu va!" Night thus assumes a sacred mantle in this title, but there is also an echo effect whereby the curious word *vat* brings to mind the noun *vivat*—perhaps in part as an accumulative result of the many occurrences of the word *vive*—and perhaps the Oriental word *wat.*

Such sleuthing is sometimes enlightening. For example, the longer poem "traces" gains stature from its opening word (*altaïr*), which provides clues to the interpretation of several passages. Littré tells us that Altaïr is a star of the first magnitude and that the word comes from the Arabic for "that which flies." Since Dib does not capitalize any words—except the word *Vive*—we do not know if he intends the name of the star or has transliterated an Arabic word. The word *altaïr,* given the way Arabic is built on consonants, brings to mind a host of things and concepts, most saliently "something that flies" (*tā'ir*), "bird" (*tair*), and, by analogy and extension, "airplane" (*tā'ira*) and "agitation/flight/female bird" (*taira*). The poem's imagery at times seems appropriate to birds, at others to airplanes, at yet others to a

Mohammed Dib (*Gil Jain*)

star, and occasionally to more than one of these ("une veilleuse qui attend").

If in certain instances one can best explain Dib's lines by plunging deep down into etymologies, one can, now and then, simply reconstruct the surface dynamics of the poet's creative wordplay, as in his use of *une/nue* in "s'il y a neige et une / pour y aller nue" or "pente / et perte," to cite but two rather obvious examples. *O Vive* paints its imagery with a very delicate line; but sensual, even erotic nuances lie behind many of the words. Dib's suite of spare poems provides a contemporary example of *trobar clus* by a brilliant, if sometimes difficult poet.

Eric Sellin

■**JOE ORTON**. *Head to Toe*. New York. St. Martin's. 1986 (© 1971). 190 pages.

Joe Orton's reputation keeps growing posthumously. Added to his hilariously shocking dramas such as *Good and Faithful Servant* and *Funeral Games,* which were not produced until after his untimely death in 1967 at the hands of his homosexual lover, is his novel *Head to Toe,* first published in Great Britain in 1971. Gombold, the

hero of this picaresque novel in the satiric tradition of Swift's Gulliver, is embarked on a strange journey, having strayed onto the head of a giant, some hundreds of miles high. Lost like Dante at the beginning of his famous journey, Gombold is frightened by strange cries and assaulted by a man he attempts to help. Innocently drawn into adventures such as the attempted assassination of a prime minister and a war between the Left Buttocks and the Right Buttocks, he is buffeted by circumstance.

Like Voltaire's Candide, whose friend may be hanged, drawn, or quartered but miraculously reappears, Gombold keeps running into former acquaintances. At one point he and his friends take refuge in the Trojan Horse. In another instance he finds himself in solitary confinement in a latrine, finally meeting up with a Doktor von Pregnant, a skeletonic Tiresias figure who in his imprisonment has written the history of man on three or four shirts which he had been able to make into paper. His phenomenal memory enables him to recall the whole of "Schoxbear, Arrispittle, Grubben, Taciturn, Saint Trim-Dinty. . .and Kneetchur." The Joycean invention of names is phantasmagoric, and he lectures Gombold on Sir Thomas Browne, Achilles, Ulysses, Petrarch, and Laura. Eventually the Doktor and Gombold tunnel their way through the sewers into the seas. The Doktor dies, and Gombold "had broken free from his chrysalis and emerged whole; he was part and parcel of the world, of the ocean, of the universe."

Finally the war between the Left and Right Buttocks is over. After a Kafkaesque trial and the executions of his former companions—Squall, Pill, and O'Scullion— Gombold reenters a forest which has been denuded. The giant is now a corpse, yet Gombold alone, having traveled head to toe, is affected by the sight of the corpse. No one comes to Gombold's rescue, and so, for the last time, he enters the forest and climbs down into his hole.

With hallucinatory effect, primal images of pissoirs, sewers, and holes vie with recognizable fragments of history, myth, and contemporary mores. Swiftian in his invective and Kafkaesque in his anguish, Orton rolls into one vivid nightmare the history of Western man, evoking along the way Homer, Dante, Voltaire, and Joyce with the brilliant grotesquerie that is his hallmark.

Susan Rusinko

■**ISAAC BASHEVIS SINGER**. *The Death of Methuselah and Other Stories*. New York. Farrar, Straus & Giroux. 1988. viii + 244 pages.

Like a vintage wine, Isaac Bashevis Singer (see *WLT* 53:2, pp. 197–201) gets better with time. The octogenarian has lost none of his vigor and lustiness and has reinforced his philosophic base with the wisdom that comes with the years. More evident than ever and far more piquant is his skepticism, his distrust of sociopolitical causes and systems. He derides their cocky yet pitiful certainty, their willingness to mortgage a relatively certain present for a promised but dubiously better future.

Whereas in more recent novels Singer has not eschewed the pitfall of repeating himself, he remains original and self-assured in the shorter genre. In his stories he retains total control, molds the same raw materials into ever-new and variable shapes. Perhaps alone among masters of the short tale, he has even individualized his narrators; few contemporaries have more creatively pitted men's knowledge of right and wrong against the seductive allure of women. In Singer the men succumb for the most part, and in *The Death of Methuselah and Other Stories* they succumb by yielding to perversions. Still, there is nothing titillating here. Singer rarely invites the reader into the bedchamber or to peep at the forbidden acts.

In the title story, not really the best in what is a superb collection, Methuselah tells us that "after you pass your 900th birthday, you are not what you used to be." Perhaps this is true of most people who have reached this age, but Methuselah still copulates successfully with a woman for whom he has lusted for centuries. He realizes, however, that the very earthy pursuits to which she reintroduces him are not for him, and after his brief final fling, he expires. I prefer "Disguised," in which a deserted wife finds her husband, a Yeshiva student, dressed as a woman and "married to a man." Singer's use of the supernatural and interest in the occult enrich several stories, not necessarily set in the Poland of past centuries. Much can be mystifying when Singer applies his sprightly imagination to what transpires in New York cafeterias, on the lecture circuit, in writers' clubs; but underlying many of his stories is the realization that man can be certain of little, that the knowledge available to him is limited, and that man fails when he makes himself more than human and allows himself to become less than human. There are no essays in Singer, though, only viewpoints emerging from brilliantly invented and brilliantly told stories. *The Death of Methuselah* may be his best prose collection since *Black Friday,* a joyous fact when renewal rather than decline so often characterizes the fiction of old age.

Lothar Kahn

1989

■**KOBO ABE**. *The Ark Sakura.* Juliet Winters Carpenter, tr. New York. Knopf. 1988. vi + 342 pages.

With the publication of the audacious novel *The Ark Sakura,* Kōbō Abe reclaims, after years of toiling in the theatrical arena, his position as one of contemporary Japan's preeminent fiction writers. The "Ark Sakura" of the title refers to an abandoned underground quarry, mammoth and mazelike, which the Mole, the novel's piggish narrator, imagines as an ark, equipped with an arsenal of electronic gadgets, armaments, foodstuffs, booby traps, and the like, that will save its inhabitants from an imminent nuclear catastrophe. The crew that assembles on the "ship," however, consists of a con artist, his shill (*sakura* in Japanese), and the shill's girlfriend, a quirky femme fatale—hardly the sort who would form, in the Mole's own words, a good "gene pool for future generations." The Mole himself harbors an unsavory past, most recently the illegal disposal of toxic waste material through the powerful toilet—capable of flushing anything, including human bodies, out to sea—that is the centerpiece of the ark.

The antics in which these tricksterlike inhabitants of the ark indulge to jockey for an advantageous position, and the way they deal with the intrusion of the Broom Brigade and the Wild Boar Stew Gang into their sanctuary, make for an outrageous story. The Broom Brigade, a self-appointed group of aggressive old men formed to sweep clean a nearby town headed by the Mole's longtime nemesis, his loutish father, is at war with the Wild Boar Stew Gang, a bunch of "real punks, the lowest of the low," for territorial rights over what the Mole had thought belonged solely to himself. The high point of the novel comes when the Mole inadvertently gets his foot caught in the toilet, thus rendering ineffectual one of the ark's prized functions.

Abe's postmodernist spirit is amply realized in *The Ark Sakura* in such ways as the irreverently humorous treatment of serious topics like survival in the nuclear age, combining (as the dust jacket puts it) "fantasy and literal-mindedness, technology and scatology, savage satire and comic precision."

Yoshio Iwamoto

■**JULIEN GRACQ**. *Autour des sept collines.* Paris. Corti. 1989. 147 pages.

Julien Gracq has long distinguished himself, together with Sartre and E. M. Cioran, as one of the few major "dissidents" of French literature who have publicly re-fused such honors as the Nobel Prize, the Goncourt Prize, or election to the French Academy. To American readers, Gracq is still known, if at all, mainly as the au-thor of *Au château d'Argol, Le rivage des Syrtes* or *Un beau ténébreux,* three strangely surrealist novels that have much in common with the Gothic fiction of over a hun-dred years earlier. Although ably translated into En-glish, Gracq's fiction has never attracted in England or America the critical attention that it deserves, in spite of the fact that Gracq is now widely acclaimed in France as one of the greatest French writers of his generation.

The author's more recent publications have includ-ed a critical study of the writings of André Breton, with whom Gracq was closely associated over a number of years as a rather marginal surrealist who still dared ex-press some admiration for the writings of Stendhal or Chateaubriand; *La forme d'une ville,* a very personal and often rhapsodic description of the city of Nantes and of its immediate environs, where Gracq had spent most of his childhood and adolescence; and now *Autour des sept collines,* an admirably written but somewhat cantanker-ous account of his reactions to Florence, Rome, and other areas of Italy. While admitting that this last book is admirably written, most of the literary critics of the French press have condemned it as if Gracq's opinions about Italy were scandalously heretical.

Breton is known to have steadfastly refused ever to cross the French frontier into Italy or to visit Greece. Gracq appears to be haunted by similarly Celtic resent-ments even two thousand years after Rome's legions conquered Gaul and defeated Vercingetorix. Twentieth-century Rome still remains to some extent much as the poet Belli once described it, a city of "princes, priests, whores, and fleas," but it has also become, like Ankara, Canberra, or Washington, a veritable warren of civil ser-vants, all too many of whom remain frustrated in their ambitions and prone to develop stomach ulcers. Few of Gracq's readers, whether in France or elsewhere, will agree with his strictures on Italy and its capital, which, like Athens, Constantinople, Paris, and Ankara, is re-puted to owe its claim to be "eternal" to the fact that it is built on seven hills. Nevertheless, this should not pre-vent anyone from enjoying Gracq's admirable style.

Edouard Roditi

■ EDNA O'BRIEN. *The High Road.* New York. Farrar, Straus & Giroux. 1988. viii + 214 pages.

Joana Russ maintains, "The one occupation of a female protagonist in literature. . .is the love story [which] in-cludes not only personal relationships but. . . exposition of character, [and] crucial learning experiences." The

High Road illustrates this statement by offering a kalei-doscopic exploration of the nature of love along a wide range of social clases. More important, however, the text focuses on the risk involved in challenging patriar-chy by sidestepping gender barriers—that is, by ques-tioning its foundation: the premise of heterosexuality.

Anna, the protagonist, who attributes her over-whelming feeling of despair to a prolonged yet unsatis-factory love affair, undergoes a rebirth process triggered by a gradual awakening of the senses that leads her to defy taboos in search of "something other-womanly, primordial," which she defines as follows:

> I felt . . . her arms around me . . . and I . . . cleaved
> to her, through her opening to life . . . tenderness,
> rabidness, hunger; back, back in time to that
> wandering milky watery bliss, infinitely safe . . .
> boundaries burst, bursting, the mind as much as
> the body borne along . . . slipping through a wall
> of flesh, eclipsed inside the womb of the world.

Young and exotic Catalina represents the vitality of a "natural woman," and this connection is reinforced by her mysterious grandmother, a witch—that is, a healer. The latter's words, "To love one must learn to part with everything," are ultimately applicable to Catalina, who gives her life for Anna.

Edna O'Brien's locale and picturesque exiles re-mind us of Hemingway, and the wry humor—especially concerning the predicament of Iris and Portia—are reminiscent of Virginia Woolf. In sum, although *The High Road* reinforces the traditional stereotypes about Spain, the text focuses on the notion of female bonding in order to arrive at a deeper understanding of the na-ture of love.

Cynthia M. Tompkins

■ CHRISTIANE ROCHEFORT. *La porte du fond.* Paris. Grasset. 1988. 250 pages.

Christiane Rochefort's Medicis-crowned novel *La porte du fond* is a chilling tale of incest, told, in conversational style and without self-pity, by the "survivor." It is the story of the person the narrator has become, because (or in spite?) of "the combat [which] lasted seven years. I lost every battle. But not the war," and of why, and how, she became a specialist in infamy. It is a tale too of broader implications about the frequent, if not general atrocities of family life in a patriarchal society, leading one to the conclusion that most, if not all of us would be better off could we but choose our relatives. It raises questions about psychology and psychologists, alluding to and agreeing or taking issue with Freud, Jeffrey Moussaïeff Masson, R. D. Laing, Françoise Dolto (who, as a woman, should most probably have known better), and others, and treats issues of psychic reality, the unreality of reality, and the possibility that disasters are only in the way one takes them.

No one—behind or in front of the door—is entirely innocent, but most particularly the narrator's parents, ill-matched in class, religion, character, and interests, are almost equally guilty. In explanation, self-defense, and self-disculpation her father uses all the shopworn arguments: it's common in families; everyone does it; you're better off learning from me; besides, I might not even be your father. Her mother neither knows nor wants to know, and nothing her daughter can do can please her. The daughter, who couldn't tell for fear it would kill her mother, for fear she herself would become an object of pity, has, during the seven-year struggle, "lost everything," including, not least of all, her illusions.

The sympathetic narrator understands childhood and (family) life without having lost all sympathy, not even for the only child of a loving family. "One communicates," she says, "not by language, but by style." Fortunately she, like Rochefort, is ever a stylist.

Judith L. Greenberg

■**WOLE SOYINKA**. *Mandela's Earth and Other Poems*. New York. Random House. 1988. vi + 72 pages.

It should never be said that Wole Soyinka is unresponsive to criticism. Attacked by Chinweizu and others as a Eurocentric modernist out of touch with Africa, Soyinka responded with *Aké: The Years of Childhood* (see WLT 56:3, p. 561), a memoir that clarified his African roots and cultural allegiances. Attacked by the same critics for overly difficult and esoteric poetry, Soyinka now responds with *Mandela's Earth,* a new volume of poetry much less enigmatic than his earlier verse and overtly Africanist in its political commitments. However, not all responses are created equal, and though *Aké* is a superb work, possibly Soyinka's greatest achievement, *Mandela's Earth* is not nearly as successful. Soyinka is a great prose writer and dramatist, whether working in an esoteric or esoteric mode, but I have never found his poetry as powerful. *Mandela's Earth,* despite its greater directness, does not make me change my mind.

The volume opens with the sequence that gives it its title, and though the political sentiments expressed there are irreproachable, irreproachable political sentiments do not necessarily make for great poetry. The problem is that Mandela has been in prison for so long that for Soyinka he has become almost completely a symbol and affords nothing concrete for the poet to come to grips with. The only part of the sequence that rises above the tone of unexceptionable sentiments is "Like Rudolf Hess, the Man Said!," which takes off from Pik Botha's statement that "we keep Mandela for the same reason the Allied Powers are holding Rudolf Hess" into a fantasy that Mandela is really Hess or even Mengele in disguise. Here is the real Soyinka, superb at turning the rhetoric of dictators against themselves in savage and funny ways. However, as if thinking that he might be misunderstood, he retreats from this satire into the tepid pieties of the rest of the sequence.

The lesson to be drawn from the successes and failures of this sequence is a simple one. Soyinka is, as Chinweizu says in disdain, a modern and individualistic poet, not a voice for a larger collectivity. These poems succeed when Soyinka's individual voice comes through; they fail when he tries to submerge that voice in a larger, public one. Still, this does not justify Chinweizu's disdain, for the voice that comes through in poems such as "The Apotheosis of Master Sergeant Doe" and "My Tongue Does Not Marry Slogans" as well as "Like Rudolf Hess, the Man Said!" is valuable because it refuses to marry slogans. Soyinka has been an important political voice in contemporary Africa precisely because of his willingness to puncture the shibboleths of those around him.

Nevertheless, there is a sense in which Chinweizu's characterization of Soyinka as essentially a private poet is correct. The best poems in the book are those in the final sequence, "Dragonfly at My Windowpane," especially the poem of that title and the closing piece, "Cremation of a Wormy Caryatid." These two poems about moments in nature perceived by Soyinka are clearly modernist in their enigmatic difficulty, though not Euromodernist, since Soyinka alone could have written them. So the final point to be made about *Mandela's Earth* is that Soyinka may have been *too* responsive to criticism. For too much of the collection, it seems as if Soyinka's tongue is trying to marry slogans. A great writer like Soyinka is better off following his own impulse, whether it leads him to write about Mandela or dragonflies and caryatids, than responding to the partial vision of others. (On Soyinka, see WLT 61:1, pp. 5–9, and 63:1, pp. 39–41.)

Reed Way Dasenbrock

■**MURIEL SPARK**. *A Far Cry from Kensington*. Boston. Houghton Mifflin. 1988. 190 pages.

"Oh, girls of slender means!" The rooming house in Kensington that housed those ladies in Muriel Spark's

1963 novel reappears now as the setting for her newest work. Mrs. Hawkins, the narrator, bears strong resemblance to the *Girls of Slender Means's* Jane Wright, a plump bookworm with a nebulous "job in publishing." Though *A Far Cry from Kensington* uses familiar scenery and characters, the twenty-five years lapsed between the two books have visibly perfected the author's technique. Her narration is more engaging, her humor quite irresistible. Spark proves, once more, her talent for making banal stories unforgettably amusing.

Mrs. Hawkins is a war widow living in a rooming house in 1954 London, protected from suitors by her enormous girth. She delivers not only the essentials of the plot but, as she goes along, dishes out sage advice on how to lose weight, find a job in times of unemployment, write a novel, start a marriage out on the right foot, and sabotage the careers of those less talented; for despite her devoutness—she recites the Angelus or Kyrie throughout the day—Hawkins harbors unbending contempt for people who cannot write. Her spontaneous hatred for one would-be author and journalist, Hector Bartlett, provides the novel's major conflict. Hector turns up everywhere with his repellent manuscripts.

Unfortunately, the *pisseur* also happens to be the protégé of an influential novelist. Mrs. Hawkins loses one job after another, partly for her refusal to edit his manuscripts, partly for becoming vulgar as she attempts to explain the chosen epithet to her superiors. Meanwhile, she also unravels a mystery involving a Polish immigrant, Wanda, who lives in the same house. Wanda receives threatening calls and letters and is secretly involved in a popular witchcraft cult called "radionics." Wanda's eventual suicide remains unexplained until Mrs. Hawkins, through a coincidence possible only in the labyrinthine world of publishing, discovers a perfidious plot concocted by—whom else?—Hector Bartlett. Mrs. Hawkins eventually loses weight and gets married; and in the end, thirty years later, she takes her acerbic verbal revenge on Hector.

Much like Doris Lessing's 1960 "documentary" *In Pursuit of the English,* Spark's *Kensington* is a nostalgic period study on daily survival in postwar England—no longer the most relevant of topics. The novel's plot is a bit trivial. No great ideas are at stake, and any attempt to paraphrase the action falls hopelessly flat, since it is only funny in context. Why then is Muriel Spark so often hailed as one of the greatest living English writers? Perhaps for this reason: her unusual and infectious wit dominates her work so completely that any inherent limitations of the subject matter become irrelevant. Spark's display of human nature, so lovable and fasci-

nating in its very banality, pervades each page and makes the book hard to put down.

Mona Knapp

1990

■ **EVELYNE ACCAD**. *L'excisée*. David K. Bruner, tr. Washington, D.C. Three Continents. 1989. 86 pages.

"Why not rebel before it is too late, before you also become an *excisée*? You have lived in war. You have seen the horror of blood spilled in the streets, on the earth, external to yourself, but if you were to encounter the blood and the shame and the horrors which you have told me about, the mutilated bodies, the sex organs ripped away, the corpses violated, if you should encounter all that internally in your very own flesh, then what would you do?" *L'excisée* is a dreamlike novel, beginning with a creation myth, rudely shattered by the violence in Lebanon, where Muslims and Christians kill one another under the watchful eyes of America and Russia, chiefly the former, whose influence is seen in the music of Elvis and the image of James Dean. The protagonist is "E."—"Elle," "Eve," "Evelyne," et cetera. The daughter of a dogmatic Christian preacher hostile to Muslims, she falls in love with a Muslim, "P."—"Palestine," the "patriarchal" system, perhaps "poet." He comes to her as James Dean, the counterpart to the Valentino Arab, and takes her to his desert home. That is where all hell breaks loose.

E. finds out about the horror of female circumcision. In fact, she had been told by an Egyptian woman aboard the ship on which she thought she was escaping about how she had been circumcised. The violence is men's way of controlling women. E. does escape, though pregnant with a girl, "Nour" (Light); Nour goes with the now-free Egyptian woman, but E. chooses to drown herself.

Such a plot summary does not do justice to the texture of Evelyne Accad's novel, but it does help explain the work's problematic nature. *L'excisée* is clearly anticolonial: Fanon's classic book (in David Bruner's translation, *The Wretched*) is on E.'s shelf. Accad wants to discover what made the violence possible; E. can do this as an outsider/insider, an Arab who is a Christian with a Swiss grandmother. However, she is unable to escape Western myths of the ugly Arab, the other side of the noble Arab. P. turns into a monster in his desert home. His honeyed words are gone; he is a sex machine, plowing her for children, spending most of his time with other women. He is now gross; he snores. What can a beguiled woman do but escape and die?

The novel thus lends itself to the idea that it is men—i.e., Third World men—who are to blame for the colonization of the Third World! This is alarming: many novels have recently been published by nonwhite women in the West implying that we, the men, colonized ourselves. The white man is thus off the hook. As Pirate Jack tells Quaw Quaw, the Indian princess he marries in Ishmael Reed's *Flight to Canada* (1989), by killing her father he became her Lincoln. A Third World man could say to E., "Get real! Don't help the colonizer in his task! Don't deny your role in history by claiming to be an innocent victim!"

So, *L'excisée* has a split personality, as its title ironically suggests. Thanks to the translator, however, the English version is a poetic work. In a world in which people are trapped by external roles and myths, the only way to see human possibility is through dream consciousness, which is the story of E.

Peter Nazareth

■ **ANTHONY BURGESS.** *Any Old Iron.* New York. Random House. 1989. vi + 362 pages.

During its planning stages, Anthony Burgess's first major novel since *Earthly Powers* (1980) must have seemed to its author an exciting opportunity to combine two themes: that of resurgent Welsh nationalism, against the backdrop of Zionism in Israel; and that of a two-generational family chronicle, in a romp through the history of the twentieth century. The narrative bogs down, however, just as Burgess's early enthusiasm for the themes seems to diminish.

Part of the problem is the writer's choice of narrator: an ironic, self-distrusting Manchester Jew, Harry Wolfson, who could not possibly "know" all the details of the story he tells. A more serious objection to *Any Old Iron* than faulty point of view is Burgess's failure to bring his characters to life. From the crusty sire of the family, David Jones, to his steely cold Russian-born wife Ludmila, to his three children—sappy-liberal misadventuring Reg, coolly promiscuous Beatrix, and fishmongering Dan—the Welsh characters seem to drift through history without much joy or enlightenment. Members of the Jewish family—conspicuously our narrator and his sister Zip (who marries Reg)—seem as confused about their roles in supporting Israel as are their Welsh counterparts in seeking a separate political destiny from England.

As symbols for Welsh separatism, Burgess uses two Jones family heirlooms: a lump of unrefined gold (mate-rialism) and an ancient piece of iron (the "any old iron" of the title, perhaps representing idealism). The iron might, or might not, be the legendary blade Excalibur (Caledvwlch), or might be the even more legendary sword of Attila. By the end of the novel neither gold nor sword helps much to prosper the Welsh; these symbols, ambiguous as Burgess's theme, fail to connect the broken links of the characters' lives.

Leslie B. Mittleman

■ **KAZUO ISHIGURO.** *The Remains of the Day.* New York. Knopf. 1989. viii + 248 pages.

Whereas the plight of "the last English gentleman" has been depicted in such works as Ford Madox Ford's *Parade's End* and Evelyn Waugh's *Handful of Dust,* among many others, Kazuo Ishiguro's *Remains of the Day* is a unique and beautifully written account of the last English "gentleman's gentleman": a stalwart, impeccably proper, consummately professional butler named Stevens, whose career in service to Lord Darlington began long before World War II. Set in the summer of 1956 and cast in the form of a travel log, the novel is both comic and poignant, affording an insightful character study of its narrator while evoking the changing society of mid-twentieth-century Britain from his (traditionally "marginalized") point of view.

With fine nuance and subtle detail, Ishiguro's first-person narrative captures the tone of a man whose life has been shaped through service. Having devoted himself wholeheartedly to a career in which success requires the inculcation of decidedly Prufrockian traits as well as an ethos of self-abnegation, Stevens is unvaryingly deferential, meticulous, and not only glad to be "of use" but actually *proud* that his profession has brought him often into the proximity of greatness. Accordingly, he contends, "a 'great' butler can only be, surely, one who can point to his years of service and say that he has applied his talents to serving a great gentleman—and, through the latter, to serving humanity." During his journey, however, as he reflects on the highlights of his career, he comes to reassess not only the nature of his employer's political activism during the inter-war period but also the pattern and meaning of his own life, during which he never allowed himself to forsake his cherished professional "dignity" even momentarily, thus preventing himself from ever achieving more intimate human relationships.

Ishiguro's novel therefore takes its place within a long-familiar and quintessentially English literary tradition. Its masterfully subtle, seemingly discursive first-person narrative is reminiscent of Henry James at his best, with certain aspects of the plot echoing "The Beast in the Jungle" in particular; Stevens's painful, retrospective revaluation of character and incident is comparable to that in Ford Madox Ford's *Good Soldier,* and Ishiguro's evocation of time, place, and class is as carefully wrought as (though on a far less massive scale than) its counterpart in Anthony Powell's *Dance to the Music of Time.* Still, because servants are incidental in the works of Powell, Ford, Waugh, and (often) James, such "marginalized" characters' perspectives have rarely if ever been considered in detail. Ishiguro's novel thus makes a new and valuable contribution to—while also managing to subvert significant conventions of—this literary tradition.

Winner of the 1989 Booker Prize, *The Remains of the Day* is the third novel by the much-acclaimed thirty-five-year-old Japanese-born author, who has lived in England since the age of six. *A Pale View of the Hills* was awarded the Winifred Holtby Prize by the Royal Society of Literature; *An Artist of the Floating World* won the Whitbread Book of the Year Award for 1986.

William Hutchings

▪ **MANUEL PUIG.** *Cae la noche tropical.* Barcelona / Mexico City. Seix Barral / Planeta. 1988/1989. 224 pages.

Breaking a six-year silence that followed the publication of *Sangre de amor correspondido* (1982), the Argentine writer Manuel Puig has published his seventh novel, *Cae la noche tropical.* This latest work by the author of *La traición de Rita Hayworth* (1975; Eng. *Betrayed by Rita Hayworth*) and *El beso de la mujer araña* (1982; Eng. *Kiss of the Spider Woman*) shows the distinctive and familiar features of his previous narrative. Puig's fiction centers on individual experiences and human relationships under limiting and oppressive social conditions. His characters tend not to be heroes but rather ordinary human beings who must often adjust to the forced disruption of their ties to family and country.

The main characters of *Cae la noche tropical* are two elderly Argentine sisters, one living in Rio de Janeiro in order to be near her only son, the other visiting her from Buenos Aires following the death of her daughter. The text includes only brief and casual allusions to the political and economic circumstances that forced many Argentines into exile, but the emotional toll of expatriation is felt through Luci's narrative voice. At age eighty-one she faces a second readaptation when her son accepts a job in Lucerne. She dies in that Swiss city, far from her sister and from the second home that she had made for herself in Rio, and even farther removed from all the places and affections of a lifetime left behind in Buenos Aires when she first emigrated at age seventy-five.

The sisters' evocation of gentler times, permeated by the pain of loss, separation, and loneliness, is mitigated by their inexhaustible interest in and concern for the problems of the other, younger people. Thus the complicated love life of a neighbor, an Argentine woman psychologist who escaped the murderous Triple A, or the Brazilian doorman's economic and family problems evoke the old women's understanding and compassion as well as their attempts to be of real help to them.

As in Puig's previous novels, we get to know the characters and their experiences without the mediation of a narrator. They are presented mostly through direct dialogue, letters, and other written documents. The author's remarkable skill in using these narrative means in a variety of forms results in a text that captures both the interest and the emotions of the reader. Once more Puig proves to be a master in conveying a concern for the limitations of the human condition through the unsophisticated materials of ordinary life.

Malva Filer

▪ **TOMAS TRANSTRÖMER.** *För levande och döda.* Stockholm. Bonniers. 1989. 38 pages.

In 1983 Kjell Espmark began his penetrating study of the poetry of Tomas Tranströmer (see *WLT* 64:1, pp. 48–49) with the observation that that poetry occupies a unique position in modern Swedish literature. During the intervening years the singularity of Tranströmer's achievement has not diminished, and *För levande och döda* (For the Living and the Dead), the first volume of poetry to appear since that assessment was made, eloquently and forcefully confirms its continuing validity. Since Tranströmer publishes only sparingly, moreover, the appearance of a new collection of verse is an occasion of interest in and of itself.

Like Tranströmer's debut collection, entitled simply *17 dikter* (1954), the slender new volume also contains just seventeen poems. In contrast to its relatively small physical size, the poetic world it evokes is spacious and informed by an arresting array of contrasting, sharply focused images. "Sex vintrar," for example, presents in six stanzas of three short lines each six highly original but at once seemingly familiar images of Swedish winters. Each one seems at the same time familiar yet somehow mysterious and unsettling. Similarly, "Gator i Shanghai" makes disarmingly immediate three contrasting impressions of what for most Swedish readers is inherently foreign, unfamiliar, and even exotic. The simultaneous evocation of the familiar and the mysterious, of the proximate and the distant, is not accomplished by the accumulation of images but by the highly concise and economical development of precisely the right image. As the title immediately suggests, Tranströmer retains the fondness for apparent antitheses—alive and dead, light and dark, high and low—that characterized so much of his earlier poetry and succeeds in suggesting that somewhere between them may lie an enigmatic center cryptically encompassing seemingly incompatible opposites.

För levande och döda is a collection that can bear—indeed invites—much rereading. The poems hold up well, remain fresh, and continue to offer surprises.

Steven P. Sondrup

■ **ELIE WIESEL**. *L'oublié*. Paris. Seuil. 1989. 318 pages.

The Holocaust and its aftermath remain powerful themes in Elie Wiesel's writings (see *WLT* 57:2, pp. 228–33, and 58:1, pp. 58–59), as he shows again with his latest novel. The *oublié* of the title refers to that which is forgotten as well to him who is forgotten, for memory, remembrance, mental and psychological forgetting are all important leitmotivs. Professor Elhanan Rosenbaum, Malkiel's increasingly sick and senile father, is fast losing his memory. To hold on to his dissolving past, he sends Malkiel to his native Carpathian village to retrace the family origins, a mission for which the son is highly qualified. As a *New York Times* reporter, Malkiel specializes in the dead, whether the victims of the Cambodian killing fields or the mighty of the obituary page.

In Nicolae Ceausescu's Romania the reporter meets a philosophical Jewish gravedigger who, through his tales told in the style of Hebraic storytellers, is at once the best witness of Nazi horrors and Jewish heroism and the repository of Jewish folklore and memory. Malkiel learns of his grandfather's self-sacrifice and of his father's courage and also that, as in so many German-occupied countries, most people actively participated in tracking and killing Jews or did nothing to save them. He also learns that the young Elhanan did not speak out while a comrade took revenge on their worst enemy by raping his widow, a silence that would haunt his father forever.

During lucid moments the father tells the son of his illegal entry into Palestine with Talia, his future wife, and of the intoxicating first days of Israel's independence, which symbolically and dramatically coincide with Malkiel's own birth and Talia's death. Woven with the moving and passionate plea not to forget the dead are Malkiel's torturing liaisons with Inge the German and Leila the Arab, each of whom revives a special

memory of hatred and pain. Tamar, his Jewish colleague and lover, on the other hand, presents him with a more difficult dilemma when she questions today's Israeli conduct and ethics.

Only through legends, stories, eyewitness accounts—in short, *le verbe*—can one hope to triumph over forgetting and ultimately over death itself. From the power of words the spinner of tales survives, and so does his message, however incomplete and lost in the fog of memory. To seize and reassemble those shattered fragments of Elhanan's failing memory, Wiesel uses various narrative devices—letters, flashbacks, journal entries, tape recordings, prayers, unspoken dialogues—complemented by parables taken from Hasidic and Talmudic scholars.

Beginning with the publication of *La nuit* in 1958, Elie Wiesel established himself as the bard of Jewish suffering. *L'oublié*, though, shines with a luminosity that was often absent from his earlier works (*Le mendiant de Jérusalem* [1968] is one exception), as if Wiesel had come out of his own Night Kingdom, scathed of course, but also full of hope and optimism. All is remembered; nothing is forgotten: "Grâce à lui [Elhanan's grandson yet to be born], je vivrai: grâce à toi, Abraham vit."

Pierre L. Horn

1991

■ **A. S. BYATT**. *Possession*. New York. Random House. 1990. 555 pages.

For some reason known only to the mysterious power that directs book buyers, in November of 1990, after a distinguished but largely ignored literary career, Antonia Byatt saw her densely intertextual fifth novel suddenly shoot to the top of the best-seller charts in the United States and win her the Booker Prize in England. It seems appropriate, then, that the full title of this publishing phenomenon is *Possession: A Romance*.

Byatt's title refers to two scholars' experience of being possessed by the commanding intellect of the writers they are studying. For all its popularity, *Possession* is about an experience restricted to dissertation writers and other haunters of archives: that of finding one's own life strangely subsumed in the life of one's subject. Roland Mitchell, drudging away in a London library on a thesis on the Victorian poet Randolph Ash, comes upon a mysterious cache of love letters by the poet. In his search for the identity of Ash's correspondent, Mitchell encounters Maud Bailey, a young professor studying another Victorian poet, Christabel La

Motte. Predictably enough, the romance between Roland and Maud develops in tandem with their investigations of the romance between Ash and La Motte.

It is a delight to watch Byatt play the variations on actual romances between Victorian writers as she develops the story of Ash and La Motte. Ash's narrative poetry (of which we are given huge samples) is Browningesque, but his character is based as well on Carlyle, Ruskin, Tennyson, and George Henry Lewes. La Motte's verse is a cross between Elizabeth Barrett Browning's and Emily Dickinson's (a cross that makes good historical sense, since Browning was Dickinson's literary model). Her character draws on Barrett Browning, Dickinson, and those legendary romantic heroines Emily Brontë, Charlotte Brontë, and George Eliot.

On the contemporary plane of her plot Byatt develops a satire on international literary scholarship that is as accurate and amusing as that of David Lodge's *Small World* and *Nice Work* (see WLT 64:3, p. 464). With the sure hand of a writer who is a veteran of academia herself, Byatt delineates the cutthroat rivalry among British and American institutions to obtain collections of papers and manuscripts, and also a wide variety of scholarly foibles, from the pedant whose slow, painstaking efforts produce no actual results, to the high-speed, high-tech scholar who publishes first and thinks later.

The beauty of Byatt's prose keeps all these cerebral details from becoming an intellectual game on the order of Umberto Eco's *Name of the Rose*. For example, in this brief description of a picnic lunch the scholars take on a walk in Yorkshire, retracing the steps of their Victorian forebears, Byatt's characteristic feel for sensuous detail makes the scene come to life: "They took a simple picnic. Fresh brown bread, white Wensleydale cheese, crimson radishes, yellow butter, scarlet tomatoes, round bright green Granny Smiths and a bottle of mineral water. They took no books."

Though without a doubt a postmodernist novel (Byatt herself defines it as one), *Possession* is a triumphant example of a new phase of postmodernism, the literature of repletion rather than the "literature of exhaustion," in John Barth's famous phrase. Byatt's primary allegiance is with the tradition of the serious, realistic novel, wherein deep sympathy for individual human beings is a central value. Whether she is probing the lives of two Victorian poets or those of two contemporary scholars, Byatt is committed to uncovering the truth about human experience. As a result, her appropriation of the past is not nostalgic but celebratory, and her satire on contemporary foolishness is tempered by an awareness that we are all time's fools.

Mary Kaiser

■ **HÉLÈNE CIXOUS**. *Jours de l'an*. Paris. Des Femmes. 1990. 277 pages.

If the prolific Hélène Cixous does not always write the same book, she does in fact write books that could be expected of her. A substantial number of critics find their great expectations for each succeeding volume fulfilled. Others, however, whose eyelids droop after a few pages, begin each book with trepidation.

Jours de l'an, which treats of the duality of Cixous as author and woman and whose principal character is "not what you thought" but rather death, will no doubt prove rewarding to the first group. It should provide them ample scope for continuing where she leaves off: meditating on her meditations, de- and reconstructing her inventions, plunging more deeply into her "subterranean" insights, interpreting and extricating the double Cixous. They can pontificate on the differences between men and women, the distinctions between the author and the living person, between what one thinks one's aim is and the end actually attained, and between the book an author wants to write and the one actually produced. Rembrandt, Clarice Lispector, and Judaism will be additional grist for their mill.

The second group, however sympathetic to Cixous's ideas, even though the book "will perhaps not be what [they] fear," will nevertheless experience a distinct sensation of déjà vu and doubtless "feel . . . an antipathy, even an anger" Cixous "was afraid of." They might indeed limit themselves to making a collection of truisms, aphorisms, and other quotations, believing that these need no commentary, being sufficient if not necessarily efficacious: "Croire est la chair de la vérité"; "Tout le monde veut être trompé, c'est tout. Voilà la vérité"; "Penser n'est pas ce que nous pensons." Et cetera, *ainsi de suite, und so weiter,* to remain true to the spirit of the text, which includes interjections in English and German.

Judith L. Greenberg

■ **GABRIEL GARCÍA MÁRQUEZ**. *El general en su laberinto*. Bogotá/Buenos Aires. Oveja Negra/Sudamericana. 1989. 288 pages.

A common phenomenon of the contemporary literary scene is the tendency to demythologize historical figures, and perhaps the greatest of these for Latin America is Simón Bolívar. In reading *El general en su laberinto* (Eng. *The General in His Labyrinth,* 1990), one gains the impression that García Márquez feels the author has no right to compose an epic concerning the founder of a nation that never truly came to be. A myth often concludes with the appearance of a new star or constellation, but in this work one of the general's companions comments that there are now fewer stars than there were eighteen years ago.

Accordingly, the author has left a key element out of the myth of Theseus that appears to underlie his text. As Theseus is about to enter the labyrinth to slay the monster that has been devouring his people, Ariadne gives him a thread to follow in order to find his way out safely. For Bolívar there is no thread; in the penultimate paragraph of the novel he exclaims, "How am I going to get out of this labyrinth!"

Throughout the work the general is haunted by news of the growing anarchy that is making impossible his dream of one great nation in the region. He is forced out of power and toward exile (although he never actually embarks for Europe) by the fragmentation brought about by General Santander and the oligarchies.

El general en su laberinto is a politically committed work. The implied narrator's stance is squarely in the present, and the contemporary sociopolitical distress of the region in question is never far below the surface of the text. The reader comes to feel that unworthy wielders of power not only crushed the Liberator but forced the writing of a demythologizing novel; this may be what García Márquez, at the end of his "Gratitudes," calls "the horror of this book." (On *El general en su laberinto,* see also pages 54–58 of this issue.)

William L. Siemens

■ **NADINE GORDIMER.** *My Son's Story.* New York. Farrar, Straus & Giroux. 1990. viii + 278 pages.

In Nadine Gordimer's novels the personal, especially the psychological and moral, intersects with and is influenced by the political. In a society so politicized the relation of the individual to the social world becomes political, and morality finds expression in terms of ideology and commitment. However, the strength of the novels has been their focus on the individual and on families and their awareness of the personal complexities, compulsions, and ironies that are the sources of political consciousness and decisions. *My Son's Story* makes the poetics of Gordimer's novels too explicit and seems too diagrammatic. It is almost as if she were explaining her fiction while showing how it can take new directions appropriate to a future South Africa. Perhaps the most difficult novel she has attempted, and filled with her personal obsessions found in previous novels (see e.g. *WLT* 56:1, p. 167, 56:2, p. 394, and 62:3, p. 500, as well as 52:4, pp. 533–38, and 62:1, pp. 76–77), it often feels contrived, manipulated, abstract, program-

matic. Too many sentences seem to be the author speaking through the narrator.

My Son's Story is an uncomfortable novel to read, for the story is told by the jealous son of a black African revolutionary hero. The son is the supposed author of the novel, which is in part about his maturation from jealous youth concerned about family loyalties to an adult who now perceives his family's actions as a heroic response to the political demands made upon the gifted by the times. The same values that made them a family make them into moral beings. There is an oppressiveness in reading of the son's sexual jealousy caused by his father's mistress (a blond white woman), the son's resentment of his father's emotional withdrawal from the family due to total involvement in the movement and his mistress, the son's perception of his father's example as being the reason for his sister's going into exile in order to work for the movement and for his mother's eventual politicization, hiding of weapons, and escape into exile. The story of the fragmentation of a black family due to politics becomes, as the son writes the novel, the story of exemplary heroism and of how life is changed by external circumstances so that the personal is given its direction by the political.

Gordimer's attempt to write about black African lives is itself a way to cross the color line, a way to claim a place in the future black-ruled South Africa. The mother even matures from passive wife to female African hero. However, the conquering of new fictional spaces has its costs. There is, no doubt consciously, none of the detailed specificity of social life, the art objects, the houses, the background, the complexities of characterization found in Gordimer's portraits of white characters elsewhere. Too much is avoided or left unknowable. There is also none of the imagining, the fantasies, the desires in conflict presented fully, of the previous fiction. It is as if she were unable to enter, or out of political correctness refrained from fully entering, the minds of her characters. Instead, conflicts are explicitly stated, and we are told how to interpret. This can be blamed on the narrator; it is his first novel, and we are told that he is writing a history of his family as an example of the personal costs of the black revolution; but the self-reflectivity of the fiction is not really a justification for turning the personal into the heroic, for the predictable way each character dedicates him or herself to the movement, or for the continual pointing to the themes by the narrator or author. Perhaps, as the ironies become clearer, *My Son's Story* will wear better on further readings.

Bruce King

▪ **ISMAIL KADARE**. *Broken April*. New York. New Amsterdam Books. 1990. 216 pages.

When the writer Bessian Vorpsi announced the destination of his honeymoon to friends and acquaintances at a dinner party in Tirana, he was met by a stunned silence. His young bride Diana was taken aback as well at the thought of spending a holiday on a desolate plateau of the northern Albanian Alps. Would not the sparkling beaches of the Albanian Riviera or Italy or even France have been more appropriate for protagonists of the upper middle class of prewar Albania's burgeoning little capital? Some friends could understand that Bessian, as a writer, was fascinated by the prospects of a journey by car into the past, among the feudal and feuding mountain tribes of the north, a primitive society as yet untouched by modern civilization. But what of his poor bride Diana? The more adventuresome envied her too: "You'll be escaping the world of reality for the world of legend, literally the world of epic that scarcely exists anymore."

Take 2: a murder. Gjorg Berisha has accomplished what all his family and relatives insisted he must do: cleanse his honor by slaying his brother's murderer from the rival Kryeqyqe clan. There was no way out of the bloody rituals of vendetta, anchored in the ancient Canon of Lek Dukagjin. Whole families had been wiped out in the "taking of blood," and now he too was obliged to follow suit, only to set himself up as the next victim. Everything was regulated by tribal law, including the thirty-day truce during which he would be allowed to spend his last days out in the sunlight and during which he would have to journey through the mountains to submit "blood money" to the feudal *geheja e gjakut* (blood steward), keeper of the records. It was on Gjorg's journey to the bleak fortress of Orosh that he was startled to see one of the rare horseless carriages he had heard of, a vehicle conveying a beautiful young lady from the city. Diana too had not failed to notice the young tribesman on their way to the "Inn of the Two Roberts." Inevitably, Bessian's morbid fascination with the bloody custom and Diana's erotic attraction to Gjorg, a growing obsession which draws her indeed into the other world, lead to the couple's estrangement.

Though the plot is set in the 1930s, *Broken April* (originally published in 1980 as *Prilli i thyer*) has little to do with Ismail Kadare's other well-known novels of twentieth-century Albania: *Gjenerali i ushtrisë së vdekur* (1961; Eng. *The General of the Dead Army;* see BA 46:1, p. 162), *Kronikë në gur* (1971; Eng. *Chronicle in Stone;* see WLT 61:4, p. 668), *Dimri i madh* (The Great Winter; 1977; see WLT 62:3, p. 493), and *Koncert në fund të dimrit* (Concert at the End of Winter; 1988; see WLT 63:2, p. 347). It must rather be ranked among the au-

thor's cycle of medieval tales (Albanian historians utilize the term *medieval* rather liberally to include events well into the eighteenth century), in which myth and legend mingle with the harsh realities of Albanian history. Among the latter novels are *Kështjella* (The Castle; 1970), *Ura me tri harqe* (The Three-Arched Bridge; 1978), and *Kush e solli Doruntinën* (1980; Eng. *Doruntine;* see WLT 61:2, p. 332). Despite its medieval flavor, *Broken April* focuses on a timeless institution, one which has been endemic to the northern Albanian tribes until quite recently. In neighboring Kosova there have been virtually thousands of families discreetly entrapped in these bloody rites to this very day, though deprived of all the romantic frills of a "blood steward," et cetera. The antivendetta campaign there, led by prominent Kosova Albanian intellectuals, has recently resulted in the "pacification" of more than nine hundred blood feuds.

Over the last thirty years Ismail Kadare (see, this issue, pp. 256–63, and WLT 58:1, pp. 40–42) has invited the reader on many a fascinating journey into curious episodes of Albanian history and into the more exotic aspects of its little-known culture. There can also be no doubt that he has contributed more than any other author to the advancement of contemporary Albanian letters, both through his works and through his candid criticism of mediocrity and politically motivated stereotyping. He has clashed publicly on several occasions in recent years with the critic Koço Bihiku, protagonist of an orthodox socialist realism, and has accused Albanian critics in general of impeding literary creativity. Most Albanian intellectuals agree with him, many of them openly now. If anyone can bring about a revolution in Albanian literature from within the political system, it will be Ismail Kadare.

Robert Elsie

▪ **DAVID MALOUF**. *The Great World*. London. Chatto & Windus. 1990. iv + 332 pages.

David Malouf's seventh work of fiction sets up a dependent and contrasting relationship between two Australian men, Digger Keen and Vic Curran, and follows their complementary but contrasting lives from their initial meeting as Pow's in Malaysia during World War II to the time of Vic's death in 1987. Rich in documentary detail and possessing a large cast, Malouf's novel records the historical events which affect the characters' lives: the Depression, the war, social change in Australia from hippies through yuppies, financial boom and bust. He is more interested, however, in what his narrator describes as "all those unique and repeatable events, the little sacraments of daily existence, movements of the heart and intimations of the close but inexpressible grandeur and terror of things, that is our *other* history." This private history forms the substance of *The Great World*.

As in earlier novels (see e.g. *WLT* 60:1, p. 174), Malouf is interested in time, in continuity, and in a character's relationship to place. While juxtaposing scenes of past and future as a kind of continuous present, he focuses in another way on his two protagonists. Digger Keen is raised at Keen's Crossing, a ferry point on the Hawkesbury where his father's family has lived for more than a hundred years. Centering in one spot, Digger, through his photographic memory which can reproduce the detailed past at will and through his close observation, understands the interconnectedness of all phenomena. Of Digger and his vision of the nature of things, Malouf writes, "Every moment was dense with lives, all crossing and interconnecting or exerting pressure on one another, and not just human lives either; the narrowest patch of earth at the Crossing, as he had known since he was two years old, was crowded with little centres of activity, visible or invisible."

In contrast, Vic Curran lives many lives: child of an alcoholic father, orphaned ward of a wealthy Sydney family, then an international tycoon and failed father. He is successful in public, alienated in private. Throughout his changing life, even at the point of his death, Vic consults his alter ego, Digger Keen. What Digger offers is a kind of balance and a witnessing that, in his various forms, Vic has a continuous and recognizable self. Like Digger, Vic also has a special relationship to time. At various points in his life, from childhood into maturity, from the Pow camp to a successful life in Sydney, Vic projects himself into his own future, recognizing the self he will become, witnessing finally the white-haired old man who cannot save himself from his own destiny.

Throughout the novel Malouf brings together several generations of Australian characters who participate in telling both a public and private history of Australia, a history segmented in time but in no sense bound by it.

Ray Willbanks

1992

■**TARIQ ALI**. *Redemption*. London. Chatto & Windus (Random House UK, distr.). 1990. vi + 280 pages.

Tariq Ali comes to fiction from a respectable writing career in politics, history, biography, and, most recently,

stage drama with a sharp focus on the contemporary world. On Christmas Eve 1989, in Paris, as the seventy-year-old Trotskyist patriarch Ezra Einstein watches on TV a Ceauşescu executioner make the sign of the cross, he seems even to forget the bliss of his late married life, he whose "fingers had rested more often on the keys and body of his antique writing aid [his fifty-five-year-old typewriter] than on the more intimate sections of the female anatomy." He issues a letter forthwith to convene a congress to discuss the world situation following the collapse of the East European regimes and the changes in the Soviet Union. As the oppressed classes have generally failed to be responsive to their program, the brigade considers changing its methods. Ezra himself proposes "that we go into these religions and fight to establish a connection between Heaven and Earth," because "one of the weaknesses of Marxism and all other isms descended from it has been a lack of understanding of ethics, morality, and, dare I say it, spirituality."

The possibility of redemption, however, is always considered tongue-in-cheek, and the gloom caused by the collapse of the Alternative System is beaten out with wit and banter. Although the new challenges include the formation of a new goulash religion called Christlamasonism and moving into the Catholic Church itself, the world congress falls short of evolving any workable theme or strategy; but there is a plenitude of jokes born of an earthy realism, as most matters are thought worthy of being "sorted out through friendly negotiations under the quilt."

While the larger issues of ideas and society are far from being resolved, solace and even blessedness (with a real halo over Ezra's infant daughter's head) are found in the formation of positive personal relations and private worlds. Ali's novel itself is a detached commentary on the enterprise. Dissentient comrade Cathy Fox refuses to attend the congress or join the excavation of Trotsky's grave in Mexico in search of some documents, but she views the dying ideological world with hope: "Something will be reborn . . . but how and when and in what shape it is impossible to predict. The whole world has to be remade." The *New Life Journal* is cited as derriding Kundera's sexist and nihilistic attitudes, and Maya, Ezra's wife, notes (in "The Chapter of Learning and Forgetting"—an obvious parody) her own reservations about the new cult novelist. The entries cited from the *Encyclopedia Trotskyana* and the narrator's comments together make up a hilarious text which is mock-learning and police work at the same time. This clever device also provides for a latter-day dramatic aside and a metafictional source of both fact and its factitious extensions. The lie about the existence of the

Trotsky letters turns out to be a truth, even if their contents are different from those presumed and announced. Although the Movement and its saints must all be seen without their robes, as well as frequently without their undergarments, all the gains are in achieving true humanity of character, with Ezra preaching plain morals and finding his peace amid his family, earnestly if comically lactating and feeding Ho, his baby. The ending, with Maya reading Ezra's journal written for Ho's tenth birthday, contains a poem, an exhortation ascribed to Goethe in which Ali, with all his riotous energy and wit, has found the right note with which to *cure* a cynical world: "Build it again, / Great Child of the Earth, / Build it again / With a finer worth / In thine own bosom build it on high! / Take up thy life once more: / Run the race again! / High and clear / Let a lovelier strain / Ring out than ever before!"

Beneath the poetic fancy, the narrative suggests screen adaptations and a simpler field-sequential of events. Surely, if Goethe and Trotsky gang up together in the "Bandung File" (BBC's Channel 4 program which Tariq Ali produced for several years), a redemption will become inevitable.

Alamgir Hashmi

■**JAMAICA KINCAID**. *Lucy*. New York. Farrar, Straus & Giroux. 1990. x + 164 pages.

With *Lucy* Jamaica Kincaid continues a story of West Indian female development. Whereas the earlier bildungsroman-style works *At the Bottom of the River;* (1983; see *WLT* 58:2, p. 316) and *Annie John* (1985; see *WLT* 59:4, p. 644) dealt with the adolescent years of a girl in the Caribbean, the new book presents a single learning year—the nineteenth—in the life of a character called Lucy, in the new setting of the United States. Lucy is an immigrant engaged to work as an au pair for a wealthy white couple and their four young daughters. Her year is complexly lived with its attendant difficult times, but it provides Lucy with learning experiences that enable her to manage the cultural change and her passage. By the end of this year she can appreciate the commitment of sisterhood (with her employer, for instance), has negotiated a social world of friends and lovers, and has embarked on an independent life provided for by a job as a photographer's helper. She has, moreover, survived the separation from her West Indian mother and upbringing, tasting an independence she has craved for many years. However, the persistence of unreconciled ambivalence toward her mother, guilt about her recently deceased father, and fears concerning her uncharted future becloud this newly gained freedom. The end of the work thus suggests a problematic future, though the fact that Lucy identifies herself as a writer—the act of inscribing her name, Lucy Josephine Potter, across the top of a journal notebook signifies this—indicates a self-authenticating, defining, and authorizing gesture of significance.

Compared to the earlier works, *Lucy* engages a thicker web of conflicts. Coming-of-age dilemmas in the preceding works involved the more limited parameters of home and small-island environment. Thus, conflicts were essentially the result of the circumstances of family (with the mother considered the most central aspect of "oppression"), of the social world of peers and adults, of the adolescent's anxieties of physical maturation and sexuality. The later work complicates these conflicts, introducing cultural and geographic change and displacement as new factors in the life experiences of the young girl. Lucy finds that she must negotiate an identity in a culture that is for all practical purposes an unknown to her, and one with operant discourses of race, class, and gender that she must quickly decipher. She focuses her alien's hostility to this culture upon Mariah, her employer. She is often enraged by the confidence of this all-American woman (whom she eventually comes to love, however), as for example in her need to wish to proclaim in great self-confidence, "I have Indian blood." Lucy considers such racial acknowledgment as transgressive; it serves to deny history. She feels that "victor and vanquished" are historically separate events of being. Contemplating her own Indian heritage—she is part Carib—Lucy tells herself that to claim Carib status would be to totemize it.

As an immigrant, Lucy bears comparison with other immigrants. Similarly, she feels threatened in the U.S. (she is, she well knows, part of an economic underclass); similarly, she is heartened by the prospects of freedom and choice there. When she first arrives, Lucy is the disappointed immigrant; the U.S. is "ordinary" and "dirty." Unusually perceptive and sensitive, however, she forgoes superficial knowledge of the culture and instead engages in a dialogic confrontation with it. Not victimlike, she expresses rather than suppresses her differences and individuality.

Lucy also makes a strong statement about the difficult terms of living under colonialism. A good example of this comes in the first chapter, when Lucy is being pressed to show admiration for daffodils. As she vehemently protests, these flowers are for her a symbol of cultural imperialism. They bring back memories of her school days in the West Indies, when she had been expected to memorize a poem about daffodils—flowers, she reminds her employer, that are not native to the islands. That foreign material (in all respects) should have been dominant in the education she received, and native material made superfluous to education, evidenced for Lucy the cultural oppression that she had endured. Negative reinforcements were the patriotic songs, such as "Rule Britannia," that tried to indoctrinate the West Indian into the discourse of European superiority and native inferiority. This past, too, Lucy seeks to escape.

The work ends with Lucy's statements, "One day I was a child and then I was not" and "Your past is the person you no longer are." The fact that Lucy gives the appearance of believing this is indication, of course, that she is barely twenty years old.

Evelyn J. Hawthorne

■ **J. M. G. LE CLÉZIO**. *Onitsha*. Paris. Gallimard (Schoenhof, distr.). 1991. 258 pages.

Once again J. M. G. Le Clézio, a novelist fascinated by the non-Western and an anthropologist respecting the Other, takes readers to a site that destroys Westerners; that is, the site either encourages their most egregious exploitative colonialism or puts them in the thrall of difference. The latter happens when the new non-Western environment casts a spell severing the Westerners from their own kind but keeping a barrier between them and the natives.

In *Onitsha* the time is the immediate postwar period, and the site is a British sub-Saharan colony about five years from independence movements. Geoffrey Allen, a distribution agent for the United Africa Company, retrieves his Italian wife Marilou and their son Fintan from their wartime refuge on the French Riviera. The twelve-year-old Fintan, Le Clézio's chief narrative consciousness here, must learn a "new" father and his language as well as an African river culture upon which the British have overlaid a colonial culture. His father is re-creating by twilight-sleep intuition the journey a fabulous black Egyptian queen must have taken to bring her people to a landmark up the river from Allen's outpost. Marilou, by another kind of intuition, connects with the female psyche of the native queen. Fintan, both intensely naïve and immensely intuitive, makes contact with but cannot become friends with two youngsters who might well be the last survivors of his father's imagined tribal royalty—if such ever existed. All three, however, must return to England when Geoffrey loses his job. At the novel's end, twenty years later in the late 1960s, Fintan, a French teacher in a British boys' school, knows that the special, troubled, riven society his family knew has been reclaimed not just by the native Africans but also by the roaring river and the overwhelming landscape, with few buildings remaining from the temporary colony.

Le Clézio, true to his method, protects himself from presumption by showing a non-Western setting from the point of view of spellbound Westerners who cannot penetrate it. It is the mystery of the unknowable Other, the Other forbidden to outsiders. The inner narratives imagined by Geoffrey are cast in the form of recorded oral history. The transitions between Fintan's traditional third-person narratives of almost understanding by a somewhat bedazzled adolescent who almost understands and Geoffrey's narratives of pseudo-oral history are made quite smoothly. The characters may be disoriented, but the readers never are. The ending, twenty years later, though a bit lame, does minister to our reader needs. All in all, an expertly managed piece of professional fiction-writing, but a little hard to take seriously.

Marilyn Gaddis Rose

■ **WISŁAWA SZYMBORSKA**. *People on a Bridge*. Adam Czerniawski, tr. London. Forest Books (Dufour, distr.). 1990. xvi + 80 pages.

Long recognized in Poland as a leading voice in contemporary Polish poetry, Wisława Szymborska has not achieved the same popularity in the English-speaking world as other poets of her generation such as Zbigniew Herbert and Tadeusz Rózewicz. Still, *People on a Bridge* is not the first introduction of Szymborska's verse to English readers. Czesław Miłosz included poems by her in his seminal anthology *Postwar Polish Poetry* (1965), and in 1981 Princeton University Press published a selection of her poems translated by Magnus Kryński and Robert Maguire (see *WLT* 56:2, p. 368). Let us hope that the present volume, a welcome addition to those earlier translations, will help bring Szymborska the recognition that she deserves.

The poems selected by Adam Czerniawski come from four different collections and span a period of twenty years. Rather than adhere to chronology, Czerniawski has grouped the poems according to recurring themes, most prominently the problem of art's relationship to time, death, and reality. Thematic unity is further emphasized by a ring composition. The poems opening and closing the book (the only two given both in English translation and in the Polish original) deal with the precariousness of human life, symbolized both times by the image of a bridge, and the inability of art—despite its futile attempt to resist the flow of time—to penetrate the mystery of death and existence.

At the center of Szymborska's attention is the disparity between the limitations of the poetic imagination and the unlimited vastness of reality: "Four billion people on this earth, / but my imagination is as it was" ("Big Numbers" The mathematical value of π comes closer to expressing the infinite richness of the universe than does the poetic imagination: "It cannot be grasped *six five three five* at a glance, / *eight nine* in a calculus / *seven nine* in imagination, / or even *three two three eight* in a conceit, that is, a comparison." Art catches only individual facts and existences, a fraction of reality. Poetry, marked by insufficiency and imperfection, is a selection, a renunciation, a passing over in silence, and a "sigh" rather than a "full breath." The poet, like anyone else, is unable to transgress his or her own "I," his own particular existence. Being himself, he cannot be what he is not.

In the opposition between reality and art, life and intellect, Szymborska declares herself on the side of reality and life. Ideas are most often pretexts to kill, a deadly weapon, whether under the guise of an artistic experiment ("Experiment"), a political Utopia ("Utopia"), or ideological fanaticism ("The Terrorist, He Watches"). Szymborska sides with reality against art and ideology, and this choice situates her in the mainstream of postwar Polish poetry alongside Miłosz, Herbert, and Bialoszewski.

Like Bialoszewski, although in a different idiom, Szymborska extols the everyday and the ordinary. Her "miracle mart" is made of barking dogs, trees reflected in a pond, gentle breezes and gusty storms, the world "ever-present." Even in dreams she appreciates most of all their ability to create the illusion of reality. In the theater she is moved by a glimpse of actors caught beneath the curtain more than by tragic tirades. Her poetry reverses the accepted view of what is important and what is unimportant; it puts forward common and humble reality at the expense of history and politics: "Pebbles by-passed on the beach can be as rounded / as the anniversaries of insurrections" ("May Be Left Untitled").

Pervaded by the spirit of contestation, Wislawa Szymborska's poetry thrives on paradox. A mixture of "loftiness and common speech" ("Unwritten Poem Review"), it is subtle, witty, and ironic.

Bogdana Carpenter

▪ **LUISA VALENZUELA.** *Novela negra con argentinos.* Hanover, N.H. Ediciones del Norte. 1990. vi + 234 pages.

Novela negra con argentinos works on diverse levels of meaning and structure. It is an Argentine novel in its main characters' speech, in a few literary references, and in the references to violence and disappearance: the protagonists act out the suffering of the body that can become manifest when mental functioning is severely blocked by fear or incomprehension. It is a detective story or murder mystery in that a murder is purported to have taken place and its agent to have been identified; yet the motive and, later, the victim are virtually erased from the text. The novelistic text thus slowly slides into the dramatic, with various fragmented scenes of eccentric characters who enter and leave the limelight as if emerging and retiring into chaotic darkness, leaving the reader/spectator with the uneasy desire to define his or her situation as pleasurable or painful yet unable to complete the diagnosis.

The nexus between the discursive and generic forms occurs on the level of the concept of writing the body, of writing (i.e., the self-conscious text) and the body which produces or acts out that text—i.e., inscribes itself on the page of life or reveals the marks by which the testimony of human experience (historical, fictional) is recorded. Taking literature too seriously gets Agustín Palant into trouble, makes him a murderer; it makes Roberta lose track of reality. She observes in a leading, perhaps overtly self-conscious and parodying way: "¿Dónde estaría el límite? Entre lo escrito y lo vivido, ¿cómo reconocer la frontera?"

Writing interpreted as reality in itself rather than as invention or representation results in the unwriting of passages or characters, or writing over them, rewriting them in contradictory ways that undermine their identity as characters in a novel. The androgynous potential of the human body, or the fluctuating traits of sexual orientation, from bisexuality, homosexuality, and heterosexual relationships, all of which may show machismo, frigidity, tendencies toward transvestism, and regression to the presexual state of the womb—these are reflected in the discourse of the text that is *Novela negra con argentinos*. Roberta is also called Robbie, Rob, and Bob, whereas Agustín's series of names progressively ridicule and purposely emasculate him.

Both characters ultimately become caricatures of themselves, victims of their author, who gives every sign of knowing exactly what she is doing with them. Unable nevertheless to achieve clear definition, they ultimately remain trapped in their connotations, nuances, and suggestive postures. They are but figures scribbled on a literary stage, signs which stand for themselves only, or perhaps not, and metaphors of the gestures made by writers, above all Argentine ones living in New York, and those who are questioning the desire, occasionally nightmarish or subtle but always Eros-bound, that informs writing as a whole—writers like Luisa Valenzuela, creator of Roberta and Agustín, of Roberta/Agustín, who seems to play her part in the novel utilizing a postmodern perspective, self-reliant and self-ridiculing. One could not ask for more succulent read-

ing than *Novela negra con argentinos,* which often savors
itself and manages to contemplate its own banquet.

Kathleen N. March

■ **YEVGENY YEVTUSHENKO.** *The Collected
Poems 1952–1990.* Albert C. Todd, James Ragan,
eds. New York. Holt. 1991. xxvi + 662 pages.

The new *Collected Poems 1952–1990* reflects Yevgeny
Yevtushenko's poetic career in microcosm: vast and uneven, sometimes irritating, often appealing, and ever astonishing in its variety. The title is somewhat misleading, since the volume offers only a selection from
Yevtushenko's extensive oeuvre, and in addition, several long poems are represented in excerpts only. Yevtushenko's allusiveness can be a problem for Western
readers; a few names and terms are explained in footnotes, but this practice could profitably have been expanded. A helpful feature is the chronological list of
poems with their Russian titles, date and place of first
publication, and location, if any, in the 1983 *Sobranie
sochinenii* (see WLT 59:4, p. 614).

Like the poems themselves, the translations by
twenty-five translators vary in quality. A few are revisions of earlier versions. Most of Yevtushenko's poems
use slant rhyme relying heavily on assonance, a practice
so closely associated with him as to be called "Yevtus-
henkean rhyme" (*evtushenkovskaia rifma*). Russian's rich
phonetic structure allows almost limitless use of this
kind of rhyme; a master of the form and clearly one of
Yevtushenko's teachers was the poet Marina Tsvetaeva.
Wisely, few attempts are made to retain this feature in
the English translations, or indeed to use rhyme at all.

From the beginning of his prolific career in the
early 1950s, Yevtushenko's poetry has been characterized by strong stances on political issues. He praises
Allende and Che Guevara, condemns the Vietnam War,
and deplores the situation in Northern Ireland. His criticism is not limited to the West, however. A popular
and privileged poet whose readings at one time filled
football stadiums and who was given unprecedented
freedom to travel abroad, he nevertheless warned
against abuses at home, castigating militarists, dishonest
bureaucrats, and toadies of all kinds. These critical
poems range from "The Heirs of Stalin" and "Babi Yar"
in the early 1960s to "Momma and the Neutron Bomb"
and poems about the dissident Andrei Sakharov and the
Afghanistan war in the 1980s. The roots of his ferocious
morality are to be found in his love for Russia, and in
his stubborn belief in the ideals of the revolution.

Even the semiofficial poet was not immune from
censorship, however. Included in the new collection are

Yevgeny Yevtushenko *(Gil Jain)*

a number of poems which were written during the sixties but for political reasons could not be published
until many years later. Among them are verses to fellow
poets Tsvetaeva (1967/1987) and Esenin (1965/1988),
"Russian Tanks in Prague" (1968/1990), and "The Ballad of the Big Stamp," a bawdy tale about castration for
the good of the party (1966/1989).

Yevtushenko is at his best when he is specific and
detailed, and this happens most frequently in poems
dealing with his native Siberia, its nature and history,
its sailors, whalers, berry pickers. These include the
long poem "Zima Junction" (1955) and a series written
in 1964 about life on the northern frontier. Yevtushenko has a strong visual sense (he is an accomplished photographer), and color often plays an important role in
his works. In the fairy-tale-like "Snow in Tokyo: A Japanese Poem" (1974), for example, a proper and repressed Japanese matron discovers the wonders of
painting and finds the courage to rebel against her stul-
tifying life through the world of color.

A thread running through Yevtushenko's work is
the importance of poetry and the responsibility of the
poet to mankind. He constantly questions his own talent and mission, thus continuing the Russian tradition
of meta-poetry. Likewise very Russian is the dialogue

between writers living and dead which Yevtushenko carries on, in poems addressed to or evoking Pushkin, Pasternak, Neruda, and Jack London, along with numerous others.

Finally, Yevtushenko's poetry is a kind of personal diary which details his extensive travels and especially his many love affairs and marriages. Remarkable love poems follow the poet from first love, to the birth of his sons, to the sadness of falling out of love again. The poems contain a rich fabric of quarrels, memories, farewells, even a conversation with his dog, who shares the poet's grief that his woman has gone. Perhaps the most attractive thing about Yevtushenko is his human breadth, his willingness to lay himself open to our reactions. *The Collected Poems* provides the reader with numerous opportunities to become acquainted with this engaged and engaging poet, one of the important, questioning voices of our age.

Patricia Pollock Brodsky

1993

■ **BLAGA DIMITROVA**. *The Last Rock Eagle*. Brenda Walker, Vladimir Levchev, Belin Tonchev, trs. Alexander Shurbanov, intro. London. Forest Books (Dufour, distr.). 1992. xi + 81 pages.

■ ——. *Noshten dnevnik*. Atanas Vasilev, ill. Sofia. Nov Zlatorok. 1992. 82 pages.

Blaga Dimitrova is a prominent, prolific author of international renown and currently the esteemed vice president of a new democratic Bulgaria. She has published twenty-three volumes of poetry, four novels, three plays, critical literary writing, and several books of political reportage, as well as verse translations from French, German, Polish, and classical Greek. Her work has been translated into several languages. *The Last Rock Eagle* is a collection of representative poems which exemplify Dimitrova's art as well as her moral and metaphysical philosophy. As the world-renowned semiologist Julia Kristeva observes, Dimitrova "can turn thought into poetry, meditation into rhythm and flavour, colours into ideas, judgement into fragrance, vision into ethical statement. Seldom has a woman's writing been at once more cerebral and more sensual."

The majority of these seventy-one pieces are short and may act upon the reader as some kind of aphorisms, pondering the difficulty, the complexity, of being. In "Experience" the poet writes: "There is no trace / of these monumental celebrations. // Everything

is transient, / but the most transient / is what we call eternal: / friendship, / fame, / power, / success, / victory. // Only the most fragile lasts: / a deep scar left by you, Love." "Fragmentation," a sort of philosophical reflection, reminds one somewhat of La Rochefoucauld's approach in his *Maximes*.

Fragmented personality divided

into together   and yet not a whole,

into yesterday   and never,

into home   and nowhere,

into name   and no one,

into face   and no entity,

into voice   and no voice,

into perhaps   and no way—

Could it ever be made whole?

In the very succinct four-line poem "Grass" the poet forcefully conveys a vital process that leads to wisdom: "I am not afraid / they'll stamp me flat. / Grass stamped flat / soon becomes a path."

When the subject matter requires, Dimitrova writes long poems with the same mastery over language, imagery, and ideas. In "Madonna from Russe," dedicated "to a mother of self-sacrifices," Dimitrova deplores the continual poisoning of the Danube waters near the town of Russe, which is located opposite a Romanian chloride plant polluting that entire area and causing congenital deformities. "Let me see the sun!" the child says. That has become impossible, however, and "a woman aborts the future."

"Sisyphus" is a fifteen-stanza poem dedicated to Václav Havel which considers the peculiarity and, in a sense, the pointlessness of human experience. "Not a boulder! but petrified history, / humiliations, battles and pain, / a petrified fate of a people." Nevertheless, in spite of mankind's awareness of the absurdity of its condition, the poet convincingly formulates the idea that only man is capable of giving significance to and creating some goal in a world devoid of perceivable meaning: "Sisyphus, with a curse / you are doomed to the stone, / so as to inspire soul into it." In "Night Diary" Dimitrova reaffirms her belief in human capacity to overcome the *néant* of our situation and to move in a direction of accomplishment: "The dead breathe life into me. / I guide myself as a blind / across chaotic crossroads. / Out of darkness will come the light."

Brenda Walker, Vladimir Levchev, and Belin Tonchev, all authors in their own right, have acquitted themselves admirably in their task as translators. Alexander Shurbanov's articulate introduction is most helpful as it assists the reader toward an understanding of the status Dimitrova has achieved in her country. Shurbanov refers to her as a "national" poet. Walker's renditions of the Bulgarian originals have preserved meaning and form and most of the uniqueness of Dimitrova's stylistic singularities. Once again Forest Books has excelled in its presentation of a quality collection. Dimitrova's beautiful photograph adorns the book's jacket, and the printing and layout of poems are impeccable from beginning to end.

Noshten dnevnik (Night Diary) comprises seventy poems (grouped under three headings), all written between 1989 and 1992. This is the most recent book Dimitrova has published, and a considerable number of poems reflect the painful social changes and political transformations that have been taking place in Bulgaria since 1989. In the first section, entitled "From One Instant to Another: The Cry of Labor Pains" (clearly alluding to the birth of new societies in Bulgaria and other East European countries), there are several poems which translate the devious means employed by communist leaders to retain their power. In "It Is Not Dignified" Dimitrova addresses herself to those who undermine the efforts of the Bulgarian people to build a democracy by setting one group of people against another: "[How can you] incite / brother against brother / like wolfhounds after bait. // [And] to divide / one's own people, / just to rule. //. . . / To foment / hatred in the back / of hope."

Similarly, in "Interrogation," written on the occasion of the arrest of several dissidents (including Dimitrova herself) in the course of May 1989, the poet asks, "Why can we not understand each other?" "What exactly do you want? / From me—what?" Later in the poem Dimitrova states, "What in reality you are looking for / Is that which does not exist." In October of that same year the communist regime fell. In "The Prague Spring Is Still Early" Dimitrova addresses herself to Václav Havel with admiration and praise, writing that "Their [the communists'] towers are hollow, for they are filled with insults and abuse." In this section are poems with such titles as "Common European Home," "The Seeker of Truth," and "The Purest Road"—all promoting justice and idealism. The subtitle of the second part, "From Fear to Laughter," contains verse composed between November 1989 and February 1990, when the communist system collapsed. The four-line "Utopia for the People" aptly characterizes the spirit of this group of poems: "Didn't we study on order / teachings for a new life? / With intoxicating Utopia / slept through half a century in a yoke," obviously referring to the forty-five years of communist rule.

The last part, entitled "From One Myth to Another," offers a variety of very long and short pieces dedicated to mythological figures such as Sisyphus, Don Quixote, and other humanists. "The Return of the Non-Returner" is devoted to Georgi Markov, murdered in London for continually exposing communist corruption in Bulgaria through broadcasts of the BBC. The tone in most of these poems is a mixture of celebration for the possibility of a brighter future ("The Earth Is Resurrecting") and the necessity and worth of service to one's country ("Fountain"), but there is also pessimism about what is to come. In "Homo Futuris" Dimitrova presents a dilemma: how a manrobot would know why and where to go.

Through her powerful and esthetically outstanding poetry, as well as through her moral rectitude, Blaga Dimitrova contributes to the shaping of a new national conscience. She is in the company of the Václav Havels of Eastern Europe.

Yuri Vidov Karageorge

■**GUILLERMO CABRERA INFANTE.** *Mea Cuba.* Barcelona. Plaza & Janés / Cambio 16. 1992. 505 pages.

Guillermo Cabrera Infante, ever the punster, has gathered here articles, essays, notes, speeches, and letters published in various international newspapers, magazines, and literary journals. They cover the period 1968–1992 yet do not include or represent all his cultural or political writings. Divided into three sections— "A propósito" (on his role in Cuban culture), "Vidas para leerlas" (purportedly biographies of Cuban authors), and "Vida única" (on Cuban and other topics)— the book is really a passionate, albeit flawed biographical assessment of Cuban cultural politics since the mid-sixties. Inimitable in style, obviously self-revealing, full of information, insight, and gossip, hilariously combative, *Mea Cuba* may well become a definitive view of one side of the t(r)opic that Cuba has become.

When this book was published in mid-November 1992, Juan Goytisolo praised it in the Spanish press as an ironic homage to Fidel Castro, the "real" father of all Cubans, whether they be in Cuba, the cemetery, prison, or exile. This sort of obsession, akin to arguing that José Martí might be the only true Cuban-American, is the source of Cabrera Infante's greatest strength and weakness in the collection. From its allusive title (which can refer either to whatever faults the author represses or to a bodily function command that his homeland is carrying out without his ranting and raving) to the now tiresome infinite play on words, these texts cover a wide and pathetic state of intellectual affairs and persecutions.

Cabrera Infante's book includes divisive propaganda parading in the guise of concerned essayistic discourse. In this sense, it is no different from the concerned scholarship published in Cuba and in the United States. However, the difference is that Cabrera Infante would never entertain a dialogue. His texts are monologues, and frequently lengthy onanisms whose irreverence is also tiresome. Thus, in the second section of the book, his portraits of Lezama Lima, Virgilio Piñera, Lydia Cabrera, Labrador Ruiz, Carpentier, Almendros, Arenas, and others are vehemently negative. It is difficult for Cabrera Infante to see wholesomeness or goodness, even among those he considers friends. The piece on Calvert Casey, for example, is representative of the homophobia the author dare not speak. Nevertheless, the telling of these unparalleled lives is the best part of the book. In spite of the author's wishes, his texts read as the ideal format for what is bandied about the United States as cultural studies. Despite one's differences with his politics, Cabrera Infante's knowledge of Cuban literariness is the broadest, liveliest, and nastiest to date.

In this regard, if we limit ourselves to the many and still ongoing imbroglios about the infamous Padilla affair, Cabrera Infante's "Mordidas del caimán barbudo" (Bites from the Bearded Crocodile) is the fullest accounting of that fiasco. This essay, the longest in the first section (and the book), shows Cabrera Infante at his best, his cruelest, and his poorest—poorest in that his puns, which somehow work better in English, have now been retranslated. Thus, many of his Groucho Marx borrowings will be lost to the general Hispanic reading public that may buy Mea Cuba once the academics are done with it. Among the various immigrant groups in the U.S. the reaction could well be dame un break, chico, since of the many Latin phrases with which he sprinkles his text, in situ (as in his not being in Cuba for twenty-seven years) never appears. The first part of the book is as historically schizophrenic and myopic as Arenas's recent sexual autobiography Antes que anochezca. Cabrera Infante traces and reviews (at times supplying contemporary addenda to pieces published in previous decades) his problems with Castroite Cuba. Trying to decide between self-hagiography and diatribe, he opts for both, with frequent dashes of invective. There should be no doubt in anyone's mind that his mastery of the Spanish language is always present, but it could be put to better use. One can sympathize with his protestations, and academic Cuban exiles may be the first to rush to his defense; but he doth protest too much, in the worst way. Nevertheless, his own defense of Latin America's "Hispanicity" in the third section of the book is well wrought and incontestable, especially from one of the only tried-and-true bilingual authors Spanish America has produced and read.

Mea Cuba is a Who's Who, What's What, Where's Where of contemporary Cuban letters. The author's eyewitness (and hearsay) account of what many of us are still fighting and writing about is difficult to circumvent or ignore. Cabrera Infante, star-struck, provides his readers with a cast of thousands; but some, like Carpentier, are struck by millions of his poisonous writerly shards, and the evidence could not be more damaging. Much like the main crystal in a kaleidoscope, Cabrera Infante manages to direct that cast of thousands for our and his enjoyment, and pain. From the very start, and throughout his book, the author states that these texts are political in nature. In this sense, paradoxically, I cannot think of a better overview of what Jorge Edwards has called "Cuban messes," but I also cannot think of a better or more personal collection of cheap shots on which to waste an extraordinary amount of talent and black humor. One will miss the exclusion of Cabrera Infante's morsels about Spanish American soap operas, popular music, or his troubles with Spanish censors (winked at here), but Mea Cuba should be read, if only to see how its protagonist became an inorganic intellectual, the author of really one well-known novel. This is so because, in naming or calling names, either feigning discretion or showing cowardice, he is seductively selective, and at times convincing.

Will H. Corral

■ **PATRICK CHAMOISEAU**. *Texaco*. Paris. Gallimard (Schoenhof, distr.). 1992. 432 pages.

In late 1992 *Texaco* was awarded France's Prix Goncourt, a much-coveted prize that usually attracts some controversy, as was the case with the first Goncourt awarded to a black writer, René Maran, in 1921. Patrick Chamoiseau, well recognized as one of the leading writers and intellectuals associated with the *créolité* movement, has not escaped some unkind comment concerning the wisdom of the jury's choice.

Nominally a novel, *Texaco* expands the traditional notions of the genre. It could qualify as an oral history of epic proportions. It is the narration by an African Martinican woman, Marie-Sophie Laborieux, to the author, who calls himself the "Marqueur de paroles" but whom Marie-Sophie occasionally addresses, with obvious relish, as "Oiseau de Cham." The author, as he explains in the post-face, first took copious notes, then resorted to a tape recorder, trying "to write life." The narrative, in mock imitation of archeological periodization, is divided into four epochs, which represent African Martinican building materials: straw, crate wood, fibrocement, and concrete. In terms of European historiography, the time span would encompass the years from circa 1823 to 1980. Biblical allusions enlarge the scope of the narrative. It begins with the sermon, not on the mount, but before old rum, and ends with Resurrection—i.e., with the author's endeavor to resurrect life, "écrire la vie."

The narrative locus starts in the city of Saint-Pierre, the cultural capital of the colony, which was annihilated almost like Sodom and Gomorrah by the eruption of Mount Pelée in 1902, and later shifts to a port in the vicinity of Fort-de-France, where tankers arrive to unload their cargoes; hence the locale's name, Texaco. Texaco becomes the refuge of the luckless poor, particularly former plantation slaves in search of urban employment. The place is considered an eyesore by the authorities, who refuse to recognize its existence and constantly harass the squatters with bulldozers and eviction notices. Amid their fight against city hall, reports from various sources indicate that Christ, like a horseman of the apocalypse, is coming to rescue the people.

Marie-Sophie, following a series of vicissitudes in her personal life, becomes willy-nilly the spokesperson for the slumdwellers. She pleads with the authorities (including "notre papa Césaire," then and still today the mayor of Fort-de-France), organizes demonstrations, and, when De Gaulle comes to visit the former colony, prepares a sumptuous feast to show him how hospitable Martinicans can be. The general, perceived as a savior figure, does not come, however. Marie-Sophie engages in a titanic struggle against the owner of the land, a *béké*—i.e., a Frenchman born in the colonies. The people persevere, and in the end, as Christ makes another appearance, the authorities recognize the squatters, install electricity, and incorporate the settlement. Even the vicious *béké* is reconciled with his enemies.

Needless to say, the novel acquires epic dimensions. Fact and fiction intertwine to weave a narrative wherein myth and history complement each other. *Texaco* evokes an ethos and also a vision which, though localized, reaches out far beyond the region.

Juris Silenieks

■ **LAURIS EDMOND**. *New and Selected Poems.* Newcastle upon Tyne, Eng. Bloodaxe (Dufour, distr.). 1992. 215 pages.

Lauris Edmond is another internationally known New Zealand poet, winner of the 1985 Commonwealth Poetry Prize. *New and Selected Poems,* her most recent and most representative collection, gives opportunity to assess nearly twenty years of publication. What gives the volume its special interest is the strong impression of a poetry and a poet in stasis.

This is traditional romantic poetry. It focuses upon the perceptions and emotions of the writer, the honey-dew eater. It is a poetry of observed nature and landscape and of straightforward feeling, as the titles suggest: "Waterfall," "Six Poplar Trees," "Before First Light," "Going to the Grampians," "The Night Burns with a White Fire," "Composition with Window and Bulldozer," "To a Grandson." Image after decorative image, word after word, epithet on "poetic" epithet could, allowing for semantic and syntactic drift, have flowed from quills two hundred years before: "Resonant harmonies," "Rapacious wind. . .the brilliant booty of the leaves," "morning's tender sky," "a dark lake bruised by the winter trees," "the moving pageant of the universe," "feel how the world rolls in its rind of mountains and seas." It is a poetry where voice is crucial, and dialogue or monologue is a favored device. And though Edmond does not employ traditional prosody—apart from a fondness for set numbers of lines to a stanza—there is seldom the echo of colloquial speech or the idiosyncratic freedom of line or sentence or the interleaving of topic or register of much contemporary verse. It is a poetry whose theme is essentially "the natural intermittent light of" the unique self, each living "in the body differently." The highest courage is to face the extinction of that self. And in a late-twentieth-century absence of search for Sublimity or Divinity in what is perceived, the perceptions and the consequent feelings of the observing-reporting-performing self are the centering, the unifying, concern.

There is, however, a second kind of stasis here. Neither Edmond's kind of poetry nor the attitudes it embodies nor the subjects it treats have developed, transmuted, or deepened over the years. She deals with the same topics in the most recent as in the earliest poetry: "Lake Idyll," "Moonshine Valley;" "Brian," "Boy"; "Midwife," "Two Birth Poems"; "The Affair," "Pas de Deux." She employs the same diction, displays the same desire to signal meaning and to impose response upon readers with the same devices.

Of course, poets may have their particular topics and voice; but the Edmond of 1992 is to a quite remarkable degree the Edmond of 1975, as if her talent, her interests, her responses, her poetic forms and language were determined at the outset of her writing career. And perhaps fittingly, the best work in the collection is one of the oldest, the sequence "Wellington Letter," where the ruminating voice movingly recollects the lost loved one. Little new material is included, only some twenty poems not contained in previous volumes, few of those unpublished. This, then, is an excellent introduction to

Edmond's poetry—and to the poetry she has yet to write.

Bernard Gadd

■ **KERI HULME**. *Strands*. Auckland. Auckland University Press (Oxford University Press, distr.). 1992. 65 pages.

Keri Hulme is internationally better known for her Booker Prize-winning novel *The Bone People* (1983) and for her short stories than for her poetry. *Strands,* a collection of work of the past decade, seems intended to present her also as a poet worth noting—and it succeeds.

The sustained major work in the volume is "Fishing the Olearia Tree," followed by a group of substantial poems, "Against the Small Evil Voices." (The title "Deity Considered as Mother Death" captures some of her concerns here.) The collection ends with "Some Wine Songs," considerably lighter and indeed so far out of kilter with the major poetry as to suggest that the publishers wanted to bulk up the collection.

Hulme employs an array of familiar contemporary techniques of impressionistic linguistic collage: the swift glides from place to place, time to time, register to register, language to language (Maori to English), focus to focus, source to source of imagery, allusion, and symbolism. She says in a prologue note: "Words mean / precisely what you want to hear them say / exactly / what you see in them." Nevertheless, this is not poststructural, postmodernist, and certainly not "language" poetry. Hulme's work is too much grounded in a specific place, New Zealand's remote Okarito Lagoon territory (whose image is suggested by the author's cover design), and in a particular people, the Maori. Her purpose too is very different. In the main poems a sustained voice meditates on death, life, their interactions—predatory or otherwise—in renewal, and on a sense both of belonging to nature and of the otherness of nature learned through life in this place and through belonging to this people. The poetry expresses her sense of the discovery, or perhaps the fashioning of, herself, and the overall tone is more earnest, more zestful than witty or verbally gaming.

For those interested to hunt them, there are interconnections with *The Bone People,* even an apparent direct reference to a reader's response; but I think these are more the result of the similarities of the source materials than of a deliberate literary playfulness. Occasionally the use of Maori strikes the ear as no more than a verbal flourish. Sometimes abrupt register switches jar pointlessly. Sometimes Hulme falls into cliché, plati-

tude, or truism. Sometimes the language is a little self-conscious, striving to make its effects. Sometimes the adjectives seem to crowd in. Sometimes the use of Maori cultural allusions may puzzle the uninitiated reader. Still, the voice encourages us to accept all these on our literary voyage with her across a persistent groundswell of romanticism, past wry reflection, the jokey, the intriguing, the beautiful, the bitter, the reminiscent, and a score of other moods and days. In the major poem the olearia tree itself is sighted again and again, affirming each time its central role as potent natural symbol.

The end of the entire collection is celebration: "Ah, sweet life, We share it / with cancers and tapeworms / with bread moulds and string beans / and great white sharks." With this work Keri Hulme at last emerges as a notable New Zealand poet.

Bernard Gadd

■ **DIANA RAZNOVICH**. *Mater erótica*. Barcelona. Robin Book. 1992. 208 pages.

There has never been any doubt as to exactly where Diana Raznovich has been going with her writing: in all three of the major genres the Argentine writer has addressed in highly imaginative ways topics relating to gender and sexual identity and has undertaken the enormous project of constructing an erotic discourse that has some sort of sociopolitical meaning to it. *Mater erótica* consists of two narratives, the first about twice as long as the second. In both cases, the fall of the Berlin Wall is the backdrop to an erotic experience. In the first case it is between the wife of a member of the East German high command and a friend of her teenage son; in the second case it is between a double agent of both Germanies who, under a death threat, lives out a sexual idyll with a sixteen-year-old woman. In both cases the story is told in the first person by the older individual; in both cases an element of bisexuality is involved; in both cases there is some element of gender role exchange; and in both cases there is reference to the climate of sexual repression that functions in all of Western society, with establishment socialism being as Draconian as capitalist democracy.

However, there is more of a narrative transgression in the case of the older woman and more of a narrative of sexual exploitation in the case of the second. What Raznovich seems to be staging here is a juxtaposition between the radical differences in perspectives. In the second narrative it is a masculinist perspective—the cynical double agent who lives out the hours before he is assassinated availing himself effortlessly of the body of an essentially powerless woman, all in the context of free and libertine Paris, the capital of "Love" in all its heterosexist mythology. In the first and longer narrative, in the context of the masculinist repression of female sexuality in an establishment socialism that is homologous to traditional Western and Christian values, a feminist discourse is forged in which the fleshquakes of an awakened sexuality foreshadow the structural earthquakes the woman produces in the society around her.

Raznovich makes use of many of the conventions of masculinist pornography, beginning with the fact that, as an Argentine, she chooses to write in an urban Peninsular dialect that provides her with a voice jarringly different from her other writings, which is much like the stilted language of her generic models. Moreover, the setting of both stories in societies that are not Spanish-speaking reinforces the otherness of her texts, although the first one is more marked than the second in this regard. From a feminist point of view, pornography (which is what Raznovich seems to be reiterating in the second, masculinist-based story) is a profound dystopia that overlaps in significant ways with the actual society of the male abuser, the female victim, and voyeuristic readers whose gender identities position them in various ways with respect to that dystopia and may even remodel it as a fantastic utopia there to lead one out of the sexual conflicts of the real world (both for those who abuse and for those who have internalized abuse as an ideal to be sought). Raznovich's proposition, in the first and feminist narrative, begins by configuring a dystopia that the noncommunist-bloc reader is asked to grasp as reduplicating capitalist society and then to accept the possibility of creating a utopian space within it based on a series of transgressions that install woman as sexual agent, with an agency that replaces feminine lack with a force capable of invalidating masculinist male phallic power. The first-person narrative underscores the greater presence of the woman who no longer speaks the stasis of the *stabat Mater* but articulates the agency of the *Mater erótica,* who will reconfigure society in a liberating and nonphallic fashion.

Despite the elements of bisexuality in both narratives, Raznovich's texts are ultimately resolutely heterosexist and genitalist, which means that her emphasis is on female/male sexual politics rather than alternate sexualities. Nevertheless, within this role frame (which also reduplicates conventional pornography), there is enough erotic delirium to demonstrate that even within traditional male/female roles there is a promise for sexual liberation.

David William Foster

1994

■**RODDY DOYLE**. *Paddy Clarke Ha Ha Ha.* New York. Viking. 1994 (© 1993). 282 pages.

"The past is a foreign country," L. P. Hartley wrote in the opening line of *The Go-Between* (1953); "they do things differently there." This observation applies not only to the collective or societal past but to the individual and psychological past as well: childhood remains—to a remarkable degree—an unexplored territory whose inhabitants have a culture comprising intricate customs and codes that are uniquely its own, seldom recorded or analyzed, usually forgotten in adulthood. Roddy Doyle's *Paddy Clarke Ha Ha Ha,* winner of the 1993 Booker Prize, is a child's-eye view of working-class life in Ireland in the late 1960s, a deft first-person narrative from the point of view of a ten-year-old who describes vividly the day-to-day cares of his boyhood world as well as his contacts with the adult world he cannot always understand. As such, it not only painstakingly evokes the particularities of its time, place, and class but also transcends them, recapturing both the wonder and the perplexity that are experienced before one nears the borders of adolescence and the far stricter boundaries of adulthood.

Unlike the decidedly adult narrative voice in Hartley's novel or in James Joyce's "Araby," for example, Paddy Clarke's is distinctively that of a child—naïve in many ways, direct and idiomatic in its simple-sentence style (similar to that of the first chapter of Joyce's *Portrait of the Artist as a Young Man*), and without precise indicators of the passage of time. Alternately comic and poignant, the novel is remarkably detailed in its portrait of the complex codes of boyhood: the rules that govern seemingly rough-and-ready play, the often gratuitous cruelties, the bonds of loyalty, the secrets and rituals that define status and power among peers. Like Alan Sillitoe's *Key to the Door* (1961), which detailed its protagonist's childhood in working-class Nottingham in the 1930s, *Paddy Clarke Ha Ha Ha* offers an unsentimental depiction of its grimly urban environment; construction sites are its playgrounds, and through the streets and shops the boys rove, fight, play, and sometimes plunder. Amid myriad details, an increasingly serious subtext can be found in the domestic silences and muffled arguments that Paddy finds inexplicably troubling and beyond his control: the words of his parents' marital discord are stifled whenever he is known to be within earshot. By the novel's end, Paddy has become sadder, wiser, more mature, and more alone—though not entirely by choice.

Best known as the author of *The Commitments* and *The Snapper,* both of which have been made into critically acclaimed films, Roddy Doyle has chronicled the working-class world of Barrytown with insight and wry humor. This novel, though relatively plotless in comparison to its predecessors, is nevertheless more masterful in its point of view, having so effectively simulated and sustained the narrative voice of a child. Along with the riotously picaresque first-person narrative of *Ceremony of Innocence* (1992) by Doyle's fellow Dubliner Anthony James Cassidy, *Paddy Clarke Ha Ha Ha* evokes the innocence and ingenuities of a modern urban preadolescent, a voice largely unheard in serious fiction heretofore.

William Hutchings

■ **ABDELKEBIR KHATIBI.** *Triptyque de Rabat.* Paris. Blandin. 1993. 139 pages.

Abdelkebir Khatibi, Abdelkebir Laâbi, and Tahar Ben Jelloun (Prix Goncourt, 1987) helped found the magazine *Souffles* in 1966. *Souffles* was a focal element in Moroccan literature written in French and was instrumental in raising Moroccan literature to its own unique status within Maghrebian literature. Khatibi has been described as a "sociologue de formation, mais aussi romancier ouvert à la métaphysique comme à la théorie des signes, poète surtout par son rapport narcissique à l'écriture." Nurtured on the Oriental tale, his language is poetic even when he is reacting as a sociologist—that is, as a decoder of life as it is lived.

The rich texture of Khatibi's prose style is an important element in creating the atmosphere of Rabat. One cannot help but compare *Triptyque de Rabat* to Durrell's *Alexandria Quartet.* As one of Durrell's characters (Darley) observes, "We are the children of our landscape. It dictates behavior and even thought in the measure in which we are responsive to it." So too in Khatibi the politics of love, the intrigue of desire, good and evil, the traditional and the modern move obscurely in the streets of Rabat, where "quelques chats errants qui dorment, de coutume, sous les voitures en *sniffant* l'odeur de l'essence. . . ."

Triptyque de Rabat is open to several interpretations: a geographic portrait, a political allegory, and/or a literary device. By definition, a triptych is a picture in three compartments, side by side. The central section is usually complete in itself, and the designs on either side are smaller and less important. Were one to divide the colonial city of Rabat under the protectorate, one would find the medina, the mellah (the Jewish quarter), and the residences of the French. Today's triptych would still include the medina and the mellah, but the third portion would remain somewhat amorphous, an ill-defined area where there is no clear direction in the labyrinth of streets. The geographic triptych is omnipresent and enhances yet another triptych: one of political activity, power, and sexuality.

In the human triptych we have three major characters: Idris, a modern functionary; Nafissa, a beautiful woman who is at the center of what is known as "L'Affaire"; and A.L., a nebulous figure who accepts the task of renewing the government. Idris is a native of Rabat, a government worker, assigned to a vaguely important position. He lives in constant fear of either losing his job or being downgraded. He is "une proie facile entre les mains de la Coterie." One day, A.L. invites him to join in the reshuffling of the government. A new Idris emerges full of self-confidence and a taste of power. When he accepts the post, he returns home, "cette nuit-là il s'allongea sur le côté droit en tournant le dos à sa femme."

"L'Affaire" occupies the second panel of the human triptych. Nafissa, a wealthy woman, is reputed to be addicted to drugs, sex, and other ingredients that can conjure a political crisis. Her mysterious death provokes rumors that involve everyone in any kind of position within the government. Nafissa and "L'Affaire" provide the political scandal, the cover-up, and the procedures so familiar to today's governments. The catalyst in the political triptych is the subtle A.L., a politician of no little skill, "un pouvoir qu'il prenait avec tact." His flair for government rests in the gift of listening: "Sa troisième oreille triait, filtrait les bruits de fond." Called to power, he is a leader "sans mépris direct pour personne. Et sur personne, pas de contrainte apparente." At his death, political power, sexuality, and strength seem to vanish into thin air.

Out of this nothingness, Khatibi creates yet another triptych. After A.L.'s death, Idris "est une tache, une image, dans cette carte, ce nouvel ordre. Saura-t-il déchiffrer cette histoire où ce sont les lecteurs qui sont pris pour personnages?" An Irish poet once said that a language is not a code to be broken but a mystery to be entered into. So too with Khatibi, he encourages us to pause and reflect on language and the magic of communication.

J. D. Gauthier, S.J.

■ **NAGUIB MAHFOUZ.** *Adrift on the Nile.* Frances Liardet, tr. New York. Doubleday. 1993. 165 pages.

Until the Nobel Prize was awarded in 1988 to Naguib Mahfouz—the first Arab writer to receive that honor (see *WLT* 63:1, pp. 5–9)—the author's works had been relatively unknown in the West. Almost overnight, many of those works began to be translated, while some already existing translations were revised for an anxiously waiting reading public. *Adrift on the Nile* (first published in Arabic as *Tharthara fawq al-nil* in 1966) is thus the latest work by the author to see its way into English.

This novel, which gained so much attention in the Arab world that it was turned into a movie some years later, perhaps epitomizes the absurdist stage that characterized Mahfouz's writing in the late sixties. Such experimentation is deeply entrenched in politics, however, as Mahfouz attempts to focus on the effect of the Nasser era in Egypt on a group of middle-class people who represent all that is left of an old and dying bourgeoisie. Most of the action takes place on a houseboat, where the protagonist Anis Zaki and a group of middle-aged men and women meet on a regular basis, smoke hashish, drink alcohol, and discuss various subjects in their attempt to situate themselves within a rapidly changing world. Most of the novel is thus recounted from a state of delirium within which many ethical and moral questions are raised and dropped. Sexual attraction and liaisons are also described in the same shifting, matter-of-fact tone that characterizes the narrative as a whole.

It is worth nothing that the translation by Frances Liardet succeeds in conveying both the colloquial nature of the dialogue among the characters and the classical tone of Mahfouz's descriptions of the various settings. The opening scene, which, in the customary Mahfouzian classical mode, describes Anis Zaki as he sits in his morbid office surrounded by dusty shelves and unfiled letters, is an example of how the author sets up a melancholy scene only to contrast it with the emotional charge of the next, where Zaki is confronted and threatened by the Director General.

It is in the last few chapters of the novel, however, that the reigning stillness and monotony of the first part of the novel is brought to crisis by a disruptive series of actions and events which cast the characters into a violent and uneasy state of sobriety. It is within this new state that the characters finally realize they can never regain their former attitude of nonchalance toward Egyptian society and the world.

Ramzi M. Salti

■**IRIS MURDOCH**. *The Green Knight*. London. Chatto & Windus. 1993. 472 pages.

Replete with familiar characters, unpredictable erotic attachments, and philosophical musings, *The Green Knight* is vintage Iris Murdoch. This twenty-fifth novel does not match the captivation and drama of its best predecessors such as *The Sea, The Sea* or *The Good Apprentice,* but it is a respectable new addition to Murdoch's repertoire of thick, wonderfully readable books about her immutable world.

Murdoch's novels are peopled by the same characters time after time, though they appear under different names. There are the affluent, middle-aged, intellectual Londoners and their identity-crisis-torn, magical children; there is the fiftyish man who abandons bourgeois life to pursue religious mysticism, and the "enchanter" figure who catalyzes other lives but despairs of his own. In *The Green Knight* we meet a large, loosely knit family consisting of the widow Louise Anderson, her three eccentric daughters (with the unlikely names of Aleph, Moy, and Sefton), Lucas Graffe, who has just killed a mugger with his umbrella, Lucas's brother Clement, and their friends Bellamy (trying desperately to join a monastery and shed all worldly ties) and Harvey, a youth destined to be bewitched by one of the three young women. We also meet the man Lucas killed, Peter Mir, who did not die after all but instead recovered, only to become obsessed with gaining entrance into this motley inner circle of strangely discontented but somehow firmly bonded beings.

Not only is Peter Mir not dead, but, it turns out, he never mugged Lucas; rather, he was an innocent passer-by whom Lucas mistakenly hit during an attempt to kill Clement (the motivation for which never becomes quite clear). Moy dubs Peter "the Green Knight," presumably come to save all of them from the "dragon," Lucas, whose heartless ways become more apparent as the plot progresses and who holds a curious power over all the others. Murdoch's image of Carpaccio's dragon—both fearsome and pathetic—applies not only to Lucas but to many other characters, and indeed to Murdoch's view of human passions. Can we love or welcome a "green knight" who reduces the magnificent dragon, "with wings spread and tail whirling," to a "miserable diminished creature. . .its wings clipped and folded"? Luckily, Murdoch appears to prefer dragons over princesses.

The intellectual, erotic, and mystical attractions (and repulsions) among all these people and a number of minor characters propel the book, which is also a feast of philosophical allusion, tidbits of foreign tongues, and beautiful imagery. Bellamy's search for religious ecstasy, divinely humorous and self-ironical, deserves special mention. With wit, wisdom, and an unparalleled eye for the subtlety of human emotion, Murdoch masterfully mixes the ridiculous and the sublime.

The book has no real conclusion. Like so many others, it drifts to an end when enough people are in love with each other and when some key players run off to America, as if to say: the tragicomedy of human lives continues, even if the book ends. The next volume will carry it on.

Mona Knapp

■**MO YAN**. *Red Sorghum: A Novel of China.* Howard Goldblatt, tr. New York. Viking. 1993. 359 pages.

Red Sorghum may be the best—surely it is the most startling—twentieth-century Chinese novel yet to appear in English translation. Belatedly it fulfills the promise that seemed to loom in Chinese literature's future when it first "thawed out" in the late 1970s but somehow got lost in the decade after. The story told here, already well known to many Americans through the film of the same name, also quells another, more recent anxiety among some critics: that famous film versions of Chinese novels by Zhang Yimou and other visually sophisticated Fifth Generation directors actually are better than the literary works on which they are based. *Red Sorghum*, in this inspired translation by Howard Goldblatt, is incomparably more interesting than the conspicuously patriotic film that followed it (as is Michael Duke's superb translation of *Raise the Red Lantern* by Su Tong, another author well served by Zhang).

Mo Yan is a young, defiantly experimental writer, and his story takes a modernist track, interweaving past and present fragments of a main plot and several subplots in a slightly mystifying yet cinematic and classically suspenseful grand narrative—cinematic because of his mesmerizing red symbolism: red sorghum (the original color of the crop; modern hybrids are colorless), red blood, red sunsets, red bridal veils, red wine. The story tells how one Yu Zhan'ao's ragtag village militia suicidally but memorably ambushed occupying Japanese troops during World War II (they felled an enemy general). This is interwoven with an even more fantastic tale of how Yu rescued, then raped (in an open sorghum field), and finally married a heroic woman destined ultimately to fall from enemy gunfire during his ambush. A second mininovel, originally a sequel to the first but now part 2 of one long *roman fleuve* (if the term may be applied to a modernist novel), tells how the couple took over a red-sorghum winery in the days before the war. The third part shows a band of orphaned children fighting for their lives against a pack of hundreds of wild dogs eager to devour the corpses with which the Japanese "refertilized" the red-sorghum fields during their My Lai–style massacre after the great ambush. (The

piece evokes *Lord of the Flies,* with the *dogs* regressing into fiendishly human cleverness.) These narratives are familiar yet eerie, for the text refers to Yu Zhan'ao as "my grandfather" and his heroic mistress as "my grandmother"; the narrator, in his flights of surrealistic and gory description, relates nearly ecstatic states of mind in his forebears that he could never have known himself or learned of from others. The novel winds up with evermore incredible and gory epiphanies in the final chapters, when "my grandmother's funeral" ends in a bloodbath, only to be outdone by the gang rape and murder of "my second grandma" (Yu Zhan'ao's second "wife").

Red Sorghum is unique among modern Chinese novels in elevating its tale to mythic proportions—though the two standard national myths engaged, filiality and patriotism, are turned on their heads, through exaggeration whose very beauty attenuates its irony, and a change in tone in the last two parts that recasts the narrator's heroic forebears as demons. Still, his unconditional love for them is never in doubt. The novel will be remembered for its inventiveness, its mythmaking, its heroism and antiheroism, its violence ("The fluids of his brain had oozed into his ears from the shattered scalp, and one of his eyeballs hung from the socket like a huge grape on his cheek"), its absurdity ("Grandma" would go on bound feet to the local dumping ground for infanticides to find lucky lottery numbers by weighing infant corpses). The "magic realism" that informs Mo Yan's work is evident not only in his plot—the first Chinese tale to demonstrate that even familiar heroic motifs can turn fantastic in the hands of one whose imagination is equal to the task—but also in the rapture of his imagery: of "crushed and broken sorghum," "sorghum corpses," "sorghum everywhere . . . crying bitterly."

Jeffrey C. Kinkley

■**MARGUERITE YOURCENAR**. *Conte bleu; Le premier soir; Maléfice.* Josyane Savigneau, pref. Paris. Gallimard (Schoenhof, distr.). 1993. 88 pages.

At the time of her death (December 1987) Marguerite Yourcenar left not only a massive correspondence but also several unpublished works. Among them were *Quoi, l'éternité* (1989), the last volume of her trilogy, *Le labyrinthe du monde* (see WLT 66:1, p. 89); a collection of essays, *En Pélerin et en étranger* (see WLT 65:1, p. 78); and three brief texts, "Conte bleu," "Le premier soir," and "Maléfice," now issued in a single volume with an excellent introduction by Josyane Savigneau, author of the meticulously researched biography *Marguerite Yourcenar: L'invention d'une vie* (1990; see WLT 65:3, p.

453). Of the latter three, only "Conte bleu" is an authentic *inédit,* the other two items appeared in periodicals in 1929 and 1933. Written when the author was still in her twenties, they offer clues to her future orientation.

"Conte bleu" recalls Yourcenar's *Nouvelles orientales* (1938). A group of (medieval?) European traders set out in search of a rich collection of sapphires, hidden in a legendary Islamic country: "Blue inscriptions trembled on the white dome of the mosque, like tattooing on a delicate breast." A slave girl leads them to a cavern where they find a lake in which the jewels are floating. The girl, letting her long hair down into the water, fishes them up in her tresses and distributes them to the greedy Europeans, who make their way back to their vessel with her. They strip the maiden and bind her to the mast, but by the next morning she has disappeared, leaving behind "a few herbs" from which rises "une fumée bleue." The jewels bring them only tragedy. Their ship is attacked and pillaged by pirates. Only a Greek merchant escapes. He jumps into the sea and is taken home by a friendly dolphin! "Conte bleu," a surrealist *poème en prose,* exalts all things azure and reflects the naïve fantasies of a young writer.

Even these early texts support an opinion of Mavis Gallant: "Wrenched out of the heart of her work, with the possibility of love, is any hope of redemption." This "hardness of heart," of which Savigneau speaks in her biography, appears in "Le premier soir," a curious piece, written "à quatre mains" by Yourcenar and her father, Michel de Crayencourt. The playboy son of a rich Lille family ("he made an art of dissipation"), he was fifty-two when she was born, the child of his second wife, who died soon after her daughter's birth. Cultivated as well as dissipated, however, he early began to occupy himself seriously with his daughter's education. He gave her a passion for reading and writing and encouraged her to be nonconformist. He had thwarted literary ambitions himself and had begun (in 1904) a novel about his second marriage. He showed the manuscript to his daughter and asked her to revise it. They worked on it together. Georges, a middle-aged man of the world who has just married an innocent *jeune file,* learns on his wedding night and without the slightest emotion that his longtime mistress has just died: "She had delivered herself from the imperfection of existing."

Yourcenar calls "Maléfice" "a realistic [?] evocation of Italian customs." The friends of Amande, who is dying of tuberculosis because she has been "bewitched," obtain the services of a healer to come and exorcise the demons. In the course of the exorcism, Algénare, who, jealous of Amande, had often wished that she were dead, realizes that she may be the witch responsible for her friend's illness. Returning home that evening, she

imagines that in the dark skies the stars formed "les lettres géantes de l'alphabet des sorcières."

These three texts, as Savigneau points out, will interest specialists. Otherwise, they may be considered as minor curiosities in the production of a great writer.

John L. Brown

1995

■ **TAHAR BEN JELLOUN.** *Le premier amour est toujours le dernier.* Paris. Seuil. 1995. 200 pages.

Winner of the prestigious Prix Goncourt, the Moroccan poet, novelist, and short-story writer Tahar Ben Jelloun differs from his francophone Maghrebian contemporaries in that his work does not highlight colonial oppression but focuses instead on the struggle within his own society, with special emphasis on love and tormented male-female relationships. His latest collection of short stories, *Le premier amour est toujours le dernier,* expounds on this dual theme.

The collection features twenty-one short stories, some published as early as 1973 and 1976. I can only applaud Ben Jelloun's persistence in exposing women's oppression and am relieved that he does not suggest Arabs are the only culprits: Spaniards and Italians are equally guilty, as illustrated in the stories "Le mirage" and "Monsieur Vito s'aime." Still, it is somewhat facile to accuse Southern Europeans of machismo. Although many of the stories are located in France, no Frenchman is depicted negatively. I am also disturbed by the subtext of these stories: all the beautiful women are tall, slender, white-skinned, and wide-eyed, with a luxurious mane of hair. Whether covered in jellabas or donning "des robes mal fermées," their perfect figure will not escape the author's gaze. They generally have "la poitrine blanche et ferme," "le sein parfait," "le sexe charnu." Above all, the most attractive are the quietest; their reserve makes men lose all control, as we can see in "L'amour fou," "Ruses de femmes," "Les filles de Tétouan," "Des robes mal fermées," and other stories. "Pudique" seems to be the greatest compliment Ben Jelloun can bestow on a woman. If she responds, she becomes "un peu envahissante et trop gourmande."

This gender stereotyping, the binary opposing of the ideally passive woman to an active man, is the very essence of sexism. And when passivity, rather than response, is equated with consent, rape is the next logical step. Thus, in "Les filles de Tétouan" a woman is asleep on the beach. A man walks by.

Il s'arrete, s'agenouille pres du corps qui reve. Sans parler, passe ses mains taillées dans la roche du mont Dersa sur la poitrine blanche et ferme de la femme qui commence a se reveiller. . . . Avec quelque precipitation, l'homme dechire la culotte large et blanche de la femme, releve sa djellaba en laine marron dont il tient le bord entre les dents et penetre en silence la femme qui ne dit rien.

Pornography has repeatedly depicted the victims of rape as "enjoying it." Is this any different? The woman begins to awake, and, "Trop heureuse pour parler, elle regarde le ciel."

Chinua Achebe convincingly argues that Joseph Conrad is "a bloody racist" even as he denounces colonialism. Similarly, at no point does the omniscient Ben Jelloun, a seasoned writer, fully dissociate himself from his male protagonists, who are frequently writers themselves. Many of the stories are framed within the first-person narrative of an Arab storyteller, resulting in an ambivalent effect of distancing/placing the author.

When Ben Jelloun was awarded the Prix Goncourt in 1987 for his novel *L'enfant du sable,* angered Arab critics accused him of pandering to foreign critics' taste for the exotic, providing them with stereotypes that do not represent the Morocco they know. Some compared him to V. S. Naipaul, praised by Europeans and rejected by many people of color. Still, *L'enfant* is to this day Ben Jelloun's most widely read and studied work, particularly outside the Maghreb. With its depiction of perverse Arab men and tormented relationships, *Le premier amour* is slated to become another such controversial, if successful, book.

Nada Elia

■YVES BONNEFOY. *La vie errante.* Paris. Mercure de France. 1993. 181 pages.

The most recent collection by one of our greatest poets (see *WLT* 53:3, pp. 364–470), gathers together the trilogy of *Les raisins de Zeuxis,* (1987), *Encore les raisins de Zeuxis* (1990), and *Derniers raisins de Zeuxis* (1993), previously available only in extremely limited edition; orchestrates them with the 1992 Maeght poems of *La vie errante* and a number of other suites, both in prose and in verse ("Lis le livre!," "De vent et de fumée," "Une pierre," "Deux musiciens, trois peut-être," and "Le canot de Samuel Beckett"); and offers us a corrected version of the 1988 "récit en rêve," *Une autre époque de l'écriture.*

To conjure in the space of a few lines the swarming nuances of this latest collection by Yves Bonnefoy is a task not easily assumed. Many texts possess a tantaliz-ingly quasi-allegorical simplicity urging upon us patient reflection and lucid reverie—and, of course, after Bonnefoy's more than forty years of prolific production in many realms, an effort, a desire, to read at once in this longer perspective yet still in utter freedom and freshness. The short prose piece entitled "La vie errante" furnishes a perfect example. Its five compact paragraphs provide no stable narration; there is no manifest contextualization, though no mystification, semantic or syntactic, either; the reference to Chateaubriand seems parenthetical despite its central location, and an intertextual reading in the optic of the Zeuxis trilogy seems to be equally feasible, even invited; there is at once a blatancy, better a transparency, about each paragraph's account, yet an exquisitely serene enigmaticalness hovers over the whole, giving to the piece mythical depth and infinite contemplatableness.

The title poem thus enacts, dynamically, what it prefers not to explain and conceptualize. It speaks, yet ever obliquely, of the tensions of purpose and recognition, persistent effort and welcome of the fortuitous. The "happiness" achievable via esthetic ordering is thrust up against the feasible joy derived from the experience of the simplicity of what spurts forth, a splash of untutored color, of pure onticity, of the mortal and the divine fused in the epiphany of being. It is less a battle with creative impotence that concerns Bonnefoy than the brilliant adequacy of what is. Chateaubriand is pictured as living this recognition of the paradox of nomination and representation. What transforms the consciousness of the poem's fictional painter is an intuition of the infinite and joyous mystery of a mere stain, a trace of our formlessness, of all that we are beyond what we think we are, a meaningless—because infinite—meaning beyond all attributable, reductive meaning, in life, in art. Such an accident of color becomes a gift received, embraced, not turned away as inadequate to the painter's desire and being. It thus "illuminates" and "saves," for it edges his, and our, awareness away from fixity, holding, pride, esthetic and mental transcendence, and toward the astonishments of experience, of presence, the freshness of the real, toward the latter's mysterious death (and beyond our mere reflections of it), toward some near-original beauty snatched away from concept, from constraining intellectualization, from deforming pretension.

All the poems and récits of *La vie errante* provoke endless, open meditation. It is an extraordinary collection in many ways, but, like all his books, Bonnefoy would not have us shut up in his words: they are there for traversal, for renewal, and for transformation.

Michael Bishop

■ **DENISE CHÁVEZ**. *Face of an Angel*. New York. Farrar, Straus & Giroux. 1994. 467 pages.

"It's a long story," Soveida Dosamantes warns us in *Face of an Angel*, Denise Chávez's first significant literary work since *The Last of the Menu Girls* (1986); but tell she must so as to stifle disturbing memories, memories like "clothes in your closet . . . you never wear . . . afraid to throw out because you'll hurt someone." Soveida works as a waitress at El Farol Mexican Restaurant, the novel evolving as literary tribute to servants: *Face of an Angel* as *Odyssey* for the working poor; Chávez as Hazel's Homer.

No Rodchenkoesque paean to the working class, Chávez's book is more Dickens *Hard Times* than Horatio Alger parable. Early on, we learn Soveida Dosamantes was named after a twenty-seven-year-old "pregnant woman with two small children" who was killed instantly in a car accident. Soveida's aptly named mother, Dolores (Spanish for "pains"), "read about it in an obituary column. . .and like[d] the name. It stuck." Here, naming serves as a microcosm for what follows.

Since *Menu Girls*, Chávez has developed her range, unveiling chapters eclectic and experimental. For instance, chapter 5 appears as two dueling prose columns retelling Soveida's parents' courtship—the form recalls more the theory of artsy French philosophers (viz., Derrida's *Glas*) than the stolid prose of American novelists (Vonnegut, true, plays with pictures). The expressionistic gap between Dolores Loera's and Luardo Dosamantes's testimony figures their fractious relationship. It also calls forth the border between men and women, between women and women (with class as allegorical emphasis), and between the United States and Mexico which found this tale. It is odd, perhaps incorrect, to imagine a border as "foundation," but for Southwest denizens it is a common truth.

Other tactical quirks await Chávez's readers as she plants two texts within *the* text: one, twelve-year-old Soveida's autobiography; the other, *The Book of Service*, Soveida's guide for El Farol waitresses. As with all books within books, one ignores them at one's own risk: Soveida's manual teaches waitressing, but structurally it is more akin to the calendar in Twain's *Pudd'nhead Wilson,* striking the novel's thematic keynotes: "Life was, and is service, no matter what our station in it. . . . It is those to whom more is given from whom more service is demanded." Chávez writes a waitresses' rejoinder to Laura Esquivel's chef-centered *Como agua para chocolate*: not recipes proper, but recipes for service. Like Esquivel's recipes, Soveida's advice serves as primer for survival in the midst of personal crisis.

Other maneuvers warrant mention. As with Toni Morrison and Alice Walker, within whose work one

find evocative tributes to such early African American storytellers as Zora Neale Hurston, Chávez laces her novel with gestures at early and contemporary Chicano/Chicana writers. When Dolores tells Soveida, "Whatever you do, don't marry a Mexican," her words echo Sandra Cisneros's story with a similar name; Chávez's chapter 27, "The House on Manzanares Street," also recalls Cisneros's early *Mango Street* novella.

When one thinks of Americans of Mexican descent, one does well to picture communities ordered by Catholicism and the family (its chief symptom). No surprise then to encounter Soveida, age twelve, ending her brief autobiography with a question worthy of Augustine: "So what am I? Saint or sinner?" Her answer, in the form of her life, is not conventional, and not very religious. The irony is hard to miss when we join Soveida in a Jesus shrine, where the son of God and man appears in a half-eaten tortilla. The Catholic Church is an easy target, but when not exposing Vatican broadcast inconsistencies, Chávez takes on the quasi-religion of Latino folklore fetishists, with Soveida eschewing sentimentality: "It's not surprising I didn't hear tales of La Llorona, La Sebastiana, El Coco . . . Papá Profe beat Mamá Lupita, Tío Todosio liked the boys . . . our ghosts were real."

Religion is out, the family dysfunctional; no long shot then that sex too is problematic; Chávez's novel soon evolves into a bestiary of sexual anomalies. Soveida's father Luardo, when not molesting her cousin Mara, is busy introducing his daughter to mechanical peepshows—one memorable opus featuring naked women washing cars. Oddly, Soveida's lascivious father proxies Chávez's position *within* the book: "Later, before I went to sleep for the night, he would tell me stories . . . about a little girl named Soveida." No room for comment on this loaded coincidence here.

Familial dysfunctions notwithstanding, the most powerful glosses in the book are on relations between women, as when Soveida describes the volatile bonds linking grandmothers, mothers, and daughters: "Only Dolores could hear the piercing decibels that brought her pain, the pain of a dog unused to certain soundless whistles. These were words from one woman to another, a mother to a daughter. . . . They were damaging[,] scarring words. Welts underneath clothing . . . from . . . one who knows your most intimate smell. Words from a woman who sees you as the man who makes love to you would. A mother."

In sum, Chávez's novel is an antisentimental family history—less *Cheaper by the Dozen* than *As I Lay Dying*. The book is an open mouth giving voice to open wounds. "This sex which is not one," Luce Irigaray put it in her landmark essay; Chávez fashions a prose sister-text. One hears also the echo of Rosario Castellanos. As the novel closes, our hardworking waitress is pregnant. Soveida calls her child "Milagro" (Miracle), one "won't be like the women I always knew: lonely, clinging, afraid."

The last word here goes not to Chávez but to Sandra Cisneros, whose witty back-sleeve promo blurb solicits the patronage of both writers: "I love this book so much it sounds like I'm lying."

William Nericcio

▪ **V. S. NAIPAUL.** *A Way in the World.* New York. Knopf. 1994. viii + 380 pages.

On the last page of V. S. Naipaul's previous novel, *The Enigma of Arrival* (1987; see *WLT* 62:3, p. 501) we read, "Men need history; it helps them to have an idea of who they are." In that novel an immigrant writer whose career runs parallel with Naipaul's discovers England as history, the center of that "real world" to which his native Trinidad was marginal. His earliest fiction and the prose work *The Middle Passage* (1962) were attacked for reflecting a superior attitude toward a Caribbean world where "nothing was created." It was historyless: yet Naipaul went far to fill that void, both in later fiction and in his own researched "history," *The Search for El Dorado* (1969). In *The Enigma* the writer/narrator acknowledges as his subject "the worlds I contained within myself, the worlds I lived in."

Now, in *A Way in the World,* another author-resembling writer-narrator amplifies and develops one purpose of *The Search* as described in *The Enigma,* "to attach the island . . . to great names and great events." Implicitly alluding to his narrative, he wonders in an aside "where in my own writings I had marked out regions of the spirit to which I was to return." *Return* is the process, to seek understanding of heritage, tradition, race, "an immense chain of events" inherited, observed, and experienced. The nine chapters of *A Way* juxtapose fictional-cum-documentary history with crucial experiences in the narrator's life, linked by a reflective investigation of meaning.

The "meaning" exposes more profoundly what in *The Search* Naipaul calls "the deeper colonial deprivation, the sense of the missing real world." The islanders "lived with the idea of disregard," their "history . . . burnt away," their mere existence dependent upon "foreign witness." Such was Raleigh, who contributed to the wiping out of the aboriginal past; yet through Raleigh's "slippery words" the narrator is helped to capture the landscape, the physical sensation of the island as a

world. In the premodern history the dominant figure of the book's longest chapter is the "quintessential colonial" Francisco Miranda, whose dream of a liberated world in Spanish Venezuela fails partly due to his blindness to the Negro presence. It is this presence that Naipaul gives new force, in the figures of Lebrun and Blair, Trinidadian revolutionaries who tell the black "people . . . about themselves."

The "sacrament" of Woodford Square (site of independent Trinidad's first prime minister's Athenian orations) endows both a new pride and an "impossible racial righteousness": this the narrator understands but sees no less dangerously limited than the deceptive romance of a Raleigh or Miranda. Still, there is no counteracting ideal order, no nostalgia for a "strong external authority." The narrator encompasses, interracially, the lives of romantics, revolutionaries, and redeemers whose ways in the world have contributed to tragic colonial history; the "racial cruelty" that created Trinidad, and finds an ironic twist in the last chapter, set in disintegrating Uganda, persists as the world's way, whoever governs.

This narrative tantalizes: much is autobiographical, but how much? Unidentified, a reproduction of the familial Lion House in Port of Spain—the Tulsis' House—appears on the dust cover; an unattributed, and rearranged, epigraph from *In Memoriam* opens. There is no disclaimer of "resemblance to persons living or dead": the modern characters are not wholly invented. An incidental sentence alludes to George Lamming's book *In the Castle of My Skin* as "autobiography."

Michael Thorpe

▪ **JULIO ORTEGA.** *Ayacucho, Goodbye; Moscow's Gold: Two Novellas on Peruvian Politics and Violence.* Edith Grossman, Alita Kelly, trs. Pittsburgh. Latin American Literary Review Press. 1994. 103 pages.

Julio Ortega is a poet, fiction writer, dramatist, anthologist, and one of Spanish America's most highly respected literary critics. In the novellas "Ayacucho, Goodbye" and "Moscow's Gold" he transforms matters of national importance—violence, betrayal, corruption, persecution, and other commonplaces of Peruvian life—into subjects of universal significance. Although the two works have some overlapping themes and both use a first-person narrator, they contrast dramatically in terms of length, style, and tone.

"Ayacucho, Goodbye" focuses on the gruesome, grotesque, and surreal aspects of Peruvian reality. The protagonist, the peasant leader Alfonso Cánepa, is reminiscent of Rulfo's dead narrators. Accused of being a terrorist and a communist, he is tortured and killed by government forces. After becoming one of Latin America's disappeared, he undertakes a journey to Lima as a kind of living corpse to reclaim his missing body parts and arrange for a decent burial for himself. Ortega's use of short chapters produces a truncated effect that mirrors Alfonso's mutilated body. The string of unsavory characters he encounters and the seriocomic scenes that form the basis of the narrative offer a highly unflattering portrait of contemporary life in a country racked by dehumanizing political intrigue and violence. Specific objects of the author's ridicule include government bureaucrats, politicians, the Shining Path, professors, and drug traffickers; but his real target is Peruvian society as a whole.

The second novella, "Moscow's Gold," subtitled "and Other Dangers Facing Adolescents on the Brink of Adult Life," is the shorter of the two pieces (covering only about twenty-five pages), although its time frame is more expansive. Set in a Peruvian port city in the 1950s, this story of the narrator's initiation into politics and adulthood—apparently based to some degree on autobiographical material—suggests parallels with Vargas Llosa. Politically naïve and sexually insecure, the unnamed narrator-protagonist is a would-be writer who feels attracted to and repelled by two high-school companions competing for his favor. Hugo, a braggart and a bully, admires the U.S. and belittles Peru's indigenous heritage. He constantly attempts to harass and brutalize Alberto, a weak and bookish type who has proclaimed himself a communist. The work chronicles the narrator's vacillation between these opposing forces and ideologies, his voracious reading habits, and his growing love for Elba, and concludes with an update on the characters after their separation following completion of high school.

The two translations flow smoothly with only an occasional bump. The lack of any kind of critical apparatus, however, is a glaring defect in an otherwise noteworthy volume. A brief foreword containing information on the author, his works, and the historical background of the two novellas would have facilitated comprehension for those unfamiliar with Peruvian history, literature, and culture. The strategic placement of notes or the inclusion of a glossary would have aided readers needing definitions of untranslated vocabulary items (e.g., *huayno, pisco, charango, soles*), clarification of allusions to famous works (*Poemas humanos* and *Amauta*), or identification of historical personages (Belaúnde, Odría, Mariátegui, et cetera).

In these two brief selections Ortega demonstrates his versatility within the genre of prose fiction with his skillful handling of black comedy and the coming-of-age story. Thanks to the translations, these works are now accessible to a wider audience. Unfortunately, his new readers will not be able to appreciate fully the richness of the texts without consulting outside sources.

Melvin S. Arrington Jr.

■ **ZINOVY ZINIK**. *One-Way Ticket*. Frank Williams et al., trs. London. Harbord. 1995. 224 pages.

Zinovy Zinik (né Gluzberg) left the Soviet Union in 1975 and came, via Israel and Paris, to London, where he now lives. The author of several comic and thought-provoking novels, he has also written many insightful stories and essays about emigration in general, and that of a Soviet émigré to the West in particular.

Readers of Zinik's works will not be disappointed by *One-Way Ticket,* a collection of nine stories written between 1987 and 1992 which directly and indirectly confront again the phenomenon of emigration in the light of the breakup of the Soviet Union and post-Soviet reality. The narrator is an intermittently fictionalized Zinik, whose relationship to the author may be compared to that of Liutov and Isaac Babel, particularly in "A Ticket to Spare," which describes the narrator's encounter with anti-Semitism in a hot and sinister Kiev.

The stories vary in their degree of literariness (all are written with elegance and rich imagery), some, like "The Refugee," ending with a Babelian epiphany. Here the narrator is pestered by a wretched refugee in Vienna (no one has better described the contrast between the squalor of the stinking Russian doss houses and the magnificence of the elegant Austrian capital); the refugee produces a stream of all the Soviet clichéd attitudes, notably the systematic nuking of the world's trouble spots, before the narrator discovers that his pathetically obsessive interlocutor is not Soviet but Lebanese.

The longest story, "The Notification," is a sad and complex reflection on the loneliness of emigration. "Mea Culpa" ends with a twist worthy of Maupassant when two Russian émigrés carefully avoid each other but end up sleeping with the same (American) woman. "Cricket" describes the author's bafflement and disillusion with the English establishment, represented by this seemingly arcane game; the liberating denouement here is Zinik's discovery that the woman he had thought the quintessence of English eccentricity proves to be of French origin, herself an alien in a strange land.

Many of the stories combine events of the present with the author's past and, particularly, his childhood. In "A Chance Encounter," untypically, belief is strained when Zinik, returning to Moscow after many years, confuses a former lover with her daughter on the "draft board of history [where] you seemed to have left the ranks, to be on eternal leave, outside time, without the problem of father and children, ancestors and progeny." The last piece, "The Face of an Age," is a remarkably frank, vivid, and touching account of the author's childhood and adolescent preparation for emigration from the Soviet Union. In an afterword Zinik offers a summary of his ambivalent yet not self-pitying attitude to his past and present, concluding with characteristic irony, "The process of ageing is perhaps the most effective literary device ever imaginable."

One-Way Ticket may be warmly recommended as a sophisticated, readable, and, above all, intellectually challenging picture of Soviet and émigré life, and especially of the no-man's land where Zinik now lives as "a vassal of the literary metropolis."

Arnold McMillin

1996

▪ **MARTIN AMIS**. *The Information*. New York. Harmony. 1995. 374 pages.

Failed novelist, book reviewer, and little-magazine editor Richard Tull deals with midlife crisis and postcolonial London decay by plotting the ruin of his closest friend, Gwen Barry, a literary superstar author of dull, uninspired novels. Richard's angst is contributed to by his many addictions, chief among which are tobacco and alcohol. Scozz, the villain in the piece, is vile and amoral, as is appropriate to the novel's gritty hipness to things sordid and illicit, but he somehow doesn't ring true. There is something contemptuous in Martin Amis's treatment of the poor and minorities that goes beyond the license of literary realism. Other characters, Richard's and Gwen's wives, are little more than cardboard stage scenery.

The Information exists somewhere between megalomania and a failed hoax, making it difficult to decide what Amis intends the reader to take seriously. The novel's theme (or is it metatheme?) seems to be the juxtaposition of the astronomical and the mundane, the cosmic and the grimy. A Eurasian dwarf walking down the street is compared to the sun, a "yellow dwarf." After describing the beauty of the solar system's gas giants, Amis concludes Pluto is "s—t." Amis sets his characters up to pronounce great transcendental truths, then has them spew forth profanity and rubbish. This fits in with Richard's ruinous vision, which also seems to be Amis's.

The higher they ascend, the farther they sink. The "information" is that voice at night that tells us we are growing older, that life is a spent and wasted starburst, that civilization is pitted and decaying. Amis is evidently listening. Amis and *The Information* seem consubstantial. You do not read his novel; you *submit* to it.

All this is according to the "postmodernist" program which the book seems to champion (assuming, of course, it really isn't a hoax). Readers can conveniently tick off the postmodernisms as Amis rattles them off. He addresses the reader directly. He inserts clips from his notebooks written four years ago, when he was Richard's age. The world is presented as a blurred rush of corporately homogenized storefronts. Amis announces that the genres have all bled together, that decorum is no longer observed, as if he expects hurrahs. Richard/Amis are not having a midlife crisis; they are still locked in adolescence, like the postmodern "movement" itself.

Language is the novel's most credible theme. Amis is actively committed to finding a language in which to express the age. Despite a tendency toward the recondite, he can write stunning prose that is fresh, precise, and beautiful—unquestionably suggestive of Nabokov. The brilliance is eclipsed, however, by the book's unreality. The world is not so base and fatal as Amis wants us to believe. Even if it is, negativity of this sort is cloying and obvious. Rather than a poet with a new vision, Amis presents the figure of a freshly divorced British Wastelander with a James Dean haircut, an American prose style, new teeth, and that famous £500,000 advance from his publisher (not a respectable, mute check but somehow coins vulgarly jingling around) in his hip pocket.

Carter Kaplan

▪ **CARLOS FUENTES**. *Diana, the Goddess Who Hunts Alone*. Alfred Mac Adam, tr. New York. Farrar, Straus & Giroux. 1995. 218 pages.

When one reads a Spanish American autobiographical novel relating the author's real-life love affair, Mario Vargas Llosa's *Aunt Julia and the Scriptwriter* (1977) inevitably comes to mind. A major difference between Carlos Fuentes's most recent novel and the one by Vargas Llosa is that the Peruvian's is far more entertaining. Fuentes's roman à clef, which has been competently translated by Alfred Mac Adam, narrates his short love affair with the American actress Jean Seberg—here called "Diana Soren"—in 1970. The plot reaches its climax when Soren rejects Fuentes for another, younger lover; Soren's suicide in the late 1970s and Fuentes's conversation with her husband "Ivan Gravet" (in reality the French novelist Romain Gary), bring the novel to its conclusion.

Replete with explicit, erotic details and allusions to pop culture (movies, directors, actors, singers, and writers), Fuentes's postmodernist novel has enjoyed considerable success in Mexico. And indeed, because he is a fine writer, some of his portraits and descriptive passages rivet the reader's imagination. For example, Diana Soren emerges as an interesting, and often pathetic, combination of free spirit (she loathes her bourgeois roots in Iowa and escapes into a cosmopolitan world of French culture and idealistic, left-wing causes) and prisoner of her past, resulting in solitude (suggested by the title) and vulnerability to drugs and sexual exploitation. She is also harassed by the FBI because of her sexual relations with a prominent Black Panther.

The portrait we glean of Fuentes is ambivalent, at least for me, because I am not sure if he is presenting himself as a parodic Don Juan or if he is nostalgically evoking a sexual episode from his past for serious literary purposes: "Literature . . . has been the filter of experience for me. . . . Sex, politics, soul—it all passes through my literary experience." On the other hand, chapter 18, which consists of an inane dialogue about keeping the bathroom door closed, mocks a love affair careening toward derailment. Because of his affair with Soren, Fuentes and his actress wife "Luisa Guzmán" separate—apparently another autobiographical element.

As in virtually all his novels, Fuentes seems compelled to articulate abstract philosophical ideas (some interesting and others too opaque to bother with) and diatribes against political and cultural enemies, his principal target here being the United States. Thus he rails against rampant racial prejudice in this country and, when an American actor mentions our loss of innocence in Vietnam, Fuentes considers American innocence a myth and launches into a listing of crimes beginning with the massacre of Indians and lasting through the Johnson and Nixon administrations. Then he invites Soren to accompany him to a gringo college, where he has been invited to lecture. I quote another reviewer who, recalling Fuentes's stint as ambassador to France, ponders, "And this man was a diplomat?"

Diana, the Goddess Who Hunts Alone is laced with flashes of brilliant writing typical of Mexico's best novelist, but it is not one of Fuentes's many outstanding endeavors.

George R. McMurray

■ **CEES NOOTEBOOM.** *The Following Story.* Ina Rilke, tr. San Diego, Ca. Harvest/Harcourt Brace. 1996. 115 pages.

The Following Story is a marvelous narrative about a man caught between two worlds. Bookish, a teacher of Latin, Herman Mussert delights in the world of words and spirit. As a classicist, he finds the icons of twentieth-century life repugnant and the dull students he faces a hopeless task. However, when Lisa d'India, a dark-haired beauty, enters his class, he finds in her a soulmate. It is she who understands not only the subtlety of his witticisms but also the spirit which infuses Horace, Ovid, and other classical authors. She is capable of entering their "now" in a way that only Mussert grasps, and a clear kinship is established between the two of them.

To his great dismay, however, he discovers that a colleague, Arend Herfst, is having an affair with Lisa. Shortly thereafter, Arend's wife, Maria Zeinstra, determines to punish Arend by having an affair with Mussert, and despite his best intentions, Mussert finds himself in love with the red-haired Maria, with whom he has little in common. As these several interweavings are uncovered, Mussert is beaten in the schoolyard by the much-larger Arend, who then physically forces Lisa to accompany him, an action which results in an auto accident and Lisa's death. The haze in which these events are recalled results in Mussert's revisiting the scene many years later to examine the defining issues of his existence.

Although the events in Mussert's life can be quite readily chronicled, the events themselves have rendered Mussert highly philosophical. In his quest to give his life more precise definition, he wrestles with issues such as temporality. Is he twenty years later inhabiting the "now" of his earlier life? Can there be a "now" in an ever-flowing stream of events? Does he in fact become part of the events which are in constant flux, and are these events separable from the temporal stream? On the other hand, Nooteboom presents his protagonist as an entity caught between antithetical forces in life. Reminiscent of Fitzgerald's Gatsby, Mussert sees his primary, ideal world destroyed by the "equally real" world of Maria and Arend. Just as Tom and Daisy leave Jay Gatsby alone and bereft, Mussert discovers his own isolation at Lisa's death, observing that Arend and his wife have moved to a distant location with no further communication with him.

Nooteboom presents the reader with a wonderfully ironic and highly allusive tale. Its complexities are carefully interwoven. It is no surprise that *The Following Story* won the European Literary Prize for Best Novel in 1993.

Arie Staal

Cees Nooteboom (*Simone Sassen; courtesy: Suhrkamp Verlag*)

■**JOSÉ SARAMAGO**. *Ensaio sobre A Cegueira*. Lisbon. Caminho. 1995. 310 pages.

In a recent interview José Saramago refers to a temporary loss of vision in 1991 to explain in part the genesis of his latest novel, an "essay on blindness." However, such an experience, no matter how unsettling, could hardly account for this story of an entire society swept by a mysterious epidemic that leaves its victims helpless when their vision is suddenly blocked by a curtain of white. The first case of such blindness concerns a motorist stricken on the novel's first page as he stops at a traffic light. A passing pedestrian helps him return to his nearby apartment, only to drive off with the man's car. But the thief is himself stricken shortly afterward as he parks the stolen vehicle. The first victim, taken by his frantic wife to the nearest ophthalmologist, leaves the doctor baffled. After alerting health officials, the doctor himself becomes sightless while researching the possible causes of the mysterious malady. At this point the alarmed authorities order the immediate internment of the afflicted, who now include the first man's wife and the doctor's regular patients, who had been exposed in his waiting room. Only the doctor's wife remains immune, but she feigns blindness to accompany her husband to an abandoned insane asylum where the epidemic is to be contained. Its first victims constitute the novel's main characters.

Guarded by terrified soldiers, the growing numbers of sightless people transform the former asylum into a scene of horror as rudimentary plumbing fails and food supplies become sporadic. When panicked soldiers shoot some inmates who venture too close in collecting their rations, the patio becomes a makeshift cemetery: there can be no contact with an outside world desperate to control the plague. A faulty transistor radio, however, tells of internment centers established throughout the country, until all programming ceases when hysterical announcers suddenly declare themselves blind.

At times Saramago's pitiless account of developing apocalypse becomes expressionistic in its excess. In the midst of a nightmare even the doctor's wife longs for blindness as she strives to keep her little group united in an institution where three hundred sightless people of all ages and conditions struggle among themselves for decaying supplies. Extortion, enforced prostitution, and, worst of all, general selfishness culminate in chaos when fire breaks out and the compound is destroyed. Only then do the survivors realize that the soldiers have disappeared, "among the last to lose their sight." They emerge into a ruined city where sightless people roam silent streets littered with abandoned vehicles as they grope for food and water amid the stench of death and decay.

Clearly, *Ensaio sobre A Cegueira* is not easy reading in any sense, and the squeamish are especially forewarned. It is equally the case, however, that the reader is struck by an air of compassion that pervades what would otherwise be unrelieved horror. Central to such compassion is the doctor's wife, who reminds her companions that "if we can't act quite like human beings, let us at least try not to live like animals," a plea that she will consider somewhat unjust when a large dog appears to lick away her tears shed in a moment of despair. After the group takes refuge in the doctor's apartment, a torrential downpour provides a welcome moment of purifying solidarity as the survivors bathe one another on the terrace above the reeking city.

The novel ends as abruptly as it begins when the first blind man regains his sight, followed by the doctor and his patients, while on the streets below there are happy cries as the epidemic recedes. The plague passes, but it is by now clear that the blindness that Saramago studies in his "essay" has been less physical than ethical. The devastation that swept away social stability and all civility resulted less from a loss of vision than from the absence of respect for communal interests based on reason. As the doctor's wife points out, "To organize is in a way to begin to see," and only the truly "blind" find hope in squares where demagogues rally their followers with appeals to "salvation through penance . . . or through a mystic vision . . . or through the power of sacred signs" and similar departures from reason. She reminds her friends that even sighted people would perish in the absence of a social order founded on rational behavior, the only guarantee of a community's survival.

The reader familiar with Saramago's earlier novels will once again find an opulent narrative where dialogue, scene, and narration are interwoven in such a way that one is tempted to read aloud, as in passages where the doctor's wife reads to her sightless little band. We are reminded specifically of *O Memorial do Convento* (1982; see *WLT* 58:1, p. 78) and *A Jangada de Pedra* (1986; see *WLT* 62:1, p. 107) as we encounter the familiar figure of the strong woman and the sympathetic dog. Also, the narrator's self-deprecation and ironic humor once again deflate any suggestion of melodrama, truly a feat in a novel like this one. Unlike Saramago's earlier fiction, though, *Ensaio sobre A Cegueira* is profoundly allegorical in structure and intent. No character is given a proper name; instead, the figures are referred to as "the first blind man," "the doctor," "the little cross-eyed boy," "the girl in dark glasses," et cetera. Equally vague are chronology (an unspecified time in the contemporary period) and place (anywhere in the industrialized world). Thus, the reader is witness to the consequences of irrational behavior that may occur anywhere and at any moment when communal interests and reason are subverted by panic and egoism. In the novel the fragile tissue of civil society is rent by the absence of understanding and a sense of shared responsibility. For the reader, the experience proves to be as harrowing as it is (one is tempted to say) insightful. (Note: While critically acclaimed, it has been pointed out that this latest novel by Portugal's best-known writer "suffers" from his growing reliance on Spanish syntax and a Castilian lexicon, the effects of Saramago's prolonged residence in the Canary Islands, where he lives with his Spanish wife.)

Richard A. Preto-Rodas

■ **NATHALIE SARRAUTE**. *Ici*. Paris. Gallimard. 1995. 182 pages.

Ici. At ninety-five, Nathalie Sarraute gives us another powerful work which shares her effort to find meaning and form in the indescribable, unformed, and perhaps unformable zone beneath all words. Who has not felt the frustration and tension of the struggle to find the correct word corresponding to the inexpressible fluid reality of sensation, of *ici*, the here-and-now we all inhabit?

Ici reconstitutes the experience of remembering a specific word, be it a name of a person, of a tree, or of a well-known artist. The closing of these *trous de mémoire* that gape before us increasingly as we age provides a certain pleasure and feeling of plenitude: "c'est ici qu'Arcimboldo a retenti avec une telle force, alors que depuis longtemps il n'était plus attendu, même le vide qu'il avait laissé derrière lui avait disparu."

Ici's dramatic action stems from these efforts and its power from Sarraute's oral style composed of dialogues, repetitions, metaphors, ellipses, and silences. Who else but Sarraute can excite and incite us with all the fixed ideas and expressions, prejudices and misunderstandings that constitute our everyday speech?

Ici also reveals the many interpretations and misunderstandings caused by the simplest and most innocent of expressions. For instance, "Est-ce que vous l'avez lu?" can hide unsatisfied desires, jealousy, and other dangerous feelings. Indeed, *Ici* explores the relationships between truth and fiction, interior and exterior, death and eternity.

Ici—even this brief title contains the repetitive contradictions and universality of Sarraute's work. Where is "here" but everywhere and nowhere? Phonetically the word suggests stability (in its redundant simplicity) but also movement (in its explosive pronouncement and in the way it returns again and again on almost every page of *Ici*). The brevity and form of the word *ici* suggest to this reader the form of the ellipsis (the three *points de suspension*) that characterizes Sarraute's writing: "Tout ce qui sort d'ici se réfléchit . . . méconnaissable, insaisissable . . . dans ses parois miroitantes."

Ici. To "review" or "analyze" this powerful work proves to be a disturbing process: any attempt appears to banalize it. My advice to any potential reader is simply "Read it!" And here I close, for—to repeat Sarraute—"ici doit rester pur de toute parole."

E. Nicole Meyer

■ **ALEKSANDR SOLZHENITSYN**. *Invisible Allies*. Alexis Klimoff, Michael Nicholson, trs. Washington, D.C. Counterpoint. 1996 (© 1995). 344 pages.

Ever since Aleskandr Solzhenitsyn started his silent—or, in some cases, quite outspoken—war against the communist regime in 1965, people often wondered how it was possible for a single individual to fight the official state machinery and remain unscathed for so

many years, until his expulsion from the Soviet Union in 1974. We have his own record of that war in a volume of recollections titled *The Oak and the Calf*, published in English in 1980, but until now the background of that campaign remained a mystery. In *Invisible Allies* Solzhenitsyn reveals for the first time not only the names of his secret allies (*nievidimki* in Russian, meaning "invisible people") but also their sometimes tragic, sometimes bizarre stories, recalling with tenderness the unselfish sacrifices they made to salvage and preserve his works, hide the manuscripts, and, in many cases, rescue the author himself from the persecution of the KGB.

The fourteen sketches making up the volume were written in Switzerland twenty years ago, immediately following Solzhenitsyn's expulsion, thus preserving fresh recollections and memories; their publication, however, was not possible at that time, since they could have compromised the safety of those "secret allies" who stood firmly behind the author during the most difficult period of his literary activities at home. Only in 1991, with the collapse of the Soviet Union, did Solzhenitsyn deem it safe to issue his personal tribute to his friends and collaborators in Russia, in the same *Novyi Mir* literary monthly which had been the arena of his struggle against the authorities in the late 1960s and 1970s.

We are given a glimpse of a tight network of people, Russians and foreign journalists or diplomats, who valiantly opposed the Soviet system and considered Solzhenitsyn their champion; we learn about their secret ways and tricks; we see how perhaps the most important Russian novels of our time were saved from annihilation or oblivion in the secret-police archives. In short, we receive a record of a relentless fight for the basic moral values mortally threatened by the Soviet regime. It is a noble and precious record, worth reading not only by those who are interested in Russian literature but also by every reader to whom those values remain dear.

And yet the account brings about some sad reflections: what has happened to all those brave folks now that the communist system has been abolished? Have they abandoned their lofty ideals and succumbed to the routine of making money in the new, seemingly free society of contemporary Russia? What has happened to the author's fighting spirit now that he has returned to his homeland? I wonder. . . .

Jerzy R. Krzyżanowski

1997

■**JULIAN BARNES**. *Cross Channel*. New York. Knopf. 1996. 211 pages.

The ten short stories collected in Julian Barnes's *Cross Channel* explore the British experience of France over the past three hundred years. From the late seventeenth century, when Irish mercenaries attempt to "convert" a Protestant village to the French King's religion (with as much cruelty as Cromwell's men had used in their homeland) to the year 2015, when a rider on the now-antiquated Eurostar train encounters football hooligans of the next millennium, these stories exhibit the finely nuanced knowledge of French culture that also characterized Barnes's much-acclaimed novel *Flaubert's Parrot*. Though the stories are not presented in chronological order, Barnes deftly and subtly establishes the distinctive period of each within its first few opening lines.

"We did not come here to disturb their lives," remarks one of two Englishwomen who buy and manage a winery in the Médoc during the 1890s in a story entitled "Hermitage"; "we came for the tranquillity of our own." Yet, like their countrymen in other stories (though their intentions are often far less benign), they encounter villagers' "pious obstinacy" and the fact that in cross-cultural conflicts and simple misunderstandings alike "tradition is [a] permission" all its own. In "Interference," the book's opening selection, the local villagers concertedly thwart the dying wish of an imperious expatriate English composer to hear one of his symphonies broadcast by the BBC. In "Junction" (in many ways the most interesting story in the collection) the encamped English workmen who build the Rouen and Le Havre Railway during the 1840s are viewed with curiosity by the citizens whose lives their creation will soon transform. "Melon" records the departure of a cricket team to play the Gentlemen of France amid the political tumults of 1789. "Brambilla" also focuses on sport, with its narrative point of view alternating between that of a cyclist entered in the Tour de France and the girlfriend who has accompanied him there.

No collection of stories about the British presence in France would be complete without an homage to the thousands who gave their lives on battlefields there, particularly during World War I. Accordingly, "Evermore" commemorates their sacrifice through a study of a commemoration of their sacrifice—a still-grieving sister's fifty-year devotion to her brother's memory and her annual visits to his grave. As a portrait of a seemingly uneventful life, the tale suggests parallels with works by Chekhov and Katherine Mansfield as well as Flaubert's classic, "Un cœur simple."

Although the final story in the collection, "Tunnel," repeats a number of leitmotivs from its predecessors, and although its final sentence attempts to unite them (as if all were written by the train traveler in 2015), they remain more memorable as a series of well-crafted vignettes than as a coherent collection.

William Hutchings

■ **CALIXTHE BEYALA**. *Your Name Shall Be Tanga*. Marjolijn de Jager, tr. Portsmouth, N.H. Heinemann. 1996. 137 pages.

Beyala's second novel, published in French in 1988 as *Tu t'appelleras Tanga,* is a story of a female friendship which overcomes racial and class boundaries, set in a prison in an unnamed country, presumably Beyala's Cameroon.

Anna-Claude is a French teacher of philosophy who comes to Africa to teach, hoping to find an African lover. She is a Jew and believes that in Africa she will find a new race, human beings "who have not invented gunpowder" and will be less prone to violence. She quickly loses the illusions inspired by Negritude. Walking the streets with a signboard protesting the disappearance of her students who had demonstrated against the government, she is arrested and imprisoned, then declared insane. She shares the lack of contact with everyday reality that Ateba shows in *The Sun Hath Looked Upon Me* (see previous review) or that Loukoum's father displays in *Loukoum, the Little Prince of Belleville* (see WLT 70:4, p. 1011).

Tanga, Anna-Claude's cellmate, is a child of the slums, thrown into the street to support her mother by prostitution. After having submitted to a clitoridectomy, she is raped by her father, who kills the resulting child. Tanga is dying when Anna-Claude is placed in her cell, but she gradually is able to recount her life, including illusions similar to Anna-Claude's that life would be better elsewhere—for her with a social-welfare government in France. At the end of the novel, as Tanga dies, Anna-Claude thinks she has become Tanga and has incorporated her story into her own soul.

The descriptions of the lives of the poor in an African city are combined with the dreams of Anna-Claude and Tanga, dreams of a better world that women might create, although both at earlier moments had hoped to find true love with an ideal man. The novel is less a direct attack on the male sex in Africa than a criticism of postcolonial society, where "air-conditioned blacks" drive past children mutilated by their parents to make them better beggars. Tanga tries to mother a crippled outcast child, Mala, and Tanga and Anna-Claude give

a motherly love to each other; but the rest of the society is cruelly lacking in any maternal sentiments. Tanga's mother wants a prize from the government for having given birth to twelve children, a prize her daughter refers to as the medal for "laying hens." The traditional role of women has been destroyed in the modern African state.

The novel alternates between conversations in the cell and long passages in which Tanga tells her story. Beyala occasionally finds striking images to convey her pessimistic vision of Africa, but her style is sometimes a rather unfortunate mixture of metaphors. Mala is given dialogue unbelievable for an abandoned, illiterate child: "No more mama. No more papa. Nothing but the hope of happiness, which is an accident of nature." As in her first novel, Beyala is more successful at creating a poetic atmosphere of suffering, and of almost insane hope for a community of women who can nurture one another, than at telling a consistent story.

Adele King

■ **SUJATA BHATT**. *Point No Point: Selected Poems*. Rolf Wienbeck, ill. Manchester, Eng. Carcanet. 1997. 148 pages.

Sujata Bhatt's *Point No Point* contains a generous selection from her three previously published books, plus one new poem which lends the volume its title. She uses free verse with delicacy, poise, and effect. Her lines are tight, her metaphors unusual, and her range of themes wide.

In her first book, *Brunizem* (1988; see WLT 68:4, p. 884), the continents in which she has lived—Asia, Europe, and North America—are used as her poetic landscapes. In "Udaylee" she explores with haunting sentiment the state of menstruating women who are deemed untouchable during that period, according to the beliefs and practices in the Gujarati community of her childhood: "Only paper and wood are safe / from a menstruating woman's touch. / So they built this room / for us, next to the cowshed." Further, she describes, "This aching is my blood flowing against, / rushing something—/ knotted clumps of blood, / so I remember fistfuls of torn seaweed / rising with the foam, rising."

Bhatt's Gujarati mother tongue figures prominently in the poems of all her books. In her second collection, *Monkey Shadows* (1991; see WLT 69:1, p. 223), the protagonist in the poem "Devibhen Pathak" says at different points "(Chaal, chaal! Sapat payhri lay!) Let's go! Put on your slippers," then later "(aray bhen, tamnay khabar nathi . . . ?) Oh bhen, don't you know . . . ?" Bhatt goes one step further by using the actual Devnagari Gujarati

script on the page. It is an aspect we have come to recognize in Bhatt's poems that highlights her inimitable style. This bilingual quality not only provides an interesting East-West tension but also flavors it with a kind of lyricism that can only be achieved when linguistic scales and registers are controlled simultaneously.

In her third book of verse, *The Stinking Rose* (1995; see *WLT* 70:4, p. 1037), Bhatt not only extends some of the themes and techniques she has used previously but also builds on them substantially. At the core of the collection is a sequence of twenty-five poems that "explores the various mythologies and the magical and practical aspects of garlic." The title poem, "The Stinking Rose," one of the many names garlic is called by, sensuously evokes warmth, passion, and beauty—all juxtaposed delicately: "Everything I want to say is / in that name / for these cloves of garlic—they shine / like pearls still warm from a woman's neck. // My fingernail nudges and nicks / the smell open, a round smell / that spirals up. Are you hungry?"

Much research has gone into considering the various aspects of garlic. Two examples are Stephen Fulder and John Blackwood's *Garlic: Nature's Original Remedy,* which provides the backdrop for the poem "Ninniku," the name adopted by the Japanese for garlic when Buddhism came to Japan in the sixth century A.D., and *Culpeper's Complete Herbal,* which provides the poem "Mars Owns This Herb" its title, where we find in the trenches "broken limbs covered / with sterilized sphagnum moss / soaked in garlic juice."

Included in *Point No Point* are poems that earlier appeared as a chapbook titled *Freak Waves.* These poems arise largely out of the poet's response and experiences while she was attached to the Creative Writing Department of the University of Victoria in Canada. Not surprisingly, many of the poems are swathed in a refractive wash of maritime color. Also, by extension, we see aspects of belonging and unbelonging, rootedness and transience, physical and mental travel, diasporic dislocation—all explored with power and poignancy. Consider the poem "The One Who Goes Away":

But I never left home
I carried it away
with me—here in my darkness
in myself . . .

We weren't allowed
to take much
but I managed to hide
my home behind my heart . . .

I am the one
who always goes
away with my home
which can only stay inside

in my blood—my home which does not fit with any geography.

World art and literature are vibrantly featured in this volume. In fact, the collection is adorned with wonderful illustrations by Rolf Wienbeck. There are several poems ("The Light Teased Me," "Cow's Skull—Red, White and Blue," "Skinnydipping in History," "Parrots," and others) that respond to the works of artists and writers such as Georgia O'Keeffe, Paula Modersohn-Becker, Jakobine von Domming, Frida Kahlo, and John Ashbery. Many of the poems in this group ingeniously and successfully employ surrealism and internal dialogue.

Point No Point is a substantial collection of poems, one that allows us to travel, dream, and learn, but one that ultimately moves us by its quietude of stance and impeccable articulation. Sujata Bhatt is an accomplished poet using her multicultural background to its fullest effect—her growing up in America, her Indian family background, and her German marriage. Her next collection, *Augatora,* is due out in England from Carcanet next year.

Sudeep Sen

▪ **JOSEPH BRODSKY.** *So Forth.* New York. Farrar, Straus & Giroux. 1996. 132 pages.

In his essay entitled "On 'September 1, 1939' by W. H. Auden," initially presented as a lecture at the Writing Division of the School of the Arts at Columbia University and published in a book of selected essays titled *Less Than One* (1986), Joseph Brodsky offers a definition of poetry: "Sorrow controlled by meter." Like Marina Tsvetaeva, whom he admired almost as much as he did Anna Akhmatova, and whose writings he analyzed in "A Poet and Prose" and "Footnote to a Poem," he voices an opinion arising from bitter personal experience: namely, that twentieth-century Russia embodies tragic destiny. In the second of the two essays on Tsvetaeva he states, "For a person . . . who has experienced the metaphysical Russian roller coaster, any landscape, including an other-worldly one, seems ordinary."

Indeed, Brodsky embarked on the ultimate roller-coaster ride when, convicted of being a social parasite (*tuneiadets*)—since "poet" was not considered by courts of law to be a profession—he was sentenced to five years of hard labor in the North. In that desolate land he was able at least to avoid the stampede of vulgarity characteristic of the Red bourgeoisie. Nor did his hardworking parents belong to the privileged class; one has only to read the deeply moving description of their family life, "In a Room and a Half."

As a schoolboy, Brodsky took his first lesson in "switching off," as he sat surrounded by the ubiquitous portraits of Lenin, Stalin, members of the Politburo, and Maxim Gorky, "the founder of Soviet literature." As to Dzerzhinsky, "the Knight of the Revolution," his countenance graced the wall of the school principal's office, as well as those of interrogation chambers. No wonder the future poet left school at fifteen to go on geological expeditions in the wilderness. An instinctive nihilist, he saved his sanity by walking out, leaving behind the clichés mouthed by the teachers, as monotonous as the "blue horizontal stripe at eye level, running unfailingly across the whole country, like the line of an infinite common denominator."

Later in his life, as a milling-machine operator in a factory which produced cannons, agricultural machinery, and air compressors, Brodsky observed the system's obsolescence, covered over by the lies fabricated by the propaganda industry. However, he says that he was lucky in having caught "the working class" in its proletarian stage, before it underwent a middle-class conversion in the fifties. Perhaps what shaped him as a poet was his contact with the direct, simple speech of the people. There was also his meeting with books, which he calls his "first and only reality." Dickens was more real than Stalin or Beria; the literary pantheon became the Central Committee of a bookish generation. In his essay "Less than One" Brodsky states: "Existence which ignores the standards professed in literature is inferior and unworthy of effort. So we thought, and I think we were right." To the French revolutionary motto "Liberté, Egalité, Fraternité," Brodsky proposes to add "Culture."

Those standards are most apparent in the present collection of Brodsky's final poems, *So Forth,* most of them translated by the poet himself from the Russian. One of his heroic tasks was to remake himself into a poet-citizen of the world, as John Bayley writes in his review for the *New York Times* (1 August 1996). In his own essay, "To Please a Shadow," Brodsky explains that he did not seek "greater estrangement like Beckett," but that his sole purpose was to find himself "in closer proximity to the man whom [he] considered the greatest mind of the twentieth century: Wystan Hugh Auden." This in fact continued after Auden's death, yet Brodsky still sought the special nearness which can only be sharing a mode of expression. In this, Brodsky says, he failed, but one cannot do more for a better man than "to continue in his vein." Indeed, for those who can read Brodsky in Russian, those who were so fortunate as to hear his bardic intonation, it is obvious that in English his voice is muffled. Still, something reaches us: an extraordinary intelligence, wit and sadness mixed, a

sense of the approaching end. Perhaps the "dear savages" addressed by the narrator of "Infinitive" are not the noble savages of swarthy shade who dwell in the tropics but rather Americans. Their ancestors were also shipwrecked on a beach. And did these blond, kind men and women consider the poet as "an island within an island"? Clearly he remained a foreigner on our shores. In a dream his father's ghost travels to Australia. "In Memory of My Father: Australia" is a deeply moving poem. A body reduced to ashes in the state crematorium can be free to travel, a right denied to Brodsky's parents, who died without ever setting eyes on their brilliant, world-famous progeny. In the poet's dream his father was free "for the first time since [he] formed a cloud above a chimney."

There are a number of lighter pieces. "A Song" dances on the page, skipping from rhyme to rhyme like a child playing hopscotch. However, it ends in a metaphysical sigh: "What's the point of forgetting / if it's followed by dying." Now that Brodsky is no longer among the living, this rhetorical question has a poignant ring. "Clouds" race in the sky, their "cirric ploys / or cumulus domus" sculpt "cupolas, peaks," raise "rent-free / castles!" Not castles in Spain, however, since the Russian poet recalls their looming presence "high in pristine / skies of the Baltic." The Centaur poems cavort. In "Centaur II" a certain (or perhaps rather uncertain) Sophie—not as full of wisdom as her name would indicate—is taken for a ride (in every sense of the word) by a beau, "two-thirds a caring male, one-third a race car."

The most affecting poem in this final collection is an ironic self-elegy written by the poet to his young daughter, the child he was reluctant to sire since he realized he would not witness her growing up. He expresses his hope that she might recall "a silhouette a contour." Although he will lose them, he plans to stand in their home, "as furniture in the corner." As in some of Baudelaire's *Spleen* poems, objects look at humans, observe them, like the trees in the sonnet "Correspondances." Brodsky warns his child that she must "keep an eye" on these pieces, as they will watch her, watch over her. Although he ends his poem by saying he addresses the child in "these somewhat wooden lines in our common language," (presumably English), there is nothing stiff about them. The poet does not give in to self-pity; rather, he echoes his mother's gesture when, pointing to a delicate set of china, one of the rare remnants of a pre-Soviet life, she says: "This will be yours when you get married."

There is a wise Russian saying, "Your wound will heal before your marriage day." Brodsky's wound at having been separated from his parents never healed; neither did the one he had to bear for his own daughter.

Still, like his parents, he does not talk about death "in the way that terrifies the listener or prods him to compassion." He mentions it casually, as his beloved mother did the china. We, however, mourn him—and mourn with him.

Rosette C. Lamont

▪ LOUIS-PHILIPPE DALEMBERT. *Le crayon du bon Dieu n'a pas de gomme.* Paris. Stock. 1996. 276 pages.

Haiti's curious political existence today is reflected in the shadowy nature of Haitian literature. The new American occupation and the charade of democracy have not cured the split between an internal literature and a literature of exile; they have only aggravated the division. The poverty and misery remain, but comprehension is lost in labyrinths of sociopolitical confusion.

Louis-Philippe Dalembert, a thirty-five-year-old Haitian poet, journalist, scholar, and now novelist, author of the volume of tales *Le songe d'une photo d'enfance* (see *WLT* 68:3, p. 620), sends his alter ego back to his birthplace, looking for Faustin the First, "nègre de Yaguana," his "big brother" and/or father figure. He is also looking for his homeland and his identity. He finds the discouraging reality of Haiti today: increased poverty, stagnation, and no jobs. As the protagonist rambles around in an old Jeep, he remembers all those who are now gone, even the missing trees.

Local color and quaint characters seem to be de rigueur today in *Créolité* and perhaps in most Third World writing. But Lord Harris, Ti-Blanc, Thibaut, and L'Homme d'Afrique remain pretty much in the background. The pathos of the story is centered on the narrator's grandmother, Pont-d'Avignon, who raised him, and on Faustin and his wife Marie. As a child, the protagonist spent many hours in his place of refuge, an old Peugeot 304 carcass, perceiving the world through the rear-view mirror, going against the will of Pont-d'Avignon, who viewed it as a "cimetière de microbes." His other delight was Faustin, who befriended and protected the orphaned child.

The focus on the joys and struggles of the newly-wed couple recalls Jacques-Stephen Alexis's *Compère général soleil,* but with a nineties twist. Since the protagonist is unable to find physical traces to correlate with his memories, he, as well as the reader, is never sure where memory shades into creative dream or invention. In any case, both levels of the story, the past and the present, well represent the current situation of Haiti, and indeed most Third World countries.

The jobs Marie and Faustin are given dramatize the oppression and degradation of work in undeveloped countries. Their housing and living conditions document the unfairness between First and Third Worlds. Eventually Faustin can no longer cope, his "mind colonized by a horde of dark spirits or zombies." The most gripping scene occurs near the end of the story: Faustin, homeless, is caught in a downpour and finds himself in the nightmare of the deluge being swept away by rushing water.

The protagonist finally decides that exile is part of the human condition—one can never go back—and that "the only country one has is the time one inhabits" (the last line of the novel). Curiously, again, Faustin comes to a happier end than the narrator, who can and does leave Haiti, again.

Hal Wylie

▪ SIMON TAY. *Alien Asian.* Singapore. Landmark. 1997. xii + 287 pages.

"Movement has not stopped: Singaporeans go to Europe and America; outsiders come in and become part of the scene," I said in my review of *Stand Alone,* a mix of prose, fiction, and poetry instead of the novel Simon Tay wanted to write (see *WLT* 65:4, p. 775). Tay's new volume, subtitled *A Singaporean in America,* is dedicated to his wife Jin Hua, "even if it is not the novel she wanted."

Having first come to America to participate in the University of Iowa's International Writing Program in 1989, Tay returned on a Fulbright to study for a Master's degree in law at Harvard, which he obtained in 1994, winning the Laylin Prize for the best thesis in international law. His book has four parts: "American Dreams," "Caning, Crime and Politics," "Country Life," and "Concluding a Continent." "I Was Born American," Tay begins. "Not in the country itself, but in its shadow. Coca-Cola and jeans were always in, no matter how the governments of Singapore and of Asia railed against 'yellow' culture in the 1960s and 1970s, or 'decadent' Western values." The book is not meant to be an objective description of America. "There is no absolute objectivity," says Tay. "Whenever something is described or reported, there is the intermediary of the person who is making the observation." That person was seen by many Americans as Chinese, yet "I was born into a Peranakan family and spoke Malay first, and then English." So at Harvard, he studied Mandarin from an American instructor who "encouraged me in a way that no Chinese could. . . . I was now convinced I could remain Peranakan and Singaporean after learning this new language."

The volume is full of experiences in and insights into America, including O.J. ("the American media is

[sic] not wholly investigative and relentless for truth as some claim . . . it can deceive and conceal as often as it reveals"), Elvis ("in Iowa, Peter—Goan and Asian, formerly of Uganda, Africa, now living in the heart of America—had found a kind of acceptance and even fame in his connection to Elvis, one of America's icons"), and arrival ("The word [aliens] suggests people from a different world, wholly different and perhaps dangerous").

And then came Fay for Tay. Michael Fay, a young American, was sentenced to caning in Singapore for vandalizing cars. Did he deserve to be caned or not? "The Larry King Show" wanted Tay but rejected him because "I was interested in exchanging views but not in mouthing opinions tailored to fit preconceived conclusions." He wrote a reply to William Safire's "sloppy, biased arguments" in the New York Times. "The American media do not always grant a right of reply," he discovers. "My reply was not published. No correspondence explained its rejection or even acknowledged its receipt. Freedom of speech in this case meant I was free to write and they were free to ignore it. There was no equal access. Without it, some like Safire were freer to speak than others, like me. The American media had spoken and, having convinced itself, seemed not to be listening to other points of view." A Harvard law journal rejected his article after first accepting it, so he had it published at McGill University, which was "sufficiently removed from the shrill political debate between the USA and Singapore to allow an Asian voice."

Tay visits Walden Pond and discusses Thoreau's Walden, pointing out that Thoreau's contemporary was Frederic Tudor, who developed a way of cutting and storing ice, some of it from the Pond, shipping it as far as Singapore. "Today, in the late 20th century, America may need more Tudors than Thoreaux," Tay observes. Yet later, Tay and his wife live in the country in Vermont, cutting wood for the fire, rather like Thoreau: "Another thing that a small community forces on you is self-reliance." Returning to Singapore, he feels uncomfortable: "There was even less of the solitude and quiet neighbourliness we had experienced in Vermont. Singaporeans talked about cars and property." Fay seemed to have stuck in Singapore's throat: "America was no longer a place of promise, a country of dreams that Singaporeans looked up to and felt empathy with. It was now seen as a place of violence and danger."

It is in the power to remove walls—Tay mentions the fall of the Berlin Wall—that we can see why the world needs an alien Asian whose work is structurally a Tudor Walden, a mediation.

Peter Nazareth

1998

■ HA JIN. *Under the Red Flag.* Athens, Ga. University of Georgia Press. 1997. 207 pages.

When Chen Jo-hsi published her collection of stories *The Execution of Mayor Yin* in 1978, Western literati were first introduced to the injustice and brutality brought about by the Cultural Revolution in China. Chen's emphasis in her stories was on the moral strength of men and women under persecution, with minor criticism of the political stigma which was the cause of their demise. Under the red flag, many of Chen's heroes and heroines, though physically subdued, arose spiritually. The human spirit prevails even in harsh conditions.

Ha Jin too writes about the Chinese in the Cultural Revolution, and he is likely the first author who has managed to do so in English—and to win the Flannery O'Connor Award for Short Fiction. However, his characters differ from Chen's in several respects: his protagonists happen to be ordinary farmers, prostitutes, poor teachers, and innocent adolescents; the stories he tells are not totally tragic per se, but rather tragicomic; and there are bitterness and tears behind the laughter. Ha Jin is a satirist, but at his best he is a writer of compassion, warmth, and love.

A farmer in his fifties has an adulterous relationship with his wife's sister. After the affair is revealed, his wife leaves him and returns to her family with their only son. But what is worse is the confession he is forced to write for the party secretary in order to show his sincerity and remorse. Since he cannot bear to write about the sexual details of the relationship, the farmer decides to cop out by becoming a monk, only to be told by the abbot that he needs the endorsement of the authorities. In disappointment, he plans to escape to Beijing, but before he can get there, his eye is caught by a beautiful young waitress at a restaurant where he is begging for food. Since he cannot produce a beggar's identification card, the police take him back to his home village, where he is again disciplined by the party secretary. In agitation, the farmer pulls out a pair of scissors, threatening to take his own life. The men laugh in his face and encourage him to be a martyr. Remembering that he already has a son, the farmer surprises everyone by severing his scrotum! After this incident, he is seen as a brave man who is sincere in his confession. His wife, feeling guilty over leaving him, returns home to take care of him, and his fellow villagers now respect him as a man. This story, "Resurrection," serves as an example of Ha Jin's style: sympathetic, humorous, and politically sensitive.

His tolerance and attraction to the poor and the insignificant in Chinese rural society remind me of another great writer, Lu Xun.

The twelve short stories gathered in *Under the Red Flag* give us the other side of life in China during the Cultural Revolution. Without sham or pretense, the author exposes the secret desires, the selfishness, and the innocence found among the common folk.

Fatima Wu

■ **PETER HANDKE**. *In einer dunklen Nacht ging ich aus meinem stillen Haus*. Frankfurt a.M. Suhrkamp. 1997. 316 pages.

Each one of Peter Handke's books—or so it seems in retrospect—has taught its readers a lesson. Where the author's youthful works contained lessons in a daredevil kind of genius, extending and jumping limits and borders of language, content and style, his later books offered firm proof of the possibility for renewal and transformation. Now, with his latest novel, Handke seems to be teaching his readership how to take wing and fly.

The recent completion of a thousand-page novel, *Mein Jahr in der Niemandsbucht* (1995; see *WLT* 69:3, p. 572) would leave any other author in a state of silence at least for a while. Handke, however, followed that book with an important theatrical play which premiered in early 1997 at the Vienna Burgtheater, and a mere few weeks later the novel under review was published. Still, there is neither a line that might sound reminiscent of the earlier magnum opus, nor a thought that would coincide with the play. Even though employing a first-person narrative form, Handke has written not an autobiographical text but rather a story, a "Rahmenerzählung" or frame narrative in the best old-fashioned sense. He seems to enjoy tremendously his new weaving of constellations and events; more than ever, he is a storyteller again. There is as much humor and positive superficiality as there is depth and seriousness in this novel with the unusual and long title ("On a Dark Night I Left My Quiet House") that in itself calls for amazement and dreams before we even read. A certain nearness to medieval epics is evoked in the hero's reading of the romance of Sir Ivain (Yvain, Ywain, Gawain).

Seemingly unimportant places such as the inconspicuous Salzburg suburb of Taxham are made central and are endowed by the author with magical centrality. Yes, Handke returns once again to the city of Salzburg, where he spent an important decade of his life and where his artistic self still seems to dwell quite substantially. The novel tells us the story of the pharmacist of Taxham—who may well exist in the flesh, even though the book's initial remark denies it—a friend of the author and of course the one who will tell his "Sommergeschichte," commanding Handke to write it down and doing so in a lovely, old-fashioned epilogue spiced with good advice: "Schreiben Sie nur noch Liebesgeschichten! Liebes- und Abenteuer-geschichten, nichts anderes!" The pharmacist does his job and otherwise seems to be a lonely man. His wife has gone on a trip, his daughter lives abroad, his son disappeared long ago. Frequently the pharmacist dines at the "Erdkellerrestaurant" near the Salzburg airport. There he encounters a former ski champion and a once-famous poet. The three get together without much discussion and set out on a journey across borders into wholly alien lands, where the pharmacist will eventually leave his two companions and embark on an adventure all his own, an adventure tinged with love or the absence thereof.

Nothing in this wonderful book can be anticipated or guessed; every page contains new surprises both in plot and in poetic style. It is of course, as always with Handke, the beauty of the singular image and sentence that transforms his prose into poetry or, to put it more aptly, shows the ultimate superiority of great prose. In this his newest novel, apparent ease, airy lightness, directness, and purity all contribute to make the reader dizzy with the pleasure of "finding" the right image and word, and eventually let us soar to new heights of sensation. There is much worldly concern, and many troublesome facts of our lives are touched upon in this weightless yet weighted story; there is much bitter truth brought forth, like the painfully relevant passage about the new relationships between men and women ("Zwischen Mann und Frau ist neuerdings Feindschaft gesetzt"), yet we find everywhere kind redemption of our common lot.

I think there is reason for gratitude as long as Peter Handke will write. Every book of his illuminates our growing confusion and makes me think of stained-glass windows in Gothic cathedrals: just as simple and yet complex are these stories, as readily available and healing to anyone stepping inside.

Erich Wolfgang Skwara

■ **ANNE HÉBERT**. *Est-ce que je te dérange?* Paris. Seuil. 1998. 138 pages.

The Québécoise writer Anne Hébert has been rewarded with important literary prizes whenever she has published a novel. *Les chambres de bois* received the France-Canada Prize, *Kamouraska* the Femina Prize, and *L'enfant chargé de songes* (see *WLT* 66:2, p. 323) the coveted Governor General Prize in 1992. The incident related in *Est-ce que je te dérange?* is out of the range of everyday experience. It is the story of a girl in the thrall of an unremitent yearning, drawn beyond reason to obtain the unattainable.

Delphine, a young Québécoise girl, is first obsessed with a need to escape from the farm of her grandmother, who collapsed and died, falling from her rocking chair on her deck. The haunting sight of the empty chair, rocking gently, pushed by the wind, impelled the girl to flee. Her obsessive, aimless, and nameless flight gathers impetus when a young commercial traveler from France picks her up. He takes her to his hotel and tries to slip out of her life after spending the night with her.

The by now pregnant girl spends all her grandmother's inheritance on the obsessive pursuit of "her" Patrick, doggedly following him to Paris and thereafter to the various cities where he is promoting his products. Patrick navigates with an ever-increasing unease between Scylla and Charybdis. The obsessive girl stages passionate scenes in her endeavor to wrench him from the clutches of his possessive, fat, well-to-do wife. However, it is this very wife who provides him with a comfortable life, an elegant apartment, and a country home.

Two young men with unimaginative jobs and dull, uneventful lives are strolling aimlessly in Paris when their gaze is riveted upon Delphine. She offers a mesmerizing sight, sitting on the edge of the Saint-Sulpice fountain, splashed by its spray, perfectly unaware of her surroundings like a vehicle of a stubborn force within herself. As if obsession were contagious, Stéphane and Edouard start to follow her absurd and tangled vision, responding meekly to her exigencies since only Delphine's point of view prevails. From the moment of encounter a symbiotic existence starts; they scrutinize timetables, escort Delphine to train stations, shop for maternity clothing.

Trapped by Delphine in every city wherever his job takes him, the cowardly Patrick finally breaks down and confesses to his wife. She takes this turn of events in her stride, wanting to keep both her husband and the yet unborn baby. The anticlimax of the novel explodes with the announcement of the nurse at the clinic where the two young men wait anxiously with the would-be parents. There is no baby! Delphine's big belly, described so lovingly throughout the novel, was filled with air. The novel could stop at this point; however, another surprise is still in wait.

Anne Hébert delves deeply into the uncanny region of obsession and its addictive thrill when ordinary people suddenly cross the border of reason, yielding to their unsuspected dark impulses and irrational desires, producing thus not a *folie-à-deux* but a *folie-à-trois*.

Maria A. Green

■ **AMOS OZ**. *Panther in the Basement*. Nicholas de Lange, tr. New York. Harcourt Brace. 1997. 147 pages.

Finish the food served you, concur with all your father's pronouncements, turn the bedroom lights out on time: what other steps could a twelve-year-old boy living in British-administered Palestine take in the summer of 1947 to help pave the way for a Hebrew state? Ask young Amos Oz.

The Oz family of three, with both parents working, had no radio, telephone, or automobile, and, only because it was essential, owned a small heater employed each winter against the Jerusalem cold. Spent matches were reused "as an economy measure for lighting the kerosene cooker from the stove or vice versa." In many ways they were apt representations of a spartan time and place. And in playing at being a warrior, Amos Oz was a typical pre-state boy. He and two other playmates formed an underground cell which plotted to menace Buckingham Palace with a bomb, thereby forcing the King of England to grant the Jews a homeland without further ado. Fantasy flourished in the hearts and minds of Jewish boys despite the austere atmosphere of Jerusalem. And although paid-for entertainment was rather rare, Amos and his friends were able to enjoy a few Hollywood movies. *Panther in the Basement,* starring Tyrone Power, especially caught Amos's fancy. It was a detective adventure in which the hero was wont "to assume and discard identities at his sole discretion."

The film's title is mentioned throughout the book, each time taking on fresh significance, casting light on the lovable, hesitant, yet impulsive Amos Oz as he struggles to know himself and to understand the adults around him. One evening Amos is caught by a British policeman as he zigzags through curfew time on his way home. His captor, Sergeant Dunlop, confounds Amos (nicknamed Proffi) by being friendly and making a date with him to meet regularly and swap English and Hebrew lessons. At this point Proffi decides to accept the offer and become a "panther in the basement," for he assumes the identity of "a secret agent disguised as a child interested in the English language."

Proffi (a little "professor" seduced by geography, languages, and the literature and history of diverse cultures) soon finds himself torn between his identification with the emerging Jewish state and his affection for one of the enemy. He has accepted anti-British stereotypes unquestioningly—his father writes slogans against the "perfidious" occupiers, slogans which appear on city walls. However, contact with Sergeant Dunlop, who is gentle, sweet, open, and learned, engenders both questions and feelings of guilt in the boy.

Worse still, talking with the sergeant puts aspects of the Bible in a new light and makes problematic the role of Jews who will soon establish a state in the Middle East. How unsettling for Proffi. Could the Bible teacher at school have gotten King David and his dynasty all wrong? And how seriously should Proffi take a prayer uttered by Sergeant Dunlop? It goes: "Oh that we might not also increase sorrow." Dunlop fears that through a military victory Jews might oppress local Arabs. The boy cannot put this utterance to rest.

Only twelve years old, Proffi struggles with guilt in a multitude of guises as childhood becomes alarmingly complex. He suffers pangs engendered by the admission that he has been spying on Sergeant Dunlop "and stealing secrets from him. Traitor, traitor. You're doomed." He has come to love the British sergeant as one would a father-teacher who complements an imperfect biological father.

Romantic love sends out a thread to further enliven this autobiography. Proffi has not only fallen in love with a nineteen-year-old neighbor, Yardena, but he also finds himself drawn to her sexually, as if he were a man. Their relationship touches on adult mysteries which both tantalize and mystify the boy.

Amos Oz has done an outstanding job here of re-creating Jerusalem in the last year of its domination by the British. More significantly, he has brought to life a household and neighborhood replete with vivid characters. Finally, he has bridged more than four decades in ways designed to beguile us. So compelling and true is the author's art that we let young Proffi Oz take us into his confidence: who can resist?

Michael Shuval

▪**CARYL PHILLIPS.** *The Nature of Blood.* New York/London. Knopf/Faber. 1997. 212 pages.

Caryl Phillips's *Higher Ground* is a triptych, the three different stories forming a thematic unity (see *WLT* 64:1, p. 518). *The Nature of Blood* is more complex in that we have the interweaving of the parts of different stories without any overt indication: the reader must identify the first-person narrators and locate them in time and space. Occasionally there is direct narration, frequently a violation of linear time, the fictional past as future, as present, and as the past: thoughts and memory make up an untidy room. For these reasons,

The Nature of Blood cannot be understood and fully appreciated at one reading. And for reasons of what it says, it is a work to be read several times.

The major story is that of young Jewish Eva, freed by British soldiers from a Nazi concentration camp at the end of the war. The reader pieces together her story: the daughter of a successful medical doctor, a father who refused to see the signs and failed to flee until it was too late. The family experiences humiliation, brutality, and then the awful train ride to forced labor and/or the gas chamber. "Liberated" Eva (in the circumstances, an ironic adjective) arrives in England and at the door of the soldier who had proposed marriage, only to find him with his wife and child. The thoughts of a deeply hurt and deranged individual make a deeply moving, though incoherent, story. Eva occasionally hallucinates, and so there are "fictions" (in the lay meaning) within the fictional mode. Her bewilderment is bewildering. The other stories are of Eva's uncle, who abandoned his wife and child in order to help in the founding of Israel; of what happened in 1480 to the Jews of Portobuffole (Venice), who were accused of ritually murdering a Christian boy; of Othello and of an Ethiopian Jew, a young woman airlifted with her family to Israel.

If blood is life, then *The Nature of Blood* is about the nature of existence, about suffering which is not the consequence of blind chance or of the impersonal elements but the result of deliberate human action. The novel is a fictionalizing of history—that is, the conveying of human experience through the invention of characters, lives, and expression set within a recognizable historical time frame. A considerable part of human suffering and pain arises from the seemingly ineradicable impulse we have to divide, to categorize on grounds of color, race, or religion, and then either to exclude or, worse, to subordinate and maltreat. As *The Nature of Blood* shows, suffering may be collectively imposed by one group upon another, but finally, *despair and pain are experienced individually,* by human beings isolated and trapped within their separate selfhood. However, as in all of Phillips's works, while one is moved, even sickened, by folly and cruelty, there is also a celebration of the human capacity to love, to make sacrifices, and to endure. All human beings are Jews (the name *Eva* takes us back to Eden and expulsion) in that we seek for a promised land upon this earth, for a more decent, humane, and happier life. We persist in this quest, in hoping and striving, despite repeated defeat and disillusionment. And so, at the end of the novel, the reader, like the Ancient Mariner in Coleridge's poem, is wiser and sadder—but not without strength and hope.

Charles P. Sarvan

■ **JAROSLAV SEIFERT**. *The Poetry of Jaroslav Seifert*. Ewald Osers, tr. George Gibian, ed. & tr. North Haven, Ct. Catbird. 1998. 256 pages.

How does one approach and treat a Nobel Prize winner, especially one venerated in his own country, whose language is spoken by barely twenty million people? The translators and editor of this excellent volume of poetry and prose selections opted for a course of honesty, avoiding laudatory rhetoric and allowing the reader to evaluate both the works and the themes and ideas of one of the Czech Republic's most admired poets. They have set the stage for Jaroslav Seifert to speak for himself.

Seifert chronicles his own development, eagerly confessing to acquiring "liberation" when he "discovered sensuality." From that momentous day on, he gloried in "the sensuality of freedom," categorically stating that he no longer was a proletarian poet and that his aim in poetry was "not to lie, that's all." Henceforth, Seifert became the conscience of his countrymen, suffering the consequences of his simple credo of freedom and honesty.

His message is loud and clear in each of his poems. The reader who knows no Czech will not be able to appreciate the whirlwind of delicate musical sounds produced in the original language by a master poet, but he will be able to share in the ideas and preoccupations of an artist who lived through the Holocaust and various tyrannies. It will come as a surprise to many that Seifert's attention was more often diverted to a woman's ankle than to a storm trooper's fists. He extolled "the myth of woman" and declared himself an inveterate "feminist." In his most intimate poem, "To Be a Poet," Seifert singles out music and poetry as being "the most beautiful things on earth"—"except for love, of course." And love is far from Platonic: it is always accompanied by "a woman's smile and / windblown hair."

Even when he is describing the horrors of war ("The Bombing of the Town of Kralupy"), Seifert concentrates on life: "I see the smiling faces / of those I love." His outcry against violence seems almost timid: "Never again, war!" But the words are drained from the heart. Poetry sometimes fails the senses: "Just then I could not think / of a single line!" In the mind of a poet, such a thing as war is unimaginable.

But love is ubiquitous. If woman is central to Seifert's poetic vision, Prague is the core of his thoughts. Whoever has visited Prague or "has seen her but once / will hear her name always ringing in his heart." Seifert was the Grand Minstrel of Prague, extolling, glorifying, and pleading a case for the world's most beautiful city. It is only natural that he referred to Prague in sensual

terms: "She is herself a song woven into time / and we love her."

George Gibian and Ewald Osers have not insinuated themselves into Seifert's work. They have allowed the singer of Prague to breathe for himself. They have provided the reader with the words: the rest is poetry, that's all.

E. J. Czerwinski

1999

■ **BÉATRIX BECK**. *Guidée par le songe*. Paris. Grasset. 1998. 442 pages.

Winner of the Goncourt Prize in 1952, eighty-five-year-old Béatrix Beck continues to write *nouvelles* (her preferred genre) by hand, her tablet resting on her knees as if poised for flight. Her stories at first glance are a frothy delight—tiny gems of intricate wordplay, sparkling with wit and imagination. Beck expresses herself in a shorthand staccato, eschewing grammar for immediacy, juggling words like a prestidigitator, reveling in alliteration and contrapuntal dialogue. Brief texts like "Etienne," "Javotte et Maximilien," and "Yvonne" are pyrotechnic displays of rhyme and wordplay: "La nabote Javotte sanglote. . . . Elle trotte par mottes et crottes jusqu'à la grotte de la Hulotte." With an arch disregard for the quotidian, characters named Deodat Lebègue, Emile Lorpailleur, Michel Ospedaletti, or Evelyn Ladigue-Mazoyer inhabit towns called Bourg-le-Bourg, Feuillard-les-Escouffes, Chognesur-Mer, or Vieux-Noufles and Noufles-Neuf.

Beck's is a fantasy world where the dead come to life, animals converse, gargoyles visit and carouse, a man turns into a cat, and a little girl is (possibly) changed into a toad. We soon realize, however, that dreams can turn to nightmares. In this surreal world, devoid of love, a spinster typist loses her heart to a lizard, and an old man cherishes a blaspheming gargoyle. The fears of childhood assume corporeal shape. Frequent biblical allusions—including the stories of Lot and Balaam recounted from the angel's point of view—question religious assumptions, undermine catechisms. Intimations of racism, sexual violence, and xenophobia underlie eccentric characterizations and equivocal relationships. "Vulgaires vies" is a tour de force of pithy representation: out of accumulated platitudes, saws, and rhymes, the author sketches the story of a man and woman who meet, marry, quarrel, rear children, and die; their uneventful but unhappy existence is rendered innocuous and inane by clichés. "Mémoires d'un illettré" is another tour de force, accomplished by expressing the thoughts of a man incapable of writing. Beck has a knack for imitating the speech patterns of criminals, children, the elderly. "Michel," with its ellipses and grammatical errors, is a murderer's rumination about the girlfriend he killed. Other "stories" are composed entirely of dialogue. Children's conversations can lead to blows, as in "Aurore"; their questions can embarrass and dismay, as in "Mise au point." The platitudes of everyday speech yield up their content of noxious hostility, as do insipid nursery rhymes and pugnacious puns. Misunderstandings arise from the misuse of speech. Words wound like spears (as Sarraute has pointed out). Although human beings are suspect, "Les bêtes n'ont aucun défaut."

Guidée par le songe is no sugar-sweet confection. Within the collection's fairy-tale atmosphere, individual lives are lonely and comfortless. The patter is amusing, but the outlook is bleak. Beauty and the beast cohabit uneasily. Like the trinkets in the "Bazar Demême," "il en faut pour tous les goûts, même du moche pour ceux qui l'aiment." Behind the cheery façade, hobgoblins lurk.

Gretchen Rous Besser

▪ANDRÉE CHEDID. *Lucy: La femme verticale.* Paris. Flammarion. 1998. 94 pages.

Born in Egypt, the French author Andrée Chedid has made Paris her home since 1946. In addition to nearly thirty volumes of poetry, she has published novels, short stories, plays, and essays, for which she has received numerous prestigious awards, most recently the Prix Albert Camus in 1996. *Lucy* falls under the rubric of *récit,* which Chedid defines elsewhere as a true story related as a fable or parable. *La femme de Job,* written in 1993 (see *WLT* 68:3, p. 524), is another example of this genre in Chedid's works.

As the title suggests, *Lucy: La femme verticale* was inspired by the female hominid skeleton known as *Australopithecus afarensis,* which was discovered by Dr. Donald Johanson in 1974 in the Hadar region of Ethiopia and has since become a cultural icon. *Lucy* is written in three parts. The first, "L'appel," introduces a recurrent theme in Chedid's works: the puissance of the "call" of an inner voice. The tale begins with Lucy's interior monologue and her response to the call that impels her to stand erect. Because Lucy lacks speech, she appropriates the voice of the female narrator at the threshold of the third millennium. This fusion, the narrator tells us, is made possible by the evolutionist perspective that all living things originated in the stars. Through her narrator, Chedid posits the alliance between "the fable

and the real": Lucy, who heretofore existed only in the narrator's dreams, will become a reality for her. At the crux of Chedid's parable lies the fundamental query of the creative artist at the turn of the millennium: do we know any truth beyond our own fictions?

In the short story "Après le jardin" (from *Mondes, Miroirs, Magies,* 1988; see *WLT* 62:4, p. 720), which was revised in an artistic collaboration as *Le jardin perdu,* Chedid explores the myth of the Fall as it relates to the question of individual autonomy. In *Lucy* she revisits the primordial world of the Garden before the birth of humankind. Lucy's response to the call of her inner voice leads the narrator to reconsider the proverbial dilemma of man's inhumanity to man. In the second part of the parable, "Le crime," the narrator plots to kill Lucy and thereby preserve the world's innocence. However, in the final section, "Le désir," she returns to the beginning of her story and rewrites it. As the narrator witnesses once again Lucy's struggle to stand, she recognizes in her simian ancestor her own aspiration to exceed the limitations of the flesh. Finally, moved by the appeal in Lucy's eyes, the narrator helps her to stand. Lucy's desire to stand upright becomes the narrator's desire for life, ultimately reflected in the dreams of the creative imagination.

The author's sonorous, forceful prose creates a rhythmic counterpoint to the struggle she depicts. With deceptively transparent imagery and a fluidity of language closer to poetry than to prose, Andrée Chedid recreates one of the important myths of Western thought, recasting it in the light of the third millennium.

Judy Cochran

▪JULIO CORTÁZAR. *Save Twilight / Salvo el crepúsculo: Selected Poems of Julio Cortázar.* Stephen Kessler, tr. San Francisco. City Lights. 1997. viii + 169 pages.

Throughout his career, Julio Cortázar (1914–84), like many fiction writers, wrote poems on the sly—on planes, in hotel rooms—but he was reluctant to publish them in book form. Toward the end of his life, however, he agreed to gather these desultory compositions for publication but made no attempt to arrange them chronologically; in fact, he suggested something of a "hopscotch" approach, the reading strategy recommended in his novel of the same name. For Cortázar, literature, like life, was a game, one in which *poemas* (poems) could become *pameos* and *meopas.* The collection finally appeared, posthumously, in a 1984 Mexican edition under the title *Salvo el crepúsculo.*

Drastically reducing the size of the original volume, translator Stephen Kessler has produced, in a bilingual, facing-page format, a sampling that conveys "the range of Cortázar's poetic accomplishment." The individual selections, which traverse the spectrum from the surreal to the mundane, from free forms to traditional ones (e.g., the sonnet), reflect the personal preferences of the translator rather than any objective criteria.

Cortázar the poet advocates living life to the fullest. His poems are meditations on such vital areas as friendship, the aging process, and nostalgia for a lost Buenos Aires and the games of youth. He writes of life's evolution from conformity to the shedding of restraints and celebrates the freedom of individual sexual expression. Many selections deal with matters of love (including its absence), especially the intensity and brevity of physical love. Readers also get a glimpse of the writer's struggles to create a poem and the exile's efforts to re-create himself. In short, the poems reveal how, for Cortázar, art and life are intimately intertwined.

Not surprisingly, Cortázar inserts several prose interludes throughout the volume. These not only display the humor and playfulness that characterize much of his work but also open a window to his thoughts on poetry ad the poetic process. These pieces prove, at least in some instances, as interesting as the poems themselves. Discounting the idea that one should not mix prose with poetry (obviously, poetry comes in diverse formats: novels, stories, songs, plays, films), he writes in these mini-essays about the writers who influenced him, the notion that an artist should be free to go against the grain, how poets should not comment on their own work (and then he proceeds to do so), and his unwillingness to trust the literary judgments of others. He concludes with a frank discussion of his battles with insomnia, how he developed a personal mandala to cope with the problem, and how dreams inevitably find their way into his writing.

In this reluctant selection Cortázar allows the reader to become intimate with his innermost thoughts and feelings. Those unfamiliar with Spanish should be grateful to Kessler for facilitating such an esthetically gratifying encounter.

Melvin S. Arrington Jr.

■ **SEAMUS HEANEY**. *Opened Ground: Selected Poems 1966–1996*. New York. Farrar, Straus & Giroux. 1998. 444 pages.

Ireland is a country of only about four million people, but in this century it has produced four Nobel Prize winners in literature: Yeats, Shaw, Beckett, and Heaney. To average one world-famous writer for every million people is a record that makes a small nation like Ireland

seem singularly blessed. Some might say its literary blessing comes at the price of a political curse, since the island has long been one of the world's trouble spots. The political curse, however, has often been a boon to Irish writers. "Out of Ireland have we come / Great hatred, little room," Yeats once remarked poetically. And James Joyce, a voluntary exile, the one indisputably great Irish writer never honored by a Nobel Prize, wrote even more bitterly about his native land, "Ireland is the old sow that eats her farrow."

Heaney can be every bit as scathing as Yeats or Joyce about the Irish character: "we slaughter for the common good," he says in one of his poems. But his gift for language, combined with his frequent quarrels with his native land, have earned him his place in the distinguished line of Irish writers. The quarrels seem more evident in the ample new collection *Opened Ground* than in the slimmer volumes which earned him the Nobel Prize in 1995 (see *WLT* 70:2, pp. 253–66). Of all Ireland's Nobel laureates, Heaney seems most consistently agitated about Irish politics, especially the still-smoldering civil war that clouds many of the poems in this ample volume, which, he insists in a foreword, is a selected and not a collected works.

Unlike Yeats and Shaw and Beckett, his Nobel predecessors, Heaney is identified with the Irish Catholic majority, even if he comes from Northern Ireland, where the majority are Protestant Irish. In Ireland, it could be argued, the minority always has the most compelling voice: Yeats was a Protestant born in the South, and Heaney is a Catholic born in the North. As Heaney notes in his Nobel Lecture, "Crediting Poetry" (printed here as a prose epilogue to the poems), "Yeats barely alluded to the civil war or the war of independence in his Nobel speech . . . he chose to talk instead about the Irish Dramatic Movement." Thus Heaney, speaking to a world audience, acknowledged an artistic as well as religious difference from Yeats, for Yeats was preeminently a lyric poet, whereas Heaney has been prevailingly a polemical poet. Yeats dramatized himself as "a sixty-year-old smiling, public man" self-critically, tracing the conflicts in Irish politics to classical and biblical roots of human imperfection; Heaney has written about the troubles around him more painfully, as proof of man's natural inhumanity to man, his "kinship" with his savage ancestors. Even when indignant, Yeats always managed somehow to sing, "and louder sing / For every tatter in his mortal dress," whereas Heaney seems obliged to speak out even when he sings.

He speaks as much as he sings in all his poems, even his most moving poems about the vast peaty wetlands that are a unique feature of the Irish landscape. They become his poetic symbol for Ireland, from "Digging," the first poem in the collection, through "Bog-land" and "The Tollund Man" and the "Bog Queen," poems which made him famous as the Poet of the Bogs. Heaney anguishes again and again over the feudal trib-alism of the Irish, who have inherited a sort of national suicide wish that threatens to catch everyone in its le-thal net. Those relatively few, early bog poems are his major legacy, eloquent in their probing of historical conscience, going below the more recent Protestant and Catholic hatreds into primeval Celtic behavior, "do-mains of the cold-blooded," where stark evidence of a murderous past has been perfectly preserved in the changeless vegetable kingdom of the bogs. Though he expresses hope in some of his poems for a gradual less-ening of Irish tensions, and though he has clearly worked hard to become a more international poet by translating passages from Dante, Virgil, and Aeschylus, the best of his later poems are, like the best of his early poems, intensely Irish, but more topical and less evoca-tive, more prosaic and less poetic, and there are in this copious collection many more of the forgettable than of the memorable.

William Pratt

▪**JAMES KELMAN**. *The Good Times*. London. Secker & Warburg. 1998. 246 pages.

The Good Times is an extremely ironic title for James Kelman's collection of twenty short stories. Much more suitable would be "Every Fucking Time," the title of a representative story whose narrator waits forever in a pub for his wife to appear, as she had promised, and finally goes home to find that she is not there either and that she has forgotten all about him. What he needs is "a bit of peace and fucking fuck knows what, just peace; peace." What he receives is frustration—every fucking time.

So do all the other protagonists in the volume, However, they do lots of talking in the process, always in the lower-middle-class lingo of Glasgow pubs.

> That wee bastard McKenzie was with them, I dont know if ye mind of him, Danny McKenzie, he went south. Good wee player but a fucking dirty little fucking bastard so he was.
>
> Dannie McKenzie? said Gus.
>
> Danny McKenzie, aye.
>
> Did he no go junior?
>
> Naw. I laughed, shook my head: Naw, he went down to England straight. [. . .] The game I'm talking about, the Possil, I'm no saying we ran rings round them, I'm no meaning that. It was just fucking. . . . Ye want to have seen Jackie Bai-ley eftir the game, I thought he was gony fucking kiss us all!

James Kelman won the Booker Prize in 1994, for *How Late It Was, How Late*. Previously, he received the James Tait Black Memorial Prize and was shortlisted for the Booker. In this volume his great accomplishment is the creation of frighteningly realistic dialogue between men (always men!) whose lives are meaningless but who nevertheless need desperately to pass the time.

In the title story a middle-aged husband, sensing his physical diminution and inescapable boredom, fan-tasizes regarding the teenagers he views on television. Yet he knows he can never be a teenager—indeed never even *was* one. The good times, indeed! In "Constella-tion" the theme is expectation sabotaged by circum-stance. A young man visits his girlfriend only to find that she is playing host to a handsome Dutch tourist be-cause his wallet has been stolen. In the sardonically en-titled "Strength," another middle-aged husband remem-bers the excitement of riding a motorcycle with his wife but is now sickly, on a regimen of pills. In "Sustenance Sustenance," which is only two pages long, the narrator meditates on cutting up carrots, leeks, and garlic in the kitchen, but of course grating his knuckles as well. In "The Norwest Reaches" a husband with a baby and a nagging wife goes out in the cold to buy bread for breakfast. He finds the bakery cozy and warm: another world where he wishes he could remain instead of re-turning to his dismal home.

Clearly, one does not need to read all these stories, for in theme and technique they are similar. A sampling is enough to convey the author's strengths.

Peter Bien

▪**GISÈLE PINEAU**. *L'âme prêtée aux oiseaux*. Paris. Stock. 1998. 221 pages.

L'âme prêtée aux oiseaux, the fifth novel by the Guade-loupean writer Gisèle Pineau, is something of a disap-pointment. The novel, which centers on the lives of three different women from three different countries during three different historical periods, is a narrative about the divisions caused by racism and exploitation, as well as the potential for overcoming such divisions. The three central characters in the novel—Sybille, a young single mother from Guadeloupe; Lila, a flamboy-ant French woman; and Jenny, a young girl from Barba-dos—are all women who have had illegitimate children as the result of a failed love relationship, and through them the novel attempts to provide a hopeful vision of the power of love.

Sybille, the first of the women to be introduced, comes to Paris with her son Marcello in order to escape from the memories of her relationship with Marcello's father. While in Paris, she befriends an elderly woman, Lila, who tells Sybille stories of her romantic adventures, and particularly of her relationship with a black American soldier shortly after the end of World War II. Eventually, Lila reveals that she bore a biracial son from her liaison with this man, but that, unable to cope with the racism of those around her, she gave up this son to his father. Consequently, Lila is a stranger to her own son, who has grown up in the United States, ignorant of her existence.

Jenny, the third woman on whom the text centers, falls in love with the son of the rich plantation owner for whom she works. Like Lila, she has a biracial son from this relationship, and just as in Lila's story, the white parent—in this case the father—is unable to confront the racism of others and embrace his own child. Jenny, however, does not abandon her son. Instead, she chooses, like Sybille, to move to another country—the United States—and raise him on her own. Jenny's son, Henry, grows up to be the soldier with whom Lila is involved after the war. Thus the lives of the three women are linked not only through their experiences, but literally through their own personal love relationships—a fact which becomes evident when Sybille falls in love with Lila and Henry's son, James-Lee.

As a result of Sybille and James-Lee's emerging love affair, the divisions of racism which have separated all the characters in the novel are erased. Woven into each of these stories are anecdotes about birds that die, or that fly away. The presence of these birds, which are clearly symbols of brokenhearted lovers, accounts for the title of the novel. The use of the birds as symbols becomes a bit overburdening quite quickly, and it is not clear that their presence adds much to the novel.

While *L'âme prêtée aux oiseaux* contains many of the elements present in Pineau's earlier novels (overlapping narratives, temporal shifts, multiple narrators), it lacks the power and magic of her best work. Unlike those novels (see e.g. *WLT* 71:4, p. 848), where the intertwining of narratives creates an air of mystery and a sense of collective destiny, *L'âme prêtée aux oiseaux* is confusing at times, overly predictable at others. Furthermore, although the work is constructed of the same poetic and multivalent prose which is characteristic of Pineau's writing in general, the text as a whole lacks the vivid realism and the almost fairy-tale magic of Pineau's earlier novels. From a lesser writer, *L'âme prêtée aux oiseaux* might have seemed like a more interesting work. However, from someone like Pineau, whose writing generally captivates and enchants while subtly raising questions as to the relationship between history and exploitation, between language and identity, between na-

tionality and subjectivity, this particular novel feels more like a first draft than a final version.

Dayna Oscherwitz

2000

■ **ISABEL ALLENDE.** *Hija de la fortuna.* Barcelona. Plaza & Janes. 1999. 429 pages.

Imagine an intricate macramé design. In order to understand its construction, you must first follow all the threads, through their intersections and knots, slowly but surely comprehending how the original unconnected strands came together to form the new, complex whole. This is how one must approach Isabel Allende's sagalike novel, *Hija de la fortuna.* She unravels the various threads that are her characters, harking back to their childhoods, or to the childhoods of people who influenced them, in order to demonstrate how they became the people they are and need to be at important junctures in the story. With so much background information on the various characters, the plot moves very slowly. Allende violates a cardinal rule of writing and allows too much of the characters' back-story to intrude on her narrative, leaving the reader confused and unsatisfied at the point the novel ends.

The three-part novel begins in Valparaíso, Chile, in 1843. There Allende introduces the transplanted British family of Jeremy Sommers, his sister Miss Rose, a spinster, and his brother John, a sea captain. The title character is Eliza, a foundling whom Rose adopts and raises as her own daughter. Since the California gold rush of 1849 forms an axis which draws many of the characters from their home countries of China, Chile, and England, one assumes from the title that Eliza will strike it rich, or that perhaps her wealthy English family will provide her with an inheritance. However, since the word *fortuna* also connotes the ideas of luck and fate, the title is inherently ambiguous.

In the end, both of these concepts—chance and destiny—help the reader understand Eliza's journey in the novel. She moves from the protected womblike environment of the Sommerses' home to the California gold fields, in search of the lover who abandoned her. Cultural and sexual identities change or are subverted throughout the book. Eliza cross-dresses first as a Chinese laborer, later as a Mexican male, denying her Chilean-British femininity. Deciding to stay in California, she uses the folk medicine she learned from her Indian nanny in Chile to work alongside the healer Tao Chi'en, who had hidden her aboard ship. Tao is the one who

Isabel Allende (*Archive Photos, Inc.*)

cares the most for Eliza, and who eventually becomes "the path" she must follow in what becomes her search for self-realization. As she travels the gold fields looking for her lover Joaquín, Eliza soon realizes that she has fallen in love with freedom instead.

By the novel's end, the characters have revealed their darkest secrets, and the reader understands that they have lived disguised even from those closest to them. Allende describes foods, odors, illnesses, costumes, rooms, et cetera, in a baroque avalanche of detail. Once the layers of characterization and description are peeled away, the reader is left with these final nuggets of wisdom: that each person must search for his or her own identity, despite the historical limitations of gender and race, despite the emotional baggage and the people standing in the way, and that sometimes the beauty is in the search itself.

Teresa R. Arrington

■ **LUIGI FONTANELLA.** *Terra del tempo e altri poemetti.* Bologna. Book Editore. 2000. 98 pages.

After an Initial Sounding, one could readily posit that the virtuosity of the poet Luigi Fontanella resides in his extraordinary abilities as a "traveler/missionary" for Italian poetry, both in America and in Europe, as the

founder of the Italian Poetry Society of America, as the disseminator of poetry written in both Italy and America by means of the international review *Gradiva,* and as the "artificer" of genuine books of poetry (his own). But as if by magic, with each new volume one is made aware of the freshness, the timeliness of his poems, some of them written nearly thirty years ago. Meanwhile his most recent poetry is like a rare hothouse flower blooming in Fontanella's garden, laid out like a golf course, with surprising bridges between pleasure and reflection which, in the end, enliven both author and readers. Fontanella is essentially the transcriber of unique lyric moments in a poetic corpus that is neither too fertile (abundant) nor too facile (redundant), yet shines with a contemporary relevance that carries it well beyond its cycles of conception and completion.

While reading *Terra del tempo e altri poemetti* (The Land of Time and Other Poems), I closed my eyes and imagined the poet's fingers as they meticulously explored the desk's drawers in search of old and more recent unedited material: for instance, the shorter narrative "New York New York," written in the winter of 1978, and "La veglia dell'ultimo soldato" (The Last Soldier's Vigil), composed in the summer of 1999. I then followed his hands as they reached up to select large and small tomes so as to extract from them, with the tender touch of a horticulturist, a few rare blossoms grown both in the garden and in the wilderness, as well as some topazes and emeralds bearing such titles as "Voyare" (Voyaging; 1970), or "Voltaluna" (Moon-Turning; 1977), or "Foglio stazione" (Station Sheet; 1989), or "Suite per mio padre" (Suite for My Father; composed in 1987 and published in 1997 and 1998).

The first previously unpublished poem presented here was composed in the winter of 1978; it is a testimonial to the poet's initial encounter with America, whose existential impact is concretized in the poem's raw linguistic toughness, which recalls the acrimonious and cutting voice of Federico García Lorca, who had visited New York in 1929–30. On one side it expresses a lyric sentiment that is tempered with European moral arrogance vis-à-vis the "cityscape" of the New World, while on the other side it exhibits a shockingly startled countenance. Although it is possible to ignore "Nocturno de Battery Place," the poem wherein Lorca describes a "paisaje de la multitud que orina" ("a cityscape where the masses urinate"), the same cannot be done with "Ode a Walt Whitman," overflowing with generic vituperative insults against America that seem to unfold with apocalyptic gravity: "Faggots of the world, murderers of doves! / Slaves of women. Their bedroom bitches." Fontanella also finds himself face to face with the "infected carcass" that is "New York New York" and asks himself: "what will become of you, turbid city-cloaca / to whom will you proffer your paper-made flowers / among the muffled yells of Central Park / and the crazed siren's screams near these unknown tourists / who don't see the hanged man who drools out his final breaths; / to whom will you flash your Credit Card and your Social Security Number / as you stand in front of that seagull confused by the waves / searching for the home that is past."

The second unpublished poem, "La veglia dell'ultimo soldato" (The Last Soldier's Vigil; 1999), recalls D'Annunzio's poem "La pioggia nel pineto" (Eng. "Rain in the Pine Forest"), evoking that torrential downpour by means of phonic seduction and delicate sensuality. The imaginary lady of these verses is not the "real" Ermione of D'Annunzio, a sensuous and fascinating creature whose "entwined leaves of grass / glisten with moonbeams / and with the silvery waves of the stream / that flow by with patience and violence / while piercing [her] hands." In Fontanella one senses a milk-like ductility, a feminine sensibility at home in the drawing room as well as on the barricades: it bewitches without corrupting us; it seeks admission without forcing its way in. In essence, his best interlocutors and interpreters are those female presences who seem profoundly co-involved with the poet as friends/lovers and mothers.

In general, Fontanella's poetry is contagious, luminous, and idea-filled, as in "Interno/Esterno," which weaves together complete opposites in a "paper-made prison" wherein the lessons of surrealism are transformed into verbal hyperreality, into a lyric instant, purely for pleasure, for the remembrance of having been alive, for the emotion that silences the voice, for the tenderness that prompts a teardrop, for the scream that both wounds and liberates. It is as if Horace's *Carpe diem* had become, for Fontanella, a clock-hand that registers the poet's quotidian instances of "leave-time" on a planet overflowing with machines, trains, and round-trip plane travel, the fluctuations of soul and body, and everything moves him toward "new discoveries": "And that is how, suddenly, / all is anew the beginning."

In the overarching constructs of virtual and real green pastures, of the remasticated and the genuinely new, the present reader of Fontanella's poetic oeuvre succeeds in seeing (even without eyeglasses) that the old revisited poetry offered in *Terra del tiempo* splendidly upholds a place of its own, side by side with the new; and the new confidently offers good company to the old, thus composing a unique entity, a complete blossom dressed in true royal hues.

Giose Rimanelli

■YASUNARI KAWABATA. *First Snow on Fuji.* Michael Emmerich, tr. Washington, D.C. Counterpoint. 1999. xiii + 227 pages.

Collected from works that originally appeared between January 1952 and January 1958, and subsequently published as an anthology a decade before Kawabata Yasunari (1899–1972) won the Nobel Prize in Literature, *First Snow on Fuji* comprises nine short stories and an unusual dramatic piece. While it borders on the trite to describe Kawabata's writings as haiku-like, lyrical, or sparsely evocative of transient beauty, so frequently are these concepts raised in discussion of his work, such descriptions are fitting for the ten stories in this collection written in the autumn of Kawabata's career, despite their hackneyed tone. In the best sense, these stories simultaneously offer confirmation of those aspects of Kawabata with which we are already familiar from his "major" works, while expanding our appreciation of the author by shedding light on nuances only hinted at previously.

The collection is wonderfully varied, and although it is difficult to identify a common thread in all the works—unless we accept Emmerich's supposition that it is simply the author's preference—there are certain themes that form linked subsets. Death is one such theme. "Chrysanthemum on the Rock" (1952) is an exquisite rumination on the nature of gravestones, while "Silence" (1953) questions what it means to die, and what its aftermath might be. Even as he warns against overreading "Silence," Emmerich playfully suggests that it obliquely adumbrates Kawabata's 1972 suicide in his Zushi studio. This self-aware irresponsibility infuses the story with the force of a cautionary tale: don't overread the author into his works.

Several stories are particularly poignant, revealing a Kawabata at the height of his art describing with trademark economy the intersections of beauty, desire, and regret. "Her Husband Didn't" (1958), "This Country, That Country" (1956)—perhaps the most engaging piece in the collection—and the title story (1952) all limn the contours of unrealized, illicit, or misdirected love. The theme uniting the three is the tenuous nature of relationships and the ephemeral nature of "solutions" to love's problems. To round out the collection, Kawabata included the enigmatic "Boat-Woman" (1954), one of only two dramatic works that he wrote during his career and his first attempt at buyō (traditional dance), as a commemoration. It evinces a very loose connection to the poetic traditions of nō drama, both in style and in taking as its antecedent the historically significant Heike clan defeat by the Genji clan during the Genpei war (1180–85).

Emmerich, through his comfortably tight translations, brings to a wider audience a facet of Kawabata's oeuvre that will certain enliven studies of Kawabata's shorter fiction. As with any translation, Emmerich has made choices that will not necessarily satisfy all people, yet in aggregate, his renderings read well with a flow that generally does not betray their status as translations. Occasional inconsistencies in romanization and omitted macrons, a mildly haphazard application of explanatory footnotes, and a lack of original date of publication for the stories are but minor quibbles in an otherwise enjoyable addition to the body of Kawabata literature in English.

Erik R. Lofgren

■ **FRANK MCCOURT.** *'Tis.* New York. Scribner. 1999. 367 pages.

If *Angela's Ashes,* this sequel's predecessor, had not been one of the most delicious autobiographies ever written, perhaps we would not be so disappointed in its successor, which, thank goodness, is not entitled *Angela's Ashes II.* The eighteenth and penultimate chapter of the earlier book ended with the nineteen-year-old Frank McCourt sailing from Cork, Ireland, into Albany, New York, looking at the lights of America twinkling, and the Wireless Officer of his freighter saying to him, "Isn't this a great country altogether?" The nineteenth and final chapter in its entirety: "'Tis." Hence the title, and the taking-off point, for these memoirs of a young American-born exile returning to his homeland after sixteen years in Darkest Ireland.

Is it because the USA did not turn out to be as great as the returned migrant expected that the deeply heartwarming enchantment of *Angela's Ashes*—impoverished Ireland as seen subjectively from within—has waned into the cool but humorous disenchantment of *'Tis,* rich America as seen objectively from without? To the contrary, McCourt's beady-eyed observations of his new society are precisely the best reasons for reading this altogether enthralling book . . . and I will return to these later.

What *does* account, then, for the undeniable drop in charm and hypnotic magnetism since the first installment? Can it be that memoirs of childhood inevitably evoke more enchantment than do memoirs of young manhood? We have had enough Châteaubriands, Casanovas, Gides, and Pepyses to know that this does not necessarily follow. Can it be that the extraordinarily well-deserved critical and commercial success of *Angela's Ashes* prompted McCourt's publishers to urge him to churn out another financial blockbuster doublequick? Did McCourt himself get tired of the whole proceedings, especially after seeing the misfired film version of his first book? Did the celebrated hullabaloo of his brothers' joining in on the exploitation of their past on paper and on stage cast a pall on Frank's private endeavor? I can't tell you.

But what I *can* tell you is that this is one splendid book despite its inevitable comparison with its predecessor, and not only for the wonderfully human tales McCourt continues to narrate (and the wonderful way he narrates them), but because he sees the differences between America and the rest of the world (including other English-speaking countries) as few Americans can see her by themselves, and knows how to communicate what he sees—and that really is where the chief value of this book exists. McCourt does not take America as the central point of reference for the rest of the world, the way the *noo* and lamentable *Encarta World Dictionary of the English Language* does. Take this early comment:

> In America a torch is called a flashlight. A biscuit is called a cookie, a bun is a roll. Confectionery is pastry and minced meat is ground. Men wear pants instead of trousers. . . . The lift is an elevator and if you want a WC or a lavatory you have to say bathroom even if there isn't a sign of a bath there. And no one dies in America, they pass away or they're deceased and when they die the body, which is called the remains, is taken to a funeral home . . . and then it's taken away in a casket to be interred. They don't like saying coffin and they don't like saying buried. They never say graveyard. Cemetery sounds nicer.

He sees through the most deep-seated American myths too, wondering, for example, how a country can consider itself "the world's melting-pot" when its cities are divided into insular neighborhoods: Irish, Italian, Chinese, Jewish, Black, Puerto Rican, et cetera. These critiques are not limited to superficial comments, and they often cut deep indeed.

There is hardly a page that does not contain incisive insights, all of which must have taken a lifetime of observation and note-taking. I particularly commend the sidelong but clear analysis of how Sergeants in our Ultra-Prussian Army speak to buck privates. It is a privilege to share in McCourt's experiences, and in his reflections on them.

Clearly, neither the treatment nor the goal of *'Tis* is the same as in *Angela's Ashes.* The main interest this time is not reliving personal suffering in a social context but observing and delineating a social context itself, the inanities of American culture as compared to other cultures, but with the unstated inference that other cultures have their inanities too. I take issue with Michiko

Kakutani, who in the *New York Times* took McCourt's observations as "resentments." I call them "illuminations" and hold them up as excellent reasons for reading this wonderful book. Just don't expect another *Angela's Ashes.* 'Tain't!

Leslie Schenk

■ **HELEN MEIER.** *Liebe Stimme.* Zürich. Ammann. 2000. 178 pages.

Since 1984 the Ammann Verlag has published six short-story collections and two novels by the contemporary Swiss author Helen Meier. She writes with wit and humor, using an elliptical style and at times a biting, devastating irony well suited to the short-story form. Much more readable than her recent novel *Die Novizin* (1995; see WLT 70:1, p. 184), *Liebe Stimme,* a collection of twenty-two stories, some as brief as two pages in length, provides a rich variety of themes and denouements revolving loosely around apprehensions and misapprehensions of love. None of the subjects is tragic or entirely absurd; rather, these are little gems of description, tolerance, and insight, reminiscent of the rhymed vignettes of Sebastian Brandt's *Ship of Fools.* With even less satiric intention than the sketches of Honoré Daumier or George Grosz, they are portraits of different kinds of modern Europeans, old and young, male and female. Although the treatments are evenhanded throughout, Meier is especially good at portraying the psyches, fantasies, and imagined in-adequacies of women.

The characters are in turn amusing, shocking, lascivious, poignant, grotesque, and sad, all described economically and with devastating honesty. Inevitably, contemporary society—its façades and its insensitivities—is also revealed in the text, often in surprising ways. An example is the disarmingly simple and also shocking two-page story which takes place on a train. It is titled "Angenehm" (Pleasant), despite a grisly accident which has taken the life of a railroad employee. Some of the tales are surreal; others make use of one striking symbol, like that of a turtle being dropped from a height by a raptor and taken to the nest to feed its young. The mutilated turtle dies only when the nestlings devour its living heart ("Lady Curzon").

Meier is especially gifted at describing the thoughts of disappointed, slightly hysterical, and often cruelly immoral middle-aged characters, such as those in "Sternennacht," but she also excels at humorous twists: for example, the discovery of the sexual proclivities of a figure in the story ironically entitled "Das Paar" (The Couple). In some stories there is no conventional human love object, but instead a mania, such as that for

building a house in "Capital Gain." This tale exposes the foolish ways in which we deceive ourselves by believing that we can have what we want, no matter how costly or unusual our desires may be. When reality intrudes, as it always does in these tales, it is the author's great gift that she does not leave the reader or the characters bitter and despairing, but instead reconciled, resigned, wiser, and even calm in their disappointment. In other stories they have missed the significance of their experiences altogether, and so they are content.

Liebe Stimme is a book of rare entertaining qualities, a joy to read, full of variety and charm, yet also tasteful, literate, well-written, and intelligent.

Erlis Wickersham

■ **RAJENDRA SINGH.** *The Shirt of Flame.* Calcutta. Writers Workshop. 1999. 314 pages.

It Is a Matter of common knowledge that epic narratives are very few in modern Indian English literature. Even the abridged versions of the *Ramayana* and the *Mahabharata* by R. C. Dutt, Sri Aurobindo's *Savitri,* and K. R. Srinivas Iyendar's *Sitayana* are all poetic retellings or revisions of age-old Hindu myths. There is hardly any epic narrative in modern Indian English literature dealing with a contemporary theme. The traditional Hindu writers are notorious for their obsession with mythic themes and hardly interested in the burning problems of contemporary or historical life. Viewed against this background, Rajendra Singh's *Shirt of Flame* is a refreshing composition filling in the long-felt desideratum. A very interesting literary experiment in Indian English literature, it is a sequence of 575 sonnets with a common theme running through it, obviously inspired by Vikram Seth's *Golden Gate.* To deal successfully with any theme at such length is indeed a remarkable achievement. Singh therefore deserves our congratulations for such a refreshing and sustained effort in his "novel in verse."

The most interesting aspect of Singh's epic sequence is its contemporary setting and its re-creation of the ethos of northern India, especially rural Uttar Pradesh, with all its cultural details. Mahatma Gandhi said that the real India is rural India, and Singh has done a wonderful job of evoking a very authentic picture of rural India, with all its flora and fauna, pastoral-agricultural atmosphere, caste problems, family feuds, social evils, politics, et cetera. The poem is epic in its canvas, alternately comic and tragic in its tone, and witty and satirical in its realism. It is the purity of the native theme that gives a remarkable freshness to the poem, which fortunately is not modeled upon some Western classic. The eighteen chapters of this sonnet sequence easily owe their allegiance to the numerological importance of the number eighteen in the Indian epics and puranas.

The Shirt of Flame deals with the struggles and successes of Harial Singh. Far from being a representative of the highest ideals of his culture—which an epic hero is—Harial happens to be an embodiment of the most practical, opportunistic, and immoral pursuits of modern life. Money, sex, power, and success are his top priorities, and morality is his archenemy. In this sense, the poem can be described as a satire on modern Indian life wherein values are topsy-turveyed. The first half of the poem deals with his personal life, whereas the latter half deals with his sociopolitical life. But in both aspects he exhibits unscrupulous opportunism, selfishness, callousness, corruption, and shamelessness. Having failed in the fourth standard, Harial takes charge of financial matters at home from his father Sardar Singh. While he dislikes his younger brother Bhopal Singh, he likes his younger brother Dalpat Singh for his sycophancy. The family's common fund for buying a he-buffalo he misappropriates for the pleasures of drinking and visiting prostitutes, and on one occasion he steals Bhopal's buffalo in the latter's absence. Following Bhopal's complaint to the police, Harial is arrested and imprisoned. Upon his release, he decides to take revenge, eventually poisoning Bhopal with a sweet dish of *halwa*.

In the latter half of the poem, Harial's evil nature extends to his sociopolitical relationships. Inspired by rural political circumstances, he runs for office and succeeds in getting elected as Pradhan of the village panchayat by systematically abducting the Harijan voters. Capitalizing on the antagonism between high-caste and low-caste Hindus, he humiliates the latter by sealing their only well, thereby creating an acute drinking-water problem. He reopens the well only after eliciting an apology from his enemy Jogi Ram. Harial achieves success by foul, immoral, and nefarious means in everything that he undertakes. Through his depiction of this contemporary "hero," the poet offers a satiric vision of Indian society wherein evil triumphs over good in all matters, from familial to social to political. He exhibits a remarkably subtle perceptiveness in showing the helplessness of good, innocent, illiterate villagers against the evil machinations of people like Harial. The imagery sparsely employed in the poem is pointed, sarcastic, and uninhibited, and the language has a freshness that is rare in Indian English poetry. Kudos to Rajendra Singh.

Basavaraj Naikar

2001

■ **AHARON APPELFELD**. *Kol Asher Ahavti*. Jerusalem. Keter. 1999. 213 pages.

The Fate of a Fractured, tragic family represented in Aharon Appelfeld's *Kol Asher Ahavti* (All That I Have Loved) mirrors the fate of many Jews in Central Europe in the late 1930s. In this modern tale of anxiety, uncertainty, and pain, a truncated family is doomed to suffer illnesses, pain, discrimination, and death.

The deep-seated sense of frustration among Jewish intellectuals in Central Europe is not a new theme for Appelfeld, having appeared in several of his earlier novels (*The Age of Wonders* among others). In this novel, the first-person narrator is a nine-year-old boy, Paul, whose point of view orchestrates the unfolding events. His young parents—a father who is a frustrated painter, art teacher, and heavy drinker, and a mother who is a beautiful schoolteacher—are divorced. The child does not attend school and focuses his obsessive dependency and love on his mother. The father appears occasionally, taking the boy out to bars and coffeehouses. Everything the young boy loves is taken away from him gradually and painfully.

Discord, silence, and tension accompany the child's existence. By means of this protagonist, Appelfeld introduces places that were seminal in his own childhood. The mother and son reside in Czernowitz, the city of Appelfeld's youth, and Stroznitz, his grandparents' village. The modern secular Jew who has lost touch with his roots is a constant marker in Appelfeld's fiction. The attraction of Christian ritual and the frustration connected with overt and covert anti-Semitism create a no-exit situation. Lurking in the background are the traditional Orthodox Jews in their black garb who fascinate the young boy. In a sense, they bespeak continuity and faith. Dreams are the boy's escape from a world of uncertainty and fear. Conversations in this novel are sparse, and the atmosphere takes center stage in creating a sense of inevitable disaster. Suppression, silence, and motion typify the characters in the novel.

The absence of memory and existential angst unite the separated parents. Both lost their own parents and were raised in an orphanage. The sensual mother and the stormy, artistic father are locked in their own dark existence. The beauty of nature in the countryside and the proximity of his mother give the young child a sense of security and solace.

When they move to a village, the mother takes a position as a teacher, and the anxiety of separation (even for a few hours) shatters his sense of self. Slowly he becomes acclimated to a local girl who takes care of him during the day. Her murder adds to the child's devastation.

The mother's conversion and marriage to a Ukrainian man throws the child into the care of his sensitive, erratic, belligerent, and depressed father. The father's persistent fight against art critics and expressions of anti-Semitism concludes in his death. The mother, whose beauty wanes eventually, succumbs to typhoid. Love and affinity exist among the three afflicted characters who inhabit this dark, sensitive novel.

Appelfeld's work evokes persistent and disturbing questions. Do his characters act out a prescribed script over which they have little control? Are they caught in a historical whirlpool? Is the loss of faith affecting their judgment? Is the loss of the sense of belonging to a tribe thwarting their judgment? These questions loom heavily over "All That I Have Loved."

Gila Ramras-Rauch

■ **CYRIL DABYDEEN**. *My Brahmin Days and Other Stories*. Toronto. TSAR. 2000. 136 pages.

The Collection *My Brahmin Days* consists of twelve short stories, almost all of them first-person narratives. Cyril Dabydeen was born in Guyana, a descendant of those Indians who were brought to the region and elsewhere under the infamous indenture system (see *Kunapipi*, 22:2, 2000), but he moved to Canada many years ago. Even before his emigration, Dabydeen had made a name for himself as a poet. The result of the first is that exile features strongly in these stories; of the second, that his poetic gift is evident in the use of figures of speech and musical elements.

Several of the stories are seamless between past and present, fantasy and reality. (In "Departure" an immigrant changes his mind and tells the officer, a deity deciding the fate of desperate arrivals, he doesn't want to stay in Canada.) Diaspora is at the heart of what he writes, and the stories are of Guyana, India, and Canada, while some are set in a plane—seemingly cut off from time and place—as the narrator journeys between these countries. A sense of at once belonging and "unbelonging" leads to heightened awareness, sensitivity and perception.

"Going to Guyana" is about flying back to what was once home but now, in many ways, is a strange land. Guyana, among other things, is associated with desiccated leaves, cowshit, sheep, fowl excrement, women walking to the village well with aluminum pails on their heads. But some have escaped from that "forest" only to end up in the Bronx ("Who Is Lee Harvey Oswald?").

The author's ancestors had come from India, and the heroic figures of his childhood had been people like Mahatma Gandhi and Jawaharlal Nehru. The voyage into indenture had taken several weeks; the narrator's flight to India, a matter of hours. And yet the narrator has something of that mixture of anxiety, fear, and hope with which the "coolies" crossed the *kala pani* (dark waters). He looks like, and is mistaken for, an Indian, yet isn't one; he no longer feels at ease in Guyana, and is conscious of his immigrant status in Canada, despite having lived there for nearly thirty years. (As Doris Lessing wrote, once you leave your first home, you've left all homes forever.) In India, he finds pettiness and pretension, but also achievement and confidence. The cruelty of caste persists ("My Brahmin Days"), while at the same time there's an eagerness for the West, for what is new.

"Burning Wood" is a complex work, an allegory of trees being cut down, burned, planted, of one from the new wave of immigrants joining a native Canadian to repair the damage which has been done, both to community and nature, to repair and heal. It is the best story in the collection, rich with symbolism, despairing and determined. Altogether, this collection strengthens Cyril Dabydeen's reputation as a significant postcolonial writer: "And I never wanted to return. . . . And somewhere my mother kept hailing me, as if only she understood my yearning for peace and bliss—in a time yet to come."

Charles P. Sarvan

■ **MARGARET DRABBLE**. *The Peppered Moth*. New York: Harcourt. 2001. 369 pages

Margaret Drabble's Latest novel is a generational epic, a family saga inspired by her own family history. It is an account of three generations of women. With her usual storytelling skill and her fertile imagination and creative ability to connect divergent elements, Drabble relates the stories of her heroines to a microbiologist's study of the family mitochondrial DNA, the discovery of a well-preserved skeleton of a prehistoric Cudworth ancestor, and evolutionary theory as illustrated by the survival of the dark moth that gives the book its title. This expansion of the theme is in line with Drabble's enduring interest in the nature/nurture question (see, for example, her 1980 novel, *The Realms of Gold*). The novel's focus on topics current in our genetic-engineering age is consistent with her concern with real-life implications of scientific discoveries. It is also a demonstration of her expressed belief that good fiction must be relevant in some way to the world around her, a belief that has led some of her critics to accuse her of trendiness.

The novel begins with the story of Bessie Bawtry, who represents Drabble's mother, Kathleen Marie Bloor, who died in 1984. Young Bessie is described as a delicate, pretty, intelligent, and ambitious child who was totally at odds with the rough, prosaic, ugly, joyless environment of Breaseborough, a Yorkshire coalmining town. Upon completion of her secondary-school education, Bessie succeeds in getting to Cambridge on a scholarship, but she is not strong enough to overcome her discomfort in the new intellectual and social milieu, or her own inertia, self-doubt, and fear of success. She returns to teach in the school that she had attended and ends in an indifferent marriage, an unhappy wife and ineffectual mother.

An account of the life of Bessie's rebellious daughter Chrissie follows, her lonely childhood, tempestuous adolescence, short career at Cambridge, a dizzying love affair with Nick Gaulden, and a short-lived marriage to him. In middle age we find Chrissie happily remarried, a professional woman, efficient, flexible, and responsible, who enjoys a close relationship with her daughter. Faro, the daughter, appears in the prime of her middle youth, all expectation and vigor. She is loving and generous, "a triumphant, confident, careless creature. As though she had come from nowhere." She is an unfinished young woman in the process of individuation seeking to terminate an affair with a manipulative young man and embarking on a new life enhancing relationship.

The Peppered Moth has attracted a great deal of attention in England because of Margaret Drabble's and her sister A. S. Byatt's position in the British literary establishment and the fact that it was publicly known, even before the publication of the novel, that Byatt disapproved of it and of the image of their mother that it projects. It is regrettable that the negative judgment of this fascinating work by many a critic has centered on the negative picture of the mother. The criticism also has stemmed in part from the fact that the author disregarded the boundary between two literary genres. In the midst of the fictional narrative, Drabble interjects: "If this story were merely a fiction, it would be possible to fill these gaps with plausible incidents." This is followed by an "afterword" that begins with the stark declaration "This is a novel about my mother. . . . I wrote the book to try to understand my mother better. I went down into the underworld to look for my mother, but I couldn't find her. She was not there."

That the two sisters differ in their view of their mother is no surprise. There is truth in Drabble's reference to Winnicott's claim that each child has a different mother. As to shared memory, we may recall Byatt's own words: "It is hard to have shared memories with another writer. So much of art is transmutation of memory, and this needs to be private not communal, or it is in danger of being destroyed." The fact that the novel crosses the boundary of one literary genre into another is in line with modern literary trends and with Drabble's own recent shift away from the Victorian tradition of realistic storytelling. Indeed, this is not the first time that Drabble interrupts the story to address the reader directly, to admonish, to answer anticipated objections, or to call attention to issues relating to the craft of the novel—a practice that has been identified as metafiction about writing fiction.

The negative image that Drabble gives of her mother need not be a determining factor in any assessment of the literary value of *Moth* as a work of fiction. The primary consideration ought to be the realism, authenticity, and psychological sophistication with which the character is described, and there is no doubt that the development of the character here is masterful and the final picture quite convincing. A very few pages into the novel, one of Bessie's earliest memories is described, a memory of her climbing steep stairs and arriving at a point where she is paralyzed by fear, unable to climb up, afraid to fall down. The memory persists and recurs in her dreams, an eloquent expression of the paralyzing fear of failure as well as fear of success that dominated her life.

The insightful, consistent, well-documented description of the development of the woman who became Margaret Drabble's mother is flawless. The family constellation, the physical environment, and the class culture provide the necessary context that brings the character to life.

What is true of the fictional Bessie Bawtry is true of a host of other characters, the least important of whom is described with attention to the minutest details of comportment, dress, and speech, bringing to life not only a wealth of individual diversity but a whole society with its stratifications, its social mores, and its particular geographic setting at a specific historical period.

One of the appeals of *The Peppered Moth* stems from its encompassing of many perspectives. The highlighting of the theme of heredity indicated by the title and the emphasis on matriarchal descent would lead the reader to expect a predominance of inherited characteristics and thus a similarity among the heroines: mother, daughter, and granddaughter, for are not daughters, according to this perspective, doomed to become their mothers? Actually the three women are different in temperament and in style, and the contributing role of their environments is quite prominent. In a work that appears to attempt to prove the possibilities of the future through the past, we find the future undetermined, open to heredity and environment, to accident and to free choice.

There is no ending to young Faro's story and no conclusion to this rich and deeply moving novel. It ends simply with an expression of hope in a future that is not severed from the past, and an affirmation of life through Faro's song in her clear voice that floods the valley.

Adma d'Heurle

■**EDOUARD GLISSANT**. *Sartorius: Le roman des Batoutos*. Paris. Gallimard. 1999. 352 pages.

From *Le Quatrième Siècle* (1964) to *Tout-Monde* (1993; see *WLT* 69:1, p. 205), Edouard Glissant pursued the saga of the Béluse and Longoué clans, those who suffered under slavery and its aftermath and those who refused to submit. In his fourth novel, *La case du commandeur* (1981), the name Odono appeared episodically and somewhat mysteriously. Marie Celat's musings, which, from the point of view of quotidian reality, appeared delusional, sometimes turned or focused on this name. The present novel sets out to contextualize the name and to justify its presence in the mind of latter-day Martinicans.

The Batutos, it turns out, are an invisible but very durable African people, located vaguely in the regions from which the majority of slaves came to the New World. As a people, they exhibit to a high degree precisely those characteristics that Glissant has praised in *Poétique de la Relation* (1990) and has attempted to illustrate in *Tout-Monde*. Odono is the name of both one of their gods and a member of this ubiquitous collectivity who willingly undertook the trials of slavery in the West. The Batutos, as Glissant imagines them here, have over time provided occult but indispensable knowledge to the descendants of New World slaves. If the reader takes seriously his utopian story of the Batutos, they appear as the ancestors of those mysterious characters whom both Glissant and Patrick Chamoiseau call *mentohs*, which Confiant sometimes writes as *Mentores*. As mentors, then, the Batutos have accompanied and supported the descendants of Africans in the New World down to the present.

The purpose of *Sartorius* seems to be a consolatory myth for those Glissant had described in *Le discours antillais* (1981) as stripped migrants. The novel suggests that, whereas Africans thrown pell-mell into the harsh world of the plantation did not enjoy the benefits of an enduring cultural tradition, they were somehow, however mysteriously, accompanied by an efficacious presence. Perhaps the greatest interest of this book, which

is not particularly successful as fiction, lies in the question: why did Glissant feel the need to write it? A quarter-century ago Glissant showed considerable interest in Afro-Caribbean syncretic religion as social pathology, which he approached from the standpoint of a collective need that could not be satisfied in the degraded existence of post-plantation societies (see *Le discours antillais*). However, religion as a positive experience, individual or collective, has been largely absent from Glissant's world view and from his fictional oeuvre.

Sartorius is a very strange book. At times one has the impression of reading Henri Michaux's fantastic prose poems from *Ailleurs,* which describe in detail the folkways of peoples who could not possibly exist. At fleeting moments, the style suggests the combination of detachment and intimate knowledge that characterizes Saint-John Perse's *Anabase*. In terms of a broader Caribbean poetics, *Sartorius* may be Glissant's belated contribution to the mythic mode of representation that Wilson Harris made his own in the 1960s. Whereas Harris's fictional universe is posited on the co-presence of spirit forces emanating from the multiple ethnic strains of American peoples—not to mention the possibility of their reincarnation or sudden apparition in the phenomenal world—in Glissant's fiction this departure raises questions that *Sartorius* does not begin to answer.

If Glissant's Babutos respond to some real need, what is its nature? On what experiential plane can the reader of *Le quatrième siècle* or even *Tout-Monde* be expected to integrate these vignettes—some thirty-four in all, ranging from two to twenty pages, mostly devoted to an individual Batuto—into Glissant's emerging world view? Why did the author of *Tout-Monde,* which pushed to the limit the principle of open-ended relation of cultures in the contemporary world, find it necessary to posit an ahistorical spiritual/cultural source that antedates slavery in Africa? Was it his intention to provide a putative, albeit fictional, unity to all neo-African cultures, a position Glissant has combatted in its expression by either Aimé Césaire or the Afro-centrists of the contemporary United States? Glissant's critics will, I predict, wrestle with these questions for some time to come.

A. James Arnold

■**CZESŁAW MIŁOSZ**. *To Kraków*. Poland. Znak. 2001. 103 pages.

Few Poets Can Compete with Czesław Miłosz these days. Ninety years old on 30 June 2001, he shows no signs of the intellectual infirmity which affects many people much younger than himself. His latest collection of verse, *To* (which may be rendered as "That"), demonstrates a keen interest in life, even if memories and self-assessments play a larger part in his poetic thinking than new experiences. Also, readers of Miłosz's poetry will recognize the recurrence of earlier themes: the poem "W mieście" (In the City) is once again about Vilnius/Wilno, the scene of the young Miłosz's first triumphs and disappointments. It is a kind of poetic confrontation with "unrealized opportunities," with a destiny that could have been his, had certain decisions been taken differently.

Miłosz's present collection is arranged in four cycles, which, though untitled, could well have been labeled as "Places," "Views," "People," and finally "Beliefs/ Mythologies." These categories sometimes overlap; while in the first cycle images of Lithuania predominate, in the second the central sequence is about paintings seen at different locations (Vienna, New Haven, Lugano), which shows how much the nonagenarian Miłosz travels these days. As he puts it sarcastically in "Voyeur," "Byłem podglądaczem wędrownym na ziemi" (I was a wandering voyeur on this earth). It is in this sequence that the confession of fundamental "alienness" occurs: in one poem Miłosz admits that wherever he travels the locals know one thing for certain: "I am not from here," which could also be rendered as "I am from elsewhere" or "I do not belong here." For Miłosz, displacement seems to be the natural state of human beings in the twentieth century.

Man may be displaced and uprooted, but he has to keep his loyalty to ideals and, what is even more important, to people. The central cycle in *To* consists of poems written about or addressed to different individuals. Among these Miłosz has particular regard for John Paul II, his great compatriot, and for his French friend Jeanne Hersch. Others, such as Marian Zdziechowski, Aleksander Wat, and Robert Lowell, all subjects of separate poems, intrigue him with their neuroses and contradictions. There are traces of arguments but also high regard expressed in poems about younger fellow-poets such as Zbigniew Herbert and Tadeusz Różewicz. The only person whom Miłosz openly dislikes is the English poet Philip Larkin; the short poem entitled "Against Philip Larkin's Poetry" reflects the Polish-American poet's unease about the self-pitying laments of "mournful Larkin," with whom he feels no affinity. Miłosz's poetry has always contained a robust affirmation of life, and for all its diversity it was also a song of praise to the Lord who works not only through the individual soul but also through History. Proof of the work of Providence is the demise of both murderous totalitarian systems of the twentieth century; Miłosz is surprised that people do not regard these developments with immense gratitude.

A moving poem of this collection is "Modlitwa" (Prayer), in which the poet confesses that he "has to believe" in God, who "guided and protected" him as if he had rendered some special service to Him. He is in fact praying to the "human-faced God," to Christ, asking forgiveness for his real and imaginary sins and ending the poem with these words: "W godzinie mojej agonii bądź ze mną Twoim cierpieniem, / Które nie może świata ocalić od bólu" (In the hour of my agony be with me with Your suffering / Which cannot save the world from pain). These words sound almost like a farewell to a world which, though full of terrible suffering, is nurtured and mysteriously upheld by divine care.

George Gömöri

■ **GAO XINGJIAN**. *Soul Mountain*. Mabel Lee, tr. Sydney. Flamingo/HarperCollins Australia. 2000. xi + 510 pages.

Gao Xingjian Was Diagnosed with lung cancer in 1982. Faced with imminent death, he began to gorge himself with sumptuous food and to immerse himself in reading in an old graveyard in a Beijing suburb. However, a second examination revoked the first diagnosis, and Gao was then returned to the human world. It was at this time that he left the city of Beijing to begin his 15,000-kilometer journey from central China to the east coast. This journey, which lasted over five months, gave birth to the book *Soul Mountain*.

The work is an account of Gao's odyssey, or a pagan's *Pilgrim's Progress*. In eighty-one chapters covering over five hundred pages, the author makes use of multiple narrators named "I," "you," "he," and "she" to iterate various perspectives of his ideas. One can regard the text as a traveler's journal recording Gao's feelings and routes, or even as a philosophical treatise on life, religion, culture, history, et cetera. It is also an extended monologue, bordering on stream of consciousness, by a writer who is eager to find himself and to make sense of the world around him. Above all, the book records one lonely individual's quest for his soul.

Soul Mountain distinguishes itself from contemporary Chinese literature in its form, content, and narrative technique. Maybe because Gao is also an artist, descriptions of nature in the narrative stand out in readers' eyes as paintings. The eighty-one chapters are held together not by plot or characters, but by the search for truth in a collective mind. When human beings are unhappy, whom or what can they blame? Religion? Politics? History? Culture? The opposite sex? Amid the philosophical discussions of life, Gao intersperses stories of love, tales of political persecution, and fables. These fictional narratives add to the meaning of life that

Gao is searching for. They reflect the world around him, the people and the suffocating environment.

Like Wordsworth, Gao perhaps finds redemption only in nature, in its beauty and serenity. Hence the quest for Soul Mountain, of whose existence no one is certain. But unlike Wordsworth, who found meaning in nature and salvation in God, Gao renounces both the Buddhist and Taoist sects while failing to reach his destination. At the end of the narrative, he proclaims, "I comprehend nothing, I understand nothing."

Gao finished this book in 1989, and by that time he had already emigrated to Paris. The seven-year quest recounted here, presented through the eyes of a poet and a painter, enhances the work's literary and visual effect. Overall, Mabel Lee's translation can be deemed superb and outstanding, revealing not only the nihilistic and frustrated mood of the narrator but also the beauty and the all-embracing arms of nature.

Fatima Wu

Notes on Contributors

■ ■ ■

This section presents names of contributors, accompanied by the titles of their essays and the section of the table of contents in which each essay appears (designated by roman numerals), followed finally by brief biographical information.

■ A

GÉMINO H. ABAD, "One Hundred Years of Filipino Poetry: An Overview," (IV). Professor of English at the University of the Philippines. Among his publications are *A Formal Approach to Lyric Poetry* (1978), *Poems and Parables* (1988), and *Orion's Belt and Other Writings* (1996).

EVELYNE ACCAD, "Assia Djebar's Contribution to Arab Women's Literature: Rebellion, Maturity, Vision," (II). Novelist and critic, Professor of French, Comparative Literature, African Studies, Women's Studies, and Middle East Studies at the University of Illinois, Urbana-Champaign. Among her publications are *L'excisée* (1982), *Sexuality and War: Literary Masks of the Middle East* (1990), and *Blessures des mots* (1993).

FERNANDO AINSA, "Juan Carlos Onetti (1909–1994): An Existential Allegory of Contemporary Man," (V). Writer and Director of Publications for UNESCO in Paris. Selected work includes the book *De la Edad de Oro a El Dorado: Genesis del discurso utópico americano* (1992).

CHINGIZ AITMATOV, "The Intellectual Crisis, the Demise of Totalitarianism, and the Fate of Literature," (VI). Russian prose writer, whose work includes *Farewell, Gulsary* (1966), *The Ascent of Mount Fuji*

(1975), and *The Day Is Longer Than a Century* (1981).

EDNA AIZENBERG, "Borges, Postcolonial Precursor," (V). Professor at Marymount Manhattan College. Among her publications are *Borges and His Successors: The Borgesian Impact on Literature and the Arts* (1990) and *Books and Bombs in Buenos Aires: Borges, Gerchunoff, and Argentine-Jewish Writing* (2002).

SAAD AL-BAZEI, "Tension in the House: The Contemporary Poetry of Arabia," (II). Professor of English and American Poetry at King Saud University in Riyadh, Saudi Arabia. His publications include *Desert Culture: Studies of the Contemporary Literature of Arabia* (1991) and *References of the Poem: Readings in Contemporary Poetry* (1998).

MOHAMMED SAAD AL-JUMLY, "Emigration and the Rise of the Novel in Yemen," (article written with J. Barton Rollins) (II). Teaches at the National Chung Cheng University in Taiwan. Scholar of Modern American and Yemeni Fiction.

ROGER ALLEN, "Arabic Literature and the Nobel Prize," (II); "Literary History and the Arabic Novel," (II); "Najib Mahfuz: Nobel Laureate in Literature, 1988," (II). Professor of Arabic Language and Literature at the University of Pennsylvania. His book publications include *The Arabic Novel* (1982) and *The Arabic Literary Heritage* (1998).

ISABEL ALVAREZ-BORLAND, "Displacements and Autobiography in Cuban-American Fiction," (III). Associate Professor of Spanish at the

College of the Holy Cross in Massachusetts. Author of *Discontinuidad y ruptura en G. Cabrera Infante* (1982) and *Cuban-American Literature of Exile: From Person to Persona* (1998).

MONA TAKIEDDINE AMYUNI, "Literature and War, Beirut 1993–1995: Three Case Studies," (II). Associate Professor at the American University of Beirut, author of articles on contemporary Arabic writers and *Women and War in Lebanon* (1999).

JEANETTE LEE ATKINSON, "Karl Ragnar Gierow: A Skeptic's Way," (VII). Scholar of Germanic languages and literatures. Author of *Traditional Forms in German Poetry, 1930–1945* (1978).

GORKA AULESTIA, "A Comparative Study of Basque and Yugoslav Troubadourism," (VI). University of Nevada, Reno. Publications include *Improvisational Poetry from the Basque Country* (1995) and *The Basque Poetic Tradition* (2000).

■ B

ASIYA BAIGOZHINA, "A Dilettante's Marginal Notes on National Literature," (IV). Scriptwriter, editor of film documentaries, and journalist for the regional newspaper, *Zvezda Priirtyshia*, in Palvodar.

ANNA BALAKIAN, "Theorizing Comparison: The Pyramid of Similitude and Difference," (I); "René Char in Search of the Violet Man," (VIII). Professor Emerita of French and Comparative Literature at New York University. Her publications include *The Symbolist Movement: A Critical*

Appraisal (1967) and *The Fiction of the Poet: From Mallarmé to the Post-Symbolist Mode* (1992).

JACQUELINE BARDOLPH, "Brothers and Sisters in Nuruddin Farah's Two Trilogies," (III). Professor Emerita of Postcolonial Literatures at the University of Nice. Author of *Le roman de langue anglaise en Afrique de l'est 1964–1976* (1981) and a monograph on Ngũgĩ wa Thiong'o (1991).

PETER BIEN, "The Predominance of Poetry in Greek Literature," (VI). Professor Emeritus in the Department of English at Dartmouth College. Translator and specialist in Greek literature. Among his publications are *Modern Greek Writers: Solomos, Calvos, Matesis, Palamas, Cavafy, Kazantzakis, Seferis, Elytis* (1972) and *Kazantzakis: Politics of the Spirit* (1989).

ROBERT BLY, "Tomas Transtrõmer and 'The Memory'," (VII). Translator and critic of Swedish literature. Publications include the collaborative compilation *Friends, You Drank Some Darkness: Three Swedish Poets, Harry Martinson, Gunnar Ekelöf, and Tomas Transtrõmer* (1975).

YVES BONNEFOY, "On the Translation of Form in Poetry," (I). French poet, essayist, translator, and art historian. Author of such studies as *The Act and the Place of Poetry* (1989) and *The Lure and the Truth of Painting* (1995). His collections of poetry include *On the Motion and Immobility of Douve* (1953) and *Words in Stone* (1965). Bonnefoy was featured at the 1979 Puterbaugh conference.

MARGARET C. BRADHAM, "Barbara Pym's Women," (VIII). Freelance writer. Areas of research interest include the work of Barbara Pym and Jean Rhys.

STEPHEN BRESLOW, "Derek Walcott: 1992 Nobel Laureate in Literature," (III). Author and playwright. Publications include *W. S. Merwin: An American Existentialist* (1978) and *A Quartet from 1812* (1992).

ANDRÉ BRINK, "Reinventing a Continent (Revisiting History in the Literature of the New South Africa: A Personal Testimony)," (III). Professor

of English Literature at the University of Cape Town and the author of works in Afrikaans and English, including the novels *A Dry White Season* (1979), *An Act of Terror* (1991), and *On the Contrary* (1993).

JOSEPH BRODSKY, "Presentation of Czesław Miłosz to the Jury," (VI). Russian poet, critic, essayist, and translator. Selected works include *A Part of Speech* (1980), *To Urania* (1988), and *So Forth* (1995). Brodsky died in 1996.

BROTHER ANTHONY OF TAIZÉ, "From Korean History to Korean Poetry: Ko Un and Ku Sang," (IV). Professor of English at Sogang University in Seoul. His translations include *The Sound of My Waves* by Ko Un (1993) and *Back to Heaven* by Ch'on Sang Pyong (1995).

CAROLYN T. BROWN, "The Myth of the Fall and the Dawning of Consciousness in George Lamming's *In the Castle of My Skin*," (III). Translator and critic of Chinese literature. Author of *Psycho-Sinology = Meng: The Universe of Dreams in Chinese Culture* (1988).

JOHN L. BROWN, "V. S. Naipaul: A Wager on the Triumph of Darkness," (III); "Brassaï, the Writer," (VIII). Poet and critic. Professor Emeritus of Comparative Literature at Catholic University. Author of *Hemingway* (1961), *Fragments from a Paris Mémoire* (1972), and *Valery Larbaud* (1981).

MARIANNE BURKHARD, "Gauging Existential Space: The Emergence of Women Writers in Switzerland," (VIII). Swiss editor and scholar. Taught German language and literature at the University of Illinois, Urbana-Champaign. Published work includes *Conrad Ferdinand Meyer* (1978) and *Gestaltet und gestaltend: Frauen in der deutschen Literatur* (1980).

MICHEL BUTOR, "The Origin of the Text," (I). French novelist and critic, author of such books as *Passing Time* (1956) and *The Modification* (1957). Other publications include *The Spirit of Mediterranean Places* (1986) and *Frontiers* (1989). Butor was featured at the 1981 Puterbaugh conference.

JANET BYRON, "Albanian Nationalism and Socialism in the

Fiction of Ismail Kadare," (VI). Freelance writer and translator. Author of *Selection among Alternates in Language Standardization: The Case of Albanian* (1976).

■ C

MATEI CALINESCU, "Romanian Literature: Dealing with the Totalitarian Legacy," (VI). Translator and critic. Professor of Comparative Literature at Indiana University. Publications include *Five Faces of Modernity: Modernism, Avant-Garde, Decadence, Kitsch, Postmodernism* (1987) and *Rereading* (1993).

GLAUCO CAMBON, "Modern Poetry and Its Prospects in Italy," (VIII). Italian translator and critic. Published work includes *Dante's Craft: Studies in Language and Style* (1969), *Eugenio Montale* (1972), and *Michelangelo's Poetry: Fury of Form* (1985). Cambon died in 1988.

MARTA CAMINERO-SANTANGELO, "Contesting the Boundaries of Exile Latino/a Literature," (V). Associate Professor of English at the University of Kansas. Author of *The Madwoman Can't Speak: Or Why Insanity Is Not Subversive* (1998).

ROBERT CANCEL, "Literary Criticism as Social Philippic and Personal Exorcism: Ngũgĩ Thiong'o's Critical Writings," (III). Associate Professor of African and Comparative Literature at the University of California, San Diego. Author of *Allegorical Speculation in an Oral Society: The Tabwa Narrative Tradition* (1989).

BOGDANA CARPENTER, "Wisława Szymborska and the Importance of the Unimportant," (VI). Professor of Polish and Comparative Literature at the University of Michigan in Ann Arbor. Author of *The Poetic Avant-Garde in Poland, 1918–1939* (1983) and *Monumenta Polonica: The First Four Centuries of Polish Poetry* (1989).

MARY ANN CAWS, "Reading, the Cast Shadows: A Reflection," (I). Professor of English, French, and Comparative Literature at the Graduate School of the City University of New York. Selected publications include *The Eye in the Text* (1982), *Textual Analysis: Some Readers Reading* (1986), and *Surrealist Love Poems* (2002).

ELLEN CHANCES, "'In the Middle of the Contrast': Andrei Bitov and the Act of Writing in the Contemporary World," (VI). Professor of Russian at Princeton University. Publications include *Conformity's Children: An Approach to the Superfluous Man in Russian Literature* (1978) and *Andrei Bitov: The Ecology of Inspiration* (1993).

KATHLEEN CHASE, "Legend and Legacy: Some Bloomsbury Diaries," (VIII). Essayist, translator, and poet. Research areas include British and American literatures and women's literature.

DOMINIC CHEUNG, "The Continuity of Modern Chinese Poetry in Taiwan," (IV). Professor of Chinese and Comparative Literature at the University of Southern California. Publications include *Chinese Arts and Literature: A Survey of Recent Trends* (1977) and *The Isle Full of Noises: Modern Chinese Poetry from Taiwan* (1987).

YING-YING CHIEN, "From Utopian to Dystopian World: Two Faces of Feminism in Contemporary Taiwanese Women's Fiction," (IV). Assistant Professor of Comparative Literature and Women's Studies at Pennsylvania State University. Author of *The Feminine Struggle for Power: A Comparative Study of Representative Novels East and West* (1987).

KANISHKA CHOWDHURY, "Revisioning History: Shashi Tharoor's Great Indian Novel," (IV). Associate Professor of English at the University of St. Thomas in St. Paul, Minnesota. Author of *Writing Histories, Constructing Identities: Postcolonial Narratives of Cultural Recovery* (1993).

RONALD CHRIST, "A Last Interview with Manuel Puig," (V). Translator and critic. Professor Emeritus of English at Rutgers University. Publications include *The Narrow Act: Borges' Art of Allusion* (1969) and *A Modest Proposal for the Criticism of Borges* (1971).

ROBERT J. CLEMENTS, "World Literature Tomorrow," (I). Specialist in Italian and in Literary Criticism and Theory. Selected publications include *Picta Poesis: Literary and Humanistic Theory in Renaissance Emblem Books* (1960) and *Comparative Literature as Academic Discipline* (1978).

DAVID COAD, "Patrick White: Prophet in the Wilderness," (IV). Lecturer in Commonwealth Studies at the Université de Valenciennes et du Hainaut-Cambrésis. Author of articles published in English and French on Australian, South African, Italian, and French literatures.

MICHAEL J. COLLINS, "The Sabotage of Love: Athol Fugard's Recent Plays," (III); "Recovering a Tradition: Anglo-Welsh Poetry 1480–1980," (VIII). Dean of the School for Summer and Continuing Education at Georgetown University, where he taught American Literature and Modern British Drama. Publications include *Teaching Values and Ethics in College* (1983).

MARYSE CONDÉ, "The Role of the Writer," (III). Guadeloupean novelist and playwright, author of such works as *Ségou: A Novel* (1987), *I, Tituba, Black Witch of Salem* (1992), and *Desirada* (2002). Condé was featured at the 1993 Puterbaugh conference.

RUFUS COOK, "Place and Displacement in Salman Rushdie's Work," (VIII). Associate Professor of English at National Cheng Kung University in Taiwan. Author of *Reason and Imagination: A Failure of Balance in Yvor Winters' Criticism* (1982).

MIRIAM COOKE, "Telling Their Lives: A Hundred Years of Arab Women's Writings," (II). Professor of Modern Arabic Literature and Culture at Duke University, author of *The Anatomy of an Egyptian Intellectual: Yahya Haqqui* (1984), *War's Other Voices: Women Writers on the Lebanese Civil War* (1988), and *Women Claim Islam: Creating Islamic Feminism through Literature* (2000).

JONATHAN CULLER, "Comparability," (I). Professor of English and Comparative Literature at Cornell University. Author of such studies as *Flaubert: The Uses of Uncertainty* (1974), *The Pursuit of Signs: Semiotics, Literature, Deconstruction* (1981), and *Framing the Sign: Criticism and Its Institutions* (1988).

■ **D**

CYRIL DABYDEEN, "Places We Come From: Voices of Caribbean Canadian Writers (in English) and Multicultural Contexts," (III). Author of poetry, fiction, and criticism, including *Black Jesus and Other Stories* (1996), *Berbice Crossing* (1996), and *Discussing Columbus* (1997).

KATHLEEN OSGOOD DANA, "Sámi Literature in the Twentieth Century," (VII). Scholar of Finnish Literature at the Center for Northern Studies in Vermont. Translator of Heidi Liehu's *Long, Long Goodbyes* (2000).

ROBERT MURRAY DAVIS, "Desperate but Not Serious: The Situation of Hungarian Literature in the Nineties," (VI); "Out of the Shadows: Slovene Writing after Independence," (VI). Professor Emeritus of English at the University of Oklahoma. Selected publications include *Evelyn Waugh: Writer* (1981) and *Playing Cowboys: Low Culture and High Art in the Western* (1992).

ROCÍO G. DAVIS, "Back to the Future: Mothers, Languages, and Homes in Cristina García's *Dreaming in Cuban*," (III); "Postcolonial Visions and Immigrant Longings: Ninotchka Rosca's Versions of the Philippines," (IV). Teaches at the University of Navarre in Spain. Author of *Transcultural Reinventions: Asian American and Asian Canadian Short-Story Cycles* (2001).

JEAN DÉJEUX, "Major Currents in North African Novels in French since 1966," (II). Author of works focusing on North African French-language literature, including *Le sentiment religieux dans la littérature maghrébine de langue française* (1986) and *La littérature feminine de langue française au Maghreb* (1994).

DAVID DER-WEI WANG, "The Literary World of Mo Yan," (IV). Professor of Chinese at Columbia University. Author of *Fictional Realism in Twentieth-Century China: Mao Dun, Lao She, Shen Congwen* (1992) and *Fin-de-siècle Splendor: Repressed Modernities of Late Qing Fiction, 1849–1911* (1997).

VINAY DHARWADKER, "Indian Writing Today: A View from 1994," (IV). Associate Professor in the Department of Languages and Cultures of Asia at the University of Wisconsin, Madison. Among his publications are the verse collection *Sunday at the Lodi Gardens* (1994) and the *Oxford Anthology of Modern Indian Poetry* (1994), edited with the late A. K. Ramanujan.

ROBERT E. DIANTONIO, "Biblical Correspondences and Eschatological Questioning in the Metafiction of Murilo Rubião," (V). Author of *The Passage from Myth to Anti-Myth in Contemporary Hispanic Poetry* (1973) and *Brazilian Fiction: Aspects and Evolution of the Contemporary Narrative* (1989).

JANET W. DÍAZ, "Spain's Vernacular Literatures in the Post-Franco Era," (VIII). Professor of Spanish at Texas Tech University. Among her publications (under the name Janet Pérez) are *Modern and Contemporary Spanish Women Poets* (1996) and *Camilo José Cela Revisited: The Later Novels* (2000).

OPHELIA A. DIMALANTA, "Philippine Literature in English: Tradition Change," (IV). Professor of English at the University of Santo Tomas in Manila. Poet and literary critic. Publications include *Philippine Contemporary Literature in English: Tradition and Change* (1993) and *Our Voices, Our Zones* (1998).

GUZINE DINO, "The Turkish Peasant Novel, or the Anatolian Theme," (II). Translator and scholar of Turkish literature, author of such studies as *Un village anatolien: récit d'un instituteur paysan* (1963) and *La Montagne d'en face; poèmes des derviches turcs anatoliens* (1986).

MICHAEL S. DUKE, "Walking toward the World: A Turning Point in Contemporary Chinese Fiction," (IV). Specialist in Asian Studies in the Center for Chinese Research at the University of Columbia. Author of *Su Tong, Raise the Red Lantern: Three Novellas* (1993).

MANUEL DURÁN, "The Nobel Prize and Writers in the Hispanic World: A Continuing Story," (V); "Octavio Paz: Nobel Laureate in Literature, 1990" (V); "Vicente Aleixandre, Last of the Romantics: The 1977 Nobel Prize for Literature," (VIII); "Fiction and Metafiction in Contemporary Spanish Letters," (VIII). Professor Emeritus of

Spanish at Yale University. Publications include *Cervantes* (1974) and *Earth Tones: The Poetry of Pablo Neruda* (1981).

KHUDAYBERDY DURDYEV, "Toward a New Maturity," (IV). Turkmen writer, essayist, and translator. Served as Minister of Culture, as Secretary of the Central Committee of the Communist Party of the Turkmen Republic, and as head of the Turkmen Writers Union.

KRZYSZTOF DYBCIAK, "The Poetic Phenomenology of a Religious Man: About the Literary Creativity of Karol Wojtyła," (VI). Polish critic and translator whose published works include *Personalistyczna krytyka literacka: teoria i opis nurtu z lat trzydziestych* (1981) and *Karol Wojtyła: A Literature* (1991).

■ E

BARBARA J. ECKSTEIN, "Nadine Gordimer: Nobel Laureate in Literature, 1991," (III). Teaches in the Department of English at the University of Iowa. Author of *Language of Fiction in a World of Pain: Reading Politics as Paradox* (1990).

UNIONMWAN EDEBIRI, "Toward a Convention of Modern African Drama," (III). Author of *Drama as Popular Culture in Africa* (1983) and editor of *Bernard Dadié: hommages et études* (1997).

NADA ELIA, "In the Making: Beur Fiction and Identity Construction," (II). Publications include *"To Be an African Working Woman": Levels of Feminist Consciousness in Ama Ata Aidoo's "Changes"* (1999) and *Trances, Dances, and Vociferations: Agency and Resistance in Africana Women's Narratives* (2001).

ROBERT ELSIE, "Evolution and Revolution in Modern Albanian Literature," (VI). Writer, translator, specialist in Albanian studies. Publications include *Dictionary of Albanian Literature* (1986) and *Dictionary of Albanian Religion, Mythology, and Folk Culture* (2001).

EZENWA-OHAETO, "Bridges of Orality: Nigerian Pidgin Poetry," (III). Teaches at the Institut für Ethnologie

at the University of Mainz in Germany. He is the author of collections of verse in English and Pidgin, including *Songs of a Traveller* (1986) and *I Wan Bi President* (1988).

■ F

HUANG FAN, "Avant-Garde Poetry in China: The Nanjing Scene 1981–1992," (article written with Jeffrey Twitchell) (IV). Editor, author of fiction and poetry. Among his publications are *Fan dui zhe* (1984) and *Caifa* (1990).

WENDY B. FARIS, "The Return of the Past: Chiasmus in the Texts of Carlos Fuentes," (V). Professor of English at the University of Texas, Arlington. Selected publications include *Carlos Fuentes* (1983) and *Labyrinths of Language: Symbolic Landscapes and Narrative Design in Modern Fiction* (1988).

ROSARIO FERRERI, "Eugenio Montale's *Diario Postumo*," (VIII). Associate Professor Emeritus of Italian at the University of Connecticut. Publications include *Le rime di G. Boccaccio e la tradizione lirica italiana* (1978) and *Innovazione e tradizione nel Boccaccio* (1980).

HELENA FORSÅS-SCOTT, "In Defense of People and Forests: Sara Lidman's Recent Novels," (VII). Senior lecturer in Swedish at University College London. Among her publications are *Textual Liberation: European Feminist Writing in the Twentieth Century* (1991) and *Swedish Women's Writing, 1850–1995* (1997).

DAVID WILLIAM FOSTER, "Camilo José Cela: 1989 Nobel Prize in Literature," (VIII). Professor of Spanish at Arizona State University. Publications include *Studies in the Contemporary Spanish-American Short Story* (1979) and *Mexican Literature: A History* (1994).

MAX FRISCH, "We Hope," (I). Swiss novelist, essayist, diarist, and playwright. Selected works include *When the War Is Over* (1949), *Homo faber* (1957), and *Triptychon* (1978). Frisch received the Neustadt International Prize for Literature in 1986.

CARLOS FUENTES, "On Reading and Writing Myself: How I Wrote *Aura*,"

(V). Mexican writer. Selected work includes the novels *The Death of Artemio Cruz* (1964), *Old Gringo* (1985), and *Christopher Unborn* (1989). Fuentes was featured at the 1983 Puterbaugh conference.

▪ G

SAMBA GADJIGO, "Social Vision in Aminata Sow Fall's Literary Work," (III). Teaches in the African-American and African Studies Department at Mount Holyoke College. Author of *Ecole blanche, l'Afrique noire: L'école coloniale dans le roman d'Afrique noire francophone* (1986).

PATRICIA GEESEY, "Algerian Fiction and the Civil Crisis: Bodies under Siege," (II). Associate Professor of French at the University of North Florida. Author of *Writing the Decolonized Self* (1991), *North African Literature* (1992), and *Autobiography and African Literature* (1997).

LEONG LIEW GEOK, "Dissenting Voices: Political Engagements in the Singaporean Novel in English," (IV). Associate Professor of English Language and Literature at the National University of Singapore. Editor of Ee Tiang Hong's monograph on the poetry of Edwin Thumboo (1997) and the anthology *More Than Half the Sky: Creative Writings by Thirty Singaporean Women* (1998).

DAVID GILLESPIE, "Russian Writers Confront the Past: History, Memory, and Literature, 1953–1991," (VI). Teaches Russian Language and Literature at the University of Bath in England. Publications include *Valentin Rasputin and Soviet Russian Village Prose* (1986) and *Iurii Trifonov: Unity through Time* (1992).

ARMANDO GNISCI, "Contemporary Italian Literature from a Comparatist's Perspective," (VIII). Professor of Comparative Literature in the Department of Italian Studies at the University of Rome. Published work includes *La letteratura del mondo* (1984), *Lettere & Ecologia* (1990), and *Ascesi e decolonizzazione* (1996).

KAREIN GOERTZ, "Transgenerational Representations of the Holocaust: From Memory to 'Post-Memory'," (VIII). Teaches in the Residential College German Program at the University of Michigan. Her publications include articles on Holocaust memoirs in Germany and France.

MARKETA GOETZ-STANKIEWICZ, "Václav Havel: A Writer for Today's Season," (VI). Professor Emerita of German Studies at the University of British Columbia. Publications include *The Silenced Theatre: Czech Playwrights without a Stage* (1979) and *Czechoslovakia: Plays* (1985).

HOWARD GOLDBLATT, "Fresh Flowers Abloom Again: Chinese Literature on the Rebound," (IV). Translator and specialist in Chinese literature. Publications include *The Columbia Anthology of Modern Chinese Literature* (1995) and *Chairman Mao Would Not Be Amused: Fiction from Today's China* (1995).

GEORGE GÖMÖRI, "Literature and Revolution in Hungary," (VI). Teaches at Darwin College, Cambridge University. Selected publications include *Polish and Hungarian Poetry, 1945 to 1956* (1966) and *Polish and Hungarian Poets of the Holocaust* (1986).

ANN GONZÁLEZ, "Fabián Dobles: Memories of a Costa Rican Novelist," (V). Associate Professor of Spanish at the University of North Carolina in Charlotte, specializing in Central American fiction. Co-author, with Bernth Lindfors, of *African, Caribbean, and Latin-American Writers* (2000).

DAVID G. GOODMAN, "The Return of the Gods: Theatre in Japan Today," (IV). Professor of East Asian Languages and Cultures at the University of Illinois, Urbana-Champaign. Publications include *After Apocalypse: Four Japanese Plays of Hiroshima and Nagasaki* (1986) and *Jews in the Japanese Mind: The History and Uses of a Cultural Stereotype* (1995).

D. C. R. A. GOONETILLEKE, "Sri Lanka's 'Ethnic' Conflict in Its Literature in English," (IV). Professor of English at the University of Kelaniya in Sri Lanka. His books include *Images of the Raj* (1988) and *Salman Rushdie* (1998).

ADMER GOURYH, "Recent Trends in Syrian Drama," (II). Syrian translator and critic, whose areas of specialization include the semiotics of theatre. Author of *The Plays of Walid Ikhlasi: A Study in Theme and Structure* (1983).

REGINA GROL, "Eroticism and Exile: Anna Frajlich's Poetry," (VI). Professor of Comparative Literature at Empire State College, State University of New York. Critic and translator of Polish literature. Her published work includes *Ambers Aglow: An Anthology of Contemporary Polish Women's Poetry (1981–1995)* (1996).

CLAUDIO GUILLÉN, "Distant Relations: French, Anglo-American, Hispanic," (I). Professor Emeritus of Comparative Literature and Romance Languages at Harvard University. Published work includes *Literature as System: Essays toward the Theory of Literary History* (1971).

RICARDO GULLÓN, "Twentieth-Century Spanish Poetry," (VIII). Professor Emeritus of Spanish and Portuguese at the University of Texas, Austin. Among his publications are *La novela lírica* (1984) and *Diccionario de literatura española e hispanoamericana* (1993). Gullón died in 1991.

GÜNELI GÜN, "The Turks Are Coming: Deciphering Orhan Pamuk's Black Book," (II). Novelist and translator. Work published includes *Book of Trances: A Novel of Magic Recitals* (1979), *On the Road to Baghdad: A Picaresque Novel of Magical Adventures, Begged, Borrowed, and Stolen from the Thousand and One Nights* (1991), and *The Black Book* (1996).

R. K. GUPTA, "Trends in Modern Indian Fiction," (IV). Teaches English at the Indian Institute of Technology in Kanpur. Author of *The Great Encounter: A Study of Indo-American Literacy and Cultural Relations* (1986).

▪ H

FREDERICK HALE, "Tor Edvin Dahl and the Poverty of Norwegian Prosperity," (VII). Specialist in Scandinavian history, literature, and religious culture. Publications include *Danes in North America* (1984) and *Norwegian Religious Pluralism: A Trans-Atlantic Comparison* (1992).

MICHAEL HAMBURGER, "The Survival of Poetry," (I). Poet, translator, and critic, author of such studies as *The Truth of Poetry* (1968) and *A Proliferation of Poets* (1983), and editor and translator of *Rilke: Poems 1912–1936* (1981) and *Goethe: Roman Elegies* (1983).

ABDEL-AZIZ HAMMOUDA, "Modern Egyptian Theatre: Three Major Dramatists," (II). Egyptian academic and literary critic, whose research interests focus on contemporary Egyptian theatre. Dean of the Faculty of Literature at the University of Cairo.

WILSON HARRIS, "Raja Rao's Inimitable Style and Art of Fiction," (IV). Writer and critic of Caribbean literature, originally from Guyana. Author of *The Womb of Space: The Cross-Cultural Imagination* (1983) and *The Guyana Quartet* (1985).

KEVIN HART, "Open, Mixed, and Moving: Recent Australian Poetry," (IV). Associate Professor of Critical Theory at Monash University in Melbourne. Poet and author of *The Trespass of the Sign: Deconstruction, Theology and Philosophy* (1989) and *A. D. Hope* (1992).

ALAMGIR HASHMI, "Poetry, Pakistani Idiom in English, and the Groupies," (IV); "'A Stylized Motif of Eagle Wings Woven': The Selected Poems of Zulfikar Ghose," (IV). Poet and prose writer. Professor of English and Comparative Literature at the Quaid-I-Azam University in Islamabad. Publications include *The Commonwealth, Comparative Literature, and the World* (1988) and *The Poems of Alamgir Hashmi* (1992).

GERISE HERNDON, "Gender Construction and Neocolonialism," (III). Director of Women's Studies and Associate Professor of English at Nebraska Wesleyan University. Her research focuses on film studies and literatures of the African diasporas.

CRISTINA PANTOJA HIDALGO, "The Philippine Novel in English into the Twenty-First Century," (IV). Professor of English and head of the Creative Writing Center at the University of the Philippines. Among her publications are *Woman Writing: Home and Exile in the Autobiographical Narratives of Filipino Women* (1994) and *A Gentle Subversion* (1998).

KEITH HITCHINS, "Theme and Character in the Azerbaijani Novel, 1930–1957," (IV). Professor of History at the University of Illinois, Urbana-Champaign. Publications include *The Idea of Nation: The Romanians of Transylvania, 1691–1849* (1985) and *Rumania* (1994).

SIDNEY HOOK, "Solzhenitsyn and Western Freedom," (VI). Philosopher and writer. Author of such works as *Religion in a Free Society* (1967), *Philosophy and Public Policy* (1980), and *Out of Step: An Unquiet Life in the 20th Century* (1987). Hook died in 1989.

RUTH A. HOTTELL, "A Poetics of Pain: Evelyne Accad's Critical and Fictional World," (II). Associate Professor of French at the University of Toledo. Author of *Gender-Based Ideology in Film and Literature: The Fantastic and Related Genres* (1987).

E. ANTHONY HURLEY, "Loving Words: New Lyricism in French Caribbean Poetry," (III). Associate Professor of Francophone Literature and Africana Studies at the State University of New York in Stony Brook. Selected publications include *Through a Black Veil: Readings in French Caribbean Poetry* (2000).

LINDA HUTCHEON, "Productive Comparative Angst: Comparative Literature in the Age of Multiculturalism," (I). Canadian Professor of English and Comparative Literature at the University of Toronto, author of *Narcissistic Narrative: The Metafictional Paradox* (1980), *A Poetics of Postmodernism: History, Theory, Fiction* (1988), and *Irony's Edge: The Theory and Politics of Irony* (1994).

■ **I**

WILMA A. IGGERS, "The World of Jaroslav Seifert," (VI). Professor Emerita at Canisius College in Buffalo, N.Y. Selected publications include *Karl Kraus: A Viennese Critic of the Twentieth Century* (1967) and *Women of Prague* (1995).

GUILLERMO CABRERA INFANTE, "Brief Encounters in Havana," (III). Cuban author of novels, essays, short stories, and film scripts, including *Infante's Inferno* (1984), *Two Islands, Many Worlds* (1996), and *Guilty of Dancing the Chachacha* (2001). Infante was featured at the 1987 Puterbaugh conference.

YOSHIO IWAMOTO, "The Nobel Prize in Literature, 1967–1987: A Japanese View," (IV); "A Voice from Postmodern Japan: Haruki Murakami," (IV). Professor Emeritus of East Asian Languages and Cultures and Comparative Literature at Indiana University. Author of *The Relationship between Literature and Politics in Japan, 1931–1945* (1964).

■ **J**

KARL E. JIRGENS, "Carnival of Death: Writing in Latvia since Independence," (VII). Associate Professor of English at Laurentian University. Among his publications are *Christopher Dewdney and His Works* (1994) and *A Measure of Time* (1995).

SOPHIE JOLLIN, "From the Renaudot Prize to the Puterbaugh Conference: The Reception of J. M. G. Le Clézio," (VIII). Assistant Professor of French Literature at the Université de Versailles-Saint Quentin. Author of *J.M.G. Le Clézio: l'érotisme, les mots* (2001).

JOHN M. JONES, "The Renaissance of Welsh Letters," (VIII). Taught in the Foreign Language Department of Rowan University from 1968 to 1990. Scholar of Welsh literature.

W. GLYN JONES, "Naïve, Naïvistic, Artistic: Some Thoughts on Danish and Swedish Diaries," (VII). Critic, translator, and writer. Selected publications include *Denmark: A Modern History* (1986) and *Hans Christian Anderson, Translation Problems and Perspectives* (1995).

■ **K**

DJELAL KADIR, "Turkish Family Romance," (II). Scholar of English, Spanish, and Portuguese literatures, Professor of Comparative Literature and Director of the Center for Global Studies at Pennsylvania State University. Author of *The Other Writing: Postcolonial Essays in Latin*

America's Writing Culture (1993). Served as director of *World Literature Today* from 1991 to 1996.

MOHJA KAHF, "The Silences of Contemporary Syrian Literature," (II). Assistant Professor in the Department of English at the University of Arkansas in Fayetteville. Author of *Western Representations of the Muslim Woman: From Termagant to Odalisque* (1999).

E. D. KARAMPETSOS, "Tyranny and Myth in the Plays of Four Contemporary Greek Dramatists," (VI). Pen name for Thomas Carabas, specialist in modern Greek theatre. Author of *The Theater of Healing* (1995).

AHMAD KARIMI-HAKKAK, "Poetry against Piety: The Literary Response to the Iranian Revolution," (IV). Associate Professor at the University of Washington. Published *An Anthology of Modern Persian Poetry* (1978) and *Recasting Persian Poetry: Scenarios of Poetic Modernity in Iran* (1995).

ALFRED KAZIN, "We See from the Periphery, Not the Center: Reflections on Literature in an Age of Crisis," (I). Literary critic and editor, Kazin has published such studies as *On Native Grounds: An Interpretation of Modern American Prose Literature* (1942), *Bright Book of Life: American Novelists and Storytellers from Hemingway to Mailer* (1973), and *God and the American Writer* (1997).

JOAN TRODDEN KEEFE, "Dwelling in Impossibility: Contemporary Irish Gaelic Literature and Séamas Mac Annaidh," (VIII). Translator and essayist, lecturer in the Celtic Studies Program at the University of California, Berkeley. Publications include the translation of Máirtín Ó Cadhain's *Churchyard Clay* (1984).

JOHN AUSTIN KERR, JR. "Some Considerations on Rodrigues Miguéis's 'Léah'," (VIII). Scholar of Portuguese literature. Publications include *Aspects of Time, Place and Thematic Content in the Prose Fiction of José Rodrigues Miguéis as Indications of the Author's Weltansicht* (1970) and *Miguéis—To the Seventh Decade* (1977).

IMAN O. KHALIL, "Arab-German Literature," (VIII). Associate Professor

of German at the University of Missouri, Kansas City. Author of *Das Fremdwort im Gesellschaftsroman Theodor Fontanes: zur literar. Unters. e. sprachl. Phänomens* (1978).

ADELE KING, "*Le premier homme:* Camus's Unfinished Novel," (VIII). Professor of French at Ball State University in Muncie, Indiana. Published work includes *French Women Novelists: Defining a Female Style* (1989) and *Camus's "L'Etranger": Fifty Years On* (1992).

BETTINA L. KNAPP, "Mishima's Cosmic Noh Drama: *The Damask Drum,*" (IV). Specialist in French and other literatures, Professor of French at Hunter College. Publications include *Gertrude Stein* (1990), *Women in Myth* (1997), and *Voltaire Revisited* (2000).

JERZY R. KRZYŻANOWSKI, "*The Captive Mind* Revisited," (VI). Professor Emeritus in the Department of Slavic Languages and Literatures at Ohio State University. His publications include *Legenda Somosierry* (1987), *Katyń w literaturze* (1995), and *Ariadne* (1998).

MARTHA KUHLMAN, "The Ex(centric) Mind of Europe: Dubravka Ugrešić," (VI). Doctoral student in Comparative Literature at New York University. Research focuses on authors from the "other" Europe, including the Czechs Josef Škvorecký, Pavel Kohout, and Milan Kundera.

MILAN KUNDERA, "1968: Prague, Paris and Josef Škvorecký," (IV). Czech writer whose publications include the novels *The Joke* (1967), *The Book of Laughter and Forgetting* (1979), and *The Unbearable Lightness of Being* (1984).

MAZISI KUNENE, "Some Aspects of South African Literature," (III). Zulu poet, translator, and critic. Teaches at the University of Natal. Author of *Zulu Poems* (1979), *Emperor Shaka the Great* (1979), and *Anthem of the Decades* (1981).

PETER KUSSI, "Milan Kundera: Dialogues with Fiction," (IV). Translator, critic, and editor, author of *Essays on the Fiction of Milan Kundera* (1978). Teaches in the Department of Slavic Languages at Columbia University.

JOHN KWAN-TERRY, "Chinese Literature and the Nobel Prize," (IV). Co-editor of *English and Language Planning: A Southeast Asian Contribution* (1994). Kwan-Terry died in 1993.

▪ L

KAI LAITINEN, "Finland and World Literature," (VII). Translator and critic of Finnish literature. Among his publications are *Modern Nordic Plays: Finland* (1973) and *Literature of Finland: An Outline* (1985). Professor Emeritus at the University of Helsinki.

AGNES LAM, "Poetry in Hong Kong: The 1990s," (IV). Poet and critic. Associate Professor in the English Center at the University of Hong Kong. Author of *Woman to Woman and Other Poems* (1997) and *Water Wood Pure Splendour* (2000).

RENÉE LARRIER, "The Poetics of of Ex-île: Simone Schwarz-Bart's *Ton beau capitaine,*" (III). Associate Professor of French at Rutgers University. Author of *New Directions in Haitian Fiction, 1915–1934* (1986) and *Francophone Women Writers of Africa and the Caribbean* (2000).

CHARLES R. LARSON, "The Fiction of Hanan Al-Shaykh, Reluctant Feminist," (II); "The Precarious State of the African Writer," (III). Professor of Literature at American University in Washington, D.C. Publications include *The Emergence of African Fiction* (1972), *Arthur Dimmesdale* (1983), and *The Ordeal of the African Writer* (2001).

K. C. LEUNG, "Literature in the Service of Politics: The Chinese Literary Scene since 1949," (IV). Professor of Chinese at San Jose State University. Translator and critic, author of *Visions of Cathay: China in English Literature of the Romantic Period* (1979), co-editor of *Hsu Wei as Drama Critic: An Annotated Translation of the Nan-tz'u hsü-lu* (1986).

ÉTAN LEVINE, "Writing in Hebrew," (II). Teaches at the University of Haifa. Among his book publications are *The Burning Bush: Jewish Symbolism and Mysticism* (1981), *The Resurrection of the Hebrew Language* (1982), and *The Aramaic Version of the Bible: Contents and Context* (1988).

SUZANNE JILL LEVINE, "Vistas of Dawn in the (Tristes) Tropics: History, Fiction, Translation," (III); "Manuel among the Stars (Exit Laughing)," (V). Critic and translator of literature in Spanish. Publications include *Latin American Fiction and Poetry in Translation* (1970) and *Manuel Puig and the Spider Woman: His Life and Fictions* (2000).

C. S. LIM, "A Survey of Malaysian Poetry in English," (IV). Professor of English at the University of Malaya in Kuala Lumpur. Essayist and critic, author of articles on Shakespeare and other subjects in such journals as *Cahiers Elisabethains* and *Southeast Asian Review of English*.

SYLVIA LI-CHUN LIN, "Between the Individual and the Collective: Gao Xingjian's Fiction," (IV). Translator and critic, teaches Modern and Contemporary Chinese Literature and Culture at the University of Colorado in Denver. Author of *The Discursive Formation of the "New" Chinese Women, 1860–1930* (1998).

DAVID LLOYD, "Welsh Writing in English," (VIII). Professor of English at Le Moyne College in Syracuse, N.Y., specializing in contemporary poetry from Wales and Ireland. He is editor of the anthology *The Urgency of Identity: Contemporary English-Language Poetry from Wales* (1994).

LUIZA LOBO, "Women Writers in Brazil Today," (V). Professor at the Universidade Federal do Rio de Janeiro. Publications include *Crítica Sem Juízo: Ensaios* (1970) and *Modernidad y modernización: Cultura y Literatura en Latinoamérica* (2002).

CELESTE LOUGHMAN, "The Seamless Universe of Ōe Kenzaburō," (IV). Professor Emerita of English at Westfield State College in Westfield, Massachusetts. Publications include *Mirrors and Masks in the Novels of John Barth* (1971) and *Hawthorne's Patriarchs and the American Revolution* (1978).

■ **M**

DOMENICO MACERI, "Dario Fo: Jester of the Working Class," (VIII). Teaches Romance Languages at Allan Hancock College in Santa Maria, California. Author of *Dalla novella alla commedia pirandelliana* (1991).

SIGURÐUR A. MAGNÚSSON, "Postwar Literature in Iceland," (VII). Icelandic poet, novelist, and critic, whose publications include *The Postwar Poetry of Iceland* (1982) and *The Icelanders* (1998).

URSULA MAHLENDORF, "Confronting the Fascist Past and Coming to Terms with It," (VIII). Professor Emerita of German and Women's Studies at the University of California, Santa Barbara. Author of *The Wellsprings of Literary Creation: An Analysis of Male and Female "Artist Stories" from the German Romantics to American Writers of the Present* (1985).

HASAN MARHAMA, "The Fictional Works of Caryl Phillips: An Introduction," (article written with Charles Sarvan) (III). Associate Professor in the Department of Foreign Languages and Literatures at the University of Bahrain. Published work includes essays on "Culture in Foreign Language Teaching and Learning" and "Poetry, English Sounds, and EFL Learners" (both 1991).

JOHN MARNEY, "PRC Politics and Literature in the Nineties," (IV). Specialist in Classical Chinese literature; specific research areas include Six Dynasties literature. Publications include *Liang Chien-wen Ti* (1976) and *Chinese Anagrams and Anagram Verse* (1993).

MURRAY S. MARTIN, "Who Is the Colonist? Writing in New Zealand and the South Pacific," (IV). New Zealander, served as head librarian at Tufts University. Author of *Reviewers: Who Needs Them?* (1977) and *Academic Library Budgets* (1999).

Z. NELLY MARTÍNEZ, "Dangerous Messianisms: The World According to Valenzuela," (V). Publications include a critical collection of the prose writings of Ernesto Sábato (1975) as well as *El silencio que habla: Aproximación a la obra de Luisa Valenzuela* (1994).

FERNANDO MARTINHO, "The Poetry of Agostinho Neto," (III). Scholar of Portuguese literature. Publications include *Pessoa e os surrealistas* (1988), *Tendências dominantes da poesia portuguesa da década de 50* (1996), and *Mário de Sá-Carneiro e o(s) outro(s)* (1999).

WILSON MARTINS, "Carlos Drummond de Andrade and the Heritage of Modernismo," (V). Professor Emeritus of Spanish at New York University. Selected publications include *The Modernist Idea: A Critical Survey of Brazilian Writing in the Twentieth Century* (1970) and *Structural Perspectivism in Guimaraes Rosa* (1973).

YAIR MAZOR, "Besieged Feminism: Contradictory Rhetorical Themes in the Poetry of Daliah Rabikovitz," (II). Professor of Hebrew Studies, and Director of the Center for Jewish Studies and the Hebrew Studies Program at the University of Wisconsin, Milwaukee. His book publications include *Farewell to Arms and Sentimentality: Reflections of Israel's Wars in Yehuda Amichai's Poetry* (1986) and *Somber Lust: The Art of Amos Oz* (2002).

ROBERT H. McCORMICK JR., "Desirada—A New Conception of Identity: An Interview with Maryse Condé," (III). Associate Professor of Literature and Freshman Composition at Franklin College in Lugano, Switzerland.

WALTER J. MESERVE, "Shakuntala's Daughters: Women in Contemporary Indian Drama," (IV). Professor Emeritus in the Program in Theatre at the Graduate School of the City University of New York. Author of *An Emerging Entertainment: The Drama of the American People* (1977).

VASA D. MIHAILOVICH, "The Karamazov Syndrome in Recent Yugoslav Literature," (VI). Professor Emerita in the Department of Slavic Languages at the University of North Carolina, Chapel Hill. Selected publications include *Contemporary Yugoslav Poetry* (1977) and *South Slavic Writers before World War II* (1995).

MONA N. MIKHAIL, "Middle Eastern Literature and the Conditions of Modernity: An Introduction," (II). Associate Professor of Middle Eastern Studies at New York University. Publications include *Studies in the Short Fiction of Mahfouz and Idris* (1992) and *Seeds of Corruption* (2002)

J. HILLIS MILLER, "'World Literature' in the Age of

Telecommunications," (I). Professor of English and Comparative Literature at the University of California, Irvine. Among his book publications are *Topographies* (1995), *Reading Narrative* (1998), and *The Disappearance of God: Five Nineteenth-Century Writers* (2000).

SIDNEY MONAS, "Words Devouring Things: The Poetry of Joseph Brodsky," (VI). Translator and critic. Professor of Slavic Literatures at the University of Texas. Selected publications include *The Third Section: Police and Society in Russia under Nicholas I* (1961) and *The Myth of St. Petersburg* (1973).

MILDRED MORTIMER, "Whose House Is This? Space and Place in Calixthe Beyala's *C'est le soleil qui m'a brûlée* and *La Petite Fille du réverbère*," (III). Associate Professor of French and Francophone Literature at the University of Colorado. Published work includes *Journeys through the French African Novel* (1990) and *Maghrebian Mosaic: Literature in Transition* (2001).

GERALD M. MOSER, "Neglected or Forgotten Authors of Lusophone Africa," (III). Professor Emeritus of Spanish and Portuguese at Pennsylvania State University. Author of *Essays in Portuguese-African Literature* (1969) and *Changing Africa: The First Literary Generation of Independent Cape Verde* (1992).

WARREN MOTTE, "Writing Away," (VIII). Professor of French and Comparative Literature at the University of Colorado in Boulder. His books include *The Poetics of Experiment: A Study of the Work of Georges Perec* (1984) and *Playtexts: Ludics in Contemporary Literature* (1995).

JOSEPH P. MOZUR, "Chingiz Aitmatov: Transforming the Esthetics of Socialist Realism," (VI). Professor of Russian at the University of South Alabama. Author of such studies as *Chingiz Aitmatov and the Poetics of Moral Prose* (1983) and *Parables from the Past: The Prose Fiction of Chingiz Aitmatov* (1995).

KLAUS MÜLLER-BERGH, "*Feijoada*, Coke and the Urbanoid: Brazilian Poetry since 1945," (V). Professor of

Spanish and Latin-American Literature at the University of Illinois at Chicago. Author of *Asedios a Carpentier: Once Ensayos Críticos sobre el novelista cubano* (1972) and *Mariano Brull: Poesia reunida* (2001).

▪ N

FRED J. NICHOLS, "Jacques Hamelink: A Man Armed with the Imagination," (VIII). Professor Emeritus of French at the Graduate Center of the City University of New York. Publications include *An Anthology of Neo-Latin Poetry* (1979).

PAUL NIZON, "Exile: Multiculturalism as Stimulant," (I). Swiss novelist and critic. Among his book publications are *Canto* (1963), *Goya* (1991), and *Die Innenseite des Mantels* (1995).

▪ O

KENZABURŌ ŌE, "Japan's Dual Identity: A Writer's Dilemma," (IV). Japanese novelist, author of such works as *A Personal Matter* (1968), *The Silent Cry* (1974), and *Teach Us to Outgrow Our Madness* (1977). Ōe was featured at the 2001 Puterbaugh conference.

ODE S. OGEDE, "Angled Shots and Reflections: On the Literary Essays of Ayi Kwei Armah," (III). Specialist of twentieth-century British poetry, oral literature, and the African novel at Ahmadu Bello University in Zaria, Nigeria. He has contributed essays on Ayi Kwei Armah's writing to such journals as *Kunapipi* and *Ariel* (both 1990).

BETTY O'GRADY, "Tchicaya U Tam'Si: Some Thoughts on the Poet's Symbolic Mode of Expression," (III). Zimbabwean specialist in Francophone African literature, particularly of the Congo.

S. E. OGUDE, "Slavery and the African Imagination: A Critical Perspective," (III). Author of works such as *Genius in Bondage: A Study of the Origins of African Literature in English* (1983) and *No Roots Here: On the Igbo Roots of Oluadah Equiano* (1989).

BRENDAN P. O HEHIR, "Re-Grafting a Severed Tongue: The Pains (and

Politics) of Reviving Irish," (VIII). Co-founder of the Celtic Studies Program at the University of California, Berkeley. Author of *A Gaelic Lexicon for "Finnegans Wake," and Glossary for Joyce's Other Works* (1967) and *Harmony from Discords: A Life of Sir John Denham* (1968). O Hehir died in 1991.

CHINYERE G. OKAFOR, "Ola Rotimi: The Man, the Playwright, and the Producer on the Nigerian Theater Scene," (III). Author of *Continuity and Change in Traditional Nigerian Theatre among the Igbo in the Era of Colonial Politics* (1988).

ISIDORE OKPEWHO, "Comparatism and Separatism in African Literature," (III). Fiction writer and critic, Professor of Africana Studies, English and Comparative Literature at the State University of New York in Binghamton. Publications include *Myth in Africa: A Study of Its Aesthetic and Cultural Relevance* (1983) and *The African Diaspora: African Origins and New World Identities* (1999).

MAKOTO ŌOKA, "Contemporary Japanese Poetry," (IV). Japanese poet and critic. Publications include *A Play of Mirrors: Eight Major Poets of Modern Japan* (1987) and *The Colors of Poetry: Essays in Classic Japanese Verse* (1991).

VALÉRIE ORLANDO, "Writing New H(er)stories for Francophone Women of Africa and the Caribbean," (III). Assistant Professor of French and Francophone Studies at Illinois Wesleyan University. Author of *Nomadic Voices of Exile: Feminine Identity in Francophone Literature of the Maghreb* (1999).

▪ P

MICHAEL PALENCIA-ROTH, "Gabriel García Márquez: Labyrinths of Love and History," (V). Professor of Comparative Literature at the University of Illinois, Urbana-Champaign. Selected publications include *Perspectives on Faust* (1983) and *Myth and the Modern Novel: García Márquez, Mann, and Joyce* (1987).

JOHN M. PARKER, "João Cabral de Melo Neto: 'Literalist of the Imagination'," (V). Translator, specialist in contemporary Brazilian and Portuguese fiction and poetry, as well as in stylistics and linguistics. Among his publications are *Three Twentieth-Century Portuguese Poets* (1960) and *Brazilian Fiction, 1950–1970* (1973).

R. PARTHASARATHY, "Tamil Literature," (IV). Poet, translator, and critic, whose works include *Ten Twentieth-Century Indian Poets* (1976) and *The Cilappatikāram of Ilankō Atikal: An Epic of South India* (1993). He is Associate Professor of English and Asian Studies at Skidmore College in Saratoga Springs, N.Y.

RAJEEV S. PATKE, "Poetry in English from Singapore," (IV). Associate Professor of English at the National University of Singapore. Author of *The Long Poems of Wallace Stevens* (1985) and co-editor, with Robert Lumsden, of *Institutions in Cultures: Theory and Practice* (1996).

OCTAVIO PAZ, "The Liberal Tradition," (I). Mexican poet, essayist, and critic, winner of the 1990 Nobel Prize for Literature. Verse collections include *Sun Stone* (1957) and *A Tale of Two Gardens* (1997). Prose and essays include *The Labyrinth of Solitude* (1950), *Conjunctions and Disjunctions* (1982), and *Convergences* (1987). He won the Neustadt International Prize for Literature in 1982. Paz died in 1998.

MARJORIE PERLOFF, "Barthes and the Zero Degree of Genre," (I); "Living in the Same Place: The Old Mononationalism and the New Comparative Literature," (I). Professor of Humanities at Stanford University. Publications include *Licence: Essays on Modernist and Postmodernist Lyric* (1990) and *Radical Artifice: Writing Poetry in the Age of Media* (1991).

JOHN OLIVER PERRY, "Contemporary Indian Poetry in English," (IV). Professor Emeritus of English at Tufts University. Publications include *Voices of Emergency: An All-India Anthology of Protest Poetry of the 1975–77 Emergency* (1983) and *Absent Authority: Issues in Contemporary Indian English Criticism* (1992).

JOHN R. PERRY, "Tajik Literature: Seventy Years Is Longer Than the

Millennium," (IV). Professor of Persian Language and Civilization at the University of Chicago. Publications include translations from Arabic, Persian, and Tajik, as well as critical studies, such as *Karim Khan Zand: A History of Iran, 1747–1779* (1979).

HENRI PEYRE, "Beyond Cultural Nationalism," (I); "Marguerite Yourcenar: Independent, Imaginative and 'Immortal'," (VIII). Peyre taught for many years at Yale University and at the Graduate Center of the City University of New York. Author of critical studies, such as *The Contemporary French Novel* (1955), *The Failures of Criticism* (1967), and *What Is Symbolism?* (1980).

DIETGER PFORTE, "Disunitedly United: Literary Life in Germany," (VIII). Director of the Department of "Literatur- und Autorenförderung" with the Berlin Senate Administration for Science, Research, and Culture. Publications include *Comics im ästhetischen Unterricht* (1974) and *Freie Volksbühne Berlin, 1890–1990: Beiträge zur Geschichte der Volksbühnenbewegung in Berlin* (1990).

PETER PIERCE, "Australian Literature since Patrick White," (IV). Senior Lecturer at the National Centre for Australian Studies at Monash University, Melbourne. Editor of *The Oxford Literary Guide to Australia* (1987) and author of *The Country of Lost Children: An Australian Anxiety* (1999).

WILLIAM PRATT, "The Great Irish Elk: Seamus Heaney's Personal Helicon," (VIII); "Brian Friel's Imaginary Journeys to Nowhere," (VIII). Professor Emeritus of English at Miami University in Ohio. Poet, translator, and essayist, whose published work includes *The Fugitive Poets* (1965) and *Singing the Chaos: Madness and Wisdom in Modern Poetry* (1996).

RICHARD A. PRETO-RODAS, "José Saramago: Art for Reason's Sake," (VIII). Professor Emeritus of Romance Languages and Literatures at the University of South Florida. His books include *Negritude as a Theme in the Poetry of the Portuguese-Speaking World* (1970) and *Dialogue and Courtly Love in Renaissance Portugal* (1971).

■ Q

TAHIR QAHHAR, "Uzbek Literature," (IV). Poet, critic, and editor. Verse collections include *White Apricot* (1980), *The Eye of the Day* (1987), and *The Flight of the Mountain* (1990).

■ R

GREGORY RABASSA, "García Márquez's New Book: Literature or Journalism?," (V); "'O Tempora, O Mores': Time, Tense and Tension in Mario Vargas Llosa," (V). Distinguished Professor of Brazilian and Spanish-American Literature at Queens College, Graduate School of the City University of New York. Translator and critic of Gabriel García Márquez, Mario Vargas Llosa, and other Spanish-language novelists.

OLGA RAGUSA, "Italo Calvino: The Repeated Conquest of Contemporaneity," (VIII). Professor Emerita of Italian at Columbia University. Selected publications include *Narrative and Drama: Essays in Modern Italian Literature from Verga to Pasolini* (1976) and *Luigi Pirandello: An Approach to His Theatre* (1980).

NASRIN RAHIMIEH, "The Quince-Orange Tree, or Iranian Writers in Exile," (IV). Professor at the University of Alberta. Publications include *Responses to Orientalism in Modern Eastern Fiction and Scholarship* (1988) and *Missing Persians: Discovering Voices in Iranian Cultural History* (2001).

MARIOS BYRON RAIZIS, "The Stream of Consciousness in Greek Fiction," (VI). Professor in the Department of English at the University of Athens. Publications include *The Prometheus Theme in British and American Poetry* (1966) and *The Poetic Manner of George Seferis* (1977).

GILA RAMRAS-RAUCH, "Aharon Appelfeld: A Hundred Years of Jewish Solitude," (I). Professor of Jewish Literature at Hebrew College in Boston. Publications include *The Arab in Israeli Literature* (1989).

ROBERTO REIS, "Who's Afraid of (Luso-)Brazilian Literature?," (V). Publications include *A Dictionary of Contemporary Brazilian Authors* (1981) and *The Pearl Necklace: Toward an*

Archaeology of Brazilian Transition Discourse (1982).

WILLIAM RIGGAN, "The Swedish Academy and the Nobel Prize in Literature: History and Procedure," (I). Joined the editorial staff of *World Literature Today* in 1974 and served in many capacities, including editor of the journal. Author of *Picaros, Madmen, Naifs, and Clowns: The Unreliable First-Person Narrator* (1981).

GIOSE RIMANELLI, "The Poetry of 'Limited' Exile and Its Revealing Trek among Italy's Small Presses," (VIII). Professor Emeritus of Italian at Suny-Albany. Selected publications are *Moliseide* (1992), *Benedetta in Guysterland* (1993), and *I rascenije* (1996).

EDOUARD RODITI, "Paul Celan and the Cult of Personality," (VIII). Poet, translator, critic. Published works include *Dialogues on Art* (1960), *Meetings with Conrad* (1977), and *Choose Your Own World* (1992). Roditi died in 1992.

J. BARTON ROLLINS, "Emigration and the Rise of the Novel in Yemen," (article written with Mohammed Saad Al-Jumly) (II). Professor of English at National Chung Cheng University in Taiwan. His articles on American poetry and fiction have appeared in *American Literature*, *Journal of Modern Literature*, and *Markham Review*.

SIDNEY ROSENFELD, "1981 Nobel Laureate Elias Canetti: A Writer Apart," (VI). Professor Emeritus of German at Oberlin College. Selected publications include *Understanding Joseph Roth* (2001).

DAVID H. ROSENTHAL, "The Poetry of J. V. Foix," (VIII). Freelance writer, translator, and critic. Author of such works as *4 Poemes* (1985) and *Hard Bop Jazz and Black Music, 1955–1965* (1992).

DALIA ROSS-DANIEL, "Memory and Reconstruction of Self in Contemporary Yiddish Literature," (I). Poet and theorist. Among her publications is a critical study, *Memory and Reconstruction of Self in Contemporary Yiddish Literature* (1985).

SVEN H. ROSSEL, "Ole Hyltoft and the Neorealistic Trends in Contemporary Danish Literature," (VII); "Gunnar Ekelöf: Poet, Visionary, and Outsider" (VII). Translator and critic, specialist in Scandinavian and Comparative Literature at the University of Washington. Author of such studies as *A History of Scandinavian Literature, 1870–1980* (1982) and *A History of Danish Literature* (1992).

LEON S. ROUDIEZ, "Michel Butor: Past, Present, and Future," (VIII). Translator, editor, and critic of French literature and theory, particularly of the work of Julia Kristeva. Professor Emeritus of French at Columbia University.

G. ROSS ROY, "The Thorn on Scotland's Rose: Hugh MacDiarmid," (VIII). Professor Emeritus of English at University of South Carolina. Critic and scholar of Scottish literature. Published work includes *Robert Burns and the Merry Muses* (1999) and *Robert Burns & America: A Symposium* (2001).

EMANUEL RUBIN, "Israel's Theatre of Confrontation," (II). Professor of Music History and Judaic Studies at the University of Massachusetts, Amherst. Author of *The Warren Collection* (1971), *The English Glee in the Reign of George III* (2001), and *Music in Jewish History and Culture* (2001).

SUSAN RUSINKO, "The Last Romantic: Henry Boot, Alias Tom Stoppard," (VIII). Professor Emerita at Bloomsburg University. Among her publications are *British Drama, 1950 to the Present: A Critical History* (1989) and *Joe Orton* (1995).

▪ S

JUHANI SALOKANNEL, "Unusual Men: Three Masters of Contemporary Finnish Prose," (VII). Finnish critic and writer, Director of the Finnish Institute in Estonia. His publications include *Linnasta Saarikoskeen: Kirjailijakuvia* (1993) and *Sielunsilta: Suomen ja Viron kirjallisia suhteita, 1944–1988* (1998).

IVAN SANDERS, "Freedom's Captives: Notes on George Konrád's Novels," (VI). Scholar and specialist of Hungarian literature. Professor of English at Suffolk County Community College. Translations include the novels of George Konrád, such as *The City Builder* (1977).

RIVANNE SANDLER, "Literary Developments in Iran in the 1960s and the 1970s Prior to the 1978 Revolution," (IV). Professor Emerita of Middle Eastern and Islamic Studies at the University of Toronto. Areas of research specialization include twentieth-century Iranian society and Persian literature.

CHARLES P. SARVAN, "French Colonialism in Africa: The Early Novels of Ferdinand Oyono," (article written with Hasan Marhama) (III); "The Fictional Works of Caryl Phillips: An Introduction," (III). Sri Lankan critic whose research specializations include African and Commonwealth literatures. He teaches English at the University of Bahrain.

JOHN SCHECKTER, "Dreaming Wholeness: David Malouf's New Stories," (IV). Professor of English at the C. W. Post Campus of Long Island University, New York. Author of *The Australian Novel, 1830–1980: A Thematic Introduction* (1998).

LESLIE SCHENK, "The Western Canon," (I). Essayist and fiction writer. Published work includes *Haystacks and Cathedrals: Selected Short Stories* (2000) and *Cory O'Lanus for President: A Novel* (2000).

PETER SCHNEIDER, "All My Foreigners," (VIII). German novelist, playwright, and essayist, whose work includes *The German Comedy: Scenes of Life after the Wall* (1991), *Couplings* (1996), and *Eduard's Homecoming* (2000).

GEORGE C. SCHOOLFIELD, "Might-Have-Beens: The North and the Nobel Prize, 1967–1987," (VII). Professor Emeritus of Scandinavian and Germanic Languages and Literatures at Yale University. Selected publications include *Swedo-Finnish Short Stories* (1974) and *Helsinki of the Czars: Finland's Capital, 1808–1918* (1996).

ERIC SELLIN, "Moloud Mammeri Returns to the Mountains," (II). Professor of French and Franco-African Literature at Temple University. Author of *The Dramatic*

Concepts of Antonin Artaud (1968) and *Reflections on the Aesthetics of Futurism, Dadaism and Surrealism: A Prosody beyond Words* (1993).

SUDEEP SEN, "New Indian Poetry: The 1990s Perspective," (IV). Poet, critic, and editor, whose publications include *The Lunar Visitations: A Cycle of Poems* (1990) and *Postmarked India: New and Selected Poems* (1997).

ALEX SEVERINO, "Fernando Pessoa's Legacy: The Presença and After," (VIII). Taught in the Department of Spanish and Portuguese at Vanderbilt University. Selected publications include *Fernando Pessoa na Africa do Sul: A formação inglesa de Fernando Pessoa* (1983) and *Fernando Pessoa e o mar português* (1988). Severino died in 1993.

BEKTASH SHAMSHIEV, "Post-Socialist Kyrgyz Literature: Crisis or Renaissance?," (IV). Kyrgyz editor and journalist. Publications include *Barpy: izildoolor, eskeruulor, arnoolor* (1994).

FRANCIS MICHAEL SHARP, "Max Frisch: A Writer in a Technological Age," (VIII). Specialist in German and Austrian literatures at the University of the Pacific. Author of *The Poet's Madness: A Reading of Georg Trakl* (1981).

MUHAMMAD SIDDIQ, "The Contemporary Arabic Novel in Perspective," (II). Research specializations include Arabic literature and language, Hebrew, and English literature. Studies published include *Man Is a Cause: Political Consciousness in the Fiction of Ghassan Kanafani* (1984).

RIMVYDAS ŠILBAJORIS, "Post-Soviet Literature in Lithuania: An Overview," (VII). Professor Emeritus of Slavic and East European Literatures at Ohio State University. Publications include *Perfection of Exile: 14 Contemporary Lithuanian Writers* (1970) and *War and Peace: Tolstoy's Mirror of the World* (1995).

EISIG SILBERSCHLAG, "Redemptive Vision in Hebrew Literature," (II). Selected publications include *Hebrew Literature: An Evaluation* (1959), *Saul Tschernichowsky* (1968), and *Hebrew Literature in the Land of Israel* (1977). He died in 1988.

SAADI A. SIMAWE, "Modernism & Metaphor in Contemporary Arabic Poetry," (II). Associate Professor of English and Africana Studies at Grinnell College. Fiction writer, editor, translator. Author of *Modern Iraqi Literature in English Translation* (1997) and *Out of the Lamp* (1999).

NORMAN SIMMS, "Maori Literature in English: An Introduction," (IV). Senior Lecturer in English at the University of Waikato. Author of *Silence and Invisibility: A Study of the Literatures of the Pacific, Australia, and New Zealand* (1986) and *Writers from the South Pacific: A Bio-Bibliographical Critical Encyclopedia* (1991).

KIRSTI SIMONSUURI, "The Lyrical Space: On the Poetry of Paavo Haavikko," (VII). Poet, essayist, and critic of Finnish literature at the University of Helsinki. Among her publications are *Enchanting Beasts: An Anthology of Modern Women Poets of Finland* (1990) and *Traveling Light: Selected Poems of Kirsti Simonsuuri* (2001).

JAN SJÅVIK, "Alfred Hauge's Utstein Monastery Cycle," (VII). Associate Professor of Scandinavian Studies at the University of Washington. Author of *Arne Garborgs Kristiania-romaner: Beretterteknisk Studie* (1985).

ANDERS SJÖBOHM, "Poverty, Pride, and Memory: On the Writings of Basil Fernando," (IV). Swedish literary critic and essayist of comparative work, including essays on Virgil, Georg Trakl, and Sri Lankan writers, such as Jean Arasanayagam.

JEAN STAROBINSKI, "On Yves Bonnefoy: Poetry, between Two Worlds," (VIII). Professor of the History of Ideas and of French at the University of Geneva. His published work includes the studies *The Invention of Liberty, 1700–1789* (1964), *Montaigne in Motion* (1985), and *Blessings in Disguise, or, The Morality of Evil* (1993).

■ **T**

JÜRI TALVET, "The State of Estonian Literature Following the Reestablishment of Independence," (VII). Poet, critic, and essayist. Teaches Comparative Literature at Tartu University in Estonia. A selection of his publications includes *The Spanish Spirit* (1995) and *Estonian Elegy and Other Poems* (1997).

MARTA TARNAWSKY, "Ukrainian Literature for the American Reader," (VI). Translator and specialist in Ukrainian literature. Professor Emerita of Law at the University of Pennsylvania. Author of an annotated bibliography, *Ukrainian Literature in English, 1980–1989* (1999).

JEFFREY TWITCHELL, "Avant-Garde Poetry in China: The Nanjing Scene 1981–1992," (article written with Huang Fan) (IV). Associate Professor at National Chung Cheng University in Taiwan. His publications focus on modernist and contemporary poetry.

■ **V**

MARIO VARGAS LLOSA, "Social Commitment and the Latin American Writer," (V). Peruvian writer whose publications include the novels *The Time of the Hero* (1962), *The Green House* (1966), *Conversation in the Cathedral* (1969), and *The Storyteller* (1987). Vargas Llosa was featured at the 1977 Puterbaugh conference.

SHOULEH VATANABADI, "Past, Present, Future, and Postcolonial Discourse in Modern Azerbaijani Literature," (IV). Teaches in the Department of General Studies at New York University. Author of *A Feast in the Mirror: Stories by Contemporary Iranian Women* (2000).

TOMAS VENCLOVA, "Czesław Miłosz: Despair and Grace," (VI). Lithuanian poet and critic. Author of *Aleksander Wat: Life and Art of an Iconoclast* (1996) and *Forms of Hope: Essays* (1999).

LOUISE VILJOEN, "Postcolonialism and Recent Women's Writing in Afrikaans," (III). Teaches in the Department of Afrikaans and Dutch at the University of Stellenbosch, South Africa. Co-author, with Ronel Foster, of *Poskaarte: beelde van die Afrikaanse poësie sedert 1960* (1997).

■ **W**

H. M. WAIDSON, "Silvio Blatter: Realism and Society in Modern

Switzerland," (VIII). Translator and critic of German and Swiss literatures. Publications include *German Short Stories, 1945–1955* (1967) and *Anthology of Modern Swiss Literature* (1984).

NGŨGĨ WA THIONG'O, "Kamau Brathwaite: The Voice of African Presence," (III). Kenyan poet, novelist, and playwright, author of such works as *Weep Not, Child* (1964), *The Black Hermit* (1968), and *Secret Lives* (1992).

ELIE WIESEL, "A Vision of the Apocalypse," (I). Winner of the Nobel Peace Prize in 1986. Among the books Wiesel has published are *Night* (1982), *Twilight* (1988), and *Sages and Dreamers: Biblical, Talmudic, and Hasidic Portraits and Legends* (1991). His memoirs, *All Rivers Run to the Sea*, appeared in 1995.

FREDERICK G. WILLIAMS, "Prodigious Exorcist: An Introduction to the Poetry of Jorge de Sena," (VIII). Professor of Luso-Brazilian Studies at Brigham Young University. Publications include the study *From Those Who Wrote: Poems and Translations* (1975) and the edition *The Poetry of Jorge de Sena* (1980).

A. LESLIE WILLSON, "Entering the Eighties: The Mosaic of German Literatures," (VIII). Professor Emeritus of German Studies at the University of Texas, Austin. Published work includes *A Mythical Image: The Ideal of India in German Romanticism* (1964) and *Contemporary German Fiction* (1996).

REUEL K. WILSON, "Stanislaw Lem's Fiction and the Cosmic Absurd," (VI). Associate Professor in Modern Languages and Literatures at the University of Western Ontario. Author

of *The Literary Travelogue: A Comparative Study with Special Relevance to Russian Literature from Fonvizin to Pushkin* (1973).

MANFRED WOLF, "On the Poetry of Albert Verwey," (VIII). Professor Emeritus of English at San Francisco State University. Among his publications are *Change of Scene: Contemporary Dutch and Flemish Poems in English Translation* (1969) and *Albert Verwey and English Romanticism: A Comparative and Critical Study, with Original Translations* (1977).

DEREK WRIGHT, "The Metaphysical and Material Worlds: Ayi Kwei Armah's Ritual Cycle," (III); "Soyinka's Smoking Shotgun: The Later Satires," (III). Author of studies on African literature, such as *Critical Perspectives on Ayi Kwei Armah* (1992), *Wole Soyinka Revisited* (1993), and *New Directions in African Fiction* (1997).

HAL WYLIE, "The Dancing Masks of Sylvain Bemba," (III). Associate Professor Emeritus of French at the University of Texas, Austin. Publications include *Contemporary African Literature* (1983) and *Multiculturalism and Hybridity in African Literatures* (2000).

SYLVIA WYNTER, "Beyond the Word of Man: Glissant and the New Discourse of the Antilles," (III). Professor Emerita in the Department of Spanish and Portuguese, as well as in African and Afro-American Studies, at Stanford University. Publications include *Jamaica's National Heroes* (1971) and *Reading, Writing, and Race* (1991).

▪Y

MO YAN, "My Three American Books," (IV). Chinese writer whose

novels include *Red Sorghum* (1993), *The Garlic Ballads* (1995), and *The Republic of Wine* (2000).

WONG MING YOOK, "Traversing Boundaries: Journeys into Malaysian Fiction in English," (IV). Writer and poet. Teaches in the Department of English at the University of Malaya. A specialist in twentieth-century British literature, as well as in postcolonial (particularly Southeast Asian anglophone) and women's literatures.

SANROKU YOSHIDA, "An Interview with Kenzaburō Ōe," (IV). Japanese scholar whose areas of specialization focus on the work of modern Japanese novelists. Professor Emeritus of Japanese at Miami University of Ohio.

LEON I. YUDKIN, "Memorialization in New Fiction," (I). Teaches Hebrew and Comparative Literature at University College London. Selected publications are *A Home Within: Varieties of Jewish Expression in Modern Fiction* (1996) and *Public Crisis and Literary Response: The Adjustment of Modern Jewish Literature* (2000).

▪Z

THEODORE ZIOLKOWSKI, "Günter Grass's Century," (VIII). Professor of German and Comparative Literature at Princeton University. His book publications include *The Mirror of Justice* (1997) and *The View from the Tower* (1998).

JOHN ZUBIZARRETA, "The Woman Who Sings No, No, No: Love, Freedom, and Rebellion in the Poetry of Forugh Farrokhzad," (IV). Associate Professor of English at Columbia College. Author of *Frost, Eliot and Modernism* (1983).

Index

Arabic numbers followed by colon (:) indicate volume number. Bold–face Arabic numbers refer to the main article on a subject. Photographs are designated by italicized Arabic numbers.

∎ A

Abdel–Qadir, Ghazi, 2:1237–1238

Abdul–Wali, Mohammed, *They Die Strangers*, 1:274–276

Abe, Kōbō, 1:570
  The Ark Sakura, 2:1594

Abraham's Promise (Jeyaretnam), 1:777, 780–781

Abroad (Bellad barrah) ('Ashour), 1:185

Absconding (Gao), 1:540–541

Absheron (Hüsein), 1:631

Abülhasan, Alekperzade
  Dostlug galasy (The Bastion of Friendship), 1:631
  Iokhushlar, 1:630–631

Accad, Evelyne, **1:231–237**
  Blessures des mots: Journal de Tunisie (Wounded by Words: A Tunisian Journal), 1:231, 234–235, 236
  Coquelicot du massacre (Poppy from the Massacre), 1:233–234, 235, 236
  L'excisée, 1:235–236; 2:1597–1598
  Sexuality and War: Literary Masks of the Middle East, 1:232–233, 236
  Veil of Shame, 1:231–232

Accidental Death of an Anarchist (Morte accidentale di un anarchico) (Fo), 2:1320, 1321n2

Achebe, Chinua, *1:286,* 286–288, 296–297
  Arrow of God, 1:297, 304
  The Healers, 1:288
  A Man of the People, 1:288
  Things Fall Apart, 1:286–287, 288
  The Trouble with Nigeria, 1:288

"Adeus à hora da largada" (Farewell at the Time of Parting) (Neto), 1:316–317

Adrift on the Nile (Mahfūz), 2:1615–1616

Afdalingen in de ingewanden (Descent into the Intestines) (Hamelink), 2:1341–1342

Africaans literature, 1:395, 401–411

African literature, **1:281–411**
  comparatism in, 1:298–302, 304–305
  drama and, 1:281–286; 2:1531–1532
  English–language writers and, 2:1528–1534
  fiction and, 2:1529–1531
  francophone writers and, 1:126–130, 154–176, 175n, 306–315, 319–324
  lusophone writers and, 1:290–294, 315–318
  poetry and, 2:1532–1534
  separatism in, 1:298, 302–304, 305
  slavery, and effects on, 1:294–298
  socio–political and economic situation of writers, 1:286–290
  South African literature, 1:383–411
  West African literature, 2:1528–1534
  women writers and, 1:121–126, 154–165, 306–315
  See also specific countries

"African Socialism: Utopian or Scientific?" (Armah), 1:335–336

Age of crisis, literature in, 1:48–55

Age of telecommunications, and world literature, 1:55–58

Agnon, Samuel Joseph, *Haknasat kallah* (The Bridal Canopy), 1:216–217

Agolli, Dritëro, 2:946

Agrestes (Cabral), 1:895–896, 897

Ahavat Tapouach Hazahav (The Love of the Orange) (Rabikovitz), 1:193

Ahl lil–hawa (Of Dust and Love) (Barakat), 1:226, 227–229, 230, 230n

Aig–Imoukhuede, Frank
  "One Wife for One Man," 1:352–353
  Pidgin Stew and Sufferhead, 1:356–372

Aitmatov, Chingiz, 1:664; *2:1045,* **1071–1075**
  I dol'še veka dlitsja den' (And the Day Lasts Longer Than a Century), 2:1073–1075
  Pegij pës, beguščij kraem morja (A Spotted Dog), 2:1072–1073
  Plakha, 2:1590–1591
  Rannie žuravli (Early Cranes), 2:1072

Alabi, Bozorg, 1:644

Alafenisch, Salim, 2:1234, 1236, 1239

Alavi, Bozorg, 1:651

Albanian literature, **2:939–949**

Albuquerque, Orlando de, 1:291

Aleixandre, Vicente, **2:1374–1379**

Alexander, Meena, 1:721–723, 726

Alexis, Andre, *Childhood*, 1:431

Alfian Sa'at, 1:788, 789

Algerian literature, **1:154–177**

Ali, Ahmed, 1:732

Ali, Tariq, *Redemption*, 2:1604–1605

Alien Asian (Tay), 2:1631–1632

Allāz, al–'Ishq wa–al–Mawt fī al–Zaman al–Harāshī (Allaz: Love and Death in Terrible Times) (Wattā), 1:142–143

Allende, Isabel, *2:1641*
  Hija de la fortuna, 2:1640–1641

Al–Rabī' wa–al–Kharīf (Spring and Autumn) (Mīna), 1:144–145

Alterman, Nathan
  Pundak Ha–Ruhot (The Inn of the Winds), 1:214